Encyclopedia of Security Management

Second Edition

Encyclopedia of Security Management

Second Edition

Edited by

John J. Fay

ELSEVIER

AMSTERDAM • BOSTON • HEIDELBERG • LONDON
NEW YORK • OXFORD • PARIS • SAN DIEGO
SAN FRANCISCO • SINGAPORE • SYDNEY • TOKYO

Butterworth-Heinemann is an imprint of Elsevier

Acquisitions Editor: Pamela Chester
Signing Editor: Jennifer Soucy
Assistant Editor: Kelly Weaver
Project Manager: Melinda Ritchie

Butterworth–Heinemann is an imprint of Elsevier
30 Corporate Drive, Suite 400, Burlington, MA 01803, USA
Linacre House, Jordan Hill, Oxford OX2 8DP, UK

Library of Congress Cataloging-in-Publication Data
Application submitted

British Library Cataloguing-in-Publication Data
A catalogue record for this book is available from the British Library.

ISBN: 978-0-12-370860-1

For information on all Butterworth–Heinemann publications
visit our Web site at www.books.elsevier.com

Printed in the United States of America

07 08 09 10 11 12   10 9 8 7 6 5 4 3 2 1

Table of Contents

I. BUSINESS PRINCIPLES   1

Age Discrimination   1
The U.S. Equal Employment Opportunity Commission

Best Practices   2
Dennis Dalton

Budgeting   5
John J. Fay

Budget Planning   8
Charles A. Sennewald

Business Ethics   9
John J. Fay

Corporate Security and the Processes of Change   15
John J. Fay

Counseling   19
John J. Fay

Deming   20
Dennis Dalton

Disability Discrimination   25
The U.S. Equal Employment Opportunity Commission

Discipline   26
Charles A. Sennewald

Equal Pay and Compensation Discrimination   28
The U.S. Equal Employment Opportunity Commission

Gramm-Leach-Bliley Act   29
Electronic Privacy Information Center

In Pursuit of Quality   31
Dennis Dalton

Internships: The Security Manager's Apprentice   32
Lonnie R. Buckels and Robert B. Iannone

Job Task Analysis   34
John J. Fay

Management: Historical Roots   36
John J. Fay

Motivation   39
John J. Fay

National Origin Discrimination   40
The U.S. Equal Employment Opportunity Commission

Organization: Formal and Informal Organizations   41
Charles A. Sennewald

Performance Appraisal   42
John J. Fay

Position Evaluation   45
John J. Fay

Pregnancy Discrimination   47
The U.S. Equal Employment Opportunity Commission

Quality Assurance   48
Dennis Dalton

Race and Color Discrimination   49
The U.S. Equal Employment Opportunity Commission

Religious Discrimination   51
The U.S. Equal Employment Opportunity Commission

Retaliation Discrimination   51
The U.S. Equal Employment Opportunity Commission

Security Services   53
John J. Fay

Sex-Based Discrimination   54
The U.S. Equal Employment Opportunity Commission

Sexual Harassment   55
The U.S. Equal Employment Opportunity Commission

Strategy   55
John J. Fay

Thriving for Quality   60
Dennis Dalton

Upward Feedback   63
John J. Fay

II. EMERGENCY MANAGEMENT PRACTICES   65

Bomb Threat Management   65
John J. Fay

Business Continuity Planning   70
Eugene L. Tucker

Data-Driven Incident Management   74
Denis O'Sullivan

Disaster Types   *79*
Federal Emergency Management Agency

Emergency Management Planning   *83*
Sal DePasquale

**High-Rise Security and Fire Life
Safety**   *85*
Geoff Craighead

Media Control in Crisis Situations   *89*
John J. Fay

**National Incident Command System
Organization**   *92*
James T. Roberts, Jr.

**National Incident Management
System**   *93*
James T. Roberts, Jr.

National Response Plan   *95*
James T. Roberts, Jr.

**Security and Life Safety in the
Commercial High-Rise Building**   *96*
Glen Kitteringham

III. INFORMATION SECURITY   *99*

Business Intelligence   *99*
John A. Nolan, III

**Business Intelligence:
An Overview**   *100*
John J. Fay

Competitive Counterintelligence   *100*
John A. Nolan, III

Competitive Intelligence   *102*
John A. Nolan, III

**Computer Security: Disaster
Recovery**   *104*
Sal DePasquale

Cookie and Spyware Blockers   *107*
Michael Erbschloe

**Digital Certificates, Digital Signatures,
and Cryptography**   *108*
Jill Allison

Economic Espionage   *109*
John A. Nolan, III

Industrial Espionage   *111*
John A. Nolan, III

**Management of Sensitive
Information**   *112*
John J. Fay

**Proprietary Information: A Primer for
Protection**   *117*
Lonnie R. Buckels and Robert B. Iannone

**Technical Surveillance Countermeasures
Inspections**   *123*
Richard J. Heffernan

Website Blocking Software   *125*
Michael Erbschloe

IV. INVESTIGATION   *127*

Arson   *127*
John J. Fay

Behavior Analysis Interview   *130*
Joseph P. Buckley, III

Burglary: Attacks on Locks   *132*
John J. Fay

Crime Analysis   *133*
Karim H. Vellani

DNA Analysis   *136*
*Bureau of Justice Statistics, U.S. Department of
Justice*

Evidence Types   *138*
John J. Fay

**Forensics: FBI Identification and
Laboratory Services**   *140*
Federal Bureau of Investigation

Human Factors in Interviewing   *153*
John J. Fay

Identity Theft   *155*
Eugene F. Ferraro

Interviewing Witnesses   *159*
John J. Fay

Kinesics   *161*
Leon C. Mathieu

Photography in Investigations   *167*
John J. Fay

Polygraph Testing   *170*
American Polygraph Association

Questioned Documents   *174*
Hans M. Gidion

Questioning Suspects   *177*
John J. Fay

Questioning Techniques   *181*
John J. Fay

Rape   *183*
John J. Fay

Reid's Nine Steps of Interrogation   *184*
Joseph P. Buckley, III

Robbery   *187*
John J. Fay

Undercover Investigations in the Workplace   *189*
Eugene F. Ferraro

White-Collar Crime   *194*
John J. Fay

Workplace Investigations   *199*
Eugene F. Ferraro

Wounds: Trauma Caused By Shooting and Cutting   *203*
John J. Fay

V. LEGAL ASPECTS   *205*

Arrest Law   *205*
Phillip P. Purpura

Business Law   *207*
John J. Fay

Concepts in Negligence   *209*
John J. Fay

Courts: Prosecution in State Courts   *211*
Bureau of Justice Statistics, U.S. Department of Justice

Criminal Justice Procedure   *213*
Phillip P. Purpura

Defenses to Crime   *214*
John J. Fay

The Deposition   *216*
John J. Fay

Detention for Shoplifting   *217*
Ken Bierschbach

Expert Witness: The Deposition   *219*
John J. Fay

Intellectual Property Rights   *220*
John J. Fay

Key Concepts in Security Law   *221*
John J. Fay

Laws Affecting Security   *224*
Phillip P. Purpura

Liability for Negligent Training   *225*
John J. Fay

Negligence in Premises Design   *229*
Randall I. Atlas

Negligent Hiring and Due Diligence   *232*
Robert Capwell

Rules of Evidence   *235*
John J. Fay

Search and Seizure   *237*
John J. Fay

Sentencing of Corporations: Federal Guidelines   *242*
John J. Fay

Testifying   *245*
John J. Fay

Tort Law   *248*
Phillip P. Purpura

Torts   *250*
John J. Fay

VI. PHYSICAL SECURITY   *253*

Acceptance Testing   *253*
Ray Bernard and Don Sturgis

Access Control: People, Vehicles, and Materials   *255*
John J. Fay

Alarm System Management   *258*
John J. Fay

Buried Line Sensors   *261*
Robert L. Barnard

CCTV: Cameras for Security   *262*
Herman A. Kruegle

CCTV: Covert Techniques   *266*
Herman A. Kruegle

CCTV: The Many Roles of CCTV in Security   *271*
Herman A. Kruegle

Exterior Intrusion Sensors   *276*
Mary Lynn Garcia

Interior Intrusion Sensors   *282*
Mary Lynn Garcia

Internet Protocol (IP) Video   *289*
Raymond Payne

Intrusion Detection: Intruder Types   *293*
John J. Fay

Intrusion Detection: System Design Coordination   *295*
Robert L. Barnard

Locks   *296*
John J. Fay

Operable Opening Switches   *298*
Robert L. Barnard

Perimeter Protection: Electric-Field
Sensors   *299*
Robert L. Barnard

Perimeter Sensor Systems: Design
Concepts and Goals   *299*
Mary Lynn Garcia

Physical Protection Systems: Principles
and Concepts   *302*
Mary Lynn Garcia

Physical Security Design   *307*
Robert L. Barnard

Proximity and Point Sensors   *310*
Robert L. Barnard

A Revolution in Door Locks   *312*
Dick Zunkel

Security Design and Integration:
A Phased Process   *314*
Richard P. Grassie

Security Design: Preliminary
Considerations   *323*
Richard P. Grassie and Randall I. Atlas

Security Program Development   *329*
Sal DePasquale

Sensors: Audio Detection   *330*
Robert L. Barnard

Sensors: Barrier Detectors   *331*
Robert L. Barnard

Sensors: Exterior Intrusion
Detection   *333*
Robert L. Barnard

Sensors: Fence Disturbance
Detection   *334*
Robert L. Barnard

Sensors: Interior Intrusion
Detection   *337*
Robert L. Barnard

Sensors: Invisible Barrier
Detectors   *339*
Robert L. Barnard

Sensors: Microwave Motion
Detectors   *341*
Robert L. Barnard

Sensors: Sonic Motion
Detectors   *342*
Robert L. Barnard

Sensors: Ultrasonic Motion
Detectors   *342*
Robert L. Barnard

Sensors: Volumetric Motion
Detection   *344*
Robert L. Barnard

VII. PROTECTION PRACTICES   345

Access Control in the Chemical
Industry   *345*
American Chemistry Council

Access Control Levels   *346*
Ray Bernard

Alcohol Testing   *348*
Carl E. King

Authentication, Authorization,
and Cryptography   *349*
Jill Allison

Best Practices in Guard
Operations   *351*
Dennis Dalton

Computer-Based Training for Security
Professionals   *354*
Robert W. Miller and Sandie J. Davies

Drug Recognition Process   *358*
National Institute of Justice

Drug Testing   *360*
John J. Fay

Drug Testing: A Comparison of
Urinalysis Technologies   *362*
National Institute of Justice

Employee Hotlines   *364*
*Eugene F. Ferraro, Lindsey M. Lee, and
Kimberly L. Pfaff*

Executive Kidnapping   *368*
John J. Fay

Executive Protection in a
New Era   *370*
Robert L. Oatman

Fair Credit Reporting Act   *373*
Electronic Privacy Information Center

Guard Operations   *375*
William R. McQuirter

National Explosives Detection Canine
Program   *378*
Transportation Security Administration

Parking Ramp Security   *379*
John R. Morris

Personal Security Mission   *380*
John J. Fay

Planning and Organizing
Training   *382*
Bronson Steve Bias

Pre-Employment Background Screening
and Safe Hiring   *384*
Lester S. Rosen

Pre-Employment Screening and
Background Investigations   *387*
Eugene F. Ferraro

Report Writing for Successful
Prosecutions   *391*
Liz Martinez

Security Group Services   *392*
John J. Fay

Security Officer Turnover   *393*
Steven W. McNally

Selecting the Security
Administrator   *396*
Bronson Steve Bias

Substance Abuse in the
Workplace   *398*
Eugene F. Ferraro and Amy L. Slettedahl

Violence Risk Assessment   *401*
James S. Cawood

Working Dogs   *402*
William A. "Tony" Lavelle

Workplace Violence Prevention and
Intervention   *404*
Eugene F. Ferraro

VIII. RISK ANALYSIS   *409*

Business Impact Analysis   *409*
Eugene L. Tucker

Quantifying and Prioritizing Risk
Potential   *411*
James F. Broder

Risk Analysis   *414*
James F. Broder

Risk Analysis of Commercial
Property   *416*
Chris E. McGoey

Risk and Sensitive Information   *420*
John J. Fay

Risk Assessment and Prevention
Strategies for the Chemical
Industry   *431*
American Chemistry Council

Risk Management and Vulnerability
Assessment   *433*
Mary Lynn Garcia

Vulnerability Assessment Process   *439*
Mary Lynn Garcia

IX. SECURITY FIELDS   *445*

Architectural Security: Integrating
Security with Design   *445*
Randall I. Atlas

Chemical Industry Security   *450*
Sal DePasquale

Hospital Security: Basic Concepts   *452*
Russell L. Colling

Lodging Security   *455*
Peter E. Tarlow

Museum Security   *456*
Steven R. Keller

Restaurant Security   *460*
Richard L. Moe

Retail Security System Design   *462*
Chris E. McGoey

Securing the Budget Motel   *465*
Robert L. Kohr

Security Consulting   *467*
Steven R. Keller

The Security Consultant   *469*
James F. Broder

Tourism Security   *473*
Peter E. Tarlow

X. SECURITY PRINCIPLES   *475*

Convergence of Physical Security
and IT   *475*
Ray Bernard

Crime Control Theories   *477*
Glen Kitteringham

Crime Prevention: A Community
Approach   *481*
John J. Fay

Crime Prevention Through
Environmental Design   *484*
Sean A. Ahrens

CPTED Theory Explained   *487*
Glenn Kitteringham

Environmental Crime Prevention and
Social Crime Prevention Theories 488
Glen Kitteringham

Incident Causation Model 490
John J. Fay

Operations Security 493
Sidney W. Crews

Security Expertise 495
Robert D. McCrie

Target Analysis 498
Sidney W. Crews

XI. TERRORISM 501

Agroterrorism 501
Andrés de la Concha Bermejillo

Chemical and Biological Weapons 503
John J. Fay

Critical Infrastructure Protection
(CIP) 507
Adolfo Meana, Jr. and James J. Zirkel

Critical National Infrastructure:
Electric Power 510
*Electric Power Risk Assessment, Information
Assurance Task Force (IATF) of the National
Security Telecommunications Advisory
Committee (NSTAC)*

Critical National Infrastructure: The
National Infrastructure Protection
Plan 514
Department of Homeland Security

Critical National Infrastructure: Role of
Science and Technology 517
*Office of Science and Technology Policy,
Department of Homeland Security*

Critical National Infrastructure:
Transportation 523
*Threats and Protection, Department of
Homeland Security*

Critical National Infrastructure:
Urban Transit 524
Transit Security, Federal Transit Administration

Critical National Infrastructure:
Vulnerability Assessment of Water
Systems 526
*Office of Water Management, Environmental
Protection Agency*

Cyberterrorism 529
United States Institute for Peace

Explosive, Radiological, and Nuclear
Weapons 531
John J. Fay

How the Federal Government Responds
to a Major Disaster 534
George D. Haddow

Intelligence and Local Law
Enforcement 538
Kathleen M. Sweet

Suicide Bombers 541
Daniel B. Kennedy

Tactics of Terrorists 542
John J. Fay

Terrorism 546
Scott A. Watson

Terrorism: Bomb Scene Search 549
Federal Bureau of Investigation

Terrorist Methods 551
Phillip P. Purpura

Terrorist Threats 558
Federal Emergency Management Agency

The Many Faces of Terrorism 560
John J. Fay

Transportation Infrastructure 563
Department of Homeland Security

Urban Transit: A Critical National
Infrastructure 565
Federal Transit Administration

Vulnerability to Cyberterrorism 566
U. S. Institute for Peace

XII. LIAISON 571

Bureau of Alcohol, Tobacco, Firearms,
and Explosives 571
*Bureau of Alcohol, Tobacco, Firearms, and
Explosives (ATF)*

The Central Intelligence Agency 581
The Central Intelligence Agency (CIA)

Defense Security Service 582
The Defense Security Service (DSS)

Drug Enforcement
Administration 584
Drug Enforcement Administration (DEA)

Federal Air Marshal Service 585
Federal Air Marshal Service

The Federal Bureau of
Investigation 586
The Federal Bureau of Investigation (FBI)

Immigration and Customs Enforcement   *591*
U.S. Immigration and Customs Enforcement

Internal Revenue Service Criminal Investigation   *603*
Internal Revenue Service Criminal Investigation

National Drug Intelligence Center   *603*
National Drug Intelligence Center

National Security Agency/Central Security Service   *605*
National Security Agency/Central Security Service

U.S. Air Force Office of Special Investigations   *606*
U.S. Air Force Office of Special Investigations

U.S. Army Criminal Investigation Division   *608*
U.S. Army Criminal Investigation Division

U.S. Coast Guard Office of Law Enforcement   *608*
U.S. Coast Guard Office of Law Enforcement

U.S. Customs and Border Protection   *609*
U.S. Customs and Border Protection

U.S. Marshals Service   *609*
U.S. Marshals Service

U.S. Naval Criminal Investigative Service   *618*
U.S. Naval Criminal Investigative Service

U.S. Secret Service (USSS)   *618*
U.S. Secret Service

Contributing Authors

Sean A. Ahrens, CPP. Senior Security Consultant with Schirmer Engineering and has more than 16 years of security experience. Mr. Ahrens has provided security threat and risk analysis, contingency planning, loss prevention, force protection planning, and design and construction administration services for government, public, and private entities that encompass the areas of telecommunications, security, closed circuit television, and access control systems. He is well-versed in the various trade and local authority issues impacting projects, and has specialized professional competence in security, access control systems, and force protection systems. Known for his technical expertise, he has been asked to sit on a variety of standard-setting panels including Underwriters Laboratories (UL) and the Security Industry Association (SIA). Mr. Ahrens is a former and founding member of the American Society for Industrial Security International (ASIS) Commission on Guidelines, where he assisted in the development and promulgation of a variety of security-related guidelines. Mr. Ahrens currently participates as an active member of the ASIS Commercial Real Estate Council (CREC) and a committee to develop Physical Security Measures Guidelines.

Jill Allison, CISSP, MBA, MIM. Enterprise Security Risk Management Consultant; CEO, Allison Consulting and Fireworks Security Ventures, Chaska, MN; former Vice President, 4Ai International LLC, Chicago, IL; former Consultant, National Biometric Security Project (NBSP) Washington, D.C.; former Smart Card Solutions Product Manager, Datacard Group, Minnetonka, MN; former Graduate Program Manager, St. Thomas University, MBA Program, Minneapolis, MN; former Vice President, Business Development, Security Design International (Cylink subsidiary, merged with Counterpane,) Santa Clara, CA; former Vice President, Marketing & Business Development, CertifiedTime, Inc.; former PKI Consultant, Science Applications International Corp. (SAIC), Annapolis, MD; former Consultant, Intellitactics, Annapolis, MD; former Vice President, Business Development, Voltaire Advanced Data Security, Inc., Vienna, VA; former Vice President, Business Development, War Room Research, LLC, Annapolis, MD; former Director, Strategic Partnering and Solutions Marketing; Pinkerton's Inc., Encino, CA; former Director, Business Development, IriScan, Inc. (Iridian), Mt. Laurel, NJ; former Consultant, Monsanto Company, St. Louis, MO; former Business Planning Graduate Intern, Apple Computer, Cupertino, CA; former Product Marketing Manager; Hypro Corporation; former Security Program Analyst; Vitro Security Engineering, Mt. Laurel, NJ. Member, American Society for Industrial Security (ASIS) and former Conference Chair, ASIS IT Security Council; Bachelor of Arts, Economics, Gustavus Adolphus College, St. Peter, MN; Master of International Management, Marketing, American Graduate School of International Management (AGSIM/Thunderbird) Glendale, AZ; Master of Business Administration, Strategic and Entrepreneurial Management, the Wharton School, University of Pennsylvania, Philadelphia, PA.

Randall I. Atlas, PhD, AIA, CPP. President of Counter Terror Design, Inc. and Vice President of Atlas Safety & Security Design, Inc., Miami, FL; Adjunct Associate Professor of Architecture, Florida Atlantic University; Technical Assistance Consultant for the National Institute of Corrections, Longmont, CO. Member, American Institute of Architects—Architecture for Justice Committee; member, American Society of Industrial Security—Security Architecture Engineering Committee; member, American Correctional Association—Design & Technology Committee; member, American Society of Safety Engineers; member, National Safety Council; member, Environmental Design Research Association; member, National Fire Protection Association; member, American Society of Testing Materials; member, Human Factors Ergonomics Society; member, American Jail Association; member, National Institute of Justice—Leadership Position; member, Security by Design—Leadership Position; member, Advisory Task Group—Leadership Position. Doctorate of Criminology, Florida State University; Master of Architecture, University of Illinois; Bachelor of Criminal Justice, University of South Florida; Bachelor of Architecture, University of Florida. Author of "Crime Prevention Through Building Codes," *Building Security*, 1981; "Crime Site Selections for Assaults in Four Florida Prisons,"

Prison Journal, 1986; "Stairs, Steps, and Slipping," *Florida Architect Journal*, 1987; "Crime Prevention Through Building Codes," *Journal of Security Administration*, 1986; "Secure Homes: The Future of Anti-Crime Technology," *Futurist*, 1988; "Designing Security for People, Information, and Property," *Florida Real Estate Journal*, 1988; "How to Protect Your Home," 1988; "Just When You Thought It Was Safe," *Professional Safety*, 1989; "Building Design Can Provide Defensible Space," *Access Control*, 1989; "Design for Safety: Building Code Update," *Florida Architect Journal*, 1989; "Security Design," a monthly featured article in *Protection of Assets Bulletin*; "Pay It Now or Pay It Later," *Security Management*, 1990; "Architect Input Among First Steps in Design," *Access Control*, 1991; "Offensible Space: Obstruction of Law Enforcement Through Environmental Design," *Security Management*, 1991; "Handicap Accessibility Affects Security," *Access Control*, 1992; "Will ADA Affect Security?" *Security Management*, 1992; "Need for Involving Security in Building Planning," *Campus Security Report*, 1992; "Security for Buildings," *Architectural Graphic Standards*, Wiley Publishers, 1992; "Post-Occupancy Evaluation of Building Security," *Post-Occupancy Evaluations*, 1993; "Impact of ADA on Corrections," *Construction Bulletin*, National Institute of Corrections, 1993; "Environmental Barriers to Crime," Ergonomics in Design, October 1994; "The Impact on Crime of Street Closures and Barricades: A Florida Case Study." Security Journal; Vol. 5, No. 3, July 1994; Special Report: Defensible Space, Engineering New Record, May 1, 1995; "Designing for Security in Courthouses of the Future," Court Review Vol. 34, No. 2, Summer 1997; American Judges Association; "Designing Security in School Environments," Library Administration and Management Spring, Vol. 11, #2, 1997; "Designing for Crime and Terrorism: CPTED Training is Essential: Security Design and Technology magazine, June 1998; "Designing Against Crime: the Case for CPTED Training for Architects," Florida Architect, Summer 1998; "Stairwell Security," Door and Hardware Magazine, May 1999, p. 55; "Secure Facility Design, Environmental Design that Prevents Crime!" The Construction Specifier, *April* 1999; "Security Design: Access Control Technology," Door and Hardware magazine, *April* 1999, p. 49; "ADA: Proposed Final Regulations for Courthouses, Jails and Prisons," Corrections Today, *April* 2000; "Design Considerations: Setting Standards in Security Architecture," Door and Hardware magazine, June 2000; "Building Security Through Design," The American Institute of Architects, Washington, D.C., 2001; "Barry University: A CPTED Case Study," *Campus Law Enforcement Journal,* June 2002; "The Sustainability of CPTED: Less Magic More Science!" *The CPTED Journal*, Vol. 1, Issue 1, July 2002; "Planting and Shaping Security Success," Security Management magazine, August 2002; "The ABC's of CPTED," a Florida case study of Barry University, *Campus Safety Journal,* August 2002; "Creating Safety," Landscape Architect magazine, September 2002; "Designing Safe Campuses," *Campus Security and Safety Journal,* December 2002; "Loss Prevention Returns to Its Roots with CPTED," Plant Safety & Maintenance magazine, *April* 2003; "How Are Criminals Using CPTED? Offensible Space," Security Management magazine, May 2003; "Defensible Space: An Architectural Retrospective," *Master Builder,* September/October 2004, Vol. 1, Number 1; "Designing Safe Communities: Strategies for Safe and Sustainable Communities," Landscape Architectural Registrations Boards Foundation, Vienna, Virginia, 2004; "Security Design Concepts," Security Planning and Design: A Guide for Architecture and Building Design Professionals, American Institute of Architects, Wiley Publishers, Washington D.C., 2004; "The Security Audit and Premises Liability," Spotlight on Security for Real Estate Managers, 2nd Edition, IREM, 2005.

Ray Bernard, PSP, CHS-III. Founder and publisher of *The Security Minute* electronic newsletter; President and CEO of security management and technology consulting firm Ray Bernard Consulting Services of Lake Forest, CA; founder and former Principal Consultant of Ray Bernard Consulting and Design, Detroit, MI; current technical editor and columnist for *Security Technology & Design* magazine; Board Certified as a Physical Security Professional by ASIS International; Board Certified in Homeland Security (Level III) by the American College of Forensic Examiners International (ACFEI). Education Chair of the ASIS IT Security Council and Education Committee member of the ASIS Physical Security Council of ASIS; participating member of ASTM International standards organization, and member of the ASTM Technical Committee E54 on Homeland Security Applications; member of the International Association of Independent Security Consultants (IAPSC); member of the Information Systems Security Association (ISSA); member of the Information Systems Audit and

Control Association (ISACA); member of IEEE Computer Society; leading author and frequent presenter at security conferences on the subject of the convergence of physical security and IT; author of over 30 major articles for leading security industry and other industry journals including *Access Control & Security Systems*, *Buildings*, *Corporate Security News*, *Engineered Systems*, *Graduating Engineer*, *Hi-Tech Security Solutions*, *Security*, *Security Management Practices*, *Security Technology & Design*, *Seguridad Latina* and *Ventas de Seguridad*.

Bronson Steve Bias, CHS, CPP, CFE, CPO. Executive Director of Protective Services, Nova Southeastern University, Fort Lauderdale/Davie, FL; Adjunct Instructor, School of Justice and Safety Administration, Miami, FL; former Director of Loss Prevention, Bi-Lo Supermarkets, Inc., Greenville, SC; former Commander of Internal Affairs, Hollywood Police Department, Hollywood, FL; member, Board Member, and Executive Committee Member, American Society for Industrial Security; member, International Association of Campus Law Enforcement Administrators; member, National Association of Fraud Examiners; life member, Florida Association of Campus Safety and Security Administrators; life member, Florida Police Benevolent Association and the Fraternal Order of Police; Chairperson, Educational Institutions Standing Committee, ASIS; former Chairperson, Miami Chapter, ASIS; past President, Florida Chapter IACLEA (FACSSA); past President, Broward County Police Benevolent Association; past President, Hollywood Fraternal Order of Police; recipient of the ASIS Region XIII Award of Merit, 1991. Bachelor of Science, Nova University. Author of cover article, *Security*, April, 1991; "Behavioral Analysis," *Security New Canada*, "Recruiting Campus Public Safety Management," Campus Law Enforcement Journal; "Police Benevolent Centurion," *Campus Security Report*, December, 1991; *School Security Report*, September 1991; and *"Campus Crime Prevention,"* chapter, Handbook of Loss Prevention and Crime Prevention, 1996 and 2003.

Ken Bierschbach, CPP. Security Assessment & Development Specialist, Meijer Stores, Grand Rapids, MI; former Loss Prevention Manager, Meijer Stores, Grand Rapids, MI; Member, ASIS International; former Chapter Chairman, Western Michigan Chapter of ASIS; former Chapter Vice Chairman, Western Michigan Chapter of ASIS; Member, Editorial Advisory Board, Private Security Case Law Reporter; Associate of Arts, Grand Rapids Community College, Grand Rapids, MI.

James F. Broder, CPP. Consultant, Confidential Management Services, Inc., San Dimas, CA; former Security Consultant, Marsh and McLennan, Inc.; former Special Agent, U.S. State Department; former Assistant and the Chairman, Investigations Sub-Committee, U.S. House of Representatives. Member, American Society for Industrial Security; member, Society of Former Special Agents of the FBI; member, Association of Former Intelligence Officers; past member, Congressional Staff Association, U.S. House of Representatives; past member, International Association of Professional Security Consultants; Legion of Merit, Vietnam; Bachelor of Arts, Criminology, University of California; author of *Risk Analysis and the Security Survey*, Butterworth-Heinemann; *Investigation of Substance Abuse in the Workplace*, Butterworth-Heinemann; *Resources Control in Counter-Insurgency*, Agency for International Development, U.S. State Department; "Case Management and Control of Undercover Operations for Business and Industry," *Professional Protection*; contributing author, *Effective Security Management*, Butterworth-Heinemann.

Lonnie R. Buckels, CPP. Deceased. Before his death, Mr. Buckels was Head, Information Security, Telecommunications and Space Sector, Hughes Aircraft Company, El Segundo, CA; former Branch Manager, Industrial Security, McDonnell Douglas Corporation, Huntington Beach, and Long Beach, CA; former part-time Instructor, Golden West College, Huntington Beach, CA; former substitute Instructor, California State University at Long Beach; member, American Society for Industrial Security; Chapter Chairman, Greater Los Angeles Chapter, ASIS; National General Chairman, 20th Annual Seminar and Exhibits, ASIS; member, National Classification Management Society; member, Research Security Administrators; member, California Association of Administration of Justice Educators; recipient of the James S. Cogswell Award, Douglas Aircraft Company, Long Beach, CA, and Hughes Aircraft Company, Torrance, CA; Silver Beaver and District Award of Merit, Boy Scouts of America; Associate in History, El Camino College, Torrance, CA; Bachelor of Arts in History, California State College at Long Beach; Bachelor of Science in Criminal Justice (Security Adminstration Option), California State University at Long Beach; Douglas Management Institute Certificate; co-author of "Is an Ex the Best Candidate?" and "The Security Manager's Apprentice," *Security Management*; author of "A Murphy's Law Corollary in Personnel Selection," "The Perils of 'P'," "The Plague of Security Misconceptions," and "Professionalism—An Impossible Task?" *Security Management*, "While Waiting for the Call That Never Came," *Greater Los Angeles Chapter Newsletter*.

Joseph P. Buckley, III. President, John E. Reid and Associates, Inc., Chicago, IL; past and present Lecturer, Northwestern School of Law, Federal Law Enforcement Training Center, Institute of Internal Auditors, American Society of Industrial Security, and numerous other professional groups; licensed Detection of Deception Examiner Committee, 1978–1982; Vice President, Illinois Polygraph Society, 1981, President in 1982 and 1983, and Chairman of the Board in 1984 of the Illinois Polygraph Society; Chairman, Public Relations Committee, American Polygraph Association, 1979–1980 and 1984–1990; member Investigations Committee of the American Society of Industrial Security, member of various professional associations including International Chiefs of Police, American Management Association, Chicago Crime Commission, Special Agents Association, Federal Law Enforcement Officers Association, International Association of Directors of Law Enforcement Standards and Training, and American Academy of Forensic Sciences; Bachelor of Arts, Loyola University; Master of Science in the Detection of Deception, Reid College of Detection of Deception; co-author of *The Investigator Anthology*, 1999; co-author of *Criminal Interrogation and Confessions,* 4th Edition, 2001; co-author of *The Essentials of The Reid Technique*, 2004; co-author "Abdominal and Thoracic Respiration Recordings in the Detection of Deception," *Polygraph*, 1972; "Relative Accuracy of Polygraph Examiner Diagnosis of Respiration, Blood Pressure and GSR Recordings," *Journal of Police Science and Administration*, 1975; "The Nine Steps of Interrogation," *Security Management*, 1983; "The Use of Behavior Symptoms in the Search for the Truth: A Tool for the Prosecutor," *Prosecutor*, 1985; "The Influence of Race and Gender on Pre-employment Polygraph Examination Results," *Polygraph*, 1991; "The Influence of Race and Gender on Blind Polygraph Chart Analysis," *Polygraph*, 1991; "Criminal Interrogation Techniques on Trial," *Prosecutor*, 1991; author of "Polygraph Technology" a chapter in the text *Modern Legal Medicine, Psychiatry and Forensic Science*, 1980; "The Use of Polygraphs by the Business Community," *Management Review*, 1986; "How Do I Know if They Told Me the Truth?" *Internal Audit Advisor*, 1986; "Nobody's Perfect," *Security Management*, 1987; "Interrogation," a chapter in the text, *The Encyclopedia of Police Science*, 1989; "The Behavioral Profile of a Liar," International Association of Credit Card Investigators NEWS, First Quarter, 1991; "The Behavior Analysis Interview," International Association of Credit Card Investigators NEWS, Second Quarter, 1991.

Robert Capwell. Founder and President, Comprehensive Information Services, Inc. (CIS). Mr. Capwell is considered one of the leading experts in the background screening industry with over 17 years of experience in the field. Mr. Capwell is a founding member and currently sits on the Board of Directors of NAPBS, National Association of Professional Background Screeners, and is also Co-Chair of the Board of Directors for the 2006 fiscal year. Robert has chaired the Public Awareness and Communications Committee and sits on the Government Affairs Committee. He has made industry presentations to various public entities and trade organizations including The Federal Trade Commission, The Department of Transportation, and Sub-Committee on Aviation. Mr. Capwell has also testified to the Pennsylvania Court Administrators and Senate Judiciary Committee staff regarding consumer privacy and data breach legislation. Robert is also the Managing Editor of an industry newsgroup. He was also employed with Equifax, Inc., serving as production supervisor, regional sales representative and field liaison before founding CIS. Mr. Capwell has a Bachelor of Science in Business Administration with a concentration in Management from Penn State University, The Behrend College. He has also served as a part-time high school economics teacher through Junior Achievement and sits on the board of the CIS corporate philanthropic initiative SymbioCIS.

James S. Cawood, CPP, PCI, PSP, CFE. President of Factor One; worked in the area of threat assessment, violence risk assessment, behavioral analysis, violence prevention, security analysis, and incident resolution for more than 20 years, and has successfully assessed and managed over 3,000 violence related cases for federal and state government agencies, public and private corporations, and other business entities throughout the United States; current Association President of the Association of Threat Assessment Professionals (ATAP); former Association 2nd Vice President and President of the Northern California Chapter (ATAP), Former Secretary of ASIS International Foundation Board, Former Chairman of the Board of the California Association of Licensed Investigators (CALI); has served on the faculties of Golden Gate University, in their Security Management degree program and the University of California, Santa Cruz extension, teaching Threat Management; first concurrent holder of all three ASIS International certifications: Certified Protection Professional (CPP), Professional Certified Investigator (PCI), Physical Security Professional (PSP), also a Certified Fraud Examiner (CFE), Certified Security Professional (CSP), Certified Professional Investigator (CPI), Certified International Investigator (CII), and Diplomate, American Board of Forensic Examiners (DABFE); authored articles and book chapters for various professional publications including *Security Management* magazine, as the original author of A Plan for Threat Management (Chapter 40) of the *Protection of Assets Manual*; Chapters 24 – Personnel Screening and Chapter 32 – Arson, Sabotage, and Bomb Threats in the *Accident Prevention Manual for Business & Industry – Security Management* volume; Chapter 32 – Security for *Safety, Health, and Asset Protection: Management Essentials, 2nd Ed*; and a co-authored chapter: Threat Management of Stalking Cases in *The Psychology of Stalking: Clinical and Forensic Perspectives*, published by Academic Press in 1998. He has also co-authored a book, *Violence Assessment and Intervention: The Practitioner's Handbook*, CRC Press 2003.

Russell L. Colling, CPP, CHPA, MS. Executive Vice President, Hospital Shared Services of Colorado, Denver, CO; Adjunct Professor, Security Management, Webster University, Denver, CO; former Assistant Vice President, Chicago Wesley Memorial Hospital, Chicago, IL; former Security Compliance Officer, Martin Marietta, Denver, CO; former Police Officer and Chief of Police, Saugatuck, MI; member, American Society for Industrial Security; founding president, charter member and life member, International Association for Healthcare Security and Safety; past Chairman/member, Metropolitan Law Enforcement Association, Denver, CO; past Chairman/member, Colorado Law Enforcement Memorial Committee; member, American Hospital Association, Ad Hoc Security Committee; member, Board of Directors, School of Criminal Justice Alumni Association, Michigan State University; member, Editorial Advisory Board, *Security Journal*; Editorial Advisory Board, *Hospital Security and Safety Management*; recipient of first Russell L. Colling Literary Award, International Association for Healthcare Security and Safety; Bachelor of Science, Michigan State University; Master of Science, Michigan State University; Editor, *Security Officer Basic Training Manual*, International Association for Healthcare Security and Safety; Editor, *Supervisor Training Manual*, International Association for Healthcare Security and Safety; author, "Hospital Security: Is the Patient at Risk," *Journal of Healthcare Protection Management*; author of *Hospital Security*, 3rd Edition, Butterworth-Heinemann.

Geoff Craighead, CPP. Head of High-Rise and Real Estate Security Services, Securitas Security Services USA, Inc., an organization that provides support for high-rise facilities throughout the United States. He has been involved in the security and life safety operations of industrial and high-rise facilities for over 20 years. He has conducted extensive security surveys and training programs, developed security policies and procedures, and written building emergency plans. Mr. Craighead is a member of the Building Owners and Managers Association (BOMA) Greater Los Angeles Board of Directors and chair of the ASIS Commercial Real Estate Council. He is certified by the Los Angeles Fire Department to provide high-rise life safety services and serves on the National Fire Protection Association (NFPA)'s High-Rise Building Safety Advisory Committee. Mr. Craighead is board-certified in security management (CPP) by ASIS International and a past president of the ASIS Professional Certification Board that administers certification programs for security professionals throughout the world. Mr. Craighead is author of *High-Rise Security and Fire Life Safety, Second Edition*, published by Butterworth-Heinemann. It is a comprehensive reference for security and fire life safety operations within commercial office buildings/skyscrapers. In addition, he has had numerous articles published in industry magazines on office security, high-rise emergency planning, and contract security for high-rise buildings. Mr. Craighead has spoken on security and emergency planning for high-rise buildings at BOMA International and the Institute of Real Estate Management (IREM) workshops. He has also spoken and at national conventions of ASIS International, the Risk and Insurance Management Society (RIMS), and The Council on Tall Buildings & Urban Habitat.

Sidney W. Crews. Adjunct instructor with the Texas Engineering Extension (TEEX), and a member of the Texas A&M University system. Mr. Crews travels the country teaching Enhanced Threat and Risk Assessment courses focusing on potential threat elements, security concepts, building systems, physical security practices and devices, and preparation/conduct of vulnerability assessments. Prior to joining TEEX, Mr. Crews was a U.S. Army Special Forces officer who served in various assignments over his 20-year career. He has been responsible for developing programs of instruction and training for approximately 5,000 personnel in seven nations. He has instructed on such topics as physical security planning and oversight, risk management, critical infrastructure and personnel protection, surveillance/surveillance detection, anti/counterterrorism procedures, dispute mediation, and intelligence gathering/investigative procedure. While serving as a Special Forces Operational Detachment–Alpha (A-team) commander Mr. Crews was hand-picked to recruit, outfit, and train a one-of-a-kind team that was responsible for conducting clandestine operations of the highest sensitivities. During Operation Iraqi Freedom, he led the detachment into Iraq, well in advance of any U.S. ground or air presence, to conduct extremely sensitive operations deep behind enemy lines. These operations included both targeting and security assessments of various operationally important compounds and facilities, as well as instructing Kurdish forces in physical security improvement measures and other operations. For his actions in Iraq, he was awarded the Bronze Star with "V" (for valor) by President George H.W. Bush. He also organized and led area studies and security assessments in other permissive and semi-permissive environments. Prior to his retirement from the Army in 2005, Mr. Crews was an Assistant Professor of Military Science at Texas A&M University. There, as a Course Director, he completely redeveloped course curriculums, training schedules and programs of instruction for the largest U.S. Army Reserve Officer Training Corps in the nation consisting of 600 students and 20 cadre members. He managed a ROTC instructional training staff that instructed approximately 200 hours of undergraduate coursework per student while personally conducting approximately 1,000 hours of classroom/lab presentations and stand-up training. Mr. Crews is a graduate of the University of Washington, where he received a Bachelor's Degree in International Study and was on the Dean's List for academic excellence for all terms and he has earned a Project Management Certificate from the University of Washington. He has received numerous military honors and is a graduate of both the U.S. Army Ranger and Special Forces qualification courses as well as many others. He holds a Department of Defense Top Secret security clearance and is a member of the American Society for Industrial Security (ASIS).

Dennis Dalton, DPA. Former Director of Academic Affairs for the University of Phoenix's Sacramento Campus. He teaches primarily for the Colleges of Graduate and Undergraduate Business and Management. He holds a Doctorate in Public Administration from the University of Southern California, a Master's Degree in Adult Education, and a Bachelor's Degree in Criminal Justice from Michigan State University. In 1987 he founded Dalton Affiliates, an international security management consulting firm for Fortune 500 companies. He is recognized as one of the country's foremost security experts, having been retained in over 250 cases, serving as the lead consultant for the World Trade Center bombing, the Empire State Building Palestinian shooting, and the Atlanta Day-Trader mass shooting. He is a former police officer, educator and administrator and served as Vice President and Director of Corporate Security for three large multinational companies. He is the author of many manuals, articles, and videos, and is a well-known speaker on management subjects. He has authored three very successful books on security management. His most recent is entitled: *Rethinking Corporate Security in the Post 9/11 Era: Issues and Strategies for Today's Global Business Community*. He is also a winner of Security Magazine's "Executive Achievement Award" and is the only person to have appeared

Contributing Authors   xix

on the magazine's cover twice. He has appeared on MSNBC, Fox News, the BBC, several radio stations, and is considered an industry spokesperson for several leading newspapers, including the Wall street Journal, the Los Angeles Times, and the San Francisco Chronicle.

Sandi J. Davies began her career in contract security in 1980 with a primary focus on personnel administration. She became deeply involved in training and was instrumental in developing Security Officer training programs for a major guard company. Her interest in security training grew, and in 1988 she joined the newly formed International Foundation for Protection Officers (IFPO) as a program administrative assistant. In 1991 she was elected executive director of the International Foundation for Protection Officers. She became a member of the American Society for Industrial Security (ASIS) in 1985 and has served in executive positions at the chapter level. Ms. Davies is also a Member of the Technical Advisory Board for the Canadian General Standards Board on Security Officer Training Standards. In addition, she is a Member of the Advisory Board for the Northwest Territories Security Officer Certification Committee. In 1999 Sandi agreed to serve on the Advisory Board of the International Foundation for Cultural Property Protection. Since 1994 Sandi has been the Chairperson for the Asset Protection Advisory Board for Mount Royal College in Calgary, Alberta Canada. Most recently, Sandi has been involved as an Associate Member of the Private Security Services Council of ASIS International. She has had numerous articles published in security publications relating to certifications and training of security personnel. In the early 1990s Ms. Davies in a cooperative effort with the IFPO Founding Director; Ronald R. Minion, co-edited the *Protection Officer Training Manual,* published by Butterworth-Heinemann. That text is now in its 7th edition. In 1994 she contributed a chapter relating to crime prevention in Canada in the *Handbook of Loss Prevention and Crime Prevention,* published by Butterworth-Heinemann. In 1995, again in a cooperative effort, Ms. Davies and Mr. Minion co-authored a Butterworth-Heinemann text entitled *The Security Supervisor Training Manual.* In July 1999 the second edition of this text was released as, *Security Supervision: Theory and Practices of Asset Protection,* again published by Butterworth-Heinemann. Sandi also edits "Protection Officer News," published by the International Foundation for Protection Officers, now in its 13th year of publication.

Andrés de la Concha Bermejillo, DVM, MS, PhD. Pathologist, Texas Veterinary Medical Diagnostic Laboratory, Texas A&M University, College Station, Texas; Consultant, National Emergency Response and Rescue Training Center, Texas Engineering Extension Service (TEEX), Texas A&M University; Associate Professor, Department of Veterinary Pathobiology, College of Veterinary Medicine, Texas A&M University; Assistant Professor and Research Project Leader, Department of Pathobiology, Texas A&M University's Agricultural Research and Extension Center, San Angelo, Texas; post-doctoral trainee, Department of Pathology, College of Veterinary Medicine and Biomedical Sciences, Colorado State University; post-graduate researcher and resident in diagnostic pathology, Department of Pathology, School of Veterinary Medicine, University of California, Davis; Professor and Chief of Service, Department of Pathology, School of Veterinary Medicine and Animal Science, National Autonomous University of Mexico, Mexico City; member of the American Society for Virology; awards and distinctions include the 2004 Robert & Virginia Lectureship, Western College of Veterinary Medicine, University of Saskatchewan; Member, Editorial Review Board, Clinical & Diagnostic Laboratory of Immunology; Member, Scientific Panel, Premio Canifarma "Dr. Alfredo Tellez Giron Rode," Consejo Nacional de Ciencia y Tecnologia (CONACYT), Mexico; National Institutes of Health Minority Investigator Award; peer-reviewed publications include *Genetic Characterization of Viruses Isolated from Various Ruminant Species of a Zoo, Genomes of Parapoxviruses, Virus and Bovine Papular Stomatitis Virus, Construction and Characterization of a Recombinant Ovine Lentivirus Carrying the Optimized Green Fluorescent Protein Gene at the dUTPase Locus,* and a book chapter of *Maedi-visna and Ovine Progressive Pneumonia.*

Sal DePasquale, CPP has over 25 years experience in the physical security field and has gained special expertise in vulnerability analysis and long term strategic planning. He is a former manager of security at Georgia Pacific and is presently a security consultant for CH2MHill, an organization that provides services to the chemical industry. In the past, he has consulted with the Department of State, Department of Energy, Honeywell, W.R. Grace, Aetna, American Airlines, AT&T, Atlanta Gas and Light, General Electric, Georgia Power, University of Virginia, Tampa International Airport, Kraft Foods, New Jersey Institute of Technology, Phillip Morris, and Spartanburg County, SC. Mr. DePasquale instructs at Georgia State University and has taught at Polytechnic University and the American Institute of Chemical Engineers (AIChE). He holds a Master of Business Administration, Mercer University, and a Master of Science, University of South Carolina. His memberships include the Physical Security Council, ASIS International; Site Security Committee, American Chemistry Council; Center for Chemical Process Safety; and a American Institute of Chemical Engineers. He has authored numerous security-related articles and has presented at a great number of seminars and workshops. Mr. DePasquale served with the U.S. Marine Corps in Vietnam.

Michael Erbschloe. Information technology consultant, educator, and author. He has taught graduate level courses and developed technology-related curricula for several universities and speaks at conferences and industry events around the world. Michael holds a Master Degree in Sociology from Kent State University. He has authored hundreds of articles on technology and several books, including *Physical Security for IT (Elsevier Science); Trojans, Worms, and Spyware (Butterworth-Heinemann); Implementing Homeland Security in Enterprise IT (Digital Press); Guide to Disaster Recovery, Course Technology,* and *Socially Responsible IT Management (Digital Press); Information Warfare: How to Survive Cyber Attacks (McGraw Hill); The Executive's Guide to Privacy Management (McGraw Hill); Net Privacy: A Guide to Developing & Implementing an e-business Privacy Plan (McGraw Hill).*

John J. Fay, CPP is the owner/operator of The Learning Shop, a provider of online courses and tests for security professionals and private investigators. He is also an Adjunct Instructor at Texas A&M University. Prior employment includes Adjunct Instructor, DeKalb Institute; Security Manager, British Petroleum Exploration; Adjunct Professor, University of Houston; Director of Corporate Security, The Charter Company; Director, National Crime Prevention Institute; Chief of Plans and Training, Georgia Bureau of Investigation; Chief of Training Standards, Georgia Peace Officer Standards and Training Council; Special Agent, U.S. Army Criminal Investigation Division; Lecturer, Police Science Division, University of Georgia; and Adjunct Professor, University of North Florida. Associate Member, Georgia Association of Professional Private Investigators. Former Certified Protection Professional (CPP), Regional Vice President, Chapter Chairman, and member of the CPP Board, American Society for Industrial Security International; Association of Chiefs of Police; Peace Officers Association of Georgia; Texas Police Association; and Houston Metropolitan Criminal Investigators Association. Honor Society, University of Nebraska at Omaha; Bronze Star Medal with Oak Leaf Cluster (Vietnam); Meritorious Service Medal (Vietnam); and U.S. Army Commendation Medal. Bachelor of General Education, University of Nebraska at Omaha and Master of Business Administration, University of Hawaii. With Butterworth-Heinemann, author of *Contemporary Security Management; Model Security Policies, Plans, and Procedures; Encyclopedia of Security Management; Drug Testing;* and *Butterworth's Security Dictionary.* Other books include *Security Dictionary,* American Society for Industrial Security International; *The Alcohol/Drug Abuse Dictionary and Encyclopedia,* Charles R. Thomas; *The Police Dictionary and Encyclopedia,* Charles R. Thomas; and *Approaches to Criminal Justice Training,* University of Georgia.

Eugene F. Ferraro, CPP, CFE, PCI. President and Chief Executive Officer, Business Controls, Inc., Littleton, CO; former chairman of the Workplace Substance Abuse Council, American Society for Industrial Security International (ASIS) and current Program Advisor for the ASIS Asset Protection Course II; former military pilot, intelligence officer and a graduate of the Naval Justice School; author of eight books, including *Undercover Investigations in the Workplace* and *Investigations in the Workplace;* past and current affiliations with professional associations include ASIS International, Association of Certified Fraud Examiners, Professional Private Investigators Association of Colorado, National

Council of Investigative and Security Services, National Association of Professional Process Servers, and California Association of Licensed Investigators.

Mary Lynn Garcia received a Bachelor of Arts in Biology from the State University of New York at Oswego, a Master of Science in Biomedical Sciences from the University of New Mexico, and a Certificate in Electronics Technology from the Albuquerque Technical-Vocational Institute. Ms. Garcia is a Senior Member of the Technical Staff at Sandia National Laboratories where she has worked for the past 16 years in international safeguards and physical security. Her past projects include development of an automated video review station, video and lighting design for a demonstration physical security system at a major U.S. airport, and project management of an integrated alarm communication and display system. She has taught classes at U.S. universities to initiate new programs in security engineering, internationally in the People's Republic of China, and to other government and industry groups. Ms. Garcia has written a textbook on the design and evaluation of physical protection systems for use in university security courses and is currently writing another text on vulnerability assessment of physical protection systems. Ms. Garcia is a member of the American Society for Industrial Security, is a Certified Protection Professional, and serves as a member of the ASIS Standing Committee on Academic Programs and the Security Architecture and Engineering Committee.

Richard P. Grassie, CPP is President of TECHMARK Security Integration, Inc., a Boston-based security design and integration firm with a wide range of Fortune 500, institutional, and government clients both in the United States and abroad. Mr. Grassie has designed and implemented complete asset protection programs for manufacturing and industrial sites, internet service provider hardware and service providers, internet start-up companies, biopharmaceutical companies, private residences, international petroleum terminals, transportation complexes, commercial office complexes, medical and educational institutions, college and university campuses, aerospace firms, publishing companies, communications centers, high rise commercial office, food processing, tobacco and pharmaceutical plants, international airports, government intelligence gathering and radar sites, military air bases and installations, court houses, vaccine research centers, high schools and middle schools, banks, and industrial parks. His systems design and integration expertise includes environmental designs, facility access controls, electronic intrusion detection, closed circuit television surveillance and assessment, local and remote site communications, networking remote sites over LAN/WAN, and computer-based central monitoring systems. He is equally well-versed in security technology, crime prevention, security awareness, policies and procedures, and security personnel. During the early stages of his career, he was a sworn police officer, an urban crime analyst and manager of technical assistance to police and prosecutor agencies for the U.S. Department of Justice's Integrated Career Criminal Apprehension Program. Mr. Grassie also served for 15 years as Director of Project Development for one of the world's leading security systems integrators and managed security design and installation projects in the Pacific Rim, South America, Middle East, and Europe.

George D. Haddow. Principal, Bullock & Haddow LLC, Washington, D.C.; Adjunct Professor, Institute for Crisis, Disaster and Risk Management, George Washington University, Washington, D.C.; former Deputy Chief of Staff and White House Liaison, Federal Emergency Management Agency (FEMA), Washington, D.C.; Bachelor of Arts, Washington College, Chestertown, MD; Masters of Urban and Regional Planning (MURP), University of New Orleans; co-Author of *Introduction to Emergency Management,* Butterworth-Heinemann; co-Author of *Introduction to Homeland Security,* Butterworth-Heinemann.

Richard J. Heffernan, CPP, CISM. President of R.J. Heffernan and Associates, Inc., Guilford, CT. Senior advisor and consultant to business and government on risk management of information, products, and people; member of Information Systems Security Association, Information Security Audit and Control Association and American Society for Industrial Security International (ASIS); Past Chairman, ASIS Information Asset Protection Council; and former member, National Counter

Intelligence Center Advisory Board; author and principal investigator of the ASIS Trends in Intellectual Property Theft Survey Report, and the ASIS Proprietary Information Loss Survey Reports, 1991–2006. Mr. Heffernan has testified before the U.S. Congress concerning espionage targeting and best practices in information security. Representing the 30,000+ members of ASIS before the U.S. Congress, his testimony was a key element in defining the need for and shaping the Economic Espionage Act.

Robert B. Iannone, CPP. President, Iannone Security Management, Inc., Fountain Valley, CA; former Adjunct Professor, School of Business, California State University, San Marcos, CA; former Adjunct Professor, Department of Criminal Justice, California State University, Long Beach, CA; former Adjunct Professor, Administration of Justice, Golden West College, Huntington Beach, CA; former Manager of Security, Hughes Aircraft Company, Torrance, CA; former Manager of Security and Investigations, Rockwell International Corporation, El Segundo, CA; former Security Inspector, Douglas Aircraft Company, Long Beach, CA; Member, American Society for Industrial Security; former Chapter Chairman, Greater Los Angeles Chapter, American Society for Industrial Security; Member, Board of Directors, Research Security Administrators; Member, International Association of Professional Security Consultants; Recipient of the James S. Cogswell Award, Department of Defense; bachelor of Science, California State University, Long Beach, CA; Master of Science, LaVerne University, LaVerne, CA; co-author of "Security, Higher Training, and Internship," *Security Management* and "Is an Ex the Best Candidate?" *Security Management*; contributing author, "Requirements Specification For An Integrated Electronic Security System," *"Risk Analysis and The Security Survey."*

Steven R. Keller, CPP is a Certified Protection Professional, and with 36 years in security related positions, he is Board Certified in Security Management. He is the former Executive Director of Protection Services and Construction Projects Advisor for the Art Institute of Chicago. Steve is the author of over 40 articles in professional publications, and is a frequent speaker at AAM and regional museum conferences. His written contributions include sections of "The Encyclopedia of Security" and sections pertaining to security technology for Microsoft's "Encarta Encyclopedia." He is a former chairman of ASIS International's Committee on Museums, Libraries, and Cultural Properties and has been a member of AAM's security committee for over 20 years. He has taught museum burglar and fire alarm design seminars at numerous venues including New York University, and was an author of "The Suggested Guidelines for Museum Security," the prevailing standard. He has been interviewed by all major TV networks, National Public Radio, and BBC on museum security issues. He is the recipient of the ASIS International's President's Award of Merit and "Security" Magazine's Executive Achievement Award. He has been a speaker at the Smithsonian's National Conference on Cultural Property Protection 19 of the past 25 years. He is Principal Consultant of Steve Keller and Associates, Inc. He recently authored "The Instant Museum Security Department Policy Manual" and a software package for managing a museum security operation, "The Security Department Knowledge Base." In 2006, Mr. Keller was inducted into the Centennial Honor Roll of the American Association of Museums.

Daniel B. Kennedy, PhD, CPP. Professor, Department of Sociology and Criminal Justice, University of Detroit Mercy, Detroit, MI; Consulting and testifying expert in premises liability, negligent security litigation, and use of force Issues; former Probation Officer and Police Academy Director. Member of American Society for Industrial Security, International Association of Chiefs of Police, and International Society of Crime Prevention Practitioners; former Chairman, Academic Programs Committee of American Society of Industrial Security; recipient of Chairman of the Year, American Society for Industrial Security; Faculty Award for Excellence, University of Detroit; Bachelor of Arts, Master of Arts, and Doctor of Philosophy, Wayne State University, Detroit, MI; graduate of the National Crime Prevention Institute and the author of seven books and over 80 professional articles appearing in such periodicals as *Security Journal, Journal of Security Administration, Security Management, Journal of Police Science and Administration, Justice Quarterly, Journal of Criminal Justice, Professional Psychology, Journal of Social Psychology,* and *Journal of Business and Psychology.* Dr. Kennedy is currently active in the design of computer security and intelligence analysis curricula in response to the war on terrorism.

Carl E. King. Chief Executive Officer, President, Akers Biosciences Houston, TX; Chief Executive Officer, Insights Corporate Selection Systems, Houston, TX; Chief Executive Officer WNCK, Inc., Houston, TX; Major, U.S. Marine Corps, Retired. Member of International Association of Chiefs of Police; American Society for Industrial Security; Private Security Services Council of American Society of Industrial Security; FBI National Academy; National Order of Battle Field Commissions; listed in *Who's Who in Finance and Industry, 1989–1992*; listed in *Who's Who in Security, 1989–1992*; named to *Inc.* magazine's 1990 list of 500 Fastest Growing Companies; finalist for Houston's Entrepreneur of the Year; recipient of two Purple Hearts, the Bronze Star, Presidential Unit Citation, and other Vietnam awards. Bachelor of Science in Criminal Justice, University of Nebraska at Omaha; Bachelor of Laws, Lasalle Extension University, Chicago, IL; Master of Arts in Business Management, Central Michigan University; graduate of the Federal Bureau of Investigation National Academy, Quantico, VA; graduate of the Military Police Officers Advanced Course. Author of "Why Test for Alcohol?," "When Is a Drug Not a Drug?," and "Alcohol Abuse on the Job," *Security Management*.

Glen Kitteringham, MSc, CPP, FIISec. Senior Manager, Security & Life Safety, Brookfield Properties Corp., Calgary, Alberta; former Internal Investigator, Hudson Bay Company; former Loss Prevention Officer, Hudson Bay Company; Member, ASIS International, International Foundation for Protection Officers (IFPO), National Fire Protection Association, BOMA Canada, International Institute of Security; former Chair, Calgary/Southern Alberta Chapter of ASIS; former Vice-Chair, Commercial Real Estate Council, ASIS; member Business Practices Council, ASIS; Vice-Chair International Advisory Board, IFPO; former Chair, BOMA Calgary Public Safety Committee, BOMA; member BOMA Canada Public Safety Committee; Director, BOMA Calgary; Fellow, International Institute of Security. Obtained Diploma in Criminology from Mount Royal College, Calgary, Alberta, 1992; Security Management Certificate from University of Calgary, Alberta, 1998; Masters of Science Post Graduate Degree from University of Leicester, United Kingdom, 2001; General Management Certificate, University of Calgary, Alberta, 2005; awarded Crime Prevention Award from Province of Alberta Solicitor General's Office, 2003; written, published or presented more than 80 times on various aspects of security management and/or life safety including six training videos with the Professional Security Training Network (PSTN); author of *Environmental Crime Control Theory; IFPO Certified Protection Officer Training Manual, 7th Ed*, Butterworth-Heinemann; contributing member *Threat Advisory System (TASR) Guideline: Guideline for Preparations Relative to the Department of Homeland Security Advisory System*, ASIS International; author of the soon-to-be published *Security Management Guidance for the Commercial Real Estate Industry*, ASIS International; author of Dissertation entitled, "A study of two types of vertical crime pattern analysis in the commercial multi-tenanted high-rise structure" for a Masters degree in Security and Crime Risk Management, March 2001. This dissertation currently resides within the National Criminal Justice Reference Service Database, a division of the United States Department of Justice. Member of a team researching Canadian Shoplifting Offenders Study, coordinated through PRCI Ltd. (U.K.) as part of a four-country study (Spain, Brazil, England, Canada).

Robert L. Kohr, CSP, CPP. Senior Consultant, Arthur D. Little, Inc., Cambridge, MA; Principal, Kohr & Associates, Mt. Airy, MD; Director of Design and Director of Technical Services for Loss Prevention, Marriott Corporation, Washington, D.C. Member, American Society of Safety Engineers; member, American Society for Industrial Security; member, American Society for Testing and Materials; member, National Safety Council; member, National Fire Protection Association; member, Building Officials and Code Administration International; member, American Hotel and Motel Association; Secretary, ASTM F13 and C21.06. Bachelor of Science, Geology, Virginia Polytechnic Institute and State University. Author of *Accident Prevention for Hotels, Motels, and Restaurants*, Van Nostrand Reinhold; "Washroom Safety, Things to Consider," and "Slip, Slidin' Away," *Safety & Health*; "Safety Factor in Bathroom Design," "Recognizing and Preventing Slip and Fall Accidents," "How Safe Are Marble

Floors?," and "It Could Be A Crime," *Lodging*; "Security By Design" and "Mastering the Challenge of Securing a Budget Motel," *Security Management*; "A Study of the Comparative Slipperiness of Floor Cleaning Chemicals," "Worker Safety in the Kitchen: A Comparative Study of Footwear versus Walking and Working Surfaces," and "Bucknell University F-13 Workshop to Evaluate Various Slip Resistance Measuring Devices," *Standardization News*; "Slip Resistance and the Designer," *Progressive Architecture*.

Herman A. Kruegle. President, Avida Inc., former President, Visual Methods, Inc.; former Section Head, Electro-Optics Division, ITT Avionics, Clifton, NJ; former Manager, Laser and Electro-Optical Systems Division, Holobeam, Inc., Paramus, NJ; former Assistant Chief Engineer, Spectroscopic and Electro-Optical Laboratory, Warner and Swasey Co. Member, Institute of Electrical and Electronic Engineers (IEEE); member, American Society for Industrial Security (ASIS); Chairman, 1992, 1993, Closed Circuit Television Manufacturers Association (CCTMA); awarded six patents in security, electro-optical, and laser fields; Bachelor of Science in Electrical Engineering, Brooklyn Polytechnic Institute; Master of Science in Electrical Engineering, New York University; Licensed New York State Professional Engineer; author of numerous publications in professional security and electro-optics journals; contributing author, *Handbook of Loss Prevention and Crime Prevention*, *Controlling Cargo Theft*, *Museum, Archive and Library Security*, Butterworth-Heinemann; author of *Lens Primer Series*, CCTV Source Book; author of *CCTV Surveillance*, Elsevier, Butterworth-Heinemann.

William A. "Tony" Lavelle. Consultant, TYH Police & Military Canine Services, Sacramento, CA; Vice President, Detection Support Services, Walnut Creek CA; Lobbyist, International Explosive Detection Dog Association, Wilmington, DE; Adjunct Professor, Division of Criminal Justice, California State University, Sacramento ("CSUS"), CA; Director of Force Protection, Travis AFB, CA; Deputy Chief of Police, Osan Air Base, Republic of Korea and Rhein-Main Air Base, Germany; National Chairman, International Explosive Detection Dog Association; Member, International Association of Bomb Technicians & Investigators, American Society for Industrial Security, Military Officers Association of America, U.S. Air Force Security Police Association, American Legion, China Post 1, Disabled American Veterans Association, International Chiefs of Police Association, and American Society of Law Enforcement Trainers. Significant career achievements include being handpicked to command a prototype force-protection rapid deployment unit created to support worldwide military special missions, with responsibilities for anti-terrorism actions and force protection command and control, safeguarding U.S. and Allied Armed Forces aircraft and ground personnel, including missions to Somalia, Haiti, and South America, Africa, and Southwest Asia. At CSUS, developed the criminal justice division's first web-based course program and the division's first professional speakers bureau; selected as the top faculty associate in the 45 member Criminal Justice Division. Established and made operational Detection Support Services (DSS), an organization that provides explosive detection services. DSS deployed 20 bomb-dog teams to Iraq to support U.S. Forces during *Operation Iraqi Freedom*. Master of Science Degree, Criminal Justice, CSUS; author of *State Terrorism and the Death Squad: A Study of the Phenomenon*, Air Force Institute of Technology, Wright-Patterson Air Force Base and University Publications of America, Bethesda, MD, 1993; co-author of *Global Mission Standard for Explosive Detection Dog Teams*, International Explosive Detection Dog Association, 2004. Infantryman, U.S. Army Airborne, with one combat tour in Vietnam; commissioned officer, U.S. Air Force Security Police. Decorations include the Bronze Star medal with "V" device; Purple Heart; U.S. Air Force Meritorious Service Medal; and the U.S. Army Combat Infantry Badge.

Lindsey M. Lee, BS, MA is an Investigative Consultant for the Investigations Department, forensic clinician on the Behavioral Sciences Team, and Account Manager for Business Controls, Inc.'s Anonymous Incident Reporting Systems, MySafeWorkplace and MySafeCampus. She is responsible for consulting and supporting undercover and special investigations, as well as the training, implementation, and supervision of undercover operatives. Additionally, Ms. Lee is assisting in the development and expansion of the Behavioral Sciences Department to include forensically-related evaluations, trainings, and other activities. She furthermore manages and supervises the call center representatives responsible for the intake of highly sensitive reports on the MySafeWorkplace and MySafeCampus systems. Related to her call center management, Ms. Lee conducts training, oversees the quality assurance program, and provides general support for all agents. She also guides the training, implementation, and rollout of the MySafeWorkplace and MySafeCampus systems for many premier organizations. Ms. Lee is a contributing editor for *Security Newsletters*, published by Business Controls, Inc. In 2002, Ms. Lee obtained a Bachelor of Science in Experimental Psychology from Millikin University in Decatur, Illinois and a Master of Arts in Forensic Psychology from the University of Denver, Denver, Colorado, in 2005. She completed a nine-month clinical internship with the Division of Youth Corrections at Mount View Youth Services Center, Denver, Colorado. Her responsibilities included assessing committed youth offenders for the presence or absence of mental health impairment, making recommendations for appropriate placement, and scheduling and conducting follow up therapeutic sessions with the most disturbed. Additionally, she wrote evaluation reports to guide the placement board in their decision-making. Prior to her arrival in Denver, Ms. Lee worked in the Division of Women and Family Services for the Illinois Department of Corrections at Lincoln Correctional Center (LCC), a medium security women's prison. At LCC, she assisted in release planning, interviewed female offenders for appropriate class placement, and co-facilitated psychoeducational groups, such as anger management and writing expression. Furthermore, Ms. Lee has extensive experience in conducting original psychological research and developing computer-based psychological experiments. Ms. Lee's professional affiliations include: The Association of Threat Assessment Professionals (ATAP) and Phi Kappa Phi National Academic Honor Society.

Liz Martínez. Author of *The Retail Manager's Guide to Crime and Loss Prevention: Protecting Your Business from Theft, Fraud and Violence* (2004, Looseleaf Law); "Using the Internet to Get a Job in the Criminal Justice Field," Chapter 12 of *Career Planning in Criminal Justice, 3rd Ed.* (1998, Anderson Publishing); editor of *Public Safety Funding Solutions* Newsletter and *Beyond the Badge* Magazine. Fiction credits include editing and contributing to the anthology *Cop Tales 2000* (2000, .38 Special Press); as well as short stories in the anthology *Manhattan Noir* (2006, Akashic Books); *COMBAT Literary Journal*; OrchardPressMysteries.com; *Civil Service Journal*; and *Police Officer's Quarterly*. Long-time contributor to domestic and international publications, including Law Enforcement Technology, Loss Prevention, Security Technology & Design, SecurityInfoWatch.com, Security Today (India), TheBackup.com, and many others; instructor, security and criminal justice, in the security management degree program at Interboro Institute, a two-year college in New York City, NY State Certified Security General Topics Instructor; retail security/loss prevention consultant and trainer; lecturer on the topics of organized crime, criminal justice, security and publishing for ASIS International, Contingency Planning Expo, Interboro Institute, John Jay College of Criminal Justice, Learning Annex, New Jersey Opticians Association, Police Writers Conference, and Vision Expo West; trained USMC officers to deal with the media during the 1994 East Coast Commanders Media Training Symposium. Former NYPD; Auxiliary Police Officer; formerly with Pre-Trial Services, Fairfax County, Virginia; Bachelor of Arts in Criminal Justice, John Jay College of Criminal Justice, New York, NY; Master of Arts in writing popular fiction, Seton Hill University, Greensburg, Pennsylvania; memberships in ASIS International, Criminal Justice Educators Association of New York State, National Native American Law Enforcement Association, Mystery Writers of America, Public Safety Writers Association, and Sisters in Crime.

Brad Mathers, MA is an Investigative Consultant and Forensic Clinician in the Behavioral Sciences Department at Business Controls, Inc. He is involved in the development and expansion of the Behavioral Sciences Department, which includes conducting forensically-related evaluations, trainings, pre-employment screening, fitness-for-duty evaluations, threat assessments, and police psychology. He is involved in the Special Investigations division at Business Controls, Inc., to include workplace investigations and corporate consulting. He is the primary editor for Security Newsletters, Business Controls, Inc.'s monthly newsletter. Mr. Mathers earned his Bachelor of Arts in Psychology from the University of Colorado, Boulder in 1999 and later earned his Master of Arts in Forensic Psychology at The University of Denver in 2002. He has been a Neighborhood Justice Coordinator for the Denver District Attorney's Office, during which his duties included the mediation of victim-offender conferences stemming from juvenile court. He has been a Forensic Clinician for the Colorado Department of Corrections in Denver County. His responsibilities included the treatment and evaluation of a population of individuals with criminal involvement and a psychological disposition. From this experience, he brings specialized knowledge concerning the psychological machinations of the criminal mind, violence and risk assessment, appropriate implementation of psychological interventions, keen diagnostic interpretation, and suicide and crisis intervention. Mr. Mathers has also been a Litigation and Jury Consultant for Courtroom Performance, Inc., a Colorado-based litigation consulting firm. As a Litigation and Jury Consultant, he assisted attorneys in developing effective presentation styles and litigation strategies, as well as selecting favorable juries. Mr. Mathers' previous clinical experiences have included administering psychological assessments and conducting clinical interviews for the purposes of creating a diagnostic model for clientele, assessing violence and risk potential, and coordinating treatment efforts with psychiatrists, psychologists, hospital staff, and correctional staff. In addition, Mr. Mathers has provided expert testimony and has participated in parole, probation, and disability hearings. Mr. Mathers' professional affiliations include the American Society of Trial Consultants and the Association of Threat Assessment Professionals.

Leon C. Mathieu, CFE. Security Director, Conocophillips Global Security, Houston, TX; former Chief of Investigations, The Charter Company, Jacksonville, FL; former Detective, Metropolitan Dade County Police, Miami, FL; former Insurance Adjuster, Employer's Service Corporation, Coral Gables, FL; former Instructor, Miami-Dade Community College, Miami, FL; member, American Society for Industrial Security; former Chapter Chairman, Jacksonville, Florida, Chapter of ASIS; Certified Fraud Examiner (CFE) member, International Society of Crime Prevention Practitioners; member, Energy Security Council, Houston, TX. Bachelor of Science, Florida International University; and Master of Science, Nova University.

Robert D. McCrie, PhD, CPP. Professor of Security Management, John Jay College of Criminal Justice, the City University of New York; founding editor and now editor emeritus of *Security Journal*. Founder and editor of Security Letter; member, ASIS International; recipient of President's Award of Merit, Urban History Association; Breslin Award, International Security Management Association; John J. Duffy Award, National Council of Investigation and Security Services; and Harvey J. Watson Award, National Association of Security Companies; Certified Protection Professional; author of *Security Operations Management*, Butterworth-Heinemann; *Readings in Security Management*, ASIS International; and numerous articles in the field.

Chris E. McGoey, CPP, CSP. President, McGoey Security Consulting, Phoenix, AZ; Publisher of security books, Aegis Books, Oakland, CA; former Security Manager, Neiman-Marcus, San Francisco, CA; former Corporate Loss Prevention and Region Security Manager, Southland Corporation, Dallas, TX; former Security Consultant, Big Bear Markets, San Diego, CA; former Security Manager, S.S. Kresge Corporation, San Diego, CA; former Criminal Investigator, Santa Clara County Public Defender's Office, San Jose, CA; member, International Association of Professional Security Consultants; member, American Society for Industrial Security; member, Retail Security Association of Northern California; member, California Crime Prevention Officers Association; member, California Association of Licensed Investigators; member, National Association of Legal Investigators; Board of Directors, International Association of Professional Security Consultants; District Governor, California Association of Licensed Investigators. Recipient of the President's Award for District Governor of the Year, California Association of Licensed Investigators; and recipient of the Governor's Crime Prevention Award, State of Nevada; associate of the Arts, Police Science, Chabot College, Hayward, CA; Bachelor of Science, Criminal Justice Administration, San Jose State University; Master of Science,

Criminal Justice Administration (12 units completed), San Jose State University; author of "Security; Adequate…or Not?," "The Complete Guide to Premises Liability Litigation," and "Premises Liability Investigation," *CALI*; "A Model of Management," and "Effective Security Design Must be Flexible," *Access Control*.

Steven W. McNally, MA, CPP, PSP, PCI, CFE. Director of Public Safety and Security, Williams Island Club and Property Owner's Association, Aventura, FL; University Adjunct Professor and Program Developer; former Deputy Administrator/Chief of Security, Wackenhut Corrections, Pompano Beach, FL; former Independent Security/Investigative Consultant/President, IntelQuest, Inc., Miami FL; former South Florida and Caribbean Regional Security Manager, McDonalds Corporation, Boca Raton, FL; former Miami-Dade County Police Officer and Detective, Miami, FL; former Corrections Officer, Michigan Department of Corrections, Plymouth, MI; former United States Air Force, Aircraft Armament System Specialist, Strategic Air Command, Wurtsmith AFB; member ASIS International, National Association of Chiefs of Police, Association of Certified Fraud Examiners, International Association of Protection Officers, Academy of Criminal Justice Sciences, and the National Fire Protection Association; Bachelor of Science in Criminology and Criminal Justice—Cum Laude, Eastern Michigan University; Master of Arts in Business and Organizational Security Management—Academic Honors; ASIS triple board certified in security management (Certified Protection Professional); physical security (Physical Security Professional), and investigations (Certified Professional Investigator); Certified in fraud examination (Certified Fraud Examiner) by the Association of Certified Fraud Examiners.

William R. McQuirter, CPO, CPOI. General Manager, Iron Horse Security, National Capital District, Ottawa, Ontario; former District Manager, Securitas Canada Limited, National Capital District, Ottawa, Ontario; former Security Manager, Digital Equipment of Canada Limited, Ottawa, Ontario; former Technical Services Manager, Atomic Energy of Canada Limited, Chalk River Nuclear Laboratories, Chalk River, Ontario; former President of Community Sentinels Company Limited, Ottawa, Ontario; former Police Officer, Ontario Provincial Police, Killaloe, Ontario; member of Algonquin College Security Management and Law and Security Program Advisory Council, charter member and Chairman of Ottawa Chapter of ASIS; former Regional Vice President of ASIS for Canada; member of CSIS; guest lecturer and presenter to RCMP, BOMA, CSIS and ASIS on various security related topics including Public and Private Policing; Certified Protection Officer Instructor with IFPO; member of Greater Ottawa Chamber of Commerce; author of a contract security article pertaining to public policing published in "Papyrus," a newsletter for the International Association of Museums and Galleries, Graduate of Law and Security, Ottawa, Ontario.

Adolfo Meana, Jr., Capt, USAF. Security Inspector, Defense Threat Reduction Agency (DTRA), Albuquerque, NM; former Chief of Concepts Division, Air Force Force Protection Battlelab, Lackland AFB, TX; former Operations Officer, 39th Security Forces Squadron (SFS), Incirlik AB, Turkey; lifetime member of the Air Force Association; Joint Service Commendation Medal with Oak Leaf Cluster; Air Force Commendation Medal with three Oak Leaf Clusters; Joint Meritorious Unit Award; Bachelor of Arts, Geography, University of Florida, Gainesville, FL.

Robert W. Miller, PhD. Dr. Miller has more than 20 years training and training development experience within Government and commercial sectors. In addition to serving as Advanced Systems Technology's Chief Knowledge Officer, he is currently serving as an Adjunct Professor and Corporate advisor at Cameron University, Lawton, Oklahoma. In that role he is providing instruction to undergraduate students in the application of distance learning technologies to governmental and commercial training situations. He is also advisor to the Multimedia Departments Curriculum committee. He has developed more than 40 computer-based training, web based training and performance improvement products. Dr. Miller holds a PhD in Instructional Psychology & Technology from the University of Oklahoma and a Master of Behavioral Science (Human Relations) from

Cameron University, Lawton, Oklahoma. Dr. Miller's publications and presentations include: *Keeping Captains "On Track": Support for the U.S. Army Combined Arms & Services Staff School Advanced Distance Learning Program (CAS3 ADL)*, Centra Summit 2004, Boston, MA, March, 2004 (co-authored with Daniel O. Pupek and Frank Colletti); *Internet-based Distance Learning: Implications of Emerging Technologies for Public Safety Training*, 2002, The Executive Forum, Illinois Law Enforcement Executive Institute 2(3), pp. 109–120; *The Shareable Content Object Reference Model (SCORM): A Primer for Small Businesses*, Oklahoma Distance Learning Association, *April* 2002 (co-authored with Dale Wheelis and Donald Aguilar); *Configuration Management for Web-Based Instructional Content*, Centra Summit '99, Boston, MA, October, 1999; *Integrating Environmental Tasks Into Job Performance*, National Association of Environmental Professionals, 1998 (co-authored with Barbara O'Keeffe); *Using Internet-Based Training to Integrate Environmental Compliance into Job Performance*, 1998, IX Congreso Internacional Sobre Tecnologia Y Educacion a Distancia, Consorcio Red De Educacion a Distancia, San Jose, Costa Rica; *Field Manual FM 20-400, Military Environmental Protection* (co-authored with Chris Conrad, Dave Neeley, Charles Okrassa, and Dana Merkoulov); *Training Circular TC 20-401, The Soldier and the Environment* (co-authored with Dana Merkoulov).

Richard L. Moe, CPP. Former Director of Assets Preservation for S&A Restaurant Corp., Dallas, TX; former Director of Assets Protection for Metromedia Steakhouses, Inc., Dayton, OH; former Security Manager for Argonne National Laboratories-West, Idaho Falls, ID; former Director of Security for Sambo's Restaurants, Inc.; Lieutenant Colonel, U.S. Army (Retired); member, American Society for Industrial Security; member, International Security Management Association; member, National Food Service Security Council (NFSSC); member, International Association of Chiefs of Police; Chairman, National Food Service Security Council; Chairman, Food Service Security Standing Committee, ASIS; Chairman, Santa Barbara Chapter, ASIS. Recipient of ASIS Standing Committee Chairman of the Year Award, recipient of NFSSC Award for Life Time Achievement in Food Service Security; Bachelor of Science, University of Arizona; and Master of Science, George Washington University.

John R. Morris. President, VIDEOTRONIX, Inc., Burnsville, Minnesota and Denver, Colorado; former Vice President of North American Video Corporation; member, American Society for Industrial Security International and Minnesota Association of Parking Professionals; author of "Plugging into the Systems," *Security Management*.

John A. Nolan, III, CPP, OCP, is a retired operational intelligence officer who served in Asia, Central Europe, and the U.S. During his 22-year career, his assignments included intelligence collection, counterintelligence and Special Operations projects. He co-founded the Phoenix Consulting Group in 1990, which provides CI collection and analysis, Competitive Assurance™ and professional development programs for client firms worldwide. Client firms range from the Fortune 50 to the Inc. 500, in electronics, utilities and telecommunications, defense and aerospace, manufacturing, food products, pharmaceuticals, and financial services. Government agencies in the U.S. and several allied countries also avail themselves of the expertise of the Phoenix cadre in efforts ranging from specialized training to studies and analyses. He and his firm have been profiled in many leading business journals, and he is a frequently invited guest speaker both here and abroad. He serves as adjunct faculty at the Defense Intelligence College and the University of Alabama. Multilingual, he received his undergraduate degree from Mount Saint Mary's College, and his graduate degrees from Central Michigan University and the University of Southern California. Military decorations include the Legion of Merit, Bronze Star Medal (2nd Oak Leaf Cluster), Air Medal, and numerous other commendation and service decorations from the U.S. and foreign nations. He has authored nearly one hundred articles and monographs, has contributed chapters to six different books, and has authored four books of his own. His professional affiliations include the Society of Competitive Intelligence Professionals (Member, Board of Directors and President), the Association for Psychological Type, American Society for Industrial Security (former chapter chairman and other offices), OPSEC Professionals Society (Member, Board of Directors), National Military Intelligence Association, and the Association of Former Intelligence Officers.

Robert L. Oatman, CPP retired as Major and Chief of Detectives from Maryland's Baltimore County Police Department. During his long and varied career, he acquired a broad range of training and experience in crisis management leadership, executive protection, and criminal investigation. He developed and commanded the first Hostage Negotiation Team formed in the State of Maryland, successfully concluding over 100 hostage taking incidents. United States Secret Service training provided the foundation of his executive protection skills, which he used to administer protective operations for a variety of local, national and international officials and dignitaries. His command of the Criminal Investigative Division gave Major Oatman the opportunity to utilize the investigative and management skills acquired during a distinguished 20-year career. Since entering the private sector, Bob Oatman has provided consulting advice, management services, expert protective and investigative support and training to multi-national corporations both in the United States and abroad. Frequently called upon to analyze standing executive protection operations, he has been responsible for restructuring major corporate security programs. He managed executive protection operations for NBC during the Olympic Games in Seoul, Korea in 1988, Barcelona, Spain in 1992, Atlanta, Georgia in 1996 and Sydney, Australia in 2000. An expert on protective operations, Mr. Oatman is the author of *The Art of Executive Protection* (Noble House, 1997) and co-author of *You're the Target*, (New World Publishing, 1989). He was also a contributing author to Volumes I and II of *Providing Protective Services*, (Winchester Printers, 1991–1994). Mr. Oatman holds a Bachelor of Science in Criminal Justice from the University of Baltimore and is a graduate of the FBI National Academy and the Federal Executive Institute. He is a Certified Protection Professional and long standing member of the American Society for Industrial Security, FBI National Academy Associates, American Society of Law Enforcement Trainers and the Maryland Chief's of Police Association.

Denis O'Sullivan, CPP. President and CEO of PPM 2000, Inc. Formerly Corporate Security Advisor to the City of Edmonton; Unit Commander, Alberta Highway Patrol; Special Branch detective with An Garda Siochana (the Irish National Police Force); Instructor University of Alberta; holds memberships in IACLEA, IAHSS, and ASIS International. With ASIS International, he held the positions of Chapter Chair, Regional Vice President, Trustee of the ASIS Foundation, member of the Professional Certification Board, member of the Board of Directors and International Vice President on the Executive Committee. Most recently served as the ASIS Senior Regional Vice President for International Development. Awarded the ASIS Canadian Region Pioneer Award and most recently received the Edmonton Chapter Chairman's Recognition Award.

Raymond Payne, CPP has 25 years experience in senior management for major Physical Security manufacturers. In these leading companies, he was responsible for product development and product management teams. Ray has been a visionary in new product solutions for physical security. In the capacity of product development, Ray has been involved in the design of security systems for major government facilities in Washington, as well as worldwide government organizations. He has been intimately involved in the requirements and design of many fortune 100 enterprise solutions. Some of the major contributions to the physical security market are first to introduce IP Video/Audio Security; integrated PC Security System; GUI interface for CCTV control systems; Solid State Cameras in CCTV Security; first to implement VPhase Switching in the industry, and numerous New Product awards through SIA, ASIS, etc. His areas of interest and expertise include transitioning facilities from analog to IP Video, evaluating existing security systems for flaws and/or improvements, IP Video and IP Audio, Video Object Processing (extracting intelligence from video and audio), integrating all aspects of Physical Security through AI to prevent security risks, solving challenging problems in Physical and IT Security, and dedicated to advancing the technology and solutions to Physical and IT Security. Mr. Payne has been intimately involved in the design of security systems for many facilities in the government and commercial sectors. Some of the government projects are the U.S. Capitol Building, White House, Secret Service Headquarters, CIA Headquarters, TVA, Panama Canal, FBI, and NSA. In the commercial sector he has worked with John Deere, Caterpillar, American Express, Apple Computer, and Compaq.

Kimberly L. Pfaff, BS, MA is the Director of Operations and Behavioral Sciences Department at Business Controls, Inc. She is responsible for managing the consultative and special investigations division relating to forensic psychology, as well as defining and enhancing the forensic assessment program to include pre-employment screening, fitness-for-duty evaluations, threat assessments, and police psychology. She has built a team of three forensic clinicians who actively assist and direct the above services. Ms. Pfaff often trains on workplace violence, substance abuse, and mental illness in educational and organizational settings. Ms. Pfaff is also responsible for the continual enhancement and management of the implementation and customer service program relating to the Anonymous Incident Reporting Systems provided by BCI, as well as directly training and monitoring the call center representatives responsible for handling MySafeWorkplace calls. Ms. Pfaff is currently working toward her doctorate in Clinical Psychology at The University of Denver. Ms. Pfaff received a Bachelor of Science in psychology with a minor in biology from Indiana University. She received a Master of Arts in forensic psychology from the University of Denver. She completed a 12-month clinical internship at The Federal Correctional Institute (FCI) in Englewood, Colorado. From this prison environment, she brings specialized knowledge concerning the psychological functioning of the criminal mind, conflict management and resolution, life-skills training, and suicide and crisis intervention. Ms. Pfaff worked as part of the psychology team that engaged daily with medium-to-high security male inmates. Her clinical duties included pre-screening (consisting of clinical interviews and/or cognitive and personality assessments) of new inmates, individual therapy (cognitive-behavioral in nature), and group therapy (stress management and relaxation training). Other duties included formulating treatment plans for chronic care patients and making referrals to health services for possible psychotropic medications. Ms. Pfaff's previous clinical experiences include working as a victim's advocate in the Douglas County Probation Department in Castle Rock, Colorado. Working as a liaison between perpetrators and their victims, she informed victims of current changes in perpetrator status and answered questions pertaining to the criminal justice system. Ms. Pfaff also worked as a co-facilitator of male domestic violence perpetrator groups, providing therapy and assessment of their psychological needs through testing and interviewing. Ms. Pfaff's professional affiliations include: American Psychological Association, ASIS International, and the Association of Threat Assessment Professionals.

Philip P. Purpura, CPP. Director, Security and Criminal Justice Institute, Florence-Darlington Technical College, Florence, SC; Expert Witness; Security Consultant; former Security Manager and Investigator; member, Academic Programs Council, American Society for Industrial Security; master of Science, Criminal Justice, Eastern Kentucky University; and Bachelor of Science, Criminal Justice, University of Dayton; author of *Terrorism and Homeland Security: An Introduction with Applications* (2006), Elsevier Pub.; *Security & Loss Prevention: An Introduction*, 5th Edition (2007), Elsevier Pub.; *Security Handbook*, 2nd Edition (2002), Delmar, Butterworth-Heinemann Publishers; *Police & Community: Concepts and Cases* (2001), Allyn & Bacon; *Criminal Justice: An Introduction* (1997), Butterworth-Heinemann Publishers; *Retail Security & Shrinkage Protection* (1993) Butterworth-Heinemann Publishers; and *Modern Security & Loss Prevention Management* (1989), Butterworth-Heinemann Publishers.

James T. Roberts, Jr., CPP, CFE. United States Marshal, United States Marshals Service, Savannah, GA; former Director, Criminal Justice Technology Studies, Augusta Technical College; former adjunct instructor in Criminal Justice, Augusta State University; former adjunct instructor, Security Management Studies, Park College; former security and emergency management consultant, Odgen Environmental and Energy Services; former emergency management consultant, Westinghouse Savannah River Company; former emergency preparedness planner, Advanced Systems Technology; former senior staff member, security protection team, Science Applications International Corporation; former law enforcement management consultant; former director of law enforcement and security, U.S. Army Medical Command; former district commander, director of investigative operations, and deputy commander, U.S. Army Criminal Investigation Command; former physical security staff officer, Office of the Chief of Army Law Enforcement; former team member and designated team chief, Commission on Accreditation for Law Enforcement Agencies; numerous presentations on emergency management and security subjects; former book manuscript reviewer, Butterworth-Heinneman, publisher; author, Military Policeman's Handbook (three printings), Tuttle, publisher; numerous articles for professional journals; Master in Education, Georgia Southern University, Bachelor in Public Administration, Virginia Tech University; former member, Professional Certification Board, former Regional Vice President and Chapter Chairman, American Society for Industrial Security; member, education and training committee, International Association of Chiefs of Police, former member, Board of directors, International Foundation of Protection Officers; member, American Society for Law Enforcement Trainers; board-approved Certified Protection Professional; Certified Fraud Examiner.

Lester S. Rosen is an attorney at law and President of Employment Screening Resources, a national background screening company located in California. ESR was rated as the top screening firm in the U.S. in the first independent industry study. He is the author of *The Safe Hiring Manual—Complete Guide to Keeping Criminals, Impostors, and Terrorists Out of Your Workplace*, Facts on Demand Press, the first comprehensive book on employment screening. He is also the author of the first professional development education course on safe hiring and background screening, including 30 hours of online training. He is also a consultant, writer, and frequent presenter nationwide on pre-employment screening and safe hiring issues. He has qualified and testified in the California and Arkansas Superior Courts as an expert witness on issues surrounding safe hiring and due diligence. His speaking appearances have included numerous national and statewide conferences. He is a former deputy District Attorney and criminal defense attorney and has taught criminal law and procedure at the University of California Hastings College of the Law. His jury trials have included murder, death penalty, and federal cases. He graduated UCLA with Phi Beta Kappa honors, and received a JD degree from the University of California at Davis, serving on the Law Review. He holds the highest attorney rating of AV in the national Martindale-Hubbell listing of American Attorneys. He is also a licensed Private Investigator in California. Mr. Rosen was the chairperson of the steering committee that founded the National Association of Professional Background Screeners (NAPBS), a 400-member professional trade organization for the screening industry. He was also elected to the first board of directors NAPBS and served as the co-chairman in 2004.

Charles A. Sennewald, CPP, CSC, CPO. Independent Security Management Consultant in Esco-ndido, CA; former Security Director for the Broadway Department Stores; former Chief of Campus Police, Claremont, CA; former Deputy Sheriff, Los Angeles County; former assistant Professor at California State University at Los Angeles; founder and first President, International Association of Professional Security Consultants (IAPSC); and former Standing Committee Chairman and member of the American Society for Industrial Security; recipient of *Security World* magazine's Merit Award and the IAPSC'S Distinguished Service Accolade; twice designated by the U.S. Department of Commerce as the Security Industry Representative on missions to Sweden, Denmark, Japan, China, and Hong Kong. Bachelor of Science, California State University at Los Angeles; author of various Butterworth-Heinemann-Elsevier books: *Effective Security Management*, 4th Edition, *The Process of Investigation*, 3rd Edition, *Security Consulting*, 3rd Edition, and *Shoplifting*. In production at the time of this writing is one ASIS book: *Shoplifting: Managing the Problem*.

Amy L. Slettedahl, BA, MA. Forensic Clinician on the Behavioral Sciences Team at Business Controls, Inc. and is responsible for helping in the development and expansion of forensic psychology related services, including assessment and training. She is also a senior coordinator of special investigations and undercover investigations, respectively. Additionally, Ms. Slettedahl manages client accounts for both MySafeWorkplace and MySafeCampus systems at Business Controls, Inc. (BCI). Ms. Slettedahl has been employed at BCI for two years and is responsible for training and managing high-caliber organizations prior to, during, and following implementation of anonymous incident reporting systems for the MySafeWorkplace and MySafeCampus. Ms. Slettedahl is a contributing editor for *Security Newsletters*, published by Business Controls, Inc. She obtained a Bachelor of Arts in psychology, with an emphasis in legal studies in 2002 from the University of Northern Colorado, and graduated with a Master of Arts in forensic psychology at the University of Denver in 2005. She completed a nine-month clinical internship with the Colorado Department of Corrections at the Denver Women's Correctional Facility (DWCF) in Denver, Colorado. Her clinical interaction with substance abusing female offenders as well as acute mentally ill offenders gives her specialized knowledge in the psychological functioning of the female criminal mind and addiction. Ms. Slettedahl was trained in the assessment and evaluation of substance abusing offenders, made treatment recommendations for incarcerated offenders, and facilitated a cognitive-behavioral/psychoeducational group with special-needs offenders. Her other clinical duties included assisting in the determination of risk/custody levels for incoming offenders, formulating community based treatment recommendations for the parole board and working with perpetrators and victims of sexual abuse. Ms. Slettedahl has specialized training in disaster response and has also worked at an inpatient, locked psychiatric facility in Greeley, Colorado. She co-facilitated inpatient treatment groups, monitored psychotropic medications and related effects, and developed discharge treatment plans. Ms. Slettedahl's professional affiliations include: Psi-Chi, National Honor Society in Psychology, and she is a Board Member for the Association of Threat Assessment Professionals (ATAP)-Colorado Chapter.

Don Sturgis, CPP. Physical Security Consultant; Senior Consultant, Ray Bernard Consulting Services; former Product Manager, Cardkey Systems, Simi Valley, CA; former Director of Marketing–Access Control Products, American Magnetics Corporation, Carson, CA; former Manager, Product Management, Rusco Electronic Systems, Inc., Glendale, CA; member, American Society for Industrial Security; Chapter Treasurer, California Inland Empire Chapter of ASIS; Mentor, ASIS Region III CPP Review Class; 2005 Recipient, Minot Dotson Award, ASIS Region III; Omicron Delta Kappa Honor Society and Student Body President, American University, Washington, D.C. Specialist, 3rd Class, U.S. Army, Scientific and Professional Program, Army Ballistic Missile Agency, Huntsville, AL; Bachelor of Arts, American University, Washington, D.C.; Master of Science and Master of Business Administration, West Coast University, Los Angeles, CA; co-inventor on three patents: bi-directional communication protocol used between computer systems and intelligent terminals; degraded mode operations for card readers; and self-contained programmable terminal for security systems; articles published in *Access Control & Security Systems Magazine*: "Product Overview—Magstripe Access Cards Attract Users," and "Security Technology Defeats Vehicle Theft and Driver License Fraud in Mexico," plus an eight-part series of articles on security system testing.

Kathleen M. Sweet is currently an Associate Professor in the Department of Aviation Technology at Purdue University, where she teaches courses in Aviation Security, Terrorism, and Strategic Intelligence. She is CEO and President of Risk Management Security Group, and is certified by the UK and Irish Department of Transport to teach air cargo security. Dr. Sweet received her undergraduate degree from Franklin and Marshall College in Lancaster, Pennsylvania, in Russian Area Studies and she has a Master's Degree in history from Temple University. She also has been admitted to the bar in Pennsylvania and Texas after graduating from Beasley School of Law, and Temple University in Philadelphia, PA. She is a graduate of many Air Force and civilian training programs. After graduating from law school, Dr. Sweet joined Wyeth International Pharmaceuticals as a legal specialist focused on licensing agreements between Wyeth and international agencies. She later joined the U.S. Air Force and initially was a member of the Judge Advocate General's (JAG) Department. She frequently served as Director of Military Justice at the Base and Numbered Air Force level. After 15 years as a JAG officer, and generally engaged in prosecuting cases on behalf of the military, she transferred to the 353rd Special Operations Wing as a military political affairs officer. She was later an intelligence officer assigned to HQ AMC as an executive officer and briefer. In 1995, she became an Assistant Air Attaché to the Russian Federation. As an attaché, she was engaged in liaison work not only with the Russian Air Force but also the Federal Security Bureau, at which time she became interested in counter terrorism efforts. Her final Air Force assignment was as an instructor at the Air War College where she taught in the International Security Studies division. She later became an Associate Professor at St. Cloud State University in the Department of Criminal Justice and an Associate Professor at Embry Riddle Aeronautical University, teaching security and intelligence related courses. She is the author of four books: *Terrorism and Airport Security*, Edwin Mellen Press, March 2002; *Aviation and Airport Security: Terrorism and Safety Concerns*, Prentice Hall Publishers, November 2003; *The Transportation Security Directory*, Grey House Publishing, January 2005; and *Transportation and Cargo Security: Threats and Solutions*, (Prentice Hall Publishers, August 2005). She is considered an expert in the field of airport, aviation, and air cargo security and has been well published in the fields of international space programs and associated treaties, space based offensive weapons, bio-terrorism, and aviation security. Her company, Risk Management Security Group (RMSG), doing business in Ireland as RMSG Ireland Ltd., engages in all aspects of consulting in transportation-related security including the preparation of threat and vulnerability assessments and security awareness training. As CEO of RMSG, she is certified by the United Kingdom and Irish Department of Transport to teach air cargo security. RMSG and RMSG Ireland Ltd. engage in all aspects of consulting in transportation-related security, including the preparation of threat and vulnerability assessments and security awareness training. She is the author of *Terrorism and Airport Security*; *Aviation and Airport Security: Terrorism and Safety Concerns*; *The Transportation Security Directory*; and *Transportation and Cargo Security: Threats and Solutions*. She has been well published in the fields of international space programs and associated treaties, space-based offensive weapons, bio-terrorism, and aviation security.

Peter E. Tarlow, PhD. Expert specializing in the impact of crime and terrorism on the tourism industry, event risk management, tourism, and economic development; PhD in sociology from Texas A&M University. Teacher of courses on crime and terrorism and tourism development; security consultant to numerous U.S. government agencies such as U.S. Bureau of Reclamation, U.S. Customs Service, U.S. National Park Service, and U.S. Bureau of Prisons; lecturer at major universities around the world. Consultant to the Royal Canadian Mounted Police, United Nation's WTO (World Tourism Organization), and the Centers for Disease Control and Prevention; speaker throughout North and Latin America, the Middle East and Europe on the sociology of terrorism, its impact on tourism security, and risk management; trainer of numerous police departments throughout the world on TOPS (Tourism Oriented Policing Skills); publisher of numerous academic and applied research articles, books, and chapters of books on security; writer and publisher of "Tourism Tidbits," an electronic newsletter on tourism and travel that appears in English, Spanish, and Turkish editions; contributor to the joint electronic tourism newsletter (ETRA) that is published jointly by Texas A&M University and the Canadian Tourism Commission; writer and publisher of numerous professional reports for U.S. governmental agencies and for businesses throughout the world. Guest on nationally televised programs such as Dateline: NBC and Dateline: CNBC; organizer of conferences around the world dealing with visitor safety and security issues. Founder and President of Tourism & More Inc. (T&M).

Eugene L. Tucker, CPP, CFE, CBCP. President, Praetorian Protective Services® LLC, Orinda, CA; Senior Consultant, The Steele Foundation; former Security and Safety Manager for several High Technology and Biotechnology Fortune 500 companies; former West Coast Practice leader for Minet Insurance Services; former coordinator of the Emergency Management program at Santa Clara University; former Director of Student Services and Head Professor for the Security and Investigations program at Barclay College, former Associate Manager for Global Business Continuity Planning, The Clorox Services Company. Mr. Tucker has appeared as a security expert in TV news interviews and was commended by the City of Berkeley, CA. Member, Physical Security Committee, American Society for Industrial Security; Board of Directors, Business Recovery Managers Association; High Technology Crime Investigation Association, Association of Certified Fraud Examiners; California Emergency Services Association; co-author of the second and third editions of *Risk Analysis and the Security Survey* by James F. Broder, CPP, CFE, ACFE, Butterworth-Heinemann; contributing author to the *ASIS Professional Practices* book, and has been quoted in, and written articles for *Security Management Magazine*.

Karim H. Vellani, CPP, CSC. Independent Security Consultant and President, Threat Analysis Group, LLC, Houston, TX; Adjunct Professor, College of Criminal Justice, Security Management Department, University of Houston—Downtown. Member, American Society for Industrial Security International

(ASIS), International Association of Professional Security Consultants (IAPSC), International Association of Crime Analysts (IACA); Professional Certification Committee Chairman for IAPSC; and Certifications Chairman for the Houston, TX, Chapter of ASIS; former CPP Chairman for Houston, TX, Chapter, of ASIS and Director of the Board for IAPSC; Bachelor of Criminal Justice, Sam Houston State University and Master of Criminal Justice Management, Sam Houston State University; author of *Applied Crime Analysis* and numerous articles, white papers, and case studies on crime analysis, threat assessment, and risk management; board certified in Security Management by ASIS; Board Certified as an Independent Security Consultant by IAPSC; and licensed as a security consultant.

Scott A. Watson, MCJ, MEd, CPP, CFE. Principal Consultant & CEO, S.A. Watson & Associates LLC, Dover NH; Executive Director, Christian Emergency Response Volunteers (CERV), Dover, NH; Adjunct Professor, Boston University, Metropolitan College, Boston MA. Adjunct Professor, American Military University, Charles Town, WV: Physical Security Specialist, TD Banknorth Corporate Security, Bedford, NH; Senior Risk Management Analyst, Liberty Mutual, Regional Area Markets, Keene, NH; Security Manager, Liberty Mutual, Special Operational Services, Boston, MA: Investigative Analyst, Fidelity Investments Corporate Security, Boston MA, Business Security Representative, Fidelity Investments Corporate Security, Boston, MA; Senior Security Representative, Fidelity Investments Corporate Security, Boston, MA; Security Representative, Fidelity Investments Corporate Security, Boston, MA: Investigator, Pinkerton Security & Investigations, Burlington, MA:, Security Officer, Pinkerton Security, Boston, MA. Senior Security Officer, Boston University's Mugar Memorial Library, Boston, MA; Security Officer, First Security Services Corporation, Boston, MA. Editorial Chairman of the ASIS Crisis Management Council, Member of the Association of Certified Fraud Examiners, Member of the New England Disaster Recovery Information Exchange (NEDRIX); Frequent speaker at professional conferences including ASIS Annual Seminar, ASIS Crisis Management Workshops, City of New York Employee Emergency Preparedness Manual Workshop, CPM East and NEDRIX. Bachelor's Degree in Political Science, Long Island University, Southampton, NY: Masters Degree in Criminal Justice Administration, Boston University, Boston, MA; Masters Degree in Education/Instructional Design, University of Massachusetts, Boston, MA; Author of *A Lesson in Training*; Security Management October 2002; Author of *Buildings with Bull's–Eyes*, Contingency Planning & Management, 2 Part Series-July/August & September/October Issues 2003; Author of *Emergency Preparedness in Nine Steps*, Continuity Insights, March/April Issues 2004; Author of: *How To Steer Your Company to Emergency Preparedness*, Continuity Insights, May/June Issue, 2004.

James J. Zirkel, Maj, USAF. Security Inspection Team Chief, DTRA, Albuquerque, NM; former Operations Officer, 377 SFS, Kirtland AFB, NM; former Chief of Security, 425th Air Base Squadron, Izmir AB, Turkey; former Missile Field, Convoy, and Training and Resources Flight Commander, 91 SFS, Minot AFB, ND; 2005 Air Force Commander-in-Chief's Special Recognition Award winner; 2004 DTRA Field Grade Officer of the Year award winner; Meritorious Service Medal with one Oak Leaf Cluster; Air Force Commendation Medal with one Oak Leaf Cluster; Joint Service Achievement Medal with one Oak Leaf Cluster; Air Force Achievement Medal with two Oak Leaf Clusters; Army Achievement Medal; Bachelor of Science, Economics, United States Air Force Academy, CO; Master of Arts, Security Management, Webster University, St. Louis, MO.

Dick Zunkel. Mr. Zunkel has been involved with electronic locking and access control systems since their development in the 1960s. He was a product designer and later an Engineering Manager in the builders' hardware industry. In the early 1980s he was General Manager of two start-up companies specializing in design-built door automation and access systems. He joined Recognition Systems, Inc. in Campbell, CA in 1995 where he was involved in sales of access controls in domestic and international markets. He is currently a security consultant with Ingersoll Rand Security Technologies in Pleasanton, CA. He wrote the chapter on hand geometry and access control in the book *Biometrics, Personal Identification in Networked Society*, published by Kluwer Academic Publications. His articles on locks, hardware, access control and biometrics appear frequently in trade journals.

Foreword

The security industry, aside from a handful of 19th century private sector investigators performing limited protective functions, didn't really come into its own until World War II, with the need to protect the war industry. Security was more commonly called "plant protection" and was an operational function, a process relatively restricted to "guarding" facilities and their contents, including war-related secrets. Following the war, the need for protection continued to grow in our industrialized society and the name evolved from plant protection to industrial security. In 1955 the American Society for Industrial Security was founded, adopting a name which generally reflected the industry's heritage, i.e., industrial.

One essential element of a "profession" is the presence of scholarly works, namely books. The earliest book on security I can find is titled *Practical Plant Protection and Policing*, written by G.W. Gocke for Charles C. Thomas Publishers in 1957, which was identified as a Monograph in *The Police Science Series*, edited by V.A. Leonard, a professor of Police Science and Administration at Washington State College. This is important because university undergraduate degree programs were emerging in this same period, which resulted in security being relegated to the backwaters in favor of a growing recognition of "police science," later to be named "criminal justice" degrees. Charles C. Thomas captured the public sector police book market and also recognized the growing security market in the private sector; as a result, *Modern Retail Security*, by S.J. "Bob" Curtis, was published in 1960. A few more security books found their way into print during that decade, but it wasn't until the 1970s that the security industry started to emerge as a true and rewarding profession. It was then that Security World Publishing Company, a division of Security World Magazine, came on the scene dedicated to publishing books for the industry.

The books during that decade included such works as Berger's *Industrial Security*, Carson's *Managing Employee Honesty*, Buzby & Paine's *Hotel & Motel Security Management*, and Blackwell's *The Private Investigator*, to name a few.

The management of people, as a unique and separate discipline, was not the focus of the industry. It was industry performance standards in the nuts and bolts of security as it related to specific environments, institutions, and enterprises that were in demand, and it wasn't until the late 1970s that the first purely *management* book was published.

With the growth of the security industry came the growing need not for security technicians but for the management of those technicians.

In the following decades, quality books on virtually every security-related topic imaginable have been produced, enhancing and upgrading our industry.

Then, in 1993, along comes John J. Fay with his *Encyclopedia of Security Management*, which immediately became recognized as an abbreviated synthesis of all our earlier works. I view his work as one of the leading contributions to the ever-growing professionalization of our industry, and this newly revised, enhanced, and expanded second edition is equally, no, more important than the original. One man, one author, John Fay, has captured and presented many voices sharing their views of our business for the edification of us all! No other singular work can be of greater value to the effective security manager of today.

Charles A. "Chuck" Sennewald, CPP, CSC, CPO
Security Management Consultant and Author

Preface

The security field continues to evolve rapidly, becoming broader and more complex with each passing year. The single common thread tying the field together is the discipline of management. This book is for and about security managers, the practitioners whose innovativeness and energy are fueling the great changes of our age.

Security management must be applied wherever protective effort is to be organized on a significant scale—in government, the military, or the business sector. The security manager in one arena can take advantage of technical advances in other arenas when the advances have been described in a useful format. This book is dedicated to that purpose.

The product of rapid evolution is specialization, which can be both positive and negative. The manager who specializes in computer security, for example, may possess great knowledge about electronic data bases but not know very much about the behavioral sciences or the traditional management functions. While this can be accepted as the price tag of progress, it presents a real problem in a discipline committed to control, direction, and elimination of complexity.

As specialization increases, the generalists decline—not because they are unneeded, but because the broadening opportunities are not present in the workplace. The usual experience of a security practitioner is to spend formative years in a relatively specialized area, such as supervising contract guard services, conducting investigations, or installing alarm systems. When promoted to a managerial level, the individual brings to the new job a limited, one-dimensional viewpoint. Saddled with enlarged responsibilities that call for proficiency in many aspects of managing, the individual is suddenly in a sink or swim situation. Some survive, in a sense overcoming the weight of specialization, to become generalists. The few that reach the very top often owe their success to personal efforts on a grand scale. We observe that these are individuals who have acquired a broad understanding of the profession and have developed strong skills in planning, organizing, directing, and controlling.

Continuous learning is required of a security manager who is determined to stay current. The area of electronic technology, with myriad security applications, has practically exploded in recent years. At the same time, steady advances have been made in the time-honored ways that human and financial resources are harnessed to the work of security organizations. The professional security practitioner needs an authoritative reference source to keep abreast.

This encyclopedia offers to the aspirant, student, or practitioner, whether at the entry or senior executive level, a collection of authoritative information that impinges directly upon the security management function as it is performed in many different industries. It proposes, for example, to make the novice aware of the opportunities that are presented in the diverse nature of security jobs; to make the retail store investigator aware of cash register auditing techniques used by his or her counterpart in the lodging industry; to make the electronic access control designer aware of group dynamics; to make the consultant knowledgeable about finance; and to give the top security executive improved insights into the work of the front-line technicians. In addition, this book endeavors to make all security practitioners aware of the truly remarkable strides that have been made in electronic technology, the forensic sciences, human motivation, and the like.

Authoritativeness has been assured by the professional standing of the individual contributing authors. The editor's contacts with professionals engaged in the subjects presented have made possible original contributions by leading authorities. In many cases, a contributing author is also the author of a recognized text or is a frequent contributor of articles to the security trade magazines and professional journals.

To the extent feasible, the authors have followed a prescribed editorial formula designed to tell the reader what the topic is all about, how it works, what it does, how it is used and the problems it solves or creates. A reader who has no substantive knowledge of a topic will, after referring to the article, obtain the basics, i.e., purpose, objectives, modes of operation, and scope. A reader whose education and experience provide at least a peripheral understanding of a topic will gain an appreciation of the potentials for applying the information to the reader's own job, business, or industry.

John J. Fay

I: Business Principles

AGE DISCRIMINATION

The Age Discrimination in Employment Act of 1967 (ADEA) protects individuals who are 40 years of age or older from employment discrimination based on age. The ADEA's protections apply to both employees and job applicants. Under the ADEA, it is unlawful to discriminate against a person because of his/her age with respect to any term, condition, or privilege of employment, including hiring, firing, promotion, layoff, compensation, benefits, job assignments, and training.

It is also unlawful to retaliate against an individual for opposing employment practices that discriminate based on age or for filing an age discrimination charge, testifying, or participating in any way in an investigation, proceeding, or litigation under the ADEA. The ADEA applies to employers with 20 or more employees, including state and local governments. It also applies to employment agencies and labor organizations, as well as to the federal government. ADEA protections include:

Apprenticeship Programs

It is generally unlawful for apprenticeship programs, including joint labor-management apprenticeship programs, to discriminate on the basis of an individual's age. Age limitations in apprenticeship programs are valid only if they fall within certain specific exceptions under the ADEA or if the EEOC grants a specific exemption.

Job Notices and Advertisements

The ADEA generally makes it unlawful to include age preferences, limitations, or specifications in job notices or advertisements. A job notice or advertisement may specify an age limit only in the rare circumstances where age is shown to be a "bona fide occupational qualification" (BFOQ) reasonably necessary to the normal operation of the business.

Pre-Employment Inquiries

The ADEA does not specifically prohibit an employer from asking an applicant's age or date of birth. However, because such inquiries may deter older workers from applying for employment or may otherwise indicate possible intent to discriminate based on age, requests for age information will be closely scrutinized to make sure that the inquiry was made for a lawful purpose, rather than for a purpose prohibited by the ADEA.

Benefits

The Older Workers Benefit Protection Act of 1990 (OWBPA) amended the ADEA to specifically prohibit employers from denying benefits to older employees. Congress recognized that the cost of providing certain benefits to older workers is greater than the cost of providing those same benefits to younger workers, and that those greater costs would create a disincentive to hire older workers. Therefore, in limited circumstances, an employer may be permitted to reduce benefits based on age, as long as the cost of providing the reduced benefits to older workers is the same as the cost of providing benefits to younger workers.

Waivers of ADEA Rights

An employer may ask an employee to waive his/her rights or claims under the ADEA either in the settlement of an ADEA administrative or court claim or in connection with an exit incentive program or other employment termination program. However, the ADEA, as amended by OWBPA, sets out specific minimum standards that must be met in order for a waiver to be considered knowing and voluntary and, therefore, valid. Among other requirements, a valid ADEA waiver must:

- Be in writing and be understandable.
- Specifically refer to ADEA rights or claims.
- Not waive rights or claims that may arise in the future.
- Be in exchange for valuable consideration.
- Advise the individual in writing to consult an attorney before signing the waiver.

- Provide the individual at least 21 days to consider the agreement and at least seven days to revoke the agreement after signing it.

If an employer requests an ADEA waiver in connection with an exit incentive program or other employment termination program, the minimum requirements for a valid waiver are more extensive.

Source   The U.S. Equal Employment Opportunity Commission. 2006. <http://www.eeoc.gov/types/age.html>

BEST PRACTICES

Pursuing quality requires making a commitment to doing things in the best possible way. In today's organizational environment we would call this "pursuing best practices." But what does this mean exactly? To properly understand the context of best practices we need to consider three fundamental realities:

- There are no absolute criteria for defining best practices within security today.
- Best practices do not have to be measurable by empirical means.
- Best practices can be common practices.

On the surface, each of the three considerations appears to fly in the face of the very essence of what best practices should be all about. Yet ironically all three embody the very essence of best practices for a security manager. Let's examine each briefly.

First, security is a non-codified profession. Unlike corporate safety with its guidelines as set forth by underwriters and regulators, the security industry has not subscribed to a set of standards. Consequently, security professionals are pretty much driven by the codes of other professional business counterparts, an occasional state requirement, an underwriter prescription, or a court decision.

Even though there may be no prescribed, empirical criteria for measuring the attainment of best practices, decision makers can determine if they are on the right track when such practices:

- Directly contribute to the bottom line.
- Add value in a demonstrable way.
- Maximize efficiency and effectiveness.

Established practices can become best practices. For example, requiring employees to display a photo identification badge is an established practice that is not always done well. When an organization enforces the established practice by use of a system of incentives and disincentives, and when statistical evidence shows that the practice contributes to cost savings, such as preventing theft, the common practice becomes a best practice.

A security manager can evaluate security practices by asking a simple question: "Am I getting the job done?" If the security manager's responsibilities include criminal investigations, the evaluation criteria can be how quickly the investigation was completed, whether the investigation succeeded in solving a crime or correcting a crime condition, the cost of the investigation, recovery of property, and a settlement from or restitution made by the offending party. In looking at the totality of investigations, the security manager can compare total costs against total recoveries and also use historical data to demonstrate that crime-related losses in previous years were higher than crime-related costs currently.

Challenging Basic Assumptions

Are the common assumptions associated with staffing levels and deployment, allocation of security systems and devices, and operating practices relevant in today's organizational culture? Or are there other opportunities available to be pursued that will yield the same result at a lower cost while actually maintaining or increasing the quality of the service delivered? As an example, with respect to criminal investigations, is it better to create a prosecutorial threshold (that is, no loss under an established value will be criminally pursued) rather than using civil litigation as a means of seeking appropriate remedies for all losses? By establishing such thresholds, both the manner in which investigations are pursued and the allocation of resources could vary significantly. Only those incidents involving a loss equivalent to a significant monetary value would be pursued from a criminal perspective, and those investigations would require an adherence to a higher standard of investigational pursuit. It is important to note that the best practice here is the establishment of a value threshold. The actual value you establish will vary depending on the type of organization and value of the assets.

Allocating Staff Resources

To "get the job done" how many staff people do you require? This is much different from the traditional approach of seeking authorized levels based on "the great what-if." Security executives, like many of their counterparts in other service-related industries, have traditionally defined levels above what is actually required. They want "the coverage." Usually they justify this judgment by pointing to their ability to provide a more rapid response or by giving the assurance that selected posts will not be left open. Unfortunately, neither of these "justifications" falls within the definition of services as "required."

Employing best practices means analyzing what it takes to meet the routine assigned tasks and then creatively identifying strategies to accomplish the non-routine incidences. To address the issue of rapid response, you may need to develop a mutual response program with neighboring facilities or organizations, similar to what is done in the public sector.

Using Appropriate Technology

Accomplishing most assigned security tasks requires the use of some technology. Against the backdrop of today's continuum of available security devices, it is easy to fall into the trap of believing that the more sophisticated and electronic the security device is, the better it is. The best practice approach speaks to addressing the problem at hand with the technological resource commensurate with resolving the need. If a simple mechanical lock and key can suffice to prevent unauthorized access into an area, as opposed to an electronic card-access system, then the use of the lock and key should be pursued. Though locks and keys may not be as "sexy" as access cards and electronic readers, there are applications where locks and keys are more cost-effective and, therefore, demonstrate a commitment to quality assurance and best practices.

Conversely, attempting to address a security issue using outmoded technology when state-of-the-art devices are available is equally inappropriate. An example would be the use of radio frequency controlled closed-circuit television surveillance systems as opposed to hard-wired configurations in selected applications. The wireless devices may be more expensive initially, but the cost of installing the wiring (that is, across parking lots, in marina locations, and so forth) for the other configuration may be more.

Challenging Basic Operating Practices

To get the job done using best practices also requires that the decision maker (e.g., generally the manager) challenge basic operating practices, especially when the common response from employees is "We've always done it this way." The best of a best practices approach recognizes that employing security's operating procedures is often the most effective and least costly way of accomplishing the security mission. By shifting the responsibility for good security practices to end users, the security management team is able to redirect limited resources to other areas requiring specific attention. Meanwhile, business unit managers and non-security employees can not only be held accountable for the security and safety of those assets charged to them, but also share in the knowledge that they have promoted the well-being of their colleagues.

Is the Service Being Delivered Effectively?

Best practices demand that the intended results be achievable. A gap can lie between what senior management expects and what the security manager can deliver. To eliminate the gap, or at least keep it from widening, the security manager has to be in tune with the expectations of senior management and the overall corporate culture. Determining what their perception of effectiveness is and how this translates into security's service delivery is critical. Not only must the end result be clearly defined by security best practices but it must also be perceived by senior management as being in accordance with cultural values. All too often the result is accomplished, but the methodology or personalities involved have alienated enough key players so as to render the actual results less obvious.

Best practices means looking for new ways to be effective. In using this strategy you assume nothing is so sacred that it cannot be improved upon—even if it means taking radical action. An example is the 180-degree rule. It says that effectiveness can be improved by approaching the problem from exactly the opposite direction. Often we find that by simply looking at the problem from a different perspective, an answer will arrive and it turns out to be better than what we might otherwise have come up with through conventional evaluation.

Is the Service Being Delivered Efficiently?

Efficiency is often synonymous with cost. Whether cost is measured in terms of time, dollars, or both, the hard fact is that dollars are spent to achieve results. Efficiency naturally translates into bottom-line performance. The best practices approach involves obtaining the best possible value in exchange for the "best" dollars spent. By definition, efficiency means "the best way of doing something in the best utilization of time." Time, of course, equates to cost such as paying people to do a job that should have been finished in a lesser period of time.

Pursuing Best Practices

Do One Thing Well. One of the myths about pursuing best practices is that to be a world-class organization all your departmental activities must be carried out from a best practices perspective. The pursuit of best practices is evolutionary. It begins with concentrating on one particular activity and doing it very well. As you develop a best practices proficiency in any one area, the lessons learned can then be carried over to other areas. In time, if you pursue best practices diligently, several, if not all, aspects of your security program will be classified as best practices.

Leverage the Good, the Bad, and the Ugly. While there are many ways to measure the activities in your organization, it is not uncommon to describe tasks as those being done well (the good); those that were initially good but for any number of reasons have failed (the bad); and

those that seem to "get the job done," but you're mystified about how it is accomplished (the ugly). Regardless of a particular outcome, there are lessons to be learned. The astute manager maintains the broad-based perspective and seeks to find the opportunities in each situation.

Develop and Maintain Employee Loyalty. In addition to empowering people, there are other techniques you can use to build employee loyalty, particularly when third-party providers are involved.

- Develop a "we will" package. Items to be included might be a packet for newcomers including coupons for discounts offered by the company, a WELCOME ONBOARD card signed by other employees, a company T-shirt, a certificate suitable for framing or a plaque for posting, promoting the idea of the employee belonging to the company family, and so forth.
- Recognize a security officer and his or her contribution with a gift certificate for $50 at Christmastime either to the nearest toy store to be spent on the officer's children or to a nearby department store.
- Give a gift certificate for two to the security officer to a local medium-priced restaurant. Include an extra $15 to $20 for babysitting money for those officers with children to assure that they will be able to take advantage of the gift certificate.
- Allow employees to leverage on your volume discounts for the laundering and dry cleaning of their uniforms by offering them discounted fees for the care of items in their personal wardrobes.
- Extend employee award programs to staff members normally not eligible, such as administrative staff and security branch officers, as a way of recognizing their support and contribution to the security program.
- Pay officers for as many as two hours per month for helping in community school activities or other charitable work programs.
- Create employee support groups, such as parents with teenagers, dealing with aging, and so forth.
- If security vehicles are used, stencil the name of the security officer of the year on the side of his or her vehicle.

These are all small examples of affordable options, yet they demonstrate to employees that management is willing to make an investment in them. Such gestures allow employees, proprietary or contract, to develop a measure of loyalty because they get a feeling of both acceptance and respect for the contribution they are making.

Quality Should Be Cultural—Not Supplanted. Quality, and therefore the pursuit of best practices, is not something that can be forced on an organization. It is something that is embraced naturally by both management and line staff. For them quality is a matter of identity and not just the latest management fad.

"We've Always Done It That Way" Is Changed to "We've Never Done That Before." The pursuit of best practices is a journey involving the pursuit of alternative ways of doing things. In the process you challenge traditional methods, not for the sake of eliminating them, but in an effort to seek other ways that are better suited for the current climate. "We've always done it this way" is an organizational cancer that needs to be surgically removed because it is indicative of complacency, a major obstacle to pursuing best practices.

Challenge Every Existing Assumption. Challenge does not necessarily equal change. Challenging the status quo simply shows a willingness to break away from the temptation to protect sacred cows or territorial boundaries that can get in the way of pursuing efficiency and effectiveness.

Define Your Operation as World-Class. Behaviorists have long taught us that you can only achieve that level to which you aspire. By defining yourself as a world-class organization you force new perspectives and a willingness to ask yourself questions such as:

- "How would a world-class organization respond?"
- "Would a world-class organization pursue this?"
- "If we do not pursue it this way, are we running the risk of losing our status as a world-class service organization?"

Only when you begin to define yourself as a world-class organization can you start to act like one.

Conclusion

The achievement of best practices requires a commitment from senior management. Without their sign-off there will be an absence of budgetary support and a lack of leadership by example. Yet, the actual implementation of best practices is the functional responsibility of those at the bottom of the organization. Without their willingness to implement and actively participate, best practices remain only a concept. In short, success can only be achieved when there is a convergence of involvement from both the top and the bottom levels of the organization.

Dennis Dalton

Sources

Dalton, D. 1995. *Security Management: Business Strategies for Success*. Boston: Butterworth-Heinemann.

Gulick, L. and Urwick, L. eds. 1937. *Papers on the Science of Administration*. New York: Institute of Public Administration.

Morehouse, D. 1992. *Total Quality Management: A Supervisor's Handbook*. Shawnee Mission: National Press Publications.

BUDGETING

A budget is a forecast of expenditures and revenues for a specific period of time. Because a budget sets priorities and monitors progress toward selected goals, it is a basic planning tool. A budget helps a Chief Security Officer make informed decisions on the management of people and assets in the Security Group. Typically, the CSO prepares the budget on the basis of estimates to meet priorities for the next fiscal year. The estimates reflect inflationary pressure and current year spending. The budget is presented to the CSO's supervisor who may modify the estimates and rearrange priorities. The supervisor delegates to the CSO formal authority to enter into financial obligations at certain agreed dollar levels. An independent body within the company, such as a financial control group, generally monitors security expenditures to ensure they are consistent with organizational objectives.

In any operation of size and complexity, budgeting will be a routine, yet essential, element of planning from year to year. Three purposes stand out:

- Estimate the costs of planned activities.
- Provide a warning mechanism when variances occur in actual costs.
- Exercise uniformity in the matter of fiscal control.

The budgeting process has four distinct stages: preparation, authorization, execution, and audit.

Preparation

An annual budget places on the CSO the responsibility for preparing Security Group estimates and coordinating them with overall company planning. The CSO and his/her supervisor meet, sometimes with key Security Group staff present, to discuss planned activities. It is not unusual to begin as early as six months in advance of the next fiscal year.

Security budget preparation begins with targets and ends with binding commitments. Outlays and spending authority are usually categorized by functions such as security officer operations, investigations, and physical security inspections. New spending requests, even when approved at the next higher level, tend to be very critically examined.

Preparation includes obtaining buy-in from groups dependent on or affected by Security Group activities. Garnering buy-in is typically informal: phone calls, e-mails, memoranda, and one-on-one meetings. The CSO's primary aim is to identify essential security services that have not already been addressed. A secondary aim is to identify objections that may surface later, when the time for patching up has passed.

Authorization

Authorization begins by obtaining supervisory approval. Preceding approval may be meetings with peers. Peers head up groups and report to the same supervisor. It is very likely that a peer will be a security services customer and therefore will have a stake in the security enterprise and a right to offer input.

The next step is to present the proposed budget to a budget review committee composed of specialists from the company's finance group. The review committee typically asks to receive the proposed budget for study in advance of one or more discussion meetings to follow. The CSO's budget proposal is detailed item by item and thoroughly documented. Details address projected activities, purposes and benefits, and likely consequences if activities are not funded adequately.

When the CSO presents the proposed budget in person, he/she uses a mild combination of negotiation and persuasion. Several such meetings ensue before the budget review committee sends the proposed budget to a higher level for final decision. The decision will certainly involve the chief financial officer (CFO) and possibly others on the executive team.

Execution

The budget begins at the start of the fiscal year. The CSO's responsibility is to ensure effective and efficient performance of Security Group functions while at the same time keeping costs in line with the budget.

At one point or another, the CSO may find it necessary to amend the budget; for example, when an unanticipated event requires the expenditure of unbudgeted funds. In the business of security, unanticipated events are the norm rather than the exception. The CSO will send a funding request up the chain of command.

Other amendments can occur. Unspent funds in one account can be moved to another account short of funds, not unlike a shopper that moves money from one pocket to another. In some cases in some organizations, the CSO can make such transfers on his/her authority. They must, however, be documented.

Although formal and closely managed, a budget is in a constant state of change, and not all changes bring added funds. In times of economic stress, the CSO may be required to cut spending.

Audit

A budget is audited during execution by the CSO and the company's accounting group. The CSO keeps track of spending almost as it occurs. Every invoice or bill signed by the CSO is copied and placed in a file.

Auditing by the accounting group is largely a matter of recording payments made to fund Security Group activities. A record is prepared monthly. When significant variances appear, the accounting group informs the CSO. When variances increase or are not corrected, the accounting group notifies the CSO's supervisor.

The Security Group's budget can also be examined by the company's audit office for one of two reasons: as a routine control measure or as a formal investigation of suspicious irregularities.

Budget Director

A budget director brings all group budgets into a comprehensible whole called the master budget. It is an overall forecast of transactions within a given period, set up in a manner that delivers to senior management timely reports of financial results. The master budget enables the preparation of financial statements such as the income statement and balance sheet.

The process of budget preparation at the group level adheres to a methodology specified by the budget director. Group leaders identify and justify their planned activities and estimate costs. The format and dollar figures of proposed budgets are developed according to a common framework. Without it, the auditing function would be hampered and the master budget difficult to comprehend.

The prescribed methodology of the common framework and the actual budget are two different things: the first is a tool and the second is the object crafted by the tool.

A budget is purpose driven and function conscious. The form of budgeting specified by the budget director will correspond to organizational goals and the functions necessary to reach them. Selection of the budgeting approach can be influenced also by history and experience (the way we've always done it), tax implications, and the preferences of the executive team and the board of directors. Major spending decisions can be made at the board level but are most often made by the executive team. The budget director reports to the chief financial officer, a member of the executive team.

Zero-Based Budgeting

Zero-based budgeting starts with an assumption that zero dollars are available. Dollars become available when proof is presented that an activity is necessary to the business. Implied in the approach is a requirement to explore alternatives for achieving the same or similar results at a lower cost. Group leaders, including the CSO, make their case by answering three questions: What is the purpose of the activity? What will it cost? What is the added value? Benefits that can be derived from the activity are weighed against cost. The CSO makes the argument that benefits will be lost or that undesirable consequences will come about if an activity is not funded or funded at a lesser level.

Zero-based budgeting forces the CSO to look at different levels of effect for performing an activity. The levels may range from minimum to optimum. At each spending level, the CSO would show the costs of the activity, the predicted value, and the effects likely to be experienced by increases or decreases in spending. The CSO could be required to describe the probable outcomes of operating a guard force at different spending levels.

Flow Directions

Directions on major budget issues flow from the top down and requests for funding flow upward. Directions passed downward tend to deal with both administrative and substantive matters. Administrative matters provide guidance as to the format of the budget document, the placement of particular costs into particular categories, the attachment of supporting documentation, and the deadlines for submitting drafts.

Limitations

Substantive matters can include limitations, such as no new hires, no purchases without prior authority, and no increase of the group budget beyond a certain level (e.g., not more than 5 percent above the total budget of the current year).

A down and then up again pattern is usually the case before a group's budget is set in stone. The CSO meets multiple times with multiple functionaries. At one meeting, the budget is okay; at the next meeting it is not okay. At every meeting, the CSO pleads his/her case. Nearly every meeting is called the "final" meeting, which turns out not to be the case. Because the CSO never knows if the next meeting will be the final meeting, he/she has to approach it as if it were a "last chance."

Cost-Benefit Ratio

A request for a major purchase may require approval by a spending authority separate from the budget committee. A major purchase not reflected in a budget is called an "exception to the budget." A preparatory step in considering a large expenditure is to determine the cost-benefit ratio, a figure computed by dividing costs by benefits. To illustrate:

- An access control system costs $500,000 to purchase.
- The service life of the system is 10 years.
- Guards replaced by the system result in a saving of $100,000 per year.
- The cost-benefit ratio is therefore 0.5:1, meaning that the cost of the purchase is half of the benefits or that the benefits are twice as great as the costs.

The ratio was arrived at by multiplying the annual guard cost savings by the number of years of useful service of the access control system. This figure ($1,000,000) represents the benefit, and is divided into the cost of the system ($500,000). Benefit versus cost is 0.5. When the ratio is less than 1, it is favorable; and unfavorable when it is higher than 1.

Controlling Costs

Apart from the process of budget preparation and approval is the day-to-day task of maintaining a budget folder. This folder is informal and a device of convenience. Placed into the folder are invoices, statements, price quotes, purchase orders, sales receipts, notes and memos concerning expenditures, and like items. Monthly, the accounting group sends to the CSO a computer-prepared summary that (1) reflects spending for the previous month and year-to-date, (2) compares those figures against the budget's planned expenditures, and (3) highlights variances. The CSO is expected to take action when actual spending exceeds planned spending by a significant amount. The action is to put a brake on spending, if possible; if not possible, the CSO submits a request to increase the budget, a request that is never warmly received.

Overspending

Overspending is frequently the result of poor planning. Failing to anticipate rises in the costs of essential products and services or incorrectly calculating how many and how much of each will be needed is somewhat forgivable. Underspending for a budget item is rarely a problem; overspending is an indication of poor money-managing skill.

John J. Fay

Source   Fay, J. *Contemporary Security Management, 2nd Edition.* 2006. Boston: Butterworth-Heinemann.

BUDGET PLANNING

Management is the coordinated application of resources to accomplish objectives. In this definition, managers carry out the functions of planning, organizing, directing, and controlling. The work activities of these functions consume resources that are purchased and are therefore measurable in dollars. The dollars planned to be expended are shown in budgets. There are many types of budgets. They can be used to show expenditures for projects that start and end, processes that never end, capital equipment purchases, a department's monthly activities, or the total organization's yearly activities. Budgets come in all sizes and shapes, serve a variety of purposes, and involve many different techniques.

All budgets have one thing in common, however; they have a close relationship with the planning function. This is so because the work activities planned to occur must be funded by dollars set aside in the budget. A budget can be viewed as:

- A plan stated in financial terms.
- An allocation of funds to meet planned objectives.
- A record of work activities in terms of monies appropriated.
- A tool for measuring the success of planned activities.

Let's use a simple situation to illustrate the relationship between planning and budgeting. Assume the security manager, in planning for the next fiscal year, concludes that a valuable work activity of the department will be to operate a rape avoidance program. The objective of the program is to minimize loss to the company resulting from lower productivity of employees who miss work or are distracted at work due to actual or perceived rape incidents. The security manager's plan is to conduct one rape avoidance presentation each quarter of the next year; the presentations will be made by a rape avoidance expert; a video tape on the topic will be purchased; and the presentations will be held in the company's learning center, using in-house audiovisual equipment. The presentations will be announced by posters placed in the coffee bars and each attendee will receive a booklet that is available for sale from the community rape crisis center. The security manager estimates that 100 employees will attend each presentation. The budget might look like this:

TABLE 1 A Very Simple Example of Computing Costs

Speaker fees		
Four @ $200 each	$ 800	
Film purchase	$ 250	
Posters		
Artwork	$ 150	
Printing	$ 100	
Booklets		
400 @ .50 each	$ 200	
Total	$ 1500	

This simple illustration does not take into account other costs, such as the security manager's time in managing the program, and the cost of the learning center and audiovisual equipment. Those costs might be rolled into other categories in the security manager's overall budget, and within that overall budget the rape avoidance project would be a very small item.

Forecasting

Work activities of today are based on yesterday's plans and tomorrow's expectations. Plans cannot be made without forecasting the future and what the future will bring. For example, a security manager's projection of growth in the company's employee population is a forecast of increased pre-employment screening activity; increased vehicle and pedestrian movement into, within, and from the premises; and increased pressure on the pass section to issue new access control badges.

It is well recognized that while forecasting is important in making rational decisions, the activity itself is more art than science. The value of a forecast is not in its relative accuracy, but in the fact that the activity requires the manager to give balanced consideration to factors that might influence the future. Because the past has never been a perfect predictor of the future, the manager is on mushy footing when making plans based solely on historical data.

Success at forecasting usually rests on a competency to judge under what conditions past occurrences can be relied upon. The manager must also be able to differentiate between new facts that are important and those that are irrelevant. The security manager cannot plan for the unknown or the unpredictable, but must instead concentrate on making an intelligent assessment of probabilities.

While the average line employee is thinking of work in terms of today, the manager is thinking about work stretched across substantially larger blocks of time. Thinking ahead is not necessarily a measure of intelligence, but of the conditioning effects of experience in meeting life's responsibilities.

Charles A. Sennewald

Source Sennewald, C. 1985. *Effective Security Management, 2nd Edition.* Boston: Butterworth-Heinemann.

BUSINESS ETHICS

Ethics in business are the standards of conduct and judgment in respect to what is perceived as right and wrong. An intrinsic element of ethics is the specification of responsibility for human actions. Ethical standards go beyond merely describing conduct that we habitually accept;

they seek to define higher goals and the means for attaining them.

The Chief Security Officer (CSO) encounters ethics in two dimensions: first, as the employer's instrument for developing business conduct policy and investigating improper conduct by others; and second, as an employee who is personally obligated to conduct business in accordance with the established policy.

The CSO knows well such unethical practices as misuse of proprietary information, kickbacks, and conflicts of interest. The controls for preventing and detecting offenses are clear cut and easily understood administrative mechanisms. It may be less clear to the CSO the expectations of senior management regarding the manager's decisions and conduct that impact the company's bottom line. For example, a CSO whose principal duties involve selling a security product may be caught between the choices of using persuasive, but deceptive, selling techniques and being scrupulously honest. How does senior management view the situation? Does the promise of profit take precedence over truth?

The continued deterioration of ethics in business should lead us to a closer examination of personal and corporate morality. Mainstream ethicists believe that an act is either intrinsically correct or incorrect, and that we have a duty to always act correctly. Others argue, however, that the reality of the human condition is that we all seek to engage in acts that derive pleasure, and acts that produce the greatest amount of pleasure for the greatest number of people are morally correct.

Code of Ethics

A traditional approach for promoting ethical conduct is the adoption of a code of ethics. Problems arise, however, due to concerns about who will create the code, who will be affected by it, what it will cover, and the sanctions that may be applied to violators.

In attempting to reconcile the various concerns about a code under development, the drafters may produce an ineffectual document. On the one hand it may be so watered down as to have no real impact on behavior, or on the other hand, include unattainable principles. In many cases it is impossible to select between competing and sometimes incompatible interests when moral questions are being examined.

A great difficulty lies in reconciling morality and profit. Realistically, a moral principle is not acceptable if it condemns business activity; as a result there is a natural tendency within business to see profit-making as a legitimate, if not moral, end in itself.

Principles of Business Conduct

A business is driven by the forces of economic reality, is constrained by the limits of custom and law, and is shaped by the human values of its workforce. A business, then, is an institution of people and ethics as well as an enterprise of profit and loss.

The ethical performance of a business is a matter of spirit and intent, as well as a matter of law. A company's business practices are the expression of management's philosophy and will often contain these basic principles:

- Businesses that succeed are those that conduct their affairs with honesty and integrity. These qualities are characterized by truthfulness and freedom from deception.
- There is no conflict between pursuit of profit and attention to ethics. Business generally will prosper in an environment that is fair, open, and morally secure.
- Employees are the key to ethical business conduct, and their behavior is strongly influenced by the way they are treated and how they view management. Ethics flourish in an environment that fosters individual self-respect, loyalty, and dedication.
- A business ethics policy will usually express these overriding principles in a more specific format, setting out personal standards, responsibilities, and sanctions. The policy provides a framework against which individual employees can measure their own personal conduct and management can establish a supportive climate by communicating the principles and setting the example.

John J. Fay

Source *Principles of Business Conduct*. 1990. Cleveland: British Petroleum America.

BUSINESS ETHICS POLICY

(SAMPLE)

General. The Company has a policy of strict compliance with laws which are applicable to its businesses, wherever conducted. In some instances, law and regulations may be ambiguous and difficult to interpret. In such cases we would seek legal advice to which we have access in each business and at the corporate level in order to assure that we are in compliance with this policy and are observing all applicable laws and regulations. Compliance with the law means not only observing the law, but conducting our business affairs so that the Company will deserve and receive recognition as a law-abiding organization.

Entertainment, Gifts, Favors, and Gratuities. The Company's guidelines governing levels of entertainment, gifts, favors, and gratuities, whether offered by employees or extended to them, are acceptable if:

- They cannot be construed as intended to affect the judgment of the recipient so as to secure preferential treatment and
- They are of such limited nature and value that they could not be perceived by anyone to affect the judgment of the recipient and
- Public disclosure would not be embarrassing to the Company or the recipient. All relations with government or public officials should be conducted in a manner that will not adversely reflect on our reputation or the official's integrity and with the expectation that all such actions will become a matter of public knowledge.

Political Contributions. Corporate contributions, direct or indirect, and of whatever amount or type, to any political candidate or party, or to any other organization that might use the contributions for a political candidate or party, are illegal at the federal level and in some states. In those states where such contributions are legal, they should be made only upon the approval of the Director, State Government Affairs. In addition, political contributions at the federal or state level by any employee who is a "foreign national" (i.e., an employee who is not a citizen of the United States or has not been admitted for permanent residence) are illegal.

We may from time to time take stands on issues of public policy, particularly those that affect the Company's interests or those of its several constituencies. In such cases, we may elect to express our views publicly and spend company funds to ensure that our position is broadly disseminated. We may also provide financial support to groups that advocate positions essentially consistent with our own. The Company encourages individual employees to participate in the political process, including voluntary contributions to the Company's political action committee and to candidates and parties of their choice. However, no influence shall be exerted by any employee on another employee to make any personal political contribution or to engage in any political activity inconsistent with that employee's own personal inclination.

Accountability. The law requires that the Company and the businesses for which it is responsible keep accurate books, records, and accounts to fairly reflect the Company's transactions and that we maintain an adequate system of internal accounting controls. Therefore, it cannot be over-emphasized that our books and records should have the highest degree of integrity. Employees should fulfill their responsibilities to assure that books, records, and accounts are complete, accurate, and supported by appropriate documents in auditable form.

All vouchers, bills, invoices, expense accounts, and other business records should be prepared with care and complete candor. No false or misleading entries and no undisclosed or unrecorded funds or assets should be permitted for any reason. No payment is to be made for purposes other than those described in the documents supporting the payment.

Antitrust Laws. The Company endorses the view that a viable free-enterprise system rests upon the fundamental proposition that free and open competition is the best way to assure an adequate supply of goods and services at reasonable prices. Therefore, in carrying out his or her duties, every employee shall strictly adhere to the letter and spirit of the antitrust laws of the United States and with competition laws of any other country or any group of countries that are applicable to our business.

It is recognized that the antitrust laws are complex and difficult to interpret. They also have application to a very broad range of activities. In these circumstances, employees should take the initiative to consult the Law Department whenever the proper course of action is in doubt. We consider compliance with the applicable antitrust laws so vitally important that neither claims of ignorance and good intentions, nor failure to seek timely advice will be accepted as an excuse for noncompliance.

Conflict of Interest. The term "conflict of interest" describes any circumstance that could cast doubt on our ability to act with total objectivity with regard to interests of our business. We not only want to be loyal to the Company, we want that loyalty to come easily, free from any conflicting interests.

While we fully respect the privacy of employees in the conduct of their personal affairs, we insist that each employee fully discharges his or her obligations of faithful service to the business. Activities which involve the unauthorized use of time, equipment, or information, which significantly interfere with business interests will be avoided. Of particular concern are situations in which our personal interests may conflict with the interests of our business in relations with present or prospective suppliers, customers, or competitors.

The use of an employee's position or the assets or influence of the organization for personal advantage or for the advantage of others is prohibited. In order to avoid potential conflicts with regard to accepting outside employment regarding consultancies, directorships, part-time or freelance activities, the employee should discuss the particulars with his or her immediate supervisor prior to accepting employment.

Generally, it is our policy that employees may not, except at the direction of the Company, undertake any discussions or activities with potential participants, lenders, advisors, or attorneys relative to the possible purchase of any business for which the Company is responsible. This applies whether or not that business has been applied for divestiture.

If an employee desires to undertake any such activity on his or her own behalf or on behalf of others, before doing so he or she should advise the Chief Financial Officer of the Company who will determine in each case whether such activity can be conducted in such a way so as to protect the best interests of the Company.

Prohibited Investments. The Company prohibits employees from purchasing or dealing, either directly or indirectly, in any:

• Interest (or option to purchase or sell interest) in any organization or concern that the employee knows is a candidate for acquisition by the corporation or is under consideration for some other business arrangement with the corporation. This provision, however, does not apply to ownership of stock or securities amounting to less than one-half of one percent of the outstanding stock of any publicly

held corporation. For purposes of this policy, a "publicly held corporation" is one whose shares are listed on a recognized stock exchange or are included in the daily over-the-counter list of quotations of the National Association of Securities Dealers and published in the Wall Street Journal.
- Interest in any supplier, competitor or customer with whom we do business.
- Contracts, options, or any other form of participation in the commodities' futures or trading markets and in any commodity which we sell.

These prohibitions apply to purchasing and dealings by members of the employee's household or by a third party if intended to benefit the employee. They apply only to "purchasing and dealing" and do not apply to acquisitions by inheritance or gift nor do they apply to employees who are members of collective bargaining units. Managers are requested to take necessary actions to ensure their employees are aware of these prohibitions.

Employees should also be urged to discuss any questions they may have pertaining to prohibited investments with their immediate supervisor or designated ethics coordinator within their operating company or staff department.

Other prohibitions, in addition to those above, may be prescribed by individual business who will make these prohibitions known to affected employees.

Use of Classified Information. Company classified information is found in many types, forms, and locations. Security measures applicable to the protection of information are to be followed.

It is our policy that all classified business information is used solely for our own purposes and is not to be provided to unauthorized persons or used for the purpose of furthering a private interest or making a personal profit.

We would ensure that all material non-public information concerning the securities, financial condition, earnings, or activities of the Company remain protected until fully and properly disseminated to the public. Examples of areas of particular sensitivity are current interim earnings figures or trends, possible acquisitions or divestitures, exploration and production plans, and new plants, products, or processes.

Procurement. We require that our employees maintain the highest ethical principles in the acquisition of goods and services. Procurement practices and procedures should:

- Provide equal opportunity to all qualified firms wanting to do business with us.
- Treat all suppliers and contractors fairly and consistently.
- Be meticulously applied.

During the bidding process, difficulties may arise when bidders offer unsolicited price reductions or other concessions after bid submission, or attempt to enter into other post-bid negotiations which go beyond the normal bid clarification process. Acceptance of such unsolicited offers during bidding is contrary to our procurement policy.

Bids are considered confidential and are never to be provided to anyone outside the Company, and, within the Company, only to authorized personnel. Further, pains must be taken to treat all bidders equally during the bid period, especially with respect to bid document interpretations and clarifications.

The Company procurement policy, reflecting ethical business practice, is issued by the Corporate Materials and Contracts Department. Businesses and staffs are expected to establish their own procedures consistent with such policies.

Non-Compliance. Compliance with this Policy carries the highest priority throughout the Company. Failure to comply with the principles of business conduct may unnecessarily expose us and our employees to risks in the form of administrative sanctions, civil proceedings, and/or criminal prosecution.

Management is responsible for instituting preventative measures, ensuring that violations of Policy are thoroughly investigated by competent professionals experienced in ensuring equal respect is given to the rights of employees and objectives of the Company and the business for which it is responsible, and taking the appropriate administrative and/or disciplinary actions consistent with the infraction.

Legal Violations. Diversion of Company assets, fraud embezzlement, theft, and intentional damage to equipment and similar events all represent criminal actions against the Company. It is our policy to seek and assist the prosecution of persons who are believed to have committed criminal acts against the Company. Particulars of the case will be presented to the appropriate law enforcement agency for a determination in pursuing prosecution. In addition, any criminal loss exceeding $75,000 requires an investigative audit with assistance from Internal Audit and Corporate Security.

Policy Violations. Violations of this policy on business conduct more often will not result in violations of law; however, they result in violating the spirit and intent of ethical behavior. These may include: unauthorized use or disclosure of classified information; accepting gifts or entertainment of material value that affects our ability to be impartial; records manipulation; and conflict of interest. Management's response to such cases usually will be handled internally and disciplinary procedures will be applied where deemed appropriate.

Follow-Through. There are two broad actions we can take to ensure that our written commitment to ethical business conduct pays off in practice.

The first is to provide a mechanism that will help us handle difficult judgment decisions in those "gray areas" where it is often hard to pinpoint right from wrong. None of us should be uncomfortable in handling a question of ethics.

When such situations arise, we must seek counsel. The system is very simple. Ask the person to whom you report.

All managers are to maintain an open-door policy with regard to questions of ethics. They are to make themselves easily available to any of us who have such questions. We are reminded that the time to bring up a question of moral standard or ethical behavior is before the fact, rather than after the fact. We must never hesitate to talk to our supervisors about a question of business conduct, no matter how small or insignificant it may seem to be.

The second action consists of several steps that will make attention to this policy an integral part of managing our business. These steps are as follows:

- The Chief Security Officer is assigned oversight of a follow-through program.
- Each business and staff group will establish a procedure to ensure that at least once a year these principles of business conduct are reviewed with their managerial employees. Additionally, each business

and staff group will designate at least one person to whom any employee may communicate freely on matters concerning the interpretation, application, or suspected violation of these principles. Such designees will, routinely, keep the Chief Security Officer apprised of activities/inquiries with respect to these principles which arise in the ordinary course of business.

- Urgent issues of this nature will be immediately communicated to the Chief Security Officer, who will consult, as appropriate, with the Audit and Law Departments as to the appropriate course of action.
- Any allegation or suspicion that unethical or illegal activities are taking place will be reported to Corporate Security and, where appropriate, will be thoroughly investigated in a competent, fair, and confidential manner, with equal respect being given to the rights of the employee and the objectives of the Company.
- The General Auditor will establish procedures to monitor management's compliance with our principles of business conduct and will annually report the results of this effort to the Chief Executive Officer of the Company and to others as he or she may direct.

CORPORATE SECURITY AND THE PROCESSES OF CHANGE

At least since the end of World War II, the security industry has been radically and rapidly evolving. The main driving forces of change have been the steady escalation of crime and the increasing inability of law enforcement to be effective in dealing with crimes against businesses. A whole new industry has risen up to meet market demands fueled by business fears, and with it we have seen the maturation of an entity that has come to be called the proprietary security organization or simply corporate security.

Corporate security's *raison d'être* has been the protection of the employer's assets against threats of crime, and the methods of protection have relied to a great extent on concepts borrowed from other fields. Intelligence gathering, crime analysis, investigating, and target hardening are examples of methods acquired from law enforcement; and from sister organizations in the business environment. Corporate security has learned how to conduct audits and inventories, how to secure confidentiality agreements, and how to track and control the movement of people and property. Corporate security has also necessarily developed an expertise in the application of electronic technology to the tasks of assets protection.

In other words, corporate security is the child of change and the product of its environment. It was born out of a need and grew up learning how to cope and survive. It is what it is and does what it does because of the dictates of external and internal forces. Carried with this condition is the inherent danger that change can become so demanding that corporate security may be unable to cope and therefore unable to survive.

A New Form of Change

A change with profound and sweeping proportions is in fact brewing now. The change has to do with human values, but first a little background.

Business organizations are turning up the pressure to improve results. It is not just that results matter more today, because results have always mattered, but what we are seeing is a shift in the way results are delivered. To be sure, change is essential if organizations are to succeed in a tough, competitive world, and organizations are being judged more harshly than ever before, both by their managements and shareholders.

Change is turning organizations into clusters of clever people doing clever things, and clever people have to be handled rather more sensitively than was the case in the good old days. The tried and true concepts of control and supervision are giving way to persuasion and to leadership. Business managers now speak of visions and empowerment. An entirely new rationale is taking shape in which traditional controls are increasingly unwelcome.

For the Chief Security Officer, the mandate is to achieve the same or a higher level of results, except go about it differently. This is neither simple nor easy. On the one hand, the organization's top leadership wants the CSO to embrace bold new concepts, yet on the other hand wants no dilution in the protection of assets. Whether the CSO likes it or not, he or she is caught up in a process of learning, adapting, and, above all, accepting the proposition that the change which has begun will continue well into the foreseeable future, and that corporate security must be a constructive part of the process.

Being a part of the process is another way of saying that the CSO will continue to adapt. Successful adaptation is to continue to be effective in protecting the organization's assets, but to apply techniques that fit the ways of the new organization. But what does the new or evolving organization look like, and what are its ways?

The Shamrock Organization

Some insights can be found in Charles Handy's excellent book, *The Age of Unreason.* Handy describes what he calls the shamrock organization. The first leaf of the shamrock is the core of professional workers. These are the managers, the high fliers, the skilled technicians, and key professionals who are absolutely critical to the organization. Without them, the business cannot possibly succeed. They work hard and long, and are paid well.

Life in the professional core is collegial, resembling that in a consultancy or a professional partnership. The core structure is relatively flat, with few layers of rank. The concept of superiors and subordinates has been replaced by that of colleagues and associates.

The size of the professional core in many corporations has gotten smaller and is continuing to shrink. Two cost-driven reasons stand out: a preference for a flat organizational structure is making many positions redundant, and more and more professional core functions are being assigned to outside contractors.

The second leaf of the shamrock organization is contractors; generally, people who do specialized work. While the work may have value, it is not necessarily critical or central to the business. Contractors are able to perform these jobs better and at lower cost than regular employees,

requiring less management time and attention in the bargain.

The third leaf is the flexible labor force, the part-time and temporary workers. They move in and out of the company as the needs of the business expand, contract, and evolve. The services are not always done conveniently and to great satisfaction, but they are economical. In many U.S. corporations, flexible labor is the fastest growing segment of their workforces.

Shamrock types of organizations have been emerging at least since the early 1980s when downturns in profits forced many major corporations to make significant reductions in human-power. Hit hardest were the professional cores. When times improved, businesses were determined not to be caught the same way twice. Work that in earlier times would have been returned to the professional core was farmed out to contractors, and some of the lower-level jobs were converted to part-time and temporary status.

Instead of one workforce, many corporations now have three. Each workforce has a different contribution to make, a different commitment to the organization, a different scheme of remuneration, and a different set of expectations. Clearly, there are a number of interesting problems associated with delivering security services in such an arrangement.

Security Problems in the Shamrock Organization

In the professional core we see more people conferring and sharing information across large expanses of geography, and the information they work with has been pulled from many centers of expertise. A greater amount of sensitive information is being generated and opened to a larger number of key players in many parts of the globe.

Business information, including the most sensitive possessed by an organization, is valuable to the extent it is put to work. Although the CSO's instinct is to keep sensitive information under lock and key, the reality is that sensitive information is widely scattered and in flux at any given time for the simple reason it is in use. Information in movement is most vulnerable to loss and compromise. The utilitarian value of the information at the moment of use may only be fractional by comparison to the cost of its loss.

In the professional core we are also seeing more people making spending decisions. This is called trust and empowerment, but the CSO knows that more hands on the purse strings can lead to spending that is dishonest.

In the second of the three-leaved workforce, corporate security has to be concerned when the organization makes sensitive materials available to contractors, especially when contractors work for competitors. Sensitive materials include things like business plans, trade secrets, proprietary processes, customer lists, and executive salaries.

There is the possibility of contractors learning how to pass through protected computer gateways that lead to valuable data or to third parties connected to the system. When the know-how of access is in the hands of a disgruntled contractor, the organization can be damaged severely. Hacking, viruses, worms, and Trojan horses are possibilities, as well as disablement of a critical system by the support contractor as the result of a contractual dispute.

With regard to the third part of the workforce, there are few reasons to believe that the part-timers and temporaries who replaced regular employees are of the same caliber. One should anticipate in this group a higher level of drug-related accidents and incidents, pilferage, vandalism, confrontational behavior, and acts of violence. The vendors of flexible labor are focused on providing human-power, not on conducting pre-employment background checks. Without screening, the professional core is likely working shoulder-to-shoulder with people that cannot be trusted.

Controls Based on Motivation

The motivations that supported ethical business conduct in the old organization are changing in the shamrock organization. A concern for assets, for example, is not a motivator to people who get their paychecks elsewhere. The sense of mutual interest found in the employee/employer relationship may not be present in service arrangements, and it would be foolish to believe that vendors will place the client's economic good ahead of theirs. While persons in the professional core may have careers, love the challenge of their work, and take pleasure when the organization succeeds, the people who work on an outsourced basis look at things much differently.

The traditional techniques of organizational control, such as locking things away, compartmentalizing information, and limiting spending authority, lose their effectiveness in organizations with cultures that stress individual trust. This is not to say, however, that all of the traditional controls will disappear. It is more likely they will be modified and new controls invented as the organization continues to evolve. A good guess is that the successful controls will be founded on principles of motivation, such as the influence of peers and informal groups. Motivation may be the only means of bridging the gap between rules and the desired human behavior.

The rapidly expanding work practices that rely on desktop computing are a case in point. The provision of personal computers (PCs) to employees is the giving of trust and empowerment to a large portion of the workforce. The autonomy inherent in desktop operations, combined with the power and flexibility of the technology, present new problems in control. Mainframe computers with large databases have physical, procedural, and technical safeguards, but this is not always the case with desktop systems. The risks include data loss and theft, use of time and equipment for unauthorized purposes, and theft of hardware and software.

Although the employer may have rules and provide training concerning desktop computing, the problem is one of compliance. The highly personalized nature of a desktop work station makes it very difficult to monitor computing activity in a non-intrusive way. While it is technically possible to monitor by connecting desktop equipment to networks, observing employees with closed-circuit television (CCTV) cameras, and providing closer overall personal supervision, these are not the accepted practices in a corporation that operates on trust.

Controls based on motivation would rely on the orientation, education, and training given to employees; the personal examples set for them; and, above all, an organizational culture which holds that when given a choice, people can be trusted to act in the best interests of the organization. The designers and implementers of the controls will come from the professional core. The CSO will be a key player in designing asset-protecting controls that on the one hand will be workable and effective, and on the other hand consistent with principles of trust and empowerment. The CSO will help gain acceptance of the controls by exercising the skills of teaching and leading.

A Best Practices Approach

The CSO in an evolving organization can take the initiative in a best practices approach, i.e., practices that are done with excellence, both in and out of the corporation. Following are three hypothetical examples.

- Corporation A switched from in-house security officer services to services provided by an outside contractor. The CSO played a central role in negotiating the contract and monitoring contractor performance. Over a period of time, the corporate security department acquired considerable knowledge about contract administration. Many lessons were learned about how to hire honest, emotionally stable, and drug-free security officers; how to organize security officer operations so that services did not get in the way of the corporation's business processes; and how to train, develop, and generally treat security officers so that in return the corporation obtained quality performance accompanied by low turnover. These best practices had value to other units in the corporation that were making the switch to contractor services.
- Corporation B did pioneer work in establishing a drug- and alcohol-free workplace for its employees in the safety-sensitive environment of petroleum exploration and production. Through trial and error, corporate security learned how to educate employees against alcohol and drugs; trained supervisors to spot the indicators of impairment; and used chemical testing as a tool for steering employees away from abuse and for bringing afflicted employees into contact with treatment professionals. Corporate security shared this competency with the corporation's most important partners–the drilling contractors. A best practices approach transferred the positive elements of the substance abuse program to the contractors; and it was in the corporation's best interests to do so because, after all, the contractors performed jobs having high criticality in terms of physical loss, personal safety, and damage to the ecology.
- Corporation C observed that the corporate security department of a competitor regularly worked with the internal audit department to conduct investigative audits of vendors. The audit methodology of the competitor contained some innovative ideas for discerning patterns of collusion. Corporation C adopted and modified the methodology as a best practice.

These examples are in the nature of finding positives and putting them to work to the corporation's advantage. A best practices approach adds value and blends very well with control functions performed by a corporate security department.

Being a Contributor to Assets

It is important to remind ourselves that questions always arise about the value of providing protective services to assets that are static or in a state of decline. When the cost of protection increases or remains steady and at the same time the value of the asset falls off or remains unchanged, there is a natural tendency to want to reduce or eliminate the protection. This is an obvious fact, but it deserves mention because in the evolving organization corporate security needs to shift its focus to the enhancement of assets. The objective should be to move from simply being the watchdog of assets to being a contributor to assets. A best practices approach could be one facet of a larger effort to find and add value to the company's bottom line.

Finally, it seems appropriate to observe that the winds of change in the last half of the previous century have produced problems for nations, companies, and people. Inevitably, the enterprise we call corporate security has been affected and has risen to meet the challenges. Even greater challenges lie ahead as business organizations continue to restructure, innovate, and take on new cultures. There is no reason to suppose that the first half of this century will bring any lessening of change, and if corporate security is to evolve in harmony with the organization, it must change the ways of protecting assets.

John J. Fay

Sources

Frank, J., Shamir, B., and Briggs, W. 1991. *Security-Related Behavior of PC Users in Organizations, Information and Management.* Amsterdam: Elsevier Science Publishers.

Green, G. and Fischer, R. 2004. *Introduction to Security, 7th Edition.* Boston: Butterworth-Heinemann.

Handy, C. 1989. *The Age of Unreason.* Boston: Harvard Business School.

COUNSELING

An inherent function of supervision is to assist employees in solving personal problems that detract from their effectiveness in the workplace. Counseling can occur in almost any situation that brings the individual employee and the supervisor together for the purpose of helping the employee overcome problems.

Guidance should serve all employees and not be seen as a negative activity related only to employees with problems. Counseling given to good employees can make them even better employees. But when guidance is focused exclusively on workers who perform below the established standards, other employees may be reluctant to willingly participate in counseling for fear of being stigmatized.

A principal purpose of counseling is to help individuals learn to deal with personal problems. To be effective at counseling, the supervisor must be able to communicate on an interpersonal basis and exercise patience and good judgment. A facet of good judgment is to recognize that for an individual to deal with a personal problem there must first be a willingness to act decisively, and that one of the cardinal sins of counseling is to make decisions for the individual. An overly directive approach is apt to encourage dependence rather than self-reliance.

The opportunities for a supervisor to counsel are frequent and varied. Certainly one of the earliest opportunities is when an employee first arrives on the job. The new employee needs to become oriented geographically, meet co-workers, and learn the formal and unwritten rules of the organization. The supervisor is a main source of information, particularly with regard to showing the employee where and how he or she fits into the pattern of work activities, explaining job standards, and answering questions. A good orientation will often prevent small initial problems of adjustment from escalating to larger problems at a later time.

More than any other individual in the organization, the direct supervisor is positioned to evaluate the productivity, attitude, and potential of subordinates. Knowing something about the subordinate both as a worker and a person is necessary if the supervisor is to assist the subordinate in meeting the organization's expectations and at the same time satisfy personal goals.

Counseling Methods

Two general methods of counseling are widely recognized: the directive and non-directive methods. A third method uses the two methods together and is called the co-analysis method.

Directive Counseling. This approach is supervisor-centered. The supervisor takes the initiative in the dialogue, with the supervisor choosing the subject. The directive approach is appropriate when the individual needs to understand requirements and to identify personal deficiencies. This approach can succeed only when the individual sincerely wants to face and correct deficiencies. Although the supervisor may be very skilled in this approach, the critical element for success lies entirely within the employee.

Non-Directive Counseling. The subordinate is the central actor in non-directive counseling. He/she is encouraged to talk, to clarify personal thinking, and to discover a solution to problems through objective examination and honest articulation. The supervisor's role is to encourage the individual to take the initiative in discovering solutions, and moving positively and constructively to implement them. This approach can be helpful in removing emotional blocks and creating motives for improvement.

Co-Analysis. This approach falls somewhere between the extremes of the directive and non-directive methods. It is intended to join the supervisor and the subordinate in a mutual effort intended to work out a problem-solving regimen. Co-analysis can only succeed when the employee accepts the supervisor as a partner and sincerely wants to change. Success will also be a function of how well the supervisor can bring the employee to a clearer understanding of the problems and to obtain agreement of the solution-oriented actions.

Conducting a Counseling Session

A counseling session cannot be effective without preparation. All pertinent information concerning the employee should be gathered and studied by the supervisor. Details that may be significant to the counseling process should be committed to memory so that the flow of the session will not be interrupted by referring to written materials. The presence of files or records and the taking of notes during the session can detract from a productive outcome.

The place of counseling should be relatively free from distractions and out of general view. An employee being counseled does not want to feel conspicuous, and the absence of privacy will inhibit the employee's willingness to open up. Seating, lighting, room temperature, and the physical setting should be comfortable for both the employee and the supervisor. Because the supervisor will need the employee's undivided attention, the employee's chair should face toward the supervisor and away from background distractions such as a window or open door.

The starting point will be critical. In the first few minutes the supervisor will set the tone of the discussions and attempt to open a two-way dialogue. This is often called establishing rapport, a subtle and important activity that can be difficult. The idea is to help the employee open up by getting a conversation going, usually about a topic of personal interest such as hobbies, achievements, or current events.

Encouraging the employee to talk and participate actively may cause the employee to feel constructively involved by describing the problem and playing a part in solving it. In the early part of the meeting, the supervisor should look for information that will define the dimensions of the problem. By asking questions that require more than yes or no answers, the supervisor can gain insights to the employee's motivations, attitudes, and dislikes. The responses may clarify the problem for the supervisor and provide clues to obtaining the employee's cooperation in taking corrective actions.

A counseling session should end on a positive note. The employee should walk away with a sense that something constructive has occurred. Even more importantly, the employee should leave with a commitment to take actions that were agreed upon in the meeting and the understanding that the supervisor will be expecting to see the evidence of them. Even if the employee is only helped to perceive the actual nature of the problem, this in itself is progress.

The supervisor will not always play a part in the problem-solving process. A supervisor's competency in recommending solutions will not usually extend to problems rooted in drug and alcohol abuse, marital and family stress, financial difficulties, and mental disorders. The role of the supervisor in these situations is to refer the employee to a specialized resource, such as an employee assistance program.

When an employee is referred to another resource, the supervisor should follow up to be sure the problem is being addressed. Specialized assistance should be regarded as a helping hand, not as a substitute for supervision. Responsibility to correct the employee's unacceptable performance remains in the venue of the supervisor even when third-party specialists provide the diagnosis and treatment.

A record should be made of every counseling session. The record should document the major discussion points, actions and deadlines agreed upon, and commitments of both the employee and supervisor. In some cases, the supervisor may want to give the employee a copy of the record for use as a reference in meeting the commitments.

John J. Fay

DEMING

Long after his death, Dr. W. Edwards Deming continues to be regarded by many as the leading quality guru in the United States. He argued that quality is measured in terms of the pursuit, yet quality is not definable. You can measure improvements in quality and you will know quality when you experience it.

Credited as one of the central figures in bringing Japan to a position of world leadership in competitive pricing and quality, Deming provided both a philosophy and a system for using statistical methods to achieve higher quality and productivity in manufacturing and management. Organizational theorists characterize his approach as being in the camp of teaching people how to fish rather than feeding them. He believed quality is 85 percent the responsibility of management and 15 percent the responsibility of employees. Deming developed his fourteen points as a "charter for management" because he saw senior management's commitment as essential to the process. It is only within the past few years that his philosophy and methods have begun to gain widespread recognition for their impact on quality and productivity in U.S. companies.

Given his growing influence, it would be helpful to briefly review the highlights of his charter and examine how they can/need to be applied in the security profession.

Develop a Strategy for Constant Improvement

Deming suggested that organizations want a "quick fix," and in pursuing this they lose sight of the longer term and fail in the near term because quality is not something that can be achieved in incremental, individual efforts. Quality is a continuous, unfolding process. He offers this advice: determine what business the company is in and adapt to changing customer needs.

As a security decision maker, have you developed a process for Continuous Quality Improvement (CQI)? Are job descriptions and performance objectives centered more on encouraging CQI as a way of doing business, for example, by keeping track of the number of doors found opened and unlocked, or the hours of investigative time spent, or the number of escorts provided?

Adopt a New Paradigm

We need to approach quality with a persistence that establishes the ultimate goal as an error-free operation. The goal is to achieve quality over time through a process of continuous improvement.

Replace Mass Inspection with Employee Troubleshooting

By their very nature, inspections have a negative connotation. The process involves an overseer acting independent of the process. Inspections

need to be replaced by employees assuming ownership for their service and/or production. As a part of assuming ownership, there is a need to develop a means of empowering employees to troubleshoot the process when errors are discovered. It's easy to put off known deficiencies, placing accountability away from oneself and saying simply, "Well it's not my job."

We know that security can't be everywhere, all the time. Unfortunately, for many years security professionals have preached that prevention begins with awareness. This is only half true. Prevention will not work until employees—including managers—assume responsibility for their awareness and translate this awareness into action (ownership).

End the Practice of Awarding Contracts on Price Alone

Instead of awarding work to the provider with the lowest bid, which is often tantamount to accepting minimal quality at best, companies need to develop long-term relationships with suppliers. Deming's view was that as long as organizations see vendors as vendors, they will remain vendors. When they see them as partners, they will become partners. Creating this new perspective requires nurturing mutual respect, trust, and responsibility, and offering rewards.

Promote Leadership and Institute Training

Managers need to understand that the title, manager, means that they are responsible for managing processes and things, not people. Managers lead people. This is a very critical, but oftentimes misunderstood difference. Leading involves supporting, delegating, and empowering people to achieve their fullest potential. Leadership involves coaching and mentoring as much as demonstrating by example and pushing people in positive ways to accomplish more. As many management theorists note, the organization is in the business it's in, but managers are in the organization business—and that means the business of developing people. A manager's final product is creating an environment in which people can make their best contributions, and consequently the organization can be productive and successful.

Leadership also involves eliminating fear. Deming noted that companies that make it "unsafe" for employees to ask questions and learn to do things right are facing tremendous economic losses on the way to their own demise. Employees who are afraid are not free to create. An environment of fear is directly rooted in traditional performance evaluations where compensation is tied to "those who toe the line" as opposed to those who dare to challenge assumptions and seek to make meaningful contributions.

Deming, along with many others, insisted that most performance problems can be traced to a lack of orientation and training programs. Management needs to set expectations for employees and demonstrate how workers can be successful in their jobs. This is especially true for people working in asset protection. Despite the emphasis that third-party suppliers put on their ability to train, educating employees is still one of their weakest links. The same can often be said for resident security programs.

In the security field, training is limited to primarily on-the-job learning. Initial officer training rarely exceeds twelve hours, and advanced officer training is done in a variety of ways, but invariably in the way determined to be the least costly. In short, the quality of training is largely determined by price, regardless of which side one considers. But real training is neither easy nor quick. Interactive communicating, group planning, and problem solving are the first stages. Deming believed that effective training is driven from the top down. When training begins at the top, managers and supervisors are aligned behind the same concepts and share a common language. Next, those in work groups or project teams on the pilot quality effort are trained in the new methods, teamwork, and statistical techniques. Eventually a training program is implemented for each area of work.

Eliminate Hype and Quotas

Deming rejected hype such as slogans, contests, targets, and other forms of internal competition. He thought that such efforts have little meaning and impact unless they originate from within the workforce. I'm not convinced that he is right here. Nonetheless, Deming contended that internal competition works against the goal of removing internal barriers. He believed that organizations

need to redirect the competitive spirit to their real competitors in the outside business world.

Deming also believed that quotas should be eliminated. This move can be particularly difficult for many businesspeople since we have all been conditioned since the advent of the Industrial Revolution to believe that businesses run on numbers. Profit and losses, production units, services provided—all share a common denominator: they are driven by numbers. Yet achieving the numbers alone does not necessarily equate with achieving quality, market share, or innovation. Workers who are held to quotas are held to yesterday's standards; they are not moving the company into the future. Worse, quotas merely guarantee that workers will do whatever it takes to make the mark. An excellent example of a counterproductive system is today's version of the old Detext guard watch tours. Although the Detext watch tours system is hailed as the definitive means to track security officers, an experienced officer can quickly figure out ways to effectively "beat the system."

Remove Barriers and Promote Continuous Quality Improvement

It is up to management to encourage the process of interactive listening. This means really listening to what employees have to say about what gets in the way of their performing well. To eliminate barriers entails making available the resources necessary to accomplish the task(s) at hand—by developing innovative operating practices, assuring proper levels of staffing, and providing the necessary technology. Deming insisted that a special top management team must develop a plan of action to carry out the quality mission. The organization is a holistic system, including all of its influencing factors—internal and external customers, suppliers, and competitors—and it needs constant perfecting.

The remaining seven points of Deming's charter are known as the Seven Deadly Sins.

1. Failing to develop a long-term purpose. American businesses are driven by quarterly and/or annual results. Success is measured based on how well you perform this quarter or this year as compared to the previous quarter or year. The lack of a longer view makes

employees and managers feel insecure in their jobs, and this problem then feeds directly into the second deadly disease.

2. Focusing on near-term profits. American businesses define their success based on quarterly earnings. Public companies are driven by expected returns from the investment community. This preoccupation with profit for the sake of profit erodes concern for and attention to the longer view. Quite often resources that are designed to feed the future are sapped for the sake of making the near-term profit.

3. Conducting annual performance reviews. Annual performance reviews rarely measure true annual performance. Instead they reflect the last "you done me wrong" or "attaboy." Employees soon discover that performance reviews involve more punishment than encouragement. Deming believed that the impact of these measurements on the morale and productivity of both managers and workers is the opposite of what is intended because performance reviews promote fear, inequities, internal competition, anger, and discouragement.

4. Not discouraging management exodus. Deming pointed out that the migration of high-level managers from one company to another is a tradition. Whether those who leave are dedicated executives who have become disenfranchised or opportunists, the fault is the company's for not developing managers with the "big picture" in mind. Over the past several years, corporations have unwittingly turned on themselves by collaborating in the wholesale elimination of middle and senior layers of management. In their pursuit of lower operating expenses and higher dividends for stockholders, they have lost both their own continuity and the talent once hired to create their future.

5. Missing the hidden value. A company's success is linked just as much to intangible values as to empirical, or "known," data. Unfortunately, many companies miss the former altogether in their pursuit of the latter. As Deming explained, some of the most important factors are "unknowable," including the multiplier effect of a happy or unhappy customer, the absence of motivated managers and workers who are willing to go the extra mile that makes all the difference, and the hours saved down the line by front-end planning and proper communication.

6. Failing to emphasize health care prevention. Even though many companies are turning to health care prevention programs, the vast majority of American businesses have yet to make the transition. The evidence clearly demonstrates that significant savings can be achieved in premiums when prevention becomes the front line. These programs include wellness programs, antismoking programs, paid workouts and/or health club memberships, and annual medical checkups.

7. Substituting Continuous Quality Improvement for warranties. It has become easy for companies to offer warranties. Yet the real value of their product and/or service is not based on "customer satisfaction guarantees." While such guarantees provide an assurance that the company is concerned about the quality of its product, the real value to the company is in establishing error-free systems altogether. Companies that commit to quality and error-free work realize savings during a warranty period because they decrease the number of nonanticipated services. In other words, the warranty is the consumers' safety net; it is not the company's substitution for CQI.

On the surface, it would appear that these seven deadly sins have applications that are easily applied to security providers. Even though each has a specific lesson for the third-party supplier, the underlying principles apply to resident security programs as well. Security decision makers need to be focused on the longer-term strategy for providing asset protection, and this has special relevance to their systems purchases. All too often, the procurement process is driven by answering the need here and now. As the company grows or alters its course, today's "new" security system quickly becomes obsolete.

Similarly, focus on short-term profits can be just as deadly to security programs, and organizations as well. In today's litigious society, premises liability has become big business for plaintiff attorneys. Companies that defer taking the proper precautions until better economic times are in swing are placing themselves at greater risk. There are many ways to creatively finance capital expenditures or to budget operating expenses. One of the more commonly overlooked approaches, for example, involves splitting the cost over a longer budget period, for example, by extending the budget cycle from twelve months to eighteen months.

Deming's belief that annual performance reviews work against the employer-employee relationship is worthy of particular note with regards to the security operation. He did not advocate that performance not be reviewed; rather, he found the approach troubling. In his judgment, peer reviews, group assessments, quality circles, demonstrable contributions, and so forth worked better.

One of the more difficult challenges facing corporate America, and in particular the security profession, is the issue of management mobility. It remains true that a company's success is linked to its ability to come up with fresh ideas and new perspectives on a regular basis. It is also equally true that a company's success is linked to its ability to maintain a balance of continuity. Longevity is not bad.

Security programs are built on earned trust and proven reliability. Whether the people are proprietary, outsourced, or a combination of the two, the success that is achieved is directly related to demonstrated capability. Such know-how is difficult to measure, but it is very much real.

Deming's last two deadly sins speak to a reliance on traditional approaches and their inherent traps. There was a time when the costs of health care benefits were an insignificant part of the compensation formula. With runaway costs, however, this is no longer the case. As opposed to shopping for lower premiums among competing carriers, companies should be changing their strategy altogether. By seeking an alternative health care approach, companies can attack at the root the cost associated with escalating expenses. The result is lower cost all around. The question to be asked is whether or not the same type of paradigm can be applied elsewhere.

In a like vein, warranties have become a standard business practice. There was a time when guarantees by their nature forced employees to think error-free. The corporation understood well the cost associated with having to redo or replace a defective product. Over time, warranties have become the employee's safety net. After all, managers will reason, the company can afford a few mistakes. Besides, how many people really go through the effort to take us up on our warranty? Such misguided and what I would term "lazy" thinking misses the very point of offering a guarantee.

Conclusion

In concluding this discussion of Deming's contribution, it is appropriate to review several obstacles he identified. These obstacles plague organizations because they are grounded in management mind-sets that work against their best interests. Yet because of America's obsession with short-term fixes, executives and business unit heads frequently find themselves heading down a path that leads straight to such obstacles, and not in the direction of success, as they had hoped. Security managers are no exception in meeting obstacles:

- The quick fix. You cannot put a quality process in place overnight.
- Reliance on technology as the great problem solver. Technology is an administrative tool. Nothing more. Real quality arrives when tools are used by skilled specialists.
- Following the leader. Organizations that wait for "the other guy" to chart a new course and then follow the other's lead will always be behind.
- Accountability for quality assurance is limited. Too often, QA programs are meaningful to QA professionals but not to the entire workforce.

Deming and his ideas have had profound effects on how managers think and act. Unlike many other management concepts, the Deming approach has a proven track record. His ideas have been a catalyst for extensive research and have been an inspiration for many of today's business leaders.

Dennis Dalton

Sources

Dalton, D. 1995. *Security Management: Business Strategies for Success*. Boston: Butterworth-Heinemann.

Gulick, L. and Urwick, L. eds. 1937. *Papers on the Science of Administration*. New York: Institute of Public Administration.

Morehouse, D. 1992. *Total Quality Management: A Supervisor's Handbook*. Shawnee Mission: National Press Publications.

DISABILITY DISCRIMINATION

Title I of the Americans with Disabilities Act of 1990 prohibits private employers, state and local governments, employment agencies, and labor unions from discriminating against qualified individuals with disabilities in job application procedures, hiring, firing, advancement, compensation, job training, and other terms, conditions, and privileges of employment. The ADA covers employers with 15 or more employees, including state and local governments. It also applies to employment agencies and to labor organizations. The ADA's nondiscrimination standards also apply to federal sector employees under section 501 of the Rehabilitation Act, as amended, and its implementing rules.

An individual with a disability is a person who:

- Has a physical or mental impairment that substantially limits one or more major life activities.
- Has a record of such an impairment.
- Is regarded as having such an impairment.

A qualified employee or applicant with a disability is an individual who, with or without reasonable accommodation, can perform the essential functions of the job in question. Reasonable accommodation may include, but is not limited to:

- Making existing facilities used by employees readily accessible to and usable by persons with disabilities.
- Job restructuring, modifying work schedules, reassignment to a vacant position.
- Acquiring or modifying equipment or devices, adjusting or modifying examinations, training materials, or policies, and providing qualified readers or interpreters.

An employer is required to make a reasonable accommodation to the known disability of a qualified applicant or employee if it would not impose an "undue hardship" on the operation of the employer's business. Undue hardship is defined as an action requiring significant difficulty or expense when considered in light of factors such as an employer's size, financial resources, and the nature and structure of its operation.

An employer is not required to lower quality or production standards to make an accommodation; nor is an employer obligated to provide personal use items such as glasses or hearing aids.

Title I of the ADA also covers:

- Medical Examinations and Inquiries. Employers may not ask job applicants about the existence, nature, or severity of a disability. Applicants may be asked about their ability to perform specific job functions. A job offer may be conditioned on the results of a medical examination, but only if the examination is required for all entering employees in similar jobs. Medical examinations of employees must be job related and consistent with the employer's business needs.
- Drug and Alcohol Abuse. Employees and applicants currently engaging in the illegal use of drugs are not covered by the ADA when an employer acts on the basis of such use. Tests for illegal drugs are not subject to the ADA's restrictions on medical examinations. Employers may hold illegal drug users and alcoholics to the same performance standards as other employees.

It is also unlawful to retaliate against an individual for opposing employment practices that discriminate based on disability or for filing a discrimination charge, testifying, or participating in any way in an investigation, proceeding, or litigation under the ADA.

Source The U.S. Equal Employment Opportunity Commission 2006. <http://www.eeoc.gov/types/ada.html>

DISCIPLINE

As a rule, the word discipline evokes an emotional reaction, both to the giver and the receiver. No one enjoys being disciplined and most supervisors would rather do anything but administer it, but the fact remains that discipline is an important part of supervision.

On the brighter side, discipline need not be totally negative. A positive approach will emphasize discipline accompanied by guidance, sanctions that are balanced with fairness, and a system of rules that apply to all employees uniformly and consistently.

The word discipline is derived from the Latin word *discipulus*, which means learning. The word *disciple* is from the same root. Early Christian disciples were considered the learners or students of Christ. The word conveys an important concept in supervision, i.e., that discipline is a mechanism for correcting and molding employees in the interests of achieving organizational goals. Punishment, the negative aspect of discipline, is tangential to the larger purpose of fostering desirable behavior.

Discipline is an act of the organization, not of a supervisor personally. The process is a legitimate means to an end and condemns the employee's unacceptable behavior without condemning the employee. The process essentially says, "You're okay, but what you did is not okay."

It is also important that discipline be swift. Coming to grips with a problem immediately is better than putting it off until later. Uncorrected problem behavior tends to worsen and takes on new dimensions over time. Instead of one problem, the dilatory supervisor may discover that he has one very large problem plus a number of new ones. Discipline that is applied without undue delay has a preventive influence if only for the simple reason that the offending employee is not given time to repeat the unacceptable conduct.

A note of caution is appropriate here: the supervisor should not rush into disciplinary action. Acting swiftly is important, but is not as important as obtaining all of the facts of the situation and weighing the facts carefully to arrive at a considered and deliberate judgment.

Discipline Can Be Difficult

Discipline is a responsibility that rests squarely on the supervisor's shoulders. It cannot be passed upward to the boss or laterally to a human resources specialist. A supervisor can find lots of reasons for not giving discipline: the employee is a friend, a good person, or will get upset; the workload is too heavy right now; wait until performance appraisal time to bring it up; and, it's not a popular thing to do. These are, of course, rationalizations for avoiding a difficult responsibility.

The fact is that most employees want to work in a well-ordered environment and they recognize that discipline is an essential element of good order. While no one wants to be the object of discipline, there is an acceptance of discipline as an expected consequence of violating a rule. Employees may wish for leniency in those situations where it is deserved but not leniency across the board. They worry that overly tolerant supervision will allow a few employees to engage in violations that adversely affect everyone.

While leniency may be somewhat negotiable between a supervisor and the supervised, there can be no compromise with respect to fairness and consistency. Even a hint of unfair or discriminatory discipline can be poisonous to the process and destructive to the supervisor's reputation.

Disciplinary Principles

Principle 1: Assume Nothing. Ensure that everyone knows the rules. Put the rules in writing; make them a regular item of discussion in formal and informal sessions; disseminate and display them prominently. An employee who does not know the rules cannot be expected to follow them, and a supervisor should not discipline an employee when there is doubt that the employee was unaware of the rule.

Principle 2: Discipline in Privacy. Receiving discipline is never a pleasant experience and can be particularly unpleasant when it is received in the presence of co-workers or others who have no legitimate role in the process. Embarrassment, anger, and resentment are the natural emotions that follow criticism given publicly. Discipline is a private matter to be handled behind closed doors or in a setting that ensures absolute privacy.

Principle 3: Be Objective. Rely on facts, not opinions and speculations. Consider all the facts and examine them with an open mind. Look for and eliminate any biases, for or against the offender. Make sure there is in fact a violation and determine the relative severity of the violation. Was the offender's act aggravated or mitigated in any way?

Principle 4: Educate the Violator. Administer discipline that is constructive. The purpose is to bring about a positive change in the violator's conduct or performance. Discipline should be a learning experience in which the violator gains new insights that contribute to personal improvement.

Principle 5: Be Consistent. Inconsistent enforcement of policy and rules should be totally unacceptable. For example, if the policy of the department is to terminate officers who sleep on the job, then all officers so caught must be terminated. To fire one and not another will breed contempt for the rules and those who set the rules.

Principle 6: Do Not Humiliate. The intended outcome is to correct, not hurt. When humiliation is made a part of the process, the offender will come away angry, resentful, and perhaps ready to fail again. Both the offender and the organization will suffer as a consequence.

Principle 7: Document Infractions. Make a record of violations. This is not to say that a negative dossier be maintained on each employee, but it does mean that instances of unacceptable performance have to be recorded. The record of an employee's failures is valuable as substantiation for severe discipline, such as termination, or as a diagnostic aid to counseling professionals.

Principle 8: Discipline Promptly. With the passage of time, an uncorrected violation fades into vagueness. The violator forgets details, discards any guilt he may have felt at the time of the violation, and rationalizes the violation as something of little importance. When opened for discussion, an uncorrected violation is likely to lead to disagreement about what "really happened" and any disciplinary action at that point can appear to be unreasonable.

Giving Clear Instructions

It is sad but true that discipline is sometimes meted out when the supervisor is partially at fault. When this occurs, it is usually not in connection with a rules violation, but with a failure of the employee to complete a task or to carry out the task in some particular way. The fault of the supervisor is in having given poor instructions.

The supervisor's instructions may not have been enunciated distinctly or presented in a logical sequence. The instructions may have been too complicated for the employee to follow, or they could have come across to the employee as intimidating or belittling. Even when an assignment is understood, it may not be completed because emotions get in the way. Asking is always better than demanding.

Following are tips on how to assign work:

- Know the assignment yourself.
- Do not assign work above the employee's ability.
- Explain the purpose of the assignment.
- Request or suggest—do not demand.
- Give brief, exact directions.
- Demonstrate if possible.
- Do not assume the employee understands perfectly.
- Do not watch every move; let the employee feel responsible.
- Let the employee know you are available to give assistance.

Most employees want to do a good job. If care is taken in giving assignments, there will be fewer failures and fewer resulting disciplinary problems.

Self-Discipline

No manager or supervisor can ever hope to discipline others effectively if he cannot discipline himself. Self-discipline is a foundation for working with other people, helping them overcome their failures, and for setting a workplace climate where good order is the norm.

Loss of temper may make a supervisor feel better for a while, but it will not improve personal performance or the performance of the supervised. Although some subordinates may quickly respond in the face of an angry outburst, the overall effect creates confusion, resentment, and loss of confidence in the supervisor as a leader.

Arguing with subordinates is a waste of everyone's time. Explaining and discussing are very necessary to good supervision because they operate to dispel misunderstanding, but when the dialogue gets argumentative, the process of communicating breaks down rapidly.

Recognizing subordinates for good work is a tried and true technique for creating harmonious working relationships. Those who use it well find that it works best when applied sparingly. Extending a great deal of recognition generally or directing it at one or a few persons reduces the effect. But certainly the greatest error in using recognition is to give the appearance of favoritism.

Consciously or subconsciously, subordinates tend to emulate their superiors. If the supervisor displays a lack of self-discipline, so will the supervised. Self-discipline in this sense goes beyond just maintaining personal composure. It deals with all manner of traits, for example, integrity, loyalty, and demeanor.

Constructive discipline is positive. It is focused on correcting unacceptable acts rather than on the personalities of the actors, and it is a process that relies more on education than on punishment. The supervisor administers discipline promptly but not hastily, objectively but leniently when appropriate, and always with fairness and consistency. Clear communications enhance the process, privacy and confidentiality cloak it, and good records provide a history.

Charles A. Sennewald

EQUAL PAY AND COMPENSATION DISCRIMINATION

The right of employees to be free from discrimination in their compensation is protected under several federal laws, including the following enforced by the U.S. Equal Employment Opportunity Commission (EEOC): the Equal Pay Act of 1963, Title VII of the Civil Rights Act of 1964, the Age Discrimination in Employment Act of 1967, and Title I of the Americans with Disabilities Act of 1990.

The Equal Pay Act requires that men and women be given equal pay for equal work in the same establishment. The jobs need not be identical, but they must be substantially equal. It is job content, not job titles, that determines whether jobs are substantially equal. Specifically, the EPA provides:

Employers may not pay unequal wages to men and women who perform jobs that require substantially equal skill, effort, and responsibility, and that are performed under similar working conditions within the same establishment. Each of these factors is summarized below:

- Skill—Measured by factors such as the experience, ability, education, and training required to perform the job. The key issue is what skills are required for the job, not what skills the individual employees may have. For example, two bookkeeping jobs could be considered equal under the EPA even if one of the job holders has a master's degree in physics, since that degree would not be required for the job.
- Effort—The amount of physical or mental exertion needed to perform the job. For example, suppose that men and women work side by side on a line assembling machine parts. The person at the end of the line must also lift the assembled product as he or she completes the work and place it on a board. That job requires more effort than the other assembly line jobs if the extra effort of lifting the assembled product off the line is substantial and is a regular part of the job. As a result, it would not be a violation to pay that person more, regardless of whether the job is held by a man or a woman.
- Responsibility—The degree of accountability required in performing the job. For example, a salesperson who is delegated the duty of determining whether to accept customers' personal checks has more responsibility than other salespeople. On the other hand, a minor difference in responsibility, such as turning out the lights at the end of the day, would not justify a pay differential.

- Working Conditions—This encompasses two factors: (1) physical surroundings like temperature, fumes, and ventilation; and (2) hazards.
- Establishment—The prohibition against compensation discrimination under the EPA applies only to jobs within an establishment. An establishment is a distinct physical place of business rather than an entire business or enterprise consisting of several places of business. However, in some circumstances, physically separate places of business should be treated as one establishment. For example, if a central administrative unit hires employees, sets their compensation, and assigns them to work locations, the separate work sites can be considered part of one establishment.

Pay differentials are permitted when they are based on seniority, merit, quantity or quality of production, or a factor other than sex. These are known as "affirmative defenses" and it is the employer's burden to prove that they apply.

In correcting a pay differential, no employee's pay may be reduced. Instead, the pay of the lower paid employee(s) must be increased.

Title VII, ADEA, and ADA

Title VII, the ADEA, and the ADA prohibit compensation discrimination on the basis of race, color, religion, sex, national origin, age, or disability. Unlike the EPA, there is no requirement under Title VII, the ADEA, or the ADA that the claimant's job be substantially equal to that of a higher paid person outside the claimant's protected class, nor do these statutes require the claimant to work in the same establishment as a comparator.

Compensation discrimination under Title VII, the ADEA, or the ADA can occur in a variety of forms. For example:

- An employer pays an employee with a disability less than similarly situated employees without disabilities and the employer's explanation (if any) does not satisfactorily account for the differential.
- A discriminatory compensation system has been discontinued but still has lingering discriminatory effects on present salaries. For example, if an employer has a compensation policy or practice that pays Hispanics lower salaries than other employees, the employer must not only adopt a new non-discriminatory compensation policy, he/she also must affirmatively eradicate salary disparities that began prior to the adoption of the new policy and make the victims whole.
- An employer sets the compensation for jobs predominately held by, for example, women or African-Americans below that suggested by the employer's job evaluation study, while the pay for jobs predominately held by men or whites is consistent with the level suggested by the job evaluation study.
- An employer maintains a neutral compensation policy or practice that has an adverse impact on employees in a protected class and cannot be justified as job-related and consistent with business necessity. For example, if an employer provides extra compensation to employees who are the "head of household," i.e., married with dependents and the primary financial contributor to the household, the practice may have an unlawful disparate impact on women.

It is also unlawful to retaliate against an individual for opposing employment practices that discriminate based on compensation or for filing a discrimination charge, testifying, or participating in any way in an investigation, proceeding, or litigation under Title VII, ADEA, ADA, or the Equal Pay Act.

Source   The U.S. Equal Employment Opportunity Commission. 2006. <http://www.eeoc.gov/types/epa.html>

GRAMM-LEACH-BLILEY ACT

Information that many would consider private—including bank balances and account numbers—is regularly bought and sold by banks, credit card companies, and other financial institutions. The Gramm-Leach-Bliley Act (GLBA), which is also known as the Financial Services Modernization Act of 1999, provides limited privacy protections against the sale of private financial information. Additionally, the GLBA codifies protections against pretexting, the practice of obtaining personal information through false pretenses.

The GLBA primarily sought to "modernize" financial services—that is, end regulations that prevented the merger of banks, stock brokerage companies, and insurance companies. The removal of these regulations, however, raised significant risks that these new financial institutions would have access to an incredible amount of personal information, with no restrictions upon its use. Prior to GLBA, an insurance company that maintained health records was distinct from the bank that mortgaged houses and stockbrokers that traded stocks. Once these companies merged, however, they would have the ability to consolidate, analyze, and sell the personal details of their customers' lives. Because of these risks, the GLBA included three simple requirements to protect the personal data of individuals:

- Banks, brokerage companies, and insurance companies must securely store personal financial information.
- The above companies must give consumers the option to opt-out of some sharing of personal financial information.
- Consumers must be advised of policies on sharing of personal financial information.

Privacy Protections

The GLBA's privacy protections only regulate financial institutions—businesses that are engaged in banking, insuring, stocks and bonds, financial advice, and investing.

First, these financial institutions, whether they wish to disclose personal information or not, must develop precautions to ensure the security and confidentiality of customer records and information, to protect against any anticipated threats or hazards to the security or integrity of such records, and to protect against unauthorized access to or use of such records or information which could result in substantial harm or inconvenience to any customer.

Second, financial institutions are required to provide a notice of their information sharing policies when a person first becomes a customer, and annually thereafter. That notice must inform the consumer of the financial institutions' policies on:

- Disclosing nonpublic personal information (NPI) to affiliates and nonaffiliated third parties.
- Disclosing NPI after the customer relationship is terminated, and protecting NPI.

"Nonpublic personal information" means all information on applications to obtain financial services (credit card or loan applications), account histories (bank or credit card), and the fact that an individual is or was a customer. This interpretation of NPI makes names, addresses, telephone numbers, Social Security Numbers, and other data subject to the GLBA's data sharing restrictions.

Third, the GLBA gives consumers the right to opt-out from a limited amount of NPI sharing. Specifically, a consumer can direct the financial institution to not share information with unaffiliated companies.

Consumers have no right under the GLBA to stop sharing of NPI among affiliates. An affiliate is any company that controls, is controlled by, or is under common control with another company. The individual consumer has absolutely no control over this kind of "corporate family" trading of personal information.

There are several exemptions under the GLBA that can permit information sharing over the consumer's objection. For instance, if a financial institution wishes to engage the services of a separate company, it can transfer personal information to that company by arguing that the information is necessary to the services that the company will perform. A financial institution can transfer information to a marketing or sales company to sell new products (different stocks) or jointly offered products (co-sponsored credit cards). Once this unaffiliated third party has a consumer's personal information, it can be shared with the corporate family. However, the corporate family cannot likewise transfer the information to further companies through this exemption.

In addition, financial institutions can disclose information to credit reporting agencies, financial regulatory agencies, as part of the sale of a business, to comply with any other laws or regulations, or as necessary for a transaction requested by the consumer.

Fourth, financial institutions are prohibited from disclosing, other than to a consumer reporting agency, access codes or account numbers to any nonaffiliated third party for use in telemarketing, direct mail marketing, or other marketing through electronic mail. Thus, even if a consumer fails to "opt-out" of a financial institution's transfers, credit card numbers, PINs, or other access codes cannot be sold, as they had been in some previous cases.

Fifth, certain types of "pretexting" are prohibited by the GLBA. Pretexting is the practice of collecting personal information under false pretenses. Pretexters pose as authority figures (law enforcement agents, social workers, potential employers, etc.) and manufacture seductive stories (that the victim is about to receive a sweepstakes award or insurance payment) in order to elicit personal information about the victim. The GLBA prohibits the use of false, fictitious, or fraudulent statements or documents to get customer information from a financial institution or directly from a customer of a financial institution; the use of forged, counterfeit, lost, or stolen documents to get customer information from a financial institution or directly from a customer of a financial institution; and asking another person to get someone else's customer information using false, fictitious, or fraudulent documents or forged, counterfeit, lost, or stolen documents.

However, investigators still can call friends, relatives, or entities not covered by the GLBA under false pretenses in order to gain information on the victim.

Source Electronic Privacy Information Center. 2005. <http://www.epic.org/privacy/glba/default.html>

IN PURSUIT OF QUALITY

Much of what is written today about quality is not very complex. Among the many themes discussed, you'll discover some old concepts hidden behind some new names, yet they're easy to miss because the current terminology sounds very technical. For example, what today is called "reengineering" is, for the most part, simply reorganizing. When asked why reengineering is necessary, organizational specialists will point out several advantages. They will begin by explaining the merits of "enhanced levels of productivity." We will read about how analyzing "cycle times"—a process initially developed for manufacturers to measure the cost associated with bringing a new product to the market—reduces costs while increasing quality. We'll also hear about structuring the workplace to achieve "added value for a greater return on investment."

These ideas and this new language may sound refreshing, but in many cases businesses are revisiting concepts and challenges that have faced managers, owners, and investors for decades.

In 1928 John Lee, controller of the Central Telegraph Office for England, addressed a group of work directors, managers, foremen, and forewomen at Oxford and detailed the pros and cons of functionalism. We can find relevance with his concepts in today's organizational gurus about the need to structure along functional lines as opposed to geographic boundaries. Many of today's Fortune 200 companies are restructuring themselves to consolidate business units based on the inner relationship of their functional utility and not demographic regions.

Simply put, today's emphasis on quality improvement is but the next step in the evolution of maximizing efficiency without diminishing effectiveness. Since early on, management theorists and practitioners have explored a wide variety of new approaches. Regardless of history or who is saying what, clearly today's emphasis is on achieving quality. In the context of customer satisfaction, quality can be pursued in a number of different ways. New concepts are being integrated with centuries-old approaches. Much of what is being advocated is an attempt to quantify quality. The mission is to establish criteria that can be measured empirically. And, in pursuing such criteria, we are somehow led to understand that we are engaging in quality efforts. Wrong! Quality is not something that can be pursued. It is an end result. Quality arrives when efficiency and effectiveness are maximized. Business executives can develop and pursue pricing strategies. They can achieve profitability and reduce production time and costs. They can do these things and more and still not achieve quality. Quality is a consequence. It has its own essence and comes only when certain elements occur in a proper alignment.

Understanding the nature of quality is critical to achieving quality. Many companies have become extremely frustrated in their attempts to pursue quality because they follow the mechanics, many of which will be discussed below. They work hard at achieving measurable, mechanical results. And when they are all done, they question whether or not their efforts were worthwhile since they fail to see quality. Others mistakenly believe that when they have completed a prescribed task list, they have achieved quality. They are convinced that completing the course means they now possess quality—whatever that means. After all, aren't they assured quality promised if they accomplish each task? Unfortunately, the answer is no.

Quality is a state of being. We know quality when we see a fine piece of furniture hand-crafted by a master carpenter. We see it in art and in the design of such things as automobiles and buildings. We also see it in service performance. One of the central principles of quality is caring. People who are quality driven will accomplish improvement in carrying out tasks because they care—they want to do a good job. They take pride in their work and like the credit given to them, but they don't necessarily seek it. After all, they know that quality will be recognized naturally, and due credit will come.

I have said that quality arrives. What exactly does this mean? Perhaps an example will help. You go to a concert or a sports event. At some point in the process of watching you find that "you are into it." You are no longer just the disengaged spectator. The performer or athlete has engaged you. It's more than just cheering or applauding; you feel the experience. You're excited. You're uplifted. You identify with what is unfolding in front of you. The athletes on the field or the performers onstage have captured you because of their professional skill. Another way of putting this is to say that because they have efficiently and effectively maximized their skills, they have brought you, the customer, truer satisfaction. You know that it is quality, but you cannot measure the quality you feel. It's there. It's very real. Quality is a phenomenon that emerges. It is the blending of the science and the art and transcends the mere mechanics of a process.

Dennis Dalton

Sources

Dalton, D. 1995. *Security Management: Business Strategies for Success*. Boston: Butterworth-Heinemann.

Gulick, L. and Urwick, L. eds. 1937. *Papers on the Science of Administration*. New York: Institute of Public Administration.

Morehouse, D. 1992. *Total Quality Management: A Supervisor's Handbook*. Shawnee Mission: National Press Publications.

INTERNSHIPS: THE SECURITY MANAGER'S APPRENTICE

Internship programs provide college students with opportunities to learn on the job while receiving degree credits. Internship programs have succeeded so well that many schools require students to complete one or more as a degree requirement, and on some campuses the number of prospective interns exceeds the number of available internships. Students are often caught in a Catch-22 situation created by a degree requirement (or a personal desire) that is unmatched by opportunities to gain relevant work experience with local companies. The problem seems to be rooted in a preoccupation of business leaders with the pursuit of business goals and a failure of college administrators to effectively promote internship programs.

As a result, students in Security Management degree programs are often denied the chance to develop insights and skills that can only come from working in a security management setting. This is a damaging result both for the development of the individual and professionalization of the security field.

Employers needing to fill entry-level positions often seek candidates who have a blend of formal education, training, and related experience. A Security Management degree fills the educational requirement. The elements of training and experience, however, are often absent in the personal portfolios of candidates. The reason is that many students were too busy pursuing their degrees to be more than superficially involved in the security profession. The internship program provides learning based on meaningful work experience.

A minimum number of hours are required from the intern for the semester. In a few cases they are paid (usually minimum wage); in most cases they are not paid. The intern is graded on participation, with the sponsor providing feedback to the school. A short-term paper describing the work is usually required and this can be reviewed by the sponsor as well.

Work and observation begins at the start of the semester and continues throughout the term. The school provides a set of expectations covering such topics as conduct, dress, and expectations of the school, supplemented by similar instructions from the sponsor. It serves a business well when internships can span two semesters. Scheduling assignments are made easier and continuity improves the quality of the work product.

A waiver can be developed addressing any inherent liability issues, if that is a matter of concern. The laws vary from state to state, and the waiver should be developed jointly with the school and the company's legal representative.

Interns should neither be used merely to supplement clerical staffing nor for mundane assignments. Obviously, there will be some duties that involve clerical effort. Interns should not be used to stand post, unless it applies specifically to their internship. They should be exposed to as many elements of the program as is permitted, including attendance at staff meetings, for example.

Interns required to comply with the National Industrial Security Program (NISP) can be processed for personnel security clearances. Since the clearance process can take several months, the interns can be exposed during the first semester to those elements of the NISP that do not require a clearance; during the second semester, after receiving clearances, they can be assigned more sensitive tasks.

Advantages and Disadvantages

The potential advantages to a business of an internship program include:

1. An intern can be a valuable contributor. This presupposes that the business has interviewed the candidate and found him/her acceptable; has placed the intern under a good supervisor; and assigned to the intern a combination of tasks that when properly performed, will result in a valuable work product or service.
2. The intern's competency and suitability for future hire as a full-time employee can be evaluated during the internship period.
3. Projects put on hold for lack of personnel can be completed through internship contributions. Projects can include conducting studies, writing procedures, and creating security awareness materials.
4. An intern program casts favorable light on the sponsoring company, both as a responsible corporate citizen in the surrounding community and as a supporter of security professionalization.

The potential disadvantages include:

1. Time devoted to the internship program may draw the sponsoring company from business objectives of greater import.
2. The sponsor may not be oriented toward training to the degree necessary to ensure good work performance by the intern and to ensure that the intern learns from the work experience.
3. Liability issues could be presented.

Joining an Internship Program

A company that agrees to participate in an internship program will need to meet the administrative requirements of the local college or university and at the same time set up its own mechanisms for selecting interns, in-processing them, assigning supervisors, reviewing their performance and learning, and returning them to the academic setting in an improved condition. Following is an outline of action steps in setting up and operating the program within the sponsoring company.

1. Interview candidates. Ensure that the company's criteria for employment can be met by the candidate. Fully discuss the company's expectations and requirements with respect to work hours, use of company equipment, care of company assets, dress, conduct, etc.

2. Obtain an understanding from the school and the intern concerning the length of the internship, the beginning and ending dates, and any days that may require the intern to be absent. Ascertain the school's requirements with respect to reports of the intern's work performance, progress, achievements, and so forth.

3. Complete all necessary paperwork, e.g., employment application, and payroll and tax forms, if applicable.

4. Subject the intern to the same pre-employment and post-employment screening processes that apply to regular employees.

5. Provide an orientation to the company and to the functions of the company's security program. Caution is needed concerning disclosure of sensitive information. Issue pertinent manuals, handbooks, procedures, guides, etc.

6. Thoroughly review safety rules, the wearing of personal protective equipment, reporting of injuries, evacuation procedures, and the like.

7. Consider an arrangement that will permit the intern to rotate within the security department to maximize his or her exposure to many functions.

8. Choose and brief a supervisor who can be counted on to obtain value for the company and the intern.

9. Take the intern on a tour of the facility to establish familiarity with parking areas, rest rooms, break areas, cafeteria, etc.

10. Introduce the intern to co-workers and other employees with whom the intern will be expected to interact.

Lonnie R. Buckels and
Robert B. Iannone

JOB TASK ANALYSIS

Reduced to its simplest level, job task analysis is a method for describing work in terms of tasks. The method is broad and includes a variety of techniques. Technique is influenced by the nature of the job and the purpose of the analysis. For example, the technique used to analyze investigative work for the purpose of determining job classifications is likely to be different from analyzing security officer work for the purpose of determining training needs.

The Task

The common factor in all techniques is the preparation of task statements. Preparation of good task statements requires having a clear understanding of the characteristics of a task. A task:

- Is visible and measurable.
- Has a clear beginning and end.
- Is of relatively short duration.
- Is always directed toward a specific purpose.
- Results in a meaningful product, service, or outcome.
- Is performed independently of other tasks.

A task is often confused with related terms, such as duty and job. A duty is a cluster of closely related tasks, and a job is a cluster of closely related duties. To illustrate, the job of security console operator is comprised of several duties, which might include evaluating alarm signals, dispatching security officers, and maintaining an activity log. Within the duty of dispatching, the console operator performs certain tasks, such as operating a radio, communicating by telephone, and prioritizing responses.

We can distinguish between job, duty, and task by applying the task definition. To operate a console cannot be a task because it has no definite beginning and end, it is not relatively short in duration, and by common understanding is a broad function. Dispatching security officers cannot be a task either because the action of dispatching involves a series of steps, such as evaluating the need to respond, setting a priority among needed responses, and deciding which officers to send. In this process, the console operator may use different pieces of equipment such as a base station radio and telephone.

Breaking a job down into its parts has the effect of finding where and how the tasks are performed. Conceptualizing how a job is carried out, determining the equipment needed for performance, and identifying the points where the job interfaces with other jobs has value. Information of this nature can be useful input to a full range of management decisions. Finding the tasks and critically examining them can help management get a fix on the tools and equipment needed to be purchased, where they should be placed, how much space will be required, what skills and knowledge will need to be possessed by the job incumbent, and what level of compensation will be needed to attract and retain an effective performer.

The Task Inventory

Tasks are identified by persons close to the job such as the incumbents or those who directly supervise the incumbents. The means for collecting the information can be by survey, questionnaire, interview, direct observation, and by studying job descriptions, job procedures, training manuals, and the like.

Each task is expressed in a written statement that has three elements, which appear in this order:

1. An action verb that describes what is done
2. An identification of what is being acted upon
3. A clarifying phrase, if needed

The task statement is declarative and understood to contain "I" or "he" or "she." In the task statement "Prepare property removal passes," the action verb is prepare and the thing being acted upon is the pass. If property removal passes are issued only to employees, a clarifying phrase could be added so that the task statement reads, "Prepare property removal passes for employees."

A task statement tells what is done, not how or why it is done. Statements are short, to the point, and leave little room for interpretation. The action verb is unambiguous. It is better to state "test the fire alarm detectors" than to leave room for doubt by stating "Arrange to test..." or "Coordinate the testing of...."

Rating the Tasks

Rating a task means to apply to it one or more questions that are important to the purpose of the analysis effort. Following are some questions and their implications:

Q: Is the task so critical that an error in performance will result in serious consequences?
A: Prospective incumbents should (1) possess a combination of skills, knowledge, and attitude commensurate to learning the task; (2) master the task in practice situations before going on the job; (3) receive intensive initial training and frequent refresher training; and (4) be compensated at a level sufficient to attract and retain.

Q: Is performance of the task hazardous to the incumbent or others?
A: The job will most probably be subject to some form of regulatory review; safety considerations must predominate; special insurance may be appropriate to reduce risk; and task mastery will be essential.

Q: Is performance of the task in this job essential to the performance of any tasks performed in other jobs?

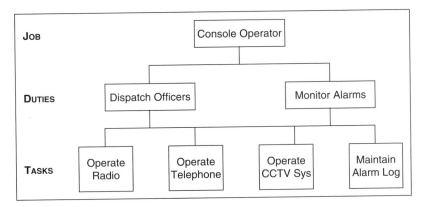

Figure 1. This chart illustrates that tasks make up a duty and that duties make up a job.

A: The incumbent will need to be informed of the relationship of the task to the work of others, and vice versa and a back-up compensating arrangement may need to be put in place.

When the question needs to be answered with more than a "yes" or a "no," the answer format can use scales, for example:

How critical is the task?

1. Not critical at all
2. Somewhat critical
3. Moderately critical
4. Critical
5. Very critical

How difficult is the task?

1. Easy
2. Easy-to-moderate
3. Moderately difficult
4. Difficult
5. Very difficult

How soon will the task be performed after the incumbent goes on the job?

1. In the first month
2. In the second month
3. In 3 to 6 months
4. In 6 to 12 months
5. After 12 months

After the persons close to the job have responded to the questions, the data are analyzed. A computer-assisted analytical procedure might be developed just for the study, or a software package might be purchased.

Task analysis can be done in a variety of ways, but all have one thing in common, i.e., they analyze jobs in terms of the ways in which work is actually performed. The approach is always objective, sometimes quantitative, and likely in many cases to lead to work improvement, which in the absence of analysis would not be possible.

John J. Fay

Sources

Fay, J. 1988. *Approaches to Criminal Justice Training, 2nd Edition*. Athens: University of Georgia.

McCormick, E. 1979. *Job Analysis: Methods and Applications*. New York: American Management Association.

MANAGEMENT: HISTORICAL ROOTS

Efforts to organize the work of people have surely existed since people started living in tribes, but few descriptions of managed work were recorded prior to about 200 years ago. Before then, work activities were fairly simple and involved relatively small groups. Typically, the workplace was tiny by contemporary standards and the workforce consisted of a single craftsman and a handful of apprentices. The craftsman was the equivalent of today's line supervisor and directly observed the work in progress. The tasks carried out by the apprentices involved relatively low levels of technology and hence were not complicated to manage.

The Industrial Revolution

In the late 18th century, the Industrial Revolution sweeping across Europe spread quickly to the United States. In his classic book, *The Wealth of Nations*, Adam Smith stole a glance into America's future when he recognized the great increases in work output offered by the use of machines.

America provided fertile ground for cultivating a system of mechanized factories. Funds needed to form manufacturing companies were willingly provided by a monied class in search of profit. The lack of tariff barriers between the states, coupled with an expanding network of roadways and waterways, facilitated large-scale movements of mass-produced goods.

Nature's generous endowment assured a large and dependable supply of raw materials. The advent of the steel plow opened the West to agricultural production, and the factories that produced farm equipment and other work-enhancing machines provided jobs that attracted large numbers of people to urban industrial centers.

The growth of the factory system led to mass employment, which in turn provided incomes that made mass consumption possible. Consumer demand for mass-produced goods enabled mass production to prosper. At the same time, improvements being made in agricultural techniques freed a large part of the work force from food production. With abundant farm land and industrial raw materials, the young American republic developed a balance of agriculture and industry.

The Industrial Revolution was essentially a shift of the production process from small workshops to large factories. Many more people were employed, each working on only one part of the manufactured article and having little contact with those who were making the other parts. Specialization of labor introduced new requirements for managing production. Coordination of separate work efforts was crucial and at the same time more difficult to achieve.

The beginning of the Industrial Revolution was marked by the absence of recorded references to management practices. While managers likely discussed common problems among themselves and thereby improved their skills, little or no exchanges of ideas in writing were circulated and passed on to succeeding managers. In the latter part of the Industrial Revolution, descriptions of management practices began to appear mainly in the professional journals of management societies. It was during this time that the faint outlines of a management movement first appeared. The movement unfolded in three phases.

The Scientific Management Era

Frederick W. Taylor observed that workers were pretty much free to carry out their job assignments at their own paces by their own methods. He used the scientific method of logical inquiry to experiment with work methods in search of better ways to perform jobs.

Although not all of the ideas that came to be known as scientific management originated with Taylor, he brought them into a comprehensible whole, put them into operation, and verified that they worked. Taylor published his findings in *Principles of Scientific Management*. He stressed that his concepts provided a method for labor and management to work together. Taylor's pioneering efforts, however, were widely misunderstood at the time.

Taylor is often referred to as the Father of Scientific Management, but he was not the only expert in this area. Among others, Frank and Lillian Gilbreth developed the principles of motion study, through which jobs were broken into component movements and studied so that wasted motions and fatigue could be reduced. Henry L. Gantt invented the "Gantt Chart" for the scheduling of work and the checking of progress against plans.

Similar management research was taking place in Europe as well. For example, Henri Fayol, chief executive of a large French mining and metallurgical firm, studied management from the top down, with emphasis on overall administration. He published widely on management practices applicable to industrial and governmental organizations.

The Human Relations Era

The pioneers of scientific management, although clearly oriented to efficiency in production, recognized the human element in management. Elton Mayo's study of workers' social needs emphasized the need to take workers' attitudes into account and to recognize them as important contributors to production.

The emphasis by Mayo and others did not downplay the prevailing interest in efficiency. It simply added a new dimension to the field of management, i.e., that management's legitimate interest in getting the work done has to be tempered with an interest in the people who do the work. Technical systems for performing work through social interactions of workers quickly evolved, and the term *sociotechnical systems* came into use to describe the merger.

The Management Science Era

Management science had its beginnings during World War II. Mathematical analyses of data led to decisions that improved the effectiveness of the war effort. In the late 1940s these analytical methods began to be applied to problems of government and industry. Management science often involves the use of models, such as equations and formulas, to describe and provide an understanding of a problem and to identify the optimum solution.

Management science brought a change in the approach to solving work problems.

Computers and other scientific tools capable of dealing with large and complex problems are routinely used for business purposes. The modern manager is expected to have strong quantitative skills.

The Age of Technology

In the early craft shop environment, tasks were performed with humans controlling the process and providing the energy to perform the work. In the transition to mass production, people controlled the operation of machines directly but the energy was provided by another source. The next improvement was automatic control in which the machine could sense its manipulations, compare them to preset requirements, and adjust accordingly. Today's automated systems provide instructions to machines, the machines comply, and provide feedback.

Without question one of the greatest triumphs of technology was the electronic computer, and business was profoundly changed as a result. Many of the early applications were to mechanize routine clerical operations, such as payroll and accounting, and as software advanced so did the use of computers in performing more difficult work tasks.

Computer-controlled equipment can make decisions based on signals generated at the points of production. For example, automatic material-handling equipment can move objects to locations depending on the signals they receive; robots can perform operations with the items being produced; and machines equipped with racks of tools and automatic tool changers can carry out commands, all without human intervention.

While technology can be used to improve efficiency and productivity, much can be gained from new management practices. The concept of just-in-time (JIT) production, which originated in Japan, is an example. JIT is founded on the simple notion that costs can be avoided by employing a minimum of inventories to make products. Companies operating in this way coordinate their operations so that one work center produces only what is required by subsequent work centers; production is timed to occur at the moment when the necessary components arrive. Successful implementation of JIT requires reliable sources of supplies and effective preventive maintenance to avoid breakdowns on the line.

Service Sector Growth

As changes have taken place in the management field, the types of operations being managed have changed as well. Operations have spread across wider geographical areas; they have come to use more and increasingly varied technologies; they have become increasingly diversified; and the aggregate mix of operations has changed, with service operations assuming increasing importance. In this century, great changes have occurred in the American workplace. The number of persons needed to produce food has decreased while the service sector has increased. The increase in service jobs was almost three times as great as the decline in other industries—enough to absorb displaced farm workers and provide many of the additional jobs required by a growing work force.

The direction of growth has been fueled by advances in technology. The shift is clearly in the direction of service operations. Among these is the increasing demand for security-related services.

Much has been said and written about the dramatic growth and the vast future potential of the security services industry. If the past 200 years can serve as an indicator of challenges to management, lively times lie ahead. Managers in the field of security can look forward to even greater changes and greater opportunities for reward.

John J. Fay

Sources
Dilworth, J. 1986. *Production and Operations Management: Manufacturing and Nonmanufacturing*. New York: Random House.

Emmons, H., et al. 1987. *Quantitative Modeling for Decision Support*. Cleveland: Case Western Reserve University.

Heyel, C. 1982. *Encyclopedia of Management, 3rd Edition*. New York: Van Nostrand Reinhold.

Levine, S. 1984. *Dow-Jones Business and Investment Almanac*. Homewood: Dow-Jones Irwin.

MOTIVATION

The success of a Chief Security Officer (CSO) in leading subordinates rests on an ability to motivate them. The CSO needs interpersonal skills that will take him far beyond being likable and popular. Leadership is not a matter of earning admiration but of inspiring people to work together constructively. The CSO's principal task is to create a climate for work in which employee efforts are organized and directed toward the goals of the organization. To effectively discharge that task, the CSO must understand the human needs, differences, and emotions of those being supervised.

The willingness of people to apply themselves to productive work activities is linked to how much personal value they find in the work itself. The CSO's challenge is to discover what satisfactions a worker finds in a job and to harness them to the objectives of the Security Group.

Maslow's Theory of Motivation

A commonly accepted theory of motivation was advanced by A. H. Maslow. It describes people as having needs in five categories: physiological, safety, love, self-esteem, and self-actualization. According to Maslow, human needs operate in an ascending hierarchy that begins with a natural striving to satisfy the physiological needs and ends with self-actualization. In this hierarchy, which can be abstracted as a pyramid, a higher need does not provide motivation until all lower, more basic needs have been satisfied. When a need is satisfied, it ceases to be a motivator.

The physiological needs are a human's basic requirements for nourishment, water, air, and rest. A person's focus will be entirely on these needs for as long as they continue to be unmet. Once met, the individual's focus shifts upward to the next level.

At the next level is a requirement to be free from harm. The safety and security of the individual dominates. Like the underlying physiological needs, this level is concerned with survival and self-preservation.

At the third level, the individual strives for love and belonging. Affection and human relationships are the focal points.

Self-esteem comes next. These needs relate to what a person thinks of himself. They include achievement, competence, independence, status, and recognition. Self-esteem needs are similar to love needs because both are social in orientation.

The highest order of needs is self-actualization. At this level the individual expresses himself through the exercise of personal capabilities. Satisfaction is derived through self-fulfillment. It is the development of one's own potentiality and the manifestation of creative urge.

The major principles of Maslow's theory can be summed up by observing that:

- A human is a continuously wanting animal. When he is fulfilled in one need, he develops desires in another.
- When a person's needs have been satisfied, they cease to motivate. A person must be confronted with a need before he is moved to initiate, change, or sustain his behavior.
- Identical needs may be satisfied in different ways. A person who needs money will be motivated to acquire it. The method of acquisition, however, could be to earn the money or steal it.
- A given style of behavior may satisfy more than one need. A person who works hard to earn money may want the money to buy food (physiological), pay the mortgage (safety), or gain prestige (self-esteem).

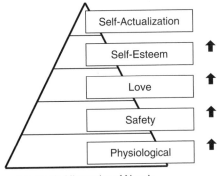

Maslow's Hierarchy of Needs

Figure 2. An individual's needs can be seen as moving upward through a series of stages.

Maslow in the Security Environment

A person's natural striving to establish human relationships and to experience self-esteem are present as much in the workplace as in any other setting. A security employee, whether working at the line level or in management, has social needs that include friendship with co-workers and acceptance within the work group. The extent and intensity of individual efforts will vary, however. An individual who satisfies social needs outside of the workplace may exhibit less striving than someone whose entire social experiences are dependent on co-workers.

Attempts to satisfy the higher needs of self-esteem are often expressed by security employees in the form of seeking recognition as a standout performer or as a valued contributor to the attainment of group goals. Most of us never stop looking for assurance that we are held in high regard by our peers, and even when we obtain that assurance today, we will seek it tomorrow and every day thereafter.

Basic to an understanding of human needs is the recognition that people respond to other people and situations as they are perceived, not as they actually are. If an employee sees work as a path to the attainment of a personal goal, he is likely to be motivated at work. A second employee may not have a goal or a goal that requires much effort and as a result will not see work as a means to realizing personal ends. A third employee may have a goal so lofty that he will view the job as an impediment.

It is not enough anymore to simply assign work. The CSO has to establish conditions, within reason, in which employees can fulfill their belonging, self-esteem, and ego needs. In some respects the CSO can be likened to a buffer that accommodates the demands of the organization and the personal needs of the employees. Using a variety of motivational techniques, the CSO can create an arrangement that allows employees to meet personal aspirations while at the same time meeting the organization's work requirements.

The CSO must appreciate that different employees will have different needs and that their needs will affect their motivations. The CSO has to recognize and assess the differences when they are manifested and to administer supervision accordingly. A critical ability in the CSO's personal inventory will be a combination of knowledge and skill that addresses the ego needs of subordinates. It is an ability resting on an understanding of motivation and a deft touch in working with people.

John J. Fay

NATIONAL ORIGIN DISCRIMINATION

Whether an employee or job applicant's ancestry is Mexican, Ukrainian, Filipino, Arab, American Indian, or any other nationality, he or she is entitled to the same employment opportunities as anyone else. EEOC enforces the federal prohibition against national origin discrimination in employment under Title VII of the Civil Rights Act of 1964, which covers employers with 15 or more employees.

> "With American society growing increasingly diverse, protection against national origin discrimination is vital to the right of workers to compete for jobs on a level playing field," said EEOC Chair Cari M. Dominguez, announcing the issuance of recent guidance on national origin discrimination. "Immigrants have long been an asset to the American workforce. This is more true than ever in today's increasingly global economy. Recent world events, including the events of September 11, 2001, only add to the need for employers to be vigilant in ensuring a workplace free from discrimination."

About National Origin Discrimination

National origin discrimination means treating someone less favorably because he or she comes from a particular place, because of his or her ethnicity or accent, or because it is believed that he or she has a particular ethnic background. National origin discrimination also means treating someone less favorably at work because of marriage or other association with someone of a particular nationality. Examples of violations covered under Title VII include:

- Employment Decisions. Title VII prohibits any employment decision, including recruitment, hiring, and firing or layoffs, based on national origin.

• Harassment. Title VII prohibits offensive conduct, such as ethnic slurs, that creates a hostile work environment based on national origin. Employers are required to take appropriate steps to prevent and correct unlawful harassment. Likewise, employees are responsible for reporting harassment at an early stage to prevent its escalation.

Language

Prohibited are:

• Accent discrimination. An employer may not base a decision on an employee's foreign accent unless the accent materially interferes with job performance.
• English fluency. A fluency requirement is only permissible if required for the effective performance of the position for which it is imposed.
• English-only rules. English-only rules must be adopted for nondiscriminatory reasons. An English-only rule may be used if it is needed to promote the safe or efficient operation of the employer's business.

Coverage of Foreign Nationals

Title VII and the other antidiscrimination laws prohibit discrimination against individuals employed in the United States, regardless of citizenship. However, relief may be limited if an individual does not have work authorization.

Source   The U.S. Equal Employment Opportunity Commission. 2006. <http://www.eeoc.gov/origin/index.html>

ORGANIZATION: FORMAL AND INFORMAL ORGANIZATIONS

The Formal Organization

The organizational structure of a department within a company will reflect a logical division of tasks and clear lines of authority and responsibility, both within the department specifically and within the organization generally.

An organizational chart is two-dimensional. On the horizontal plane the chart indicates the division of work, and on the vertical plane it defines levels of authority or rank. Although all charts will reflect these two dimensions, organizational charts will differ in widely varying degrees. This is true because organizational structures are the products of the human intellect reacting to the pressures of efficiency, economy, politics, and other variables.

The reality of organizational structure is the inevitable conflict between rational and irrational issues. It might, for example, be rational, based on considerations of productivity and cost, to place a particular function in Department A. Irrational issues, such as internal politics and opportunities for personal advantage, might dictate placing the function in Department B. Conflicts and compromise are not alien to organizational charts.

A tendency in structuring an organization is to build functions around people rather than determine the functions and then fill in the boxes with qualified individuals. This tendency can be overwhelming to the security manager who is told that he has no choice except to use existing humanpower to carry out work functions, even when the functions have changed in response to crime threats. Because the existing humanpower is unequal to the real tasks, the security manager assigns functions on the basis of ability rather than genuine work needs. When this occurs, it is testimony to the questionable belief that it is easier to tinker with the organization's structure than to change the abilities of people.

The ideal structure is developed by identifying the functions that are necessary to the attainment of organizational goals, arranging the functions into logical work units, and staffing the work units with qualified people.

An organizational chart depicts what is called the formal organization, i.e., an arrangement of people designed and formally approved by management to operate in furtherance of organizational goals. An equally important arrangement of people is called the informal organization.

The Informal Organization

The informal organization also sets goals, has a hierarchy of functions and of people, and communicates among its members. Its goals and functions, however, will often conflict with those of the formal organization, and leadership will rest on qualities other than the assignment of authority from management.

Some organizational theorists will refer to the informal organization as the "real" organization. A more accurate description might be to call it the engine that makes the formal organization work. Although the engine has been designed by management to work in particular ways, it is cantankerous and chooses to chug along in other ways that are at least tolerable and in some instances superior to expectations.

Examples of activities by the informal organization in a security organization include subordinates taking problems around the supervisor to employees they believe are better qualified even though lacking in authority, obtaining supplies and equipment through channels not officially approved, and operating "grapevine" communication networks.

Informal organizations, and there may be many within a single formal organization, exist whether management likes it or not. Some are quite obvious and even demand recognition, albeit unofficial, and others are subtle and may not even be known to or understood by management. Enlightened managements have recognized and even encouraged informal organizations. A security manager would make a serious mistake to ignore them because their opposition to security could defeat even the best practices.

Charles A. Sennewald

PERFORMANCE APPRAISAL

Performance appraisal is the ongoing process of setting objectives and assessing individual and collective behavior and achievements during a finite period of time. It is primarily about counseling and feedback on ways to improve performance at an individual and team level, and the quality of work relationships. Performance improvement results from people being clear about priorities and objectives, what skills need to be enhanced, and which types of behavior can help to this end. This comes from open, positive, and constructive discussion between supervisors, individuals, and teams, and agreement on how to focus on doing the job better.

In the appraisal process, a security manager evaluates, coaches, counsels, and develops subordinates on a continuing basis throughout the reporting period, usually 1 year. In the conduct of these activities, the manager's performance is subject to appraisal, as well.

Setting Objectives

Near the close or at the very beginning of the reporting period, the manager and his direct subordinates, individually or as a team, meet for the purpose of setting performance objectives. Objective setting ensures that the manager and the people to be rated are in agreement as to what should be achieved.

The objectives are specific, measurable, relevant, and time-related. Although firm when formulated, they can be amended and supplemented throughout the reporting period. Objectives will vary according to the type of work involved, but will normally relate to business results and expected standards of performance. Objectives can also relate to personal development. For example, the security manager may encourage a subordinate to attain the Certified Protection Professional (CPP) designation. While attainment of an objective along these lines is not directly related to a specific work output, few can dispute the job relatedness of skills and knowledge acquired in pursuit of CPP status.

To the uninitiated, objective setting may appear to be more trouble than it is worth. Objectives can be difficult to formulate and sometimes impossible to agree on. They cause problems when the manager and subordinates cannot come to terms because the objectives are irrelevant, unchallenging, or overly demanding. The manager might reject a subordinate's suggested objectives on the grounds they lack sufficient work value, are not in line with business goals, or are simply too easy. The subordinate may resist the manager's objectives (especially when they are passed down from above like Moses' tablets) because they appear inflexible or carry the risk of failure.

Posing certain questions may be helpful to manager and subordinate alike in formulating an objective:

- Does the objective make good sense? Is it important to the subordinate, the manager, the department, and the company?
- Does it mesh with departmental or organizational goals?

- Does the objective fall within the manager's area of responsibility and authority?
- Does it carry risks operationally? Financially? Politically?
- Will top management support it?
- Will the subordinate (and others who may contribute) have the knowledge, skill, and resources to complete the objective?
- Can achievement of the objective be verified in some measurable way?

For most jobs, six to eight objectives will be sufficient, and it is possible that some or all of them will change or evolve as work progresses. Objectives will sometimes be contingent upon factors beyond the manager's ability to control, such as higher-level approval of a planned project, availability of funds or equipment, and a dependence upon the work of others outside the manager's supervision.

In determining objectives, it is useful to focus on the action steps required for achievement of expectations. A single objective can incorporate several action steps. If the objective is to "develop and administer a training module for entry level security officers," the action steps could include writing a lesson plan, preparing or acquiring audiovisuals, constructing a test to measure learning, setting a training schedule, arranging for the place of training and needed training equipment, preparing certificates of completion, and making a record of attendance and scores. Time frames or deadline dates can be established for each action step, they can be programmed to occur in a particular sequence, and they can be assigned to several individuals in a team effort.

Objectives can be of two types: base and stretch. A base objective involves tasks that are integral to the job and sometimes routine in nature. Writing a report of investigation is an integral part of a security investigator's job and is fairly routine, at least to the investigator. A productivity gain might be possible by performing this task in a different manner. The manager and his investigator may agree on an objective calling for the investigator to revise the report writing method. A stretch objective goes beyond the norms of job expectations. It typically addresses a major problem, challenge, or opportunity. Achievement of the objective, if it can be done, will bring a substantial reward to the organization. It may seek to raise quality, increase productivity, reduce costs, create new markets, etc.

Once the objectives are set, they need to be put into writing, and any later changes to them should also be written down and acknowledged by the manager and subordinates with signatures or initials.

Reviewing Performance

On a continuing basis and at pre-established intervals, the manager and subordinate meet to review progress. The subordinate is invited to comment on performance with respect to the agreed objectives, highlighting areas of success, improvement, and difficulties encountered. The manager coaches and counsels as needed. A review meeting is also a time for revising, canceling, or creating objectives in light of experience.

The meeting is often documented, sometimes with the use of a form. The subordinate may be invited to comment, such as offering suggestions about how performance on particular objectives could be improved. The documentation can serve as a discussion point at the next review meeting. The usual practice is to not make any formal rating of the subordinate until the final review meeting of the reporting period.

The Performance Appraisal Cycle

Evaluation of performance is a process that continues uninterrupted. While significant events relating to performance may occur at points over time and are certainly worthy of consideration, they are not the sole criteria for making an overall judgment.

The process described here operates cyclically, that is, it transitions to a starting point from the ending point of a previous period, passes through one or more phases marked by pre-set time intervals, and moves to the starting point of the next cycle.

The Starting Point. Manager and subordinate agree on objectives for the upcoming cycle, agree on the measures that will be used to evaluate performance, and agree to meet on or about particular dates for the purpose of reviewing

PERFORMANCE APPRAISAL CYCLE

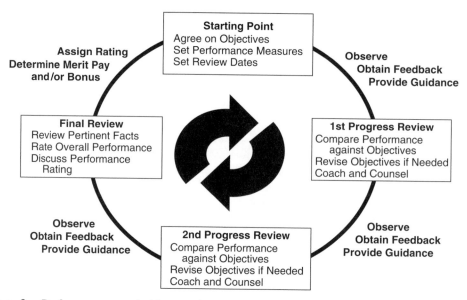

Figure 3. Performance appraisal is a continuous process with stopping points for communication between the appraiser and the person being appraised.

progress. Between progress reviews, the manager observes the subordinate's performance, obtains feedback from the subordinate, and provides appropriate guidance or assistance.

Progress Reviews. On specified dates, usually at the end of the first, second, and third quarters of the reporting period, manager and subordinate meet to compare performance against the objectives. The objectives are revised, if needed, and the subordinate is coached and counseled, if needed. During the final progress review, the subordinate's overall performance is considered, forming a foundation for a written rating.

The Ending Point. The end of one cycle and the start of the next tend to blur. Between the final progress review and the end of the cycle, the manager selects a performance rating; writes the performance report and obtains the subordinate's comments and signature on the report; determines the subordinate's merit pay increase or bonus, if any; and begins to develop with the subordinate a new set of objectives for the upcoming cycle.

Merit Rating

A chief purpose of performance appraisal is to administer salary in a manner that takes into account the separate contributions of individual employees. Through a systematic rating procedure, usually called merit rating, a manager is able to make equitable decisions regarding salary awards based on appraisal records. Despite constant complaints about the imperfections of procedures that link performance to pay, such procedures are usually objective and provide information that often cannot be obtained in any other way.

Merit ratings are designed to replace subjective, general impressions with judgments that are formed from empirically derived evidence. Generally, the evidence is quantitative in nature, capable of analysis, and collected over a period of time, such as 1 year. When soundly developed and systematically administered, merit ratings can stimulate the person being rated, particularly when the rating methodology provides opportunities for manager and subordinate to discuss ways and means for focusing performance on meaningful work outputs. This aspect of appraising is in the nature of making a "reality check."

A merit rating system requires the rater to make objective judgments and present supporting evidence. The rater is confronted with two questions: "What is the standing of the rated person, relative to others, in terms of receiving a financial reward for work contributions?" and "What proof is there to support that standing?"

Unfortunately, the appraisal process is sometimes used only as a tool for making merit, salary, and promotion determinations, as opposed to harnessing the process to the larger issue of improving productivity. In some organizations, supervisors have come to view the appraisal process as a necessary evil to be endured. They admit the process may have some value to the human resources staff but little value to the tasks of supervision or to the enhancement of work output. Appraising becomes nothing more than filling out forms.

Conducted casually, performance appraisal can be destructive. Without a clear focus and a commitment at all levels, the process can poison supervisor-subordinate relationships and seriously detract from optimum productivity. The rater and the rated person can be soured on the process and management's credibility damaged.

Evaluating human performance in the workplace is both essential and difficult. Evaluating is essential because it provides the data for making important decisions—decisions that affect the profitability of the organization and the aspirations of employees. Evaluating is difficult because it is continuous, complex, and fraught with hazards at every turn. The negative outcomes of an imperfectly administered program can be substantial, but so also are the positive outcomes.

John J. Fay

Sources

Performance Appraisal and Goal Setting. 1991. Management Paradigms, Plano, TX.

Guidance Notes on the Performance Appraisal Process. 1991. Guidance Notes, British Petroleum, London.

POSITION EVALUATION

Position evaluation is the determination of an appropriate grade level for a specific position or job. In this context, the evaluation process is focused on the nature of the job, not on the qualities of the job incumbent. Because grade level is the chief determinant of salary or wage

and other job benefits, the process of position evaluation is both critical and sensitive.

Certain key pieces of information are necessary to make an accurate determination:

- The nature and function of the job
- How the job fits into the organization
- The extent of accountability built into the job, including the dimensions and quantity of accountability

Grade level determination is an attempt to systematize or make objective what would otherwise be a subjective endeavor. The employer, in trying to sort out and make sense of the comparative values of different work functions in the organization, recognizes that the best he can do is introduce some order into making what are essentially human judgments. Although many evaluation schemes use numbers and other seemingly objective criteria, the process is more art than science.

The Position Description

The basic work of evaluating positions is done by managers who assemble and analyze information about the positions to be rated. This activity often produces a document called a position (or job) description.

Although position description documents come in many sizes and varieties, the form will typically contain particular items.

Identifying Details. These include job title, department, major business unit, location, and so forth.

Nature of the Position. A description is made of the overall purpose and chief objectives of the position and the nature of activities, such as guard force management, investigations, or special projects. The description, presented in a narrative style, might begin with, "The incumbent is responsible for…," or words to that effect.

Organizational Relationships

In this section will be an identification of the person to whom the position reports, those reporting to the position, and those who hold

☐ Position Revision/Update   **POSITION DESCRIPTION**
☐ New Position

To Be Filled Out by HR Staff
Job Number _____
Approved By _____
Date Approved _____

Position Title _____ Manager of Security _____

Name of Person _____ John Q. Doe

Department _____ Administration

Location _____ Houston, Texas

Reports to: (Name) _____ William J. Anderson _____ (Title) _____ Chief Executive Officer

---

NATURE OF POSITION

Responsible for planning, leading, organizing, and evaluating security operations at all Company locations. Identifies exposures to crime-related loss, damage, or compromise of assets, and recommends corrective actions. Carries out proactive prevention strategies, and counsels the chief executive officer and other senior managers concerning significant loss exposures and deviations from established controls. Directs investigations of criminal activity directed against the Company and unethical conduct on the part of Company employees. Maintains working relationships with peers in private sector organizations and criminal justice agencies.

This key position is responsible for providing a wide range of assets protection services which include protecting executives, implementing physical and procedural safeguards, overseeing security officer operations, and promoting security awareness among employees at all levels.

Decisions are frequently required in matters that involve complex legal and business issues. The incumbent must necessarily possess a blend of business knowledge, analytical skill, decisiveness, and practical field experience.

The major emphasis and challenge is for the incumbent to maintain an effective security program without incurring declines in efficiency and productivity.

ORGANIZATIONAL RELATIONSHIPS

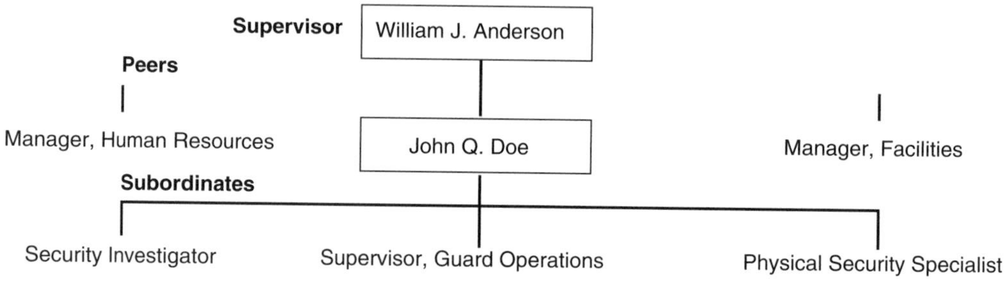

Supervisor | William J. Anderson |

Peers

Manager, Human Resources | John Q. Doe | Manager, Facilities

Subordinates

Security Investigator   Supervisor, Guard Operations   Physical Security Specialist

---

POSITION DATA

Annual Budget $1.5 million   **Number of Employees Supervised**   18

Education and Experience Required   Baccalaureate, MBA highly desired. CPP highly desired.
Five years experience in an equivalent or lead-in position.

Figure 4. A position description form describes the job, not the person holding the job.

comparable positions. These are often displayed in the style of an organizational chart. The position titles are almost always identified and, in some organizations, the names of the incumbents are included.

In evaluating a position, it may be helpful to identify the equivalent jobs, i.e., the peers of the job holder. The salary grades of the equivalent jobs can be used as a baseline for determining the grade of the position being evaluated.

Position Data

The pertinent data for this section of the form would include the annual budget of the activity performed, the number of employees supervised, the nature and amount of funds that are affected by the incumbent, licensing, education, and experience requirements, and the extent and nature of contacts maintained by the incumbent. For example, it might be pertinent to reflect that the position of security manager requires Certified Protection Professional status, an advanced degree in business administration, and five years of responsible experience in security management or administration.

Principal Accountabilities

This section usually consists of a list of the major job tasks that the incumbent performs in accomplishing the overall purpose and chief objectives of the job. The task statements are often listed in the order of importance or frequency.

John J. Fay

Sources

Heyel, C. 1982. *Encyclopedia of Management, 3rd Edition*. New York: Van Nostrand Reinhold.

"Position Description Preparation Guide." 1992. *BP America*.

PREGNANCY DISCRIMINATION

The Pregnancy Discrimination Act is an amendment to Title VII of the Civil Rights Act of 1964. Discrimination on the basis of pregnancy, childbirth, or related medical conditions constitutes unlawful sex discrimination under Title VII, which covers employers with 15 or more employees, including state and local governments. Title VII also applies to employment agencies and to labor organizations, as well as to the federal government. Women who are pregnant or affected by related conditions must be treated in the same manner as other applicants or employees with similar abilities or limitations.

Title VII's pregnancy-related protections include:

- Hiring. An employer cannot refuse to hire a pregnant woman because of her pregnancy, because of a pregnancy-related condition or because of the prejudices of co-workers, clients, or customers.
- Pregnancy and Maternity Leave. An employer may not single out pregnancy-related conditions for special procedures to determine an employee's ability to work. However, if an employer requires its employees to submit a doctor's statement concerning their inability to work before granting leave or paying sick benefits, the employer may require employees affected by pregnancy-related conditions to submit such statements.

If an employee is temporarily unable to perform her job due to pregnancy, the employer must treat her the same as any other temporarily disabled employee. For example, if the employer allows temporarily disabled employees to modify tasks, perform alternative assignments, or take disability leave or leave without pay, the employer also must allow an employee who is temporarily disabled due to pregnancy to do the same.

Pregnant employees must be permitted to work as long as they are able to perform their jobs. If an employee has been absent from work as a result of a pregnancy-related condition and recovers, her employer may not require her to remain on leave until the baby's birth. An employer also may not have a rule that prohibits an employee from returning to work for a predetermined length of time after childbirth.

Employers must hold open a job for a pregnancy-related absence the same length of time jobs are held open for employees on sick or disability leave.

Health Insurance

Any health insurance provided by an employer must cover expenses for pregnancy-related conditions on the same basis as costs for other medical conditions. Health insurance for expenses arising from abortion is not required, except where the life of the mother is endangered.

Pregnancy-related expenses should be reimbursed exactly as those incurred for other medical conditions, whether payment is on a fixed basis or a percentage of reasonable-and-customary-charge basis.

The amounts payable by the insurance provider can be limited only to the same extent as amounts payable for other conditions. No additional, increased, or larger deductible can be imposed.

Employers must provide the same level of health benefits for spouses of male employees as they do for spouses of female employees.

Fringe Benefits

Pregnancy-related benefits cannot be limited to married employees. In an all-female workforce or job classification, benefits must be provided for pregnancy-related conditions if benefits are provided for other medical conditions.

If an employer provides any benefits to workers on leave, the employer must provide the same benefits for those on leave for pregnancy-related conditions.

Employees with pregnancy-related disabilities must be treated the same as other temporarily disabled employees for accrual and crediting of seniority, vacation calculation, pay increases, and temporary disability benefits.

It is also unlawful to retaliate against an individual for opposing employment practices that discriminate based on pregnancy or for filing a discrimination charge, testifying, or participating in any way in an investigation, proceeding, or litigation under Title VII.

Source   The U.S. Equal Employment Opportunity Commission. 2006. <http://www.eeoc.gov/types/pregnancy.html>

QUALITY ASSURANCE

The pursuit of quality initiatives has taken hold in every business sector. Over the past few years many of the security giants have also developed their own programs. Others have professed to adhere to "high-quality standards" and aggressively position their marketing efforts around the theme of quality. These companies would fall into the category of "talking the talk." What makes it possible to come to this conclusion? A company is only talking the talk if it has no mechanism in place to promote quality continuously throughout the company. Regardless of how an organization frames its program, it needs to develop the following elements in order to have a true QA program:

- An articulated set of quality values
- An action plan for accomplishing each quality value
- A mechanism for soliciting customer expectations and needs
- A program that actively involves employees at each level in the decision-making and feedback process
- A program for training all employees, including managers and supervisors, in the principles of best practices and quality customer service tailored to meet the customer's needs and expectations
- A customer satisfaction program that measures satisfaction and includes a complaint resolution component
- A timely customer feedback mechanism
- A data analysis strategy that provides a springboard for continuous improvement

These eight components serve as the basic framework. If any one is missing, the program is incomplete. One of the clearest ways to test whether such a program is in place is simply to try to describe each of the components in clear language. If the descriptions are generally anecdotal, this strongly suggests that the program is either in the initial phase of development or does not include QA at all.

Asking security providers about their QA program is especially important because they may have developed a program that is limited in that it serves only those clients that require a QA program. This means that pursuit of QA is not really an integrated part of their corporate culture; instead the provider may view QA as something that is client specific and therefore a commodity rather than a process for seeking continuous quality improvement. To determine whether a company is committed to QA or not, test its ability to demonstrate that values have been identified, action plans developed, feedback received, results measured, and that plans for revision or adjustment are in evidence.

Many high-tech companies implement very elaborate programs. Unfortunately, some fall victim to the advice of so-called QA specialists who subscribe to a philosophy that says, "If it can't be measured, graded, and forced into some formula, it can't be worth much." Tragically, their approach is fundamentally flawed when it comes to implementing the quality process. This may appear to be a somewhat harsh judgment. Unfortunately for those companies, it is. Their misguided pursuit of quality assurance has caught the attention of many critics, and rightfully so. These companies unknowingly have put themselves out of touch with what their customers want. This is because total quality management programs are more often run by technocrats.

It's also interesting to note that those who seem more likely to miss the mark are those who profess an allegiance to the Malcolm Baldrige process, a methodology used by the U.S. Department of Commerce to give recognition to companies that subscribe to rigorous criteria in implementing quality improvement. Named after a former commerce secretary, the Baldrige process has become synonymous with excellence in customer service—at least according to one school of thought. The problem for many companies is the misconception as to who is the true customer.

Rarely is security the customer. Security is the conduit for delivering a service to customers. For some reason security managers—whether they employ a resident staff or rely on external partners—believe that they are the end user. Their error is further exacerbated when they measure success in terms of turnover, response time, e-mail messages and pages received, and so forth. Although these factors are critical to achieving operational success, they reflect infrastructure issues and not true QA.

As the end users of security, internal customers want to know that their expectations and needs are being met. But are these expectations realistic? If one of the customer expectations is that each security officer will know the name of certain employees, then that becomes a QA measure. If officers don't know certain names, dinging them for not knowing is unfair and unrealistic.

This leads us to another aspect of a misguided QA program—namely, the way in which programs are measured. Some companies implement grading systems that have been taken right out of the classic high-school grading system; they evaluate security personnel using numeric scores that are converted to letter grades such as A plus through D minus.

Other companies use grading systems that do not allow for failure. This is not a point to take lightly. Such a perspective, taken to its logical end, would mean that if a security officer deliberately stood by and watched while a customer/client was brutally attacked and did nothing at all, the officer would not have failed to provide quality customer service. Failure is part of the continuous improvement process and should therefore be built into the QA program. Failing to recognize failure limits the value of the program and undercuts the seriousness of the effort.

Dennis Dalton

Source Dalton, D. 1995. *Security Management: Business Strategies for Success.* Boston: Butterworth-Heinemann.

RACE AND COLOR DISCRIMINATION

Title VII of the Civil Rights Act of 1964 protects individuals against employment discrimination on the bases of race and color, as well as national origin, sex, and religion. Title VII applies to employers with 15 or more employees, including state and local governments. It also applies to employment agencies and to labor organizations, as well as to the federal government.

Equal employment opportunity cannot be denied any person because of his/her racial group or perceived racial group, his/her race-linked characteristics (e.g., hair texture, color, facial features), or because of his/her marriage to or association with someone of a particular race or color. Title VII also prohibits employment decisions based on stereotypes and assumptions about abilities, traits, or the performance of individuals of certain racial groups. Title VII's prohibitions apply regardless of whether the discrimination is directed at Whites, Blacks, Asians, Latinos, Arabs, Native Americans, Native Hawaiians and Pacific Islanders, multi-racial individuals, or persons of any other race, color, or ethnicity.

It is unlawful to discriminate against any individual in regard to recruiting, hiring and promotion, transfer, work assignments, performance measurements, the work environment, job training, discipline and discharge, wages and benefits, or any other term, condition, or privilege of employment. Title VII prohibits not only intentional discrimination, but also neutral job policies that disproportionately affect persons of a certain race or color and that are not related to the job and the needs of the business. Employers should adopt "best practices" to reduce the likelihood of discrimination and to address impediments to equal employment opportunity.

Recruiting, Hiring, and Advancement

Job requirements must be uniformly and consistently applied to persons of all races and colors. Even if a job requirement is applied consistently, if it is not important for job performance or business needs, the requirement may be found unlawful if it excludes persons of a certain racial group or color significantly more than others. Examples of potentially unlawful practices include: (1) soliciting applications only from sources in which all or most potential workers are of the same race or color; (2) requiring applicants to have a certain educational background that is not important for job performance or business needs; (3) testing applicants for knowledge, skills, or abilities that are not important for job performance or business needs.

Employers may legitimately need information about their employees' or applicants' race for affirmative action purposes and/or to track applicant flow. One way to obtain racial information and simultaneously guard against discriminatory selection is for employers to use separate forms or otherwise keep the information about an applicant's race separate from the application. In that way, the employer can capture the information it needs but ensure that it is not used in the selection decision.

Unless the information is for such a legitimate purpose, pre-employment questions about

race can suggest that race will be used as a basis for making selection decisions. If the information is used in the selection decision and members of particular racial groups are excluded from employment, the inquiries can constitute evidence of discrimination.

Harassment/Hostile Work Environment

Title VII prohibits offensive conduct, such as racial or ethnic slurs, racial "jokes," derogatory comments, or other verbal or physical conduct based on an individual's race/color. The conduct has to be unwelcome and offensive, and has to be severe or pervasive. Employers are required to take appropriate steps to prevent and correct unlawful harassment. Likewise, employees are responsible for reporting harassment at an early stage to prevent its escalation.

Compensation and Other Employment Terms, Conditions, and Privileges

Title VII prohibits discrimination in compensation and other terms, conditions, and privileges of employment. Thus, race or color discrimination may not be the basis for differences in pay or benefits, work assignments, performance evaluations, training, discipline or discharge, or any other area of employment.

Segregation and Classification of Employees

Title VII is violated where employees who belong to a protected group are segregated by physically isolating them from other employees or from customer contact. In addition, employers may not assign employees according to race or color. For example, Title VII prohibits assigning primarily African-Americans to predominantly African-American establishments or geographic areas. It is also illegal to exclude members of one group from particular positions or to group or categorize employees or jobs so that certain jobs are generally held by members of a certain protected group. Coding applications/resumes to designate an applicant's race, by either an employer or employment agency, constitutes evidence of discrimination where people of a certain race or color are excluded from employment or from certain positions.

Retaliation

Employees have a right to be free from retaliation for their opposition to discrimination or their participation in an EEOC proceeding by filing a charge, testifying, assisting, or otherwise participating in an agency proceeding.

Source The U.S. Equal Employment Opportunity Commission. 2006. <http://www.eeoc.gov/types/race.html>

RELIGIOUS DISCRIMINATION

Title VII of the Civil Rights Act of 1964 prohibits employers from discriminating against individuals because of their religion in hiring, firing, and other terms and conditions of employment. Title VII covers employers with 15 or more employees, including state and local governments. It also applies to employment agencies and to labor organizations, as well as to the federal government.

Employers may not treat employees or applicants more or less favorably because of their religious beliefs or practices—except to the extent a religious accommodation is warranted. For example, an employer may not refuse to hire individuals of a certain religion, may not impose stricter promotion requirements for persons of a certain religion, and may not impose more or different work requirements on an employee because of that employee's religious beliefs or practices.

Employees cannot be forced to participate— or not participate—in a religious activity as a condition of employment.

Employers must reasonably accommodate employees' sincerely held religious practices unless doing so would impose an undue hardship on the employer. A reasonable religious accommodation is any adjustment to the work environment that will allow the employee to practice his religion. An employer might accommodate an employee's religious beliefs or practices by allowing: flexible scheduling, voluntary substitutions or swaps, job reassignments and lateral transfers, modification of grooming requirements and other workplace practices, policies, and/or procedures.

An employer is not required to accommodate an employee's religious beliefs and practices if doing so would impose an undue hardship on the employer's legitimate business interests. An employer can show undue hardship if accommodating an employee's religious practices requires more than ordinary administrative costs, diminishes efficiency in other jobs, infringes on other employees' job rights or benefits, impairs workplace safety, causes co-workers to carry the accommodated employee's share of potentially hazardous or burdensome work, or if the proposed accommodation conflicts with another law or regulation.

Employers must permit employees to engage in religious expression, unless the religious expression would impose an undue hardship on the employer. Generally, an employer may not place more restrictions on religious expression than on other forms of expression that have a comparable effect on workplace efficiency.

Employers must take steps to prevent religious harassment of their employees. An employer can reduce the chance that employees will engage in unlawful religious harassment by implementing an anti-harassment policy and having an effective procedure for reporting, investigating, and correcting harassing conduct.

It is also unlawful to retaliate against an individual for opposing employment practices that discriminate based on religion or for filing a discrimination charge, testifying, or participating in any way in an investigation, proceeding, or litigation under Title VII.

Source The U.S. Equal Employment Opportunity Commission. 2006. <http://www.eeoc.gov/types/religion.html>

RETALIATION DISCRIMINATION

An employer may not fire, demote, harass, or otherwise "retaliate" against an individual for filing a charge of discrimination, participating in a discrimination proceeding, or otherwise opposing discrimination. The same laws that prohibit discrimination based on race, color, sex, religion, national origin, age, and disability, as well as wage differences between men and women performing substantially equal work, also prohibit retaliation against individuals who oppose unlawful discrimination or participate in an employment discrimination proceeding.

In addition to the protections against retaliation that are included in all of the laws enforced by EEOC, the Americans with Disabilities Act (ADA) also protects individuals from coercion, intimidation, threat, harassment, or interference in their exercise of their own rights or their encouragement of someone else's exercise of rights granted by the ADA.

There are three main terms that are used to describe retaliation. Retaliation occurs when an employer, employment agency, or labor organization takes an **adverse action** against a **covered individual** because he or she engaged in a **protected activity**. These three terms are described below.

Adverse Action

An adverse action is an action taken to try to keep someone from opposing a discriminatory practice, or from participating in an employment discrimination proceeding. Examples of adverse actions include:

- Employment actions such as termination, refusal to hire, and denial of promotion.
- Other actions affecting employment such as threats, unjustified negative evaluations, unjustified negative references, or increased surveillance.
- Any other action such as an assault or unfounded civil or criminal charges that are likely to deter reasonable people from pursuing their rights.

Adverse actions do not include petty slights and annoyances, such as stray negative comments in an otherwise positive or neutral evaluation, "snubbing" a colleague, or negative comments that are justified by an employee's poor work performance or history.

Even if the prior protected activity alleged wrongdoing by a different employer, retaliatory adverse actions are unlawful. For example,

it is unlawful for a worker's current employer to retaliate against him for pursuing an EEO charge against a former employer.

Of course, employees are not excused from continuing to perform their jobs or follow their company's legitimate workplace rules just because they have filed a complaint with the EEOC or opposed discrimination.

Covered Individuals

Covered individuals are people who have opposed unlawful practices, participated in proceedings, or requested accommodations related to employment discrimination based on race, color, sex, religion, national origin, age, or disability. Individuals who have a close association with someone who has engaged in such protected activity also are covered individuals. For example, it is illegal to terminate an employee because his spouse participated in employment discrimination litigation.

Individuals who have brought attention to violations of law other than employment discrimination are NOT covered individuals for purposes of anti-discrimination retaliation laws. For example, "whistleblowers" who raise ethical, financial, or other concerns unrelated to employment discrimination are not protected by the EEOC enforced laws.

Protected Activity

Protected activity includes:

- Opposition to a practice believed to be unlawful discrimination.
- Opposition to informing an employer that you believe that he/she is engaging in prohibited discrimination. Opposition is protected from retaliation as long as it is based on a reasonable, good-faith belief that the complained of practice violates anti-discrimination law; and the manner of the opposition is reasonable.

Examples of protected opposition include:

- Complaining to anyone about alleged discrimination against oneself or others.

- Threatening to file a charge of discrimination.
- Picketing in opposition to discrimination.
- Refusing to obey an order reasonably believed to be discriminatory.

Examples of activities that are NOT protected opposition include:

- Actions that interfere with job performance so as to render the employee ineffective.
- Unlawful activities such as acts or threats of violence.
- Participation in an employment discrimination proceeding. Participation means taking part in an employment discrimination proceeding. Participation is protected activity even if the proceeding involved claims that ultimately were found to be invalid. Examples of participation include:
  - Filing a charge of employment discrimination.
  - Cooperating with an internal investigation of alleged discriminatory practices.
  - Serving as a witness in an EEO investigation or litigation.

A protected activity can also include requesting a reasonable accommodation based on religion or disability.

Source The U.S. Equal Employment Opportunity Commission. 2006. <http://www.eeoc.gov/types/retaliation.html>

SECURITY SERVICES

Security services do not produce tangible outputs, although tangible products, such as access control hardware, are often provided or operated as an element of service. Security services are always customer-centered. The customer often has some contact with the service provider, although the customer does not have to be present when the service is actually being delivered. Each type of security service operation has its unique characteristics. When viewed in sufficient detail, a security service operation can be seen as changing through time.

Three characteristics of security service operations are known:

- Productivity generally is difficult to measure because the products of service operations are somewhat intangible. Intangible products are difficult to evaluate because they cannot be held, weighed, or measured.
- Quality standards are difficult to establish and to evaluate. No one knows for certain the amount of loss that was avoided because a security officer was present as a psychological deterrent or because the officer acted in a particular way to discourage or prevent a criminal act.
- Persons who provide security services generally have contact with the customers. The marketing and customer relations aspects of the service often overlap the operations function. For example, the relationship between the security services account representative and the client contact is often considered to be a very important component of the total services.

Managers of Security Services

Some companies have executives with titles such as vice president of operations, director of investigations, and account manager. In a good-size security services company, many persons serve in managerial positions, representing disciplines in planning, financing, marketing, and so forth. A company's management team, from the top executive right down to the supervisors of line workers, is at the center of directing and controlling services.

In working through others, managers exercise skills in two dimensions: technical competence and behavioral competence.

Technical Competence

Since managers make decisions about the tasks that other people are to perform, they need a basic understanding of the processes and technologies that drive the company's internal systems, and they need adequate knowledge of the work they manage. Technical competence is usually obtained through training and experience.

Behavioral Competence

Since managers work through others, their work necessarily involves a great deal of interpersonal contact. A good manager will have the ability to work with other people. Managers, and those being managed, often work in groups. Groups exist because people find they can achieve more, both in output and in social satisfaction, by working together.

Managers are responsible for seeing that their companies are successful. A successful security services company will meet at least three basic requirements. The services will be:

- Suited to the company's capabilities and the market's demand.
- Delivered with consistent quality at a level that appeals to customers and serves their needs.
- Provided at a cost that allows an adequate profit and a reasonable sales price.

The operations function plays a major role in accomplishing all of these requirements. Managers at the senior level must ensure that company objectives are consistent with operational capabilities and that the appropriate strengths are developed within operations to be consistent with broad, companywide strategy. In many companies the operations function consumes the greatest portion of company resources, thereby strongly impacting cost and price. Since the operations function produces services, it is largely responsible for quality.

Quality and productivity are two factors frequently mentioned as challenges facing security service companies. Achievement of high quality relates very closely to productivity. Providing a service that has to be repeated because of inadequate performance is both a quality and productivity issue. Consistently providing poor quality services leads to certain death in the services industry.

The idea of productivity is broader than just achieving high output per worker hour. It means balancing all factors of operations so that the greatest output is achieved for a given total input of all resources.

Even when security service companies offer the same menu of services, each company will be a uniquely different entity. Many factors account for the differences but the factor that clearly stands out is called management.

A security services company spends a great percentage of income and employee effort carrying out activities that stem from decisions made by managers. As these activities progress and evolve, they determine the current worth and the potential destiny of the company. A company's achievements can be enormous when all of its separate parts work in harmony and pull together to meet carefully established goals.

John J. Fay

Sources

Dilworth, J. 1986. *Production and Operations Management: Manufacturing and Nonmanufacturing*. New York: Random House.

Heyel, C. 1982. *Encyclopedia of Management, 3rd Edition*. New York: Van Nostrand Reinhold.

SEX-BASED DISCRIMINATION

Title VII of the Civil Rights Act of 1964 protects individuals against employment discrimination on the basis of sex as well as race, color, national origin, and religion. Title VII applies to employers with 15 or more employees, including state and local governments. It also applies to employment agencies and to labor organizations, as well as to the federal government.

It is unlawful to discriminate against any employee or applicant for employment because of his/her sex in regard to hiring, termination, promotion, compensation, job training, or any other term, condition, or privilege of employment. Title VII also prohibits employment decisions based on stereotypes and assumptions about abilities, traits, or the performance of individuals on the basis of sex. Title VII prohibits both intentional discrimination and neutral job policies that disproportionately exclude individuals on the basis of sex and that are not job related.

Sexual Harassment

This includes practices ranging from direct requests for sexual favors to workplace conditions that create a hostile environment for persons of either gender, including same sex harassment.

Pregnancy Based Discrimination

Title VII was amended by the Pregnancy Discrimination Act, which prohibits discrimination on the basis of pregnancy, childbirth, and related medical conditions.

The Equal Pay Act of 1963 requires that men and women be given equal pay for equal work in the same establishment. The jobs need not be identical, but they must be substantially equal. Title VII also prohibits compensation discrimination on the basis of sex. Unlike the Equal Pay Act, however, Title VII does not require that the claimant's job be substantially equal to that of a higher paid person of the opposite sex or require the claimant to work in the same establishment.

It is also unlawful to retaliate against an individual for opposing employment practices that discriminate based on sex or for filing a discrimination charge, testifying, or participating in any way in an investigation, proceeding, or litigation under Title VII.

Source The U.S. Equal Employment Opportunity Commission. 2006. <http://www.eeoc.gov/types/sex.html>

SEXUAL HARASSMENT

Sexual harassment is a form of sex discrimination that violates Title VII of the Civil Rights Act of 1964. Title VII applies to employers with 15 or more employees, including state and local governments. It also applies to employment agencies and to labor organizations, as well as to the federal government.

Unwelcome sexual advances, requests for sexual favors, and other verbal or physical conduct of a sexual nature constitute sexual harassment when this conduct explicitly or implicitly affects an individual's employment, unreasonably interferes with an individual's work performance, or creates an intimidating, hostile, or offensive work environment.

Sexual harassment can occur in a variety of circumstances, including but not limited to the following:

- The victim as well as the harasser may be a woman or a man. The victim does not have to be of the opposite sex.

- The harasser can be the victim's supervisor, an agent of the employer, a supervisor in another area, a co-worker, or a non-employee.
- The victim does not have to be the person harassed but could be anyone affected by the offensive conduct. Unlawful sexual harassment may occur without economic injury to or discharge of the victim.
- The harasser's conduct must be unwelcome.

It is helpful for the victim to inform the harasser directly that the conduct is unwelcome and must stop. The victim should use any employer complaint mechanism or grievance system available.

When investigating allegations of sexual harassment, EEOC looks at the whole record: the circumstances, such as the nature of the sexual advances, and the context in which the alleged incidents occurred. A determination on the allegations is made from the facts on a case-by-case basis.

Prevention is the best tool to eliminate sexual harassment in the workplace. Employers are encouraged to take steps necessary to prevent sexual harassment from occurring. They should clearly communicate to employees that sexual harassment will not be tolerated. They can do so by providing sexual harassment training to their employees and by establishing an effective complaint or grievance process and taking immediate and appropriate action when an employee complains.

It is also unlawful to retaliate against an individual for opposing employment practices that discriminate based on sex or for filing a discrimination charge, testifying, or participating in any way in an investigation, proceeding, or litigation under Title VII.

Source The U.S. Equal Employment Opportunity Commission 2006. http://www.eeoc.gov/types/sexual_harassment.html

STRATEGY

Three observations about security management are in order. First, the chief security officer (CSO) operates in a rapidly changing business world. The fast-paced and highly competitive nature of business is forcing companies to continually find new ways to be productive at lower cost. The new ways of doing business bring new security risks.

Second, every important decision made by the CSO depends upon technical knowledge. Important security decisions are never risk-free, and technical knowledge is often a critical factor in arriving at the best possible decision.

Third, international terrorism is on the scene in a very serious way. It can take many forms, is shrouded in secrecy, and threatens critical assets essential to the operation and viability of national infrastructures.

Strategic Planning

In most of the previous century, planning carried out by senior management was called long-range planning. In today's high-tech environment, it is deserving of a fancier name: strategic planning. Large companies everywhere plan strategically, and smaller companies in increasing numbers are following suit. Indeed, it can be said that in the fast-paced and intensely competitive marketplace of the new millennium any corporation worth its salt cannot afford to operate without strategic planning. According to Christopher Hoenig, a leadership guru, an organization has no choice except to engage in strategic planning. The real issues are how much planning to do, how to do it well, and when to do it.

Strategic planning underscores a point sometimes forgotten, i.e., that a business organization has two types of management. That which is done at the top is called strategic management. Everything else is operational management. Planning done at the top is strategic in nature, and planning below the top is tactical in nature. The CSO is always a developer of operating (tactical) plans, but is only sometimes involved in the development of strategic plans.

The proposition that a CSO should have a basic understanding of strategic planning rests on a number of simple observations. One is that strategic planning is a consistent element in companies that are successful. Another is that strategic planning is clearly a part of managing. Every leader is expected to understand the nature of planning and to be comfortable in its design

and execution. Yet it's a fact that some leaders have such a fuzzy understanding of planning or feel threatened by it. The gains to be made to a leader personally and to his/her subordinates can be lost when the leader is excluded from strategic planning. A leader who shies away is apt to be viewed as a non-player, particularly when the planning involves the leader's sphere of operations.

Hoenig in his excellent article, "The Master Planner" (CIO, May 1, 2001) identifies what he calls Strategic Planning Elements.

- *Measurable Goals.* Specific tasks that lead to measurable goals and assign personal accountability
- *Incentives.* Rewards that make people want to carry out the plan
- *Realistic Estimates.* Ambitious outcomes grounded in reality
- *Incremental Efforts.* A division of work that organizes a big plan into achievable chunks
- *Landmarks.* Results-oriented milestones that signify progress according to plan
- *Flexibility.* A forward view that allows alternative paths and modified expectations
- *Focus.* A keen eye on the course and a steady hand at the wheel
- *Value Perspective.* A view that looks at the cost of plan execution as an investment

Policy and Planning

The relationship between policy development and strategic planning can be described as totally intimate. You can't have one without the other, and although the functions are distinguishable, they are at the same time inseparable.

A policy establishes the arena in which the actions of the business are to occur. It provides a vision for the business and, as such, serves as a guide for action. Planning, on the other hand, is the architecture of the arena; it is specific and detailed. But the main point here is that a policy broadly defines the universe of action, whereas planning is concerned with what happens inside.

Policies abound in the corporate environment. They cover staffing, growth, planning, managerial authority, conflicts of interest, marketing, production, finance, facilities, and many more. There are also the qualitative differences in policies. Some are simply more important than others, giving credence to the term "high-level policy."

The badge of honor in the corporate environment is often the extent to which a leader is involved in policy development. The higher the policy and the more the leader shares in the decision is a determinant of status in the formal, corporate organization.

It helps to think of policies as many trees in an orchard. The gardener is the CEO. The roots of the security tree spread deep into the organization. Each root is a separate element such as security officer operations, physical security, and investigations. All roots collectively draw nutrients from the soil in the form of funding for labor and equipment. The gardener is ever watchful for blooms that produce the fruit. If the security tree does not bear fruit, the gardener will investigate and, where appropriate, change the composition of the soil, prune the unproductive limbs, or remove the tree entirely.

The CSO and Strategic Planning

Strategic plans send ripples throughout the whole of the organization. Negative ripples impacting the CSO can be lessened to the extent that the CSO participated in developing the plan. The degree of involvement by a CSO tends to be determined by three factors. First is where the CSO sits on the organizational chart. If at the lower end of the pecking order, he/she won't have much input. Second is the shape of the organization. If it is a flat organization with only few levels separating the chairman from the frontline workers, the chance for a lower-level manager to contribute is increased. Third is the personality of the CSO. If perceived as being inept or uncaring about strategic planning, he/she won't be invited to participate, no matter where located on the organizational chart and no matter the shape of the organization. If perceived as having something meaningful to contribute and willing to contribute, the CSO may be invited into the upper, upper realm.

Core and Support Activities

Nearly every business of size is organized along lines that permit simultaneous management of two main activities: the core activities at the heart of the enterprise and the support activities that contribute to the core. The core work, being essential to the business and having value that demands protection, is usually assigned to proven and trusted employees. The support work, while important to some degree, usually does not produce a significant or sustainable advantage to the business. The support staff tends to be varied, running the gamut from unskilled to highly skilled.

In a fast-evolving market where new technologies are emerging, the knowledge and skills of individuals are very limited. The technologies themselves may be proprietary and not available on the open market. If organizations can attract the knowledge and skills base of technologies, they have an advantage.

An often under-appreciated skill is the anticipation of the effect that a particular management strategy will have on the provision of security services. In the development of a company strategy, the CSO can be a key contributor by proposing measures to close security-related exposures that may arise when the strategy is implemented.

While potential exposures are not easy to detect and even more difficult to prevent or mitigate, the CSO can at least rely on the common sense observation that security risks rise when adjustments are made to the manner of work performance. A shift in strategy can move through the organization like a slow moving earthquake. Formal and informal controls on people performance that have been set in place by tested practice can be broken. Tiny fissures on the surface signal large disturbances below, foretelling eruptions that carry high risk. Loss events are waiting to happen, and it is the CSO's function to anticipate and prevent them.

Technical Knowledge

Although it is unreasonable to expect the CSO to possess a comprehensive range of technical knowledge, it is quite reasonable to expect him/her to know where to find it and to have it available on demand. Technical knowledge can be viewed as a dimension of business that operates in three human competencies: access, quality, and teamwork.

Access implies that the CSO knows where to find the right information, service, or product at the best price. It often means building sound relationships with actual and potential vendors and networking with peers. The transfer of "best practices" among security practitioners in different companies and industries is an example of accessing technical knowledge.

Quality is the optimal balance between cost and technical excellence. It includes quality control and quality assurance. Quality control is the responsibility of the supplier; quality assurance derives naturally from confidence in the relationship. In a mature connection between client and vendor, cost and quality will occur together, to the advantage of both parties.

Teamwork is the bringing together of people who each contribute from complementary specialties. It is a competency which also gives to the players the right information, service, or product. A team or teams may be the security group or the security group in tandem with various product suppliers and consultants. Team composition will vary according to the mission, with each member contributing a different set of skills and abilities. Teamwork calls for sustained leadership and goal orientation.

Strategy and Risk

The ability to predict and quantify a full menu of risks is the CSO's highest mark of excellence.

To predict risk, which is restricted by the limitations of human understanding and available technology, is to identify the nature of threats confronting the organization and assess the probability of their occurrence.

To quantify risk is to measure potential consequences through the application of science and experience. To control risk is to logically and flexibly manage resources in ways that offset threats.

The genuinely competent CSO will obtain through continuous self-development an ability to deal with evolving threats, know where to find the technical assistance sufficient to counter them, and be positioned to acquire that assistance when it is needed.

The reader may detect the outlines of a security strategy taking shape. Integral to it are six mutually-reinforcing imperatives:

- Improve on quality and cost.
- Forge close links to customers.

- Establish close relationships with suppliers.
- Make effective use of technology.
- Operate with minimum layers of management.
- Continuously improve the security staff.

Improve on Quality and Cost. The measuring stick of security performance is high quality at reasonable cost. The facets of quality are excellence, reliability, and speedy delivery of services. The successful security operations are those that strive to be the "best in class" in all the main performance activities. A characteristic of the leading performers is an emphasis on competitive benchmarking, i.e., comparing personal and unit performance with the industry's leaders, and setting goals to measure progress.

Forge Close Links to Customers. Successful CSOs make concerted efforts to develop close ties with their customers. A customer is the user of security services. Who are the users? They are all of the persons within the organization that employs the CSO, a fact that too many CSOs lose sight of.

Forging a link is less like making friends through public relations and more like getting into "the mind" of the customer. It can happen that the CSO will know what should be in the customer's mind even before the customer becomes aware of it. Having that mental connect allows the CSO to respond rapidly and appropriately to the users of security services.

Strategy in any business context is meaningless without reference to customers. The dominant aim of strategy is to deliver superior value to customers. A persistent and unavoidable challenge of the CSO in the battle to enhance and sustain superior value is to stay one or more steps ahead of security groups that support competitors. Simply emulating what others do cannot lead to superior performance.

Establish Close Relationships with Suppliers. Too often, cooperation with suppliers is achieved through the coercive power of the buyer. The alternative described here, however, is the creation of partner relationships in which price is not always the single most important factor. Coordination with external vendors is crucial to a CSO in acquiring technical assistance in whatever form that assistance might take, e.g., electronic countermeasures, forensic examinations, surveillance, undercover operations, etc.

If a key element of strategy is to position the in-house security staff to be a leader in using technical advances in support of the mission, it follows that the CSO will be active in developing partnerships with the suppliers of technology. The idea is to select a small number of capable suppliers and work with them. A partnership arrangement has little room for second-guessing and beating suppliers down to the last penny.

When a vendor provides contracted guard services, the CSO should forge a positive working relationship with the guard company's account manager. An understanding between them can help both parties find a balance between assuring high guard performance and recognizing the guard firm's right to supervise its own employees. If guard performance is inadequate, the CSO has a duty to offer constructive direction and the account manager has an obligation to listen and respond within reasonable limits. None of this is possible without a solid working relationship.

Make Effective Use of Technology. A security strategy linked to technology will demand of the CSO knowledge of work-enhancing technologies available in the marketplace and a skill in using them wisely. Being wise about technology involves recognizing that newer is not always better, and even when a technology is in fact superior, the final payoff has to exceed the costs of applying it. In short, technology must earn its way.

In looking for a technological solution, the CSO should not try to reinvent the wheel but at the same time not have a closed mind to a it. Common mistakes are to reject a technology that is not totally applicable but is workable in important respects, and to expect more than a technology can deliver. Very important also is to get the solution right the first time because retrofitting can be costly.

Another consideration is the working relationship between the security employees and the equipment or routines that make up the technology. This is not so much a matter of ergonomics but of the symbiotic linkage of man and machine. In companies where technology is routinely applied, the security employees are better able to adjust when a new or more complicated technology is acquired for their use.

Operate with Minimum Layers of Management. Organizational structure, i.e., the horizontal distribution of departments and the vertical arrangement of managerial layers, varies considerably from company to company. Today's trends favor greater functional integration and fewer layers of management, both of which promote speedy delivery of services and a strong responsiveness to customer needs. These are virtues to be cherished by any prudent CSO.

Execution of the security strategy in a flat, lean organization will in most cases rely upon a small, yet well-rounded staff of the highest quality, working in partnership with suppliers who bring to the arrangement a broad array of technical competencies. The competencies that stand out are in the job domains of computer security specialists, anti-surveillance technicians, auditors, architects, access control specialists, and others. The security profession, although very broad and mature, is surprisingly innovative when it comes to harnessing special talent.

Continuously Improve the Security Staff. The first five strategy elements require departures from the conventional way of dealing with employees. The changes call for developing a new mindset, a new commitment, and strong leadership. Progress will seldom be comfortable as old ideas are cast off and refashioned.

The improvement of security staff depends on the infusion of large doses of meaningful, useful knowledge. The modes of teaching can include counseling, formal classroom instruction, and on-the-job coaching. The constant in the process is unending development of employees, not merely development to get the strategy up and going, but development throughout the employees' working lifetimes.

The outcome of staff development will be technical competency, quality output, teamwork, and a flexibility that permits the acceptance of daunting challenges.

No Absolutes in Strategic Planning

Strategic planning has common elements in all competitive human endeavors, yet there is no such thing as a standard or universal system for strategic planning. It's not possible to transfer the strategic planning mechanism of one company to another and expect it to work properly. Business organizations, even when in the same line of work, will be different in many key respects, including differences in the nature and the how of planning.

It is no accident that geniuses often occupy senior executive chairs; these are leaders whose intuition and intelligence bring them like cream to the top. Their success is seldom the result of developing a written plan and sticking to it without deviation. They tend to fly on the seat of their pants and make snap decisions intuitively, often relying on a past experience, a gut feeling, or a flash of brilliant insight. If an organization is managed by a genius, and there are many examples in the high-tech businesses of today, formal strategic planning will likely suffer, and that may be just as well. But if the CEO is not the intuitive type, strategic planning can be "set in stone." This is not altogether bad and very appropriate for mature organizations. Planning will be formalized, highly documented, based on research and input from many sources, and involve the participation of many people.

Strategy and Change

A change in strategy precipitates changes in policy which precipitates changes in plans which precipitate changes in work practices. The strategy change begins as a snowball that gets larger and larger as it rolls downhill, producing change all along the way.

The CSO must anticipate resistance to change in the security group. "But we've always done it this way" is a common cry heard when work practices change. The old ways of doing things may be so entrenched that even the best-laid preparation will falter. Engineering change even under the best of circumstances is hard work. It requires imagination, analytical ability, and fortitude.

To sum up, every company has a strategic management at the top and operational management below. Strategic plans are extensions of policy. Policy and plans are not always created with input from the CSO, but without exception, the CSO is impacted by them.

John J. Fay

Sources

Fahey, L. 1999. *Competitors.* New York: John Wiley and Sons.

Fay, J. 2006. *Contemporary Security Management.* Boston: Butterworth-Heinemann.

Hoenig, C. "The Master Planner" *CIO magazine,* May 1, 2000. 76 and 78.

Maurice, F. 1999. *Strategic Outsourcing: A Structured Approach to Outsourcing Decisions and Initiatives.* New York: American Management Association.

THRIVING FOR QUALITY

A security manager can demonstrate an ability to think beyond the limits of asset protection in several ways. One way is to propose to senior management ideas for recognizing employees and enriching their lives. Those ideas might be:

1. A charity day one day a year when employees volunteer to work for free (on one of their days off). The proceeds of their day's pay are dedicated to a charity of their choice.
2. Leverage on the distribution of payroll checks to employees by enclosing promotional items granting employees discounted prices on the company's products.
3. Negotiate discounted prices with local handymen, electricians, plumbers, and so forth, for company employees.
4. Likewise, depending on the size of the organization, senior managers, through their procurement process, could negotiate volume discounts with local merchants such as snow and water ski rental companies, bicycle companies, camping suppliers, and so forth.
5. Leverage your professional network. Whether you are a proprietary security manager or a contract provider, think of the added value that inures to you if you are able to arrange a reciprocal agreement with other security directors for your employees or clients to take advantage of the other company's services or products at a discounted rate. For example, you might know the security director of the local

museum. What a wonderful idea it would be if your employees or clients could take in a local museum show at a discounted rate by virtue of their association with you and your connections with the security director of the museum. Similar discounted rates might apply for high-tech companies, entertainment centers, and even supermarket chains.

6. Create a charity fine program. Getting employees to wear photo identification badges can be both difficult and frustrating. One way to encourage full participation is to assess a "charity's fine" for non-compliers. Anytime an employee is found not wearing his or her photo identification badge, the violating employee would be assessed a $1 fine, or more, the proceeds of which would be donated to a local charity at the end of the year.

7. Review the top twenty-five versus the bottom twenty-five. For a number of years now Wal-Mart stores have assembled the top twenty-five performing stores within a district along with the bottom twenty-five stores every Saturday. As a company they celebrate the performance of the top companies and work on ways in which they can improve the performance of the bottom twenty-five. For contract providers, there is a significant lesson in quality assurance and customer service to be learned here. Those units that are not meeting performance expectations are able to learn both successful techniques and obstacles associated with bottom-line profitability and performance.

8. Create forgiveness notes. Great organizations understand that the freedom to fail and try again applies to both operations and customer service. Success is built on failures. Some companies distribute to all of their employees GET OUT OF JAIL FREE cards. When an employee makes a mistake in his or her attempt to deliver outstanding service, he or she goes to a corporate executive, discusses what he or she has learned from the experience, turns

in the GET OUT OF JAIL FREE card, and is forgiven. Think what could happen in your department if your employees realized that they had an opportunity to make an honest mistake without punishment.

9. Nordstrom's golden rule. The Nordstrom Department Store Company has developed one performance rule: Use your good judgment in all situations. Almost as an afterthought, they have attached a rider to this rule: "There will be no additional rules." In other words, employees are expected to always use good judgment, and as a result there is little reason to develop the typical three-inch binder of additional rules and regulations.

10. Got an idea? Give it away. One of the principles behind thriving is continuously striving to do something different. By encouraging your suppliers or employees to give away their best ideas, this forces them to push the envelope to try out new ideas. In other words, you cannot become complacent, since eventually you will become but one in a sea of penguins. By giving ideas away, you make room for bold thinking, thereby creating an opportunity to thrive in unsettling times.

11. Sometimes career development means moving on. As organizations trim down, more and more demands are being placed on the surviving staff. Companies need to be able to expand beyond the limits for which employees were originally hired. For some, the transition will be made regardless of whether it is easy or difficult. Unfortunately for others, the transition will never be made. Consequently, a thriving-oriented manager owes it to those struggling employees to suggest that their professional development may be better enhanced by moving on to another organization.

12. Create a professional library for others. One Atlanta based security services provider developed an extensive library, which they made available to their clients and local college students. It is an excellent way for the company

to demonstrate added value to its clients and a concern for the surrounding community.

13. Ask "Why not?" An executive for one of the country's largest radio station networks wanted to offer worldwide live broadcasting on the Internet. As he began to explore the possibilities, he was continuously confronted by specialists saying, "Well, we can't do it that way." Each time he received that answer, he responded by asking the question "Why not?" The specialists eventually began to relent and ask themselves the "Why not?" question. It didn't take long for the specialists to realize that the goal was achievable. Within a period of months, the radio station became the world's first to live-broadcast on the Internet. The lesson for security managers is that gains can be made by continuously challenging traditional approaches by asking the great "Why not?"

14. The brain problem syndrome. Thriving means having the ability to translate past mistakes into learning opportunities. I recently had an opportunity to work with a security director in the development of a new program for his company. As a contract provider, he had managed to bridge the perception of being an outside provider and was seen, for all practical purposes, as a member of his client's management team. In the process of implementing the operation of a closed-circuit television monitoring function, we discovered that a number of his officers were unfamiliar with the equipment. Initially I was surprised because the officers involved were veteran employees with an average tenure in excess of five years. When confronted with this situation, the security manager said that he would look into the matter and report back to me shortly. Later that afternoon he sought me out to report that the problem seemed to be rooted in what he termed a "brain problem syndrome." When I asked him to explain, he stated that he had made the assumption that tenured officers

were experienced in the operation of CCTV systems, so he had not included them in the initial training program. This ability to acknowledge basic mistakes and quickly correct them when they were brought to his attention reinforced my perception that he was a thriving-oriented manager; a perception that was also shared by his clients.

15. Create on-line teams. With the explosion of electronic mail and the Internet, staff members located anywhere from a few feet to thousands of miles away can be electronically connected and communicate at rapid speed. The thriving-oriented manager fully understands the power associated with the ability to communicate with his entire staff, irrespective of physical distance. By putting an issue out on the Internet or company e-mail system and soliciting feedback from a variety of staff resources, the manager is able to take advantage of the multiplicity of resources available in the resident staff.

16. Creating reserve resources. As companies experience fluctuation in their labor pools, retaining experienced staff can sometimes be challenging. Consider the value of actively participating in helping employees seek temporary work assignments outside of the organization. The strategy is to position valued employees so that when circumstances change you'll have the opportunity to reintroduce them into the organization. By working out alliance relationships with companies that have high turnover rates, security companies can move their employees between employers to the advantage of everyone. The security department literally cross-trains employees with another profession, thus enabling both employers to take advantage of swings in their business cycles.

These sixteen examples illustrate how security managers, whether proprietary or external, can integrate themselves and their programs into the overall business plan of the organization. They underscore the fact that success is tied directly to an ability to demonstrate an aptitude for thriving as opposed to struggling to survive in uncertain times.

Dennis Dalton

Source Dalton, D. 1995. *Security Management: Business Strategies for Success.* Boston: Butterworth-Heinemann.

UPWARD FEEDBACK

Upward feedback is a communication process between managers and their subordinates that can be mutually beneficial. Upward feedback has four objectives: (1) improve communication between the manager and his or her team, (2) improve teamwork, (3) identify management practices where change will result in managing people more effectively, and (4) create an action plan to which all members of the team commit.

Upward feedback is marked by open thinking, personal impact, empowerment, and networking. It can be a key tool in helping a manager understand his or her abilities to lead others.

Research into the responses of managers receiving feedback reveal a sequence of reactions called SARAH. The sequence begins with Shock, followed by Anger and Rejection, moves to Acceptance, and concludes with a request for Help.

A natural instinct is to react to what first appears to be personal criticism. When a manager is able to get past the initial surprise, annoyance, and rationalization, he or she is ready to accept the feedback as valid and then to accept help.

The Upward Feedback Process

The process usually begins by distributing a questionnaire to the persons who report to the manager. The questionnaire is anonymous and contains questions relating to management practices that are widely held to be supportive of effective teamwork. (The person filling out the questionnaire will be asked to rate each practice in certain dimensions; for example, the relative importance that the respondent places upon the practice and the degree to which the manager uses the practice.)

The Upward Feedback Process

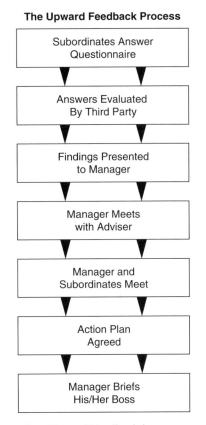

Figure 5. Upward Feedback is a process that involves three levels of employees.

The completed questionnaires are sent to a third party, such as an outside consultant or a specialist within the organization's human resources department. The questionnaires are scored, with significant variances noted. An example of a significant variance might be that the respondent considered conflict resolution within the team to be highly important but rated the manager very low in effectively resolving conflict. A report is generated in the scoring process and it may present findings in the form of numerical data, such as bar charts, and short narratives describing outstanding strengths and weaknesses.

The report provides a snapshot of team members' perceptions. The report is provided to the manager. A one-to-one meeting between the manager and an upward feedback adviser assists the manager in moving through the SARAH process. In this meeting, the manager sizes up the information, raises issues and questions with the adviser, identifies areas that need to be clarified, and develops an agenda and a plan to meet with the team to review the findings of the report.

The next step is to hold a team meeting chaired by the manager, with the adviser present to facilitate the process. The adviser's role also includes easing the comfort level of the manager and the team, and serving as an objective third party. The role of the manager is to actively solicit observations and examples pertinent to the feedback report, listen carefully and probe for understanding, and look for improvement opportunities. The desired outcomes are that the manager will gain from the team members a clearer, truer understanding of the feedback and determine a foundation for action.

Immediately following the team meeting, the manager and the adviser confer privately. They review and obtain clarity on what was said. The adviser provides objective commentary and assists the manager in "reading between the lines." The manager is led to explore areas where change is appropriate and to make a personal commitment for improvement steps. In this regard, the manager develops a draft of a realistic action plan that incorporates personal and team objectives.

Finally, the manager sets up a meeting with his or her boss to identify ways to fully support achievement of the objectives in the action plan. Included on the agenda can be a discussion of the training, education, or other resources that may be needed to carry out the plan. The manager should circulate the agreed action plan to team members. This helps confirm that the feedback has been heard at a level higher than the manager and that commitments have been made to act on the key areas.

Following is a list of team building practices:

- Meeting frequently with employees to review their overall individual performance

- Working with people to determine realistic personal development plans
- Accurately representing the views, opinions, and feelings of staff up the line
- Anticipating future business opportunities and requirements, and planning ahead to meet them
- Maintaining the right balance of skills within the work team to meet the team's objectives
- Making problems and their cases clear so that they may be corrected
- Being effective at initiating and sustaining change
- Resolving conflicts
- Understanding and clarifying the best interests of the Company and the business unit
- Involving others in decisions where necessary
- Maintaining high standards for the team's work
- Relating the total reward system to the excellence of job performance
- Agreeing on challenging and achievable performance objectives with employees
- Sharing power in the interest of common goals
- Managing time effectively
- Providing equal development and advancement opportunities to all employees
- Creating a sense of enthusiasm about the work team's direction
- Encouraging employees to be innovative to improve the business
- Being innovative and creative in responding to changing business conditions
- Supporting and helping employees
- Making tough decisions
- Setting team and individual goals

John J. Fay

II: Emergency Management Practices

BOMB THREAT MANAGEMENT

The proposition is well accepted that the organization's chief security officer is invested with the main responsibility for managing bomb threats. Even when there has been no history of threats and no reason to believe the organization has become a target, the chief security officer must anticipate the possibility and have a program in place.

Prevention Activities

Being ready to respond to a bomb threat is one thing; taking preventive action is another. A balanced program for the management of bomb threats will include proactive steps, for example:

- Coordinate with intelligence collection units of law enforcement agencies to learn the operating locales of criminal and terrorist groups known to use bombs; stay current with new developments in bomb construction and the methods of operation of groups that use them; and determine if the organization is a potential target.
- Confer with security counterparts to learn the bomb incident experiences of other organizations. Set up information sharing agreements.
- Liaise with bomb disposal experts who can be helpful to the organization in conducting training programs for plan respondents, for employees generally, and for certain employees whose duties would bring them into contact with mail bombs. This last group would comprise mail room employees and executive secretaries.
- Control suspect packages entering the workplace. Considerations can include examining packages at an offsite location that poses minimum danger in the event of

an explosion; using bomb detection equipment; and training the package examiners in the visual techniques for spotting the indicators of package bombs.
- Maintain a positive means of identifying and channeling people who enter and move within the workplace.
- Educate employees to look for and report strangers in the workplace, and educate employees and visitors alike to not leave personal items, such as briefcases and gym bags, unattended in public areas of the facility.
- Conduct periodic inspections of the workplace to identify areas where a bomb could be planted with minimum chance of detection and at the same time cause major property damage or personal injuries. The areas to think about are the facility's power plant, flammable storage rooms, telephone switching center, computer room, and executive offices.
- Educate employees, generally, and security and maintenance personnel, specifically, to be alert for suspicious persons and activities in areas that are accessible to the public, offer bomb concealment opportunities, and are sensitive in terms of damage and/or injury.
- Require security officers during each tour of duty to make random checks of public areas to look for unauthorized persons who may be hiding in or reconnoitering the facility.
- Ensure physical protection of key assets. Fire resistant safes and vaults can protect sensitive documents, cash, small valuables, magnetic media, and similar materials against bomb damage.
- Educate fire wardens and other emergency respondents to look for and report unusual activities that might signal the early stage of a bombing attempt.

An intelligent and determined adversary is likely to find a chink in even the best defensive armor. Without considering the elaborate schemes, some of the readily available means for introducing a bomb into a workplace are: on the person of an employee, by postal or commercial delivery service, and by motor vehicle into the facility's garage. Once inside, placement of a bomb is mainly a matter of the attacker's nerve and knowledge of the premises. The attacker might choose to place the bomb in a rest room, janitor's closet, stairwell, receiving platform, lobby, or elevator.

Security management must regard, as a top priority, the degree of control exerted by the security force at access points. Control at the perimeter is the first and most important line of defense in a proactive strategy. Although most bomb threats prove to be hoaxes or are resolved by disarming the bomb before detonation, we cannot rule out the skilled attacker intent upon inflicting maximum harm without warning. The best preventive course in such a case is to deny access.

The Bomb Threat

A bomb threat is rarely made in person and sometimes is transmitted in writing. A bomb threat in writing should be handled carefully, touched by as few persons as possible, and the envelope or any other accompanying materials preserved as evidence. Observing these simple precautions can be extremely helpful to a post-incident investigation.

Nearly all bomb threats are made by telephone. Two reasons can be attributed to a bomb threat call:

The caller has certain knowledge that a bomb has been or will be placed. The caller wants to minimize personal injury or property damage by alerting persons at the target area. The caller is likely to be the bomber or an accomplice.

The caller wants to disrupt the normal activity and cause inconvenience. In most cases this type of call will not involve placement of anything, although in some few cases a simulated bomb will have been placed.

When prior preparation and practice have not been made, panic can result from a bomb threat call. Panic is an infectious fear capable of spreading quickly, and when present, the potential for injury is substantially increased. One of the ways that the potential for panic can be minimized is to train persons in how to receive a bomb threat call. Training would teach the recipient of a bomb threat call to:

- Keep the caller talking for as long as possible. Ask the caller to repeat the message.

Take notes. Try to take down the exact words used by the caller.
- Ask the caller to specifically state where the bomb is located and when it is set to detonate.
- Ask what part of the facility should be evacuated first.
- Ask for a description of the bomb. What does it look like? How is it packaged? What is it made of and how does it work?
- Ask why the bomb was placed and what group is responsible. Ask the caller if he or she was the person who placed the bomb. Ask where the caller is now.
- Tell the caller that the facility is occupied and that a detonation could result in death and serious injury to many innocent people.
- Listen closely to the caller's voice. Is the caller male or female? Calm or excited? Accent? Speech impediment?
- Pay attention to background noises that may give a clue as to the caller's location. Traffic sounds, music, and voices heard in the background may be important.
- Keep the line open after the call has ended. It may be possible to trace the call.
- Notify the Security Department immediately after the caller hangs up. Be ready to be interviewed by a security representative and to pass over the notes made during the call.

A checklist form for receiving a bomb threat call can be very helpful. The form can be made a part of the training and distributed to employees for posting close to the telephone.

Formal training in how to receive a bomb threat call should be supplemented by informal refreshment through an ongoing program of security awareness and education. The objective is to condition the employees (most particularly telephone operators, receptionists, executive secretaries, and security officers) to properly receive and report a bomb threat call. The initial report triggers a cascade of notices.

Evaluating a Bomb Threat Call

The very first task of the chief security officer who has been informed of a bomb threat is to evaluate it. Interviewing the person who received the call

BOMB THREAT NOTIFICATION CHART

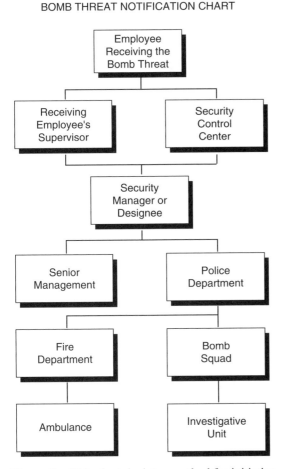

Figure 6. This chart depicts a method for initiating responses in a bomb threat situation.

was that "it seems like a good idea." In this case, the chief security officer may conclude that the call is probably a hoax.

In another case, the chief security officer may be looking at entirely different indicators, such as nervousness in the caller's voice, an expressed grievance against the organization, knowledge of the workplace or of persons who work there, and knowledge of bomb construction. The conclusion here is that the threat is probably or most probably real. When the indicators are not clear cut, the chief security officer has to act as if the threat were real.

The senior managements of many organizations will insist, as a matter of policy, that bomb threat evaluation be a shared process in which the chief security officer presents his findings to one or more senior executives before decisions are made to search or evacuate.

Search and Evacuation Options

Some organizations will require, even when searching and evacuating are deemed unnecessary, that all employees be informed of the receipt of a bomb threat and those that wish to leave may do so without penalty. The concern appears to be with the liability that may arise if a bomb explodes after the management received a warning that it chose not to disclose.

Three possible options proceed from a judgment of the threat: (1) to search without evacuating; (2) to evacuate partially or fully, and then search; and (3) to fully evacuate and not search.

Searching without Evacuating. This option is appropriate when the bomb threat call is judged to be a hoax or probable hoax. Immediate and total evacuation would at first glance seem to be the only possible response to a bomb threat. Upon close analysis, however, we can note at least two factors that operate against automatic evacuation. First, there is the matter of safety. Even the most orderly evacuation can produce injuries from tripping and falling. There is also the risk of moving large numbers of people along designated exit routes where a bomb might be planted or assembling them in an area where even a small explosive device would cause many casualties.

Evacuation is also disruptive to work. While the protection of life certainly outweighs

and examining the notes taken during the call are preliminary to making any judgment. The evaluation takes into account the details and characteristics of the call itself, prior calls, and similar threats that have been made in the community or against counterpart organizations.

Evaluation is essentially a process of judging the credibility of the threat. Is the call a hoax or is it real? In this process, absolutes are not possible. The chief security officer is weighing probabilities and if an error is to be made, it has to be made on the side of caution. For example, in looking at the details of a call, the chief security officer may learn that the caller was a young female, probably a teenager; giggling sounds and music were heard in the background; and the caller's answer to the question as to motive any economic loss, repeated threats and evacuations would soon escalate productivity losses to an unacceptable level.

Evacuating Partially or Fully and Then Searching. This option is appropriate when the call is assigned a greater degree of credibility. For example, if the caller indicates that the bomb is in a particular area, employees from that area and surrounding confines would be evacuated. Similarly, full evacuation would be appropriate if the caller is credible and indicates multiple bomb locations or refuses to name any specific location.

Fully Evacuating and Not Searching. This option is rarely taken because it is only appropriate when the call is given a high degree of credibility and when not enough time is available to conduct a search. In selecting this option, management is essentially saying it is better to get out and wait until the bomb goes off, if it goes off at all, or wait until more than sufficient time elapses to permit a conclusion that the threat was false.

These three options represent preliminary courses of action that can be changed as circumstances change. The option to search without evacuation might be upgraded if a second bomb call increased the credibility of the threat, or if during the search a suspect bomb was discovered. The size and location of a suspect bomb will influence the extent of evacuation. For example, a suspect bomb about the size of a cigarette pack that is found in a non-safety sensitive area might not require a total evacuation.

As a general rule, at least 300 feet of lateral area around a suspect bomb should be cleared of all non-essential response personnel. The vertical areas above and below a suspect bomb should also be cleared. If a suspect bomb is found on a floor of a multi-story building, the floor involved plus the floors immediately above and below should be cleared.

Does total evacuation mean that every person must leave? The answer is always yes when there is reason to believe a discovered bomb is capable of inflicting damage or injury. In the absence of that belief the answer could be no. Some persons, such as security officers and maintenance employees, may remain to perform essential life-protecting and shutdown duties when the risk to them appears to be low.

Searching Considerations

Bomb searching is in most cases conducted by persons familiar with the workplace and almost never by police officers. Public safety policy often discourages the participation of police department personnel in bomb searches on private property, unless probable cause exists to believe that a bomb is in fact present. Probable cause can be established by the details of the bomb threat call or by the discovery of a suspect bomb. With a belief established, the police are more likely to want to be actively involved in making or directing the search. Although employees at the workplace will have a greater familiarity with the possible places of bomb concealment, officers trained in bomb disposal will know how to avoid booby traps and mistakes that can lead to detonation.

Three key points need to be emphasized: (1) that the search be thorough; (2) that the search be careful; and (3) that when a suspect bomb is found, it be approached only with great caution.

Putting the key points into practice means that: (1) for a search to be thorough it is best to do it with people familiar with the physical environment, i.e., security officers, maintenance workers, and other employees who know the nooks and crannies; (2) that for a search to be careful it should be done by people who are trained, i.e., that the organization give training to its bomb searching personnel; and (3) that the dangerous nature of bomb disposal requires people with highly specialized qualifications, i.e., that a suspect bomb be approached and handled only by duly authorized and certified bomb disposal technicians.

A search team's thoroughness will be affected by the size and configuration of the workplace to be searched. It might be fair to say that making a thorough search is not easy in any working environment. Even small environments uncomplicated by multiple workstations, equipment, and labor-intensive activities will present problems. Large and complex environments, such as manufacturing plants and high-rise office buildings, are searchable on a genuinely thorough basis only with substantial expenditure of effort and time. A 20-story office building, for example, might require 48 hours of uninterrupted looking with a 20-person team before it can be said that every conceivable hiding place has been examined.

It will seldom be possible in a large and complex environment to conduct a comprehensive search because time will not allow looking into false ceilings, examining every file cabinet, and removing panels from equipment. Neither will it be acceptable to disrupt or shut down work operations for two full working days while a search is in progress. A practical solution might be to prioritize, as part of the planning process, those places that should be thoroughly searched within the time available for searching. Note that the principle of searching with thoroughness remains uncompromised but that selectivity is introduced with respect to what should be searched.

Probability and criticality stand out in prioritizing the search effort. How probable is it that a bomber would be able to penetrate the organization's security defenses, and if the probability is high, how probable is it that a bomb or bombs would be placed in some areas as opposed to others? An evaluation of probability might lead to a search priority that concentrates on areas that are outside the umbrella of high security control, such as lobbies, garages, and other areas easily accessible to the public.

An evaluation of criticality might establish a priority for searching in areas where greatest damage can be done to the organization's most valuable assets. Criticality, however, needs to be balanced by probability. For example, it may not be sensible to set a high priority on searching the computer center when the probability is low that a bomb could be brought into the computer center without detection.

A technique associated with the prioritization of searching is the use of a card system. Each area or object to be searched is represented by a card that describes its location and other details, such as a particular telephone number to be called when the search has been completed. The cards are coded or numbered according to priority and are kept by the chief security officer or other person responsible for directing search team activities. At the search team briefing that precedes the starting of a search, the cards are handed out to team members. At the end of the search, checkmarks or signatures on the cards can provide a quick reference for ensuring that no areas were overlooked.

Search Methods

As mentioned earlier, the time requirements and the disruption of a comprehensive search make that method impractical in most cases. Two other general search methods present themselves for consideration: the non-evacuation method and the post-evacuation method.

The Non-Evacuation Method. The decision to not evacuate would be based on a judgment that the bomb threat call is a hoax and that persons in the workplace are not in danger. But because a bomb threat call is never judged to be absolutely false, a search should be made even when evacuation is not deemed appropriate.

The non-evacuation method is performed in a "walk-through" manner, but not in a cursory manner. A searcher is typically working alone, and is making searches of one or more specific areas that are likely to be occupied by employees who may or may not have been informed of the bomb threat. The searcher is typically a security officer, maintenance worker, or other person known to the employees.

The searcher moves in a steady, unhurried pace looking for objects that seem to not belong. Employees can be a source of information in determining if an object is really suspicious or simply not in its proper place. In areas where there are few or no employees present, the searcher can give closer attention to containers, closets, and areas that are out of direct sight.

The Post-Evacuation Method. When employees are absent, such as following an evacuation or during non-working hours, the searcher can move into workstations, offices, and conference rooms to examine shelves, waste baskets, storage bins, and the like. Even though each searcher can move faster when employees are not in the way, the time gained is expended in looking with more intensity. Also, if the post-evacuation search is conducted after hours, the search team will not be at full force because maintenance employees and other day workers who would normally assist in the search are likely to be off duty.

Discovery of a Suspicious Object

One of the fundamentals is to not touch a suspicious object. A searcher, however, will need to do a certain amount of touching in the routine course of looking into, behind, and under the many items that can conceal a bomb. But at the instant a suspicious object is seen, all touching should stop. The searcher then needs to alert persons nearby to leave the area.

The next step is to notify the chief security officer or other person coordinating the search. The responsive actions that can follow include:

- Questioning employees who may be able to account for the presence of the suspicious object.
- Ordering a partial or full evacuation.
- Notifying the bomb disposal team.
- Notifying the fire department.
- Readying first aid supplies and calling for standby medical personnel and equipment.
- Asking the police to assume command of the situation.

The bomb disposal team leader or the fire officer in charge may ask for further information, such as the location of the suspect device relative to stored fuels, chemicals, flammables, power plant, and fire exits. Requests may be made to identify other possible hiding places, to open doors or windows for the purpose of dissipating blast effects, and to establish traffic control around the facility to permit free movement of emergency vehicles.

Command and Control

The chief security officer will find it advisable to pre-designate a location where the response coordinators can assemble at the outset of a bomb threat. The pre-designated location should be easily accessible to bomb incident response personnel, contain the applicable bomb threat response procedures, and have adequate communications, such as a radio network and telephones that can quickly connect to key persons inside and outside of the organization.

John J. Fay

BUSINESS CONTINUITY PLANNING

Business continuity planning is defined in many different ways, each reflecting its author's particular slant on contingency planning. Many of these definitions attempt to combine the definitions of continuity planning and of a continuity plan. There is an important distinction between the two.

Business continuity planning is a process that identifies the critical functions of an organization and that develops strategies to minimize the effects of an outage or loss of service provided by these functions. The most common strategies involve some type of third-party data center or alternate, off-site processing and alternate workspace to restore operations to a minimally acceptable level. In today's business environment, it is no longer acceptable to return to, or to achieve a minimum level of, service after a disaster.

These companies wish to, or need to, maintain operations at the current level or to take advantage of the disaster by the existence of the plan to gain market share over the competition. Disaster recovery planning is really synonymous with business continuity planning, but the term is a product of the data center. It represents the idea that recovery planning is important only to telecommunications and data centers. Business continuity planning implies recovery planning for all the critical functions or business units of an organization. Today, these terms are increasingly drifting apart. Disaster recovery refers to the reestablishment or continuity of information technology and data systems; business continuity refers to the recovery or continuity of business unit operations (systems versus people).

A business continuity plan is a comprehensive statement of consistent action taken before, during, and after a disaster or outage. The plan is designed for a worst-case scenario but should be flexible enough to address the more common, localized emergencies, such as power outages, server crashes, and fires. Although the actions listed in the plan contain sufficient detail to implement strategies designed to recover critical functions, they are more guides than inflexible dictates. Because it is not practical to plan for every type of contingency, and because each disaster has its own set of conditions, the ability to modify the plan must be incorporated.

Although a recovery plan is important, it is the planning process that returns the greatest value. This distinction is often missed by both planners and end users of continuity plans. The identification of critical functions, the thought and analysis behind the development of the strategies designed to recover the functions, and the knowledge of why one particular strategy was selected over another are not always apparent from simply reading the plan. This is valuable knowledge when last-minute decisions are required to adapt the plan to a particular situation. The planning process is also a training exercise. The participants must think through contingencies, so that the actions required to recover from them will be already familiar. Reading the plan for the first or second time just after the disaster will provide for a less than effective recovery. This is assuming, of course, that the plan is not buried under a hundred tons of rubble.

Why Plan?

Responsibility for continuity planning often resides with the risk manager, the chief financial officer (CFO), or the data center manager. Security managers are, however, increasingly taking the role of plan developers. Their experience with the protection of assets, involvement in the identification and the mitigation of risk, and emergency response duties makes them logical choices for this role. The ability to work effectively with all levels of management is a required trait for security managers, a trait that all successful continuity planners must possess.

Some types of businesses, such as financial institutions and industries regulated by toxics laws, are required to maintain continuity plans. Businesses are increasingly regulated by laws and standards, many differing widely in their approach and requirements. Some are intended to be industry specific and others broad based. Some use differing terminology, or try to package the same methodologies in different looking boxes.

Without continuity planning, the organization may lose its competitive advantage, valuable employees, and future research. Organizations cannot insure against lost customers or a diminished public (customer) image. History consistently shows that between 35 and 50 percent of businesses never recover after major disasters.

The Planning Process

The basic steps involved in business continuity planning are simple, although their implementation can be complex and time consuming. The critical functions of the organization are identified and ranked according to their value to the organization or to their interdependencies with other critical components. Cost-effective strategies for recovering the critical functions to an acceptable level are evaluated. Once the recovery strategies are chosen, a plan is developed to implement the strategies. The plan is tested (the proper term is exercised or simulated), and provision for maintenance of the plan is established.

Before these steps commence, it is important to identify physical or procedural hazards that could cause an outage or delay the recovery process. When dealing with multiple sites, the planner should visit each location and conduct an inspection for these hazards. This inspection should identify single points of failure in critical systems, and it should produce a set of recommendations to mitigate the results of the hazards identified in the business impact or risk analysis. This is often included as part of the business impact analysis (BIA).

Next, the organization must prepare to respond to the disaster or to the emergency when it happens. The goals of emergency response are to protect the health and safety of employees, guests, and the community and to minimize damage to the organization by stabilizing the situation as quickly as possible. Response planning is not continuity planning, but the two plans can be integrated.

Once the disaster or emergency is stabilized, recovery and restoration will begin. The terms recovery, resumption, and restoration refer to separate phases of the organization's return to pre-disaster service levels (although some planners use them interchangeably).

Resumption embraces the initial, short-term strategies and steps to get back into production as quickly as possible. Moving to a hot site (a separate building or office area with duplicate, or equivalent, equipment already installed, waiting for emergency use) and transferring production to a satellite facility are examples. Recovery and restoration refer to the long-term strategies and steps the company will follow to reestablish its normal goals, service, or production levels. The replacement of a production line, installation and testing of replacement equipment, and the construction of new facilities are examples.

Project Management

Business continuity planning projects, if not properly managed, will lose momentum, languish, and die, or assume such a negative tone that the participants become hesitant to complete the project. Information and the strategic mission of an organization can rapidly change, so that once the project is started, any significant delay will cause the end product—a business continuity plan—to be outdated before it is completed.

Project management is a major skill, and it is required of anyone who undertakes responsibility for business continuity planning. It is a partnership between members of management, outside services and vendors, employees, and sometimes regulatory agencies. The ability to schedule and manage resources, time, and people will help bring the project to a successful conclusion.

Components of business continuity planning are briefly described as follows.

Identify the Planning Coordinator. A person within the organization is designated as the planning manager, coordinator, leader, or other appropriate title. This person is responsible for the management of the project (that is, the completion of the plan) and possibly for coordinating or leading the recovery effort subsequent to a disaster. The coordinator may also have major responsibilities for plan activation. Ideally, this person should be a management-level employee who has good people and project management skills and a good understanding of the organization, and is detail oriented.

Obtain Management Support and Resources. No planning effort or project will be successful without the support of upper management. This support must be communicated to all levels of management. Most agree that the development of a business continuity plan is a noble project, but all too often other priorities take precedence if participants are not held accountable to time lines and milestones. Its timely completion should be included in the goals and objectives for all expected participants.

Define the Scope and Planning Methodology. It can be a daunting, if not impossible, task to produce plans for a large, worldwide corporate structure unless the job is accomplished in small pieces. Narrow the scope of the project to a single division, site, or building, something small enough to allow a positive outcome. A successful project will add momentum for the completion of subsequent projects throughout the remainder of the organization.

Conduct Risk Identification and Mitigation Inspections. The more hazards and risks you can identify and mitigate beforehand the more you will minimize the effects of the disaster, allowing for a faster recovery.

Inspect the buildings, grounds, and community for any hazard that may injure employees, damage equipment or facilities, or cut off the supply of materials, resources, or services. When searching for these hazards, the techniques learned from scenario planning are useful. Think through the causes and effects of likely scenarios and offer recommendations to mitigate their effects.

Conduct a Business Impact Analysis. When relevant risks and hazards have been identified, submit a report to the steering committee, senior management, or the sponsor of the project outlining recommendations to mitigate the hazards. This report can be combined with the results of the BIA, especially if the analysis has been completed informally, as is too often the case.

Identify Critical Functions. The identification of critical functions is a major result of the BIA. Many planners believe it is a waste of time, effort, and resources to include in the plan functions that are not critical to the organization. Equipment and space at a hot site or other alternative location are expensive and limited; therefore, priority is given to the most important functions and employees. Remember that recovery operations are time sensitive. In many cases, there must be a logical sequence (order) of recovery actions, especially on the information technology side. Others argue that if a function is not critical, it should not be a part of the organization in the first place. I believe that every function should have a plan, but not necessarily a seat at the alternate site. Generally speaking, a critical function can be a process, service, equipment, or duty that would have one of the following impacts on the company if the function were lost or if access to it were denied:

- Affect the financial position of the company
- Have a regulatory impact
- Reduce or destroy public or customer image or confidence or sales

Develop Recovery Strategies. The number and nature of recovery strategies are determined by the nature of the business. Following are brief descriptions of some strategy choices.

- Hot, Cold, and Warm Sites. A hot site is an alternative recovery location prepared ahead of time, in this case with computers, servers, or a mainframe, and related equipment such as hardware and telecommunications. Hot-site vendors exist to provide this service on a first-come, first-served basis. The hot sites typically include a limited number of workstations and both data and voice communications infrastructure, enabling the organization to relocate employees temporarily. A cold site consists of an empty facility or leased space where computer hardware, telecommunications, and furniture would be delivered to construct a temporary processing capability. At a cold site, nothing is prewired or ready for immediate operation. Obviously, this is a less expensive strategy, but because of the time required for setup, it may not be a practical solution. Something in between a hot and cold site is a warm site.
- Relocation. Another common strategy is to simply relocate from one part of a damaged building or site to another. Executive suites, hotel rooms, client and vendor offices, empty warehouses, or mobile home trailers are other options to consider to relocate some or all of your business functions. The use of circus-type tents is generally not a good strategy.
- Work at Home. Many employees, given the proper resources ahead of time, can work effectively at home. This may free office or work space for those who can't.
- Telecommunications. Many of the strategies used to recover data systems are also used for telecommunications. These include emergency service and replacement agreements, divergent routing, radio systems (radio frequency and microwave),

mobile switches, third-party call centers, and hot sites.
- Third-Party Manufacturing. Identify sole-source suppliers and take action to find alternatives far ahead of such problems. If the operation uses "just in time" manufacturing, arrange to warehouse a sufficient quantity of material to allow for delay caused by a disaster or contingent interruption. Some distributors will warehouse materials at your location, retaining ownership until the material is removed and used.
- Data Systems. Data recovery strategies include hot sites, spare or underutilized servers, the use of non-critical servers, duplicate data centers, replacement agreements, and transferring operations to other locations. Ahead of time, identify the critical applications and prioritize the order in which they are restored. If applications or operating systems are dependent on others, restore them first. Servers that are on the same network (or can be easily connected) and that have excess capacity can be pressed into service to rescue a server that has failed. Some organizations keep spare, preconfigured servers in storage for immediate replacement if a primary fails. Unfortunately, this is a very costly strategy.
- Revert to Manual Methods. More and more functions rely on automated systems to perform their work. When the automated systems fail, businesses can revert to the manual methods used before the system was automated.
- Workforce Management. Working extra shifts with the existing workforce or with temporary personnel is a simple strategy to recover from a short-term outage, especially when employees are cross-trained to perform a variety of functions.
- Reciprocal Agreements. Excess capacity at other sites, similar industries, or even competitors can be used to remain in production until damaged facilities are repaired or replaced. The protection of proprietary information, disruption of the host's operations, and fluctuations in the amount of excess capacity can make this a difficult strategy.
- Equipment Rental. If equipment is damaged or destroyed, many plans call for

their temporary replacement with rentals. List this equipment and its sources in the plan. Whenever possible, have the rental company pre-configure the equipment to your specifications. Remember that other firms may be after the same equipment, so have alternate or out-of-town sources available. Arrange for priority agreements when possible.

- Rescheduling Production. A priority task for many companies after a disaster is to determine the expected length of the outage and compare this to remaining capacity, current production schedules, critical deadlines, and pending product releases. Decide whether production schedules should be changed to concentrate on the most critical products or to eliminate others.
- Reallocation of Resources. Similar to rescheduling production, firms should reexamine the assumptions, strategies, and critical time frames and compare them to the extent of the disaster. As necessary, reallocate resources among teams, functions, or sites.
- Service-Level or Quick-Ship Agreements. Enter into agreements with manufacturers, suppliers, and repair companies to deliver replacement items and provide services within 24 hours.

Recovery Teams. Form individual recovery and continuity teams arranged along departmental lines or drawn from several departments with similar functions (and therefore with similar recovery strategies). Large departments or teams may contain sub-teams that focus on particular issues.

Train Recovery Teams. All employees are trained in some aspect of the plan, even if it is to simply make them aware of its existence. The planning process should accomplish most of the orientation and training required to implement the plan. Those with an active role in the recovery should understand all aspects of their duties and all components of the plan.

Exercise the Plan. No plan is complete until every element has been subjected to some type of testing, exercise, or simulation. Simulating the plan will validate the effectiveness of strategies, ensure the accuracy of information, and increase the preparedness of the individuals who will execute the plan. It will pinpoint areas that need attention or improvement and reveal gaps in instructions, misplaced or absent assumptions, or the need for better strategies and tasks.

Maintain the Plan. These plans must be "living documents." Employee and vendor contact numbers change often and must be kept current in the plan. This information must be reviewed quarterly. The plans must be reviewed annually to determine whether they still match the overall strategic direction of the organization, and be changed accordingly.

Review

Business continuity planning is a process that identifies a company's critical functions, develops cost-effective strategies to recover those functions if they are lost or if access to them is denied, and lists the instructions and resources necessary to implement the strategies. Systems, applications, products, and processes are prioritized and recovered in a logical manner that will allow the firm to remain in business and to retain or gain market share over competitors that don't have a continuity capability.

Eugene L. Tucker

Source Broder, J. and Tucker E. 2006. *Risk Analysis and the Security Survey, 3rd Edition.* Boston: Butterworth-Heinemann.

DATA-DRIVEN INCIDENT MANAGEMENT

Businesses and organizations today face enormous consequences from crime, especially "white-collar crime." Fraudulent and other illegal acts by company executives have in recent years caused billions of dollars in lost shareholder value. These high profile cases have caused legislated and internal controls that place greater responsibility on the boards of directors of publicly traded corporations to know what is going on and to take all reasonable steps to protect shareholder value. Many companies and organizations that are not affected by legislation, such as the Sarbanes Oxley Act, voluntarily comply with the requirements simply because they make sense.

Good corporate governance is the watchword of today. At the core of good corporate governance is appropriate response to incidents that include injuries to employees and visitors and criminal acts that negatively impact a corporation's reputation and shareholder value. It does not matter if the perpetrators are internal or external. Successful security directors understand the role professional security management plays in good corporate governance.

It should be obvious that the massive amounts of relevant data that cross security managers' desks must be turned into corporate intelligence. The only way this can be achieved is by using the power of computerized database management to track incidents, determine their root causes and their disposition. The answers to who, what, when, where, and how enable trend and relationship management which, in turn, facilitates corrective action and justifies any countermeasures. Additionally, any automated system must allow for performance measurement; as Peter Drucker stated, "If you can't measure it, you can't manage it." Most importantly, introducing measurement allows for accountability.

If an organization requires additional motivation to become serious about reputation management, all they have to consider is the vast sums of money that may be awarded by juries in cases where companies are found negligent. Good records are of paramount importance when defending against negligence, especially records that show the company to be a good corporate citizen. A demonstrable commitment to collecting and constructively acting on the information is at the heart of mitigating liability when the prosecution argues that the defending organization could have foreseen and prevented violent and other damaging events.

The types of incidents that a company or organization must document and respond to include:

- Business crime. Misappropriation of funds, corporate espionage, theft of PCs and other equipment, hijacking of high-tech products. These acts harm thousands of corporations every year.
- Violent crime. Senseless shootings on school campuses and violent attacks on fellow employees in offices and plants. These incidents cause extreme disruption, personal loss, and huge lawsuits.
- Hotels and hospitals. Aggravated assaults, rape, and murder, cause terrible human suffering as well as extensive litigation, costly settlements, and jury awards.
- Retail establishments. Chronic shoplifting, money laundering, violent robberies, and accidents of every type and level of severity.
- Financial institutions. Fraud, embezzlement, theft, robbery, and money laundering.
- All institutions. International terrorism, such as bombing buildings. Domestic terrorism includes arson and bombings at abortion clinics and vivisection research laboratories, damaging and destroying equipment that harm the ecology, planting booby troops in forests undergoing harvesting, sending chemical, biological, and explosive materials through the mail, and tampering with products.
- Computer and Internet crime. Cybercrime and cyberterrorism are increasing in number and frequency. They can and do cause enormous economic losses both to individuals (as in cases of identity theft) and businesses (as in cases of online fraud and theft of trade secrets).

Finding Information

Today's business world is a data-centric world. Decisions based on carefully analyzed data are not only more likely to be correct and bring results, they are also more readily accepted and trusted. The term "knowledge-based decisions" has gained currency as a term that describes decisions based on knowledge and insights that come from information gleaned from raw data.

Corporate security professionals need to know about and relate to these trends and capabilities, in particular, they need to think about and be sensitive to how this reality impacts their departments' operations and even their careers.

The daunting challenge for security professionals is to develop measures that protect a world of data that is growing exponentially and becoming increasingly complex. In our wired and networked world, turning on and off electronic devices, e-mailing correspondence, and faxing documents leave electronic trails and send sensitive information to what are called "data dumps."

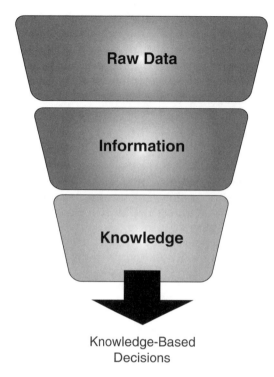

Raw Data

Information

Knowledge

Knowledge-Based
Decisions

Figure 7. Information gleaned from raw
data establishes a body of knowledge which
becomes a foundation for intelligent decision-
making.

The World of Incident Management

Incident management represents the single best
opportunity for security departments to:

- Achieve "break through" status in terms of
  positive upper management visibility and
  peer respect.
- Not only justify budgets, but to also demonstrate tangible and intangible value and

ROI to "stakeholders" within and outside
the organization.
- Leverage the power of information to
  defend the organization against accusations of inadequate security and to foresee
  danger.

However, much progress must still be made in
mindset change and the practical integration
of incident management technology into daily
security operations.

Challenges. For the sake of fairness, it must be
pointed out that, while the incident data-
information-knowledge equation is a powerful
driver of best-class business performance, it is
not without its challenges. Incident management practices do not happen without conscious
and conscientious commitment and discipline.

For security departments, and indeed other
functional departments, there are challenges to
be recognized and overcome before true incident management can be realized. Meeting the
challenges involve:

- Outlining or "mapping" the collection,
  organization and useful purpose of incident data that streams into a security
  department from multiple sources on a
  24X7 basis.
- Understanding and ensuring the quality of
  incident data and the processes of data collection.

In a typical security department—and indeed in
most other functional business departments—
data is generated and delivered in multiple
media and formats (including hand-written and
word-processed documents, spreadsheets, videos, and audio or electronic transaction logs)
from systems scattered throughout a site and
across multiple sites. Incident reports generated

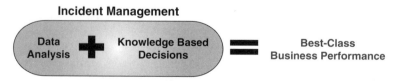

Figure 8. Superior performance in the management of incidents is the result of decisions
based on meaningful knowledge.

by a monitoring station operator are often substantially different from those filed by a security supervisor or patrol officer. The formatting and completeness of security officer incident reports can vary according to the officers' skill and enthusiasm for reporting incidents.

To be really meaningful, incident data must be resident in a relational database so that it can be sorted and analyzed intelligently in order to identify patterns and trends that can point both to root causes and to the emergence of serious issues and problems. It is obvious that repeated incidents of petty cash theft in a particular department should lead to the introduction of procedural and physical measures to reduce or eliminate the thefts. On the other hand, incidents of repeated attempts by a disgruntled ex-employee to make contact with a former manager could presage a much more serious threat.

Another major challenge related to how security data is put to use is that functional "silos" within security departments can create data-collecting and data-sharing. Security can be porous and decision making erratic without established procedures for sharing data received from different systems.

A New Age of Security Management

There is a strong, if somewhat slow, trend in security management to strengthen and make more consistent the management of security information. This trend is driven, in no small measure, by the much broader corporate interest in data analysis and knowledge-based decision making. There is also relentless pressure to improve the speed and quality of decision-making, reduce costs, improve productivity, and demonstrate a commitment to best practices.

Data-Driven Security Myths. While it may be relatively easy to appreciate the macro-level, idealistic virtues of incident management automation, the change such technology causes can be unsettling. It is also true that a new, high-tech approach to such old problems as crime is not a panacea. Nonetheless, change in the security industry is deep and broad. The trend can, and must, be understood and used for good advantage—and doing so requires an understanding of the myths, realities, and emerging benefits that change offers.

Disclosure and Foreseeability. At professional conferences and in customer meetings, the question is sometimes asked, "Could actually knowing what we currently do not know end up hurting us?" The short answer is that, as with most issues in life, it is better to know than not know. For example, the courts have held in some cases that there is a duty to know. Also, potentially damaging information in a matter being litigated can be uncovered through the process of legal discovery despite attempts to hide or ignore the information.

An ancillary, but significant, benefit to having a data-driven, automated incident management program is that a company has more control of its destiny in a lawsuit that alleges failure to establish reasonable security measures to prevent foreseeable injury or damage to others. Company counsel stands a better chance of shaping, and even limiting, a court-ordered demand for information related to an allegation of negligence.

Compliance, Risk Management and Insurance. It is sometimes pointed out that one of the curiosities of the security industry is that it is virtually unregulated and follows no independent standards. The finance and accounting professions follow a myriad of government and professional standards, practices, and reporting requirements. Most human resource policies and procedures are likewise shaped by legislative mandates and regulations. In the realm of safety, there have long been OSHA guidelines, industry standards, and fire codes that influence the ways in which security is operated and managed.

An increasingly important driver of change in the security industry will be heightened levels of government regulation and the emergence of recognized professional standards for security that will inevitably trigger compliance and disclosure requirements. Even the foremost world security association, ASIS International, has acknowledged the requirement for standards by establishing a program for articulating standards for basic security processes.

Clearly, the ability of security managers to prepare such disclosures will require the adoption of data-driven security practices. Incident management and reporting will be at the heart of both regulatory compliance and, more importantly, the ability of organizations and corporations to improve their security and reduce losses.

We would also point to the obvious relevance and expanding interaction among security departments, corporate risk management departments, and insurance companies. The risk management profession has, over many decades, built a substantial body of knowledge that has been drawn primarily from the mathematical, statistical, and actuarial sciences. It is now possible to quantify all kinds of corporate business risk. This allows companies to "finance" as much risk as they can afford; for example, entering into risky yet seemingly profitable business ventures and covering potential losses by purchasing insurance policies.

In an environment of serious, and potentially costly, risk caused by high-stakes crime and terrorist attacks, documented security practices and incident management reports can be a powerful, proactive risk management tool. Because a professional security program can prevent, or at least minimize, many types of losses, companies can make their security programs a positive element in negotiations with insurers.

Conversely, insurers have begun to require that certain coverage—including kidnap and ransom and premises liability converge—requires companies to engage the services of security consultants and to install reasonable safeguards.

Return on Investment (ROI)

Incident management is the keystone in the architecture of a data-driven security program. Without this capability, security management will remain mired in the conventional model of intuitive and reactionary decisions that lead to erratic practices. Security managers will continue to struggle to deliver management reports that reflect an understanding of the company's business. A date-driven security program can aid budget development and justify security expenditures.

Today's incident management practices make possible a "closed loop" of security program design, budgeting, implementation, measurement, and improvement. Rather than relying on intuitive and anecdotal assessments of security program effectiveness, security executives can generate crisp management reports that capture specific reductions or increases in all incident categories.

Figure 9.   Incident management practices move in a five-step cycle.

Incident management systems also can project adverse incidents and their costs. Using factual data:

- Security resources can be more effectively deployed, thereby maximizing ROI.
- The relative effectiveness of individual security safeguards and a mix of safeguards can be tracked and measured, allowing for cost-effective improvements over a given period of time at various locations.
- Return on a company's investment in its security program can be discussed in more precise business, financial, and risk management terms.
- Security program effectiveness and budgeting can be discussed using the same logical, organizational, and analytical techniques used by other corporate departments.

Conclusion

This article makes the argument that incident management is a critical element of protecting businesses and other organizations against crime, violence, and the losses they cause. In a real way, security management is similar to the management of any other business function. Data-based (or knowledge-based) decisions can be a security professional's credibility within the organization. The challenge is to adopt a data-driven mindset, acquire the necessary software tools to manage the data, and galvanize security department employees to accept and operate using the principles, practices, and disciplines of incident management.

Denis O'Sullivan

DISASTER TYPES

On March 1, 2003, the Federal Emergency Management Agency (FEMA) became part of the U.S. Department of Homeland Security (DHS). FEMA's continuing mission within the new department is to lead the effort to prepare the nation for all hazards and effectively manage federal response and recovery efforts following any national incident. FEMA also initiates proactive mitigation activities, trains first responders, and manages the National Flood Insurance Program.

National Response Plan

The National Response Plan establishes a comprehensive all-hazards approach to enhance the ability of the United States to manage domestic incidents. The plan incorporates best practices and procedures from incident management disciplines—homeland security, emergency management, law enforcement, firefighting, public works, public health, responder and recovery worker health and safety, emergency medical services, and the private sector—and integrates them into a unified structure. It forms the basis of how the federal government coordinates with state, local, and tribal governments and the private sector during incidents. It establishes protocols to help:

- Save lives and protect the health and safety of the public, responders, and recovery workers
- Ensure security of the homeland
- Prevent an imminent incident, including acts of terrorism, from occurring
- Protect and restore critical infrastructure and key resources

- Conduct law enforcement investigations to resolve the incident, apprehend the perpetrators, and collect and preserve evidence for prosecution and/or attribution
- Protect property and mitigate damages and impacts to individuals, communities, and the environment and
- Facilitate recovery of individuals, families, businesses, governments, and the environment

FEMA has more than 2,600 full-time employees. They work at FEMA headquarters in Washington D.C., at regional and area offices across the country, the Mount Weather Emergency Operations Center, and the National Emergency Training Center in Emmitsburg, Maryland. FEMA also has nearly 4,000 standby disaster assistance employees who are available for deployment after disasters. Often FEMA works in partnership with other organizations that are part of the nation's emergency management system. These partners include state and local emergency management agencies, 27 federal agencies, and the American Red Cross.

Types of Disasters

Dam Failure. There are 75,900 dams in the United States, according to the 2005 update to the National Inventory of Dams. Approximately one-third of these pose a "high" or "significant" hazard to life and property if failure occurs.

Dam failure or levee breeches can occur with little warning. Intense storms may produce a flood in a few hours or even minutes for upstream locations. Flash floods occur within six hours of the beginning of heavy rainfall, and dam failure may occur within hours of the first signs of breaching.

Other failures and breeches can take much longer to occur, from days to weeks, as a result of debris jams or the accumulation of melting snow.

Earthquake. One of the most frightening and destructive phenomena of nature is a severe earthquake and its terrible aftereffects.

Earthquakes strike suddenly, violently, and without warning at any time of the day or night. If an earthquake occurs in a populated area, it may cause many deaths and injuries and extensive property damage.

Although there are no guarantees of safety during an earthquake, identifying potential hazards ahead of time and advance planning can save lives and significantly reduce injuries and property damage.

Fire. Each year, more than 4,000 Americans die and more than 25,000 are injured in fires, many of which could be prevented. Direct property loss due to fires is estimated at $8.6 billion annually.

Fire spreads quickly; there is no time to gather valuables or make a phone call. In just two minutes, a fire can become life-threatening. In five minutes, a residence can be engulfed in flames.

Heat and smoke from fire can be more dangerous than the flames. Inhaling the super-hot air can sear lungs. Fire produces poisonous gases that make a person disoriented and drowsy. Instead of being awakened by a fire, the victim may fall into a deeper sleep. Asphyxiation is the leading cause of fire deaths, exceeding burns by a three-to-one ratio.

Wildfire. The threat of wildland fires for people living near wildland areas or using recreational facilities in wilderness areas is real. Dry conditions at various times of the year and in various parts of the United States greatly increase the potential for wildland fires.

Advance planning and knowing how to protect buildings in these areas can lessen the devastation of a wildland fire. There are several safety precautions that can be taken to reduce the risk of fire losses. Consideration has to be given to the fire resistance of the home, the topography of the property, and the nature of the vegetation close by.

Flood. Floods are one of the most common hazards in the United States. Flood effects can be local, impacting a neighborhood or community, or very large, affecting entire river basins and multiple states.

However, all floods are not alike. Some floods develop slowly, sometimes over a period of days. But flash floods can develop quickly, sometimes in just a few minutes and without any visible signs of rain. Flash floods often have a dangerous wall of roaring water that carries rocks, mud, and other debris and can sweep away most things in its path. Overland flooding occurs outside a defined river or stream, such as when a levee is breached, but still can be destructive. Flooding can also occur when a dam breaks, producing effects similar to flash floods.

Hazardous Materials. Chemicals are found everywhere. They purify drinking water, increase crop production, and simplify household chores. But chemicals also can be hazardous to humans or the environment if used or released improperly. Hazards can occur during production, storage, transportation, use, or disposal. An entire community is at risk if a chemical is used unsafely or released in harmful amounts into the environment.

Hazardous materials in various forms can cause death, serious injury, long-lasting health effects, and damage to buildings, homes, and other property. Many products containing hazardous chemicals are used and stored in homes routinely. These products are also shipped daily on the nation's highways, railroads, waterways, and pipelines.

Extreme Heat. Heat kills by pushing the human body beyond its limits. In extreme heat and high humidity, evaporation is slowed and the body must work extra hard to maintain a normal temperature.

Most heat disorders occur because the victim has been overexposed to heat or has over-exercised for his or her age and physical condition. Older adults, young children, and those who are sick or overweight are more likely to succumb to extreme heat.

Conditions that can induce heat-related illnesses include stagnant atmospheric conditions and poor air quality. Consequently, people living in urban areas may be at greater risk from the effects of a prolonged heat wave than those living in rural areas. Also, asphalt and concrete store heat longer and gradually release heat at night, which can produce higher nighttime temperatures known as the "urban heat island effect."

Hurricane. A hurricane is a type of tropical cyclone, the generic term for a low pressure system that generally forms in the tropics. A typical cyclone is accompanied by thunderstorms, and in the Northern Hemisphere, a counterclockwise circulation of winds near the earth's surface.

All Atlantic and Gulf of Mexico coastal areas are subject to hurricanes or tropical storms. Parts of the Southwest United States and the Pacific Coast experience heavy rains and floods each year from hurricanes spawned off Mexico. The Atlantic hurricane season lasts from June to November, with the peak season from mid-August to late October.

Hurricanes can cause catastrophic damage to coastlines and several hundred miles inland. Winds can exceed 155 miles per hour. Hurricanes and tropical storms can also spawn tornadoes and microbursts, create storm surges along the coast, and cause extensive damage from heavy rainfall.

Hurricanes are classified into five categories based on their wind speed, central pressure, and damage potential. Category Three and higher hurricanes are considered major hurricanes, though Categories One and Two are still extremely dangerous and warrant full attention.

Landslide and Debris Flow (Mudslide). Landslides occur in all U.S. states and territories. In a landslide, masses of rock, earth, or debris move down a slope. Landslides may be small or large, slow or rapid. They are activated by:

- Storms
- Earthquakes
- Volcanic eruptions
- Fires
- Alternate freezing or thawing
- Steepening of slopes by erosion or human modification

Debris and mud flows are rivers of rock, earth, and other debris saturated with water. They develop when water rapidly accumulates in the ground, during heavy rainfall or rapid snowmelt, changing the earth into a flowing river of mud or "slurry." They can flow rapidly, striking with little or no warning at avalanche speeds. They also can travel several miles from their source, growing in size as they pick up trees, boulders, cars, and other materials.

Landslide problems can be caused by land mismanagement, particularly in mountain, canyon, and coastal regions. In areas burned by forest and brush fires, a lower threshold of precipitation may initiate landslides. Land-use zoning, professional inspections, and proper design can minimize many landslide, mudflow, and debris flow problems.

Nuclear Power Plant Emergency. Nuclear power plants use the heat generated from nuclear fission in a contained environment to convert water to steam, which powers generators to produce electricity. Nuclear power plants operate in most states in the country and produce about 20 percent of the nation's power. Nearly 3 million Americans live within 10 miles of an operating nuclear power plant.

Although the construction and operation of these facilities are closely monitored and regulated by the Nuclear Regulatory Commission (NRC), accidents are possible. An accident could result in dangerous levels of radiation that could affect the health and safety of the public living near the nuclear power plant.

Local and state governments, federal agencies, and the electric utilities have emergency response plans in the event of a nuclear power plant incident. The plans define two "emergency planning zones." One zone covers an area within a 10-mile radius of the plant, where it is possible that people could be harmed by direct radiation exposure. The second zone covers a broader area, usually up to a 50-mile radius from the plant, where radioactive materials could contaminate water supplies, food crops, and livestock.

The potential danger from an accident at a nuclear power plant is exposure to radiation. This exposure could come from the release of radioactive material from the plant into the environment, usually characterized by a plume (cloud-like formation) of radioactive gases and particles. The major hazards to people in the vicinity of the plume are radiation exposure to the body from the cloud and particles deposited on the ground, inhalation of radioactive materials, and ingestion of radioactive materials.

Radioactive materials are composed of atoms that are unstable. An unstable atom gives off its excess energy until it becomes stable. The energy emitted is radiation. Each of us is exposed to radiation daily from natural sources, including the Sun and the Earth. Small traces of radiation are present in food and water. Radiation also is released from man-made sources such as X-ray machines, television sets, and microwave ovens. Radiation has a cumulative effect. The longer a person is exposed to radiation, the greater the effect. A high exposure to radiation can cause serious illness or death.

Thunderstorms. All thunderstorms are dangerous. Every thunderstorm produces lightning. In the United States, an average of 300 people are injured and 80 people are killed each year by lightning. Although most lightning victims survive, people struck by lightning often report a variety of long-term, debilitating symptoms. Other associated dangers of thunderstorms include tornadoes, strong winds, hail, and flash flooding. Flash flooding is responsible for more fatalities—more than 140 annually—than any other thunderstorm-associated hazard.

Dry thunderstorms that do not produce rain that reaches the ground are most prevalent in the western United States. Falling raindrops evaporate, but lightning can still reach the ground and can start wildfires.

Tornado. Tornadoes are nature's most violent storms. Spawned from powerful thunderstorms, tornadoes can cause fatalities and devastate a neighborhood in seconds. A tornado appears as a rotating, funnel-shaped cloud that extends from a thunderstorm to the ground with whirling winds that can reach 300 miles per hour. Damage paths can be in excess of one mile wide and 50 miles long. Every state is at some risk from this hazard.

Some tornadoes are clearly visible, while rain or nearby low-hanging clouds obscure others. Occasionally, tornadoes develop so rapidly that little, if any, advance warning is possible.

Before a tornado hits, the wind may die down and the air may become very still. A cloud of debris can mark the location of a tornado even if a funnel is not visible. Tornadoes generally occur near the trailing edge of a thunderstorm. It is not uncommon to see clear, sunlit skies behind a tornado.

The following are facts about tornadoes:

- They may strike quickly, with little or no warning.
- They may appear nearly transparent until dust and debris are picked up or a cloud forms in the funnel.
- The average tornado moves Southwest to Northeast, but tornadoes have been known to move in any direction.

- The average forward speed of a tornado is 30 MPH, but may vary from stationary to 70 MPH.
- Tornadoes can accompany tropical storms and hurricanes as they move onto land.
- Waterspouts are tornadoes that form over water.
- Tornadoes are most frequently reported east of the Rocky Mountains during spring and summer months.
- Peak tornado season in the southern states is March through May; in the northern states, it is late spring through early summer.
- Tornadoes are most likely to occur between 3 p.m. and 9 p.m., but can occur at any time.

Tsunami. Tsunamis (pronounced soo-ná-mees), also known as seismic sea waves (mistakenly called "tidal waves"), are a series of enormous waves created by an underwater disturbance such as an earthquake, landslide, volcanic eruption, or meteorite. A tsunami can move hundreds of miles per hour in the open ocean and smash into land with waves as high as 100 feet or more.

From the area where the tsunami originates, waves travel outward in all directions. Once the wave approaches the shore, it builds in height. The topography of the coastline and the ocean floor will influence the size of the wave. There may be more than one wave and the succeeding one may be larger than the one before. That is why a small tsunami at one beach can be a giant wave a few miles away.

All tsunamis are potentially dangerous, even though they may not damage every coastline they strike. A tsunami can strike anywhere along most of the U.S. coastline. The most destructive tsunamis have occurred along the coasts of California, Oregon, Washington, Alaska, and Hawaii.

Earthquake-induced movement of the ocean floor most often generates tsunamis. If a major earthquake or landslide occurs close to shore, the first wave in a series could reach the beach in a few minutes, even before a warning is issued. Areas are at greater risk if they are less than 25 feet above sea level and within a mile of the shoreline. Drowning is the most common cause of death associated with a tsunami. Tsunami waves and the receding water are very destructive to structures in the run-up zone.

Other hazards include flooding, contamination of drinking water, and fires from gas lines or ruptured tanks.

Volcano. A volcano is a mountain that opens downward to a reservoir of molten rock below the surface of the earth. Unlike most mountains, which are pushed up from below, volcanoes are built up by an accumulation of their own eruptive products. When pressure from gases within the molten rock becomes too great, an eruption occurs. Eruptions can be quiet or explosive. There may be lava flows, flattened landscapes, poisonous gases, and flying rock and ash.

Because of their intense heat, lava flows are great fire hazards. Lava flows destroy everything in their path, but most move slowly enough that people can move out of the way.

Fresh volcanic ash, made of pulverized rock, can be abrasive, acidic, gritty, gassy, and odorous. While not immediately dangerous to most adults, the acidic gas and ash can cause lung damage to small infants, to older adults, and to those suffering from severe respiratory illnesses. Volcanic ash also can damage machinery, including engines and electrical equipment. Ash accumulations mixed with water become heavy and can collapse roofs. Volcanic ash can affect people hundreds of miles away from the cone of a volcano.

Sideways directed volcanic explosions, known as "lateral blasts," can shoot large pieces of rock at very high speeds for several miles. These explosions can kill by impact, burial, or heat. They have been known to knock down entire forests.

Volcanic eruptions can be accompanied by other natural hazards, including earthquakes, mudflows and flash floods, rock falls and landslides, acid rain, fire, and (under special conditions) tsunamis.

Active volcanoes in the U.S. are found mainly in Hawaii, Alaska, and the Pacific Northwest. Active volcanoes of the Cascade Mountain Range in California, Oregon, and Washington have created problems recently. The danger area around a volcano covers approximately a 20-mile radius. Some danger may exist 100 miles or more from a volcano, leaving Montana and Wyoming at risk.

Source Federal Emergency Management Agency. 2006. <http://www.fema.gov/about/index.shtm>

EMERGENCY MANAGEMENT PLANNING

Emergency planning has been the beneficiary of renewed interest, post September 11, as business and government have sought to adapt to new exposures made evident in 2001. An avalanche of material has been produced on emergency planning. This article will not add new material, but hopefully will encapsulate key concepts within the context of security planning.

Before creating Emergency Plans, it is imperative that a formal Security Program be developed based on a formal Risk Analysis process. Data derived in this analysis is essential for Emergency Planning. The Risk Analysis data highlights key resources, the consequences of an attack, the process by which an attack may take place, and the points of vulnerability that may be exploited by an adversary.

In reviewing the Security Risk Analysis consider the following:

1. How thoroughly did the analysis address single points of failure?
   a. Infrastructure services, such as power, water, telecommunications
   b. Critical operating systems or human resources
2. Did the Risk Assessment recommendations include any of the following:
   a. Mitigating single points of failure by introducing redundancy
   b. Application of security measures to harden the potential target to make it less attractive to an adversary

On the basis of this foundation data, the Emergency Planning process may commence. The objective is to define in step by step detail how the organization should respond, if an adversary (criminal, natural disaster, or accident) succeeds in an attack. The plan should address response protocols for implementation at each of the following stages of an event:

1. Warning: Some emergency events are preceded by a warning. If a warning is received, what protocols should be implemented?
   a. Example: Workplace Violence Event
      i. Receive notice of a domestic dispute involving an employee in which a threat is issued against

the employee by the estranged spouse

    ii. Protocol may be to initiate the Temporary Restraining Order process, alert security officers and local law enforcement authorities

2. During the Event: When an event is in progress, protocols may be implemented to minimize the exposure to harm.
   a. Example: Bomb threat
      i. Receive threat
      ii. Conduct search
      iii. Locate suspicious device
      iv. Notify police
      v. Apply bomb blanket
      vi. Evacuate immediate area
      vii. Keep people disbursed
      viii. Keep traffic arteries open for emergency response personnel

3. Immediate Post Event: When the event has ended, protocols should be implemented to care for the injured, notify authorities, preserve evidence, and minimize any future damage or harm that may result in the aftermath.
   a. Example: Critical system sabotage, resulting in a fire and shutdown of operations.
      i. Keep area inhabitants in sheltered positions, while facility engineers shutdown power systems (also, keep inhabitants in place to minimize exposure to falling debris and other structural exposures)
      ii. Attend to the injured with first aid
      iii. Rescue personnel remove remaining inhabitants
      iv. Rope off crime scene area
      v. Control access to the area
      vi. Preserve evidence

4. Clean-Up and Resumption of Operations: When law enforcement authorities have released the crime scene, begin the clean up process.
   a. Example: Continuation of above
      i. Photograph crime scene
      ii. Tag and photograph all evidence
      iii. Plot evidence location on a site floor plan
      iv. Establish evidence log and log custodian

    v. Establish evidence storage container
    vi. Interview witnesses
    vii. Physically clean up area
    viii. Repair system damage
    ix. Document and repair structural damage

These are simply examples to highlight the type of information required for each stage of an event. More importantly, the planning process should highlight issues that require resolution so they may be resolved before an event occurs.

An administrator should be selected for management of the emergency response protocols. The administrator should develop training plans, table top exercises, and other creative methods to ensure the facility population knows what to do in the event of an emergency.

When security human resources are deployed, the emergency response protocols should be incorporated into the Post Orders clearly defining the tasks to be performed by security in an event.

The Emergency Plan also must consider the magnitude of a terrorist attack and the extreme response protocols that may be necessary. Consider this: emergency response protocols for a hazardous material event usually are structured for response to an industrial level accident in which a vessel is punctured resulting in a leak. In contemplation of a terrorist attack, it may be suggested that the attack may result in much more than a puncture leak; it may result in a completely ruptured vessel. The magnitude of the release may far outstrip response protocols structured for an accident, rendering them not applicable.

This will require a considerable adjustment for traditional emergency planners. Across the country many first responders, in preparation for terrorist attacks, applied for grants to procure more training and equipment to plug leaking vessels. New exposures require new approaches. It is imperative that today's emergency planning efforts not be constrained by what has been done in the past, but use the past as a springboard for confronting new challenges.

Sal DePasquale

HIGH-RISE SECURITY AND FIRE LIFE SAFETY

According to the *Protection of Assets Manual*, ASIS International, a high-rise structure is a building "that extends higher than the maximum reach of available fire-fighting equipment. In absolute numbers, this has been set variously between 75 feet (23 meters) and 100 feet (30 meters), or approximately seven to ten stories, depending on the slab-to-slab height between floors." The exact height above which a particular building is deemed a high-rise is specified by the fire and building codes in the area in which the building is located. When the building exceeds the specified height, fire must be fought by fire personnel from inside the building rather than from outside using fire hoses and ladders.

High-Rise Assets

Assets in the high-rise setting may be tangible or intangible. Tangible assets include the people using the facility, the building itself, its fittings, and its equipment. This equipment consists of the electrical, gas, mechanical, heating, ventilating, air conditioning, lighting, elevator, escalator, communication, security, and life safety systems. In addition, within offices there is equipment such as telephones, computers, word processors, printers, typewriters, FAX machines, photocopiers, audiovisual equipment, general-use items (coffee machines, vending machines, refrigerators, microwaves, ovens, furniture) and sometimes antiques and works of art, cash, and negotiable instruments. Also, vehicles parked in the building's parking garage are tangible assets. Intangible assets include the livelihood of building users; intellectual property and information stored in paper files, reference books, photographs, microfilm, x-rays, and within computer systems and peripherals; and the reputation and status of the facility, including the ability of tenants to conduct business.

Threats to Security and Fire Life Safety

For the purposes of discussion and to address issues in a systematic way, this chapter treats security and fire life safety in high-rise structures as two different disciplines. However, at times, these subjects are so closely interwoven that they appear to be one. Before identifying security and fire life safety threats to high-rise buildings, it is important to understand what these terms mean.

Security is a noun derived from the Latin word *securus*, which means, "free from danger" or "safe." The New Webster Encyclopedic Dictionary defines security as "the state of being secure; confidence of safety; freedom from danger or risk; that which secures or makes safe; something that secures against pecuniary loss." In *Introduction to Security*, Robert J. Fischer and Gion Green write, "Security implies a stable, relatively predictable environment in which an individual or group may pursue its ends without disruption or harm and without fear of such disturbance or injury."

Public security involves the protection of the lives, property, and general welfare of people living in the public community. This protection is largely achieved by the enforcement of laws by police funded by public money.

Private security, on the other hand, involves the protection of the lives and property of people living and working within the private sector. The primary responsibility for achieving this rests on an individual, the proprietor of a business employing an individual, the owner or agent of the owner of the facility where a business is conducted, or an agent of the aforementioned who specializes in providing protective services. In *Security and Administration: An Introduction to the Protective Services*, Richard S. Post and Arthur A. Kingsbury write, "In providing security for specific applications, the purpose of private security may be described as providing protection for materials, equipment, information, personnel, physical facilities, and preventing influences that are undesirable, unauthorized, or detrimental to the goals of the particular organization being secured."

Safety is a noun derived from the Latin word *salvus*, which means "safe" (salvation is also from this root). The New Webster Encyclopedic Dictionary defines safety as "the state or quality of being safe; freedom from danger." Obviously, there is very little distinction between the terms security and safety. Fire life safety, fire and life safety, fire safety, and life safety are four synonymous terms commonly in use in high-rise structures.

Security Threats

A threat is any event that, if it occurs, may cause harm or destruction of assets. In the high-rise setting, security threats come in many forms. Threats to people include murder, manslaughter, robbery, assault, assault and battery, mayhem, and sex offenses (including rape, sexual harassment, and lewd behavior). Threats to property include vandalism, trespass, burglary, larceny, sabotage, espionage, arson, and disorderly conduct.

Security threats to both people and property include fire, bombs, riots, civil disorder, hazardous materials, chemical and biological weapons, nuclear attack, and natural disasters. Some of these threats may involve terrorism.

Life Safety Threats

In the high-rise setting, life safety threats include fires, workplace violence, hostage and barricade situations, medical emergencies, trip-slip and falls, power failures, elevator malfunctions and entrapments, traffic accidents, labor disputes, demonstrations, riots, civil disorder, bombs and bomb threats, hazardous materials, chemical and biological weapons, nuclear attack, aircraft collisions, and natural disasters. Again, some of these threats may involve terrorism.

According to the *Protection of Assets Manual*, ASIS International, "The most critical threats in high-rise structures include fire, explosion and contamination of life-support systems such as air and potable water supply. These threats can be actualized accidentally or intentionally, and because they propagate rapidly, can quickly develop to catastrophic levels."

In addition to these threats, an individual may exhibit aberrant behavior, such as that caused by substance abuse. Such conduct may be a threat not only to the personal safety of the individual involved but to others as well. Also, people may attempt to deliberately injure themselves or take their own lives. Because of their very height, the possibility exists that people may jump from a high-rise, particularly if they are successful in reaching the roof. High-rises, particularly major ones, may attract people who view them as a means to gain attention for themselves. For example, protestors may attempt to drape large banners promoting their *raison d'être*

over the front of a building or daredevils may perform outlandish feats to achieve notoriety.

Security of Modern High-Rise Buildings

The changes in the design and construction of high-rises since their first appearance have affected the security needs of these facilities. Modern high-rise buildings have inherent security hazards different from the earliest high-rises because of the following:

- Open-style floors with little compartmentation and fewer individual offices that can be secured have made it easier for a potential thief to gain access to business and personal property. The advent of modern telecommunications, with answering machines, portable phones, and services, has meant that the presence of a tenant receptionist to screen persons entering the office is now not always the standard. The open-style floor has also made it easier for an unauthorized person, having once gained access, to move unchallenged throughout the entire floor.
- The higher number of occupants per floor in a modern high-rise means a greater concentration of business equipment and personal items and therefore a more desirable target for a potential thief.
- The concealed space located above the suspended ceiling on each floor of many high-rises has provided a possible means of ingress to a tenant office. This space could also be used to hide unauthorized listening or viewing devices, such as microphones or cameras. The central heating, ventilating, and air conditioning (HVAC) system has provided a similar means for unauthorized listening and viewing.
- The greater number of occupants per floor means the increased potential for these individuals to be perpetrators or targets of a crime and an increased likelihood that some of these people could be injured or killed, particularly by an incident occurring close to them.

In addition to these changes, other factors have added to the security risks of modern high-rise buildings. For one thing, the tenant offices in modern high-rises are often the headquarters of highly successful corporations that have designed and furnished their places of business in a style to reflect their status. This has resulted in very high-quality furnishings, including, in some instances, expensive works of art, and state-of-the-art business systems. The tenant employees themselves are generally well paid, often carry cash and valuables, and tend to drive and park expensive vehicles in the building parking garage. Hence, these facilities are a potential target for criminal activity.

Next, the computer revolution with its proliferation of compact business machines (such as personal data assistants and personal, laptop, and notebook computers) has resulted in equipment and proprietary information that can be carried away relatively easily by a potential thief. The computer, in itself, presents a unique set of risks because crimes can now be committed without the perpetrator ever setting foot on the premises where information is stored.

Finally, the development in the mid-1950s of completely automatic control systems for the operation of elevators eliminated the need for elevator attendants and, in effect, did away with an important access control and screening measure for high-rise buildings. With the elevator attendant gone, it is often possible for people to travel unchecked throughout a structure once they have entered an elevator. Such unchecked travel can be curtailed by the use of other security measures such as security personnel, locking off certain "secured" floors from elevator access and the installation of modern electronic access control systems in elevator cars and lobbies.

The technological advances that have occurred in the security field, particularly over the past 40 years, have mitigated some of these security risks. Centralized, microcomputer-based control of security and elevator systems has considerably extended and improved the application of basic security measures, such as some of the following:

- Locks and locking systems
- Access control devices: electronic keypads, card readers, and biometric readers
- Lighting systems
- Communication systems: intercoms, handheld radios, pagers, and portable telephones

- Closed-circuit television systems and audio/video recording equipment
- Intrusion detection systems
- Patrol monitoring devices
- Better-trained security officers

These changes have all contributed to improved and better-designed security programs.

Fire Life Safety of Modern High-Rise Buildings

Buildings constructed after World War II began to include fire safety enhancements such as fireproofing insulation sprayed directly onto steel columns, floor beams, and girders to protect these structural members from distortion due to heat. It is applied in accordance with the requirements of the local building code. If the insulation is not correctly applied (for example, if the steel is rusted and the surface has not been properly prepared or if the insulation has not been applied at the specified thickness or density) or if the insulation has been dislodged during construction or high winds, heating an exposed steel floor beam to high temperatures can cause vertical deflection (because the secured beam has no space to move horizontally when it elongates) and failure of the connection used to secure the beam to other beams or to the main girders.

In the modern core construction high-rise built of lightweight steel or reinforced concrete frames, skin-type curtain walls that support none of the weight of the building are usually found on the outside of the structure. According to Mark Gorman of URS Corp., "They are like a shower curtain—designed to keep the rain out. These curtain walls are usually glass and stone cladding supported on the structure by lightweight metal frames. Skin-type refers to a continuous wall that covers the surface like skin on a body."

In addition, curtain walls may be attached to the exterior wall columns, sometimes creating an empty space (of width varying from 6 to 12 inches) between the interior of these walls and the outer edges of the floors. If there is such a gap, it is usually filled with fire-resistant material to restrict the vertical spread of fire.

Suspended ceilings, the most common type of ceiling in high-rise buildings, create a concealed space that often extends throughout an entire floor area. Apart from mandatory fire-walls extending from a base floor slab to the floor slab of the floor above and in restrooms and corridors where fire-rated plasterboard ceilings are used for fire protection, these ceilings lack fire-stopping material. This uninterrupted space is about 30 inches in depth and consists of noncombustible acoustical ceiling tiles that are supported in a metal grid hung on metal hangers attached to the floor above. It often is used to house electrical, plumbing, and ducting systems, as well as telephone wiring conduits and computer wiring for that particular floor. In some buildings, it is also used as a return plenum for the heating, ventilating, and air-conditioning (HVAC) systems. According to Mark Gorman of URS Corp., "Hotels often do not have a suspended ceiling—the concrete floor slab above is the ceiling below, and all the electrical is cast in the slab."

Floor beams and girders are often covered with corrugated steel panels or plates and then covered with a layer of concrete to form the floor itself. According to John Seabrook, "The floors in most of the high-rise buildings erected since the sixties are much lighter in weight than the floors in the older buildings. In a typical high-rise office floor, 3 to 4 inches of concrete covers a corrugated-steel deck, whose weight is supported by I-beams or, in the case of the [World Trade Center] Twin Towers, by long 'trusses'—lightweight strips of steel that are braced by crosshatched webs of square or cylindrical bars that create a hollow space below each floor surface. This space allows builders to install heating and cooling ducts within the floors, rather than in a drop [suspended] ceiling below them—an innovation that allows the developer to increase the number of floors in the entire building."

Multiple stairwells provide primary and secondary means of egress and are often equipped with automatic stairshaft pressurization and smoke evacuation systems. Because these stairwells are located in the central core area, they are less distant from each other than those in pre-World War II buildings. Stair and elevator shaft openings are equipped with protective assemblies and horizontal openings are protected.

Floor areas tend to be larger and have a generally open-plan design, with little compartmentation using floor-to-ceiling walls and

barriers. Aluminum-framed, cloth-covered foam partitioning is often used to construct cubicles to be used as individual offices. This partitioning is cheaper than the hardwood partitioning used in the past and just as effective as a sound barrier; however, it is more combustible.

The number of occupants tends to be high, and results in a high concentration of business and personal property, and hence high fire or fuel load. Much of this property (including office supplies, plastic wastepaper baskets, files, paper, and the personal computer systems that now equip most workstations) is made of synthetic materials that are flammable; they produce toxic gases that become components in the resulting smoke and gas. In the *Fire Protection Handbook*, Brian L. Marburger writes, "Over the past several years, there have been many changes in the furnishings put into buildings. At one time, desks and chairs were routinely wood. Then metal became popular. Now, any combination of wood, metal, thermoplastics, and foamed plastics can be found. In addition, the increased use of computers has also added to the fuel load." To mitigate against this threat to life safety, office furniture and interior furnishings in all offices, conference and waiting rooms, and reception and assembly areas should be of fire-resistive quality and treated to reduce combustibility.

There is the potential during fires for stack effect. In the *Fire Protection Handbook*, Wayne D. Holmes writes, "The stack effect results from temperature differences between two areas, which create a pressure difference that results in natural air movements within a building. In a high-rise building, this effect is increased due to the height of the building. Many high-rise buildings have a significant stack effect, capable of moving large volumes of heat and smoke through the building." In contrast, in *Building Construction for the Fire Service*, Francis L. Brannigan notes that pre-World War II, "Windows could be opened in buildings of this era. This provided local ventilation and relief from smoke migrating from the fire. The windows leaked, often like sieves, therefore, there was no substantial stack effect." Modern high-rise building windows provide some resistance to heat and are often made of tempered safety glass; they usually cannot be opened and are well insulated. In the *Fire Protection Handbook*, Wayne D. Holmes writes, "No manual firefighting techniques are known to counter stack effect or to mitigate its effect during a fire….The only way to mitigate the potential of stack effect is to design and construct the building to minimize the effect."

Automatic fire detection systems and automatic fire suppression systems are often incorporated into building design. According to Francis L. and Maureen Brannigan, "Most new high-rise office buildings have sprinklers installed. The huge losses suffered in such fires as Philadelphia's One Meridian Plaza and Los Angeles' First Interstate Tower [First Interstate Bank Building] leave little room for argument. But there is still much opposition to any requirement for retroactive installation of sprinklers in existing buildings. While much of the opposition is financial, the specious argument that such requirements are unconstitutional has found some favor. This argument is without merit with respect to United States law. Much of the cost, particularly of a retroactive installation, is caused by hiding the sprinkler system. If the argument of overall sprinkler cost is an issue, the opposing argument is that safety requires only the cost of a bare bones system. Aesthetic costs such as hiding the sprinklers and the piping are the option[s] of the owner, not a fire protection requirement."

Summary

High-rise buildings contain many valuable assets. The terms security and fire life safety are synonymous but can be addressed separately for the purposes of systematic analysis and discussion. There are many potential security and life safety threats to the people who use these facilities on a daily basis and to the businesses, property, and information contained within them.

Geoff Craighead

Sources

Abbott, R. 1994. *Comparison of Design and Construction Techniques, Class 'E' High-Rise Office Buildings*. New York: Fire Science Institute.

Brannigan, F. 1992. *Building Construction for the Fire Service, 3rd Edition*. Quincy: National Fire Protection Association.

Brannigan, F. and Brannigan, M. Statements in a letter to the author regarding building construction for the fire service. Mar. 1995.

Fischer, R. and Green, G. 1998. *Introduction to Security, 6th Edition*. Boston: Butterworth-Heinemann.

Gorman, M. Comments to author in an e-mail regarding core and tube construction of high-rises. Mar. 2002.

Holmes, W. 2003. *Fire Protection Handbook, 19th Edition*. Quincy: National Fire Protection Association.

Marburger, B. 2003. *Fire Protection Handbook, 19th Edition*. Quincy: National Fire Protection Association.

Post, R. and Kingsbury, A. 1991. *Security Administration: An Introduction to the Protective Services, 4th Edition*. Boston: Butterworth-Heinemann.

Protection of Assets Manual. 2006. Arlington: American Society for Industrial Security International.

Seabrook, J. "The Tower Builder: Why Did the World Trade Center Buildings Fall Down When They Did?" *The New Yorker* Nov. 19, 2001.

Thatcher, V. ed. 1980. *New Webster Encyclopedic Dictionary of the English Language*. Chicago: Consolidated Book Publishers.

MEDIA CONTROL IN CRISIS SITUATIONS

An organization is much like a living organism in the sense that it reacts to external stimuli, and when the stimuli are unpleasant, as would be the case during a crisis, the organization experiences stress. An external stimulus contributing to an organization's stress in a crisis is the uncompromising search by the news media for information. A significant incident affecting the organization, such as a major accident or crime, will stimulate public interest and consequently set the news media on the trail.

At the outset of a crisis, the organization faces two critical tasks simultaneously: first, deal with the crisis, and second, communicate the facts. Great pressure is on the organization to launch an effective response and at the same time intelligently present the details of what happened and what is being done in response. The target of communications set by the organization is the public broadly, and the vehicles for getting to the target are television, radio, and press agencies.

Business people are learning to be aware of public concerns when commenting on broad issues in which corporate interests are involved. Executives generally look ahead when making public statements. They do so to avoid the impression of not caring for public health or safety when company profit may be at risk. This can be difficult when liability is a possible outcome and legal counsel urges management to be careful in avoiding language that suggests culpability. However, if management is overly circumspect, the business may suffer public relations losses. Losses of this type include damage to public confidence and increased regulatory restrictions imposed by legislators responsive to the public mood. The long-term costs of political and regulatory responses are likely to greatly outweigh the short-term costs of accepting responsibility when it is due.

Interacting with the Media

Certain problems of a security nature can be anticipated in dealings with the media. They include access control at the scene of the incident, disruption of business operations resulting from attempts by the media to acquire information, and unauthorized release of information from sources within the organization. Also, when the chief security officer is a central persona in responding to contingencies, which is almost always the case, he or she will be sought after by the media.

Being responsive to media requests for information is especially important during emergency response operations. The usual procedure is for media inquiries to be channeled to one office or person, typically called the Public Information Office or PIO. A PIO representative is designated in advance to speak for the organization, to meet with news representatives, and to arrange and be present at media interviews of company employees. The PIO is often sensitive to the needs of the news media, particularly with respect to time. While the media are racing to report the news, the PIO is concerned about releasing details that are both accurate and considerate of the organization's view.

Incidents involving death, serious injury, substantial property loss, damage to the environment, and risk to the public constitute significant news. The PIO serves as a "control valve" for preventing the release of distorted versions and providing some modicum of protection against disclosures that may be harmful to the organization or its individual employees.

Whether business likes it or not, the media will present news in a manner intended to attract attention, and in the process will make news reporting more important than the news itself. The outcome can be distortion of facts.

When an incident of any magnitude arises, the news media will want, indeed demand, the facts. Oftentimes they will be asking for details even before the organization's management is aware of the incident. Through arrangements with governmental response agencies, such as police and fire departments, media employees learn of incidents on a real-time basis. Television, radio, and press reporters are likely to arrive at the incident scene with the first responders.

When the organization's headquarters is located a considerable distance from the site of the incident, which will frequently be the case, senior management will expect a knowledgeable manager at the scene to act as the organization's spokesperson, at least until arrival of more senior persons. The on-scene spokesperson can initially provide all available details as quickly as possible. Of concern in accidents will be precisely what happened, how, when, and where; the number of persons involved and their names; the nature and extent of deaths and injuries; and the nature and extent of property damage, including non-organizational property and the environment.

A chief security officer, especially one who also has operational safety responsibilities, may be called upon to perform spokesperson duties. Direct media contact with an operational manager is usually better, at least from the media's point of view, than contact through a PIO representative or other intermediary. Misunderstandings frequently develop whenever a critical incident is being developed by the media, and an absence of personal contact between the media and persons close to the situation contribute to misunderstanding and distrust.

A chief security officer tabbed for interview must be wary of offhand remarks that could give a wrong impression, and should also avoid leaving out important details. Being quoted out of context can be minimized by speaking in short sentences and repeating constantly the key phrases that convey the organization's point of view. This requires rehearsing, and is particularly important in television interviews where reporters are obliged to select only the briefest, most salient comments from an interview that may have taken an hour or more to tape. If at all possible, a PIO representative should be present to listen objectively and intervene to correct errors on the spot.

Rumor and exaggeration are the organization's nemesis in a time of crisis. Accuracy, although difficult to maintain in the very early stages of an incident, is a priority. Information flowing from the scene has to be carefully weighed as to the extent of casualties and damage. A golden rule is to not release the names of persons killed or injured until the next of kin have been notified, to not speculate as to the causes of the incident, and to not mention dollar amounts concerning damage and loss. Another rule is to avoid saying "no comment." Corporate counsel may like this response because it closes off a line of questioning that could be troublesome, but use of the term suggests to the media and the public that the organization has something to hide.

The organization and the media each have a right to be wary of deception. The organization may feel it has an overriding and legitimate reason to be reserved in its response, and the media know from prior experiences that businesses have engaged in denials and half-truths. Good reporters usually can see through a lie and have it in their power to make the organization look worse for it. Reporters hungry for a headline story may be more attuned to negatives than positives. Some may have an anti-business bias or be ignorant of business needs. Fortunately, most reporters genuinely want to present a responsible view and will work with an organization that deals squarely with them.

If saying the wrong thing can hurt the organization, why not impose a policy of silence? The problem with this approach is that speculation, conjecture, and rumor take the place of facts. Fiction and fantasy rapidly fill the vacuum of official silence. By saying nothing, the organization makes itself vulnerable to unfounded perceptions. Perception takes on a reality all its own in a world strongly influenced by mass communications.

The principal cause of tension between business and the media is their different perspectives. Business operates through policies it believes are proper and is resolute in defending policies in the face of criticism. Executives are resentful when taken to task by reporters who do not understand the policies and the reasons for them. Reporters, on the other hand, feel that their function is to report what they find, even when their findings run counter to long-established business practices and beliefs.

On-Scene Functions

The PIO's contingency plan will customarily call for sending a representative to the scene of a major incident. When the incident is significantly destructive, such as an oil spill or plant explosion, the representative will almost certainly be accompanied by one or more senior managers, possibly including the organization's chief executive officer. Virtually no crisis incident is too small or unimportant to warrant senior management attention.

Some of the media-related functions that require prompt attention at the scene are:

- Verifying key details, such as casualties and damages
- Meeting and escorting reporters
- Setting up and making announcements at press conferences
- Updating and reporting developments as they evolve
- Clearing the statements and comments of management

To the extent that circumstances permit, the PIO representative will set up a press center at or close to the scene of the incident. The center could be on the organization's premises, at a hotel nearby, or at any safe and reasonably convenient place having telephone facilities. It is not necessary or even appropriate for the PIO to provide food or refreshments at press center meetings, but it is a given that news personnel will receive honest answers with least possible delay. The answers are delivered courteously and in a manner ensuring that all news personnel receive information the same way at the same time.

Verbal announcements are often supplemented with written materials designed to facilitate accurate reporting. Working from written materials, the PIO spokesperson is able to focus on facts that are fully known. Dangerous conjecture, which will sometimes arise in the face of insistent questioning, can be avoided by commenting only on what has been put into writing.

Also, in the case of releasing the names of persons injured or killed, the chances of word-of-mouth name errors are reduced by providing a written list.

As an incident winds down, the PIO may hold one or more follow-up meetings with the news media. By then, the causes of the incident and the extent of damage may be known and open to discussion. Positive messages would include assurances to the community with respect to safety and the restoration of jobs destabilized by the incident; progress reports on assistance given to families and repairs made to property and the environment; the effectiveness of the organization's preventive and responsive actions; and credit to local response agencies that assisted in bringing the emergency under control.

The Role of the Chief Security Officer

The chief security officer has a full plate during a major incident. Depending on the nature of the incident, there can be requirements to provide first-responder medical assistance, establish access control at the incident scene, and protect people and assets exposed to continuing risk. Meeting these requirements involves coordination with many persons inside and out of the organization. Within the organization, and surely this will be a key element in contingency planning, the chief security officer interfaces with the PIO.

The services performed by a chief security officer that relate narrowly to the media fall generally under access control. Three services stand out:

- Preventing entrance to an unsafe incident scene by unauthorized personnel. After an incident has been declared safe, the chief security officer may be involved in escorting media representatives interested in taking pictures, making notes, and in some controlled situations, interviewing employees at the scene.
- Preventing close-in access to PIO representatives and senior managers at meetings

with the press. Distraught relatives of victims and issue-oriented persons antagonistic to the organization may use a press meeting to physically attack the organization's spokespersons.

- Preventing access to travel conveyances utilized by senior managers. A person, deranged or motivated by revenge and/or the desire to gain attention to a cause, may attempt to place a bomb aboard or otherwise sabotage the plane or automobile used to transport key members of the organization.

The chief security officer must be prepared to support the important functions carried out by the organization's PIO during times of crisis. Security support to the PIO cannot be properly executed if it is based on a misunderstanding of the PIO function or if there is insufficient preparation in crisis management. A chief security officer simply cannot wait until an emergency occurs to determine and fill PIO needs. All of the planning for the handling of public information matters must be done well in advance.

The quality of security support is examined, to the chief security officer's credit or discredit, at the conclusion of a crisis when the organization summarizes the lessons learned. A manager who puts effort into learning PIO needs and in developing a support capability assures a quality response for the organization and a creditable rating personally.

John J. Fay

NATIONAL INCIDENT COMMAND SYSTEM ORGANIZATION

The national structure of incident management establishes a vertical progression of coordination and communication from local to state and regional to the national level. Security professionals, for the most part, will be coordinating planning issues with the local emergency operations center personnel typically located at the county or parish level. During an incident, however, security management personnel may be coordinating with or supporting incident response organizations.

Most daily incidents are handled by the local public safety authorities through established command and control protocols. They use the ICS concept when they respond to major local incidents such as chemical spills, large fires, explosions, and other disaster situations. The first command and control entity is the incident command post and is usually under a single command element such as the fire department. When there are multiple locations that are part of the response, local leadership may activate additional incident command posts. To control the operations of the multiple numbers of incident command posts, a unified command entity may be established. This occurs when more than one agency has incident jurisdictional responsibilities or the incident crosses political jurisdictions. The agencies or local jurisdictions provide liaison representatives to the unified command location to participate in the decision-making process. The unified command entity carries out short-term operations, planning, logistics, and finance/administration functions and is focused on establishing common objectives and strategies for the execution of a single incident action plan.

When the area command is activated it usually oversees multi-incidents being managed by ICS first responders or conducts management of large incidents that cross jurisdictional boundaries. The area command does not have the direct operations responsibility that is identified with the unified command concept. It has the responsibility to set overall strategy, identify priorities, allocate critical resources to meet those priorities, and to ensure that incidents are properly managed through objectives and strategies accomplishment. The area command may develop more than one incident action plan and may become a unified area command when required. The incident command post commanders report to the area command for support and guidance.

Both the unified command and area command provide information to the local emergency operations center. That center is a full-time organization with a nucleus of personnel responsible for long-term planning and exercise production; communication operation; operational information sharing; and resource coordination, dispatching, and tracking in support of on-scene efforts. When activated to support an incident, the center is manned by state and local public and private sector liaison representatives. This additional augmentation assists in coordinating the center's activities and needs with state, federal,

and appropriate private sector emergency operations centers and support sectors.

James T. Roberts, Jr.

NATIONAL INCIDENT MANAGEMENT SYSTEM

Private-sector emergency preparedness and responses of today are integrated with local community preparedness measures. Local resources and responses identified during the planning process are often available for use on a larger scale. Security planners may be tasked to work with government emergency management planners and coordinate support at different levels to ensure that their company resources assist in the most efficient and effective manner. All private sector organizations, especially those who represent critical infrastructure or key resource materials or technology, are encouraged (or required in some cases) to develop detailed emergency response and business continuity plans to include information-sharing and incident reporting measures that are compatible with the National Incident Management System (NIMS).

Homeland Security Presidential Directive/HSPD-5, issued in 2003, directed the establishment of NIMS. As developed, this system is based on incident management best practices developed by public safety practitioners at the local, state, and federal levels. The NIMS goal is to provide common nationwide command and control methodology for use by all government and non-government emergency management and public safety elements. Using the interoperability and compatibility approach fine-tuned by firefighters, hazardous materials teams, rescuers, and emergency medical teams since the 1970s, NIMS permits organizations to use core sets of concepts, principles, terminology, and technologies to jointly prepare for, respond to, and recover from domestic events regardless of the cause, size, and complexity. It establishes an organizational structure that focuses on the incident command system (ICS), multi-agency coordination systems, and unified command models. Other parts of NIMS address training; identification and management of resources; qualifications and certification; and the collection, tracking, and reporting of incident information and incident resources.

The ICS manages major incidents through focus on five major functional areas: command, operations, planning, logistics, and finance/administration. A sixth function of intelligence gathering, analysis, and sharing may be assigned based on the type of incident being addressed by the responders. ICS gives users an on-scene, integrated, all-hazard management system which can be used for single or multiple incidents. Where the incident transcends geographical or governmental jurisdictions, use of a unified command structure may be warranted. This integration of multi-agency personnel permits coordination of and joint decisions for incident objectives, strategies, plans, priorities, and public notifications.

The strength of the ICS management stems from the characteristics of the system. These characteristics are:

- Common terminology. Standardized key terms, titles, facility and unit designations, and definitions that are used in planning, operations, and communications at all levels
- Modular organization—use of the building block concept to add needed pre-planned command, operational, and administrative elements required to meet the level of complexity for successful incident control and recovery
- Chain of command and unity of command. NIMS is based on a distinct vertical chain of command that facilitates assignment of authority and responsibility for decision-making, coordination, and issuance of orders based on information and requests that flow up and down the chain. At each level, one individual is designated as the decision-maker for all elements responsible for addressing an incident at his or her level and subordinates report to only one person.
- Establishment and transfer of command. The formal identification of who is in command of an incident, operations center, or higher command center. Shift transfer is a formal process where the incoming commander is briefed by the outgoing commander as to threat, operations, resources and other items important to the successful completion of the mission. Command staff conduct the same briefings in their respective areas to ensure continuity of operations.
- Manageable span of control. The effective span of control that varies between three and five elements with the most desirable being one supervising element for five reporting elements
- Unified command—established when there are two or more agencies with incident jurisdiction or when incidents cross political jurisdictions. Agency-designated incident commanders work from a single incident command post through an agreed upon common set of objectives, strategies, and single incident action plan.
- Management by objectives. The systematic and organized approach used by leadership to focus on achievable goals, establish specific objectives, and target the use of available resources to obtain the best results possible
- Reliance on incident management planning. The use of the continuous planning cycle that addresses prevention, preparedness, response, and recovery actions
- Comprehensive resource management. The management of those tasks that establish systems for describing, inventorying, requesting, and tracking resources; activating those systems prior to, during, and after an incident; dispatching resources prior to, during, and following an incident; and deactivating or recalling resources during or following an incident
- Pre-designated mobilization locations and facilities. The use of the planning process (or on-scene identification) of sites where operational and logistical elements are marshaled for future mission assignment and deployment
- Accountability of resources and personnel. The use of measures that require check-in of all materials, personnel, and equipment regardless of agency affiliation to a central person or section that can, in turn, advise the incident commander, area commander, or multi-agency coordination center manager of assets that are available for use
- Deployment. The orderly movement of identified elements and resources from a home base, base camp, heliport, or marshaling point to a specific operational location

- Integrated communications and information management—the use of pre-identified equipment that allows for multi-agency interoperability and is compatible vertically and horizontally
- Information and intelligence management—the establishment of an awareness system that ensures the continual process of collecting, analyzing, and disseminating intelligence, information, and knowledge to allow organizations and individuals to anticipate requirements and to react properly

Daily ICS operations are governed by the development of incident action plans (IAP) that are based on the objectives identified by leadership. The plans, usually covering a 12 hour period, provide the overall incident objectives for operational and support elements. IAP objectives are used to develop and make assignments, plans, procedures, and protocols. At the end of each period, operational results are documented and fed back into planning for use in the next 12 hour period.

James T. Roberts, Jr.

NATIONAL RESPONSE PLAN

Security practitioners that are tasked with planning for or responding to emergency incidents, whether local or national, are affected by the National Response Plan (NRP).

The NSP, released by the Department of Homeland Security in December 2004, is the central document that provides domestic emergency management guidance for all federal departments, state, and local agencies. The guidance is aimed at seamless management and coordination between departments in their actions to prevent, prepare for, respond to, and to recover from terrorism, major natural disasters, and other national emergencies. The NRP is the result of Homeland Security Presidential Directive 5 (HSPD-5) which ordered the development of new guidance that aligned all federal coordination structures, capabilities, and resources into a unified, all-discipline, all hazards approach to major incident responses.

Included in the plan are the roles and responsibilities of state, local, and tribal governments; non-governmental and volunteer organizations,

the private sector, and citizen involvement. The NRP is written to generally recognize that incidents are best handled at the lowest jurisdictional level possible. As those first responder jurisdictions at the local level determine that they lack the capability to control the incident, they request additional resources from mutual aid pact agencies and the state under the first line of emergency response and support concept. When the state recognizes that the incident is beyond its long term response, it may request federal assistance. The plan also recognizes that there may be incidents of national significance where the federal government will quickly initiate actions to prevent, prepare for, respond to, and recover from those situations. In the latter case, actions will be taken in coordination with those government, non-government, and private sector entities affected.

The plan establishes the common organizational structure from incident command to local emergency operations centers to regional centers to national multi-agency coordinating centers. This structure is based on the National Incident Management System (NIMS). NIMS was initially developed for use by the fire services to determine common command and control measures that could be used by one or more agencies in incident command response. The system is now the model for use by all public safety agencies. An example of one temporary organization is the Joint Field Office (formally the FEMA disaster field office). This locally activated multi-agency center has the responsibility for coordinating federal, state, local, tribal, non-governmental, and private sector response to the following: natural disasters, national public health incidents, incidents of national significance (e.g., massive oil spills, etc.), and national special security events. The plan also establishes the parameters for requesting federal assistance under Stafford Act or non-Stafford Act circumstances.

The key components of interest to the private sector are found in the three groups of annexes to the plan. The emergency support functions (ESF) annexes are: transportation; communications; public works and engineering; firefighting; emergency management; mass care, housing, and human services; resource management; public health and medical services; urban search and rescue; oil and hazardous materials response; agriculture and natural resources; energy; public safety and security; long-term community recovery and mitigation; and external affairs. Support annexes cover: financial management, international coordination, logistics management, private-sector coordination, public affairs, science and technology, tribal relations, volunteer and donation management, and worker safety and health. The incident annexes provide specific guidance on: biological incidents, catastrophic incidents, cyber incidents, food and agriculture incidents, nuclear and radiological incidents, and terrorism incident law enforcement and investigation.

Of particular interest for security practitioners, is Emergency Support Function #13, Public Safety and Security. This annex outlines the federal to federal and federal to state and local coordination and support tasks. It discusses non-investigative and non-criminal law enforcement, public safety, and security capabilities and resources available during potential or actual Incidents of National Significance.

Private sector entities support national response initiatives stemming from emergency support actions that are noted in the plan's ESF annexes. The primary agencies are mandated to work with, and coordinate actions with their private sector partnership committees to develop a seamless industry relationship. Individual organizations share vital information with the government, identify tasks to be accomplished, perform vulnerability assessments, develop emergency response and business continuity plans, enhance corporate readiness, implement appropriate prevention and protection plans, and provide assistance necessary to respond to and recover from an incident.

James T. Roberts, Jr.

SECURITY AND LIFE SAFETY IN THE COMMERCIAL HIGH-RISE BUILDING

The variety of ownership formulas and tenant occupancies associated with commercial high-rise buildings presents challenges in the delivery of security and life safety services. Buildings can be owned and managed by single organizations, owned by one party and managed by another, owned by groups of business entities, owned by a tenant and managed by the property manager, etc. Different organizations have differing standards of risk acceptance and differing perspectives on the very nature of security

and life safety. What they share in common is an overriding concern with costs. The natural results are that the practices of security and life safety in commercial high-rises are inconsistent and poorly funded.

A commercial high-rise is defined by the National Fire Protection Association (NFPA) as "a building greater than 75 feet (23 meters) in height where the building height is measured from the lowest level of fire department vehicle access to the floor of the highest occupiable story (Section 3.3.25.6, 2000)." The Building Owners and Managers Association (BOMA) provides a less technical description. It classifies a building according to work performed within it, tenant base, size, location, structural composition, and other factors. Small commercial properties can occupy tens of thousands of square feet and have hundreds of occupants while large properties can occupy millions of square feet, hold tens of thousands of occupants, and consist of several buildings.

Persons inside a building can be numerous and varied: employees, temporary employees, visitors, contractors, vendors, people "just passing through," and undesirables such as vagrants and criminal opportunists. The internal operations of buildings vary. A tenant that provides information technology services will use equipment, materials, and supplies different from a tenant that provides counseling services.

Commercial high-rises often have retailers that provide products and services to tenants and the general public. They are usually at ground level and consist of department stores, boutiques, theaters, restaurants, fast-food shops, bars, health clubs, banks, and visitor parking areas. Great difficulties confront a security and life safety program that is mandated also to provide services to the ancillary operations.

These varying factors prevent uniformity in the operation of security and life safety programs. A program in place at one facility is certain to be different at another. There can be variances within the program as well. For one tenant, the services may not be wanted at all and for another tenant the services may be very much desired. Adding to the mix are complaints and irrational demands.

The security component of a program is concerned with protecting tenants against crime such as physical assault and theft of vehicles in the underground parking lot, theft of materials arriving at and moving from a loading platform, receipt of package bombs in the mailroom, internal theft, and employee-to-employee violence. Typically, protection is achieved through a combination of physical safeguards and security officers working in ways specified by plans and procedures.

The life safety component is concerned with preventing and/or responding to life-threatening incidents such as fire, major accidents, hazardous materials releases, and acts of nature such as earthquakes, windstorms, and flooding. The life safety component addresses building evacuation, sheltering in place, administration of first aid, and assisting the handicapped.

Many commercial properties have critical infrastructure capabilities such as:

- Fire detection and suppression equipment
- A system for delivering water to fire-affected areas
- An uninterrupted power supply system
- Backup power generation
- Air handling system
- Pressurized stairwells
- Automatic shutdown of interfering utilities
- Emergency communication

For business continuity purposes, a commercial property can have infrastructures that provide:

- Fresh water and dispel waste water
- Work areas isolated from danger
- Heating and cooling
- Means for communicating internally and externally
- Power hookups for critical equipment such as computers
- Protection of critical business records

The regular operations of a security and life safety program are influenced by:

- Life safety and construction codes
- Budgetary restrictions
- Standards and guidelines
- What tenants say, want, expect and, most importantly, what they are willing to pay
- What the building owners want
- What the building management wants
- Findings of building vulnerability and threat/risk assessments
- Local, regional, and national concerns

- Signature status of the building
- High-profile tenants
- Proximity to high profile buildings and landmarks

The manager of a security and life safety program focuses on issues of concern to tenants. These can be incidents that have relatively low importance but occur regularly such as loitering, minor theft, and graffiti. Other incidents have high importance but occur infrequently such as fire, power blackouts, hazardous materials releases, and violent crimes.

The resources that are available to the security and life safety program manager to deal with incidents of concern fall into three categories: personnel, physical/electronic systems, and documentation. The personnel category can include security officers, contractors that service security equipment, staff employees in the building management office, maintenance and engineering employees, and tenant employees. External to the building are persons that provide first-responder services such as police officers, firefighters, and emergency medical technicians.

Tenant employees are sometimes overlooked as resources or not thought to be resources at all. The reality is that all building occupants play a part in security and life safety; for example, reporting and correcting hazardous conditions, reporting suspicious persons and activities, and helping mitigate the effects of a major disaster. Tenants often designate certain of their employees to perform these types of functions on a regular basis. Persons in this group are often called floor or fire wardens.

The physical/electronic systems category can include fences, gates, lights, bollards, locks, reinforced doors, access control systems, intrusion detection systems, CCTV systems, fire detection/suppression systems, HVAC systems, elevator systems, etc.

The documentation category can include mutual aid agreements, security and safety policies and standards, emergency management plans, notification lists, standard operating procedures, post orders, incident reports, training manuals, and manuals for operating and calibrating security hardware. Sometimes overlooked are as-built plans and engineering documents that identify critical locations such as air intake and exhaust openings, shutoff points for power and water, and electrical conduits.

Of the three categories just mentioned, the people category is most important, and within that category, security officers are most important. This is because security officers are often the first to learn of a crisis impending or in progress; they alert others to danger, summon first-responders, intervene to contain an incident and mitigate its effects, and assist persons in need of emergency care. When a major incident occurs after hours, which is often the case, security officers take on the duties of absent persons such as building management staff, maintenance and engineering personnel, and floor wardens.

Security officers are important for another reason: without them, the electronic systems serve no valuable purpose. Worth cannot be found in a CCTV system that has no human to monitor images, or a fire alarm that has no human to hear it, or an intrusion detection system that has no response force.

In conclusion, a security and life safety program for a commercial high-rise building has to be managed competently, coordinated internally, configured to meet the full range of anticipated contingencies, and sufficiently resourced.

Glen Kitteringham

III: Information Security

BUSINESS INTELLIGENCE

"Business Intelligence" is a major phrase in today's competitive marketplace; it means many things to many people—usually for marketing purposes. Definitions range from software packages to data mining techniques to technology solutions to difficult problems. In this definition, however, we deal with the operational, business process that derives largely from the experiences of intelligence professionals who translate skills, tools, techniques, and approaches from national and international intelligence operations.

Business intelligence includes competitive intelligence (CI) and competitive counterintelligence (CCI). Both specifically include the nature of competition, for it is the purpose of both to assist the firm in gaining and maintaining competitive advantage through the application of established principles not normally found in the business community.

CI and CCI have been successfully characterized and applied using cyclical approaches. They operate as interlocked cycles which both begin and end at the decision maker. The decision maker, in need of the best information possible, uses CI processes to define the actual requirements to be satisfied through legal, ethical, and effective means; to have the information evaluated and analyzed and provided in a format sufficient to take competitive actions on time.

This same decision maker is also responsible for determining those elements of competitive advantage which sets the firm apart from adversaries and commissioning those steps necessary to protect that advantage. This process includes the identification of the competitor set, their capabilities and competencies in order to paint as effective a portrait of the threat to the firm's business as possible. Once that picture emerges, testing of the firm's actual vulnerabilities to such external threats is conducted, and countermeasures developed that are consistent with the firm's environment, culture, and requirements. This process also includes an ongoing analysis of the efficacy of such selected approaches and regularly advises the decision-maker about needful changes consistent with different approaches undertaken by competitors once they encounter the countermeasures designed to thwart their intelligence collection efforts.

John A. Nolan, III

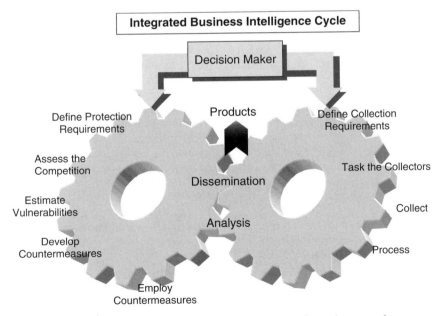

Figure 10. Information is processed as it moves through two cycles.

BUSINESS INTELLIGENCE: AN OVERVIEW

Business intelligence is both a product and a process. As a product, it is information with use and value that can be applied by decision makers to the organization's particular purposes or goals. As a process, it is a combination of ethical and legitimate activities that involve the collection, evaluation, analysis, integration, and interpretation of data obtained from open and covert sources. Industrial espionage is a loose, generic term that describes the harnessing of the business intelligence process in a manner that may or may not be entirely legitimate or which involves the use of a legitimately developed intelligence product to achieve an illegal end.

Open sources of business information are publicly available. They include information presented by the news media, public records, government reports, and reports issued by business competitors, such as annual reports and stock offerings. On the gray fringe are the competitors' internal newsletters, proposals to prospective clients, and similar documents that are usually not confidential and which would be impossible for the authoring organizations to control in any meaningful way.

For the user of open information, the caveat is extreme caution because the data is often a potpourri of fact, fiction, half-truths, and deliberate distortions. The challenge to the collector of publicly available information is to ferret out the factual portions and combine them with pieces of data obtained from other sources.

Covert sources of information include informants, paid and unpaid, witting and unwitting. They may be the targeted organization's regular, temporary, and contractor employees, as well as suppliers, vendors, clients, and other competitors. They may also be the wives, children, or friends of these individuals.

Also included are the collector's operatives who may be in-house employees or outside contractors, and may range in skill from amateur to veteran professional. Operative activities can consist of recruiting and directing informants, going undercover into the targeted organization, intercepting written communications to and from the target, maintaining visual and photographic surveillance of the target's activities, conducting audio surveillance with the use of covert listening devices, and posing as headhunters to possibly acquire from the target's key employees sensitive information that may be inadvertently leaked during a bogus job interview. The more odious tasks involve searching the competitor's trash, breaking and entering, and blackmailing the vulnerable.

The information sought by industrial spying is usually proprietary in nature, i.e., it is information owned by a company or entrusted to it that has not been disclosed publicly and has value. Trade secrets, patents, business plans, research and development discoveries, and the like are examples. Proprietary information is generally under the owner's protective shield, except when it is also classified government data entitled to protections afforded by the government.

The dark side of business intelligence has only recently come to be acknowledged as a serious threat to the viability of a business and, in a larger sense, to entire industries and national economies. As companies, industries, and nations move to dependence on technologically intense products and services, as is the case in the United States, business spying will expand and intensify. Adding fuel to this fire is the availability of national spying infrastructures that can be converted from military to business objectives.

John J. Fay

COMPETITIVE COUNTERINTELLIGENCE

Competitive Counterintelligence (CCI) is an organized and coherent process that is characterized by anticipatory and proactive steps designed to identify and neutralize attempts to obtain that intellectual property and other proprietary information which contribute materially to a firm's competitive advantage.

Just as counterintelligence as practiced by national agencies rarely seeks criminal prosecution as an outcome, CCI is also focused largely on prevention and active intervention rather than ex post facto investigation and other actions that typically must adhere to strict legal protocols. Indeed, CCI seeks not only to prevent illegal attempts to compromise a firm's information, but also to deal with the far more prevalent legal and ethical—yet just as potentially problematic—methods employed by aggressive businesses world-wide.

The Competitive Counter Intelligence Cycle

CCI is most often depicted in a circular form comprised of seven major elements:

Identification of the Critical Elements. Rather than attempting to safeguard everything, all the time, this part of the process seeks to identify those elements that provide a competitive advantage from several perspectives—what must be protected, for how long, from whom it must be protected and where it's located. This allows a focused, and concentrated picture upon which the remainder of the process depends and allows prioritization and resource allocations.

Assessment of the Adversary(ies). Here, an in-depth analysis of those companies or other actors in the marketplace (e.g., an environmental protection group that attempts to subvert sympathetic employees of an oil company into providing information that can be used to damage the firm) and the capabilities, approaches, techniques that they have been known to use— or which they can be reasonably expected to use—in gathering information about the firm. Fundamentally, this requires an understanding of how aggressively the firm operates with its internal counterintelligence assets, which kinds of constraints they place on internal or external collectors of information, and the origins of those collectors (which can range from aggressive and talented former government intelligence officers to fairly benign librarians). This assessment also takes into consideration the relationship that the opposing firm has with its own domestic (national) intelligence service and the degree of cooperation they enjoy, as well as the differences in attitudes, principles, and actions between countries and regions of the world.

Testing of the Firm's Vulnerabilities. Once there has been an identification of what might plausibly be at risk within the firm and the extent that it may be sought after—and the approaches that a business rival are known or can be reasonably postulated to undertake—the firm will attack itself by replicating such approaches as nearly as possible, thus gaining an accurate picture of the

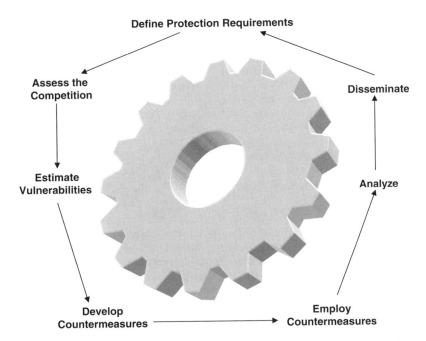

Competitive Counterintelligence Cycle

Figure 11. The competitive counterintelligence cycle is a process that begins by identifying company holdings that need to be protected; characterizes threats against the holdings; identifies weaknesses in the scheme that protects the holdings; devises protective methods for reducing or eliminating the weaknesses; implements the protective methods; evaluates the effectiveness of the protective measures; and on a regular basis informs the company's leadership of changing threat conditions. The need to adjust starts the cycle again.

extent to which present protective measures and processes need improvement or initiation. Typically, this "penetration testing" is performed by a trusted, yet outside supplier of such services in order to provide as realistic an appraisal as possible, uncontaminated by suggestions that inside knowledge of vulnerabilities has compromised the integrity of the process.

Design of Appropriate Countermeasures. Once there is a clear picture of the actual vulnerabilities, appropriate countermeasures are developed and presented with recommendations for implementation. And, beyond the obvious practical, financial, and procedural conditions, other factors such as the culture of the organization are taken into account when selecting the appropriate countermeasures.

Implementation of Countermeasures. Countermeasures take many forms and can range from very inexpensive yet effective (mostly procedural) to educational, physical and electronic or a combination. An important element of the countermeasures is the development of performance metrics that help to determine the efficacy of such standards.

Analysis of the Countermeasures. As surely as electricity will always seek and find the paths of least resistance, so too will business rivals that are intent on obtaining proprietary information. Once roadblocks are placed in their way, they will seek alternatives, thus changing the threat picture in accordance with the countermeasures arrayed against them. Regular testing and measurement according to the metrics established earlier help guard against false expectations of effectiveness.

Dissemination of the Analyses. Having started with the leadership that defined the corporate holdings that are needful of protection, the circle is completed with regular reporting as to the threat conditions as they relate to the protection of the firm's competitive advantages.

The ability of a firm to demonstrate that it has taken appropriate countermeasures to protect its intellectual property and other information assets—countermeasures consistent with the threat environment—plays a large part in any misappropriation litigation. Should there be a loss, and the firm is unable to show that they fully appreciate the value of their information and have

taken such reasonable measures, the chances of being able to prevail are dramatically reduced.

CCI closely mirrors the Competitive Intelligence Cycle and when the two are combined into an integrated set of protocols, as is the case with many modern, sophisticated businesses, they are referred to as Business Intelligence. See separate entries under Business Intelligence, Competitive Intelligence, Economic Espionage, and Industrial Espionage.

John A. Nolan, III

COMPETITIVE INTELLIGENCE

Competitive Intelligence (CI) is a formalized business process that seeks to advance a firm's advantages through an increased understanding of the various forces present in, and influencing, their marketplace. CI is focused on supporting the defined intelligence needs of a decision maker, characterized in modern use as "actionable." Actionable intelligence means that which arrives in time, with the requisite degree of accuracy, and absence of bias or prejudice in order to take the most effective actions.

Fundamentally, CI has its origins in national and military intelligence principles, practices, and processes which have been under development and modification for literally thousands of years. The business applications of these processes, however, have only been recognized as a discipline since the early 1980s. Large and medium sized firms across many different industrial sectors and across much of the world have established CI functions and units. Generally speaking, the more competitive and resource-intensive the industry, the greater is the likelihood that a firm will have an established CI organization. For instance, the pharmaceutical industry houses many of the benchmark units since the risks are so great. Bringing a new drug to market may require an investment of $800–900 million and take ten years from identification of the molecule to introduction of the pill.

Most CI practitioners, whether embedded within a corporate structure or employed by the numerous consulting firms around the world, follow a well-established intelligence operational cycle. The cycle is comprised of a six-phase protocol, beginning with the *requirements definition* that defines and describes what the decision-maker needs and when it is needed. Next, the requirements are distributed as *tasking* to those who are in a position to collect the information. The *collection activities* are then undertaken according to standards of the firm, the country, or other professional standards. In many parts of the world, the Code of Ethics of the Society of Competitive Intelligence Professionals (Alexandria, Virginia, www.scip.org) provides a framework for these collection activities. Once the information is collected, it is *processed and reported* either orally, in writing, or in an electronic format to those who can collate it and make sense of it. The *analysis* is undertaken in ideal circumstances by specialists with a unique understanding of issues that are separate and distinct from the understanding of those who collected the information. Analysts are responsible for the removal of biases, prejudice, and misconceptions which may have been present in the reporting prior to making judgments as to the implications of the intelligence and *disseminating* those estimates to the decision maker—thus completing the cycle.

In the U.S., for example, approximately 360 of the Fortune 500 have installed CI practices at organizational levels from the corporate (strategic) to the business unit (tactical), providing the intelligence needed by business leaders to make long- or short-range decisions, avoid—or at least mitigate—surprises, and to monitor the activities of significant players in the marketplace.

CI is not solely limited to information about competitors. Instead, the focus of virtually every sophisticated CI unit is quite wide and satisfies intelligence requirements about nearly every element that influences competitiveness. An easy way to depict the differences is to suggest one or two of the literally thousands of questions that relate to a company's ability to survive and prevail in the marketplace:

- *Competitor Intelligence*: What is our competitor doing today, or planning to do tomorrow that will take away market share from us?
- *Financial Markets Intelligence*: How do key investors view us and our competitors, against the conditions of the marketplace? How will changes in monetary practices in Country X affect our ability to operate there?
- *Legislative Intelligence*: What is the impact of current legislation that is being formulated

Competitive Intelligence Cycle

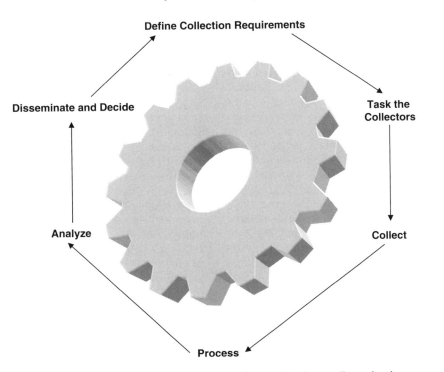

Figure 12.   Information moves in a cycle from collection to dissemination.

in State Y on our operations? What can we do to influence that legislation?

• *Regulatory Intelligence:* How are planned rules issued by a state or federal regulatory agency going to affect our industry and our company? How must we change our business processes, products, or practices in order to avoid compliance problems? What will be the financial impact of those changes?

• *Customer Intelligence*: How much money has our customer set aside for this purchase? Who will make the actual decision about buying from us? How does he make his decisions and how can we get inside his decision-cycle and influence him toward us?

• *Supplier/Vendor Intelligence*: How reliable is supplier X compared to Y? How old is his manufacturing line? How financially reliable is the firm? How effective are their quality control measures? How many delivery dates have they missed in the past five years? What are their actual capacities? How well will they safeguard our proprietary information as they manufacture the sub-components of our system?

CI can be easily and broadly differentiated from other business processes such as market research, corporate libraries, data mining, and knowledge management. CI is most often about what will happen, not what has happened, thus there is little potential for literature—whether in print or electronic form—to describe what is going to happen. Rarely is CI statistically based, such as the results of a market research focus group study might be, since there are rarely multiple sources with access to the same kind of information—indeed, there may only be one such source. Uniqueness, however, does not disqualify a single source or the information as unreliable. Indeed, the aggregation and analysis of small, perhaps even unremarkable bits of information from diverse sources—none of which may represent or provide the entire answer by itself—can represent other differentiating elements. Data, information, and intelligence are compared not only in relative amounts, but also in the processes generally associated with each.

Competitive Intelligence is also different from Industrial Espionage and Economic Espionage, which cross the lines of legal and ethical practices.

John A. Nolan, III

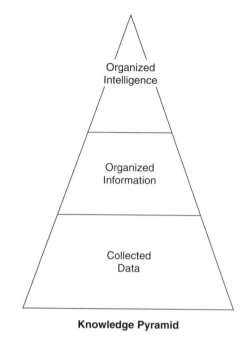

Knowledge Pyramid

Figure 13.   Mass is reduced and refined as data move up.

COMPUTER SECURITY: DISASTER RECOVERY

The focus of the disaster recovery business has been in a state of change since the mid-1980s. In past years, the industry had concentrated almost exclusively on backup capabilities that could be called into service, should a disaster occur. Now, the focus is on mitigating points of vulnerability that could result in a system loss. Finding the single point of failure, or the weakest link in the chain, is the central objective.

The disaster recovery industry has had a relatively short history that has evolved with the advent of computerization. As businesses have become dependent on systems and could not revert quickly to manual practices, it has become evident that system downtime could prove catastrophic. In the early days of disaster recovery, the emphasis was placed on establishing backup facilities; today, that is not enough.

During the past two decades, computer operations have shifted from batch processing operations to real-time environments. This shift has coincided with the concepts of "just-in-time" manufacturing and with the trend toward drastic reductions in inventory. In batch processing environments, business operations simply required a backup operating system for disaster recovery. In real-time, however, downtime is intolerable.

In contrast to the focus on backup data procedures, today's planners must analyze the total infrastructure of computer operations, identify single points of failure, and develop strategies to mitigate exposures. This requires extensive analysis.

Computer operations require power, environmentally controlled operating facilities, telecommunications services, and skilled operating personnel, among a litany of other supporting functions. Failure of one component may mean compromise of the entire system. For businesses of today, that could mean catastrophe.

Disaster Recovery Analysis

An analysis begins by defining operating components. If the focus is computer operations, which it is in most cases, this would include each component of hardware, software, database, operating personnel, telecommunications, and the supporting infrastructure of power and environmental controls. Each component must be listed and categorized based on criticality.

Possible threats are defined next and placed in categories based on the probability of occurrence. Threats include natural disasters, accidents, criminal events, and even operational threats such as mismanagement of the system or of the people operating it. Threats are correlated with each element of the system and an order of priority established, so the most vital elements are considered first. This correlation notes which threats are applicable to specific system components and which are not.

The vulnerability of each element is defined by outlining the process by which a specific element may be subject to a specific threat. Through this process, the Achilles heel of the overall operation is identified.

In the final phase of analysis, countermeasures are selected to mitigate the exposures noted in the vulnerability analysis. This involves eliminating single points of failure and providing substantial backups for critical system components that may compromise the entire operation. Exposure mitigation may be considered the single most important aspect of disaster recovery planning.

Emergency Plans

Of course, exposures can never be completely eliminated. Consequently, emergency plans are needed that define procedures for actions to take in the event of a system loss, despite the effort to mitigate exposures. These procedures can be subdivided into the following phases as outlined below.

Phase 1: Prewarning
   a.   Evacuation procedures
   b.   System shutdown procedures
   c.   Identification of shelter facilities

Phase 2: During the Event
   a.   Endurance techniques
   b.   Survival techniques

Phase 3: Immediately After the Event
   a.   First aid accommodations
   b.   System shutdown procedures
   c.   Notification of response authorities
      1.   Police
      2.   Fire
      3.   Rescue
      4.   Utility crews
   d.   Security of the scene
      1.   Control of access
      2.   Preservation of evidence
   e.   Traffic control
   f.   Removal of injured
   g.   Notification of regulatory agencies
   h.   Summon emergency management team
   i.   Implement containment strategy

Phase 4: Post-Event
   a.   Clean-up
   b.   Repair
   c.   Alternate site operation
   d.   Notification to next of kin
   e.   Legal services
   f.   Mental health services

Phase 5: Resumption of Normal Operations
   a.   Plan for return to facilities and operation restart

Data Gathering

Following is an outline of tasks essential for developing the content of the plan:

1. Conduct interviews within the organization in order to:
   a. Identify key systems.
   b. Define shutdown and evacuation requirements.
   c. Examine feasibility of alternate site operation.
   d. Identify chain of command and succession of authority.
   e. Identify likely issues that management will need to address during the event.
   f. Define regulatory agency reporting requirements.
2. Meet with response agencies (such as police, fire, rescue services, the emergency management agency, and public utilities companies) in order to:
   a. Determine the methods of interagency communication.
   b. Note who is to be called.
   c. Identify the needs of emergency response forces.
   d. Identify routes to, from, and within the site.
   e. Define utility needs.
   f. Define action steps and responsibilities for preserving the scene.
   g. Identify key safety considerations.

Formal Document. The collected data should be presented in a formal document that addresses the following issues.

Plan Coordinator. One person should be identified as responsible for preparing the plan document, communicating it to interested parties, revising and updating the plan, and organizing training to facilitate proper execution.

Management Authority. The plan should delineate the chain of command that will apply in the carrying out of plan functions, provisions should be made for succession of authority, and the duties of key figures will be described so as to leave no doubt concerning personal accountability. This portion of the plan might also take note of legal and corporate restrictions.

Security Response. This plan element defines the tasks to be performed by security, such as facilitating access by public authorities, directing traffic, controlling spectators, preserving the scene, rendering first aid, coordinating evacuation, and making notifications to emergency response personnel.

Communications. The plan should spell out the methods for establishing and maintaining communications among the various agencies involved in responding to a disaster. A number of separate networks are likely to be utilized in moving critical messages simultaneously.

Agency Notifications. The plan should include a detailed listing of agencies that are required to be notified in a disaster. The nature of the disaster will determine the agencies to be contacted and the order of contact. The agencies likely to be identified in the plan include the Federal Emergency Management Agency (FEMA), Federal Aviation Administration (FAA), Environmental Protection Agency (EPA), and Occupational Safety and Health Administration (OSHA).

Support Services. These include hazardous waste cleanup, fire salvage, office repair, cleaning, and other specialized services that may be required to remove materials left in the wake of a major disaster. This part of a plan also addresses the use of specialized professionals such as psychologists and lawyers.

Public Relations

A strategy for dealing with news media and making next of kin notifications should be included. It will assign responsibilities for prompt collection of information of interest to the media and identify the authorized spokespersons. Families of persons injured or killed in the disaster will be informed quickly, according to procedures that respect privacy needs.

Disaster Response Equipment and Facilities. The plan should identify the equipment and facilities that will be fully or partially dedicated to disaster-response activities. These include an emergency management center, first aid-triage center, salvage and storage areas, media center, and alternate operating site. The technicians who provide the related services, such as communications coordinators and paramedics, might also be mentioned in this section of the plan.

Alternate Site. The plan might include provisions for moving employees and equipment to an alternate location in order to maintain continuity of essential business operations. In this event, the company will need to include as response agencies (although not as emergency responders) the vendors who will provide the alternate site, transport to and set up equipment at the alternate site, provide temporary backup equipment, prepare the alternate site for operation, and so forth.

Resumption of Normal Operations. The plan should give guidance for resuming normal operations. Points to be considered include cleaning up, restoring utilities, ensuring that safety risks have been removed, and obtaining public authority approval for a return to business as usual.

Sal DePasquale

COOKIE AND SPYWARE BLOCKERS

The most widely used monitoring tool on the World Wide Web is the cookie. A cookie is a small file that generally holds some unique identifying information. When computer users visit cookie-powered websites a cookie file or several cookie files are downloaded into the cache of the web browser. The cookie identifies the computer user to the website during each visit.

Cookies were designed to help computer users by saving them time when they visited websites that require registration or a login process. The website developer also benefited by being able to serve the visitor faster and to track the frequency of visits and the preferences that a user has in browsing, shopping, or researching. The website is able to match the visitor with their profile information stored on a server.

Examples of benefits for both the user and an e-commerce site are functions like speedy check out or quick purchasing. The visitor saves time and the website saves resources by not having to serve up numerous pages to get an order for merchandise processed.

Many web marketing companies utilize cookies to bring targeted advertising methods

to cyberspace. These cookies can be identified by every website that uses the services of the marketing company and data can be collected over a period of time to create a profile of individual Internet users. This allows websites to selectively display banners for products or services that the visitor had expressed interest in during their visits to various websites. Cookie-blocking software packages provide a variety of functions including:

- The ability to add servers and cookies to file and designating them as always accept, accept for session-only, or reject.
- Automatically being able to accept or reject cookies received from unspecified servers without user interaction based on designation or expiration date.
- Automatically being able to accept or reject certain types of cookies without user interaction.
- Maintenance of a list of the cookies accepted and rejected from all servers for current sessions.
- Classification of cookies already stored on the computer.

In addition to cookies are several types of invasive parasitic programs designed to install and maintain themselves on a computer without the permission of the computer user. These include web bugs, spyware spybots, adware, malware, browser hijackers, and keyloggers. Web bugs are often unseen graphic files that load with a web page. Once installed they can track activities and gather information about computer usage and send that information back to a server someplace on the Internet.

There are several symptoms that indicate a computer may have been infected with parasitic code; for example, unusually slow Internet connection, computer freezing or hanging, frequent system crashes, an unusual long time to boot-up, and an unusual level of bandwidth usage. In addition, unauthorized websites may have added an icon to the desktop or added themselves to the browser's list of favorite Internet websites.

Anti-virus and firewall protection is often bypassed by parasitic software because many of these programs are small and very stealthy. In addition, manual removal is often difficult for computer users that do not have technical skills.

There are several software products on the market to protect computers against parasitic code. The annual costs for these products range from $30 to $50. Bear in mind, as with all protective products, staff time will be required to install and maintain the software. The functionality of anti-invasive software products can include:

- Automatic review and removal of all various forms of parasitic software.
- Automatic updates of the software with new threat detection profiles.
- Detection and removal of registry entries made by parasitic software.
- Interception of parasitic file downloads.
- Monitoring and logging of parasitic software that tries to install on computers.
- Quarantine of infected or suspicious files.
- Removal of objects or modules that hijack Internet browsers.
- System scanning to detect parasitic software.

Michael Erbschloe

Source Erbschloe, M. 2004. *Trojans, Worms, and Spyware: A Computer Security Professional's Guide to Malicious Code*. Boston: Butterworth-Heinemann.

DIGITAL CERTIFICATES, DIGITAL SIGNATURES, AND CRYPTOGRAPHY

Cryptography is the study and practice of protecting information by data encoding and transformation techniques. It includes means of hiding information (encryption) and means of proving that information is authentic and has not been altered from its original form (such as a digital signature).

In the physical world, a key is the device used to open or close a lock. Thus, in cryptography the information used to "lock" data to protect it is called an encryption key, a cryptography key, or sometimes just a key when the context allows it.

The primary means of cryptographic key protection is based upon pairs of very large numbers which have a special relationship to each other, whereby you encode with one number

and can only decode with the other, and vice versa. Yet you cannot figure out one number if you have the other number. These two cryptographic keys are known as a Public Key/Private Key pair, because the user makes one key public and keeps one key private. This means of protection is called Public Key cryptography, or Asymmetric Cryptography, because a different key is used to decode the information than was used to encode it. Since no secret keys are shared, public key cryptography allows two parties (or two systems) to securely communicate with each other without prior contact.

Digital Signatures

Another application of Public Key cryptography is Digital Signatures. To sign an e-mail message, a user can employ cryptographic software to perform a calculation involving the user's Private Key and the message. The result of the calculation is called a digital signature and is attached to the message. Anyone who has the user's Public Key can decode it, ensuring that the information is not altered and is indeed sent from the owner of the Private Key.

Thus, a digital signature is used to perform two types of authentication: it authenticates the sender of the message by proving who the sender was (or party to a transaction), and authenticates the information by proving that it hasn't been altered.

A digital signature is additional data that is appended to data in transit or storage. It functions similarly to a written signature to check and verify who the sender is. Second, similar to a tamper evident seal on a package, checking the digital signature also reveals whether or not the data has been altered since it was signed.

Digital Certificates and PKI

To verify a digital signature, the verifier must have access to the signer's Public Key and assurance that it corresponds to the signer's own Private Key. However, public and private key pairs are just numbers. Some scheme or strategy is necessary to reliably associate a particular person or organization to a particular key pair. The solution is the use of one or more trusted third parties to associate an identified signer with a specific public key. That trusted third party is referred to as a Certificate Authority (CA), because it issues electronic certificates known as digital certificates.

A digital certificate is a specially formatted block of data that among other things: (1) contains the certificate's serial number, (2) identifies the certificate authority issuing it, (3) names or identifies the certificate's subscriber, (4) identifies the period of time for which the certificate is valid, (5) contains the subscriber's public key, and (6) is digitally signed by the certificate authority issuing it. By digitally signing the issued certificates, the certificate authority guarantees the authenticity of the data held in them.

The publication of digital certificates is what enables two parties (or systems) to use certificates to communicate securely without prior contact. The international standard governing digital certificates is X.509, a specification for digital certificates published by the ITU-T. FIPS 201 requires X.509 certificates.

A Public Key Infrastructure (PKI) is a security management system including hardware, software, people, processes, and policies (including Certificate Authorities (CAs) and Registration Authorities (RAs), dedicated to the management of digital certificates for the purpose of achieving secure exchange of electronic information. The term PKI is also sometimes loosely used as a reference to public key cryptography.

Digital Certificate Verification

A digital certificate is no longer valid if it has expired or been revoked. There are two methods of determining if a certificate has been revoked: checking a locally stored certificate revocation list (CRL) issued by a CA, and using the online certificate status protocol (OCSP) to obtain the real-time status of the certificate.

FIPS 201 Cryptographic Keys, Digital Certificates, and Digital Signatures

Prior to FIPS 201 (the U.S. Federal Personal Identity Verification program), the use of cryptography in physical access control systems was for encryption of Ethernet network traffic (front end system to panels, front end system to workstations, and panels to readers). FIPS 201 introduces the additional elements of digital certificates and digital signatures to provide strong authentication of the card, the data elements on the card including biometric data, and also of the individual card management's system.

FIPS 201 specifies that, at a minimum, the Personal Identity Verification (PIV) Card must store one asymmetric private key called the PIV authentication key and a corresponding public key digital certificate, and perform cryptographic operations for authentication (such as "challenge and response"). The FIPS standard states that this key must only be available through the contact interface of the PIV card, and a PIN must be provided by the user before cryptographic operations can be performed. The card must hold the X.509 digital certificate for each asymmetric key on the PIV card.

FIPS 201 requires that the generation, handling, and physical security relating to all PIV cryptographic keys shall meet certain specific requirements.

Jill Allison

Source   D'Agostino, S., Engberg, D., Sinkov, A. and Bernard, R. 2005. "The Roles of Authentication, Authorization and Cryptography in Expanding Security Industry Technology," *SIA Quarterly Technical Update*.

ECONOMIC ESPIONAGE

Economic Espionage is typically practiced by professionals employed by the national intelligence services of the country where a company is domiciled. For example, a domestic French company desiring information about a competitor in another country enjoys access to the world-wide operations of the French government's intelligence services to help satisfy those information requirements.

Many, although not all, modern nations employ their intelligence services in this way. Indeed, in terms of cooperative assistance from intelligence services, countries operate across the spectrum from being wholly and actively engaged to those which keep an arms-length relationship with most businesses unless absolutely necessary for the survival of an industrial sector, to those countries (such as the United States of America) where such cooperation has a long history of being illegal and discouraged. For example, Clinton Administration attempts during the 1990s to change the laws in order to enable American firms to obtain assistance from national resources were almost universally rebuffed by companies, the Congress, and the intelligence community itself.

Most countries that do participate in such activities base their degree of cooperation on a simple premise: if economic power and influence are fundamental to the national security, embodied by its commercial and industrial interests, then it naturally follows that resources of the state should be available to assist those companies. Beyond the philosophy, there is clear economic value to using a nation's intelligence service: by comparison with the risk, the gain is enormous. The further and further behind a country is (or is becoming) technologically, the greater the temptation to use illicit means to steal the information that represents the competitive advantage that another holds.

In its simplest formulation, consider that Company A has invested $100 million in developing and bringing to market a new technology; enjoying "first-to-market" advantage, it hopes to capitalize its second generation with revenue from the first generation's dominance. Company B, in the same industry, uses its country's intelligence service to obtain the discriminating information for $500,000. Company B can use any considerable portion of the $99.5 million difference to their own Research and Development, and leapfrog Company A by bringing the second generation to market before Company A's original investment has been repaid.

In cases such as these, there is usually a clear *quid pro quo*. Not only does the intelligence service provide assistance to its companies, it also expects and typically receives the cooperation of employees of those serviced companies when they reside in or travel to other countries and can be expected to report on matters of interest.

Countries can offer a panoply of services for their domestic companies, including but not limited to the use of human assets, overhead platforms, or signals intercepts, or a combination of all three for collection. Government analysts also assist those firms in determining the accuracy and/or utility of the information obtained by the national means and resources.

Countries that subscribe to, and practice, this close linkage between their intelligence services and business interests include Russia, China, Taiwan, Korea, India, Japan, Brazil, Israel, and France.

The amount of support by foreign intelligence services to their domestic firms reached such proportions that American industry lobbied very hard in the middle of the 1990s for protection at the national level. Most companies realized that their own, organic security apparatus was overwhelmed by the complexity and sophistication of intelligence services threats to their intellectual and proprietary information; they also realized that there was little deterrent value under the civil Trade Secrets laws; or the desire or ability of local law enforcement officials to become effectively involved in any attendant criminal prosecutions that might arise from a misappropriation.

The result was the enactment of the Economic Espionage Act of 1996, which both federalized and criminalized such conduct by foreign intelligence services representatives. Under this legislation, the U.S. Justice Department initiates investigations through the federal Bureau of Investigation and any subsequent prosecutions in federal court; and with a combination of jail time and fines in the millions of dollars range.

An unintended consequence of the Act, in which the U.S. State Department's suggested that there be penalties for domestic misappropriation by one company from another, is that there have been a greatly disproportionate number of prosecutions of American individuals and firms than there have been against foreign enterprises. By 2006, of the nearly 60 cases brought, only three have been focused on foreign intelligence services.

There is frequently a direct relationship between the closeness and resulting efficacy—with the level of dedication and sophistication of counterintelligence practices. Simply, they recognize what has worked for them and wish to keep what they have from others. Thus, the aforementioned Economic Espionage Act in the USA is not alone on the world stage. Indeed, some countries such as Korea and Japan are far more draconian in their punishment provisions.

John A. Nolan, III

INDUSTRIAL ESPIONAGE

Often considered the catch-all phrase to describe intelligence operations in the business world, industrial espionage is actually differentiated on several levels from other approaches to obtaining information about another company.

Industrial espionage is typically sponsored by companies that push the envelope—either wittingly or unwittingly—past the limits of acceptable, ethical, or even legal conduct. In this regard, industrial espionage can range from "gray" to "black."

Gray operations include a variety of approaches that are considered to be on the fringe of ethical activities but which do not rise to the level of illegality. Examples include:

- Ruse interviews designed to trick employees of a target firm into providing information to an outsider by using social engineering techniques that capitalize on a range of vulnerabilities, e.g., a lack of employee sophistication, low level of security awareness, and a desire to assist. In a telephone call, the interviewer can pretend to be a fellow employee from another department of the same firm or a disgruntled customer, to name a few.
- Dumpster diving in which the information collector seeks to capitalize on the tendency of employees to simply throw documents or materials into the trash, with no expectation that anyone would attribute value to the trash. Constitutional constraints on unlawful search and seizure by law enforcement are well-known and cause popular beliefs that such activities are illegal. In fact, however, when private actors (not law enforcement officers) search or take trash, the Principle of Abandonment applies: throwing material into the trash clearly shows that the owner believes it no longer has any value and thus, taking something of no value is not a crime. While certainly unsavory and generally odiferous, dumpster diving is not illegal. Entering a company's property in order to gain access

to a dumpster may constitute criminal trespass, yet even that is compromised when a number of companies in a building or office park use a common dumpster.

Black aspects of industrial espionage are those areas which clearly move into the range of illegal conduct. Examples are:

- Bogus employees being placed inside a competitor firm for the express purpose of stealing information, plans, intentions, products, or committing sabotage.
- Hacking into computer systems to either steal information, corrupt data files, degrade a firm's ability to conduct business, or any of the other nefarious options that systems afford in modern business.
- Bribing a knowledgeable employee into providing information that is not otherwise available through legal means.
- Blackmailing or co-opting a knowledgeable individual, usually after making the individual vulnerable to blackmailing or co-option.
- Clandestine interception of communications. These can take many forms ranging from compromising a telephone to bugging conference rooms, invading videoconferences, and the like.

Industrial espionage can be found on the domestic and international levels. The usual practitioner is not in an intelligence service or someone with an intelligence background. Depending on the degree of operational intensity, industrial espionage is practiced by various actors ranging from private investigators to outright criminals. Typically, such persons are employed by aggressive, perhaps naïve, managers at lower levels of an organization; the acts are usually not commissioned or encouraged by senior management. The objectives are usually short-term and tactical as opposed to strategic issues that are the concern of people at the top of the organization. Ethical considerations are often in the eye of the beholder.

The availability of advanced technology, to even the smallest company, has made information collection possible in myriad ways on a grand scale. Many of the new and technical collection methods exist outside of the law, and methods that were once illegal are now less so. An example is the matter of aerial photography.

A 1980s Texas ruling barred handheld photography from aircraft flying over a plant. The ruling is now essentially moot because satellites routinely and legally take photographs from the air, and do so with state-of-the-art photographic equipment.

John A. Nolan, III

MANAGEMENT OF SENSITIVE INFORMATION

Information Is Expansive

Unlike other business resources, information is expansive, with limits imposable only by time and the thinking capabilities of humans. Information may age but will not deplete; it reproduces rather than diminishes. Information is compressible and transportable at very high speeds, and can impart advantages to the holder. Many work endeavors, such as research and development, education, publishing, and marketing, are very highly dependent on information.

Information Protection Requires Barriers

In ancient times the walled city was man's way of protecting himself and his property. Walls were a key defense against armies, they kept roving bands of robbers at bay, and at night, when the gate was closed, they blocked the escape of criminals. After the sack of Rome, walls became a way of life. During the next one thousand years, which we call the Middle Ages, men and their property found refuge behind walls. It was not until the Renaissance brought a period of renewed interest in art, science, and commerce that men began to venture out from their walled cities.

The ancient walled city is analogous to the modern business corporation. Starting in the middle of the last century, when computers began to play a commanding role in processing and storing information, a businessman could feel safe because information assets were behind electronic barriers inside centrally controlled equipment located within the protected confines of a computer room—sort of like a city with three walls. Then came the computer Renaissance. Many companies moved from a centrally based approach to a system of widely dispersed personal computers, which we call a LAN or local area network.

In a typical LAN, nearly every employee has a PC at his or her work station; many have company-owned PCs at home; and some employees carry portables everywhere they go. Instead of holding information at one central location, in the custody of a handful of trusted technicians, information is made available to nearly every employee. In companies where this is the case, information assets have moved out from behind protective barriers.

Information Is Costly and Important

Information is deserving of protection for at least two reasons: (1) it is costly to acquire and maintain, and (2) it is important to the success of the business enterprise. Information fuels a business and has value in much the same sense that people, physical property, and financial assets have value. Information that an enterprise assembles for making a major business decision or developing a new product may cost many millions of dollars and be absolutely essential to viability. For example, an oil exploration company can easily spend in excess of a hundred million dollars just to get to a point that allows a sensible decision to be made about where to place the drill bit. If the decision proves correct, oil producing operations are assured, and the company stands a good chance of recouping its investment many times over.

Information Is Coveted

And, like anything of value, information is coveted. When something has value, count on the certainty that someone will be looking for an opportunity to take it away. The bad guys are not thugs and common sneak thieves; they are intelligent, clever, and ruthless people such as the professional spy that steals information without the owner ever knowing it, the executive that defects to a competitor carrying a briefcase full of proprietary secrets, or the disaffected scientist that sells R&D data.

Information Has a Limited Life

Efforts to safeguard information assets in an open environment are made difficult by a host of realities. Chief among these is a recognition that a piece of information has a limited life, i.e., that at some point in time, which is usually sooner than later, the information will lose all or most of its value. Within the time frame of value, the owner of the information will want to extract from it the maximum worth possible. This means making the information available to users whose special talents can exploit it. Oftentimes the users of the information are numerous and are spread across a global landscape. In these circumstances, the information has been duplicated repeatedly and transmitted widely by a variety of communications media. During the time information is in a state of flux, the opportunities for compromise are many and diverse. Worse still, when compromise occurs it is difficult, if not impossible, to detect.

Information Is Difficult to Protect

Problems in protection are compounded when a company finds it necessary to share its information with outsiders, such as joint venture partners and contractors. As an example, a joint venture's operational information, which is routinely available to all partners, may be of a nature that if released to the public would affect stock prices, a result that might be good for some partners but not for other partners. When sharing information with contractors, two examples of exposures stand out. First is the risk that sensitive information entrusted to the contractor will leak out, a likelihood that increases when the contractor works for competitors. The second type of exposure is present when an outsourcing arrangement puts the contractor in control of a company's critical business data or of the systems that massage the data. In a like sense, the arrangement called partnering, which brings a company and a vendor into a mutually rewarding relationship, can result in both organizations sharing each other's sensitive business data.

Information Is Voluminous

Another reality is that companies are dealing in larger volumes of information than ever before. Great amounts of raw data are needed to make fully developed analyses, and the judgments that flow from them produce not just a favored recommendation but a range of options, each with its own set of variables and predicted outcomes. Of even greater moment is the reality

that the criticality of information is increasingly on the rise. Not only is there more information, but it is high-impact information.

Factor in the reality that the means of communication are changing. The fax machine, cellular telephone, electronic mail, modem, and voice answering device are examples of changes in the way companies communicate. All of these have serious security vulnerabilities. The task of protecting information is daunting to say the least.

Operations Security (OPSEC)

Operations Security (OPSEC) is the name of a program initiated and used for the most part by the Department of Defense (DOD). Due mainly to the terrorist threat, the program moved into high gear and is now generating a considerable degree of interest on the part of security professionals in the private sector. An OPSEC program differs from an information security program. Its focus is on the concealment of sensitive activities as opposed to the protection of sensitive information.

OPSEC Process

OPSEC is the process of:

- Denying to potential adversaries information about DOD capabilities and/or intentions by identifying, controlling, and protecting evidence of plans and practices related to sensitive activities.
- Analyzing unfriendly attempts to penetrate the protective shield surrounding sensitive information.
- Concealing in-house activities that if known to an adversary would have a detrimental effect on national defense.
- Identifying seemingly innocuous information exposures that if collected by an adversary over time would have a detrimental effect on national defense.
- Finding and eliminating vulnerabilities.

The attractiveness of OPSEC to CSOs is a "get tough" approach. For the business organization it means having strict information security rules, enforcing the rules and meting out punishment for violations, and making referrals to the criminal justice system for egregious offenses.

The OPSEC approach can be harnessed to three business-survival imperatives:

- Prevent loss or compromise of privately owned technology
- Prevent business competitors from learning the intentions of the organization
- Prevent terrorist groups from characterizing the organization's most critical assets and assessing weaknesses in the protection of them

Sensitive Information

Security professionals use the term "sensitive" when referring to information that has value and is protected. The main forms of sensitive information are:

- Proprietary business and technical information
- Personal data concerning applicants, employees, and former employees
- Proprietary information owned by partners and obtained through an agreement

Access to or knowledge of sensitive information is based on a need-to-know connection to job tasks. An employee whose job is to invoice vendors does not need to know the CEO's plan to spin off a subsidiary. Jobs and groups of jobs are compartmental by nature; confining sensitive information to compartments helps prevent information leaks.

Information protection is also afforded by avoiding careless talk outside the compartment, being careful on the telephone and in sending e-mail messages, placing sensitive information in secure containers when not in use, and ensuring that sensitive documents are turned over or distributed to authorized persons only.

A few simple steps can save a very big headache. For example:

- Be suspicious of unexpected messages, especially those with a teasing subject header.
- Be leery of attachments. If in doubt, don't open.
- Don't answer SPAM or forward chain letter messages.
- Don't use vacation messages that can tip off criminal opportunists.

- Close your e-mail application when it is not in use.
- Save sensitive messages in a secure folder.
- Choose a hard-to-guess e-mail password.

Classification

Organizations assign classifications to their sensitive information. The usual classification model is a three-tiered hierarchy. The names assigned to the tiers vary from organization to organization and include SECRET, RESTRICTED, CONFIDENTIAL, PRIVATE, and PERSONAL. The names are sometimes emphasized with preceding terms so that they appear, for example, as TOP SECRET or HIGHLY CONFIDENTIAL. For the purpose of discussion here, the three tiers from top to bottom are SECRET, RESTRICTED, and PRIVATE.

SECRET. This is information the unauthorized disclosure of which could cause serious damage to the organization's business. Its use and access to it are strictly limited. Examples include:

- Trade secrets
- Plans to merge, divest, acquire, sell, or reorganize
- Information that could affect the price of shares
- Information with high political or legal sensitivity
- Information prejudicial to the interests or reputation of the organization

RESTRICTED. This is information of such value or sensitivity that its unauthorized disclosure could have a substantially detrimental effect on the organization's business. Examples include:

- Marketing strategies
- Customer files
- Agreements and contracts
- Contentious or litigable matters

PRIVATE. This is information relating to employees. Examples include:

- Salaries, bonuses, and wages
- Health and medical matters
- Disciplinary actions
- Job performance

For convenience, sensitive information can be referred to in a project context, e.g., a project to construct a new building might be called Project Phoenix, and information related to that endeavor might be called Project Phoenix information. In this example, only certain types of information, such as financial data, are classified. Another project might be so hush-hush that all information relating to it is classified.

Sensitive information can also be regarded as falling under the "ownership" of a particular employee such as the originator, the person who assigned a classification to it, or the person who holds primary responsibility for putting the information to work.

Ownership carries with it a responsibility to change or remove the classification as needed. (Ownership does not mean that an employee has rights to the information.)

An important task of the CSO is to learn which information is sensitive and which is not. The CSO has to know which is which because classification is assigned to sensitive information only. The classification program will collapse of its own weight if overburdened. If all of an organization's information was declared sensitive, there would be no need for classification, and to the extent that non-sensitive information is given a classification, the effectiveness of the classification program is diminished.

The CSO's task of separating the sensitive from non-sensitive cannot be done without input from managers and supervisors. This is the case because the CSO, like all other employees, has access to sensitive information on a need-to-know basis. The CSO does not need to know where a drill bit is to be placed, only that a body of information exists concerning drilling. Using the three-tiered matrix discussed earlier, the manager or supervisor has decided if classification is merited and if so, selected the appropriate classification level. The CSO merely verifies that the process was followed and that the body of information still merits protection.

A CSO will think what would happen if particular information was to fall into unfriendly hands. A number of possible scenarios can lead the thinking process to an identification of what should be protected, the adversaries, the probable nature of attempts by adversaries to acquire the information, the exposures of the information to the hypothesized attempts, and an estimate in dollars of the value of the information.

Marking. Classified information, regardless of form, is marked, distributed, copied, mailed, transported, stored, and destroyed in accordance with established procedures. The procedure for marking a document might require every page to bear in the top right corner the word "RESTRICTED," stamped in upper case letters, red in color, and not smaller in height than one-half of an inch and not taller than one inch.

Awareness. The operation of an awareness program is within the purview of the CSO. The program is continuous, uses many forums, reaches out to employees at all levels, and emphasizes the duty of everyone to protect the organization's sensitive information. An awareness program sometimes includes an orientation session before an employee is granted access to classified information, one or more refresher sessions throughout the duration of the employee's access, and a debriefing at the time the employee's access is removed. These sessions, which are ordinarily conducted by the employee's supervisor, can include the signed acknowledgments by the employee and warnings as to personal consequences of violations.

The awareness program is also directed at preventing careless talk and release of details about plans, strategies, and other sensitive matters. Prior approval may be required when an organizational matter is to be discussed by an employee in a speech, article, or presentation.

Clean Desk Policy. A clean desk policy is the name given to a work rule that requires employees to:

- Place classified materials under lock and key when not in use. Materials of chief concern are classified correspondence, maps, photos, diskettes, and compact disks.
- Not leave keys unattended or hidden.
- Destroy unneeded classified materials.
- Switch off, disconnect, or lock PCs when not in use.

Confidentiality Agreement. This safeguard is intended to prevent unauthorized disclosure of classified information by employees, consultants, contractors, and other outside parties that have business ties to the organization. Confidentiality agreements can be crafted to apply to sensitive information generally or to certain forms of information specifically.

Non-Competition Agreement. A non-competition agreement grants protection to an employer from the unauthorized use of the employer's intellectual property by a current or former employee. It typically incorporates one or more of three basic conditions:

- Restrictions on competition by departing employees
- Definitions of what constitutes property that the employer can legally protect from use by others
- Requirements that employees are obligated to cooperate with the employer in efforts to protect its intellectual property

Proprietary Information

Proprietary information is information owned by a company or entrusted to it that has not been disclosed publicly and has value. Information is considered proprietary when:

- It is not readily accessible to others.
- It was created by the owner through the expenditure of considerable resources.
- The owner actively protects the information from disclosure.

Very critical forms of proprietary information are intellectual properties. Most countries recognize and grant varying degrees of protection to four intellectual property rights: patents, trademarks, copyrights, and trade secrets.

Patents. These are grants issued by a national government conferring the right to exclude others from making, using, or selling the invention within that country. Patents may be given for new products or processes. Violations of patent rights are known as infringement or piracy.

Trademarks. These are words, names, symbols, devices, or combinations thereof used by manufacturers or merchants to differentiate their goods and distinguish them from products that are manufactured or sold by others. Counterfeiting and infringement constitute violations of trademark rights.

Copyrights. These are protections given by a national government to creators of original literary, dramatic, musical, and certain other intellectual works. The owner of a copyright has the exclusive right to reproduce the copyrighted work, prepare derivative works based upon it, distribute copies, and perform or display it publicly. Copyright violations are also known as infringement and piracy.

Trade Secrets. These can be formulas, patterns, compilations, programs, devices, methods, techniques, and processes that derive economic value from not being generally known and not ascertainable except by illegal means. A trade secret violation in the vocabulary of the law is a misappropriation resulting from improper acquisition or disclosure. The key elements in a trade secret are the owner's maintenance of confidentiality, limited distribution, and the absence of a patent.

The Paris Convention is the primary treaty for the protection of trademarks, patents, trade names, utility models, and industrial designs. Established in 1883, the convention is the oldest of the international bodies concerned with the protection of intellectual properties. It is based on reciprocity, i.e., it grants the same protections to member states as those granted to its own nationals, and provides equal access for foreigners to local courts to pursue infringement remedies.

Data Protection

Data are a valuable corporate asset. Consider these examples:

- In the minerals extraction industry, finding ores depends on data. It is no exaggeration to say that before a single shovel is placed into the ground, hundreds of millions of dollars will have been spent collecting and interpreting seismic and other scientific data.
- Hotels routinely build patron-oriented information databases that enable them to provide personalized service.
- Retailers collect data to help their managers monitor the flow of products moving from manufacturing plants to warehouses, stores, and ultimately purchasers. The process makes sure that sellable items are on

the shelves in the right stores, at the right time, and in the right quantities.

- Transportation firms routinely track movement of packages, even to the extent of allowing customers to access the information.
- Manufacturers have refined data-dependent "just in time" techniques to ensure that source materials reach the beginning of the production line not a day sooner or later than required and that the final products leave the plant already sold.

Today's successful organizations are very competent at collecting and making good use of data. Only a few, however, are fully competent in protecting their data assets. These are growing in value and volume. In some circles information moves from owner to owner, not unlike the way money moves in financial markets. Three dynamics seem to be at play: knowledge has become an economic resource, information technology is expanding, and the number of people familiar with information technology is growing by leaps and bounds.

Knowledge is emerging as an economic resource. Production in the United States is moving away from a dependence on capital, natural resources, and blue-collar labor. One hundred years ago, the Nation's wealth derived from oil, coal, minerals, ores, and farmlands. Today's wealth derives from the creation and use of knowledge, and the raw materials that create knowledge are in the form of data.

A second dynamic is information technology. New computer hardware and software come on line every day in dazzling arrays. All functions and sub-functions of business are addressed in the information technology marketplace. The Internet, company intranets, and multi-company extranets open doors wide for the collection and dissemination of huge volumes of information. Critical data, such as client lists and strategic plans, are moved around the globe in the blink of an eye by e-mail, fax, and cellular phone.

A third dynamic is the increasing ability of the average employee to work competently and comfortably with data. Add to this a very large and rapidly growing new employee class called information workers. In some companies, the entire workforce consists of people who work only with data.

Data protection is a challenge not easily met. For example, how does an organization balance the need to use data and the need to protect it from harmful disclosure? The clash between use and protection is problematic. An operations manager will consider data an essential resource to be fully exploited, therefore requiring it to be accessible at all times. He/she will say, "If data can't be used, our bottom line suffers." The manager is right; the value of the data is directly related to its use.

The CSO may agree with the operations manager but feel compelled to point out: "If our data are damaged, lost or compromised, the company may fail." The CSO's concern appears valid in light of at least one study. An insurance company found that 40 percent of companies that experienced major data loss as the result of disaster (e.g., fire, flood, hurricane, and terrorist action) never resumed business operations and a third of the companies that initially recovered went out of business within two years.

The CSO can enhance data protection by following commonsense suggestions:

- Stay on top of the issue
- Keep pace with data-related technology, not necessarily at the detail level, but certainly at a level that permits a clear understanding of the risks
- Look for countermeasures that take advantage of new techniques and leading edge technology
- Maintain a frank and ongoing dialogue with data managers about risk avoidance, and don't be preachy or harp on a shortcoming unless you have a solution in mind
- Spread the word among supervisory employees that data protection is their responsibility

John J. Fay

PROPRIETARY INFORMATION: A PRIMER FOR PROTECTION

In 1780, a drunken pattern maker working for James Watt, the inventor of the steam engine, bragged at the local pub that circular motion could be obtained from a reciprocating engine. When challenged, the man chalked a rough sketch on the bar top. James Pickard, a button maker,

NON-DISCLOSURE AGREEMENT

Effective Date:_____

Participant: _____

In order to protect certain confidential information that may be disclosed by Discloser ("DISCLOSER") to the "Participant" above, they agree that:

1. The confidential information disclosed under this Agreement is described as:_____
   _____
   _____

2. The Participant shall use the confidential information received under this Agreement for the purpose of:____
   _____

3. The Participant shall protect the disclosed confidential information by using the same degree of care, but no less than a reasonable degree of care, to prevent the unauthorized use, dissemination, or publication of the confidential information as the Participant uses to protect its own confidential information of a like nature.

4. The Participant shall have a duty to protect only that confidential information which is (a) disclosed by DISCLOSER in writing and marked as confidential at the time of disclosure, or which is (b) disclosed by DISCLOSER in any other manner and is identified as confidential at the time of the disclosure and is also summarized and designated as confidential in a written memorandum delivered to the Participant within 30 days of the disclosure.

5. This Agreement imposes no obligation upon the Participant with respect to confidential information that becomes a matter of public knowledge through no fault of the Participant.

6. The Participant does not acquire intellectual property rights under this Agreement except the limited right of use set out in paragraph 2 above.

7. DISCLOSER makes no representation or warranty that any product or business plans disclosed to the Participant will be marketed or carried out as disclosed, or at all. Any actions taken by the Participant in response to the disclosure of confidential information by DISCLOSER shall be solely at its risk.

8. The Participant acknowledges and agrees that the confidential information is provided on an AS IS basis.

   DISCLOSER MAKES NO WARRANTIES, EXPRESS OR IMPLIED, WITH RESPECT TO THE CONFIDENTIAL INFORMATION AND HEREBY EXPRESSLY DISCLAIMS ANY AND ALL IMPLIED WARRANTIES OF MERCHANTABILITY AND FITNESS FOR A PARTICULAR PURPOSE. IN NO EVENT SHALL DISCLOSER BE LIABLE FOR ANY DIRECT, INDIRECT, SPECIAL, OR CONSEQUENTIAL DAMAGES IN CONNECTION WITH OR ARISING OUT OF THE PERFORMANCE OR USE OF ANY PORTION OF THE CONFIDENTIAL INFORMATION.

9. Upon DISCLOSER's written request, the Participant shall return to DISCLOSER or destroy all written material or electronic media and the Participant shall deliver to DISCLOSER a written statement signed by the Participant certifying same within 5 days.

10. The parties do not intend that any agency or partnership relationship be created between them by this Agreement.

11. All additions or modifications to this Agreement must be made in writing and must be signed by both parties.

12. This Agreement is made under and shall be construed according to the laws of the State of Massachusetts.

DISCLOSER

_____
Authorized Signature

_____
Name

_____
Title

PARTICIPANT

_____
Authorized Signature

_____
Name

_____
Title

_____
Address

Figure 14.   This is an example of an agreement between a "discloser" (the owner of confidential information) and a "participant" (such as a partner, contractor, or vendor).

realized the possibilities and obtained a patent ahead of Watt. The case was eventually heard in the courts, and Pickard's claim was upheld, although there was no doubt that Watt was the inventor. This early example supports the security manager's often stated thesis that proprietary information is subject to compromise when protective measures are not in place or not being followed. The loss of proprietary information can have a direct relationship to the bottom line, and when loss is severe it can mean the difference between success or failure of the organization.

Legal scholars tell us that in order to recover damages resulting from the theft of proprietary information, it must be demonstrated that the owner:

- Clearly regarded and identified the information as proprietary in nature
- Had a clear policy that required employees to treat the stolen information as proprietary
- Actively took steps to protect the information

A first step, then, is to identify the genuinely critical information. Too often, the more sensitive critical information is ignored while costly measures are directed at protecting information that has little value. A rigorous approach is appropriate when determining what types of information are worth safeguarding.

A good way to start is to think what would happen if particular information was to fall into unfriendly hands. A number of possible scenarios can lead the thinking process to an identification of what should be protected, the adversaries, the probable nature of attempts by adversaries to acquire the information, the exposures of the information to the hypothesized attempts, and an estimate in dollars of the value of the information.

This thinking process asks probing questions that relate to criticality and vulnerability. What information, in what form, is critical to the company or to a key operation? How much of that information is vulnerable to exploitation? In what ways is the information vulnerable and to whom? What is the worth of the information, what are the replacement costs and the costs of lost business opportunity? How much is the company willing to spend to protect information?

The answers will not be arrived at easily. They will emerge only after key managers have been interviewed, pertinent business data have been collected and analyzed, and an estimate made of threats and threat capabilities.

Information Classifications

When the truly sensitive information has been differentiated from non-sensitive information, an understanding of it will be helped by defining it in one or a very few categories and assigning to each category a descriptive designator. The designators can be anything, except that companies involved in safeguarding government classified information are not authorized to utilize the government's designators, i.e., TOP SECRET, SECRET, and CONFIDENTIAL, or any combination thereof, e.g., "Company Confidential."

In setting up a classification scheme there will be a temptation to keep it simple, which is certainly sensible, but the aim for simplicity should not go so far as to dictate that every form of sensitive information will be placed in a single classification. If one looks at the sum of all sensitive information residing in a business organization, at least two major groups stand out: that which deals with purely business matters and that which deals with matters relating to employees on a personal level. Thus, a two-level system would be a good choice, especially since it would be relatively easy to differentiate between business information and personal information.

If we look, however, at the business information category we may see that certain types of information (e.g., trade secrets) are clearly more important than others. The information that we perceive to have a lesser sensitivity may still be too sensitive to exclude from protection. Thus, a three-level system may be a better choice than the one- or two-level systems.

Systems that use a single classification level tend to be inflexible, and those that use more than two classification levels tend to be complex and difficult to manage. If there is a need for security protections that cannot be provided within the organization's existing system, the answer may be to use code names, such as Project X or Operation A, to denote the special protections that apply to those very limited groups of information applicable to the project or operation.

Designations and definitions for a three-level scheme might be as follows:

ABC SENSITIVE. Information that, if revealed in any manner to unauthorized persons, could unquestionably damage the operational, competitive, or financial position, or public image of the company or any other party to which the company owes a duty of protection. Examples include production figures, takeover or merger plans, litigation strategies, trade secrets and formulas, and marketing plans.

ABC RESTRICTED. Information that, if disclosed in an unauthorized manner, would be prejudicial to the interests of the company or which would cause embarrassment to or difficulty for the company. This category of information would include information of commercial value, or which is subject to legal or confidential agreement, or contains controversial or contentious views. Examples include financial statements, bid proposals, succession plans, and reports of investigation.

ABC PRIVATE. Information that is private to the individual and is only to be opened by the addressee. Examples include personal health reports, salary data, and performance ratings.

Proprietary Information Program

The authority for administering protection to information is derived from policy, that is, a statement of management. A policy will state the business necessity for information protection, the goals and objectives of the policy, the means for achieving the goals and objectives, and will identify the entities and positions affected by the policy. A policy is broad, provides direction, and sets a tone. A policy is carried out by directives, commonly referred to as procedures, that are much more specific and detailed. The activities generated by the policy and the procedures can be called a program; in this case, a proprietary information program. The major elements of the program could include the following:

Access. Decisions will need to be made as to the entitlements or privileges of access. Will access be limited to the need to know or will there be some flexibility in making proprietary information accessible for some other reason? Choices on access may not be controllable if the information falls within the purview of the National Industrial Security Program. In this case, that proprietary information to which some recipients do not have a need to know should be placed in an addendum that can be protected in the proprietary information program.

How will access rights be documented and how often will they be reviewed? Will job applicant and employee screening be a decision point in granting access? A consideration will be the reality that the likelihood of compromise increases as the number of persons having access increases. On the other hand, information is valuable to the organization to the extent it is used. A balance must be struck between the protection of information and the use of it.

Accountability. The program may impose accountability on persons and on supervisors of persons. Receipts, log books, a numbering system, and periodic inventories may be instituted for all or just the more sensitive categories. A missing item should automatically trigger an investigation, a report of investigative findings, and recommendations to prevent recurrence.

Classification and Declassification. Who will have classification authority? The choices can be the originator of the information, the head of the department in which the information originated, a manager one level above the originating department, a classification of information coordinator, a classification team representing a number of organizational interests, and so on. For reasons of stability and continuity, the classification authority should be vested in positions as opposed to persons because positions tend to be constant whereas persons are subject to attrition and turnover.

Other issues to be settled are whether or not classification authority can be delegated; and what criteria are to be used in determining if classification is warranted and, if so, determining the appropriate classification level. In this latter regard, strict rules should be in force to prevent non-sensitive information from being classified and sensitive information from being assigned inappropriately high classifications.

Declassification should be automatic when the information is no longer sensitive. The same mechanisms in place to apply classifications would be correct for removing them. Periodic review of classified holdings can help in purging materials that should no longer be subject to special handling and control. A related consideration is downgrading and upgrading of classifications. The management may find it helpful to lower or raise classifications relative to changes in sensitivity.

Communications and Transmissions. The unnecessary distribution of proprietary information outside the circle of those members of staff directly concerned with it wastes time and effort, and leads inevitably to compromise and possible damage to the organization's interests. For this reason, the distribution of proprietary information must be kept as low as possible. This can be helped by circulating one copy among the essential addressees, using the established transmission controls (e.g., receipting, numbering, marking, sealing, double-enveloping, and encrypting) suitable to the classification, rather than by distributing to each addressee a separate copy.

Detailed instructions should be prepared and followed with respect to the distribution of proprietary information via mail channels within the organization, postal and non-postal channels outside of the organization, electronic mail, telex, facsimile, and computer systems that communicate with one another.

Computer Systems. Organizations are increasingly dependent upon computer systems, and the data these systems store, process, and transmit can be of vital importance. The policy and practices for protecting proprietary information will need to reflect the differences in computer systems, which can range from small and simple desktop devices to large and complex mainframe equipment.

Protection is more than just physically safeguarding the hardware, software, and data storage media; it involves backup and recovery, and passwords for accessing files and moving through protected computer gateways and networks.

The manner of protecting computer-related proprietary information can also be influenced by data protection legislation. Obtaining protection under a law designed to protect owner rights might require the owner to register or to meet standards concerning computer access,

data retrieval, and storage. This can vary between jurisdictions, therefore a review by the company's legal function would be in order.

Destruction. The general rule is to destroy classified documents by burning, shredding, or pulping when no longer required. Printing ribbons, cassette tapes, microfiche, microfilm, and the like should be destroyed as efficiently as documents. With proper equipment, destruction can be done entirely in-house, it can be contracted to an outside vendor (whose integrity should be verified), or by a combination of both approaches. Generally speaking, the more sensitive categories are destroyed in-house while less sensitive proprietary information is destroyed by vendors (if volume is an issue).

Education and Awareness. The proprietary information policy must be clear and unambiguous. It must be thoroughly announced when initiated and be continuously reinforced thereafter. The methods for developing awareness can include orientations at time of hire, formal initial training, refresher training, newsletters, posters, and verbal reminders by supervisors at meetings and in discussions with subordinates.

Enforcement. The protection of the proprietary information program will be crippled when it does not have a means for enforcing policy and taking action against violators. Those persons given enforcement responsibilities must accept them, must be able to spot violations, must be able to intervene to correct the violations, and must be able to document the violations and refer them to management for the appropriate disciplinary action. Disciplinary actions should correspond to the severity of the violation.

Legal Review. The policy and implementing procedures should be reviewed initially and periodically by legal counsel to ensure that the program protects ownership rights to proprietary information and that liabilities to the organization are not created by the manner of administering the program.

Management Support. The program can be only as good as the support it receives from management. Support is evidenced when management treats proprietary information according to the rules followed by other employees, affirms enforcement and disciplinary actions, and speaks in support of information protection. For the program to succeed, enforcement must be effective; and for enforcement to be effective, management must be entirely supportive.

Marking. The practice of marking can include applying to the sensitive material a stamp or legend that identifies the classification, a number or code, or other distinctive mark; placing a classified document into a specially marked folder or covering the front page of the document with a specially marked cover sheet; and numbering the pages of the document. Related to marking is the preparation of classified documents for transmittal by using a return receipt method, inserting inner envelopes within outer envelopes, and sealing envelopes and packages with tamper-resistant and tamper-revealing tape.

A stamp or legend should be applied regardless of format, i.e., documents, drawings, transparencies, film, or tape. It should be carefully constructed as to form and legal content to ensure no misunderstanding about ownership.

Non-Disclosure Agreements. Employees, contractors, and others who will have access to proprietary information in the normal course of their employment should be required at time of hire (and periodically thereafter) to sign an agreement pledging them to not violate the organization's rules regarding proprietary information. The agreement may relate to protection of such information generally and/or it may relate to a particular kind of information, such as work on a research project.

When a signatory to an agreement leaves employment, a debriefing is made to remind the individual of non-disclosure obligations that may continue. It is helpful at the debriefing to obtain a signed acknowledgment of the continuing obligations. Implied in this step is the prospect of legal action for a failure to comply.

Policy and Procedures Review. A review of the policy and its associated procedures should be made at regular intervals to bring them in line with changes that may have occurred since the policy and procedures were first written or last reviewed. Changes can be forced upon the program by external forces, such as the enactment of a law, or by internal forces, such as a major shift in the management's philosophy.

Releases of Information. The disclosure of proprietary information through the press, radio, television, publications, teaching, public speaking, and the like may be permitted by policy providing, of course, that permission is obtained in advance.

Requests for releases of information should be channeled to a knowledgeable person or designated office so that a review can be made of the information to be released. The information is likely to be in the form of financial and operating reports, technical papers, and promotional materials for use at trade shows and seminars.

Reproduction. Unsupervised copying machines present an opportunity for the unauthorized reproduction of proprietary information. Reasonable steps should be taken to guard against improper use of copying equipment. When proprietary information is being copied according to the existing rules, a responsible member of the department charged with protection of the information should oversee the copying operation to ensure that no extra copies have been left on the machine or in trash bins nearby. Other questions come into play: Should subcontractors be hired to reproduce proprietary information? Who can approve reproduction? Should in-house copying be done in one or a few designated areas?

Storage. Generally speaking, proprietary information not in use is stored in containers that correspond to their classification levels as established in the company's proprietary information policy. For example, materials with the highest classification might be stored in a steel safe fitted with a combination lock, materials in the second highest classification stored in a metal filing cabinet fitted with a locking bar, and materials in the lowest classification stored in a locked desk or credenza. The composition and construction of storage containers can be adjusted in relation to whether the facility is protected around the clock by roving security officers or whether the facility is equipped with an intrusion-detection system.

For large volumes of proprietary information, such as might be the case in an organization involved in research, a central library may be appropriate. The library holdings might be recorded on computers, and check out of files by authorized users might be managed by a computer-assisted technique, such as bar coding.

Lonnie R. Buckels and
Robert B. Iannone

(Note: Since co-authoring this article, Lonnie Buckels passed away.)

TECHNICAL SURVEILLANCE COUNTERMEASURES INSPECTIONS

Intense competition and rapidly evolving markets are just a few of the external forces that are changing the ways we do business. Upper managers are pushing decision situations down the corporate ladder to operational managers, the operational managers are spread across large expanses of geography, and the decisions they make are based on great amounts of detail pulled from many centers of expertise. Businesses are working hard to generate meaningful information, to open the information to greater numbers of key players, and to maintain a working dialogue with affected groups in widely separated places.

Business information, including the most sensitive possessed by an organization, is valuable to the extent it is put to work. Although a security manager would like sensitive information to be constantly kept under lock and key, the reality is that information exists to be used. Further, in a fast-track environment many types of information will have a relatively short life span, meaning that it must be put to advantage fairly quickly in order to wring value from it.

The security dilemma is that when information is in the process of being used, with attendant value flowing from such use, it is most vulnerable to compromise. The attendant loss flowing from compromise can be many hundreds of times greater than the utilitarian value attached to the moment of use. This is the problem and the challenge to the security manager.

When is sensitive information at greatest risk? Experience tells us that those who are determined to acquire someone else's secrets will focus on two opportunities: when secrets are brought into the open for discussion, such as at a conference, and when they are transmitted from one place to another, such as messages across an electronic network. In short, sensitive information is at risk when it is being communicated.

The risk is considerably heightened when the business sphere is global. The dollar stakes are higher and political aims are often intertwined. We see, for example, the extraordinary ambitions of Eastern Bloc countries and former Soviet republics to establish business ties with the non-Communist world. The newcomers to Western-style democracy are discovering that capitalism is fueled by technology and until they develop a technological base and become producers and suppliers instead of consumers, they will be junior partners in the economic alliances they wish to forge.

A picture can be drawn that the American business sector, situated as a major repository of technology, is a natural target for those who desperately need technology to become competitive but lack the time and the resources to develop it on their own. An era of industrial espionage on a global scale is being ushered in, and the United States is among the few who have the greatest to lose.

The communications networks that support international commerce are notoriously vulnerable to surreptitious attack, and although efforts have been undertaken by governments to establish some modicum of secure transmissions, the principal protection must come from the network users. Self-protection has even more validity with respect to sensitive information disclosed at conferences and meetings. The owner of the information is the exclusive protector.

This section discusses a form of self-protection called the TSCM inspection, that is, making an organized search for technical surveillance devices. The places of search are typically at corporate offices and off-site meeting places. They include at the corporate offices the chief executive officer's suite, executive conference and dining rooms, the telecommunications center, and the telephone switching room, and off site the search activity might be of the facilities at a resort hotel where a senior management meeting has been scheduled. Findings from the inspection become the basis for taking steps to counter actual or potential surveillance attempts.

A handful of major corporations retain on staff one or a few technicians whose primary duties involve making TSCM inspections. The technicians are usually highly trained and are supplied with an array of electronic sensing equipment. Most companies, however, choose to obtain the inspection service from a TSCM provider. The guidance here is applicable to either situation, although written for the security manager who engages a provider.

The first contact made by the security manager to the TSCM provider should be via a communications medium separate from the site that is to be inspected. The idea is to not disclose to those targeting you that you are about to inspect the phone line or area that has been compromised.

The TSCM provider will want certain details in advance of the inspection. For example:

- The number of phones, identity of manufacturer, and model numbers
- The number and size of rooms
- The location of rooms relative to each other
- The number of floors and buildings involved
- The type of ceiling, for example, fixed or moveable
- The types of audiovisual and communications devices, computers, and other special electronic equipment on site
- The forms of electronic communications and networks in use at the place to be inspected, including local area networks, microwave links, and satellite teleconferencing facilities

The security manager should expect the TSCM provider to supply all equipment required to carry out a comprehensive inspection. The equipment used should be the products of manufacturers that are recognized by TSCM professionals. The following described pieces of equipment should be expected of any TSCM provider selected for consideration:

- Time domain reflectometer capable of evaluating telephone systems cables, terminals and equipment utilized by the telecommunications system to be examined
- Tuneable receiver or spectrum analyzer with sufficient sensitivity to be capable of detecting extremely low powered devices and continuous coverage from 10 kilohertz to 21 gigahertz and a capability to analyze power lines, and provide a panoramic visual display of any video signal present, with a capability to extend frequency cov-

erage as may be required by circumstances. Older equipment with frequency coverage that does not extend coverage to 5 gigahertz and above is obsolete to address current and evolving threats.

- Non-linear junction detector for detecting hidden tape recorders, non-operating transmitters, and remotely controlled transmitters. This instrument can also aid in detecting devices that use transmission techniques that go beyond the frequency range of countermeasures receivers.

Thermal imaging equipment for thermal signature spectrum analysis is used for locating operating video and audio transmitters though ceiling tiles and sheet rock walls by detecting their thermal (heat) signature. Additionally this methodology can help detect differences in ceiling and wall construction with the potential to indicate current or previous placement of pin-hole cameras, microphones, etc. Thermal imaging equipment can also help evaluate AV systems components to insure system components are not powered up when the system is deactivated. Thermal imaging equipment utilized must have sufficient sensitivity to resolve thermal signatures of eavesdropping devices through standard sheet rock walls.

TSCM technicians must be thoroughly grounded in countermeasures work, be current in their knowledge of state-of-the-art equipment, and be schooled and experienced in telephone systems to be examined. All detected signals must be identified as either legitimate or suspect. The source of a legitimate signal might, for example, be an FM broadcast station. A suspect signal would be one that is found to emanate from the area being inspected and cannot be attributed to a legitimate source.

Electronic emissions from computers, communications equipment, and teleconferencing facilities should be evaluated to determine their vulnerability to interception. The TSCM provider must be sufficiently competent to both detect readable emissions and formulate sensible, cost-effective recommendations to prevent exposure of sensitive data to unauthorized parties.

Telephones and telephone lines within the area under inspection should be examined with a time domain reflectometer, a TSCM audio-amplifier, and other specialized analyzers as required. These instruments check for compromises to telephone cables and terminals as well as devices that allow listening of conversations over the telephone and within the office or area nearby, even when the phone is not in use. Telephone satellite terminals and frame rooms, as well as station and distribution cables in the areas of concern should be inspected. Telephone systems should be evaluated for potential programming problems.

A thorough physical search should be made, with particular attention to areas adjoining rooms where sensitive communications occur. The walls between the rooms require careful inspection, and exiting wires need to be examined, including in some cases, electrical testing of wires for audio signals. Ceilings, radiators, ducts, electrical outlets and switches, picture frames, furniture, lamp fixtures, and plants all deserve the TSCM technician's attention.

All walls, ceilings, and furniture need to be evaluated with thermal imaging equipment to detect heat signatures from operating eavesdropping devices as well as differences in wall or ceiling density that may indicate current or previous pinhole camera, microphone or other device placement. All AV equipment needs to be evaluated to insure that powered down systems do not have components that have been compromised to remain on picking up room conversations that may be routed out of the area of concern.

Selected objects, such as desks, tables, chairs, and sofas, can be examined with a non-linear junction detector. This instrument uses a low-power microwave beam to detect energy reflected from electronic components such as diodes, transistors, and integrated circuits. These components are integral to radio transmitters, tape recorders, and other eavesdropping devices. Also, microwave transmitters, remotely activated transmitters, and transmitters that operate on infrared and ultrasonic principles can be spotted with a non-linear junction detector.

At the conclusion of the inspection, the TSCM provider should meet with the security manager to verbally discuss the work performed, the findings, and the recommendations. A fully detailed written report should be submitted within 10 days.

Safeguarding proprietary information is a concern for all companies of substance. TSCM inspections can be a security manager's tool for reducing the organization's exposure to loss or compromise of valuable information as well as providing assurance to management, customers, partners, and regulators concerning their information protection efforts.

Richard J. Heffernan

WEBSITE BLOCKING SOFTWARE

There are several good reasons to block certain types of websites. Pornography websites, for example, are notorious for planting web bugs on the computers of people that visit sites. Other types of sites have been blamed for spreading worms and viruses including many websites in Russia and China. Other websites have been known to collect information about visitors by placing spyware on their computers and then selling that information to marketing companies.

Many organizations have had problems with employees visiting pornographic websites during working hours. There have been situations where this behavior has resulted in sexual harassment lawsuits being filed by female employees.

Although there are many good reasons to use website blockers there can also be unintended consequences for using blocking software. One of the more famous incidents involved blocking websites that had the word breast on any of the pages. This resulted in dozens of websites offering information about breast cancer being blocked.

The technology that supports the popular website blockers and Internet filters that parents use to keep their kids from visiting inappropriate websites, such as those offering pornographic images, has found its way into many organizations. Website blocking software is relatively inexpensive and can be installed on a computer for as little as $30 per year. Bear in mind, however, that installation and maintenance does require staff time which can drive up the per computer costs rather dramatically.

Website blockers allow system administrators to block websites in a number of ways including:

- Setting blocking preferences on specific categories.
- Blocking websites by creating a list of allowed or blocked sites.
- Checking for offensive text based words and phrases.

The Internet usage patterns of employees can be tracked and recorded in an event log that keeps a list of websites that each user visited or attempted to visit. This information can be reviewed by supervisors or IT staff. Website blocking software packages offer several features that make administration easier and less time consuming including:

- Filters and lists can be updated automatically on a subscription basis.
- Supervisors or other designated personnel can be authorized to override blocked websites.
- Administration functions and responsibilities can be delegated and assigned.
- Many products have an easy to use web-based interface.
- Administrators can create custom categories of websites to be blocked.
- Filters can be set for specific users or groups just like file access is set.
- Filters can be set to be turned off or on based on a schedule for times of the day or days of the week.
- Blocking functions can be set to a monitor only mode and provide a warning to users about the appropriateness of the website they are visiting.
- Some products support several languages including English, French, Italian, Spanish, Danish, Swedish, German, Dutch, Portuguese, and Japanese.

Website blockers and content filters generally provide administrators with a wide variety of reports to analyze web surfing activities and e-mail usage. Reports can be provided in a format that can be viewed on a computer screen or printed. Administrators can use pre-configured reports or customize their own reports. Some products allow reports to be produced on-demand or administrators can be scheduled to run during off-peak hours and then can be e-mailed to designated recipients in various file formats. The content of reports can include the following items:

- AOL Chat Rooms and IRC chat usage
- AOL Instant Messenger, MSN Instant Messenger, Yahoo Messenger usage
- Attachments that are viewed or opened
- Bandwidth consumption by user or time-of-day
- Blocked activities by category or with extensive detail
- Blocked connections
- Filtering categories by user or time-of-day
- Filtering modes by user or time-of-day
- FTP requests and session details
- Hotmail, Yahoo email, AOL Internet e-mail, NetZero web-based e-mail, ATT Worldnet web based e-mail, and Netscape web based e-mail usage
- Kazaa & Kazaa Lite, Gnucleus, Limewire, and other peer to peer system usage
- Microsoft Exchange usage
- Most active users
- Most popular file types, FTP sites, newsgroups, and secure websites
- Newsgroups participation
- Reports for usage by individuals, departments, or other groups
- SMTP/POP3 e-mail usage
- Specific URLs visited
- The name of all files downloaded using peer to peer systems
- The text of all searches conducted within peer to peer systems
- The total number of visits to specific websites
- Top 10 blocked users
- Top sites requested by user or time-of-day
- Visits to secure websites

Michael Erbschloe

Source   Erbschloe, M. 2004. *Trojans, Worms, and Spyware: A Computer Security Professional's Guide to Malicious Code.* Boston: Butterworth-Heinemann.

IV: Investigation

ARSON

In most types of crime, an investigation will follow the known fact that a crime was committed. Arson is an exception. An investigation must take place before it is even known that arson occurred.

Arson Motives

Willful and malicious intent is an essential element in proving the offense of arson. The establishment of a motive adds weight to evidence tending to prove intent. Common motives are fraud, crime concealment, revenge, jealousy, spite, sabotage, intimidation, suicide, excitement, and pyromania.

Proving the element of intent in a building fire can be advanced when the following questions are answered through the inquiries of the investigator:

- Were alarms or communications systems tampered with?
- Was property removed prior to the fire?
- Were interior and exterior doors and windows open or closed?
- Was the ventilating system tampered with?
- Was the fire department called immediately?
- Were flammable materials in the building?
- Was internal fire fighting equipment in working condition?
- Was there any evidence of tampering?

In respect to proving intent regarding an automobile fire, the investigator needs to address these questions:

- Were payments being made regularly?
- Was the lien holder or finance company about to repossess the vehicle?
- Was the vehicle the subject of a domestic problem, such as divorce?
- Was the owner dissatisfied with the vehicle?
- Were accessories removed from the vehicle prior to the fire?
- Did the owner or prior owner have an insurable interest?

Accelerant Indicators

The detection, recovery, and analysis of fire accelerants are of major concern to the arson investigator. The areas most likely to contain residue of liquid fire accelerants are floors, carpets, and soil, since, like all liquids, they run to the lowest level. In addition, these areas are likely to have the lowest temperatures during the fire and may have had insufficient oxygen to support the complete combustion of the accelerant. Porous or cracked floors may allow accelerants to seep through to the underlying earth. Other places where accelerants may be discovered are on the clothes and shoes of the suspect.

Because scientific laboratory equipment cannot always be brought to the scene of a suspected arson, the investigator must rely upon a personal ability to detect the possible presence of accelerants through smell and sight. The sensitivity of the human nose to gasoline vapor appears to be on the order of 1 part per 10 million. As such, the nose is as sensitive as any of the currently available vapor detection equipment. Experienced arson investigators will agree that their noses are as sensitive to gasoline as the equipment available to them. However, not all flammable liquids are gasoline. A factor called olfactory fatigue and the possibility of an arsonist using a strong smelling substance to mask the presence of an accelerant are further reasons why a determination of arson should not rest solely upon detection by smell.

In addition to the sensitivity of the human nose, there are certain visual indicators of arson. These indicators reflect the effects on materials of heating or partial burning, which are used to indicate various aspects of a fire such as rate of development, temperature, duration, time of occurrence, presence of flammable liquids, and points of origin. The interpretation of burn indicators is a principal means of determining the causes of fires. Interpretation of burn patterns is a most common method of establishing arson.

Alligator Effect. This is the checkering of charred wood, giving it the appearance of alligator skin. Large, rolling blisters indicate rapid, intense heat, while small, flat alligator marks indicate long, low heat.

Crazing of Glass. This indicator is seen in the formation of irregular cracks in glass due to rapid, intense heat. Crazing suggests a possible fire accelerant.

Depth of Char. The depth of burning wood is used to determine length of burn and thereby locate the point of origin of the fire.

Line of Demarcation. This is the boundary between charred and non-charred material. On floors or rugs, a puddle-shaped line of demarcation is believed to indicate a liquid fire accelerant. In the cross section of wood, a sharp, distinct line of demarcation indicates a rapid, intense fire.

Sagged Furniture Springs. Because of the heat required for furniture springs to collapse from their own weight and because of the insulating effect of the upholstery, sagged springs are believed possible only in either a fire originating inside the cushions or an external fire intensified by a fire accelerant.

Spalling. This is the breaking off of pieces of the surface of concrete, cement, or brick due to intense heat. Brown stains around the spall indicate the use of a fire accelerant.

A tool for helping the arson investigator cover all bases is a comprehensive checklist.

Arson Checklist

Information that can be used to establish the fact that a fire occurred:

- Date and time of the burning
- Address or location where burning occurred
- Description of the building structure or premises, including the kind of construction material; the age or approximate age; the dimensions or approximate dimensions
- Fire station that received the alarm
- Time that the fire station received the alarm
- Fire apparatus, if any, that attended the fire, and the time that the fire apparatus was officially in operation
- Time that the fire apparatus was withdrawn from the burning, or the time that

the fire department declared the burning extinguished
- Official designation of the incident by fire department records

Information that establishes a loss and ownership:

- Value of the property
- Insurance coverage on the property, or of items and articles of particular value; data as to mortgages, liens, loans, and the financial status of the suspect; and any action, pending or past, against the suspect or against any member of the suspect's family
- Inventory of stock, fixtures, equipment, and other items of value within the premises, and the damage as a result of the fire
- Name of the occupant at the time of the fire; and if the dwelling was vacant, the length of time that the premises had remained unoccupied
- Alterations or changes made in the building while it was occupied by the last tenant, such as the addition of partitions, electric wiring, or stoves
- Evidence that any articles were removed from the premises or were recently repaired, altered, or adjusted in any way
- Evidence indicating who was responsible for the security of the building: who possessed the keys to the building, and who could have had additional keys made
- Information as to whether windows or doors were normally closed and locked; whether some windows were, of necessity, left unlocked although they were closed; or whether some, or all, of the windows were normally left open
- Name of the owner of the property
- Name of the insured

Information and evidence that can be used to establish that arson occurred:

- Name of the person who discovered the fire and the person's observations concerning the location(s) in the building where burning or smoke were observed
- Time that the fire was discovered
- Circumstances under which the fire was first discovered

- Name of the person who turned in the alarm
- Means by which the fire was reported
- Time interval between the discovery of the fire and the report to the fire department
- Weather data, such as the atmospheric temperature and the direction of the wind at the time of the burning, and information concerning any electrical storms that may have occurred at that time
- How the burning occurred, if known
- Type of burning, e.g., flash fire, explosion, smoldering fire, or rapidly spreading fire; the approximate intensity of the burning; and whether there were separate fires
- Presence, color, and odor of smoke during the fire
- Color, height, and intensity of the flames
- Direction of the air currents within the building during the burning, as deduced from partially burned wallpaper, depth of charring, or soot deposits
- Quantity of air within the building during the fire, as revealed by the heaviest concentrations of smoke and soot
- Direction in which the burning spread
- Significant noises that were noticed before or during the burning
- Name of the person who was in the building at the time of the burning or who was in the building last
- Area that suffered the greatest damage
- Physical evidence discovered
- Evidence of possible devices or means by which the burning was started, e.g., candle, match, timing device, or flammable material (mechanical, electrical, chemical, or combination of the three)
- Blistered paint, charred wood, melted metal, glass, or other material that may be found at the suspected or known point of origin
- Presence among the debris of peculiarly colored ashes and clinkers, or traces of paraffin, saturated rags, waste, excelsior, or other fire spreaders
- Identification of the material burned, e.g., oils or chemicals. (Laboratory examination of samples of soot may supply this information.)
- If a death occurred, all pertinent data and facts revealed by the autopsy

- Photographs or sketches of the scene, interior and exterior, taken during the burning and after the burning was extinguished, supplemented with notes and evidence
- Photographs and impressions of evidence of forced entry at any of the doors, windows, hatches, skylights, or other points of entry
- Condition and location of fire-fighting equipment, such as hoses, extinguishers (full or empty), damaged alarm mechanisms, and sprinkler systems
- Information from inspections of the premises that may have been made prior to the fire. (Such data may be obtained from city or local fire departments, insurance carriers, city or local construction permits and accompanying inspections, and from insurance underwriting groups.)
- Evidence of the careless storing or placing of flammable materials such as gasoline, paint, oils, chemicals, lighter fluid, and cleaning fluid
- Location and condition of all electric lights, drops, extensions, appliances, and fuses
- Condition of electric wiring, including exposed wiring; evidence of recent repairs, inside and outside; evidence of splices, connections or alterations, and when, if known, such alterations were made and by whom; load carried by the wires; prescribed load of the fuses through which the lines were fed; and testimony as to whether or not heat was ever noticed in the wires or terminals before the fire
- Number and type of machines, if any, in the room or building; when they were last used; the amount of power they consumed; and when they were last tested and serviced
- Number of electric motors in the room or building; how they were safeguarded against dust, debris, and tampering; their horsepower, voltage, and purpose; whether they were of the "open" or "sealed" type; the length of time they were generally in operation, and their defects, if any
- Condition of gas pipes, bottled gas pipes, steam pipes, air pipes, and water pipes
- Number and type of stoves within the room or building; whether fires were in the stoves; the kinds of fuel used; the locations of the sources of fuel in relation to the stoves;

whether the stoves were self-insulated; when the ashes were last removed; where removed ashes were placed; when the stoves were last cleaned or serviced; and whether they had pilot lights or similar continually burning flame
- Glass objects that may have accidentally caused the fire by concentrating the rays of the sun
- Facts pertaining to any suspicious items or devices that may have been found among the debris
- Methods used to extinguish the burning, e.g., water, foam, and carbon dioxide

Conclusion

Unfortunately, arson investigations are sometimes inadequate or not performed at all. This is often due to a shortage of arson-trained investigators generally. Even when a skilled investigator is on the case, evidence of the crime is likely to have been destroyed by the fire or by the suppression of the fire. As a result, many fires are declared to have innocent origins when in fact they were deliberately set.

John J. Fay

BEHAVIOR ANALYSIS INTERVIEW

Every investigator evaluates the behavior displayed by the person being interviewed (whether a victim, witness, or suspect) and draws some conclusion as to that person's truthfulness. This article profiles the behavioral characteristics indicative of a person who is telling the truth, as well as those characteristics that are suggestive of a person who is withholding information. Before describing the typical behaviors exhibited by truthful and deceptive subjects, some cautions must be emphasized. There is no single verbal or nonverbal behavior that automatically means that a person is lying or telling the truth. Each behavior displayed must be considered in the context of the environment and in comparison to the subject's normal behavior patterns.

The evaluation of behavior symptoms should take into consideration the subject's intelligence, emotional and psychological health, sense of social responsibility, and degree of maturity. Judgment as to a subject's truthfulness or deception should be based on the overall behavioral pattern displayed, and not upon any single observation or activity.

Nonverbal and Verbal Behavior

With these cautions in mind, the nonverbal and verbal behavior of a person during questioning may provide very valuable and accurate indications of truthfulness or deception.

Attitude. Truthful individuals usually display an attitude that can be characterized as concerned, composed, cooperative, direct, spontaneous, open, and sincere. On the other hand, a person who is lying may appear to be overly anxious, defensive, evasive, complaining, guarded, or, in some cases, unconcerned.

Posture. In a non-supportive environment, one in which the investigator and subject are sitting in chairs facing each other about 4½ to 5 feet apart, without any desk or barrier between them, the truthful subject is likely to sit upright (but not rigid or immobile) and frontally aligned with the investigator. The truthful subject will oftentimes lean forward as a sign of interest and participation, and when the subject changes posture the movement is usually casual and relaxed. By contrast, the deceptive subject may maintain a very rigid and immobile posture throughout the interview. There may be a lack of frontal alignment, slouching in the chair, and a closed, barriered posture with arms folded across the chest and legs crossed. In som e cases, the deceptive subject may exhibit very rapid and erratic posture changes.

Significant posture changes are likely to occur when key questions are introduced and deceptive answers given. The deceptive subject's movements are attempts to relieve or reduce internal anxiety experienced when confronted with questions that pose a personal threat and when making untruthful responses that are potentially detectable as lies. The truthful person will not usually experience this same level of high anxiety and will therefore not exhibit these same pronounced posture changes.

Gestures. In addition to significant posture changes, deceptive suspects also engage in a variety of other tension-relieving activities that include grooming gestures and supportive gestures. Examples of grooming gestures include stroking the back of the head, rearranging jewelry or clothing, dusting the pants or lint picking, and adjusting or cleaning glasses. Supportive gestures consist of placing a hand over the mouth or eyes when speaking, hiding the hands, and holding the forehead with a hand for an extended period of time. Deception may be indicated when a suspect repeatedly engages in any of these nonverbal activities while making verbal responses.

Eye Contact. Deceptive persons oftentimes do not look directly at the investigator when they answer critical questions—they look down, over to the side, or up at the ceiling. They feel less anxiety if their eyes are focused somewhere else than on the investigator. Truthful persons, on the other hand, are not defensive and can easily maintain eye contact with the investigator.

Verbal Indicators. Generally speaking, a truthful person will answer questions in a direct, spontaneous, and sincere manner. The truthful subject will use realistic words, such as steal, embezzle, and forge, while the deceptive person will use euphemisms such as take, misuse, and write. The truthful person will exhibit a reasonable memory, not qualify the answers, and volunteer helpful information. Conversely, the deceptive subject may delay a response or repeat the question before giving the answer. The deceptive suspect may also anticipate a question and offer an answer quickly, even before the question is completed. The deceptive person will oftentimes exhibit a remarkable memory (remembering too much or too little detail) and preface answers with such phrases as "To tell you the truth," or "As far as I can recall," or "To the best of my knowledge."

Behavior-Provoking Questions

The Behavior Analysis Interview (BAI) combines the use of traditional investigative questions as well as a series of behavior-provoking questions. The BAI was developed by John E. Reid and Associates, Inc., Chicago. Theoretical models were developed, statistically tested, and validated for the predicted differences in the responses given by truthful and deceptive

subjects to the behavior-provoking questions. More than 30 behavior-provoking questions have been developed and utilized in the BAI technique.

First, let's differentiate between behavior-provoking questions and investigative questions that are routinely asked as part of the investigative process. These routine investigative questions are designed to elicit factual information with respect to the who, what, when, where, why, and how of the matter under investigation. The behavior-provoking questions are intended to ascertain the subject's perspective of the issue under investigation, as well as to identify areas of anxiety that will be manifested in visible and detectable signals.

As the suspect responds to each investigative question, the investigator should carefully record and evaluate the suspect's version of events. Simultaneously, the investigator will be looking for nonverbal and verbal signals (as outlined above) that accompany these questions to identify areas of anxiety and possible deception that will require further inquiry or investigation.

To illustrate the behavior-provoking questions, five of these questions are presented in a hypothetical investigation into the theft of credit cards from a bank's mail room.

1. The purpose question: "What is your understanding of the purpose for this interview?" The truthful responder will provide an accurate description of events; may use descriptive language such as steal; and may mention numbers of cards stolen and/or victims' names, if known. The deceptive subject's response may be vague and nonspecific. The response may include non-descriptive language, such as "the incident," or "something happened," or qualifiers, such as "apparently" or "evidently" or "may have." Details are absent concerning the number of cards stolen or victims' names.

2. The you question: "Over the past several weeks we have had a number of credit cards disappear from the bank; specifically, the mail room. If you had anything to do with stealing these missing credit cards, you should

tell me now." A truthful response is likely to be a direct, contracted, and unequivocal denial, e.g., "No, I didn't steal any credit cards." Broad, all encompassing language may be used: "Absolutely not! I haven't stolen anything from here." The deceptive response may be a non-contracted and unemotional denial ("I do not know anything about this") or an evasive response ("I didn't even know credit cards were missing") or an objection ("Why would I risk my job by doing something like that?").

3. The knowledge question: "Do you know for sure who did steal any of the missing credit cards?" A truthful subject will often volunteer information, "Not for sure, but I have some ideas." Concern or anger may come out, "I wish I did know, but I just don't have any idea." The deceptive subject may give an unemotional denial, "No, I do not." The subject does not offer spontaneous thoughts or feelings.

4. The suspicion question: "Who do you suspect may have stolen these missing credit cards?" The truthful subject will give the question careful thought, and when offering a suspicion, will cite a reason for the suspicion. A deceptive response is "I don't have any idea." without giving the question any careful thought. The deceptive person may name improbable suspects, such as employees without opportunity or access.

5. The vouch question: "Is there anyone who you work with that you feel is above suspicion and would not do anything like this?" The truthful subject will give the question thought and typically eliminate possible suspects. The deceptive subject will not vouch for others because in so doing the field of suspects is narrowed, which would have the effect of increasing the suspect's chance of exposure.

Joseph P. Buckley, III

Source Inbau, F., Reid, J., Buckley, J., and Jayne, B., ed. 2001. *Criminal Interrogation and Confessions, 4th Edition*. Gaithersburg: Aspen.

BURGLARY: ATTACKS ON LOCKS

A door lock is usually all that prevents movement into a protected area, whether commercial or residential. Occasionally, a door lock will be supplemented with a padlock. Most door locks are key-operated. They consist of a cylinder or other opening for inserting a key that mechanically moves a bolt or latch. The bolt (or deadbolt) extends from the door lock into a bolt receptacle in the door frame.

The cylinder part of a lock contains the keyway, pins, and other mechanisms. Some locks, called double-cylinder locks, have a cylinder on each side of the door and require a key for both sides. With a single-cylinder lock, a thief may be able to break glass in or nearby the door and reach inside to turn the knob to release the lock. The disadvantage is that a key to the lock on the inside of the door must be readily available for emergency escape, such as during a fire.

The key-in-knob lock works on the same principles as the cylinder lock except, as the name implies, the keyway is in the knob. In the single key-in-knob lock the keyway is almost always on the outside door knob and a push or turn button for locking/unlocking is on the inside knob. The double key-in-knob lock has a keyway on the outside and inside knobs, which increases security but also decreases safety.

From the standpoint of forced entry, the cylinder lock is somewhat resistive in that it cannot be ripped easily from the door because it is seated flush or close to the surface. One model of the cylinder lock features a smooth, narrow ring around the neck of the cylinder. The ring moves freely so that even if it can be grasped by a tool, it cannot be twisted. The cylinder lock is vulnerable to a burglary tool called the slam hammer or slam puller. The device usually consists of a slender rod with a heavy sliding sleeve. One end of the rod has a screw or claw for insertion into the keyway. The other end has a retaining knob. When the sleeve is jerked away from the lock, striking the retaining knob, the lock cylinder or keyway is forcibly pulled out.

By contrast, the key-in-knob lock is somewhat more vulnerable because the knob itself can be hammered off; pried off with a crowbar; or pulled out by a grasping tool, such as channel lock pliers. Once the inner workings of the lock are exposed, the burglar can retract the bolt to open the door.

Probably one of the simplest attack techniques is slip-knifing. A thin, flat, and flexible object, such as a credit card, is inserted between the strike and the latch bolt to depress the latch bolt and release it from the strike. Slip-knifing of sliding windows is accomplished by inserting a thin and stiff blade between the meeting rail (stile) to move the latch to the open position; slip-knifing of pivoting windows is done by inserting a thin and stiff wire through openings between the rail and the frame and manipulating the sash operator.

Springing the door is a technique in which a large screwdriver or crowbar is placed between the door and the door frame so that the bolt extending from the lock into the bolt receptacle is pried out, enabling the door to swing open. A 1-inch bolt will hinder this attack.

Jamb peeling is the prying off or peeling back the door frame at a point near the bolt receptacle. When enough of the jamb is removed from the receptacle, the receptacle can be broken apart or removed, allowing the door to swing open. A metal or reinforced door frame is the antidote.

Sawing the bolt is inserting a hacksaw blade between the door and the door frame and cutting through the bolt. The countermeasure is to use a bolt made of a saw-resistant alloy or a bolt that is seated in such a way that it will freely spin on its side, thereby taking away the resistance needed for the saw blade to gain purchase.

Spreading the frame involves the use of a jack, such as an automobile jack, in such a way that the door jambs on each side of the door are pressured apart to a point where the door will swing free from the bolt receptacle. A reinforced door frame and a long deadbolt are countermeasures.

Kicking in the door is a primitive, but effective technique. In this case, the attack is against the door so that even the best locking hardware will have little deterrent effect. The countermeasure is a metal door or a solid wood door, at least 1¾-inches thick, installed in a wooden door frame at least 2-inches thick, or a steel door frame. An escutcheon plate can be used to shield the bolt receptacle.

A more sophisticated attack technique is lock picking. It is seen infrequently because of the expertise required. Lock picking is accomplished by using metal picks to align the pins in the cylinder as a key would to release the lock. The greater the number of pins, the more difficult it is to align them. A cylinder should have at least six pins to be resistive to lock picking.

The high-security form of the combination lock requires manipulation of one or several numbered dials to gain access. Combination locks usually have three or four dials that must be aligned in the correct order for entrance. Because only a limited number of people will be informed of the combination, the problems associated with compromised mechanical keys and lock picking are removed. Combination locks are used at doors and on safes, bank vaults, and high-security filing cabinets; in most cases, the combination can be changed by the owner on an as-needed basis.

With older combination locks, skillful burglars may be able, often with the aid of a stethoscope, to discern the combination by listening to the locking mechanism while the dial is being turned. Another attack method is for the burglar to take a concealed position at a distance from the lock and with binoculars or a telescope observe the combination sequence when the lock is opened.

The combination padlock has mostly low-security applications. It has a numbered dial and may be supplemented with a keyway. On some models, a serial number impressed on the lock by the manufacturer will allow the combination to be determined by cross-checking against a reference manual provided by the manufacturer to dealers. Although a convenience, it is a risk to security.

In a technique called padlock substitution, the thief will remove the property owner's unlocked padlock and replace it with a similar padlock. After the property owner locks up and leaves, the thief will return, open the padlock and gain entry. The preventive measure is to keep padlocks locked even when not in use.

John J. Fay

Sources

Fennelly, L.J. 1982. *Handbook of Loss Prevention and Crime Prevention*. Boston: Butterworth-Heinemann.

Purpura, P.P. 1984. *Security and Loss Prevention*. Boston: Butterworth-Heinemann.

CRIME ANALYSIS

What cannot be measured cannot be managed. This is a commonly accepted business paradigm, yet its acceptance within the security industry is not as far reaching as one would expect. Data-driven security is fast becoming an accepted business practice and refers to using measurable factors to drive a security program. While not all elements of a security program lend themselves to measurement, many components can be measured effectively. A key component of a data-driven security program is the quantitative threat assessment, or more specifically, a crime analysis. Crime analysis is key to successful operational management as it broadens management's vision and increases its effectiveness with a wealth of information.

Statistics are used in planning for the future. Crime and security statistics guide security surveys, help in the selection of countermeasures, measure program effectiveness, and alleviate the risks and costs relating to those risks. The use of information regarding crimes and other security incidents helps security decision makers plan, select, and implement appropriate security measures that address the actual risks of the facility. Security decision makers, after assessing the crime problem, can select the most effective countermeasures including the cost of implementation and maintenance.

Budget justification is also accomplished through the use of statistics since effective security measures will reduce the risks, and a return on investment can be calculated. Typically, internal security incident reports are used to determine security weaknesses and problem areas, as well as to select crime countermeasures, calibrate countermeasure effectiveness, and consider future budget needs. Crime statistics, available from local law enforcement agencies, are also utilized extensively in determining concrete security risks. Though internal security reports and police crime data may overlap, it is incumbent upon security decision makers to consider both in determining a facility's true risk.

Security decision makers need not be mathematicians to fully utilize statistical information; rather they need only a basic understanding of the various methods to use such data along with a touch of personal computer and spreadsheet software knowledge. A common application of statistics in the security arena is the use of security reports and crime data to determine the risks to a facility, including its assets and personnel.

The use of statistics extends beyond planning security at an existing facility. Statistical data may also be used to select and plan security at new facilities. For example, the real estate department of a company may provide the security decision maker with a list of potential new sites, one of which will be selected based on, among other things, the risks posed at the location. In this role, the security decision maker serves as an advisor to the real estate department by conducting crime analyses of the proposed sites as well as performing security surveys to select the location that poses the least or a tolerable level of risk. In this scenario, the security decision maker will gather and analyze crime data for similar businesses in the area surrounding each site to determine the security problems. The sites that have the least crimes can be evaluated further by means of a security survey. After the sites have been narrowed down by risk and surveys completed, the security decision maker has the necessary information to advise the real estate department.

Threat assessments are the backbone of security surveys and risk analysis and often define the scope of work to be performed in a security survey. Before conducting a security survey, security decision makers will have a thorough understanding of the crime and security-incident history of the facility. This information guides the security decision maker as he conducts the survey and looks for crime opportunities that can be blocked with security measures.

Crime analysis is the logical examination of crimes which have penetrated preventive measures, including the frequency of specific crimes, each incident's temporal details (time and day), and the risk posed to a property's inhabitants, as well as the application of revised security standards and preventive measures that, if adhered to and monitored, can be the panacea for a given crime dilemma.

While the above definition of crime analysis is holistic, it can be dissected into three basic elements:

- Logical examination of crimes which have penetrated preventive measures
- Frequency of specific crimes, each incident's temporal details (time and day), and the risk posed to a property's inhabitants
- Application of revised security standards and preventive measures

Examining crimes perpetrated at company facilities is commonplace in today's business environment. In larger companies, there may be a person or group of people working under the risk management or security departments who are solely dedicated to the function of crime analysis. In smaller companies, the crime analysis function is carried out by someone who also has other security management duties. Crime analysis may also be an outsourced function, whereby company personnel simply utilize crime data that a contractor has collected, entered into a database, and possibly provided some analytical work up or the tools to do so.

The second element is the analytical component. Crimes are analyzed in different ways depending on what one is trying to accomplish. Most commonly, facilities are ranked based on the crime level or rate. Generally, facilities with more crime or a higher crime rate are given a larger piece of the security budget, while less crime-prone sites are given less money. Crimes are also analyzed on a facility-by-facility basis allowing security decision makers to select appropriate countermeasures.

Crime analysis is used to assess and select appropriate countermeasures. Crimes that are perpetrated on a property can usually be prevented using security devices or personnel; however, it should be noted that all measures are neither cost effective nor reasonable. Certainly, a criminal perpetrator would be hard pressed to steal an automobile from a small parking lot patrolled by 20 security officers, though that type of security extreme is not reasonable, nor inexpensive. Crime analysis guides security decision makers in the right direction by highlighting the types of crimes perpetrated (crime specific analysis), problem areas on the property (spatial analysis), and when they occur (temporal analysis) among others. Using this information, it is much easier to select countermeasures aimed directly at the problem.

Why would a security decision maker need to know how crime occurs? By understanding the factors that lead to crime, coupled with a comprehensive study of crime on the property, security personnel can be assisted in blocking opportunities for crime and creating effective crime prevention programs.

Crime analysis seeks to answer the questions: What? Where? When? Who? and How?

Answers to these questions help us better understand the particular nature of crime on a given property and formulate specific responses.

The *What* question tells us what specifically occurred. For example, was the crime against a person or property, violent or not, completed or attempted? The *What* also distinguishes between types of crime that require different solutions such as whether a reported robbery was actually a burglary.

Where answers the location-specific question. Did the crime occur inside the walls of the location, in the parking lot, in the alley way behind the site? If the incident occurred inside, did it occur in a public area or a controlled area? Determining the precise location assists property managers in creating additional lines of defense around targeted assets. For example, if the crime analysis indicates that a vast majority of loss at a small grocery store is occurring at the point of sale, then little will be accomplished by installing a lock on the back office where the safe is located. In this example, the crime analysis will rule out certain measures, but by the same token, crime analysis will also spotlight certain solutions, such as increased employee training or updated accounting systems at the point of sale.

The answer to the *When* question gives us the temporal details of each incident. Knowing when crimes are most frequent helps in the deployment of resources, especially costly security measures such as personnel. Temporal details include the date, time of day, day of week, and season that a crime occurred.

Who answers several important questions that help a property manager create an effective crime prevention program. Who is the victim and who is the perpetrator? Knowledge of the types of criminals who operate on or near a given property assists property managers select the best measures to reduce crime opportunities. For example, gambling casinos have used closed circuit television (CCTV) for some time to track known gambling crooks. Also important are the potential victims of crime. Ted Bundy and Jeffrey Dahmer, like other more common criminals, select particular types of victims. Thus, an understanding of the people that may be targeted focuses a property manager's attention. For example, a residential apartment complex that caters to recently released hospital patients has larger responsibility to provide a safe environment given the fact that the clientele is not usually capable of self-protection. The oldest example of the *Who* question dates back to premises liability law where innkeepers were often found to be responsible for the safety of a guest when crime was foreseeable. People on travel are usually not aware of the area in which they are staying and they also have little control over the security measures that they can take to protect themselves inside a hotel room.

How is the most consequential question to be answered by the crime analysis. How a crime is committed often directly answers the question, "How can the crime be prevented in the future?" More specific *How* questions may also be asked. How did the criminal access the property? If we know that a criminal has accessed the property via a hole in the back fence of the property, efforts can be taken to immediately repair the fence. Other specific questions reveal the method of operation (MO). How did a criminal enter the employee entrance of an electronics store to steal a television? How did a burglar open the safe without using force? How did the car thief leave the gated premises without knowing the exit code? Obviously, the list of examples is unlimited and property managers need to ask many questions about the criminal's actions as soon as possible to learn the most effective solutions. It is true that often the *How* will be the most difficult question to answer. This leads into a problematical area as crime sources can be divided into two categories, internal and external. Internal sources of crime can be employees and other legitimate users of the space such as tenants. They are called legitimate users of the space as they have a perfectly valid reason for attending the location, but in the course of their regular activities, they also carry out criminal activities.

With these answers, security decision makers are better armed to attack the crime problem. Some would argue that security is more of an art than a science. While they are correct, the business of security is not an art. The security department is a business unit, not unlike other business units within a company that must justify their existence. Crime analysis is a critical component for demonstrating a return on security investments.

In today's corporate environment, it is important for all departments to show bang for the buck, and this philosophy applies to the security organization all too much as often their budget is among the first to be cut. Showing a

return on investment simply means that security measures are either paying for themselves, or better, adding to the bottom line. Return on investment is important as it helps the security decision maker justify costs and obtain future budget monies. Some security programs will not pay for themselves while others actually become a profit center. Regardless of a security measure's ability to be quantitatively assessed, security decision makers should strive to calculate a return on investment.

Karim H. Vellani

DNA ANALYSIS

DNA is the basic genetic material within each living cell that determines a person's individual characteristics. Since the early 1980s, DNA testing has been used in AIDS and genetic disease research, bone marrow transplants, and in anthropological investigations. In forensics, DNA testing is typically used to identify individuals, using only small samples of body fluids or tissue—such as blood, semen, or hair—left at a crime scene.

DNA Testing Methodologies

DNA testing includes two major components when used for forensic purposes. The first involves the molecular biological techniques that allow analysts to directly examine a DNA sample. The second component has to do with population genetics—how to interpret DNA tests to calculate the degree to which different samples are associated. Such population studies help to determine the results of the analytical work.

DNA tests investigate and analyze the structure and inheritance patterns of DNA. Many methodologies exist, and new ones are constantly being developed. The particular test used will depend on the quantity and quality of the sample, the objective of the test, and the preferences of the laboratory conducting the procedure. All tests, however, are designed to isolate certain nucleotide sequences—the polymorphic segments of the DNA molecule carrying marked, recurring distinctions—and these variable segments provide the basis for discriminating among individuals' DNA.

In a forensic environment, two common analytical methods used to detect the polymorphic DNA in human samples are the Restriction Fragment Length Polymorphism (RFLP) and Polymerase Chain Reaction (PCR) techniques. The RFLP method identifies fragments of the DNA chain that contain the polymorphic segments, produces a DNA "print" of the fragments, and measures the fragment lengths. The PCR-based methods seek to determine the presence of specific alleles (alternative forms of genes that occur in different individuals), thus indicating specific genetic characteristics.

Restriction Fragment Length Polymorphism. RFLP requires the presence of as little as 50 to 100 nanograms of DNA—an amount of DNA that may be present in a single hair follicle. The distinct stages in developing a DNA print using RFLP will be portrayed here by describing the analysis of a blood sample.

First, white cells containing the DNA are separated from the blood sample by use of a centrifuge, and the cells are ruptured to extract the DNA strands. The DNA strands are then cut, or digested, using restriction endonucleuses (REs)—enzymes derived from bacteria that catalyze the cutting process. A particular enzyme will cut the DNA strands at the same nucleotide sequence (restriction site) each time. By cutting a person's DNA in the same place, the several alternate forms (alleles) of a gene are separated from each other. A specific allele will be of the same size and molecular weight as others of its type. The polymorphism, or individuality, of a person will be detected on the basis of differences in DNA fragment lengths.

At this point in the process, all of the DNA fragments are mixed together. Using a technique called electrophoresis, the polymorphic fragments are separated by length. The DNA is placed at one end of a plate containing agarose gel, with a positive electrode placed at the other end. DNA carries a negative electrical charge; therefore the DNA will move toward the positive electrode. The distance that an individual fragment of DNA travels depends on the amount of its electrical charge, which is determined by its length and molecular weight. Thus, fragments of the same length and weight will travel the same distance while large DNA fragments will move more slowly than smaller fragments. This process sorts the DNA into bands based on length

and weight and these length-dependent bands are the basis for DNA identification.

After electrophoresis, the next step calls for transferring the DNA fragments in the gel to a nylon membrane. In a technique called "Southern blotting," a chemical reagent (such as sodium hydroxide) acts as a transfer solution and a means to separate the double-strand fragments into single-strand fragments.

Using the zipper analogy, the strands are unzipped, exposing the building blocks. The unzipped DNA fragments are now fixed on the nylon membrane, where they are exposed to radioactive DNA probes—laboratory-developed (thus, known sequences), DNA nucleotide fragments which carry a radioactive "marker." The probes seek out the sequence that they match and attach themselves to the complementary split DNA strands.

The probes are made radioactive so that the DNA sequences to which they become attached can be visibly tracked. The nylon membrane is placed against a sheet of X-ray film and exposed for several days. When the film is developed, black bands will appear at the point where the radioactive DNA probes have combined with the sample DNA. The result, called an "autoradiograph" or "autorad" looks much like the bar codes found on items in supermarkets and department stores.

The final step is the band pattern comparison. Genetic differences between individuals will be identified by differences in the location and distribution of the band patterns, which correspond to the length of the DNA fragments present. The actual measurement of the band patterns being compared can be done manually or by machine, but often DNA identification depends upon expert judgment.

Polymerase Chain Reaction-Based Techniques. PCR is not only an analytical tool, but also an amplification technique often used when the available amount of DNA material is insufficient for proper analysis, or when the sample is degraded by chemical impurities or damaged by environmental conditions. PCR is an in vitro process that causes a specific sequence to repeatedly duplicate itself, mimicking its natural replication process. Short pieces of purified DNA, called primers, are used to build a foundation upon which the sample DNA can build. The primers must have sequences that complement the DNA flanking the specific segment to be amplified. The sample DNA is heated to separate the double helix, producing two single strands. By then lowering the temperature, copies of the primers bind to the DNA sample's flanking sequences. A heat-stable DNA polymerase (an enzyme) is then introduced to the DNA sample causing the primers to synthesize complimentary strands of each of the single strands. This process is repeated for generally 25 cycles, amplifying the original DNA sequence approximately a million times. The amplified DNA can then be analyzed by any one of several methodologies.

Functions of DNA Testing

DNA testing provides a basis for positive identification, but it is not expected to become a suitable technology for validating identification in security settings. DNA analysis would be inappropriate in situations where a nearly immediate determination must be made as to whether a person seeking entry to a particular area, or seeking to conduct a particular transaction is, in fact, authorized to do so. The chemical analysis required to make a DNA comparison takes weeks, not minutes. DNA testing is increasingly used to determine paternity and, in forensic settings, it has been most prolifically and successfully used to identify or exonerate a suspect.

Paternity Determinations. In determining paternity, DNA has proven to be extraordinarily useful. Each chromosome contains nucleotides identical to those of each parent, as well as the nucleotides that distinguish the individuality of the person. If samples from the child and from one of the parents are available, the nucleotides of the child that are different from the known parent's DNA must have come from the unknown parent's DNA. If a sample from the suspected, but unknown, parent supplies all the "missing" nucleotides without any superfluous nucleotides, one can conclude that the suspected individual is, in fact, the other parent.

Identification of Suspects. The forensic promise of DNA typing is substantial. Samples of human skin, hair follicles, blood, semen, or saliva containing cells or other tissues found on a crime victim or at a crime scene can be examined to identify the DNA pattern. That pattern can be compared with DNA from a suspect to make a "positive identification," or to exonerate a suspect. DNA examination techniques sometimes permit the use of extraordinarily small samples of human tissues or fluids, such as a few hairs or a single spot of blood. Moreover, DNA is durable and is relatively resistant to adverse environmental conditions such as heat or moisture. DNA degrades slowly in a decomposing body, lasting sometimes for years and allowing samples to be analyzed for some time after the death of an individual. Although some experts debate the percentage of usable tissue and fluid samples that are retrieved from all crime scenes, DNA analysis will have the greatest effect on violent crime cases, such as murder and rape, where hair, blood, semen, or tissue evidence is frequently found.

Source "Forensic DNA Analysis." 1991. *Bureau of Justice Statistics, U.S. Department of Justice.*

EVIDENCE TYPES

Physical Evidence

Evidence is anything that tends to prove or disprove a fact. Within that general definition, physical evidence is any material substance or object, regardless of size or shape. Generally, there are three categories of physical evidence.

- Movable Evidence. Items that can be transported or moved, such as weapons, tools, and glass fragments.
- Fixed or Immovable Evidence. Items that cannot easily be removed, such as walls of a room, trees, and utility poles.
- Fragile Evidence. Items that are easily destroyed, contaminated, or will easily deteriorate.

Evaluating Physical Evidence. In many cases the success or failure of an investigation depends on the investigator's ability to recognize physical evidence and derive understanding from it. This process of evaluation begins with the initial report of a crime and concludes when the case is adjudicated. Evaluation is usually carried out in concert with laboratory technicians, a prosecuting attorney, other investigators, experts in certain fields, and other persons whose knowledge contributes to a better understanding of physical evidence and its relationship to the many facets of the case.

Identification. Evidence must be marked for identification as soon as it is received, recovered, or discovered. Identification markings help the investigator identify the evidence at a later date. Markings are normally made by placing initials, time, and date on the items. If it is not practical to mark evidence, it is placed in an appropriate container and sealed. The container is then marked for identification.

Identification markings are supplemented by the use of an evidence tag. An evidence tag is filled out at the time the evidence is acquired. Entries on the tag are made in ink, and the tag accompanies the evidence from the moment it is acquired until it is relinquished. An evidence tag is not a substitute for marking evidence, but is an administrative convenience for locating evidence while it is in custody.

Chain of Custody. Chain of custody begins when an item of evidence is received. The number of persons who handle an item of evidence should be kept to a minimum. All persons who handle an item are considered links in the custody chain and such persons must receipt for each item whenever a transfer is made. An investigator in possession of evidence is personally liable for its care and safekeeping.

Three factors influence the introduction of evidence at trial:

- The object must be identified.
- Relevancy must exist.
- Continuity or chain of custody must be shown.

Rules of Evidence

The rules for presenting evidence in a criminal investigation are as varied as the types of evidence. Let us look at them.

Opinion testimony is a conclusion drawn by a witness, hence the term opinion testimony. Another form of testimonial information is hearsay evidence. Hearsay is a statement that is made other than by a witness. Hearsay cannot be entered into evidence unless the maker of the statement can be cross-examined.

Privileged communication is confidential information between two persons recognized by law as coming within the so-called privileged relationship rule. The following relationships are generally recognized: a husband and wife, an attorney and client, a physician and patient, and a law enforcement officer and informant.

Character evidence is evidence introduced by either defense or prosecution witnesses to prove the accused's good or bad character. Character evidence is usually introduced only when the defense raises the issue of the accused's character.

Direct evidence is evidence presented by a person who actually witnessed something. Contrast this with circumstantial evidence, which is evidence that proves other facts from which a court may reasonably infer the truth.

Admissibility is a characteristic or condition of evidence. To be admissible, evidence must be material, relevant, and competent. Evidence is material when it plays a significant part in proving a case. Examples of material evidence might be fingerprints of the accused that were found on the murder weapon, an eyewitness account of how the accused committed the crime, or stolen property found in the possession of the accused. Evidence is relevant when it goes directly to the proof or disproof of the crime or of any facts at issue. Examples of relevant evidence might be a death certificate or a medical examiner's report. Evidence is competent when it is shown to be reliable. Examples of competent evidence might be accurate business records or the testimony of an expert fingerprint examiner.

Burden of proof is a rule which holds that no person accused of a crime is required to prove his or her innocence. The prosecution must prove the guilt of a defendant beyond a reasonable doubt. Reasonable doubt means the jury must believe the charges to be true to a "moral certainty." On the other hand, the accused must prove his or her contentions. Such defenses as self-defense, insanity, and alibi are affirmative defenses that must be proved by the accused.

A presumption is a conclusion that the law says must be reached from certain facts. Presumptions are recognized because experience has shown that some facts should be accepted or presumed true until otherwise rebutted. For example, defendants are presumed to be sane at the time the crime was committed, and at the time of trial, in the absence of proof to the contrary. Presumptions are of two classes: conclusive and rebuttable. A conclusive presumption is one that the law demands be made from a set of facts, e.g., a child under 7 years of age cannot be charged with a crime. A rebuttable presumption can be overcome by evidence to the contrary, e.g., presumption of death after being unaccounted for and missing for 7 years.

Rules of Exclusion

In general, rules of exclusion deal with conditions in which evidence will not be received. They limit the evidence a witness may present to those things of which he had direct knowledge, i.e., what he saw, smelled, tasted, felt, or heard.

All evidence, direct and circumstantial, if relevant, material, and competent is admissible provided it is not opinion testimony, hearsay evidence, or privileged communication. There are exceptions regarding the admissibility of opinion testimony and hearsay evidence. An exception to the rule against opinion testimony can be made when no other description could be more accurate. For instance, a witness is allowed to testify on such matters as size, distance, time, weight, speed, direction, drunkenness, and similar matters, all of which require the witness to state an opinion. There is no requirement for the witness to be an "expert" when testifying to facts such as these.

Exceptions to the rule against hearsay can be made for the dying declaration and the spontaneous declaration. The admissibility of a dying declaration is limited to homicide cases. Because of the seriousness of homicide, a dying declaration is an exception. A dying declaration is admissible either for or against the accused. The statement must have been made when the victim believed he was about to die and was without hope of recovery. The admissibility of the declaration will not be affected as long as the victim dies; otherwise, the issue would not arise since there would be no charge of homicide.

The spontaneous declaration, a statement made under conditions of shock or excitement, may be admitted as another exception to the hearsay rule. Normally, such a statement is made simultaneously with an event or act and there

is not time or opportunity to fabricate a story. It is generally accepted that the statement will be admitted if it precedes, follows, or is concurrent with the act. The statement cannot have been made in response to a question and must pertain to the act that produced it. The spontaneity of the statement is sufficient guarantee of truthfulness to compensate for the denial of cross-examination.

In prosecutions for sexual offenses, evidence that the victim made a complaint within a short time after the offense occurred (i.e., a fresh complaint) is admissible in certain cases. The fact that the complaint was made is relevant for corroborating the testimony of the victim. The statement may relate only to who and what caused the conditions, and merely indicate the credibility of the victim as a witness.

An official statement in writing made as a record of fact or event by an individual acting in an official capacity (called a "business record") is admissible to prove the truth of a matter. Records are of two types: private and public. To introduce private records, someone associated with the business must introduce them. He must show that the company kept records, that the record produced was one of these records, and that the record was the original or certified copy of the original. Public records are usually introduced by presenting certified copies.

A confession is a statement or complete acknowledgment of guilt. An admission is a statement which does not amount to a complete acknowledgment of guilt, but links the maker with a crime. Admissions are forms of hearsay. A court is inclined to apply the same rules of admissibility to admissions as for confessions.

John J. Fay

FORENSICS: FBI IDENTIFICATION AND LABORATORY SERVICES

The FBI's Identification Division contains the largest collection of fingerprint identification data in the world available to law enforcement agencies. Services of the division include furnishing standard forms, such as fingerprint cards, for submitting identification data; searching of fingerprint cards; making name checks to locate identification records; sending fugitive notices to enforcement agencies; making latent print examinations; examining fingers of deceased persons for possible identification; and assisting in the identification of persons killed in major disasters.

The Laboratory and the Technical Services Divisions of the FBI have capabilities in a wide range of forensic sciences: (1) document analysis, (2) scientific analysis, and (3) analysis of audio/video recordings and electronic devices. Competent expert testimony and technical assistance are provided in special situations, such as kidnapping cases, airline disasters, and photographic problems.

These divisions maintain standard reference files and collections of typewriter standards, automotive paint, firearms, hairs and fibers, blood sera, safe insulation, shoe prints, tire treads, watermark standards, safety paper standards, checkwriter standards, office copier standards, and National Motor Vehicle Certificate of Title File.

Files of questioned material consist of the National Fraudulent Check File, Bank Robbery Note File, Anonymous Letter File, National Motor Vehicle Certificate of Title File, Pornographic Materials File, National Stolen Art File, and National Stolen Coin File.

In the laboratory's National Automobile Altered Numbers File (NAANF) are surface replica plastic impressions of altered vehicle identification numbers found on stolen cars, trucks, and heavy equipment. The purpose of this file is to have a central repository for specimens of altered numbers so that comparisons can readily be made to identify recovered stolen vehicles and to link such vehicles with commercialized theft rings.

A related reference file is the National Vehicle Identification Number Standard File (NVSF), which contains standards of Vehicle Identification Number (VIN) plates from each factory of the major manufacturers of American automobiles. The purpose of the file is to enable the FBI Laboratory to determine whether or not a submitted VIN plate is authentic. Additionally, it gives the laboratory the capability, in the event that bogus VIN plates are being prepared in an automobile factory, to identify the factory and the machine used in making the bogus plates.

Engineering Section Capabilities

The Engineering Section of the Technical Services Division is responsible for the development, procurement, and deployment of many types of technical equipment used in support of the FBI's investigative activities. In addition, this section has the capability of examining evidence of an electrical or electronic nature, conducting analysis of magnetic recordings, and providing expert testimony regarding findings. Engineering Section capabilities include the following.

Authenticity Determination. This analysis is made in cases involving allegations of tape tampering and/or alteration by a defense expert, and when the legitimacy of the recording cannot be established through chain of custody and testimony.

Signal Analysis. In this test, various analyses are conducted to identify, compare, and interpret non-voice sounds on original tape recordings, including telephone dialing, gunshots, and radio transmissions.

Speaker Identification. This test uses the spectrographic (voice-print) technique to compare the recorded voice of an unknown individual to a known recorded voice sample of a suspect. Decisions regarding speaker identification by the spectrographic method are not considered conclusive, since there is limited scientific research regarding the reliability of the examination under the varying conditions of recording fidelity, interfering background sounds, sample size, voice disguise, restrictive frequency range, and other factors commonly encountered in investigative matters.

Sound Recording Comparisons. This is an aural examination to determine if a recovered "bootleg" tape recording contains the same material as a copyrighted commercial tape.

Tape Duplication. This service provides standard format copies of unusual or obsolete tapes or disc recordings.

Tape Enhancement. This is the selective suppression of interfering noise on audio recordings, or the audio track of video recordings, to improve the voice intelligibility.

Telephone toll fraud examinations are made to identify:

- "Blue Box" and "Black Box" devices, which receive toll-free long distance telephone calls.

- "Red Box" devices, which allow free pay telephone calls.

Interception of Communications Examinations include identification of:

- Wire tap devices attached to telephone lines, which monitor, record, or transmit telephone conversations as a radio signal to a remote location.
- Infinity transmitter devices, which allow a room conversation to be monitored by a remotely activated microphone on a telephone line.
- Telephones which have been modified to monitor a room conversation when the telephone is not in use.
- Miniature transmitters, concealed microphones and recorders designed to surreptitiously intercept oral communications.

Other examinations include identification of devices used to defeat "burglar alarm" systems, FM radio transceivers, scanners and tracking devices, and electronic devices of unknown use or origin believed to have been used in the commission of a crime.

The FBI's services in these areas are available to all federal agencies, U.S. attorneys, military tribunals, in both civil and criminal matters, and to all duly constituted state, county, and municipal law enforcement agencies in the United States in connection with their official criminal investigative matters only. These services, including the loan of experts if needed as expert witnesses, are rendered free of cost to the contributing agency.

As a general rule, Laboratory Division examinations are not made if the evidence is subjected elsewhere to the same examination for the prosecution. Additionally, in order to more effectively and efficiently utilize its resources, the laboratory will not accept cases from other crime laboratories that have the capability of conducting the requested examination(s).

Because of the nature of the evidence submitted for fingerprint examinations, the previously mentioned Laboratory Division restriction does not apply. Therefore, the Identification Division will examine fingerprint evidence even if it has been or will be subjected to examination by other fingerprint experts.

Blood and Other Body Fluids

Forensic serology involves the identification and characterization of blood and other body fluids on items associated with a crime or crime scene. Evidence from violent crimes, such as murder, rape, robbery, assault, and hit-and-run usually bear body fluid stains.

Blood examinations aid investigations:

- By locating the possible crime scene. Identification of human blood similar in type to that of the victim can assist investigators in identifying the crime scene.
- By discovering a crime. Occasionally, the identification of human blood on a highway, sidewalk, porch, or in a car is the first indication that a crime has occurred.
- By identifying the weapon used. The grouping of human blood found on a club, knife, or hammer can be of considerable probative value.
- By proving or disproving a suspect's alibi. The identification of human blood on an item belonging to a suspect who claims that the blood is of animal origin refutes an alibi, whereas the identification of animal blood can substantiate the alibi.
- By eliminating suspects. The determination that the human blood on items from the suspect is different in type from that of the victim may exculpate the suspect. Blood similar to that of the suspect can help corroborate a suspect's claim of having a nosebleed or other injury.

Testing can determine whether visible stains do or do not contain blood. The appearance of blood can vary greatly depending on the age of the stain and the environmental conditions (such as temperature, light, and humidity) to which it was subjected. Chemical and microscopic analyses are necessary to positively identify the presence of blood in a stain and to determine whether blood is of human or non-human origin, and if non-human, the specific animal family from which it originated.

Human blood can be classified according to the four groups of the International ABO Blood Grouping System and other blood grouping systems, including red blood cell enzyme and serum protein systems, which are analyzed by electrophoresis.

The age of a bloodstain or the race of the person from whom it originated cannot be conclusively determined, and using conventional serological techniques it is not possible to identify human blood as having come from a particular person.

An investigation can also be aided by the examination of semen, saliva, and urine.

Semen. The identification of semen by chemical and microscopic means on vaginal smears, swabs, or on the victim's clothing may be of value in corroborating the victim's claims. Enzyme typing is possible on semen stains of sufficient size and quality.

DNA analysis may allow for positive personal identification of the semen source. If DNA analysis is unsuccessful and the depositor is a secretor, grouping tests may provide information concerning the depositor's ABO blood type.

Saliva. A saliva sample from a known source may be used in conjunction with the liquid blood from the same source to establish the secretor status of the individual. Saliva from a questioned source may provide information as to ABO blood type of the depositor.

Known saliva samples should be submitted from both the suspect(s) and victim(s) in sexual assault cases, and in cases where a saliva examination may provide probative information (e.g., a cigarette butt found adjacent to a homicide victim's body).

Urine. Urine may be qualitatively identified by chemical testing. Absolute identification of a stain as urine is not possible; however, no routinely reliable forensic techniques are available that provide blood group information from urine.

Secretors and Secretor Status. Secretors (which represent approximately 75 percent of the U.S. population) are individuals who have in their non-blood body fluids (e.g., semen, saliva, and vaginal fluid) detectable amounts of substances that are chemically similar to the antigens located on red blood cells, which confer ABO blood type.

It is because of this that the ABO blood type of a secretor can often be determined from a non-blood body fluid stain from that individual. Nonsecretors (the remainder of the population)

do not exhibit these blood group substances in their non-blood body fluids.

The Lewis blood grouping system can be utilized to determine secretor status from a liquid blood sample. If, however, the secretor status cannot be determined from the known blood, then the known saliva sample can be examined.

Limitations on Seminal and Saliva Stains. Sometimes semen is mixed with urine or vaginal secretions from the victim. This can make interpretation of grouping tests more difficult inasmuch as the blood group substances from the victim's body fluids could mask the blood group substances in the semen.

To make a meaningful comparison of grouping test results on questioned semen and saliva stains, the investigator will need to obtain known liquid blood and known dried saliva samples from the victim and suspect.

Saliva on cigarette butts is often contaminated with dirt. Saliva on cigar butts is not groupable. Ash trays should not be simply emptied into a container. Rather, individual cigarette butts should be removed from the ash and debris, and packaged separately. In view of the difficulties involved in cigarette saliva grouping and the circumstantial nature of any successful result, it is often more judicious for the investigator to request latent fingerprint examinations of cigarette butts in lieu of serological examinations.

It is not necessary to submit known semen samples from the suspect in rape cases because the information necessary to make comparative analyses can be gleaned from the suspect's known blood and known saliva samples.

Rape Case Considerations

In light of recent developments in forensic DNA technology, the collection and preservation of serological evidence in a rape case warrants special consideration The forensic serologist can often provide the investigator with information beyond the fact that "semen is present" on an item if the proper samples are obtained, preserved, and submitted to the laboratory in a timely manner.

Body cavity swabs should be collected from the victim as expeditiously as possible following the assault. Once dried and packaged, these swabs should be frozen until they are submitted to the laboratory.

DNA Examinations

Deoxyribonucleic acid (DNA) is analyzed in body fluids and body fluid stains recovered from physical evidence in violent crimes. DNA analysis is conducted utilizing the restriction fragment length polymorphism (RFLP) method or other appropriate DNA methods. Evidence consists of known liquid and dried blood samples, portions of rape kit swabs and extracts, and body fluid stained cuttings from homicide, sexual assault, and serious aggravated assault cases.

The results of DNA analysis on a questioned body fluid stain are compared visually and by computer image analysis to the results of DNA analysis on known blood samples as a means of potentially identifying or excluding an individual as the source of a questioned stain. As such, this technique is capable of directly associating the victim of a violent crime with the subject or the subject with the crime scene, similar to a fingerprint. The implementation of this technique in the laboratory represents a significant advance in forensic serology.

Chemicals

Toxicological Examinations. A toxicological examination looks for the presence of drugs and/or poison in biological tissues and fluids. The toxicological findings show whether the victim of a crime died or became ill as the result of drug or poison ingestion, or whether the involved persons were under the influence of drugs at the time of the matter under investigation.

Because of the large number of potentially toxic substances, it is necessary (unless a specific toxic agent is implicated prior to examination) to screen biological samples for classes of poisons.

Examples of these classes and the drugs and chemicals that may be found within these classes are as follows:

- Volatile compounds, e.g., ethanol, carbon monoxide, and chloroform
- Heavy metals, e.g., arsenic, mercury, thallium, and lead
- Inorganic ions, e.g., cyanide, azide, chloride, and bromide
- Non-volatile organic compounds, e.g., most drugs of abuse and other pharmaceuticals, as well as pesticides and herbicides

Drug and Pharmaceutical Examinations. The forensic laboratory will determine if materials seized as suspected drugs do in fact contain controlled substances. In addition, the laboratory can examine a wide variety of items, such as boats, aircraft, automobiles, clothing, luggage, and money, for the presence of trace quantities of cocaine, heroin, phencyclidine (PCP), etc. A pharmaceutical examination will identify products for the purpose of matching recovered products with stolen products, or for proving that pharmaceuticals were switched.

Arson Examinations. The gas chromatography technique is used to determine the presence of accelerants or other substances introduced to a fire scene to facilitate destruction. Debris collected from the scene of a suspected arson can be analyzed to learn if a distillate was used to accelerate the fire and, if so, testing can classify the distillate by product, such as gasoline, fuel oil, or paint solvent. Debris most suitable for analysis will be absorbent in nature, e.g., padded furniture, carpeting, plasterboard, and flooring.

General Chemical Examinations. Qualitative and quantitative analyses can be made of miscellaneous chemical evidence. Quality analysis is helpful in cases involving theft or contamination of chemical products, malicious destruction, and assault. Analysis of writing inks can match questioned documents with known ink specimens obtained from typewriter ribbons and stamp pads. In consumer product tampering cases, analysis can determine the presence and nature of contaminants, adulterants, and alterations to containers. Chemical examinations can be useful in evaluating tear gas and dyes in bank robber packets, constituents determination in patent fraud cases, and flash and water soluble paper in gambling and spy cases.

Document Examinations

The questioned document field includes examinations of handwriting; hand painting; typewriting; mechanical impressions, such as checkwriter imprints, embossed seals, rubber stamps, and printed matter; photocopies; paper; altered documents; obliterated writing; indented writing; charred documents; and others.

Handwriting and Hand Printing. Writers can be positively and reliably identified with their writings. Other characteristics, such as age, sex, and personality, cannot be determined with certainty from handwriting. A handwriting identification is based upon the characteristics present in normal handwriting. It is not always possible, therefore, to reach a definite conclusion in the examination of handwriting. Some of the reasons for inconclusive results are:

- Limited questioned writing.
- Inadequate known samples.
- Lack of contemporaneous writing, such as when a long period of time has elapsed between preparation of the questioned writing and the known samples.
- Distortion or disguise in either the questioned writing or the known writing. In this situation, the normal handwriting characteristics are not present.
- Lack of sufficient identifying characteristics in spite of ample quantities of both questioned and known writing.

Three types of forged writings are commonly examined:

- Traced Forgery. Produced by tracing over a genuine signature, this forgery cannot be identified with the writer. A traced forgery can, however, be associated with the original or master signature from which the forgeries were traced if it is located.
- Simulated Forgery. Produced by attempting to copy a genuine signature, this forgery may or may not be identifiable with the writer, depending on the extent to which normal characteristics remain in the signature. Samples of the victim's genuine signature should also be submitted for examination.
- Freehand Forgery. Produced in the forger's normal handwriting with no attempt to copy another's writing style, this forgery can be identified with the writer.

Typewriting Examinations. Questioned typewriting can be identified with the typewriter that produced it. This identification is based upon individual characteristics that develop on the type face and on other features of the machine during the manufacturing process and through use.

Photocopier Examinations. Photocopies can be identified with the machine producing them provided samples and questioned copies are relatively contemporaneous. Two sets of questioned photocopies can be identified as having been produced on the same machine, and possible brands or manufacturers can be determined by comparison with a reference file maintained at the laboratory.

Mechanical Impression Examination. Questioned printed documents can be compared with genuine printed documents to determine if counterfeit. Two or more printed documents can be associated with the same printing, and a printed document can be identified with the source printing paraphernalia such as artwork, negatives, and plates.

A checkwriter impression can be identified with the checkwriter that produced it, and examination of a questioned impression can determine the brand of checkwriter producing it. A rubber stamp impression can be identified with the rubber stamp producing it, and an embosser or seal impression can be identified with the instrument that produced it.

Paper Examinations. Torn edges can be positively matched, the manufacturer can be determined if a watermark is present, and paper can be examined for indented writing impressions. Indentations not visible to the eye can be brought up using appropriate instruments. Some watermarks provide dating information, indicating the date of manufacture of the paper.

Writing Instruments. Chemical analysis can determine if the ink of two or more different writings is the same or different formulation. The same analysis can be conducted with an ink writing and a suspect pen. The examinations do not identify a specific pen, only that the inks are the same formulation. Ink dating examinations can also show the earliest date a particular ink was produced.

True Age of a Document. The earliest date a document could have been prepared may sometimes be determined by examination of watermarks, indented writing, printing, and typewriting. Chemical analysis of writing ink may determine the earliest date the formulation was available.

The Federal Bureau of Investigation (FBI) Laboratory maintains reference files of known standards that can be compared with questioned materials submitted for analysis.

Typewriter Standards. These consist of samples of many styles of both foreign and domestic; they permit determination of possible brands or manufacturers of typewriter from examination of questioned typewriting.

Watermark Standards. This file is an index of watermarks found in paper; it enables determination of the paper manufacturer.

Safety Paper Standards. These are samples of a variety of safety papers which enable determination of paper manufacturer when used in production of fraudulent documents, such as checks and birth certificates.

Checkwriter Standards. Sample impressions from many checkwriters allow determination of checkwriter brand or manufacturer from examination of questioned impression.

Shoe Print and Tire Tread Standards. A collection of sole and heel designs and tire tread designs helps determine the manufacturer of shoes and tires from prints or impressions left at the crime scene.

Office Copier Standards. A collection of samples from and information about many brands of photocopiers and office duplicating machines assists in determining possible brands and manufacturers of a questioned photocopy.

Explosives Examinations

Explosives examinations are visual and microscopic analyses of bomb remains, commercial explosives, blasting accessories, military explosives, and ordnance items. Tool mark examinations of bomb components are also possible.

Bomb remains are examined to identify bomb components, such as switches, batteries, blasting caps, tape, wire, and timing mechanisms. Also identified are fabrication techniques, unconsumed explosives, and overall construction of the bomb. Instrumental examination of explosives and explosive residues are carried on in conjunction with bomb component examinations. All bomb components are examined for tool marks, where possible tools used in constructing the bomb are identified for investigative purposes.

Explosive Reference Files. The FBI Laboratory maintains extensive reference files on commercial explosives, blasting accessories, and bomb components. These files contain technical data plus known standards of explosive items and bomb components, including dynamite, water gels, blasting agents, blasting caps, safety fuse, detonating cord, batteries, tape, switches, and radio control systems.

Firearms

Firearms identification is the study by which a bullet, cartridge case, or shotshell casing may be identified as having been fired by a particular weapon to the exclusion of all other weapons.

The firearms examiner will provide one of three conclusions: (1) that the bullet, cartridge case, or shotshell casing was fired by the weapon; or (2) was not fired by the weapon; or (3) there are not sufficient microscopic marks to make a positive identification.

Bullets. Marks on bullets can be produced by rifling in the barrel of the weapon by a flash suppressor or possibly in loading. When a bullet and/or fragment bearing no microscopic marks of value for identification purposes is encountered, it is often useful to perform a quantitative analysis and compare the results to the similarly analyzed bullets of any recovered suspect ammunition (e.g., cartridges remaining in the suspect firearm, cartridges in suspect's pockets, partial boxes of cartridges in suspect's residence, etc.). When two or more lead samples are determined to be compositionally indistinguishable from one another, a common manufacturer's source of lead is indicated. Lead composition information, in conjunction with other circumstantial information, is often useful in linking a suspect to a shooting. Compositional analysis of shot pellets and rifled slugs can provide similar useful circumstantial information.

Cartridge Cases or Shotshell Casings. Marks on a fired cartridge case or shotshell casing can be produced by breech face, firing pin, chamber, extractor, and ejector with a fired cartridge case. The examiner may be able to determine the specific caliber, type, and, possibly, make of the weapon that was fired. A fired shotshell casing can reveal gauge and original factory loading. Wadding can indicate gauge and possibly manufacturer. From shot, the examiner can determine size.

Extractor or ejector marks on a fired cartridge or casing that match with a specific weapon means only that the cartridge or casing had been loaded into and extracted from that specific weapon. To conclude that the cartridge or case was actually fired by the specific weapon, the examiner must rely on a firing pin impression or breech face and chamber marks.

Gunshot Residues. Gunshot residues on clothing may be located, depending on the muzzle-to-garment distance, in two ways: (1) by microscopic examination of the area surrounding the hole for gunpowder particles and gunpowder residues, smudging, and singeing; and (2) by chemical processing to develop a graphic representation of powder residues and lead residues around the hole. Test patterns can be compared with those produced at various distances using the suspect weapon and ammunition like that used in the case.

When a person discharges a firearm, primer residues can be deposited on that person's hands in varying amounts. These amounts are dependent upon the type, caliber, and condition of the firearm, and the environmental conditions at the time of the shooting. Residue samples can be collected from a suspect's hands and analyzed for the presence of the chemical elements antimony, barium, and lead, which are components of most primer mixtures. The analytical technique used to analyze these hand samples is dependent upon the type of hand samples collected from the suspect's hands.

Washing the hands and various other activities on the part of the shooter can remove substantial amounts of residue. Therefore, it is imperative to obtain samples as soon after the shooting as possible. Samples obtained more than 6 hours after a shooting are generally of little value and normally will not be analyzed.

Samples obtained from the hands of victims of close-range shootings (within approximately 10 feet) are generally of no value since it is not possible to differentiate between residues deposited on the hands of a shooter and victim of a close-range shooting. Therefore, samples from the hands of victims are not normally accepted for analysis.

Shot Pattern. The distance at which a shotgun was fired can be determined. It is necessary to fire the suspect weapon at various distances using the same type of ammunition involved in the case being investigated.

Hairs and Fibers

Hair and fiber examinations are valuable in person-to-person violence cases, such as rape and murder cases, because they can assist in placing the suspect at the scene of the crime by determining the interchange of hairs or fibers between the victim and suspect. Similarly, these examinations can be helpful in connecting a suspect to surreptitious crimes, such as burglary and auto theft, and in identifying the scene of the crime. Hairs or fibers found on knives, jimmy bars, and the like can identify the weapons or instruments of crime, as well as automobiles involved in hit-and-run cases. Victim and witness testimony can also be corroborated by the discovery of hairs and fibers.

Hairs. Examination of a hair can determine if it is animal or human; if animal, the species from which it originated (dog, cat, deer, etc.), and if human, the race, body area, how removed from the body, damage, and alteration (bleaching or dyeing).

The finding from a hair examination is good circumstantial evidence, but not positive evidence. An examination can conclude whether or not a hair could have originated from a particular person based on microscopic characteristics present in the hair. Age cannot be determined, but gender may be determined depending on the condition of the hair's root.

Fibers. Examination of a fiber can identify the type of fiber, such as animal (wool), vegetable (cotton), synthetic (human-made), and mineral (glass). The usual purpose of a fiber examination is to determine whether or not questioned fibers are the same type and/or color, and match the microscopic characteristics of fibers in a suspect's garment. Like hairs, fibers are not positive evidence, but are good circumstantial evidence.

Fiber examinations can include analyses of fabrics and cordage. A positive identification can be made if a questioned piece of fabric can be fitted to the known material. Composition, construction, color, and diameter of fibers are the points of comparison. Cordage or rope left at the scene of the crime may be compared with similar materials, and in some cases the manufacturer can be identified if the material contains a unique tracer.

The same principles of examination can be applied to botanical specimens, where plant material from a known source is compared with plant material from a questioned locale.

Finally, identifications can be made through comparisons of teeth with dental records and X-rays with corresponding bone structures. Examinations may be made to determine if skeletal remains are animal or human. If human, the race, sex, approximate height and stature, and approximate age at death may be determined.

The presence of a suspect at the crime scene can be established from a comparison of wood from the suspect's clothing or vehicle, or possession of wood from the crime scene. The specific wood source can be determined from side or end matching and fracture matching.

Miscellaneous Examinations

Related examinations include button matches, fabric impressions, glove prints, feathers, knots, and identifying the clothing manufacturer through a label search.

Materials Analysis

These examinations entail the use of instrumentation, such as infrared spectroscopy, X-ray diffractometry, emission spectrometry, and gas chromatography/mass spectrography (GC/MS), for identification or comparison of the chemical compositions of paints, plastics, explosives, cosmetics, tapes, and related materials.

Automobile Paints. It is possible to establish the year and make of an automobile from a paint chip by use of the National Automotive Paint File, which contains paint panels representing paints used on all makes of American cars and many popular imported cars such as Mercedes Benz, Volkswagen, Porsche, Audi, BMW, Renault, Honda, Subaru, Datsun, and Toyota. A very careful search of the accident or crime scene should be made to locate small chips because:

- Paint fragments are often found in the clothing of a hit-and-run victim. Therefore, the victim's clothing should be obtained and submitted to the laboratory whenever possible.
- Paints may be transferred from one car to another, from car to object, or from object to car during an accident or the commission of a crime. Occasionally it is better to submit an entire component, such as a fender or bumper, if the paint transfer is very minimal.

Non-Automobile Paints. Paint on safes, vaults, window sills, door frames, etc., may be transferred to the tools used to open them. Therefore, a comparison can be made between the paint on an object and the paint on a tool.

Cosmetics. Unknown or suspected cosmetics and/or makeup can be compared with a potential source in assault cases, such as rape. The investigator should be alert to the possible transfer of such materials between victim and suspect.

Plastics/Polymers. It is not possible to specifically identify the source, use, or manufacturer of plastic items from composition alone, but comparisons such as the following can be made:

- Trim from automobiles, depending upon the uniqueness of the composition, is compared with plastic remaining on property struck in a hit-and-run type case.
- Plastics comprising insulation on wire used in bombings, wiretapping, and other crimes are compared with known or suspected sources of insulated wire.
- Plastic/rubber tapes from crime scenes are compared with suspected possible sources.
- Polymers used in surgical cloth-backed tape are compared with sources.
- Miscellaneous plastic material from crime scenes is compared with possible sources.

Tape. A positive identification can be made with the end of a piece of tape left at the scene of the crime and a roll of suspect tape. If no end match is possible, composition, construction, and color can be compared as in other types of examinations.

Metallurgy

Metals or metallic objects may be metallurgically examined for comparison purposes and/or information purposes. Determinations to ascertain if two metals or two metallic objects came from the same source or from each other usually require evaluations based on surface characteristics, microstructural characteristics, mechanical properties, and composition.

Surface Characteristics. These are macroscopic and microscopic features exhibited by a metal surface, including fractured areas, accidental marks or accidentally damaged areas, manufacturing defects, material defects, fabrication marks, and fabrication finish. The fabrication finish reveals part of the mechanical and thermal histories of how the metal was formed, e.g., if it was cast, forged, hot-rolled, cold-rolled, extruded, drawn, swaged, milled, spun, or pressed.

Microstructural Characteristics. These are the internal structural features of a metal as revealed by optical and electron microscopy. Structural features include the size and shape of grains; the size, shape, and distribution of secondary phases; non-metallic inclusions; and other heterogeneous conditions. The microstructure is related to the composition of the metal and to the thermal and mechanical treatments that the metal has undergone; it therefore contains information concerning the history of the metal.

Mechanical Properties. These characteristics describe the response of a metal to an applied force or load, e.g., strength, ductility, and hardness.

Composition. This is the chemical element makeup of the metal, including major alloying elements and trace element constituents. Because most commercial metals and alloys are non-homogeneous materials and may have substantial elemental variation, small metal samples or particles may not be compositionally representative of the bulk metal.

Broken and/or mechanically damaged (deformed) metal pieces or parts can be examined to determine the cause of the failure or damage, i.e., stress exceeding the strength or yield limit of the metal, material defect, manufacturing defect, corrosion cracking, and excessive service usage (fatigue). The magnitude of the force or load that caused the failure can be determined, as well as the possible means by which the force or load was transmitted to the metal and the direction in which it was transmitted.

Burned, heated, or melted metal can be evaluated to determine the temperature to which the metal was exposed; the nature of the heat source that damaged the metal; and whether the metal was involved in an electrical short-circuit situation.

Rusted or corroded metal can be examined to estimate the length of time the metal has been subjected to the environment that caused the rust or corrosion, and the nature of the corrosive environment.

Cut or severed metal can be tested to identify the method by which the metal was severed—sawing, shearing, milling, turning, arc cutting, flame cutting (oxyacetylene torch or "burning bar"), etc.; the length of time to make the cut; and the relative skill of the individual who made the cut.

Metal fragments can be analyzed to reveal the method by which the fragments were formed. If fragments had been formed by high-velocity forces, such as an explosion, it may be possible to determine the magnitude of the detonation velocity. It may also be possible to obtain an identification of the item that was the source of the fragments. In bombings, timing mechanisms can often be identified as to type, manufacturer, and model; determinations are sometimes possible as to the time displayed by the mechanism when the explosive detonated and as to the relative length of time the mechanism was functioning prior to the explosion.

Examination of nonfunctioning watches, clocks, timers, and other mechanisms can be revealing as to the condition responsible for causing the mechanism to stop or malfunction, and whether the time displayed by a timing mechanism represents a.m. or p.m.

For items unidentified as to use or source, it may be possible to identify the use for which the item was designed, formed, or manufactured, based on the construction of and the type of metal in the item. The manufacturer and the specific fabricating equipment utilized to form the item might be revealed, as well as the possible sources of the item if an unusual metal or alloy is involved. Lamp bulbs that are subjected to an impact, such as from vehicles involved in an accident, can be examined to determine whether the lights of a vehicle were incandescent at the time of the accident.

Objects with questioned internal components can be exposed to X-ray radiography to non-destructively reveal the interior construction and the presence or absence of defects, cavities, or foreign material.

Mineralogy

Mineralogy includes materials that are mostly inorganic, crystalline, or mineral in character. Comparisons will, by inference, connect a suspect or object with a crime scene, prove or disprove an alibi, provide investigative leads, or substantiate a theorized chain of events. These materials include glass, building materials, soil, debris, industrial dusts, safe insulation, minerals, abrasives, and gems.

Glass Fractures. Glass, a non-crystalline, rigid material, can be excellent physical evidence. Fracture patterns can provide valuable information as to direction of breaking force. A physical match of two pieces of glass results in an opinion that they came from a common source to the exclusion of all other sources.

Penetration of glass panes by bullets or high-speed projectiles produces a cone pattern from which the direction and some idea of the angle of penetration can be determined. The type of projectile can also sometimes be determined. By an examination of stress lines on radial cracks near the point of impact, the direction of the force used to break the glass can be determined. This determination depends on identification of the radial cracks and the point or points of impact. By fitting glass pieces together with microscopic matching of stress lines, the laboratory examiner can positively identify the pieces as originally having been broken from a single pane, bottle, or headlight. If pertinent portions of a bottle, headlight, or taillight can be fitted

together, the manufacturer and type may be determined for lead purposes.

When a window breaks, glass particles shower toward the direction of the force 10 feet or more. Particles, therefore, can be found in the hair and on the clothing of the perpetrator. Particles can also become embedded in bullets and/or objects used to break windows. Particles of broken glass from a hit-and-run vehicle are often present on the victim's clothing; many times the driver of a hit-and-run vehicle will emerge from the vehicle to determine what was hit or how seriously the victim was injured; consequently, broken glass from the accident may often be found embedded in the driver's shoes.

By microscopic optical and density comparisons, glass particles can be identified or compared with glass from a known source. The laboratory expert cannot identify the source to the exclusion of all other sources; however, it can be stated and demonstrated that it is highly improbable that the particles came from a source other than the matching known source; if two or more different known sources can be matched, the conclusion is greatly enhanced.

Soils, Dust, and Debris. Soil is any finely divided material on the surface of the earth and may contain such human-made material as cinders, shingle, stones, glass particles, paint, and rust. Soil, as a category, includes debris and industrial dusts, as well as natural soils.

Soil varies widely from point to point on the surface of the earth and even more with depth. For example, industrial dust specimens or soil near factories are often distinctive, and debris may contain particles characteristic of a specific area. Soil cannot be positively identified as coming from one source to the exclusion of all others, but the laboratory expert can associate questioned soil with a most probable source, conclude that a source cannot be eliminated, or that a point or area could not be the source of the questioned soil. Such conclusions have proven extremely valuable in the proof of criminal cases. Soil specimens will often consist of shoe prints, tire marks, burial sites, or mud taken from an area where a transfer of soil to the suspect is logical.

Safe Insulation and Building Materials. Safe insulation is found between the walls of fire-resistant safes, and in vaults and safe cabinets. It is readily transferred to tools and clothing.

Samples of insulation collected at the scene can be compared to apparel, shoes, and tools confiscated from the suspect. The same principles apply where unlawful entry through a roof or wall may cause particles to adhere to the suspect or the tools used.

Photographic Examinations

Infrared, ultraviolet, and monochromatic photography can be utilized to assist in rendering visible, latent photographic evidence that is not otherwise visible to the unaided human eye. Examples of this type of evidence include alterations and obliteration to documents, invisible laundry marks, and indented writing.

Bank Robbery Film. The laboratory can examine this film to:

- Attempt enhancement of poor quality photographic exposures and/or prints.
- Compare in detail the unknown subject's clothing as depicted in the film with the clothing obtained from a suspect.
- Determine the individual's height as depicted in the film. Height is determined preferably from a height chart, but it can also be done mathematically, often to within an inch.
- Compare facial features of the unknown subject in the film with those in a known photograph of a suspect.

Miscellaneous Photographic Examinations. Various other types of photographic examinations can be conducted such as:

- Comparison of film or prints to determine if they were taken by a specific camera.
- Determine the type and date of Polaroid film, as well as preparing a print from the "throw-away" portion.
- Determine if photographs have been altered.

Considerable information can usually be obtained from photographic evidence, using hundreds of various techniques. If photographic materials are in question, they should be forwarded to the laboratory with a clear narrative as to what information or examination is desired.

Reference Files

The FBI Laboratory maintains a number of reference files that can be used for comparison purposes in the evaluation of forensic evidence.

National Motor Vehicle Certificate of Title File. Samples of genuine state motor vehicle certificates of title, manufacturer's statement of origin, and vehicle emissions stickers assist in determination of authenticity of questioned certificates. This file contains photographs of fraudulent documents to assist in association of questioned material from different cases with a common source.

National Fraudulent Check File. A computerized file contains images of fraudulent and counterfeit checks, which helps associate fraudulent checks from different cases with a common source and assists in identification of fraudulent check passers.

Anonymous Letter File. A computerized file contains images of kidnapping, extortion, threatening, and other anonymous communications. This file is matched with questioned documents from different cases with a common source.

Bank Robbery Note File. Images of holdup notes are used to link notes used in various robberies with a common source.

National Stolen Art File. This is a listing of stolen and recovered artwork, mostly paintings, reported by law enforcement agencies. Because artwork does not bear a serial number, entries in the file are based upon a description of the artwork. When available, an image of the artwork is stored, which can be recalled for reference. During a file search, both data and image will appear simultaneously. The minimum value of stolen and recovered artwork for inclusion in the file is $2,000.

National Stolen Coin File. This is a computerized listing of stolen and recovered coins reported by law enforcement agencies. Because coins do not have serial numbers, entries in the file are based upon a description of the coin along with a photograph when available. During a file search, both data and image will appear simultaneously. The minimum value of stolen and recovered coins for inclusion in the file is $2,000.

Pornographic Materials Files. A collection of evidentiary pornographic materials, printed and video, helps in determining proof of interstate travel of pornographic material, and assists in determining production and distribution channels, as well as identity of actors.

These consist of materials submitted in connection with investigations of violations of the White Slave Traffic Act, Interstate Transportation of Obscene Materials, and sexual exploitation of children statutes. This computerized file contains over 50,000 records of commercially produced pornographic materials, and the inventory of items is in every medium including video tapes, 8-millimeter movies, books, magazines, and photographs.

These files provide reference materials for laboratory examiners, data searches for investigations (investigative lead information regarding subject, companies, or specific pornographic products), and "charge out" materials for limited courtroom use and undercover operations.

Shoe Print and Tire Tread Evidence

Shoe print and tire tread evidence found at the scene of a crime can provide important evidence for investigation and eventual prosecution of a case. For three-dimensional impressions, casts should always be made immediately following appropriate photography of the impressions. For two-dimensional impressions, the original impression is most valuable and should be retained and preserved whenever possible and practical, such as when the impression is on glass, paper, or some other retrievable surface.

Shoe and tire reference materials are maintained in the laboratory to assist in the determination of the make or manufacturer of a shoe or tire that made a particular impression. This is useful in some cases to help locate suspects or suspect vehicles.

When known shoes or tires are obtained, comparisons are made between those items and the questioned shoe prints or tire impressions. Comparisons can be made between the physical size, design, manufacturing characteristics,

wear characteristics, and random accidental characteristics. If sufficient random characteristics are present, a positive identification can be made.

Tool Mark Identification

Tool mark examinations are microscopic studies to determine if a given tool mark was produced by a specific tool. In a broader sense, they also include the identification of objects that forcibly contacted each other, were joined together under pressure for a period of time and removed from contact, and were originally a single item before being broken or cut apart. The inclusion of these latter areas results from the general consideration that when two objects come in contact, the harder object (the tool) will impart a mark on the softer object. Saws, files, and grinding wheels are generally not identifiable with marks they produce.

The tool mark examiner can conclude that: (1) the tool produced the tool mark, (2) the tool did not produce the tool mark, or (3) there are not sufficient individual characteristics remaining within the tool mark to determine if the tool did or did not produce the questioned mark.

Several comparisons can be made between a tool and a tool mark. Examination can be made of the tool for foreign deposits, such as paint or metal; for comparison with a marked object; establishment of the presence or nonpresence of consistent class characteristics; and microscopic comparison of a marked object with several test marks or cuts made with the tool. Examination of the tool mark can determine the type of tool used (class characteristics); the size of tool used (class characteristics); unusual features of the tool (class or individual characteristics); the action employed by the tool in its normal operation, and/or in its present condition; and most importantly, if the tool mark is of value for identification purposes.

Fracture Matches. Fracture examinations are conducted to ascertain if a piece of material from an item, such as a metal bolt, plastic automobile trim, knife, screwdriver, wood gunstock, or rubber hose, was or was not broken from a like damaged item available for comparison. This type of examination may be requested along with a metallurgy examination if questioned items are metallic in composition.

Marks in Wood. This examination is conducted to ascertain whether or not the marks in a wood specimen can be associated with the tool used to cut it, such as pruning shears and auger bits. This examination may be requested along with a wood examination.

Pressure/Contact. Pressure or contact examinations are conducted to ascertain whether or not any two objects were or were not in contact with each other, either momentarily or for a more extended time.

Plastic Replica Casts of Stamped Impressions. Plastic replica casts of stamped numbers in metal, such as altered vehicle identification numbers, can be examined and compared with others, as well as with suspect dies.

Locks and Keys. Lock and key examinations can be conducted to associate locks and keys with each other. Such associations are useful in establishing a conspiracy or link of commonality between or among individuals. It is often possible to illustrate this through their possession of keys that will operate a single, lockage instrumentality (e.g., vehicle, safe house, or padlock). Laboratory examination of a lock can determine whether an attempt has been made to open it without the operating key.

Restoration of Obliterated Markings. Obliterated identification markings are often restorable, including markings obliterated by melting of the metal as evidenced by welding marks or "puddling."

Obliterated markings can also be restored on materials other than metal, such as wood, plastics, and fiberglass. Because different metals and alloys often require specific methods for restoration of obliterated markings, the laboratory should be contacted for number restoration procedures for field processing of items too large or heavy for submission.

Conclusion

FBI experts will furnish testimony regarding evidence they have examined. In the interest of economy, however, their testimony should not be requested if it is to be duplicated by another prosecution expert. It is realized that exceptions to this general policy may be required in a given instance.

Source "Laboratory Services." 1992. *Federal Bureau of Investigation.*

HUMAN FACTORS IN INTERVIEWING

Human factors strongly influence interviews. The skilled interviewer recognizes this critical point and strives to understand and deal with the motives, fears, and mental makeup of the interviewee. The line of questions and interview techniques are selected on the basis of an assessment made by the investigator of the interviewee's psychological makeup.

Perception

The average person does not possess strong perceptive skills, and among different people are different skill levels. This point has been illustrated many times in controlled situations where a single event is observed by several persons. As each person recounts his/her observations of the event, we are surprised at how many different versions are offered of the same incident. Why is this so? Psychologists tell us that perception is conditioned by:

- Differing abilities to see, hear, smell, taste, and touch.
- The location of the viewer in relation to the incident at the time of occurrence. Distance and geographical perspective affect vision.
- The amount of time intervening between occurrence and interview.
- The number and nature of events that occur during the interval between occurrence and interview.

What are the implications of these factors? Well, for one thing, the interviewer should attempt to discover if the person being interviewed has physical disabilities that impair the senses. If it is known, for example, that a witness has a vision problem, the investigator should be careful in accepting at full value statements that are based on what the witness saw. It is far better to discover problems in a witness's perception at the outset of an investigation than to have such problems exploited at time of trial by the defendant's lawyer.

It might be helpful during an interview for the investigator to ask the interviewee to place himself or herself on a map or a sketch that depicts the physical layout of the scene at the time of the incident. The position of the interviewee in relation to other persons and objects can help the investigator evaluate how much the person could have seen, heard, or smelled. This technique also discourages fanciful elaboration by the person being interviewed.

Because human memory erodes over time, interviews should be conducted as quickly as practical. Memory not only fades, but becomes colored, either consciously or unconsciously, by what the witness is exposed to after the incident. Remarks made by other witnesses or newspaper accounts may cause an interviewee to fill in memory gaps with inaccurate details. A witness may form an own opinion of guilt or innocence and shape his/her testimony accordingly. This possibility is reduced when the interview is conducted soon, that is, before the witness has time to form personal judgments that distort the truth. Prompt interviewing also affords a suspect less time to formulate an alibi or to "get the story straight" with fellow accomplices.

A person who is subjected to stressful, exciting, or injurious events after observing an incident is likely to forget details. To illustrate, assume a pedestrian observes a speeding motorist strike another pedestrian and drive away from the scene. The witness is caught up in a series of actions, such as giving first aid assistance to the injured, that interfere with recollection.

Prejudice

It is not unreasonable to expect every interviewee to be prejudiced to some degree. The strength and targets of prejudice vary among people. The investigator should be alert to prejudice and deal with it when it surfaces. One way to keep information from being distorted by prejudice is to require detailed, specific answers during an interview. If allowed to talk in generalities, a prejudiced person will make statements that are partially accurate and partially misleading. By remaining within a narrow line of discussion aimed at a specific issue, the investigator forces the interviewee to respond with information that is free of bias.

Hostility

Suspects are naturally reluctant to talk, and we expect them to be uncooperative and resistive to interviewing. Sometimes we are surprised (and dismayed) when we discover that witnesses and even victims show an unwillingness to talk. Finding the reason for hostility is a first step in overcoming it.

Fear of Self-Involvement

The fear of self-involvement is a common obstacle to information collection. Many citizens are unfamiliar with investigative methods and are afraid to assist. Also, a person may have committed a separate offense at some previous time and is fearful it will come to light. Some persons think that crimes that do not happen to them directly are not their business, or they believe that the misfortunes that befall victims are of the victims' own making. Many people are very private, disliking publicity in general, and some people fear reprisal. The investigator who knows the underlying reason for resistance is better able to work around it.

Inconvenience

Disruption of lifestyle is not pleasant. We are all pretty much animals of habit and we dislike it when the routines of our daily lives are upset because we are kept waiting or inconvenienced by an unexpected event. Some people will actually disclaim knowledge of criminal matters because they wish to avoid questioning. We are also aware of witnesses being required to wait several days in courthouse hallways and then not be called to the stand. Even when a witness is compensated for lost time, there is a residue of resentment against a process that penalizes citizens in the name of civic duty.

Resentment

With some people resentment runs deep and wide. It may manifest itself in a dislike for authority generally. Resentment can appear in the form of blind loyalty to the accused person. We are talking here not of the American tradition that pulls for the underdog, but of the unreasoning attitude that criminals are victims of a repressive society.

Personality Conflicts

Occasionally an interviewee and interviewer will get along beautifully right from the start. More often an interviewing session will begin with mixed feelings and, through the normal give and take of interpersonal communications, a foundation of mutual respect and cooperation will develop. Sometimes, but infrequently, interviewer and interviewee will for one reason or another find it impossible to communicate at all. When this happens the conflict usually has its roots in the attitudes of the interviewee. A successful interviewer will compensate by demonstrating friendliness, showing respect for the interviewee, and using the right words at the right time. In those cases where the investigator is unable to overcome a basic personality conflict, the best course of action is to voluntarily withdraw in favor of another questioner. This should not be regarded as failure, but recognition of a human factor that must be accommodated in the interest of achieving a successful investigative outcome.

John J. Fay

IDENTITY THEFT

According to the Federal Trade Commission over 11 million consumers had their identities stolen and misused in 2004. While the number of victims in 2005 has not yet been officially tallied, it is estimated that one in every 31 consumers was a victim. According to James Van Dyke of Javelin Strategy & Research Inc., a California-based research firm, contrary to popular wisdom the Internet is not the problem. Van Dyke and others objectively argue that the Internet may be a consumer's best fraud-fighting tool. His study reveals that the Internet has gotten a bad rap and the risk it poses to consumers may be grossly exaggerated. "The very thing consumers are most afraid of is actually the thing that makes [them] safer," reports Van Dyke. Those who noticed the fraud quickly by viewing their accounts online usually were able to cut their losses. Van Dyke's study also showed that consumers who spot fraud online suffer an average theft of only about $500 while consumers who spot the problem by other means suffer average losses closer to $4,500.

Van Dyke's study also suggests personal data is most often stolen offline—from an employer or trash bin. Only 12 percent of the victims in his study reported they believed their information was stolen electronically. Stolen or lost wallets, checkbooks, and mail remain the principal mechanisms by which thieves obtain the identities of others. FTC attorney Lois Greisman said, "The crime [identity theft] is not growing" and that "We're seeing a leveling off and that's where you're going to see your first signs of improvement. I'd like to say this is a positive signal."

Fraud investigators have long known that most identity thieves do not typically use public records or computers to steal identities. Moreover, while the crime itself is particularly offensive, under most circumstances the victims suffer little to no harm until the thief uses the stolen identity to commit a more serious crime. Thus, to many it seems that fighting identity theft by restricting access to public records is like attempting to stop telephone fraud by eliminating the public's access to telephones.

Historical Perspective

Identity theft is not a new crime. For centuries criminals have assumed the names and identities of others to hide and escape the long arm of the law. Over the ages, smugglers, pirates, and political revolutionaries have used aliases to protect their true identities and further their endeavors. The use of physical disguises and false identities continues to aid criminals to this day. However, only during the last two decades has the crime of identity theft entered our lexicon and captured our attention. Only since the advent of the desk-top computer and the Internet has identity theft been easy and profitable.

While losses due to identity theft are estimated to be in the billions of dollars, the actual economic impact is difficult to calculate. The Federal Trade Commission (FTC), along with other researchers, frequently lumps ID theft and credit card fraud together. For example, in the

FTC 2002 survey ID theft victims were defined as those who had suffered a stolen and misused credit card, lost money from a personal checking/savings account by way of fraud, or had at any time been the victim of a telephone, Internet, or insurance fraud. Such broad definitions tend to distort reality and limit meaningful analysis. Adding additional complexity is the fact that many victims never report the crime. Businesses particularly are hesitant to make public disclosures when losses occur. In many cases only when it is absolutely necessary is any disclosure made at all. Moreover, the media is rarely sympathetic to the business that becomes a victim, further disincentivizing the well-meaning enterprise. The press abounds with shocking tales of hapless employers who lose personal information on employees, customers, and even shareholders.

It is easy to see that large losses of personal information cause problems for both the individual whose information is lost but also the party that lost it. In some instances, it would appear, the public relations damage to the organization can far exceed the sum of the hard dollar losses suffered by the individual victims. It is also apparent that as small computers and other similar technologies play a greater role in business and are able to hold greater and greater amounts of information, the potential exposure will continue to grow.

How Identity Theft Occurs

In 2002 Ernst & Young reported that over 47 percent of surveyed organizations had been significantly affected by fraud in the previous year. The study concluded that 13 percent of the losses were over $1 million. "Corporate scandals ripped from today's headlines are forcing executive management worldwide to take a closer look at the policies and procedures they have in place to control and mitigate incidents of fraud," said David L. Stulb, in a study conducted by Ernst & Young's North American Global Investigative Services Group. The study says that 51 percent of the organizations surveyed were recovering a greater proportion of fraud-related financial losses than in prior years, an increase from 29 percent. The report also revealed that 60 percent of reporting companies had trained their staff on guide-

lines relating to fraud-related behavior, but a third of those responding to the survey admitted that their staffs would not actually be able to recognize fraudulent activity if confronted with it. The report also disclosed that over half of the surveyed organizations had established policies and guidelines for dealing with fraud-related behavior. This is an important finding. While the number of victim organizations is still significant, more organizations are doing more about it.

Troubling, however, was the study's findings that some 85 percent of the worst frauds were by insiders on the payroll. This corresponds to the experience of this paper's author regarding large-scale identity theft. What seems to be true is that the more access employees are granted, the greater potential exposure of losses for the employer. The reader will be served remembering this when designing a prevention strategy.

Identity thieves often work in one or more of the following ways:

1. They open new credit card accounts, using the victim's name, date of birth, and Social Security number. When they use the credit card and don't pay the bills, the delinquent account is reported on the victim's credit report and collection efforts against the victim ensue.
2. They call the victim's credit card issuer and, pretending to be them, change the mailing address on the credit card account. Then the imposter runs up charges on the account. Because the bills are being sent to an incorrect address, the victim may not immediately realize there's a problem.
3. They establish cellular phone service in the victim's name or use the victim's identity to rent or purchase real estate.
4. They open a bank account in the victim's name and write bad checks on that account.

Regardless of what is done with stolen identity, the criminal must first obtain it. As indicated above, the Internet is not the primary source of identities that are stolen and misused. Most are stolen from employers. Because employers typically maintain personal information on large numbers of people (usually employees), attractive targets exist. Employers are also sometimes careless. Improperly storing information or failing to properly protect it, will give thieves easy access to large volumes of personal information without incurring significant risk. Stealing from employers also does not require one to disguise an IP address, redirect e-mail, recruit and trust an unscrupulous Internet Service Provider, or slink around in an electronic underworld. In many instances, the thief needs only access to the data and a means to remove it.

Once removed, the data is then repackaged or parsed. It ultimately finds its way to the criminals that misuse it. To the surprise of many, criminal networks exist that broker and distribute such information at the wholesale level. Eventually, the personal data is "retailed" to someone capable of using it to commit criminal mischief.

Identity Theft Terminology

Flagging. Identity thieves look for the raised flags on mailboxes. They take letters addressed to creditors that may contain checks and personal information. The thieves then "wash" checks and write their own name into the "Pay to the order of" line, and cash the check. It may take months to discover this form of identity theft.

Skimming. Skimming involves the use of a small electronic device to capture personal account information from debit or credit cards. Skimmers can be hand-held or affixed to ATM machines.

Dumpster Diving. Identity thieves search discarded trash for pre-approved credit card applications or other personal financial documents, and then use the information therein to make purchases.

Phishing. These attacks use 'spoofed' e-mails and fraudulent websites designed to fool recipients into divulging personal financial data such as credit card numbers, account usernames and passwords, Social Security numbers, etc. By hijacking the trusted brands of well-known banks, online retailers, and credit card companies, phishers are able to convince up to 5 percent of recipients to respond to them. The responding

party is then asked to provide passwords and/or personal information which are then later used to commit crimes.

Prevention

While it appears clear that ID theft is pervasive and costly, it seems unclear what to do about it. While lawmakers hastily write new laws restricting access to public records, security professionals suggest that the key to preventing ID theft is already in the hand of the many potential victims.

Here is what the leading security experts recommend:

1. Keep credit cards, personal identification, and passwords in a safe place.
2. Never carry more credit cards or cash with you than you need at any particular time.
3. Report the theft of credit cards or personal identification immediately.
4. Carefully examine your credit card bills and look for charges that may not be yours.
5. If you must give your credit number over the telephone, ensure no one is eavesdropping.
6. Secure your mail. Obtain a mailbox which locks and is tamper-proof.
7. Destroy or safely store all credit card offers, receipts, and bills when finished with them. Shred documents containing sensitive information.

Although the public's concern about ID theft and the information they share while online is well placed, security experts say consumers should also be concerned about what they put in the mail. Here's what to do to protect yourself and your checks:

1. Never make checks payable to *Cash*.
2. Protect deposit slips. A common scam is to deposit worthless checks into your account and get some of the deposit back as cash.
3. Order your checks from your bank. Mail-order checks are often less expensive but typically are easier to alter than bank checks.

4. Pay all bills electronically. Most major banks offer electronic payment services. The convenience is safe and saves time and money.
5. Take your mail containing checks directly to the Post Office. Do not leave them in your mailbox for pickup.
6. Sign checks with indelible black ink. Do not use felt-tip pens or pencil.
7. Keep unused checks in a safe place. Destroy all unused checks from closed accounts.
8. Review your bank statements carefully. Notify your bank immediately if you suspect someone has altered or forged one of your checks.
9. Protect your signature. Use your real signature for checks and important documents; use another for forms, questionnaires, and other routine documents.
10. Report suspicious transactions to your bank immediately. The sooner the bank is aware of problem, the sooner it can investigate it and take corrective action.

Protecting Computers

Combine a readily available cracking application with a simple dictionary file and chances are any hacker could crack most of the passwords protecting your computer. As simple as it sounds, this type of "brute force" attack is one of the most common among hackers.

Password cracking doesn't always have to take a high-tech approach to be successful. Finding a sticky note on a computer or under a keyboard is fairly simple. Because most passwords are so simplistic, crackers often use tools that literally try every word in the dictionary. Add a hybrid module and this same program starts adding numbers and symbols to these words. According to security experts at Carnegie Mellon University, well over a million passwords have been stolen on the Internet.

Ineffective passwords include common words, the same words spelled backwards, or words with numbers added at the end. Users who are comfortable with a password will often start off with the word, and when prompted monthly to change their password, will simply add a digit. So what starts in January as

"Snoopy" ends up in December as "Snoopy 12." Avoid family members' names, pets' names, and Social Security numbers.

An effective strategy is to use a combination of upper and lower case letters in conjunction with symbols and numbers. Some examples might be:

Time + effort = $

IThinKThere4Im!

$howMeThe$

Protecting E-mail

Most cyber-users know e-mail messages are neither secure nor private. But privacy advocates have recently issued a new warning that e-mail may be less confidential than people thought. A recent First Circuit Court of Appeals decision suggests that e-mail's mode of transmission—hopping from computer to computer—does not fit the definition of "electronic communications" in federal wiretap laws. If so, the privacy protections that were once thought to exist when using e-mail may not exist at all. In response, security and legal experts have issued their own warnings:

1. Do not send messages that, if compromised, would embarrass you or your organization.
2. Read your e-mail service provider's privacy statement. Ensure it promises that your messages will not be read by the provider or shared with others without your permission.
3. Consider using encryption software. A Google search while writing this paper for the term, *encryption software* yielded approximately 3,030,000 results.
4. Do not use instant messaging (IM) for confidential communications.
5. Before giving away an old computer, remove the hard drive and destroy it.

Summary

Identity theft is less likely to occur from online activities than by traditional means, such as losing or having your wallet stolen, stolen mail, or dumpster diving. Researchers report that computer crime accounts for only 11.6 percent of all identity theft in 2004, while 68 percent occurs from paper sources. And while employers are not expected to provide an impenetrable island of safety for their employees or those with whom they do business, they should take reasonable and appropriate steps to protect personal information.

Organizations should create policies and practices that protect sensitive information. Supervisors and managers should enforce those policies consistently and investigate all credible allegations of theft or other misconduct. Employers should use training and education to inform employees of their responsibilities and obligations. Individuals should also take more responsibility for protecting their personal information.

Eugene F. Ferraro

INTERVIEWING WITNESSES

A witness is any person, other than a suspect, who has information concerning an incident. Victims, complainants, accusers, laboratory experts, and informants are simply types of witnesses.

The Victim

In some instances the nature of an incident or the victim's condition as a consequence of the incident can prevent an interview, at least a timely interview. When a business is the victim, an interview is made of a person representing the business. In almost every case, the person interviewed will be the person in charge of the department affected by the incident such as the custodian of a stockroom from which valuable computer equipment disappeared.

Although we can normally expect a victim to be cooperative, we cannot expect the information to be highly reliable. A victim may be overly eager to please, or may inflate the severity of the incident as a means to obtain sympathy or a larger insurance payoff. The investigator also has to guard against the possibility that a victim may be the guilty party.

When a victim is not cooperative, it may be due to fear of retaliation by the offender. Uncooperativeness can also stem from fear of publicity, or a belief that the amount of personal effort in cooperating exceeds the value of bringing an offender to justice.

Direct and Indirect Witnesses

A direct witness is an eye-witness, i.e., a person who saw the incident under investigation. Eyewitnesses are not always known or easily available. It may be necessary to learn the person's name, find him, and then hope he will cooperate. The investigator's task is made more difficult when an eye-witness actively seeks to avoid identification or contact.

An indirect witness is a person who did not see the incident but has valuable information such as the whereabouts of a suspect before and after a violation was committed, or heard the suspect make certain remarks, or knows the location of physical evidence.

Forensic specialists are indirect witnesses. These are persons that evaluate physical evidence and are qualified to give expert and impartial testimony in court. As a general rule, forensic specialists prepare their own statements, which are in the form of laboratory reports. These reports become addenda to the investigator's final report of investigation. When a laboratory report is unclear, the investigator should interview the specialist that made the examination.

A special kind of witness is the informant. Informants are persons who, for pay or other consideration, furnish information. The identity of the informant is usually protected. Interviewing an informant is done much differently than with other witnesses. The place of the interview is likely to be clandestine and the details are taken down in notes as opposed to a formal written statement.

The Complainant

The person who makes the initial report is called a complainant. A complainant can be the victim or a person close to the victim. The motivation of a complainant may not always be honorable. A person may make a report for revenge, to divert suspicion, or self-glorification.

Conducting the Interview

The rule rather than the exception is that an investigator will have very little time to prepare for interviews of non-suspect persons. Persons who are not immediately contacted after the occurrence of an incident may become entirely unavailable at a later time, and when the interval is long, details begin to slip from memory.

The investigator should fix in mind all that is currently known, pay particular attention to specific details, especially those that have not become public knowledge and may therefore be known only to the offender.

Background knowledge of the person to be interviewed will enable the investigator to select a suitable questioning technique. An understanding of the interviewee's connection to the incident helps the investigator evaluate the accuracy and truthfulness of information offered. Knowing something about the interviewee also helps the investigator establish rapport. Examples of background facts include age, place of birth, nationality, address, educational level, habits, companions, prior arrests and convictions, and hobbies.

If the incident is a criminal violation, an investigator who knows the elements of proof for the crime is better prepared to ask questions that bring out the relevant facts. For example, if the law requires that proof be shown of the suspect's use of a dangerous weapon, the investigator is alerted to the need to obtain a detailed description of the weapon in order to establish that a weapon was used and that it was capable of causing serious injury. In complex cases, the investigator can prepare a set of questions to consult during the interview. The questions should be formulated to reveal critical points but still allow the interviewee to freely talk.

Care should be taken not to overestimate or underestimate the interviewee as a potential source of information. Preparation in the context used here is essentially self-preparation, especially of the mind. The investigator readies himself for an encounter with an individual who may be friendly or hostile, communicative or reticent, full of facts or devoid of facts, truthful or lying. The best start that an investigator can make is to have a thorough grasp of case facts, know something about the person, and know what information is necessary to bring the case to a successful conclusion.

Although it is always useful to talk to a witness as soon as possible after an incident, it is sometimes more valuable to postpone an interview until other facts have been determined. Interviews that are scheduled in a logical sequence will permit the investigator to build upon information obtained previously and to avoid re-interviewing persons in order to fill missing gaps or remove contradictions.

Generally, cooperative witnesses can be interviewed first with uncooperative witnesses put on hold until a fuller understanding of the case has been obtained. Also, it might be desirable to delay an interview until physical evidence has been examined or records checked.

It is appropriate to interview witnesses at times and places of their convenience, except when there's a chance the witness may be a suspect or accomplice. The relaxed, psychologically comfortable atmosphere of the witness's office may help the investigator obtain valuable information in a paced, unrushed interview. There is, of course, no objection to conducting a non-suspect interview at the investigator's office if that is the desire of the witness.

The situation is different with hostile and reluctant witnesses. If resistance is anticipated, it is to the investigator's advantage to conduct the interview in an environment psychologically comfortable to him. When an uncooperative witness objects to being interviewed at the investigator's office, a neutral meeting place might be in order.

At the start of an interview, the investigator should make a courteous introduction using his/her correct name and title. The interviewee should be asked to do the same. If there's any doubt about identity, picture identification should be requested.

A quick introduction gives an appearance of haste. A few minutes spent in a proper introduction can pay off. Of even greater importance is the fact that an introduction provides an ideal opportunity for the investigator to assess the interviewee and select an appropriate interviewing technique. A good introduction also affords the interviewee time to overcome nervousness and relate to the investigator as a person.

The closing moments of the introduction should be used to make a general statement about the case without disclosing any of the specific facts. This not only sets the stage for discussions which follow, but also removes the possibility that the interviewee will later claim to be uninformed as to the nature of the inquiry.

What is meant by rapport? In the context used here, rapport is the condition of harmony or agreement that allows a free flow of communication.

The attitude and actions of the investigator during the initial moments of an interview will determine success or failure. The first few minutes almost certainly determine the tenor of the session. The investigator should be friendly, but professional. The objective is to get the interviewee into a talkative mood, and to guide the conversation toward the interviewee's knowledge of the case. Where possible, the interviewee is encouraged to tell the complete story without interruption.

There is usually no requirement to have an observer present during a non-suspect interview. When an investigator feels, however, that the person to be interviewed may have some guilt, it is appropriate to have another person present. When a woman is interviewed, either as a suspect or non-suspect, it is good practice to have another person present (preferably a female) or hold the interview in an open room or semi-public area. This affords some protection from a later accusation of sexual impropriety.

An interview observer should remain neutral, unless planned otherwise. Too many persons present during an interview, or even a single antagonistic person, can cause a statement to be later challenged on the grounds it was obtained under duress.

Conclusion

In the business environment, interviewing is the rule where interrogating is the exception. The term "interrogation" can conjure up visions of coercion and intimidation, and is largely unacceptable for that reason alone. Experienced corporate investigators typically care less; for them, a well conducted interview can be just as productive as an interrogation.

John J. Fay

KINESICS

Kinesics is the study of body language and is based on the behavioral patterns of nonverbal communication. Body language can include any non-reflexive or reflexive movement of a part or all of the body. Body language can be particularly revealing when a person communicates an emotional message to the outside world. It is said that actions speak louder than words, and it's not what you say, but how you say it that counts.

To understand this unspoken body language, kinesics experts often have to take into consideration cultural and environmental differences. The average man, unschooled in cultural nuances of body language, often misinterprets what he sees.

Some have called body language an unconscious signal, such as widening of the pupil when the eye sees something pleasant. Often the swiftest and most obvious type of body language is touch. The touch of the hand, or an arm around someone's shoulder, can spell a more vivid and direct message than dozens of words, but such a touch must come at the right moment in the right context.

We act out our state of being with nonverbal body language. We lift one eyebrow for disbelief. We rub our noses for puzzlement. We clasp our arms to isolate or protect ourselves. We shrug our shoulders for indifference, wink one eye for intimacy, tap our fingers for impatience, slap our forehead for forgetfulness. The gestures are numerous. While some are deliberate and others almost deliberate, there are some, such as rubbing under our noses for puzzlement or clasping our arms to protect ourselves, that are mostly unconscious.

No matter how crowded the area in which we humans live, each of us maintains a zone or territory around us, an inviolate area we try to keep for our own. How we defend this area and how we react to invasion of it, as well as how we encroach into other territories, can all be observed and charted, and in many cases used constructively. These are all elements of non-verbal communication. This guarding of zones is one of the first basic principles. How we guard our zones and how we intrude into other zones is an integral part of how we relate to other people.

When you are at close intimate distance you are overwhelmingly aware of your partner.

For this reason, if such contact takes place between two men, it can lead to awkwardness or uneasiness. It is most natural between a man and a woman on intimate terms. When a man and a woman are not on intimate terms, the close intimate situation can be embarrassing.

We use body language to communicate approval of someone's closeness. Aside from the actual physical retreat of going somewhere else, there will be a series of preliminary signals such as rocking, leg swinging, or tapping. These are the first signs of tension, which are saying, "You are too near, your presence makes me uneasy."

The next series of body language signals are closed eyes, withdrawal of the chin into the chest, and hunching of the shoulders. They say, "Leave me alone. You are in my space." When these signals are ignored, the person will usually move to another location.

Many people who act violently have said that their victims "messed around with them," although the victims had done nothing but come close to them. The victim had intruded on the assailant's personal space.

Defending personal space involves using the proper body language signals or gestures and postures, as well as a choice of a location. Body language and spoken language are dependent on each other. Spoken language alone will not give the full meaning of what a person is saying, nor for that matter will body language alone give the full meaning. If we listen only to the words when someone is talking, we may get as much of a distortion as if we listened only to the body language.

An awareness of someone else's body language and the ability to interpret it create an awareness of one's own body language. As we begin to receive and interpret the signals others are sending, we begin to monitor our own signals and achieve greater control over ourselves, and in turn function more effectively. Research suggests there are no more than about 30 traditional American gestures. There are even fewer body postures that carry any significance in communication and each of these occurs in a limited number of situations.

Of all parts of the human body that are used to transmit information, the eyes are the most important and can transmit the most subtle nuances. While the eyeball itself shows nothing, the emotional impact of the eyes occurs because of their use and the use of the face around them.

The reason they have so confounded observers is because by length of glance, by opening of eyelids, by squinting, and by a dozen little manipulations of the skin and eyes, almost any meaning can be sent out.

The most important technique of eye management is the look, or the stare. With it we can often make or break another person, for example, by giving him or her human or non-human status. Simply, eye management boils down to two facts. One, we do not stare at another human being. Two, staring is reserved for a non-person. We stare at art, at sculpture, at scenery. We go to the zoo and stare at the animals. We stare at them for as long as we please, as intimately as we please, but we do not stare at humans if we want to accord them human treatment.

With unfamiliar human beings, when we acknowledge their humanness, we must avoid staring at them, and yet we must also avoid ignoring them. To make them into people rather than objects, we use a deliberate and polite inattention. We look at them long enough to make it quite clear that we see them, and then we immediately look away. We are saying, in body language, "I acknowledge you," and a moment later we add, "But I won't violate your privacy." A look in itself does not give the entire story, even though it has a meaning. A word in a sentence has a meaning too, but only in the context of the sentence can we learn the complete meaning of the words.

If we are to attempt to interpret body language, then we must assume that all movements of the body have meaning. None are accidental. Extreme caution must be used to avoid misinterpretation of behavior. We cannot rely on any one instance to make a valid inference. All the body signals must be added up to a correct total if we are to use body language effectively.

Perhaps scratching the nose is an indication of disagreement, but it may also be an indication of an itchy nose. This is where the real trouble in kinesics lies, in separating the significant from the insignificant gestures, the meaningful from the purely random, or from the carefully learned.

We must approach kinesics with caution and study a motion or a gesture only in terms of the total pattern of movement, and we must understand the pattern of movement in terms of the spoken language too. The two, while sometimes contradictory, are also inseparable.

There is a surprising lack of uniformity in body movement. Working class people will give certain interpretations to movements, and these interpretations will not apply in middle class circles.

A body movement may mean nothing at all in one context, and yet be extremely significant in another context. For example, the frown we make by creasing the skin between our eyebrows may simply mark a point in a sentence or in another context it may be a sign of annoyance or, in still another context, of deep concentration. Examining the face alone will not tell us the exact meaning of the frown. We must know what the frowner is doing. No single motion ever stands alone; it is always part of a pattern. We must examine other cues accompanying a particular movement to accurately assess its meaning. Body language can serve as a means of communications if we have the ability to understand it.

Kinesics and Interrogation

With respect to interrogation, the psychological assumptions underlying the kinesics technique are:

- The deceptive person who experiences physiological changes resulting from his fear of detection will regard the interrogation as a threat, i.e., an intensification of fear.
- The deceptive person's fears intensify during interrogation at moments when questioning focuses on investigative details having the greatest immediate threat to the person's self-preservation.
- The deceptive person is aware of physiological changes occurring in the body and may do or say things as a means to disguise the changes.
- The deceptive person who does not experience fear during an interrogation will not exhibit any of the body movements that can be associated with deception.

The guilty subject has a general fear of an investigation. When the investigation calls for an interrogation of the guilty subject, the fear intensifies. During the interrogation, the guilty subject's immediate anxieties and apprehensions are directed toward those questions that present the greatest threat to exposure. In other words, a guilty person's fear of detection increases as the investigation proceeds from the general to the specific.

The deceptive person will tune in on questions that indicate trouble or danger. His mental attention and sensory organs are anticipating particular questions. There is a tendency to tune out questions that are of a lesser threat and to concentrate on questions that lead to exposure.

The interrogator cannot always know what questions will produce fear in the guilty subject. As the line of questioning moves closer to the issues having the greatest psychological threat to the subject, there is likely to be an increase in the number and intensity of deceptive behaviors.

Following are tips for spotting deceptive behaviors:

- Determine the demeanor or combination of demeanors that represent a "normal" pattern for the individual being interrogated. Look for changes in the pattern.
- Look for consistency of behavioral signals. One quick change in behavior is not conclusive. Repeated changes from the "normal" pattern may be indicative of deception.
- Look for timing of behavioral signals. Look for deceptive signals or changes from the "normal" pattern when a fear-provoking question (stimulus) is asked. Anticipate a body language response, keeping in mind that it might be a delayed response.
- Interpret deceptive signals in clusters rather than as single observations.
- Look, listen, and follow intuition. Concentrate on watching and listening, and don't be afraid to follow your "sixth sense" in evaluating your observations.
- Compare the suspect's behavior in relation to case details and evidence. Ask yourself, "Is the outward personality of the suspect consistent with the nature of the offense, the manner in which the offense was committed, and the motive?"
- Do not challenge the suspect by telling him the specific indicators of deception you have observed. Although it may be a good practice to point out the forms of personal behavior that contradict a suspect's denial, this should be done in a general way without getting into specific detail. This tends to sidetrack the interrogation and give the suspect an opportunity to explain the symptoms as innocent phenomena.

- Prepare a checklist for recording deceptive signals. As soon as possible following or during a break in the interrogation, the checklist can be used to record the deceptive signals. The checklist can help the interrogator remember behavioral signals which otherwise would have gone unremembered and can serve as a guide in conducting further interrogation.

The interrogation must be planned, and modified during execution, so as to move the line of questioning toward issues that have the greatest threat. A successful interrogation is dependent to a very large degree upon the ability of the interrogator to force the guilty subject to focus upon specific, self-threatening issues.

Not all persons who react deceptively are in fact deceptive or guilty. Some people will respond with deceptive behavior signals when subjected to accusatory questions regardless of guilt. A person of this type is sometimes referred to as a guilt complex reactor. The guilt complex reactor is extremely rare. The basic emotionality of the subject being interrogated must be taken into consideration in determining his or her potential for reaction. Generally speaking, the severity of the offense is proportional to the reaction potential of the guilty subject.

At the beginning of an interrogation the subject will undergo a temporary heightening of the emotional state. This is true whether the subject is guilty or not guilty. As the interrogation proceeds, the heightened emotional state of the innocent subject will decrease.

The reaction potential of a deceptive subject is conditioned by the number and intensity of previous interrogations; and the reaction potential of the deceptive subject may be low or beyond observation if emotional fatigue is present. The innocent apprehensive subject (not necessarily the guilt complex reactor) may give random erratic reactions.

Physiological Roots of the Kinesics Technique

The human body is composed of cells. The cells are organized into tissues, organs, and systems.

The general composition of the human body is specialized both structurally and functionally to accomplish the basic life processes. These processes are: ingestion, digestion, absorption, respiration, excretion, growth, and reproduction.

There are nine major systems of the body. You can be assisted in remembering the nine major systems by the acronym MCRENDERS. The letters of this acronym are the first letters of the major systems of the body, i.e., muscular, circulatory, respiratory, endocrine, nervous, digestive, excretory, reproductive, skeletal.

The nervous system consists of conscious functions and unconscious or autonomic functions. The autonomic functions are actions that occur without our conscious knowledge. They control the actions of the intestine and other digestive organs, the heart and blood vessels, the adrenal glands and the sweat glands. The autonomic functions are performed by motor fibers only. There are no sensory nerve fibers involved.

The autonomic functions are of two types, sympathetic and parasympathetic, which are carried out through nerve fibers in certain body organs. If an organ has sympathetic nerve fibers, it also has parasympathetic fibers. The effects of the two types of fibers operate in exact opposition. For instance, the operation of the heart is accelerated by sympathetic nerves and slowed by parasympathetic nerves. The principal purposes of the autonomic subsystem are to direct the ordinary housekeeping of the body (parasympathetic) and to prepare the body for stress (sympathetic).

The sympathetic function strengthens the defenses of the body against various dangers such as lack of water, temperature extremes, and enemy attacks. By preparing the body to fight or run, the sympathetic function produces certain

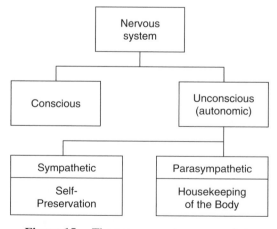

Figure 15.   The nervous system responds to various stimuli.

physiological reactions over which the individual has little control.

The parasympathetic function causes the body to slow down, and in general manages body organs that permit the body to operate under normal, non-stressful conditions. With respect to interrogation, the significance of the parasympathetic function is that a person under stress (for example, a guilty subject) will very likely exhibit deceptive signals that are identifiable.

Deceptive Signals

What is meant by the term deceptive signal? It may be helpful to think of a deceptive signal in terms of the stimulus/response or action/reaction concept. The interrogator provides a stimulus or action that produces a response or reaction from the person being interrogated. The stimulus might be a verbal statement, a remark, a question, or the showing of a photograph or piece of evidence, or even a nonverbal message sent by the interrogator in the form of a gesture or facial expression. For every stimulus or action, one should expect a response or reaction. Sometimes the response is barely perceptible or entirely concealed. Even when the response is small or hidden, the interrogator can draw from this observation some indication of deception. The capacity for deceptive signals is present in every deceptive subject; it is up to the interrogator to provoke the signals through skillful interrogation and then to interpret the signals as he or she sees them.

Now that we know the origin of deceptive signals, what are they and what do they look like? Deceptive signals are varied and numerous. A few examples are: finger tapping; licking the lips; movement of the Adam's apple; rapid speech, stammering; eye movement; changes in pitch, tone, and volume of the voice, etc. You should note that the foregoing examples include signals that are delivered in two modes: a visual mode and an audio mode. It is not correct to think of deceptive signals as being in the visual mode only. Many strong signals are sent through speech and it is not the content of speech that is always significant, but the manner of speech. Deception may be indicated not in terms of what is said, but in the way it is said.

General Demeanor. This term has meaning with respect to the person being interrogated.

A general demeanor is the outward manner, attitude, or bearing of a person in relation to other persons. For our purposes, we can regard a general demeanor as the attitudinal framework within which deceptive signals are manifested. For example, a nervous demeanor is manifested by such deceptive signals as wringing of the hands, slurred and rapid speech, knee jerking, fidgeting, and nail biting. In other words, it is the totality of behaviors (deceptive signals) that convey a general demeanor. Finally, it is possible for one or more demeanors to be exhibited simultaneously or in transition. It is possible for a person to be nervous, fearful, and angry simultaneously, or be in the process of making a transition from these attitudes to demeanors that are defensive, evasive, and complaining. These demeanors are consistent with each other and reflect a discernible pattern. Some demeanors, however, are not consistent. Demeanors that are apologetic and overly polite are inherently contradictory to demeanors that exhibit fear and anger. A shift of this type would represent a radical change in behavior worthy of notice by the interrogator.

Major Body Movements. Many of the gestures and mannerisms of the deceptive subject are somewhat difficult to detect because they are of short duration and hard to catch. This is not the case with gross body movements in which the subject may shift his entire body, move within the interrogation room, or even attempt to leave the room.

TABLE 2. Body Movements Are Easy to Spot but Not Always Easy to Interpret

When a Suspect Displays	
These facial expressions…	These may be the meanings…
Fear	Deception. May be difficult to question
Anger	Truthful person wrongly accused
Defiance	Deception. Difficult to interrogate
Acceptance	Progress is being made
Pleasure	Nervousness or flippant defiance
Blank	Deception. Suspect is careful and wary

Smaller gestures or mannerisms, such as facial expressions, occur at the same time a major body movement is occurring. In fact, the subject may undertake a major body movement at the moment he is aware of a revealing facial expression; the body movement is meant to mask an expression he wishes to hide. Sometimes a body movement will be used to thwart a growing physiological change which, of course, is the product of a threat posed by the interrogator and the line of questioning.

A deceptive subject is likely to want to place his chair as far as possible from the interrogator without giving the impression that he fears the interrogator. The deceptive subject will also want to place some substantial object between him and the interrogator; for example, position his chair so that a desk or table separates the interrogator from the suspect. The intervening object becomes something of a psychological barrier behind which the suspect finds some degree of protection.

Preparation of the interrogation room in advance will help the interrogator maintain control over major body movements of the suspect. These arrangements can include:

• Seat the suspect between the interrogator and the interrogator's partner, and away from the exit door.
• Place the suspect's chair close to the interrogator's chair.
• Select for the suspect a chair that is not too high, too wide, nor too comfortable.

The timing of a major body movement is important. What was asked or what was said immediately prior to the major body movement may have significance with respect to fears of the suspect. Keep in mind that sitting postures are preceded and followed by major body movements. The major body movements may also be revealing, especially when interpreted in conjunction with a sitting posture.

Gestures. A gesture is an activity created by the suspect to reduce tension. Most gestures are unconsciously performed. A deceptive person is likely to perform gestures without realizing it.

Some gestures are consciously initiated and deliberate. A conscious gesture may be an attempt by the deceptive subject to mislead the interrogator; it may be a gesture meant to mask an emotion the suspect wishes to conceal. Consciously controlled gestures should be viewed with suspicion. They are also indicative of a clever, willful, and self-controlled person who is determined to prevail over the interrogator.

Gestures are numerous and varied. As a group, they outnumber other forms of nonverbal communication. Gestures can be a rich source of information concerning the true feelings of a person, and can be placed into four categories: those that symbolize, those that relieve tension, those that mask inner tension, and those that protect.

Facial Expressions. A single facial expression by itself should not be interpreted to conclusively indicate deception. More meaning can be derived by observing the variety of facial expressions displayed by a person being interrogated, especially as the expressions relate to particular questions.

The main value of facial expressions is the help they give in identifying the emotional state of the person being interrogated. They can be likened to road signs that guide the traveler to the desired destination. The interrogator watches for them and alters the route to the final destination.

A problem with interpreting facial expressions is the difficulty of differentiating between genuine and false expressions. Also, a person has greater conscious control over the face than any other part of body. The interrogator should ask himself if a particular facial expression is appropriate to the question posed, or if the expression is consistent with similar questions posed previously.

TABLE 3. All Facial Expressions Have Meaning

When the Deceptive Subject Performs	
These major body movements…	These may be the meanings…
Shift of the torso and gross movement of head and limbs	Internal conflict or fear of the subject being discussed
Stand up	Desire to change the subject
Attempt to leave	A bluff tactic
Move chair away	Retreat from fear

Of the several features constituting the face, the eyes are most important simply because of the large number and variety of eye expressions. Some researchers suggest that about 90 percent of all facial expressions come from the eyes.

When two people are engaged in a normal conversation, between 30 and 60 percent of the time is maintained in eye contact. The implication of this fact is that abnormal or unusual eye contact occurs below or above the 30 to 60 percent range. For the professional investigator, interrogation is a normal, sometimes routine function. For the deceptive subject, interrogation may be a first-time or occasional experience. The deceptive subject therefore finds himself in an abnormal situation. Excessive eye shifting and looking away from the interrogator indicate deception. Prolonged eye contact may suggest that the suspect is aware of eye signals as body language and is over-compensating.

Also, a deceptive subject who is uncooperative and arrogant may stare at the interrogator to show his defiance and throw the interrogator off balance.

Eye contact is related to unwritten social rules. The character of eye contact will vary among persons of varying cultural and ethnic backgrounds. What could be regarded as deceptive eye contact by a person during questioning may in fact be perfectly normal within the person's cultural and ethnic environment.

The best way for an investigator to develop expertise in recognizing nonverbal language by cultural and social type is to study the many varieties of people engaged in routine daily activities. Although different cultures have different rules that govern eye contact, studies indicate that most cultures have these points in common:

- An extended gaze between two persons is normally a challenge and an invasion of privacy.
- Emotionally disturbed persons have abnormal eye contact.
- Strangers will look at each other longer in conversations than persons who know each other.
- The speaker in a conversation is regarded as having dominance and has greater freedom in keeping or breaking eye contact with listeners.

A study of body language is a study of the mixture of all body movements from the very deliberate to the completely unconscious, from those that apply only in one culture to those that cut across all cultural barriers. We are born with the elements of a nonverbal communication. We can make hate, fear, amusement, sadness, and other basic feelings known to other human beings without ever learning how to do it. Nonverbal language is partly instinctive, partly taught, and partly imitative.

Leon C. Mathieu

Sources

Archer, D. and Akut, R.M. "How Well Do You Read Body Language?" (*Psychology Today*, October, 1977).

Goleman, D. People Who Read People. (*Psychology Today*, July, 1979).

Goleman, D. The 7,000 Faces of Dr. Ekman. (*Psychology Today*, February, 1981).

Inbau, F.E. and Reid, J.E. 1967. *Criminal Interrogation and Confessions*. Baltimore: Williams and Wilkins Company.

O'Hara, C.E. 1970. *Fundamentals of Criminal Investigation*. Springfield, IL: Charles C. Thomas.

Plutchik, R. A Language for the Emotions. (*Psychology Today*, February, 1980).

Schurenberg, E. Sheepish Smiles Don't Hide Embarrassment. (*Psychology Today*, November, 1981).

Specter, A. and Ketz, M. 1967. *Police Guide to Search and Seizure, Interrogation and Confession*. Philadelphia: Chilton Books.

Swanson, C.R., Chamelin, N.C., and Territo, L. 1977. *Criminal Investigation*. Santa Monica, CA: Goodyear Publishing Company.

Tobias, M.W., and Peterson, R.D. 1972. *Pretrial Criminal Procedure*. Springfield, IL: Charles C. Thomas.

PHOTOGRAPHY IN INVESTIGATIONS

Photography is an essential tool for the investigator. As a tool it enables the investigator to record the evidence of a crime. Photographs made of a crime can be stored indefinitely and retrieved when needed. There is no other process that can record, retain, and recall criminal evidence as effectively as photography.

Photographs are also a means of communication. They tell something about the objects photographed or the scene of a crime that is helpful in clarifying the issues when testimony is given in court. Because photographs are meant to communicate information honestly, the investigator-photographer has a great responsibility. His photographs must portray a situation as it would be observed by anyone who stood in the same position as the camera and viewed the scene from where the photograph was made.

Photographs by themselves are not substantive evidence. Photographs accepted in court must be attested to by a person who saw the scene and can truthfully state under oath that the photographs accurately represent what the person saw at the scene. In the ordinary, nonlegal field of photography, only the finished photographic print is of interest, but in criminal investigative work, all photographic procedures are subject to review and inspection by the court. Obviously, this rigid requirement makes it imperative that investigative photography conform to high standards of quality and ethics.

Photographic Techniques

The most frequent factor contributing to inferior photographic results is over exposure of the negative. This produces soft, grainy images of low contrast and brightness. Exposure recommendations for any given film are based upon the requirement for a so-called average subject. This is a photographic subject that contains light, medium, and dark tones. If a photographic subject consists of all light tones, the subject would be very low in contrast and high in brightness. If the recommended speed for a given film for use with a so-called average subject were ASA 80, the fact that the photographic subject contained all light tones means that less exposure is required. If, on the other hand, the subject consisted of all dark tones, the subject is low in contrast and is therefore reflecting very little light. In this case the investigator-photographer adjusts his equipment to provide more exposure. For example, less exposure would be called for when the photographic subject is a nude body of a white bleached blonde lying on white sand; or at the other extreme, highly blackened wood at the scene of arson will require greater exposure than an average subject in order to obtain

shadow detail. In short, the investigator must learn to evaluate his photographic subject by contrast and brightness, and to make appropriate adjustments.

Another common difficulty is a dirty lens. Dirt and oxidation may form on the back surface of the lens, as well on the front. Both the outer and inner surfaces of the camera lens should be checked frequently and cleaned when necessary.

Loss of detail in photographic prints is a common problem. This is usually caused by movement of the camera at the time the shutter is released. This problem can be reduced through the use of a rigid tripod and a fast shutter speed.

Sharpness, or image definition, suffers when the diaphragm of a lens is stopped down, i.e., adjusted from its largest opening to its smallest opening. When a lens is stopped down, three things happen:

- The aperture is reduced and less light passes through during a given period of time.
- The depth of field increases.
- The image definition improves to a point (although in a few special cases the definition softens at the smallest apertures).

To obtain good definition the following general rules apply:

- Use a tripod whenever possible.
- For outdoor photography with a handheld camera, set the aperture as required by film and light conditions, and use a faster shutter speed.
- For flash pictures use an electronic flash.

Photography plays a vital part in establishing points of proof for certain types of crime, particularly crimes involving physical violence. The characteristics and location of relevant objects need to be captured in accurate detail and permanently recorded until presented at trial. If a crime scene is altered through carelessness or haste, it can never be restored to its exact original condition, and as a consequence, vital elements of proof may be lost forever. In addition, the significance of certain aspects of a crime scene may not be apparent, although later they may powerfully affect a guilty or innocent conclusion. The first step in the investigation of any crime is to photograph completely and accurately all aspects of the scene before any of the objects of evidence are removed or otherwise disturbed. Photographs should also be made after victims have been removed. It is much better to take too many photographs rather than not enough.

When taking photographs at a scene, the objective should be to record the maximum of usable information in a series of photographs that will enable the viewer to understand where and how the crime was committed. The term *crime scene* refers not just to the immediate locality in which the offense occurred, but relates also to adjacent areas where important acts took place immediately before or after the commission of the offense. The number and types of photographs will be determined by the total circumstances of the crime.

Photographs of the broad area of the locale of the crime scene should be supplemented by closer shots of portions of the crime scene so that important details are made apparent. Each object within an area should be photographed so that it can be located readily in the overall pictures, thus enabling the viewer to gain a clear picture of its position in relation to other objects at the scene and to the overall scene.

Procedures. At an indoor crime scene location at least four photographs will be required to show the room adequately. Moving in a clockwise direction, each photograph will overlap a portion of the preceding photograph so that 360 degree coverage is made of the area. Obviously, when an area is large or contains many pieces of evidence, the number of photographs will be far in excess of the minimum four. Medium-distant, as well as close-up, photographs should be made of important objects. Two lenses are usually sufficient for crime scene photography. A wide-angle lens is useful for interior photographs and a normal angle lens for outdoor photographs.

Lighting. Indoor lighting is rarely satisfactory for photographic purposes. The investigator must take into account the need for additional illumination. Depending upon the size, shape, and location of a crime scene, the investigator may elect to provide additional illumination through photoflood, photoflash, or electronic flash equipment.

Markings in the Field of View. Because a court may object to the presence of rulers or similar measuring devices in a crime scene photograph, it is recommended that the photographs be taken first without the marker and then with the marker. Measuring devices that are used to show the relative size of and distances between objects should be placed in such a manner that they will not obscure any important part of the evidence.

The final determination of the admissibility of photographs is made in court and often depends upon legal points that have little to do with the investigator-photographer. The investigator's contribution to the admissibility of photographs relates mainly to their accuracy and to the custody of them prior to trial.

All evidence must be protected and accounted for from the time it is found until it is offered in evidence. The law requires that the person presenting physical evidence in court be prepared to prove such evidence could not have been altered or replaced. This means that an investigator must be able to account for negatives and prints at all times. This does not present any great problem when photographs taken by the investigator are developed, printed, and secured within in-house resources. Problems can arise, however, when film is processed or placed into the custody of an outside agency. When this occurs, chain of custody procedures must be followed.

To be admissible, a photograph must be verified by a person who viewed the scene, object, or person represented in the photograph, and is able to state that it is an accurate and truthful representation. In other words, the photograph must be a fair and accurate representation of the scene of the crime. Depending on the desires of the court, this issue can be addressed through testimony given by the investigator who took the photographs or by some other competent witness present at the time the photograph was taken.

An investigator who is required to give testimony regarding photographs he or she took at a scene should be prepared to testify regarding safekeeping of negatives and prints, and to explain the details of the photographic procedures followed. An understanding of the rules of evidence and an application of common sense is usually sufficient to ensure that photographs taken in connection with a crime will be admissible in court.

John J. Fay

POLYGRAPH TESTING

The term "polygraph" literally means "many writings." The name refers to the manner in which selected physiological activities are simultaneously recorded. Polygraph examiners may use conventional instruments, sometimes referred to as analog instruments, or computerized polygraph instruments.

A polygraph instrument collects physiological data from at least three systems in the human body. Convoluted rubber tubes that are placed over the examinee's chest and abdominal area record respiratory activity. Two small metal plates, attached to the fingers, record sweat gland activity, and a blood pressure cuff, or similar device records cardiovascular activity.

A typical polygraph examination will include a period referred to as a pre-test, a chart collection phase, and a test data analysis phase. In the pre-test, the polygraph examiner completes required paperwork and talks with the examinee about the test. During this period, the examiner discusses the questions to be asked and familiarizes the examinee with the testing procedure. During the chart collection phase, the examiner administers and collects a number of polygraph charts. Following this, the examiner analyzes the charts and renders an opinion as to the truthfulness of the person taking the test. The examiner, when appropriate, will offer the examinee an opportunity to explain physiological responses in relation to one or more questions asked during the test. It is important to note that a polygraph does not include the analysis of physiology associated with the voice. Instruments that claim to record voice stress are not polygraphs and have not been shown to have scientific support.

Users of the Polygraph

The three segments of society that use the polygraph include law enforcement agencies, the legal community, and the private sector.

Law Enforcement Agencies
- Federal law enforcement agencies
- State law enforcement agencies
- Local law enforcement agencies, such as police and sheriff's departments

Legal Community
- U.S. attorney offices
- District attorney offices
- Public defender offices
- Defense attorneys
- Parole and probation departments

Private Sector
- Companies and corporations that fall under the restrictions and limitations of the Employee Polygraph Protection Act of 1988 (EPPA)
- Private citizens in matters not involving the legal or criminal justice system
- Attorneys in civil litigation

Critics of Polygraph

One of the problems in discussing accuracy figures and the differences between the statistics quoted by proponents and opponents of the polygraph technique is the way that the figures are calculated. At the risk of over simplification, critics, who often don't understand polygraph testing, classify inconclusive test results as errors. In the real life setting an inconclusive result simply means that the examiner is unable to render a definite diagnosis. In such cases a second examination is usually conducted at a later date.

To illustrate how the inclusion of inconclusive test results can distort accuracy figures, consider the following example: If 10 polygraph examinations are administered and the examiner is correct in 7 decisions, wrong in 1 and has 2 inconclusive test results, we calculate the accuracy rate as 87.5 percent (8 definitive results, 7 of which were correct). Critics of the polygraph technique would calculate the accuracy rate in this example as 70 percent (10 examinations with 7 correct decisions). Since those who use polygraph testing do not consider inconclusive test results as negative, and do not hold them against the examinee, to consider them as errors is clearly misleading and certainly skews the figures.

Pre-Employment Test Accuracy

To date, there has been only a limited number of research projects conducted on the accuracy of polygraph testing in the pre-employment context, primarily because of the difficulty in establishing ground truth. However, since the same physiological measures are recorded and the same basic psychological principles may apply in both the specific issue and pre-employment examinations, there is no reason to believe that there is a substantial decrease in the accuracy rate for the pre-employment circumstance. The few studies that have been conducted on pre-employment testing support this contention.

While the polygraph technique is not infallible, research clearly indicates that when administered by a competent examiner, the polygraph test is one of the most accurate means available to determine truth and deception.

Polygraph Screening in Police Agencies

The Employee Polygraph Protection Act of 1988 (EPPA) prohibits most private employers from using polygraph testing to screen applicants for employment. It does not affect public employers such as police agencies or other governmental institutions.

False Positive and False Negative Errors

While the polygraph technique is highly accurate, it is not infallible and errors do occur. Polygraph errors may be caused by the examiner's failure to properly prepare the examinee for the examination, or by a misreading of the physiological data on the polygraph charts. Errors are usually referred to as either false positives or false negatives. A false positive will occur when a truthful examinee is reported as being deceptive; a false negative when a deceptive examinee is reported as truthful. Some research indicates that false negatives occur more frequently than do false positives; other research studies show the opposite conclusion. Since it is recognized that any error is damaging, examiners utilize a variety of procedures to identify the presence of factors which may cause false responses, and to insure an unbiased review of the polygraph records; these include:

Protection Procedures

- Assessment of the examinee's emotional state

- Medical information about the examinee's physical condition
- Specialized tests to identify the overly responsive examinee and to calm the overly nervous
- Control questions to evaluate the examinee's response capabilities
- Actual analysis of the case information
- Pre-test interview and detailed review of the questions
- Quality control reviews

Remedies

If a polygraph examinee believes that an error has been made, several remedies are available:

- Request a second examination
- Retain an independent examiner for a second opinion
- File a complaint with a state licensing board
- File a complaint with the Department of Labor under EPPA
- File a request for the assistance of the American Polygraph Association

Prohibited Inquiries

Personal and intrusive questions have no place in a properly conducted polygraph examination. Many state licensing laws, the Employee Polygraph Protection Act, as well as the American Polygraph Association, have stated that an examiner may not inquire into any of the following areas during pre-employment or periodic employment examinations:

- Religious beliefs or affiliations
- Beliefs or opinions regarding racial matters
- Political beliefs or affiliations
- Beliefs, affiliations or lawful activities regarding unions or labor organizations
- Sexual preferences or activities

In a law enforcement pre-employment polygraph examination, questions can only focus on job related inquiries, such as the theft of money or merchandise from previous employers, falsification of information on job applications, use of illegal drugs during working hours, and criminal activities. The test questions are limited in the time span they cover, and all are reviewed and discussed with the examinee during a pre-test interview. There can be no surprise or trick questions.

In a specific issue polygraph examination, the relevant questions focus on the particular act under investigation.

Use of Results

According to the various state licensing laws and the American Polygraph Association's Standards and Principles of Practice, polygraph results can be released only to authorized persons. Generally those individuals who can receive test results are the examinee, and anyone specifically designated in writing by the examinee, the person, firm, corporation, or governmental agency that requested the examination, and others as may be required by law.

Employee Polygraph Protection Act

On December 27, 1988, the Employee Polygraph Protection Act (EPPA) became law. This federal law established guidelines for polygraph testing and imposed restrictions on most private employers. This legislation only affects commercial businesses. Local, state and federal governmental agencies (such as police departments) are not affected by the law, nor are public agencies, such as a school system or correctional institution. In addition, there are exemptions in EPPA for some commercial businesses. These are:

- Businesses under contract with the federal government involving specified activities (e.g., counterintelligence work).
- Businesses whose primary purpose consists of providing armored car personnel, personnel involved in the design, or security personnel in facilities which have a significant impact on the health or safety of any state. Examples of these facilities would be a nuclear or electric power plant, public water works, or toxic waste disposal.
- Companies that manufacture, distribute, or dispense controlled substances.

In general, businesses cannot request, suggest, or require a job applicant to take a pre-employment polygraph examination. A business can request a current employee to take a polygraph examination or suggest to such a person that a polygraph examination be taken but only when specific conditions have been satisfied. However, the employer cannot require a current employee to take an examination, and if the employee refuses, the employer cannot discipline or discharge the employee based on the refusal alone.

Guidance for the Employer

The American Polygraph Association conforms to U.S. Department of Labor guidance relating to polygraph tests for employees. This information is intended to assist in complying with the EPPA. Employers are encouraged to develop their own forms, use forms that bear their company name, and have the forms approved by legal counsel. When the polygraphist is a private sector person, the employer should demonstrate that the investigation is specific to the loss. In addition, the employer should:

- Show that the investigation is currently in progress.
- Show there is an identifiable economic loss to the employer.
- Abide by the EPPA.
- Provide the employee with a written statement that includes an identification of the company and the working location of the employee.
- Describe to the employee the incident under investigation.
- Name the location of the loss.
- Name the specific amount of the loss.
- Name the type of loss.
- Determine that the employee had access to the loss. (Access alone is not sufficient grounds for polygraph testing.)
- Have a valid reason to suspect the employee.
- Give to the employee a written statement signed by a person authorized to legally bind the employee. The binding statement must be retained by the employer for at least 3 years following the investigation. Read the statement to the employee. Have the employee acknowledge understanding

of the statement. If the employee agrees, the employee should then sign a timed and dated statement in the presence of a witness.

- Notify the employee in writing not less than 48 hours in advance (exclusive of weekends or holidays) as to the time and date of the scheduled polygraph test. If the test is to be conducted at a location other than the place of employment, directions to the location should be provided in writing.
- Conduct a follow-up interview of the employee before an adverse action is taken, during which the employee is told why the adverse action is to be taken.
- Keep all records for at least 3 years.
- Do nothing to require or otherwise coerce the employee to waive his or her right to refuse taking the polygraph test.

When the investigation is loss-related and conducted by a public sector employee, such as a law enforcement or government agent, all of the above apply before conducting a polygraph test. Test results cannot be released to the employer when the test is conducted by a public sector agency.

A $10,000 penalty can be applied for each violation of the EPPA. For this reason alone, the employer should verify that the polygraphist is licensed (if applicable) and possesses professional and experiential competence.

Guidance for the Polygraph Examiner

- Give to the employer a copy of EPPA guidelines and explain it in a face-to-face conference.
- Do not participate with the employer in determining if there is reasonable cause to believe a loss has occurred and who should or should not be tested.
- Prior to interviewing or conducting a polygraph exam, obtain from the employer copies of the relevant documents such as the advance notice and explanation of rights. Also obtain photo identification of the person to be tested.
- At the time and place of a polygraph test, give to the examinee a verbal and written explanation of polygraph test procedures. Obtain from the examinee a written acknowledgment of same.

- Read and explain the examinee's right to refuse taking the test. Obtain from the examinee a written acknowledgment of same.
- If the test is to be taped or viewed, such as through a one-way mirror, advised the examinee of these conditions.
- When one or more tests are conducted in the context of the EPPA, conduct not more than 5 polygraph tests in one day.
- When one or more tests are conducted in the context of the EPPA, keep a log of the company name, examinee names, and times of polygraph tests conducted in the course of one day.
- Administer a single test for not longer than 90 minutes.
- Give to the examinee a form that identifies the questions to be asked during the test. Ask the examinee to answer the questions in writing and sign the form. Retain the original of the form.
- If so required, possess a license issued for use in the state where the test is to be conducted.
- Inform the examinee of test results and allow the examinee to give reasons for the results.
- Inform the examinee in writing of your opinion as to deception or non-deception.
- Base your opinion on test results, and not behavior.

Inform the employer of your opinion but only in the context of the matter under investigation. Do not include extraneous information.

- Keep all documentation for at least 3 years.
- Provide a copy of charts and questions, and an original report to the employee upon request.
- Provide a copy of charts and questions, and an original report to the employer when test results indicate deception.
- Provide the U.S. Department of Labor and other authorized agencies with a copy of charts and questions, and an original report within 72 hours upon request.
- Carry a minimum of $50,000 or equivalent professional liability coverage.

Even when an employer holds an exemption to the EPPA, the EPPA guidelines should be followed.

REQUIREMENTS IMPOSED ON THE PRIVATE SECTOR EMPLOYER

1.   The polygraph test must be relevant to an ongoing specific investigation involving an economic loss to the employer.

2.   The employee must have had access to the property, money, or area central to the investigation. Access can mean physical presence or special knowledge, such as the combination to a safe.

3.   The employer must have a reasonable suspicion that the employee was involved in the incident under investigation. Reasonable suspicion goes beyond having access, and incorporates such factors as a witness's statement, suspicious behavior on the part of the employee, or contradictions between the employee's statements and documented records.

4.   At least 48 hours prior to the examination the employer must give to the employee a written statement which describes the nature of the loss and the investigation, as well as the basis for the employer's "reasonable suspicion."

5.   The Employee Polygraph Protection Act (EPPA) requires that the polygraph examiner follow certain procedures in the administration of the examination. Examples of these include a minimum duration of 90 minutes for the examination, and reading a statement to the employee that enunciates certain rights under the Act.

6.   The employee to be tested cannot be required to take the test.

Qualifications of a Polygraph Examiner

A person is qualified to receive a license as a polygraph examiner when he or she:

- Presents evidence of good moral character.
- Has passed an examination to determine competency.
- Holds an academic degree at the baccalaureate level from an accredited educational institution.
- Has satisfactorily completed 6 months of study in the detection of deception, as prescribed by applicable rule.

Sources

American Polygraph Association. 2006. <http://www.polygraph.org/faq.htm>

Employee Protection Act. 2006. http://www.admpoly.com/eppahome.htm

U.S. Department of Labor. 2006. http://www.dol.gov/esa/regs/compliance/posters/eppa.htm

QUESTIONED DOCUMENTS

A set of absolute rules cannot be applied to the conduct of any investigation, and no two cases involving questioned documents will be exactly alike. The implication? Use the information in this section as a guide and be prepared to season it with liberal amounts of common sense.

An exemplar is a collected writing obtained from an individual at the request of another, usually an investigator. It is a sample of an individual's handwriting or hand printing, and relates to a case under investigation in which the individual is somehow involved. A standard is a known writing made during the normal course of an individual's activity, usually prior to the incident under investigation. Hand-printed entries on an employment application form and signatures on canceled checks are examples of standards.

Standards are particularly valuable to the document examiner because they allow comparison with characteristics that appear in exemplars. If a disguise is attempted by the writer of exemplars, the examiner may be able to detect the attempt in the examination of standards. Exemplars and standards are often called known writings because authorship is known.

In addition to linking a suspect to the questioned text or signature, exemplars and standards are often used to eliminate the victim from consideration as the author. They are also valuable in determining attempts to simulate or trace the writing of the victim. Exemplars and standards should be collected from the victim in every case, even when the indications of guilt point strongly elsewhere.

Obtaining Known Writings

Exemplars are made from dictation without allowing the writer to view the questioned document. No assistance should be given to the writer as to spelling and punctuation. An error in spelling or punctuation that appears in both the questioned document and an exemplar would be noteworthy. As each exemplar is completed, the investigator removes it from the writer's sight. The objective is to not make it easy for the writer to create a consistent disguise among all the exemplars by copying one after the other.

Each exemplar is placed on a separate piece of paper. The shape and size of the paper corresponds to the shape and size of the questioned document. The writer is directed by the investigator to place the exemplar in the same area or space as it appears on the questioned document. If the questioned writing is on a form, such as a credit application, the investigator would want to obtain a quantity of the same credit application stock. Blank forms would be handed one at a time to the writer. An absolutely incorrect procedure would be for the writer to put all of the exemplars on one piece of paper, one immediately below the other.

Exemplars need to be made of all writings that appear on the questioned document. For example, if a check is the questioned document, the writer should be asked to write not only the maker's signature, but the "Pay to the Order of" entry, the date, and the check amount in words and numbers. A point to keep in mind is that a document may bear writings made by more than one person. Because a person did not write a questioned signature does not mean he or she did not write some other portion of the document. In check cases, it is not unusual for one person to fill out the check and get an accomplice to sign it.

How Much Is Enough?

This question is answered with the observation that the chances for obtaining a definitive opinion increase relative to the number of exemplars provided to the questioned document examiner. Case circumstances will sometimes dictate a need for collecting a large number of exemplars and standards. Consultation with a document examiner is recommended before making the collections. As a general rule, a greater number of known writings is required for analysis when the questioned writing is meager, and vice versa. Also as a general rule, the collected standards should reflect a mix of writings that were made just prior to and shortly after the time frame of the document in question. A signature made 10 years before or after a signature in doubt will not be very meaningful to the examiner.

Typically, a questioned signature will require the investigator to obtain 12 to 15 signature exemplars, plus 12 to 15 known signature standards. A note or letter to be examined will require two to three repetitions, depending on length, and an address on an envelope or package will require about 25 exemplars. If the questioned document is typewritten and lengthy, such as a letter, two to three repetitions of the exact text should suffice, but if the typewritten text is short, such as a signature block, at least 25 exemplars will be needed.

Because some people can write equally or nearly as well with either hand, the investigator should ask the writer at the beginning of an exemplar collecting session to provide one or two samples from each hand. If the investigator is satisfied that the writer is proficient with only one hand, further exemplars by the weak or "unaccustomed writing hand" will not be necessary. If the investigator is not satisfied on this point, exemplars from both hands should be collected. When the questioned writing appears to have been made by the weak hand, the investigator will want to obtain a sufficient number of samples made with that hand.

A questioned writing that is illegible or unreadable is called an abbreviated writing. Generally, an abbreviated writing occurs when the author writes with speed so as to save time. A person with a long name who writes the name many times a day is likely to develop an abbreviated signature. When an abbreviated signature is questioned, the investigator should attempt to acquire standard signatures that would have been made under conditions that called for speedy writing, and also obtain exemplars under similar conditions. An investigator wanting to introduce speed into the exemplar-taking process can dictate rapidly or require so many exemplars that the writer may resort to abbreviation.

Original Documents Are Critical

A properly conducted analysis requires the examiner to work with the original document. Although remarkable advances have been made in the technology of document reproduction, the examiner cannot make definitive judgments based on a copy. Particular characteristics present on the original are simply not transferred to a copy. Indications of pressure of the writing instrument on the paper and constituents of ink are examples of characteristics that lie outside the examiner's analysis when working from a copy. A good examiner will not render unqualified opinions in such cases, and many examiners will refuse to accept work or give opinions involving reproductions.

It will happen, however, that the original of a questioned document has been lost or destroyed, leaving only a reproduction. The examiner may be asked to make an analysis with the understanding that the finding could be inconclusive, qualified, or limited.

An original is sometimes not readily available for analysis because it is an official record entrusted to a custodian whose authority does not extend to allowing replacement of an original with a certified true copy. The investigator will need to direct his request for the original to a higher level in the custodian's organization or petition a court. An alternative solution, although decidedly less desirable, would be for the examiner to conduct the analysis at the place of custody. Because the examiner utilizes equipment that is not easily transported, this approach is like bringing the hospital to the patient.

In addition to giving the examiner materials to evaluate, the investigator needs to provide certain details such as the writer's date of birth and date of death, if applicable; whether the writer was left-handed or right-handed; the duration of formal schooling of the writer; the profession of the writer; the country where the writer learned to write; the state of the writer's health on the date the questioned document was executed; the dates of execution for standards; and the date exemplars were obtained.

Selecting a Document Examiner

A Chief Security Officer or investigator in need of forensic document examination services has to differentiate between examiners who apply scientific-based techniques in the analysis of questioned writings and people who assess personalities based on handwriting. So-called graphologists and graphoanalysts will sometimes claim, often in public advertisements, the ability to judge questioned documents. More art than science, their techniques focus on writing characteristics that purport to reveal the writer's personal traits such as deceit and dishonesty.

A competent document examiner will hold diplomate status conferred by the American Board of Forensic Document Examiners (ABFDE), which is the only recognized national certifying board in this discipline. Recognition of the ABFDE is derived from the field, principally two professional organizations: the American Academy of Forensic Sciences and the American Society of Questioned Document Examiners. The ABFDE diplomate will:

- Possess a baccalaureate degree.
- Have completed a 2-year, full-time training program at a recognized document laboratory.
- Have completed an additional 2 years of full-time independent document work.
- Practice forensic document examination on a full-time basis.
- Have passed a comprehensive written and/or oral examination.

A professionally concerned examiner will attend seminars, workshop, and training courses to maintain or enhance competency. Some of the better specialized courses are offered by the U.S. Secret Service and the Federal Bureau of Investigation (FBI). Participation in professional associations is an indicator of professional commitment. National associations of interest include the Questioned Document Section of the American Academy of Forensic Sciences, the American Society of Questioned Document Examiners, and the International Association for Identification.

A qualified examiner will own or have access to a professional library of forensic document literature and an assemblage of technical equipment such as a stereoscopic binocular microscope and hand magnifiers, an electrostatic detection apparatus for detecting and visualizing indentations on paper, a video spectral comparator for detecting differences in inks, test grids for detecting alterations to typewritten documents, and a variety of special cameras and films for documenting the examiner's findings. Finally, a very important qualification is the recognition extended to a forensic document examiner by civil and criminal courts and administrative bodies for the provision of expert witness testimony.

Checking out the credentials of prospective examiners and making a careful selection before authorizing the work may very well be the most critical activity in a case. It could mean the difference between establishing the truth of the situation in doubt, and if taken to court could mean the difference between winning and losing. At stake may be large sums in litigation costs, awards, and punitive fees. The best advice to the Chief Security Officer or investigator charged with making an inquiry is to do the homework necessary to choose a competent examiner.

Hans M. Gidion

QUESTIONING SUSPECTS

Questioning suspects requires careful planning and skillful execution. Although questioning should not follow an inflexible, predetermined script, a general "game plan" can be very helpful. Knowledge of the case enables the investigator to determine what information needs to be obtained and how much the suspect can be expected to possess. The investigator may want to prepare a list of questions and to arrange topics of discussion in a logical sequence so that the questioning session will progress smoothly and important points will not be overlooked.

Statements of witnesses and facts derived from physical evidence are carefully examined for the purpose of re-constructing the offense mentally and anticipating the suspect's admissions and denials.

The general rule is that witnesses and suspects should be interviewed as soon as possible after commission of the offense. With respect to witnesses, the value of timely interviews lies in the freshness of details and the opportunity for the investigator to obtain productive leads. Early questioning of a suspect reduces the chances for fabricating an alibi and for keeping accomplices from synchronizing their separate stories.

While speed may be helpful, hasty preparation can be counterproductive. The timing of a questioning session cannot be fixed by some absolute rule that applies in all situations. Rather, it is conducted at a time of maximum advantage to the investigator.

The session is scheduled so that other activities do not interfere. Questioning is paced and unhurried. A session can be long but not so long that duress is suggested. Duress includes conditions also such as the need for food, water, personal hygiene, and sleep.

Ideally, questioning is conducted at a place where:

- Facilities are available for recording the session.
- Secretarial assistance is available if needed.
- Observers are available if needed.
- Control of the physical environment is ensured.
- Interruptions are minimal.
- Privacy is guaranteed.

A room specifically designed for questioning is typically plain but comfortably furnished, devoid of pictures or items that can distract attention. It will have recording devices and a two-way mirror. The room will be neither so hot nor so cold as to raise contentions that information was extracted through physical discomfort. Furniture will consist of three chairs and a small table large enough to write on, but not large enough for the suspect to hide behind. Pens, pencils, forms, wastebaskets, and like items should be in place prior to beginning. If the room is equipped with a telephone, it should be disconnected or removed for the purpose of reducing possible interruptions. Most important, any article or item in the room that might serve as a weapon should be removed.

The suspect should be seated at the side of the table. This removes a physical barrier and enables the investigator to fully observe the suspect's body language. If there is a window in the room, chairs should be arranged so that window light falls on the face of the suspect rather than the investigator. Chair arrangement should also preclude the suspect from being able to gaze out of a window.

Establishing Control and Rapport

At the beginning of the session, it must be made very clear that the investigator is in charge. This can be done in a variety of ways, for example: demonstrating an air of confidence, authority and professionalism; telling the suspect where to sit; calling the suspect by his/her last name; telling the suspect that smoking and tobacco or gum chewing is not permitted.

Establishing control and establishing rapport are two different techniques, yet they complement one another. Control, of course, is established first. After the ground rules have been laid, the process of establishing rapport can begin. Study of case materials prior to the questioning session usually reveals at least some personal aspects of the suspect such as place of residence, places frequented, marital status, job held, and perhaps an avocation or hobby. Any of these can provide opportunities to open the suspect to two-way communication. "I understand you like fishing," could be a starting point, assuming the investigator knows something about fishing.

Assessing the Suspect

With rapport comes the opportunity to assess the suspect. Productive questioning depends in large measure upon the investigator's ability to size up the suspect and choose a general approach for getting the suspect to cooperate and dealing with resistance should it arise. If the first approach does not succeed, an alternate approach should be tried. All of this is in the nature of sparring; two contestants testing and appraising each other. The investigator

has the advantage for two reasons: control and familiarity with the process.

The ability to assess others is largely a matter of practical experience, even though a lack of experience can be compensated for by pure native ability and keen psychological insight. While the "sizing-up" of a suspect is essentially a subjective process, there are usually a sufficient number of facts known to the investigator that can help in judging probable guilt prior to questioning. A person can fall under suspicion through the examination of physical evidence and statements of witnesses. On the other hand, a lack of essential facts will cause some doubt or uncertainty as to probable guilt.

The Questioning Session

Once the questioning begins, the investigator and suspect are locked into a contest. The investigator will use his/her knowledge of human behavior to find a chink in the armor of the suspect. The suspect will resist and try to avoid traps set by the investigator.

At the outset, the investigator will use everything known about the suspect to form a preliminary judgment as to involvement. The tradition of questioning provides two convenient categories: the apparently guilty person and the person whose guilt is uncertain.

The Apparently Guilty Person. A direct approach is normally used to question a suspect in this category. The investigator assumes an air of complete confidence with regard to evidence or witness statements that point to the suspect; incontrovertible proof implicates the suspect beyond any doubt. The investigator assumes a brisk, accusatory manner, displays a complete belief in the suspect's guilt, and acts as if a statement is not really important because the quantity and quality of evidence already on hand is more than enough to bring the investigation to a conclusion—a conclusion that places the suspect in a difficult position. The purpose of the interview, according to the investigator, is not to establish that the suspect committed the offense—because that has already been determined—but to learn why. The meeting is nothing more than an opportunity for the suspect to tell his/her "side of the story."

The Person Whose Guilt is Uncertain. A person in this category is best questioned using an indirect approach. Questioning is designed to establish a detailed account of the suspect's activities before, during, and after the time of the offense. Facts that are definitely known can be used to test the suspect's reactions. Guilt is indicated when the suspect lies regarding a known fact. If, as the questioning progresses, the investigator becomes increasingly convinced of the suspect's guilt, the direct approach is merited.

Tactics and Techniques

The number and kinds of possible tactics and techniques are limited only by the investigator's imagination, within reason however. There are limitations to what an investigator can do or say. Constitutional safeguards, case law, appellate decisions, and a variety of other rules or procedures apply to suspect rights. A good rule of thumb to follow when deciding to employ a particular questioning tactic is to internalize this question: "Does a possibility exist that the action I take could result in an admission of guilt by an innocent person?" If the answer to the question is "yes," the tactic is out of bounds. To illustrate, assume that questioning is about to take place of a suspect whose guilt is uncertain and the offense involves a degrading act. It would be wrong for the investigator to imply that a failure of the suspect to confess would require interviewing the suspect's family and friends. If such a tactic were employed, a possibility exists for the truly innocent person to confess out of concern for family and friends.

Following are descriptions of the more common questioning tactics. In them the reader will see their applicability to different kinds of suspects in different kinds of situations.

Sympathy. A person who has committed an offense in the heat of passion is normally responsive to a sympathetic and understanding attitude. Violent offenses have emotional overtones; they are generally committed by people acting from the heat of passion, anger, revenge, or mental aberration. In the mildest of such instances, the investigator can treat offenders as rational people who, under the pressure of circumstance or extreme provocation, committed acts that are out of keeping with their true personalities. The investigator should present a rationalization of the crime by pointing out that "it could happen to anyone" and minimize the moral seriousness of the act by alluding to the frequency by which such crimes occur. The investigator can attempt to gain the confidence of the suspect, for example, by referring to similarities of good citizenship that appear to exist between them.

Sympathy can be mixed with confidence by pointing out the evidence linking the suspect to the incident. Signs of stress and nervous tension can be pointed out to the suspect as indicators of guilt.

Repugnant acts and low motives can be treated as "out of character" for the suspect. The idea is to help the suspect "save face" by putting forth an excuse. Euphemisms should be used in place of emotion-laden words like "stab" and "steal."

The sympathetic technique is also particularly useful in dealing with the first offender. A person who has not been in trouble previously is likely to respond to an understanding attitude. It is natural for a first offender to experience feelings of regret and penitence. A skilled investigator will play upon these feelings by acting considerate and helpful. In fact, a showing of warm feelings is not always false. There have been many cases where investigators, through compassion and understanding, have turned first offenders away from disrespect for laws.

Reasoning. In this technique the suspect is told that guilt is already established, or that it will be established soon, and that there is nothing else to do but make an admission. The investigator points out the futility of denying guilt. Every denial is met with logic and facts that refute the suspect's assertions. Laboratory reports, photographs, fingerprint lifts, and similar items can be very useful in convincing a suspect that lying is useless. The thrust of this technique is to appeal to the suspect's common sense.

Point Out the Symptoms of Guilt. Demeanor and verbal expressions can place a suspect in a vulnerable situation. A person who knows that the signs of guilt are apparent may be moved one step closer to an admission.

Nonverbal symptoms of guilt can be very revealing. Kinesics, the study of nonverbal communications, teaches us that the body can communicate what we are not saying. Body positions, motions, gestures, and facial expressions are forms of silent language that convey inner thoughts. Some people find it easy to use words to mask their true feelings, but no one can completely control the body's natural reaction to intense inner feelings. While the brain can learn to lie, the body cannot.

Documenting the Session

Documenting a questioning session consists of three main phases: note taking, electronic recording, and obtaining a written statement.

Note Taking. The traditional method for documenting a questioning session is note taking. Notes do more than just create a record, they help the investigator keep track of what has been asked and answered, what remains to be asked, and what needs to be asked again. Electronic devices are far superior to note taking for recording a session but have no value in the give and take of questioning.

Handwritten notes are subject to examination by opposing counsel at a legal proceeding, and for that reason must be understandable to others. Notes that are confusing to understand or appear to be out of character for a professional, can discredit an otherwise excellent investigation.

Because suspects are inclined to conceal the truth, it bothers them to observe note taking. This can be overcome by using a third party to take notes out of the suspect's sight.

The suspect should be permitted to tell the story at least once before the investigator lifts pencil to paper. Notes are seldom taken in a fully narrative form. They tend to consist of key words that denote salient points, common abbreviations, and words compressed with the use of apostrophes. Points notated while the suspect talks usually become points for later questions that can amplify guilt or clarify facts.

Electronic Recording. The preferred recording device is the video/recorder. Video leaves little doubt as to the identification of persons present, objects examined or handled, the environment, the activities of persons present, and words said.

Video allows parties of interest to see the offender nod, shrug, and make other telling movements that convey guilt. Video can be used to capture images of the suspect re-constructing the offense through physical actions such as the way in which a security container was pried open.

The video recording should be preceded and concluded with acknowledgments by the suspect that he/she understands the purpose of the questioning and is free to leave at any time. The recorder should have a time and date generator.

Video recordings should be carefully kept in their entirety, along with a chain of custody form. Except for chain of custody, the same is true for notes and any other recordings such as stenographic transcripts.

Written Statements. The most convincing type of statement is the one in which a suspect personally writes the confession and signs it. Statements exclusively prepared by suspects are relatively uncommon because of the difficulty in persuading suspects to write them.

On the other hand, the investigator may not wish a suspect to write the statement because in so doing critical points can be omitted. The investigator may prefer instead to prepare a typed statement and have the suspect sign it.

When preparing a typed statement, common sense is called for. The text of the statement should reflect the general vocabulary of the suspect. A confession obtained from a suspect having a sixth grade education deserves skepticism when it includes large words and highly complex sentences. If a suspect speaks with profanity, the typed statement should contain profanity. As much as possible, the actual sentences spoken are included, although they may not necessarily appear in the same order given by the suspect.

It sometimes happens that a suspect will refuse to sign a statement of any type, even though an understanding may have been reached prior. If the suspect declines to sign, the investigator should try to obtain a verbal acknowledgment in the presence of an observer. If the suspect refuses to do even this, the investigator should prepare a personal statement that describes the entire session in detail. For this task, notes are essential.

Conclusion

Questioning skill is acquired through training, practice, and experience. For some, the skill comes with difficulty and for others it comes easily. The important point is that it can be acquired.

Skill is not simply verbal. It requires study prior to the questioning session, making good choices as to when and where to hold the session, assuring that the questioning environment is arranged to personal advantage, "reading" the suspect, concentrating on what is important, taking notes, closing the session with a signature or acknowledgment, and assuring that recordings are marked for identification at a later time.

John J. Fay

Sources

Bennett, W. and Hess, M. 1998. *Criminal Investigation, 5th Edition*. New York: West/Wadsworth.

Berg, B. 1999. *Policing in Modern Society*. Boston: Butterworth-Heinemann.

Inbau, F. and Reid, J. 1967. *Criminal Interrogation and Confessions*. Baltimore: Williams and Wilkins.

Montgomery, R. and Majeski, W. 2002. *Corporate Investigations*. Tucson: Lawyers and Judges Publishing.

O'Hara, C. 1970. *Fundamentals of Criminal Investigation*. Springfield: Charles C. Thomas.

Sennewald, C. and Tsukayama, J. 2001. *The Process of Investigation, 2nd Edition*. Boston: Butterworth-Heinemann.

Specter, A. and Katz, M. 1967. *Police Guide to Search and Seizure, Interrogation and Confession*. Philadelphia: Chilton Books.

Stuckey, G. 1968. *Evidence for the Law Enforcement Officer*. New York: McGraw-Hill.

Swanson, C., Chamelin, N., and Territo, L. 1997. *Criminal Investigation*. Santa Monica: Goodyear Publishing.

Tobias, M. and Peterson, R. 1972. *Pre-Trial Criminal Procedure*. Springfield: Charles C. Thomas.

QUESTIONING TECHNIQUES

Security professionals like to make a distinction between "interview" and "interrogation" and, of course, there are differences. For example:

- An interview is non-accusatory; the interrogation is.
- An interview has a free-flowing dialogue; the interrogation does not.
- An interview can be held at many places; the interrogation is done in an environment controlled by the questioner.
- An interview does not have to be perfectly private; the interrogation does.
- Interviewing is the mode for questioning cooperative non-suspects; interrogating is the mode for questioning suspects and hostile witnesses.
- An interview is not lengthy; an interrogation can be.
- An interview is characterized by friendliness; an interrogation is often hostile.
- An interview is unstructured; an interrogation is highly structured.
- An interview requires some planning; an interrogation requires extensive planning.
- In an interview, note taking is okay; in an interrogation it may not be.

An interview is the questioning of a person who has or is believed to have facts of official interest. The person questioned usually gives an account of the incident under investigation or offers information concerning a suspect. The person being interviewed is usually a witness, victim, or complainant. An interrogation, on the other hand, is the questioning of a person suspected of having committed an offense, or of a person who is reluctant to make a full disclosure. The person being interrogated is a suspect, or may be a reluctant witness.

Both definitions have one thing in common; each seeks to obtain information through questioning. The differences arise in the manner of questioning and the type of person being questioned. It is not unusual for an information-gathering session to switch back and forth between interview and interrogation, depending on the degree of cooperation or hostility encountered.

The most consistently available and most valuable sources of information in the majority of inquiries are the people involved. The inquiry obtains information from people for a variety of reasons; initially to establish the facts of an incident, including determination of whether or not an incident actually occurred. During initial phases it is important to verify information given by other persons connected with the case, or tie in facts gleaned from an examination of physical evidence. Information collected from the victim, complainant, or witnesses may lead to identification of offenders and accomplices.

Prompt and properly conducted interviews can produce investigative leads, additional physical evidence, and develop background information regarding motives, habits of the offender and other details that contribute to a fuller understanding of the incident. Interviews can also lead to a discovery of unreported offenses, or connect other persons to other incidents. The function of interviewing has many important uses.

An investigator charged with conducting an investigation of a criminal act must become thoroughly familiar with the elements of proof pertaining to the crime committed. A working knowledge of criminal law helps the investigator formulate questions, the answers to which will satisfy the elements of proof. In the questioning of a suspect, for example, knowledge of what is required to establish criminal intent will assist the investigator to steer questioning toward motivation and premeditation.

The Questioning Session

After rapport has been established and the interviewee is communicating, the investigator must guide the conversation in productive directions. For those interviewees who require no stimulation to continue talking, the investigator can wait until the story has been told, review it out loud, and ask clarification of confusing points. Matters that were not touched upon can be covered at the end. For some persons, occasional prodding is necessary to keep a conversation moving. A common mistake of the fledgling interviewer is the tendency to interrupt or dominate a conversation to such a degree that the interviewee is not permitted to tell the story. Knowing when to ask a question is every bit as important as knowing what to ask and how to ask. Following are some questioning techniques for non-suspects.

Ask One Question at a Time. Too many questions at one time can be confusing for any person. Questions should be segregated one from each other, and the investigator should not proceed to the next question until the fullest answer possible has been obtained. It is important also to pose questions intermittently. A constant series of questions is less desirable than a conversation punctuated by occasional questions inserted to clarify or stimulate.

Use Simple Questions. Long and complex questions lead to confusion and irritation. Legal terms and security jargon are unfamiliar to many people. If the person being interviewed does not understand the question, the answer cannot be accurate. Also, some people when confronted with a misunderstood question will become defensive and difficult to deal with.

Avoid Implied Answers. There is not much point in asking a question that provides its own answer. Suggesting answers defeats the whole purpose of the interview. An example of a question with an implied answer is "Was the weapon a caliber 0.38 revolver?" A better question might be "What kind of a weapon was it?"

Avoid "Yes" and "No" Questions. The idea in interviewing is to encourage elaboration. Short answers can omit valuable facts. While a "yes" or "no" reply is very specific, they are not always absolutely accurate and can be misleading in the absence of details.

Avoid Embarrassment to the Interviewee. Remarks, gestures, or facial expressions that can be interpreted as ridiculing should be avoided. When dealing with the non-suspect interviewee, it is usually not difficult to separate deliberate misrepresentation from unintentional mistakes. If honest errors are made, they should be resolved with tact and courtesy.

Control Digressions. While it is extremely important to get an interviewee to talk, it is equally important to confine talking to the issues at hand. Long, rambling discourses are time consuming and unproductive. The investigator must keep the discussion from drifting into irrelevant matters and excessive detail. The use of precise questions is effective in limiting the range of information being offered. Questions that are highly specific require answers that are not easily shifted to side issues. A technique called shunting can also be useful in controlling digression. A shunting maneuver allows the investigator to bring the interviewee back to the original line of discussion. A shunt might occur by saying, "Let's return to that point where you said the suspect was wearing a baseball cap." The shunt is an inoffensive interruption because it appears to rise out of an interest in what the person has said.

Radiate Confidence. How many times have we been infected by the enthusiasm of others? People who think and act in positive ways influence those around them. The investigator who looks and acts in a confident manner projects an image of competence. The comments and questions of the investigator are expressed in positive terms and avoid negative comments like, "I don't know if there is much we can do in this case, but I need to talk with you anyway." Comments of that type practically guarantee failure. It would be far better to say, "I intend to get to the bottom of this matter, and I am sure you will be able to help."

Concluding the Session

When the investigator terminates the interview of a non-suspect person, it is appropriate to display appreciation for cooperation received. This applies not only to interviewees who have been completely cooperative from the very start, but also to those who initially or occasionally had to be motivated to furnish information. It is not unusual during the closing phase of an interview for the individual to request confidentiality of information provided. Although it is never a good practice for an investigator to release official information, absolute assurances can never be given concerning releases of information.

The closing of an interview is not necessarily the termination of communications between the investigator and the interviewee. On the contrary, an effective closing can result in the acquisition of valuable information. A person who may not have been fully cooperative during the body of the interview may feel safe in saying something after questioning has apparently ceased. Pertinent facts that may have been suppressed during the interview might be disclosed as the interview is being ended. Details that escaped the investigator earlier can be brought to the surface even while making a farewell hand-shake.

John J. Fay

RAPE

The security professional holds a special responsibility for helping employees prevent being assaulted. Rape is a particularly odious form of assault. Fortunately, it is a crime susceptible to prevention, largely through engaging in avoidance tactics and knowing what to do if attacked.

Although the legal definition of rape will vary from state to state, it is generally accepted that rape is first and foremost a crime of force. The rapist uses or threatens to use violence in what is essentially an exercise of power. The primary motive of the rapist is not to attain sexual pleasure, but to feel a sense of superiority by dominating the victim.

Rape has no boundaries. Males have been victims as well as females. Anyone, regardless of age, race, economic status, and physical appearance can be victimized. Victims have included infants, mentally retarded persons, and the elderly.

Rape is also unlimited as to time and place of occurrence. It is not something that happens mainly at night or in ghetto areas. Rapes occur at all times of the day in the poorest and wealthiest sections of cities, suburbs, and rural areas all across America.

Many rapes take place in the victim's home and frequently the rapist is there by invitation. This is so because the rapist is likely to be a friend, relative, or work associate. In some cases, he is an estranged husband or lover, and in about 9 of every 10 reported cases, is of the same race as the victim.

Violence is an element of the act and only about 3 of 10 incidents will involve the use of a weapon. Only very infrequently will a rape end in murder. This is not to suggest that the crime is any less serious, but it does point to the high probability that the victim will survive.

There has never been any truth to the notion that rape is an invited crime, meaning that the victim invited rape because of the way she dressed or behaved. The idea that the rapist was provoked by the victim's sexual advances reflects a dishonored and mistaken view that rape is motivated by sexual desire.

There is also little evidence to support the proposition that women use accusations of rape as a means of obtaining revenge. On the contrary, there is evidence to show that women accusers often suffer further harm by being stigmatized in their communities and abandoned by friends and loved ones.

Another disturbing reality is that a rapist will usually continue to rape until caught and removed from society. The only effective remedy is for the victim to report the crime and assist in the investigation and prosecution. This can be difficult and unpleasant for the victim, but is essential in preventing repeat occurrences of the crime.

Setting Up Personal Defenses

The rapist, like most criminals, will prefer the "easy target," that is to say, a woman who has the appearance of vulnerability. If the rapist can be made to believe that a particular woman would be difficult to overcome, he will look elsewhere for easier prey. A good defense, then, is to display strength—not in the physical sense, but in character and personality. How is that done? It is done through expressions of self-confidence, capability, and control of events. Strength can be shown by actions and appearance. It is also manifested in what is said and how it is said.

Assertiveness is one of the most powerful indicators of strength. It is largely verbal in nature and is an excellent weapon to use when confronted with a threatening situation. A verbal response that says "no" without any doubt or hesitation could be all that's required to defuse a potentially dangerous encounter.

If a simple refusal is not sufficient, a woman should not be afraid to make a scene. Embarrassment is an acceptable alternative to the risk of the possible consequences of giving in. A woman can use her voice to attract attention, to make people nearby aware of her need for help, and to tell them how they can help, such as by staying close or calling the police.

From childhood, people are taught to be courteous and friendly. These are valuable teachings, but they should not have priority in situations that pose danger. Traits that are trusting and passive give encouragement to the rapist.

John J. Fay

REID'S NINE STEPS OF INTERROGATION

An interview is a non-accusatory information gathering conversation during which the investigator develops investigative and behavioral information that will help to assess the veracity of the statements made by a suspect, victim, or witness. When the results of the interview and subsequent investigation indicate that the subject is withholding information, then an interrogation may be appropriate. However, it is very important to conduct a non-accusatory interview before any interrogation takes place for a number of reasons. During this interview process the investigator gains important insight with respect to the subject's psychological characteristics; possible reasons or motives for committing the act in question; fears or concerns regarding the discovery of their participation; and, the process allows the investigator to establish an image of professionalism and competency by giving the subject the opportunity to tell their story to an objective listener. An interrogation should only be conducted when the investigator is reasonably certain that the subject has not told the truth during the interview.

In contrast to the interview process, interrogation is an accusatory procedure designed to persuade the subject to tell the truth about information that they are believed to be withholding. While interrogation is most often used with an individual suspected of committing a crime, a victim who is believed to be fabricating a crime or a witness who is believed to be withholding relevant information may also be the subject of an interrogation. The process seeks to obtain an acknowledgment that the person did not tell the truth in an earlier statement to conceal guilt or to protect the guilty party.

Privacy is one of the principal psychological factors contributing to the successful outcome of an interview or interrogation. Typically, the investigator and the subject sit in similar chairs, directly facing each other approximately 5 feet apart and without any physical barrier (such as a desk) between them. The investigator should minimize distractions, such as phones ringing, the disturbance of others interrupting the session, open views out of windows, etc.

The Accusatory Interrogation

As a result of many years experience, primarily on the part of the staff of John E. Reid and Associates under the guidance of the late John E. Reid, the interrogation process has been formulated into nine structural components—the nine steps of criminal interrogation. These nine steps are presented in the context of the interrogation of suspects whose guilt seems definite or reasonably certain. It must be remembered that none of the steps is apt to make an innocent person confess and that all of the steps are legally as well as morally justifiable.

The Positive Confrontation. Following the non-accusatory interview, the investigator leaves the room. After several minutes, the investigator returns carrying an investigative file, opens it, and confronts the subject with facts that clearly point to the subject's deception. ("Jim, the results of our investigation clearly indicate that you did [issue].") This type of accusation is made only when the subject's guilt is very apparent. Otherwise, the statement should be less direct. ("Jim, the results of our Investigation indicates that you have not told me the complete truth about [issue].") Following the confrontation, the questioner pauses to evaluate the subject's reaction to the statement, then repeats the statement. Following this, the questioner places the investigative file aside, sits down directly opposite the subject, and makes a transition from being an accuser to a sympathetic and understanding person.

Theme Development. The next step is to present themes that are "moral justifications" for the subject's criminal behavior. One way of doing this is to place moral blame for an illegal activity on another person or an outside set of circumstances. This appeals to a basic aspect of human nature. Most people tend to minimize responsibility for their actions by placing blame on someone or something else. In a credit card fraud case, for example, the questioner might suggest that the subject was not paid enough by the employer or that someone left the card out where it was an open invitation to use. Other moral justifications include unusual family expenses, desperate financial circumstances, a friend came up with the idea, retribution for an argument, and drug or alcohol dependence.

The questioner presents the moral justification in a sympathetic and understanding way. An interest in working with the subject to resolve the problem breaks the ice. The justification is presented in an unbroken monologue that minimizes the subject's opportunity to voice denials.

Handling Denials. In fact, the more often the subject denies guilt, the more difficult it becomes for the subject to admit guilt later. Therefore, during theme development the questioner interjects a blocking statement whenever the subject attempts to verbalize an "I didn't do it" plea. Denials from the guilty subject are often preceded by permission phrases such as, "Can I say one thing?" or "If I could only explain" or "But sir, if you'll just let me talk." Each of these permission phrases will be followed by the denial, "I didn't do it." When the investigator hears these permission phrases he should interject a comment, such as, "Jim, hold on for one second" or "Sue, wait just a minute" and then return to the development of the theme.

Innocent subjects rarely use permission phrases before denying guilt. Instead, the innocent subject will, with any display of etiquette, promptly and unequivocally maintain innocence. An innocent subject remains steadfast in the assertion of innocence and never moves past the denial stage. On the other hand, many guilty subjects will abandon the strategy of denial, which is a defensive tactic, and move to an offensive strategy that offers objections.

Overcoming Objections. An objection is a stated reason why a subject would not or could not have committed the crime under investigation. Most guilty subjects will make objections that fall into general categories. The first of these are trait objections such as, "I wasn't brought up that way" or "I'd be too scared to do something like that." The other category of objections includes factual objections that allege lack of opportunity or access to commit the crime. Examples of factual objections are, "I don't even have the combination to the safe," "I don't own a handgun," and "I was with my girl friend that night."

While both types of objections offer feeble reasons supporting a claim of innocence, most objections will have some basis in fact. For example, the subject in fact was probably not brought up to rob gas stations and in fact was probably with his girl friend at some point in time on the night of the robbery. Because of the factual basis for most objections, the questioner generally does not refute them. To do so would only encourage an argument or discussion that would break the flow of theme development. Rather, when the subject offers an objection the questioner first rewards it, perhaps with a statement such as "I'm glad you said that" or "You're absolutely right, I was aware of that before I talked with you about this." The objection is then incorporated into the theme. For example, a subject who states, "I'd be too scared to do something like this" could be told, "I'm glad you said that because it tells me that this crime was out of character for you and that you probably had never done anything like this before in your life." By handling objections in this manner the subject is made to realize that this offensive tactic will be ineffective in convincing the questioner of innocence. At this stage most subjects psychologically withdraw and begin to focus mentally on the prospects of impending punishment.

Keeping a Subject's Attention. Following the objection stage, the guilty subject often becomes pensive, apathetic, and quiet. It is most important during this stage that the questioner procure and focus the subject's attention on the theme (i.e., the psychological justification for the subject's behavior). Through this process the subject's thoughts will be diverted away from the impending punishment (which only serves to reinforce the resolve to deny guilt). To procure the subject's attention, the questioner draws nearer to the subject. A closer physical proximity helps direct the subject's thoughts to what the questioner is doing and saying. The questioner now begins to channel the theme down to the probable alternative components.

Handling a Subject's Passive Mood. At this stage, the subject may cry, which is often an expression of remorse. Many other subjects do not cry, but express their emotional state by assuming a defeatist posture—slumped head and shoulders, relaxed legs, and a vacant stare. In order to facilitate the impending admission of guilt, the questioner intensifies the theme presentation and concentrates on the psychological justification for the unlawful act.

Presenting an Alternative Question. The alternative question is one in which the questioner presents two incriminatory choices concerning some aspect of the crime. Elements of the alternative are developed as logical extensions of the theme. If the theme focuses on contrasting behavior that is impulsive or spur-of-the-moment versus planned or premeditated acts, the alternative question is, "Did you plan this thing out or did it just happen on the spur of the moment?" Either choice is an admission of guilt. The alternative

question should be followed by a statement in which the investigator indicates he believes the good side of the alternative: "I'm sure it was just on the spur of the moment, wasn't it?" The alternative question should be based on an assumption of guilt, not on a yes or no proposition, such as, "Did you do this or didn't you?" A misphrased question invites denial. The first admission of guilt is established when the subject accepts either of the offered alternatives. The way now stands clear to develop the admission into a corroborated confession.

Having the Subject Relate Details. Once the alternative question is answered, the investigator responds with a statement of reinforcement such as, "Good, that's what I thought all along." Essentially, this is a statement that acknowledges the subject's admission of guilt. Following this, the objective is to obtain a brief oral review of the basic sequence of events, while obtaining sufficient detail to corroborate the subject's guilt.

Questions asked at this time should be brief, concise, and clear, calling only for limited verbal responses from the subject. It is premature to ask all-encompassing questions like, "Well, just tell me everything that happened." Furthermore, questions should be open-ended and devoid of emotionally charged terminology. Once the subject has offered a brief verbal statement about the crime sequence, the questioner should ask detailed questions to obtain information that can be corroborated by subsequent investigation. After this full verbal statement is complete, it may be necessary to return to the subject's choice of alternatives or to some other statement previously made. Discussions along these lines tend to shed light on the subject's motive, purpose, and intent at the time of the crime.

Converting an Oral Confession. In this step, the investigator tells the subject he has to leave for a few moments to check on something. The investigator leaves the interrogation room and then returns with a partner who the investigator introduces as someone who has been working on the investigation. The actual function of the partner is to be a witness to the subject's confession. The investigator then goes over the essential details in a manner that would allow the witness to testify to the correctness and voluntariness of the confession. The questioner is now ready to convert the oral confession into a written or recorded confession. One of four formats can be used:

- A statement handwritten by the subject
- A statement written by the questioner, and read and signed by the subject
- A statement taken down by a secretary or stenographer and transcribed into a typed document for the subject to read and sign
- A tape-recorded or video-recorded statement

Fundamental guidelines should be followed. In a custodial setting, even though Miranda warnings may have been given and the appropriate waiver obtained, it is advisable to repeat the warning at the beginning of the confession, referring to the fact that the subject had received them earlier.

The statement of guilt must be readable and understandable by someone who is not familiar with what the subject has done. Leading questions should be avoided, the confessor's own language should be used, and full corroboration should be established. Any errors, changes, or crossed-out words should be initialed with an "OK" written in the margin by the subject. The statement should reflect that the subject was treated properly, that no threats or promises were made, and that the statement was freely given by the subject. When the subject has completed reading the written statement, the questioner says, "Write your name here" while pointing to the place of signature. The questioner avoids saying "Sign here" because "sign" connotes a degree of legalism that may cause the subject to back out of making a written confession. The subject signs each page of the statement in front of the questioner and the witness, who also add their signatures.

Obtaining the written confession at the end of the interrogation is, of course, not the capstone. Every effort should be made to verify the statement and obtain the support evidence necessary for trial.

Joseph P. Buckley, III

Source Inbau, F., Reid, J., Buckley, J., and Jayne, B., ed. 2001. *Criminal Interrogation and Confessions, 4th Edition.* Gaithersburg: Aspen.

ROBBERY

The crime of robbery is a serious offense capable of being carried out by a variety of means. Crime statistics show that robbers are not always men and come from a wide range of age, racial, social, economic, and occupational groups. The robber's principal motive is usually to obtain money, or property that is easily converted to cash. Robbery is also a crime that is sometimes committed in conjunction with another crime, such as murder or rape, and because robbery is a form of larceny that uses violence as its means, the investigative techniques used in larceny and assault cases have application to robbery cases.

Types of Robberies

Mugging. Mugging is a type of robbery committed by the muffling of the victim's mouth (or by choking) while forcibly taking property from the victim's possession. The amateur or inexperienced mugger will usually act on the earliest opportunity to victimize a lone person. He will act on the spur of the moment, usually with little or no preparation, and is acting in response to some urgent need for money, as for example the drug addict in early withdrawal who needs money to buy his next fix. At the other extreme is the experienced mugger who usually selects his target carefully and formulates a plan that includes a concealed location and an unobstructed escape route. His victims are chosen on the basis of the valuables they are expected to be carrying. The experienced mugger looks for high return at low risk. When a particular mugging method proves successful over a period of time, the experienced mugger will establish a modus operandi or pattern of activity.

A common example of a mugger's operandi is the yoking technique. The largest of a group of two or three muggers subdues the victim from behind by a strangle-hold on the neck. If there are three or more muggers the victim's arms are pinned while the last mugger, usually the smallest, searches the victim's pockets and removes valuables. Other similarities in the mugger's method of operation might include use of the same or similar locations such as parking lots or stairwells; weapons used, if any; the manner of approach; opening statement to the victim or other conversation leading up to the incident; and the use of violence inflicted in certain ways upon the victim. A particularly dangerous type of mugger is the sadist-flagellant robber whose primary motive is sexual gratification through inflicting injury on his victim. The theft aspect of the crime is a secondary consideration.

Robberies of Places. Banks, stores, and residences are common robbery targets. As is the case with mugging, this type of robbery can be committed by amateurs or professionals. The amateur robber is capable of traveling to and from the place of robbery in his own car or with a leased car, sometimes leased in his own name, or may travel on foot or even by bicycle. Because the inexperienced robber is certain to be nervous during the commission of the crime, he is apt to use violence unnecessarily. The experienced robber is likely to retain his composure and is comforted by the preparation and planning that has preceded the act. He knows what he is doing, is operating on a schedule, and realizes the risk of causing injury. He will usually use a stolen car, which he later abandons, or he might rent a car in a false name and use stolen plates.

Vehicle Robberies. The target of the crime is frequently a commercial-type vehicle carrying cash or high-value cargo. Vehicle robberies are more likely to be committed by experienced, professional robbers because of the requirements to obtain "inside" information concerning the valuables being transported, the schedule of the vehicle, and its defense capability. A vehicle robber needs also to stop his target, extricate the valuables, and safely get away.

Investigative Techniques

Robberies that are committed on the spur of the moment by amateurs or robberies that are committed by professionals only after long and intricate planning have at least one thing in common: they are both difficult to solve. Many robberies are committed during hours of darkness or under conditions that make it difficult for the robber's features to be seen by the victim. Adding to this is the fact that the attention of the victim is frequently focused on the weapon, thereby making it difficult for the victim to provide a good description of the suspect.

A robbery is usually reported fairly soon after it has happened. The investigator who is called to the scene of the robbery should follow the basic steps of crime scene processing. The crime scene is usually larger than the normal crime scene because it covers that territory where a robber may have lain in wait for his victim, the approach routes of the suspect and victim, the place of the robbery, and the escape route of the suspect. Persons who were present immediately before, during, and after the incident are potential witnesses. The investigator should question witnesses, as well as the victim, to determine the following:

- A description of the robber to include words used, voice peculiarities, gestures, mannerisms, and clothing
- The direction and type of approach used by the suspect
- A description of valuables taken
- The victim's action prior to the robbery
- The direction traveled by the robber when he left the scene and the method of travel

After the victim has had time to recover and the investigator has had time to make a careful examination of the crime scene, a second interview should be conducted. The victim may remember details after he has settled himself emotionally and the investigator may have to ask specific questions to clarify details or develop leads on the basis of evidence discovered. The second interview can also be used as an opportunity to prepare a composite likeness of the suspect.

If an automobile is involved in the robbery, the investigator should obtain a detailed description of it from as many persons as possible. In addition to making a routine stolen vehicle check, the investigator should contact car rental agencies. When a rental automobile is used in the commission of a robbery, it is possible that a description will be obtained from the clerk who handled the rental transaction. If and when an abandoned vehicle used in a robbery is located, latent fingerprints and items recovered from it will provide valuable leads. Items of clothing found in the car or close to it should be checked for laundry marks or other peculiarities that may provide leads to the identity of the suspect. Footprints at the scene of an abandoned stolen vehicle should not be ignored. Valuable leads can also be developed from discarded items such as newspapers, matchbooks, and cigarette butts that are inside or around the vehicle.

When a robbery has occurred indoors, there should be an intensive search for latent fingerprints. Furniture, counter tops, and anything else that could have been touched by the robber should be processed for latent prints. Notes handed to a teller, discarded deposit slips, or counter checks not only provide opportunities to obtain fingerprints, but can also link the robber to the crime through handwriting analysis.

Some robbers feel a need to restrain their victims using such items as rope or adhesive tape. When rope has been used and to the extent that it is possible to do so, the investigator should obtain the rope with any knots still intact. The type of knot used by the robber may provide a link to him and to other crimes he may have committed. It may also be possible to trace the type of rope to a particular dealer. Adhesive tape has an especially high potential as evidence because it may be possible to obtain fingerprints from either side of it. It may also be possible to match the torn edge of the tape to the end of a roll of tape found in the possession of the suspect.

When interviewing witnesses or victims, the investigator should concentrate on determining the exact words used by the robber. The use of particular words or groups of words is valuable in matching the crime against previous robberies. The speech, gestures, and mannerisms of the robber are sometimes the only leads an investigator may be able to develop.

Any discussion of robbery is not complete without mention of the critical importance that informants can play in the identification and arrest of robbery suspects. While there is no replacement for hard work in developing physical evidence and testimony from people having knowledge of a robbery, there is tremendous value in obtaining the right piece of information from a confidential source that is in a position to know or acquire information beyond the influence of the investigator.

John J. Fay

UNDERCOVER INVESTIGATIONS IN THE WORKPLACE

While undercover is one of the most powerful forms of workplace investigation, it is also the most complicated. Successful undercover investigations require the investment of time, patience, and resources. An employer that is unwilling to make the required investment should not contemplate this form of investigation. The chief distinction between undercover and other forms of investigation is that the undercover investigator does not conceal his or her presence or attempt to pass unnoticed. What is concealed is the investigator's true identity or purpose. Other than interviewing, undercover investigation is the only form of interactive investigation. This unique quality allows the skilled undercover investigator (properly identified as the operative) to not only gather information concerning a workplace problem, but to learn the "how" and "why" behind the actions of those under investigation.

When Should Undercover Be Used?

Undercover enables the collection of information and ultimately the solving of problems not possible by other means. The shape and form of the investigation, and the way it unfolds will be dictated by the nature of the information sought. Consequently, it is widely held that undercover operations are not a panacea and should only be used in the most aggravated circumstances. Undercover investigation should be the exception, not the rule. Undercover should only be contemplated when no other options are available.

The following are situations which typically lend themselves to the use of undercover:

1. When there is consistent, reliable information suggesting employee misconduct or criminal activity but insufficient detail to permit prevention or the identification of those involved
2. When losses are known to occur in a specific area, but there is no information as to how they occur or who is responsible
3. When there is a strong suspicion or actual indicators of on-the-job alcohol or drug abuse and/or drug dealing in the workplace
4. When there is a strong suspicion or actual indicators of on-the-job impairment due to alcohol or drug abuse, yet

supervision is non-responsive or incapable of intervening

5. When it is necessary to compare actual practices with required or stated prac-tices and routine auditing is not possible
6. When there is a high probability the use of undercover will produce significant results and all other reasonable options have been ruled out

Undercover operations are not appropriate for:

1. The investigation of protected union activities.
2. The investigation of any activity per-mitted or protected by any governmen-tal statute, rule, or regulation, or otherwise protected by a union agree-ment or contract.
3. Fact-finding that will likely produce the same results while consuming less time and resources.

It should be noted that simply because a work-force is unionized, the use of undercover should not automatically be ruled out. It is permissible for an employer to use undercover and even place undercover investigators into a unionized workforce as long as the investigation does not impinge upon the lawful and protected activi-ties of the union or its membership.

Clearly, undercover should not be used to gather or collect information of a personal or confidential nature or offensively intrude into private lives where a reasonable expectation of privacy exists. Such efforts are actionable and may give rise to legal claims against the employer and its investigators.

The Undercover Investigative Process

Workplace undercover investigations have pot-entially several distinct outcomes. Categorically, when employee misconduct is uncovered these outcomes include: employee discipline; employee prosecution; and restitution. The orga-nization must select the desired outcome(s) and then engineer the investigation to achieve it. To do so, the organization must contemplate past practices, precedent, organizational policies, labor contracts (should they exist), the criminal-ity of the suspected activity, employee relations,

potential public opinion, the organization's cul-ture and its reputation, and the potential return on investment. Sometimes competing, these considerations must be thoroughly analyzed and weighed before realistic objectives can be decided.

Next, the organization must select the investigative team. At a minimum the team should include a corporate decision maker, a representative from human resources, a cor-porate security professional, and an attorney familiar with state and local employment law. Once constituted, the team should then seek a vendor that can provide the undercover inves-tigator and conduct the investigation. Because undercover is so complex and fraught with such enormous liability, it is best to hire only experts.

Although law enforcement can conduct workplace undercover investigations, most often law enforcement has neither the time or resources to conduct an investigation prop-erly or for any useful duration. As such, most employers turn to private agencies that special-ize in undercover. Consider the following when selecting an undercover agency:

- Licensing: In all but several states, private investigators and their agencies must be licensed.
- Training: The agency selected should pro-vide professional training and rigorously screen its investigators.
- Experience: Ensure the agency as well as the employees they assign to the investi-gation have the experience necessary to do the job properly.
- Reputation: Reputations vary widely in the industry. The best agencies are well known in the business community and are active in their trade associations. Find out about the firm's litigation and claims experience. A reputation of sloppy work, high profile lawsuits, and big settlements could spell trouble.
- Willingness to Testify: All undercover investigators must be willing to testify and see their cases through to their fullest com-pletion. Sometimes that means testifying in court or before an arbitrator.
- Reports: Reports are an important part of every investigation, not just undercover. As such, detailed reports should follow

all investigative efforts. The information provided in a report should be complete, concise, and correct.

- Insurance: All quality agencies carry general liability insurance. In fact most states that license investigators require insurance. Bonding is not enough protection. In order to be safe, require the agency under consideration to provide a Certificate of Insurance naming your organization as an additional insured. Also ensure the coverage is occurrence not claims-made.
- Willingness to Involve the Police: Employee prosecution is not always necessary. It is complicated and often expensive. As such, the decision to prosecute should be made for business reasons only. However, a good agency knows its limitations and when to involve the authorities. Investigations involving illegal drugs for example can not be done without the assistance of the police. Also ask the vendor about their success with prosecution. The answer will provide some idea as to how many cases the agency has run, and how complicated they were. A low prosecution ratio should not patently disqualify an agency. Instead examine the organization in its totality before making your selection.
- Attorney Involvement: All experienced undercover agencies insist on the involvement of their client's attorneys. The attorney's role is an important one and the attorney should be an active participant during most of the investigation. Sophisticated undercover firms know the attorney will contribute to the smooth running of the investigation and coincidentally protect its interests as well as the interests of the client.

Once an agency is selected, the next step is to select the investigator. Undercover investigators come in all shapes, sizes, and colors. They also vary in experience and ability. Some of the best positions for the undercover are in:

- Materiel handling and expediting.
- Shipping and receiving.
- Mailrooms.
- Customer service.
- Uniformed security.
- Some on-site contractor capacity.

The professional operative must also have strong communication skills. Not only must he make daily written reports detailing his day's activities, he must be able to effectively communicate verbally with his supervisor and occasionally with the employer-client. The successful operative will also eventually have to testify. His cases may eventually yield criminal prosecutions, terminations, and other employment actions. Compelling testimony is essential for successful prosecution and winning civil actions, and is a skill that must usually be taught. In order for the investigation to be successful, the operative must be able and willing to testify effectively and professionally.

Once selected, the undercover investigator should not be placed in a position for which he does not have the requisite credentials, prior experience, or documentation. The operative should also have the skills required for the job he will be performing. If he lacks the necessary skills, sometimes remedial training can be provided before he is inserted into the job. In some instances, it is easier and more cost-effective to simply select another investigator.

Consequently, for these and other reasons a position should not be created for the investigator if possible. To do so might bring unnecessary suspicion upon him and will likely lengthen the duration and expense of the investigation. Regardless of the circumstances, the undercover investigator should be treated like any other employee and not receive any preferential treatment or special considerations.

The Cover Story

The operative should also have a plausible cover story. The cover story is the explanation of the investigator's identity and how he or she came to obtain the job. In some situations, the level of detail may be quite superficial and in other cases, the history may be quite involved. Generally, the more intimate the personal association between the investigator and members of the target group, the greater depth of the cover story.

The cover must not only explain the investigator's qualifications for the particular job, but must also offer a convincing account of how the job was obtained and something about the investigator's past. Routine documents supporting the cover story should be carried if possible. However, no documentation indicating the investigator's actual identity should ever be carried while on the assignment.

Once the investigator has been successfully placed into the target workforce, he or she will first engage in what is commonly called the relationship-building phase. During this phase the operative will learn the job, become familiar with the surroundings, and make acquaintances. The investigator should resist the temptation to press for information or appear too inquisitive. To do so will create suspicion and will hamper the collection of useful information later.

Law enforcement plays an important role in most workplace undercover investigations. In cases involving illegal drugs, no drug purchases should take place without the approval of law enforcement. In other types of cases law enforcement may provide resources, manpower, and intelligence, and in some instances actively participate in the supervision of the operative.

However, law enforcement's role should be limited. As the line between private corporate investigation and public law enforcement begins to blur, legal responsibilities and liability begin to shift. The more law enforcement becomes involved in the undercover investigation the more "police-agent-like" the operative becomes. If agent status is bestowed upon the investigator, the rights of the investigated persons are expanded. Significant among those rights is that of due process and Miranda. Furthermore, if agent status is achieved the criminal defendant may be able to escape prosecution using the entrapment defense.

Aside from the telephone, written reports are the most fundamental form of communication used in undercover. Even before the operative is placed, generation of reports should begin. Although practices vary from agency to agency, most firms require their operatives to make daily reports. These daily reports in their most basic form detail the who, what, when, where, how, and why of the investigator's daily observations and experiences. Generated by the operative at the end of his workday, the reports are then transmitted to his case manager for review and dissemination. The formats for these reports are as varied as the agencies that generate them. However, most are chronological and begin with the operative's arrival at work and conclude with his return home at the end of the

work day. Whatever the format selected, reports must be easy to read and use, and above all accurately describe the observations and experiences of the operative.

Employee Prosecution

It is logical that those who are caught violating the law be punished. In fact it is the mission of law enforcement to enforce public law and bring to justice those who violate it. For example, if the objective of the investigation is elimination of workplace substance abuse the investigative team must then articulate how prosecution will help achieve that objective. In most places, only dealers can be prosecuted. The criminal justice system generally does not have the capacity to prosecute every user. In workplace drug investigations, the users are almost never prosecuted. Prosecution is expensive and problematic. Although counterintuitive, prosecuting employees may not be the best action to take. Prosecution is expensive, time consuming, and often exasperating. Even before a trial date is set, documents, photographs, notes, sketches, and physical evidence may have to be produced, pre-trial conferences may be necessary, and witnesses may have to be interviewed. Then, after lengthy and costly preparation, the defendant's attorney negotiates a settlement with the prosecuting attorney that very frequently amounts to nothing more than a slap on the wrist.

Buy-Busts and Sting Operations

The buy-bust is nothing more than arranging the arrest of the perpetrator at the moment he is committing the crime. Usually the other party to the transaction is a member of law enforcement or a designated agent. Upon some prearranged signal, the suspect is confronted and arrested on the spot. In theft cases, the technique works best toward the end of the investigation. By necessity or design, the true identities of the undercover operative and law enforcement agents can be revealed at the time of the bust because the bust culminates the investigation. By arresting the offender(s) at this point reduces the chance that valuable evidence will disappear or that accomplices will escape. Chasing down a fleeing felon can be dangerous.

A sting operation is similar to a bust but is typically longer, more complicated, and more expensive. A sting usually involves an elaborate setup such as an apparently legitimate store where thieves can sell or trade stolen goods. A sting requires considerable planning, preparation, coordination, and skillful operative performance.

Recoveries

Recoveries can be a big part of theft investigations. Because undercover investigations permit a high degree of interactivity with the offenders, they permit the gathering of information not generally otherwise obtainable. Of obvious value is the determination of who is stealing and what it is they are taking. But of equal value is why are they stealing and how the property is stolen and disposed of. If other parties are receiving the property, civil recovery may be possible. A properly conducted investigation should reveal the identities of third parties and to what degree they are involved. Once identified, the investigation can be engineered to allow recovery from them as well as the principal perpetrators. Not only can property or consideration for the property be recovered, but also so can some of the costs of the investigation. A recovery of costs will significantly increase the return on investment of any investigation, not just undercover.

Case Closure

Every undercover investigation eventually evolves to where the production of useful information reaches the point of diminishing return. In some instances, the investigative effort has met every objective and the undercover investigator identified every perpetrator. More common, however, is something short of this idealistic outcome. Typically, the investigation simply reaches the point where it has yielded enough information to permit the removal of the operative and allow the rest of the investigative team to take over. Generally, the properly engineered investigation has anticipated this eventuality and has designated and allocated the sources necessary to properly close the investigation. The next phase of the investigation is called Verification and Analysis and it usually involves interviewing the offenders.

Interviews

Interviews of the guilty are key to any successful workplace investigation. In fact, the undercover portion of the investigation could be considered only a vehicle by which the investigative team reaches the point where interviews are likely to be successful. In other words, the information developed by the operative serves as the seed information, which enables the proper selection of candidates for interview. However, unlike most general investigations where the interview process over time closes in on the perpetrators, these interviews begin with those most involved and work toward those less involved. Interviews are the most critical component of the entire undercover investigation. To not conduct employee interviews following the efforts of a productive undercover is the equivalent of professional negligence. For those who use this powerful tool will attest, most of the information gleaned during the investigative process comes from interviews. When it is all said and done, only a fraction of the useable information is actually developed by the undercover. Investigative agencies that don't effectively interview are not properly serving their clients.

Investigatory interviews are interviews in which the subject is either known to have committed the offense in question or the interviewer has very good reason to believe that he has. Investigatory interviews are complex and can be fraught with liability even when properly conducted. For tactical reasons, the most serious offenders should be interviewed first. These individuals are usually the easiest to obtain admissions from and very often the most cooperative. Thus the skilled interviewer (or team in some cases) will start at the top and work down the list of interviewees, such that each subsequent interviewee is less involved than the one prior. This procedure also allows the interviews to be concluded at any time without the concern of someone claiming discrimination, bias, or disparate treatment. Theoretically, by this process the initially interviewed persons were believed to have committed more serious offenses than persons that were interviewed later.

Operative Extraction

The timing of the removal of the operative is one of the most frequently debated subjects among undercover supervisors. However, the answer is a simple one: the operative should be kept in as long as possible. In instances where interviews follow the undercover effort, the operative should stay in place until he is named as a co-offender by enough actual offenders that they would expect the operative to be interviewed. To remove the operative sooner will only bring suspicion upon him. If he is removed before the interviews begin, it will appear clear to everyone that he was an informant.

If the undercover investigator is not compromised or otherwise exposed he can be very valuable if left in place. Often after the disciplinary and corrective action is taken, offenders who have not been caught will sometimes become complacent. Some offenders will even brag of their cunningness and of having slipped through management's grasp. These individuals are easy targets for the operative.

The Administration of Disciplinary and Corrective Action

Following the interviews the investigative team should compile all of the information gleaned during the investigation and separate it by individual. The team can then guide the employer's decision makers through the information, examining each offender and the totality of information regarding them. Clearly, if an employee made an admission against interest, it would serve as the best evidence against him. If the admission was properly obtained, no other evidence is needed to take disciplinary action such as termination. Unlike the criminal justice system, which requires substantial evidence and a long waiting time for trial, an admission is all that is needed to make the case. In some instances, it is wise for the employer to disregard all of the other evidence in favor of an admission. In doing so, the disciplined employee can only challenge his admission. Because nothing else from the actual investigation (including the information developed by the undercover) has been used, he cannot challenge any of it. In other words, he cannot challenge the undercover operative and those who provided incriminating information about him. If the employer exclusively relied upon the subject's admission and nothing else, the subject will have difficulty challenging the employer's disciplinary decision.

Once all of the discipline and corrective actions have been taken, the entire case file must be provided to the custodian of record for storage and safe-keeping.

Eugene F. Ferraro

Source Ferraro, E. 2000. *Undercover Investigations in the Workplace*. Boston: Butterworth-Heinemann.

WHITE-COLLAR CRIME

The term "white-collar crime" is a general descriptor that relates broadly to a wide variety of specific crimes. It may take the form of consumer fraud, illegal competition, deceptive practices, check and credit card fraud, tax evasion, bankruptcy fraud, bribes, kickbacks, pay-offs, computer-related crime, pilferage, insurance fraud, fencing stolen property, securities fraud, and similar offenses.

The white-collar criminal can be a bank executive who embezzles or a shipping clerk who pilfers. The essential characteristic of white-collar crime, however, has more to do with the nature of the offense rather than the status of the offender. White-collar crime is a non-violent crime; it involves deceit, corruption, or breach of trust. The offense frequently involves lying, cheating, or stealing through misrepresentation. It can be committed against private individuals, business corporations, non-profit organizations, and government units.

A problem in addressing white-collar crime is the absence of valid measures for determining if criminal activity is present and to what extent. A difficulty in detecting its presence is the fact that a victim is not aware that he is being victimized, and when discovery is made, it may be too late to take effective action against the offender. In a sense, white-collar crime is an invisible crime.

The invisibility of the crime is complicated by two other factors: an unwillingness of the public to vigorously prosecute white-collar criminals and the failure of investigators to keep pace with increasingly complex schemes.

The Nature of White-Collar Crime

In most crimes there is a "crime scene," but with white-collar crime the offense is not readily apparent and is usually in progress. The investigator needs to detect the crime and work backwards to identify the principals. Following are general characteristics of white-collar offenses:

- Detection is frequently accidental.
- Offenses are frequently reported anonymously.
- There is usually no complainant.
- The scheme has been in existence over a long period of time.
- The crime tends to cover a large geographical area, often spanning several prosecutorial jurisdictions.
- The scheme tends to involve several specific violations of law.
- The principals are usually well known, respected, intelligent and, in some cases, influential.
- The scheme is sometimes difficult to decipher.
- Evidence tends to get "lost or destroyed" when the principal learns that an investigation is in progress.

Types of White-Collar Crime

Following are brief discussions of the more common types of white-collar crime.

Advanced Fee Schemes. These are designed to obtain fees in advance for services the promoter has no intention of providing. They usually occur when the offender claims to have means of obtaining buyers for one's business, property, securities, or other assets, or to have access to sources of loan financing. These usually occur when property is hard to obtain.

Pyramid Schemes. These are investment frauds by which an individual is offered a distributorship or franchise to market a particular product. The contract also authorizes the investor to sell additional franchises. Promoters represent that the marketing of the product will result in profits, but that the selling of franchises will result in quicker return on investment. Therefore, investors expend greater energies on selling franchises than on sale of products. Finally, a point is reached where the supply of investors is exhausted, leading to the collapse of the pyramid. Often, too, the product itself is overpriced,

and no real effort is made by promoters to sell the product.

Chain Referral Schemes. These involve sales of grossly overpriced products through false representation that the cost will be recovered by commissions the promoter will pay on sales to the purchaser's friends, if only the purchaser will permit them to be contacted with the same proposition.

Ponzi Schemes. These are basically investment frauds. Operators solicit investors in a business venture, promising extremely high financial returns or dividends in a very short time. The operator never invests the money in anything, but does pay "dividends" to the investor by giving him back some of his original investment. This is done as an inducement to investors to put up additional funds, or to solicit others to do so. During the early stages, the investor may even be able to liquidate his investment if he wishes, plus interest. This makes the operation more credible to others. When the operator has accumulated sufficient funds for his purposes, he flees the area.

Business Opportunity Schemes. These are a number of schemes and deceptions concocted to attract victims into participating in an allegedly lucrative business venture. They may appear in almost any type of financial dealing, e.g., vending machines, product dispensing, distributorships in limited areas, multi-level sales organizations, etc. The schemes may differ in form, but may have basic identifiable similarities, such as:

- Financial investment by the victim in advance.
- The victim's investment is "covered" by company inventory, buy-back agreements, or escrow accounts.
- The promoter convinces the victim that the company will work closely with him to ensure success. This usually includes management and marketing aids, training, and saturation advertising.

The best way to identify potentially fraudulent business opportunity schemes is to attempt to identify the misrepresentation. Some of the common indicators of misrepresentation are:

- Claiming affiliation or association with a larger or well-known company.
- Presenting a misleading credit rating, such as a false Dunn & Bradstreet report.
- Citing false business and personal references (e.g., Better Business Bureau, Chamber of Commerce, and well-known individuals).
- Inflating marketing experience and national sales.
- Misreporting the size of the firm.
- Promoting a unique product or service that has a high public demand and need.
- Projecting unrealistic sales and profits.
- Presenting doctored marketing surveys.
- Claiming easy selling, working during spare time and/or at home, such as filling orders for retail stores and selling via direct mail.
- Offering exclusive territory with leads and potential customers furnished.
- Offering a re-purchase or buy-back option.
- Providing free training, free servicing, and repair of the product to be marketed.
- Representing that the manufacturer or sponsor will provide saturated advertising.
- Advising that the offer to "get on board" will soon expire.
- Changing the contract or deleting clauses before signing.

Planned Bankruptcy Schemes. This is a merchandising swindle based on the abuse of credit that has been established, either legitimately or fraudulently. The scheme usually consists of:

- Overpurchasing of inventory on credit
- Selling or other disposing of the merchandise obtained
- Concealing the proceeds
- Not paying the creditors
- Filing a bankruptcy petition, either voluntarily or involuntarily

The new company is organized, a bank account opened, and operating space is leased. The company begins making purchases from a number of suppliers and making payment promptly to establish credit. The operators then use this credit to find other suppliers and order more merchandise, while slowing payments to the original suppliers.

The orders for goods from all suppliers are increased while the goods are sold to fences below cost. The operators now either abscond or gut the business and file bankruptcy. This can also be accomplished in one step by buying a business with a good credit rating. Organized crime has been particularly active in this type of scheme.

Merchandising Schemes. Many times these schemes are visible, blatant, and occur in the retail marketplace. All are frauds based on a twisting of the truth for increased profits. Some include:

- Bait and Switch. A product or service is promoted with no intent to sell it as advertised. The customer is lured to the seller by an extraordinarily good buy and upon arrival the salesperson tries to induce the customer to buy a higher-priced product or service. Hence the name, "bait and switch."
- Phony Sales. The unscrupulous businessperson relies on the customer's desire for a bargain. These may take the form of fire, liquidation, or going out of business sales. The advertising must be shown to be fraudulent.
- Deceptive Sales Contest. Through a variety of means, the deceptive businessperson promotes a contest in which the victim is led to believe that the chance of winning is much greater than it really is.
- Short Weighing. This practice involves substantially more than simply cheating a customer in the weighing of produce in a grocery store. Producers at the packaging stages of production can fill containers of their product 9/10 the capacity and charge retailers for the entire amount. Investigative efforts directed at a package-by-package basis seems a waste, but considering mass marketing practices, this can be extremely lucrative for the dishonest firm.

Service and Repair Schemes. Since in the affluent society many of our appliances, automobiles, or other mechanical devices need repair from time to time, this can be a very lucrative scheme. Repair schemes, regardless of the product involved, give dishonest repairpersons the chance to "lowball" the customer. Lowballing occurs when a customer takes a product in for repair, and is quoted a ridiculously low bid for the repairs. The operator has no intention of fixing the product at this price, but the lowball price will induce the customer to authorize the repairs.

Once the repairperson has the product in his possession, he tends to discover other malfunctions or worn parts, and the repair price is adjusted upward.

The most difficult element to prove is that from the beginning the repairperson intended the original estimate only as an enticement to obtain the repair job under false pretenses.

Land Schemes. Increasing in frequency, land schemes are marked by high-pressure sales tactics in which many misrepresentations are made, such as the location of the land, value, utilities available, title validity, prospect for future profitable sale, the installation of roads, or other improvements. The land is often sold sight unseen with the use of deceptive photographs, appraisal reports, and false promotions as to free bonuses, refunds, and closing costs. Targets are usually retirees, middle-income families seeking vacation resort property, and investors lured by promises of lucrative returns.

Home Improvement, Debt Consolidation, and Mortgage Loans. In recent years, all of these have been combined into one overall scheme. Homeowners already heavily burdened with debt have been the victims. The homeowner is offered a loan sufficient to pay off all other debts, as well as finance a home improvement, and is promised that the one monthly payment is less, or at least no larger, than the combined payment now being made. The large amount of the loan offered may stem from the criminal's intention to quickly sell the note at a discount to a finance company. To do so profitably he knows the amount borrowed must sufficiently exceed the cost of the home improvement work so as to offset the discount. The finance company, a third party, assumes legal possession of the promissory note, collects the monthly payments as a holder in due course, and disowns all responsibility for any misrepresentations that may have been made in its creation. In this type of scheme, promoters rely on the bewildering terms of the signed documents and numerous put-off tactics to forestall serious consequences when the home improvement falls in arrears, is poorly done, or is not done at all.

Home Solicitation Schemes. In this type of scheme, the operator represents that an individual may receive a product at no cost because the operators wish to showcase the product in the neighborhood. He will often say that the person was selected because of his reputation in the community. The victim is then asked to sign a contract that supposedly reflects the terms of the oral agreement. It is, in fact, a long-term sales contract that requires the consumer to make additional purchases for as long as 10 years.

Personal Improvement Schemes. Promoters prey on the victim's need to improve himself. These may come in the form of joining a health spa, attending a trade school, computer dating service, losing weight, learning to dance, becoming more attractive, etc.

Medical Frauds. In these illegal activities are found a number of schemes that involve defrauding of government-sponsored medical programs:

- *Double Billing.* Others billed include the patient, Medicare, Blue Cross, Medicaid of another county or state, or state insurance (Workers' Compensation).
- *Over-Billing and Billing for Services Not Performed*
- *Billing for Services Provided by Another.* This is done by gaining access to another provider's records and billing for the other's as yet unbilled services. This frequently occurs where many doctors work at the same location and records are centrally maintained.
- *Ping-Ponging.* The victim is given unnecessary treatment at the same time needed services are performed.

Welfare Frauds. These involve the acquisition of public assistance funds by those not entitled to such funds, for example:

- Receiving payments while employed.
- Receiving payments with an undisclosed source of support that would otherwise disqualify the person from receiving funds.

- Receiving funds for individuals no longer residing in the household.

Food Stamp Frauds. The individual may improperly receive food stamps in much the same way that welfare frauds are committed. The following are examples:

- Misrepresenting current income or property
- Receiving support from an undisclosed source
- Trafficking in the sale of stamps for cash

Official Corruption. Many times the investigation of other white-collar type crimes, such as bid-rigging or fraud in government programs, have corrupt public officials at the core. Often the only way to identify these frauds is when they are brought to the attention of the investigator by informants. To succeed, these investigations must be discreetly conducted.

Bid-Rigging. Generally, large public contracts are awarded by means of competitive bidding. Sometimes providers of the bids will agree on which one will submit the lowest bid, and although it is the lowest bid received, it is usually inflated because of the rigging. Oftentimes, this is very difficult to prove because the rigging is the result of a tacit understanding rather than a provable conspiracy. Sometimes the bidders may have divided the public market among themselves, or the competitors may rotate the lowest bids. Either way, the competitive bidding process is no more than a sham.

Commercial Bribery. This includes payments, kickbacks, and rebates. Through the offer of a bribe, a responsible corporate official may be persuaded to purchase inferior supplies from one firm, or to overlook deficiencies or irregularities by a contractor and thus certify payment for unsatisfactory work. The cost of the corruption is ultimately passed on to the consumer.

Insurance Fraud. This type of fraud basically occurs in four ways:

- Fraud Committed by Insurance Agents. Agents who become involved in this type of fraud usually practice a form of the Ponzi scheme. They are normally independent, travel large territories, and sell a variety of types of insurance. They purport to represent legitimate insurance companies, and often use forms and promotional materials of the major companies. Since all premium payments, policy changes, and claims are processed through the agent, the agent simply fails to forward the payment to the company. Barring a rash of claims at once, the agent can operate successfully over a number of years by simply paying the claims out of the premiums. State insurance agent licensing laws makes this type of fraud fairly easy to detect, but this has not seemed to decrease the incidence of this fraud.
- Fraud Committed by Claim Adjusters. An adjuster's investigation is the basis for insurance settlements. The most common fraud is when the adjuster conspires with claimants or repairpersons. Exclusive dealing arrangements and falsely inflated bills are the hallmark of this type. They also often substitute claimants.
- Fraud Committed by Individual Policy Holders. False customer claims are the largest source of insurance fraud. Sometimes this involves the "staging" of accidents.
- Fraud Committed by Organized Rings of Phony Claimants. Although many times an individual will commit frauds involving "staged" accidents, an increasing number of false claims are the result of organized rings of economic criminals who work together. The annual loss suffered by legitimate insurance companies is enormous in terms of fraudulent accident and health claims—losses that impact increasingly on the rising cost of insurance to the general public.

Computer-Related Frauds. Most computer crime is not detected and most of what is detected is not reported. This type of fraud is very difficult for the investigator because of lack of expertise and because the computer can be programmed to wipe out the evidence of a crime. Many schemes involve fraudulent conversion of confidential information stored within the memory banks. For this type of criminal, data is money and power.

Credit Card Frauds. Several distinct crimes are included in this classification.

- Falsely acquired credit cards by misrepresentation, including identity, age, employment, etc.
- Use of the card to defraud merchants or other providers
- Professional credit card rings who deal in counterfeit, lost, stolen, or misdelivered credit cards

These losses are in the millions annually. As always, the economic consequences are borne by the honest consumer in terms of increased prices.

Charity Frauds. The most common form of this type of fraud involves solicitation of money for an ostensibly worthwhile cause by an individual who has no intention of turning the money over to the organization if, in fact, one does exist. Also, professional fund raisers solicit donations for legitimate charities but fail to disclose that because they are professional they take for themselves a large percentage of the funds.

Check Kiting. This is the practice of drawing checks on accounts whose balances consist substantially of uncollected funds (checks that have not cleared). Using two different banks, the kiter can cover checks drawn on one bank by checks drawn on the other. The key to the scheme is the time required for the bank to actually collect deposited funds (checks).

John J. Fay

WORKPLACE INVESTIGATIONS

Workplace investigations are complex affairs, each one unique to another. A workplace investigator must have a comprehensive understanding of criminal, civil, and employment law. Workplace investigations also require a considerable investment of time, money, and patience by the employer. And finally, to ensure success, the process must be highly structured and flawlessly executed. Even the most sophisticated organization or experienced investigator can find the task consistently challenging.

Every organization at any level inevitably finds itself in need of an internal investigation. Workplace misconduct occurs in every type of organization, and at every level. Every organization is eventually confronted with the need to gather evidence, interview suspects, and uncover the truth. With the ability to muster the necessary resources, deploy skilled fact-finders, and adhere to a disciplined process, an organization can conduct a successful investigation. The investigator that is able to assist the employer in conducting a successful investigation is an invaluable asset to that organization.

Predictably, workplace investigations are fraught with liability. These considerations significantly add to the complexity of the fact-finding process and the manner in which the subject may respond to the investigation's findings and management's corrective actions. For the unsophisticated and hapless employer, a workplace investigation is a virtual legal minefield. An investigator familiar with the legal issues can be of vital assistance.

Necessary Elements of Investigative Success

A successful workplace investigation provides many dividends for the employer. In addition to uncovering facts and essential information needed to solve problems, a successful investigation helps restore order. It provides the employer the opportunity to analyze process and system failures and re-engineer them to prevent future problems. For an investigation to be successful, it must have:

- Management commitment.
- Meaningful objectives.
- A well-conceived strategy.
- Properly pooled resources and expertise.
- Lawful execution.

An investigation will undoubtedly fail when the investigator is confronted with a management that is dysfunctional or cannot make decisions. Failure in this case has nothing to do with the actual workplace problem, but with the resolve and commitment of the employer.

An investigation without meaningful, practical objectives cannot succeed. Success will be denied also when objectives constantly change and when efforts to achieve the objectives are allowed to wane and shift.

A well-conceived strategy is essential. A strategy explicates how the investigation will proceed; the objectives are the intended outcomes of the strategy. The employer's role is to define the objectives, such as to identify guilty parties and recover stolen property; it is the investigator's role to determine how the objectives are to be met.

Knowing what needs to be done and how it is to be done is one thing; having the expertise and tools is another. Before taking a first step, the investigator must possess the requisite talent and have access to resources, which can include human, logistical, and financial resources.

One of the dangers in conducting a workplace investigation is the natural urge to cut corners, an urge that is often encouraged by an employer that wants to cut costs. The risk is defeat in the courtroom. A single unlawful act, particularly one that violates a constitutional right, can cause havoc. From it can come judicial problems, negative publicity for the employer, and damage to the investigator's professional reputation.

The Investigative Framework

In order to be successful, any workplace investigation should be conducted within a logical framework that provides process to the investigator and attainable goals to the organization. This framework specifies the objectives of most any workplace investigation:

- Seek out and identify the true nature and scope of the problem
- Identify who is involved and why
- Gather any and all information in such a fashion as to allow the proper distribution of appropriate disciplinary and/or corrective action
- Orchestrate the process in such a fashion that is least disruptive to the organization and its operations
- Achieve the best possible return on investment

An investigator who does not understand the true nature and scope of the problem may focus on one area or one individual related to misconduct, while failing to notice other critical elements of misconduct. Identifying who is involved is key to any investigation, and a seasoned investigator can often learn through skillful interviewing the identities of other employees previously unknown. Gathering information in

an investigation is very important, but being able to properly present it to the client is of paramount importance. A skilled investigator may uncover mountains of actionable information, but it must be presented coherently and in such a way that the client can exact appropriate disciplinary and/or corrective action. An organization can be adversely affected by employee misconduct, but a careless investigator can also be worse than the disease and inflict damage to the organization.

Process of Investigation

Most workplace investigations unfold incrementally. That incremental, yet dynamic process is called *The Process of Investigation*. It includes five distinct phases. They are:

- Planning and Preparation
- Information Gathering and Fact-Finding
- Verification and Analysis
- Determination and Disbursement of Disciplinary and/or Corrective Action
- Prevention and Education

Every proper workplace investigation requires the investigator to structure his or her investigation such that it systematically contemplates each phase. To do otherwise is insufficient, unprofessional, and possibly even negligent. The investigator who imposes process and structure on his investigation obtains better results and does so with more efficiency. What's more, it differentiates him as a professional. It affords him and his employer or client the benefit of ease in assessing and analyzing the result. As in the scientific community, process also permits peer review. In the community of employer-employee relations, others may review the investigator's efforts and are able to easily and accurately reconstruct that which the investigator found and how he found it. The ability to reconstruct the process and demonstrate its integrity and propriety lends it credibility. That credibility is the foundation on which all facts rest. An investigative process without credibility is fatally defective. That defect potentially imposes a bar to the admission and ultimate use of otherwise admissible and actionable evidence. It is the implementation and ultimate integrity of this process that is the hallmark of the professional investigator.

Methods of Investigation

Fundamentally, there are six basic methods of investigation available to those who conduct workplace investigations:

- Physical surveillance
- Electronic surveillance
- Research and internal audit
- Forensic analysis
- Undercover
- Interviewing and interrogation

Physical surveillance is likely the oldest investigative technique and is nothing more than observing people, places, or things. Electronic surveillance is the use of electronic technology to enhance the investigator's observations and overcome limitations of physical surveillance. Research and audit is the review and examination of documents and records, both of public record and internal to the organization. Forensic analysis is the application of modern science and scientific technology in the gathering of information. Undercover investigation is the surreptitious placement of an operative into the workplace to gather information. Interviewing and interrogation is an interactive investigative technique that requires little more than an interviewer and an interviewee. An effective interview should always contain some semblance of methodology and offer the interviewee the element of due process.

Every workplace investigation uses one or more of these methods. The challenge then for the professional investigator is to select the method(s) most suitable for his particular circumstances and deploy them properly and efficiently. In many instances, the investigator will find that he must combine the methods in some fashion or mix and match them. It is only with knowledge and experience can the investigator know which methods to use and when. It is this unique ability to combine these methods properly and efficiently that separates exceptional investigators from good investigators.

Due Process

As with many other facets of workplace investigations, oftentimes the investigator should engage in practices that not only produce the desired results in terms of the goals of the investigation, but that are defensible to legal challenge. Among these considerations is that of due process. Among other things, due process includes: the right to know the offense(s) and crime(s) of which one is accused; the right to view and examine the government's evidence; the right to face one's accusers and examine them as well as any and all witnesses; the right to competent representation; and protection against self incrimination.

Employers must be careful. Although they have no legal duty to provide the subjects of internal investigations any due process, some triers of fact and jury sometimes think otherwise. The appearance of treating the subject unfairly and the failure to comply with the reasonable requests of the subject may expose the employer to considerable liability. Even absent the rights of due process, it is expected that all people be treated fairly and provided all reasonable accommodations while under suspicion or when accused of misconduct.

Burden of Proof

Ultimately, when one is conducting or supervising a workplace investigation, it is critical to understand the burden of proof that is applicable to the investigation and equally important for the investigator to be able to educate and communicate to management the differentiation between the perceived and actual burden of proof in a workplace investigation.

It is very common for members of management to assume that the standard of proof in building a case against an employee who is engaging in workplace misconduct is the same as it would be in a civil or criminal arena; most of the time, the burden of proof is actually lower and more attainable.

As most people know, the burden of proof in a criminal case is "beyond a reasonable doubt," which is the highest level of proof in any case. In mathematical terms, beyond a reasonable doubt equates to being approximately 99 percent sure of a decision. In most civil cases, the burden of proof is a "preponderance of the evidence." A preponderance of the evidence means that a trier of fact is swayed to one side more than the other given the facts of the case. One may see the "clear and convincing" burden of proof in certain types of civil cases or matters involving civil fraud. Clear and convincing evidence falls between preponderance of the evidence and beyond a reasonable doubt, and contains evidence so clear and weighty in terms of quality, and convincing as to cause the trier of fact to come to a clear conviction of the truth of the precise facts in issue.

Employers, however, need only to meet the "good faith investigation/reasonable conclusion" burden of proof. As it states, management must only reasonably conclude that misconduct occurred after conducting a good faith investigation.

Reporting

Another important consideration, fraught with pitfalls, is the question of to whom the investigator reports during a workplace investigation. Ideally, in the planning stages of an investigation, a distinct and select group (or individual) is identified who is in the "need to know" group. This group should contain individuals who can be a point of contact for the investigator, a management representative for employees (and union stewards, if applicable), who can exact disciplinary or corrective action if necessary, and who can assist the investigator in coordinating certain logistics of the investigation and obtain critical records. Involving the appropriate legal counsel, whether internal, external, or both, can be helpful to management, especially when deciding what to do with the investigative results. Legal counsel should always be involved in undercover investigations without exception. Involving too many members of management or non-essential members can have a negative impact on the process of investigation and, ultimately, the entire investigation's outcome.

Litigation Avoidance

Workplace investigations have precedent in the arena of employment law to help guide the investigator and employer through litigation avoidance. *Noble v. Sears, Roebuck & Co.*, 33 Cal. App. 3d 654 (1973) held that an organization that hires an investigator can be held liable for violations of law made by the investigator which the employer authorized, either implicitly or expressly. Similarly, *Solis v. Southern Cal. Rapid Transit Dist.*, 105 Cal. App. 3d 382 (1980) held that employers may be held liable for the tortuous invasion of privacy when investigators conduct an "unreasonably intrusive investigation."

Organizations must also be sensitive to the federal requirements regarding discrimination. According to the Americans with Disabilities Act, employers may test for drug use but may not discriminate against a person who has successfully completed a drug rehabilitation program and who no longer uses illegal drugs. Title VII of the Civil Rights Act of 1964 states that employers must avoid disparate or different treatment and/or disparate impact in regards to an employee's race, gender, color, religion, or national origin. The Civil Rights Act of 1991 affects workplace investigations in that employers must be nondiscriminatory in investigating suspicious activity, be consistent applying discipline to all levels of the organization, and offer consistent rehabilitation opportunities. Furthermore, organizations must be diligent in ensuring that sexual harassment does not exist in the workplace and that claims of sexual harassment are dutifully investigated.

Labor Union Involvement

In a unionized workplace environment, considerations must be given to union employees when involving them in a workplace investigation. Failure for the employer (or investigator) to afford such consideration could result in heavy fines and sanctions to the offending employer, not to mention having to take back employees involved in misconduct. Under no circumstances may any employer (or its agents) conduct surveillance or monitor employees' union activities. In the *Weingarten* ruling [*NLRB v. Weingarten, Inc.*, 420 U.S. 241 (1975)], the Supreme Court ruled that an employee is entitled to ask for and receive union representation at an employer's interview if the employee reasonably believes that the interview might result in disciplinary action against them. An employer who disciplines or terminates an employee for refusing to participate in an interview without a union representative present is in violation of *Weingarten*.

Invasion of Privacy

While law enforcement enjoys the power to search people and seize property, the closest thing to it in the private sector is the ability of an employer to search its own property. Workplace searches of desks, computers, lockers, and other work areas are permissible only where an employee does not have a reasonable expectation of privacy. The employer can substantially reduce the expectation of privacy by: advising employees that such areas are subject to inspection, with or without notice; restricting private use of these areas by issuing its own locks and retaining duplicate keys; and by crafting policies that limit workers' expectation of privacy and permit searches under any circumstances. An organization can broaden its ability to search by creating company policy and advising employees that there is no privacy associated with specific aspects of work or workplace locations. It is important for the organization in this instance to document employee notification of those policies and to apply the policies without discrimination. For the investigator, considerations around invasion of privacy include limiting the use of the methods of investigation in those areas where an employee could conceivably have an expectation of privacy.

Entrapment

Employers shy away from undercover investigations for many reasons. But among the most common and unnecessary is the fear of entrapment. Employers and sometimes the lawyers that represent them fear entrapment because they don't understand it. Contrary to popular belief, entrapment is not a crime. It is not something bad employers do to innocent employees. Entrapment is not something for which one might be punished or even admonished. Entrapment is nothing more than a criminal defense. Because entrapment is a criminal defense, only the government can entrap. What's more, the defense of entrapment can only be used after a defendant admits to the commission of the crime.

Eugene F. Ferraro and Brad Mathers

WOUNDS: TRAUMA CAUSED BY SHOOTING AND CUTTING

In gunshot cases, a bullet entrance wound is usually a neat, round hole made by a bullet entering the body. The shape of an exit wound will vary according to where it exits (whether through a fleshy or bony structure), the shape of the bullet as it exits (whether pristine or flattened), and the motion of the bullet (whether spinning or tumbling). Exit wound shapes include marks that are stellate (star-like), slit-like, everted (inside-out), and irregular.

A bullet exit wound is typically a ragged or torn hole made by a bullet leaving the body and is usually much larger than the size of the bullet.

An abrasion collar is a narrow ring around the entry of a bullet hole in the skin. The skin, being resistant and elastic, will be stretched by the impacting bullet. A narrow ring around the bullet hole is formed by the abrasive action of the bullet. The ring may also contain residues from the surface of the bullet.

A contact or tattooed gunshot wound is a close-range wound characterized by gunpowder tattooing in and around the bullet hole. The tattooing consists of charring at the entry point, and powder grains and combustion products embedded in the skin. The wound results when the muzzle of the gun has been firmly applied to the skin at the instant of firing. When the muzzle is against a bony structure, such as the head, the blast causes a lacerated, charred wound that shows flame burns of the skin and hair from the rapidly expanding explosive gases. Smudges from carbon deposits appear within the subcutaneous tissue, muscle, and bone. A distinct abraded and contused imprint, with the laceration in the shape of a star, will very likely appear on the skin. When the muzzle is in contact with soft flesh, such as the abdomen, the star-shaped laceration and flame burns are not present because the exploding gases of the muzzle blast are dispersed without resistance into the abdominal cavity.

A near-contact gunshot wound results when the muzzle, at time of discharge, is approximately 2 inches or less from the victim but not in contact with the skin. The wound is rounded with inverted abraded edges, surrounded by a zone of scorching, soot deposits, and compact tattooing from powder grains embedded in the skin.

A close-range gunshot wound is a wound caused when the muzzle, at time of discharge, is 2–24 inches from the victim. As the distance between a gun and the skin is increased, the flame burns diminish and powder grains embedded in the skin (tattooing) are spread in a widening circle around the bullet entry hole. Eventually, the tattooing effect disappears. When a bullet fired at close range first passes through clothing or some other substance, the tattooing effect may not be visible at all, thereby giving the appearance of a distant shot.

A distant wound is a wound caused by a bullet that traveled in excess of at least 2 feet from muzzle to victim. A distant wound is apparent by the absence of flame, smoke, and tattooing marks characteristic of a shot made in contact or in close contact with the victim. When a bullet penetrates the body perpendicular to the skin, it produces a round wound with abraded margins, called a collar abrasion. When a bullet penetrates the skin at an angle, the direction from which it enters the skin is indicated by a triangular abrasion and undermining of the skin. A bullet that grazes but does not penetrate the skin will produce a rectangular abrasion of the skin, called a bullet rub.

A beveled wound or a tangential gunshot wound results when the skin is penetrated at an angle. One margin of the wound is beveled and the other margin overhangs it. A residue track may be visible.

Marks from shotgun wounds have similar characteristics and are potentially classifiable as to the distance separating the victim and the shotgun muzzle at time of discharge. Four classifications are generally recognized: (1) the direct contact wound, which shows an imprint of the muzzle on the skin or which indicates contact by massive destruction of bone and tissue; (2) the up-close or loose-contact wound, which shows a small diameter entry pattern having abraded edges surrounded by a zone of considerable scorching, soot, and powder residue; (3) the close-range or near-range wound, which has a larger diameter entry pattern consistent with a discharge at 4–6 feet and shows abraded, scalloped margins, wad-impact abrasion, and wide dispersal of powder residue, soot, and smoke stains; and (4) the distance wound, which has a very large-diameter entry pattern consistent with a discharge at greater than 6 feet and shows scattered, small, round pellet holes with abraded margins.

In cutting and stabbing cases, a cleavage line wound is a gaping wound produced by cutting or stabbing perpendicularly to a cleavage line. The wound will appear to have been caused by a large blade or a deep cutting action. The gaping aspect, however, results from a distortion of the muscle fibers that provide a normal tension to the skin. Defense wounds are often found on the victim's hands and arms. The wounds evidence the manner in which the victim maneuvered to fend off the attacker. Wounds made by cutting instruments are called incised wounds.

A wrinkle wound results from a cutting or stabbing action that produces multiple cuts or punctures along the line of the blade, with interspersed areas of uninvolved skin. Wrinkle wounds are usually associated with obese or elderly victims.

John J. Fay

Source   Fay, J. 1987. *Butterworths Security Dictionary*. Boston: Butterworth–Heinemann.

V: Legal Aspects

ARREST LAW

Because our justice system places a high value on the rights of the individual citizen, private and public officers cannot simply arrest, search, question, and confine a person by whim. A consideration of individual rights is an important factor. The Bill of Rights of the U.S. Constitution affords citizens numerous protections. If we examine the Fourth and Fifth Amendments of the Bill of Rights, we can see how individual rights are safeguarded during criminal investigations.

Amendment IV: "The right of the people to be secure in their persons, houses, papers, and effects, against unreasonable searches and seizures, shall not be violated, and no warrants shall issue, but upon probable cause, supported by oath or affirmation; and particularly describing the place to be searched, and the person or things to be seized."

The Fourth Amendment stipulates guidelines for the issuance of warrants. Public and private police obtain arrest and search warrants from an impartial judicial officer. Sometimes immediate action (e.g., chasing a bank robber) does not permit time to obtain warrants before arrest and search. In such a case, an arrest warrant is obtained as soon as possible. Private police should contact public police for assistance in securing warrants and in apprehending suspects.

Amendment V: "… nor shall [any person] be compelled in any criminal case to be a witness against himself, nor be deprived of life, liberty, or property, without due process of law."

The Sixth, Eighth, and Fourteenth Amendments are other important amendments frequently associated with our criminal justice process. Briefly, the Sixth pertains to the right to trial by jury and assistance of counsel. The Eighth states that "excessive bail shall not be required, nor excessive fines imposed, nor cruel and unusual punishments inflicted." The Fourteenth bars states from depriving any person of due process of law or equal protection of the laws.

Probable Cause

A key factor to support a legal arrest and search is "probable cause," which means that there are reasonable grounds to justify legal action. An eyewitness viewing of a crime would support probable cause in an arrest warrant.

Knowledge of arrest powers is essential for those likely to exercise this authority. These powers differ from state to state and depend on the statutory authority of the type of individual involved. Generally, public police officers have the greatest arrest powers. They are also protected from civil liability for false arrest, as long as they had probable cause that the crime was committed. Those in the private sector have arrest powers equal to citizen arrest powers which means that they are liable for false arrest if a crime was not, in fact, committed—regardless of the reasonableness of their belief. An exception is apparent if state statutes point out that these personnel have arrest powers equal to public police only on the protected property. If private sector personnel are deputized or given a special constabulary commission, their arrest powers are likely to equal those of public police.

Whoever makes an arrest must have the legal authority to do so. Furthermore, the distinction between felonies and misdemeanors, for those making arrests, is of tremendous importance. Felonies are considered more serious crimes and include burglary, armed robbery, murder, and arson. Misdemeanors are less serious crimes such as trespassing, disorderly conduct, and being drunk in public. Generally, public police can arrest someone for a felony or a misdemeanor committed in view. Arrest for a felony not seen by the public police is lawful with probable cause; arrest for a misdemeanor not seen by the public police is unlawful, and a warrant is needed based upon probable cause. On the other hand, private police have less arrest powers (equal to citizen arrest powers). Basically, citizen arrest powers permit felony arrests based upon probable cause, but prohibit misdemeanor arrests.

A serious situation evolves when, for example, a private officer mistakenly arrests a person for a misdemeanor thinking that the offense was a felony, or when the jurisdiction in which the arrest occurred does not grant such authority. Many employers in the private sector are so afraid of an illegal arrest, and subsequent legal action, that they prohibit their officers from making arrests without supervisory approval. It is imperative that private sector personnel know state arrest law.

An illegal arrest may lead to civil and/or criminal prosecution of the arrestor. False arrest may be grounds for a civil action for damages. If an illegal arrest has resulted in the death of the arrestee, an arrestor can be prosecuted for homicide.

Force

During the exercise of arrest powers, force may be necessary. The key criterion is "reasonableness." Force should be no more than what is reasonably necessary to carry out legitimate authority. If an arrestee struggles to escape and is subdued to the ground, it would be unreasonable for the arrestor to step on the arrestee's face. Although jurisdictions vary, "deadly force" is usually reserved for life-threatening situations. Unreasonable force can lead to difficulties in prosecuting a case, besides civil and criminal litigation.

Searches

A legal arrest is a prerequisite to a search. Ordinarily, a public police officer conducts a search of an arrestee right after arrest. This has been consistently upheld by courts for the protection of the officer who may be harmed by a concealed weapon. However, evidence obtained through an unreasonable search and seizure is not admissible in court; this is known as the "exclusionary rule." In reference to private sector officers, who generally have citizen arrest powers, the law is not clear and varies widely. Generally, a search is valid when consent is given and where, in a retail environment, a shoplifting statute permits the retrieval of merchandise. A search for weapons may be justified through common law, which states that citizens have the right of self-defense. The recovery of stolen goods as the basis for a search is typically forbidden, except in some state shoplifting statutes.

Though the law of searches by private police is not as well developed as for public police, court cases are evolving that are changing this situation. In the California Supreme Court decision *People v. Zelinsky*, 24 Ca. 3d.357, handed down in 1979, the court ruled, in essence, that the exclusionary rule applies to private security officers.

This decision involved a shoplifting case in which Virginia Zelinsky placed a blouse in her purse without paying for it. She was stopped outside the store and escorted to the security office. When the officers opened her purse and found the blouse, they also discovered a vial of heroin. She went to trial on a charge of possession of narcotics. Zelinsky requested the judge to suppress the heroin because it had been seized illegally. The judge denied her request stating that store detectives are not governed by the prohibition against unreasonable searches. On appeal, the California Supreme Court disagreed. What was also significant about this case was that the court had ruled that when private security officers investigate crimes, their acts are "government actions," so the full force of the Constitution governs those acts.

Questioning

An important clause of the Fifth Amendment states that a person cannot be compelled in any criminal case to be a witness against himself. What constitutional protections does a suspect have upon being approached by an investigator for questioning? Here again, the law differs with respect to public and private sector investigations.

Basic criminal law states that a person about to be questioned about a crime by public police must be advised of:

1. The right to remain silent.
2. The fact that statements can be used against the person in a court of law.
3. The right to have an attorney present, even if the suspect has no money.
4. The right to stop answering questions at any time.

These rights, known as "Miranda rights," evolved out of a 1966 Supreme Court case known as *Miranda v. Arizona*. If these rights are not read to a person (by public police) before questioning, the statements or a confession of the accused will not be admissible as evidence in court.

Are private police required to read a person the Miranda warnings prior to questioning? The courts have not yet required the reading.

However, any type of coercion or trick during questioning is prohibited for private as well as public police. A voluntary confession by the suspect is in the best interests of public and private investigators. Many private sector investigators choose to read suspects the Miranda warnings as a protection against legal challenge.

Philip P. Purpura

Source Purpura, P.P. 2002. *Security and Loss Prevention, 4th Edition*. Boston: Butterworth-Heinemann.

BUSINESS LAW

Business and law are inextricably linked; the law determines who may engage in business, how business is to be carried out, and the penalties that apply when the law is broken. An understanding of the law as it relates to business is indispensable to the security manager.

An understanding of business law means knowing the origins of law, how they have changed and are continuing to change, and how they are currently applied. The particular areas of interest to the security manager are constitutional law, statutory law, case law, administrative law, and the role of ethics in influencing business conduct.

Sources of Law

Law acts as an instrument of social control and of change. Many of the laws that regulate business, for example, have evolved in response to societal demands. In responding to the will of society, the law is in a constant state of flow, ebbing and rising in relation to pressures from many different sources. We see this, for example, in restrictions designed to protect ecological systems. Clearly, law has a profound impact on the decisions of managers in all disciplines and at all levels in a business organization.

The security manager's view of the law will necessarily be both broad and purposeful. It will be broad in the sense that the law expresses concepts that generally ascribe to the notion that for civilization to be functional there must be a body of rules enforced by the government for the good of the people. The security manager's view will be purposeful because it will focus on functional purposes, such as prevention of crime, maintenance of order, investigation of crime, and apprehension of violators. This view acknowledges that the law is not just a statement of rules of conduct, but also the mechanism for dealing with violations and affording remedies.

American law has four sources: (1) the U.S. and state constitutions, (2) legislation or statutory law, (3) judicial decisions or case law, and (4) the rules and regulations of governmental agencies or administrative law. The general priority among the various sources of law is that constitutions prevail over statutes, and statutes prevail over common-law principles established in court decisions. Courts will not turn to judicial decisions for law if a statute is directly applicable.

The rules and principles that are applied by the courts fall into three groups: (1) laws that have been passed by legislative bodies; (2) case law, derived from cases decided by the courts; and (3) procedural rules, which determine how lawsuits are handled in the courts and include matters such as the rules of evidence. The first two groups are used by the courts to decide controversies. They are often called substantive law. The third group, known as procedural law, provides the machinery whereby substantive law is given effect and applied to resolve controversies.

Substantive law defines rights, whereas procedural law establishes the procedures by which rights are enforced and protected. For example, Jones claims that Smith should reimburse him for losses sustained in a burglary at the apartment that Jones rented from Smith. The rules that provide for bringing Smith into court and for the conduct of the trial constitute procedural law. Whether Smith had a duty to protect Jones against burglary and whether Jones is entitled to damages are matters of substance that would be determined on the basis of the substantive law.

Private law pertains to the relationships between individuals. It encompasses the subjects of contracts, torts, and property. The law of torts is a chief source of litigation. A tort is a wrong committed by one person against another or against his property. The law of torts holds that people who injure others or their property should compensate them for their loss.

Constitutional Law

The Constitution of the United States and the constitutions of the various states form the foundation of our legal system. All other laws must be consistent with them. A federal law cannot violate the U.S. Constitution; all state laws must conform to the federal Constitution, as well as with the constitution of the appropriate state.

Statutory Law

Much of law is found in legislation. Legislation is the expression of society's judgment and the product of the political process. Legislative bodies exist at all levels of government. Legislation is created by Congress, state legislatures, and local government bodies. Legislation enacted by Congress or by a state legislature is usually referred to as a statute. Laws passed by local governments are frequently called ordinances. Compilations of legislation at all levels of government are called codes. For example, we have city fire codes that cover fire safety, state traffic codes that regulate the operation of motor vehicles, and, at the federal level, we have the U.S. Code consisting of statutes that regulate general conduct.

Substantial differences in the law exist among the various states simply because each state has its own constitution, statutes, and body of case law. Two methods of achieving uniformity in business law are possible: (1) having federal legislation govern business law, and (2) having uniform state laws for certain common business transactions. The latter method has produced more than 100 model uniform laws concerning such subjects as partnership, leases, arbitration, warehouse receipts, bills of lading, and stock transfers. The most important development for business in the field of uniform state legislation has been the Uniform Commercial Code (UCC).

Case Law

A very substantial part of law is found in cases decided by the courts. This concept of decided cases as a source of law is generally referred to as case law and has been a predominant influence in the evolution of the body of law in the United States. Case law is important because of the great difficulty in establishing law in advance of an issue being raised.

When a case is decided, the court writes an opinion. These written opinions, or precedents, make up the body of case law. The concept of precedent is linked to a doctrine called *stare decisis*, which means "to stand by decisions and not to disturb what is settled." *Stare decisis* holds that once a precedent has been set, it should be followed in later cases involving the same issue. In this way, the law takes on certainty and predictability. *Stare decisis* is also flexible. If a court, especially an appeals court, finds that the prior decision was wrong or that it is no longer sound under prevailing conditions, it may overrule and change the decision. Although *stare decisis* introduces some degree of consistency, the system is far from perfect. Precedents (and statutes) vary from state to state. In some states the plaintiff in a negligent security case must be completely free of fault in order to recover damages; in most other states the doctrine of comparative negligence is used, so that a plaintiff found to be 10 percent at fault can recover not more than 90 percent of his damages.

Administrative Law

Administrative law is concerned with the many administrative agencies of the government. This type of law is in the form of rules and regulations promulgated by an administrative agency created by a state legislature or by the Congress to carry out a specific statute. For example, in a variety of statutes the Congress gives authority to the U.S. Department of Transportation (DOT) to regulate the nation's transportation systems (air, maritime, highway, railroad, pipeline, and metropolitan transit). The rules put into effect by DOT are in the nature of law to the regulated parties, e.g., the air, sea, motor, and rail carriers engaged in interstate transportation.

The powers and procedures of the administrative agencies do not always correspond exactly to the general intent of the legislature. By its very nature, most legislation is general, and interpretation is necessary to carry out the intent of the legislative body when it passed an act. The rules that implement a legislative act are often the interpretation of a government administrator. Since it is not possible to precisely express legislative intent in words that mean the same thing to everyone, the rules and regulations are often approximations that, when implemented, are quickly challenged by the affected parties.

Ethics

Ethics play a part in influencing conduct and regulating the behavior of individuals and businesses. Concern for the consequences of one's actions is clearly a powerful motivator. For example, as security professionals we are concerned about the damage to our reputations that would follow if we were found to have engaged in practices that were unethical or immoral, although not necessarily illegal. Business entities have similar fears based on economic consequences. Personal and institutional ethical standards are having an ever-increasing impact on decisions. Almost every publicly held business has adopted a code of ethical conduct for its employees; the federal government has one for its employees; and nearly all trade and professional associations, including the American Society for Industrial Security, adhere to ethical codes. While these codes are not laws, they are usually enforced and provide penalties for non-compliance.

Ethical conduct is based on a personal commitment to do what is correct and to not do what is wrong. Ethical standards articulate values that go beyond what the law specifically demands and proscribes. The law provides a floor above which ethical conduct rises. Although ethical standards are usually considered to be extensions beyond the law, they are sometimes enacted into law when legislatures bring the law into alignment with society's views of right and wrong.

In the business environment, ethical conduct normally exists at a level well above legal minimums. It often means doing more than the law requires or less than it allows. Codes of ethics adopted by businesses can be thought of as internal work rules for all persons subject to them. Typically, they are based on fairness and honesty, and most provisions only require disclosure of facts to superiors in particular situations, while a few may dictate certain decisions and conduct. Codes of ethics state a collective sense of right and wrong, usually in the broadest of terms.

John J. Fay

Source   Corley, R. and Shedd, P. 1989. *Principles of Business Law, 14th Edition.* Englewood Cliffs: Prentice-Hall.

CONCEPTS IN NEGLIGENCE

Negligence is the doing of that thing which a reasonably prudent person would not have done, or the failure to do that thing which a reasonably prudent person would have done in like or similar circumstances. It is the failure to exercise that degree of care that reasonably prudent persons would have exercised in similar circumstances.

Tort law has attempted to refine the concept of negligence by subdividing it into narrower categories. Degrees of care and degrees of negligence are closely related but separate approaches in refining negligence. Degrees of care is the amount of care that is reasonable for a given situation. It depends on various factors, including the relationship between the parties and the nature and extent of the risk inherent in that situation. For example, transporting school children requires a higher degree of care than hauling watermelons.

Degrees of negligence embraces the idea that negligence may be classified as slight or gross. This has been a persistent theme in tort law and criminal law. There are statutes in which the term negligence is preceded by some adjective, such as "slight" or "gross." In most cases, the statute applies only to a particular situation or activity.

Slight negligence is the failure to exercise great care. It is not a slight departure from ordinary care. Technically, it is the failure to exercise greater care than the circumstances would ordinarily require. On the other hand, gross negligence is something more than ordinary negligence but only in degree. It is less than recklessness, which is a different kind of conduct showing a conscious disregard for the safety of others. The distinction is important since contributory negligence is not a defense to wanton misconduct but is to gross negligence. A finding of reckless misconduct will usually support an award of punitive damages whereas gross negligence will not.

Contributory negligence is an act or omission amounting to want of ordinary care on the part of a complaining party, which, concurring with the defendant's negligence, is the proximate cause of injury. Contributory negligence generally applies to a condition of employment, either express or implied, with which an employee agrees that the dangers of injury ordinarily or obviously incident to the discharge of required duties will be at the employee's own risk.

Negligent conduct is an element of various tort causes of action. The components of the cause of action for negligence are: (1) a duty owed by the defendant to the plaintiff, (2) a violation of that duty by the defendant's failure to conform to the required standard of conduct, (3) sufficient causal connection between the negligent conduct and the resulting harm, and (4) actual loss or damage. The plaintiff's contributory negligence, if any, will reduce or defeat a claim. In many jurisdictions, contributory negligence is a defense to be pleaded and proved by the defendant, but in some jurisdictions the plaintiff must allege and prove his freedom from contributory negligence as a part of his case.

Negligent conduct can be alleged in an employer's hiring practices. The term *negligent hiring* refers to a concept that holds an employer directly liable for an employee's harmful conduct after the employer failed to exercise reasonable care in hiring the employee. Although similar to *respondeat superior*, this concept can extend to situations that occur outside of the workplace. For example, assume that during working hours a security officer makes a date with a female employee. During the date (off the employer's premises and during non-working hours) the officer rapes the other employee.

She learns that the employer was aware that this same officer had assaulted other women whom he had met at work, but had hired him anyway without warning her or other female employees. The employer can be charged with failure to exercise reasonable care in the hiring and retention of a dangerous employee.

The "reasonable person" concept applies objective standards of reasonableness when judging whether conduct is negligent. The law does not make special allowance for the particular weaknesses of a person acting negligently. Conduct that creates an unreasonable risk of harm is no less dangerous because the actor lacked the capacity to conform to an acceptable level of performance. While it may seem unfair to hold some people to standards they cannot always meet, it would be more unjust to require the innocent victims of substandard conduct to bear the consequences.

The standard is usually stated as reasonable care, ordinary care, or due care, and is measured against the hypothetical conduct of a hypothetical person, i.e., the reasonable human of ordinary prudence. Such a person is not the average or typical person, but an idealized image. He is a composite of the community's judgment as to how the typical citizen ought to behave in circumstances where there is a potential or actual risk of harm. The reasonable person is not perfect or infallible. He is allowed mistakes of judgment, of perception, and he may even be momentarily distracted. Above all, he is human and prone to errors, but such errors must have been reasonable or excusable under the circumstances.

The law of negligence distinguishes between liability for the consequences of affirmative acts (misfeasance) and liability for merely doing nothing (nonfeasance).

Almost any inaction can be characterized as misfeasance if the court is so disposed, and often inaction is substantially the equivalent of active misconduct. The failure to repair defective brakes may be seen as active negligence. A fundamental question is whether there is a sufficient relationship between the one who failed to act and the one injured as a result.

A common example is the absence of a duty to go to the aid of someone needing help (when such help is not required by some preexisting status or relationship). A person skilled in administering cardiopulmonary resuscitation is not required to aid a victim needing such assistance, unless the person happens to also be a paramedic hired for that purpose.

Duties of affirmative action that would not otherwise exist may be voluntarily assumed. It is commonly held that one who freely undertakes to render aid to another assumes a duty to act with reasonable care, and once the duty is assumed it may not be abandoned. This rule is thought by many to have the negative effect of discouraging rescuers.

John J. Fay

Source   Fay, J. 1987. *Butterworths Security Dictionary: Terms and Concepts*. Boston: Butterworth-Heinemann.

COURTS: PROSECUTION IN STATE COURTS

A chief prosecutor is the attorney who advocates for the public in felony cases, as well as in a variety of other cases. A prosecutor's responsibilities are limited geographically. A prosecutorial district follows county lines and typically consists of a single county but may include two or more.

In the recent past half of these officials had the title of either district attorney or county attorney. A chief prosecutor may have a staff of "assistant prosecutors," attorneys who do much of the actual case work.

The prosecutor usually does not know of a felony matter until a law enforcement agency made an arrest. Because 95 percent of prosecutors receive felony cases from three or more arresting agencies, an opportunity exists for considerable variation in the time between arrest and notification of the prosecutor's office. About 73 percent of law enforcement agencies in the United States are state or local police departments and 18 percent are county sheriff's departments; the remainder are special agencies such as transit police or campus police.

Some prosecutors are notified only after the arresting agency has filed papers in a special or "lower" court. This court conducts necessary pre-trial events, such as informing the accused person of the charges, setting bail, and assigning defense counsel.

When a staff attorney handles all phases of a criminal case, the processing is known as "vertical" case assignment. A career-criminal unit is an example of a vertical case assignment in which certain assistant prosecutors handle repeat offenders from the targeting stage onward. "Horizontal" assignment means that different assistants specialize in different phases—drafting complaints, conducting trials, or doing appellate work.

Indigent Defendants

The U.S. Constitution guarantees rights to citizens as they relate to the federal government and federal criminal prosecutions. Such rights are not automatically applicable to state governments and state criminal prosecutions. In lawsuits concerning specific rights, the U.S. Supreme Court decides the applicability of such rights to the states.

The Sixth Amendment to the U.S. Constitution establishes the right of a criminal defendant to have assistance of counsel for his or her defense. The Supreme Court has ruled that counsel must be available to any defendant who is at risk of a federal or state sentence of incarceration. This right extends to indigent defendants unable to pay a lawyer. If an indigent defendant who faces a penalty of incarceration wants a lawyer, the state must either provide a lawyer or seek a lesser penalty.

Filing

After a document charging a person with a crime is submitted to the felony court, an event known as a case "filing," the court takes control of the case. Most felony cases begin with the filing of an indictment issued by a grand jury. In most other felony cases, the charging document is an "information" filed by the prosecutor. Either type of document states who the accused person is and what illegal acts were committed. To proceed on the basis of an information rather than an indictment, the prosecutor normally must present the case in a preliminary hearing, which in some places occurs in a lower court. In a preliminary hearing, the judge reviews the facts and circumstances of the case to determine whether there are reasonable grounds ("probable cause") to believe the accused person committed the crime for which he or she is being charged. The accused person may waive any right to have the matter reviewed by grand jury. Such waivers often occur, particularly when the accused decides to plead guilty early in the case.

The Fifth Amendment to the Constitution establishes that a citizen accused of a felony has the right to have a grand jury, rather than the prosecutor, decide whether he or she shall be prosecuted. Except in cases that could involve a death sentence, the accused may waive this right. The grand jury right does not apply to prosecutions in state courts. About half of the states, however, have laws allowing or requiring the use of grand juries in felony cases.

Where grand juries are used, an indictment takes precedence over the prosecutor's view of whether probable cause exists in a case. The court rather than the prosecutor convenes grand juries. In districts with grand juries, however, judges of a lower court or a felony court often screen cases for probable cause, providing for greater grand jury efficiency.

Criminal History Data

When a person is arrested or brought before a court on a criminal charge, usually a government agency keeps a permanent official record of the event. These records enable prosecutors to find out about a person's "criminal history." That knowledge can help prosecutors make proper decisions.

Plea Negotiation

In a vast majority of felony convictions, the defendant pleads guilty rather than requests a trial. The high percentage of guilty pleas is a key factor in minimizing case backlogs. Guilty pleas often result from negotiations: the defendant agrees to plead guilty to a lesser charge or to a charge for which the prosecutor recommends a reduced sentence. The court may impose deadlines on negotiations when responding to requests for extensions of time or continuances. Requests for more time to negotiate a plea agreement are sometimes made on the day of trial, even when witnesses, juries, and court personnel have already assembled.

Speedy Trial

The Sixth Amendment of the U.S. Constitution guarantees to the accused in a criminal trial, whether federal or state, the right to a speedy trial. In recent years legislatures and courts have established limits on the time following an arrest that a prosecutor has to bring the case to trial. Such speedy trial requirements often apply when a defendant is held in custody, but do not apply when the defendant has been granted pre-trial release.

Jury Trial

The Sixth Amendment to the U.S. Constitution gives state and federal felony defendants the right to trial by jury. This right may be waived in favor of trial by judge. An estimated 4 percent of all felony convictions are the result of a judge trial.

In some jurisdictions the prosecutor also has the right to have a case tried by a jury. In such jurisdictions, the jury may be used even if the defendant prefers a judge trial, although how the proceedings are carried out is decided by the trial judge. The prosecutor may exercise this right to a jury trial for many reasons, including belief that

- A jury is more likely than a particular judge to convict.
- A jury is likely to impose or recommend a desired sentence.
- A jury trial will attract more public attention to a defendant's heinous conduct.

Policies and Practices after Trial

A convicted defendant remains under the court's jurisdiction until sentencing. Between conviction and sentencing, information is often gathered to enable the judge to impose an appropriate sentence. In most districts the judge requests a pre-sentence report containing information about the defendant, family and employment circumstances, mental or physical health problems, and history of drug or alcohol abuse. This information may have an important bearing on the choice between a sentence of confinement and a sentence of probation.

A convicted defendant may appeal to a higher court, asking it to review any defect in the proceedings of the original trial. Only certain major issues, such as the sentence or what trial evidence was admitted or excluded, will serve as a basis for the appeals court accepting the appeal. Under some circumstances the prosecutor may also appeal. The special conditions for a prosecutorial appeal usually do not include the prosecutor's view of the determination of guilt in a particular case.

An appeal involves two main activities: preparing the written document (brief) that explains both the case and the defects complained of, and presenting this material verbally to the appeals judges (oral argument).

Source "Special Report." *Bureau of Justice Statistics.* 1992.

CRIMINAL JUSTICE PROCEDURE

The criminal justice system operates as a process. Following is a brief and generalized description of the process.

1. The purpose of an arrest is to bring the person into the criminal justice system so that he/she may be held to answer the criminal charges.
2. A citation is frequently used by public police instead of a formal arrest for less serious crimes (e.g., traffic violation). If the conditions set forth in the citation are not followed, a magistrate of the appropriate court will issue a misdemeanor warrant.
3. All arrests must be based on probable cause which is stated in arrest warrants. Probable cause, which is more than mere suspicion, is reasonable grounds to justify legal action. A viewing of an assault would be good probable cause.
4. Booking takes place when an arrestee is taken to a police department or jail so that a record can be made of the arrested person's name, the date, time, location of offense, charge, and the arresting officer's name. Fingerprinting and photographing are part of the booking process.
5. Because our system of justice has a high regard for civil liberties as expressed in the Bill of Rights, the accused is informed, usually right after arrest, of the Miranda rights.
6. After booking, and without unnecessary delay, the accused is taken before a magistrate for the "initial appearance." At this appearance the magistrate has the responsibility of informing the accused of constitutional rights, stating the charge, and fixing bail (if necessary).
7. Also after booking, the arresting officer will meet with the prosecutor or prosecutor's representative to review evidence. A decision is made whether to continue legal action or to drop the case. A case may be dropped by the prosecutor for insufficient evidence or when the case can be better handled by another agency, such as a mental health agency.
8. The prosecutor prepares an "information" when prosecution is initiated. It cites the defendant's name, the charge, and is signed by the complainant (e.g., the person who witnessed the crime). An arrest warrant is prepared by the proper judicial officer. The defendant may already be in custody at this point.
9. At the initial appearance, the magistrate will inform the defendant about the right to have a preliminary hearing. The defendant and the defense attorney make this decision. The hearing is used to determine if probable cause exists for a trial. The courtroom participants in a preliminary hearing are a judge, defendant, defense attorney, and prosecutor. The prosecutor has the "burden of proof." Witnesses may be called by the prosecutor to testify.
10. Federal law and the laws of more than half the states require that probable cause to hold a person for trial must result from grand jury action. The Fifth Amendment of the Bill of Rights states such a requirement. When probable cause is established, the grand jury will return an "indictment" or "true bill" against the accused. A "presentment" results from an investigation initiated by a grand jury establishing probable cause. Based on indictment or presentment, an arrest warrant is issued.
11. At an "arraignment" the accused enters a plea to the charges. Four plea options are: guilty, not guilty, *nolo*

contendere (no contest), and not guilty by reason of insanity.

12. Few defendants reach the trial stage. Plea bargaining is an indispensable method to clear crowded court dockets. Essentially, it means that the prosecutor and defense attorney have worked out an agreement whereby the prosecutor reduces the charge in exchange for a guilty plea. Charges may also be dropped if the accused becomes a witness in another case.

13. Pre-trial motions can be entered by the defense attorney prior to entering a plea at arraignment. Examples: A motion to quash an indictment or information because the grand jury was improperly selected. The defense attorney may request a continuance because more time is needed to prepare the case. A change of venue is requested when pre-trial publicity is harmful to the defendant's case. The defense hopes to locate the trial in another jurisdiction so that an impartial jury is more likely to be selected.

14. The accused is tried by the court or a jury. The prosecutor and defense attorney make brief opening statements to the jury. The prosecutor presents evidence. Witnesses are called to the stand to testify; they go through direct examination by the prosecutor, followed by defense cross-examination. The prosecutor attempts to show the defendant's guilt "beyond a reasonable doubt." The defense attorney strives to discredit evidence. Redirect examination rebuilds evidence discredited by cross-examination. Recross-examination may follow. After the prosecutor presents all the evidence, the defense attorney may ask for acquittal. This motion is commonly overruled by the judge. The defense attorney then presents evidence. Defense evidence undergoes direct and redirect examination by the defense, and cross- and recross-examination by the prosecutor.

Next, the judge will "charge the jury," which means that the jury is briefed by the judge on the charge, and how a verdict is to be reached based on the evidence. In certain states, juries have responsibilities for recommending a sentence after a guilty verdict; the judge will brief the jury on this issue. Closing arguments are then presented by opposing attorneys.

The jury retires to the deliberation room, a verdict follows. A not guilty verdict signifies release for the defendant. A guilty verdict leads to sentencing. Motions and appeals may be initiated after the sentence.

Philip P. Purpura

Source Purpura, P. 2002. *Security and Loss Prevention, 4th Edition*. Boston: Butterworth-Heinemann.

DEFENSES TO CRIME

The law allows many defenses to charges of crime and it is the right of the accused to use any and all of them. The concept of defenses against prosecution may be viewed from two aspects: the basic capacity of the accused to commit the crime charged, and the applicability of certain specifically accepted defenses.

Capacity Defenses

The concept called "capacity to commit crime" demands that a person should not be held criminally punishable for his conduct unless he is actually responsible for it. Young persons and mentally afflicted persons, for example, may be recognized as not having the capacity to commit crimes, because they lack a sufficient degree of responsibility.

The infancy defense holds that children are incapable of committing any crime below a certain age, that at a higher age there is a presumption of incapacity to commit crime, and at an even higher age certain crimes are conclusively presumed to be beyond the capability of a child. For example, it may be presumed that a toddler is incapable of stealing and a 10 year old is incapable of committing the crime of rape.

The corporation defense holds that because a corporation is an artificial creation, it is considered incapable of forming the requisite criminal intent. This defense has been largely overcome in recent years. Some crimes, such as rape, bigamy, and murder, cannot logically be imputed to a corporation.

The insanity defense holds that a person cannot be held liable for his criminal act if he was insane at the time of the act. The defense goes to the heart of the fundamental principle of intent, or guilty mind. If the accused did not understand what he was doing or understand that his actions were wrong, he cannot have criminal intent and, without intent, there is no crime.

The intoxication defense is similar to that of the insanity defense. It argues that the accused could not have a guilty mind due to intoxication. The fact of voluntary intoxication is generally not accepted as a defense. Involuntary intoxication produced by fraud or coercion of another may be a defense, and insanity produced by intoxicants may be acceptable.

Intoxication can also be offered as evidence that an accused was incapable of forming the intent to commit a crime, e.g., the accused was too drunk to entertain the idea of breaking and entering into a house at night for the purpose of committing an offense.

Specific Defenses

The alibi defense seeks to prove that because the defendant was elsewhere at the time the offense occurred, the defendant cannot be accused.

The compulsion or necessity defense argues that a person should not be charged with a crime when the act was committed in response to an imminent, impending, and overwhelmingly coercive influence. For example, a person who is ordered to drive a getaway car under the threat of immediate death would not be punishable as a principal to the crime.

The condonation defense is used in some rare cases where the law allows an accused not to be prosecuted if certain conditions are met. For example, a charge of seduction might be dropped if the parties involved subsequently marry.

The immunity defense grants protection from prosecution in exchange for cooperation by the accused. The required cooperation might be a full disclosure of all facts and testimony at trial.

The consent defense may be used when consent of the victim is involved. Where consent is offered as a defense, the consent must have been given by a person legally capable of giving it and it must be voluntary.

The entrapment defense argues that an accused should not be charged if he was induced to commit a crime for the mere purpose of instituting criminal prosecution against him. Generally, where the criminal intent originates in the mind of the accused and the criminal offense is completed by him, the fact that a law enforcement officer furnished the accused an opportunity for commission does not constitute entrapment. A key point is that where the criminal intent originates in the mind of the officer and the accused is lured into the commission, no conviction may be had.

The withdrawal defense may sometimes be used in a prosecution for conspiracy. A conspirator who withdraws from the conspiracy prior to commission of the requisite overt act may attempt a defense based on withdrawal.

The good character defense may seek to offer evidence that the accused is of such good character that it was unlikely he/she committed the act. This is not a defense as a matter of law, but an attempt to convince a jury it was improbable for the accused to have committed the crime.

The defense of ignorance or mistake of fact argues that the accused had no criminal intent. This defense seeks to excuse the accused because he was misled or was not in possession of all facts at the time of the crime. For example, this defense might be used in a case where a homeowner injured someone who he thought was a burglar in his home, but who in fact was the invited guest of another member of the family. This defense is based on the grounds that a defendant did not know certain essential facts, that he could not have been expected to know them, and that there could be no crime without such knowledge. Mistake of law is a rarely allowed defense offered by an accused that he did not know his act was criminal or did not comprehend the consequences of the act.

The statute of limitations defense seeks to prevent prosecution on the grounds that the government failed to bring charges within the period of time fixed by a particular enactment. Not all crimes have time limitations for seeking prosecution, and some crimes, such as murder and other major crimes, have no limits whatsoever.

Irresistible impulse is a legal defense by which an accused seeks to be fully or partially excused from responsibility on the grounds that although he knew the act was wrong, he was compelled to its execution by an impulse he was powerless to control.

Necessity is the defense of justification of an otherwise criminal act on the ground that the perpetrator was compelled to commit it because a greater evil would have ensued had he failed to do so. Thus, one could plead necessity if he committed arson to destroy official documents that would otherwise have fallen into the hands of a wartime enemy.

The self-defense or defense of life rule is derived from English common law, which authorizes the use of deadly force in self-defense and in order to apprehend persons committing or fleeing from felonies. In many jurisdictions, the rule has been narrowed by statute so that the use of weaponry is limited only to defense of life situations and to some specific violent felonies, for example, murder, rape, aggravated assault, arson, or burglary. This protection against prosecution relies on the premise that every person has a right to defend himself from harm. A person may use, in self-defense, that force which, under all the circumstances of the case, reasonably appears necessary to prevent impending injury.

Diminished capacity is the decreased or less-than-normal ability, temporary or permanent, to distinguish right from wrong or to fully appreciate the consequences of one's act. It is a plea used by the defendant for conviction of a lesser degree of a crime, for a lenient sentence, or for mercy or clemency.

Former jeopardy is a plea founded on the common law principle that a person cannot be brought into danger of his life or limb for the same offense more than once. The former jeopardy defense is founded on the principle that a case once terminated upon its merits should not be tried again.

Double jeopardy can only be claimed when the second prosecution is brought by the same government as the first. When the act is a violation of the law as to two or more governments, the accused is regarded as having committed separate offenses.

The "but for" rule or the sine qua non rule holds that a defendant's conduct is not the cause of an event if the event would have occurred without it.

Related to legal defenses is the bill of particulars. It is a statement by the prosecution filed by order of the court, at the court's own request or that of the defendant, of such particulars as may be necessary to give the defendant and the court reasonable knowledge of the nature and grounds of the crime charged, such as the time and place, means by which it was alleged to have been committed, or more specific information.

The concept can also apply to the defendant; for example, a defendant who intends to rely on an alibi defense may be required to furnish the prosecuting officer with a bill of particulars as to the alibi. This bill sets forth in detail the place or places the defendant claims to have been, together with the names and addresses of witnesses upon whom he intends to rely to establish his alibi. The purpose of this procedure is to prevent the sudden and unexpected appearance of alibi witnesses whose testimony in the latter stage of a trial could cast reasonable doubt on the state's case.

By compelling advance notice, the prosecutor is afforded time to investigate the alibi, as well as the credibility of the alibi witnesses, and, in so doing, establish a position for refuting the alibi defense.

John J. Fay

Source Fay, J. 1987. *Butterworths Security Dictionary: Terms and Concepts.* Boston: Butterworth-Heinemann

THE DEPOSITION

A deposition is a legal proceeding conducted for the purpose of preserving the testimony of a witness for use in court. In this case, we are talking about a witness who is an expert witness. The deposition is usually held in a reasonably comfortable and private setting, very often the conference room of an attorney's office. The persons present are the witness, a notary public to administer an oath, a court reporter (usually a notary), and lawyers for all parties. The parties themselves or their representatives have a right to attend but seldom choose to do so.

The deposition begins by administering an oath to the witness. The lawyers take turns in asking the witness questions. A lawyer may skip a turn or take more than one turn. The proceeding is relatively informal, although serious to the outcome of the lawsuit. The reporter takes down everything said and the reporter's record will later be typed and bound in a document called a deposition or a transcript. The deposition is essentially a tool for opposing lawyers to discover what a witness' testimony will be at trial. For example, the plaintiff's lawyer in deposing an expert witness for the defense:

- Will want to discover what the expert knows concerning the facts involved in the matter being litigated. The search here is for evidence that the expert will present in support of the defendant.
- Will want to discover if the expert knows of any facts that may be damaging to the defense, e.g., that the defendant may have been careless or failed to do something.
- Will want to commit the expert to the statements made under oath so that at trial the expert's testimony cannot be changed (at least not without difficulty and damage to the defense).
- Will look for ways to discredit the expert's testimony or to use the expert's testimony to discredit the testimony of other defense witnesses. Minor contradictions among witnesses are inevitable, while major contradictions or the appearance of them can be damaging.
- Will attempt to learn the basic theory and strategy that the defense will rely on at trial. The plaintiff's attorney may decide that the defense will be formidable against the claim as stated and that the claim needs to be changed.

Although a deposition can embarrass or even damage the reputation of an expert witness, this is not a legitimate purpose of the proceeding. When it happens, it is often the result of inadequate preparation by both the expert witness and the attorney that engaged the witness.

The expert witness has three fundamental obligations. First, is to tell the truth, even if the truth will hurt. This is an obligation that sits above the outcome of the lawsuit. Second, is to be fair. This does not mean that the witness has to give equal favor to both sides, only that the witness not overstate or color the facts. Third, is to be accurate, and this is where the expert witness plays a critical part in helping the judge and jurors fulfill their responsibilities in seeing that justice is carried out.

John J. Fay

Source Baker, T. 1992. *Operator's Manual for a Witness Chair*. Kansas City: Baker and Sterchi.

DETENTION FOR SHOPLIFTING

In the fight against shoplifting, merchants and their employees are directly on the front line. The statistics can vary widely, but it's safe to say that hundreds of thousands of individuals are detained for shoplifting each year in the United States, and although anti-shoplifting technology continues to improve, there will always be a need to detain shoplifters. Shoplifting is usually thought of as the concealment and subsequent theft of merchandise from a merchant, but shoplifting language can also include price-switching of merchandise, refunding for unpaid merchandise, and "sweet-hearting" of merchandise at the point of sale. The majority of shoplifting offenses are misdemeanor crimes unless a specific dollar amount is reached. In most states, this dollar amount falls within the $300 to $500 range, but in some states the value can be in excess of $1,000 before shoplifting becomes a felony crime.

A shoplifting detention is multi-faceted and should only be attempted by trained personnel. The many factors that must be considered include knowledge of the criminal elements that constitute a crime, the merchant's policy on detaining shoplifters, and strategies on how to make a detention as safely as possible. Additional considerations include how to respond to a problematic or violent person and how best to communicate with the person in order to obtain cooperation. While recovering property is the primary goal of any detention, it is important for employees to remember that safety should never be compromised. In addition to their own safety, employees should also consider the safety of bystanders. Liability to the merchant is an additional factor that needs consideration.

Necessary Elements

Prior to making a detention, a set of proofs, or elements, must be established, If not done, the merchant faces potential liability. It is generally acceptable for employees to detain suspected shoplifters based on probable cause.

Care, however, should be taken to avoid behavior that could lead to civil action. Such behavior can include making accusations in the hearing of others, unnecessary touching, unnecessary use of force, detaining the individual for a lengthy period of time, intimidating or browbeating the individual, denying the individual water or the use of a restroom, not calling the police immediately when it appears that arrest is the proper course of action, and being untruthful when giving details to the police or writing an incident report. For these reasons, many merchants require that their employees use standards higher than probable cause before detaining a suspected shoplifter.

Since shoplifting is simply "theft" or "larceny," the elements required are the same as for any other theft crime. Those elements being that the item in question has a value; that a taking and carrying away of the merchandise has occurred (i.e., selection); that there was no permission granted to take the merchandise; that the merchandise belonged to the merchant and that the person had the intent to permanently deprive the merchant of the merchandise. It's this last element of intent that is the most important and can be the most difficult to prove. This is why most, if not all, merchants require that the person has actually passed the last point of sale before allowing a detention. While not an actual element of the crime, this policy assists greatly in helping to prove the element of intent to permanently deprive. While concealment is also a great indicator of intent, shoplifters don't always conceal their merchandise. An employee must be aware of the fact that some shoplifters will simply walk out of the store with the merchandise.

Detention is appropriate only when an employee actually sees the selection and conversion of the merchandise through concealment or other means. The suspect should then be constantly watched. If the merchandise is discarded inside the store, detention is not appropriate. If the suspect is in possession of the merchandise after leaving the store, it is appropriate to stop the suspect. The employee making the stop should anticipate that the suspect will flee or offer resistance, including physical violence. The loss of merchandise is acceptable in lieu of injury to the employee or others.

Detention Strategies

No two detentions are ever the same and approaching a shoplifter with the intent to detain is not a task that should be taken lightly. The primary goal of a detention should be the safe recovery of the merchandise. Subsequent goals include identifying the person and possibly bringing criminal charges against them

Several considerations should be taken into account before actually approaching the shoplifter. The first of these is the behavior of the shoplifter. While it's impossible to exactly predict what a shoplifter will do, paying attention to certain behavioral indicators can help in planning the approach. Does the person appear to be nervous or confident? Did the person take a long time to actually conceal the product or did the person do it quickly? Consideration also needs to be given to the assistance that might be needed. Does the person's size, appearance, or demeanor indicate a type of reaction? If there's a feeling that the person might resist or run, a decision needs to be made to either obtain additional assistance or to simply avoid approaching the individual.

Ideally, shoplifters should be approached with an assertive and confident posture. The tone of voice should be matter of fact but polite. Trigger words such as "thief," "jail," and "police" should be avoided so as to better attain the cooperation of the individual. The approach should be as private as possible, should never be confrontational, and treated simply as a situation that needs resolving. Employees should be prepared for and know what to do if the person resists or runs.

The location of the detention also needs to be considered. If the person resists, is there a possibility of injury to bystanders? What exit routes exist for the person? What exit routes exist for the employee should the person become violent? Are there shopping carts strewn about the entry or other barriers that could make the approach difficult?

By evaluating the totality of circumstances, an employee is better able to decide how to handle the situation.

Making the Detention

Once the decision is made to approach the shoplifter, care must be taken in the way the approach is made. It is recommended that a minimum of two people should make an approach. The employee should maintain a distance of approximately 6 feet from the shoplifter, and should never stand directly in front. This distance can be closed once the shoplifter's cooperation is attained. The employee should identify himself and invite the individual to a private location to discuss the matter. The employee should be prepared to deal with a reaction such as shock, denial, anger, and bargaining.

To obtain compliance, the employee should have a polite but firm business-like tone and not be diverted from the situation at hand. The employee should not take personally anything the shoplifter might say and avoid arguing or reacting negatively. The employee should expect the shoplifter to attempt to take control of the situation and should simply restate the purpose of the detention. It is crucial to maintain continual observation of the shoplifter throughout the detention process. This cannot be underestimated. Without continual observation, shoplifters have the ability to discard stolen merchandise, become violent, or escape.

Encountering Resistance

Resistance to being detained can be either verbal or physical. A merchant should have a sound and clearly understood policy as to how employees should handle a suspected shoplifting situation. A situation involving resistance can easily get out of control. When it happens, the risk of injury greatly increases. If force is allowed by policy, it should be the minimum amount of force necessary to bring the person under control. In the case of verbal resistance, only verbal control techniques should be utilized. Physical control techniques should be a choice of last resort and should only be undertaken if the employee is trained in physical control techniques. Additionally, the employee should be trained in how to apply handcuffs if their use is allowed by policy. Physical control techniques must be avoided for safety and liability reasons. Lastly, physical control techniques should be abandoned if at any time the employee loses control of the individual.

Processing the Subject

Once the detention has been carried out, the suspect must be processed according to the merchant's policy. A merchant has two choices: recover the merchandise and release the subject with a warning or call for police assistance and make a complaint. It is essential that the employee take notes and later enter them into an incident report. Of importance are actions made and words spoken by the suspect. Of greater importance is a written statement in which the suspect makes an admission or confesses. Everything said and done by the employee and the suspect will be closely scrutinized if the suspect is prosecuted. The same applies if the suspect files a civil action alleging negligence, false arrest, false imprisonment, or mistreatment.

Conclusion

Detention of a shoplifter is far more difficult than it might seem. Many issues are involved: safety, recovery of property, use of force, police arrest, and prosecution. An employee dealing with a suspected shoplifting must follow procedures that are set out by a sound policy and obey the law.

Ken Bierschbach

EXPERT WITNESS: THE DEPOSITION

A deposition is a legal proceeding conducted for the purpose of preserving the testimony of a witness for use in court. In this case, we are talking about a witness who is an expert witness. The deposition is usually held in a reasonably comfortable and private setting, very often the conference room of an attorney's office. The persons present are the witness, a notary public to administer an oath, a court reporter (usually a notary), and lawyers for all parties. The parties themselves or their representatives have a right to attend but seldom choose to do so.

The deposition begins by administering an oath to the witness. The lawyers take turns in asking the witness questions. A lawyer may skip a turn or take more than one turn. The proceeding is relatively informal, although serious to the outcome of the lawsuit. The reporter takes down everything said and the reporter's record will later be typed and bound in a document called a deposition or a transcript. The deposition is essentially a tool for opposing lawyers to discover what a witness' testimony will be at trial. For example, the plaintiff's lawyer in deposing an expert witness for the defense:

- Will want to discover what the expert knows concerning the facts involved in the matter being litigated. The search here is for evidence that the expert will present in support of the defendant.
- Will want to discover if the expert knows of any facts that may be damaging to the defense, e.g., that the defendant may have been careless or failed to do something.
- Will want to commit the expert to the statements made under oath so that at trial the expert's testimony cannot be changed (at least not without difficulty and damage to the defense).
- Will look for ways to discredit the expert's testimony or to use the expert's testimony to discredit the testimony of other defense witnesses. Minor contradictions among witnesses are inevitable, while major contradictions or the appearance of them can be damaging.
- Will attempt to learn the basic theory and strategy that the defense will rely on at trial. The plaintiff's attorney may decide that the defense will be formidable against the claim as stated and that the claim needs to be changed.

Although a deposition can embarrass or even damage the reputation of an expert witness, this is not a legitimate purpose of the proceeding. When it happens, it is often the result of inadequate preparation by both the expert witness and the attorney that engaged the witness.

The expert witness has three fundamental obligations. First, is to tell the truth, even if the truth will hurt. This is an obligation that sits above the outcome of the lawsuit. Second, is to be fair. This does not mean that the witness has to give equal favor to both sides, only that the witness not overstate or color the facts. Third, is to be accurate, and this is where the expert

witness plays a critical part in helping the judge and jurors fulfill their responsibilities in seeing that justice is carried out.

John J. Fay

Source   Baker, T. 1992. *Operator's Manual for a Witness Chair.* Kansas City: Baker and Sterchi.

INTELLECTUAL PROPERTY RIGHTS

Most countries recognize and grant varying degrees of protection to four basic intellectual property rights: patents, trademarks, copyrights, and trade secrets.

Patents are grants issued by a national government conferring the right to exclude others from making, using, or selling the invention within that country. Patents may be given for new products or processes. Violations of patent rights are known as infringement or piracy. An example of patent protection is the Process Patent Amendments contained in the Omnibus Trade and Competitiveness Act of 1988. The Act treats unlicensed importers, distributors, retailers, and even consumers of standard products as patent infringers, if an unpatented product was produced by a U.S. patented process. The amendments apply to foreign and domestic manufacture and also to end products that are protected by U.S. process patents.

Trademarks are words, names, symbols, devices, or combinations thereof used by manufacturers or merchants to differentiate their goods and distinguish them from products that are manufactured or sold by others. Counterfeiting and infringement constitute violations of trademark rights.

Copyrights are protections given by a national government to creators of original literary, dramatic, musical, and certain other intellectual works. The owner of a copyright has the exclusive right to reproduce the copyrighted work, prepare derivative works based upon it, distribute copies, and perform or display it publicly. Copyright violations are also known as infringement and piracy.

Trade secrets are information such as formulas, patterns, compilations, programs, devices, methods, techniques, or processes that derive economic value from not being generally known and that cannot be ascertained by unauthorized persons through proper means because they are subject to reasonable efforts to maintain their secrecy. Trade secret violations are known as misappropriation and result from improper acquisition or disclosure. Distinguishing between trade secret safeguards and patent or copyright protection can be difficult. The key elements in a trade secret are the owner's maintenance of confidentiality, limited distribution, and the absence of a patent.

A non-competition or non-disclosure statement is a written agreement that grants protection to an employer from the unauthorized use of the employer's intellectual property by current or former employees. A non-competition statement will typically incorporate one or more of three basic conditions: (1) restrictions on competition by departing employees, (2) definitions of what constitutes property that the employer can legally protect from use by others, and (3) requirements that employees are obligated to cooperate with the employer in efforts to protect its intellectual property.

The Paris Convention is the primary treaty for the protection of trademarks, patents, service marks, trade names, utility models, and industrial designs. Established in 1883, the convention is the oldest of the international bodies concerned with the protection of intellectual properties. It is based on reciprocity: (1) the same protections in member states as that state grants to its own nationals, and (2) equal access for foreigners to local courts to pursue infringement remedies.

Three elements of protection must be in place for the owner to claim violation of intellectual rights: (1) the information is not readily accessible to others, (2) it was created by the owner through the expenditure of considerable resources, and (3) the owner sought to keep the information confidential.

John J. Fay

KEY CONCEPTS IN SECURITY LAW

Corpus Delicti

The term corpus delicti means "body of the crime." It is often used erroneously to describe the body of a victim. Actually, the term relates to the essence of an offense and thus implies that every offense must have a corpus delicti.

In proving an accused's guilt of a specific crime, the prosecution establishes three general facts:

- That an injury or loss particular to the crime involved has taken place.
- That the injury or loss was brought about by somebody's criminality, meaning that the injury or loss resulted from a criminal act as opposed to an accident or other cause.
- That the accused, possessing the requisite state of mind (i.e., intent), was the person who caused the injury or loss.

The first two facts constitute the corpus delicti. The third fact simply establishes the identity of the offender. For example, the corpus delicti in a larceny would be (1) the loss of property (2) by an unlawful taking. In an arson offense, it would be (1) a burned house (2) that was deliberately set on fire.

Criminal Intent

Criminal intent is a clearly formulated state of mind to do an act that the law specifically prohibits, without regard to the motive that prompts the act, and whether or not the offender knows that what he or she is doing is in violation of the law.

It is generally regarded as falling into two categories: general criminal intent and specific criminal intent. General criminal intent is an essential element in all crimes. It means that when the offender acted, or failed to act, contrary to the law, he or she did so voluntarily with determination or foresight of the consequences. For example, general criminal intent is shown in the offense of assault and battery when the offender voluntarily applies unlawful force to another with an awareness of its result. In larceny, general criminal intent (often called larcenous intent) is shown by intent to knowingly take and carry away the goods of another without any claim or pretense of right, with intent wholly to deprive the owner of them or to convert them to personal use.

Specific criminal intent requires a particular mental state in addition to that of general criminal intent. The laws relating to certain crimes may describe an additional, specific mental purpose. For example, the crime of murder has a general criminal intent in that the offender voluntarily applies unlawful force with an awareness of its result. In addition, the crime of murder in a particular jurisdiction may require a showing that the offender acted with premeditation to commit murder.

The terms *overt act* and *malice* are often associated with criminal intent. An overt act is an outward or manifest act from which criminality may be inferred; for example, an act done to carry out a criminal intention. In the crime of conspiracy, the overt act is an essential element of proof.

Malice is a mental state accompanying a criminal act that is performed willfully, intentionally, and without legal justification. The term malice aforethought is the state of mind or attitude with which an act is carried out, i.e., the design, resolve, or determination with which a person acts to achieve a certain result. In the death of another, it means knowledge of circumstances that according to common experience would indicate a clear and strong likelihood that death will follow the contemplated act. Malice aforethought is usually coupled with an absence of justification for the act.

Motive and intent are separate concepts in criminal law. Motive is the desire or inducement that tempts or prompts a person to do a criminal act. Intent is a person's resolve or purpose to commit the act. Motive is the reason that leads the mind to desire a certain result. Intent is the determination to achieve the result.

Motive is an important investigative consideration, but is not an essential element of a crime. Intent must be established for a crime to exist. A good motive (as might be represented in a mercy killing) does not keep an act from being a crime, and an evil motive will not necessarily make an act a crime. Furthermore, an accused would not be acquitted simply because a motive could not be discovered.

The basic urge that led the offender's mind to want the result of the forbidden act is immaterial as to guilt. Proof of motive, however, may be relevant and admissible on behalf of either side at trial. Motive can be especially pertinent where the evidence in a case is largely circumstantial. In some statutes, proof of motive may be required.

Federal Offenses

There can be no federal crime unless Congress first makes an act a criminal offense by the pas-

sage of a statute, affixes punishment to it, and declares what court will have jurisdiction. This means that all federal crimes are statutory. Although many of the statutes are based on common law, every federal statute is an express enactment of Congress. Nearly all crimes are defined in Title 18 of the U.S. Code.

Generally speaking, federal crimes fall into three large areas: crimes affecting interstate commerce, crimes committed in places beyond the jurisdiction of any state, and crimes that interfere with the activities of the federal government.

Crimes affecting interstate commerce are described in a variety of acts, e.g., the Mann Act, the Dyer Act, the Lindbergh Act, the Fugitive Felon Act, etc. They cover a wide variety of offenses over which Congress has plenary control.

Crimes committed in places beyond the jurisdiction of any state might include, for example, murder on an American ship on the high seas or on a federal enclave such as a military reservation ceded to the United States by a state. It should be noted that when an offense, not covered by a federal statute, is committed on a federal enclave, the case can be tried in a federal court under the laws of the state where the enclave is located. The offense of murder, for example, is not defined in a federal statute. If murder occurs on a military reservation in Texas, the federal government can prosecute the case using the Texas statute covering murder. This procedure is authorized by the Assimilative Crimes Act.

Crimes that interfere with the activities of the federal government include fraudulent use of the mails, robbery of a federal bank, violations of income tax laws, espionage, and many similar offenses. Federal courts have no jurisdiction over crimes against the states, and vice versa. It can happen, however, that an offense will violate both a state law and a federal law, e.g., robbery of a federally insured state bank. In such a case, both the federal and state court will have jurisdiction.

Federal death penalty laws include these violations:

- Espionage by a member of the Armed Forces in which information relating to nuclear weaponry, military spacecraft or satellites, early warning systems, war plans, communications intelligence or cryptographic information, or any other major weapons or defense strategy is communicated to a foreign government.

- Death resulting from aircraft hijacking.
- Murder while a member of the Armed Forces.
- Destruction of aircraft, motor vehicles, or related facilities resulting in death.
- Retaliatory murder of a member of the immediate family of a law enforcement official.
- Murder of a member of Congress, an important executive official, or a Supreme Court justice.
- Espionage.
- Destruction of government property resulting in death.
- First degree murder.
- Mailing of injurious articles with the intent to kill or resulting in death.
- Assassination or kidnapping resulting in the death of the President or Vice President.
- Willful wrecking of a train resulting in death.
- Murder or kidnapping related to robbery of a bank.
- Treason.

Parties to Crime

Persons culpably concerned in the commission of a crime, whether they directly commit the act constituting the offense, or facilitate, solicit, encourage, aid or attempt to aid, or abet its commission are called the parties to the crime. In some jurisdictions, the concept is extended to include persons who assist one who has committed a crime to avoid arrest, trial, conviction, or punishment.

The parties to a felony crime fall into four categories: (1) principals in the first degree, (2) principals in the second degree, (3) accessories before the fact, and (4) accessories after the fact.

Generally, a principal in the first degree is the actual offender who commits the act. If the offender uses an agent to commit the act, the offender is still a principal in the first degree. There may be more than one principal in the first degree for the same offense.

A principal in the second degree is one who, with knowledge of what is afoot, aids and abets the principal in the first degree at the very time the felony is being committed by rendering aid, assistance, or encouragement. A principal in the second degree is typically at the crime scene, nearby, or situated in such a way as to render assistance. Under the concept of "constructive presence," a principal in the second degree could be a considerable distance removed from the crime while it is being committed. An example might be a lookout that monitors police radio communications at a remote location and calls burglar accomplices at the crime scene to alert them of police patrol movements.

An accessory before the fact is a person who, before the time a crime is committed, knows of the particular offense contemplated, assents to or approves of it, and expresses a view of it in a form that operates to encourage the principal to perform the deed. There is a close resemblance between an accessory before the fact and a principal in the second degree. The difference relates to where the accessory was and the nature of the assistance rendered at the time the crime was committed. If a person advises, encourages, and gives aid prior to the act, but is not present at the act and not giving aid at the time of the act, the person would be regarded as an accessory before the fact.

An accessory after the fact is a person who, knowing that another has committed a felony, subsequently aids the felon to escape in any way or prevents arrest and prosecution. The person may help the felon elude justice by concealing, sheltering, or comforting the felon while a fugitive, or by supplying the means of escape or by destroying evidence. An accessory after the fact must have an intention to assist the felon and must actually do so. Mere knowledge of the felon's offense and a failure to report it does not make a person an accessory after the fact.

Preliminary Offenses

There are three crimes that are preparatory in nature and serve as part of a larger purpose. Each of them is a means of reaching a criminal end. These so-called preliminary crimes are: solicitation, attempt, and conspiracy.

Solicitation consists of the offender's oral or written efforts to activate another person to commit a criminal offense. The essence of the crime is to incite by counsel, enticement, or inducement. The offense of solicitation is complete if the offender merely urges another to violate the law and otherwise does nothing himself.

Attempt has two elements. First, there must be a specific intent to commit a particular offense, and second, there must be a direct ineffectual overt act toward its commission. There must be some act moving directly toward the act. Mere preparation, such as obtaining tools or weapons, may be insufficient to establish the crime, especially when made at a distance in time or place.

Conspiracy is the combination of two or more persons working in some concerted action to accomplish some criminal or unlawful purpose, or to accomplish some purpose in a criminal or unlawful manner. If there is a common understanding among the participants to achieve a certain purpose or to act in a certain way, a conspiracy exists without regard to whether there is any formal or written statement of purpose, or even though there is no actual speaking of words. There may be merely a tacit understanding without any express agreement.

John J. Fay

LAWS AFFECTING SECURITY

Our system of justice places a high value on the rights of citizens. The loss prevention practitioner's work activities in requesting arrests, collecting evidence, interviewing and interrogating witnesses and suspects, preparing reports, seeking prosecution, and recovering company assets places the practitioner within the scrutiny of our justice system. Should the practitioner violate a citizen's rights, he or she may be held personally accountable, and where the violative act was performed as a job duty, the practitioner's employer may also be accountable. When the violative act is a crime, the issue can be decided in a criminal court and the punishment may be imprisonment and/or a fine; and when the violative act is a civil wrong, the issue may be decided in a civil court and redress made through monetary awards.

Criminal law deals with crimes against society. The states and the federal government maintain a criminal code that classifies and defines offenses. Felonies are considered more

serious crimes, such as burglary and robbery. Misdemeanors are less serious crimes, such as trespassing and disorderly conduct.

Civil law adjusts conflicts and differences between individuals. Examples of civil law cases in the security field are false arrest, unlawful detention, negligent training of security officers, and inadequate security that results in death or injury. When a plaintiff (i.e., a person who initiates a lawsuit) wins a case against another party, monetary compensation commonly results.

Law Origins

Three major sources of law are common law, case law, and legislative law. English common law is the major source of law in the United States. Common law is an ambiguous term. Generally, it refers to law founded on principles of justice determined by reasoning according to custom and universal consent. The development of civilization is reflected in common law. Specific acts were, and still are, deemed criminal. These acts, even today, are referred to as common law crimes: treason, murder, robbery, battery, larceny, arson, kidnapping, and rape, among others.

Common law is reinforced by decisions of courts of law. After this nation gained independence from England, the common law influence remained. Nineteen states have perpetuated common law through case law (i.e., judicial precedent). Eighteen states have abolished common law and written it into statutes. The remaining states have either adopted common law via ratification or are unclear about exactly how it is reflected in the state system.

Case law, sometimes referred to as "judge-made law," involves the interpretation of statutes or constitutional concepts by federal and state appellate courts. Previous case decisions or "precedent cases" have a strong influence on court decisions because they are used as a reference for decision making. Since the justice system is adversarial, opposing attorneys refer to past cases (i.e., precedents) that support their individual contentions. The court makes a decision between the opposing parties. Societal changes are often reflected in decisions. Since the meaning of legal issues evolves from case law, these court decisions are the law. Of course, later court review of previous decisions can alter legal precedent.

The U.S. Constitution provides the authority for Congress to pass laws. Likewise, individual state constitutions empower state legislatures to pass laws. Legislative laws permit both the establishment of criminal laws and a justice system to preside over criminal and civil matters. A court may later decide that a legislative law is unconstitutional; this illustrates the system of "checks and balances," which enables one governmental body to check on another.

Philip P. Purpura

Source   Purpura, P. 2002. *Security and Loss Prevention, 4th Edition*. Boston: Butterworth-Heinemann.

LIABILITY FOR NEGLIGENT TRAINING

Contract security officers, their employers, and the clients they serve continue to be named in lawsuits alleging a wide variety of civil violations. Two factors appear to be at work. First is the increasingly litigious nature of society, and second is an expanding social conscience that favors the little guy. The pattern that emerges from civil actions reveals a pronounced targeting of persons in authority positions, such as security officers and the people who hire and manage them.

Because misconduct litigation is a prominent and highly profitable specialty in the practice of law, there are many who seek careers in it. Seminars on the subject are offered around the country, and how-to manuals are available to guide the novices. Expert witnesses, many of them current and former security professionals, are paid to testify for plaintiffs.

The usual path of pursuit in civil litigation is the negligence theory. In this approach the argument is not that the injurious conduct was malicious in nature, but that the injury and damages resulted from a failure to perform a duty with due care. Liability is the result of negligence or failure to give proper attention or care to one's duty. For the liability to be recognized, it must be the cause of a deprivation of rights secured by the Constitution.

Within the negligence theory, there is a particular vulnerability to accusations of improper training. The courts have consistently ruled in favor of plaintiffs who can show injury caused by negligence resulting from the absence of training or the administration of faulty training. The citizenry and the law impose an affirmative duty upon employers to provide their employees with requisite knowledge and skills. When jobs contain the potential for abuse and injury, as is the case with many jobs in security, the affirmative duty to provide training is expected to be met without qualification.

More often than not, the injured party will file suit against the offending officer, as well as the officer's superiors. The plaintiff's charge will frequently allege that the officer acted intentionally to cause injury and that the superiors should also be held accountable for being negligent in failing to take preventive action.

When a suit is pursued along these lines, the officer and superiors are very apt to come into sharp and bitter disagreement. The officer will argue that his or her actions conformed with policy, procedures, and the training provided by superiors. The superiors will argue that their subordinate's actions were inconsistent with the standards established for the officer. The conflict is certain to weaken their separate defenses and cast a shadow of doubt in the minds of jurors.

The damages that may be assessed in a negligence case are of three types: direct, punitive, and nominal. Direct damages may include such things as medical expenses, lost wages, and the costs of replacing or repairing property. Punitive damages are usually assessed when an element of fraud, malice, or oppression is present. The third type is called nominal damages. If assessed, the amount is usually set at $1, hence the term nominal.

In the concept of proximate cause, a single wrongful act may be caused by two or more persons acting at different points in time. For example, a security officer might make an unlawful arrest. The officer says his action was based on knowledge imparted to him through training given by the officer's employer. The concept of proximate cause supports the plaintiff's charge against the officer and any other persons who contributed to the unlawful arrest. In this example, the contributing persons could be the instructor, the officer's supervisor, and so on right up to senior management.

Lawsuits that allege insufficient instruction serve as reminders that the days of training on a catch-as-catch-can basis are over. Today the techniques of quality control have as much meaning in the classroom as in any work environment where excellence is the minimum standard. Further, the general public holds high expectations concerning training. The media have helped shape public perceptions, and when training expectations fall short, the community is angered and the injured parties seek justice through the courts.

Any response strategy to counter the potential for civil litigation should be aimed at eliminating in the training domain any conditions that might contribute to charges of improper instruction. Even the finest training operation must anticipate that negligent training lawsuits will be charged. The best answer to charges will be a positive defense based on accurate and detailed documentation.

Five tactics should be included within the strategy:

- Validate training.
- Administer training to specifications.
- Evaluate the trainees.
- Keep training records.
- Impose instructor standards.

Validate Training

Validation means to ensure through an objective process that the training provided corresponds to duties associated with the job. The key objectives of validation are to verify that: (1) doctrinal content and skills development are correct, (2) instructional methods are appropriate and effective, and (3) training is relevant to the workplace and answers the day-to-day needs of job incumbents.

One of the more objective and commonly used techniques of validation is task analysis. Information drawn from task analysis gives to the curriculum designer a wealth of facts obtained from incumbents and others close to the job. The data reveal with high accuracy and specificity the nature and conditions of the trainees' future work environment.

A curriculum constructed from task analysis data will establish the baseline tasks of the job and will highlight tasks that, if not performed or performed incorrectly, could lead to litigation. Further, the task analysis approach uncovers the knowledge and skills that support each task. For example, if a task requires a security

officer to use his revolver in defense of human life, the officer must be taught how to handle and fire the revolver (skills), and he must know the deadly force law and be able to differentiate between threatening and non-threatening situations (knowledge). The curriculum will require each officer-trainee to perform the skill part of the task, demonstrating a competency to predetermined standards. The knowledge part of the task might be tested by written examination, again in accordance with high standards.

By far, the most important specifications are the tasks. They serve as the focal points and basic framework of instruction. Other course specifications, such as practical exercises and tests, are derived from and influenced by tasks. When a curriculum has been validated (i.e., determined objectively to be job relevant) and when instructional activities have been executed according to plan, the opportunities for negligence are largely, if not entirely, removed and a strong defense is constructed against accusations of improper training.

Administer Training to Specifications

A minimum of logic must prevail for a training course to be made resistant to charges of negligence. Logic tells us that the success of a training operation cannot exceed the combined capacity of its component parts. The instructors, the logistics, and the students might all be top notch, but the training will be less than successful if the program is poorly conceived or carried out haphazardly.

The curriculum can be the training supervisor's most valuable tool for planning, organizing, and controlling. If the tool is ignored or used without skill, the training will suffer. Sadly, some training supervisors regard a curriculum as something to be merely tolerated, deserving not much more than lip service, and certainly not something to be followed. After all, they might argue, the curriculum was put together by people who have no real appreciation of the problems that confront trainers.

Serious implications are present in a situation where control is lacking over what is being taught and learned. When a training supervisor ignores a curriculum, so will the instructors. It does not take much imagination to speculate on the variety of civil liability risks that are created when instructors and their supervisors are allowed to teach according to their own dictates. The appropriate remedy is to make clear that curriculum specifications are not negotiable and that if the curriculum requires a change, for whatever reason, it will be done through an established process.

Training that is in progress can be monitored in several ways to ensure that the curriculum is being followed. Trainees can be asked if they personally participated in certain programmed activities; classrooms and training areas can be visited to verify that trainees are engaged in activities that support the training objectives; and tests, scores, critique sheets, and other written materials that reflect the details of training can be examined.

It is far better to discover imperfections during training than to wait until the imperfections produce undesirable consequences on the job. Mistakes noted as they happen are easier to correct and are free of the potential for complaints and redress in the courts.

Evaluate the Trainees

Students are evaluated in two dimensions, general and specific. Generally, they are appraised in terms of personal appearance, demeanor, attitude, motivation, and similar characteristics. In the specific dimension, students are evaluated in objective terms, that is, by the administration of tests. Two types of tests are appropriate in security officer training programs: written examinations to measure knowledge attained, and performance examinations to measure skill development.

Since every task (or training objective) is either knowledge-oriented or skill-oriented, determining the appropriate type of test is not a problem. If the task is to "name the limitations on the use of deadly force," the test is by written examination, and if the task is to "operate a handy-talky radio," the test is by performance or doing.

A written examination may contain one or more classes of questions such as essay, write-in, matching, true/false, and multiple choice. The questions can range from subjective to objective, and operate from the principles of discrimination, recall, and recognition. Subjective questions have a lesser value in entry-level training programs because most knowledge-oriented tasks are either performed correctly or incorrectly, with no tolerance for "in-between" responses. Subjective questions are also difficult to grade and depend on the interpretations and judgments of the grader. By contrast, objective questions do not have these limitations and lend readily to task-centered training.

In testing important knowledge, more than one question needs to be asked, not just to convey importance to the student, but to obtain assurance that the student really possesses the knowledge and did not guess the answer.

The issue of whether or not a question is easy or hard is not a consideration. Certainly, a question should not give away its own answer. The purpose is to determine fairly if the student has attained the required knowledge. Testing is not a contest of wits between the test writer and the student.

Everything that is taught should be tested. Testing some tasks and not others is not an acceptable practice. Neither is testing extraneous and nice-to-know information or information not included in the curriculum. Testing all and only what has been taught is an effective, direct approach.

The testing concept is the same for the skill-oriented task, but with conditions and standards spelled out. For example, if the task being tested is to operate a handy-talky, the test might require the student to turn the radio on, adjust for squelch, and send a message using the 10 series code. Grading would focus on the time required to perform the task and the number of errors made in turning the radio on, adjusting it, and speaking the message using the correct code numbers.

Testing a skill-oriented task is especially demanding of an instructor's time, energy, and resourcefulness. The instructor has to find a testing location and furnish it with the required equipment, recruit assistants, organize the students and get them to the testing location, and conduct the tests.

Instances of instructors allowing some students to pass without being tested or without achieving the minimum competency levels are most likely to occur in the performance examinations. The preventive steps are to make sufficient time available for testing, precede testing with lots of practice, provide plenty of help to the primary instructor, and give slower learners special attention prior to and during the testing.

Establishing a spread among learners or comparing learners against each other is not necessary. The idea is to find out if the student has reached an acceptable level of competence. This is what we would call a pass/fail situation. It is both pointless and misleading for a grade to be assigned to a task. Why even try to compute a task grade or even a composite grade when the only measurement that really counts is whether or not the student has satisfactorily performed the task?

Keep Training Records

Because documentation can serve as a strong defense to a charge of negligent training, keeping records of every aspect of a student's progress from start to finish makes very good sense. At the front end are documents which reflect the qualifications that a student brings to the course. Licenses, entrance examination scores, aptitude and psychological test scores, high school and college transcripts, and certificates of prior training are examples. These items are indicators of the student's entering abilities and predictors of course performance.

If a course applicant does not meet prerequisites but is nonetheless allowed to enter, a record should be made of who granted the waiver and why. This should serve as a red flag, not to stigmatize the student but to alert the staff to a need for special teaching attention. Whatever extra efforts are expended by the staff and the student to overcome the deficiency should be made a matter of record.

Documents associated with course administration run the gamut from the opening day schedule to the graduation agenda. Within this large collection of written materials are two broad classes: documents that relate to training activities generally, and documents that relate to students individually. One way to organize what can surely be a very large mass of paperwork is to place the general documents in a single, large file and the student documents in separate dossiers.

The general file is for documents from one single course offering, not all offerings of the same course. The general file can be broken down into subcategories such as correspondence and memoranda, course announcement and sched-

ule, curriculum or program of instruction, lesson plans, student handouts, class roster, attendance sheets, etc. Related to the file, but maintained apart from it for security reasons, are the written examinations.

Lesson plans and handouts are excellent documents for refuting negligent training claims. They reflect what the instructors taught and what the students were expected to learn. For example, a lesson plan on self-defense tactics would require an instructor to emphasize the risk of injury to a person being restrained by a choke hold. The student handout would reinforce that important teaching point. The lesson plan and handout would directly rebut a claim of improper training of the choke hold. One note of advice: put preparation/revision dates on lesson plans and handouts.

The attendance sheets can also be important. If the officer in the example just given falsely represents that he was not in class on the day the lesson was taught and the handout distributed, thereby imputing negligence to the training agency, the attendance sheets provide an opportunity for refutation.

A student's dossier contains items that reflect entry into the course, participation in it, and departure from it. There might be evidence of registration, issuance of supplies, disciplining, counseling, academic problems, absences, makeup and remedial training/re-testing, special honors earned, and test results.

From the standpoint of potential civil liability, test results are extremely significant because they substantiate that important, job-related tasks were learned by the trainee. It also helps when the test results are recorded in a format that describes the tasks tested, the names of the evaluator and approving official, whether re-teaching and re-testing were needed, and the initials or signature of the trainee in acknowledgment of the record's entries.

Impose Instructor Standards

Without good instruction, it will not matter if students are bright and eager, facilities first-rate, and the administration efficient. All of these elements are important, but the controlling element will certainly be the competency of instructors.

Instructor qualifications are typically fixed by legislation in states where security officer training is mandated. A certification process will accompany enforcement in almost every case. Instructor certification may specify minimums that relate to education and training accomplishments, field experience in the subject area to be taught, and successful completion of an approved instructor training course.

An instructor's competency can be judged in two areas: knowledge of subject, and ability to teach. If either area is deficient, it is reasonable to expect that the instructor's performance will be correspondingly deficient.

Each of us at one time or another has been the victim of the knowledgeable instructor who, despite good intentions and best effort, was just not able to get his message across. By contrast, the instructor who is weak in the subject area but strong as a teacher is apt to be less noticeable. Through superior communications, a small amount of information can be stretched a long way.

The exceptional instructor will be solidly proficient in both subject matter knowledge and teaching abilities. The average instructor will have a combination of strengths and weaknesses in each area, and the below-average instructor will be significantly weak in at least one area. If required to select a below-average instructor, a training director would not want the instructor's weakness to be in topic knowledge. This is a problem that cannot be corrected easily or quickly. An instructor who lacks a solid command of his or her subject needs to return to the field and gain more knowledge through job experience and self-development.

The instructor who knows the topic to be taught but cannot teach very well can be improved with much less difficulty and in a reasonable period of time. A certain amount of improvement will inevitably result from the teaching experience itself, and from the process of instructors interacting and learning from one another. Surely the most dramatic improvement can result from attendance at an instructor training course.

A training course for instructors is typically 1 or 2 weeks long and covers topics such as learning theory, instructional strategies and methods, learning aids, lesson plan writing, and development of practical exercises. The 1-week course has only enough time to explain basic teaching concepts; the 2-week course will additionally allow the trainee to make one or more graded presentations using lesson plan materials, learning aids, and handouts developed while in the course.

Where instructor training is required as a condition of certification, the certifying agency will most likely conduct or make available a range of approved courses. In addition to a course that prepares an instructor to teach generally, specialized instructor training courses in firearms may be provided.

The absence of legislated requirements should not be seen as a rationale for not upgrading instructors, and under no circumstances should it be seen as a legal defense to complaints of incompetent instruction. Even where minimum standards prevail, a very persuasive argument can be made that such standards are, after all, only minimums. There is no law against establishing instructor standards where none exist or in setting standards above what are minimally expected. Having no instructor standards or choosing to operate with minimums is an assurance of mediocrity.

Chief security officers need to reduce risks associated with inadequate and poorly operated training programs. A question to be asked is not whether an organization can afford quality training, but whether it can afford not to have it.

John J. Fay

NEGLIGENCE IN PREMISES DESIGN

Criminologists have studied the causation of criminal behavior for the last three hundred years, and have usually associated crime with urban centers. However, the flight from the cities to suburbia over the last three decades has created lucrative magnets of crime in the suburbs such as office parks, apartment complexes, industrial sites, and multi-unit residential properties. The courts are finding the owners liable for criminal acts that occur on their property.

The primary function of security professionals employed by premises owners and operators is to prevent criminal incidents that result from security negligence. This primary function obligates a security professional to:

- Identify the level of criminal activity in the site and the neighborhood. The evaluation should include a three-year history, with periodic annual reviews. The radius of area for review will vary from site to site but typically will cover a half-mile radius.

• Conduct a security audit that identifies the assets to be protected, the threats, vulnerabilities, and recommendations for security improvement. The principal assets in premises liability are people and their property; the threats are criminal events; the vulnerabilities are security measures that are needed but not in place; the recommendations are those actions that must be taken to eliminate the vulnerabilities. The audit should be factual, well documented, and in writing. It is both a report of findings and a plan of action. The recommended actions should be prioritized according to magnitude of consequences and probability of occurrence.

• Develop a security delivery system that conforms to the findings of the audit. The system will be a combination of three components: (1) physical safeguards, such as locks, fences, and lighting, (2) people, such as security officers and on-site employees, and (3) procedures that guide the people component in using/operating the physical safeguards component. To function at maximum efficiency, the three components must operate in harmony.

In addition to developing and ensuring efficient operation of the security delivery system, the security professional should pose to the owner/operator pertinent questions:

a) Do you maintain good relations with the local police agency and are able to get copies of crime reports of events happening on your property?

b) Do you maintain active membership associations that have strong national standards?

c) Have you established procedures for notifying tenants or residents of crime problems and what to do when suspicious activities are spotted?

d) Do you record incidents and keep them on file for possible later use in defending against civil actions?

e) Have you clearly stated the essential security functions, job duties and tasks, emergency response plans, and security operating procedures?

f) Are you able to provide or ensure that sufficient training is given to security and non-security staff on the proper practices of security?

g) Do you review, update, and document policies and procedures at least annually?

h) Do you ensure that all employees are issued their own copies of procedures and sign off that they have read and understand them?

i) Can you ensure that all locks and locking devices are of sufficient quality and quantity to protect tenants from unauthorized entry?

j) Have locking devices on doors and windows been inspected at least annually, and reviewed as tenants move out and move in?

k) Has periodic testing been done of intercom, security alarm, fire safety, and CCTV systems?

l) Is there adequate lighting in exterior parking areas, walkways, and entries that meet industry standards of the Illumination Engineering Society of North America or local building codes?

m) Is repair and maintenance performed on physical safeguards such as fences, gates, and lighting?

n) Do residential units have door viewers?

o) Are vacant spaces and units kept secured?

p) Are keys inventoried, issued with controls, and kept under lock and key?

q) Is foliage around the grounds and building perimeter trimmed to eliminate hiding spaces and allow exterior lighting penetration?

r) Are roof, basement, and utility and mechanical room doors kept locked?

s) Are fire-escape doors equipped with release hardware?

t) Are visitors, guests, and other non-residents screened at points of entry?

u) Is protection afforded to utilities such as direct electrical power, emergency power, gas lines, HVAC, and water supply?

v) Do advertising and marketing materials accurately represent the security delivery system?

w) Are rental agents, managers, and staff truthful when describing the security delivery system?

x) Are disclaimers included in lease agreements and contracts, and security warnings posted in common areas such as pools, parking areas, and mail areas?

y) Are tenants and residents kept informed of changes in security and criminal events that require warning?

z) Are employees thoroughly screened prior to employment?

These questions will be the first questions asked when negligent security is alleged. Every question that cannot be answered in the owner's favor is a question that will be damaging at trial. As the number of unfavorably answered questions rises, the amount of compensatory and punitive damages can proportionally rise.

Examples of actual security negligence cases:

- A man is robbed in an apartment lobby left unguarded in the afternoon.
- A woman is attacked in a parking lot of a design showroom.
- A faulty door allows a rapist to enter an apartment building and rape a tenant.
- A faulty stairway design allows for a serious injury to an elderly visitor at a condominium.
- A hotel room balcony facing an open atrium is wide enough to allow a child to slip through and fall ten stories.
- An inmate hangs himself from an air return grille over the toilet that is not properly secured.
- A secretary walks into a sliding glass door that had no window markings on it.
- An entry rug in a bank buckles when the doorjamb hits the edge of the carpet and trips an elderly tenant.
- A child is shot inside an apartment walkway by a stray bullet fired during a drug deal.

These are just a few examples of cases litigated under premises' liability case law.

According to a study published in 1984 by Professor Lawrence Sherman, a professor of criminology at the University of Maryland at College Park, the number of major awards reported nationwide each year in security liability cases increased 3000 percent between 1965 and 1982. The average dollar amount awarded in those cases increased by 5000 percent. Moreover, the study suggests that almost half the major awards are from four states: New York, New Jersey, Florida, and the District of Columbia. Security negligence lawsuits are one of the fastest growing civil torts in the United States currently.

To protect against lawsuits, it is wise to hire a security/safety expert to look for vulnerabilities using a risk analysis approach. An expert will look for deviations from fire codes and similar standards, develop crime demographics, and point out the potential for crime and accidents. The expert can also provide counsel on reasonable steps that should be taken to remove the potential, and when those preventative actions are set in place the issue of foreseeability in litigation is removed.

A type of risk analysis approach is the security audit. It is a systematic search for and examination of factors that can lead to adverse events such as rape, robbery, burglary, theft, and accident-related injury. The audit gives direction to the owner for reducing the probability of adverse events through the implementation of sensible, cost-effective countermeasures. When the countermeasures are in place, the owner has met the reasonable standard of care, an extremely important issue in defending against a charge of negligence.

Foreseeability is a key issue in security and safety liability cases. For example, foreseeability is present when a premises has a history of crime, particularly like crimes such as robbery and assault. The owner of the premises knows, or should know, that a problem exists and that reasonable steps must be taken to prevent future robbery and assault. Liability increases dramatically when preventative actions are not taken.

Court decisions have consistently held that the owner/operator of premises, such as an apartment building, has certain duties that cannot be ignored. Among these are (1) a duty to provide reasonable care for tenants and guests and (2) meet contract requirements such as those stipulated in a rental agreement.

Many courts make decisions using a doctrine called "totality of circumstances." All circumstances, not just one major circumstance, are considered. A case that does not have a major circumstance but has several minor circumstances can be decided in favor of the plaintiff when the "totality of circumstances" doctrine is applied. The more common circumstances in premises liability include:

- Prior crime on the premises.
- Prior crime in the immediately surrounding neighborhood.
- Preventive measures not taken when preventive measures have been taken at like premises nearby.
- Absence of physical security safeguards such as fences, locks, and lights.
- Absence or inadequate maintenance such as broken fence gates and burned out bulbs in hallways and stairwells.
- No security officers or not enough security officers.
- Untrained and poorly supervised security officers.
- No response or poor response to incidents in progress.
- No warnings to tenants of accident hazards or of recently committed crimes.
- Non-compliance with codes, statutes, etc.
- Reduction of security and safety measures such as cutting back on the number of security officers, canceling the roving patrol function, or eliminating the position of lifeguard.

The security professional can be of great help in identifying problematic conditions, hopefully in time to prevent litigation. When preventative steps have not been taken and litigation occurs as a result, the owner/operator can expect to see a security professional working for the plaintiff. Every action not taken by the defendant will be thoroughly exploited.

It needs to be understood that the term "security professional" is a general descriptor. Not all security professionals possess expertise in risk analysis, vulnerability assessment, security design, and expert witness credentials. And the individuals that qualify in these categories are not of equal caliber. The owner/operator has to recognize the distinctions.

Many sites have architectural features that facilitate criminal opportunities. These can include blind spots in a parking lot, malfunctioning access control devices, and CCTV cameras mounted in wrong places.

Such features are often the result of not using the services of a security professional when the site was constructed or retrofitted. Left to their own devices, design professionals will in almost every case choose esthetics over security.

Design features that facilitate security in vulnerable areas include clear sight lines, overlapping illumination, sturdy fences, barrier-landscapes, buildings arranged in a pattern that makes criminal intrusion visible, and vehicle/pedestrian pathways that channel traffic away from critical assets.

"Adequacy" of security is subjective, judgmental. Adequacy defined by the plaintiff will be wildly different than adequacy defined by the defendant. An accurate assessment of adequacy is best made by a non-vested consultant having impeccable security credentials. The cost of the service is minuscule in comparison with monetary damages.

A mistake often made by an owner/operator is to hire a consultant that works for a company that sells a security product or service. A prime issue for the consultant will be to help sell the product or service. An owner/operator's biggest mistake would be to accept a "free" consultation.

In summary, security professionals can help the owner/operator avoid civil liability. Nearly all occurrences of negligent security are rooted in dollars. It is sad irony when a failure to pay a few extra dollars upfront to ensure a reasonable level of security leads at a later time to an enormous dollar loss. The security audit, or vulnerability assessment, can be an extremely valuable tool in the hands of the knowledgeable practitioner. The audit identifies security weaknesses and provides a blueprint for remedial action.

Randall I. Atlas

NEGLIGENT HIRING AND DUE DILIGENCE

The threat of negligent hiring litigation is at an all time high. Employers large and small are troubled by lawsuits that allege negligence, workplace violence, and employee theft. A comprehensive background check can arm an employer with a clear picture of a candidate's past work history, education, general character, criminal history, and propensity to harm others.

The fear of negligent hiring and retention are primary concerns of human resources managers and risk managers. Since 1970 negligent hiring torts have resulted in settlements and awards at the multi-million dollars level. A payout of this magnitude can cripple an organization financially or push it into bankruptcy.

Before fully understanding the risks of not conducting background checks, employers need to understand two very important principles: due diligence and negligent hiring. In the context of pre-employment screening, due diligence refers to the duty of care an employer must take to ensure that persons selected for employment do not pose a threat to others. The employer's duty to exercise due diligence in a hiring situation can be met by conducting a thorough background investigation.

Negligent hiring is the employment of a person that poses danger to others. Negligence is shown when the employer failed or did not try to know of an applicant's undesirable background at time of hire, and at a later time the hired person caused harm to another.

Together, due diligence and negligent hiring can be thought of as a "risk barometer." Due diligence is at the lower end of the barometer. It signifies low risk because applicants are screened before hiring, therefore lowering the risk of harm. Negligent hiring is at the top end of the barometer. It signifies high risk because reasonable steps, such as a background investigation, were not taken to filter out high-risk applicants.

Respondeat superior, or let the master answer, is a premise for negligent hiring claims. An employer (the master) can be held liable under certain circumstances for the wrongful act of an employee (the servant). Many allegations of negligent hiring are based on the *respondeat superior* concept. For example:

- A Florida jury awarded damages of $2,500,000 in Tallahassee Furniture Co., Inc. v. Harrison. An employee of the company savagely attacked a woman customer in her home. According to the facts of the case, the employee had a history of criminal violence, which would have easily been discovered during a background check.

- In Artis vs. Wayside Baptist Church, a Dade County, Florida, jury awarded the plaintiff $6,700,000 which included $2,500,000 in punitive damages. The church's youth minister had molested a boy over a 2.5-year period. Verification of the minister's past employment would have revealed the risk.

An employer should look for application and résumé fraud when conducting background screening. Applicants have several tricks up their sleeves when it comes to crafting a competitive résumé. From lying about past work history and education credentials, to falsifying professional licenses, applicants have thought of just about every way imaginable to place themselves above other job candidates.

Several industry studies indicate that a great many applicants lie on their résumés. A majority of embellishments are in education and employment such as claiming to have a college degree or claiming to have worked in a particular position or at a senior management level. False claims range from stretching the truth to flat out lies.

Information available online at *www.resumefraud.com* indicates that applicants continue to utilize online diploma mills to obtain fictitious credentials. The U.S. Department of Education defines a diploma mill as "an organization that awards degrees without requiring students to meet educational standards for such degrees."

In a recent study, Comprehensive Information Services, Inc. (CIS) purchased from a diploma mill a Bachelor of Business Administration degree in Human Resource Development and Management with a 3.5 grade point average. It cost $519.00 and arrived in a package sent from an overseas company. The package contained an authentic-looking diploma, transcripts, a certificate of participation in the school's student council, and an award of excellence. To make things even more realistic, the package included an alumnus bumper sticker and window decal.

Another tactic used by dishonest job seekers is "date stretching." This ploy is used when a candidate fears that a past employer will not give a favorable opinion. The candidate will stretch the end date of the immediately preceding employment to the start date of the immediately following period of employment, thus concealing the middle period.

Background checks come in many shapes and sizes. A background check to determine a person's suitability for hire is a special type if only because it is subject to the Fair Credit Reporting Act (FCRA). The FCRA effectively controls the methods by which background screening firms operate. The FCRA, regulated by the Federal Trade Commission (FTC), sets out specific requirements and procedures with regard to notification, authorization, consumer privacy, and the use of a consumer report (background investigation) in making a hiring decision. A consumer report (CRA) generally includes information as to a consumer's credit worthiness, character, general reputation, personal characteristics, and mode of living. This type of screening includes information gathered from credit reports, criminal histories, verification of education credentials, and past employment information. An "investigative consumer report" is one that digs deeper into the applicant's past such as by interviewing persons familiar with the applicant. Both types of screening are conducted by a consumer reporting agency, i.e., a third party hired by the employer to conduct the investigation.

Several federal regulations and state statutes mandate background screening in a variety of industries such as healthcare, finance, and transportation. The Department of Transportation, for example, requires screening of pilots and other persons holding safety-critical positions.

Apart from federal and state mandates, employers have their own options. They can choose to screen all applicants, some applicants, or no applicants, and they can choose to go with bare-bones screening, intermediate level screening, or thorough screening. But before making any choices, the employer should weigh the risk potential. In the simplest sense, the employer can ask, "What risk do I face if I don't screen this type of applicant?" For a person applying for a job in the accounts receivable department, the risk may be embezzlement; for a person applying for a job as a cashier, the risk may be theft from the register; for a person applying for a job that involves stress and close proximity to others, the risk may be violence; and for a person applying for a job as a heavy equipment operator, the risk may be serious accidents. Each risk has its own parameters and not all risks should

be measured in dollars alone. The employer has to consider loss of talent, loss of morale, and loss of reputation.

Employers should first develop a preemployment screening policy that ensures compliance with the FCRA and other applicable laws such as the Americans with Disabilities Act (ADA) and regulations established by the Equal Employment Opportunity Commission (EEOC). The policy can call for a narrow, limited program, such as screening applicants for a single class of work, or a comprehensive program for screening all or most all applicants. Some jobs will stand out as critical. For example, a job that places an employee in close contact with children is a critical job. Background screening program for a job of this type would include ruling out that an applicant is using a false name, making comprehensive searches and examinations of criminal records, and matching the applicant's name against sex offender registries. The human resources department should also administer a battery of psychological tests.

The natural urge to control costs can lead an employer to ineffective screening practices such as making Internet searches or purchasing database searches. Due diligence requires much more. It means accessing the best information sources available, using professionals to extract the relevant information, and making the information available to the person(s) making the hiring decision.

An important information source is the criminal records office at a county courthouse. When it comes to the search of criminal records, employers have many options. For proper due diligence, a search should be conducted at the county of residence for at least the past seven years. Searching criminal records at the county level provides accurate and up-to-date information but care should be taken because many counties have different courts of jurisdiction that handle different types of cases.

A closer look should be taken when considering searching records at the state level. Only a handful of states provide comprehensive databases. Many counties and reporting jurisdictions do not submit their criminal files in a timely manner or may not even send in reports at all. Employers should always consider other database resources such as a national criminal database as a tool to enhance a records search. In addition, some private and public background screening firms gather electronic information from county, state, and federal repositories and place the information in databases. A single database can have millions of records and be amenable to specialized searches such as for sexual predators.

A disadvantage with databases is that they often have "holes" and contain information that is out-of-date, inaccurate, or only partially accurate. A professional screening firm can verify database information. This practice can provide accurate and current information.

The National Association of Professional Background Screeners (NAPBS) was founded to provide standards, education, and best practices for its members. A recent NAPBS study revealed that there are currently 500-plus screening firms operating in the United States. They come in all shapes, sizes, and capabilities. An employer looking to contract with a screening company would be well advised to closely examine credentials. The two main attributes are quality of work and compliance with the law, most especially the FCRA.

Many states have implemented laws on the collection and use of criminal records as a guide in selecting job applicants. Obtaining arrest and conviction information may also be restricted by use, depending on the income level or earning potential of a candidate. State laws have also been put into place to provide fair treatment of lower income individuals and minorities. Before engaging in any kind of pre-employment screening, an employer must determine and understand the applicable laws of the jurisdiction.

Many screening firms accept online requests for service and provide quick turn-around. For the online work to proceed, the employer must provide certain data such as the applicant's name, date of birth, social security number, and other identifiers. A reputable, well established screening firm will protect the identifying data, usually as well as or better than the employer. Assurance is demonstrated when the screening firm uses standard protections such as passwords, firewalls, and encryption. A less reputable, fly-by-night screening firm may not have any procedures in place to shield the employer's data from prying eyes. While a screening firm's services and prices can be satisfactory, there is a risk that sensitive information is open to exposure.

Human error can account for information that is lost, stolen, damaged, and misfiled. The FBI, which prides itself on quality, has its share of human-error problems. The National Crime Information Center (NCIC) is operated by the FBI in cooperation with state law enforcement agencies. The NCIC maintains a national database of criminal information that is accessible to law enforcement. A study conducted in one state (Florida) revealed errors in 11.7 percent of 93,274 background checks. Even worse, 5.5 percent of more than 10,000 criminal records were in error because the individuals involved had never been convicted of a crime.

Employers need to understand that there are different roadblocks throughout the screening process. Many courts still utilize non-automated and antiquated ways of maintaining criminal records. Restrictions such as "clerk courts" or courts that do not provide public access to records may slow the process and make employers reconsider due diligence. Applicants are not always cooperative. They give partial or inaccurate information that makes it difficult to verify simple facts such as past employment and previous addresses.

A concern to a company is the possibility of a lawsuit alleging invasion of privacy because a former employee's performance information was released to another company that had the former employee under consideration for hire. The practical result is that a former employer will release nothing more than the former employee's dates of employment and job description.

In conclusion, employers are responsible for providing a safe and secure working environment for their employees and others on their premises. This is called duty of care and the duty can be met by due diligence practices such as screening out job applicants that have a history or propensity for violence or dishonesty. The methods of screening are limited to those approved by law such as the FCRA. To obtain the best available information in accordance with the law requires the use of professionals skilled in conducting background investigations.

Robert Capwell

RULES OF EVIDENCE

The rules for presenting evidence in a criminal investigation are as varied as the types of evidence. Let us look at them.

Opinion testimony is a conclusion drawn by a witness, hence the term opinion testimony. Another form of testimonial information is hearsay evidence. Hearsay is a statement that is made other than by a witness. Hearsay cannot be entered into evidence unless the maker of the statement can be cross-examined.

Privileged communication is confidential information between two persons recognized by law as coming within the so-called privileged relationship rule. The following relationships are generally recognized: a husband and wife, an attorney and client, a physician and patient, and a law enforcement officer and informant.

Character evidence is evidence introduced by either defense or prosecution witnesses to prove the accused's good or bad character. Character evidence is usually introduced only when the defense raises the issue of the accused's character.

Direct evidence is evidence presented by a person who actually witnessed something. Contrast this with circumstantial evidence, which is evidence that proves other facts from which a court may reasonably infer the truth.

Admissibility is a characteristic or condition of evidence. To be admissible, evidence must be material, relevant, and competent. Evidence is material when it plays a significant part in proving a case. Examples of material evidence might be fingerprints of the accused that were found on the murder weapon, an eyewitness account of how the accused committed the crime, or stolen property found in the possession of the accused. Evidence is relevant when it goes directly to the proof or disproof of the crime or of any facts at issue. Examples of relevant evidence might be a death certificate or a medical examiner's report. Evidence is competent when it is shown to be reliable. Examples of competent evidence might be accurate business records or the testimony of an expert fingerprint examiner.

Burden of proof is a rule which holds that no person accused of a crime is required to prove his or her innocence. The prosecution must prove the guilt of a defendant beyond a reasonable doubt. Reasonable doubt means the jury must believe the charges to be true to a "moral certainty." On the other hand, the accused must prove his or her contentions. Such defenses as self-defense, insanity, and alibi are affirmative defenses that must be proved by the accused.

A presumption is a conclusion that the law says must be reached from certain facts. Presumptions are recognized because experience has shown that some facts should be accepted or presumed true until otherwise rebutted. For example, defendants are presumed to be sane at the time the crime was committed, and at the time of trial, in the absence of proof to the contrary. Presumptions are of two classes: conclusive and rebuttable. A conclusive presumption is one that the law demands be made from a set of facts, e.g., a child under 7 years of age cannot be charged with a crime. A rebuttable presumption can be overcome by evidence to the contrary, e.g., presumption of death after being unaccounted for and missing for 7 years.

Rules of Exclusion

In general, rules of exclusion deal with conditions in which evidence will not be received. They limit the evidence a witness may present to those things of which he had direct knowledge, i.e., what he saw, smelled, tasted, felt, or heard.

All evidence, direct and circumstantial, if relevant, material, and competent is admissible provided it is not opinion testimony, hearsay evidence, or privileged communication. There are exceptions regarding the admissibility of opinion testimony and hearsay evidence. An exception to the rule against opinion testimony can be made when no other description could be more accurate. For instance, a witness is allowed to testify on such matters as size, distance, time, weight, speed, direction, drunkenness, and similar matters, all of which require the witness to state an opinion. There is no requirement for the witness to be an "expert" when testifying to facts such as these.

Exceptions to the rule against hearsay can be made for the dying declaration and the spontaneous declaration. The admissibility of a dying declaration is limited to homicide cases. Because of the seriousness of homicide, a dying declaration is an exception. A dying declaration is admissible either for or against the accused. The statement must have been made when the victim believed he was about to die and was without hope of recovery. The admissibility of the declaration will not be affected as long as the victim dies; otherwise, the issue would not arise since there would be no charge of homicide.

The spontaneous declaration, a statement made under conditions of shock or excitement, may be admitted as another exception to the hearsay rule. Normally, such a statement is made simultaneously with an event or act and there is not time or opportunity to fabricate a story. It is generally accepted that the statement will be admitted if it precedes, follows, or is concurrent with the act. The statement cannot have been made in response to a question and must pertain to the act that produced it. The spontaneity of the statement is sufficient guarantee of truthfulness to compensate for the denial of cross-examination.

In prosecutions for sexual offenses, evidence that the victim made a complaint within a short time after the offense occurred (i.e., a fresh complaint) is admissible in certain cases. The fact that the complaint was made is relevant for corroborating the testimony of the victim. The statement may relate only to who and what caused the conditions, and merely indicate the credibility of the victim as a witness.

An official statement in writing made as a record of fact or event by an individual acting in an official capacity (called a "business record") is admissible to prove the truth of a matter. Records are of two types: private and public. To introduce private records, someone associated with the business must introduce them. He must show that the company kept records, that the record produced was one of these records, and that the record was the original or certified copy of the original. Public records are usually introduced by presenting certified copies.

A confession is a statement or complete acknowledgment of guilt. An admission is a statement which does not amount to a complete acknowledgment of guilt, but links the maker with a crime. Admissions are forms of hearsay. A court is inclined to apply the same rules of admissibility to admissions as for confessions.

John J. Fay

Source Fay, J. 1987. *Butterworths Security Dictionary: Terms and Concepts*. Boston: Butterworth-Heinemann.

SEARCH AND SEIZURE

The Fourth Amendment to the Constitution of the United States guarantees the right of the people to be secure in their persons, houses, papers, and effects against unreasonable searches and seizures. The words used in the Constitution are directed at unreasonable searches and seizures conducted by the government. Unfortunately, however, the Constitution does not go on to define what is meant by the term "unreasonable," nor does the law discuss any provision for punishment of persons who violate the Fourth Amendment. It has been left up to the U.S. government and the various states to create definitions of search and seizure violations, and to provide suitable punishment when violations are proven. At the federal level, Title 18 of the United States Code provides fines and imprisonment for persons found guilty regarding searches. Most states have tended to model their search and seizure laws in conformance with the federal law. Where differences might exist between a particular state and the overall guiding federal law, the difference is more likely to be a matter of semantics rather than spirit or intent of the law.

In addition to possible criminal prosecution for violations of law regarding illegal search and seizure, the offending person is likely to be charged in a civil suit for damages resulting from the violation. A defense is possible, however, if it can be shown that the searching official was acting in good faith, according to an official duty. An official who uses bad judgment and conducts an illegal search has an excuse, but when the search is conducted illegally by intent, or not in connection with official duties, then the official can be charged with a violation.

Search

The term "search" denotes the examination of an alleged or suspected offender or his house or other building or property. The examination must be conducted in the normal course of enforcing the law or maintaining order. The examination must have a purpose of looking for some specific item or items. Items looked for will fall into one or more of the following categories: contraband, tools of a crime, fruits of a crime, or incriminating evidence. For an examination to be properly called a "search," the person conducting the examination must have some legal status. Not only must the searcher be duly empowered by law to make searches, but he must also possess a specific authority for conducting a particular search at a particular place at a particular time to look for particular items. There are several ways for a searching official to demonstrate his authority to search. Most common among these is the search warrant. The term "search" does not include other kinds of "looking" functions. For example, an inspection of a place with a view towards reducing fire hazards is not a search. The close examination of an entry pass by a security officer is not a search.

The plain view doctrine is a rule of law that states it is not a search within the meaning of the Fourth Amendment to observe that which is open to view, provided that the viewing officer has a lawful right to be there. No warrant is required to seize items in plain view. Plain view exists when an officer who had justification for intrusion in the course of official duties inadvertently comes into contact with contraband in open view, and prior to the discovery was unaware of the existence of the contraband before coming upon it unexpectedly. The doctrine relies on the presumption that the officer has a right to be in a place where evidence or contraband is seen in an area open to plain viewing. An example would be an officer who is called to the scene of an assault and observes cocaine on a coffee table. The officer is legally on the premises and can seize the cocaine. However, if the cocaine was viewed by an officer observing through an open window, not in connection with official police business, the plain view doctrine would not apply. In this case, a search warrant would be required to make a search and seizure.

Seizure

The term "seizure" denotes the taking of contraband, fruits of a crime, tools of a crime, or incriminating evidence. The person taking the items must be empowered to make the seizure, and the items seized must be protected until disposed of in some proper fashion. If, for example, the item seized is a stolen ring, the ring will be safeguarded as evidence until the trial is completed. When the judicial action against the offender is ended, the ring will be returned to the owner. For some kinds of seized items, final disposition might be destruction. Narcotics, certain kinds of weapons, and illegal

whiskey are examples of items that are usually destroyed after court action has ended.

Search Warrant

The term "search warrant" means a written order issued by competent legal authority that directs a search to be conducted. The warrant specifies who is to conduct the search, who or what place is to be searched, and the items to be looked for during the search. The warrant is made valid for only a certain limited period of time. In some cases a warrant might direct that the search be made at some particular time of night or day, but a warrant is never prepared so that the searcher can wait many days or weeks before deciding to carry out the warrant. A warrant is issued on the basis of a need that exists at the time the warrant is requested. The need cannot be interpreted to spread out over a long period of time. It should also be noted that the word "warrant" itself means an order. Although the person or agency carrying out the warrant was the requester of the warrant in the first place, it is the issuing judge who gives the order for a search to be conducted. A warrant is therefore not simply a permit granted to someone to conduct a search, it is an order to do so. That order is very specific in what must be done. The warrant will name a person or small number of persons who will carry out the warrant. The warrant will name the person, place, or property to be searched. Knowing the details of the area to be searched is sometimes of great importance to the requester of a warrant. For example, it might be very important to know that the building to be searched has a separate shed. Unless the shed is included in the warrant, it cannot be lawfully searched. It might be that the items to be looked for are in the shed. A little advance knowledge on the part of the searcher is important in getting a properly worded warrant. Along the same line, it is important that the warrant include mention of all items that are useful as evidence. If the case involves a search for an automatic rifle, the person requesting the warrant would want to include mention of ammunition, ammunition clips, magazines, or parts pertaining to the type of automatic rifle involved. If the warrant simply names the rifle as the item to be looked for, the searcher cannot technically seize anything except the rifle and misses the chance of getting other pieces of evidence related to the same crime. Advance preparation in the wording of a warrant is therefore important.

A warrant is specific in one other regard. The judge's order will direct that any seized property be taken to some designated place or agency. Seized items are sometimes regarded as property of the court until such time as the items are properly disposed of, with disposition instructions normally issued by the court in writing. The proper safeguarding of seized property requires that the property be inventoried at the time it is seized. The inventory is placed into writing, usually on a receipt type of form that lists all items taken. The copy of the receipt is given, with the search warrant, to the person from whom the items were taken. If no such person is available, the receipt and search warrant are left at the place of seizure. The original copy of the receipt remains with the seized items and is used to account for the property from the time of seizure until the time of final disposition.

Affidavit

The term "affidavit" describes a written document that is used to support or justify the issuance of a search warrant. An affidavit is nothing more than a written statement made under oath. It sets forth details that provide the issuing judge with enough information for him to conclude that a crime was committed and that a search of a certain place will probably reveal the presence of some evidence pertaining to that crime. The affidavit therefore provides the type of information that is sometimes called "probable cause."

An affidavit might read as follows:

> I, John Doe, having been duly sworn, on oath depose and state that at 11:30 p.m., July 1st, 2006, at the premises of ABC Company, 1000 Main Street, Houston, Texas, a person unknown did steal a carton containing a Carrier air-conditioning unit, model X, serial number 123456, valued at $800.00. The affiant further states that Alfred Aware, a security officer at the premises, reported that at 11:30 p.m., July 1st, 2006, he observed a person exit a rear loading door of the building and place a large carton into the rear of a station wagon.

> Before Mr. Aware could reach the scene, the station wagon fled the area. Mr. Aware did, however, note the license plate number of the station wagon. A check with the license plate bureau revealed the owner of the suspect station wagon to be Billy Badguy, a tenant at 1115 North Street, Houston, Texas. An interview with Mrs. Betty Busybody, landlady at 1115 North Street, revealed that after midnight on July 1st, 2006, she observed Mr. Badguy carry a large carton into his rented room. She described the carton as having writing that said the carton contained a Carrier air-conditioning unit. In view of the foregoing, the affiant requests that authorization be issued for a search of rooms at 1115 North Street, Houston, Texas, that are rented and controlled by the person identified as Mr. Badguy, and that such authorization include seizure of a Carrier air-conditioning unit, serial number 123456.

> Signed, John Doe

> Sworn to and subscribed before me this Third Day of July 2006, at Houston, Harris County, State of Texas.

> Signed, Lawrence Law, District Attorney

In this fictionalized sample of an affidavit, the most important pieces of information were provided by a security officer. The security officer provided the time, date, place, a description of the property stolen, and certain other details that led to an identification of the suspect.

In other words, the security officer observed and made notes as to the who, what, when, where, and how elements of an offense. It is this kind of basic information that will add up to a total picture so as to provide probable cause for a judge to issue a search warrant. The basic information in the affidavit demonstrates firstly that a crime happened. The affidavit then leads to a reasonable conclusion that some evidence of that particular crime will probably be found at a certain place. When these requirements are satisfied, a judge will likely grant the request for a search warrant.

A few other terms need to be explained regarding searches. We have already mentioned the terms "contraband," "fruits of the crime," "tools of the crime," and "incriminating evidence." Items to be looked for and seized in connection with a search will fall into one or more of these four categories.

Contraband

Contraband is any item that, by itself, is a crime to have. Bootleg whiskey is contraband because possession of it is against the law. The same holds true for certain types of firearms, explosives, illegal narcotics, marijuana, pornographic materials, and counterfeit money. Search warrants are issued to cover the seizure of contraband when it is known in advance that contraband is present at a certain place. If such contraband is seized without getting the search warrant, the seizure is illegal; however, contraband that is discovered accidentally can be seized without a warrant. In regard to contraband, it can always be seized. How it was seized will determine whether the contraband can be used as evidence against the person responsible for it.

Fruits of the Crime

This is a term referring to that advantage which is derived by the criminal who commits a crime. A stolen television set and swindled money are all examples of fruits of crime.

Tools of the Crime

This term refers to the devices used in the commission of the illegal act. Tools in this sense obviously include burglary devices such as a jimmy, lock pick, bolt cutter, and so forth. Tools also include a worthless check, a false document, or even a fraudulent advertisement.

Incriminating Evidence

The term "incriminating evidence" covers a wide range of items. In this category are items that tend to show involvement of a suspect or an accomplice in a criminal activity. The item could be a shirt bearing blood stains acquired during the crime, it could be a diary containing references to a crime, it could be a photograph showing some relationship to a crime, or it could even be a tape recording of accomplices discussing a crime.

Reasonableness

An understanding of the foregoing terms will be of assistance in understanding further concepts associated with search and seizure. One other term, which is common to everyday language, should be looked at in respect to the matter of legal searches. The term "reasonable" is sometimes used to describe the nature of a search conducted with authority of a search warrant. Since probable cause has to be present for a search warrant to be issued, it can be said that the search was reasonable. The term reasonable then becomes almost identical with words like "constitutional," "lawful," or "legal." The term "unreasonable" is therefore just the opposite of "reasonable" in meaning. "Unreasonable" has often been used to describe searches that were conducted without benefit of a search warrant. An example of an "unreasonable search" would be an examination of a place for the purpose of finding any kind of evidence that might possibly be used against a person. This type of search is unreasonable because it is not specific in terms of what item or items are expected to be found. Such a search is exploratory and is in the nature of a fishing expedition.

Search Without a Warrant

This does not mean that only searches conducted with warrants can be properly called reasonable. A search with a warrant is certain to be reasonable, but other searches can be considered reasonable, if they are conducted under certain conditions. Let us look at those situations in which it is possible to conduct reasonable searches without the use of a search warrant.

Search Incidental to Arrest

Perhaps the most common type of search is the search made in connection with an arrest. A check of a person's possessions at the time he is taken into custody is mainly intended to discover the presence of weapons that can be used against the arresting person. The arresting person has a right to protect himself from attack by a weapon concealed on the body of the arrested person. A search at the time of arrest is mainly directed toward this consideration. A second consideration for the arresting person is to see if the offender has any evidence on his person that is connected with a crime. It is important that the evidence be taken before the suspect has an opportunity to destroy or discard it. A frisk or wall search will normally reveal the presence of weapons or destructible evidence. The frisk and wall search are called precautionary searches because they are designed to take precautions against attack and against the chance of losing valuable evidence. Property in the possession of the arrested person can be searched. This would include packages, brief cases, and the like. The place under immediate control of the arrested person can be searched for evidence connected to the crime. Thus, when a person is arrested in his private office, the unlocked areas of the office can be legally searched. If the arrest is made in a building lobby, the lobby cannot be searched because it is not under immediate control of the suspect at the time of arrest. Vehicles driven by an arrested person can be searched, but only those areas of the vehicle that are controlled by the suspect. The trunk of a vehicle is not considered to be under control of the suspect at the time of arrest. If it is felt that a search of the trunk will probably yield evidence connected to a crime, a search warrant can be requested. If the arrested person is a woman, the search can include only the purse, coat, parcels, baggage, or other articles not worn by her.

The Emergency Search

Another type of lawful search and seizure is the looking for and taking of criminal goods before those goods can be disposed of. This form of search is in the nature of an emergency action that is taken to prevent the removal, destruction, or further hiding of property illegally held by a suspect. To illustrate, assume a company employee discovers that three rolls of 25-cent pieces are missing from a box containing the company's petty cash fund. The employee calls the security office and explains that he knows the missing rolls of quarters were in the box minutes prior to the time the cleaning man had access to the cash box, and the cleaning man is getting ready to leave the company premises. Under circumstances like this, a search of the cleaning man would be justified. A search is justified because facts show that a crime was committed, that the stolen property is probably in the possession of the suspect, that the suspect is leaving and there is no time to obtain a search warrant,

and that to recover the stolen property it is necessary to take emergency action before the suspect can leave with the stolen money.

Search with Consent

Another kind of search not requiring a warrant is search by consent. The consent must be freely and intelligently given. Consent cannot be obtained through the use of threats or trickery. The person giving permission to search his person or property must do so in a completely willing manner. For the consent to be intelligently given, the person must be able to recognize the consequences of permitting a search. A person who is too young, too old, too drunk, retarded, ill, or insane cannot intelligently give consent to a search. Also, mere submission or giving in to a request for consent is not the same as giving a free consent. In order to demonstrate that consent to search was freely and intelligently given, the security officer should obtain the consent in writing. The writing itself, the words used, and the physical act of writing help to demonstrate that the consent was properly obtained.

Any consent obtained must be obtained from the person who has a right to give the consent. A hotel manager cannot give consent to search a paying guest's hotel room. A person sharing an apartment cannot give consent to a search of another person's property within the apartment. This is an important point to remember when asking for consent to conduct a search.

Purposes of a Search

It can be said that a search and seizure action has two overall purposes. One is to discover and obtain evidence that will bring the criminal to justice. The other is to recover property that belongs to another person. A search and seizure that achieves both these purposes is what we strive for.

Sometimes, because of improper methods in a search, the goal of justice is not realized. Evidence is inadmissible in a court of law if it was obtained as the result of an unlawful search or seizure. The law also goes on to provide that other evidence obtained later, quite lawfully, cannot be used if it was connected in any way with a preceding unlawful search. For instance, assume that an unlawful search resulted in the discovery of a notebook containing information that led to the identification of other accomplices and hiding places of stolen property. Any evidence discovered from lawful searches made of the accomplices and the hiding places cannot be made in court. For this reason it is important to keep in mind the major points of law dealing with search and seizure.

John J. Fay

SENTENCING OF CORPORATIONS: FEDERAL GUIDELINES

In 1984 the Sentencing Reform Act established the U.S. Sentencing Commission. The Commission's mandate was to create guidelines designed to eliminate disparity in sentences being meted out by federal courts. The idea was to replace a very loose sentencing approach with an approach that would be consistent and impose punishments equal to the crimes committed.

In creating the Commission, Congress was making it clear that indeterminate sentencing had grown excessively lenient and that a tougher stance on crime was needed. Congress instructed the Commission to "insure that the Guidelines reflect the fact that, in many cases, current sentences do not accurately reflect the seriousness of the offense." The Commission's response to Congressional concern was its stated objective to "avoid unwarranted sentencing disparities among defendants with similar records who have been found guilty of similar criminal conduct while maintaining sufficient flexibility to permit individualized sentences when warranted by mitigating or aggravating factors not taken into account in the establishment of general sentencing practices."

Accordingly, the Commission established Guidelines for determining sentences, including whether to impose a sentence of probation, fine, or imprisonment, and if so, how long and/or how much; whether the defendant should be placed on supervised release after imprisonment; and whether multiple sentences should run concurrently or consecutively. Most observers agree that the Guidelines have generated more and longer prison terms and heavier fines.

In 1988, the mandate of the Commission was expanded to include development of Guidelines for the sentencing of corporations. The stated purposes were to (1) substantially increase most of the fines imposed on companies convicted of crime, (2) introduce a concept of "corporate

probation," and (3) call for self-reporting of crimes discovered by corporate management. The interesting and important part is that a corporate defendant's culpability can be mitigated by having a program in place to detect violations and by self-reporting of offenses prior to investigation. In effect, a corporate defendant has a measure of control over the leniency or severity of its sentence by its own action taken before and after its violation of the law. The Guidelines provide strong incentive for compliance and self-policing. Indeed, the U.S. Sentencing Commission has said that the purposes of the Guidelines are to "provide just punishment, adequate deterrence, and incentives for organizations to maintain internal mechanisms for preventing, detecting and reporting criminal conduct."

On November 1, 1991, the Guidelines became law. If the same tough stance that has been applied in individual sentencing is carried over to business organizations, corporate management should be concerned. A sense of foreboding can be found in the new corporate Guidelines in the statement that the "goals and purposes of sentencing for organizations are identical to those for individuals."

At present, the impact of the law on corporate behavior is uncertain, but many commentators anticipate that because sentences will be defined and judicial discretion reduced, punishment for corporate crime will be more predictable. It is certain, however, that the intent of the government is to seek increased penalties against companies for anti-trust and other violations. The Department of Justice is on record about its intent to vigorously pursue corporate offenders.

Guidelines

Prevention and Detection. The Guidelines call for a credible effort to detect and deter crime. The elements of a compliance program are spelled out. Anything less will expose a corporation and its officers to substantial punishment.

Remedies. A convicted organization must notify the victims of the crime and take appropriate action to compensate them or remedy the harm. Full restitution either as part of the sentence or as a condition of probation is provided, trust funds for victims may be ordered, and community service is an option.

COMPLIANCE POLICY: CONCERNING CORPORATE CONDUCT

(Sample)

The Company and each of its subsidiaries will establish and maintain an effective compliance program that conforms to the standards established in the Sentencing Guidelines promulgated by the U.S. Sentencing Commission. The program will be designed, implemented, and enforced with the purpose of being effective in preventing and detecting criminal conduct.

The Company will exercise due diligence in attempting to prevent and to detect criminal conduct by its employees and agents. To those ends the Company will establish and maintain the policies and practices set forth as follows:

1. The Company will determine the likelihood that there is a substantial risk that certain types of criminal offenses may occur.

2. The Company will establish and maintain compliance standards and procedures to be followed by its employees and agents which are reasonably capable of reducing the prospect of criminal conduct.

3. Specific high-level individuals within the Company shall be assigned overall responsibility to oversee compliance with such standards and procedures. Division and subsidiary presidents and vice presidents in charge of corporate staff functions are hereby assigned such responsibility for their respective divisions, subsidiaries, and departments.

4. The Company will not delegate substantial discretionary authority to any individual it knows, or through the exercise of due diligence should have known, had a propensity to engage in illegal activities.

5. The Company will take reasonable steps to communicate effectively its standards and procedures to all employees and other agents.

6. The Company will take reasonable steps to achieve compliance with its standards. Such reasonable steps include the establishment of monitoring and auditing systems that are reasonably designed to detect unlawful conduct by employees and agents, and establishing, monitoring, and publicizing a reporting system whereby employees and other agents can report abuse by others within the organization without fear of retribution.

7. The Company will consistently enforce its standards through appropriate disciplinary mechanisms, including, as appropriate, discipline of individuals responsible for the failure to detect an offense.

8. If a criminal offense is detected, the organization must take all reasonable steps to respond appropriately to the offense and to prevent similar offenses.

9. Each division and subsidiary will establish one or more committees to assist the president of the division or subsidiary in the implementation and enforcement of this program.

10. These compliance statements are intended to establish a procedural framework; they are not intended to set forth in full the substantive compliance programs and practices of the Company and its subsidiaries. Additional standards for compliance are established and maintained by virtue of the practices, procedures, and policies of the Company and the form of organization that manages the Company, and those additional practices, procedures, policies, and organization are an integral part of the compliance program.

Fines. Fines are assessed using a complicated formula that considers the seriousness of the offense and the culpability of the offending organization. The first step is to determine a base fine that is the greater of the dollar value of the gain to the offender/loss to the victim, or an amount determined by a table of fines set out in the Guidelines.

The second step is to determine a "culpability score" based on aggravating and mitigating factors. Aggravating factors might be foreknowledge by management, concealment of the offense, and a history of prior offenses; mitigating factors might be the existence of a compliance program, prompt reporting of the offense, and cooperation in the investigation. The culpability score is cross-referenced to minimum and maximum multipliers.

In the third step, the multiplier is applied to the fine. A low culpability score can lead to a fine smaller than the base fine while a high culpability score may lead to a fine many times larger.

To illustrate, assume that the victim's damages were $100,000 and that the court used this amount as the base fine. The judge noted that the culpability score is 10 points based on aggravating factors. In looking at the Guidelines table, the minimum multiplier is 2 and the maximum is 4. The judge can set the fine no lower than $200,000 and no higher than $400,000.

Probation. In addition to requiring payment of damages and a fine, the judge can place a company on probation for up to 5 years. Probation is mandatory if at the time of sentencing the company does not have in place an acceptable compliance program. When this happens, the court will impose a program that it will periodically monitor.

Developing a Compliance Program

The first objective of a compliance program is to keep from violating criminal laws; the second objective is to achieve the lowest possible culpability score if the first objective is not met. A compliance program to meet these two objectives will include:

- Written policy, directives, and procedures to guide employees.

- The assignment to specific senior management of responsibilities for the proper execution of the compliance program.
- Steps to prevent giving discretionary authority to individuals whom the company knew or should have known had a propensity to engage in illegal acts.
- An education component for informing employees of their personal responsibilities under the program.
- A monitoring and auditing system to detect deviations from compliance, including a mechanism for employees to report suspected criminal conduct without fear of retribution.
- Consistent enforcement of compliance standards with appropriate disciplinary sanctions.
- Steps to prevent recurrence of offenses, including needed changes to the program.

The Federal Sentencing Guidelines add a new dimension to corporate accountability by emphasizing compliance programs, self-policing, and reporting of offenses. The sentencing judge is bound to a highly defined, essentially mathematical scheme when determining sentences. The result in many cases will be heavy fines and invasive probation.

John J. Fay

Sources

"Amendments to the Sentencing Guidelines for United States Courts." 1992. *Federal Register*, Vol. 57, No. 91, 1992.

Fett, L. 1991. *New Corporation Sentencing Guidelines: Perils and Possibilities of Compliance Programs and Self-Policing*. Washington: American Corporate Counsel Association.

Machlowitz, D. 1991. *Designing and Implementing Corporate Compliance Policies*. Lyndhurst: General Instrument Corporation.

Murphy, J. 1989. *Corporate Compliance Programs: Counsel's Role*. Washington: American Corporate Counsel Association.

Nord, N. 1991. "Sentencing Guidelines Up the Ante for Corporate Compliance Programs." *American Corporate Counsel Association Docket*, Fall, 1991.

Olson, J. and Mahaffey, D. 1992. *Criminal Exposure in the Corporate Environment*. Washington: American Corporate Counsel Association.

"Sentencing Guidelines and Policy Statements for Federal Courts." *Federal Register*, Vol. 57, No. 1, 1992.

TESTIFYING

The person who has investigated a case is often the most important witness in the trial of that case. He may be the only person with a comprehensive understanding of a crime sufficient to give a complete, coordinated view of what happened. He is, therefore, the main communications system through which evidence of a crime is transmitted to the finder of fact at trial.

The importance of a good presentation by the investigator on the witness stand cannot be overemphasized. Hours and hours of the most competent investigation and preparation may be wasted if the results are improperly presented in court. The trier of fact (usually the jury) comes into court having no prior knowledge of what happened or who is guilty or innocent. The picture the jury gets depends largely on the ability of the investigator to testify truthfully and accurately, and to do so in a manner that impresses everyone present that he is intelligent, honest, competent, and fair. The defense attorney will do everything legally permitted to twist the evidence in his client's favor. If the investigator is confused, hazy, or unsure of important facts, the jury will be similarly confused and hazy. However, if he presents a clear-cut report containing all elements of proof in a calm, unprejudiced manner, the jury will see the case in the same light.

Furthermore, a verdict of guilty accomplishes little if an investigator has testified so poorly that he affords the accused good grounds for a new trial or for a reversal on appeal. Neither does a guilty verdict accomplish the good it should unless the trial has been conducted in such a manner that everyone in the courtroom has been impressed with the dignity and justice of the proceedings. Public confidence in our system of justice is essential to its proper function.

Preparation before Trial

Effective testimony in court depends to a large extent on preparation. Preparation begins with the first notification that a possible crime has been committed. All facts, observations, and actions having to do with the case should be carefully recorded in notes, reports, and photographs, keeping in mind that the information may eventually be introduced in court. Proper investigative procedures cannot be stressed strongly enough, because there are often long delays between the investigation of a case and the trial, and unless information is recorded, much of it is sure to be forgotten in the interim.

Knowledge of the Case. As the time of trial draws near, the investigator should make a complete review of the case and refresh his memory of the facts by carefully reading through all notes and reports. He should also examine physical evidence that has been collected, in the event that it has to be identified or referred to in court. Then he should put his thoughts together so he can visualize the whole case in the sequence in which it happened. Testimony presented to a jury as a chain of events in the order that they occurred is both interesting and convincing.

An investigator may be allowed to refresh his memory on the witness stand by referring to his notes or reports. However, if he does, the defense counsel has a right to examine these notes and question him about them. Therefore, the investigator should discuss with the prosecuting attorney the advisability of taking notes to the witness stand.

Also, the prosecuting attorney may want to confer with the investigator about the facts of the case at a pre-trial session. At this session, the prosecuting attorney may try to re-awaken the investigator's senses to recall parts of the investigation that he deems essential to the case and to go over the investigator's testimony. This is entirely proper and, at this time, the investigator should make sure that the prosecuting attorney knows all the facts of the case, whether favorable or unfavorable to the defendant. The prosecuting attorney may not, however, tell the investigator what to say or influence the investigator to deviate from the truth in any way.

Knowledge of the Rules of Evidence. Besides knowledge of the case being tried, the investigator testifying in court should have a basic knowledge of the rules of evidence. This knowledge will help him to better understand the proceedings and enable him to testify more intelligently, removing the opportunities for delay and confusion that can occur in the mind of the investigator when placed under pressure in the courtroom.

Appearance and Attitude. When an investigator appears in court, he must observe the highest standards of conduct. The minute he walks to the witness stand, he becomes the focal point of interest and observation by the public.

The key thing for an investigator to impress in his mind when testifying in court is that he is engaged in a very solemn and serious matter. He should look and act accordingly. While waiting to testify, the investigator should not linger outside the door of the courtroom smoking, gossiping, joking, laughing, or engaging in other similar conduct. This distracts attention from the proceedings and shows little regard for the serious nature of the occasion. Rather, the investigator should be seated quietly in the courtroom while awaiting his turn to take the stand, unless he is directed to wait in the witness room.

An investigator's appearance while testifying should be neat and well-groomed. He should wear a clean suit, tie, and shined shoes. Neither should he wear dark glasses, smoke, chew gum, or generally fidget around while on the witness stand. A favorable impression is created if the investigator sits erect but at ease in the witness chair and appears confident, alert, and interested in the proceedings.

Testimony during Trial

Our system of securing information from a witness at a trial is by the question and answer method. The questioning by attorneys on direct examination serves merely to guide the witness in his testimony and to indicate the information that is required. After direct examination, the witness may be subject to cross-examination by the opposing counsel. The questions on cross-examination will have the opposite purpose of those asked on direct examination. Cross-examination questions may be devious, deceptive, or innocent in appearance, masking the opposing counsel's real objective, which is to discredit or minimize, to as great an extent as possible, the effect of the witness's testimony. The investigator is usually a witness for the state. Direct examination is by the prosecuting attorney, with cross-examination by counsel for the defense.

There are no definite rules for testifying effectively in court because each case has its own peculiarities. However, there are general guidelines for answering questions that should be followed in most cases and some specific suggestions designed to aid the witness on cross-examination.

Answering Questions on the Witness Stand

When taking the oath, the investigator should be serious and stand upright, facing the officer administering the oath. He should say "I do" clearly and positively and then be seated to wait for further questioning.

The investigator should listen carefully to the questions asked and make sure he understands each question before answering. If he does not understand, he should say so, and ask to have the question repeated. He should then pause after the question long enough to form an intelligent answer and to allow the attorneys and judge time to make objections.

Answers to questions should be given in a confident, straightforward, and sincere manner. The investigator should speak clearly, loudly, and slowly enough so that all in the courtroom can hear, and he should avoid mumbling or covering his mouth with his hand while talking. He should look at the attorney asking the questions but direct his answers toward the jury. Simple conversational English should be used, and all slang and unnecessary technical terms avoided. Most importantly, the investigator should be respectful and courteous at all times despite his feelings toward the people involved in the case. He should address the judge as "Your Honor," the attorney as "Sir," and the defendant as "the Defendant."

The essential rule to be observed above and beyond all others is to always tell the truth, even if it is favorable to the defendant. Facts should not be distorted or exaggerated to try and aid a conviction, nor should details be added to cover up personal mistakes. Once it has been shown that an investigator has not truthfully testified as to one portion of his investigation, no matter how small and inconsequential, the jury may reject the truthfulness of all other testimony which he may offer. On the other hand, an investigator's testimony will appear strong if it is a truthful recital of what he did and observed, even though it reveals human error on his part and favors the defendant in some parts.

Answers to questions should go no further than what the questions ask for. The investigator should not volunteer any information not asked for. If a question requests a "yes" or "no" answer and the investigator feels it cannot properly be answered in this manner, he should ask to have the question explained or re-worded, or request the right to explain his answer. He may state that he cannot answer the question by "yes" or "no." This should alert the prosecuting attorney to come to his assistance.

Answers to questions should be given as specifically as possible. However, figures for time, distance, size, etc., should be approximated only, unless they were exactly measured by the investigator.

When an investigator is referring to a map or plan in his testimony, he should identify the point on the map as clearly as possible so it becomes part of the trial record. For example, he should say "the northwest corner of the room" rather than just point to the spot and say "here" or "there." If the investigator does not understand the map or plan that is to be used at trial, he should tell the prosecuting attorney before trial and go over it with the person who prepared it.

If a wrong or ambiguous answer is given, it should be clarified immediately. It is far better for an investigator to correct his own mistakes than to have them pointed out to the jury by the defense attorney or a subsequent witness.

If a judge interrupts or an attorney objects to an investigator's testimony, the investigator should stop talking instantly. However, he should not anticipate an objection when a difficult question is asked but should only pause long enough to form an intelligent answer.

Under no circumstances should an investigator memorize his testimony. It will only sound rehearsed and false, and will not inspire the confidence of the jury. Instead, the investigator should have a thorough knowledge of the facts of the case and organize them in his mind so he can recite them as a narrative. If a particular fact or circumstance becomes hazy or is forgotten, the investigator may be allowed to refresh his memory from his notes as long as this does not become a habit. It is worth noting that if an investigator does refer to notes, they may be examined by the opposing counsel. If

for any reason, the judge criticizes an investigator's conduct in court, the investigator should not allow it to disturb his composure. The best policy is to ask the court's pardon for the error committed and proceed as though nothing had occurred.

Cross-Examination

In a criminal trial, it is the duty of counsel for the defendant, as an officer of the court and as an attorney, to use every legal means to secure the acquittal of the client or the best possible verdict under the circumstances. Since the investigator is often a chief witness for the state, the defense attorney, in order to win, must normally discredit or nullify the investigator's testimony, or at least minimize its importance in the eyes of the jury. To do this, he may use every device legally available to him. He may attempt to show that the investigator did not have the proper opportunity to observe the facts, or that he was inattentive or mistaken in his observations. He may try to make it seem like the investigator is lying or leaving out facts which are favorable to the defendant. In trials of crimes that happened some time ago, the defense counsel may try to show that the investigator's recollection of the entire event is bad and that he knows nothing without his notes. He may even try to show that the investigator has a grudge against the defendant. One of the ways of doing this is to goad the investigator into losing his temper to give the appearance of being personally antagonistic to the defendant. Under the proper circumstances, all these approaches are legal and available for the use of defense counsel.

The best defense against the techniques and devices of the defense attorney is thorough preparation. If the investigator has carefully observed the facts at the time of their occurrence, made complete and sufficient notes, reviewed his notes and reports carefully to fix the events in his memory, and testified truthfully, he need have no fear of cross-examination. Nevertheless, there are a few important suggestions regarding cross-examination that help prevent the investigator from falling into the traps laid by a clever defense attorney. Some of these suggestions have been mentioned previously and others apply exclusively to cross-examination.

- The investigator should not become angry or argumentative with the defense attorney. This is exactly what the defense attorney wants. Rather, the investigator should stick to calmly answering all questions unless an objection is sustained by the judge.
- The investigator should make very clear by his attitudes and statements that he has no personal feelings against the accused. If an accused has been nasty, insulting, or even has assaulted the investigator, the defense attorney may make much of such occurrences to persuade the jury that the investigator has a personal grudge in the matter and is "out to get" the accused. Jurors, being only human, are quick to resent any evidence of overbearing conduct or personal animosity on the part of the witness. The investigator, in this situation, should make clear that such things are common occurrences in his line of work and that they have no bearing on the matter as far as the facts are concerned.
- The investigator should not be afraid to admit mistakes made either in his investigation or his prior testimony. No one is perfect and an investigator admitting his errors himself will give defense counsel less fuel for attacking his credibility.
- If a defense attorney's question is not clear, the investigator should tell the court and ask to have it re-stated. An answer to an ambiguous question may very likely be a setup for a contradiction later on.
- The investigator should never be afraid to admit that he had discussed his testimony before trial with the prosecuting attorney, his superiors, or other investigators. This is entirely proper and accepted procedure. However, defense counsel, in the way he asks the question, may try to make it seem improper, and thereby trick the witness into a lie.
- If defense counsel seeks to cut off an investigator in the middle of his testimony, the investigator may turn to the judge and request an opportunity to explain his answer. This request will usually be granted.

Conduct after Trial

When an investigator leaves the witness stand, he should do so quickly and quietly, and return to his seat or leave the courtroom if no longer needed. He should not linger to talk to the prosecutor. If he should have additional information or ideas to tell the prosecutor, they should be written down and passed to the prosecutor with a minimum amount of display. When an investigator leaves the courtroom he should not loiter to talk or gossip with others and, most important, he should not talk to jurors if it is a jury trial.

Convincing and effective testimony by the investigator is essential to successful operation of the criminal justice system and depends on proper preparation, approach, and experience. The suggestions outlined previously are designed to familiarize the investigator with court procedure and improve his testimony as a witness. The preparation and individual effort required in this endeavor is a minimum expectation.

John J. Fay

Source Fay, J. 1979. *Special Agent Manual.* Atlanta: Georgia Bureau of Investigation.

TORT LAW

Public police officers have greater powers than private sector officers. In conjunction with police powers, public officers are limited in their actions by the Bill of Rights. On the other hand, private officers, who possess lesser powers, are, for the most part, not heavily restricted by constitutional limitations. Authority and limitations on private officers result from tort law.

Tort law is the body of state legislative statutes or court decisions that governs citizen actions toward each other and allows lawsuits to recover damages for injury. Tort law is the foundation for civil actions in which an injured party may litigate to prevent an activity or recover damages from someone who has violated his/her person or property. Most civil actions are not based on a claim of intended harm, but a claim that the defendant was negligent. This is especially so in cases involving private security officers. Tort law requires actions that have regard for the safety and rights of others; otherwise negligence results. The essence of the tort law limitations on private officers is fear of a lawsuit and the payment of damages.

The primary torts relevant to private sector police are as follows:

1. False Imprisonment. The intentional and forceful confinement or restriction of the freedom of movement of another person. Also called "false arrest." The elements necessary to create liability are detention and its unlawfulness.
2. Malicious Prosecution. Groundless initiation of criminal proceedings against another.
3. Battery. Intentionally harmful or offensive touching of another.
4. Assault. Intentional causing of fear of harmful or offensive touching.
5. Trespass to Land. Unauthorized entering upon another person's property.
6. Trespass to Personal Property. Taking or damaging another person's possessions.
7. Infliction of Emotional Distress. Intentionally causing emotional or mental distress in another.
8. Defamation (Libel and Slander). Injury to the reputation of another by publicly making untrue statements. Libel refers to the written word; slander to the spoken word.
9. Invasion of Privacy. Intruding upon another's physical solitude, the disclosure of private information about another, or public misrepresentation of another's actions.
10. Negligence. Causing injury to persons or property by failing to use reasonable care or by taking unreasonable risk.

Civil action is not the only factor that hinders abuses by the private sector. Local and state ordinances, rules, regulations, and laws establish guidelines for the private security industry. This usually pertains to licensing and registration requirements. Improper or illegal action is likely to result in suspension or revocation of a license. Criminal law presents a further

deterrent against criminal action by private sector personnel. Examples are laws prohibiting impersonation of a public official, electronic surveillance, breaking and entering, and assault.

Union contracts can also limit private police. These contracts might stipulate, for instance, that employee lockers cannot be searched, and that certain investigative guidelines must be followed.

Contract Law

Torts often result from the failure of a party to meet the requirements of a contract. A contract is basically an agreement between parties to do or to abstain from doing some act. The law may enforce the agreement by requiring that a party perform its obligation or pay money equivalent to the performance. These court requirements are known as remedies for breach of contract. Specific circumstances may create defenses for failure to perform contract stipulations. Contracts may be express or implied. In an express contract—written or oral—the terms are stated in words. An implied contract is presumed by law to have been made from the circumstances and relations of the parties involved.

There are several areas in the security/loss prevention field relevant to the law of contracts. The company that provides a service or device to a client company may be liable for breach of contract. Also, a contract usually states liabilities for each party. For instance, if a third party is harmed (e.g., a person illegally arrested on the premises by a private officer from a contract service hired by a client company), the contract will commonly establish who is responsible and who is to have insurance for each risk. However, in third-party suits, courts have held a specific party liable even though the contract stipulated that another party was to be responsible in the matter.

In the common law principle of *respondeat superior* (i.e., let the master respond), an employer (master) is liable for injuries caused by an employee (servant). Typically, the injured party will look beyond the employee—to the employer—for compensation for damages. Proper supervision and training of the employee can prevent litigation.

Another form of contract is the union contract. If a proprietary force is employed on the premises, a union contract may be in existence. As stated earlier, union contracts for regular employees may have certain guidelines for locker searches and investigations.

Philip P. Purpura

Source   Purpura, P. 2002. *Security and Loss Prevention, 4th Edition*. Boston: Butterworth-Heinemann.

TORTS

A crime is a public wrong and a tort is a private wrong. A public wrong is remedied in a criminal proceeding and a private wrong is remedied in a civil proceeding. A single act in some instances will constitute both a crime and a tort. For example, if a person commits an assault and battery upon another, he commits a crime (a public wrong) and a tort (a private wrong). The law will seek to remedy both wrongs, but it will do so in different ways.

The state will move on its own authority to do justice by bringing a criminal action against the offender. The victim is also entitled to bring action against the offender in a civil suit. Tort law gives the victim a cause of action for damages in order that he may obtain sufficient satisfaction. The victim, however, pursues a civil remedy at his own discretion and in his own name. Whether the victim wins his lawsuit or not, the judgment will not prevent prosecution of the offender by the state.

The civil injuries involved in tort cases usually arise from acts of negligence. The fact that by his own negligence the victim contributed to the harm done may afford the offender a defense in a civil action of tort, but it does not constitute a defense to the offender in a criminal prosecution.

The single characteristic that differentiates criminal law from civil law is punishment. Generally, in a civil suit the basic questions are:

- How much, if at all, has the defendant injured the plaintiff, and
- What remedies, if any, are appropriate to compensate the plaintiff for his loss?

In a criminal case, the questions are:

- To what extent has the defendant injured society, and
- What sentence is appropriate to punish the defendant?

Tort Law Purposes

Tort law has three main purposes:

- To compensate persons who sustain a loss as a result of another's conduct
- To place the cost of that compensation on those responsible for the loss
- To prevent future harms and losses

Compensation is predicated on the idea that losses, both tangible and intangible, can be measured in money.

If a loss-producing event is a matter of pure chance, the fairest way to relieve the victim of the burden is insurance or governmental compensation. Where a particular person can be identified as responsible for the creation of the risk, it becomes more just to impose the loss on the responsible person (tortfeasor) than to allow it to remain on the victim or the community at large.

The third major purpose of tort law is to prevent future torts by regulating human behavior. In concept, the tortfeasor held liable for damages will be more careful in the future, and the general threat of tort liability serves as an incentive to all persons to regulate their conduct appropriately. In this way, tort law supplements criminal law.

Damages: Compensatory and Punitive

When one person's tortious act injures another's person or property, the remedy for the injured party is to collect damages. The common law rules of damages for physical harm contain three fundamental ideas:

- Justice requires that the plaintiff be restored to his pre-injury condition, so far as it is possible to do so with money. He should be reimbursed not only for economic losses, but also for loss of physical and mental well-being.

- Most economic losses are translatable into dollars.
- When the plaintiff sues for an injury, he must recover all of his damages arising from that injury, past and future, in a lump and in a single lawsuit.

If the defendant's wrongful conduct is sufficiently serious, the law permits the trier of fact to impose a civil fine as punishment to deter him and others from similar conduct in the future. Punitive damages (also called exemplary or vindictive damages) are not really damages at all since the plaintiff has been made whole by the compensatory damages awarded in the same action. Punitive damages are justified as:

- An incentive for bringing the defendant to justice.
- Punishment for offenses that often escape or are beyond the reach of criminal law.
- Compensation for damages not normally compensable, such as hurt feelings, attorneys' fees, and expenses of litigation.
- The only effective means to force conscienceless defendants to cease practices known to be dangerous and which they would otherwise continue in the absence of an effective deterrent.

The Intentional Tort of Intrusion

Interference with the right to be "let alone" can be grouped into four categories: intrusion, appropriation of one's name or likeness, giving unreasonable publicity to private facts, and placing a person in a false light in the public eye. The latter three of these are founded upon improper publicity, usually in the public press or electronic media. They are beyond the scope of this concept and will not be discussed.

Intrusion is an intentional tort closely related to infliction of emotional distress. Both torts protect a person's interest in his mental tranquility or peace of mind. A person has a basic right to choose when and to what extent he will permit others to know his personal affairs. Essentially, intrusion is an intentional, improper, unreasonable, and offensive interference with the solitude, seclusion, or private life of another. It embraces a broad spectrum of activities. It may consist of an unauthorized entry, an illegal search or seizure, or an unauthorized eavesdropping, with or without electronic aids.

The tort is complete when the intrusion occurs. No publication or publicity of the information obtained is required. It is, of course, essential that the intrusion be into that which is, and is entitled to remain, private. Additionally, the harm must be substantial. The intrusion must be seriously objectionable, not simply bothersome or inconvenient.

John J. Fay

Source   Fay, J. 1987. *Butterworths Security Dictionary: Terms and Concepts*. Boston: Butterworth-Heinemann.

VI: Physical Security

ACCEPTANCE TESTING

Technology continues to advance and physical security systems advance with it. Today's security systems are becoming more and more complex. The introduction of information technology into physical security systems has made the pace of technological change so rapid that physical security components moving along the assembly line can almost become obsolete before they reach the shipping dock. In the rush to get products to end-users, some manufacturers begin shipping "the next version" of products and systems before they have been fully tested. This one fact alone is reason enough for end-users to require extensive testing of physical security systems prior to accepting them.

Does the System Work Correctly?

For the end-user the important issue is not whether each of the long list of security system features will work properly; the interest is in the specific system features that address the user's security needs. The important questions in the end-user's mind will be:

- Do the features of the system support my security objectives?
- Are these features set up correctly?
- Do these features operate correctly?
- Do they operate the way I expect them to operate?

The last three questions can only be answered by testing. What follows is a baseline of best practices for acceptance testing.

System Testing

System testing is a primary element of on-schedule and in-budget security system projects. The larger the project, the more critical the testing becomes—but testing is important in a project of any size. An electronic security system integrates multiple components such as alarms, access control, and CCTV. In some cases, the components were acquired from more than one manufacturer, yet they are interdependent and communicate with each other. A system can have almost any combination of components for the simple reason that almost all facilities have different security needs. A mix of components can also result from adding or changing out the components of an existing system.

A separate circumstance that affects testing is bringing a newly acquired system into operation before testing can be done or even started. This often occurs when installation of a new system runs behind schedule and a deadline must be met.

Scenario-Based Testing

A purpose of scenario-based testing is to ensure that the system will operate according to the organization's security plans and procedures such as those that deal with responses to various emergencies. This form of testing is also used to evaluate the system's efficiency under normal, routine conditions. An emergency scenario could be the simulation of a serious fire or an attempt to breach the facility's outer fence line. A routine scenario could be a test to determine if an access control point is capable of admitting a certain number of people in a certain length of time.

What to Test?

Testing can be defined as "a process of ascertaining if a certain thing will perform as expected." Expectations are determined by the user. The user prepares, often with help from a consultant, a written functional requirements document, which says in plain language what these expectations are.

The system provider uses this document to develop a complete specification and equipment list along with descriptive design information that explains how the offered products will meet or exceed expectations. Descriptive materials such as product brochures, data sheets, and specification sheets are usually included in proposals submitted with bids.

In the bidding context, the prospective client's expectations are clearly detailed in specifications that are given to the system provider.

Specifications can be expressed in a variety of documents:

- A functional requirements document.
- Architect and engineer (A&E) documentation. An A&E describes in technical terms the user's requirements. The system provider will make a strong argument that equipment capabilities perfectly match or exceed what the end-user wants.
- A hardware or equipment list that names certain products desired by the end-user.

The end-user clarifies the specifications with the use of a facility walk-through that allows the bidders to see where the system will be installed. Typically, the end-user will show where equipment is to be placed, for example: a console at a security control center, card readers on certain doors, motion detection sensors on a perimeter fence, or CCTV cameras on the top of a building.

If the system to be purchased is complex, a walk-through may not answer all of the bidders' questions. Further clarification can be made by the functional requirements document, which says in plain language what the system should do and how. A bidder can use the functional requirements document to develop a proposal that in part will use plain language to describe how the features of the proposed system will perform the needed functions.

There can be only one basis for testing the operation of a purchased and installed system. That basis is the written information given by the end-user to the system provider. If a system fails to meet a specification, the system provider is at fault; if a system fails to perform a function that is required but not stated in a specification, the end-user is at fault. An installed system is most likely to perform to the satisfaction of the end-user when the end-user has provided detailed, clear specifications.

Acceptance Testing Phases

Four phases of acceptance testing, plus ongoing operational testing, are recommended for a large multi-site physical security system. The tests are described as follows.

Factory Acceptance Test (FAT). A FAT is not necessarily conducted where system compon-

ents are manufactured. It can be done at an assembly facility or even at the end-user's facility. For this test, all of the major system components are assembled in one place. Although the final, installed system may extend to widely dispersed sites, the FAT will test the system in one manageable area. Using simulations, the test can evaluate the system's network, redundancy, backup/restore, and other functions. The purpose of the FAT is to ensure that the system works to the satisfaction of the provider and the end-user.

Some system providers will try to avoid the FAT because they believe it to be costly, time consuming, and unnecessary. Others will view the FAT as an opportunity to demonstrate system quality and efficiency. These system providers usually know their products well and have high confidence that the FAT will work to their advantage.

The FAT can be important to an end-user because it is the last chance to gain assurance about the critical elements of a system before installation work begins. Depending on contract specifications, the end-user can demand that any glitch, small or large, must be corrected by the system provider before the system can be said to have passed the FAT. A failure to correct a glitch in a pre-agreed time frame can be sufficient justification for the end-user to cancel the contract (a very rare occurrence).

As systems become more and more complex, the FAT becomes more and more important. However, given today's level of technological sophistication, there is little reason for a system to fail a FAT if the system provider performs the appropriate preparations and test setup.

Site Acceptance Test (SAT). The SAT is performed in the "field" and for that reason is sometimes called a field acceptance test. A SAT is used to test system components that are located apart from the main system. A single system can have multiple SATs. It is not uncommon for a SAT to be conducted on an ad hoc basis. The result will be dissatisfaction when an unscheduled SAT reveals problems that could have been avoided by prior planning.

System-Wide Acceptance Test (SWAT). The SWAT is performed after sub-systems at all sites are up and running. It consists of end-to-end testing under normal and emergency conditions. The central monitoring function is tested when all of the sub-systems are fully operational. In addition to scenario-based testing, the system is also subjected to maximum usage and worst-case conditions. This is extremely important for networked systems, especially security video systems. The network infrastructure must be managed to maintain the availability of the network bandwidth (amount of data the network can transmit) that is required by the security system for its highest anticipated network load even though day-today operations may only require a small portion of the larger network capacity. Where service companies provide a portion of the network infrastructure, benchmarking network requirements during the SWAT provides important input for network Service Level Agreement (SLA) requirements.

Operational Acceptance Test (OAT). This test, sometimes called a field reliability test, usually consists of inspections made of the system in operation over a 30-day period. The purpose of the OAT is to ensure that the system can operate reliably for an extended period of time. Performance exercises are included if normal operations are not expected to sufficiently challenge the system. The OAT can include SATs when other sites are part of the system.

Because the OAT is lengthy compared to other tests and uses a variety of testing techniques, it is fair to call it a test phase.

Ongoing System Operational Test (OSOT). This testing, like some others, has an alternate name; it is sometimes called ongoing maintenance testing. The OSOT is not a single specific test; it is testing performed periodically throughout the life of the system. Ideally, ongoing testing will also test system operators, such as security officers, and the plans and procedures that guide the operators.

The frequency of the periodic testing varies significantly from one facility to another. The cause of schedule variation can be a built-in system requirement, customer or regulatory requirements, or even factors related to a maintenance schedule. Frequency can also be related to the preference of management.

Testing Techniques

All of the previously described tests can be conducted using various techniques, the names of which indicate how the tests are conducted.

- Functionality Testing
- Security Scenario Testing
- Performance Testing
- Stress Testing
- Load and Capacity Testing
- Fault Tolerance Testing
- End-to-End System Testing

Physical security system testing is never simple and easy to do. When done properly, the payoff can be substantial such as savings that result from preventing security-related losses, productivity increases that result from facilitating the movement of people, vehicles, and property, cost reductions that result from automatically turning off lights and the HVAC system when they are not needed, and lastly, money saved by reducing the operating costs of the physical security system.

Ray Bernard and Don Sturgis

ACCESS CONTROL: PEOPLE, VEHICLES, AND MATERIALS

Access controls regulate the flow of people, vehicles, and materials into, out of, and within a protected facility. They apply to many categories of people: employees, visitors, contractors, vendors, service representatives, etc. Access controls apply to vehicles, such as employee automobiles entering and leaving parking lots, and trucks moving to and from shipping and delivery platforms.

Access controls can be applied to materials, such as raw goods moving to the production line and finished goods moving to the shipping department or warehouse. Although access controls are most often in place as a means for protecting assets (which include the people being regulated), they play an important part in facilitating movement in a manner that meets the operating needs of the protected facility.

People Control

Employees. The basic tool for controlling the movement of employees is an identification card. The use of an employee identification card depends on the number of employees and the sensitivity of the protected facility. A workplace with a few employees in a low security situation will not require an access control system or one that is elaborate in any meaningful respect. A location containing many employees will have difficulty operating without some form of access control. This will be especially true when there is a need also to control access to restricted areas within the protected facility. Large or small, simple or sophisticated, for the system to operate efficiently, it must be clearly understood by those affected by it and be supported by management.

Visitors. A variety of techniques are applicable to visitor access control; for example, a visitors lounge, appointments made in advance and registered with a receptionist, personal vouching by employees, positive identification of the visitor, search of items carried into the premises by the visitor, screening by metal detector, escort while on the premises, and temporary badges that self-destruct.

Relevant information collected at the time of issuing the badge would be the name of the visitor, date of visit, time entering and leaving, purpose, specific location visited, name of sponsoring/escorting employee, and temporary badge number. In a safety-sensitive environment, visitors may be required to be briefed and to wear special protective equipment, such as a helmet, safety glasses, robe, or steel-reinforced footwear. A record or log of visits is wise. In some situations, contact between employees and visitors should be discouraged; for example, on the loading dock where larcenous conspiracies may evolve between truck drivers and employees of the shipping and receiving departments.

Electronic Access. Systems for controlling access by use of electronic technology are appropriate in highly populated working environments and where asset protection is essential. The typical approach is to issue to each authorized person a sturdy key card that contains coded information capable of being read by electronic devices placed at the entry/exit points.

Three traditional types of key cards are the magnetically encoded card, the magnetic pulsing card, and the proximity card. The first has small magnets within the card. When the card is brought into contact with a reader device at the entry point door, the card's magnetically encoded data are transmitted to a computer processor. If the card's data corresponds to the access requirements, entry is granted; if not, entry is denied. Magnetic pulsing works in a fashion similar to the magnetically encoded card. Magnets and wires encased in the card emit positive and negative pulses that are sensed by the reader device at the entry point.

The proximity card contains circuits tuned to a radio frequency emitted by the reader at the point of entry. When the card is brought within the detection range of the radio frequency, the reader will sense the unique characteristics of the card and transmit these data to the computer. If the data meet the entry criteria, the lock mechanism at the entry point disengages. This type of key card is called a proximity card because it does not have to be brought into physical contact with a reader, such as by inserting or swiping, but by placing it in the proximity of the reader.

Then there are the biometric access control systems. They offer a variety of personal identification principles based on fingerprints, signature recognition, voice characteristics, retinal patterns, and hand geometry. Also available are applications that incorporate in a single system two or more biometric principles such as fingerprint, facial, and iris recognition.

Among the biometric choices, fingerprint systems are widely used. They work well and are relatively inexpensive to purchase and install. Also new in the marketplace are access control systems that use radio frequency identification (RFID) and so-called "spoof protection" that can trigger automatic responses to suspected intrusion attempts. To guard against compromise, the system itself can be protected with encrypting software.

Access control systems are used in many facilities such as airports, offices, computer centers, factories, special weapons depots, warehouses, jails, prisons, police stations, courthouses, Federal buildings, U.S. intelligence offices, border crossing points, and military installations. Many locations that are separated by great distances can be protected by a single system.

However, systems that record time and attendance are not control-oriented. The principal users are human resources and payroll departments.

In this category also are systems devoted to investigation. They are linked to closed circuit television systems that can help the user spot crimes in progress, identify the culprits, and visually demonstrate vulnerabilities that need to be eliminated. Forgery can be detected and the forger apprehended with a combination of signature recognition and a live-sensing and communicating capability.

Traffic Control

In comparison to people control, traffic control can be relatively simple yet extremely frustrating. This is because automobiles can, for some individuals, be an emotional issue. Where employees park and how they park, although uncomplicated, can be difficult to manage.

Traffic control at a protected facility can begin at points outside of the property line. Whether the control is administered by local police officers or security officers who have been deputized for the limited purposes of traffic control, the essential point is that some degree of influence can be brought to bear on vehicles before they cross the property line or enter the facility. Once inside the facility, control of vehicles can be enhanced through pre-designed roadway features such as gates, jersey barriers, median dividers, one-way travel, signage, traffic signals, and bollards. Uniformed security officers at traffic control points can be an added feature.

Multiple entrances, especially to restricted areas, can require multiple security officers. Management may decide that during times of high vehicle traffic, typically the morning and evening rush hours, normally closed entry/exit points at non-restricted areas can be opened without having an officer present at every one. Electrically operated gate arms can be set to automatically open during rush hours without presentation of access cards, and to operate in the normal mode during other hours.

From the standpoint of theft prevention, traffic control around the facility's loading dock is important. To ensure that the vehicles and drivers in the loading dock are there on legitimate business, the access control system may feature closed-circuit television (CCTV) cameras to monitor activity; a loading dock door that can be operated remotely from an interior location, such as the security center; an intercom for drivers to obtain notice of arrival and opening of the loading dock door; and the presence of a security officer to monitor and/or inspect departing cargo.

Traffic control may also involve control of vehicles moving within the protected facility. An out-of-doors holding area for cargo received at a seaport may, for example, have trucks and heavy loading and stacking machinery moving simultaneously throughout a relatively large and congested area. Control in this situation can be directed at both theft prevention and accident prevention.

Materials Control

An access control system can be engineered to regulate free movement and tracking of materials such as the mail, supplies and raw goods that feed the business, unfinished products being created within, and finished goods leaving. Included in this capability are the tools used by the business such as computers, manufacturing equipment, and vehicles.

Three physical security features have been found to be successful: metal-detectors at entrances, RFID or similar technologies that monitor materials moving inside the facility, and controlled barriers at exits.

Inspection of Entering Packages. This method of access control is intended to prevent introduction to the premises of dangerous or undesirable items such as bombs and handguns. Packages are inspected visually and with devices such as metal detectors and x-ray machines. The inspection point is usually a gate outside the blast zone (that area in which property and life are at risk from an explosion). Packages can be briefcases, purses, backpacks, mail bags, and courier-delivered containers.

Inspection is usually made by security officers that have been trained in how to use detection equipment, spot the visual indicators of bombs and chemical/biological agents, evacuate people, and notify first-responders. Ideally, the place of inspection will be isolated and if indoors will be entirely enclosed and have its own air conditioning system. Inspection will be focused on detecting mass destruction weapons and may include attention to other undesirable items such as illegal drugs and alcohol.

Accounting for Property Removed. In this method, the employer is attempting to exercise control of company-owned property leaving the protected facility. The arrangement usually involves cooperation between supervisory personnel and the security officer force. Supervisors authorize subordinates to remove company property from the premises for a business-related purpose, such as taking a personal computer home to work on a word processing project, and security officers inspect departing property to insure that removal authority has been given. Typically, a property removal pass, signed by the supervisor, describes the property to be removed; the supervisor keeps a copy of the pass; the employee presents the original and a copy of the pass to the security officer at the exit point; the security officer compares the pass against the property, retains the copy of the pass, and allows the employee to proceed; and the security department holds its copy of the pass as a record of property having left the premises. When the employee returns the property, the supervisor signs and files the original copy held by the employee.

Inspection of Departing Vehicles. This method is also intended to control removal of company property. In some industries, removal of property is based on safety considerations such as in the chemicals industry where the taking of a toxic chemical would constitute a hazard to public safety. Whatever the industry and whatever the reason for making inspections, management will have observed certain necessary prerequisites: ensuring that the inspection program will not violate laws, contracts, or agreements with a bargaining unit or the employees; ensuring that the employees, visitors, or others affected by the inspection program have been informed; and training the security officers to conduct the inspections in a manner that will not violate constitutional protections and reasonable standards of fairness and privacy.

Management may decide that inspection need not be made of all departing vehicles but at an inspection rate high enough to discourage attempts to leave the premises with restricted material. When this option is taken, the method for selecting the vehicles to be inspected is based on random selection. If the objective is to inspect 20 percent of departing vehicles, a random selecting device at the exit point will keep count and an enunciator, such as a horn, will let the security

officer know that that the next vehicle should be inspected. A driver immediately behind a vehicle undergoing an inspection has no assurance that his vehicle will not be inspected.

John J. Fay

ALARM SYSTEM MANAGEMENT

Alarms are tools that make security incident response possible. Management of alarms is shared by the chief security officer (CSO) and the end user, i.e., the CSO's employer. A third player is the alarm consultant, a person with expertise in designing an alarm system, integrating it with other systems, and solving problems that arise.

The CSO is concerned with:

- Ensuring that the alarm system meets the security needs of the organization.
- Ensuring that the alarm system operates in harmony with other systems.
- Ensuring that the alarm system's components are of high quality, installed correctly, and perform as intended.
- Ensuring that the alarm system does not interfere with business operations.
- Ensuring that the costs to purchase and maintain the alarm remain within the boundaries of the budget.
- Ensuring that the alarm system is cost-effective, i.e., that the value of benefits derived from the system are at least equal to the costs of the system.

The Human Component

The effectiveness of an alarm system cannot exceed the competency of the persons that monitor and operate it. Included in the word "competency" is (1) knowing the purpose of the system and its functional arrangement; (2) knowing how to turn the system on and off and how to correct minor, anticipated glitches; and (3) knowing the meaning of alarm signals, i.e., differentiating between fire, intrusion, duress, and touching or tampering.

The enemy of competency is lack of knowledge. Too often, alarms are misinterpreted, resulting in a failure to initiate a response when response was essential or initiating a response inappropriate to the alarm-reported condition. Misinterpretation can occur, for example, when the system operator thinks that a signal indicating an open door to a restricted area is the result of an employee propping the door open and for that reason ignores the signal, or when the system operator initiates a full-blown response when the signal was clearly the result of a nuisance such as a small animal tripping an intrusion sensor on the outer perimeter.

When a security program is in effect at a protected facility, the system operators are almost always security officers. This places a responsibility on the alarm system designer and/or installer to thoroughly teach the officers how to operate the system prior to final acceptance of it. The CSO's responsibility is to ensure that security officers are proficient in system operation prior to and following acceptance.

Alarm Points

Alarm point is a misnomer because an alarm is the result of a sensor activating. For example, a smoke detector will activate when it detects smoke indicative of fire. Activation of the detector sends a signal. The signal is the alarm and the signal is manifested in a way that can be registered by humans. The ululating sound of a siren is registered in the human consciousness as a message that says fire is nearby. A flashing red light on a console tells the alarm system controller that an intrusion has occurred or that something which should not be touched has been touched.

Alarm points are essentially substitutes for security officers. If a certain place requires protection, such as a door that provides access to valuable property, the CSO can either place a guard at the door or install an alarm point at the door. The less expensive of the two options is the alarm point. Qualitative differences are arguable.

The selection of an alarm point is influenced by:

- Normal operations of the protected organization, i.e., an alarm should not interfere with the orderly conduct of work.
- A protection need, e.g., a critical asset that needs to be protected against theft, damage, or destruction.
- A detection need, e.g., a place that presents an opportunity for unauthorized entry.
- A safety need, e.g., fire sprinklers in a high-rise office building.

An alarm point is often an element of a physical safeguard or countermeasure. A fence is a physical safeguard. A vibration sensor mounted on a fence is an alarm point. Alarm points can be coded to facilitate human understanding, and the codes can be associated with zones. For example, the northeast section of an out-of-doors storage area has three alarm points. The codes for the alarm points are NE-1, NE-2, and NE-3. A map viewable to the alarm system operator depicts the precise locations of the alarm points. In another example, a protected building has alarm points on doors, windows, and interior rooms. The code for the main entrance door is D-1, the rear door D-2, etc. A window on the 2nd floor is 2W-1 and a room on the 3rd floor 3R-1. Using codes in lieu of geographic descriptions helps the system operator communicate quickly and accurately when dispatching a response unit and the response unit is aided in figuring out which asset may be in jeopardy.

Further, in the case of intrusion, an alarm point activated at a particular spot on a fence line, followed by an alarm point activated at a particular spot inside the fence line, followed by an alarm point activated at the entry point to a particular building can possibly reveal to the alarm system operator the path of the intruder and the speed at which the intruder is moving.

The locations of alarm points correspond to the organization's overall security plan. They do not determine the design of the plan; the opposite is true. From the point of view that the vulnerability assessment process determines the security plan, the security plan incorporates countermeasures that offset vulnerabilities. In turn, countermeasures incorporate alarms.

Alarm Communication and Display

The heading of this section means exactly what it says: an alarm is communicated and it is displayed. Communication begins when a sensor activates, it moves to a computer that assesses the activation, and communication ends when the assessment reaches the monitoring station such as a security control center. Display is the presentation of information to the alarm system operator in a meaningful format.

A meaningful format could be a red light on a panel board, with red meaning that a sensor has activated; a yellow light meaning that a certain sensor is in the off mode; and green meaning that the sensor is active and stable. The positioning of lights on the panel and/or adjacent labels can indicate the type of alarm and its location.

The format, whatever it may be, has to tell the operator: (1) the nature of the alarm, (2) the place where the alarm went off, and (3) when the alarm happened.

Communication from the sensor to the monitoring station moves through a wire or fiber-optic cable. (A wireless connection may be acceptable in a low-security situation. When wireless technology reaches a level of reliability equal to hard wires, it will be suitable for high-security situations. When that point is reached, hard wires will go the way of the dinosaur.)

An alarm system is worthless if the wire or cable is severed. It does not matter if the break is accidental or intentional, the effect is the same. To guard against a break, the wire or cable needs to run inside a conduit and, if possible, the conduit should be buried. Because sensors tend to be added later, it makes sense to place extra wires and cables inside the conduit when the system is initially installed.

A function called line supervision monitors the link between the sensor and the monitoring station. A break in the link or an indication of tampering sends a warning signal to the system operator. Supervision can be static or dynamic. In static supervision, a secure condition is represented when a supervising signal remains constant. In dynamic supervision, a secure condition is represented when the supervising signal is continually changing.

Assessment

A secure communicating method is essential, so also are qualitative characteristics of the information being transported. These include:

- Quantity of data.
- Reliability that the data will reach the assessing computer intact and uncontaminated.
- Speed at which the data moves.

The assessing computer analyzes the alarm data and sends to the monitoring station the appropriate message, which could be a report of fire in the southwest quadrant of the 16th floor or interruption of a photoelectric beam in Room 304 or the pressing of a duress button in the executive suite. The assessing computer can send messages to display devices in multiple locations within the protected facility and to outside locations such as the fire department, police department, or medical emergency agency.

The Alarm History File

A step in managing an alarm system is to set up and maintain a file that records the history of alarm initiations. The file is maintained by the CSO or a person responsible to the CSO. The file is organized so that each alarm has an individual record. A record will reflect:

- When the alarm went off.
- The sensor that triggered the alarm.
- The cause of the alarm.
- Actions taken in response to the alarm.
- The name of the system operator when the alarm went off.

The CSO's examination of the file might reveal:

- Alarms and/or sensors that are in need of calibration, repair, or replacement.
- Malfunctioning ancillary equipment such as a lock that will not fully engage.
- Alarms and/or sensors that do not operate well due to environmental conditions such as extreme temperatures, rain, heavy winds, and ground vibrations.
- A frequency of enunciation indicating that an alarm is asynchronous to the security program; for example, a receiving dock door that is in the active alarm mode when the dock is in use.
- A correlation between alarm frequency and the identity of the person operating the alarm system at that time.
- A correlation between alarm frequency and a security operation; for example, an alarm that activates whenever a roving patrol passes nearby.
- A discrepancy between the criticality of the alarm and the nature of the response.
- A discrepancy between the performance of an alarm and the alarm manufacturer's

and/or the alarm system designer's representations.
- Poor alarm performance at highly critical locations.

The alarm history file can include multiple forms of documentation such as security department incident reports, complaint reports from end-user employees, and computer printouts generated whenever an alarm is activated.

John J. Fay

Source Garcia, M. 2001. *The Design and Evaluation of Physical Protection Systems*. Boston: Butterworth-Heinemann.

BURIED LINE SENSORS

Buried line sensors protect an area along the ground just above the sensor transducer cable or sensors by detecting anyone crossing the protected zone. Someone who crosses the sensitive area induces both seismic energy and exerts pressure in the ground. Buried sensors are available that detect strain and seismic energy. Another type of buried line sensor is available that detects the presence of ferrous metals being carried or worn by the person crossing the transducer cable, as well as detecting local induced pressure.

Piezoelectric transducers are used primarily to detect short-range pressure disturbances in the ground, and geophones are primarily used to detect longer-range seismic waves. These are basically the same devices used for the fence disturbance sensor transducers, and in some cases they are the same device.

Geophone Transducers

Buried geophones detect the low-frequency seismic energy induced in the ground by someone crossing the protected area above the sensors, and convert this energy into electrical signals. The electrical signals correspond to the frequency of the induced seismic energy, and they are proportional in amplitude to the magnitude of the energy. These induced signals are sent to the signal processor, where they are filtered before entering the signal processor. The band-pass of the filter corresponds to the seismic energies with frequencies or signatures typical of someone crossing the geophone sensors. When the characteristics of the induced signals satisfy the processor alarm criteria, an alarm is initiated.

A geophone consists of a movable spring-balanced coil of fine wire suspended around a permanent magnet. The coil of fine wire is cylindrical to slide over the magnetic rod fixed to the geophone housing. When the geophone is acted upon by the seismic energy, the permanent magnet vibrates with the geophone housing at the frequency of the induced energy. The vibrating magnet moves in line with the coil of fine wire, which tends to stay near rest. It stays near rest because the fine spring holding the wire coil in suspension around the magnet offers very little resistance to the moving geophone housing. As the magnet vibrates in the coil, the magnetic lines of force associated with the permanent magnet induce an electromotive force (emf) in the coil. This emf, or electrical signal, is the signal that is monitored by the signal processor.

Geophones are very sensitive to detecting even low-level seismic energies generated by moving objects anchored in the ground such as trees, fences, light poles, or telephone poles. When these objects are subjected to wind loads, the overturning forces are absorbed by the ground. As the winds vary, the objects move, inducing seismic energy in the ground. To help reduce the need for the signal processor to differentiate between these energies and valid intrusion signals, the geophones should be installed a reasonable distance from this type of object. A reasonable distance is difficult to define because of all the varying parameters in any given installation. However, the following minimum distances can be used as guides: about 30 feet from tree-drip line, 10 feet from fences, and a distance about equal to the height of the light pole or telephone pole away from the pole.

Piezoelectric Transducers

Piezoelectric transducers detect the stresses or pressure induced in the ground by anyone crossing the protected area above the sensor line. The transducer consists of a quartz crystal that is secured to the transducer case such that when an external pressure is applied to the transducer the crystal generates a voltage. In operation, when someone steps on the ground above the transducer, the pressure from the person's weight stresses the piezoelectric crystal. The stressed crystal generates an electrical signal that is proportional to the applied pressure. When the characteristics of the signal satisfy the processor alarm criteria, an alarm is initiated.

Strain/Magnetic Line Sensors

The combined strain and magnetic line sensors detect both the pressure or strain induced in the ground by someone crossing the sensor line and the presence of ferrous material carried or worn by the person crossing. The sensor consists of a passive transducer cable and an alarm electronics module. The passive transducer cable uses a magnetic material wound with a pair of sense coil windings. This assembly is wrapped with a stainless steel jacket and covered with an outer plastic jacket. The two sense windings are wound on the magnetic core and connected together in a manner to cancel far-field seismic and magnetic disturbances.

In operation, the residual flux density of the ferromagnetic core material and the flux density of the earth's magnetic field remain constant during normal circumstances. The weight of anyone crossing the sensitive area above the transducer cable stresses the ferromagnetic core material. The induced stress alters the magnetic flux that

generates a voltage in the sense winding overlay around the coil. A voltage is also induced in the sense winding when someone crosses the transducer cable carrying or wearing ferrous material. In this case, the ferrous materials distort the earth's magnetic field. The changing magnetic field alters the coil magnetic flux density, generating a voltage in the sense winding. Signals resulting from either the mechanical stresses or from the presence of ferrous materials, or these combined signals, are processed and analyzed by the signal processor in the alarm electronics module. Before the signal is analyzed and when their characteristics satisfy the established alarm criteria, an alarm is initiated. The purpose of the dual-channel signal processing is to reduce false alarms from wind and electrical interference.

Robert L. Barnard

Source   Barnard, R. 1988. *Intrusion Detection Systems, 2nd Edition*. Boston: Butterworth-Heinemann.

CCTV: CAMERAS FOR SECURITY

The closed-circuit television (CCTV) camera's function is to convert the focused visual (or infrared) light image from the camera lens into a time-varying electrical video signal that contains the intelligence in the scene image. The lens

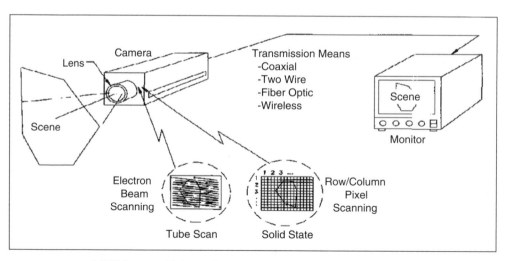

CCTV System with Lens, Camera, Transmission Means, and Monitor

Figure 16.   This diagram shows how scene images are captured, processed, and sent to a monitoring station.

collects the reflected light from the scene and focuses it onto the camera image sensor. The camera processes the information from the sensor and sends it to a viewing monitor via coaxial cable or other transmission means.

There are two generic types of CCTV sensors: (1) tube and (2) solid-state. The solid-state type represents the majority of existing security installations. The tube cameras use electron beam scanning techniques while the solid-state cameras use the charge coupled device (CCD) or the complementary metal-oxide device (CMOS) sensor.

Camera Scanning Function

The monochrome or color television camera in the security CCTV system analyzes the scene by scanning it in a series of closely spaced lines in the case of a tube camera, or picture elements (pixels) in the case of a solid-state camera. This technique generates the codes and electrical signal as a function of time so that the scene can later be reconstructed on the monitor.

Unlike film cameras or the human eye, or low-light-level television image intensifiers that see a complete picture one frame at a time, a television camera sees an image point by point until it scans the entire scene. In this respect the television scan is similar to the action of a typewriter where the type element starts at the upper left-hand corner of the page, moves across the page to the right-hand corner, and in this way a single line of type is completed. The typewriter carriage then returns to the left-hand side of the paper, moves down to the third line (skips a line), and starts over again. At the left-hand side the typewriter carriage again moves from the left to the right, typing out another line, then returns and moves down again, with this action continuing until the typewriter has reached the bottom of the page. This completes one field or half the television picture. If the page is then moved back so that the typewriter begins typing on the second line at the left just below the first line and the same action continues again, moving down two lines at a time, each line in-between the originally typed lines is filled in, and by the time the typewriter gets to the bottom of the page, the full page is completely typed. This completes two fields and is equivalent to one full video frame.

Scanning is accomplished in the tube camera, through the use of magnetic or electrostatic deflection of an electron beam whereas in the solid-state camera electrical clocking circuits are used to scan the sensor pixel array.

The television camera consists of: (1) an image sensor, (2) some form of electrical scanning system with synchronization, (3) timing electronics, (4) video amplifying and processing electronics, and (5) video signal synchronizing and combining electronics to produce a composite video output signal. The camera has synchronizing signals so that a monitor, a recorder, a printer, or other CCTV routing or processing equipment can be synchronized to produce a stable display or recording.

In operation, the lens forms a focused image on the camera sensor. In the tube camera the television picture is formed by extracting the light information on the target area as the electron beam moves across the light-sensitive area of the tube in a process called linear (or raster) scanning. The entire picture is called a frame and is composed of two fields. Each frame contains 525 horizontal lines in the U.S. National Television System Committee (NTSC) system based on the 60-Hz power line frequency and duration of 1/30 second per frame (30 frames/second). The European system, based on a 50-Hz power line frequency, has 625 horizontal lines and 1/25 second per frame. In the NTSC system the electron beam scans the picture area twice, with each scan producing a field. Each field contains 262-1/2 television lines with the two fields producing a complete frame having 525 television lines total. A 2:1 interlaced scanning technique is used to reduce the amount of flicker in the picture and improve motion display. This scanning mode is called two-field, odd-line scanning.

For the solid-state camera, in place of the moving electron beam in the tube, the light-induced charge in the individual sites—picture elements (pixels)—in the sensor are clocked out of the sensor into the camera electronics. The time-varying video signal from the individual pixels clocked out in the horizontal rows and vertical columns generate the two interlaced fields.

Sensor Types

The most popular tube type sensor used for many years was the vidicon. Now the most popular type cameras use solid-state type sensors: charge transfer devices (CTD), charge coupled device (CCD) and complementary metal-oxide semi-conductor (CMOS), and charge injection device (CID) solid-state types. The most widely used are the CCD and the CMOS.

In LLL applications these tube and solid-state sensors are combined with image intensifiers to produce the silicon intensified target (SIT), intensified SIT (ISIT), and intensified CCD (ICCD) cameras. The most commonly used is the ICCD.

Solid-State Cameras

The solid-state camera uses a silicon array of photo-sensor sites (pixels) to convert the input light image into an electronic video signal, which is then amplified and passed on to a monitor for display.

Most solid-state sensors fall into the category of devices called charge transfer devices (CTD), which can be subdivided into three groups depending on the manufacturing technology used: (1) charge coupled device (CCD), (2) complementary metal-oxide semiconductor (CMOS), (3) charge priming device (CPD), and (4) charge injection device (CID). By far the most popular devices used in security camera applications are the CCD and CMOS. The CID is reserved primarily for military and industrial applications. The solid-state imaging devices used in security CCTV applications are small, light weight, rugged, and consume low power.

Solid-State Sensor

The solid-state sensor CCTV camera performs a function similar to that of the tube camera, but the sensor and scanning system is significantly different. It has no electron beam scanning of the visual image on the sensor area, and an area array of pixels replaces the camera tube. The typical sensor has hundreds of pixels in the horizontal and vertical directions equivalent to several hundred thousand pixels over the sensor area. A pixel is the smallest sensing element located on the sensor that converts the light energy into an electrical charge and signal.

Scanning and Timing. The CCD imager works by a process called charge coupling. It is the collective transfer of the electrical charges produced by the image stored in the CCD storage element (pixel) and moved to an adjacent storage element by the use of external synchronizing or clocking voltages that, in effect, push out the signal, line by line, at a precisely determined clocked time and produce the video signal. The signal represents the light intensity at each pixel location, which is the intelligence in the picture.

Typical device parameters for a CCD available in the market today are 488 by 380 pixels (horizontal × vertical) in formats of 1/4-, and 1/3-inch, in a 4 × 3 (H × V) aspect-ratio television presentation.

The CMOS-type sensor exhibits high picture quality but has a lower sensitivity than the CCD. In the CMOS device the electric signals are read out directly through an array of MOS transistor switches, rather than line by line as in the CCD sensor.

The CID device differs from all other solid-state devices in that any of the pixels can be addressed or scanned in a random scan sequence rather than in the row/column sequence used in the other sensors. The advantage of this capability has not been realized in the security field but is used in industrial and military applications where non-raster scan sequences or patterns offer advantages.

Most CCD image sensors have wide spectral ranges and are usually useful over the entire visible range and into the near infrared (IR) spectral region above 800 to 900 nanometers.

One of the significant advantages of charge coupled image sensors over vacuum tube sensors is the precise geometric location of the pixels with respect to one another. In a camera tube the video is "read" from a photosensitive material by a scanning electron beam.

The position of the beam is never precisely known because of some uncertainty in the sweep circuits resulting from random electrical noise, variations in power supply voltage, or other variations.

CCTV Resolution

CCTV resolution is a critical measure of the television picture quality; the higher the resolution, the higher the level of information.

CCTV resolution is measured by the number of horizontal and vertical television lines that can be discerned in the monitor picture.

The U.S. NTSC standard provides a full video frame composed of 525 lines, with 504 lines for the image, and a vertical blanking interval composed of the remaining 21 retrace lines. The television industry has adopted the practice of specifying horizontal resolution in television lines per picture height. The horizontal resolution on the monitor tube depends on how fast the electron beam can change its intensity as it traces the image on a horizontal line.

With the 525-line NTSC system, the maximum vertical resolution achievable in any CCTV system is approximately 353 television lines. The 625-line system can produce a maximum vertical resolution of 438 television lines. While the vertical resolution is determined solely by the number of lines chosen (U.S. standard 525 lines), the horizontal resolution is dependent upon the electrical performance bandwidth of the individual camera, transmission, and monitor system.

Most standard cameras with a 4.5-MHz bandwidth produce a horizontal resolution of 550 television lines. The traditional method of testing and presenting CCTV resolution test results is to use the Electronic Industry Association (EIA) resolution target.

One comparison made between the solid-state and tube camera is resolution, i.e., how much detail is seen in the picture. The resolution for a good tube security camera is 500 to 600 television lines. Solid-state data sheets often quote the number of picture elements (pixels) instead of television lines of resolution. However, unless the number of horizontal pixels is converted into equivalent television lines, the horizontal resolution is not known.

To approximate the horizontal resolution from the horizontal pixel count, multiply the number of horizontal pixels by 0.75. Only recently have solid-state sensors been available that can match the resolution of average tube cameras.

Low-Light-Level Sensors

LLL cameras such as the SIT, ISIT, and ICCD share many of the characteristics of the tube and solid-state types described previously but include means to respond to much smaller light levels found in scenes illuminated by natural moonlight, starlight, or some other very LLL artificial illumination. These cameras use image intensifiers coupled to imaging tubes or solid-state sensors, and can amplify the available light up to 50,000 times and view scenes hundreds to thousands of feet from the camera under nighttime conditions. Complete SIT tube and ICCD camera systems have sufficient sensitivity and automatic light compensation to be used in surveillance applications from full sunlight to overcast moonlight conditions.

The ICCD camera is a new LLL camera class whose sensitivity approaches that of the best SIT cameras and eliminates the blurring characteristics of the SIT under very LLL conditions. The ICCD camera combines a tube or micro-channel plate (MCP) intensifier with a CCD image sensor to provide a sensitivity similar to that of an SIT camera.

For dawn and dusk outdoor illumination, the best CCD cameras can barely produce a usable video signal. SIT and ICCD cameras can operate under the light of one-fourth moon with one 0.001 foot candle (FtCd) of illumination. The ISIT camera can produce an image from only 0.0001 FtCd, which is the light available from stars on a moonless night. SIT, ISIT, and ICCD offer a 100 to 1,000 times improvement in sensitivity over the best CCD cameras because these cameras intensify light whereas the tube and CCD cameras only detect it. By contrast, the best CCD camera has a minimum sensitivity of 0.00093 FtCd.

Format Sizes

There are four existing image format sizes for solid-state and tube sensors. These are 1/4-, 1/3-, 1/2-, and 2/3-inch. All sensor formats have a horizontal × vertical geometry of 4 × 3 (H × V) aspect ratio as defined in the EIA and NTSC standards. For a given lens, the 1/4-inch format sensor sees the smallest scene image (smallest angular field of view) and the 2/3-inch sees the largest. The 1/4- and 1/3-inch solid-state formats are presently the most popular, with the direction going toward the smaller sensors. The SIT tube cameras using the 1-inch tube to provide LLL capabilities are likewise being replaced by their solid-state counterpart, the ICCD.

Color Cameras

Solid-state color cameras developed for the consumer video cassette recorder (VCR) and camcorder use a single solid-state sensor with an integral three-color filter and automatic white balancing circuits. These sensors incorporated into a CCTV camera provide a stable, long-life color camera with good sensitivity suitable for indoor and outdoor security application.

There are presently two techniques to produce the color video signal from the image sensor produced by the color visual image from the lens: (1) single sensor and (2) triple sensor with prism. Most color cameras used in the security industry are of the single sensor type. The single sensor camera has a complex color imaging sensor with three integral optical filters on the image sensor to produce the three primary colors—red, green, and blue (R, G, B). These colors are sufficient to reproduce all the colors in the visible spectrum.

Solid-state CCD and MOS color cameras are available in 1/3-, 1/2-, and 2/3-inch formats. Most of those used in security applications have single-chip sensors with three-color stripe filters integral with the image sensor. Typical color sensitivities for these cameras range from 0.7 to 1.4 FtCd (7 to 15 lux) for full video, which is less sensitive than their monochrome counterpart. The resolution of most color cameras ranges from 350 to 410 television lines.

Cameras with higher resolutions of 420 to 470 television lines are available for use with the higher resolution digital video recorders (DVR), S-VHS, and Hi-8 (8-millimeter) recorders. Color cameras with a 1/2-inch format producing 250 to 350 television line resolution require an array with 780 (H) × 490 (V) (380,000 pixels).

Most color cameras incorporate automatic white balance compensation as an integral part of the camera so that when the camera is initially turned on, it properly balances its color circuits to a white background as determined by the type of light illuminating the scene. The camera constantly checks the white balance circuitry and makes any minor compensation for variations in the illumination color temperature (spectrum of colors in the scene it is viewing).

The availability of solid-state color cameras has made a significant impact on the security CCTV industry. Color cameras provide enhanced television surveillance because of the increased ability to identify objects and persons when using color rather than monochrome.

Lens Mounts

All security cameras have a lens mount in front of the sensor to mechanically couple whatever objective lens or optical system is used to image the scene onto the camera.

The two widely used lens mounts in the CCTV industry are the C and CS mounts. Until recently, all 1-, 2/3-, and 1/2-inch cameras used an industry standard mount to couple the lens to the camera called the C mount. This camera mount has a 1-inch diameter hole with 32 threads per inch (TPI). The lens has a matching thread (1-32 TPI) that screws into the camera thread. The distance between the lens rear mounting surface and the image sensor for the C mount is 0.69 inches (17.526 millimeters).

A second new mount adopted by the CCTV industry for 1/3- and 1/2-inch sensor format cameras is the CS mount, in which the camera has a 1-inch diameter hole with a 32 TPI thread (same as the C mount) and the lens has a matching thread. The distance between the lens rear-mounting surface and the image sensor for the CS mount is, however, 0.492 inches (12.5 millimeters), which is 5 millimeters (0.2 inches) shorter than for the C mount. This shorter distance means that the lens collecting light for the sensor is closer to the sensor by 5 millimeters and can be made smaller in diameter for an equivalent FOV.

A C mount lens can be used on a CS mount camera if a 5-millimeter spacer is interposed between the lens and the camera, and the lens format covers the camera format size. The advantage of the CS mount system is that the lens is smaller, lighter, and less expensive than its C mount counterpart.

Herman A. Kruegle

CCTV: COVERT TECHNIQUES

Overt closed-circuit television (CCTV) security equipment is installed in full view of the public, and is used to observe action in an area while simultaneously letting the public know that CCTV surveillance is occurring. This technique often has the effect of deterring crime. Covert CCTV is used so that the offender is not aware he or she is under surveillance and to produce a permanent recording on a digital video recorder (DVR) or a video cassette recorder (VCR), for later use in confronting, dismissing, or prosecuting the person committing the offense. The covert camera and lens are out of view of anyone in the area under surveillance, and therefore unsuspecting violators are viewed on CCTV, their actions recorded, and often are apprehended while committing the illegal act. Although the camera uses small optics and is hidden, the result can be a high-quality CCTV picture of the area and activity.

An independent reason for using covert CCTV is to avoid changing the architectural aesthetics of a building or surrounding area. Covert CCTV cameras are concealed in common room objects or are located behind a small hole in an opaque barrier such as a wall or ceiling. Cameras are camouflaged in common objects such as lamps and lamp fixtures, table and wall clocks, radios, books, etc. A very effective covert system uses a camera and lens camouflaged in a ceiling-mounted sprinkler head.

A small-diameter front lens can view a scene through a 1/16-inch diameter hole. These lenses have a medium to wide field of view (FOV) from 12 to 78 degrees to cover a large scene area, but still permit identification of persons, and monitoring activities and actions. Other special pinhole lens variations include right angle, automatic iris, sprinkler head, and fiber optic, and small pinhole cameras combining a mini-lens and sensor into a small camera head and other complete miniature cameras.

In low-light-level (LLL) applications, a charge coupled device (CCD) camera with a very sensitive sensor and infrared (IR) light source or an image intensifier are used. Since many covert installations are temporary, wireless transmission systems are used to send the CCTV camera signal to the monitor, VCR, or video printer.

CCTV lens and camera concealment is accomplished by having the lens view through a small hole, a series of small holes, or from behind a semi-transparent window.

A number of suitable lens and camera locations include: (1) ceiling, (2) wall, (3) lamp

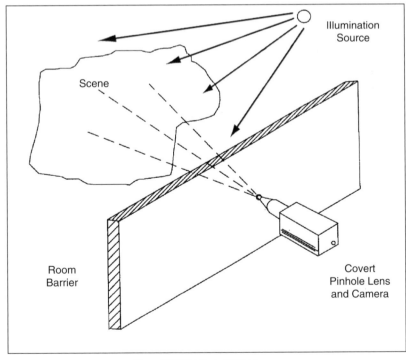

Covert CCTV Surveillance

Figure 17. A CCTV camera hidden behind a wall can reveal and record suspicious activities.

fixture, (4) furniture, and (5) other articles normally found in a room. CCTV cameras are installed in one or more locations in the room, depending on the activity expected.

Since the diameter of the front lens viewing the scene must, by necessity, be small to hide it, these lenses are optically fast, and collect and transmit as much light as possible from the reflected scene to the television sensor. As a consequence, small-diameter lenses, referred to as pinhole lenses, are used. The term pinhole is a misnomer, as these lenses have a front diameter anywhere from 1/8 to 1/2 inch.

The lens/camera requirement is to receive reflected light from an illuminated scene, have the lens collect and transmit the light to the camera sensor, and then transmit the video signal to a video monitor and/or VCR and video printer.

The hole in the barrier is usually chosen to be the same diameter (d) or smaller than the pinhole lens-front lens element. When space permits, the straight-type installation is used. In confined or restricted locations with limited depth behind the barrier, the right-angle pinhole lens/camera is used. In both cases to obtain the full lens FOV, it is imperative that the pinhole lens-front lens element be located as close to the front of the barrier as possible to avoid "tunneling" (vignetting). When the pinhole lens-front element is set back from the barrier surface, the lens is, in effect, viewing through a tunnel, and the image as viewed on the camera sensor has a narrower FOV than the lens can produce. This is seen on the monitor as a porthole-like (vignetted) picture.

Pinhole Lenses

Pinhole lenses and cameras can be mounted behind a wall, with the lens viewing through a small hole in the wall. A generic characteristic for almost all pinhole-type lenses is that they invert the video picture and therefore the camera must be inverted to get a normal right-side-up picture. Some right-angle pinhole lenses reverse the image right to left and therefore require an electronic scan reversal unit to regain the correct left-to-right orientation.

Pinhole lenses have been manufactured for many years in a variety of focal lengths (FL) (3.8, 4, 5.5, 6, 8, 9, 11 millimeters), in straight, right angle, manual-, and automatic-iris configurations.

The focal length (FL) of most of these lenses can be doubled to obtain one-half the FOV by using a 2× extender. The 16- and 22-millimeter FL are achieved by using a 2× magnifier on the 8- and 11-millimeter lenses, between the lens and the camera. This automatically doubles the optical speed or f/number (F/#) of each lens (halves the optical speed). In many applications, the required FL and configuration are not known in advance, and the user must have a large assortment of pinhole lenses, or take the risk that the job will be done using an incorrect lens. This dilemma has been solved with the availability of a Pinhole Lens Kit.

With this kit of pinhole lens parts, eight different FL lenses can be assembled in either a straight or right-angle configuration in minutes. An additional four combinations can be assembled for a disguised sprinkler head covert application. All lenses have a manual iris (automatic-iris optional).

Mini-Lenses

Mini-lenses are small fixed focal length (FFL) objective lenses used for covert surveillance when space is at a premium. The lenses will typically have focal lengths of 3.8, 5.5, 8, and 11 millimeters and front barrel diameters between 3/8 and 1/2 inch, making them easy to mount behind a barrier or in close quarters. These small lenses do not have an iris, and therefore, should be used in applications where the scene light level does not vary widely or with shuttered cameras. Mini-lenses, like other FFL lenses and unlike standard pinhole lenses, do not invert the image on the camera.

Mini-lenses have only three to six optical lens elements, fast optical speeds of f/1.4 to f/1.8. Pinhole lenses, on the other hand, are 3 to 5 inches long, and have as many as 10 to 20 optical elements and optical speeds of f/2.0 to f/4.0. This makes the mini-lens approximately five times faster (five times more light) than the pinhole lens.

Small Covert Camera

The most compact covert CCTV installation uses a flat board CCD camera and integral mini-lens. The complete camera is only 1.38 × 1.38 × 2.2

inches long. The 11-millimeter FL lens extends 0.3 inches in front of the camera. The camera operates directly from 12-volt DC, requires only 2.5 watts of power, and produces a standard composite video output.

Sprinkler Head Pinhole Lens

A very effective covert system uses a camera and lens camouflaged in a ceiling-mounted sprinkler head. Of the large variety of covert lenses available for the security television industry (pinhole, mini, fiber-optic), this unique lens hides the pinhole lens in a ceiling sprinkler fixture, making detection of it extremely difficult for an observer standing at floor level. This unique combination of pinhole lens and overhead ceiling-mounted sprinkler head provides an extremely useful covert surveillance television system.

The covert surveillance sprinkler installed in the ceiling in no way affects the operation of the active fire suppression sprinkler system; however, it should not be installed in locations that have no sprinkler system so as not to give the false impression to fire and safety personnel that there is a real and active sprinkler system.

The only portion of the system visible from below is the standard sprinkler head and the small (3/8 × 5/8 inch) mirror assembly. In operation, light from the scene reflects off the small mirror which directs it to the front of the pinhole lens. The 11- or 22-millimeter pinhole lens in turn transmits and focuses the light onto the camera sensor. The small mirror can be adjusted in elevation to point at different scene heights. To point in a particular azimuth direction, the entire camera-sprinkler lens assembly is rotated with the mirror pointing in the direction of the scene of interest.

If the sprinkler head assembly is removed from the right-angle lens, all that protrudes below the ceiling is a small mirror approximately 3/8 × 5/8 inch. This technique provides

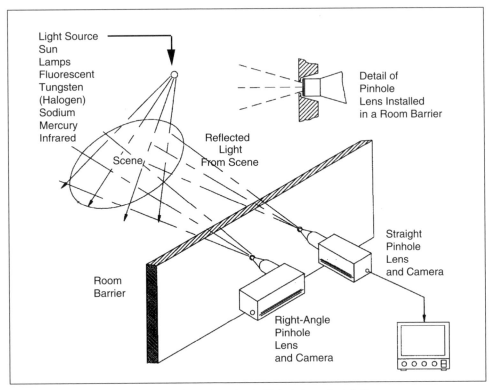

Straight and Right-Angle Pinhole Lens Installations

Figure 18. A sprinkler head unit is an investigative tool because it is difficult to see.

a very low profile and is difficult to detect by an observer at ground level.

The pinhole/mirror system provides an alternative to some dome applications. The system can be fixed or have a 360-degree panning range, or a limited pan, tilt, and zoom capability, depending on the design.

Fiber-Optic Lenses

In applications where it is required to view a scene where the camera is located 6, 8, or 12 inches behind a thick concrete wall, a rigid coherent fiber-optic conduit or a borescope lens is used to extend the objective lens several inches to several feet in front of the camera sensor.

Difficult television security applications are sometimes solved by using coherent fiber-optic bundle lenses. They are used in surveillance applications when it is necessary to view a scene on the other side of a thick barrier or inside a confined area.

The lens is installed behind a thick barrier (wall) with the objective lens on the scene side, the fiber-optic bundle within the wall, and the camera located on the protected side of the barrier. The lens viewing the scene can be a few inches or a few feet away from the camera. The rigid fiber version is a fused array of fibers and cannot be bent.

The fiber-optic lens should not to be confused with the single or multiple strands of fiber commonly used to transmit the time-modulated television signal from a camera over a long distance (hundreds of feet or miles), to a remote monitor site. The fiber-optic lens typically has 200,000 to 300,000 individual fibers forming an image-transferring array.

A minor disadvantage of all fiber-optic systems is that the picture obtained is not as "clean" as that obtained with an "all lens" pinhole lens. There are some cosmetic imperfections that look like dust spots, as well as a slight geometrical pattern caused by fiber stacking. For most surveillance applications the imperfections do not result in any loss of intelligence in the picture.

Configuration

In the case of the rigid fiber-optic bundle, the individual fibers are fused together to form a rigid glass rod or conduit. The diameter of the rigid fiber-optic bundle is approximately 0.4 inch for a 2/3-inch format sensor, 0.3-inch diameter for a 1/2-inch format, and 0.2-inch diameter for a 1/3-inch format. The rod is usually protected from the environment and mechanical damage by a rigid metal tube (0.5 inches in diameter for 2/3-inch format). It should be noted that the image exiting the fiber-optic lens is inverted with respect to the image produced by a standard objective lens. This inversion is corrected by inverting the camera.

Infrared (IR) Sources

There are numerous commercially available thermal lamp and light-emitting diode (LED) IR sources for covert CCTV applications. They vary from short range, low power, wide-angle beam to long range, high power, narrow-angle beam types.

A single IR LED emits enough IR energy to produce a useful picture at ranges up to 5 or 10 feet with a CCD camera. By stacking many (several hundred) LEDs in an array, higher IR power is directed toward the scene and a larger area at distances up to 50 to 100 feet may be viewed.

Special Configurations

CCTV cameras and lenses are concealed in many different objects and locations. Examples of some objects include an overhead track lighting fixture, emergency lighting fixture, exit sign, table top radio, table lamp, wall or desk clock, shoulder bag, attaché case, etc.

The emergency lighting fixture operates normally and can be tested for operation periodically. The fixture's operation is in no way affected by the installation of the CCTV camera.

The exit light fixture is another convenient form for camouflaging a covert CCTV camera system. The right-angle pinhole lens and CCD camera are located inside the unit and view out of either arrow on the exit sign, providing an excellent covert CCTV camera system.

A large wall-mounted clock is an ideal location for camouflaging covert CCTV camera/lens combination. The lens views out through one of the black numerals. In this case, the flat camera (approximately 7/8-inch deep) and right-angle mini-lens is mounted directly behind the numeral 11 on the clock. The camera uses offset optics so that the camera views downward at approximately a 15-degree angle even though the clock is mounted vertically on the wall.

Wireless Transmission

Covert CCTV applications often require that the camera/lens system be installed and removed quickly from a site, or that it remain installed on location for only short periods of time. This may mean that a wired transmission means cannot be installed and that a wireless transmission means from camera to monitor (or VCR) is necessary. This takes the form of a VHF or UHF radio frequency (RF), microwave, or lightwave (IR) video transmitter of low power mounted near the television camera. The RF transmitters are of low power—from 100 milliwatts to several watts—and transmit the video picture over ranges from 100 feet to several miles.

Microwave transmission systems operate in the 2- to 22-gigahertz range and require FCC licensing and approval, but can be used by government agencies and commercial customers as well. One condition in obtaining approval is to have a frequency search performed to ensure the system causes no interference to existing equipment in the area. Most microwave systems have a more directional transmitting pattern than for the RF transmitters. Most microwave installations are line of sight, but the microwave energy can be reflected off objects in the path between the transmitter and the receiver to direct the energy to the receiver. The higher frequency of operation and directionality makes microwave installation and alignment more critical than the RF transmitters.

Pinhole lenses are used for surveillance problems that cannot be adequately solved using standard FFL or zoom lenses. The fast f/#s of some of these pinhole lenses make it possible to provide covert surveillance under normal or dimly lighted conditions. The small size of the front lens and barrel permit them to be covertly installed for surveillance applications.

A large variety of mini-, pinhole, fiber-optic, and borescope lenses are available for use in covert security applications. These lenses have FL ranges from 3.8 to 22 millimeters, covering FOVs from 12 to 78 degrees. Variations that include manual and auto iris, standard pinhole, mini and off-axis-mini, fiber optic, and borescope provide the user with a large selection from which to choose.

Herman A. Kruegle

CCTV: THE MANY ROLES OF CCTV IN SECURITY

Closed-circuit television (CCTV) is a reliable, cost-effective deterrent to crime and a means for the apprehension and prosecution of offenders. In view of high labor costs, CCTV more than ever before has earned its place as a cost-effective means for expanding security and safety, reducing asset losses and reducing the cost of security. Most safety and security applications require several different types of equipment including CCTV surveillance, fire and intrusion alarm, and access control.

Theft Reduction

Thievery causes loss of assets and time, and is a growing cancer in our society. It reduces the profits of all organizations, be they government, retail, service, manufacturing, etc. CCTV is effective in counteracting these losses in small and large companies alike, thereby increasing corporate profits. The public at large has accepted the use of CCTV systems in public and industrial facilities while the reaction by workers to its use is mixed.

The integration of CCTV with a properly designed security system can be an extremely profitable investment to any organization. One objective of the CCTV system should be to deter crime so as to prevent thievery. It has been shown that CCTV is an effective psychological deterrent to crime. If an organization or company can prevent an incident from occurring in the first place, the problem has been solved.

A second objective is the apprehension of offenders and successful dismissal or prosecution of them. A successful thief needs privacy in which to operate and it is the function of the CCTV system to prevent this. The number of thefts cannot be counted exactly, but the reduction in shrinkage can be measured.

Theft takes the form of removing valuable property and/or information from a facility.

Lost information takes the form of computer software, magnetic tape and disks, optical disks, microfilm, data on paper, etc. Real property losses include vandalizing and defacing buildings; graffiti on facilities and art objects; and destroying furniture, business machines, or other valuable equipment. CCTV surveillance systems provide a means for successfully deterring such thievery and/or detecting or apprehending the offenders.

Management Function

The protection of assets is a management function. Three key factors that govern the planning of an assets protection program are: (1) preventing losses from occurring, (2) providing adequate countermeasures to limit actual losses and to limit unpreventable losses, and (3) obtaining top management support.

The Role of CCTV in Assets Protection

CCTV plays an important role in the protection of assets by permitting detection of unwanted entry into a facility beginning at the perimeter location and by monitoring internal activity.

The CCTV security system consists of an illumination source, lens, camera, transmission, switching, recording, and printing means. To make best use of all aspects of CCTV technology, the practitioner and end user must understand the lighting sources needed to illuminate the scene, the CCTV equipment and its capabilities, and the surveillance limitations during daytime and nighttime operation.

Videocassette recorders (VCRs) and hard-copy video printers provide CCTV security with a new dimension, i.e., going beyond real-time camera surveillance. This archiving ability is of prime importance since it permits permanent identification of activities and personnel necessary for dismissal or prosecution of an offender in a court of law at a future time.

Color vs. Monochrome

Most CCTV surveillance applications use monochrome equipment, but the solid-state camera has made color systems practical. The driving functions responsible for the accelerated development and implementation of the excellent CCTV equipment available today has been the widespread use of CCTV by consumers, made

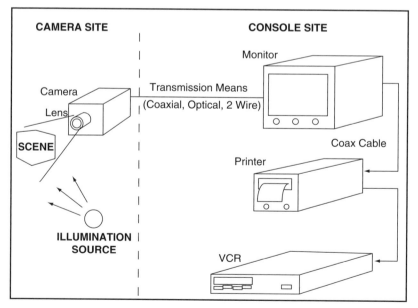

Single Camera System

Figure 19. A single camera system has multiple components and relies on a source of illumination.

possible through technological advances and the resulting availability of low-cost VCRs and associated camera equipment. Solid-state color cameras for the consumer VCR market accelerated the availability of reliable, stable, long-life color cameras and time-lapse VCRs for the security industry. Color is important in surveillance applications because objects that are easily identified in a color scene are difficult to identify in a monochrome scene. For this reason, color cameras will replace most monochrome types as the sensitivity and resolution increases, and the cost decreases.

CCTV as Part of the Emergency and Disaster Plan

An organization should have a method to alert employees in the event of a dangerous condition, and a plan to provide for quick law enforcement, fire and/or emergency response. Every organization regardless of size should have an emergency and disaster control plan that includes CCTV as a critical component. CCTV can:

1. Protect human life by enabling security or safety officials to see remote locations, to view what is happening, where it is happening, what action is most critical, and what areas to attend to and in what priority.
2. Warn of an oncoming disaster.
3. Prevent or at least assess document or assets removal by intruders or unauthorized personnel.
4. Document via VCRs the equipment and assets in place prior to the disaster for comparison to the remaining assets after the disaster.
5. Help in restoring the organization to normal operation and procedures.
6. Reduce exposure of physical assets and optimize loss control.

Documentation of the Emergency

CCTV can aid in determining whether machinery, utilities, boilers, furnaces, etc., have been shut down properly, whether personnel must enter the area to do so, or whether other means must be taken to take it off-line. It can be used to verify that all personnel have left a potentially dangerous area.

The use of CCTV is an important tool that can be used to monitor assets during and after a disaster to ensure that material is not removed and that it is monitored. After the emergency situation has been brought under control, CCTV and security personnel provide the functions of monitoring the situation and maintaining the security of assets.

For insurance purposes, and for critique by management and security, documentation provided by CCTV recordings of assets lost or stolen and personnel injuries or deaths can support that the company was not negligent, and that a prudent emergency and disaster plan was in effect prior to the event.

CCTV can play a critical role in evaluation of a disaster plan to identify shortcomings and to illustrate correct and incorrect procedures to personnel.

Stand-By Power and Communications

It is likely that during any emergency or disaster, primary power and/or communications from one location to another will be disrupted. Stand-by power will keep emergency lighting, communications, and strategic CCTV equipment on line as needed during the emergency. When power is lost, the CCTV equipment is automatically switched over to the emergency power backup equipment (gas-powered generator) or uninterruptible power supply (UPS). A prudent security plan anticipating an emergency will include a means to power vital safety and security equipment to ensure its operation during a crisis event. Since critical CCTV and audio communications must be maintained over remote distances during such an occurrence, an alternate means of communication (signal transmission) from one location to another should be supplied either in the form of protected auxiliary hard-wired cable or a wireless system.

Security Investigations

CCTV is used for covert security investigations where the camera and lens are hidden from view by any personnel in the area so that positive identification and documentation of an event or person's actions can be made. Lenses and cameras can be discreetly hidden in rooms, hallways, and specific objects in indoor or outdoor locations to provide such surveillance.

Safety

CCTV equipment is used for safety purposes whereby security personnel can identify unsafe practices to prevent accidents or respond to those needing immediate attention. CCTV cameras should be distributed throughout a facility, in stairwells, loading docks, and other potentially dangerous locations to permit security and safety personnel to respond to safety violations and accidents.

CCTV is used when an area is evacuated to determine if all personnel have left the area and are safe. Security personnel can use CCTV for pedestrian and vehicular traffic monitoring and control, to locate high traffic areas, and how to best control them.

CCTV plays a critical role in public safety to monitor vehicular traffic on highways, city streets, truck and bus depots, public rail and subway facilities, and airports.

Guard Role

A guard using CCTV can significantly increase security effectiveness. CCTV represents a low capital investment and low operating cost as compared with the overall cost for a guard. A guard can often be replaced with CCTV equipment when monitoring remote sites.

Training of Employees and Security Personnel

CCTV is an effective training tool for management, security personnel, and employees that improves employee efficiency and increases productivity. It is in widespread use because it so vividly and conveniently demonstrates security procedures for the trainee to implement. Actual, real-life situations demonstrate to the trainee what can happen when procedures are not followed, and the improved results obtained

when plans are properly executed by trained personnel.

Scenes from actual exercises can demonstrate good and poor practices, breaches of security, unacceptable employee behavior, and proper guard reaction. Training videos are used for rehearsals or tests of an emergency or disaster plan. At a later time all members of the team observe their response and are critiqued by management or other professionals to improve their performance.

Synergy Through Integration

CCTV equipment is most effective when integrated with other security hardware to form a coherent security system. The hardware used in synergy with CCTV is electronic access control, fire and safety alarms, intrusion detection alarms, and communication channels.

Functionally, the integrated security system can be regarded as a design-coordinated combination of equipment, personnel, and procedures that utilizes each component to enhance every other component to assure optimum achievement of the stated objective.

Each element chosen is analyzed to determine how it will contribute to prevent loss or protect assets and personnel. As an example, if an intrusion occurs, at what point should it be detected, what should the response be, and by what means should it be reported and recorded? In a perimeter-protection role, CCTV can be used with other intrusion detection devices to alert the guard at the security console that an intrusion has occurred.

When an intrusion occurs, multiple CCTV cameras located throughout the facility follow the intruder to permit implementation of the planned response by guard personnel or designated employees. Management determines the specific guard reaction and response. If the intruder has violated some form of barrier or fence, the intrusion-detection system should be able to determine that a person passed through the barrier and not an animal, bird, insect, leaves, debris, etc. (false alarms). CCTV provides the most positive means for making this determination and communicating it to the security personnel reaction force, with enough information to permit them to initiate a response.

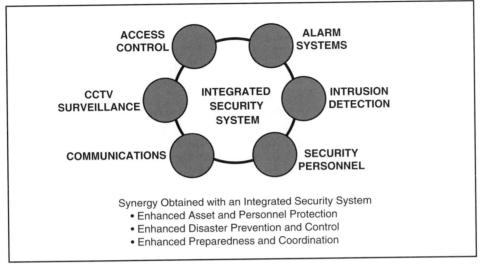

Integrated Security System

Figure 20.   An integrated security system can synergize prevention, mitigation, and control.

The synergistic integration of CCTV, access control, alarms, intrusion detection, and security guards into a system increases the overall security of the facility and maximizes assets protection and employee safety.

Fire and Safety

The greatest potential for CCTV is its integration with other safety-related sensing systems (smoke detectors, alarms), and its use to view remote areas having potential safety problems or fire hazards. In the case of a fire, CCTV cameras act as real-time eyes at the emergency location, permitting security and safety personnel to send the appropriate reaction force. Having CCTV cameras on location before personnel arrive shortens the reaction time to a fire or other disaster. A CCTV camera can quickly ascertain whether an event is a false alarm, a minor alarm, or a major event. In a fire alert, the automatic sprinkler and fire alarm system alerts the guard to the event, but the CCTV "eye" views the scene and permits more effective use of personnel and ensures that they are not diverted to false alarms unnecessarily. The synergistic combination of audio and CCTV from a remote site enhances the intelligence received from the remote site.

Security Surveillance Applications

CCTV applications are broadly classified into indoor or outdoor: those suitable for a controlled indoor environment, and those suitable for harsher outdoor environments. The indoor location requires the use of artificial lighting, which may or may not be augmented by daylight entering the viewing area, and is only subjected to mild indoor temperature and humidity variations, dirt, dust, and smoke. The outdoor location uses sunlight during daytime and artificial lighting during nighttime, and can encounter environmental precipitation (fog, rain, snow), wind loading, dirt, dust, sand, and smoke. Some typical safety and security applications for which CCTV provides an effective solution include:

1. Overt observation of hazardous areas with the potential for life threatening or injurious situations, including toxic, radioactive, high fire or explosion potential, X-ray radiation, or other nuclear radiation.
2. Visual observation of a scene that must be covert (hidden) is accomplished by means of a small camera and lens rather than locating a person in the area.

3. Where significant events must be viewed or recorded when activity occurs, at a normally low-activity area such as at a perimeter or other location.

4. Simultaneous surveillance of many locations by one person from a central security location to trace the entry and path of a person or vehicle through a facility from the entry point to the final destination in the facility or interdiction by the security force.

5. Provide a high-quality hard-copy print-out of unauthorized entry, activity, or event using a VCR and/or printer system.

CCTV Access Control

CCTV access control uses television to remotely identify a person requesting access, whether as a pedestrian or in a vehicle. Identification is accomplished by comparing the person's face with a photo on an identification card carried by the person. The live and replicated facial image is displayed side-by-side on a split-screen monitor. If the two images match, the security guard unlocks the door and allows entry. The CCTV access control system can be combined with an electronic access control system to increase security and provide a means to track all attempted entries.

For medium- to low-level access control security requirements, electronic card reading systems are adequate after a person has first been identified at some exterior perimeter location. To provide higher security than a simple identification card and electronic card reading system can provide, it is necessary to combine the electronic card reader with either biometric descriptors of a person, and/or CCTV identification. For the highest level of access control security, the video image of the person and other pertinent information is stored in a video image file and then retrieved and used as part of the identification process.

The synergy of a CCTV security system implies the following functional scenario:

1. An unauthorized intrusion or entry or attempted removal of equipment is detected at the time of the event by some alarm sensor.

2. A CCTV camera located somewhere in the alarm area is pointed manually or automatically (from the guard site) to view the alarm area.

3. The alarm sensor and CCTV camera information is transmitted immediately to the security console and monitored by personnel and/or recorded for permanent documentation.

4. The security operator receiving the alarm information acts according to a security plan to dispatch personnel to the location or to take some other appropriate action.

5. After appropriate action the guard resumes normal security duties to view any future event.

The use of CCTV plays a crucial role in the overall security plan. During an intrusion or theft, the CCTV system provides information to the guard to make an assessment of the security problem and provide an appropriate response. Suitable alarm sensors and CCTV cameras permit the guard to follow the progress of the event and assist the response team by providing tactical information.

With an intrusion alarm and visual CCTV information, all the elements are in place for a reliable transfer of information to the security officers in a timely fashion. For proper effectiveness, all parts of the security system must work properly: the alarm, CCTV, and guard response.

The motivation for an organization to justify expenditures on security and safety equipment is that there must be a positive return on investment, i.e., the value of assets not lost must be greater than the amount spent on security. Experience has shown that CCTV does play a crucial role in the success of a security and safety plan. A well-planned security and safety system has the potential to reduce thefts, protect assets, and save lives. When disaster strikes, an organization should have an emergency and recovery plan in place.

Herman A. Kruegle

EXTERIOR INTRUSION SENSORS

Intrusion detection systems consist of exterior and interior intrusion sensors, video alarm assessment, entry control, and alarm communication systems all working together. Exterior sensors are those used in an outdoor environment, and interior sensors are those used inside buildings.

Intrusion detection is defined as the detection of a person or vehicle attempting to gain unauthorized entry into an area that is being protected by someone who is able to authorize or initiate an appropriate response. The intrusion detection boundary is ideally a sphere enclosing the item being protected so that all intrusions, whether by surface, air, underwater, or underground, are detected. The development of exterior intrusion detection technology has emphasized detection on or slightly above the ground surface, with increasing emphasis being placed on airborne intrusion.

Performance Characteristics

Intrusion sensor performance is described by three fundamental characteristics—probability of detection (PD), nuisance alarm rate, and vulnerability to defeat. An understanding of these characteristics is essential for designing and operating an effective intrusion sensor system.

Probability of Detection. For the ideal sensor, the PD of an intrusion is one (1.0). However, no sensor is ideal, and the PD is always less than 1. The way that PD is calculated does not allow a PD of 1. Even with thousands of tests, the PD only approaches 1. For any specific sensor and scenario (for example, a specific facility at night, in clear weather, a crawling attacker), the two values PD and confidence level (CL) are used to describe the effectiveness of the sensor. The sensor will detect the intrusion with probability of detection PD for confidence level CL. This means that, based upon test results and with probability CL, the sensor's true, but unknown, probability of detection is at least PD. For an ideal sensor the PD would be 1.0 with a CL of 1.0 or 100 percent. In reality, a PD or a CL equal to 1.0 will not occur, because complete knowledge of a sensor's effectiveness is never achieved. Also, the pair (PD, CL) is not unique; based upon the same test results, it is possible to calculate different PDs for different CLs. Most commonly, values of 90 percent, 95 percent, or even 99 percent are used for CL, although a value of 99 percent would require very extensive testing. Although technically incorrect,

manufacturers will often state values of PD without stating the corresponding value of CL. When this happens, it is reasonable to assume that they are inferring a value of at least 90 percent for CL.

The probability of detection depends primarily upon:

- Target to be detected (i.e., a walking, running, or crawling intruder; tunneling; etc.)
- Sensor hardware design
- Installation conditions
- Sensitivity adjustment
- Weather conditions
- Condition of the equipment

Nuisance Alarm Rate (NAR). A nuisance alarm is any alarm that is not caused by an intrusion. Nuisance alarm rate is a function of the number of nuisance alarms over a given time period. In an ideal sensor system, the nuisance alarm rate would be zero (0.0). However, in the real world all sensors interact with their environment, and they cannot discriminate between adversary intrusions and other events in their detection zone. This is why an alarm assessment system is needed—not all sensor alarms are caused by intrusions. This is also why it is ineffective to have the guard force respond to every alarm. Assessment, then, serves the purpose of determining the cause of the alarm, and whether or not it requires a response. This is why we say that detection is not complete without assessment.

Usually nuisance alarms are further classified by source. Both natural and industrial environments can cause nuisance alarms. Common sources of natural noise are vegetation (trees and weeds), wildlife (animals and birds), and weather conditions (wind, rain, snow, fog, lightning). Industrial sources of noise include ground vibration, debris moved by wind, and electromagnetic interference.

False alarms are those nuisance alarms generated by the equipment itself (whether by poor design, inadequate maintenance, or component failure). Different types of intrusion sensors have different sensitivities to these nuisance or false alarm sources.

As with PD, it is important to specify an acceptable nuisance alarm rate (NAR) and false alarm rate (FAR). For example, the FAR for the total perimeter intrusion system shall not average more than one false alarm per week, per zone, while maintaining a PD of 0.9. This statement is much more meaningful than a higher FAR and NAR may be tolerated if this does not result in system degradation. In this case, system degradation takes on a very subjective meaning and so becomes harder to measure. Establishing specific values for FAR and NAR also helps the operator determine when a sensor should be reported to maintenance personnel.

Vulnerability to Defeat. An ideal sensor could not be defeated; however, all existing sensors can be defeated. Different types of sensors and sensor models have different vulnerabilities to defeat. The objective of the PPS designer is to make the system very difficult to defeat. There are two general ways to defeat the system:

- Bypass—Because all intrusion sensors have a finite detection zone, any sensor can be defeated by going around its detection volume.
- Spoof—Spoofing is any technique that allows the target to pass through the sensor's normal detection zone without generating an alarm.

Sensor Classification

There are several ways of classifying the many types of exterior intrusion sensors. In this discussion, five methods of classification are used:

- Passive or active
- Covert or visible
- Line-of-sight or terrain-following
- Volumetric or line detection
- Application

Passive or Active. Passive sensors detect some type of energy that is emitted by the target of interest, or detect the change of some natural field of energy caused by the target. Examples of the former are mechanical energy from a human walking on the soil or climbing on a fence. An example of the latter is a change in the local magnetic field caused by the presence of a metal. Passive sensors utilize a receiver to collect the energy emissions. Passive sensor technologies include those based on vibration, heat, sound, and capacitance.

Active sensors transmit some type of energy and detect a change in the received energy created by the presence or motion of the target. They generally include both a transmitter and a receiver and include microwave, infrared, and other radio frequency (RF) devices.

The distinction of passive or active has a practical importance. The presence or location of a passive sensor is more difficult to determine than that of an active sensor since there is no energy source for the adversary to locate; this puts the intruder at a disadvantage. In environments with explosive vapors or materials, passive sensors are safer than active ones because no energy that might initiate explosives is emitted. Active sensors, because of their stronger signals, more effectively eliminate nuisance alarms.

Covert or Visible. Covert sensors are hidden from view; examples are sensors that are buried in the ground. Visible sensors are in plain view of an intruder; examples are sensors that are attached to a fence or mounted on another support structure. Covert sensors are more difficult for an intruder to detect and locate, and thus they can be more effective; also, they do not affect the appearance of the environment. Visible sensors may, however, deter the intruder from acting. Visible sensors are typically simpler to install and easier to repair and maintain than covert ones.

Line-of-Sight or Terrain-Following. Line-of-sight (LOS) sensors perform acceptably only when installed with a clear LOS in the detection space. This usually means a clear LOS between the transmitter and receiver for active sensors. These sensors normally require a flat ground surface, or at least a clear LOS from each point on the ground surface to both the transmitter and receiver. The use of LOS sensors on sites without a flat terrain requires extensive site preparation to achieve acceptable performance.

Terrain-following sensors detect equally well on flat and irregular terrain. The transducer elements and the radiated field follow the terrain and result in uniform detection throughout the detection zone.

Volumetric or Line Detection. Volumetric sensors detect intrusion in a volume of space. An alarm is generated when an intruder enters the detection volume. The detection volume is generally not visible and is hard for the intruder to identify precisely.

Line detection sensors detect along a line. For example, sensors that detect fence motion are mounted directly on the fence. The fence becomes a line of detection, since an intruder will not be detected while approaching the fence; detection occurs only if the intruder moves the fence fabric where the sensor is attached. The detection zone of a line detection sensor is usually easy to identify.

Application. In this classification method, the sensors are grouped by mode of application in the physical detection space. These modes are:

- Buried line, in which the sensor is in the form of a line buried in the ground.
- Fence-associated, in which the sensor either is mounted on a fence or forms a sensor fence.
- Freestanding, being neither buried nor associated with a fence, but mounted on a support in free space.

Sensor Technology

Sensors are grouped by their modes of application. The table below summarizes the different exterior intrusion sensor technologies according to the different sensor classification schemes.

Many sensor technology reviews have been published and supplement the material presented here.

As shown in the above chart, exterior sensors are grouped according to their characteristics.

Buried-Line Sensors

At present there are four types of buried-line sensors that depend on different sensing phenomena: pressure or seismic sensors, magnetic field sensors, ported coaxial cable sensor, and fiber-optic sensors.

Pressure or Seismic. Pressure or seismic sensors are passive, covert, terrain-following sensors that are buried in the ground. They respond to disturbances of the soil caused by an intruder walking, running, jumping, or crawling on the ground. Pressure sensors are generally sensitive to lower frequency pressure waves in the soil, and seismic sensors are sensitive to higher frequency vibration of the soil.

A typical pressure sensor consists of a reinforced hose that is filled with a pressurized liquid and connected to a pressure transducer.

A typical seismic sensor consists of a string of geophones. A geophone consists of a conducting coil and a permanent magnet. Either the coil

TABLE 4. Types and Characteristics of Exterior Sensors

Types of Exterior Sensors and Characteristics	Passive or Active	Covert or Visible	LOS or Terrain-Following	Volumetric or Line Detection
Buried Line				
Seismic Pressure	P	C	TF	L
Magnetic Field	P	C	TF	VOL
Ported Coaxial cable	A	C	TF	VOL
Fiber-Optic cables	P	C	TF	L
Fence-Associated				
Fence-Disturbance	P	V	TF	L
Sensor Fence	P	V	TF	L
Electric Field	A	V	TF	VOL
Freestanding				
Active Infrared	A	V	LOS	L
Passive Infrared	P	V	LOS	VOL
Bistatic Microwave	A	V	LOS	VOL
Dual Technology	A/P	V	LOS	VOL
Video Motion Detection	P	C	LOS	VOL

or the magnet is fixed in position, and the other is free to vibrate during a seismic disturbance. Many sources of seismic noise may affect these sensors and cause nuisance alarms.

Magnetic Field. Magnetic field sensors are passive, covert, terrain-following sensors that are buried in the ground. They respond to a change in the local magnetic field caused by the movement of nearby metallic material. Thus magnetic field sensors are effective for detecting vehicles or intruders with weapons.

This type of sensor consists of a series of wire loops or coils buried in the ground. Movement of metallic material near the loop or coil changes the local magnetic field and induces a current. Magnetic field sensors can be susceptible to local electromagnetic disturbances such as lightning. Intruders who are not wearing or carrying any metal will be able to defeat this type of sensor. Magnetic field sensors are primarily used to detect vehicle traffic.

Ported Coaxial Cables. Ported coaxial cable sensors are active, covert, terrain-following sensors that are buried in the ground. They are also known as leaky coax or radiating cable sensors. This type of sensor responds to motion of a material with a high dielectric constant or high conductivity near the cables. These materials include both the human body and metal vehicles.

The name of this sensor is derived from the construction of the transducer cable. The outer conductor of this coaxial cable does not provide complete shielding for the center conductor, and thus some of the radiated signal leaks through the ports of the outer conductor. The detection volume of ported coax sensors extends significantly above the ground: about 1.5 to 3.0 feet above the surface, and about 3 to 6 feet wider than the cable separation.

Fiber-Optic Cables. Optical fibers are long, hair-like strands of transparent glass or plastic. These transparent fibers guide light from one end to the other. As light travels through the fiber, it remains in the clear plastic core by reflecting off the surface of cladding material that has a different refraction index. Thus the fiber becomes a "light-pipe."

The fiber does not have to be straight since light reflects off a curved or straight surface. The light diffraction (speckle) pattern and the light intensity at the end of the fiber are a function of the shape of the fiber over its entire length. Even the slightest change in the shape of the fiber can be sensed using sophisticated sensors and computer signal processing at the far end (100 yards or more). Thus a single strand of fiber-optic cable, buried in the ground at the depth of a few centimeters, can very effectively give an alarm when an intruder steps on the ground above the fiber (Wolfenbarger, 1994). To ensure that an intruder steps above the fiber, it is usually woven into a grid and buried just beneath the surface.

Fence-Associated Sensors

There are three types of intrusion sensors that either mount on or attach to a fence or form a fence using the transducer material: fence-disturbance sensors, sensor fences, and electric field or capacitance sensors.

Fence-Disturbance Sensors. Fence-disturbance sensors are passive, visible, terrain-following sensors that are designed to be installed on a security fence, typically constructed with chain-link mesh. These sensors are considered terrain-following because the chain-link mesh is supported every three yards with a galvanized steel post, and thus the fence itself is terrain-following.

Fence-disturbance sensors can detect motion or shock. Thus they are intended to detect primarily an intruder who climbs on or cuts through the fence fabric. Several kinds of transducers are used to detect the movement or vibration of the fence. These include switches, electromechanical transducers, strain sensitive cables, piezoelectric crystals, geophones, fiber-optic cables, or electric cable.

Sensor Fences. Sensor fences are passive, visible, terrain-following sensors that make use of the transducer elements to form a fence itself. These sensor fences are designed primarily to detect climbing or cutting on the fence.

Taut-wire sensor fences consist of many parallel, horizontal wires with high tensile strength that are connected under tension to transducers near the midpoint of the wire span. These transducers detect deflection of the wires caused by an intruder cutting the wires, climbing on the wires to get over the fence, or separating the wires to climb through the fence. The wire is typically barbed wire, and the transducers are mechanical switches, strain gauges, or piezoelectric elements.

Electric Field or Capacitance. Electric field or capacitance sensors are active, visible, terrain-following sensors that are designed to detect a change in capacitive coupling among a set of wires attached to, but electrically isolated from, a fence.

The sensitivity of electric field sensors can be adjusted to extend up to 1 meter beyond the wire or plane of wires. A high sensitivity typically has a trade-off of more nuisance alarms. Electric field and capacitance sensors are susceptible to lightning, rain, fence motion, and small animals. Ice storms may cause substantial breakage and damage to the wires and the standoff insulators. Good electrical grounding of electric field sensors is important to reduce nuisance alarms.

Freestanding Sensors

The primary types of freestanding sensors currently used for exterior intrusion detection are infrared, microwave, and video motion detection sensors.

Active Infrared. The infrared (IR) sensors used for exterior intrusion detection are active, visible, line-of-sight, and freestanding sensors. An IR beam is transmitted from an IR light-emitting diode through a collimating lens. Collimating lenses are used in active infrared sensors to convert the divergent beams of IR light into parallel beams, resulting in an efficient collection of the signal at the receiver. Without this lens, the light would disperse and provide a weaker signal at the receiver. The beam is received at the other end of the detection zone by a collecting lens that focuses the energy onto a photodiode. The IR sensor detects the loss of the received infrared energy when an opaque object blocks the beam. These sensors operate at a wavelength of about 0.9 microns, which is not visible to the human eye.

Although single-beam IR sensors are available, multiple-beam sensors are normally used for high-level security applications because a single IR beam is too easy to defeat or bypass. A multiple-beam IR sensor system typically consists of two vertical arrays of IR transmitter and receiver modules (the specific number and configuration of modules depends on the manufacturer). Thus the IR sensor creates an IR fence of multiple beams but detects a single beam break. Multiple-beam infrared sensors usually incorporate some electronics to detect attempts at spoofing the beams with an alternative IR source.

Passive Infrared. Humans emit thermal energy due to the warmth of their body. On average, each active human emits the equivalent energy of a 50-watt light bulb, and passive infrared (PIR) detectors sense the presence of this energy and cause an alarm to be generated. For years this technology was only usable in an interior application because the changes in heat, emitted by the ground as clouds passed overhead, caused too many false alarms. Current models, however, compare the received thermal energy from two curtain-shaped sensing patterns. A human moving into one area and then the other would cause an imbalance. Weather-related temperature changes such as the increases in temperature during a summer day would affect both areas equally and would not cause an alarm.

Bistatic Microwave. Bistatic microwave sensors are active, visible, line-of-sight, freestanding sensors. Typically, two identical microwave antennas are installed at opposite ends of the detection zone. One is connected to a microwave transmitter; the other is connected to a microwave receiver that detects the received microwave energy. This energy is the vector sum of the direct beam between the antennas and the microwave signals reflected from the ground surface and other objects in the transmitted beam. Microwave sensors respond to changes in the vector sum caused by objects moving in that portion of the transmitted beam that is within the viewing field of the receiver.

Monostatic Microwave. Microwave detectors are also available in monostatic versions. In this configuration, the transmitter and receiver are in the same unit. Radio-frequency energy is pulsed from the transmitter, and the receiver looks for a change in the reflected energy. Motion by an intruder causes the reflected energy to change and thus causes an alarm. These sensors are range-gated, meaning that the site can set the range beyond which motion can occur without an alarm.

Dual-Technology Sensors

In an effort to reduce nuisance alarms, dual-technology sensors are becoming more popular for security use. An example of dual technology would be to place both a passive infrared and a monostatic microwave in the same housing. The theory behind these devices is that the sensor will not give an alarm until both sensors have detected, thus avoiding common nuisance alarms from each of the technologies and only initiating an alarm for an actual intruder. In this mode the sensitivity of each sensor could be set very high without the associated nuisance alarms. The reduction in nuisance alarms, however, is accompanied by a decreased probability of detection (PD) since an intruder must only defeat one sensor to bypass the detector.

Video Motion Detection. Video motion detectors (VMDs) are passive, covert, line-of-sight sensors that process the video signal from closed-circuit television (CCTV) cameras. These cameras are generally installed on towers to view the scene of interest and may be jointly used for detection, surveillance, and alarm assessment. Lighting is required for continuous 24-hour operation.

VMDs sense a change in the video signal level for some defined portion of the viewed scene. Depending on the application, this portion may be a large rectangle, a set of discrete points, or a rectangular grid. Detection of human body movement is reliable except during conditions of reduced visibility, such as fog, snow, heavy rain, or loss of lighting at night.

Mary Lynn Garcia

Sources

Barnard, R. 1988. *Intrusion Detection Systems, 2nd Edition*. Boston: Butterworth Publishers.

Cumming, N. 1992. *Security, 2nd Edition*. Boston: Butterworth-Heinemann.

Fennelly, L. 1996. *Handbook of Loss Prevention and Crime Prevention, 3rd Edition*. Boston: Butterworth-Heinemann.

Williams, J. 1988. "Exterior Alarm Systems." pp. 1–25. *SAND88–2995C*.

Wolfenbarger, F. 1994. "A Field Test and Evaluation of Exterior Fiber-Optic Intrusion Detection Sensors." pp. 1–39. *SAND94–1664*.

INTERIOR INTRUSION SENSORS

There are several ways of classifying the types of intrusion sensors. The following methods of classification are used for interior intrusion sensors:

- Passive or active
- Covert or visible
- Volumetric or line detection
- Application

Active or Passive

A useful way of looking at interior sensors and their interaction with the environment is to consider the sensors in two categories: active and passive. Active sensors transmit a signal from a transmitter and, with a receiver, detect changes or reflections of that signal. The transmitter and the receiver may be separated, in which case the installation is called bistatic, or they may be located together, in which case the installation is called monostatic. The principal point is that these active sensors generate a field of energy when the sensor is operating, and a very sophisticated adversary could use this field to detect the presence of the sensor prior to stepping into the active sensing zone.

Passive sensors are different from active sensors in that they produce no signal from a transmitter and are simply receivers of energy in the proximity of the sensor. This energy may be due to vibration (from a walking man or a truck), infrared (from a human or a hot object), acoustic (sounds of a destructive break-in), or from a change in the mechanical configuration of the sensor (in the case of the simpler electro-mechanical devices). The distinction of passive or active has a practical importance. The presence or location of a passive sensor can be more difficult to determine than that of an active sensor; this puts the intruder at a disadvantage.

Covert or Visible

Covert sensors are hidden from view; examples are sensors that are located in walls or under the floor. Visible sensors are in plain view of an intruder; examples are sensors that are attached to a door or mounted on another support structure. Covert sensors are more difficult for an intruder to detect and locate, and thus they can be more effective; also, they do not disturb the appearance of the environment. Another consideration, however, is that visible sensors may deter the intruder from acting. Visible sensors are typically simpler to install and easier to repair than covert ones.

Volumetric or Line Detection

The entire volume or a portion of the volume of a room or building can be protected using volumetric motion sensors. An advantage of volumetric motion sensors is that they will detect an intruder moving in the detection zone regardless of the point of entry into the zone.

Forcible entry through doors, windows, or walls of a room can be detected using line-type sensors. These sensors only detect activity at a specific location or a very narrow area. Unlike volumetric sensors, line sensors only detect an intruder if he or she violates a particular entry point into a detection zone.

Application

Sensors may be grouped by their application in the physical detection space. Some sensors may be applied in several ways. There are three application classes for interior sensors:

- Boundary-penetration sensors detect penetration of the boundary to an interior area.
- Interior motion sensors detect motion of an intruder within a confined interior area.
- Proximity sensors can detect an intruder in the area immediately adjacent to an object in an interior area or when the intruder touches the object.

Boundary-Penetration Sensors

This class of sensors includes vibration, electromechanical, infrasonic, capacitance proximity, and passive sonic sensors.

Vibration Sensor. Boundary-penetration vibration sensors are passive line sensors and can be either visible or covert. They detect the movement of the surface to which they are fastened. A human blow or other sudden impact on a surface will cause that surface to vibrate at a specific frequency determined by its construction. The vibration frequencies are determined to a lesser extent by the impacting tool.

Glass-break sensors that mount directly to the glass are vibration sensors. These are specifically designed to generate an alarm when the frequencies more nearly associated with breaking glass are present.

The more recent models of fiber-optic intrusion sensors also detect vibration. These are passive, line sensors, and can be either visible or covert. Fiber-optic sensors of this type detect microbending of fiber-optic cable. Microbending is caused by cable movement or bending, even minute movement of the cable such as vibration of the surface to which the cable is attached.

Electromechanical Sensors. Electromechanical sensors are passive, visible, line sensors. The most common type is a relatively simple switch generally used on doors and windows. Most of these switches are magnetic switches, which consist of two units: a switch unit and a magnetic unit. The switch unit, which contains a magnetic reed switch, is mounted on the stationary part of the door or window. The magnetic unit, which contains a permanent magnet, is mounted on the movable part of the door or window, adjacent to the switch unit. With the door or window closed, the spacing between the switch unit and magnet unit is adjusted so that the magnetic field from the permanent magnet causes the reed switch to be in the closed (or secure) position.

A relatively new type of magnetic switch is known as a Hall effect switch. This switch is totally electronic without mechanical reed switches. It contains active electronics and requires power. It is intended to provide a higher level of security than balanced magnetic switches. Similar to other magnetic switches, it consists of a switch unit and a magnetic unit. Operation of the switch is based on Hall effect devices in the switch unit that measure and monitor the magnetic field strength of the magnetic unit. The Hall effect is a phenomenon that occurs when a current-carrying wire (or metallic strip) is exposed to an external magnetic field. In this state, the magnetic field causes charge carriers to be accelerated toward one side of the wire, resulting in a charge separation across the wire.

Another electromechanical sensor, the continuity or breakwire sensor, is usually attached to or enclosed in walls, ceilings, or floors to detect penetration through many types of construction materials. The sensor consists of small electrically conductive wires and electronics to report an alarm when the conductor is broken. The wires can be formed in any pattern to protect areas of unusual shape. Printed circuit technology can be used to fabricate continuity sensors if desired.

Breakwire grids and screens can be used to detect forcible penetrations through vent openings, floors, walls, ceilings, locked storage cabinets, vaults, and skylights. Nuisance alarm rates for this class of sensor are very low since the wire must be broken to initiate an alarm. The principle is the same—the optical fiber must be broken or damaged enough to stop or significantly reduce light transmission. These are considered fiber-optic intrusion sensors, but are very different and much simpler than the fiber-optic intrusion sensors described earlier under vibration sensors.

Capacitance Sensors. Capacitance sensors are most commonly proximity type sensors; however, they can be applied for boundary penetration detection. They establish a resonant electrical circuit between a protected metal object and a control unit, making them active sensors. The capacitance between the protected metal object and a ground plane becomes a part of the total capacitance of a tuned circuit in an oscillator. The object to be protected is electrically isolated from the ground plane. The capacitive dielectric is usually the air that surrounds, or is between, the protected object and the ground plane. The tuned circuit may have a fixed frequency of oscillation, or the oscillator frequency may vary.

Humans very close to or touching the protected object will change the capacitance.

Infrasonic Sensors and Passive Sonic Sensors. Infrasonic sensors are a class of intrusion sensors that operate by sensing pressure changes in the volume in which they are installed. A slight pressure change occurs whenever a door leading into a closed room is opened or closed, for example. They are passive sensors that can be centrally located in a building some distance from exit doors. Air blowing into the closed volume can cause nuisance alarms with an infrasonic sensor. These sensors are best used in environments where there is only occasional access, such as a storage area.

Passive sonic sensors are passive, covert, volumetric sensors. They are one of the simplest intrusion detectors, using a microphone to listen to the sounds generated in the area within range of the microphone. It is possible to make the sensor respond only to frequencies in the ultrasonic frequency range. This kind of sensor is then termed a passive ultrasonic sensor.

Active Infrared Sensors. Active infrared (IR) sensors are active, visible, line sensors. These sensors establish a beam of infrared light using an infrared light source or sources (mated with appropriate lenses) as the transmitters and photodetectors for receivers. Several transmitters and receivers are usually employed to provide a system with multiple beams, and the beams are usually configured into a vertical infrared fence. A pulsed, synchronous technique may be used to reduce interference and the possibility of defeat by other sources of light. Infrared light is invisible to the human eye.

Fiber-Optic Cable Sensors. These sensors are passive line detectors and can be either visible or covert. They can be applied as either a boundary penetration or a proximity sensor. A fiber-optic sensor typically consists of a length of fiber-optic sensing cable and an alarm processor unit. Both ends of the fiber are usually connected to the processor unit, which has a light source, a light receiver, and signal alarm processing electronics. Fiber-optic sensors can be separated into two major categories: continuity-type sensors and microbend-type sensors.

A fiber-optic continuity sensor is primarily sensitive to damage or breaks in the fiber loop, which causes a severe loss of signal amplitude at the receiver. The signal alarm processor detects the loss of signal and then initiates an alarm.

A microbend fiber-optic sensor is sensitive to both applied pressure and movement of the cable. Pressure and movement cause microbends in the fiber cable, which are detected.

Interior Motion Sensors

Sensors that use several different types of technology fall into this category of motion sensors.

Microwave Sensors. Microwave sensors are active, visible, volumetric sensors. They establish an energy field using energy in the electromagnetic spectrum, usually at frequencies on the order of 10 GHz. Interior microwave motion sensors are nearly always in the monostatic configuration with a single antenna being used both to transmit and receive. Intrusion detection is based on the Doppler frequency shift between the transmitted and received signal caused by a moving object within the energy field.

Bistatic and Monostatic microwave work on different principles. Bistatic uses vector sum of reflected energy, while monostatic is a Doppler shift device. The Doppler shift requires a sufficient amplitude change and duration time to cause an alarm. In practical terms, this means that the microwave transmitter sends out a known frequency and if a higher or lower frequency is returned to the receiver, this is an indication that a target is moving closer or further away from the sensor. Due to this operating principle, optimum detection for microwave sensors is achieved when the target is moving towards or away from the sensor, not across the detection zone. Placement of microwave sensors should then be made so that the adversary is forced to move in this manner.

The shape of the detection zone is governed by the design of the antenna and is roughly similar to an elongated balloon. The antenna is typically a microwave horn but may be a printed circuit planar or phased array.

The fact that microwave energy can penetrate walls has both advantages and disadvantages. An advantage occurs when an intruder is detected by the microwave energy penetrating partitions within a protected volume; but detecting someone or something moving outside the protected area, or even outside the building, is then a disadvantage and would cause a nuisance alarm.

Other advantages of microwave detectors include:

- Invisible and inaudible detection pattern
- Reliable low maintenance device
- Low cost for area of coverage
- High probability of detection
- Immune to high air turbulence, temperature and humidity changes
- Variety of detection patterns available

For all of their good qualities, there are a few disadvantages to the use of microwave sensors, in addition to those described above. These are:

- Require a completely rigid mounting
- Susceptible to pattern drift
- Tendency to reflect off metallic objects
- Extra considerations are required when considering installing in an area with light construction (glass, plaster board, wood)

Monostatic microwave devices can also be used as point sensors to provide limited coverage of a point or area in which other sensors may provide inadequate coverage or may be vulnerable to tampering. A common commercial application of monostatic microwave sensors is the automatic door openers used in supermarkets and airports.

Ultrasonic Sensors. Ulltrasonic sensors are active, visible, volumetric sensors. They establish a detection field using energy in the acoustic spectrum typically in the frequency range

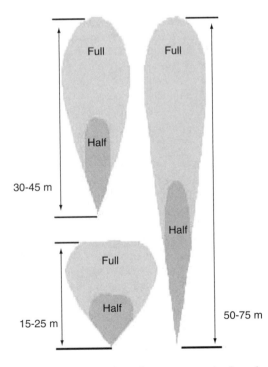

Figure 21.   The detection pattern varies based on antenna design.

between 19 and 40 kHz. Ultrasonic sensors may be monostatic, and as is the case with monostatic microwave sensors, detection is based on the frequency shift between the transmitted and received signal caused by the Doppler effect from a moving object in the beam.

Most common solid materials such as walls, cardboard, and windows will stop or deflect ultrasonic waves. Large objects in a protected volume, such as bookcases, desks, and partial wall partitions, will create shadow zones. Coverage of a volume by several sensors can usually overcome this problem.

A feature of ultrasonic energy is that it will not penetrate physical barriers such as walls; therefore, it can be easily contained in closed rooms. Since acoustical energy will not penetrate physical barriers, the walls of the protected room will either absorb or reflect the energy. Because most walls absorb very little ultrasonic energy unless they are covered with a very soft material, such as heavy drapes, most of the energy is reflected. This reflected energy helps fill the detection zone, making it more difficult for an intruder to escape detection.

Active Sonic Sensors. Sonic sensors are active, visible, and volumetric. They establish a detection field using energy in the acoustic spectrum at frequencies between 500 and 1,000 Hz. These units can be used in monostatic, bistatic, or multistatic modes of operation. Since a much lower frequency is transmitted, good reflections are obtained, and standing waves will be established in the protected volume even in the monostatic configuration. For proper operation, it is necessary to establish standing waves to prevent drastic reduction of the detection range.

Passive Infrared Sensors. Passive infrared (PIR) sensors are visible and volumetric. This sensor responds to changes in the energy emitted by a human intruder, which is approximately equal to the heat from a 50-watt light bulb. They also have the capability to detect changes in the background thermal energy caused by someone moving through the detector field of view and hiding in the energy emanating from objects in the background if there are sufficient differences in the background energy. These systems typically employ special optical and electronic techniques that limit their detection primarily to an energy source in motion; therefore, reliance on background energy change for detection is discouraged.

Optics in the sensor provide a single long conical field of view or a multi-segmented field of view. Long single-segment sensors are used to protect corridors, and those with multi-segments are used to protect large open areas.

There are four major characteristics of infrared radiation. First, all objects emit infrared radiation. The intensity of the infrared is related to the object's temperature. Second, infrared energy is transmitted without physical contact between the emitting and receiving surfaces. Third, infrared warms the receiving surface and can be detected by any device capable of sensing a change in temperature. Fourth, infrared radiation is invisible to the human eye.

The passive infrared sensor converts this radiation into an electrical signal. The signal is then amplified and processed through logic circuits, which generally require that the source of radiation move within the field of view of the sensor. If the signal is strong enough and the required movement occurs, an alarm is generated.

PIRs offer several advantages, including:

- Totally passive device
- Well-defined detection zones
- No interaction between multiple devices
- Low to moderate cost
- Relatively few nuisance alarms

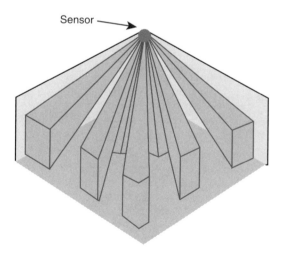

Sensor

Figure 22. As a person passes across the detection segments, each segment will detect an increase or decrease in temperature, which will trigger an alarm.

The disadvantages of PIRs include:

- Moderate vibration sensitivity
- Sensitivity changes with room temperature
- It is a line-of-sight device and the field-of-view is easily blocked.
- Sources of rapid temperature change are potential nuisance alarm sources.

Dual-Technology Sensors. This sensor is active and passive, visible, and volumetric. This sensor type attempts to achieve absolute alarm confirmation while maintaining a high probability of detection. Absolute alarm confirmation is ideally achieved by combining two technologies that individually have a high probability of detection and no common nuisance alarm-producing stimuli. Currently available dual-channel motion detectors (dual-technology) combine either an active ultrasonic or microwave sensor with a passive infrared sensor.

Dual-technology sensors usually have a lower nuisance alarm rate than single technology sensors—when the detectors are properly applied and assuming each has a low nuisance alarm rate.

Ultrasonic and microwave detectors have the highest probability of detecting motion directly toward or away from the sensor, but infrared sensors have the highest probability of detecting someone moving across the field of view. Therefore, the probability of detection of the combined sensors in a single unit will be less than if the individual detectors are mounted perpendicular to each other with overlapping energy patterns and field-of-view. To optimize the probability of detection for combined sensors, separately mounted, logically combined sensors are recommended. For high-security applications, a single dual-technology sensor should never be used in place of two separately mounted sensors. If dual-technology sensors are to be used, multiple sensor units should be installed, with each unit offering overlap protection of the other.

Video Motion Detection. A video motion detector (VMD) is a passive sensor that processes the video signal from a CCTV camera. A single camera installed to view the scene of interest can be jointly utilized for detection, assessment, and surveillance. Generally speaking, there are two types of VMDs: analog and digital. Analog VMDs are the older technology. This type monitors the camera signal and detects changes in brightness in the video scene. The size of this detection area can usually be varied over a wide range as a percentage of total camera field-of-view. A change is detected when the brightness is either higher or lower than a stored reference. An external alarm is generated at the time of the change or after additional conditions (such as time) are satisfied. Once an alarm is generated, the section where detection has occurred is highlighted on the CCTV monitor.

Digital VMDs are more sophisticated than analog VMDs and have allowed broader use of VMD because of their ability to reduce nuisance alarms. Digital VMDs convert the camera signal into a digitized format so that digital processors can be used for video signal processing.

The assessment camera is an integral part of a VMD sensor. Camera characteristics affect both detection capability and nuisance alarm rate. A low-contrast output from a camera reduces detection capability. High noise levels from a camera can cause nuisance alarms. Enough light is required for proper operation of CCTV cameras, and the light must be uniform to avoid excessively dark or light areas.

Many VMDs are effective for interior use, because nuisance alarm sources like snow, fog, traffic flow, and clouds are not present. The following factors should be considered before selecting a VMD:

- Consistent, controlled lighting (no flickering)
- Camera vibration
- Objects that could cause blind areas
- Moving objects such as fans, curtains, and small animals
- Changing sunlight or shadows entering through windows or doors

Proximity Sensors

This class of sensors includes capacitance and pressure sensors.

Capacitance Proximity Sensors. Capacitance proximity sensors are active, covert line sensors. They can detect anyone either approaching or touching metal items or containers that the sensors are protecting. These sensors operate on the same principle as electrical capacitors. A capacitor is an electronic component that consists of two conductor plates separated by a dielectric medium. A change in the electrical charge or dielectric medium results in a change in the capacitance between the two plates. In the case of the capacitance proximity sensor, one plate is the metal item being protected, and the second plate is an electrical reference ground plate under and around the protected item. The metal item in this application is isolated from ground by insulating blocks. This leaves only air around and between the metal object and ground, so air is the dielectric medium.

Variable frequency oscillators use a phase-locked loop and use the correction voltage for sensing. This type of capacitance proximity sensor generally balances itself in a short time (usually less than two minutes) after being connected to the conductive metal object to be protected. Once the sensor is balanced, any change in capacitance between the object to be protected and ground will disturb the balance condition, thereby causing an alarm.

For applications where the object to be protected must be grounded, the object can be considered the ground plane. This requires the fabrication of a capacitance blanket for draping over the protected object. If the blanket is made large enough to cover the object entirely, any access attempts will cause blanket movement, capacitance change, and alarm. This can also be useful to keep the object out of plain sight, as for some classified components or proprietary equipment.

Pressure Sensors. Pressure sensors, often in the form of mats, can be placed around or underneath an object. These sensors are passive, covert, line detectors. Pressure mats consist of a series of ribbon switches positioned parallel to each other along the length of the mat. Ribbon switches are constructed from two strips of metal in the form of a ribbon separated by an insulating material. They are constructed so that when an adequate amount of pressure is exerted anywhere along the ribbon, the metal strips make electrical contact and initiate an alarm.

As shown above, interior sensors are classified according to their characteristics.

Wireless Sensors

The most common wireless sensors are the RF transmission type. A typical RF wireless sensor system consists of sensor/transmitter units

TABLE 5. Classification of Interior Sensors

	Passive or Active	Covert or Visible	Volumetric or Line
Boundary-Penetration Sensors			
Electromechanical	P	C/V	L
Infrared	B[*]	V	L
Vibration	P	C	L
Capacitance	P	C	L
Fiber-Optic Cable	P	C/V	L
Interior Motion Sensors			
Microwave	A	V	V
Ultrasonic	A	V	V
Sonic	A	V	V
Passive Infrared	P	V	V
Proximity Sensors			
Capacitance	A	C	L
Pressure	P	C	L

[*]Both Active and Passive

and a receiver. The sensor/transmitter unit has both the sensor and transmitter electronics integrated into one package and is battery powered. In order to conserve battery power, the transmitters are in a sleep mode until an event requires a transmission. Events consist of alarms, tampers, and state-of-health messages. Alarms and tampers are transmitted when they occur. State-of-health messages verify that the sensor is still present and operating. The receiver is programmed to expect state-of-health messages at the specified intervals. If they are not received, the receiver will indicate a fault condition.

Most wireless systems use PIR, microwave, dual-technology, and magnetic switches as sensor types. They also typically have what is known as a universal transmitter. The universal transmitter allows interfacing to other sensors or controls by monitoring the alarm contacts of the separate sensor.

Testing to verify good transmission path and possible interference sources prior to final location and installation of transmitters and receivers is recommended and can also help reduce problems.

Mary Lynn Garcia

Sources

Adams, D. 1996. "Operational Tips for Improving Intrusion Detection Systems Performance." *SAND96-0468C*.

Barnard, R.L. 1988. *Intrusion Detection Systems, 2nd Edition*. Stoneham, MA: Butterworth Publishers.

Cumming, N. 1992. *Security, 2nd Edition*. Boston: Butterworth-Heinemann.

Graham, R. and Workhoven, R. 1987. "Evolution of Interior Intrusion Detection Technology at Sandia National Laboratories." *SAND87.0947* 1–10.

Rodriguez, J., Dry, B., and Matter, J. 1991. "Interior Intrusion Detection Systems." *SAND91–0948*.

Sandoval, M.W. and Malone, T.P. 1996. "Evaluations of Fiber-Optic Sensors for Interior Applications." *SAND96–0514 1996*.

Vigil, J.T. 1993. "An Evaluation of Interior Video Motion Detection Systems." *SAND92–1987*.

Vigil, J.T. 1994. "An Evaluation of Fiber-Optic Intrusion Detection Systems in Interior Applications." *SAND94–0020 1994*.

INTERNET PROTOCOL (IP) VIDEO

What Is IP Video?

Standard closed circuit television (CCTV) video is transported in an analog format that requires a dedicated coax or fiber cable to transport it. This results in a closed circuit (dedicated cable) video system. The term CCTV (closed circuit television). Digital video describes a digitized version of analog video, which results in a stream of 1s and 0s (digital format). Digital video offers a number of advantages over analog video, one being the ability to transport the real-time video on a standard network. The industry term for this networked real-time video is IP video. Other terms used interchangeably are streaming video and networked video. The term streaming video refers to the concept that the video is constantly being sent on the network, streaming data, since it is real-time. The term IP video stands for Internet Protocol, which is the network communications protocol used on the Internet and on Local and Wide Area Networks (LANs and WANs). In IP video, the video image information is transmitted over the network using IP messages.

Why IP Video?

Video surveillance is an effective tool for physical security. The use of CCTV for video surveillance in the physical security market has been one of the fastest growing segments of physical security over the years. CCTV offers remote eyes for the security staff and provides a recorded visual history of events. CCTV has a family of products developed for the security market. The major components of a CCTV system are:

- Camera including lens, housing, and motorized platforms (Domes/PTZ)
- Switcher/Multiplexer
- VCR (video cassette recorder)
- Distribution amplifiers, video amplifiers, RF modulators

Fiber Transmitters and Receivers and Microwave

IP video eliminates many of the disadvantages of CCTV and brings many new advantages not possible with analog video.

Advantages of Digital and IP Video

IP video has multiple advantages over its analog predecessor. A major advantage of IP video is that it is less costly to install and maintain. In most cases, there is little or no new wiring since the IP devices need only to be connected to an existing network, eliminating the need for dedicated cabling for each camera running to a central location. An additional advantage with IP video is that the video can be transported to any location in the world through LAN and WAN connections. This is not possible with analog video.

IP video is far more efficient in the recording of the video. IP video can be stored on standard network storage systems (hard drive arrays). The video information can be indexed on time-date, as well as tied to alarms or events. With indexing, information can be retrieved rapidly by going directly to the specific incident instead of having to visually search using fast forward viewing, as is the case with analog VCR systems.

Digital video offers a new advantage commonly called "Intelligent Video Processing." With digital video, it is possible to apply computer algorithms to process the video data. Some of the popular algorithms being deployed are:

- Intelligent motion detection, i.e., monitoring the flow and direction of traffic or people or objects
- Object left or theft, i.e., monitoring objects appearing/disappearing in the field of view
- Object recognition
- Video stabilization
- People counting
- Behavior algorithms

These functions can automatically initiate recording and/or raise an alarm or alert to notify management of incidents often prior to a compromise. With these monitoring functions, manpower can be more efficiently applied.

IP video is a major enabler toward "convergence." Convergence is a catchall phrase in the physical security market that defines the union of physical security and information technology (IT). There are major forces driving the industry to be IT-centric. The cost savings and efficiencies through convergence are well defined in the industry. IP video is one of the early adopters of convergence.

The key technology that has made this paradigm shift possible is improved video compression algorithms. Prior to being able to reduce the size of the video signal, each camera required its own dedicated wire to connect back to the monitoring and recording equipment. By turning video signals into computer data, data compression techniques can be applied. High compression ratios have made it possible to easily stream multiple cameras on a single Ethernet cable. Compression also means that the recorded video takes up much less storage space on computer hard drives. With the cost of bandwidth on networks dropping and the cost of hard drives dropping, IP video and digital video are now cost effective.

IP and Digital Video Evolution

In the 1990s the convergence process began to put video on the internet. During this early stage, the security market was also demanding changes in CCTV. The first and most obvious change needed was in recording video because VCRs have many shortcomings:

- VCRs are costly to maintain.
- Tapes are expensive and do not last more than several cycles.
- Tapes require manual intervention to replace and store.
- Searching tapes for past incidents is very time consuming.

The first implementation of digital video was driven by the need to replace older VCR technology. This move resulted in the DVR (digital video recorder) and DVMR (digital video multiplexer/recorder). DVMR offered the ability to store the video on hard drives, including indexing of the video information at a much lower cost. This resulted in rapid access to needed information. Data can be archived to other media and mass storage. Another advantage is the ability to transport (send) the video via network infrastructures (including the Internet) to any location in the world.

In addition to DVRs and DVMRs, other solutions were being offered in the form of

CODECs and Network Recorders. CODEC is an acronym for Compression/Decompression. A CODEC takes in the analog video signal, converts it to a digital format, compresses the signal, and readies the stream to go on the network. CODECs can perform as encoders (converting analog video to the network) or decoders (converting IP video back to analog video).

Camera manufacturers began building the CODEC circuitry into cameras, eliminating the need for external CODECs. Today we have available an assortment of IP cameras, IP domes, IP PTZs, network recorders, and video servers that replace older analog counterparts (see the chart below).

With streaming cameras, video can be recorded on a standard network video recorder (NVR) (Hard Drive Array). The NVR can be placed anywhere on the network and can be accessed from anywhere on the network (assuming user authorization).

CCTV Components Moving to Digital Components

Below is a table of CCTV components and their digital replacements.

The new paradigm products offer many distinct advantages over their analog predecessors. DAs and VAs are analog video devices that distribute and amplify analog video. These and the coax cables, or fiber, are being replaced with a network infrastructure of CAT-5, hubs, switches, and network management tools that now allow the video to be transported anywhere in the world. In this context, the term closed circuit does not apply.

TABLE 6. Paradigms

Old Paradigm	New Paradigm
Analog Cameras, Domes, & PTZs	IP Cameras, Domes, & PTZs
VCRs and Multiplexers	IP DVRs
VCRs	NVRs
Matrix Switchers (hardware)	IP Switching (software)
DA, VA, Microwave, Fiber	Network Infrastructure, hubs, switches, etc.

The New IP and Digital Video Products

Below is a brief description of the new IP and digital video products.

DVR. The first product family to move to IP video was the multiplexer family. Multiplexing has always been a driving force in CCTV systems. The term, however, means different things to different people. To clarify, multiplexing began as an attempt to save VCR space in recording multiple cameras. Multiplexing from an engineering standpoint is short for time multiplexing. In common language, the system can handle 4, 8, or 16 cameras, capturing portions of scene from each camera, and insert them on a video tape.

As multiplexers evolved, the manufacturers created circuitry to display all 4, 8, or 16 cameras in a cameo on a single monitor. Thus multiplexing can be thought of as a means of reducing up to 16 cameras to a single VCR and a single monitor.

Today, the analog multiplexer has evolved to a digital multiplexer. In this case, the video is converted to digital inside the box and stored on a hard drive. These units are commonly called DVRs. The advantages of DVRs over the older analog multiplexers are significant. A DVR:

- Eliminates tape, which wears out and requires constant replacement.
- Eliminates the need to manage the changing of tapes, thus reducing costly manpower.
- Eliminates the mechanical problems endemic in VCRs.
- Provides the ability to go directly to an incident in the stored video. This is done through indexing by time/date and event.
- Can copy stored incidents on DVDs or memory sticks and be given to others to review. In fact, DVRs can email the event since the recorded video is in a digital format.

IP Cameras, Domes, and PTZs. The next major step in the new paradigm has been the introduction of IP cameras, domes, and PTZs. Most of the major camera manufacturers have a family of cameras and domes that connect directly to the network. These devices are assigned an IP address, which allows video to be streamed to any location on the network, including NVRs.

CODEC Encoders/Decoders. A key element in IP video is the technique used to compress the video signal. Video signals, analog and digital, are very large. There is a great deal of data in a single field of video. Live video is 60 fields per second so our eyes view what appears as continuous, real-time visual information. A standard digital video signal can be as large as 250Mbs. Standard Ethernet has only 6Mbs of bandwidth in normal TCP/IP transmission. (Note: 40 percent of the network bandwidth is dedicated to packet signaling to insure delivery.) Given this, a standard Ethernet 10BaseT could not handle a fraction of a single camera's signal. In order to fit real time video on a standard network, the signal must be compressed using a CODEC.

Today, several compression techniques are being used. They are defined in industry standards. The most common are MJPEG, Wavelet, and MPEG4. Each of these formats has advantages and disadvantages. Unfortunately, the market is very confused by the data sheets and specs applied to these compression algorithms. To correct the problem, most manufacturers are moving to MPEG4 as a *defacto* standard.

Video Encoders. Video encoders are boxes that convert analog cameras to an IP camera. Most manufacturers have boxes with 1 to 4 camera inputs. In addition, the boxes usually have one analog audio channel and a data channel. In addition, most of the manufacturers support a few alarm inputs and/or relay outputs for local controls. These boxes are valuable tools for customers who have cameras already installed and wish to convert their system to IP video. The boxes allow the customer to plug in the cameras and PTZ or other data driven devices, converting them to an IP system.

Video Decoders. Video decoders are the reverse of video encoders. They are most often used by customers that want to take IP video (streaming video) off the network and display it on a standard analog monitor. Again, these are useful tools for converting an existing analog system to an IP video system.

NVRs. These are typically network storage arrays. Network storage arrays are devices with multiple hard drives that allow terabytes of storage. Most network component manufacturers provide network based mass storage systems. These devices, when connected to the network, can store the video real time from a large number of cameras.

The question always arises as to how many cameras can be stored on an NVR. Most manufacturers have calculators for their customers to estimate the amount of video that can be stored on a gigabyte of storage medium. Many of the storage arrays today are measured in terabytes. NVRs are used in installations using IP cameras/domes and/or video encoders that stream the cameras.

IP Switching. Once a system has been developed with streaming video, the user can purchase video management software for virtual matrix switching. (Virtual matrix switching has the same functionality of analog video switching but there is no switching hardware—it is virtual.) With this software, the user can switch any camera to any user. The IP switching eliminates the need for costly analog matrix switchers. There are a number of sources for Virtual matrix software. Each manufacturer's product has its own feature list, which the user must review prior to selecting one for a video security application.

Implementation of IP Video

Because IP video is still video, it shares the camera lens and area lighting requirements of analog video systems with regard to lighting, camera motion, etc. The video camera market has advanced over the years. In addition to IP cameras, there are day/night cameras and intelligent cameras. These new advancements make it easier for the video system designer.

Network Issues

There are a number of barriers preventing a more rapid movement to IP video. First, the CCTV industry (manufacturers, consultants, dealers, and integrators) is not comfortable with the network technology. There are concerns IP video will bog down or crash existing networks. However, IP video with today's compression technology is easily managed on network infrastructures.

New Systems

If one is designing a new video security system, it is advantageous to use IP video for the total design. The cost is much less than that of analog. This is especially true from a cabling standpoint.

The video system designer needs to work with the customer's IT staff or department in specifying the new design. It behooves the designer as well as the security manager to get the buy-in of the IT department.

The components used in new designs will be:

- IP cameras, IP domes, and/or IP PTZs
- NVRs for recording
- Virtual matrix switch for management and control

Old Systems

Existing systems should consider CODECs for conversion to IP video. The boxes and cages available today can plug in to the network. The designer can change over to IP switching by designing out the customer's old matrix switch.

Raymond Payne

INTRUSION DETECTION: INTRUDER TYPES

It is safe to say that no two intrusion-detection systems (IDS) can ever be exactly the same. Each IDS is unique in the sense that it will be designed with careful attention to a number of variables: the nature of the threat, the assets at risk, the layout and structures of the protected area, the operating processes and culture of the organization, the characteristics of supplemental systems, such as security officer operations, and the security manager's personal philosophy and supervisory style. External forces, such as geography, law, governmental regulation, and politics, may also impact an IDS.

Although systems will vary considerably, each will at least carry out four interacting functions: delay, detect, alert, and respond. Delay is provided by the presence of physical barriers around the assets, such as safes, vaults, walls, ceilings, and fences. Detection is accomplished by sensors that pick up the presence of an intruder. The alert function is provided by alarm equipment that annunciates the place of intrusion. The respond function is executed by a trained response force.

Threat Analysis

The nature of the threat is a key variable in the design of a system. We can look at the threat variable from at least two perspectives. The first is experiential because it is concerned with past and present occurrences. We can apply labels to these two dimensions of experience: traditional and contemporary.

From the second perspective we can look at threat in terms of source. Again, two dimensions stand out: internal and external. The internal threat is sourced within the employee population, including part-timers and contractors; the external threat is sourced within elements of the population outside of the organization and they run the gamut from unskilled criminals to highly skilled ideological groups and revenge-motivated individuals.

Another way to organize our thinking about threat personalities is to apply labels. The traditional threat personalities are the insider, the opportunist, and the professional. Overlaying the traditional threat are contemporary types that we may call the ideologue and the avenger. Let's look at them.

Traditional Threats

The Insider. The inside threat is typically manifested in theft, destruction, damage, and disruption. A combination of physical and procedural safeguards is valuable in thwarting the inside threat. Access controls, at least those that regulate movement of people through perimeter and second-level defenses, will not significantly impede the insider. Barriers and sensors at the critical points of protection (i.e., the places where critical assets are kept), in conjunction with procedures followed by security personnel and the law-abiding employees, will be effective in minimizing insider-related losses.

Designing an IDS to protect against internal threat requires considerable insight and careful deliberation. The insider can be expected to have access to lock combinations and keys, to have a good working knowledge of security equipment and operating procedures, and to enjoy freedom from excessive restraint and suspicion.

The Opportunist. More often than not, an IDS is set up with the external threat in mind. The opportunistic intruder tends to follow the path of least resistance in attempting to breach security defenses and is hoping to act upon whatever opportunities may be presented. The opportunistic intruder is typically a petty, common criminal lacking in sophistication, intelligence, and skill. Once inside the protected area, he or she will move about looking for targets of opportunity, e.g., easily convertible assets such as cash, jewelry, small appliances, desktop computer equipment, and automobiles. Some intruders in this class are oriented to sexual assault crimes; they look for chances to victimize the helpless. Most IDS are designed to deter the opportunistic intruder at the outermost boundaries.

The Professional. A third type of external threat is the skilled professional who has a particular target in mind, possesses technical knowledge of security devices and how to defeat them, and has a plan of action and the resources for carrying out the plan. The skilled intruder is often patient, is willing to abort an intrusion attempt that goes awry, has a back-up plan, an escape route, a plausible story if caught, and the good sense to concentrate efforts on soft targets as opposed to those that have been hardened by countermeasures. Most security systems are not effective in keeping the skilled intruder out, although many systems will feature second- and third-level safeguards, such as proximity sensors and safes, designed to detect and delay.

Contemporary Threats

The Ideologue. The ideologue seldom operates alone; although it is not uncommon for an individual to act alone, the act is usually supported morally or materially by a group. Ideologies spring from many sources: religion, nationalism, human rights, animal rights, environmental protection, etc. Each group will have its own set of targets, an agenda and avenues for achieving goals, and a support base. Material greed and unmet psychological needs for power/sexual satisfaction are not motivators for ideological groups, although groups have a history of resorting to robbery and kidnapping to acquire operating revenue.

Group tactics can range from highly terroristic acts, such as bombings and assassination, to purely symbolic acts, such as splashing blood on walls or burning a flag on the front steps. The ideologue may or may not be skilled, is likely to be intelligent, very likely to be strongly committed and dedicated, and willing to take chances and suffer the consequences of being caught. The issue-oriented intrusion is likely to be made by several or many intruders simultaneously, causing the initial response capability at the protected area to be overwhelmed. The capacity of the security system to deal with this threat can be significantly expanded when the security manager adjusts the IDS in relation to intelligence data concerning likely adversaries, their capabilities, probable methods of attack, and determination.

The Avenger. The number of incidents involving violence by an employee (or former employee) against co-workers and supervisors has increased dramatically in recent years. The number of injuries and deaths at work has also increased. When robbery-related shootings are factored in, workplace killings are a leading cause of on-the-job deaths.

Workplace homicides are often the result of an unstable employee being laid off or terminated; the worker returns with a gun and kills the supervisor and others who get in the way. When layoffs and terminations rise, violence also rises.

Employees who are likely to release frustration through acts of violence are also likely to have a history of violence and likely to indicate their growing frustration by changes in behavior at work. The implication here is that background checks can be helpful in identifying applicants who bring a potential for violence into the workplace, and that supervisors during periods of layoffs and terminations should be alert to radical changes in employee attitudes and performance.

The security manager should also move quickly to remove the access privileges of employees who have been let go and to set up with remaining workers and security officers an early warning system that will signal the return to the workplace of a released employee. Even more important, the security manager should have a plan and procedures for dealing with violent episodes at work.

John J. Fay

INTRUSION DETECTION: SYSTEM DESIGN COORDINATION

The designer of an intrusion detection system should thoroughly coordinate the contemplated operating and maintenance concepts with those individuals who will be affected by their implementation. These are the individuals who must operate and maintain the facility's performance within any restrictions that might be imposed by the security system.

The designer should also be concerned about those individuals who are responsible for the safety of the employees and other occupants of the premises. These are the same individuals who are usually forgotten until the security system is already installed or in the process of being installed. The designer's dread is to hear the operations manager say, "You can't install that equipment there because ..." or the safety manager say, "That door can't be locked during the day because ..." This is when the designer's problems really begin.

This type of problem can be virtually eliminated if the security system design is properly coordinated before the fact. Another benefit is that the individuals who participate in the system design will have personal interest in its implementation and acceptance by both the employees and management. Management support is needed for the security system to be successful. Management must set an example by following the security procedures themselves, as well as insisting that all security procedure be followed by others and all systems maintained in operations.

Operations is defined as the group composed of people who manufacture the products, refine the minerals, generate the electricity, operate the department store, manage the office building, etc. In other words, these are the people who are directly involved with the assets that the intrusion-detection system is being designed to safeguard. Therefore, time should be taken to understand their requirements and to review the proposed system design with them. As obvious as this recommendation appears, many systems have been designed without consideration to the operator or user. The design review should start with the initial system concept and continue through the final system design and installation. Follow-up reviews after installation will alert the designer to system problems that could be detrimental to the maximum effectiveness of the system if they are not corrected. These include not only hardware and operating problems, but also problems associated with management and employee acceptance of the intrusion-detection system.

A general training session should be conducted before the system is operational to apprise employees of the need for the security system, acquaint them with the equipment, and instruct them regarding proper system operations. The training session could be highlighted by a tour of the facility to demonstrate, if possible, the operation of each piece of equipment. A well-conducted training session will eliminate many day-to-day operational problems and improve employee acceptance of the system. The acceptance might be enhanced even more if a responsible individual from management attended the training session and addressed the importance of the security system.

Additional training may be required for those employees who must comply with special operating procedures as a result of the new security equipment. For instance, if an access control system is installed to limit access to controlled areas, the employees affected by this system would require special training on its operation.

Fire and Safety Officers

Since the fire and safety officers are responsible for the safety of occupants of the facility, they should be included in the system design coordination. Both the fire and safety officers will be concerned about the types of locking and access control systems, and bars and grilles installed on windows and doors.

Maintenance Department

Probably the most overlooked department with respect to being consulted on system design is the maintenance department. Yet these are the individuals who will be given the responsibility for maintaining the equipment after it is installed. Therefore, rather than just handing them the responsibility for maintaining security equipment, they should be given the opportunity to contribute to the system's design. They should participate in selecting the equipment location within the facility, routing the equipment's interconnecting cables, and selecting the system's maintenance concept, including the confirmation of estimated maintenance costs.

Quite often the plant drawings are not kept up-to-date to depict latest equipment locations, additions, or deletions, or they do not show the new wall or the fact that new plumbing has been added—and the list goes on and on. Sometimes these changes, especially the obvious ones, can be noted during a walk-through survey; but many of the subtle changes, such as the additional plumbing or cable trays, will probably be overlooked. The maintenance people will probably be familiar with most of these changes and additions, and therefore will be helpful in locating the security equipment and especially helpful in selecting the best cable routes.

The maintenance supervisor should certainly be consulted with regards to selecting the most appropriate maintenance concept for the intrusion-detection system. The supervisor understands his employees and knows their technical qualifications and skills. However, the supervisor will sometimes misjudge their ability to maintain the security equipment. The usual first impression is that anything containing electronic circuitry is too complicated to properly maintain. The supervisor may be right; but more often than not, the department can perform the maintenance if given sufficient training.

If the maintenance department has qualified electricians or electronics technicians who can operate a volt/ohm meter and have the manual dexterity to work with small electronics modules, then they should be able to perform most maintenance on equipment using the modular replacement concept. Sometimes it is helpful to demonstrate the equipment operation and perhaps give the supervisor a hands-on demonstration on how to trouble-shoot and repair the equipment. Another suggestion is to offer additional training for the maintenance personnel or hire an electronics technician who could perform the maintenance.

It sometimes happens that out of a sense of apprehension the maintenance supervisor will recommend that the maintenance be contracted. Quite often, however, the supervisor will experience a change of mind after witnessing the system's actual maintenance needs.

Robert L. Barnard

Source　Barnard, R. 1988. *Intrusion Detection Systems, 2nd Edition*. Boston: Butterworth-Heineman.

LOCKS

A door lock is usually all that prevents movement into a protected area, whether commercial or residential. Occasionally, a door lock will be supplemented with a padlock. Most door locks are key-operated. They consist of a cylinder or other opening for inserting a key that mechanically moves a bolt or latch. The bolt (or deadbolt) extends from the door lock into a bolt receptacle in the door frame.

The cylinder part of a lock contains the keyway, pins, and other mechanisms. Some locks, called double-cylinder locks, have a cylinder on each side of the door and require a key for both sides. With a single-cylinder lock, a thief may be able to break glass in or nearby the door and reach inside to turn the knob to release the lock. The disadvantage is that a key to the lock on the inside of the door must be readily available for emergency escape, such as during a fire.

The key-in-knob lock works on the same principles as the cylinder lock except, as the name implies, the keyway is in the knob. In the single key-in-knob lock the keyway is almost always on the outside door knob and a push or turn button for locking/unlocking is on the inside knob. The double key-in-knob lock has a keyway on the outside and inside knobs, which increases security but also decreases safety.

From the standpoint of forced entry, the cylinder lock is somewhat resistive in that it cannot be ripped easily from the door because it is seated flush or close to the surface. One model of the cylinder lock features a smooth, narrow ring around the neck of the cylinder. The ring moves freely so that even if it can be grasped by a tool, it cannot be twisted. The cylinder lock is vulnerable to a burglary tool called the slam hammer or slam puller. The device usually consists of a slender rod with a heavy sliding sleeve. One end of the rod has a screw or claw for insertion into the keyway. The other end has a retaining knob. When the sleeve is jerked away from the lock, striking the retaining knob, the lock cylinder or keyway is forcibly pulled out.

By contrast, the key-in-knob lock is somewhat more vulnerable because the knob itself can be hammered off; pried off with a crowbar; or pulled out by a grasping tool, such as channel lock pliers. Once the inner workings of the lock are exposed, the burglar can retract the bolt to open the door.

Probably one of the simplest attack techniques is slip-knifing. A thin, flat, and flexible object, such as a credit card, is inserted between the strike and the latch bolt to depress the latch bolt and release it from the strike. Slip-knifing of sliding windows is accomplished by inserting a thin and stiff blade between the meeting rail (stile) to move the latch to the open position; slip-knifing of pivoting windows is done by inserting a thin and stiff wire through openings between the rail and the frame and manipulating the sash operator.

Springing the door is a technique in which a large screwdriver or crowbar is placed between the door and the door frame so that the bolt extending from the lock into the bolt receptacle is pried out, enabling the door to swing open. A 1-inch bolt will hinder this attack.

Jamb peeling is the prying off or peeling back the door frame at a point near the bolt receptacle. When enough of the jamb is removed from the receptacle, the receptacle can be broken apart or removed, allowing the door to swing open. A metal or reinforced door frame is the antidote.

Sawing the bolt is inserting a hacksaw blade between the door and the door frame and cutting through the bolt. The countermeasure is to use a bolt made of a saw-resistant alloy or a bolt that is seated in such a way that it will freely spin on its side, thereby taking away the resistance needed for the saw blade to gain purchase.

Spreading the frame involves the use of a jack, such as an automobile jack, in such a way that the door jambs on each side of the door are pressured apart to a point where the door will swing free from the bolt receptacle. A reinforced door frame and a long deadbolt are countermeasures.

Kicking in the door is a primitive, but effective technique. In this case, the attack is against the door so that even the best locking hardware will have little deterrent effect. The countermeasure is a metal door or a solid wood door, at least 1-3/4-inches thick, installed in a wooden door frame at least 2-inches thick, or a steel door frame. An escutcheon plate can be used to shield the bolt receptacle.

A more sophisticated attack technique is lock picking. It is seen infrequently because of the expertise required. Lock picking is accomplished by using metal picks to align the pins in the cylinder as a key would to release the lock. The greater the number of pins, the more difficult it is to align them. A cylinder should have at least six pins to be resistive to lock picking.

The high-security form of the combination lock requires manipulation of one or several numbered dials to gain access. Combination locks usually have three or four dials that must be aligned in the correct order for entrance. Because only a limited number of people will be informed of the combination, the problems associated with compromised mechanical keys and lock picking are removed. Combination locks are used at doors and on safes, bank vaults, and high-security filing cabinets; in most cases, the combination can be changed by the owner on an as-needed basis.

With older combination locks, skillful burglars may be able, often with the aid of a stethoscope, to discern the combination by listening to the locking mechanism while the dial is being turned. Another attack method is for the burglar to take a concealed position at a distance from the lock and with binoculars or a telescope observe the combination sequence when the lock is opened.

The combination padlock has mostly low-security applications. It has a numbered dial and may be supplemented with a keyway. On some models, a serial number impressed on the lock by the manufacturer will allow the combination to be determined by cross-checking against a reference manual provided by the manufacturer to dealers. Although a convenience, it is a risk to security.

In a technique called padlock substitution, the thief will remove the property owner's unlocked padlock and replace it with a similar padlock. After the property owner locks up and leaves, the thief will return, open the padlock and gain entry. The preventive measure is to keep padlocks locked even when not in use.

John J. Fay

Sources

Fennelly, L. 1982. *Handbook of Loss Prevention and Crime Prevention*. Boston: Butterworth-Heinemann.

Purpura, P. 1984. *Security and Loss Prevention*. Boston: Butterworth-Heinemann.

OPERABLE OPENING SWITCHES

Operable openings are doors, windows, gates, hatches, and other openings that present opportunities for gaining access to restricted areas. Hence, operable opening switches are devices that detect unauthorized passage through the openings. The switches used for this purpose are called balanced magnetic, magnetic, mechanical contact, and tilt switches.

An important consideration in selecting a switch for a door is to evaluate the durability of the door itself. Doors range in durability from very substantial vault doors to easily defeated hollow-core doors. The durability of the door is an important consideration because an intruder who cuts or breaks through to gain access will not cause the operable opening switch to activate for the simple reason that the door remains in the closed position.

Another consideration with respect to doors and windows is that they should be tight against their surrounding frames in order to prevent false alarms induced by wind, rain, and similar innocent forces.

A switch used to protect a door should be installed along the top near the leading edge, if possible. In this position there is greater displacement between the door and door frame than at any other position. Because the displacement is greater at the leading edge, the sensitivity of the switch is not as critical in terms of alarm position, and the switch will not be as sensitive to small displacements if the door is slightly loose.

Balanced Magnetic Switch

A balanced magnetic switch is an assembly containing a balanced magnet usually mounted to a door or window frame. The electrical contact is a three-position reed switch mounted adjacent to an adjustable biasing magnet in the assembly. The reed switch is held in the balanced or center ("no alarm") position by two interacting magnetic fields. The primary field is generated by the balancing magnet and the secondary field by a small biasing magnet. As long as the magnetic field remains balanced around the reed switch, the contacts remain in contact in the center position. If the balancing magnet is moved or the magnetic field is unbalanced by an external magnet, the switch becomes unbalanced and initiates an alarm.

Contact Switches

The magnetically and mechanically activated contact switches are commonly used to detect the opening of protected doors and windows. Magnetic contact switches are similar to balanced magnetic switches only inasmuch as they are both magnetically activated.

The magnetic contact switch is a two-position reed switch held either in an open or closed position when the door or window is closed. The no-alarm contact position depends on whether the signal monitoring circuit recognizes an open or closed contact to initiate an alarm. In a circuit where the monitor recognizes an open circuit as an alarm condition, the switch would be installed such that when the door is opened the switch opens and initiates an alarm.

In general, the contact switch is mounted on the door frame with the activating magnet mounted on the door.

Mechanically activated contact switches are available with either pushbutton or lever actuators. Pushbutton switches are normally mounted in the hinge side of the door frames. When a door is opened, the switch contact opens and initiates an alarm.

Since the pushbutton switch is mounted on the hinge side of the door frame, the position where the door is opened far enough to initiate an alarm is critical. If the door can be opened far enough to slide a thin piece of metal over the pushbutton, the switch can be defeated. Lever-type switches are usually installed on a door frame along the top of the door so that when the door is closed it holds the switch closed. When the door is opened, the lever opens, allowing the switch contacts to open.

Robert L. Barnard

Source Barnard, R. 1988. *Intrusion Detection Systems, 2nd Edition*. Boston: Butterworth-Heinemann.

PERIMETER PROTECTION: ELECTRIC-FIELD SENSORS

Electric-field sensors generate an electrostatic field between either a pair or an array of wire conductors and detect distortions in the field caused by anyone approaching the sensor. The electrostatic field is generated by an alternating current induced on the "field" wire by a crystal-controlled generator. That portion of the electrostatic field coming in contact with or close to the "sense" wires induces electric signals in these wires that are monitored by the signal processor. Under normal operating conditions, the induced signals are constant; however, when someone approaches the sensor, the electrostatic field is distorted, thus altering the induced electrical signal. When the characteristics of the altered signal satisfy the processor alarm criteria, the detector initiates an alarm.

The signal processor is part of the control unit located in or near the electric-field sensor. Signals from the sense wires enter the signal processor and are passed through a band-pass filter. The filter rejects the high-frequency signals that might be caused by wind vibrating the field and sense wires, and the low-frequency signals that might be caused by foreign objects striking the fence wires. The signals must also simultaneously satisfy several signal processing criteria before an alarm will be initiated. The first criterion is that the amplitude of the signal must exceed a certain pre-set level that is a function of the intruder's size and proximity to the fence. This criterion is imposed to discriminate against small animals that might otherwise cause false or nuisance alarms. A second criterion is that the movements of the intruder approaching the sensor must be in the frequency range of the band-pass filter to be accepted by the signal processor. As already mentioned, this criterion is imposed to alleviate alarms from wind and blowing debris. The third and final criterion is that the signal must be present at the processor for a pre-set period of time. This pre-set time criterion minimizes false alarms caused by electromagnetic fields generated by lightning and also provides additional protection against nuisance alarms caused by objects blowing or birds flying through the sensor wires.

Another feature of the signal processor is that it has a self-adjusting circuit that automatically adjusts the detector sensitivity to compensate for objects moved close to the sensor. This means that cars, buses, or other metal equipment could be located near the electric-field sensor for protection. Anyone who attempts to move the object will initiate an alarm.

Excessive movement between the wire conductors or between the conductors and the fence fabric would induce low-frequency signals on the sense wire that might be interpreted by the signal processor as valid intrusion alarm signals. For the same reason, the chain-link fence fabric should be tight to reduce the relative motion between the fence and sensor. Line supervision for the wire conductors is provided by a terminator installed between the sense and field wire at the end of the electric-field sensor. Two terminators are required for three-wire sensor configurations.

Electric-field sensors can provide perimeter protection for many industrial and commercial installations. An application feature is that the sensors will follow the ground contour and perimeter configuration. If they are mounted to the perimeter fence, the sensors do not occupy a lot of space inside the fence. When the electric-field sensor is mounted on the perimeter fence, it has a high probability of detecting anyone climbing over or cutting through the fence and a fair probability of detecting a low-crawling intruder attempting to crawl under the fence and detector. Therefore, if the intruder can be expected to lift the fence fabric and crawl under, the bottom of the fence fabric should be secured either to the ground or to a bottom rail to prevent it from being easily lifted. This will increase the difficulty to enter under the fence, forcing the intruder to climb over or cut through the fence fabric.

Robert L. Barnard

Source   Barnard, R. 1988. *Intrusion Detection Systems, 2nd Edition.* Boston: Butterworth-Heinemann.

PERIMETER SENSOR SYSTEMS: DESIGN CONCEPTS AND GOALS

Before the detailed design and implementation of a perimeter sensor system are considered, some basic design principles and concepts should be understood.

Continuous Line of Detection

By definition, a perimeter is a closed line around some area that needs protection. A design goal is to have uniform detection around the entire length of the perimeter. The perimeter is divided into sectors to aid in assessment and response. This requires that sensors form a continuous line of detection around the perimeter. In practice this means configuring the sensor hardware so that the detection zone from one perimeter sector overlaps with the detection zones for the two adjacent sectors. Also, in areas where the primary sensor cannot be deployed properly, such as a gate, an alternate sensor is used to cover that gap.

Protection-In-Depth

As applied to perimeter sensor systems, the concept of protection-in-depth means the use of multiple lines of detection. Thus a minimum of two continuous lines of detection is used in high-security systems. Many perimeter sensor systems have been installed with three sensor lines, and a few have four. For example, a perimeter sensor system might include a buried-line sensor, a fence-associated sensor, and a free-standing sensor. Multiple sensor lines provide additional detection, increased reliability, and in case of hardware failure, will fail-secure (i.e., still provide protection, although to a lesser degree). In this scheme, any single sensor can fail without jeopardizing the overall security of the facility being protected. Elimination of single-point or component failures is a major advantage in any security system, as this will assure balanced protection even in adverse conditions and will prevent the introduction of vulnerabilities based on the failure or defeat of only one component by the adversary.

Complementary Sensors

Significantly better performance by the perimeter sensor system can be achieved by selecting different and complementary types of sensors for the multiple lines of detection, for example, microwave and active infrared. In this way, different sensor technologies, with different PD, NAR, and vulnerabilities are combined to increase the effectiveness of the exterior perimeter intrusion detection system. Complementary sensors enhance the overall system performance because they use the best features of a particular technology, while at the same time providing effective backup in case of environmental change, component failure, or successful attack by the adversary. This design philosophy results in detection of a wider spectrum of intruders, allows operation of at least one sensor line during any conceivable environmental disturbance, and increases the difficulty of the task for the covert intruder attempting to defeat the system.

Use of complementary sensors is an effective alternative to the use of dual-technology sensors since the individual sensors will perform at their maximum levels and not be compromised by co-location and filtering. While implementation of complementary sensors may be more expensive, they will also afford a higher protection level. Due to the higher protection provided by complementary sensors, they are the preferred method in high-security applications.

Examples of exterior complementary sensors include microwave/infrared, microwave/ported coaxial cable, and ported coaxial cable/infrared combinations. The important point is that the detection patterns must overlap for the sensors to be complementary. For example, a microwave/fence sensor combination is not complementary because the detection patterns can't overlap without serious nuisance alarm problems. In addition, bistatic/monostatic microwave combinations are not complementary since both are susceptible to the same defeat methods and nuisance alarm sources.

Priority Schemes

One disadvantage of multiple sensor lines is that more nuisance alarms will have to be processed. System effectiveness has not been increased if the system operator is overwhelmed with nuisance alarms. The probability of detection decreases as the time to assess alarms increases. The assessment subsystem should aid the operator in evaluating alarm information. Many different methods have been used to deal with the alarm data from a combination of sensors. A recommended method currently in use requires the system operator to assess all alarms with the aid of a computer that establishes the time order of assessment for multiple simultaneous alarms. The computer sets a priority for each alarm based on the probability that an alarm event corresponds to a real intrusion. The alarms are displayed to the operator in order of decreasing priority; all alarms are eventually assessed. The alarms priority is typically established by taking into account the number of sensors in alarms in a given sector, the time between alarms in the sector, the order in which the alarms occur in relation to the physical configuration of the sensors, and alarms in the adjacent sectors.

Combination of Sensors

It is desirable that a sensor or sensor system have a high probability of detection (PD) for all expected types of intrusion and a low nuisance alarm rate (NAR) for all expected environmental conditions. No single exterior sensor presently available meets both of these criteria; all are limited in their detection capability and all have high NARs under certain environmental conditions.

The nuisance alarm rate can be reduced significantly by combining sensors. A seismic sensor and an electric field sensor do not give correlated alarms, for example, because they respond to different things. If both are activated at about the same time, it is probable that they have detected an intrusion. Since a single intrusion attempt will not activate two or more sensors simultaneously, a system can be designed to generate an alarm if two or more sensors are activated within a pre-selected time interval. A long time interval is desirable to assure detection of intruders moving slowly, but if the interval is too long, the NAR may not be reduced enough. By installing sensors so they cover the same general area, thereby providing redundant coverage, the time interval can be kept small.

Clear Zone

A perimeter intrusion detection system performs better when it is located in an isolated clear zone (or isolation zone). The purpose of the clear zone is to improve performance of the perimeter sensor system by increasing detection probability, reducing nuisance alarms, and preventing defeat. The clear zone also promotes good visual assessment of the causes of sensor alarms. Two parallel fences extending the entire length of the perimeter usually define the width of the clear zone. The fences are intended to keep people, animals, and vehicles out of the detection zone. The area between the fences is usually cleared of all above-ground structures, including overhead utility lines; vegetation in this area is also removed. After the zone between the fences is cleared, only the detection and assessment hardware and associated power and data lines are installed in the area. When clear zones bounded by two parallel fences are used, no sensors should be placed on the outer fence. This will reduce nuisance alarms from blowing debris and small animals and will eliminate the possibility of an adversary defeating the fence sensor without being seen by the video assessment system. Video assessment of anything outside the fence will be difficult due to the inability of the camera to see through the fence fabric. Clear zones, and the associated use of multiple complementary sensors, is generally reserved for use at high-security facilities, such as nuclear plants, prisons, military bases, or other government installations.

Sensor Configuration

The configuration of the multiple sensors within the clear zone also affects system performance. Overlapping the detection volumes of two different sensors within each sector enhances performance by creating a larger overall detection volume. Thus, defeat of the sensor pair is less probable because a larger volume must be bypassed or two different technologies must be defeated simultaneously. A third sensor can even further enhance performance, not by overlapping with the first two, but by forming a separate line of detection. Physically separate lines of detection can reveal information useful for determining alarm priority during multiple simultaneous alarms. In particular, the order of alarms in a sector (or adjacent sectors) may correspond to the logical sequence for an intrusion.

Site-Specific System

Each site requiring physical protection has a unique combination of configuration and physical environment. Thus, a physical protection system designed for one site cannot be transferred to another. The physical environment will influence the selection of types of sensors for perimeter sensor systems. The natural and industrial environments provide the nuisance alarm sources for the specific site. The topography of the perimeter determines the shapes and sizes of the space available for detection, specifically the clear zone width and the existence of flat or irregular terrain. These factors generally help determine a preferred set of sensors. Although understanding of the interaction between intrusion sensors and the environment has increased significantly in recent years, it is still advisable to set up a demonstration sector on site using the possible sensors before making a commitment to a complete system. This test sector located on site is intended to confirm sensor selection and to help refine the final system design.

Tamper Protection

The hardware and system design should incorporate features that prevent defeat by tampering. This means the system should be tamper-resistant and tamper-indicating. Sensor electronics and junction box enclosures should have tamper switches. Above-ground power and signal cables should be installed inside metal conduit. Alarm communication lines should use some type of line supervision, which detects lines that have been cut, disconnected, short-circuited, or bypassed. The receiver electronics of bistatic sensors are generally more vulnerable to defeat than the transmitter electronics. In this case the sensors can often be placed so that an intruder must be in or pass through the detection volume to approach the receiver.

Self-Test

To verify normal operation of a perimeter sensor system, its ability to detect must be tested regularly. Although manual testing is recommended, manpower requirements are usually restrictive. A capability for remote testing of trigger signals can be provided and initiated by the alarm communication and control system. Typically this is a switch closure or opening. In an automatic remote test procedure, the central computer control

system generates at a random time a test trigger to a given sensor. The sensor must then respond with an alarm. The control system checks that an alarm occurred within a specified time and cleared within another specified time. Failure to pass the test indicates a hardware failure or tampering and produces an alarm message.

Pattern Recognition

The field of sensor technology is in a period of major change, caused by the development of inexpensive, powerful computers. These computers can now receive signals from sensors and analyze the signal pattern, looking for patterns that are particularly characteristic of an intruder. Using neural network or artificial intelligence software, the computers can actually learn these intruder signal patterns and then avoid nuisance alarms. Any sensor or combination of sensors that returns a signal other than just off-on can have their signals analyzed by a small computer and can in some cases sense whether or not an intruder is present.

Mary Lynn Garcia

PHYSICAL PROTECTION SYSTEMS: PRINCIPLES AND CONCEPTS

This article addresses the use of principles and concepts when conducting a vulnerability assessment (VA). The main purpose of this article is to examine:

- Physical protection systems (PPS) functions of detection, delay, and response.
- Basic principles of an effective PPS design.
- Performance measures used for each PPS function.

Physical Protection Systems Overview

The designer must determine how best to combine such elements as sensors, fences, barriers, procedures, communication devices, and security personnel into a PPS capable of achieving the protection objectives. The resulting PPS design should meet these objectives within the operational, safety, legal, and economic constraints of the facility. The primary functions of a PPS are detection of an adversary, delay of that adversary, and response by security personnel (guard force). These functions and some of their components are shown in Figure 23.

Certain guidelines should be observed during the PPS design. A PPS performs better if detection is as far from the target as possible and delays are near the target. In addition, there is close association between detection (exterior or interior) and assessment. It is a basic principle of security system design that detection without assessment is not detection, because without assessment, the operator does not know the cause of an alarm. If the alarm is the result of trash blowing across an exterior area or lights being turned off in an interior area, there is no need for a response, because there is no valid intrusion (i.e., by an adversary). Another close association is the relationship between response and response force communications. A response force cannot respond unless it receives a communication call for a response.

Physical Protection System Design

A system may be defined as a collection of components or elements designed to achieve an objective according to a plan. The ultimate objective of a PPS is to prevent the accomplishment of overt or covert malevolent human actions. Typical objectives are to prevent sabotage of critical equipment, theft of assets or information from within the facility, and protection of people. A PPS must accomplish its objectives by either deterrence or a combination of detection, delay, and response. Listed here are the component subsystems that perform these functions.

Detection
- Exterior/Interior Intrusion Sensors
- Alarm Assessment
- Alarm Communication and Display
- Entry Control Systems

Delay
- Access Delay
- Response
- Response Force
- Response Force Communications

The system functions of detection and delay can be accomplished by the use of either hardware or guards. Guards usually handle response, although automated response technologies are under development. There is always a balance between the use of hardware and the use of guards. In different conditions and applications, one is often the preferable choice.

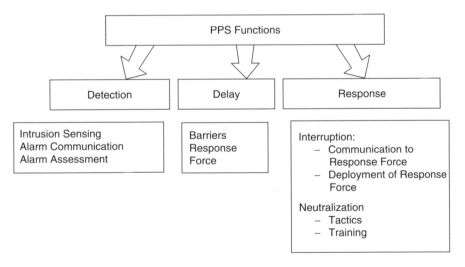

Figure 23. PPS functions include detection, delay, and response. These functions must occur in this order and can be evaluated to determine the vulnerability of an existing or proposed PPS to a specified threat. From *Vulnerability Assessment of Physical Protection Systems*, by Mary Lynn Garcia, p. 34. Butterworth-Heinemann, 2006. Reprinted by permission.

Detection, delay, and response are all required functions. They must be performed in this order and within a length of time that is less than the time required for the adversary to complete his task.

PPS Functions

The primary PPS functions are detection, delay, and response. It is essential to consider the system functions in detail, as a thorough understanding of the definitions of these functions and the measure of effectiveness of each is required to evaluate the system. It is important to note that detection must be accomplished for delay to be effective. For a system to be effective at this objective, there must be notification of an attack (detection), and then adversary progress must be slowed (delay), which will allow the response force time to interrupt or stop the adversary (response).

Detection. Detection is the discovery of an adversary action. It includes sensing of covert or overt actions. To discover an adversary action, the following events need to occur:

1. A sensor reacts to a stimulus and initiates an alarm.
2. Information from the sensor and assessment subsystems is reported and displayed.
3. A person assesses information and judges the alarm to be valid or invalid. If assessed as a nuisance alarm, detection has not occurred. Therefore, detection without assessment is not considered detection. Assessment is the process of determining whether the source of the alarm is due to an attack or a nuisance alarm.

Detection is not an instantaneous event. Included in the detection function of physical protection is entry control. Entry control allows entry to authorized personnel and detects the attempted entry of unauthorized personnel and material. The measures of effectiveness of entry control are throughput, false acceptance rate, and false rejection rate. Throughput is defined as the number of authorized personnel that are allowed access per unit time, assuming that all

personnel who attempt entry are authorized for entrance. False acceptance is the rate at which false identities or credentials are allowed entry, and false rejection rate is the frequency of denying access to authorized personnel.

The measures of effectiveness for the detection function are the probability of sensing adversary action, the time required for reporting and assessing the alarm, and nuisance alarm rate. A sensor activates and then at a later time a person receives information from the sensor and assessment subsystems. The probability of detection decreases as the time before assessment increases. A long time delay between detection and assessment lowers the probability of detection. The more time required in making an accurate assessment, the less likely it will be that the cause of the alarm is still present. For example, if sensor alarms are assessed by sending a guard to the sensor location, by the time the guard arrives, there may no longer be an obvious alarm source. In this case, the delay between sensor initiation and assessment can be so lengthy that no assessment could be made.

Response force personnel can also accomplish detection. Guards at fixed posts or on patrol may serve a vital role in sensing an intrusion. An effective assessment system provides two types of information associated with detection: information about whether the alarm is a valid alarm or a nuisance alarm and details about the cause of the alarm—what, who, where, and how many. Even when assisted by a video assessment system, however, humans do not make good detectors. Studies have shown that brief instances of movement are missed by 48 percent of human observers using video monitors.

An additional performance measure of sensors is the nuisance alarm rate. A nuisance alarm is any alarm that is not caused by an intrusion. In an ideal sensor system, the nuisance alarm

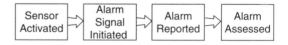

Figure 24. Detection starts with sensor activation and ends with assessment of the alarm to determine the cause. From *Vulnerability Assessment of Physical Protection Systems*, by Mary Lynn Garcia, p. 36. Butterworth-Heinemann, 2006. Reprinted by permission.

rate would be zero. In the real world, however, all sensors interact with their environment, and they cannot discriminate between intrusions and other events in their detection zone. Common sources of natural noise are vegetation (trees and weeds), wildlife (animals and birds), and weather conditions (wind, rain, snow, fog, lightning). Industrial sources of noise include ground vibration, debris moved by wind, and electromagnetic interference. False alarms are those nuisance alarms generated by the equipment itself (whether by poor design, inadequate maintenance, or component failure).

Delay. Delay, the second function of a PPS, is the slowing down of adversary progress. Delay can be accomplished by people, barriers, locks, and activated delays. The response force can be considered elements of delay if they are in fixed and well-protected positions. The measure of delay effectiveness is the time required by the adversary (after detection) to bypass each delay element. Although the adversary may be delayed before detection, this delay is of no value to the effectiveness of the PPS, as it does not provide additional time to respond to the adversary. Figure 25 summarizes the delay function.

Response. The response function consists of the actions taken by the response force to prevent adversary success. Response, as it is used here, consists of interruption. Interruption is defined as a sufficient number of response force personnel arriving at the appropriate location to stop the adversary's progress. It includes the communication to the protection force of accurate information about adversary actions and the deployment of the response force. The measure of response force effectiveness is the time between receipt of a communication of adversary action and the interruption of the adversary action (response force time). The PPS response function is shown in Figure 26.

The effectiveness measures for response communication are the probability of accurate communication and the time required for communication. The time after information is initially transmitted may vary considerably depending on the method of communication. After the initial period, the probability of valid communication begins to increase rapidly. The probability of correct and current data being communicated is increased. There can be some delay in establishing accurate communication caused by human behavior. On the first attempt to communicate, the operator is alerted that there is a call, but may not have heard all the relevant information. Then a request for a second transmission is made to repeat the information, and finally, the operator understands the call and asks for clarification.

Deployment describes the actions of the protective force from the time communication is received until the force is in position to interrupt the adversary. The effectiveness measure of this function is the probability of deployment to the adversary location and the time required to deploy the response force.

Relationship of PPS Functions

The total time required for the adversary to accomplish the goal depends on the delay

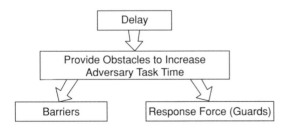

Figure 25. Delay components include barriers and members of the response force. Barriers include active and passive barriers. From *Vulnerability Assessment of Physical Protection Systems*, by Mary Lynn Garcia, p. 38. Butterworth-Heinemann, 2006. Reprinted by permission.

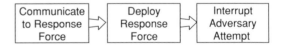

Figure 26. Response components include communication, proper deployment of the response force, and interruption of the adversary before attack completion. For some threats, interruption by the response force may not be enough to counter the attack. From *Vulnerability Assessment of Physical Protection Systems*, by Mary Lynn Garcia, p. 38. Butterworth-Heinemann, 2006. Reprinted by permission.

provided by the PPS. The adversary may begin to act some time before the first alarm occurs. After the alarm, the alarm information must be reported and assessed to determine if the alarm is valid. At this time the location of the alarm must be communicated to the members of the response force. Further time is then required for the response force to respond in adequate numbers and with adequate equipment to interrupt adversary actions.

Characteristics of an Effective PPS

The procedures of the PPS must be compatible with the facility procedures and integrated into the PPS design. Training of personnel in policies, procedures, and operation of equipment is also important to system effectiveness. Security, safety, and operational objectives must be accomplished at all times. A well-engineered PPS will exhibit the following characteristics:

- Protection-in-depth
- Minimum consequence of component failure
- Balanced protection

Protection-in-Depth. Protection-in-depth means that, to accomplish the goal, an adversary should be required to avoid or defeat a number of protective devices in sequence. For example, an adversary might have to defeat one sensor and penetrate two separate barriers before gaining entry to a process control room or a filing cabinet in the project costing area. The actions and times required to penetrate each of these layers may not necessarily be equal, and the effectiveness of each may be quite different, but each will require a separate and distinct act by the adversary moving along the path. The effects on the adversary by a system that provides protection-in-depth will be to:

- Increase uncertainty about the system.
- Require more extensive preparations prior to attacking the system.
- Create additional steps where the adversary may fail or abort the mission.

Minimum Consequence of Component Failure. It is unlikely that a complex system will ever be developed and operated that does not experience some component failure during its lifetime. Causes of component failure in a PPS are numerous and can range from environmental factors (which may be expected) to adversary actions beyond the scope of the threat used in the system design. Although it is important to know the cause of component failure to restore the system to normal operation, it is more important to provide contingency plans so that the system can continue to operate. Requiring portions of these contingency plans to be carried out automatically (so that redundant equipment automatically takes over the function of disabled equipment) may be highly desirable in some cases, for example, the presence of back up power at a facility. In the event that an adversary disables the primary power source, generators or batteries can be used to power the security system. Some component failures may require aid from sources outside of the facility to minimize the impact of the failure. One example of this was the use of National Guard units to supplement airport security personnel after the terrorist attacks at the World Trade Center and the Pentagon on 9/11. In this case, the component failure was the temporary lack of sufficient response forces under new threat conditions.

Balanced Protection. Balanced protection means that no matter how an adversary attempts to accomplish a goal, effective elements of the PPS will be encountered. Consider, for example, the barrier surface that surrounds a room. This surface may consist of:

- Walls, floors, and ceilings of several types.
- Doors of several types; equipment hatches in floors and ceilings.
- Heating, ventilating, and air conditioning openings with various types of grilles.

For a completely balanced system, the minimum time to penetrate each of these barriers would be equal, and the minimum probability of detecting penetration of each of these barriers should be equal; however, complete balance is probably not possible or desirable. Certain elements, such as walls, may be extremely resistant to penetration, not because of physical protection requirements, but because of structural or safety requirements. Door, hatch, and grille delays may be considerably less than wall delays and still be adequate.

Design and Evaluation Criteria

Any design process must have criteria against which elements of the design will be evaluated. A design process based on performance criteria will select elements and procedures according to the contribution they make to overall system performance, which is the effectiveness measure of the system. By establishing a measure of overall system performance, these values may be compared for existing (baseline) systems and upgraded systems and the amount of improvement determined. This increase in system effectiveness can then be compared to the cost of implementation.

A feature criteria (or compliance-based) approach selects elements or procedures to satisfy requirements that certain items are present. The effectiveness measure is the presence of those features. The use of a feature criteria approach in regulations or requirements that apply to a PPS should generally be avoided or handled with extreme care. Unless such care is exercised, the feature criteria approach can lead to the use of a checklist method to determine system adequacy, based on the presence or absence of required features. This is clearly not desirable, as overall system performance is of interest, rather than the mere presence or absence of system features or components. The performance measures for the PPS functions are:

Detection
- Probability of detection
- Time for communication and assessment
- Frequency of nuisance alarms

Delay

- Time to defeat obstacles

Response

- Probability of accurate communication to response force
- Time to communicate
- Probability of deployment to the correct location
- Time to deploy
- Response force effectiveness after arrival at the correct location

When performing a VA, the general purpose is to evaluate each element (people, procedures, and technology) of the PPS. Once this is done, an estimate of overall system performance is made. The key to a good VA is accurately estimating element performance by considering specific degradation factors for each element. When using a quantitative approach, this can be done by starting with a tested performance value for a particular PPS element, such as a sensor, and degrading its performance based on how the device is installed, maintained, tested, and integrated into the overall PPS. For qualitative analysis, we would degrade performance of each element based on the same conditions, but we would represent the performance of the device by assigning a level of effectiveness such as high, medium, or low, rather than a number. Operation of all elements must be evaluated under all weather conditions, facility states, and considering all threats.

Additional Design Elements

An effective PPS will combine people, procedures, and equipment into an integrated system that will protect assets from the defined threat. People and technology components are important design tools that often form the basis for protection systems. The use of procedures as protection elements cannot be overstated. Procedural changes can be cost-effective solutions to physical protection issues, although, when used by themselves, they will protect assets from only the lowest threats. Procedures include not only operational and maintenance procedures but also training of facility personnel in security awareness and of guards or other response forces on when and how to stop an adversary.

Mary Lynn Garcia

Source   Tickner, A. and Poulton, E. 1973. "Monitoring Up to 16 Television Pictures Showing a Great Deal of Movement." *Ergonomics*, 16(4), 381–40.

PHYSICAL SECURITY DESIGN

A threat analysis is a prerequisite to the security system design of a planned facility. A comprehensive survey will take into consideration the range of possible threats, including both natural and man-made, and the vulnerabilities of the facility's site. The professional conducting the survey will be concerned with such elements as likely adversaries and their capabilities, probability and frequency of threat occurrence, and the criticality of the assets to be protected within the facility. Also of concern will be the physical and psychological factors that can contribute to or detract from the protective scheme.

Physical factors, such as fences, locks, walls, and doors, should be regarded as opportunities for enhancing protection. They are fairly easy to evaluate because their effectiveness can be measured in discrete terms, such as in the minutes of delay afforded against intrusion. By contrast, the effectiveness of psychological factors is relative and arguable. They include uniformed guards, television surveillance cameras, lights, and signage that discourage unwanted entry.

Asset Value

The protection given a particular asset should be in keeping with its value. Value in this context is both extrinsic and intrinsic. Extrinsic value represents monetary worth as well as replacement cost. It can also incorporate the cost of lost business opportunity when an asset cannot be sold because it has been stolen or destroyed. Intrinsic value corresponds to assets (which may also have extrinsic value) that are irreplaceable, unique, or of such great psychological worth that protection of them is absolutely essential. Nuclear weapons, highly toxic substances, rare paintings, and the like fall into this category because they cannot be measured in dollars alone.

Asset Protection

The selection of locations and safeguards for the protected assets will be influenced by the needs of the business to have use of them and the convertibility of the assets to personal use. Cash in a retail facility, for example, is somewhat dispersed among cashiers and is highly convertible. Sensitive information in a research facility, on the other hand, tends to be compartmented, closely held, and not very convertible to personal use. The locations of retail cashiers

and the physical and procedural safeguards for protecting cash will be markedly different than those used for protecting information in the research setting.

Location also refers to a number of proximities, i.e., nearby structures and access roads, human activity in and around the facility, and the nearness of the response force to the installation. Nearness of other buildings or neighboring businesses could be an advantage if there is a mutual sense of concern. Conversely, nearby premises or business activities could serve as a magnet in attracting crime that could spill onto the protected site.

Roads around the site also carry advantages and disadvantages. For a fenced compound containing stored materials, highly traveled roads with close-up visibility will be an advantage because the protection scheme will rely upon the deterring effect of passing motorists and law enforcement patrols; for a rare metals laboratory, nearby roads may be a disadvantage because they create easy in and out access for robbers and burglars.

Nearness of human activity is pertinent because if there is activity near the assets, the security system might be effective with a combination of locks, barriers, and locally annunciated audible alarms.

The proximity of the security or law enforcement force to the location of assets will determine the timeliness of response. Physical barriers to intrusion provide delay and intrusion sensors provide notice. These are essentially useless safeguards unless reinforced by the neutralizing effect of a human response.

Physical Barriers

Delay of the intruder can be provided by structural barriers such as fences, gates, walls, roofs, floors, doors, windows, or vaults, and natural barriers such as rivers, lakes, cliffs, or any natural obstruction that is difficult to cross. Unsophisticated intruders, whose modes of operation are limited to forcible entry through doors and windows, will probably be discouraged by structurally sound barriers secured with high-security locks. These barriers are minor obstacles to the sophisticated intruder.

The length of time required for an adversary to penetrate the physical barriers is a function of its penetration resistance and the breaching method used. The time required to penetrate a physical barrier should be considered in tandem with the response time. If the barrier can be penetrated before an effective response can be mounted, the system should be modified to either increase barrier resistance time or give earlier detection of a penetration attempt.

Fences. Fences are used to channel personnel and vehicles through designated entrances during normal operations and to discourage or deter entrance into the fenced area during non-working hours. Fences may be considered a barrier to an unskilled intruder, but they are only minor obstacles to a more skilled or agile intruder. Fences are, however, usually considered the first level of protection in a security system. For this reason, fences are quite often protected with fence disturbance sensors.

The most common type of fences are chain-link fences like those installed on the perimeter of most industrial sites, utilities, and government installations. These fences are typically 7-foot high, woven metal fabric supported by steel posts, usually topped with either three or six strands of barbed wire. A single arm outrigger supports three strands of barbed wire and a V-shaped outrigger supports six strands with three strands on each arm. The barbed-wire topping increases the effective height to 8 feet.

A structurally sturdy, well-maintained fence provides a better barrier for fence disturbance sensors and will psychologically discourage intruders and resist penetration more effectively than a loose, poorly maintained fence. Some maintenance measures that should be taken are: keep the fence-line free of brush and bushes; eliminate washouts under the fence that allow easy access by crawling; remove any objects from along the fence that could be used for gaining entrance by climbing; and secure all gate-hinges hardware so that the gate cannot be easily removed even though locked.

Sometimes the major advantage of a fence is that after the intruder crosses it to get in, he must retreat through or over the fence with the assets he is trying to steal. For some assets this may not be difficult, but if the intruder is trying to steal bulky materials or large objects, the fence may impede retreat, limiting the thief as to how much he can take without opening the gate

or cutting through the fence. Therefore, chain-link fences have some value in protecting bulky assets, assuming that the area is patrolled; otherwise, the intruders would be undisturbed to execute their objective.

Overall, fences serve a useful purpose by defining legal boundaries, deterring the general public, and eliminating interference from wanderers and lowly motivated intruders. Defining the legal boundary around an installation is important. If, for instance, a guard or responding police officer finds someone inside the fenced compound, there can be little doubt that the person knowingly trespassed. The effectiveness of the boundary is enhanced when it is properly posted.

Walls. Exterior walls are usually considered the first level of protection for buildings not enclosed by a fence. Depending on the type of building, the exterior walls may vary from wood siding to thick granite walls. However, the most common types of exterior walls are constructed from cinder block, brick, concrete, pre-cast concrete, or combinations of these materials. Concrete and pre-cast concrete walls offer the greatest penetration resistance, but even these are vulnerable to penetration.

Operable Openings. Operable openings are doors, windows, transoms, and similar devices that can be opened or closed to allow or prevent passage of people, air, or light. They are the usual points of entry for intruders, especially at ground level and in concealed and semi-concealed locations. Operable openings are also the hardest points to protect, simply because they are designed for passage.

The first consideration in protecting an operable opening is to determine if the opening is really needed. Many buildings, especially older ones, have windows and doors that are no longer used. The problem of protecting obsolete windows or doors can be eliminated by simply sealing them permanently in a manner that maintains the penetration resistance of the wall containing the opening. For instance, if the door to be eliminated is mounted in a brick wall, the door assembly should be removed and the opening bricked up, taking care to properly anchor the new construction. When an operable opening is less than 18 feet from the ground or less than 14 feet from another structure, it should be either physically covered with bars or grilles equipped with intrusion detection devices, or both.

Ground-level doors, especially the accessible ones, are used for gaining entrance into a facility more than any other openings. Therefore, the door locks, mounting hardware, and construction of the door assemblies should be in keeping with the integrity of the surrounding walls. Because of the high probability of an intrusion through a door, all exterior doors should have intrusion-detection devices that will detect anyone opening the door. Since ground-level windows also allow easy access, they too should be physically secured and protected with intrusion-detection devices.

Deterrents

Deterrents can be classified as either physical or psychological. Physical security deterrents are highly visible devices or barriers that are designed to delay the entry of an intruder long enough to effectuate an apprehension. A deterrent is effective only to the extent it is believed by the potential intruder to be effective. A hollow core door has less deterrent value than a steel reinforced door because the potential intruder will understand the difference in time delay and will accordingly gauge his prospects for success.

The same is true for psychological deterrents, such as uniformed security officers, watchdogs, lighting, closed-circuit television (CCTV) cameras, mirrors, etc.

The effectiveness of physical deterrents can be quantitatively measured in terms of penetration times and ranked as to the likely effect on deterring or delaying an intruder, but their effectiveness as psychological deterrents cannot be quantitatively measured. Qualitative pronouncements can be made and interpolations based on crime rates can be put forward convincingly, but assessment is subjective at best. Nonetheless, the conventional wisdom is that the tried and true security safeguards do act as important deterrents to crime.

Robert L. Barnard

Source   Barnard, R. 1988. *Intrusion Detection Systems, 2nd Edition*. Boston: Butterworth-Heinemann.

PROXIMITY AND POINT SENSORS

Proximity and point sensors are available that detect persons approaching, touching, or attempting to remove valuable items or attempting to penetrate areas containing valuable items.

Proximity Sensors

Capacitance Proximity Detectors. These protect metal items such as safes and file cabinets. They detect changes in the electrical capacitance between the item being protected and an electrical ground plane under the protected item. Capacitance detectors can also be used to protect valuable items such as art objects by mounting the detectors on a metal surface isolated from the ground plane.

A capacitor is an electronic component that consists of two conductor plates separated by a dielectric medium. A change in the electrical charge or dielectric medium results in a change in the capacitance between the two plates. One plate is the metal item being protected and the second plate is an electrical reference ground plane under and around the protected item. The metal object is isolated from the ground plane by insulating blocks. This leaves only air around and between the metal object and ground. Therefore, air is the dielectric medium.

In operation, the metal objects are electrically charged to a potential that creates an electrostatic field between the metal object and reference ground. The strength of the field is certainly non-lethal but is adequate enough to cause a detectable change in the capacitance if anyone approaches or touches the protected object. The electrical conductivity of the intruder's body alters the dielectric characteristics. The dielectric changes result in a change in the capacitance between the protected item and the reference ground. When the net capacitance change satisfies the alarm criterion, an alarm is activated.

The detector sensitivity can be adjusted to detect an intruder approaching a protected item or adjusted to a lesser sensitivity level requiring the intruder to actually touch the item. Although some detectors can be adjusted to detect an intruder at a distance up to 4 or 5 feet from the protected object, this level of sensitivity is not recommended unless it is required for some specific application. The level of sensitivity should be limited to detect the intruder at a distance of about 6 inches or even require him to actually touch the protected item in order to initiate an alarm.

A lower sensitivity will not affect the response time but will help reduce false alarms. If the detector sensitivity is adjusted to detect an intruder 4 feet from the protected item, the electrostatic field close to the item would be very sensitive, perhaps sensitive enough to cause false alarms, even to changes in humidity.

The sensitivity of capacitance detectors is affected by changes in relative humidity and the relocation of other metal objects closer to or farther away from the protected item. Changes in the relative humidity vary the air dielectric characteristics. An increase in the relative humidity causes the air conductivity to increase and reduces the capacitance. Conversely, a decrease in humidity or a drying of the air reduces the conductivity. When a metal object is moved close to a protected object, it is electrically coupled to the protected object by the electrostatic field. The object basically increases the size of the capacitor plate and reduces the capacitance monitored by the detector.

The capacitance detector signal processor is basically a balanced bridge circuit with the protected metal object as part of the bridge. Anyone approaching or touching the protected object changes the capacitance, thus unbalancing the circuit and initiating an alarm. Initially, the circuit must be adjusted either automatically or manually to balance the bridge. If the circuit is manually adjusted, then every time metal objects are moved close to or away from the protected object, the circuit must be rebalanced. Sometimes at the change of seasons the manually adjusted sensors need readjusting to compensate for changes in humidity.

Pressure Mats. These can be used as proximity detectors to detect anyone approaching valuable objects and as barrier detectors to protect entrances leading to areas requiring protection. Pressure mats are available as individual mats for multiple application purposes and as continuous runners that can be cut to any length. Individual mats are typically used for protecting small areas such as at entrances, under windows, or on steps. Runners are installed under carpets to cover larger areas such as in the area of a safe.

Pressure mats consist of a series of ribbon switches positioned parallel to each other approximately 3 inches apart along the length of the mat. Ribbon switches are constructed from two strips of metal in the form of a ribbon separated by an insulating material. It is constructed so that when an adequate amount of pressure, depending on the application, is exerted any place along the ribbon the metal strips make electrical contact. Individual ribbon switches are available in lengths up to 20 feet, but the switches used in pressure mats or runners are about 2 to 3 feet long. The series of switches forming the mat are electrically wired in parallel, and the assembly is sealed between two plastic sheets or molded in rubber to form a durable, weatherproof mat.

Point Sensors

Pressure Switches. These can be mechanically activated contact switches or single ribbon switches used in pressure mats. An open switch becomes a point sensor when the item requiring protection is placed on the switch, thus closing the contacts. Anyone lifting the item causes the switch to open and initiate an alarm.

Mechanical Vibration Transducers. These are secured to the item being protected rather than to the mounting surface like most mechanical contact switches. When the protected object is moved, the forces required in the act of movement will cause the vibration transducer to initiate a series of open-circuit pulses. These pulses are detected by the supervisor circuit and initiate an alarm. Items being protected by vibration transducers should be physically secured to their mounting surfaces to ensure that adequate force is required to initiate an alarm as the item is being removed. Signal wires to the transducer should be kept short and well-secured.

Robert L. Barnard

Source Barnard, R. 1988. *Intrusion Detection Systems, 2nd Edition.* Boston: Butterworth-Heinemann.

A REVOLUTION IN DOOR LOCKS

In the early 1970s two technologies came together that forged a revolution in door locks. Intel Corporation was looking for applications for its new generation of microprocessors, a quantum leap in solid state technology. Meanwhile, Pitney Bowes Inc. was seeking to license the electronic access technology they had developed to increase security on their postage machines.

The Birth of the Electronic Hotel Lock

Yale Lock and Hardware negotiated a license agreement with Pitney Bowes as the platform for an electronic hotel lock. Using an Intel processor, Yale developed a lock that would read data to a magnetic stripe card on two tracks, one for access and one for programming the lock. This technology allowed hotels to re-combinate guest room locks without having to send a locksmith to the door. When a guest went to his or her room, the card used to unlock the door voided the previous user's card, authorized it for the current guest, and programmed it for the next guest.

The early development was archaic compared to today's computer technology. The first prototype locks were connected to a timeshare computer via acoustical modem. Data came via teletype machine. Later, Yale's prototype lock connected to a circuit board about the size of a flatbed scanner through an "umbilical cord." Finally, Yale packaged the card reader, battery pack, and circuit board with the Intel processor into an enclosure that looked remarkably like a commercial mortise lock.

Then, during the "salad days" of computer technology, Intel introduced the 8088 microprocessor, the heart of the desktop computer. The IBM XT was small and affordable, compared to the monster servers that required their own environmentally controlled rooms to process data that fits in today's PDA. The PC would allow front desk personnel to manage the access system while guests checked in, thus making the concept feasible.

Yale launched its revolutionary lock in the late 1970s, though it was not the first to manufacture an electronic hotel lock. A small New York manufacturer, Ellison Co. (not related to Ellison Bronze Co.) sold recombinating hotel locks in the New York metro area in the early 1970s. As is often the case, the first to introduce a new technology is not successful, and Ellison did not survive.

Problems and Upgrades

At first, hotel owners scoffed at the idea of paying money to replace good old, reliable mechanical locks with these new-fangled electronic gadgets. However, when large hotel owners saw the savings they could achieve by replacing nickel silver keys with plastic cards, they warmed up to the idea. Las Vegas casino owners saw a huge benefit in being able to retrieve an event history from a guest's lock. This resolved many disputes about "stolen" valuables. After security reviewed an audit trail retrieved from a complaining guest's room lock, stolen valuables often became "lost" valuables. Ultimately, hotel owners rushed to purchase the cost-saving technology, but Yale found itself surrounded by competitors and withdrew from the hotel lock business. The company returned to the market through acquisition years later.

The concept of credential-reading locks with an event memory soon found its way into the commercial security market. However, commercial access control is quite different from hotel lock security. In commercial buildings, it is seldom necessary to change coding data daily. Conversely, the locks must hold hundreds of users, not just one or two hotel guests and a few service personnel. Advanced access control technology includes assignable time zones and master keying structures by user and location. Entering such complex data for each user through a card or keypad is impractical at best, so manufacturers moved to programming locks at a remote computer and uploading the data through a portable computer or PDA. This concept of networking by walking around (also commonly known as sneaker-net) remains common today.

The practicality of maintaining access control data in a host computer and programming stand-alone locks on a tour depends on the quantity of locks and the frequency of changes required. For example, touring a dozen locks with a hand-held computer only takes a few minutes if the locks are near each other. However, reprogramming 100 or more locks located in several buildings could take all day. Touring remains cost effective compared to re-keying mechanical cylinders if the tour is infrequent. However, the administrative cost of reprogramming many locks frequently, such as in a college dormitory, can be significant.

Seeing this as an opportunity, several manufacturers introduced modified versions of the electronic hotel lock. Security personnel can pre-program the locks with access control data, such as time zones, and group access levels with a tour. Programming a new user code when a user loses his or her card or when the occupancy changes is simply a matter of issuing a new card. On the first use, the new card voids the previous card, authorizes the user card, and programs the lock for a future user. The user card holds user data on one track and access control programming information on another. Using a read/write encoder, security administrators can reprogram cards or add access control data to existing cards. Still, these locks do not allow real-time monitoring and control.

Network Systems

Network access control systems offer three distinct advantages over stand-alone smart locks. They allow security personnel to remotely lock and unlock doors, monitor events, and retrieve event information, all in real time. Responding to these requirements, several smart lock manufacturers adapted their products to communicate with network access controls. Recognition Source LLC developed wireless point-to-point data communication systems that allow battery-operated locking devices to communicate data with each other and a central access control panel. The company offers a series of traditional mechanical lock configurations that link to their wireless communication modules. The result is a system of battery-powered stand-alone locks that interface with network access control systems. Ingersoll Rand Corp recently acquired Recognition Source and re-branded the products as Schlage Wireless locks. The locking hardware incorporates Schlage's D (cylindrical) and L (mortise) lock chassis.

Wireless access control is not a new concept. However, security consultants and systems integrators have traditionally stayed with hard-wired systems. The emergence of computer communications and addressable components has greatly simplified network applications. However, they still require multi-conductor or fiber optic cables to link components together. The exponential popularity of wireless communication (cell phones) caused systems designers to seriously consider wireless access control an acceptable alternative to wired systems. Integrating locking hardware with wireless communication drastically reduces the labor cost of pulling wire and installing locking hardware, request-to-exit switches, intrusion sensors, and separate card readers. Wireless locks ultimately connect to an access control panel that is grid powered, but installers can place hard-wired components in easily accessible locations.

A wireless lock has a battery powered integral credential reader, lock releasing motor, memory chip, and microprocessor for making access decisions, either offline or upon a command from the access control panel. In addition, it contains a request-to-exit switch, door status monitor. It communicates with a Panel Interface Module (PIM) that is hard-wired to the access control panel. The distance between a wireless lock and the PIM can be up to 200 feet, and is not required to be "line of sight." Line of sight applications, such as outdoor gate locks, can work up to 1000 feet or more with repeaters. The distance between locks within a building can be up to 400 feet with the PIM is centrally located. The locks communicate over a multi-channel frequency that will transmit through common building materials such as cinder block, plaster board, wood, and concrete. However, "chicken wire" embedded plaster, rebar and steel studs can affect signal strength. To ensure reliable communication, installers check signal strength with a reduced power pre-installation test kit. If the system tests OK with reduced power, it is virtually assured that it will work at the lock's full output power.

Several manufacturers offer battery-operated locks that maintain user codes and feature a variety of functions including time-controlled access levels and audit capability. Ever-shrinking microprocessors and memory chips allow for more compact locking hardware. Product designers continually strive to stretch the service intervals of battery-powered locks through the use of micro-motors and miserly processors. Kaba Ilco adapted a power-generating technology first used in high-security safes. The Kaba PowerLever® lock features advanced access control functions in a unique lock that gets its power from the user. Each time a user presents a valid magstripe, proximity, or PIN credential and turns the lever, an internal dynamo generates electricity that it stores to maintain system memory and operate the unlocking mechanism. The technology virtually eliminates battery replacement while offering computer-linked access control.

As building owners increasingly purchase computer-based locking hardware, systems integrators seek alternative energy sources. One emerging technology that shows promise is photovoltaic glass. Schott North America Inc. offers a unique glazing product that provides sun screening using solar cell technology in a glass laminate. As this technology finds new and unique applications, it will be possible to power smart locks from the vision light in the door. Because the solar panel is a lamination, it can be used in security glazing.

Schlage Lock Div. of Ingersoll-Rand Corp. took a different approach with its VIP series locks. They receive power and data from external access control systems. A four-wire connection through the hinge to an interface board links the lock to a third-party access control terminal. The interface board receives its power from an independent power supply, thus the power required to lock and unlock several doors does not tax the access control power supply. Each interface board connects to four locksets using four conductors for each lock. Since the locks receive their power from an external source, there are no batteries to replace. The interface board translates card data and forwards it to the host access control.

Upon verification, the host access control system sends a lock or unlock command to the interface board, which sends power to the locking mechanism. User access levels and event information reside in the host access control system. The Schlage VIP series locks support magstripe and HID proximity configurations. In addition to the locking hardware, the lock includes a door monitor switch and request-to-exit switch linked to the secure side lever. The lock sends a signal to the host when there is a legal exit, forced door, or propped door condition. The host system records unknown cards and access attempts outside user access levels.

An optional internal switch within the lock detects and logs the use of a mechanical override key.

The hardware cost—locking hardware, request-to-exit switch, door monitoring, and card reader—is comparable to systems with these components installed separately and linked by wiring. However, the installation cost of network-compatible locks is considerably less because there is only one hardware preparation and single cable termination. The lock installs using standard door reinforcement and ANSI (American National Standards Institute) door preparation. The wired hinge or pivot requires only four wires for data and power transfer.

A network integrated lockset is of particular value on fire rated doors, particularly on remodel projects. Current building codes prohibit field modification of rated fire doors and frames by personnel other than the door manufacturers' technicians. Metal doors with internal raceways pre-built into the door structure allow technicians to install network compatible locks without voiding the testing laboratory labels. Listed frame assemblies do not require modification for electric strikes and remain intact.

Stand-alone battery-operated locks will continue to enjoy strong sales due to their advanced access control capabilities at low initial cost. Building owners and managers who need the features of real-time monitoring and control will find that integrated access control locks and alternative energy sources will provide reliable solutions to their security challenges.

Dick Zunkel

SECURITY DESIGN AND INTEGRATION: A PHASED PROCESS

Introduction

Critical assets can offer extremely attractive targets for a variety of threats. Threats can range from unsophisticated activist groups to highly sophisticated, well-armed and trained professional career criminals or narco-terrorists. While the nature of the threat is key to security design and integration efforts, in many cases the consequences of loss for a small or medium firm due to even a medium-level threat can be catastrophic when a key business asset has been compromised.

Security managers are becoming increasingly convinced that the best defense against dynamic threats and potential catastrophic loss is a fully integrated security program that carefully and effectively blends architectural, technological, and operational elements into a flexible, responsive system. The design and integration process described below is one approach that can be employed by security managers to effectively counter threats and substantially reduce risk or consequence of loss. The process is generic and requires that the manager overlay his or her own security problem in order to arrive at an effective design solution.

Some security organizations place undue emphasis upon the selection and application of security personnel or equipment alone without equal consideration of the full range of options and countermeasures that comprise a totally integrated security system. Security managers must avoid the tendency to emphasize a single solution or approach and they must strive to achieve a virtually seamless mix of security countermeasures designed specifically to address anticipated threats and risks. More important, soaring humanpower and equipment costs coupled with the risk posed by the ominous insider threat demand the effective application of state-of-the-art security countermeasures at key locations to reduce asset vulnerability and keep operational costs under control.

The Design and Integration process applies equally to the security manager as system user and the architect/engineer as system designer. This approach will ensure the proper selection and combination of humanpower, procedures, information, facilities, and equipment into a fully responsive and operationally effective system at a reasonable cost.

System Objectives

Simply stated, a security system is an integrated combination of barriers, technologies, personnel, and procedures designed to safeguard personnel, property, and operations. System objectives generally address deterrence, denial, detection, delay, assessment, and response options based upon a precise definition of threat and user requirements.

It is essential that the security manager recognize that complete systems incorporate a wide range of measures to achieve stated objectives. In the case of a fully integrated security system, protection objectives are achieved through the selection and integration of protective measures from the following range of subsystem options:

- Facilities, architectural barriers, and space definition to deter and delay the movements of an adversary
- Physical security equipment designed to detect, assess, and, in some cases, respond to intrusion attempts and unauthorized activities
- Communications and control and display networks to collect, integrate, transmit, and display alarm and other data for operator response and to control activities of the response force
- Security personnel to conduct day-to-day security program operations, management and system support, and response to non-routine events
- Security procedures to guide security operations and provide overall security program direction and control

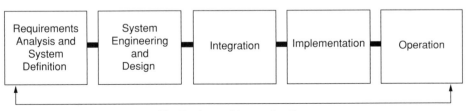

The Design and Integration Process

Figure 27. Designing and integrating a security system moves in logical stages.

The Design and Integration Process

The essence of design is to invent an order or arrangement of components and details of a system in accordance with a plan. In all cases, whether for security or any other function, a system is designed for a purpose. In the case of security design, the plan is to select and incorporate the various physical elements, personnel, and procedures into a unified system that reduces and controls vulnerability based upon an identified threat.

Engineering design usually involves six project stages, namely: study and report, preliminary design, final design, bidding or negotiation, construction, and operational. While these engineering stages are familiar to the architect and engineer, for the security manager, some adjustments are necessary in order to arrive at a process that includes not only the functions of engineering design, but also the integration of tangible and intangible elements resulting in a responsive protection system design.

The essence of integration is to make a whole by bringing together individual parts. For the security manager, system integration is the art of fusing security equipment, facilities, personnel, and procedures together seamlessly in a manner that produces pro-active asset protection.

The end result is a fully integrated security system that responds effectively to dynamic threats and risks during crisis conditions and, at the same time, functions imperceptibly during normal conditions. Whereas design results in the various security elements responding to a threat or risk, integration fuses them into a workable, day-to-day strategy for effective asset protection.

Security system design and integration begins with a thorough requirements analysis and concept definition. Facility and site protection plans are always based on the identification of critical assets requiring protection and the identification of appropriate countermeasures for each asset. Barriers, electronic hardware, personnel, and procedures are selected to interplay at key locations within the design scheme to form an integrated subsystem protection scheme.

The system concept is formed through the collection of integrated approaches at each asset, facility, and group of facilities sharing a common boundary. Given the diverse missions found in organizations, the integration of protective measures and resources does not involve a static set of environments. Because threat is normally dynamic at each asset or facility requiring protection, the fully integrated system concept must allow for various scenarios, system redundancy based on criticality, and collective management of available resources in order to achieve the best possible protective design solution. The security manager is always the final authority on system options based on requirements stated early in the process and resource constraints.

Based on the approved concept, the System Engineering and Design phase brings the system through the various phases of design steps from preliminary to final design. The end result is a complete system solution. The integration function that follows the design phase is merely a design review phase where the final design and integration solution is formally reviewed by the security manager based upon previously stated requirements.

This Integration phase is absolutely critical for the security manager to be ensured that the integrated design solution addresses all stated requirements. More importantly, design solution validation is essential before hardware is acquired and construction is begun. Once validated, the system is ready for the final phases of Implementation and ultimate Operation by the end user. Feedback on the effectiveness of the system, which is based upon the dynamics of threat and changing missions, is continuously fed into the front-end requirements phase.

Requirements Analysis and System Definition

Experience has shown that the System Design and Integration process must be front-loaded in order to arrive at a valid security concept. This means the process cannot be expected to yield sufficient results unless it is based upon a thorough analysis of threats and risks, and the relative exposure of individual assets to these conditions. Thus, the Requirements Analysis phase is critical to develop an optimum system configuration and to determine the relative cost-effectiveness of various physical security options.

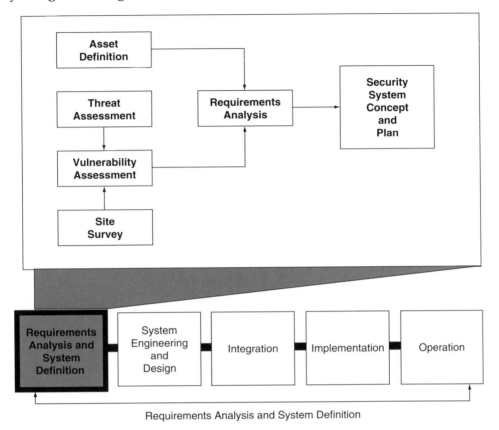

Figure 28. Determining what is needed will determine the nature of the security plan.

Initially, assets that need protection are identified and their criticality determined. Next, the attractiveness of these assets to potential threats and their likely modes of attack are evaluated. Finally, areas in which existing security measures do not adequately address the threat are identified as vulnerabilities.

Based on the results of the on-site requirements analysis, asset-specific countermeasures are applied at various locations on and around the asset to be protected. Selection of individual countermeasures is made by the designer based upon an initial statement of system objectives and functional requirements, such as detecting unauthorized entry and controlling access. The designer and security manager must consider the full range of potential countermeasures, to include architectural barriers, intrusion detection, access control, and assessment subsystems, as well as procedural and personnel intensive countermeasure combinations appropriate to each asset.

Finally, the security concept or design solution is reached through the selection of the best combination of individual, complementary countermeasures for specific assets. The accumulation of the various countermeasure selections for each asset are considered collectively in terms of total protection afforded and potential for unnecessary redundancy.

The overall concept for protection of all grouped assets is then factored into a cohesive design solution and preliminary life cycle cost estimates are prepared.

The security manager is the final arbiter of which conceptual design solution is offered for more detailed consideration and design in the next phase.

Design solution documentation that forms the basis for subsequent engineering and detailed design includes basic schematic representations or drawings, basic level of specifications, and a preliminary "order of magnitude" cost estimate of subsystem and overall system costs in equipment, materials, and labor.

The conceptual design drawings will usually include an overall site plan, a building footprint, building elevations, and a system block diagram that depicts the major components and their connections that will form the total protection system.

System Engineering and Design

The System Engineering and Design phase uses the system's conceptual design as a basis and results in a detailed engineering design solution. The security manager is responsible for providing the designer with an established system goal, a full set of functional requirements upon which the design can be based, and a complete system concept that clearly defines how the total system and its elements will function to counter identified threats and reduce vulnerabilities. These are all expected outputs of the initial conceptual design phase incorporated in a security plan.

The engineering design consists of both a preliminary and final design. The preliminary design defines the total project through construction and operation and includes preliminary design drawings, outline specifications, a design analysis, and a total project cost estimate. The final design results in complete design documentation to include detailed drawings, specifications, cost estimate, bid requirements, contract forms, and contract conditions. The engineering design also addresses and resolves all of the integration issues

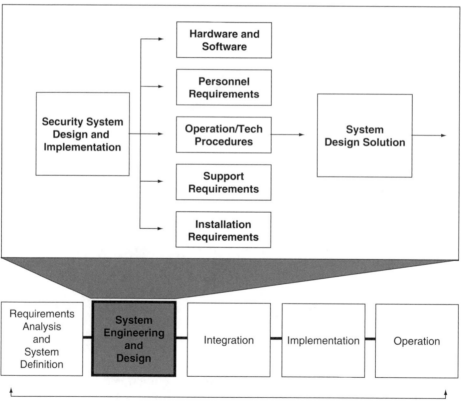

Figure 29. Hardware, software, system operators, operating procedures, and the requirements for support and installation are determined individually and in concert with one another.

associated with the resultant total system and its key elements. Apart from the identification of equipment and subsystem interface, the engineering design also addresses a concept of operations that describes in clear terms the interplay of personnel and procedures with equipment.

The system designer leads a team effort that concentrates on the development of asset-, facility-, organizational-, and site-specific protective measures to deter, delay, deny, detect, assess, and respond to a variety of threats. Typical protective measures detailed in the engineering design phase include architectural barriers, interior and exterior detection technology, closed circuit television (CCTV) assessment/surveillance equipment and associated support lighting, data transmission and communication, alarm and signal field collectors, and annunciator equipment for control and display. The security manager must consider appropriate response procedures along with security force weapons and equipment sufficient to counter the design basis threat.

These protective measures must be identified in terms of their individual characteristics and overall contribution to facility/asset protection from an integrated perspective. For example, the delay capabilities of selected architectural barriers may modify the designer's choice of associated sensor and access control subsystem elements. The determining criteria applied in this case would be to measure the delay/denial capability of the barrier in conjunction with an appropriate sensor keyed to the threat scenario and to sufficient response force reaction time. In essence, the availability and operational capabilities of the security response force will dictate the optimum selection, configuration, and placement of various protective measures.

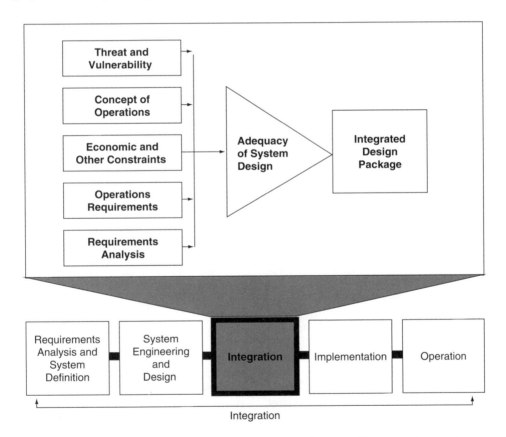

Figure 30. The design of an integrated security system will reflect considerations given to threats against assets, vulnerability of assets to the threats, an overall protective scheme to counter the threats, constraints that may affect system operations, essential requirements for effective operations, and analysis to determine if the system will operate according to design.

In another example, the designer may focus on the combination of specific technologies such as microwave and infrared sensors to ensure maximum probability of detection using complementary technologies. Each of the various protection options available to the security designer represent a complete inventory of choices that may be selected and combined with other protection options to form a completely integrated physical security system.

Considered individually, countermeasures likely offer little in the way of complete protection for critical assets. Collectively, a carefully chosen combination of measures keyed specifically to facility and site-unique requirements comprise a wholly effective, integrated approach to asset protection. Selection of the best measures is based on the designer's determination of individual and collective performance, reliability, maintain-ability, cost, and vulnerability reduction potential.

The designer's principal function is to select the various components, elements, and subsystems and integrate them into a complete system design. In all cases, selecting and balancing combinations of asset protection measures according to perceived threat and desired results is the key to design integration.

System Integration

System design and integration has been presented as a complete process accomplished by the security manager and security architect/engineer. Although the integration function is exercised by both in every phase of the process, it is also a major phase between design and implementation. Upon completion of the system engineering design, both the security manager and design engineer need to carefully review the designed system and ask the critical integration question: How do all of the selected protection measures and components required for their operation fit together for total system effectiveness?

Integration is singled out as a major phase to emphasize the importance of reviewing and balancing the engineering design according to validated requirements and constraints before proceeding to the costly later phases of construction and operation. In effect, the Integration phase is really a formal, detailed final design review elevated to a major phase in the process.

While not normally recognized as a major design phase, System Integration is an essential step between final design and implementation where the security manager validates the system design in accordance with previously established requirements. It is at this point that the security manager considers the adequacy of the complete final system design solution in terms of previously determined threats and vulnerabilities, the security manager's concept of security operations, economic and other constraints, organizational operations, and overall system requirements. In effect, system integration is really the final design review elevated to a major phase.

The Integration phase confirms the primary objective of the earlier design process to incorporate the various subsystem elements (architectural barriers, sensors, data transmission media, controllers, CCTV, etc.), with personnel and procedures resulting in an integrated approach to asset protection. During Integration, each subsystem, along with its associated component(s), needs to be evaluated by the security manager and the designer according to its individual contribution to vulnerability reduction and contribution to the total system protection effort. Each measure offers trade-offs in terms of costs and benefits. Subsystem integration reflected in the final design represents the culmination of choices appropriate to individual asset protection decisions.

The end result of the Engineering Design phase is a completely integrated security system consisting of various subsystems and their associated elements, which collectively counter an adversary with a high degree of reliability and assurance.

System Implementation

Implementing the security system involves preparing facilities, acquiring hardware, installation, testing and evaluation, training, and establishing a comprehensive logistics and maintenance support system.

In terms of eventual system performance, proper completion of the steps in this phase, namely system installation, will to a large extent determine successful operation and responsiveness of the final system.

It is at this crucial phase that the security system designer can lose control of the desired results. Project controls need to be exercised with respect to the design specifications to ensure quality control. The security manager has overall responsibility for quality assurance, test, and acceptance issues. On-site quality control of system installation is essential to successful system performance. The designer plays a key role in this phase by carefully considering key installation activities when on-site inspection can confirm that design requirements are being met.

The designer must be completely familiar with the devices being installed and ensure that all items, right down to cable connectors, meet the design specifications and are appropriate for the conditions and environment in which they will be used.

Quality assurance representatives are responsible for monitoring compliance with technical design requirements and they must be given the authority to stop the project upon determining that the system will not meet the requirements and objectives established at the beginning of the process.

Field system checkout and performance tests need to be monitored closely. The system test results, prepared at the end of each test phase, should be documented fully by the testing agency and verified by user security representatives. Likewise, shop drawings and other engineering submittals required by the specifications and statement of work need to be reviewed for acceptability.

Formal acceptance of the installed system should be made only after the user has confirmed that all quality control provisions have been satisfied.

System-level training for operators, maintainers, and supervisors should also be scheduled at the conclusion of this phase.

System Operation

The System Operation phase is put into operation by the user organization. Key aspects of

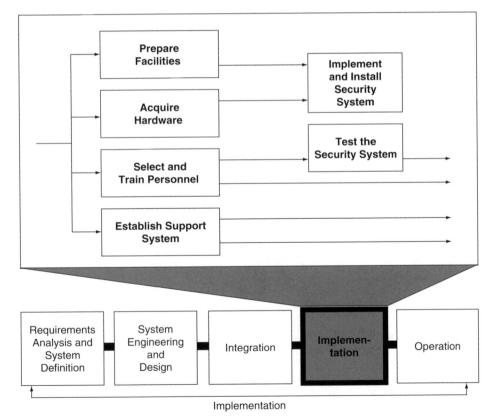

Figure 31.　The security system is put into place and tested.

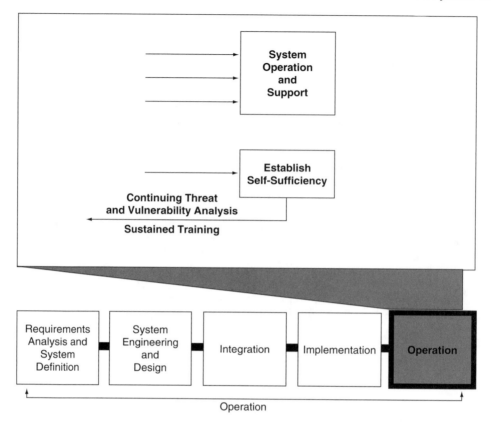

Figure 32. The security system goes into operation under control of the user organization. Evaluation is made of its ability to counter the postulated threats and its capacity to function as designed. The process does not end, however. Changes in threats and vulnerability trigger a new cycle.

this phase include preparing and submitting as-built drawings, and the final receipt of technical manuals for system operation and maintenance. A principal element of this phase is the assumption by the user of responsibility for system support.

One pricing option involves the forming and training of a dedicated maintenance team to perform the routine preventative and trouble-shooting procedures on a regular basis. Another option is to contract out all maintenance to a qualified firm.

Regardless of the option chosen, all maintenance personnel need to understand system operation and be able to test, troubleshoot, and replace modular components and repair certain components. In some cases, multiplex control and display manufacturers offer diagnostic software to troubleshoot system, subsystem, and component failures.

All operational systems should be evaluated on a regular basis—at least yearly—based on a continuing threat and vulnerability analysis, and changes in organizational missions. System hardware should also be tested regularly to verify that system performance has not been degraded. Some experts recommend repeating original system-level acceptance tests semi-annually. Lastly, sustained training of all system personnel, including operators, maintenance, and supervisory personnel, is mandatory.

Effective security system integration not only includes security hardware selection and application, but also must take into consideration existing procedures, architectural measures, and security resources. This requires a thorough understanding of the System Design and Integration process, as well as the roles and responsibilities of each member of the project team.

Adherence to the phased steps of the process is critical to effective system design and operation. After selecting assets deemed critical for protection, the security manager must systematically determine potential threats and their characteristics, the attractiveness of critical assets to threats, potential attack modes, and potential attack severity. Finally, with the aid of a project team that understands that the most effective, flexible, and economical security system is one that has an appropriate blend of personnel, procedures, and technology, an integrated security system can be designed.

Richard P. Grassie

SECURITY DESIGN: PRELIMINARY CONSIDERATIONS

Security is a topic on the minds and budgets of a growing number of owners, as is evidenced by the rapidly expanding supply of security technology and the increased attention being paid to the cost-effective integration of facility monitoring systems. The demand for more secure facilities, coupled with computerized technology and its growing integration capabilities, is making access control and intrusion detection a science of its own. Unfortunately, the design of a system incorporating these security functions far too often emphasizes the technological aspects of access control and intrusion detection rather than the basic design considerations associated with the system's intended use.

Security needs and requirements must be determined early in the project programming and definition process. Burglary, industrial espionage, shoplifting, riots, vandalism, assault, rape, murder, and employee theft are crimes that imperil lives and drive up the cost of doing business.

As crime increases, owners and their architect/engineers alike are being called upon to address security problems by incorporating security into the design and construction in all building types.

Designing a facility without security in mind can lead to expensive lawsuits, injuries, and retrofitting of protection measures after the facility is complete. The designer needs to consider a number of factors: objectives of the security system, physical and operational environment, and the anticipated complexity and responsiveness of the system under design. These factors need to be considered early in the design process, regardless of whether the goal is to construct a new system or upgrade an existing system.

Determining System Objectives

Security concerns need to be defined by the owner, with subsequent assistance in formulating system objectives and design details provided by a security architect/engineer. With the proliferation of security devices, along with rapid advances in system technology, security planning requires specialists with a working knowledge not only of the devices themselves, but also of the various integration possibilities for joining discrete systems for increased facility monitoring effectiveness. Electronic intrusion detection, perimeter protection, surveillance, and access control techniques are contributing elements in a total security system and design approach. Each technique has distinct technological and operational characteristics, and environmental reactions, along with differing requirements for installation and maintenance.

In order to determine what security strategy is most cost-effective and appropriate, the following questions should be answered by members of the project team:

- What is the purpose of the system? For example, is the system designed to prevent escape or intrusion? For high or low security? Profile security? Interior or exterior detection or both? What are the methods of responding to alarms? Length of delay from time of criminal entry? To justify the use of an electronic access control system, the owner will need to know what assets and areas are to be protected along with what the potential loss or damages will cost. Each security situation is unique; there are no package solutions.
- What are the operational aspects and priorities? The type of alarm system needs to be defined, as well as the allowable false alarm rate tolerance. The proposed transmission system from sensors to alarms needs to be considered; for example, radio waves, hard wired, dedicated circuits, or multiplexed fiber-optic systems. What is the backup system in power and

hardware? How are the alarms to be assessed for effectiveness, e.g., with closed-circuit television (CCTV), lights, horns, bells, or printed records? Should the system have tamper alarms, self-tests, or lightning protection? Each security system requires careful forethought on subsequent implementation and operation.

- What are the environmental impacts? Examples are weather, water surfaces, wildlife, vegetation, corrosive condition of acid rain, or salt. Information is needed on topographic conditions of the site and humanmade impacts such as physical structures, traffic patterns, and industry controls.

Answers to these questions will allow the owner and designer to focus on the best strategy for asset protection within budget and operational constraints. Arriving at the best security strategy for the intended environment requires that they also factor in the preliminary considerations.

Preliminary Considerations

The security design process is a key element in the overall project development plan. Most designers perform their design and integration tasks according to specific phases. Generally, these phases of the design process include, in order of accomplishment:

- Survey and Report
- Conceptual Design
- Preliminary and Final Design
- Bid and Construction
- Turnover and Operation

It is imperative that the system's requirements be incorporated at the earliest possible phase of planning. Determining requirements for security systems is the principal responsibility of the owner/user. They are often part of the conceptual design and characterized in the initial survey and report. They form the basis for quality control and review during the more detailed phases of engineering and system implementation planning. Establishing and baselining system requirements early-on in the design process can allow the design team to avoid the costly oversight and disruptive consideration of

security requirements at later phases of major design and construction.

Each site or facility to receive a security system will offer the designer unique differences in local circumstances and conditions. As a result, the requirements for individual facility protective measures must be evaluated on a case-by-case basis. Specific factors that need to be evaluated when designing integrated systems include:

- The mission criticality of the facility and its assets.
- The threats anticipated for each of the assets, including current threat assessments and owner concerns.
- The vulnerability and consequence of loss for each asset to be protected given the anticipated threats.
- Local security response force capabilities.
- Design constraints such as monetary, operational, and environmental limitations.

The previous list of preliminary considerations leads the designer to a determination of functional requirements for each facility to be protected. Once the functional baseline of the system has been established, other considerations become the basis of selecting appropriate security measures. These include the physical and operational environment, the need for protection-in-depth, and the complexity and sensitivity of the subsystems to be employed. The system designer must consider these factors in the analysis of proposed security measures, including upgrade efforts.

Security System Selection

Each type of security system is intended to perform a specific function within a total system design. Basic factors to be considered in selecting security measures include, but are not limited to, the physical environment, operational environment, and the need for protection-in-depth of critical assets. The end results of the failure of the designer to consider these factors are a nonresponsive system, an ineffective system, and an unacceptable level of false and nuisance alarm occurrences. A discussion for each of these basic design considerations will follow.

The meanings of the terms *false* and *nuisance* alarm are important to our discussion. Without a proper understanding of these terms, the designer is likely to overlook important sources of system degradation.

A false alarm is an alarm indication that results from the malfunction anywhere in the system hardware or software between the outermost sensor and the control and display central annunciator. A nuisance alarm is an alarm condition that is caused by sensor system response to outside stimuli such as environmental conditions, vehicle traffic, electrical power line disturbances, electromagnetic interference, and vibration-causing machinery, to name a few.

Both sources of system degradation, false alarms and nuisance alarms, demand that the designer carefully consider the physical environment and operational environment, as well as the most effective protection-in-depth schemes.

Physical Environment. The state-of-the-art of electronic security systems presents a series of options for the designer that will result in the selection of best, acceptable, or unacceptable technology and other countermeasure options. In particular, sensor and CCTV elements are designed to perform within specific environmental parameters and failure to adhere to accepted application requirements for each technology will lead to degraded performance, excessive nuisance alarms, or both. In addition to the real system performance costs associated with a degraded detection and assessment capability, hidden costs of such misapplication are in the real dollar cost of repair/retrofit and in the loss of owner confidence in the system.

The security system designer needs to carefully analyze the physical environment to determine and document the host of physical environment variables that may adversely affect the performance of electronic components. In the exterior physical security environment these include the factors of wind, temperature extremes, fog, foliage, salt, rain/standing water, condition of fence fabric, location of underground utilities, and other environmental influences that would cause sensor and other technologies to not respond within specified performance limits. The selection and placement of interior sensors must consider the heating, ventilating, and air conditioning (HVAC) location; heat sources; transient light; vibration; moving machinery; dust; and moisture/humidity. The assignment and positioning of CCTV must consider the aspects of sun glare, even and sufficient distribution of artificial light, temperature, wind, and the monitoring location.

Thus, the most critical consideration for the security designer is that the initial requirements analysis phase of system design should identify all potential sources of environmentally generated stimuli which could adversely impact overall system performance. The subsequent preliminary design phase will then be able to accommodate these design constraints through the selection of the appropriate technology, combining technology with other measures and/or modification of the environment.

Another aspect of the physical environment to be considered by the designer is the notion of security control through environmental design. This concept involves a review of the physical environment to be protected and the use of facility and site design concepts to reduce the inclination of the physical environment to support criminal behavior. Environmental design strategies include the use of natural access control through placement of walkways, natural surveillance through the elimination of unsafe areas, and the use of improved lighting. Included within the environmental design approach are concepts of individual territoriality, effective use of space, and manipulation of the natural environment to deter potential threats.

Operational Environment. Operational issues place two types of constraints on the architect and engineer as designers: physical and owner-required. An example of the former is a facility perimeter that must adapt to site constraints, property availability, or usage. Owner-required issues include the need to compartmentalize certain operations, limitations on location and design of access control portals, and placement of handicapped access. Distinct owner groups must maintain their own separate operations that include their own safety, efficiency, and a variety of other mission performance criteria within which the security system must adapt.

Each of these unique requirements may result in selection or rejection of specific security system solutions. Rejection of a technology is usually due to an inability to operate effectively within the operational environment or as a result of a potential for impeding routine organizational operations. Specific examples of these instances include rejection of CCTV assessment in the manufacturing environment and rejection of access control portals at a key entrance gate.

Protection-In-Depth. Depending upon the criticality of the asset in terms of mission or replacement value, the security designer attempts to establish a series of integrated protective measures around the asset(s) to be protected. The strategy of forming layers of protection is known as designing for protection-in-depth. The purpose of the protective layers is to make it progressively more difficult for an intruder to reach critical targets and to escape undetected. These protection-in-depth schemes also build time delays into the intruder's path to the asset, calculated to allow for arrival of the response force and neutralization of the threat before reaching the asset.

Technology selection and placement is critical to forming effective protection-in-depth schemes and must be made in such a pattern as to maximize the potential that the intruder will pass through the desired detection pattern. A well-conceived security system should detect penetration attempts as far away from the asset to be protected as is practical, and at several points along the path of the intruder to the asset.

The area where the system detects an intrusion is defined as a zone or line of detection. A comprehensive system protecting highly critical assets may require multiple lines or zones of detection. The security designer determines the number of zones to be implemented and their configuration according to the perceived degree of protection required to ensure a rapid response. Also considered are the possible intrusion schemes that might be launched against the defense and the neutralizing capacity of the security forces.

Security System Performance

The security system designer must constantly strive to make the probability of detecting and assessing the nature of an intrusion 100 percent and the potential for nuisance and false alarms 0. Both objectives in their extremes are ideals and most likely unattainable given our relevant inability to absolutely control the environment, technology limitations, and unexpected threat capabilities. Probability of detection of individual sensors

and detection configurations is the ratio of the total number of successful test intrusion detections to the total number of attempted test intrusions. Probability of detection can be expressed in terms of individual sensors or as an indication of the complete security system, considering all of its individual components together.

Most commercially available interior systems individually claim a probability of detection (PD) of 0.95 (being capable of detecting greater than 9 out of 10 intrusions), while other sensors designed to operate in harsh or outside environments generally are rated to have a PD of 0.90 for each sensor. This latter rating is usually based upon tests of actual intrusions by relatively knowledgeable intruders into the sensor field in a controlled environment. A higher overall system rate can be obtained by combining sensors in a protection-in-depth scheme. Combining sensors in a protection scheme can increase the likelihood of intruder detection and correspondingly the probability of detection.

In any event, PD ultimately needs to be evaluated as a system *performance goal* rather than as a measure of *individual sensor performance*. The probability of successfully detecting an intrusion will depend upon the inherent performance of the component, the method and appropriateness of technology deployment, the type and number of sensors deployed, the environment in which the technology operates, the individual sensor PD, and the competence and knowledge of the intruder.

False and Nuisance Alarms. Security systems should be designed and installed to generate the absolute minimum number of nuisance and false alarms per unit of time. As mentioned previously, false alarms are differentiated from nuisance alarms in that the former are caused by non-intrusion internal phenomena inherent to the system, such as a malfunction, while the latter are valid alarms generated by physical stimuli or environmental phenomena.

Careful equipment selection, system design, and effective installation can substantially minimize nuisance (and false) alarms to an acceptable level. Because nuisance alarms are so dependent upon controlling the environment or reducing the sensitivity of the sensing equipment and cannot be completely controlled in the typical installation, the technique of assessing alarm annunciations through CCTV or direct visual observation covering the sensor field is normally used. When properly configured, CCTV permits automatic assessment of a sensor zone in a state of alarm. The design requirement to maximize system probability of detection and protection-in-depth within constraints does not mean that the designer should saturate a building or site with sensors, cameras, or other technological devices. The designer must perform the critical integration function of determining an acceptable level and mix of electronic, physical, and procedural measures that will work together to maximize intruder delay, detection, assessment, and speed of response. While this mix will be unique for each site or facility, cost trade-off analyses conducted during the initial design phase will force the selection of certain countermeasures against a perceived threat.

Although nuisance alarm sources must be considered in an overall negative light, they nevertheless do provide an actual test of the system to respond to various phenomena. Ideally, all sources of false alarms should be eliminated from the system by the designer and installer, although it is often operationally difficult to differentiate between false and nuisance alarms. The security system designer needs to establish acceptable levels of nuisance alarm criteria and false alarm rates, and take particular note of these requirements in the design specifications, subsequent installation, and test of system components.

Integration Considerations

A decade ago, the security manager's portfolio of protective technology options was limited to relatively simple sensors, basic yet expensive CCTV, archaic photo identification systems, and unidimensional access control systems. Access control systems in particular relied more on humanpower than technology. In cases where technology was integrated with personnel and procedures for access control, managers were faced with reliance on complex processing systems that had limited applications and required major capital expenditures. Today, the security industry offers a wide assortment of capable protective technologies and integrated systems at affordable prices.

Integrated protective systems can include: guard personnel, responsive procedures for contingencies, detection sensors, automated access control elements, CCTV, fiber-optic communication and transmission lines, and multiplexed control and display equipment to tie all the various elements together into one central monitoring location. Ultimately, integrated security systems are designed to detect and communicate intrusions and other alarm conditions to a central control location for response.

Thus, the adequacy of the security force response depends largely upon the ability of the security command and control function to assess reliably the nature of the alarm, and to communicate the circumstances and conditions in the alarm zone to the available response force. The use of CCTV, which is tied into the sensor annunciation system, permits the security system operator to immediately view the alarming sector, to validate the alarm, and to communicate relevant information to the response force. The designer must consider the most cost-effective means to accomplish this system objective.

The advantages of employing integrated systems are obvious. Integrated security systems can be used to reduce the cost of providing essential security services. Integrated systems permit more economical and efficient use of humanpower usually assigned to building patrols and fixed guard posts. Integrated intrusion detection and access control systems have become electronic extensions of the security organization by permitting remote monitoring of critical locations at a lower initial equipment cost vs. continuing humanpower expenditures.

In addition, integrated security technology can be used in place of other physical security measures that cannot be employed because of safety regulations, operational requirements, appearance, layout, cost, or other reasons. Security technology can augment guard personnel to provide additional protective measures at critical entry points or within a building's high security or sensitive areas. Technology can also provide increased protection-in-depth where the use of multiple protective measures for increased system reliability is considered essential by the owner.

Upgrades. The system designer should ensure that future expansion or upgrades, such as adding new alarm points and electronic access controls, and expanding CCTV coverage, are included in initial system designs and that future upgrades do not force the retrofit of costly control and display equipment. Most state-of-the-art alarm and video control systems are modularly expandable and permit future growth. The integrated system should have an expansion capability sufficient to accommodate modular additions throughout the life cycle of the installed system. A 7- to 10-year life cycle is generally accepted as a baseline for off-the-shelf commercial systems. The designer should consider maximum enhancements projected over this period based upon the continual reassessment of threats and resultant effectiveness of installed countermeasures.

Simplicity and Maintainability. The security system designer also must keep the system as simple as possible, and carefully consider the interaction of people and hardware. How will an alarmed area be assessed? What throughput rates must be accommodated for controlled entrances? Who is available to monitor a simple alarm system for a small protected area? In particular, at the alarm control and monitoring location, it is important to know the operational limitations imposed on the system design in terms of operator sophistication and the inventory of functions to be performed while monitoring the alarm and display.

System and component maintainability is also a critical concern for non-redundant items, as is the probability that an item can perform its intended function for a specified interval under stated conditions.

As a common system descriptor, mean-time-between-failure (MTBF) is a basic measure of reliability for repairable hardware items. MTBF is the mean number of life units during which all parts of the hardware item perform within specified limits, during a particular time interval under defined conditions. Mean-time-to-repair (MTTR) is a basic measure of maintainability, defined as the sum of corrective maintenance times at any specific level of repair, divided by the total number of failures within an item repaired at that level. The designer must keep these two concepts in mind when preparing the initial and final security designs with specific technologies selected on the basis of these and other criteria.

Alarm Zone Configurations. Unless carefully specified in design and construction documents, system installers may often connect sensors in series to simplify the installation task and to reduce installation costs. This may result in the annunciation of each device in the series as one alarm at the control and display annunciator, without giving the console operator the benefit of knowing which device in the area is causing the alarm. This type of sensor integration is called daisy-chaining. The opposite is called point-for-point integration, where each sensor is wired separately to a common control unit and, upon alarm, the sensor is readily identifiable as the source of the alarm by the control operator.

Where direct point-for-point annunciation is a design goal, care should be taken in designing and specifying the control network so that the control console will display an individual sensor zone, CCTV sector, or specific point, as well as facilitate troubleshooting and maintenance. For example, all sensors in a single room may be combined on a single zone because it may not seem important for the system operator to know which window or door was penetrated. From the response management point of view, it may be important that each sensor be annunciated individually so that the point of intrusion can be determined and the response force directed accordingly.

Different types of sensors may be annunciated separately by sensor zone so that the security system operator can differentiate between sensor types and location. For example, door contact switches would annunciate attempted entry from one approach, the microwave or infrared sensors would annunciate when the intruder enters the room, and the capacitance sensor would annunciate when the intruder attempted to penetrate a given asset (e.g., a safe). This has the added advantage of providing operator assessment of intruder progress across or through the sensored area.

Additionally, at some level within the system, the identification of individual sensor alarms must be possible to enable maintenance personnel to expeditiously identify sensors for maintenance or repair. Wiring sensors individually to the control unit substantially eases troubleshooting, and reduces maintenance cost, as a trade-off against initial increased wiring costs.

Codes and Regulations. Finally, the designer must ensure that the security system hardware complies with the applicable codes, standards, and regulations that are in effect for a specific site at the time the design is prepared. This includes safety and legal protective measures such as posted notices. Additionally, security system components located in areas where fire or explosion hazards may exist due to flammable gases or vapors, flammable liquids, combustible dust, or ignitable fibers must be made intrinsically safe. Intrinsically safe components are those that are incapable of releasing sufficient energy to ignite a specific atmospheric mixture under normal operating conditions. Methods of accomplishing intrinsic safety include either limiting the level of voltage and current, or housing components within sealed conduit or enclosures that prevent the release of hazardous energy.

System integration of protective measures is the primary objective of the security system design process. The designer must effectively combine all physical protective measures with security personnel and procedures. The designer's selection of which security measures are more effective depends upon several factors, e.g., the availability and capability of the security force to respond within a specific time, the value of the asset, the criticality of the mission, the capabilities of the adversary, budgetary constraints, and a host of other factors. These are all basic considerations factored into the design effort from the beginning.

System integration is totally within the hands of the security manager as he or she ponders the choices appropriate to individual asset protection schemes. Principal design considerations include the physical and operational environment, and the need for the designer to base his or her protection scheme on the need for protection-in-depth. Whether the security system designer is working with the design of a relatively small system with detection and control display devices or a large system with multiple elements, all the subsystems must be integrated into a total systems approach.

Richard P. Grassie and Randall I. Atlas

SECURITY PROGRAM DEVELOPMENT

In the wake of the tragedy now commonly known as September 11, businesses and government were compelled to examine their security posture within the context of a new and ever more dangerous threat that was clearly dem-onstrated on that fateful day. Although there had been previous attacks, the magnitude of September 11 reached an unprecedented scale.

Previous attacks were met with assorted security improvements, mostly as a means for demonstrating a degree of diligence. But the events of 2001 were too substantial to respond with mere window dressing. Although concerns about terrorism are not new, the attack demonstrated a portentous character and lethality beyond imagination. Leaders of government and commerce had to accept a new reality of engaging in war with a determined and skilled foreign adversary.

Business and government, however, have sought moderation in response to security concerns. Developing a security program geared at defending against a terrorist attack requires a dramatic rethinking of the security function. Indeed, traditional security structured for traditional exposures, such as street criminals, internal saboteurs, and thieves, simply is impotent against the skills and determination of an adversary seeking to wage war. Security measures aimed at controlling common street crime simply do not suffice.

The prospect of what might be necessary for adequate security is daunting. Substantial barriers, sophisticated intrusion detection and surveillance systems, and armed security officers may be the appropriate prescription, but these are costly and disruptive to normal operation. Before embarking on this road business and government have pursued mechanisms for conducting an objective analysis and constructing reasonable approaches for response.

To be sure, this has been difficult. Whatever approach is taken, criticism is sure to follow, faulting leadership for either under, or over protecting a specific asset. From a business perspective, investments in technology and capital system expenditures have been preferable to expenditures on people. In a business environment in which workforce reduction is the goal of the time, adding staff for security has been a least attractive solution. In some cases, however, the use of security personnel was unavoidable.

How to assess exposures and determine appropriate course of action has been elusive at best, leaving industry wanting for some mechanism to compile data for management decision making. The following outlines a process that frames the issues for management decision making.

The process begins with an understanding of the business or institutional enterprise and a priority listing of the resources essential for the enterprise to function. Each resource, albeit tangible or intangible, represents a potential target subject to attack by an adversary. Prioritization establishes which assets are more important than others so resources may be channeled against the most significant assets.

The next step is to evaluate the threats that are the most applicable to the facility and its operations. Threats may be viewed broadly to include a wide range of criminal threats, natural disasters, accidents, and legal sanctions that may result from inadequate security. Each threat should be correlated with specific assets creating pairs or protection sets (Asset/Threat) and preparing the data for a Vulnerability Analysis.

The Vulnerability Analysis is structured for e creation of scenarios defining how an adver-ry may attack a potential target. Using a team roach with members drawn from operations, iness management, and others, the vulner-ty analysis draws upon the vast wealth of nal knowledge to create plans for attack n the parameters of the Protection Sets.

ttack scenarios highlight specific points erability. Using extensive inside knowl-e team assumes the role of the adversary ines in step by step detail the process for ; the facility. Each scenario is evaluated sis of the following:

er
w, lausibility: Is the scenario under con-
er, leration based on a subjective assess-
er, nt?
ital
to nsequence: If the scenario was a real
t, what would be the likely conse-
ron- ce?
enre
the Number of people killed and/or
ever, jured
ble. perational impact, measured in
ne an wntime and/or losses
ive, at pact on public relations, reputa-
echa- and image
ecision tional tolerance for risk:
ss that worth taking
ecision worth a minimal investment
gation
orth a substantial invest-
mitigation

These three judgments highlight the issues for management's resolution and set the stage for applying security measures.

Security measures consist of the following:

1. Policies and procedures
2. Use of electronic security system
3. Use of physical protective barriers
4. Use of security personnel

Each should be applied in a complementary and supportive manner. The recommended security measures should be viewed as a program and not merely an ad-hoc deployment of assorted security systems and practices. By following the process methodically and deliberately, the resulting recommendations may be focused on the most significant exposures and applied strategically to meet the specific needs of the organization.

The process is logical and linear. It is not prescriptive and it does not mandate any outcomes. It accommodates control by management so decisions may be reached on risks that are worth taking and those that are not.

The process, however, does not validate that it is exercised faithfully. Indeed, the process may be used to justify poor security practices and operations. The process is only effective if senior management understands and embraces the approach. If not, a risk analysis may be little more than telling people what they want to hear, nor what they need to hear. If exercised diligently, the process may effectively highlight key exposures and allow management to direct resources where they may be best invested.

Sal DePasquale

SENSORS: AUDIO DETECTION

Audio detectors are not motion detectors in the same sense as are active or infrared detectors. They do not generate an energy pattern to detect motion, nor do they detect thermal energy emanating from someone in the protected area, as do infrared detectors. Audio detectors listen for audible noises generated by an intruder's forced entry into the protected area or for noises from destructive activities within the area. Since they are often used to detect forced entry, audio detectors can be classified as penetration detectors. However, they are classified here as motion detectors because any noise that satisfies the detector alarm criteria, whether it is associated with penetration or movement, will initiate an alarm.

Audio detectors consist of a number of microphones strategically located within the protected area to listen for sounds in the audio frequency range. These sounds are sent to the signal processor in the control unit. The signal processor includes a manual sound level adjustment for setting the sound level alarm threshold above the normal audible background sounds in the protected area.

In certain applications it is difficult to satisfactorily adjust the sound level threshold for the prevailing background sound levels. If the threshold is set too high above the normal sounds in the protected area, actual intrusion sounds may not be detected. If the threshold is set just above the normal background sounds, exterior noises might exceed the alarm threshold and cause false alarms.

Two signal processing techniques are used to minimize such false alarms from exterior noises. One technique is to use an adjustable pulse counting circuit; the second technique is to use cancellation microphones. Pulse count circuits can be set to initiate an alarm only after counting a selected number of noise bursts or pulses within a specific time period. If there are not a sufficient number of noise pulses within the designated time period to satisfy the alarm criteria, the accumulated pulses will be cancelled after about 10 minutes. The count circuit will then be ready to start counting the next series of noise pulses. This feature reduces false alarms from noises that exist for only a short time such as thunder or back-firing vehicles.

The second technique to reduce false alarms from exterior noises or common interior noises is to use cancellation microphones. Cancellation microphones are installed outside the protected facility or near any interior noise sources to listen for sounds that could be received by the microphones. Signals received by the cancellation microphones are used to cancel the corresponding signals received by the detection microphones. This signal cancellation is accomplished in the signal processor. Typical outside noises that could be cancelled are those from trucks, airplanes, trains, etc., while inside noises might be from compressors, generators, and fans.

Although the pulse count circuits and cancellation microphones do not appreciably affect the detection effectiveness against a low-skill-level intruder, they do reduce the probability of detecting the intruder with a higher skill level. An unskilled intruder, such as someone entering a facility for vandalism, will usually generate sufficient noises while breaking and entering to satisfy the signal processing alarm criteria. However, the more serious threat will be made by an intruder who moves very quietly by exercising patience and caution. In such a case, the intruder may escape detection. This is especially true if cancellation microphones are used and the intruder strikes during the occurrence of loud outside noises such as thunder and high wind.

Audio detectors are available that detect only high frequency sounds generated during forced penetration through masonry construction materials such as cinderblock, brick, and concrete. They can also detect torch cutting or hacksawing through expanded steel grills and steel bars. These materials generate energies over a broad frequency range when they are subjected to forced penetrations or cutting. The frequencies generated during these attacks extend well into the ultrasonic frequency range.

One of the limitations in the application of audio detectors is that audible energies or noises are likely to cause them to go into alarm when they should not. To reduce this vulnerability, these audio detectors use bandpass filters that pass only high frequency signals above 20KHz to the signal processor. Because these detectors will not detect low frequency energies, they should not be used to detect penetrations through soft materials such as sheet rock and wood. Forced penetrations through soft materials may not generate a sufficient quantity of high frequency energy to be detected.

Robert L. Barnard

Source   Barnard, R.L. 1982. *Intrusion Detection Systems*. Boston: Butterworth-Heinemann.

SENSORS: BARRIER DETECTORS

Barrier detectors are used in intrusion detection systems across entrances leading into protected areas and across probable routes an intruder would take inside the protected areas.

Photoelectric detectors are the most popular inside-barrier detector. The newer, active infrared detectors form an invisible beam of light in the infrared frequency range between a transmitter located on one side of the area requiring protection and a receiver located on the opposite side. When anyone interrupts or breaks the beam, the infrared energy is blocked from the receiver, thus initiating an alarm.

Trip-wire devices are also in use as barrier detectors, but they are becoming unpopular because they must be set up and taken down at closings and openings. This task quickly becomes a nuisance, especially if the protected area has more than one or two trip-wire devices.

Barrier detectors can be easily avoided, especially if they are visible or the intruder is aware of their existence, because the barrier usually consists only of a single beam or trip-wire. The beam or trip-wire is installed about 30 inches from the floor. At this level, if the intruder can see it, the intruder can simply crawl under the beam undetected. If the beam is lower than 30 inches, the intruder can probably step over it.

Therefore, any barrier detector should be concealed or disguised to minimize its vulnerability to defeat; at least two beams should be used to reduce the vulnerability to an intruder crawling under the barrier.

Photoelectric Detectors

Photoelectric beam detectors consist basically of a light transmitter and a separate receiver. The light transmitter is located on one side of the entrance or area requiring protection, and the receiver is positioned on the opposite side of the entrance to receive the radiant energy from the transmitter. In earlier photoelectric detectors, an incandescent lamp was the light source in the transmitter. The light, radiating from the lamp, passed through a lens that columnated the light source. The light then passed through a red filter to reduce its visibility. The columnated beam was projected onto a photoelectric cell in the receiver. The photoelectric cell converted radiant energy into an electrical signal that was amplified for the detector processor.

In actual application, the photoelectric detector initiated an alarm when interruption of the radiant energy incident on the photocell sat-isfied the alarm criteria. The red beam of light, formed by the incandescent lamp, was visible and therefore easy to bypass.

Photoelectric detectors are used for many applications other than as intrusion detection devices. Some of these applications include automatic door openers, automatic feed packaging systems, safety barriers, and many other similar automatic systems. In these types of applications, the visible light beam does not affect the function of the device.

But for the photoelectric device to be an effective intrusion detection barrier, the light beam should be virtually invisible to the naked eye. The gallium arsenide light-emitting diode (LED) is now being used because it generates a beam of light in the infrared frequency range that is virtually invisible to the naked eye. Thick fog and smoke in the area of the beam will scatter the light particles, making the beam visible, especially near the transmitter. Gallium LEDs are solid-state devices that are highly shock- and vibration-resistant and they have about a ten-year life expectancy.

Photoelectric detector light beams should be modulated to minimize the possibility of an intruder defeating the detector with another light source. Modulating the light beam requires only that the light beam be pulsed at a specific frequency. The results of the modulation is that the intensity of the light source is recognized by the detector processor. This feature makes it very difficult for an intruder to substitute another light source, even a pulsed light source, to compromise the detector.

An added benefit of modulation is that detectors, using modulated light beams, are less susceptible to false alarms from sunlight or other light sources. Both the constant beam and the modulated beam photoelectric detectors should initiate an alarm when 90 percent or more of the beam is interrupted for a period of no greater than 75 milliseconds.

The detector's obscuration time is the time the light beam is obscured from the receiver. The momentary interruption caused by an intruder moving at a rapid speed through the light beam would be detectable.

Trip-Wire Devices

A trip-wire device consists of a spring-loaded switch and spring-loaded wire that can be stretched across the entrance to a protected area or across any path an intruder might take after entering the area. The trip-wire is connected to the switch that initiates an alarm if the wire is bumped, stretched, or retracted. When anyone comes in contact with the wire, the wire stretches, disconnecting the switch that initiates an alarm. The wire is also part of a supervised circuit to detect cutting. Some trip-wire devices have the wire attached to a retractable spool for storing the wire when the area is open. An advantage of a trip-wire is that it will not initiate an alarm unless someone or something comes in contact with the wire. Therefore, false alarms from trip-wire devices are minimal.

Robert L. Barnard

Source   Barnard, R. 1988. *Intrusion Detection Systems, 2nd Edition*. Boston: Butterworth-Heinemann.

SENSORS: EXTERIOR INTRUSION DETECTION

Exterior intrusion detectors can be used for both outside and inside applications. When used out-of-doors, they must be designed to withstand the rigors and unique demands of outside conditions and must, of course, also reliably detect intrusion. Among the design considerations will be climate, weather, terrain, animals, traffic and similar forces, and stimuli.

The basic concept is to detect an intruder's movement across a boundary around the area under protection. In this sense, the concept is often called perimeter intrusion detection. Detecting an intrusion at the perimeter provides time advantages by allowing the protective force to mount a response and at the same time tighten interior safeguards surrounding critical assets.

Types of Detectors

The boundary of a protected area can be defined either by physical barriers, such as walls and fences, or natural barriers, such as a lake, river, forest, or mountain. The boundary can also be defined as an imaginary, unmarked border that delineates property lines. The types of detectors used at boundaries are fence disturbance sensors, invisible barrier detectors, buried line sensors, and electric-field sensors.

Fence Disturbance Sensors. Chain-link fences typical of the type installed around the perimeter of military installations, industrial sites, and utility complexes can be augmented with fence disturbance sensors. These devices detect mechanical forces induced in the fence by an intruder either by climbing over, cutting through, or crawling under. Regardless of the intruder's method, the act of penetration will impact the fence, creating vibrations that are larger in amplitude and usually higher in frequency than vibrations induced by naturally occurring phenomena such as wind and small animals.

Invisible Barrier Detectors. Exterior perimeters with level ground can be protected by using invisible barrier detectors that generate a narrow invisible beam of electromagnetic energy. The energy is formed by a transmitter that emits a beam of either microwave or infrared energy; the beam moves through space on a line-of-sight path and is captured by a receiver. An intruder who runs, walks, or crawls through the beam will interrupt or distort the energy pattern. When the disturbance of the pattern satisfies the alarm criteria, the detector initiates an alarm. Separation between transmitter and receiver is a function of the detector application, terrain, operating environment, and certainly the types of detector (infrared or microwave). Under ideal operating conditions, infrared detectors can protect zones between 300 and 1,000 feet; and microwave detectors can protect zones between 500 and 1,500 feet, depending on the individual detector model.

Buried Line Sensors. Perimeter boundaries can be protected by buried line sensors. These sensors form a narrow sensitive area along the ground above the buried sensor line and detect intruders crossing the sensitive area. Buried line sensors are available to detect seismic, pressure, and magnetic phenomena. The seismic sensor reacts to propagated energy induced in the ground by an intruder crossing the buried sensor; the pressure sensor reacts to soil deformation produced by the weight of the intruder moving across the sensitive area; and the magnetic sensor reacts to ferrous materials either worn or carried by the intruder. Each of these buried line sensors can protect a zone at least 300 feet long.

Electric-Field Sensors. These sensors generate an electrostatic field along a combination of parallel field and sense wires. The field and sense wires are either secured to separate fence posts to form a stand-alone electric-field fence, or they are secured to stand-offs mounted to existing fence posts to form a protected barrier that is part of the existing fence. As an intruder approaches the electric-field sensor, his body distorts the electrostatic field generated by the field wire. These field distortions alter the normal electrical signals on the sense wire. When the change in the signals' characteristics satisfies the detector alarm criteria, an alarm is initiated. Depending on the sensing configuration, a single detector can protect a boundary section as long as 750 to 1,000 feet.

Robert L. Barnard

Source   Barnard, R. 1988. *Intrusion Detection Systems, 2nd Edition*. Boston: Butterworth-Heinemann.

SENSORS: FENCE DISTURBANCE DETECTION

Fence disturbance sensors detect the act of an intruder either climbing over or cutting through a fence, or lifting the fence fabric to crawl under. These acts of penetrating the fence generate mechanical vibrations or stresses in the fence fabric that are usually higher in frequency and have larger acceleration amplitudes than the vibrations or stresses generated by naturally occurring phenomena such as wind and rain. These fence vibrations are detected by electromechanical switches, piezoelectric and geophone transducers, and electret transducer cables. Electrical signals from the transducers are sent to the signal processor where they are analyzed.

Fence disturbance sensors can best detect cutting, climbing, and lifting when the fabric is reasonably tight and the fence posts are well anchored. If the fabric is loose, the high-frequency vibrations and mechanical noises might be attenuated in the fence fabric before they reach the sensors, reducing the probability of detection.

Another phenomenon that can cause false alarms is the wind-induced vibration from loose objects striking the fence. All loose signs, especially metal signs, should be removed from or secured to the fence so they cannot rattle. Rattling induces high-frequency vibrations in the fence similar to a cutting penetration. Since the sensors cannot differentiate between high-frequency vibrations caused by rattling signs, loose gates, vegetation, or any other objects banging or rubbing against the fence, the fence sensors can alarm to these stimuli.

Some fence disturbance sensor transducers can be installed on every third fence fabric section or fence post. The caution is that the probability of detecting an intruder penetrating the fence is a function of the sensor sensitivity and the sensor spacing along the fence. In other words, these sensors might be able to detect many types of penetrations at this spacing, but the farther apart they are spaced, the lower their probability of detecting all penetrations. This is especially true if an intruder cuts the fence fabric or lifts the fabric to crawl under midway between the sensors. Therefore, areas requiring a high degree of security should install the individual transducers on every fence fabric section or fence post. Installing the sensors closer together, however, will increase cost, a fact to be considered in relation to the anticipated threat.

The major objection to using fence disturbance sensors to detect penetrations through perimeter fences is that an intruder can either tunnel under or bridge over the fence without being detected. But the fence effectiveness can be enhanced to reduce these threats.

The threat of tunneling under the fence can be reduced by extending the bottom of the fence into the ground, by installing another barrier in the ground along the bottom of the fence, or by captivating the bottom 2 to 4 inches of the fence fabric in an asphalt or concrete sill. An asphalt sill that extends from the fence approximately 1/2 to 1 foot on each fence side reduces the tunneling threat while facilitating mowing operations along the fence. However, adequate drainage must be provided under or over the asphalt to eliminate erosion and standing water.

The threat of bridging the fence can be reduced by extending the effective height of the fence with additional fencing, or by adding barbed wire or rolls of barbed tape on top. Adding barbed tape to the fence improves the deterrent effect of the fence but it could make the fence sensors more susceptible to false alarms in the wind.

If the intruder is not likely to tunnel under or bridge over the fence, there are several advantages to protecting the perimeter fence with fence disturbance sensors. A definite advantage is that the fence sensors are mounted directly to the fence; therefore, they do not require additional space inside the protected area as do invisible barrier detectors, buried line sensors, and electric-field sensors. Another advantage is ease of installation. The sensors and interconnecting cables can be mounted directly to the fence, following the fence contour up and down hills and around corners.

It is recommended that the fence sensors be installed in sealed electrical junction boxes and that the interconnecting cables be installed in sealed conduit, provided the conduit or junction boxes will not interfere with the operation of the sensor. Although it is initially more expensive, the conduit provides additional tamper protection and electromagnetic shielding for the sensors and signal cable. Tamper protection exists because anyone trying to cut through the conduit for access to the cables will be detected by the sensors just like an intruder cutting through the fence. The conduit also protects the cable and sensors against weathering and day-to-day abuse, thereby reducing considerable long-term maintenance problems.

Electromechanical Transducers

Electromechanical fence disturbance transducers are usually normally closed switches; however, normally open switches are also available. Normally closed switches initiate an open-circuit pulse when the switch is acted upon by accelerations generated in the fence fabric during penetration. Forces with adequate accelerations cause the electromechanical switch to momentarily open and close in a series of short pulses. The pulse rate corresponds to the frequency of the induced vibration. The number of pulses and the pulse rate depends on the attack method and the time required for the intruder to penetrate the fence. For instance, if the fence is cut there will be a number of distinct pulses,

one for each time the fabric is cut. If the fence is climbed over, there will be several seconds of continuous open circuit pulses. These pulses can either be recorded in a pulse count accumulator circuit or they can activate an alarm circuit directly. Pulse accumulators are recommended because they will minimize the number of false alarms from single impacts on the fence such as when debris blows against the fence.

There are two basic types of electromechanical switches. One type uses mechanical inertia switches and the second uses mercury switches. A mechanical inertia switch consists of a single- or double-metal seismic mass that rests on two multiple contact rods or two or three electrical contacts in the normal or no-alarm position, creating a normally closed switch. The switch assembly is enclosed in a plastic case that captivates the movable mass, restricting its movement so that it always returns to rest on the contacts. The plastic case also seals the switch mass and contacts from moisture. To prevent corrosion and ensure a long contact life, the contacts and seismic mass are gold plated. The movable seismic mass in the inertia switch reacts to the minute accelerations in the vibrations generated in the fence during a forced penetration. In some inertia sensors, the seismic mass is unrestricted so that it can react to forces slightly greater than its own weight. In other inertia sensors, the movable mass is restricted by some internal force, therefore requiring a larger force to move the mass off the contacts. Inertia switches with the restricted mass are not as sensitive as the unrestricted movable mass switch, and are therefore used to protect fence gates or fence sections that have excessive movement where the undamped sensor might be susceptible to false alarming.

The mercury switch is a normally closed switch that momentarily opens on impact. It consists of a glass vial containing a small amount of mercury with electrical continuity between the two conductors. Each switch assembly is enclosed in a small tamper-protected case mounted in a near-vertical direction on the fence to function satisfactorily. On impact to the fence, the mercury is displaced from the contacts, generating a momentary open circuit or pulse.

The mechanical fence disturbance switches can either activate an alarm circuit directly or they can be connected to a pulse count accumulator circuit. An accumulator circuit counts the open-circuit pulses and activates an alarm after it has accumulated the pre-set number of pulses in a specific time period. Depending on the intruder's method of penetration, the act of intrusion will generate a large impact on the fence, such as when cutting the fabric. Some accumulator circuits can respond to both the long-duration pulses generated with a hurried climb and the short-duration pulses generated when cutting. The circuit initiates an alarm momentarily after only several long duration pulses while a greater number of short-duration pulses are required to initiate an alarm. Regardless of the counting method, the circuit should automatically bleed off the pulse counts accumulated if an insufficient number of pulses are not accumulated within the present alarm time period.

Piezoelectric Transducers

The piezoelectric transducer converts the mechanical impact forces generated in the fence during a penetration attack into electrical signals. Unlike the mechanical switches that respond to the mechanical forces by generating a series of open-circuit pulses, piezoelectric transducers generate an analog signal. The analog signal varies proportionally in amplitude and frequencies to the amplitude and frequency of the mechanically induced vibrations. The analog signals from each transducer are collectively processed and analyzed in the signal processor.

The piezoelectric crystal, which converts the mechanical forces into proportionate electrical signals, is usually a thin slab of quartz. The quartz material is physically ground to a thickness that will respond to the vibrational frequencies generated in the fence during an intrusion. This thin crystal is secured to the transducer enclosure so that it can respond to the mechanically induced forces. The induced mechanical stresses distort the crystal, generating an electrical signal that is proportional to the induced stresses. The resulting signals are amplified and sent along the interconnecting cable to the signal processor.

Typically, signals from the transducers enter the signal processor through a bandpass filter. The filter passes only those signals that correspond to the energies with vibration frequencies characteristic of the vibrations generated during a fence penetration attack. The bandpass of the filter is selected by the manufacturer after con-

ducting penetration tests and measuring the resulting frequencies. The filter is then designed to pass those corresponding signals with the best signal-to-noise ratio. Filtering reduces the susceptibility of false alarms resulting from low-frequency vibrations induced by low velocity winds, but higher-velocity winds, above about 20 to 25 mph, generate high-frequency vibrations that are within the bandpass of the input filter. Since the processor cannot always differentiate between the valid intrusion signals and the wind-induced signals, false alarms can result.

Geophone Transducers

Geophone transducers detect the mechanical vibrations generated in the fence during a forced penetration and convert these energies into analog electrical signals that are proportional to the induced forces. A geophone transducer consists of a tubular shaped seismic mass wound with a coil of fine wire and a cylindrical permanent magnet. The magnet is fixed to the geophone housing and the seismic mass is suspended in spring balance around the magnet. When the geophone is acted upon by external mechanical forces, accelerations from these forces displace the housing and permanent magnet, while the seismic mass remains at rest. As the permanent magnet moves through the coil, the windings cut the magnetic lines of force. As the windings pass through the magnetic field, an electromotive force (emf) is induced in the coil. The induced analog signal is proportional to the external accelerations. These signals are then amplified and sent to the signal processor for analysis. When the signal amplitude and duration satisfy the alarm criteria, an alarm is activated.

Electret Cable Transducer

The electret cable transducer is a specially sensitized coaxial cable. The cable center conductor is covered with a low-loss dielectric material processed to carry a permanent electrostatic charge. A braided wire shield encloses the dielectric material. This cable assembly is covered with a weather-resistant plastic jacket. When the cable is subjected to mechanical distortions or stresses resulting from the fence penetration, electrical analog signals are induced in the transducer cable proportional to the mechanical stresses.

These signals are sent along the transducer cable to the signal processor that is usually mounted to the fence at the beginning of a detection zone. Incoming signals pass through a bandpass filter that passes only those signals characteristic of fence penetration signals. The frequency band of the bandpass filter was selected by the manufacturer based on frequency measurements made while conducting forced penetration tests. Processing only those signals within the bandpass of the input filter improves the signal-to-noise ratio. Improving the signal-to-noise ratio of the processed signal improves the detector detection capability and reduces its susceptibility to false alarms.

An optional feature is available that will enhance the central station operator's ability to verify actual intrusions. It allows the operator to listen to the fence noises causing the alarm to determine if they are naturally occurring sounds from wind or rain, or if they are actual penetration sounds. Some sounds, such as an animal climbing or bumping the fence, will be difficult to differentiate from penetration sounds, but a trained operator can differentiate between most naturally occurring noises and the noises generated during an actual penetration. The listening feature is made possible because the transducer cable is microphonic, that is, it acts like a microphone.

Taut-Wire Switches

Taut-wire switches do not detect mechanical disturbances in chain-line fences like the mechanical, piezoelectric, and geophone transducers. They are used in conjunction with barbed-wire barriers to detect anyone penetrating the barrier. Taut-wire switches consist of a movable center rod that forms one contact of a normally open switch and a cylindrical conductor that forms the other contact. In the neutral or no-alarm switch position, the center rod conductor is in the center of the switch, not touching the cylindrical contact, thus forming the normally open switch.

The switches are installed in line with individually supported strands of barbed wire configured to form the barbed-wire fence barrier. Anyone cutting, pulling, or stepping on the individual strands of barbed wire will pull the switch-center conductor rod in contact with the cylindrical conductor, closing the switch, and initiating an alarm.

A unique feature of the taut-wire switch is that the switch assembly is supported in the housing by a pliable plastic material. This material exhibits cold-flow properties that allow the switch assembly always to assume a neutral force-free position when the switch housing is acted upon by gradual external force. External stresses could be caused by the fence settling or moving during the freezing and thawing seasons. This feature prevents the switches from becoming pre-stressed, altering their response to intrusion by changing the relative separation between the switch movable center conductor and the fixed cone-shaped conductor.

Robert L. Barnard

Source   Barnard, R. 1988. *Intrusion Detection Systems, 2nd Edition*. Boston: Butterworth-Heinemann.

SENSORS: INTERIOR INTRUSION DETECTION

Interior intrusion detectors can be classified as active and passive volumetric motion detectors, barrier penetration detectors, operable opening switches, proximity detectors, and barrier detectors. These detectors, as the title implies, are designed for interior applications, except when explicitly indicated by the manufacturer. Should consideration ever be given to utilizing interior intrusion detectors in exterior environments, extensive testing will be necessary to determine that the detectors will function properly. The primary reason for not using interior detectors outside is that they are not weatherproof or rugged enough to survive out-of-doors conditions. Another reason is that some of the detectors are very susceptible to false alarms in the outside environment, especially volumetric motion detectors. Their detection techniques are influenced by moving animals, grass, trees, etc.

Volumetric Motion Detectors

The whole volume or just a portion of the volume of a room or building can be protected using volumetric motion detectors. Whether the whole volume or just part of the volume is protected depends on the facility detection requirements. Again, depending on the requirements, motion detectors can be used to provide the primary intrusion detection for a building, or they can be used in conjunction with other interior detectors such as barrier and proximity detectors to satisfy the detection requirements. An advantage of volumetric motion detectors is that they will detect an intruder moving in the detector's zone of detection independently of his point of entry into the zone. For example, a store could use volumetric motion detectors to detect motion in the interior of the store along with magnetic door switches to detect anyone opening the entrance doors, and glass break detectors to detect breaking the showcase glass. In this type of application, an intruder coming into the store through a hole in the wall or ceiling will be detected by the volumetric motion detector just as though he had entered the store through a protected door.

The amount of volumetric coverage along with the configuration of the volume requiring protection dictates the number of detector transducers required to detect motion in the volume. A transducer, sometimes referred to as a sensor head, is the device that responds to an event or stimulus within the detection zone and produces an electrical signal for processing. The detector processor analyzes the electrical signal and activates an alarm circuit when the signal characteristics satisfy the alarm criteria.

Volumetric motion detectors consist of either a single transducer with a self-contained signal processor, or multiple transducers connected to a common signal processor. While some of the single transducer detectors have a large zone of detection, detectors with multiple transducers can be positioned to form a patterned zone of detection. This pattern can be configured to protect a specific item or to protect the most probable entrance route of an intruder. The decision to use a large-volume, single transducer detector or detectors with multiple transducers is only one of many tradeoffs that should be considered when selecting volumetric motion detectors.

There are two basic types of volumetric motion detectors—active and passive. Active detectors fill the protected volume with an energy pattern and recognize a disturbance in that pattern when an intruder moves within the zone of detection. Ultrasonic detectors fill the volume

with inaudible acoustical energy, microwave with electromagnetic energy, and sonic with audible acoustical energy. While active detectors generate their own energy pattern to detect an intruder, passive detectors detect the energy generated by the intruder either by sensing the body heat or thermal energy in the infrared frequency range emanating from the intruder, or by sensing changes in the thermal energy background as a result of the intruder shadowing the background while moving through the protected zones. Audio detectors detect the presence of an intruder by simply listening for the noises generated by a forced entry into the protected facilities or the noises generated as the intruder carries out his objective inside the protected area.

Barrier Penetration Detectors

Forcible entry through perimeter barriers, walls, ceilings, and windows can be detected by barrier penetration detectors. There are several types of penetration detectors including vibration, heat, breakwire grids, foil tape, and security screens. Vibration detectors are available that detect low-frequency vibrations generated by a physical attack on a structural wall or ceiling, and high-frequency vibrations generated by breaking glass. The high-frequency vibration detectors are often referred to as glass breakage detectors. As the name implies, they are used to protect glass windows such as display or showcase windows.

Heat sensors are sometimes used as intrusion detectors to detect unusual thermal activity. An example of such activity would be a torch cutting through a metal barrier such as a safe and vault. Foil tape has been used for many years to protect glass windows, but it can also be installed around perimeter walls and ceilings to detect penetration. Breakwire grids are constructed with slotted wooden dowel rods lined with a fine wire that breaks if the frame is cut or broken. They are used to detect penetrations through windows or any other human-size openings, such as heating and ventilating ducts, leading into a protected area. Breakwires can also be installed in a grid pattern directly on the perimeter barrier to detect penetrations. Since the foil tape and breakwire installed directly on the perimeter barriers break easily, they should be protected against day-to-day abuse. Foil tape on windows can be protected with a clear, hard plastic coating material; however, sheet materials such as plywood or gypsum board installed directly over the breakwire patterns installed on perimeter barriers will provide lasting protection. Security screens can be used as barriers to detect penetrations through windows. Foil tape, breakwire grids, and security screens are connected directly to a control unit or signal transmitter that recognize an open circuit as an alarm. An intruder who penetrates the protected barrier breaks the foil tape or wire and thereby initiates an alarm.

Operable Opening Switches

Several types of switches are available to detect entries through operable openings such as doors and windows. These include balanced magnetic, magnetic, mechanical contact, and tilt switches. In a typical door installation, a switch detects movement between the door and the door frame. The switch is usually mounted on the door frame and the activating device, if required, is mounted on the door. When the door is opened, the activating device either opens or closes the switch contacts, thereby initiating an alarm. Operable opening switches can be connected directly to a control unit that recognizes either an open or closed circuit as an alarm condition, depending on whether the switch is normally open or normally closed.

Interior Barrier Detectors

The entrance or the most probable avenue an intruder would take when entering or moving through a protected area can be protected by interior barrier detectors. The actual barrier can be either an invisible infrared beam or a trip-wire device. The infrared beam, generated by an infrared source in the transmitter, is projected onto a photoelectric cell in the receiver. When the beam is interrupted, the incident infrared radiation projected onto the photoelectric cell is interrupted and the detector initiates an alarm. A trip-wire, as the name implies, consists of a thin wire or cord and a spring switch for terminating the trip-wire. In an actual application, the trip-wire is stretched across the entrance to the protected area and fastened to the termination

switch. An intruder who comes in contact with the wire trips the termination switch and initiates an alarm.

Proximity Detectors

Anyone coming in close proximity to, touching, or lifting a protected item can be detected by proximity detectors. They are used for protecting metal safes, art objects, jewelry on display, etc. Probably the most popular proximity device is the capacitance detector used to protect metal devices, such as safes and file cabinets. They detect changes in the electrical capacitance between the protected metal objects and the ground plane formed by the surrounding surfaces and floor. Pressure mats and tilt switches can also be used as proximity detectors. Pressure mats detect an intruder who steps on the mat installed in the vicinity of the protected item. They are also used as barrier detectors to protect entrances and the probable route through the protected facility. Although tilt switches are primarily used to protect operated openings, they can also be used as proximity detectors. In such applications, the tilt switches are fastened to valuable movable items such as paintings and other art objects. Thereafter, if a protected item is tilted, the switch initiates an alarm. This is another example of how detection devices can be used for alternate protection applications.

Robert L. Barnard

Source Barnard, R. 1988. *Intrusion Detection Systems, 2nd Edition*. Boston: Butterworth-Heinemann.

SENSORS: INVISIBLE BARRIER DETECTORS

Invisible barrier detectors generate a narrow invisible beam of electromagnetic energy and detect a disturbance or reduction of the energy caused by an intruder running, walking, or crawling through the protected zone. The energy barrier is formed by a transmitter emitting a beam of energy to a corresponding receiver, moving along a line-of-sight path aligned with the transmitter, at the opposite end of the zone. The distance between the transmitter and receiver pair is a function of the type of detector, the application, and the operating environment. The primary application requirement for an invisible barrier detector to be effective is that the terrain between the detector transmitter and receiver be flat and free of obstructions, such as vegetation. Ground shrubbery and the like must be maintained at a height of not more than about 4 inches to prevent interruption of the beam.

There are two general types of active invisible barrier detectors: one operates at microwave frequencies and the other operates in the infrared frequency spectrum.

Microwave Detectors

Exterior microwave transmitters generate a narrow beam of microwave energy that is received by a corresponding receiver located in line-of-sight of the transmitter at the opposite end of the beam. Anyone passing through the beam will cause the receiver to react to the perturbations in the energy pattern, initiating an alarm when the resulting signals satisfy the detection alarm criteria. The maximum separation between the detector transmitter and receiver to achieve reliable detection is primarily a function of the antenna configuration.

The Federal Communications Commission (FCC) has allocated five frequency bands for operating exterior microwave detectors. These are the same frequency bands allocated for interior detectors. Of the five available frequencies, the exterior detectors presently available operate at next to the highest allocated frequency, 10,525 plus/minus 25 megahertz. This frequency is used because the higher-frequency microwave energy is more directive than the lower-frequency energies, and the energy pattern is less affected by moving or blowing grass in the area between the transmitter and receiver. Detectors operating at 10,525-megahertz frequency are restricted to a maximum field strength level of 250,000 microvolts per meter at a range of 30 meters for unlicensed use.

The narrow shape of the microwave energy beam and the maximum separation between the transmitter and the receiver is a function of the antenna size and configuration. The various detector antenna configurations being used by the microwave detector manufacturers include parabolic dish arrays, waveguide horns, stripline arrays, and slotted arrays. The maximum range of detection varies from approximately 200 feet to 1,500 feet. A 1,500-foot range is difficult to cover, except perhaps for upright walkers.

Infrared Detectors

Exterior infrared detectors generate a multiple-beam fence-like pattern of infrared energy and initiate an alarm when a beam or a combination of beams is interrupted. Since the infrared energy frequency band lies just below the color red in the visible light spectrum, infrared energy is too low in frequency to be visible to the naked eye. The infrared energy is generated in the detector transmitter by a solid-state infrared source. A commonly used light source is the gallium arsenide light-emitting diode (LED). In operation, the light source should be modulated and pulsed at a specific frequency to reduce the possibility of an intruder substituting another infrared source in an attempt to compromise the detector. Modulating the beam also reduces the susceptibility of the detector alarming from sunlight or other light sources.

Energy radiating from the infrared light source passes through a co-luminating lens that forms and directs a beam of energy that is directed toward the receiver at the opposite end of the zone. Energy reaching the receiver passes through a collecting lens that focuses the radiant energy onto a photoelectric cell. The photoelectric cell is a semiconductor device that converts the radiant infrared energy into electrical signals proportional to the radiant energy. The receiver monitors the electrical signal and initiates an alarm when its magnitude drops below a preset alarm threshold for a specific period of time. The alarm threshold should correspond to at least a 90 percent blockage for a period of about 75 milliseconds. The blockage reduces the probability of false alarms from birds flying or debris blowing through the beams. Some detectors require a loss of signal from at least two receivers to initiate an alarm. This technique reduces the susceptibility of the detectors alarming to birds and debris; however, the bottom receiver alone should initiate an alarm if it is interrupted. Otherwise, low-crawling intruders will not be detected.

The infrared fence beam patterns are formed between two separate detector columns. One column is located at one end of the protected zone and the other column is located at the opposite end. Since the exterior infrared detectors are line-of-sight devices, the area between the columns must be level and clear of any obstacles that might interfere with the transmitted energy. The separation between the two detector columns ranges from a few feet to protect entrance gates to zones as long as 1,000 feet. Weather conditions, such as heavy rain, fog, snow, or even blowing dust particles, attenuate infrared energy and can affect the operating range. In areas where these weather conditions occur, the detector range might have to be reduced to 100 or 200 feet, depending on the density of the particles.

Infrared detectors can provide perimeter penetration detection for industrial and commercial installations with level grounds that can accommodate detection zone lengths of at least 300 feet long. Infrared detectors have a high probability of detecting anyone running, walking, or attempting to jump over the infrared beams if the detector columns are at least 4 to 6 feet high. They also have a high probability of detecting anyone crawling through the energy barrier, if the ground is level between the detector columns and the lowest beam is no greater than 6 inches above the ground.

Robert L. Barnard

Source   Barnard, R. 1988. *Intrusion Detection Systems, 2nd Edition*. Boston: Butterworth-Heinemann.

SENSORS: MICROWAVE MOTION DETECTORS

While ultrasonic motion detectors generate inaudible acoustic energy patterns and recognize a disturbance in those patterns caused by a moving intruder, microwave motion detectors generate an electromagnetic energy pattern that serves the same function. Also, ultrasonic motion detectors consist of a single control unit with multiple transducers. However, most microwave detectors are self-contained units; that is, the detector antenna, signal processor, and power supply are contained in a single unit. Microwave detectors are, however, available with multiple transceivers connected to a common control unit. Even though each of the multiple transceivers contains its own signal processing circuit, they share the same power supply and alarm relay in the control unit. With multiple transceiver detectors, each transceiver usually generates a smaller energy pattern than the single unit detectors. In application of the multiple transceiver detectors, additional transceivers are required to protect large volumes; however, each detector can be directed to cover a specific area.

Microwave energy has the distinct ability to penetrate glass, wood, and even cinder block walls to some extent, depending on the frequency and antenna direction. Therefore, microwave motion detectors can be used where the volume of the facility to be protected is large, and when it is advantageous to detect intruders through internal partitions and walls. Microwave detectors can also be used in place of ultrasonic motion detectors for volumetric detection when air turbulence in the area requiring protection might cause false alarms with ultrasonic detectors.

The microwave motion detectors described here are for indoor applications only. Indoor microwave detectors should never be used outdoors unless they are designated for outside use by the manufacturer; however, outdoor microwave detectors can certainly be used indoors. The reason indoor detectors should never be used outdoors is that indoor units recognize a Doppler frequency shift produced by a moving target to detect intruders. Moving trees and waving grass can produce Doppler frequency shifts similar to those produced by a moving intruder. This type of motion can cause serious false alarm problems.

Although the resistance to higher-frequency microwave energy passing through wood, sheetrock, and brick is greater than for the lower-frequency energy, the energy can penetrate the walls. The fact that it can penetrate walls has both advantages and disadvantages. An advantage occurs when an intruder is detected by the microwave energy penetrating partitions within the protected volume; but, if it detects someone or something moving outside the protected area, or even outside the building, that is a definite disadvantage. The fact that microwave energy is difficult to contain should be considered in locating and directing the detector-transmitted energy within the area requiring protection.

The shape of the transmitted energy pattern is a function of the antenna configuration. Detectors are available with antennas that generate both omni-directional and directional energy patterns. Omni-directional antennas generate a circular donut-shaped, hemispheric, or ellipsoid energy pattern, while directional antennas generate broad teardrop-shaped patterns to protect long corridors.

Robert L. Barnard

Source   Barnard, R. 1988. *Intrusion Detection Systems, 2nd Edition*. Boston: Butterworth-Heinemann.

SENSORS: SONIC MOTION DETECTORS

Sonic motion detectors are similar to ultrasonic motion detectors inasmuch as they both use air as their signal transmission medium. The primary difference between the two is that sonic detectors fill the volume requiring protection with energy in the audible frequency range (typically 800 hertz) instead of with ultrasonic energy (above 20 kilohertz). Since the audible energy is lower in frequency than inaudible ultrasonic energy, the audible energy has longer wavelengths and, consequently, is less sensitive to air currents that might distort ultrasonic energy patterns.

It is also less sensitive than ultrasonic motion detectors to small moving objects in the zone of detection such as insects, cats, or rodents. This sensitivity difference results from the fact that the wavelength of sonic energy is much longer than ultrasonic energy. Therefore, the distortions generated by the small animals are not as significant as they are with the ultrasonic detector.

Sonic detectors consist basically of a control unit that contains the power supply and signal processor, and the central unit can operate from one to eight transceivers. The transmitter section of these units fills the area requiring protection with acoustical energy, while the receiver section collects the reflected acoustical signals for the signal processor. The transmitted acoustical energy is reflected by the walls and other objects within the protected area, thus generating standing wave patterns of acoustical energy. Any disturbance in these energy patterns that satisfies the detector alarm criteria initiates an alarm, as is the case with the ultrasonic and microwave motion detectors.

Sonic motion detectors monitor the received acoustic energy for both a change in the amplitude of the received energy and a Doppler frequency shift in the standing wave pattern. These changes can be detected by comparing the frequency spectrum of the reflected signal with that of the transmitted signal. When both the standing wave amplitude change and the frequency shift satisfy the detector alarm criteria, an alarm is initiated.

Robert L. Barnard

Source   Barnard, R. 1988. *Intrusion Detection Systems, 2nd Edition*. Boston: Butterworth-Heinemann.

SENSORS: ULTRASONIC MOTION DETECTORS

A basic ultrasonic motion detector consists of a transmitter, receiver, and control unit. The control unit contains the signal processor, power supply, and standby battery. In operation, the detector transmitter generates an acoustical energy pattern that fills the zone of detection. Energy reflecting from the walls, ceiling, and floor, and objects within the energy pattern and entering the receiver's field of acceptance, is processed and analyzed by the signal processor. As long as the reflected energy is at the same frequency as the transmitted energy, there is no alarm; but anyone moving in the energy pattern produces a Doppler frequency shift that changes the reflected signal. When the signal characteristics satisfy the processor alarm criteria, the detector initiates an alarm.

Most ultrasonic detectors operate at a specific frequency in the frequency range between 19 and 40 kilohertz. Acoustical energy generated at frequencies above 19 kilohertz is considered inaudible to the average human ear and is defined as ultrasonic energy. A feature of ultrasonic energy is that it will not penetrate physical barriers such as walls; therefore, it can be easily contained in closed rooms. Since acoustical energy will not penetrate physical barriers, the walls of the protected room either absorb or reflect the energy. Since most walls absorb very little ultrasonic energy unless they are covered with a very soft material, such as heavy drapes, most of the energy is reflected. This reflected energy helps fill the zone of detection, making it more difficult for an intruder to escape notice.

There are two basic ultrasonic motion-detector configurations. The first configuration consists of a number of transceivers connected to one common control unit. A transceiver is a single unit that has a transmitter and receiver in one housing. In case of an ultrasonic transceiver, it has a separate transducer that transmits and receives ultrasonic energy. The second detector configuration consists of a number of separate transmitters and receivers also connected to one common control unit. The number of individual transceivers or separate transmitters and receivers in a specific installation depends primarily on the size and configuration of the area requiring protection. The limiting factor on the number of transceivers or receivers and transmitters connected to a single control unit is the maximum allowable number of units designated by the manufacturer.

Piezoelectric and magnetostrictive transducers are used in ultrasonic motion detectors to convert electrical energy into acoustical energy and vice-versa. In the piezoelectric transducer, the crystal is mounted in the center of a circular diaphragm mounted in the front of the transducer housing. When an alternating current is applied to the crystal, it physically expands and contracts at the frequency of the alternating current. This expansion and contraction causes the mounting diaphragm to vibrate, which in turn causes the air in front of the diaphragm to vibrate. This vibrating air is the acoustical energy. Conversely, reflected acoustical energy exerts an external force on the receive transducer, causing the crystal mounting diaphragm to vibrate. These vibrations stress the crystal, which generates an output signal for the signal processor. The signal is proportional to the strength of the reflected energy.

Piezoelectric transducer crystals are optimized to operate over a rather narrow-frequency band. Although they operate very well at these frequencies, their ability to transmit and especially to receive energy at frequencies much above or below their design frequency is marginal. Although the piezoelectric transducer frequency response is considered narrow, the transducers are quite capable of receiving an ample signal to detect a moving intruder. A moving intruder produces a Doppler frequency shift containing frequency components that range between 20 to 800 kilohertz on either side of the primary operating frequency. The amplitude and range of the frequency shift depend on the moving intruder's size, speed, and direction. The

"speed" is not just the velocity of the intruder's body; it also includes the velocities of swinging arms and legs.

Magnetostrictive transducers perform the same functions as the piezoelectric transducers; but, instead of a vibrating crystal, the magnetostrictive transducer uses a laminated nickel rod wound with a wire coil. When the coil around the nickel rod is excited by an alternating current, the resulting magnetic field expands and contracts the rod at twice the frequency of the impressed field—twice the frequency because it expands and contracts the rod on both halves of the alternating electromagnetic field.

A permanent magnet is used to bias the coil and cancel out the flux generated on one half-cycle of the impressed electromagnetic field. Removing one half-cycle of the impressed field, or halving the frequency, reduces the transducer frequency to the original alternating current frequency.

In the piezoelectric transducer, the crystal mounting diaphragm excites the air medium, but in the magnetostrictive transducer the nickel rod is connected to the base of a hemispherical-shaped aluminum shell or to some other shaped diaphragm that excites the air medium. When the nickel rod expands and contracts, it vibrates the hemispherical shell or diaphragm that generates the acoustical energy pattern.

The receive transducer is identical in configuration to the transmitting transducer. Reflected acoustical energy impinging on the hemispherical shell or diaphragm stresses the nickel rod in compression and expansion at the frequency of the reflected energy. The compression and expansion of the nickel rod generates a signal for the processor that is proportional to the strength of the reflected energy.

Most ultrasonic motion detectors are designed to operate at lower ultrasonic frequencies because low-frequency acoustical energy is less affected by air currents. The lower operating frequencies, approximately 19.6 kilohertz for the magnetostrictive type transducers and 25 kilohertz for the piezoelectric transducers, are also compatible with the construction characteristics of the individual transducers.

Although the detector operating frequencies have been described as low frequencies, the acoustical energy at these frequencies is still out of the audible frequency range for most human ears.

However, the frequencies are high enough so that the detector operation is not affected by common audible noises occurring in the protected areas. Resorting to higher operating frequencies above 25 kilohertz to further isolate the detector from common noises would result in a loss of coverage due to the resistance air imposes on the propagation of ultrasonic energy.

Robert L. Barnard

Source   Barnard, R. *Intrusion Detection Systems, 2nd Edition*. Boston: Butterworth-Heinemann.

SENSORS: VOLUMETRIC MOTION DETECTION

Active Detectors

Active volumetric motion detectors generate their own energy pattern and analyze the disturbance in that pattern for that portion of the energy reflected back to the receiver from a moving intruder. The disturbance in the energy pattern is referred to as a frequency shift or, in particular, a Doppler frequency shift. A Doppler frequency shift can best be explained by the classic example found in most elementary physics books. A person standing near a railroad track observing an approaching train and hearing the blowing whistle will first hear an increase in the pitch of the whistle and then hear a distinct lowering in the pitch as the train passes. Pitch increase is a result of the compression of the whistle sound waves as the train approaches and the decrease in the pitch is a result of the expansion of the sound wave as the train moves away from the observer. The change in the whistle pitch illustrates a wave principle that was discovered by the Austrian physicist Christian Doppler and it is applicable to all wave motion.

The most popular active volumetric detectors using the Doppler principle are the ultrasonic and microwave motion detectors. As already mentioned, ultrasonic motion detectors generate an inaudible acoustic energy pattern and process the Doppler frequency shift caused by an intruder moving in the detection zone. Microwave motion detectors basically operate by the same principle, except that they generate an energy pattern of electromagnetic energy. Because they do transmit electromagnetic energy, the detector operating frequencies and power output are regulated by the Federal Communications Commission (FCC). The FCC has allocated five operating frequencies for microwave motion detectors. The lowest frequency is 915 megahertz and the highest is 22,125 megahertz; however, most microwave detectors operate at a 10,525-megahertz frequency.

Another, but less popular, active volumetric motion detector is the sonic detector. Unlike ultrasonic detectors, sonic detectors generate an audible instead of an inaudible acoustic energy pattern and detect phase changes in the energy pattern, as well as Doppler frequency shifts caused by someone moving in the detection zone. Audibility of the sonic energy is probably the reason for the limited application of sonic motion detectors; however, there are applications where the sound is not a problem and in fact it could be a deterrent against an intruder who might otherwise consider entering the protected area.

Passive Detectors

Passive motion detectors detect energy generated by the intruder. In other words, passive detectors do not generate their own energy patterns. They detect the presence or change in energy as a result of the intruder's presence, or they detect energy generated during the intrusion. Two types of passive volumetric motion detectors are the infrared motion detector and the audio detector.

Infrared motion detectors detect a change in the thermal energy pattern resulting from a moving intruder and initiate an alarm when the change in the energy satisfies the detector alarm criteria. Audio detectors are not motion detectors per se. They depend on the intruder to generate noises, either breaking in or moving within the protected area. When the noise level reaches the detector alarm threshold, an alarm is activated.

Robert L. Barnard

Source   Barnard, R. 1988. *Intrusion Detection Systems, 2nd Edition*. Boston: Butterworth-Heinemann.

VII: Protection Practices

ACCESS CONTROL IN THE CHEMICAL INDUSTRY

The term "access control" generally refers to physical or behavioral measures for managing the passage of personnel and vehicles into, out of, and within a facility. An access control plan strives to exert enough control to protect the facility while still allowing employees enough freedom of movement to work effectively.

The appropriate level of access control varies significantly from facility to facility. It depends on the number of employees, hazards of materials present, level of pedestrian and vehicular traffic into and out of the facility, degree to which facility operations are controversial, attractiveness of the facility as a target of various threats, proximity of the facility to populated areas, and many other factors.

The following are just a few of the measures that security managers may wish to consider for the purpose of controlling access into, within, and out of a chemical facility:

- Post "No Trespassing" and "Authorized Access Only" signs, along with signs stating that vehicles and visitors are subject to search.
- To the extent feasible, employ natural surveillance by arranging reception, production, and office space so unescorted visitors can be noticed easily.
- Install appropriate locks on exterior and interior doors.
- Keep publicly accessible restroom doors locked and set up a key control system. If there is a combination lock, only office personnel should open the lock for visitors. Keep closets locked.
- Require visitor sign-in logs and escorts.
- Pay close attention to access control at loading and unloading areas.
- Install appropriate, penetration-resistant doors and security hinges.
- Install secure windows with appropriate locks, perhaps using unbreakable plastics instead of glass and employing window bars.

- Institute a system of employee and contractor photo ID badges. Train employees to challenge persons who are not wearing badges.
- Establish a system for determining which cars, trucks, rail cars, marine vessels, and other vehicles may enter the site, through which gates, docks, or other entrances, and under what conditions. Such a system may be part of the pedestrian access control system, relying on key cards carried by vehicle operators, or it may be an independent system relying on staffed security posts.
- Install an electronic access control system that requires the use of key cards at main entrances and on other appropriate doors and that provides an audit trail of ingress and egress. Consider electronic access control for entry to motor control centers, rack rooms, server rooms, telecommunication rooms, and control rooms.
- Install a closed-circuit television system to monitor key areas of the facility. Where appropriate, employ motion sensors that mark the video recording and alert security staff when someone enters a restricted area.
- Institute a system of parcel inspection (using magnetometers, X-ray screening, or explosives detectors). Require the use of property passes for removal of property from the site.

Perimeter Protection

Controlling the movement of people within a facility is important, but it is far better to stop intruders—whether they be terrorists, saboteurs, vandals, thieves, protesters, or disgruntled former employees—at the edge of a facility's property, long before they reach vital assets and operational areas.

Perimeter protection includes such measures as these, which managers can consider and implement as appropriate:

- Fences and exterior walls that make it difficult for intruders to enter the site
- Bollards and trenches that prevent vehicles from driving into the site at points other than official entrances
- Vehicle gates with retractable barriers

- Personnel gates and turnstiles
- Setbacks and clear zones that eliminate hiding places near the site's perimeter, making it difficult for intruders to approach the site unnoticed
- Lighting that makes it easier for employees and even passersby to observe and possibly identify intruders

Security Officers

Security officers can provide a range of useful security services, such as touring a site to look for intruders or irregularities, staffing site entrances to check IDs, maintaining entry and exit logs, handing out trucker safety lists, reminding employees and contractors of security and safety policies, and assisting in emergencies. Some security officers also have first aid and CPR training, boosting their companies' emergency response capabilities.

If it is deemed appropriate for a site to have security officers, managers should consider whether the officers will tour the site or remain at fixed posts; whether they will be contract or in-house officers; and what training and licensing they should receive.

Managers should also develop "post orders," which are written directions informing security officers what they should do on the job.

Security personnel help chemical facilities with access control and emergency response, but they can also help in other ways. Because they patrol areas that may be unoccupied in the evenings and weekends, security officers can prevent problems that might otherwise go undetected until too late.

Backup Systems

From a security standpoint as well as a safety and operations standpoint, it may be appropriate for chemical facilities to secure such utilities as electricity, communications (telephone and computer), water, sewer, and gas. Crucial communications equipment and utility areas can be protected with locks and with alarms that ring to a location that is staffed around the clock. Wiring can be protected by being placed in rigid conduit so it cannot easily be cut.

Such key resources as control centers, rack rooms, computer servers, and telecommunications equipment may warrant a backup power source, such as a generator.

Other Considerations

At a chemical facility, managers should keep in mind that any physical security hardware must be safe for use in that particular facility. For example, closed-circuit television cameras and access control card readers may need to be specially selected so they are safe and effective in corrosive or flammable areas.

In addition, any site redesigns should be done with security in mind. For example, plants should generally be laid out so that the most vulnerable or important locations are hardest for adversaries to reach.

A few general physical steps that managers may wish to take include these:

- Keep offices neat and orderly to identify strange objects or unauthorized people more easily. Empty trash receptacles often.
- Open packages and large envelopes in executive offices only if the source or sender is positively identified.
- Keep closets, service openings, and telephone and electrical closets locked at all times. (Author's note: This article is based in large part on the document cited below.)

John J. Fay

Source   Site Security Guidelines for the U.S. Chemical Industry, American Chemistry Council. 2006. <www.chlorineinstitute.org/Files/PDFs/SecurityguidanceACC1.pdf>

ACCESS CONTROL LEVELS

Criticality of the protected asset determines the level of accessibility to it. We traditionally assign labels to the various levels. Following are examples of the labels and what they mean in terms of access control.

- Top Security. Physical security with monitored and audited control must be implemented to the maximum degree available using the most current automated and/or manned technologies. ID verification is critical and thus biometric technologies are often employed. Cost, aesthetic appearance, traffic flow and operational impact are of secondary importance to the control of access to personnel and property.

- **High Security.** Unauthorized access is not physically possible, or if possible is deterred by visible armed security personnel or police. The building or area can be manually or automatically placed in a completely secure mode, under which entry or unalarmed exit are not physically possible without extreme injury (such as exit by breaking through a non-ground floor window). Access is monitored and can be audited by personal ID. The cost factor is balanced against the aesthetic requirements and any impact on operations.

- **Medium Security.** Door control includes one or more security advantages not normally found in a door secured by standard commercial key locks alone. Manned response would be either instantaneous unarmed response or delayed armed response. Access is granted based upon ID verification determined by human or electronic examination. The degree of security is balanced against aesthetic appearance, operational impact, and cost and maintenance requirements.

- **Low Security.** Control mechanisms are used to indicate restricted access. Access is generally regulated by time, ticket, or personal or group ID. Low security requires only a low degree of difficulty to obtain unauthorized access. It utilizes inconvenience and the threat of high attention or observation (including flashing lights, sirens, or cameras) to deter a would-be violator. Appearance is usually balanced against cost. In most commercial buildings, automated access control has meant the fitting of access control hardware onto standard doors.

Top, high, medium, and low loosely characterize security products relative to the level of protection appropriate for a building, people, operations, and the surrounding environment.

The increasing importance of building security and the emergence of doors and gates designed specifically for the access control purpose, make it worthwhile to invest additional thought in the design of the building's total access control scheme. It's important to know the new types of doors now available and how they fit into a facility's security and its operational requirements.

High security access control doors are the norm where unattended access control is necessary. They allow traffic flow and yet conform to the facility's aesthetic requirements. The fit of appearance and functionality are sometimes balanced against cost factors, but a suitable combination can usually be found in an acceptable cost range. The four-wing security revolving door that comes to rest in the x-position can prevent the easy passage of items through the door. Such doors can be installed with sensors that limit passage to one person at a time, and can prevent passage of a person carrying a box or large stack of material. These doors can also be built with bulletproof glass, yet still match a variety of highly aesthetic decors.

Medium security is common but not always appropriate. Most access control systems provide medium security access control, mainly because they employ standard doors for entry and exit control. When an authorized user is granted access through a standard door, the burden of access control temporarily passes over to that user when the door is opened. This is where access violations occur. The most common security violation is one borne out of courtesy, where the authorized user holds the door open to permit entry by another who has also approached the door. If the person looks vaguely familiar, is carrying packages, or if the weather is inclement, courtesy prevails over security concerns. Also, it may not be a safe move to personally confront a "piggy-backing" individual.

Although many systems provide a duress or panic signal, it won't be activated unless the authorized person is absolutely sure that the other individual is unauthorized. The next most common access violation is where authorized users prop a door open to carry boxes or other materials in or out. This permits others to come and go while the door is open, and enables theft of equipment and material. To prevent these violations, video cameras and some level of manned security are often used in conjunction with medium security automated access control.

Until recently the common options for low security access control were unaesthetic turnstiles, wooden railings with electrically controlled gates, or half-height walls with electrically controlled half-doors. Now many types of turnstiles and glass gates exist that are easily installed, blend well with modern architectures, and can handle a steady flow of traffic.

Buildings generally have mixed security requirements. For example, a single floor or suite in a building can have high-security requirements, while the rest of the facility has only a medium security requirement. If high security access control is used for building entry and exit, often medium-security and low-security access control can be used throughout the inside of the facility.

Ray Bernard

ALCOHOL TESTING

Alcohol's cost to society is staggering. The Research Triangle Institute of North Carolina reports alcohol abuse was responsible for $50.6 billion in reduced productivity in 1988, compared with $25.7 billion in losses from drug usage. Our nation spent $9.5 billion in health care costs for alcohol-related problems, compared with $1.2 billion for drug-related problems.

The Employee Assistance Society of North America reports that absenteeism among alcoholics and problem drinkers is as much as 8.3 times higher than for other employees. Alcohol abusers also have a two to three times greater risk of being involved in industrial accidents.

The Society's studies show that up to 40 percent of industrial fatalities and 47 percent of industrial injuries are due to alcohol abuse. Even nonalcoholic members of an alcoholic's family will use as much as 10 times more sick leave than will other employees.

Alcohol problems are not limited to the workplace. The U.S. Department of Health and Human Services reports that alcohol was involved in half of all highway deaths last year, resulting in 25,000 fatalities. It is also a factor in 50–70 percent of all murders, fatal accidents, and fire death; and in over half of all arrests. Considering alcohol's impact on our nation and our businesses, alcohol testing should be considered a part of a responsible drug screening program.

Blood Alcohol Content

Law enforcement agencies have long used breath tests to measure the level of alcohol in the blood of persons suspected of committing crimes. Most states have set 0.10 percent blood alcohol content (BAC) as the maximum level of alcohol a person may have in the body system while operating a motor vehicle. Some states use a 0.08 percent BAC standard. The Department of Transportation recently set limits of 0.04 percent BAC for pilots, bus and truck drivers, train crews, and marine crews.

Loss of driver attention and control is generally understood to occur at BAC levels of 0.03 percent and 0.04 percent. Studies show that some impairment may be measured with any detectable level of alcohol, and for this reason there is a growing consensus that the acceptable level should be lowered or that zero tolerance be applied. The relatively high BAC level of 0.10 percent comes from an earlier period in which the professional community was in general agreement that any person exhibiting a BAC at that level was unquestionably intoxicated to operate any dangerous machinery.

In the industrial setting, where impairment is known to increase the risk of accidents, the rule of thumb is that 0.04 percent should be the highest acceptable BAC level for employees operating equipment.

The several methods of analyzing blood for alcohol content can be divided into two basic categories: pre-evidentiary and evidentiary testing. Pre-evidentiary tests produce preliminary or presumptive test results. They are like field tests or screening tests designed to indicate the need for more definitive testing conducted in a laboratory environment. Evidentiary tests are the definitive, highly analytical tests whose findings are widely recognized in the scientific community and accepted as evidence in a court of law.

Pre-Evidentiary Testing

Three types of pre-evidentiary tests stand out. Two are based on the application of scientific principles to the examination of body substances (i.e., breath and saliva) and the third is based on the empirical observations of a person trained in the identification and interpretation of physiological symptoms associated with alcohol-induced impairment.

Breath Tests. Hand-held, disposable breath testers are inexpensive, accurate, and easy to administer. Where it is necessary to test for alcohol abuse—such as at the scene of an accident or when an employee appears to be intoxicated—a disposable breath tester can provide nearly instant visual proof that the subject should be further tested.

A positive breath test provides a "reasonable cause" justification for conducting a more definitive test, such as a blood test. Since disposable breath testers are priced at only a few dollars each, they are cost-effective.

A variety of disposable breath testers are on the market. One brand works as follows. The test administrator squeezes a tube containing silica gel granules. The squeezing action breaks a small glass ampule of potassium dichromate inside the tube. The subject then blows through the tube for a period of 12 seconds. If alcohol is present in the breath, the granules in the tube change color.

Testers can be purchased that are factory-calibrated for BAC levels at the 0.02 percent, 0.04 percent, 0.05 percent, 0.08 percent, and 0.10 percent ranges. When using the 0.10 percent tester, the color change becomes distinct in most of the granules when the BAC is higher than 0.05 percent and the color change becomes complete when the BAC exceeds 0.10 percent.

Saliva Tests. In these tests a sterile swab is used to collect a sample of saliva from the subject's mouth. The swab is then directly rubbed against a sensitized plate. A color change on the plate indicates the presence of alcohol. Unfortunately, the test materials have a limited shelf life and must be kept cool. On the positive side, the saliva test costs less than the breath test.

Observational Tests. Observational tests are almost exclusively limited to motor vehicle traffic enforcement. A driver suspected of driving while under the influence of alcohol is examined by a law enforcement officer specially trained (and sometimes certified) in the administration of such tests. The tests usually involve a combination of psychomotor exercises, such as touching the nose and walking a line, and a systematic search for physiological indicators, such as dilated pupils and irregular eye movements, e.g., strabismus and nystagmus. Although these techniques can be applied to making fitness-for-work determinations, they are not generally accepted in the workplace.

Evidentiary Testing

The methods of evidentiary testing for alcohol are different from drug testing due to the rapid breakdown of alcohol, both in the body and in any sample collected.

Because alcohol moves through the kidneys and is held in the bladder until expelled, a urine test can report an alcohol level in the danger zone even though the subject is no longer affected by the intoxicant.

Conversely, it's possible for the urine to show very little alcohol while the blood contains a great deal. Another potential problem with urinalysis is the evaporation rate of alcohol during transportation, leading to a discrepancy between the alcohol content at the time of collection and at the time of testing.

Blood testing is the most accurate method of proving excess alcohol content, but it is intrusive and costly. It is also inconvenient because the person to be tested must be transported to a medical facility and the collected blood sample must then be transported to a forensic drug testing laboratory. In the case of a highly intoxicated subject, the BAC is likely to drop significantly during the time spent getting to a blood collecting facility.

Blood and urine tests should be conducted by a forensic laboratory that specializes in such tests, such as a laboratory certified by the National Institute on Drug Abuse. An NIDA-certified laboratory will use testing methodologies and chain-of-custody procedures capable of withstanding intense court scrutiny.

Breath analysis machines, such as the Breathalyzer and Intoximeter, are evidentiary testing devices that work with high accuracy and are usually recognized in judicial proceedings. These devices are extensively used by law enforcement officers but are only rarely used in the private sector. They are costly, require certified operators, and must be calibrated continuously, making them difficult for use by the average company.

Carl E. King

AUTHENTICATION, AUTHORIZATION, AND CRYPTOGRAPHY

Authentication (verifying identity) and authorization (verifying that the identified person is permitted the requested access at that moment) have typically been performed by physical access control systems as a single step; present a valid access card, and authentication and authorization are instantly performed.

Cryptography (the science of providing security for information through the transformation of data) initially used encryption as a way to protect passwords and other sensitive information in an access control system's databases. Then manufacturers began to use encryption in system and network communications. Today, information security requirements for enterprise-scale integrated security systems utilize additional cryptographic techniques to establish trusted system connections, and to ensure that transmitted data is authentic and unaltered.

Authentication, authorization, and cryptography were initially built into single systems to protect physical and information security assets by restricting individual access to them. These technologies have now become the enablers and protectors of critical business processes and commercial transactions. Due to the extremely large scale of enterprise-wide identity and access management systems and the complexity of integration requirements, entire systems have been developed to provide these functions as a service to other systems.

Identity Management

Within the context of a business system or security system, identity generally has one of two meanings. First, it refers to identity information (such as an identifying name or number) that is unique within the system, plus additional information that usually includes one or more of the following: identifying characteristics, which individuals and systems will use to perform an identification; system or organizational role, used to determine specific rights and authority granted; and the period of time for which the identity information can be relied upon. Second, identity can refer to a person, artifact such as a security smart card, data object (such as a biometric signature on a card), or computer system that is being verified as authentic by the system.

Strictly speaking, identity management is the identification of authorized users and their enrollment in a system that is used to manage their identity information. However, the management of identity information is not an end in itself — it is used to facilitate business activities such as physical access control, information systems access control, and workflow automation in accordance with business policies. This identity management is an integrated system of business processes, policies, and technologies.

An identity management system (IDMS) identifies individuals in a system and controls their access to resources within that system by associating user rights and restrictions with each identified individual. The FIPS 201 standard (see below) requires that an identity management system be used to manage the identity information required for the Personal Identity Verification process specified in the standard.

User Provisioning

Provisioning means to provide users (such as the cardholders in an access control system or the users of a computer-based information system) with two things: (1) a means to *authenticate* themselves (such as a card and PIN, or name and password), and (2) *access privileges*. Those two elements combined are what enable access to protected assets.

FIPS 201

Federal Information Processing Standard (FIPS) Publication 201, commonly known as FIPS 201, governs the Personal Identity Verification (PIV) of U.S. Federal Employees and Contractors. It specifies the architecture and technical requirements for a common identification standard to achieve appropriate security assurance for multiple applications by efficiently verifying the claimed identity of individuals seeking physical access to federally controlled government facilities and electronic access to government information systems.

The standard contains two major sections. Part one describes the minimum requirements for a Federal personal identity verification system that meets the control and security objectives of Homeland Security Presidential Directive 12, including personal identity proofing, registration, and issuance. Part two provides detailed specifications that will support technical interoperability among PIV systems of Federal departments and agencies.

Personal Identity Verification (PIV) in FIPS 201 refers to the processes and technologies involved in (a) *identification*: verifying the identity of an individual at the time of initial identification and enrollment into the identity management system, and (b) *authentication:* verifying the identity of the individual for purposes of physical and information systems access control.

Role-Based Access Control

The basic concept of Role-Based Access Control (RBAC) is that within an organization, roles are created for various job functions, and personnel are assigned a specific role. Corresponding roles are created in the access control system, and access privileges are assigned to the roles (as opposed to being assigned directly to personnel). Thus, personnel acquire access privileges by being assigned a role. This use of roles facilitates policy-based management of access control that mirrors the actual job requirements of an organization's personnel.

The purpose of RBAC is to enable and enforce policy-based access control in an auditable manner, and to allow access roles to align with actual personnel roles within the organization. In contrast to typical group access control schemes, RBAC has the following features when properly implemented:

- Privileges are assigned to roles. This contributes to scalability, since in most large organizations more than one person has the same role (sales person, accountant, auditor, receptionist, and so on).
- Roles are assigned to cardholders. Roles are designed to parallel actual organizational roles, which simplifies management and allows role assignment to be accurately done as part of the Human Resources personnel enrollment process.
- Only one role is assigned to one cardholder. This facilitates simple audit of access against organizational policy, since individual privileges don't have to be examined to determine the scope of a cardholder's access. The assigned role states it.
- Roles are hierarchical—they can inherit privileges from other roles. This is required in order to parallel real-world organizational functional roles, and to make it possible to implement the "one role per user" rule.

As RBAC has become the single most effective approach to managing large-scale access control, the American National Standards Institute (ANSI) adopted it as a standard in 2004. Many Federal agencies are adopting, or have already adopted, RBAC for information security. A significant opportunity exists to improve the management of physical security by leveraging existing RBAC initiatives.

RBAC can be used to unify the management of physical and information systems access. The same organizational roles can be used by physical security and information security to establish appropriate role privileges, based upon organizational policy and job function needs. This allows policy-based information security to be implemented easily for both physical and electronic forms of information.

By utilizing physical and information access control systems that implement RBAC, physical and information security can be synchronized based upon policy even if the access control systems themselves are not integrated. However, the greatest return on investment and business process improvement would come from integrating the physical and information access control systems with an Identity Management System used to manage roles for the entire organization.

Jill Allison

Source D'Agostino, S., Engberg, D., Sinkov, A., and Bernard, R. 1997. "The Roles of Authentication, Authorization, and Cryptography in Expanding Security Industry Technology," *SIA Quarterly Technical Update, Dec. 2005.*

BEST PRACTICES IN GUARD OPERATIONS

The Commodity Syndrome

A security program can make a value-added contribution to an organization because the business of protecting assets can be critical to the survival and success of the organization as a whole. Just as we would not think of the function of marketing or personnel management as a product that can be contracted out to the lowest bidder, the same needs to be understood about the function of security. Unfortunately, many proprietary security directors and third-party providers seem unable to break away from defining their services as if they were commodities. The best illustration is in the procurement process, in which the overwhelming majority of agreements are reached following a process of identifying the provider who will provide the service for the lowest price. The very notion of competitive bidding suggests a lock on what I refer to as the commodity syndrome.

Best Practices and Change

Organizations are dynamic. The same can be said for the environments in which they operate and serve. It is only reasonable to expect, therefore, that the way in which security conducts its business needs to be characterized in fluid terms. Organizations that remain static discover that it doesn't take long before they are behind the curve and are at risk of losing more than they gain. The very nature of best practices connotes a desire to continuously evaluate your practices through established feedback mechanisms and to adapt accordingly. Best practices require the perception "We're in it for the long haul." Those who pursue best practices understand that it takes time not only to effect change, but also for change to have a measurable impact on the rest of the company. To be world-class requires an investment of both time and resources. Just as it requires more time to build a custom home or assemble an automobile by hand, the same can be said for pursuing strategies that are designed to assure that end users receive the best in quality service. The most visible component of a security program is guard operations. The end users rate the entire security program on what they see security officers do or not do.

Legal Counsel and Human Resources

Best-in-class practitioners understand the role of resource specialists and will draw upon them much as they would any other management tool in the decision-making process. The function of legal counsel is to avoid risks and the function of human resources is to assure compliance with corporate policies and the rules of regulatory agencies. These two organizational functions are inherently risk averse; they follow strategies that limit liabilities that can arise from security officers performing unlawful acts and not performing duties according to policy. The best-in-class security manager views legal counsel and human resources in much the same way the head coach of a football team views assistant coaches. Regardless of their input, it is the head coach who makes the final decision.

Benchmarking

Benchmarking is a method that a security manager can use to improve guard operations. The method compares a questionable operation against an operation known to be excellent. From the comparison, the security manager of the questionable operation is able to see opportunities for improvement, which may relate to the nuts and bolts of the operation or the manner in which the operation is supervised and managed. The security manager can also use benchmarking to compare his or her management practices against the practices of peers within and outside of the organization. Whether done in-house or out-of-house, benchmarking can serve as a barometer for determining what works best under what circumstances.

Best Practices Is a Continuous Loop

The pursuit of best practices is not done in a vacuum. It is a four-step process configured as a continuous loop. It begins with the identification of the end user's needs and expectations, which is often referred to by management theorists as the research phase.

The identification step is followed by an articulation of operational strategies capable of meeting or exceeding the needs and expectations of end-users. The development of a strategy can begin with bold ideas suggested by the security manager's staff, testing the strategy through trial and error, collecting and examining data internal to the strategy, and using comparative data obtained from external sources.

The third phase of the process consists of soliciting and receiving feedback from end users. Even though the security manager may believe that best practices are being achieved, the real measure of improvement is reflected in end-user feedback.

The fourth step is to make changes based on feedback. These are changes in operations, not changes on paper. A few notes of caution are merited. Make sure the feedback is not the result of a knee-jerk reaction, that it is the product of careful examination by the end user, and that you do not misinterpret the feedback.

This four-step process is called a continuous loop because it never ends. Lessons learned in the fourth step are used to reformulate strategies. Hopefully, reformulation will be in the nature of tweaking as opposed to major overhaul.

Cost Is a Primary Driver

It is easy to get caught up in the process of bold thinking. Exploring new ideas is invigorating and exciting. The reality, however, is that putting new ideas into action must be done against the backdrop of cost-effectiveness. In a world of highly competitive markets, it is paramount that today's security managers keep a sharp eye on the bottom-line contribution. If bold thinking and new ideas cannot be framed within the context of profitable performance, then senior management, despite their enthusiasm and initial support, will reluctantly withdraw support in deference to the pressures of cost containment.

Security Is Measurable

When pursuing best-in-class practices, assume that any support function can break its contributing parts down to activities that are measurable. The same holds true for corporate security. Although many security managers attempt to take solace in the mistaken belief that there is more art to security management than science, in reality there is nothing within the operational management of asset protection that cannot be measured in one way or another.

In guard operations, the security manager can look at tasks performed by security officers. For example, the number of visitors processed, the number of visitors turned away due to invalid entry privileges, the amount of time required to process one visitor, the number of security officers assigned to visitor processing in a single tour of duty, and dollar numbers associated with security officer labor, tools of the job, and supplies required. These numbers tell the security manager what has been done and at what cost. The most important number is one that can be found by comparing historical data against current data, which in this instance is the number of dollars lost to the company as the result of less-than-acceptable visitor management in the immediately preceding period, the number of dollars lost for the same reason in the current period, and the differential. The security manager will pray that the differential is positive. A positive differential is then compared to the cost of the visitor management function. If the dollar cost is less than the differential (which is dollars saved), the security manager has hard data demonstrating that a contribution has been made to the company's bottom line.

Expectations and Realities

It is easy for a security manager to disregard an end user's expression of needs and expectations. The manager may rationalize that the end user knows little about the security function, does not accurately perceive risk and threat, and would be better served by just letting security do its job. While all of this may be true, the reality is that the end user is the ultimate authority.

Another reality is that the end user's expectations can exceed the capacity of the security function. The end user may want a service or a bundle of services that simply cannot be provided given the resources available to the security function. This reality can be a source of rancor between the security manager and the end user; also, it can cause the security function to be less effective. In the attempt to placate an unhappy end user, the security manager may agree to take on a new set of tasks, and in so doing eliminates or diminishes the quality of other equally important tasks.

What is the connection to best practices? A security manager committed to best practices will see the end user's reality and move it closer to the security reality. There should be little difference between what the end user expects and what the security function is able to deliver. However, when the difference is large and resists closing, the security manager has to make it clear to the end user that expectations are out of sync with capacity.

Here's a quick example to illustrate the point. Department heads are quick to challenge security managers when an unauthorized person is found walking through a restricted area without an escort or a valid reason to be there. Non-security managers assume that as long as security is responsible for access control, it is security's responsibility to ensure that an unauthorized person will not be allowed to leave a public area such as the main lobby and enter into a restricted work area. While the non-security manager's perception is that security is responsible for access control, the reality may be that there are competing elements operating within the lobby that make it impossible for the security officer to control access into restricted areas 100 percent of the time. Such demands on the officer's attention can range from responding to radio transmissions to answering telephones to registering visitors or conversing with regular employees who have forgotten or lost their access control cards. Given these competing demands, it is not unreasonable to expect that unauthorized persons will at times slip by the security officer unnoticed.

Instead of being defensive when such a breach occurs, the security manager can use the incident as an opportunity to explain limitations and ask for a budget increase to fund hiring of an additional security officer. The increase may not be forthcoming but the security manager will have made an important point.

Conclusion

It is far easier to pursue those things with which we are most comfortable. Over time we become proficient in those things we do every day and are lulled into a false state of satisfaction. Being proficient in everyday tasks is not the end point. A person that manages with best practices will seek opportunities to perform beyond his or her current level of expertise, and at the same time transfer acquired best practices to others.

Dennis Dalton

COMPUTER-BASED TRAINING FOR SECURITY PROFESSIONALS

Introduction

For millennia humans have used a variety of instructional media to allow instructors to reach out to students that were separated from them in time or space. The instructional media may have employed high technology media such as satellite broadcasts or less sophisticated media such as correspondence courses, but they still attempted to connect instructors with students that were not physically located in their presence. In fact, it is highly likely that many cave drawings and petroglyphs most likely served to pass on important knowledge to future generations, long after the authors departed. As new instructional media emerged, so too did supporters and opponents. For example, Julius Caesar decried the role of books in the Roman educational system because they reduced the requirement to memorize volumes of information. On the other hand, Thomas Edison proclaimed that movies would soon replace books and teachers within most educational settings. As computer technologies proliferate throughout the home, the school, and the workplace, supporters and opponents of computer-based training each make claims concerning the value of this emerging approach for training delivery. This article will provide a general description of computer-based training, review the scientific research on its effectiveness, and then discuss considerations for its use within the security professional's workplace.

What is Computer-Based Training?

Computer-based training (CBT) is an instructional form that has existed since the 1960s. This article uses the term "CBT" in a very broad sense to refer to any use of the computer to deliver and/or manage training. If any training professional finds this use onerous, no harm is intended. There are simply too many terms used to describe the spectrum of CBT and the subtle distinctions between them are best discussed in other venues. These terms include computer-assisted instruction (CAI), computer-managed instruction (CMI), multimedia training, e-learning, web-based training (WBT), and interactive multimedia instruction (IMI). All these terms refer to the use of computers to deliver and/or manage training that is provided directly to students. The only distinction between types of CBT that this article will make is between programmed and unprogrammed CBT.

In some instances, the training provided to the students is unprogrammed; that is, it connects the learners directly to live instructors that deliver their instruction through the computer. For example, applications such as chat rooms, instant messaging, or Centra Live™ allow instructors and students to interact with each other through computers. In these instances, the instructor controls the pace and content of the lesson just as they would in a classroom.

However, the vast majority of current CBT offerings employ programmed (self-paced or automated) instruction to the learners. In these instances, there is no instructor communicating with the learner. Instead, the learner interacts with a computer program that delivers the lesson content. The computer program controls the lesson pace and content. The same computer program may also check on the student's progress using questions, quizzes, and tests. For the purposes of this article, computer-based instruction (CBT) refers to the delivery of *programmed* instruction to learners through a computer. Subsequent articles will address other ways in which CBT can support training delivery and management.

A computer is not an instructional technology any more than a book or a video. However, the computer's "…unmatched ability to manage information with such speed and accuracy" makes it an inviting tool for the delivery of instruction. In the early days of CBT, lessons were generally limited to text displays. However, with advances in technology, CBT lessons can now include graphics, animations, audio, video, and even interactive simulations. More importantly, programmed CBT can guide one hundred students through each lesson as easily as one student. The computer never gets tired, never forgets to cover a key point, and never gets exasperated with students. Furthermore, by "de-linking" the instructor from the training delivery process CBT can provide 24-hour-by-7-day availability without incurring overtime.

This is not to say that CBT can cure poor quality training or a flawed training program. As this author's mentor once proclaimed, "Delivering bad training with CBT just makes bad training more expensive." CBT can be expensive to develop; sometimes as much as $45,000 per delivered hour. Cost factors dictate that CBT provide accurate content, learning activities that allow students to develop skills (not just watch the screen), and an evaluation strategy that informs the student immediately when he/she is not making adequate progress.

Is CBT Effective?

As with all instructional technologies, CBT has its avid supporters and rabid opponents arguing that CBT is instructionally superior or inferior to instructor-led training. Since the 1960s, considerable research has been conducted on CBT. The vast majority of studies have found little or no difference in student achievement when comparing CBT to instructor-led training.

A multiyear, multimillion dollar research project conducted by The National Science Foundation of America (NSF) of two CBT solutions (i.e., PLATO and TICCIT) concluded that CBT was as effective as instructor-led training. In another instance, researchers reviewed fifty-nine independent studies of college level CBT projects and noted that CBT made small but significant contributions to course achievement when compared to instructor-led training. Furthermore, they noted that CBT substantially reduced the amount of time needed for instruction. Some of these same researchers later analyzed the results from fifty-one independent evaluations of CBT in grades 6–12. They also noted substantial savings in learning time. Rigorous studies of the effectiveness of CBT conducted at the University of Michigan also reported positive (but modest) effects of CBT.

Noted author and researcher Brandon Hall provides what is probably the most salient summary of research into CBT's effectiveness to date. He notes that:

1. There is very strong evidence that computer-based training reduces the total cost of training when compared to instructor-led training.
2. There is very strong evidence that computer-based training requires less time for training compared to instructor-led training. Reductions range from 20 to 80 percent with most commonly reported reductions ranging from 40 to 60 percent.
3. There is strong evidence to suggest that computer-based training results in equal or better quality learning as instructor-led training.

Advantages to the Use of CBT

CBT does not require simultaneous communication between people. A computer-based lesson on how to collect DNA evidence, whether delivered over the Internet or with a CD-ROM, is a good example of this approach. CBT provides students with a common curriculum of tutorials and references. References may consist of instructor notes, online articles, or texts converted to online formats. Individual lessons contain automatically scored evaluations to assess student progress within the lesson's framework. These evaluations may occur in the form of pretests, embedded questions, or posttests. Remediation is usually supported using branching, a technique that allows students to review material previously presented, or to receive additional instruction on material. This approach is well suited for subjects that employ written tests.

A significant advantage to programmed CBT is that it paces itself to each student, individually. By employing pre-tests of student knowledge, CBT can allow students to skip material that they have already mastered and concentrate their time on areas in which they are weakest. For several years studies have consistently noted that computer-based training that follows this training approach tends to yield "substantial savings of student time." Citing these studies, Brandon Hall notes, "There is very strong evidence that computer-based training requires less time for training compared to instructor-led training. The amount of reduction ranges from 20–80 percent, with 40–60 percent being the most common. Time reduction for multimedia training is usually attributed to a tighter instructional design, the option for participants to bypass content not needed, and the opportunity for participants to focus on those sections of the course not yet mastered."

Another advantage to this approach is that the program delivering the instruction will perform consistently for all students. Unlike instructors, it will not tire, become irritable, or forget to cover every point in the lesson. When training programs address content that is based on compliance requirements (e.g., security, environmental compliance, sexual harassment) CBT's ability to both deliver consistent content and to document student achievement makes a compelling business case for its use. However, CBT is only interactive with the student to the extent allowed in the program. This limits interactivity to the program design. Weak program designs fail to accommodate even the most common

student requirements for additional feedback or assistance. CBT appears to be most effective when learners interact with the CBT program to solve problems and to practice skills.

What Types of Interactivity Can CBT Provide?

The level to which students interact with a CBT product can best be described in terms of four levels of interactivity ranging from passive to real-time participation. Several different descriptions of interactivity exist, but the four-level approach provided by the Department of Defense (MIL-HDBK-29612-3A, 31 August 2001) is most common.

Level 1 Interactivity—Passive. At this level of interactivity the learner is essentially passive. Learner activity is limited to advancing the display to the next screen (i.e., turning pages). While CBT lessons with level one interactivity cost little to produce, they may fail to provide students with adequate feedback. Additionally, the absence of quizzes, tests, or exams may leave management asking whether the lesson achieved its intended purpose.

Level 2 Interactivity—Limited Participation. This level of interactivity provides the learner with limited participation through drill and practice exercises that provide feedback on learner responses. These drill and practice exercises do more than present questions to students; they provide remediation when the student fails the exercise. To provide this remediation, the CBT employs branching strategies that link the exercise to additional content. In the event the student fails the exercise, the CBT program informs the student of the correct response and displays the additional information. Because timely remediation ensures that errors are corrected immediately it is a significant factor in CBT's demonstrated ability to reduce overall training time. CBT offering level two interactivity should also provide self-scoring tests and examinations, which is important to any organization that employs written tests. Rather than waiting hours or even days for test results, CBT with level two interactivity offers organizations the ability to determine student achievement as soon as the test is complete.

Level 3 Interactivity—Complex Participation.
At this level of interactivity, CBT should provide complex branching paths based on student selections and responses. Rather than evaluating the response as simply correct or incorrect, CBT with this level of interactivity can provide tailored responses that address different types of student errors. At this level of interactivity CBT may also provide a limited capability for real-time simulation of tasks performed in the workplace (e.g., operating simple switch panels). Testing and examination at this level should include all of the previous level's capabilities and add predictive test items.

Level 4 Interactivity—Real-Time Participation.
At the most interactive level, CBT should allow real-time simulation of performance in the operational setting employing state-of-the art technology for simulation and communication.

What Are the Organizational Considerations for Using CBT?

Support and reporting requirements for training delivery suggest that managers should consider organizational requirements for using CBT. The skills sets typically required for development and distribution of CBT include information technology management, audio and video production, graphic design, subject matter expertise, writing ability, and project management. Assembling this diverse set of skills within one organization is often challenging, at best. One option many organizations consider rather than obtaining the necessary skills sets is outsourcing to specialty firms or requiring vendors to provide these services.

Deploying and supporting CBT suggests significant requirements for organizational change. The change is not revolutionary, but evolutionary. However, managers should assess their organizations' adaptability. The organizational implications extend beyond the students' ability to use computers and the availability of computers within the organization. CBT may generate significant amounts of student performance data (e.g., scores, certifications, course selection, individual schedules, and completion data). In many ways, the data management requirements resemble those of an instructional institution. Managers should pay close attention to the collection, security, and integration of student performance data if they are to avoid information overload. Even more importantly, managers should be completely familiar with the CBT's lesson content and the operation of the CBT product.

Summary

Computer-based training is NOT a silver bullet—it is one of many training tools that security professionals should consider. As such it is the means to an end, not an end in itself. Training decisions should focus first on the organization's training and training management requirements, the target audience requirements, and then the delivery infrastructure. Employed correctly, computer-based training can provide the training flexibility and cost effectiveness that security professionals require.
Robert W. Miller and Sandi J. Davies

Sources
Bangert-Drowns, R., Kulik, J., and Kulik, C. 1985. "Effectiveness of Computer-Based Education in Secondary Schools." *Journal of Computer-Based Education*, 12, 59–68.

Department of Defense. 2001. *Department of Defense Handbook MIL-HDBK-29612-3A, Development of Interactive Multimedia Instruction (IMI) (Part 3 of 5 Parts).*

Edwards, J., Norton, S., Taylor, S., Weiss, M., and Dusseldorp, R. 1975. "How Effective is CAI? A Review of the Research." *Educational Leadership* 33(2), 147–153.

Hall, B. 1995. "Return on Investment and Multimedia Training (Research Study)." *Brandon Hall Multimedia Training Newsletter.*

Heinich, R., Molenda, M., and Russell, J. 1989. *Instructional Media and The New Technologies of Instruction, 3rd Edition.* New York: Macmillan.

Jamison, D., Suppes, P., and Wells, S. 1974. "The Effectiveness of Alternative Instructional Media: A Survey." *Review of Educational Research*, 44, 1–68.

Kulik, A., Bangert, R., and Williams, B. 1983. "Effects of Computer-Based Training on Secondary School Students." *Journal of Educational Psychology*, 75, 19–26.

Kulik, C. and Kulik, J. 1986. "Effectiveness of Computer-Based Education in Colleges." *AEDS Journal*, 19, 81–108.

Kulik, C. and Kulik, J. 1991. "Effectiveness of Computer-Based Instruction: An Updated Analysis." *Computers in Human Behavior*, 7, 75–94.

Kulik, C., Kulik, J., and Shwalb, B. 1986. "The Effectiveness of Computer-Based Instruction in Adult Education: A Meta-Analysis." *Journal of Educational Computing Research*, 2, 235–252.

Kulik, J. 1994. "Meta-Analytic Studies of Findings on Computer-Based Instruction." In Baker, E.L and O'Neil, H.F. (Eds), *Technology Assessment in Education and Training*. Lawrence Erlbaum Associates.

Kulik, J., Kulik, C., and Bangert-Drowns, R. 1985. "Effectiveness of Computer-Based Education in Elementary Schools." *Computers in Human Behavior*, 1, 59–74.

Kulik, J., Kulik, C., and Cohen, P. 1980. "Instructional Technology and College Teaching." *Teaching of Psychology*, 7, pp. 199–205.

Miller, R. 2002. "Internet-Based Distance Learning: Implications of Emerging Technologies for Public Safety Training." *The Executive Forum, Illinois Law Enforcement Executive Institute*, 2(3), pp. 109–120.

DRUG RECOGNITION PROCESS

The Drug Recognition Process is a systematic, standardized evaluation. It is systematic in that it is based on a variety of observable signs and symptoms, known to reliably indicate drug impairment. The conclusion is based on the complete analysis, not on any single element of the evaluation. The process is standard in that it is conducted in the same way for every person.

The recognition techniques include the evaluation of specific physical and behavioral symptoms (examination of eyes and vital signs, scrutiny of speech and coordination) that indicate if a person:

- Is currently under the influence of drugs (substances actively circulating in the blood).
- Has recently used drugs (within the last 3 days).

The evaluation can also provide information about the category of drug used. The evaluation will not identify the exact drug or drugs a person has used. The process permits the pres-

ence of drugs to be narrowed down to certain broad categories (for example, central nervous system stimulants), but not to specific drugs such as cocaine. It can be determined that a person probably used a narcotic analgesic but not whether it was morphine, codeine, heroin, or some other substance.

The evaluation does not substitute for chemical testing of persons who exhibit signs of drug influence or recent use. The process will usually supply accurate grounds for suspecting that a particular category of drugs is present in urine or blood, but sample collection and analysis must still be done if scientific or legal evidence is needed.

The evaluation process can suggest the presence of seven broad categories of drugs, distinguishable from each other by observable signs they generate in users:

1. Central nervous system (CNS) stimulants, such as cocaine and amphetamines
2. CNS depressants, such as alcohol, barbiturates, and tranquilizers
3. Hallucinogens, such as LSD, peyote, and psilocybin; but not phencyclidine (PCP)
4. Narcotic analgesics, such as Demerol, codeine, heroin, and methadone
5. Phencyclidine (PCP) and its analogs
6. Cannabis, such as marijuana, hashish, and hash oil
7. Inhalants, such as model airplane glue and aerosols

Recognition Techniques

Professionals who implement the drug recognition techniques should follow these 12 steps, in the given order:

1. Take a drug history. Ask a structured series of questions concerning prior drug involvement. The drug history may reveal patterns of usage that will be of assistance in the evaluation.
2. Administer a breath alcohol test. With a breath-testing device, it can be determined if alcohol is contributing to the person's observable impairment and whether the concentration is sufficient to be the sole cause of that impairment.

An accurate and immediate measurement of blood alcohol determines the person's blood alcohol concentration (BAC). If the BAC is not sufficient to produce the observed level of impairment, the evaluation is continued to detect the presence of other drugs. The BAC is also useful in determining if a person is in need of immediate medical treatment or other special attention.

3. Perform the preliminary examination (pre-screen). Ask a structured series of questions, make specific observations, and have the person perform simple tests that provide the first opportunity to examine the person closely and directly. Determine if the person is suffering from an injury or some other condition not necessarily related to drugs. Begin also to systematically assess appearance and behavior for signs of possible drug influence or drug use, as well as screening out persons who do not exhibit signs of drug use. For asymptomatic persons, no further evaluation or drug testing is necessary.

4. Examine the eyes. The inability of the eyes to converge toward the bridge of the nose suggests the presence of certain drugs, such as cannabis. Other categories of drugs can induce horizontal-gaze nystagmus, an involuntary jerking that may occur as the eyes gaze to one side or as they are elevated. CNS depressants (alcohol, barbiturates, tranquilizers) will typically cause horizontal-gaze nystagmus.

5. Administer the divided-attention psychophysical tests. These include the Rhomberg Balance, the Walk and Turn, One-Leg Stand, and Finger to Nose. Specific errors of omission or commission can point toward specific categories of drugs causing impairment. For example, a person who is under the influence of a CNS stimulant (cocaine or amphetamines) may move very rapidly on the Walk and Turn test, but may exhibit a distorted sense of time on the Rhomberg Balance test (such as estimating 15 seconds to be 30).

6. Perform the dark room examination. Make systematic checks of the size of the pupils, the reaction of the pupils to light, and evidence of drugs taken by nose or mouth. Certain categories of drugs affect the eyes, especially the pupils, in predictable ways. For example, a person under the influence of a CNS stimulant or hallucinogen will have dilated (enlarged) pupils. A person under the influence of a narcotic analgesic, such as heroin, will have extremely constricted (small) pupils, which will exhibit little or no response to the presence or absence of light.

7. Examine vital signs. Perform systematic checks of the blood pressure, pulse rate, and temperature. Certain categories of drugs (including stimulants) will elevate blood pressure and pulse rate, raise the body temperature, and cause breathing to become rapid. Other drugs, including narcotic analgesics, have the opposite effects.

8. Examine for muscle rigidity. Certain categories of drugs, such as PCP, can cause the muscles to become hypertense and very rigid.

9. Look for injection sites. Some users of certain categories of drugs routinely or occasionally inject their drugs. Evidence of hypodermic needle use (scars or "tracks") may be found in veins along the arms, legs, or neck. Injection sites are frequently found on users of narcotic analgesics.

10. Interview the person and make observations. Based on the results of the previous steps, at least a suspicion can be formed about the category or categories of drugs that may be involved.

11. Form an opinion. Based on all the evidence and the observations, it should be possible to reach an informed conclusion about whether the individual is under the influence of drugs or has recently used drugs, and if so, the category or categories of drugs that are the probable cause of the impairment.

12. Request a toxicological examination. Chemical tests provide scientific, admissible evidence to substantiate conclusions. Generally, urinalyses are performed (90 percent of the time); in some cases, blood tests are ordered also.

Source   "Drug Recognition Process." 1990. *National Institute of Justice*, Report No. 221.

DRUG TESTING

Testing of job applicants and employees has long been used to ensure that workers are free of medical conditions that might interfere with safety and productivity. The rise of drug abuse in the United States has prompted many employers to establish pre-employment and in-service drug testing programs. These programs are proving to be an effective tool for managing drug abuse problems in the workplace.

The drug testing proposition essentially means that applicants will not be hired and employees will be disciplined when drug test results indicate current use of illicit substances. Possible legal challenge of a positive test result should be of special concern to management.

A principal focus of management should therefore be the selection of a qualified drug testing laboratory. The U.S. Department of Health and Human Services (DHHS) certifies laboratories that meet stringent standards relating to personnel qualifications, equipment and instrumentation, analytical methods, and quality assurance. In addition to these critical standards, the laboratory's customer will expect services that give attention to chain of custody, confidential reporting and recordkeeping, secure storage of positive specimens for later testing, and, if needed, expert witnesses to testify in court and present drug testing evidence.

The DHHS program for certifying drug testing laboratories is by far the most exacting of the various certification programs and has come to be regarded by the courts as a standard for judging workplace drug testing activities. Although many employers in the private sector fall outside regulatory purview and are therefore not required to use a DHHS-certified laboratory many elect to do so because they recognize the advantages of high accuracy and reliability of tests and the value that courts place upon testing that meets high standards.

The major assurance of accuracy is the series of checks built into the testing system. Two types of errors are of concern. First is the administrative error such as incorrect transcription of test results, incorrect recording of donor identification number, and failure to maintain chain of custody. Second is the analytical error related to the precision of analysis, calibration of equipment, and interpretation of test results. In the case of administrative error, the single test result involved may or not have to be discounted, but with analytical error more than one test result may be faulty because the error may have affected other specimens tested in the same batch.

Gas chromatography/mass spectrometry (GC/MS) is a technique used mainly to confirm the positive results of screening tests. It is generally considered to be the most conclusive method of determining the presence of a drug in urine. GC/MS combines the separating power of gas chromatography with the high sensitivity and specificity of spectrometry.

An immunoassay seeks to detect in urine the presence of a drug or drug metabolite. It is based on the principle of competition between labeled and unlabeled antigens for binding sites on a specific antibody. An antibody is a protein substance to which a specific drug or drug metabolite will bind.

In the enzyme immunoassay technique, the label on the antigen is an enzyme that produces a chemical reaction that allows for the detection of a drug or its metabolite. The concentration of the drug present in the urine is determined by measuring the extent of enzymatic activity. The radioimmunoassay technique looks at the reaction produced by the injection of a radioactive-labeled substance. The presence or absence of the drug being looked for is indicated by the amount of radioactivity found. The immunoassay techniques are used mostly for screening urine samples. They are not really suitable for confirming positive test results.

Positive test results are frequently reported quantitatively in measurements called nanograms and micrograms. The concentration of the drug is expressed as a certain amount per volume of urine. Urine concentrations may be expressed as nanograms per milliliter or as micrograms per milliliter. There are 28 million micrograms in 1 ounce and 1,000 nanograms in a microgram.

A positive test that has not been confirmed by an alternate and at least equally sensitive test is called a presumed positive. For example, a specimen that has been screened by an immunoassay and found to be positive is only presumed to be positive until a second test confirms or refutes the initial finding. When the second test is by an alternate test having an at least equally sensitive technique (such as GC/MS), the test is called a confirmation test. A positive result on the second test is called a confirmed positive.

When the second test is a repeat of the first test or uses a less sensitive or essentially similar technique, it is called a verification test, and a positive result is called a verified positive. A verification test falls far short of a confirmation test, especially a confirmation test by GC/MS.

The sensitivity limit of a test is the lowest concentration at which the test can detect the presence of a drug in a urine specimen. The sensitivity limit is inherently determined by scientific capabilities. The cutoff level, on the other hand, is an administrative mechanism for distinguishing a positive result from a negative result. The absence of a drug concentration or a concentration below the cutoff level yields a negative result, whereas one above the cutoff limit yields a positive result.

The immunoassays are subject to an interference called cross-reactivity. Because immunoassays rely on immune reactions, a certain degree of interference occurs among the various drug metabolites and structurally similar compounds of a particular drug. For example, methamphetamine cross-reacts with some over-the-counter medications, such as diet pills and decongestants, and ibuprofen (the main ingredient in Advil, Motrin, Medipren, and Nuprin) has been found to interfere and cause positives for marijuana.

A few screening tests will occasionally produce positive results caused by the interference of certain foods, such as poppy seeds. Since poppy seeds come from the opium plant, a positive for opiates is possible. However, the interfering substances are well known to drug testing laboratories and are easily resolved with alternate screening techniques. The possibility of interference during screening is a very good reason for all positive screens to be confirmed.

Urinalysis

Testing for drugs is almost always done through the analysis of urine. The objective is to identify any evidence of drugs or drug metabolites in the urine. Some drug classes, such as the opiates class, can be identified directly by the presence of the drug itself. Other drug classes, such as the cannabinoids (marijuana), are identified indirectly by the presence of metabolites.

A metabolite is a compound produced from chemical changes of a drug in the body. It is a by-product resulting from the body's natural process of converting the drug to waste matter. A urine specimen that tests positive for marijuana will contain marijuana metabolites.

Urine testing is done in two steps: a screening test and a confirmatory test. When a specimen shows negative in the screen, the specimen is declared to be free of drugs and is destroyed. When a specimen shows positive in the screen, it is subjected to the confirmatory test. If the confirmatory is negative, the specimen is declared negative and destroyed. If positive, a positive finding is issued.

In some instances a second confirmatory test may be conducted, and many employers regard a positive test result as only presumptively positive until verified by a medical review officer (MRO). An MRO is a specially trained medical doctor who evaluates a positive test result in light of further evidence obtained from a physical examination of the individual, an interview of the individual, or a review of the individual's medical history. The MRO seeks to determine if the positive finding could have some other medical explanation, such as the innocent use of a legally prescribed drug.

Screening tests are most often conducted using immunoassay techniques. Immunoassays are designed to detect traces of drugs or metabolites; they lend themselves well to automation, and are accurate at the 95 percent level and higher. Two types stand out: enzyme immunoassay and radioimmunoassay.

Confirmatory tests are most often conducted using the GC/MS technique, which is widely considered to be the most conclusive method for confirming the presence of a drug in urine.

Certainly a most serious problem in drug testing is that of false positives. A false positive occurs when a drug or drug metabolite is reported in a urine specimen but is actually not present. False positives can be categorized into three groups:

- Chemical False Positive. This is the result of another substance in the sample being mistakenly identified as a drug. Chemical false positives sometimes occur when donors contaminate their specimens at the collection site.
- Administrative False Positive. This is the result of one person's positive test

result being attributed to another person. Improper labeling and inaccurate chain of custody documentation are the usual causes.

- Operator Error. This is the result of a mistake by a laboratory technician during an analytical procedure. Inadequate operator training, poor supervision, and failure to follow testing protocols are usually at the root of operator error.

Collecting Urine Specimens

Employers who regularly administer urine drug testing have learned that administrative or human error is more likely to occur during the urine collection process than at any other time in a drug testing program. The following precautions were born out of experience.

- The written policy that authorizes drug testing should be available at the urine specimen collection point for reading by the specimen donor prior to giving a specimen.
- At the collection point, the specimen donor should provide positive identification, such as a photo-bearing driving license.
- Written consent should be obtained from the donor at the collection point.

Steps against contamination should include:

- Using a specimen container of the type that is packaged at the point of manufacture in a protective plastic envelope.
- Allowing nothing to be introduced (e.g., thermometer, litmus paper) into the specimen or its container at the collection point.
- After the donor has voided into the container, asking the donor to place tape across the container cap, sign the label, put the container in a plastic envelope, place tape across the envelope sealing flap, and sign the tape.

Blind specimen testing is an integral part of the continuing assessment of laboratory performance. A percentage of the specimens sent to the laboratory are spiked with drugs and metabolites that the laboratory routinely looks for, and the laboratory is expected to detect the spiked drugs in concentration ranges that correspond to what can be expected in the urine of recent drug users. The idea is to imitate the type of specimens that a laboratory normally encounters both in terms of content and appearance. The laboratory, of course, has no way of differentiating between the blind specimens and the actual specimens.

Passive Inhalation

A number of defenses have been put forward to explain positive test results. Passive inhalation or inadvertent exposure to marijuana is frequently cited, but clinical studies show that it is unlikely that a non-smoking individual can passively inhale sufficient marijuana smoke to result in a high enough concentration for marijuana to be detected at the cutoff level of the standard urinalysis methods. It is extremely improbable that a person who was not smoking would be exposed to the level of smoke and for the length of time required to produce a positive test result.

John J. Fay

Source Fay, J. 1991. *Drug Testing*. Boston: Butterworth-Heinemann.

DRUG TESTING: A COMPARISON OF URINALYSIS TECHNOLOGIES

Employers interested in conducting drug tests often ask critical questions:

- How accurate are the technologies? Does one particular technology result in more false positive or false negative errors than others?
- Do the federal guidelines for drug testing in the workplace, especially for cutoff levels, meet the needs of the private sector?
- Is one technology consistently accurate enough to eliminate the need for routine confirmation by an alternative method?

These questions were answered in a study conducted under the auspices of the Bureau of Justice Assistance and the National Institute of Justice.

Accuracy of the Technologies

The study involved tests made of the five drugs examined in the federal testing program: marijuana, cocaine, phencyclidine (PCP), opiates, and amphetamines. The technologies included EMIT (the enzyme multiplied immunoassay test, manufactured by the Syva Company, Palo Alto, CA), TDx (the trade name for the fluorescent polarization immunoassay test, manufactured by Abbott Laboratories, Chicago, IL), RIA (the radioimmunoassay test, also called Abbuscreen, manufactured by Roche Diagnostic Systems, Nutley, NJ), TLC (the standard thin layer chromatography test), and GC/MS (the gas chromatography/mass spectrometry test).

Questions have been raised within the business, scientific, and legal communities concerning the accuracy of TLC relative to other testing procedures. Test results showed a clear difference between the accuracy of the immunoassays as a group (EMIT, TDx, and RIA) and TLC. TLC performed poorly in identifying the presence of illegal drugs.

A concern frequently voiced about drug testing is the possibility that a test will label as positive a urine specimen from an individual who has not used drugs. These errors are known as false positives. The study's average false positive rate, combining results for the five drug types and using the National Institute on Drug Abuse (NIDA) cutoff levels, was about 1-2 percent, based on the screening test, without GC/MS confirmation.

The study also examined the extent to which the current screening technologies miss the presence of drugs in urine; that is, the extent of false negatives. For the three immunoassays, the average false negative rate for the five drug types was about 20 percent, using the NIDA cutoff levels. Screening tests are designed to minimize false positive results and, as a consequence, a larger number of false negative results will occur.

The magnitude of the false negative rate was determined by the screening and confirmation cutoff levels, which followed the NIDA guidelines. The data revealed that the immunoassay cutoffs were partly the reason for the technology's failure to identify the specimens designated as positive by GC/MS. Many of the false negative specimens contained some amount of the drug, but not at concentrations high enough for the immunoassays to label the specimens positive. Accordingly, the false negative rate would be reduced by lowering the cutoff levels of the immunoassays.

Adequacy of Cutoff Levels

The study also looked at whether the current NIDA cutoff levels are appropriate, considering the strong likelihood that lower cutoff levels could lead to the detection of a greater number

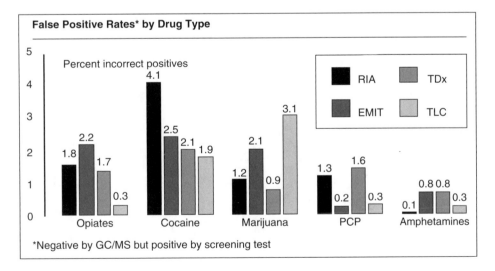

Figure 33. The percentage of positive test results varies by drug type.

of drug users. To accomplish this, screening and confirmation cutoffs were selected for marijuana, cocaine, and opiates that were lower than those specified by NIDA.

The study concluded that if the cutoff levels for marijuana were lowered to 50 nanograms/milliliter, approximately one-third more users might be identified. For cocaine and opiates, lowering the cutoffs to 200 might increase detection of drug use by 10 to 20 percent. The potential impact on an employer's drug testing program could be considerable. On the up side, it would eliminate from consideration many more drug-using job applicants and identify drug-using employees who represent accident risks and higher operating costs. On the down side, it would drive up the employer's costs with respect to increased use of drug treatment and an increased need for additional supervision of drug-using employees.

The Issue of Confirmation

Immunoassay technologies are not error-free. The study concluded that an average of 1 to 2 specimens may test positive in every 100 specimens, when examined by one immunoassay technology. When more than one immunoassay technology is applied to the same 100 specimens, the number of false positives may decrease, although not disappear entirely. Repeat testing by the same method or by a similar technology most probably will not eliminate all erroneous results on a long-term basis.

GC/MS confirmation of positive results, however, would eliminate virtually all false positive errors. GC/MS provides the best protection against legal challenges and gives assurance of accuracy to persons affected by drug testing.

Sources Visher, C. and McFadden, K. 1991. "A Comparison of Urinalysis Technologies for Drug Testing in Criminal Justice (An Executive Summary)." *National Institute of Justice.*

EMPLOYEE HOTLINES

The Association of Certified Fraud Examiners' (ACFE) 2004 *Report to the Nation* revealed that the majority of fraud schemes within organizations are discovered through the receipt of employee tips. With organizational losses amounting to approximately $660 billion annually due to fraud, and in the wake of the Sarbanes-Oxley Act of 2002, many organizations have implemented anonymous reporting mechanisms in recent years. The ACFE maintains that such reporting systems can potentially reduce these losses by as much as 50 percent. The exposure of corporate scandal in the early years of this century has certainly eroded the public faith in American business and organizations are learning difficult lessons in the aftermath.

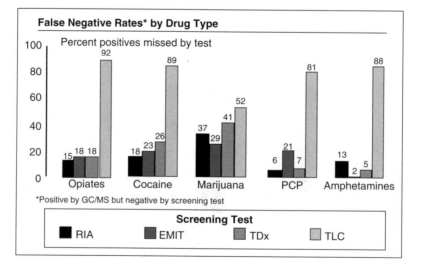

Figure 34. The percentage of negative test results varies by drug type.

While organizations have scrambled to provide new avenues to receive employee reports of misconduct, there is evidence to suggest that it remains difficult for employees to bring forward their concerns and information. The fear of retaliation and reprisal still impedes employees from making a report, especially in an environment with limited reporting mechanisms in place. The implementation of anonymous incident reporting systems has served to curb some of that fear because employees have the opportunity to make a report while remaining completely anonymous. Gone are the days in which employees felt comfortable enough to walk into the office of their supervisor or manager to report concerns of misconduct. Open-door policies are not enough to ensure an organization is equipped with the knowledge necessary to prevent and detect corporate crime, misconduct, and fraud.

Applicable Legal Mandates

The passage of the Sarbanes-Oxley Act of 2002 naturally resulted in an upsurge of the implementation of fraud hotlines within organizations. Among other things, this mandate requires all publicly traded companies to establish a confidential means by which questionable accounting or auditing activities can be reported anonymously by employees, customers, vendors, etc. Organizations are further charged with ensuring proper "receipt, retention, and treatment of complaints." Therefore, it is not enough for organizations to simply put a reporting mechanism in place, but retention and treatment activities must also be documented.

While Sarbanes-Oxley technically applies only to public sector organizations, private organizations are not legally exempt from implementing a program for the detection of employee misconduct. *Any* organization with 50 or more employees is subject to the Federal Sentencing Guidelines of 1991. Established by the United States Sentencing Commission, the Federal Sentencing Guidelines of 1991 addressed the rising issue of corporate crime and had a huge impact on the culture of corporate America. The U.S. government lacked a clear sentencing and enforcement policy regarding organizational criminals. As a result, the guidelines were created essentially as a manual for judges to consider in determining the most appropriate sentencing disposition for organizational defendants.

The guidelines stipulate that organizations must institute procedures for the detection of criminal conduct within the organization and, once it discovers such conduct, the organization must take all reasonable steps to appropriately respond and ensure such violations do not occur in the future. The guidelines do not provide specific guidance regarding the structure of such a detection program, but many organizations responded by enhancing or creating corporate ethics programs, some including enhanced reporting mechanisms such as employee hotlines.

While American law clearly dictates the need for anonymous incident reporting mechanisms within organizations, it cannot adequately address the special needs posed by international organizations. Recent decisions in France and Germany make the already difficult task of corporate compliance even more challenging. Without certain precautions in place, employee hotlines that provide anonymous reporting can be considered unlawful in those countries. These conflicting legal mandates across various countries likely reflect cultural attitudes toward "whistle-blowers" and the role they play within organizations. European countries have historically felt uneasy over the concept of employees anonymously reporting the behavior of other employees, delaying the opportunity for the accused to respond. While the true impact of such conflicting mandates is yet to be revealed, it is likely that multinational organizations faced with such compliance difficulties will have to request special relief from U.S. Regulators. While it is beyond the scope of this article to provide specific practical guidance around international compliance issues, more information can be found in the World Data Protection Report published by BNA International, Inc. in 2005.

Employee Hotlines, Early Warning Systems

Besides allowing organizations to maintain legal compliance, the implementation of an anonymous employee hotline makes good business sense for a variety of other and possibly more valuable reasons. Such a reporting mechanism allows for fraudulent activity and other employee misconduct to be detected sooner than it might otherwise be, enabling organizations to effectively manage the problem before significant losses accrue and the organization's reputation is tarnished. Establishing an anonymous employee hotline provides another avenue by which other forms of employee misconduct, such as harassment, discrimination, and/or theft, can be reported as well, thereby further limiting the organization's exposure and liability.

Human Resources and Risk Management professionals have quickly realized the benefit of receiving reports of employee misconduct through hotline mechanisms. They now have the ability to detect safety concerns and criminal activity as it is "brewing" and manage it before safety is compromised and the organization faces a huge liability. What's more, the costs associated with the implementation of an anonymous employee hotline are minimal in comparison to the potential losses incurred through long-term fraudulent activity or litigation resulting from the inappropriate treatment of human resources-related complaints.

Establishment of an anonymous incident reporting solution further communicates to employees that their concerns are taken seriously and that the organization is committed to ensuring the safety and security of their employees. Such a system encourages employees to act when they discover coworkers behaving inappropriately. Furthermore, it helps create an organizational culture that values ethical behavior and honesty and instills a level of confidence in employees that the organization will respond when reports of fraud or other problems are received. Management cannot act in response to activity of which they are not aware, and research indicates that employees are more likely to bring forth information if they have the ability to do it confidentially and anonymously (Author unknown, 2005). Therefore, anonymous reporting systems increase an organization's ability to identify and appropriately manage issues as they arise.

Many of the third-party systems that are available enable immediate documentation of all reports and report-related activity. Such documentation potentially limits an organization's liability should a reported issue end up in litigation in the future. The organization has the ability to document all steps taken to ensure the appropriate disposition and outcome of all issues reported. Such activity limits claims that the organization failed to comply with any one or more legal mandates in place regarding corporate ethics programs.

While the advantages are clearly substantial, organizations must be aware of the potential drawbacks of such a hotline program. For example, because employees have the opportunity to remain completely anonymous if they so choose, the organization may be limited in their ability to follow up with reporting employees regarding the matters disclosed. Many systems rely solely on the reporting employee taking the initiative to call back and the organization has no way of directly contacting him or her. Some investigations may be delayed or extremely restricted due to this inability to proactively follow up with reporting employees.

Organizations should be aware that, while thorough documentation of all complaints and investigative steps taken assure compliance can be demonstrated, all documentation is potentially discoverable in any future legal proceedings. Employers must balance both sides of this legal conundrum in the interests of protecting the organization's assets while simultaneously instilling a sense of security among their employees.

Furthermore, organizations may find themselves in legal difficulty if they fail to warn reporting employees of the potential risks associated with reporting concerns while remaining completely anonymous. While it is not likely in the best interests of an organization to attempt to deduce, however simple or complex, the identity of the anonymous whistle-blower, evidence indicates that this is done with alarming frequency and as many as 70 percent of employee whistle-blowers experience some form of retaliation (Jernberg, 2003). Anonymous reporting employees will find it difficult to demonstrate a causal link between their report and the retaliatory action. However, providing a broad warning about the potential risk associated with reporting anonymously would significantly diminish employees' confidence in the reporting mechanism. The experienced and knowledgeable vendor will provide a system, however, that addresses most, if not all, of these potential pitfalls.

Selecting a System

The mandates of Sarbanes-Oxley limit an organization's ability to provide strictly internal reporting mechanisms and there are many advantages to outsourcing anonymous incident reporting hotlines. First of all, vendor technology capabilities typically tend to exceed those of the typical organization. For example, third-parties have the ability to develop and maintain highly specialized software and web-reporting tools that requires only minimal set-up and resource investment by the organization. Engaging a third-party to provide hotline services allows organizations to offer not just a hotline employees can call, but also a web portal by which employees can report their concerns directly. Additionally, third-party vendors generally employ better trained call takers and collect the data most pertinent to the issue being reported so that the client organization has the information necessary to pursue their investigation and find an appropriate resolution. Many reporting employees find comfort in knowing that a third-party is responsible for gathering all the initial information, while the issue will still be reported and managed by their organization.

Some of the more sophisticated third-party vendors further have the ability to instantaneously notify organizational managers of issues as they are being reported in real-time. The organization, therefore, has the ability to swiftly and effectively manage all issues, especially those concerning the immediate safety of their employees. Traditional internal hotlines rely on the availability of typically one or two human resource managers who cannot be expected to field all calls at all hours of the day and night. Furthermore, these managers are responsible for a whole host of other duties that make it impossible to devote all attention to the receipt, retention, and treatment of employee complaints. Most third-party systems provide live around-the-clock coverage, 365 days per year in multiple languages.

Probably one of the greatest advantages to outsourcing an employee hotline lies in the issue of confidentiality and anonymity. A traditional internal hotline is managed directly by an employee of the organization. Therefore, the reporting employee only has the option of disclosing or not disclosing his or her identity to the organization. Even when employees choose to remain anonymous, there is often fear that their voice may be recognized by the person answering the phone or voicemail message. A third-party can offer a third level of anonymity that an internal hotline cannot. With a third-party vendor, the employee may have the opportunity to remain completely anonymous to his or her organization but provide contact information to the third-party only. That way, should the organization need to follow up with the reporting employee but find it difficult to

do so, the third-party can follow up on behalf of the organization while continuing to keep the reporting employee's identity anonymous.

A third-party vendor also has the ability to assist the organization in effectively rolling out and communicating the hotline solution to their employee base. Experience shows that anonymous incident reporting solutions are destined to fail if they are not effectively communicated to the employees who are the intended users of the service. Third-party vendors specialize in such communication and can ensure each organization's very specific objectives in implementing the solution are met. The responsible vendor will further take all steps necessary to assist the client organization in avoiding litigation and liability exposure.

Summary

There are clearly very good reasons for organizations to implement anonymous incident reporting systems and, further, very good reasons to outsource such services. Successful and effective corporate ethics programs incorporate anonymous ethics reporting mechanisms as part of their commitment to compliance and principled corporate governance. Employee hotlines clearly provide organizational management with insight into their organization they likely would not otherwise have, providing them the opportunity to capitalize on their strengths and swiftly manage their areas of weakness. All of this effectively increases the bottom lines and ensures the security of the organization for the long-term. Implementing an anonymous ethics hotline for employees helps them realize the stake they have in their organization and their ability to help the organization protect its assets, ultimately protecting their own job security and safety.

Eugene F. Ferraro, Lindsey Lee, and
Kimberly Pfaff

Sources

Author unknown. (2005). "Best Practices in Whistleblower Systems." Accessed on December 7, 2005 from http://www.itcinstitute.com/display.aspx?id=931.

Jernberg, D. V. (2003). "Whistle-Blower Hotlines Carry Own Risks." *Business Insurance*, 37. p. 10.

EXECUTIVE KIDNAPPING

U.S. business, both at home and overseas, is a target for kidnapping and other acts of violence. Terrorists use violent methods to force changes to business practices, to shape public opinion, and to bargain with governments for relief from prosecution and incarceration of their brothers-in-arms. Terrorists, as well as ordinary criminals, also use kidnapping as a means for acquiring money.

A first step in an organization's defense against executive kidnapping is to obtain approval of the protection program. Approval in most cases will be made at the Board of Directors level and will involve consideration of kidnap insurance, ransom payments, and a crisis management team (CMT). The Board's decisions will set the framework for an overall policy. The policy promulgated by senior management, with input from the chief security officer, is written into a kidnap plan that is cascaded down through the organization in the form of directives, procedures, and the like.

If kidnap insurance is purchased, the carrier will require absolute secrecy with respect to that fact and to any premeditation concerning intent to pay ransom demands. The carrier may also dictate who is to do the negotiating of ransom payments, require that the organization's response be conducted in accordance with applicable laws of the United States and other nations, and that prompt and full notification be given to law enforcement. A failure by the organization to meet the carrier's requirements can render the coverage null and void or reduce the carrier's obligations to pay.

Planning

Although the organization's plan for dealing with kidnapping is a highly sensitive matter, it cannot be developed with such great secrecy that it will reflect the thinking of one or a few individuals who may not have all the right answers. An initial planning group consisting of in-house and outside experts can be helpful in hitting all the bases. In addition to the chief security officer, who should play a key role within the group, the members might include a representative of the Federal Bureau of Investigation (FBI), an attorney, a counter-terrorism expert, a political analyst familiar with the nation or region where

kidnapping is anticipated, a kidnap insurance specialist, a professional hostage negotiator, a public affairs specialist, an electronics communication expert, and a human resources specialist. Members of the initial planning group are also likely to be members of the CMT.

The early planning effort should clearly evaluate the capabilities of persons or groups who may direct kidnapping at the organization, the vulnerabilities of the organization with respect to the kidnapping threat, the current capacity of the organization to resist the threat, and the range of additional countermeasures that are necessary to lower the threat to an acceptable threshold of risk. The output of the initial planning group would become the working materials for the chief security officer in preparing a kidnap plan and its implementing procedures.

Plan Execution

Carrying out the plan is more than just responding to an incident. Plan execution is getting ready, paying attention to details day in and day out, rehearsing, learning from the rehearsals, and improving on procedures.

The kidnap plan will be an integral part of the organization's overall security program. The plan will be reflected in the overall program in many ways: controls on access to the executive suite and the executive's vehicle, panic alarms and closed-circuit television (CCTV) cameras in the executive reception area, bullet- and bomb-resistant materials inside the walls surrounding the executive suite, and an alarm center for monitoring sensors installed in the office (and home) environment.

The same considerations apply where the executive resides. A survey of the executive's home should be conducted and, in all probability, it will uncover weaknesses that may be corrected through investing in simple, inexpensive safeguards, such as trimming the shrubs and adding some outside lights, to more expensive and intrusive safeguards, such as watch dogs and security officers. Thought in the survey should be given to the time needed to respond. When a rapid response is not always certain, protection of the occupants can be enhanced by creating in the home a concealed room that features a highly resistive door, a panic button, and a telephone. A weapon inside the room is an option.

Following are brief discussions of actions that support plan execution.

Preparation. An important administrative step is to set up a file on the protected executive. The file will contain details about close friends, relatives, servants, and other persons who live with, work for, and frequently visit the executive; physicians, dentists, and required medications; the places where the executive and his family frequently visit, e.g., country club, church, vacation spot, weekend retreat, and the executive's favorite haunts when on the road; and proof-of-life information, e.g., a name known only to the executive and his significant other (such as the name of the family's first dog). The file can also be supplemented with photographs, handwriting samples, fingerprint cards, and voice tapes. This file can be of enormous value in launching a search for the protected executive and when communicating with kidnappers.

Being prepared also means being properly staffed and equipped. Protective staff can include a bodyguard, a chauffeur, and house and garden help. Screening and training of these persons is essential. Equipment appropriate for close-in executive protection includes defensive firearms, bulletproof wear, communication devices, and armor-plated vehicles.

Training. The protected executive, his or her family members, and protective staff are in the top priority for training. The next priority includes house servants and office workers. The training topics would focus on the tactics of kidnappers, the early warning signals of an attempted kidnapping, how to respond, and, if abducted, how to survive.

Low Profile. The protected executive should be informed of the advantages of maintaining a low profile by not unnecessarily revealing personal identity, company affiliation and position, travel plans, and planned social activities. Care should be taken when communicating with others on the telephone, in restaurants, and in public areas where conversations can be monitored. Written information of a sensitive nature should be given confidential protection and shredded when no longer needed.

Predictable Patterns. Routes to and from work and the automobiles used should be frequently and randomly changed; the times, dates, and places of out-of-office business meetings should not follow a discernible pattern; and family and social routines should be varied.

Alertness. A group intending to kidnap or harm the protected executive may attempt to gain entry to the residence or office through pretext. The target may be the executive's child and the method may be trickery in effecting a release of the child from the custody of a babysitter, child care center, or school. The best guidance is to anticipate possible scenarios, take pre-emptive steps, and look for and react to the early warning signals.

Abduction

The value of planning is immediately evident in the aftermath of abduction. Preparations will be made to receive contact from the kidnappers. Contact will most likely be made directly by telephone, although it could be made indirectly through another party, such as a newspaper or radio station, or in writing. If contact is by telephone, certain protocols are in order: express a willingness to cooperate, ask to speak to the victim, and ask for the proof-of-life code. The call should be recorded.

If contact is in writing, the document and its envelope or outside container should be carefully protected so that forensic analyses (e.g., examinations for fingerprints, handwriting, and saliva on the flap or stamps) will not be adversely affected.

Contact by the kidnappers should be immediately reported to the FBI. Notifications to law enforcement agencies of other countries that have jurisdiction should also be made without delay. Attempts to handle the situation without recourse to government authorities are likely to fail. Success depends too heavily on having extensive capabilities in intelligence gathering and negotiating for the release of hostages.

By the time the kidnappers have made contact, the CMT will have been activated. The CMT leader, to whom considerable decision-making authority has been delegated, will be the key persona in coordinating major issues with law enforcement and a variety of other parties of interest. The CMT members will be variously going about the pre-planned tasks assigned to them in the plan. These tasks may include notifying next of kin, dealing with the news media, setting up a command center, establishing a rumor control function, coordinating with the kidnap insurance carrier, and conferring with the head negotiator.

John J. Fay

Sources

Fuqua, P. and Wilson, J. 1978. *Terrorism: The Executive's Guide to Survival.* Houston: Gulf Publishing.

Purpura, P. 2002. *Security and Loss Prevention, 4th Edition.* Boston: Butterworth-Heinemann.

EXECUTIVE PROTECTION IN A NEW ERA

The United States is at war now, fighting terrorists around the globe. For many, this is a high-risk era. It is a time to keep one's guard up, carrying out the fundamentals of executive protection (EP) while opening one's mind to additional techniques against a wider range of threats.

The Islamic terror attacks in the first years of the 21st century can clearly be viewed as a major trend and continuing risk. Other recurring threats—some reported more widely than others—include attacks by radical environmentalists and animal rights supporters, kidnappings, and workplace violence. Is it right, then, for executives and those who protect them to get used to such attacks? The answer is yes, but only in the specific sense of concluding that such dangers are real, and lasting, and must be intelligently avoided.

Executive protection supports an organization's mission in two ways: (1) it preserves a key asset by keeping the executive alive and well, and (2) it makes the most of that asset by freeing him or her from the need to worry about personal safety, making it possible to concentrate more on business.

This article examines several key themes in executive protection, viewed through the prism of today's conditions:

- Guiding principles
- Threat assessment
- Information and coordination: the advance
- Reduction of travel risk

- Countersurveillance
- Role of firearms
- Security awareness training

This article does not attempt to cover all aspects of EP but instead touches briefly on those that are most needed—and most altered—in the current risk climate.

Guiding Principles

Three guiding principles may help EP specialists organize their thinking and their protective efforts:

Be systemic, not symptomatic. This principle urges EP specialists to understand the complete picture of risks and protective measures, address all relevant elements of protective operations, avoid the urge to plug small holes without solving underlying problems, and apply simple, sometimes basic measures consistently across many domains.

Be proactive, not reactive. This principle encourages EP specialists to look forward and outward. That means conducting threat assessments, weighing and managing risks, appropriately applying resources, and performing countersurveillance. The opposite approach—event-driven response—can result in excessive security measures, over-engineering, inflated deployment of security personnel, and unnecessary inconvenience to the protectee.

React with flight, not a fight. The primary purpose of EP is not to capture or kill attackers but to protect the executive. Experience shows that, in this context, escaping from an attack leads to better outcomes than standing one's ground and fighting back. Therefore, the EP specialist should develop plans that emphasize getting the protectee away from danger or else finding cover. Preparing for a safe escape requires detailed advance preparation, including site surveys and training for a near-automatic execution of the exit strategy.

Threat Assessment

Executives face both greater and lesser threats than the average person. They tend to inhabit statistically safer neighborhoods, but they are more desirable targets for criminals. They use safe means of travel, but their high frequency of travel increases their exposure to accidents and attacks. Their jobs put them at little risk of workplace injury, but they are symbolic, attractive targets of persons seeking to harm the company.

To determine (1) whether the executive needs protection and (2) how to provide it intelligently, the EP specialist must conduct threat assessment. This is the process of studying the executive's risk-attracting characteristics, looking at crime rates for places he or she frequents, tracking threats made against the company, assessing travel habits and conditions, surveying home and office security, and so on.

To learn about specific threats the executive faces, the EP specialist should take the following steps, among others:

- Interview the executive, his or her spouse, and key staff about past incidents or concerns.
- Examine the company's threat file—that is, the record of threatening letters, phone calls, and incidents.
- Obtain information on crime levels and types from local police contacts or state crime analysis experts.
- Read about crimes against people who match the executive's profile.
- Examine any information about the executive that is available to the public. Sources include annual reports, company promotional materials, newspaper and magazine articles, industry directories, the Internet, and even waste paper sent to unsecured trash bins. By finding out what a potential adversary could learn, the EP specialist may be able to stay a step ahead in planning a defense.

After conducting the threat assessment, the EP specialist can determine whether the executive needs special protection and just what he or she needs to be protected from.

Information and Coordination: The Advance

One of the most important measures in EP, the advance is an effort to learn about an executive's route and destination. In effect, it is a preemptive strike against confusion and exposure. Advance work requires that the EP specialist actually go to the destination and prepare for the executive's arrival. By performing trial runs and evaluating transportation, lodging, and places at which the executive will conduct business, one smooths the executive's path. The result is both safer and more convenient travel. The foreknowledge that comes from an advance allows the EP specialist to eliminate many problems and steer the protectee clear of various dangers.

Advances should be conducted before visits to hotels, meeting rooms, convention centers, theaters, airports, and most other places the executive goes. Advances require gathering a significant amount of detail. For example, in performing a hotel advance, the EP specialist would visit the hotel; take photos or video footage to familiarize other security staffers with the site; determine the best way to enter and exit, along with alternate paths; meet with the manager to make special arrangements and obtain names of secondary contacts; meet with the director of security, doorman, bell captain, *maître d'*, valet parking manager, and others; inspect the hotel's safety features; determine the range of hotel services; gather information about restaurant and recreational facilities; and determine the location and phone numbers of the nearest fire department, police department, and rescue squad. That requires a significant effort, but it is only half the job: a thorough advance covers two hotels in each city to be visited—in case one suddenly becomes unavailable (due to fire) or unsuitable (due to changed conditions in the area around the hotel, such as civic unrest).

Smooth connections, check-ins, pick-ups, and drop-offs can easily give the executive an extra two hours per day of work time or rest time. Movement facilitation also reduces the executive's exposure to attacks. For example, if hotel check-in, billing, baggage handling, parking, and other matters are worked out in advance, then the executive can step out of the car at the hotel's front door, walk straight through the lobby to the elevators, and arrive quickly at the room.

Reduction of Travel Risk

It is useful to develop a relationship with the executive's administrative assistant, travel planner, or other person who arranges the schedule. The EP specialist should ask to be notified of upcoming trips so that he or she can assess the threats faced at the destination. If the threat level is especially high, the EP specialist may have to recommend that the executive refrain from taking the trip. In some cases, it may make more sense for others to come to the executive than for the executive to travel to a dangerous location.

In the current risk environment, it is advisable for executives to use private aircraft whenever possible. Commercial air travel presents risks both on the ground and in the air. On the ground, at large, busy airports, inconvenient delays can occur during pickup and drop-off; the executive may be recognized and bothered by other travelers; airport lobbies (on the non-secure side) are notorious terrorist targets; and passing through busy security checkpoints can create opportunities for loss of personal property, missed flights, and awkward or embarrassing searches.

By contrast, private air travel is not packed with people who would bother the protectee and is generally more oriented to customer service. Further, the small lobbies of general aviation FBOs (fixed-base operators) are not prime targets for terrorists who wish to draw attention to their cause. Flying via general (private) aviation reduces the likelihood of being in the wrong place at the wrong time—that is, of happening to be at a major public airport during a significant attack.

In the air, in commercial air travel, the executive and the EP specialist have no way of knowing whether a dangerous person is aboard the plane. By contrast, in private aviation, it is likely that the protectee will personally recognize every passenger on the aircraft, or at least that the passengers will be known to someone on the aircraft. Overall, an executive is less likely to be accessible to adversaries if he or she uses private aircraft.

Countersurveillance

Surveillance is the covert observation of places, persons, and vehicles for the purpose of obtaining information on the identity or activities of a subject. Countersurveillance consists of observing the persons who are conducting surveillance. It is sometimes called "watching the watchers."

When and where the threat level is relatively high, it makes sense for the protective operation to conduct countersurveillance. For example, observers can be planted in a crowd to which the executive is giving a speech, or they can drive "follow cars" to watch for adversaries who might be observing the executive and his or her protective measures.

Countersurveillance may detect an act that is in the planning stage and enable the EP specialist to increase protection before the attack. Countersurveillance is usually kept hidden, but if the effort is discovered, the potential attackers may conclude that their target is too well protected and thus change their plans.

Role of Firearms

The cyclist Lance Armstrong wrote a book titled, "It's Not About the Bike." The corollary in EP would be, "It's not about the gun." Firearms have a role in EP, but not the central role. In extreme cases, it may be necessary to take cover and return fire. However, it is important not to become reliant on firearms. They may discourage an EP specialist from the preferable response, which is to quickly move the protectee out of harm's way. Moreover, training exercises at the Oatman School of Executive Protection show that it is rare for an EP specialist to be able to draw a gun fast enough: an attacker is likely to enter the scene "gun ready" (under a coat, with a finger on the trigger), while the EP specialist has his or her firearm tucked away in a holster.

Other challenges include the perishability of an EP specialist's firearms skills (which need constant refreshing), and the almost overwhelming complications involved in bringing firearms across state lines. Thus firearms, though useful in some circumstances, must not be considered the primary means of protection.

Security Awareness Training

In today's environment, executives are likely to know that security is important. However, security is not their primary concern: performing their job is. Because personal security depends so much on making smart decisions and being aware of one's surroundings, an EP specialist can provide a great service to the executive merely by raising and refining the executive's security awareness.

There are several ways to put EP on the executive radar screen:

- Periodically brief executives and, if possible, their family members on current threats. Teach them about such practices as positively identifying visitors, screening packages, and minimizing the amount of personal information they release.
- Offer to arrange defensive driving training for executives and their families.
- Offer to conduct a security assessment of executive homes (both primary and secondary).
- Conduct research on the executives and show them how much information an outsider could discover about them—information that could be useful for planning an attack.
- Provide executives with information on attacks against people similar to them.

This article addresses the high points of EP in today's environment. However, many other key issues must also be considered, such as executive home security, workplace violence exposure, local travel procedures, use of protected vehicles, and personal protection choreography, among many others.

Robert L. Oatman

Source   Oatman, R., 2006. *Executive Protection: New Solutions for a New Era*. New York: Noble House.

FAIR CREDIT REPORTING ACT

The Fair Credit Reporting Act (FCRA) was enacted in 1970 to promote accuracy, fairness, and the privacy of personal information assembled by Credit Reporting Agencies (CRAs). These are sometimes referred to as "credit bureaus."

CRAs assemble reports on individuals for businesses, including credit card companies, banks, employers, landlords, and others. The FCRA provides protections for credit reports, consumer investigatory reports, and employment background checks. The FCRA is a complex statute that has been significantly altered since 1970 by Congress and the courts. The Act's primary protection requires that CRAs follow "reasonable procedures" to protect the confidentiality, accuracy, and relevance of credit information. To do so, the FCRA establishes a framework of Fair Information Practices for personal information that include rights of data quality (right to access and correct), data security, use limitations, requirements for data destruction, notice, user participation (consent), and accountability.

FCRA Provisions

The FCRA establishes rights and responsibilities for "consumers," "furnishers," and "users" of credit reports:

- *Consumers* are individuals.
- *Furnishers* are entities that send information to CRAs regarding creditworthiness in the normal course of business.
- *Users* of credit reports are entities that request a report to evaluate a consumer for some purpose.

A consumer reporting agency (CRA) is an entity that assembles and sells credit information and financial information about individuals. There are three national CRAs in the United States: Experian (formerly TRW), Trans Union, and Equifax (formerly Retail Credit Co.). There are also many smaller credit reporting agencies that usually concentrate on reporting on individuals living in certain regions of the country.

Inspection bureaus, companies that sell information to insurance companies and assist in performing background checks, often are considered CRAs as well. Tenant screening and check approval companies are also considered CRAs. Depending on the nature of the operation, other companies can be considered CRAs.

Courts have held that private investigators, detective agencies, collection agencies, and even college placement officers can be CRAs under the law.

Consumer Credit Reports and Investigative Consumer Reports (ICRs)

Consumer credit reports contain information on financial accounts, and include credit card balances and mortgage information. Credit reports are used for evaluating eligibility for credit, insurance, employment, and tenancy; the ability to pay child support; professional licensing (for instance, to become an attorney); or for any purpose that a consumer approves.

A consumer credit report will contain basic identifying information (name, address, previous address, Social Security Number, marital status, employment information, number of children) along with:

- Financial information: Estimated income, employment, bank accounts, value of car and home.
- Public records information: Such as arrests, bankruptcies, and tax liens.
- Tradelines: Credit accounts and their status. This will also include the data subject's payment habits on credit accounts. Collection items: Whether the data subject has unpaid or disputed bills.
- Current employment and employment history.
- Requests for the credit report: The number of requests for the data subject's report and the identity of the requestors.
- Narrative information: A statement by the data subject or by the furnisher regarding disputed items on the credit report.

Investigative Consumer Report

CRAs can also prepare ICRs. These are dossiers on consumers that include information on character, reputation, personal characteristics, and mode of living. ICRs are compiled from personal interviews with persons who know the consumer. Since ICRs include especially sensitive information, the FCRA affords greater protections for them. For instance, within three days of requesting an ICR, the requestor must inform the consumer that an ICR is being compiled. The consumer also can request a statement explaining the nature and scope of the investigation underlying the ICR.

The Credit Header

A credit header is identifying information from a credit report. It includes name, mother's maiden name, birth date, sex, address, prior addresses, telephone number, and the Social Security Number. Credit headers are used for location of

individuals and for target marketing. They are sold in bulk by the CRAs and can be purchased online.

Permissible Uses of the Credit Report

The FCRA limits the use of the credit report to certain purposes. They are:

- Applications for credit, insurance, and rentals for personal, family or household purposes.
- Employment, which includes hiring, promotion, reassignment or retention. A CRA may not release a credit report for employment decisions without consent.
- Court orders, including grand jury subpoenas.
- "Legitimate" business needs in transactions initiated by the consumer for personal, family, or household purposes.
- Account review. Periodically, banks and other companies review credit files to determine whether they wish to retain the individual as a customer.
- Licensing (professional).
- Child support payment determinations.
- Law enforcement access: Government agencies with authority to investigate terrorism and counterintelligence have secret access to credit reports.

Specific prior consent is required before consumer reports with medical information can be released.

Background Checks

Since September 11, 2001, many employers have either begun or expanded background check programs on current employees or new hires. Because they have become so prevalent, simple background checks can now be done for under $20, and more complex investigations may be hundreds of dollars.

Employers can request standard consumer credit reports or investigative consumer reports (ICRs) on their employees. Employers request the reports for hiring, promotion, reassignment, or retention decisions. In doing so, the employer must certify to the CRA that it will comply with the FCRA. The employer must also gain the individual's written consent before obtaining the report.

The Fair and Accurate Credit Transactions Act of 2003, which updated the FCRA, excluded additional categories of employee investigation data from credit reports, thus eliminating protections offered by the FCRA. If the investigation is of suspected misconduct relating to employment, compliance with the law, or compliance with preexisting written policies of the employer, such information is not regulated by the FCRA. However, if the employer takes an adverse action due to such investigations, the employee has a right of notice.

The FCRA also prohibits the provision of reports that contain medical information for employment purposes without notice and explicit affirmative consent for release of the health data.

It is important to note that the FCRA does not apply to investigations performed by companies or individuals who are not CRAs.

Right to Correct Inaccurate Information

Individuals may dispute inaccurate information that appears in a credit report. CRAs are required to investigate disputes and provide a report back to the consumer. If the CRA cannot resolve the dispute, the individual can add a statement to the credit report. Inaccurate or unverifiable information must be removed within 30 days of notice of the dispute. FACTA requires that investigation be "reasonable," although this standard is much lower than the requirements in creating the credit report which specify that there be "reasonable procedures to assure maximum possible accuracy."

Individuals may also dispute inaccurate information with the furnisher. If an individual disputes inaccurate information with a furnisher, that furnisher cannot report the information to a CRA without also including a notice of the dispute. If a furnisher determines that the information is inaccurate, it must block that information from being re-reported to CRAs—a common and major problem in the credit reporting industry.

The FCRA limits the length of time some information can appear in a consumer report. For instance, bankruptcies must be removed from the report after 10 years. Civil suits, civil judgments, paid tax liens, accounts placed for collection, and records of arrest can only appear for 7 years. Records of criminal convictions can remain on the report indefinitely.

Consumers may now directly dispute fraudulent transactions with the furnisher, the result of another FACTA amendment. Previously the FCRA required a furnisher to not report information that it "knows or consciously avoids knowing that the information is inaccurate." The FCRA now requires that a CRA not report information that it "knows or has *reasonable cause to believe* is inaccurate." On the "other end," when a CRA determines that transaction information is fraudulent, it must notify the furnisher that the information has been modified or deleted.

Accountability

The FCRA affords individuals a private right of action that can be pursued in federal or state court against CRAs, users of credit reports, and furnishers. In certain circumstances, individuals can obtain attorney's fees, court costs, and punitive damages. Additionally, the FTC can enforce provisions of the act. Criminal penalties can be brought against those who knowingly and willfully obtain a consumer report under false pretenses.

The statute of limitations for bringing an action for a violation of the FCRA is two years from the date of discovery of the violation by the consumer, although the action must be brought within five years of the date of the actual violation.

Source Electronic Privacy Information Center. 2005. http://www.epic.org/privacy/fcra/

GUARD OPERATIONS

The issue of selecting a supplier vs. using proprietary staff has long been a challenge for entities that require the services of a human security presence. I believe that this can be done relatively easily if you remember that security is a very simple business and you approach it on that basis.

Remember, only use security staff where electronics or technology will not meet your needs.

The First Step

Before you do anything else, you need to understand the risks and why you need security at all. Carry out a complete and professional threat risk assessment or comprehensive security audit. Once that process is complete and you have reviewed the report, you will be in a much better position to move forward effectively.

The Decision. Once you have the information and you determine that you need a human security presence, the choice can be made between proprietary, contract, or a combination of both.

A number of factors are set out for your consideration.

The Proprietary Choice. If your threat risk assessment or security audit reveals a significant risk to proprietary technology or equipment which is critical to the success of your entity, a proprietary force or a combination is a wise choice. This will give your Security Manager more direct control in all of the areas critical to the security operation such as hiring, training, administering discipline, enforcing policy and procedures, etc.

While a total proprietary force is the ultimate, affordability can be an issue and under these circumstances a combination of proprietary and contract is an option. The proprietary staff can be assigned to deal with all of the more critical areas while contract staff can deal with the more routine security matters.

But, not all is roses. Proprietary security can present a number of challenges. For example:

- You must manage the employer/employee relationship and all that it entails.
- Convincing management to pay a premium can be challenging.
- Additional headcount is required for sickness, vacation, special leave, etc.
- Dealing with headcount fluctuations when business needs change can be difficult to say the least.
- Total cost can be 40 percent to 50 percent higher than a contract staff.

The Contract Choice. Care must be taken in awarding a contract. Although the award process can be somewhat mechanical and involve other persons, such as representatives from purchasing, legal, and finance and administra-

tion, you will be the person who will have to live with the ultimate decision. As a security professional, you will need to be involved every step of the way. There is also a belief (often unfounded) that a negligent act by a contract security officer frees the client from liability. This is but one more reason to have a strong voice in the ultimate choice of supplier.

You can greatly enhance your chances of achieving a satisfactory result if you approach the decision properly and methodically.

Some guidelines:

- Qualify or screen the companies you invite to submit a proposal.
- Ask for and verify proof of financial viability.
- Ask for a list of past and current clients. Ask these clients about the quality of the contractor's services.
- Examine a sampling of "Client Service Evaluations" and verify.
- Review biographical sketches of key personnel that would be assigned to your contract. Such person should be the Account Manager, On-site Manager, Shift Supervisor, etc.
- Determine the value-added technology each offers and the cost of each. Ask for a list of current sites where this technology is in use and verify use and value.
- Examine turnover rates. High turnover rates generally mean dissatisfaction.
- Verify benefits and incentives paid to security staff. Low pay and poor or nonexistent benefits will lead to low quality in performance ultimately.

Based on an examination of this information, you can then select a number of companies that will be able to meet your security needs and they should be invited to submit a full proposal covering all of the areas set out above.

Request for Proposal (RFP)

The RFP should cover a number of areas, but in particular the following:

- Specific services required
- Equipment required and who is responsible for providing same

- Training and be very specific as to the level such as CPO, CGSB, CPP, etc.
- Location where services are to be provided
- Any specific site or performance condition such as standing, lifting, etc.
- Standards of performance, time elements, turnover rates, minimum pay rates for staff assigned, and benefits for staff assigned
- Quality control methodology
- Contract cancellation terms
- Vendor review process and penalties
- Continuous Improvement Teams and expectations
- Post Order preparation and acceptance
- Recordkeeping and acceptability
- Frequency of supplier/client contact and at what levels

Set a closing date for all proposals and set a time for a bidders meeting and a site walk-through. This will give all bidders an opportunity to ask any questions they may have. All responses should be in writing and go to each bidder.

- Invite each bidder to make a presentation based on the proposal, using the person that would administer the contract if awarded.
- Visit the bidder's office and speak to key personnel.
- Review training material or consider sitting in on a training session.
- Determine if the bidder's training program conforms to a recognized regimen such as training standards promulgated by the American Society for Industrial Security, Canadian Society for Industrial Security, Canadian General Standards Board, or the curriculum of a training academy or community college.

As soon as possible following the cutoff date, all bids should be evaluated using objective criteria. Using price vs. performance criteria, a number of key factors are identified such as financial stability, program quality, value-added technology, training, supervision, management, etc. These factors are then rated as to importance and given a total potential score based on that rating. As an example, financial stability may have a potential score of 50, while training may have a score of 200.

A minimum acceptable score is set so that bidders who do not achieve this minimum score do not move on to the pricing exercise which follows.

When totaled, a bidder may have a total score of 1080 out of a possible total of 1200 and surpasses the minimum required of 900 points.

All bidders then have their pricing added to the exercise and each bidder's score is divided into the total bid price submitted. While price is certainly important, it is not the only consideration. With this process, as an example, Bidder A submits a price of $130,000.00 and achieves a score of 1080. His final number is 120.37. Bidder B submits a price of $125,000.00 and achieves a score of 890. His final number is 140.44.

Our first instinct is to say that Bidder B is the winner with a lower price and a higher score. The reality is that the lower the score the better the bid. Bidder A is the clear winner with a lower score. This method ensures that quality is considered as well as cost in the final decision. This system, if applied properly, is fair to all involved.

The Contract

If everything is done correctly, the contract will be more than just a control document. It will be a blueprint that provides an excellent opportunity for success. Success is made possible when you:

- Strive to achieve a strategic partnership with your supplier.
- Consider a long-term contract to allow your partner to amortize their investment over a number of years.
- Consider a mutual cancellation clause, 30 days for you and 90 days for your supplier.
- Set minimum pay rates and benefits for all staff to be assigned.
- Include clear and concise language around expectations.
- Accept pricing which is realistic and will allow a reasonable return for your partner.
- Include a vendor review process as part of the contract.
- Insert a Continuous Improvement process in the contract.
- Provide for a contract staff member removal at your request and be specific around timing.

Contracting for security services, or for that matter any other kind of service, should be more than nuts and bolts methodology. To be sure, the company client needs to be protected if the client/contractor relationship goes sour, and that's why dotting the i's and crossing the t's is important. But also important is the opportunity to form a strategic partnership based on trust and respect that will bring benefits for both parties.

William R. McQuirter

NATIONAL EXPLOSIVES DETECTION CANINE PROGRAM

On March 9, 1972, a Trans World Airlines jet bound for Los Angeles took off from JFK International Airport in New York. Moments into the flight, the airline received an anonymous phone call warning there was a bomb onboard. The aircraft returned to JFK where passengers were evacuated and a bomb-sniffing dog named Brandy was brought on board to search. Brandy found the explosive device just 12 minutes before it was set to detonate. That same day, then-President Nixon directed the Secretary of Transportation to use innovative means to combat the problems plaguing civil aviation. The result was the creation of a unique federal project—the FAA Explosives Detection Canine Team Program—designed to place certified teams at strategic locations throughout the nation so that any aircraft receiving a bomb threat could quickly divert to an airport with a canine team. After the Transportation Security Administration (TSA) was formed, the Explosive Detection Canine Team Program transferred to the new agency and has experienced rapid growth, including plans to deploy canine teams to other modes of transportation in early 2006.

The National Explosives Detection Canine Program (NEDCP) exists to deter and detect the introduction of explosive devices into the transportation system. In addition, bomb threats cause disruption of air, land, and sea commerce, and pose an unacceptable danger to the traveling public and should be resolved quickly. Explosives Detection Canine Teams (EDCT) are a proven reliable resource to detect explosives and are a key component in a balanced counter-sabotage program. The use of highly trained EDCTs is a proven deterrent to terrorism directed towards transportation systems and provides a timely and mobile response support to facilities, rail stations, airports, passenger terminals, seaports, and surface carriers.

Partnership

Because the explosives detection canine teams combine excellent mobility with reliable detection rates, their use today has evolved to include searching areas in response to bomb threats in aviation and mass transit systems, as well as serving as general deterrents to any would-be terrorists or criminals.

NEDCP is a partnership with industry in which airports and mass transit systems voluntarily participate and are supported by federal funds to the tune of $40,000 per year, per canine team. The TSA pays to purchase and train the dogs, trains the canine handlers, and partially reimburses each participating agency for costs associated with maintaining the teams. Associated costs include handlers' salaries (handlers are usually airport police or local law enforcement personnel), food and veterinarian costs. In turn, the local jurisdiction agrees to utilize TSA canine teams at least 80 percent of the time in the transportation environment and to maintain a minimum of three certified teams available for around-the-clock incident response.

The canine program has expanded significantly over recent years as a result of recommendations by the White House Commission on Aviation Safety and Security, the Security Baseline Working Group of the Aviation Security Advisory Committee, the tragic events of September 11, 2001, and the London and Madrid train bombings. The commission said that an increase in the number of well trained dogs and handlers would make a significant and rapid improvement in security, while the working group recommended placing at least two canine teams at all of the nation's largest airports. With the $8.9 million Congress provided for the program in the Omnibus Consolidated Appropriations Act of 1997, the number of teams rose from 87 at 30 airports in 1996, to about 174 teams at 39 airports in 1999. The program has continued to grow steadily thanks to Congressional funding and we expect to field over 400 teams at over 80 airports by year's end. Additionally, 30 teams will be deployed to 10 mass transit systems in early 2006.

For the first time in the history of this program, TSA-certified explosives detection canine teams are stationed at each of the nation's largest airports. These highly trained teams are used several times each day to search aircraft and terminals, to check out suspect bags or cargo, and to deter terrorist activities.

Training

Each canine team, composed of one dog and one handler, undergoes 10 weeks of intensive training at the Transportation Security Administration Explosives Detection Canine Handler Course at Lackland Air Force Base in San Antonio, Texas. Once the teams are certified by the TSA, they undergo several hours of proficiency training each week in their operational environment, which includes all the smells and distractions associated with a busy airport or mass transit system. The TSA also requires each team to go through an intensive three to four day annual re-certification to demonstrate they continue to meet TSA-certification standards. These standards are some of the most stringent in the nation and include demonstrated performances in searching aircraft, luggage, terminals, cargo, and vehicles. These evaluations test the team's abilities to perform their day-to-day mission—protecting transportation systems for the traveling public.

To ensure quality training takes place, the TSA provides canine explosives training aids and magazines used to store the aids. TSA mandates strict standards for accountability, safe handling, and transportation of these canine training aids. In addition, a special data system called the K-9 Training Aid Reporting System was created to document and track the teams' training.

Breeds

The TSA primarily uses German Shepherds, Belgian Malanois, and Labrador Retrievers that usually are obtained from breeders and canine vendors from across the United States and Europe. These breeds are chosen for their temperament and keen sensory capabilities. Individual dogs selected for the program must undergo exacting pre-acceptance screening to prove they are healthy, smart, highly motivated, and able to detect the necessary odors. The TSA also operates a breeding program of Labrador Retrievers at Lackland Air Force Base in San Antonio, Texas. This program is modeled after the world-class Australian Custom's Service Breeding Program. Puppies are raised in "foster families" in the San Antonio area until they are entered into formalized training. The Australian government has provided TSA with more than 20 puppies to accelerate the program and to assist in the worldwide effort to thwart terrorist activities. TSA dogs are kenneled at the homes of their handlers and many retire to the handlers' homes after 10 to 12 years of explosives detection work.

Research and Development

The TSA continues to lead the "pack" in initiating research and development projects within the canine community. These collaborative efforts include projects with other federal agencies, such as the Technical Support Working Group, industry, and academia. Current projects include, but are not limited to canine olfaction studies, evaluating the performance of canine duty cycles, generalization of explosives odors, handler selection criteria, and selection of the right breed of dog for the task at hand.

(Author's note: This article is based in large part on the document cited below.)

John J. Fay

Source National Explosives Detection Canine Program (NEDCP), Transportation Security Administration. 2006. <www.tsa.gov/public/display?theme=32>

PARKING RAMP SECURITY

With the ever increasing security problems occurring in parking ramps, security managers are constantly looking at new ways to improve their physical security systems. Usually there is no single remedy to answer all the problems.

There are pros and cons to all current working systems and new systems that are being considered for increased protection. As an example, many parking ramps and parking lots are increasing the number of security officers both to tour the facility and provide escort service for customers. Although this practice should reduce greatly the perceived dangers that many customers have regarding parking ramps, it is a very costly remedy that would be impossible to accommodate during peak hours. Also, when touring a ramp, it is impossible for a guard to be everywhere at once.

Another suggested remedy is adding closed-circuit television (CCTV) equipment. Although this remedy is less costly than guard service, it cannot provide the same feeling of security that is projected by a live guard. Also, it is virtually impossible for CCTV equipment to cover every nook and cranny of a parking ramp due to columns and low-ceiling height.

A third remedy is to install a sound system in the parking ramp proper to monitor activities that go beyond what would be considered the normal threshold level. Some systems are effective in stairwells, elevator lobbies, and in elevators where noise can be monitored easily. Sound systems are, however, somewhat limited in the ramp proper where noises made by cars and birds can be confusingly similar to the human scream.

An alternative remedy might be a combination of security officers, CCTV, and sound systems. Additional security personnel working on a structured guard tour and connected by radio to a security center would provide deterrence, rapid response, and an enhanced comfort level for customers.

To enhance the performance of the security personnel, strategically located CCTV camera locations should be provided and monitored by personnel at the central site. From this location, a second tour of the facility can be accomplished quicker and provide backup to the live guard tour. This puts security personnel in every location of the ramp every minute of the day.

By adding a sound system, a method is created in which the central monitoring personnel can both monitor remote activities and respond immediately to let people know that help is on the way. If this sound system is augmented with the public address announcements regarding security at a regulated time interval, it would further enhance the security comfort level of customers.

In addition to the previous remedies, certain things such as painting walls, increasing the lighting and videotaping at critical entrance and exit locations can add to the overall security.

On a final note, the owners and operators must be cognizant of the fact that liability and exposure is greater with a security system that is not working vs. having no security system at all. Whatever the decision, a structured check of new and existing systems performance should be done on a routine basis and system maintenance should be performed throughout its life.

John R. Morris

PERSONAL SECURITY MISSION

The success of a personal security mission depends on many considerations. The key consideration is planning. Planning requires attention to the following details:

- Coordination with other agencies
- Importance of the dignitary
- The probable threat against the dignitary
- Equipment required
- Means of communication
- Emergency procedures
- Contingency or alternate procedures
- Orientation of security personnel concerning the assignment
- Relations with new media

The Security Detail

When the protected person is highly important, it is likely that he or she will have a security detail permanently assigned for protection. A security detail frequently consists of the person in charge, a personal security officer, an advance team, a residence team, and a baggage team.

Person in Charge. The person in charge of the personal security detail has overall responsibility for accomplishing the objectives of the assignment. He or she coordinates such matters as itinerary, protocol, press policies, and the amount of exposure to the public desired by the principal. The person in charge establishes liaison with supporting intelligence and law enforcement agencies.

The person in charge also coordinates the utilization of resources of manpower and equipment, and approves the security plan formulated for the assignment.

Personal Security Officer. This person is somewhat like a bodyguard who provides close-in protection for the principal and normally accompanies the principal away from the office or residence. The personal security officer is the principal's main liaison with the personal security force and with the security personnel provided by the responsible protective agency. The personal security officer communicates with the person in charge and, whenever possible, with the advance team on a daily basis. The personal security officer is usually the person to brief the principal concerning the security arrangements established for the assignment.

Advance Team. This team is responsible for conducting on-site security inspections before the arrival of the principal and his party to determine and complete personal security arrangements. The advance team is usually tasked to:

- Initiate working relationships with the responsible protective agency and its project officer.
- Initiate liaison with appropriate intelligence and police agencies.
- Examine arrival and departure terminals, and make appropriate security arrangements to ensure security of the principal and his party.
- Conduct a reconnaissance of local travel routes and establish necessary security and traffic control points. Also, make recommendations regarding the speed, composition, and order of a motorcade if appropriate.
- Initiate working relationships with management and security personnel at the place where the principal will reside during the period of the assignment.
- Inspect the buildings and grounds selected as the sites for functions involving the principal, and, on the basis of the inspection, establish appropriate security arrangements.
- Coordinate transportation and arrange for the security of baggage of the principal and his party.
- Inspect the principal's vehicle and conduct a security briefing for all drivers.
- Prepare sketches, maps, and photographs as may be required to fully inform the person in charge and the personal security officer.

Residence Team. This is a security team that provides protection at the principal's place of stay on a 24-hour-a-day basis. This team maintains a log and various registers, screens telephone calls, checks packages, and exercises control over visitors.

Baggage Team. This team is responsible for maintaining the security of the baggage of the principal and his official party when in transit. This team may accompany the official party, or it may be drawn from resources under the control of the responsible protective agency. The baggage team does not personally handle the baggage of the official party, but supervises such details. The baggage team conducts baggage counts and answers directly to the personal security officer.

Every detail of security in the performance phase of the assignment must be carefully planned in advance. There is always, however, the possibility of sudden changes of plans. This requires that flexibility be an important element in planning for the personal security assignment. Contingency for alternate plans must be prepared in the event circumstances cause deviation from the original plan. Factors that must be weighed in the development of plans include the importance of the protected person; the amount, duration, and nature of exposure desired by the principal or required by the circumstances; the factors of geography; and modes of transportation.

Persons assigned to personal security duties should recognize that within the democratic framework it is virtually impossible to provide absolute personal protection. Protective security officers must accept the legal and sociological constraints and within those limits reduce the opportunity of kidnap or assassination to the extent possible. A chief operational concept in creating protection is in-depth deployment of the protective force. The potential attacker is forced to penetrate layers of protection before reaching the target. A single-layered security shell, no matter how resistant, will crack when struck with sufficient force, thereby losing the protection it was designed to provide. The shell around the principal should consist of a number of protective layers, each of which becomes increasingly difficult to penetrate as an attacker moves inward toward the target.

Concentric protection, or defense in depth, can be thought of as a pattern of rings radiating out from the protected person. At a minimum, concentric protection consists of an inner and outer ring. The concept is applicable whether the principal is at home, at work, or in travel. In high-risk situations, the number of rings may be increased, made mobile, or supplemented with extra equipment. Under routine circumstances, the concentric pattern remains fairly fixed, but the protective screen exists at all times.

After-Action Report

An after-action report is made as soon as possible after the operation. It is written in narrative style, with emphasis placed on problems encountered and procedures used to resolve them. The after-action report should include detailed recommendations for improvement of performance in future personal security missions. The report provides a history file and is a valuable document for planning future security missions of a similar nature.

John J. Fay

PLANNING AND ORGANIZING TRAINING

Chief security officers (CSOs) often have dual training responsibilities; first to train employees that work in the security group, and second to train employees generally. The training of security group employees can be done fairly easily. The CSO can ensure that the audience will be at the place of training, such as the security group's conference room, and be there at a certain time on a specific date. The CSO has the needed training equipment on hand or easily accessible. The training topic is stable because it is specific to tasks performed by the group's employees. There are few surprises, and those that arise can be handled quickly and with little difficulty.

In the other half of the CSO's training responsibilities are employees from all groups that make up the company. When the full employee population is located at a single site, the CSO can have problems, though minor. The problems are usually correctable because the CSO knows who has responsibility for what. A phone call or a face-to-face visit is usually all that is needed to keep the training plan on track.

However, and it is a big however, training that occurs off-site can be nothing except one large sack full of problems. At first, when the training event is scheduled and the trainees identified, everything is rosy. But as the training date nears, problems begin to pop up, they multiply quickly, and they go from minor to major. Imagine a CSO setting off on a one-month tour of fifteen company properties where he or she is to give a four-hour presentation every second day. Will the CSO run into problems? You already know the answer.

The number and magnitude of training-related problems at an off-site location can be mitigated by developing a sensible, workable plan and organizing to carry out the plan. Decide what you are going to do, get ready to do it, and make sure you have all the equipment you will need plus backups just to make sure.

Getting ready to conduct an off-site training event should really begin about one year ahead of time. This is the case because more likely than not your preparation will be hampered for a variety of reasons such as moving from one location to another, acquiring a new boss or new subordinates, changes in company policy, budget crunches, outsourcing, and myriad other reasons.

The only effective way to ensure that the event will succeed is to plan it thoroughly and then organize it to plan. It would be nice if the original plan turns out to be the final plan and that the original organizational setup turns out to be just the way you intended from day one. Such is never the case, however. The plan will be changed several times before the event and probably during the event. And, of course, every change in plan will require a change in organization. For example, the original plan was to hold the training in an auditorium equipped with a rear-view projector. One day before the event you learn that the place of training has been switched to a conference room that has no projector and no screen. The plan and organization for it has to be modified, and quickly.

Apart from the logistics of a training event are academic considerations. What is it precisely that the attendees need to learn? What instructional method will facilitate the learning? What is the intended learning outcome? For example, if the learning outcome is an ability to make an unannounced cash drawer audit, the instructional method could very well be a demonstration followed by hands-on and performance-oriented exercises. If the learning outcome is to make cashiers aware of procedures to be followed during a robbery, the instructional method might be a combination of lecture, slides, and a video. The instructional method will determine the equipment and materials that need to be brought to the training site.

The equipment to be used has to be set up in advance. If the equipment fails, there will need to be time available to repair or replace the equipment. Nothing can be more embarrassing and competency-damaging than to begin a training session only to discover that the projector's bulb has burned out.

Materials might need to be distributed to attendees. These can be enrolment forms, instructor evaluation forms, participant manuals, desk signs, scratch pads, and pencils. For some training sessions, student learning materials might need to be sent in advance so that all students start off with the same level of knowledge.

The trainer has to be attentive to attendee needs. Periodic breaks and sufficient time for lunch are the minimums. Refreshments, although not necessary, can add a little pleasure.

Three Essential Elements

Every training endeavor, regardless of purpose, has three key elements: the people to be trained, the subject to be learned, and the people that do the training.

People. The people to be trained can vary widely. For example, an organization can have people that work at the line level such as clerks, warehousemen, drivers, and security officers. Above them in the organizational hierarchy can be human resource staffers, auditors, accountants, and supervisors. One level up is managers and department heads. At the top level is the executive group. In this example, the organization has four levels: line, staff, managerial, and executive.

The general training approach will vary for each level and the topics to be covered will vary as well. The trainer's communication style with line level employees will be different than the style used with executives. The topics taught to line level security officer employees are often intended to develop psychomotor skills such as operating a security console or directing traffic. The language, appearance, and demeanor of the trainer with these employees are down-to-earth. The executive level employee is taught intellectual skills such as competitive intelligence and industrial espionage. The language, appearance, and demeanor of the trainer are considerably different at the higher level. An even different training approach is used when all levels are brought together for a security awareness presentation at a town hall meeting.

Training Subject. Irrespective of employee status, the training subject has to be purposeful, meaningful, and agreed by the employees to be important to their work. It is accurately said that the selection of a training topic is limited only by one's imagination. A CSO, for example, would have no difficulty in conjuring up a security-related topic. But the real purpose is not to put the imagination to work but to choose a topic that is significant to the moment at hand. To inform employees in June of Christmas season crime risks has no value nor is it purposeful to teach employees how to keep tools from being stolen when the company's greatest asset is information.

Training subjects change as events change. Subjects taught post-9/11 are distinctly different than subjects taught pre-9/11. That single event changed the entire security landscape, and along with it the training topics and modalities of the security industry worldwide.

People That Do the Training. The CSO is the primary trainer for security-related topics. Secondary trainers in the security area can be people that report to the CSO. If a hot topic has to do with theft, the secondary trainer may be the security group's investigator. In some cases, the CSO will bring in an outside trainer such as a specialist to train mail room employees in how to spot parcel bombs.

The most important attribute of an effective trainer is subject knowledge. Next, and almost nearly important, is the trainer's ability to transfer that knowledge to the learner. We all know brilliant people that know a subject inside and out but have no capacity to pass the knowledge along.

A third attribute is making the information relevant to the trainee. Every person in training is thinking: How can this help me personally? The thought is not: How can this help the company? A trainer knows this and knows that every trainee can be shown personal value such as "knowing this can help me get promoted" or "knowing this can help me from being fired."

Some will argue that a fourth element in the training equation is a facilitator. There is truth to the argument but only when the training format is a seminar or workshop. A facilitator can be invaluable in keeping the attendees' focus on the issue at hand. The facilitator knows where the "train should go" and keeps the train moving in the right direction. The facilitator writes pertinent points on an easel, asks questions, provides answers when needed, and generally keeps track of what is going on.

A facilitator is not an instructor in the true sense of the word. The facilitator takes the lead of the instructor, amplifies and clarifies key points, and provides tutorial help during practical exercises.

Other Factors

When the training event is off-site, such as at a hotel or conference center, the CSO might have to attend to details such as:

- Setting up sleeping room arrangements.
- Coordinating with local/campus police to facilitate a higher level of patrol activity.
- Informing attendees of nearby areas to avoid such as high-crime neighborhoods and traffic hazards.
- Ensuring that the meeting room has the correct number and mix of audiovisual equipment.
- "Sweeping" the meeting room if extremely sensitive information is to be discussed.
- Inspecting sleeping rooms after attendees have checked out so that sensitive written information is not left behind.

Conclusion

The CSO engages in a wide range of training activities. Events held at the "home base" are somewhat manageable but the opposite is true when training is delivered off-site.

Planning and organizing are absolutely essential to the success of a training event. They are not one-time activities but activities that evolve from the moment of inception to moment of delivery, and even beyond.

Effective training relies on a right mix of attendees, purposeful and meaningful information, and skilled teachers.

Bronson Steve Bias

PRE-EMPLOYMENT BACKGROUND SCREENING AND SAFE HIRING

In today's economic environment, firms cannot afford to be side-tracked by employee problems such as workplace violence, theft, false resumes, embezzlement, or lawsuits for negligent hiring, harassment, or trumped-up injury claims.

Employers of all sizes across all industries have increasingly turned to pre-employment screening as a critical risk-management tool to try to avoid hiring problem employees in the first place. Lawsuits for negligent hiring are among the fastest growing types of litigation in the U.S., and employers who fail to demonstrate due diligence can be hit hard by juries. Nationally, the cost of human capital is usually the largest single line item in any firm's budget, responsible for a third of business costs. With employees as their biggest source of risk, firms that fail to exercise due diligence in their hiring practices put their future at risk.

By utilizing professional pre-employment screening techniques, employers, security professionals and human resources departments can attempt to minimize and even avoid financial and legal repercussions due to hiring a person with an unsuitable criminal record, falsified credentials, or some other issue that makes them dangerous, unqualified, or unfit for their position.

Pre-employment screening has four goals. First, a screening program can demonstrate that an employer utilizes due diligence in hiring. Every employer has a legal duty of care to take reasonable steps to avoid hiring workers who pose a foreseeable risk of harm to co-workers, the public, or vulnerable individuals. Failure to exercise that duty can lead to lawsuits for "negligent hiring," where employers can face substantial financial exposure. The duty of care is higher for employers engaged in business with higher risk, such as firms that send workers into homes. Second, effective screening obtains factual information about a candidate, supplementing the impressions obtained from an interview alone. It is also a valuable tool for judging the accuracy of a candidate's resume or application. Third, effective pre-employment screening serves to discourage applicants with something to hide. An applicant with serious criminal convictions is less likely to apply at a firm that announces it conducts pre-employment background checks. Finally, a background-screening program should encourage applicants to be very honest in their applications and interviews. Since applicants are told there is a background check, they are motivated to reveal information about themselves they feel may be uncovered with a check.

A pre-employment screening program looks at four categories of information.

Public records

The primary source of public records is criminal records. Screening industry statistics suggest that even among applicants who consent to screening and know they are going to be screened, the "hit" rate for uncovering criminal records can be as high as 10 percent.

Contrary to popular perception, criminal records are not available by computer nationwide. The FBI database (NCIC) is restricted to employers who have specific governmental authorization, and even that search is subject to various errors. For private employers, a search must be conducted by examining the public records at each individual county courthouse that is potentially relevant. Since there are over 10,000 courthouses in America, the search is usually conducted in jurisdictions relevant to the applicant, as determined by reviewing their employment history and utilizing a search called a Social Security Trace that provides past addresses and names associated with a Social Security Number in records maintained by credit bureaus and other databases. In some courts, the court clerk conducts the search and the accuracy depends upon the court clerk. Federal courts are a separate system that can also be searched.

As with any process that depends upon humans for accuracy, there is always the possibility of error. If there is a possible criminal record, it is critical to carefully review the underlying court documents to locate identifying information to determine if the criminal record in fact belongs to the subject of the search. The criminal record must also be examined to determine the details of the offense and whether the criminal matter is reportable. There are numerous legal restrictions on employers utilizing certain information such as arrests not resulting in convictions, certain minor offenses, expunged cases, or cases where there is a form of delayed adjudication.

Employment cannot be automatically denied based upon a criminal record; employers must show a sound business-related reason. Under federal and state EEOC rules, an employer must consider the nature and gravity of the offense, the age of the offense, and the nature of the job.

Another criminal tool is statewide and multi-jurisdictional databases that contain millions of criminal records. Criminal records database searches are valuable because they cover a much larger geographical area than traditional searches performed at the county level. It is critical to understand that these criminal database searches are a research tool only and under no circumstance is its use a substitute for a hands-on search at the county level. Databases in each state are compiled from a number of various sources and the information may not be complete or timely. Because of the potential for errors, the appearance of a person's name on a database is not an indication the person is a criminal any more then the absence of a name shows they are not a criminal. Any positive match must be verified by reviewing the actual court records. However, a database is a valuable supplemental tool for a background screening since it may point to additional jurisdictions to search.

In a number of states, employers can also obtain information from sexual offender registrations. These should also be treated with the same caution used for other databases, since each state varies in what information is assembled and released—some states do not release identifying details and some states limit the types of offense made available. There can be large gaps in these databases since studies show that many sexual offenders fail to register.

Another example of public records is drivers' records. "Driving for work" is very broadly defined in most jurisdictions and is not limited to driving positions. A drivers' record and license status may give insight into an applicant's level of responsibility by showing if an applicant keeps commitments to appear in court or pay fines, or has a drug/alcohol problem.

Private Records

Private records are primarily maintained by the credit bureaus. Credit reports can help determine whether an employee is suitable for a position involving cash or the exercise of financial discretion. Credit reports are a possible way to gauge trustworthiness and reliability as well. A credit report should only be requested when it is specifically relevant to a job function and the employer has appropriate policies and procedures in place to ensure that use of credit reports is relevant, fair, and protected against unauthorized viewing. Of all the screening tools available, a credit report is probably the most sensitive, so caution should be used.

Credential Verification

Verifying past employment is one of the most important tools for an employer. Some employers make a costly mistake by not checking past employment because past employers may not give detailed information. However, even verification of dates of employment and job title is critical because an employer must be concerned about unexplained gaps in the employment history. Although there can be many reasons for a gap in employment, if an applicant cannot account for the past seven to ten years, that can be a red flag. It is also important to know where a person has been because of the way criminal records are maintained in the United States; searches must be conducted at each relevant courthouse. If an employer knows where an applicant has been, it increases the accuracy

of a criminal search and decreases the possibility that an applicant has served custodial time for a criminal offense. Finally, documenting an attempt to obtain references demonstrates due diligence.

Verification of educational accomplishment and licenses is also critical for confirming whether an applicant has the required credentials, licenses, or education claimed. There is a high rate of fraudulent education claims. Employers need to be aware of "diploma mills" that grant worthless degrees. If a licensing agency or school cannot verify data, the applicant should be given an opportunity to explain before assuming the applicant has lied, since there can be an explanation for a discrepancy.

Reference Checks

In addition to confirming dates of past employment, an employer may want to contact past employers and supervisors to obtain information about the employee's job performance. Past job performance can be an important predictor of future success. Despite laws in forty states that protect employers who respond to such request in good faith with factual and job-related information, many employers have a policy of limiting past employment information to dates of employment and job title only. Reference checks can be conducted on sources that have been "supplied" by the applicant, and on other sources "developed" during interviews with the supplied references.

Legal and Practical Issues on Background Checks

Employment screening differs from an investigation. In a pre-employment background screening program, employers are typically looking to either verify known information—such as past employment or education—or checking public records, having been supplied with the applicant's consent and personal data. A screening program is utilized to look for red flags on a number of applicants. A screening program may not detect every potential problem with applicants but it is a cost-effective means of screening large numbers of applicants and demonstrating due diligence. By comparison, investigations are typically more in-depth and more focused on an individual, and seek to develop information that is unknown to the investigator. It is often much more expensive.

Another issue is whether background checks can be conducted in-house or be outsourced to a professional third-party background screening firm. The trend among profitable and efficient organizations is to outsource services that, although vital, do not represent the company's core competency and can be done effectively by a third-party professional. In addition, background screening requires specialized knowledge, expertise, and software. A background firm can typically provide the service at less cost and within an average of three days or less. As a general rule the cost of a background check is less then the employees' first day salary.

Another consideration is that employee background screening is a heavily regulated area, subject to a number of employment, discrimination, and privacy laws both on the federal and state levels. A federal law known as the Fair Credit Reporting Act (FCRA) regulates background screening performed by third-party background firms, also known as Consumer Reporting Agencies. The FCRA balances the right of employers to know whom they hire with an applicant's right of disclosure and privacy. Under FCRA law, the employer first obtains the applicant's written consent to be screened and clearly disclose information about the screening on a standalone document. In the event negative information is found, the applicant must be given an opportunity to correct the record. Qualified background screening firms can assist employers with legal compliance. The FCRA rules apply equally to private investigators as well as background firms if the report is being prepared for an employer by a third party for purposes of evaluating a consumer for employment. A PI license does not negate FCRA requirements.

Some employers justify in-house screening on the basis that the FCRA only applies to third parties who perform screening. However, an in-house program can potentially trigger the FCRA requirements if it accesses databases not available to the public, or if a third party is hired to obtain court records. In addition, in California, in-house background screening carries some of the same requirements imposed on third-party screening.

In selecting a screening firm, an employer should apply the same criteria that it would use in selecting any other provider of critical professional services. For example, if an employer were choosing a law firm for legal representation, it would not select the cheapest—it would clearly want to know it is selecting a firm that is competent, experienced, and knowledgeable as well as reputable and reasonably priced. The same criteria should also apply to critical security and human resource services. A screening firm should have an understanding of the legal implications of background checks, particularly the federal Fair Credit Reporting Act and applicable state laws. In addition, employers are well advised only to deal with screening firms that have evidenced a professional commitment by joining the national trade association of the screening industry—the National Association of Professional Background Screeners.

Finally, employers and security professionals should understand that background checks are just one part of an overall safe hiring program. Employers also need pay attention to the entire hiring process. One example is the employment application. It is critical that an employment application put an applicant on notice that a background check will be conducted on finalists in order to promote honesty and discourage applicants with something to hide. The application should ask applicants in the broadest language permitted by law about past criminal conduct, and caution applicants that any false statements or material omissions are grounds to terminate employment no matter when discovered. The application should be carefully reviewed to look for red flags such as unexplained employment gaps or missing information.

Lester S. Rosen

PRE-EMPLOYMENT SCREENING AND BACKGROUND INVESTIGATIONS

Practical experience reveals that many job applicants misrepresent or exaggerate their experience and accomplishments to increase their chances of getting the job they seek. Statistics from the Bureau of Justice reveal that up to half a million criminal offenders are released every year, and recidivism rates can be as high as 67.5 percent. And as most employers recognize, workplace violence, employee theft, and substance abuse remain serious problems. Never before has the need to better screen job applicants been greater. Today's employers that do not have effective employment screening practices and do not routinely perform background investigations of those they choose to hire, will be likely to hire their competitors' rejects tomorrow.

The objectives of an effective pre-employment background investigation should (1) verify the accuracy and completeness of statements made by the applicant and (2) develop additional relevant information concerning the applicant to assist the prospective employer make an informed decision regarding the applicant's overall suitability.

However, federal, state and local laws impact what the employer can and cannot do when conducting pre-employment background investigations. Some of the provisions are complicated, and penalties for violating these laws can be stiff. As a result, many employers decide not to perform background investigations at all. The price of doing nothing can be immeasurable, possibly leading to unwanted workplace crime, substance abuse, and violence and eventually lawsuits.

Specific Statutory Prohibitions and Restrictions

Title VII of the Civil Rights Act of 1964, the Americans with Disabilities Act, the Equal Employment Opportunity Act, the Fair Credit Reporting Act, and the Employee Polygraph Protection Act, regulate how and under what circumstances an employer can conduct pre-employment background investigation. For example, employers are prohibited in most instances from making any oral or written employment inquiry that directly or indirectly identifies personal characteristics such as age, race, color, national origin, ancestry, sex, sexual orientation, marital status, pregnancy, religion, creed, disability, or recognized handicap. The mere consideration of any such characteristic by an employer is considered in and of itself discriminatory. Employers are even barred from discriminating against an applicant who perceives he or she has a handicap. Direct questions about an applicant's protected status and the use of indirect inquiries that disproportionately screen out job candidates of a protected group are strictly prohibited. Those violating the law may

be subject to both civil and criminal penalties. Federal and State handicap laws (Rehabilitation Act of 1973 and Americans with Disabilities Act) regulate the manner in which an employer can conduct a pre-employment drug test or physical test. In most instances, such tests may only be requested after an offer of employment has been made.

Although the U.S. Constitution provides no specific privacy protections, an assortment of state statues and federal court decisions have created the "right to privacy" which today protects applicants and employees against intrusions into their privacy by employers. Employers should not gather or collect information of personal or confidential nature or offensively intrude into the private lives of anyone where a reasonable expectation of privacy exists. Visiting an applicant's home or interviewing an applicant at his residence could constitute an invasion of privacy. Such efforts are actionable and may give rise to legal claims against the employer and its agents.

Arrest and Criminal Records

It is unlawful for most private employers to ask a job applicant to provide information concerning an arrest or detention that did not result in a conviction. Employers can ask about any arrest with respect to which the individual is out on bail or personal recognizance. There are exceptions applicable to health facilities regarding arrests for sex offenses and possession of narcotics. However, the Equal Employment Opportunity Commission (EEOC) has ruled that an employer's use of arrest records, although lawful under some circumstances, has an adverse impact on classes of minorities and that the use of such records is, in fact, discriminatory. For the purposes of pre-employment screening, employers should only use actual conviction records, not arrest records.

Unfortunately (and contrary to the claims of many database vendors), there is no nationwide public repository for criminal conviction records. Publicly available criminal conviction records are maintained either at the state or county level. Most statewide criminal databases that are available online (including those that offer instant criminal record searches) are often incomplete, unreliable, and should be used cautiously. Many of these databases draw their data from the state's Department of Corrections and contain arrest records which have not been updated or are incomplete. Today, there is no statewide database for criminal records that can guarantee complete and accurate information. There is also no publicly available technology for employers to screen applicants by means of fingerprints. Many states prohibit employers from requesting or using applicant fingerprints or photographs.

What Can Be Done

What employers are left with is the search of public records. A vast amount of information is available and for the most part, the information is reasonably accessible and inexpensive. Additionally, there are many private sources of information, including credit bureaus such as Equifax, Experian, and TransUnion. Accessed through designated licensees or resellers, they and other information providers can be extremely helpful to those conducting pre-employment background investigations. Following are useful sources:

Criminal Courts

Criminal conviction records can be an invaluable source of information. For the most part, these records are public and available to anyone. In most instances these records can be obtained from the county criminal court clerk's office. Convictions for minor infractions to major felonies are found here. Files include full details of the case and ultimate disposition. As stated earlier, statewide databases are unreliable and should be used with caution. Criminal convictions records are best searched by hand at the county level, and full names, with dates of birth, should be used as much as possible to confirm a positive identification.

Civil Courts

These records are indexed by the name of the plaintiff and defendant. They can be obtained from the county court clerk's office. Uncovered will be civil actions, judgments, notices of default, and unlawful detainers. Many employ-

ers have learned that litigious applicants often become litigious employees.

Driving Histories

These records are maintained at the state level and are typically accessible to employers through the state department of motor vehicles. This is an excellent place to search for a history of substance abuse and other problems. Revealed will be convictions for driving under the influence of alcohol and/or drugs, suspensions due to child support issues and failure to provide insurance, convictions for lesser violations, and vehicle registration information and accident histories.

Other Public Records

Corporations and other business entities are registered at the offices of the Secretary of State. Filings include the names of officers, street addresses, and agent for process of service. This is a particularly good place to search if the applicant is a corporate officer or is suspected of being one. Also found on the state level are the licensing boards for the various professions. Nurses, doctors, building contractors, and even mattress re-builders must be licensed in most states. If the job requires a license, it is often worth the effort to check and see if the applicant is properly licensed.

Federal Bankruptcy Court

All bankruptcies are handled in Federal Court. These records are public and often reveal valuable information about one's ability to handle his or her financial affairs. However, in the case of a pre-employment investigation, Federal Bankruptcy Code prohibits an employer from considering a past bankruptcy when making an employment decision.

What Should Be Searched?

Search strategies and procedures vary, however, the process should always be well thought out. In order to avoid discrimination claims, all applicants should be screened similarly. It is suggested that an "applicant screening checklist" be used as part of the screening process. The checklist should be attached to the other application materials and retained for future reference. Using such a system helps prevent disparate treatment claims and the potential of hiring an undesirable individual.

The items and their order on the checklist should be given much thought, based upon the goals of the screening process and needs of the organization. For example, not all employers need to search bankruptcy records. However, if the organization manages other people's money, the applicant's financial affairs history could be important. At the very least, employers should check the applicant's criminal and driving histories.

Verification of Prior Employment

Verification of prior employment begins with the job application. It is not enough to ask for the name of the applicant's former supervisor. Screeners and interviewers should ask for the names of other people with whom the applicant worked or supervised. Experience reveals that subordinates will more likely cooperate and provide useful information than personnel managers or former supervisors. Former co-workers also can be very helpful. Unfortunately, due to a growing concern about the potential of defamation claims, employers have been increasingly reluctant to provide valuable information. Today, many former employers provide little more than dates of employment and job descriptions. Unfortunately, many organizations have adopted policies that restrict the information to be released and the persons authorized to make the release.

Other Valuable Searches

For sensitive positions, more in-depth investigations are recommended and may be tailored to the position. Exercising care up front can prevent many problems later. Other searches may include:

- Personal credit history
- Verification of education
- Verification of current address
- Business ownership
- Fictitious business name filings

- Real estate ownership
- Vehicle and aircraft ownership
- Corporation ownership or officership
- Sexual offender registries
- Consumer credit reports

Section 604 of the Fair Credit Reporting Act (FCRA) details the permissible uses and access of consumer credit reports. Many employers find consumer credit reports useful, particularly if the applicant will be handling money or have financial responsibilities. However, due to the complexity of these reports and the potential that their use will give rise to discrimination claims, they may be more trouble than they are worth for many employers.

Verification of Education

Typically, colleges and universities provide education verification over the telephone. Very few require signed releases or verify only by mail. Contact the admissions office or the registrar's office first. Some of the larger schools have offices that do nothing but verify student and graduate information. In recent years, more and more colleges and universities subscribe to third-party verification systems such as Degreechk.com or the National Student Clearinghouse. For a fee these organizations provide verification of education and other credentials.

Selecting a Vendor to Conduct Pre-Employment Backgrounds

Today's employers have many choices in selecting a pre-employment screening and background investigation vendor. Many vendors offer their services via the Internet. These vendors offer a wide range of services but may or may not offer personalized service. A vendor should not be selected by price alone. An acceptable vendor will:

- Be properly licensed where necessary. Many states require a background screener to have a private investigator license. Ensure the vendor has the licenses it needs to provide the services offered.
- Be properly insured. Remarkably, several well-known vendors do not have

any general liability or "errors and omissions" insurance. Require a certificate of insurance and verify that the coverage is "occurrence," not "claims-made."

- Have the professional and technological resources necessary to do the job. Though many vendors claim to possess the resources to consistently provide quality results, most do not. Even some of the largest Internet vendors use primitive database management systems and outdated computer technology.
- Be professionally involved in the industry and related trade associations, such as ASIS International (formerly the American Society for Industrial Security) and National Association Professional Background Screeners. Involvement allows the vendor to keep abreast of changing laws and new technology.

The vendor selected should be familiar with and compliant to current laws and regulations, especially the Fair Credit Reporting Act.

Summary

Effective pre-employment screening and background investigation practices are an essential component of a healthy and productive organization. It is widely accepted that an organization that invests in the proper screening of applicants will enjoy less turnover, greater productivity, and fewer employee problems than those that do not.

Eugene F. Ferraro

REPORT WRITING FOR SUCCESSFUL PROSECUTION

A well-written report can mean the difference between a successful prosecution and a civil liability lawsuit for false arrest.

A good report contains the five Ws and one H (who, what, when, where, why, and how), but those basic elements are broader than one might think. The objectivity of the report is also a key element. By leaving out relevant information or including emotionally loaded words or opinions, security practitioners can destroy the chances of successfully prosecuting what would otherwise be a good case.

Many personnel at the guard level have challenges when it comes to proper report writing. The task thus falls to security supervisors, managers, and executives to train front-line officers in report-writing skills. In addition, professional security practitioners are often charged with reviewing subordinates' reports. They then must have the report writers fill in missing information in incomplete reports and/or correcting errors.

The following information provides useful guidelines for report preparation. Although some examples given below pertain to retail businesses, the principles of good report writing apply to all areas of security.

The Building Blocks

Every report is built on the foundation of the five Ws and one H. In a good report, these categories include more than just the obvious.

The first element of the complaint to address is who the complaining party is, as well as the identity of the victim, the suspect, the witnesses, and any involved law enforcement personnel. In the case of a retail operation, these parties are not always so clear as they may seem.

The store security officer(s) who make the apprehension must be named, of course, and so should the suspect(s). And while the complainant is often the store itself, the victim can be other than the store. Large stores, for example, often contain small separate stores, such as jewelry concessions or optical shops. These stores-within-a-store can appear to be owned by the department store but in reality are owned and operated by a totally separate company. Ownership must be clearly spelled out in the report, or the case may not be successfully prosecuted.

Identifying information about persons involved should include home and work addresses, including corporate contact information, telephone numbers, e-mail addresses, physical descriptions, and occupations.

The report should describe not only what was stolen, but also what evidence was found. An explanation should be included of what was done with the evidence and what individual(s) or police agency or agencies responded to the scene. It is also important to clarify what agency has jurisdiction and to specify what section or officer(s) will follow up. The contact information for the prosecutor's office or prosecutor assigned to the case should also be listed. In addition, the report should spell out what is expected of the security officer who made the apprehension, including testimony, submission of written reports, and so forth.

The time frame is also important information. The report should describe when the incident occurred. If known, information about when the suspects arrived, how long they stayed, and when they left should also be included.

Data regarding the time frame of the police response should also be included. Specify when the law enforcement officer(s) arrived and when they had contact with the security officers, the witnesses, or other parties to take their statements.

Location must also be accurately addressed in the report. Aside from where the incident occurred specifically, the locations and activities of the loss prevention team should also be recorded. In addition, where the witnesses and suspects were interviewed is important. Where the evidence was collected, marked, and stored is another aspect of the investigation that should be included in the report, as is the location where the police questioned and arrested the suspect.

How the offense was committed is also important information. It is critical to identify whether the crime was committed by an organized theft ring with several players, each of whom had a specific role, or whether the crime was carried out by a professional, such as a shoplifter who wore a booster coat or carried a booster bag. If a juvenile was the actor, whether working alone or with friends, that fact should also be noted. Answering these questions helps establish a pattern both within the business and within the area.

How the security officer identified the suspect, the merchandise and the witnesses should also be noted.

The "why," or the motive for the incident, may be the most difficult foundation question to answer in a report. The security staff may never discover the reason behind a crime. Nevertheless, prosecutors and jurors like to have a motive because it helps them understand the crime.

Should a suspect offer a reason—"My friends dared me" or "It was stupid, just a spur-of-the-moment thing," or even "I heard this store was an 'easy steal'"—then the officer should include it in the report. But if a motive cannot be established, the report writer must never make one

up for the sake of writing a "complete" report. Fabricating information only weakens a case; it doesn't strengthen it.

Objective Reporting

Including answers to the building-block questions helps ensure that there are no gaps or missing pieces of information. When security supervisors review guards' reports, they want to find completeness as well as correct grammar and spelling.

A report that states "The dude stole and I caught him" is not going to lead to a successful prosecution. The reader should be able to find answers to all the foundation questions within the report. However, security managers must work with guards to ensure that they understand that brevity is also desirable. The reader should never have to wade through unimportant details in order to find pertinent information.

In reviewing reports, supervisors also need to make sure that guards have written them objectively. Accuracy also means that the report is free of opinions, guesses and other non-factual information.

Objectivity includes avoiding the use of emotionally charged words in favor of words with a neutral connotation. A security officer would not be correct to say, for example, "I saw this lowlife come into the store." Rather, the report should include the information that led the officer to draw the conclusion that the person was not a pillar of society without using any derogatory or slang terms: "When the man entered the store, I saw that his clothing was torn and dirty and his hands and face were streaked with dirt."

By painting a picture of the incident for the reader, the report has a greater impact than when using negative, subjective language.

In the words of *Dragnet* star Jack Webb, incident reports should include "just the facts"—but all the facts should be included.

Liz Martínez

SECURITY GROUP SERVICES

Security Group services are always customer-centered. The customer is the company that employees the Security Group, which is managed by the Chief Security Officer (CSO).

Security Group services are marked by three characteristics:

- Productivity generally is difficult to measure because the results of service operations are intangible. Intangible results are difficult to evaluate because they cannot be held, weighed, or measured.
- Quality standards are difficult to establish and to evaluate. No one knows for certain the amount of loss that was avoided because the presence of a security officer deterred a criminal act or because the CSO implemented a procedure for controlling access to the company's computer center.
- Company employees have varying types and degrees of contact with the Security Group but they are not always present when Group services are actually delivered such as patrolling during a midnight shift or operating a security console behind locked doors.

The Chief Security Officer

A good-size security company will employ a person to manage loss preventing activities. That person is generally called the Chief Security Officer and the loss preventing activities are the output of the company's Security Group. The effectiveness of the Security Group relies on the competence of the CSO in two dimensions:

- Technical Competence. The CSO must have a basic understanding of the processes and technologies that drive the company's internal systems. Technical competence is usually obtained through training and experience.
- Behavioral Competence. The CSO works through others, both in the Security Group and in the company at large. A mix of leadership, communication, and interpersonal skills is required.

The Security Group is expected to deliver services that are:

- Suited to the company's core processes and functions.
- Delivered with consistent quality.
- Provided at a reasonable cost.

The CSO plays the major role in ensuring that security services meet these requirements. In so doing, the CSO establishes work objectives that are consistent with the operational capabilities of the Security Group and consistent with company goals.

Quality and output are intertwined factors that face the CSO. Poor quality services cannot meet output demands and unrealistically high demands for output lowers the quality of services. Bringing the two factors into alignment at an acceptable level at a reasonable cost is the challenge.

John J. Fay

Sources

Dilworth, J. 1986. *Production and Operations Management: Manufacturing and Nonmanufacturing*. New York: Random House.

Heyel, C. 1982. *Encyclopedia of Management, 3rd Edition*. New York: Van Nostrand Reinhold.

SECURITY OFFICER TURNOVER

Given the extremely high rate of reported security officer turnover, estimated at 100 to 400 percent, it is imperative that security professionals have a thorough understanding of the factors that cause turnover. And since the costs associated with turnover are also extremely high, it's equally incumbent upon managers to understand the strategies to counter turnover.

Of course, organizations must first know their historical turnover numbers and rates. Then current surveys, intertwined with proven retention strategies, will better enhance organizational success and profitability.

Documenting historical retention/ turnover performance establishes a benchmark to gauge and predict future performance. The security executive can then set goals to measure the effects of any attempted turnover remedies. Still, turnover rates must be continually recorded and monitored to ensure that high retention remains a goal of the organization.

Once turnover rates have been identified, managers should conduct a written, anonymous survey to gather officer opinions on issues that matter most to them such as what they believe contributes to their retention, and conversely, their voluntary separation. Since the variables that contribute to turnover have direct and negative organizational consequences, the exact identification, extent, analysis, and understanding of any issues can result in an initial well-founded starting place to develop retention strategies as well as to measure the effectiveness of solutions.

Survey results can then combine with retention strategies while measuring success or failure in future surveys.

Turnover Costs

The costs of employee turnover are measured in both financial and operational terms. When an employee resigns, is involuntarily terminated, or retires, there is a direct and negative affect to the bottom line as well as adverse organizational performance consequences.

Financial estimates vary by industry and compensation levels, but reports of turnover costs generally range from 25 to 200 percent of the employee's annual salary. For example, a 30 percent estimate for an employee who earns $22,000 a year would result in $6,600 turnover cost. Turnover costs encompass advertising, interviewing time, background checks, hiring, new employee processing and training. Furthermore, there is a related cost of covering terminated employees' hours—frequently at an overtime rate. There is also the loss of employee productivity to consider as a newly-hired officer simply is not as knowledgeable and therefore not as productive as an experienced worker.

Turnover Factors

The effects of turnover are not only felt on the bottom line, but operationally as well. According to Michael Goodboe, Ed.D., CPP, a vice president of training for the Wackenhut Training Institute, "high turnover is inherently dangerous in an industry charged with the security and safety. Clearly, when employees don't stay long enough to become proficient at the job, overall performance suffers." Dr. Goodboe also pointed out that many security personnel earn less than the federal poverty level, and that "paying low wages that lead to high turnover is penny wise, pound foolish." Stated another way, high employee retention equates to greater customer satisfaction, contented employees, and satisfied customers and employers.

There are numerous reasons to explain why employees opt to voluntarily terminate their employment. The following is a self-explanatory list of many causal factors that influence employees to resign.

- Competition
- Lack of recognition or reward
- Lack of teamwork
- Incompatible management style
- Quality of life issues
- Stress
- Pay versus effort
- Poor recruiting
- Lack of orientation
- Lack of training
- Ineffective supervision
- Lack of leadership
- Boredom
- Lack of job security
- No opportunities for advancement
- Not enough hours
- Lack of benefits
- Lack of standards
- Lack of respect
- Lack of feedback
- Personal reasons

There also are overarching causes such as the local economy, industry trends, organizational characteristics, company performance, company culture, communications, and job performance.

There are as many, if not more, retention strategies as there are factors that cause an employee to resign.

- Recognize and praise—little things mean a lot.
- Help officers grow—encourage professional growth.
- Ask for ideas—they are in the best position to sometimes know what works best, and they need to know employers are listening.
- Reward ideas—demonstrate how valuable the employee's ideas are.
- Improve skills—invest in their future.
- Invest—in screening profiles to select better employees.
- Get officers as involved with the company—the better they understand, the more they can offer.

F. Leigh Branham, author of "Keeping the People Who Keep You in Business" and "Six Truths about Employee Turnover," offers strategies with a twist.

Twelve Ways to Keep Good Employees

1. Don't always hire the best, but hire the "best fit."
2. Have the insight to realize that, no matter what the job, not just anyone can do it well.
3. Focus on matching a person's strengths to the right challenge and the right role, not on improving weaknesses to the point that every employee is well-rounded.
4. Build a culture of trust by giving people free reign to achieve outcomes in their own way, instead of insisting they do things the way you would do them.
5. Manage different people differently. Know that not all people have the same motivations.
6. See yourself as serving your people, and not the other way around.
7. Be tolerant of diversity, but intolerant of nonperformance.
8. Surround yourself with the talented people and don't feel threatened by them.
9. Care about your people and take a personal interest in what is going on in their lives.
10. Let your people move on to a growth assignment outside the team instead of blocking the move.
11. Give feedback, praise, and recognition on the spot.
12. Know when to confront nonperformance and redesign the job so that it fits the individual, reassign the person to a better-fitting job, or terminate when necessary.

Security should hire for a culture fit—spend more time in the selection process. Provide better new employee orientation and on-going training—set the stage and maintain the focus. Ensure a competitive salary and benefits package by reviewing salaries and benefits to ensure market competitiveness. Evaluate the effectiveness of supervisors and managers—remember the saying that people do not quit companies, they quit their bosses.

In this regard, supervisors and managers must:

- Set clear expectations.
- Train and develop employees.
- Flex their management style to the situation and the needs of each officer.
- Provide positive and constructive feedback.
- Evaluate and document performance.
- Resolve conflict situations productively.
- Communicate effectively and proactively.
- Intervene and resolve performance issues before they get out of hand.
- Treat all officers fairly, objectively, and humanely.
- Relate to a diverse workforce.
- Weed out non-performers who are demotivating to productive employees.
- Sell and re-sell the company.
- Conduct employee opinion surveys and exit interviews, which can be enlightening.
- Beef up the communication efforts—people assume the worst and when there is no communication employees think the worst.
- Offer soft benefits and pass out psychological paychecks while taking the time to determine what is really important to each officer.

Compensation

A review of various studies and reports concludes that the top reason for early termination versus long-term employment is unsatisfactory compensation. However, other proven causal factors include recognition, poor supervision, lack of growth opportunities, and poor communication. Here are some ways to address these compensation concerns.

Ensure competitive wages and benefits by reviewing hourly rates and benefits to make certain of the organization's market competitiveness for quality employees. Conduct annual market analyses of similar companies with similar or identical security positions and, when you can, make necessary adjustments in pay and benefits.

Offer soft benefits and pass out psychological paychecks by determining what's really important to each employee. Supervisors know their officer better than the manager. They should take advantage of this knowledge in a positive manner to appropriately reward the employee. This suggestion could mean many different things to many different supervisors and officers, but the concept is simple and may not "cost" anything.

Recognize and praise—little but important things mean a lot. Reward ideas by demonstrating how valuable employees' ideas are. Setup or continue an Officer of the Month/ Year program. Recognize staff by promoting their accomplishments throughout the organization-newsletter, special announcements, and prominent photographic display of the organization's top performers. Praise in public; criticize in private.

Conclusion

Security operations cannot continue forever with high turnover rates. Failure to address the causes of high turnover will affect the operational efficiency and eventually limit the financial well-being of the security function. So it's essential that security professionals with responsibility to manage a security staff have an extensive understanding of the factors that cause turnover as well as the strategies to remedy employee turnover. Managers must be aware of their historical turnover rates while prepared to survey employees to identify issues that are contributing to high turnover. Combining survey-acquired insight and proven industry retention strategies can significantly contribute to low turnover rates and greater organizational efficiency, viability, and a competitive edge.

Steven W. McNally

SELECTING THE SECURITY ADMINISTRATOR

Making the best choice among candidates for the position of security administrator can be a difficult and critical step in providing for the protection of an organization's assets. The selection process should begin with an understanding of what constitutes the profile of a good candidate.

Examining the Main Qualifiers

There are four main areas of consideration when selecting a security administrator:

- Organizational fit
- Skills and knowledge
- Education
- Experience

Although organizational fit is obviously important, it cannot be applied as a disqualifier based on subjective considerations, such as the applicant's race, gender, or sexual preferences. Organizational fit is an appropriate selection factor; for example, when the applicant is expected to perform within a highly structured work environment where extremely inflexible lines of authority and responsibility prevail. Not every applicant will be able to survive under those conditions. Making the right selection has consequences both to the efficiency of the organization and to the needs of the applicant.

Generally recognized also as standard measurements of an applicant are skills, knowledge, and abilities. Education and experience, which are facets of these standards, can be fairly easily determined by verification of the applicant's academic and work credentials. Technical skills and knowledge, which tend to be objective and precision-oriented, can be measured through performance and written examinations, but the so-called "soft" or managerial abilities are somewhat elusive to precise assessment. Very often, the evaluation of these elements is made through the traditional process of applicant interviewing.

The Resume and the Application

Information communicated to the organization in the resume and the application form is essentially one-sided and flows in one direction. These evaluation devices are also one-dimensional because they portray the applicant abstractly. Although they often serve as discussion point reminders during interview of the applicant, their real value may lie in using them during the background investigation process to verify the applicant's representations with respect to education, training, certifications, licenses, professional affiliations, publications, prior employment, and work experience. A candidate's resume is designed to illustrate and promote their best attributes.

A job application, properly designed and administered, is useful to help evaluate the whole professional. A resume would not be as detailed in regard to a number of choice variables such as: dates of employment, salary at each company/position, and more specific information.

Interview Preparation

A good applicant interviewer will bring to the interview session a blend of objective and intuitive judgment. Objectivity will ensure fairness, consistency, and similar positive outcomes that will benefit both the employer and the candidate. Intuitiveness can allow insights and perceptions that go beneath the surface of the image presented by the candidate during the relatively short "sizing up" period afforded by the interview. The seasoned interviewer will be sensitive to "red flags" that may signal problems known to the interviewer through past work experiences, and the really skilled interviewer will use behavior-provoking questions to elicit the nonverbal and verbal indicators of internal anxiety that may be associated with deception.

Preparation for the interview can begin with a checklist that identifies factors for facilitating an analysis of the candidate's nonverbal behaviors. Such a checklist might be as follows:

- Ensure that the interview room will be private.

Arrange the interview room so that the space between the interviewer and the candidate will not be blocked by a desk, table, or other objects that might interfere with face-to-face communications.

For example:

- Ensure that the chairs of the interviewer and candidate are of the same height and provide equivalent comfort.
- Provide the interviewee with a chair that is not so relaxing as to induce slouching or

leaning, such as placing the chair next to a table.
- Position the chairs about 3 to 4 feet apart.

By developing a package of pre-assembled notes, the interviewer will prepare questions to be asked, a checklist for recording answers, important points to be emphasized, and materials that were submitted by the candidate such as the resume and application. In the interviewer's package there may also be a written agenda for providing structure and direction of the interview.

A Structured Interview

The agenda is likely to reflect a step-by-step progression that begins with a greeting, comfortable small talk, an explanation of the organization and the department and their respective missions, and the nature of the position to be filled.

After the preliminaries are out of the way, the interviewer may move to a series of questions that probe the specifics of the candidate's qualifications. The questions will be job related, that is, they will relate to the skills, knowledge, and abilities that the job incumbent must exercise in order to be effective in the job.

In addition to taking notice of the candidate's answers with respect to the demands of the job, the interviewer will be evaluating the candidate's personality. If one accepts the notion that the principal objective of the candidate will be to persuade the interviewer that the candidate is the best person for the job, the candidate's ability to persuade will be a dimension worth observing closely. Is persuasive ability a job-related skill for a security administrator? You bet it is. Other dimensions of the candidate's personality will bear watching as well, such as poise under fire, quick thinking, and verbal articulation.

Modern security management has evolved from an ancillary necessity to a universally recognized business profession. The profession is constantly undergoing change, with more and more requirements being placed on security administrators. The ordinary definition of a generalist security administrator now includes many organizational skills such as budgeting, data processing, and business forecasting, which until recently were considered specialties outside of the security realm. The process of selecting a security administrator must take into account the changing nature of the job and include an objective and detailed examination of the candidate's skills, knowledge, and abilities as they relate to the employer's expectations.

Bronson Steve Bias

SUBSTANCE ABUSE IN THE WORKPLACE

The pervasiveness of substance abuse in America and its impact on society should not be underestimated. According to the United States Drug Enforcement Agency (DEA) the international illicit drug trade is a $300 billion industry, which knows no national borders, deals almost exclusively in cash, and increasingly enforces its policies with violence. Ever more, illicit drug use is entering the workplace, with an estimated 75 percent of all illicit drug use in America by those with jobs. According to the National Household Survey on Drug Abuse (1998) rates of drug use remain highest among persons aged 16 to 25—coincidentally, the age group entering the work force most rapidly.

In 1990 the National Institute on Drug Abuse (NIDA) estimated that 23.8 percent of all full-time working males in the United States had used an illegal drug at least once in the 60 days prior to their polling. More recently, the National Institutes of Health reported that alcohol and drug abuse cost the economy $246 billion in 1992. Drug use costs organizations, not only monetarily, but also by decreasing productivity and morale, increasing turnover and absenteeism, increasing the likelihood of workplace accidents, increasing insurance costs, and by increasing consumption of unnecessary benefits while decreasing profitability. Sadly, workplace substance abuse robs organizations of talent, vitality, and enthusiasm and instead, destroys teamwork and cooperation. Workplace substance abuse is indeed a billion dollar competitor.

People do not simply check their substance abuse problems at the door when they enter the workplace. Employees caught up in drug abuse tend to be absent from the job up to 16 times more often, claim three times as many sickness benefits, and file five times as many workers' compensation claims as non-abusers. Abusers are also more likely to be laid-off or fired. Drug abuse also breeds dysfunctional relationships as is often evident in their relationships with managers and coworkers. They tend to withdraw from friends and be more secretive, spending less time at home and work. For the employer, they become less productive and frequently represent the 20 percent who consume 80 percent of management's time.

Illicit drug use in the workplace is best described as a progressive, debilitating disease, which if left unaddressed by supervisors and managers can have severe detrimental effects in the workplace. No one ever aspires to be a drug addict or chemically dependant. Drug abuse is the use of a drug for something other than its intended medical or social purpose. Abuse results in an impaired physical, mental, and emotional sense of well-being. Abuse can often easily lead to addiction and/or chemical dependency. Mental illness also increases the risk for substance abuse and addiction. According to epidemiological studies, as many as 6 in 10 people who abuse drugs and alcohol also suffer from mental illnesses.

Abuse also can create personal, familial, and financial problems beyond the abuser's control. Involvement with drugs usually begins with experimentation, and typically involves introduction to the drug by a friend, co-worker, or family member. If the drug produces an enjoyable or desirable effect, experimentation most often leads to a pattern of irregular use, usually amidst social settings. However, if the progression is uninterrupted, the user begins to select and develop relationships with friends and co-workers who share the same interest with the drug(s) as they. As these relationships solidify, former friends and co-workers are increasingly shut out. The user's appearance, behavior, interests, and relationships all begin to change, and it is not uncommon for the user to withdraw from their social circles entirely. Paranoia, persistent suspicion, and the invariable desire to keep their drug use a secret are all aggravating factors in the progression of social isolation.

The user's relationship with the drug also changes, and they become protective of it. It is not uncommon for the user to defend the drug's benefits, value to society, and the constitutional right to use it. They frequently think about it, study it, and talk about it whenever they have an opportunity. They engage in rituals while preparing it and consuming it such as, "two cubes of ice, not four...fill it to here, not there...hold it in your lungs longer and let it out slower...I always do it like this." Other things change too. The user's on-the-job performance deteriorates in many ways. They develop attendance problems usually with recognizable patterns, such as constantly being absent on a Friday or Monday in an attempt to recover from their drug use over the weekend. They appear less focused and begin to have more personal problems. They use drugs more frequently and irresponsibly. Drinking and driving, smoking marijuana or being impaired while hunting, or while handling firearms, or consuming drugs in public places with people they don't even know are behaviors typical of the seasoned substance abuser.

Ultimately, they begin to even use drugs while on the job. At first their use is discrete, but then it becomes quite brazen. In fact, some of the excitement is seeing how bold and flagrant the consumption at work can become, while remaining undetected by managers and supervisors. Employee abusers will drink in the employee parking lot during lunch and breaks, and smoke marijuana in restrooms and locker rooms. They will consume cocaine or speed at their desks or workstations, and will use drugs in company-owned vehicles or while out of town on business. Given the opportunity, they may even use drugs with the organization's customers and vendors. They will keep drugs in their desks, lockers, and toolboxes. They will use the company mailroom or shipping department to distribute drugs, and use inter-office mail, company pouches, and over-night delivery services to move and receive drugs. They'll hide drugs in safes, furniture, trash containers, hazardous material containers, beverage containers, lunch boxes, briefcases, purses, shoes, coats, raw materials, and finished goods. Employee drug abusers are notorious for being resourceful, cunning, and deceitful.

Dealers will also secretly sell right in front of non-abusers, supervisors, and managers. In some instances the trafficking of drugs and contraband make it impossible to understand how any real work is ever accomplished. Dealers tend to socialize more than others and are constantly networking while feverishly trying to avoid detection. They are frequently not where they belong or absent while on the job. They tend not to make trouble and generally avoid interaction with management whenever possible. When accused of misconduct, they become belligerent and quickly anger.

They tend to like to support employee causes and enjoy creating strife between management and labor. Employee drug dealers resist team building, pursue secret agendas, and resent authority.

So why do employees bring drugs into the workplace? For the drug abuser, the workplace abounds with opportunity unlike other settings and there are several reasons why. First, the element of *better quality*; in most cases users would have to go to the source to obtain drugs in better quality than typically found in the workplace. Workplace dealers want repeat customers and they recognize high quality drugs keeps the users coming back for more. Second, *fairer quantity*; illegal drugs are expensive. Often sold in quantities as small as a 1/4 gram, accuracy in weight is important to the user/buyer. Again, workplace dealers recognize the importance of repeat business and resultantly tend not only to sell high quality drugs to their co-workers, but in fair and accurate quantities as well. Third, *low risk*; unfortunately the perception by many employee abusers and dealers is that the workplace is a safe place to use and sell drugs largely in part because they perceive supervisors and managers as unable to detect or stop them. Rarely do they see a drug abuse issue addressed or even talked about. In many instances the security policies and practices of an employer that are intended to protect assets and people, also protect the abusers and dealers. Walls, fences, and security doors not only keep out unwanted outsiders but also protect employees from the peering eyes of management and law enforcement. Fourth, *high return of investment*; that is employees who choose to sell drugs at work often do it as a means to obtain drugs for themselves. Others do it for profit. Lastly, the *ability to buy and sell on credit*; in the workplace it is known as a *front*. The drugs are sold to the employee user under the agreement that they will be paid for later, typically resulting in a specified payday. For this service to be employed, dealers generally charge a small premium, which commonly takes the form of keeping a small amount of the drug exchanged. This practice is commonly referred to as *pinching*. However, abusers win too because fronting allows them to obtain and use drugs even when they don't have the cash to buy them.

Once drug abusers have exhausted their discretionary income, they have no other choice but to purchase their drugs on credit. However, once their credit lines are exhausted, they generally are obliged to either deal drugs or steal. If they become dealers, they will most often sell to their co-workers at work. If they choose to steal, their principal victim will be their employer. Drug abuse related employee theft often begins with stealing food from co-workers. It eventually leads to the theft of petty cash, cash receipts, office equipment, and the personal valuables of co-workers. Left unchecked, the drug abuser will eventually steal to the extent the system will allow. The stolen goods may range from scrap, raw materials, and finished goods and even intellectual property. To the desperate abuser, nothing and no one is sacred.

Employee drug abusers also steal from customers and vendors. Shorting a shipment to an important customer, while keeping and selling the balance is unfortunately one of but many scenarios. They may accept kickbacks for miscounting, allowing overages, double shipping, approving improper or unauthorized credits, or diverting a vendor's delivery. The impact on the employer can be devastating. Business relationships may be destroyed and, as a result, valuable vendors may withhold service or necessary materials. Customers may cancel contracts, refuse payment, or take legal action. Unfortunately, the employer's problems don't end here.

In addition, productivity and profitability are also affected by drug use. Drug abusers are more likely to have accidents and get injured. They file more health claims and consume more than their share of the benefits provided them. More illnesses and injuries yield higher insurance costs. The resulting absence of the injured or sick drug abuser may result in lower productivity for the organization hence affecting the organization's bottom line. Their absence is disruptive and can be costly. Furthermore, it may necessitate recruiting, hiring, and training replacements. While real claims cost real money, fraudulent claims cost money as well. Substance abusers are also more prone to file false claims and feign on-the-job injuries. As the abuser's burden grows and their performance begins to slip, some form of progressive discipline begins. Missed deadlines and careless mistakes are rarely terminable offenses. However, repeat offenders are not as readily forgiven and are usually punished. With each subsequent transgression the punishment is enhanced.

The role of the employer has never been more important as organizations have come to accept that substance abuse is a workplace problem that must not be overlooked. The foundation of all doctrine and practices in the workplace rests upon policy. For the creation of a drug free workplace, a policy is absolutely necessary. The policy must be practical, functional, and enforceable. Additionally, the policy must be written, effectively communicated, and equitably enforced. An effective policy should:

- Make a clear statement of the company's objective to create a drug-free workplace, and why a drug-free workplace is important to all employees.
- Explain why substance abuse (including alcohol use) at work or on the job is unacceptable.
- Give a clear definition of what constitutes an infraction of the policy and describe the consequences.
- Explain that drug problems and abuse are treatable and spell out the availability of treatment and rehabilitation options.
- Answer any questions that might be asked about drug abuse, the policy, or policy enforcement that might be unique to the organization or the industry.

Once the policy has been established, it is the role of supervisors and managers to communicate and enforce that policy. One of the most significant deterrents against employee drug abuse that supervisors and managers have is communicating their familiarity with the policy and their willingness to enforce it. In doing so, management clearly defines behavioral and performance boundaries. Expectations of employees can clearly be defined and the consequences of not meeting those expectations can be explained. More than ferreting out drug abuse and employee drug abusers, management must also monitor performance. Supervisors and managers are not expected to catch employees using and selling drugs. Rather, they are expected to evaluate employee performance and be able to take remedial action when performance is not adequate or is substandard. Management that is able to do this avoids the destructive effects of enabling and codependent relationships. It creates a healthier and more productive work environment and forces employees to take accountability for their actions.

Workplace substance abuse is an issue all employers need to address. Moreover, it is a problem that can be successfully prevented if supervisors and managers are willing to put forth the effort required. Taking steps to raise awareness among employees about the impact of substance use on workplace performance, and offering the appropriate remedial resources and/or assistance to employees in need, will not only improve worker safety and health, but also increase workplace productivity and overall market competitiveness.

Eugene F. Ferraro and Amy L. Slettedahl

Sources

"National Household Survey on Drug Abuse." 1998. *U.S. Department of Health and Human Services.*

"The Economic Costs of Alcohol and Drug Abuse in the United States." 1992. *National Institute on Alcoholism and Alcohol Abuse.*

VIOLENCE RISK ASSESSMENT

Violence risk assessment is a behavioral assessment process for determining the potential violence risk posed by an individual or defined group of individuals to a particular target or targeted population. It is a process that can be used on a variety of violence related problems including workplace violence, school violence, domestic violence, correctional system violence, domestic terrorism, and international terrorism. The value of violence risk assessment, like all forms of risk assessment, is that by sorting out those that make threats or act in ways that raise concern, from those that actually pose an immediate risk of significant harm, it allows appropriate allocation of resources (time, budget, material, and personnel) to those situations that pose the greatest risk to the target(s) of aggression, thereby increasing safety and minimizing disruption.

This process is different from behavioral investigative analysis (profiling). Behavioral investigative analysis was developed to identify an unknown subject's behavioral and personal characteristics by behavioral analysis of physical evidence found at particular types of crime scenes (e.g., arson, bombings, serial killings, rapes, etc.). This methodology was designed to aid in the elimination of possible suspects from an investigation, thereby narrowing the investigation to a more concentrated group of suspects. Violence risk assessment is used to predict, with a substantial level of accuracy, whether a known individual or defined group of individuals may pose a significant risk of violence to a particular target or target population. The violence risk assessment is an information-driven process that requires comprehensive information about the aggressor's past behavior across a wide range of areas and an insight into the aggressor's current personal perspectives, emotions, stress levels, and environmental factors.

The range of historical information of interest includes: medical and mental health history, criminal history, history of violence or conflict, family history, history of substance use and abuse; history of interest, training, possession, and use of weapons; relationship history, employment history, educational history, hobbies, and history of the aggressor's interest in, connection to, or relationship with the target or target population.

This information can be obtained from public records, employment records, law enforcement records, medical providers, family members, friends, co-workers, neighbors, and the aggressor themselves.

After the information is gathered it can be most effectively assessed by first organizing a chronology of the aggressor's life. This chronology will aid analysis of cause and effect relationships between life events and the choices of behavior the aggressor has made to those events. Once a thorough analysis is done of the intertwining life events and behavioral choices that were made, a working hypothesis can be developed concerning the range of behaviors most likely to be chosen by the aggressor when stimulated by specific future events. The guiding principle which allows this process of behavioral assessment to work is expressed in the widely accepted statement made in a vast range of psychological research that "the best predictor of future behavior is past behavior." Though the original author of this statement is unknown, this widely accepted concept is based on both research and reality. Human beings have a tendency to act in a way similar to past behavioral choices in circumstances that they perceive to be similar, because the past behavior choice allowed them to survive and provided a reasonably acceptable outcome. That is why we feel "comfortable" doing things we have done before and less comfortable doing new things. That is also why all humans develop habits. Habits develop to simplify life by providing repeated safe and effective outcomes. Thus, once established, habits, both good and bad ones, are hard to break. This same genetically reinforced mechanism allows assessors, that possess a large quantity of behavioral data about an aggressor, to predict with accuracy, substantially above chance, what an aggressor may do when presented with certain life events, both those that are uncontrolled by the assessor and those that are.

Another vector to look at in this data is the "control vector." All violence by human beings, against other human beings, is driven by the desire to establish or re-establish the perception of control. It does not matter if we are talking about a domestic abuser, a stalker, an armed robber, a workplace aggressor, a school shooter, a serial killer, or a terrorist. All of these aggressors act out against others based on their perceived need to control the people or re-establish control over the people in the situation. Even suicides are a form of proof that the person may not be able to control the circumstances of their lives, but they can re-establish control by choosing when to end it. So, the assessor might ask:

- How desperate is this aggressor to establish control?
- What have they done to establish control in the past?
- What might they be willing to do now?

The assessment gleaned from the hypothesis developed around the answers to these questions might reveal the velocity of the situation, the methodology the aggressor might use, and the precise target that they may act against. These answers may not be as obvious as previously thought. For example, an aggressor is stalking a former love interest. He or she is communicating, "If I can't have you, no one can have you." It seems fairly obvious on the surface that the former love interest would be the target. But does the aggressor want to control the victim or destroy the victim? What is the assessment if the aggressor has a history of attacking people or objects precious to the victim or prior victims and that has caused the victim to relent and reunite with the aggressor; now what might the assessment be?

The second method that can be used to increase the accuracy of a violence risk assessment is to take the developed behavioral information and apply a validated violence risk assessment tool or instrument to the data. This type of tool or instrument, such as the Spousal Assault Risk Assessment Guide (SARA), the HCR-20 version 2, the Assessment/Response Grids, the Association of Threat Assessment Professionals (ATAP) Risk Assessment Guide Elements for Violence (RAGE-V), and Violence Risk Appraisal Guide (VRAG), provides a method to gain an objective understanding of the potential for violence by mapping the behavior of the aggressor in the immediate case against a tool or instrument that has been tested against a wide sample of similar individuals and found to provide accurate assessments with a significant degree of accuracy above chance. Over a large sampling of assessments, the accuracy rate found using best process, as described here, of comprehensive data collection and a tool or instrument, hovers around 85 percent depending on the study and the appropriateness of the tool or instrument used for the individual or population being tested.

It is important to understand that even with effective and comprehensive data collection, development of an accurate chronology, and the use of a valid assessment tool or instrument, the accuracy of the violence risk prediction will have a short time span and its ongoing accuracy will be dependent upon updated information and continuous assessment of that information. Circumstances change, people's perceptions change with them, and the assessment needs to evolve with the development of new events over time. Consequently, the "shelf life" of a violence risk assessment can be as short as a few days or, at most, as long as several months, without seeking new behavioral data and assessing what, if any, changes need to be made, given the new information.

James S. Cawood

WORKING DOGS

History

Homo sapiens started domesticating dogs about 130,000 years ago, first by eating them, then by using them to help hunt for bigger food animals. Dogs are the only domesticated working animal still used by humans. Working dogs, as opposed to pets, are professionals in many specialties. Working dogs were used by the Egyptians to help build pyramids. The Romans used large armor-wearing Mollosian Hounds, the larger cousin to the Rottweiler, to break the enemy's ranks during battle. The Germans were the first to train modern police and military working dogs; the Swiss trained search and rescue dogs; the British were first to develop the explosive detection dog, which was later adopted by the U.S. Armed Forces. Today, in many countries, thousands of dogs are doing specialty work for organizations in law enforcement, national defense, corporate security, search and rescue, and public health.

Working Dog Specialties

Working dogs fall into certain categories according to the major functions they perform. The categories overlap in many cases, meaning that a single dog can be used in more than one venue; for example, a dog used by airport security to detect explosives in baggage can do the same for law enforcement at a bomb scene or for the military in detecting land mines. The major categories and subcategories are:

Law Enforcement

- Detecting explosives
- Detecting drugs
- Detecting accelerants in debris
- Finding human remains
- Tracking criminals on foot
- Conducting routine patrol
- Searching and rescuing in major emergencies
- Defending against attack
- Protecting public figures

Security

- Protecting employees, property, and premises
- Searching premises during a bomb threat
- Detecting drugs on the premises
- Detecting weapons on the premises
- Detecting explosives, incendiaries, and biological agents such as those sent though the mail or by courier
- Deterring intrusion and criminal attempts

- Protecting executives
- Patrolling a perimeter fence line, parking lot or garage, and exterior restricted areas
- Searching for people in buildings during the hours of darkness such as criminals that hide inside a retail store just before closing
- Detecting odors that might indicate hazards such as incipient fire, gas leak, and spillage of chemicals

Military

- Detecting explosives such as land mines
- Detecting drugs such as those used or distributed
- Reconnoitering and scouting
- Tracking the enemy on foot
- Performing ambush patrol
- Detecting and deterring on-foot enemy attack

Search and Rescue

- Tracking humans and animals in a variety of terrains and environments
- Searching for victims, both dead and alive
- Searching for missing persons
- Searching for hazardous materials

Public Health Assistance

- Guiding the blind and partially blind
- Aiding physicians in detecting the indications of some medical conditions such as tumors, diabetes, and cancer

Working Dog Training

A dog being considered for work must first undergo testing that is designed to reveal if the dog is trainable, and if so, the type of work the dog is best suited for. Other factors are considered as well: breed, gender, age, health, and adaptability to the environment such as working nearby people, working in unsafe conditions, working in extreme temperatures, working where odors might be distracting such as a chemical factor.

Dogs have personalities. Dog evaluators and trainers understand this. It does not take very long for a dog to be identified as suitable or non-suitable. And like other high-order mammals, dogs vary in intelligence, enthusiasm, industriousness, and controllability.

Depending on the work the dog is to perform, training will run between 6 and 16 weeks, or more if necessary. Again, depending on the nature of the work, a dog will undergo refresher training. In all cases, dogs are trained by professionals. Typically, the training is done by a vendor; for example, a company that specializes in breeding/selecting and training dogs for work-related purposes. When a dog is ready, it can be sold or leased. In other instances, the agency that makes use of the dog will develop the dog from start to end. This tends to be the case with police departments that are large and have the necessary resources.

Certification

Field training usually follows on-site training. When the handler is confident the dog can perform the intended function, "certification" is issued. Certification means that the "team" is qualified to go on the job. In some cases, the certification is issued by an independent third party such as an accrediting agency. The team is tested annually and if the test is passed, the team is re-certified. The certification automatically ends when the team is broken up such as transfer of the handler to another dog or to another job.

The Dog Handler

Dogs are able to carry out their work to the extent that the dog handler is competent. A handler may be incompetent when he/she has not been trained, is inexperienced, lacks the ability to "bond" with the dog, or does not have and cannot develop skill sets essential to dog handling. Handlers usually spend 10 to 16 weeks in training. A good handler will be able to see and interpret the dog's body language and above all else, be patient.

Dog handlers have a career path. The typical progression is:

- Apprentice Handler
- Journeyman Handler
- Senior Handler
- Entry-level Trainer

- Experienced Team Trainer
- Trainer-Instructor
- Certification Officer

Persons that can perform all of the above described jobs tend to carry titles such as Working Dog Unit Manager/Commander or Kennel Master. These persons are supervisors or managers.

The use of working dogs, particularly dogs that work in the security venue, tend to be regulated in one way or another and at various levels of government. Some states have well-defined rules; others have poorly defined rules; and some have no rules at all. Security professionals wishing to use dog services are well advised to learn if rules apply and what they are.

Rules exist within the working dog industry. For example, dogs used for bomb detection must meet 50 different training and testing standards.

William A. "Tony" Lavelle

Sources
Information contained in this article was obtained variously from the International Explosive Detection Dog Association, National Police Canine Association, National Guidelines of the Scientific Working Group on Dog Orthogonal Grouping, Auburn University, and the Canine and Detection Research Institute.

WORKPLACE VIOLENCE PREVENTION AND INTERVENTION

Workplace violence touches everyone. It affects the way we think, feel, and behave. The threat of workplace violence affects the emotional stability and productivity of our employees, and ultimately our profitability. Although the incidence of actual physical violence at work is relatively low, workplace violence affects the lives of thousands of innocent Americans each year. These unfortunate and often preventable crimes can destroy people, families, and businesses. Even when the act of aggression is only psychological, it can be painful and costly.

More locks and guards are not the answer, however. Employers need strong policies, effective security protocols, and a well-conceived strategy to confront the potentially violent employee and prevent workplace violence.

Employers have a moral duty and a statutory obligation under federal and state laws to provide and promote a safe and non-violent work environment. Illustrative of these responsibilities are the requirements under the Occupational Safety and Health Act (OSHA) and state workers' compensation laws. Employers also have responsibilities to the public. Either vicariously or directly, employers may be liable for the harm brought to others by workplace violence. Moreover, employers have additional legal obligations to job applicants.

This intricate web of statutes, standards, rules, and regulations creates a legal minefield for supervisors and managers. Wading through that minefield is precarious at best; employers must protect employees and other parties without infringing on anyone's rights. Rarely has the challenge for employers been greater. Fortunately, there are solutions.

Characteristics of an Aggressor

Research shows that workplace aggressors follow a typical sequence of behavior, called a progression, which in many cases ultimately leads to violence. They usually suffer a traumatic, insoluble (or so they believe) experience and they project the blame for that experience on others. Egocentric by nature, they typically believe that everyone is against them and the world is out to get them. Unable to resolve personal, interpersonal, and work-related problems, these individuals usually resort to violence.

Progressions can be detected, though predicting an aggressor's behavior is a considerable challenge. Experts agree that without careful evaluation and analysis it is reckless and dangerous to attempt to predict future violent behavior. Without the help of an experienced clinician or other qualified professional, it is impossible for the typical supervisor or manager to psychologically assess an emotionally troubled employee and determine his or her fitness for duty. However, many workplace aggressors share certain characteristics. They often relate poorly to people, have difficulty getting along with others, strongly believe they have been wronged, have recently been adversely influenced by something or someone outside of their control, and have a history of violence (domestic, public, or workplace).

Though no two aggressors are alike, they share some common characteristics and behaviors:

- Withdrawn and considered a loner
- Few interests outside work
- Self-esteem depends heavily on job
- Strong sense of injustice to self or beliefs
- Externalizes and projects blame
- Poor people skills, difficulty getting along with others
- History of substance or alcohol abuse
- History of violence (domestic, public and work)

Motivation toward Violence

We are a culture steeped in violence and a society burdened with enormous economic pressures. The threat of corporate downsizing, restructuring, and potential layoff looms over many of us. As a result, many have rid themselves of traditional values and chosen to accept less personal responsibility while expecting more from their employers and government. People are afraid and angry. Truly, the sanctity of the workplace is being challenged.

Research reveals that perpetrators of workplace violence generally fall into six motivational typologies. They are:

1. Economic. The aggressor believes the target is responsible for undesirable economic conditions affecting him, his family, or a particular group.
2. Ideological. The aggressor believes that the target is endangering principles the attacker considers extremely important.
3. Personal. The aggressor possesses distorted feelings of rage, hate, revenge, jealousy, or love.
4. Psychological. The aggressor is mentally unbalanced or clinically psychotic, a condition often exacerbated by drugs or alcohol.
5. Revolutionary. The aggressor obsessively desires to further political beliefs at any cost.
6. Mercenary. The aggressor is motivated by opportunity for financial gain.

Behavioral Changes

Those who commit workplace violence do not simply snap without warning. Research has shown that aggressors tend to exhibit inappropriate and disruptive behavior prior to committing an act of violence. To the observant supervisor or manager, this behavior serves as a warning sign and allows time for preventative action. Listed below are characteristics and behaviors that might signal a potentially violent employee:

- Inappropriate emotional outbursts
- Intense mood swings
- Overreaction to criticism
- Unusual paranoia
- Inappropriate statements or comments
- Rambling, incoherent speech
- Isolation from others
- Volatile, antisocial personality
- Obsessive-compulsive personality
- Uncontrollable romantic obsession
- Distorted values
- Devaluation of other people
- Reckless impulsiveness/destructiveness
- Exaggerated self-importance and value to the organization

Aggressors generally exhibit several of these behaviors over a period of time. The aggressor tends to display a progression toward a violent outburst, with his or her behavior becoming increasingly inappropriate. This incremental escalation, or ramping up, is typical and should serve as a warning to the observant supervisor or manager. Once set in motion, rarely does a progression reverse without intervention. Supervisors and managers must recognize inappropriate behaviors and interrupt the progression before it is too late.

Recognizing and Overcoming Denial

Supervisors, managers, and even organizations engage in denial. Supervisors and managers may deny that an employee has a problem, even in the face of irrefutable proof. They may refuse to admit that someone for whom they are responsible could be violent or dangerous to others and excuse or overlook the employee's inappropriate behavior. By denying the exis-

tence of a problem, they are also denying the employee help.

Companies engage in denial by failing to create sound policies, failing to enforce the policies they have, and failing to respond to incidents suggesting the potential for violence when they occur. Out of fear and unwillingness to confront the truth, employers deny the troubled employee the help they need. In so doing, they not only participate in the progression toward violence, but also incur what may be immeasurable liability.

Redefining Boundaries

When recognizing danger, supervisors and managers must act appropriately and quickly. That action is called intervention. Intervention is the process of returning the employee to a structured work environment and helping the employee regain control of his or her life. To successfully intervene, management must have the will to redefine boundaries and overcome the aggressor's base of power. The intervention process must be well planned and executed. Nothing should be left to chance.

Upon recognizing inappropriate or disruptive behavior, management must act immediately and put the employee on notice. If a progression is identified early enough, the first warning by the organization is usually oral. Verbal warnings often suffice to cause behavioral changes and halt further aggression. When such warnings are not enough, written warnings should follow. If the progression continues, the aggressor may be referred to the company's employee assistance program (EAP) or an outside resource for counseling. Monitoring performance and addressing behaviors is called performance-based management. It provides structure to the work environment while at the same time, offers the employee choices.

In extreme cases, progressive discipline and professional counseling may not be enough. Under these circumstances, termination, a temporary restraining order, hospitalization, or prosecution may be the only solutions available.

Threat Management

Intervention is not possible without a well-conceived plan. That plan or strategy is developed and implemented by what is often called the threat (or incident) management team. Depending upon circumstances, the threat management team will consist of professionals from the following areas or disciplines:

- Executive management
- Human resources
- Security/executive protection
- Employment/labor law
- Public law enforcement
- Clinical psychology/psychiatry
- Incident/crisis management

Though each member of the team has an important role, the role of the clinician is probably the most critical. The clinician provides powerful insight into the psychological and emotional makeup of an individual. The clinician is typically a licensed psychological or psychiatric professional at a Ph.D., Psy.D., or MD level. He or she should have experience in dealing with the psychology of criminal behavior, conducting hostage negotiations, and facilitating trauma management.

Once the members are identified, the team will meet and decide on preliminary objectives based on available information. Lacking adequate information, the team will be unable to make decisions. When this situation occurs, one or more team members can be assigned to collect the necessary information. That process may involve discreetly interviewing the target, witnesses, co-workers, supervisors, former employers, or family members.

A proper background investigation of the aggressor may also be in order. The typical background investigation includes the detailed examination of the following records:

- Criminal history
- Driving history
- Civil indices
- Notices of default
- Judgments
- Tax liens
- Bankruptcies
- Ownership or registration of weapons

Additionally, the aggressor's personnel file (if available) should be reviewed. Treating physicians, law enforcement officials, and other professionals can also be contacted for collateral data whenever possible. As in all employment situations, the privacy of all parties should be respected. To ensure that the balance between need and privacy is adequately struck, the team attorney should be consulted during the entire information gathering process.

After gathering all reasonably available information, the incident management team should review it and make an assessment. That assessment will form the basis for the strategy to deal with the aggressor. With the information available, the team will determine the seriousness of the threat, an appropriate course of action, and possible outcomes.

If termination, hospitalization, or prosecution is appropriate, the team will strategize and do all that is practical to achieve that result without provoking a violent response. Even if management intends to work with the troubled employee, the threat management team must still create a workable strategy. That strategy should redefine performance and behavior boundaries for the aggressor, as well as tolerance thresholds for management.

In summary, the threat management team will, whenever practicable and possible:

- Conduct a thorough and comprehensive investigation of the aggressor and the allegations against him (or her).
- Have the aggressor professionally assessed and determine the potential for violence.
- Decide the best course of action with the information available.
- Implement all appropriate safety and security precautions, making sure to protect people before property.
- Coordinate with local law enforcement and access all available outside resources.
- Review, rehearse, and refine the plan.
- Review legal implications and potential liability.
- Make contingency plans and communicate with the intended target.
- Meet face-to-face with the aggressor and disclose actions intended by management.
- Determine future safety and security needs.
- Notify law enforcement of outcomes.
- Take appropriate legal action (e.g., obtain a restraining order).
- Debrief target and tie up loose ends.
- Provide professional counseling to those in need.

- Hold employee communication sessions that are forthright, but respectful of the rights of the target and the aggressor.

The Five-Step Safety Plan

Employees can help protect themselves and their co-workers by exercising the following simple steps:

- Plan ahead and prepare for the unexpected.
- Treat co-workers with respect and dignity.
- Respect clients and customers.
- Be aware of strangers and their surroundings.
- Report inappropriate behaviors and activities.

Prevention

Though an employer cannot be expected to provide an impenetrable island of safety for its employees, the organization's supervisors and managers can be expected to do as much as possible to promote safety and prevent workplace violence. Supervisors and managers must enforce company policies fairly and consistently. The organization also has an obligation to implement an avenue in which employees can voice complaints and grievances. When unstable individuals are not able to resolve personal, interpersonal, and work-related problems, they may turn to violence as a solution. In order to prevent this escalation, supervisors and managers must provide employees the opportunity to resolve their problems in a safe and confidential manner.

Training and education are also important in creating a safe and non-violent workplace. Employees must understand what is expected of them to create a violence-free work environment. Every employee must also understand that violence or the threat of violence will not be tolerated and may result in immediate termination and/or prosecution.

Summary

According to the 2004 Federal Bureau of Investigation report on workplace violence, the majority of workplace incidents are not multiple homicides, but lesser cases of assaults, stalking, threats, harassment, and physical and/or emotional and psychological abuse that occur on a daily basis. More alarmingly, homicide is still the leading cause of injury and death for women in the workplace, as reported by the Bureau of Justice Statistics in 2005.

In conclusion, supervisors and managers must:

- Treat all people with respect and dignity.
- Listen to those who come and seek help.
- Recognize and document inappropriate behaviors.
- Properly enforce company policies.
- Hold subordinates accountable.
- Document performance.
- Keep management and human resources informed.
- Never hesitate to call for help.

Eugene F. Ferraro

Sources

Ferraro, E. 2006. *Employer's Guide to Workplace Violence Prevention*. Denver: Business Controls.

"Workplace Violence: Issues in Response." 2004. *Federal Bureau of Investigation*.

VIII: Risk Analysis

BUSINESS IMPACT ANALYSIS

A business continuity plan that is not predicated on or guided by the results of a business impact analysis (BIA) is at best guesswork, is incomplete, and may not function as it should during an actual recovery.

The BIA will help a company establish the value of each business unit and business process as it relates to the organization and not to itself, illustrating which functions need to be recovered and in what order.

It identifies the financial and subjective consequences to the organization of the loss of its functions over time and highlights interdependencies.

BIA results are used to determine which functions are the most critical, at what times they are critical, and which strategies are the most cost-effective.

It is fundamental to an understanding of the amount of risk to retain, transfer, or mitigate, and it will assist management to make timely decisions about future business issues. This is accomplished by examining impacts over significant blocks of time (hours or days) on service objectives, cash flow and financial position, regulatory requirements, contractual issues, and competitive advantage.

The BIA presents management with a financial basis for selecting the most cost-effective recovery strategies.

A risk analysis and a BIA can greatly reduce the cost of insurance by identifying and quantifying a potential loss, thereby allowing the risk manager to avoid overinsuring or underinsuring the risk. A BIA will also help to accomplish the following:

- Identify which processes and computer applications are critical to the survival of the organization.
- Identify critical resources of the organization.
- Gain support for the recovery process from senior management.
- Increase management's awareness of the issues and resources required for a workable program, as well as introduce a basic planning structure to the management group.
- Potentially satisfy regulatory requirements and standards.
- Potentially reveal inefficiencies in normal operations.
- Help to justify or better allocate recovery planning budgets (cost/benefit).

Risk Analysis and Business Impact Analysis

A BIA is often thought of as another name for a risk analysis. Some contingency planners believe a risk analysis is a process that focuses solely on physical assets and that a BIA focuses solely on business processes. A close examination will reveal that this belief is not correct.

A BIA is a means of assessing the impact of a disruption in any functional area or on the operations of the enterprise as a whole. It can be considered a subset of a risk analysis, in that it places an "asset value" on business functions and focuses on the criticality of a disruption over various time periods. The source or cause of the disruption, or a detailed understanding of the probability of its occurrence, is relatively unimportant when conducting an impact analysis and is not considered. Therefore, the BIA focuses much less on hazard identification (some say there should be no focus on hazard identification).

Listing all the hazards that might befall an operation may be useful in understanding the conditions, environment, and special needs required when selecting recovery strategies (such as the inability to move large pieces of equipment across town after an earthquake or the amount of time required to remove bodies, complete an on-site police investigation, and remove the carnage after a workplace homicide), but it adds little to the understanding of financial or subjective loss to the operation over time.

The approach taken to initiate and manage a BIA is very similar to that used in a risk analysis. It must begin with senior management's commitment. Because a top-down approach provides the fastest and often most accurate results, management must emphasize that this is a task not to be delegated downward in the organization.

The planners' discussions with these managers in the process of collecting impact data will help to build relationships that will be useful later on if the business continuity planning process becomes stalled, or if resistance is encountered.

Business Impact Analysis Methodology

Plans based on intuitive analysis are often too generalized or miss details important to an effective recovery. A comprehensive analysis often reveals interdependencies and outage tolerances that are not obvious even to those with intimate knowledge of the company's operations. The BIA, if conducted in a structured manner, can help guarantee the success of the entire business continuity process. Different methods exist to accomplish this task. Whatever method is used, certain steps must be completed if the planner is to avoid obstacles commonly encountered in the analysis. The major elements of a BIA include the following:

- Project planning
- Data collection
- Data analysis
- Presentation of data
- Reanalysis

The following initial steps should be taken in the development of a BIA:

- Management commitment
- Definition of the scope of the analysis
- Identification of the participants
- Deciding how to collect the data
- Arranging interviews or distributing questionnaires

The biggest single predictor of the success or failure of the business continuity planning process is the level of senior management commitment. Most often, this commitment is gained only after management becomes fully aware of the potential harm to the company from the loss of its ability to deliver service or products.

To get the BIA process started, the planner must find or convince someone in senior management to sponsor the project. Often, this is the chief financial officer (CFO) who may take an interest if only because he or she is legally responsible for the protection of certain corporate documents. The CFO is usually high enough within the organization to drive the project and to help the planner both collect and interpret the data. Lower managers usually do not have the "big picture" of the impact that loss of their functions could have on the objectives of the organization.

Normally, the scope of the BIA will mirror that of the business continuity planning project, but management or the planner can tighten the scope to an individual division, site, or location. Many planners make the mistake of including in the analysis only those departments or business functions they believe are critical without the understanding that a major goal of the BIA is to determine what is, and what is not critical. At this juncture, assume that all functions are critical at some point in time, or under certain circumstances, and include them in the analysis.

In addition to the CFO, the risk manager is an important resource for:

- Determining what perils and property are excluded in existing policies.
- Ascertaining the period of indemnity for business interruption and contingent business interruption, and estimating the time delay in reimbursement.
- Calculating the value of the physical assets and identifying lead times for the replacement of assets.

Critical functions can include "mission critical" processes, equipment, and applications. It is extremely important at this point to also meet with the information systems director to determine the impact of losing IT functions and other vital communication links.

Data for the analysis are best collected through interviews with business unit leaders. This approach helps to gain their buy-in for the project more effectively than if they were simply to respond in a questionnaire. It may be necessary to meet later with the next-lower level of management to validate impacts. The interview should determine:

- How the business unit fits in with the overall mission of the organization.
- The primary service objectives of the business unit.
- The business unit's processes and dependencies.

The business unit leader should:

- Estimate the maximum loss if the function is out of service, out of operation, or access to it is denied for 30 days or more.
- Determine how this maximum loss is allocated over the following times: day 1, day 2, day 3, day 4, day 5, week 2, week 3, and week 4.
- Estimate any extraordinary expenses the unit may incur if the function is lost.
- List the impact on any contractual or regulatory obligations the outage will cause.
- Indicate how cash flow will be affected by the outage.
- Rate the loss of goodwill or damage to the corporate image.

During or soon after the interview, the business unit leader will add a deeper level of detail by filling out a questionnaire.

Presentation of the Completed Data

Data presentation to management could be the most important step in the BIA process. Credibility is attached to findings when the business unit leaders are identified and the data collection process described succinctly. Pie and bar charts can help. Attendees should leave with a written report in hand.

Summary of Key Points

BIA should not be a "one-shot deal." The information in recovery plans must be updated regularly and the basic strategic framework of the plan reviewed annually. It is logical that the impact to the organization will change as the structure and strategic direction of the business changes. The impact analysis will help to identify these changes.

A BIA identifies the financial and subjective loss of business functions over time. Some definitions say it identifies the loss of "critical" business functions, but it is the BIA that determines whether they are critical or not.

A BIA differs from a risk analysis in important ways, i.e., it is not concerned with the cause, probability, or effect of consequences. The BIA

has no focus on hazard identification, at least from the standpoint of pure risk.

Many believe the BIA is the most critical part of the continuity process because it forms the basis for future decisions and develops momentum and support for the project.

It is important that data and conclusions are valid and accepted, and that findings are included in a presentation and report to management.

Eugene L. Tucker

Source Broder, J. 2006. *Risk Analysis and the Security Survey, 3rd Edition*. Boston: Butterworth-Heinemann.

QUANTIFYING AND PRIORITIZING RISK POTENTIAL

As with any complex chain of interrelated issues, overall strength is measured by the weakest link. Very strong security in one area will not compensate for very weak security in another. To proceed to correct conclusions and then to recommendations for corrective action, it is necessary to quantify and prioritize all the loss potentials identified. For the professional, here lies one of the most difficult tasks in the survey process—the task of measurement, or quantification, of exposures. Given adequate historical or empirical data, loss expectancy can be projected with a satisfactory degree of confidence. On the other hand, when there are insufficient data for reliable forecasting because the data either have not or cannot be collected, one is left with the nagging suspicion that conclusions will be nothing more than an exercise in educated guessing—not that there is anything wrong in that.

Many risks may be classified as things that might happen but that have not yet occurred. Such risks can either be accepted or minimized, using prescribed preventive measures. Acceptance assumes that the risk is not sufficiently serious to justify the cost of reduction, or that recovery measures will ensure survival, or that cessation of operations, if the risk should occur in its most serious magnitude, is an acceptable alternative. Minimizing the risk assumes that the risk exposure is or may be serious enough to justify the cost of eliminating or reducing the possibility of its occurrence, and that recovery measures alone will not always be effective in ensuring survival. Also, it postulates that the remaining alternative—cessation of operations—is unacceptable.

It is at this juncture that quantifying or prioritizing the loss potential becomes the hallmark of the true professional. We have often told clients that it does not take much talent to prescribe an 85 percent solution for a 15 percent problem. Real talent comes into play when one is able to diagnose client problems correctly and recommend necessary countermeasures to solve them without engaging in overkill. Granted, when we err, it must be on the side of prescribing more rather than less security, but not to the level that turns a college campus, hospital, or resort hotel into a Stalag 17 prisoner-of-war camp.

There are always several tradeoffs when one considers the implementation of a new or improved security program. Cost is the most obvious. Less obvious and often overlooked are the inconveniences new security systems cause to personnel and the probable impact on employee morale. This is especially true if the employees perceive (rightly or wrongly) that the inconvenience caused them is greater than the threat. This type of "solution" can cause more harm than if management had done nothing at all. As an example, we observed that when excessive access-control systems were installed in a computer department of an airline reservations center, it resulted in employees' propping doors open for simplicity of movement during working hours. When queried, employees said, "The inconvenience was a bigger problem than unauthorized access."

Assessing Criticality or Severity

Some authors refer to this stage of the survey as assessing criticality or severity of occurrence. Regardless of what one calls the process, it is vital to search for and locate the proper benchmark to adequately approximate dollar values for the loss probabilities previously identified. Once this is done, the task of comparing the cure to the disease becomes self-evident. One can then develop a list of meaningful solutions with priorities based on a common denominator—the dollar. One technique in use is the three-stage approach, involving prevention, control, and recovery. Prevention attempts to stop

undesirable incidents before they get started. Control seeks to keep these incidents from affecting assets, or, if impact occurs, to minimize the loss. Recovery restores the operation after assets have been adversely affected.

Many professionals take the approach that prevention is sufficient, and yet they opt for the installation of various control measures. It is one thing to install fire alarms that signal a serious situation; it is another to respond to and control a fire, and then recover from its effects. Similarly, it may behoove corporate management not only to have adequate security in place to prevent kidnapping attempts but also to design a contingency plan to deal with the kidnapping event, should preventive measures fail and the event become an actuality. In addition, nothing mentioned previously—prevention, detection, control, or contingency planning—precludes the necessity of having adequate insurance to help recover from a serious fire or successful kidnapping, extortion, and ransom event.

Another technique for assessing security is to prepare a segmented schedule of overhead, installation, and operating costs for the security project. All costs identified must be directly chargeable to expected benefits. In this process, it is crucial to show that the benefits (risk prevention or reduction) will outweigh the cost. This is referred to as a cost/benefit summary and is useful for both existing and proposed security programs and projects.

The Decision Matrix

Another simple technique for prioritizing loss potential is the use of a frequency and severity loss matrix as an aid in making decisions about handling risk. The following matrix uses the adjectives high, medium, and low as factors to measure both frequency and severity of loss.

The quantification and prioritizing of loss potential should take into account the fact that there are both "intuitive" security control concepts, such as the installation of a burglar alarm at a warehouse, and security control concepts based on detailed cost/benefit analysis. An example of the latter is a multiple-stage electronic card-access control system for the research and development laboratory of a computer chip manufacturer. The procedures for both approaches take into full consideration the following:

TABLE 7. Steps Taken to Reduce a Loss-producing Event Are Determined by the Frequency and Severity of the Event

Decision Matrix: A Risk-Handling Decision Aid

Severity of Loss	Frequency of Loss		
	High	**Medium**	**Low**
High	Avoidance	Loss prevention and avoidance	Transfer via insurance
Medium	Avoidance and loss prevention	Loss prevention and transfer via insurance	Assumption and pooling
Low	Loss prevention	Loss prevention and assumption	Assumption

- Available information resources
- Reliable probability relationships
- Minimum time and resource requirements and availability
- Maximum incentives for management cooperation
- A realistic evaluation of existing or planned security control effectiveness

The means of protection designed must always be tailored to the specific risk in the real day-to-day working environment of the specific entity being studied. The application of controls simply because they are recommended by some vague standard or acceptable practice, without regard to risk in the real-world environment, often results in controls that are inappropriate, ineffective, and costly. Worse, as so often seen with inappropriately planned closed-circuit television (CCTV), such controls may generate a false sense of security on the part of management. For example, I was once asked to review the installation of a CCTV security system for a newly constructed newspaper plant in California. The CCTV system had been designed for the corporation by a building and facilities engineer. The plant was located in a newly developed industrial park. The CCTV system had apparently been planned without regard to environmental considerations. Upon review, it was determined that the CCTV system—complete with zoom, tilt, and pan lenses as well as video cassette tape-recording functions, all very costly to install and maintain—was operating in an area that had heavy fog about 6 months of the year during nighttime hours. Further, the fence line, at its nearest point to the building, was 350 yards away from the closest camera lens! To the question, "Why install CCTV at this location?" the answer was, "We have used CCTV successfully at all our other plants and it just seemed the natural thing to do here."

They did have CCTV at their other plants, but in the plants that I inspected, the CCTV systems were more often than not inoperative, in whole or in part, because of inadequate maintenance and repairs needed on cameras, monitors, and video recording units. The CCTV systems were regarded by operations personnel as expensive toys that added little to the security of the facility. Management, however, was proud of its security program, having been lulled into a false sense of security by the presence of the CCTV cameras.

This technique has become generally reliable. However, in our experience, the entire exercise of estimating risks for a specific installation or complex is at best imprecise. Defining risks by using highly specific numbers has not always been validated by experience. Several well-known authorities have concluded that order-of-magnitude expressions, such as low, moderate, and high, to indicate relative degrees of risk are more than adequate for most risk-control surveys.

The terms low, moderate, and high equate roughly with probability ranges of 1 to 3, 4 to 6, and 7 to 10, respectively. One is cautioned here to remember that even a low risk should be taken seriously if the potential damage (or danger) is assessed as being moderate to high. An example would be the kidnapping for ransom of a high-profile business executive in a foreign country. We may regard the risk to be nearly nonexistent (low), but the potential danger and the impact on the company of such an unfavorable event should always be rated as high.

James F. Broder

Source   Broder, J. 2006. *Risk Analysis and the Security Survey, 3rd Edition*. Boston: Butterworth-Heinemann.

RISK ANALYSIS

Risk is associated with virtually every activity one can think of, but in the present context it is limited to the uncertainty of financial loss, the variations between actual and expected results, or the probability that a loss has occurred or will occur. In the insurance industry, the term *risk* is also used to mean "the thing insured," for example, the XYZ Company is the risk. Risk is also the possible occurrence of an undesirable event.

Risk should not be confused with perils, which are the causes of risk and are things such as fire, flood, and earthquake. Nor should risk be confused with hazard, which is a contributing factor to perils. Almost anything can be a hazard: a loaded gun, a bottle of caustic acid, a bunch of oily rags, or a warehouse used for storing paper products. The end result of risk is loss or a decrease in value.

Risks are generally classified as "speculative" (the difference between loss or gain, for example, the risk in gambling) and "pure risk," a loss or no-loss situation, to which insurance generally applies.

The divisions of risk are limited to three common categories:

- Personal (having to do with people assets)
- Property (having to do with material assets)
- Liability (having to do with legalities that could affect both of the previous categories, such as errors and omissions liability)

What Is Risk Analysis?

Risk analysis is a management tool, the standard that is determined by whatever management decides it wants to accept in terms of actual loss. In order to proceed in a logical manner to perform a risk analysis, it is first necessary to accomplish some basic tasks:

- Identify the assets in need of being protected (money, manufactured product, and industrial processes to name a few).

- Identify the kinds of risks that may affect the assets involved (internal theft, external theft, fire, or earthquake).
- Determine the probability of risk occurrence. Here one must keep in mind that such a determination is not a science but an art—the art of projecting probabilities.
- Determine the impact or effect, in dollar values if possible, if given loss does occur.

A risk assessment analysis is a rational and orderly approach, and a comprehensive solution to problem identification and probability determination. It is also a method for estimating the anticipated or expected loss from the occurrence of some adverse event. The key word here is *estimating*, because risk analysis will never be an exact science. Nevertheless, the answer to most, if not all, questions regarding one's security exposures can be determined by risk analysis.

Analysis provides management with information on which to base decisions, such as: Is it always best to prevent the occurrence of a situation? Should the policy be to contain the effect a hazardous situation may have? Is it sufficient simply to recognize that an adverse potential exists, and for now do nothing but be aware of the hazard? The eventual goal of risk analysis is to strike an economic balance between the impact of risk on the enterprise and the cost of protective measures.

A properly performed risk analysis has many benefits. It can:

- Show the current security posture (profile) of the organization.
- Highlight areas where greater (or lesser) security is needed.
- Help to assemble some of the facts needed for the development and justification of cost-effective countermeasures (safeguards).
- Serve to increase security awareness by assessing the strengths and weaknesses of security to all organizational levels from management to operations.

Risk analysis is not a task to be accomplished once and for all time. It must be performed periodically in order to stay abreast of changes in mission, facilities, and equipment. Since security measures designed at the inception of a system have generally proved to be more effective than those superimposed later, risk analysis should have a place in the design phase of every system. Unfortunately, this is seldom the case.

The major resource required for a risk analysis is humanpower. For this reason, the first analysis will be the most expensive as subsequent ones can be based in part on previous work and the time required will decrease to some extent as experience is gained. The time allowed to accomplish the risk analysis should be compatible with its objectives. Large facilities with complex, multi-shift operations and many files of data will require more time than the single-shift, limited production locations. If meaningful results are expected, management must be willing to commit the resources necessary to accomplish this undertaking.

The Role of Management in Risk Analysis

The success of any risk analysis undertaking will be strongly contingent on the role top management takes in the project. Management must support the project and express this support to all levels of the organization. Management must delineate the purpose and scope of risk analysis. It must select a qualified team and formally delegate authority, and management must review the team's findings.

Personnel who are not directly involved in the analysis process must be prepared to provide information and assistance to those who are conducting the analysis and, in addition, to abide by any procedures and limitations of activity that may ensue. Management should leave no doubt that it intends to rely on the final product and base its security decisions on the findings of the risk analysis team. The scope of the project should be defined and the statement of scope should specifically spell out the limitations of the analysis. It is oftentimes equally important to state specifically what the analysis is not designed to accomplish or cover. This will serve to eliminate any misunderstandings at the start rather than at the conclusion of the exercise.

At this point it may be well to define and explain two other terms that are sometimes used interchangeably with risk. They are: *threats*, anything that could adversely affect the enterprise or the assets, and *vulnerability*, weaknesses, flaws, holes, or anything that may conceivably be exploited by a threat. Threats are most easily

identified by placing them in one of three classifications or categories: natural hazards, accidents, or intentional acts. Vulnerabilities are most easily identified by collecting information from interviewing persons employed in the facility, by field observation and inspection, by document review, and, in the case of hardware or electronics, by conducting tests designed to highlight vulnerability and expose weaknesses or flaws in the design of the system.

Threat occurrence rates/probabilities are best developed from reports of occurrence or incident reports whenever this historical data exist. Where the data do not exist, it may be necessary to reconstruct them by conducting interviews with knowledgeable persons.

Risk Exposure Assessment

Before any corrective action can be considered, it is necessary to make a thorough assessment of one's identifiable risk exposure. In order to accomplish this, it is essential that three factors be identified and evaluated in quantitative terms.

The first is to determine the types of loss or risk that can affect the assets involved. Here examples would be fire, burglary, robbery, or kidnapping. If one of these were to occur, what effect would the resulting disruption of operations have on the company? If the chief executive officer, on an overseas trip, were to be kidnapped by a terrorist group, who would make the day-to-day operating decisions in his absence? What about the unauthorized disclosure of trade secrets and other proprietary data? After the risk exposure potentials are identified, one must then proceed to evaluate those threats that, should they occur, would produce losses in quantitative terms.

To do this we proceed to the second factor: estimate the probability of occurrence. What are the chances that the identified risks may become actual events? For some risks, estimating probabilities can be relatively easy. This is especially true when we have documented historical data dealing with identifiable problems. For example, how many internal and external theft cases have been investigated over the past year? Other risks are more difficult to predict. Sabotage, industrial espionage, kidnapping, and civil disorder may never occur or may occur only on a one-time basis.

The third factor is quantifying loss potential. This is measuring the impact or severity of the risk, if in fact a loss does occur or the risk becomes an actual event. This exercise does not become final until one develops dollar values for the assets previously identified. This part of the survey is necessary to set the stage for classification evaluation and analysis of the comparisons necessary to the establishment of countermeasure priorities.

Some events or kinds of risk with which business and industry are most commonly concerned are as follows:

- Natural catastrophe (tornado, hurricane, earthquake, volcanic eruption, and flood)
- Industrial disaster (explosion, chemical spill, structural collapse, and fire)
- Civil disturbance (sabotage, labor violence, and bomb threats)
- Criminality (robbery, burglary, pilferage, embezzlement, fraud, industrial espionage, internal theft, and hijacking)
- Conflict of interest (kickbacks, trading on inside information, and unethical practices)
- Miscellaneous risks, threats, or loss factors (bookkeeping errors, unaccounted for inventory losses, traffic accidents, alcohol and drug abuse, absenteeism, gambling, and improper leave or time clocking)

Admittedly, some of the listed events are unlikely to occur. Also, some are less critical to an enterprise than others. Nevertheless, all are possibilities and are thus deserving of consideration.

James F. Broder

Source   Broder, J., 1984. *Risk Analysis and the Security Survey*. Boston: Butterworth-Heinemann.

RISK ANALYSIS OF COMMERCIAL PROPERTY

Any commercial property that is open to the public should be evaluated to determine its exposure to crime. The crime history of a property is the best indicator of crimes likely to occur on the property in the near future. The second best indicator is the crime rate in the surrounding neighborhood and at similar properties nearby. The results of a crime risk analysis can help the property owner make informed decisions about

security measures needed to counter the risks of harm to people and property.

Crime Record Research

An examination of the crime history of a property can reveal the characteristics of perpetrators; the times and days they strike; the targets they prefer; the methods, weapons, and vehicles they use; and their routes of approach and departure. These, and other details like them, are called crime demographics.

Crime demographics can be gathered from many sources. People sources can include crime victims, witnesses, complainants, property managers, police patrol officers and supervisors, police criminal intelligence specialists, informants, and neighbors. People sources can also include customers, vendors, maintenance and janitorial people, trash collectors, and just about anyone familiar with the property.

Paper sources can include security incident reports and logs, security investigation reports, police initial reports, police investigation reports, newspaper reports, property insurance claims, workers' compensation claims, and just about any record containing data about the property, the area surrounding the property, and the people who live in or frequent the area.

The "paper" sources are not always paper. Frequently, they are electronic blips inside a computer system. Knowing the capabilities of the computer system and knowing how to retrieve the data from the system are essential to developing accurate demographics. Also, a computer system can be used to process collected information.

Crime record research involves more than gathering crime data. It involves assembling the data logically, examining it for meaningful connections and trends, and projecting those findings against the property in question.

Standard Crime Data

In addition to the sources just mentioned, the person conducting the risk analysis can look at two standard sources of crime data: the Uniform Crime Report (UCR) and the National Crime Survey (NCS). The UCR and NCS reflect the occurrence of certain serious crimes in the

United States over a period of one year. General conclusions can be made from these reports; for example, the rate of rise or fall of murder during the year reported. The data in these reports are at least one year old when published and are of such a general nature that they are likely to be of little use in predicting a particular crime at a particular property in a particular neighborhood at a particular time on a particular day. This does not mean the UCR and NCS are useless; it only means that for gathering grass roots demographics they are less valuable than police and security reports and statements of knowledgeable persons. Even still, it is worth knowing something about these two reports.

Uniform Crime Report (UCR)

The UCR program was conceived in 1929 by the International Association of Chiefs of Police to meet a need for reliable, uniform crime statistics for the nation. In 1930, the FBI was tasked with collecting, publishing, and archiving those statistics. The UCR focuses on eight main offense classifications, known as Part I crimes. These are the violent crimes of murder and non-negligent manslaughter; forcible rape; robbery; aggravated assault; burglary; larceny-theft; motor vehicle theft; and arson. UCR data reach the FBI either from local law enforcement agencies or state-level agencies, often called state criminal intelligence centers.

UCR crime statistics are collated by region, geographic division, state, and city. The number of incidents reported is divided into the area population and indexed as the crime rate per 100,000 persons. Problems with these statistics arise because certain population rates can be estimated only. In some instances the methods for classifying crime vary from place to place. Also, cities and towns with populations of less than 25,000 have to extrapolate their numbers to fit the UCR reporting requirements.

Although the UCR permits interesting trend comparisons, it offers little benefit for determining actual risk.

National Crime Survey (NCS)

The NCS is a victimization survey that began in the mid-1960s and has grown since. The NCS is people-oriented because data are collected from people over the telephone, by mail, or in person. The people queried are crime victims.

The NCS has concluded that only about half of all felonies are reported to the police. Much can be learned from having information about the sex, age, race, and income level of victims. The NCS has often produced crime trends different from the UCR for the same time periods. The NCS is informative, but provides little practical benefit in evaluating commercial property crime risks.

Law Enforcement Records

Law enforcement agencies are the principal repositories of crime-related records. They are convenient and useful to the person making the risk analysis because the records are not far away and contain a wealth of information. However, the quality and quantity of records can vary within and between jurisdictions because of variations in the technologies used to collect and manage information. Other disadvantages are department policies and legal constraints that prohibit the release of police information for non-police purposes.

Computer-generated information, to the extent it is accessible, gives the advantage of acquiring a large amount of data in a short period of time. A single printout that is generated in 10 minutes can produce information that would require ten weeks to collect. In addition, computer software allows the presentation of data in meaningful categories such as type of crime; residential, retail and commercial targets; proximity of the crime site to getaway routes; victims; weapons or tools used; assets taken and damaged; time, date, and location of occurrence; arrest and conviction; and ethnicity of the criminals.

A small law enforcement agency tends not to have a computer system. Records can take the form of paper files and microfiche. Considerable time and persistence are required to sift through documents and operate microfiche equipment. One advantage is records that have been retained over an extended period of time. The relevant records, whether available in a computer or on a dusty shelf, can be helpful for going back in time to develop the crime history of a building or the community in which the building is located. Knowing what happened in the past and present can be a predictor of what is likely to happen in the future. However, records that are very old can have negligible value. A two-year time span between the event and the present is generally appropriate.

Cost is always present when people and equipment are utilized. When the utilization is not police-related, fees can be levied against the collector. In the instance of obtaining one copy of a single incident report, the charge can be $5.00. At some point or other the question of cost-effectiveness arises. Costs can be eliminated or reduced when the person making the analysis has working relationships with police department personnel. This point underscores the importance of police liaison and networking with people in the right positions. However, some police departments prohibit outside release of information for any reason and punish violators severely. No amount of friendship and networking can overcome this restriction.

Calls for Service

A little known police record is the call-for-service record, which is most often made and maintained by dispatch operators or a computer-assisted dispatch system that electronically captures and stores verbal communications made by police units and a dispatch center. A call-for-service record reflects the name of the officer and/or the identity of the patrol unit dispatched. The communication modes are usually radio and cell phone. The communicated messages describe the response to an incident such as assault, robbery, or burglary in progress.

Call-for-service records can reveal information pertinent to the commercial property that is being evaluated for risk. They answer such questions as to the number of times the police were called to the site, the reasons for the calls, and the actions taken by the responding officers. Electronically recorded messages have two drawbacks: messages transmitted in the heat of an incident can be erroneous or defective, and call-for-service records have a relatively short life span due to the need to free up memory space.

In-House Security Reports

Another source of information about a commercial property is security logs and incident reports kept on file by the guard force protecting the property. A hard and fast rule in guard operations is to make a record of every unusual incident. The guard force procedure is similar to the police procedure: the officer that handled the incident prepares a report; a supervisor reviews the report and assigns an administrative number to it; the number on the report, along with the name of the incident, is entered in a log book; and when the incident is serious (as defined by the client or guard company management), the report is distributed, usually to persons in positions with authority to correct the causes underlying the incident. In some cases, an "action taken" report is returned to the guard force and appended to the record on file.

For a reason difficult to understand, security files often escape the attention of the person conducting the risk analysis. When a security incident involved a call for law enforcement assistance, a police record was created. The person making the assessment can use the security incident data to find the corresponding police report without much difficulty.

Security records can be extremely valuable because the report preparer is familiar with the incident site; the report is one part in a continuous, chronological chain; and the chain goes back for as many years as the guard force has been in operation. However, at some locations, such as a shopping mall, a crime committed against a shopper can be reported directly to the police without the security officer on duty having any knowledge of the incident.

A large commercial property with multiple locations would logically keep separate records at each location. For example, the business might have a seaport for receiving crude oil, a refinery for converting the oil to gasoline, a tank farm for storing the gasoline, a truck terminal for distributing the gasoline to service stations, and a regional network of service stations where the gasoline is sold. The security files for each location provide the risk assessor with an opportunity to make comparisons between the separate locations.

Proximity and Similarity

In the preceding example, the risk assessor might decide not to make one risk analysis for all locations because they are too far apart and dissimilar operationally. The assessor's decision could be the opposite if the company to be assessed was in the convenience store business. The business might have multiple locations that are not far apart within a defined region and have similar if not identical operations. In this case, security reports obtained at all locations can help the assessor discover common risks and make store-to-store comparisons. The assessor might be able to see that the common risk of robbery is much higher at Store A than Store B and that Store C has the lowest robbery risk among all stores. Crime demographics can probably explain the differentiations. For example, Store A might be in a neighborhood with a high overall crime rate, the majority of the store's customers live in the neighborhood, the neighborhood has five taverns, a robbery occurs at the store every two months on average, a robbery usually takes place one or two days prior to the payday for most neighborhood residents, the crime is committed by one person brandishing a revolver and wearing a black ski mask, the robber appears to be a young African-American male, the store clerk and customers are told to lay face down on the floor while the robber rifles the cash drawer, the robber arrives and departs in a vehicle that is always different, police patrolling in the area is spotty and infrequent, and the store is adjacent to the on ramp of an interstate highway.

In a very simple sense, the assessor is now able to comprehend the robbery dynamics at Store A and compare the dynamics against other stores. The assessor is able also to identify mitigation measures to reduce or prevent robbery at Store A and to make a reasonable judgment that robbery at Store A is inevitable for as long as the mitigation measures are not implemented. A situation of this type is at the core of the foreseeability doctrine which holds that when the owner of a property frequented by the public knows (or should know) that persons on the property are at risk of harm and does not take reasonable steps to prevent the risk, the owner can be held liable for harm to persons on the property.

Field Interviews

It is impossible to evaluate crime risk from behind a desk. Visits to the site and surrounding area at different times and days of the week are required. Factors to be looked for include traffic flows; establishments in the surrounding area such as shopping centers and sport venues; the presence of gangs, prostitutes, and persons that appear to be selling drugs; and nighttime illumination. All such circumstances need to be identified and considered in the overall risk analysis process.

In addition to looking, it can be helpful to talk with people in the area such as neighbors, employees of local businesses, and police patrol officers. The nature and tenor of the assessor's questions should be friendly, down-to-earth, and non-threatening. To corroborate information obtained from other sources can be helpful but the main purpose of interviewing is to learn what has not already been learned. The perspectives of people who live and work in the area will be much different than the perspectives of police officers and other authority figures.

Interviewing is important for another reason: it may be the only way to acquire the needed information such as when police reports cannot be released, police officers are not permitted to talk about their work, and organizations are reluctant to talk about crime. A local Chamber of Commerce and realty businesses are examples.

Environmental Change

Crime statistics will change when the local environment changes. Changes can include constructing new buildings, two-way streets becoming one-way, new businesses moving in and old businesses moving out, apartment complexes converting to condominiums, housing projects closing or opening, store hours changing, increasing or decreasing the number of police patrols, and the passage of laws or ordinances that impact the site and/or the surrounding area.

Summary

A well conducted crime risk analysis will produce a clear picture of risks presently confronting a particular commercial property and of risks that appear to be on the horizon. The analysis will provide actionable information, i.e., security steps that can and should be taken to offset crime risk. The assessor's responsibilities are to analyze and recommend; the owner's responsibilities are to consider the recommendations and act upon them.

Chris E. McGoey

Sources

Crime Doctor. 2006. <www.crimedoctor.com>

"Crime in the United States." *Uniform Crime Reports*. Washington, D.C.: Federal Bureau of Investigation.

"Criminal Victimization in the United States." *National Crime Survey. Bureau of Justice Statistics*. Washington, D.C.: U.S. Department of Justice.

McGoey, C., *Security: Adequate…or Not? The Complete Guide to Premises Liability Litigation*. Murrieta, CA: Aegis Books, Inc.

RISK AND SENSITIVE INFORMATION

Organizations are increasingly reliant on automated and interconnected systems to perform key information-processing functions. The benefits of such systems are enormous yet they carry with them risks of data loss and damage, fraud, and disruption of productivity. Information systems have long been at risk from malicious actions, inadvertent user errors, and natural disasters. The risk rises relative to complexity, interconnectivity, and the accessibility of the systems to a larger number of individuals. Fueling the risk are the increased number and skills of hackers and the motivations that spur them.

With grinding repetition, the news media report breakdowns in the security of automated systems. A recurring theme is the failure of the system's management to take a risk-based approach in determining what needs to be protected and how to go about it. The intelligent use of resources requires management to consider factors such as the value of the system at

Risk Assessment Model

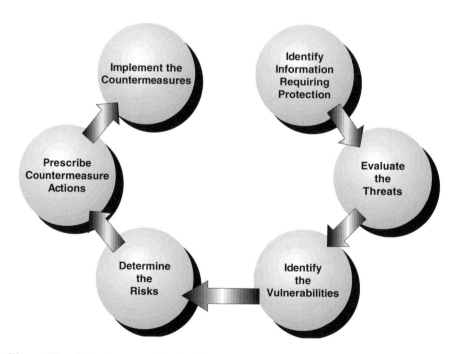

Figure 35.   As is the case with other key assets, risk assessment applies to information.

risk, the threats to it, its vulnerabilities, and the protective safeguards in place.

Assessing risk is one step in a broad stairway of risk management activities. Other elements include establishing a central management focal point, implementing policies and procedures, promoting awareness, and monitoring and evaluating the effectiveness of controls.

A risk assessment, whether pertaining to information or other type of asset, can provide decision makers with:

- An understanding of events and circumstances that can negatively influence operations.
- Options for preventing and mitigating risks.

The risk management function is performed widely: mortgage bankers manage the risk of loan defaults, nuclear power plant engineers manage the risk of nuclear emissions, and pharmaceutical officials manage the risk of product contamination. As reliance on computer systems and electronic data has grown, loss of information has joined the list of business risks that merit careful management.

Several key actions go into making an effective risk assessment:

- Obtain support from the top.
- Designate focal points.
- Build a consensus.
- Communicate.

Senior management support helps ensure that:

- Resources are made available to conduct risk assessment.
- Assessment activities and findings are taken seriously at lower levels.
- Resources are made available to implement changes recommended in the assessment.

Top-level support is evident when senior managers assist in determining the scope of the assessment and handpicking the key participants. Next is agreement with the assessment's findings and approval of an action plan. Finally, and most importantly, support is shown when senior management funds the action plan.

Designate Focal Points. A focal point is a person, a team, or a group of individuals charged with assessment tasks. A focal point will often possess expertise: the CSO is an expert in security, a planning group has expertise in planning, and the head of the information technology department understands the complexities of the information system. A focal point will sometimes be an employee who has been a champion of the very change that is needed to reduce risk. Very importantly, one or more focal points will be "big picture" people who can assure that organization-wide issues are addressed.

Build a Consensus. A risk assessment is a mechanism for reaching consensus on which risks are the greatest and what steps are appropriate for mitigating them. Consensus building involves encouraging discussions of the issues, resolving dissonance, and obtaining agreement on controls necessary to carry out the action plan.

Communication from beginning to end is essential. The matters to be communicated include:

- Rationale or business necessity for the risk assessment.
- Goals and objectives of the assessment.
- Identification of participants.
- How employees can help.
- Milestones and progress.
- Findings.
- Schedule of actions planned.
- Actions completed.

A summary of the risk assessment report can be a helpful communication tool. A caveat, one to be made by the CSO, is to be silent on vulnerabilities. There's nothing to be gained by letting adversaries know the system's weak points.

The organization's information security policy provides the framework and tone of the risk assessment. A policy lays out requirements. Generally, the requirements specify the frequency of assessments, a plan and procedures for conducting an assessment, disruption categories, unacceptable risks, distribution of the risk assessment report, and responsibilities for corrective actions.

An assessment of the security scheme that protects information assets is appropriate:

- Prior to or immediately following a significant change to the scheme.

- After a serious security incident.
- Whenever a new significant risk factor is introduced.
- At least once every 2 or 3 years.

An information security plan and procedures will typically:

- Name the objectives and methodology of the assessment.
- Assign assessment responsibilities to positions, teams, groups, and departments.
- Identify assessment team size and composition.
- Identify modes for ensuring compliance and administering punishment for non-compliance.

The policy will set parameters of loss, damage, or business disruption, for example:

- Category I: Loss of or severe damage to critical proprietary information or serious disruption to the system.
- Category II: Loss of or serious damage to non-critical proprietary information or disruption of the system.
- Category III: Loss of or serious damage to non-critical, non-proprietary information or minor disruption of the system.

Some risks are acceptable and some are not. Determinations are made by senior management and take into account many variables, e.g., threats and their probability, history of loss, financial strength of the organization, and others. Also considered will be the extent to which the organization will go to remove unacceptable risks.

The information protection policy may specify the job positions that are to receive the report. These are positions that have been assigned responsibilities for the protection of information.

A policy cannot predict weaknesses identified by risk assessment, but it can set requirements for correcting them when they are identified. Corrective actions can include acquiring needed equipment or material; improving knowledge and skills; and making changes to plans, procedures, and practices. Correction can be avoided with a few simple actions:

- State a business necessity for the policy. Explain how IT contributes to the company's

mission and how violations of IT security detract from the mission.
- Identify job positions subject to the policy, e.g., regular, temporary, contract, and sub-contract employees. My view is that anyone with access privileges should be subject to the policy.
- Assign responsibilities. A responsibility not assigned is a responsibility not performed.
- Name activities prohibited by the policy, e.g., prohibitions against not protecting passwords, using IT equipment for other than company business, and e-mailing sensitive company information in non-encrypted modes.
- Name the enforcement actions. Describe the controls in place to detect policy violations, e.g., mention that supervisors will look for unattended PCs that have not been shut down, and that during non-business hours security guards will look for hidden notes showing employee passwords.
- Identify the penalties for violations. Specify the range of disciplinary actions. You'll need to confer with HR on this issue.

Cyber Offenses

A cyber offense is a premeditated criminal attack against information, computer systems, computer programs, and data. When the criminal act is minor, such as an attack that uses a nuisance virus or results in a denial of service, the commonly accepted (and frequently misused) term is hacking. When the act is greater than minor, such as a malicious attack that results in damage or destruction, the term cybervandalism seems appropriate, and when the purpose of the act is to steal, such as acquire identification data that results in the taking of another's property, the usual term is cybercrime. When a cybercrime is politically motivated and results in violence against non-combatant targets, the appropriate term is cyberterrorism. All of these crimes involve information technology and the Internet.

The Internet

The Internet is a massive collection of computers located around the world, all of which are linked together and accessible from anywhere. The Internet is often called the Information Superhighway because it works like a path leading to the information desired. It is therefore very useful as a source of business information, a means of communication, and a facilitator of electronic commerce. Significant benefits accrue from having access to the Internet, but a companion of access is risk.

Chief security officers understand that attacks launched from the Internet can have devastating effects. It is fortunate that a majority of computer system penetrations are carried out by non-malicious hackers. It is also fortunate that anti-virus software programs are effective at deflecting many hacker attacks.

On the unfortunate side of the ledger is the short shrift given to computer security by companies in a hurry to get their e-commerce applications up and running. Because hacker damage in the historical perspective has been relatively benign, some companies are choosing to assume the risk of hacking rather than install costly protections. Another reason to expect more frequent and more spectacular hacker events is the growth of computer literacy in the population as a whole. Computer-savvy criminals, terrorists, and others with an inclination to damage are learning the mechanics and use of a powerful weapon. Especially at risk are companies and consumers who meet on the Internet for commercial purposes.

Attacks on major commercial web sites reveal collaboration among hackers of varying types, e.g., virus writers, Trojan Horse bombers, and e-mail spammers. A collaborative or mixed attack occurs when a hacker places an undetectable program on a network. The program monitors important information passing along the network, and copies small chunks of data over an extended period of time. The chunks, which might be social security numbers or bank account numbers, accumulate. The hacking activity has now moved from a minor crime to a major crime. The final step is to download the stolen data and use it for a criminal purpose such as identify theft or theft of funds from bank accounts.

Hackers have been depicted in the media as fun-loving teenagers and technical whiz kids acting out "teens-will-be-teens" scenarios. Their only crime, apologists will say, is an intellectual fulfillment attained from entering the protected portals of the electronic world. A more accurate depiction might be to think of lunatics swinging baseball bats inside a china shop. The damage is done quickly, easily, and with stunning results; putting the broken pieces back together is nearly impossible. With hackers of various stripes working together, a difficult challenge is presented to CSOs. The challenge can be met, at least in part, when the CSO communicates to employees a number of don'ts.

- Don't connect to the Internet except on connections provided by the employer.
- Don't download software from an Internet source of questionable reliability.
- Don't download from an Internet source without scanning for viruses.
- Don't ignore licensing and export restrictions on software and shareware obtained through the Internet.
- Don't change the security settings on your PC or web browser.
- Don't use for the Internet the same passwords you use for other services.
- Don't open electronic mail attachments that appear suspicious.
- Don't mix internal and external e-mail addresses in a single distribution list.
- Don't include embarrassing information in e-mail messages.
- Don't auto-forward the organization's e-mail address to an external e-mail service.
- Don't send sensitive information on the Internet without first encrypting.
- Don't send or forward chain letters.
- Don't unnecessarily send or download large files.
- Don't browse inappropriate web sites.
- Don't import inappropriate material.

Restrictions on Internet Use

The CSO shares responsibility with information technology leaders for controlling unacceptable employee behaviors when they are on the Internet. Ways to control Internet behavior can include:

- Limit use to official business.
- Monitor Internet use and admonish/punish those who use the company's time and equipment for personal purposes.

- Prohibit viewing, downloading, or distributing obscene or abusive material.
- Prohibit employees from advertising on or participating in illegal or unethical Internet activities.
- Require respect of copyright laws.
- Prohibit communication of sensitive information via the Internet.

An intranet is a collection of web sites owned and operated by the organization. Although an intranet operates on the Internet with standard browser software, it is open only to designated persons such as employees, partners, and contractors. Passwords, firewalls, and other protective methods help keep an intranet secure from outsiders.

Following a few guidelines can help maintain the integrity of a company's intranet. For example:

- Information that is classified at the highest level (e.g., SECRET information) must not be placed on the Intranet.
- Information that is classified at the next lower level (e.g., RESTRICTED information) may be placed on the Intranet but only with access restrictions.
- Information that is personal employee information (e.g., PRIVATE information) should not be placed on the Intranet.
- Other information, although not classified but of a sensitive nature, should not be placed on the Intranet.
- Information displayed on the Intranet should be accompanied by a notice of viewing privileges.
- Partners and contractors must be informed of their Intranet viewing and publishing responsibilities.

The chief purpose of an intranet is information sharing. Large amounts of useful information (although not necessarily sensitive) can be stored in the intranet's servers. Many different types of information are typically available: policies, plans, procedures, rules and regulations, standards, phone and address lists, maps, technical drawings, travel advisories, etc. The CSO, for example, might access the intranet to determine the engineering department's standards for perimeter fence construction; an employee planning to travel to Bogota might use the intranet to identify hotels and restaurants that provide good security; and a clerk preparing to type a classified document might go on the intranet to be refreshed on procedures for marking and distributing a classified document.

An intranet is a means for sharing information and facilitating business processes. It can be helpful to companies large and small, and is particularly beneficial to organizations that are highly dependent on information. However, like other information facilities, an intranet is accompanied by risk.

The need to protect information riding the intranet can be quite high in some situations. For example, information moving between the executive team and a joint venture partner may be so important as to require extra protection. However, the extra protection is meaningless when the joint partner's receiving portal is unprotected.

A large responsibility for intranet security lies with the provider of the information. Authors, owners, and custodians of information are charged with assessing the sensitivity of the information and determining the appropriate readership. It is not excusable to ignore security precautions for the sake of information flow. The correct approach is to make the information available, yet secure.

Passwords provide a modicum of security. A password is a sequence of characters that gives an authorized user access to a computer system. A password should not be easy to guess. A good password contains a combination of characters, numbers, and symbols that do not form a word. Computer systems usually limit the number of attempts to enter a correct password.

An auxiliary feature is a hand-held device called a password authenticator. During logon, the computer displays a challenge number, the user enters the challenge number into the password authenticator, and the authenticator replies directly to the computer. If the reply is correct, logon is granted.

Another access-control device is the token, a tamper-resistant plastic card embedded with a microprocessor chip containing a stored password that automatically and frequently changes. When a computer is accessed using a token, the computer reads the token's password, as well as a password entered by the user. Access is granted when the computer finds a correct match of the passwords.

State-of-the art logon systems combine passwords and biometric readings of fingerprints and retinal patterns. DNA profiles are on the horizon.

Firewalls are to a computer network what castle walls are to a king's home; they keep invaders out and keep insiders a safe distance from the king. Friends can get through the outer wall when they present proper identification at entrance points, and the king's attendants can move past inner walls depending on trust given them by the king. The analogy makes an important point: firewalls protect against intrusion from both external and internal sources. Damage caused by outside hackers is costly and well understood; damage caused by employees is even more costly and not widely acknowledged. Employees should be educated to:

- Determine the risks and choose measures to control them.
- Place your web site on a server different than your internal network servers.
- Enforce the rules on passwords.
- Control access to hardware.
- Stay abreast of hacker methods and viruses.
- For a critical system, use more than one security method, e.g., passwords, separate servers, and firewalls.
- Check regularly for vulnerabilities; use penetration tests.
- Encrypt sensitive information before sending it over the Internet.
- Require your online partners to take the same precautions you do.
- Take advantage of up-to-date expertise and technology.

A firewall can be constructed within hardware, by software, or through a combination of both. The so-called network firewall will block incoming messages that are infected by viruses, sent from unwelcome sources, or fail to meet certain entry criteria. An application firewall prevents messages from moving directly between networks.

Firewalls are often complemented with equipment that looks for pre-defined "attack signatures" and then sends out an alert to the security network administrator. The equipment can be set up to automatically cutoff a connection that appears suspicious.

A secure server provides relatively safe connections between networked computers and outside systems such as database storage and printing facilities. These outside systems use encryption in what is called the handshaking process, i.e., an electronic exchange in which two systems confirm each other's authority to connect.

Encryption is the process of converting messages, information, or data into a form unreadable by anyone except the intended recipient. Encrypted messages must be deciphered, or decrypted, before they can be read. The coding and de-coding functions are performed using mathematical formulas (algorithms) and secret public keys.

Some of the newer encrypting techniques are nearly unbreakable; they are highly complex, guarded very carefully by their owners, and resistant to most code-breaking techniques. They use public-key encryption in which the authorized user gets two keys: a public key for encrypting and a private key for decrypting. It is virtually impossible to determine the private key, even when the public key is known.

Industrial Espionage

Industrial espionage is the secret collection of proprietary business information. The owner or possessor attaches a value to the information and takes steps to protect it.

The term espionage most commonly relates to government security and generally has a national security connotation. Industrial or business espionage is associated with economic and marketplace advantages. Although the venues and motives differ markedly, the methods of espionage are fairly standard.

Espionage has been romanticized by the mass media, but in truth is a dirty game played out of sight. Spying involves recruitment of operatives, encouragement of disloyalty, wiretapping, bugging, electronic and photographic surveillance, bribery, coercion, intimidation, fraud, and plain old stealing.

Industrial espionage has flourished in America since the birth of the Industrial Revolution. The founding in 1789 of Slater's Mill in Pawtucket, Rhode Island, is the earliest known example. Samuel Slater had memorized the plans of the layout of an English textile mill where he had worked as an apprentice. Under the then prevailing English law, the export of factory plans was forbidden as was the emigration of textile workers. Slater nevertheless managed to slip out of the country and find passage to the New World, where he established a textile mill from the plans he had committed to memory.

Espionage has always been a vital tool of politics, diplomacy, and war, and in recent years a tool of business. Today, nearly every large corporation engages in strategic planning, a function heavily reliant on information about the marketplace and competition. Corporate leaders are undeniably interested in the plans and objectives of their competitors. Despite laws against and public disapproval of industrial espionage, spying practices are routinely carried out. Because industrial espionage is difficult to detect and prove, the law against it is infrequently enforced.

Operating a business in today's highly competitive environment places demands on businesses to collect and use large amounts of information, which in turn spawns new technological tools. These same information-handling tools are vulnerable to compromise. Not surprisingly, businesses turn to their CSOs for protection. The duty cannot be taken lightly since survival of the business may be at stake.

The clandestine nature of industrial espionage rules out making a reliable identification of those engaged in it. However, it can be said with some degree of accuracy that in certain countries industrial espionage is government sponsored. The FBI estimates that loss due to theft by foreign governments of U.S. technology and sensitive economic information is in the range of one hundred billion dollars annually.

Industrial espionage is acknowledged as a serious threat to the viability of a business and in a much larger sense to entire industries and national economies. As companies, industries, and nations move to dependence on technologically intense products and services, business spying will continue to expand and intensify.

Information targeted by industrial spying is usually proprietary in nature, i.e., it is information owned by a company or entrusted to it that has not been disclosed publicly and has value. Trade secrets, patents, business plans, research and development discoveries, and the like are examples. Proprietary information is generally under the owner's protective shield, except when it is also classified government data entitled to protections afforded by the government.

Industrial espionage moves through five stages: decide the information to be collected, collect the targeted information, refine it, and distribute it to the end user where a decision is made to use or not use the information.

Decide the Information To Be Collected. The focus of interest may be long-term and broad, such as to learn and track a competitor's overall research and design capability, or short-term and narrow such as to learn the details of a new product launch.

Collect the Targeted Information. In this stage, the espionage apparatus learns where the information is located, how it is protected, and how best to obtain it. The information may be collectable overtly, such as paying attention to newspapers, books, articles, and speeches, or it may be collectable through covert means such as planting a mole, subverting an employee, or installing electronic listening devices.

Refine the Collected Information. This step is like working a jigsaw puzzle. Information is organized and evaluated to arrive at an answer to the question initially asked, e.g., is the competitor about to introduce a new product?

Distribute the Refined Information. The processed information is given to the decision maker and/or the people who can make use of it. To be useful, the information must be timely, accurate, and understandable.

Ignore or Act on the Information. The users have two choices: ignore the information or act on it. Undesirable consequences may follow when the information happens to be accurate and is ignored, or happens to be faulty and is acted upon.

Industrial Espionage Spies

Cloak and dagger is not a term appropriate for industrial spies. Neither are they of the same ilk.

Professional. The most effective among espionage spies are professional agents. They operate from various motives.

- Greed
- Financial need
- Revenge
- Ambition
- Political, religious, or cultural ideology
- Belief in a cause

Professional agents (often self-promoted as legitimate consultants) earn hefty fees and are inclined to dismiss greed as a primary motive. Many are former government or military intelligence officers, private investigators, or security consultants. Other types of paid collectors are persons who have been carefully recruited and enticed into cooperation by the promise of reward.

Professionals sometimes pose as head hunters to engage in conversation with key employees of the targeted organization. Bogus job interviews can be a rich source of inside information. The more odious tasks performed by hired hands are searching trash, breaking and entering, and blackmailing the vulnerable.

The industrial spy follows a unique thought process.

- How can I get access to the targeted company's paper trash?
- Who are the targeted company's contractors, vendors, suppliers, and lenders? Can I obtain those details from watching the loading dock and reading license plates in the visitor parking area?
- Who in the targeted company possesses or has easy access to the information I'm after?
- Can I get access to these key employees by e-mail, telephone, and mail? What will be my cover story?
- Have any of the key employees submitted papers to or are scheduled to speak at industry symposia? How do I get the papers? How best to make personal contact? What will be my cover?
- Will a bogus job offer get me in contact with key employees? What questions can I ask that will not raise suspicions, yet lead to an inadvertent leakage of sensitive information?
- Should I make contact as a job applicant, a bidder, or a prospective vendor or repairperson?
- Where does the executive team meet when making major decisions? Is the meeting place vulnerable to electronic surveillance?

Informant. The use of informants, paid or unpaid and witting or unwitting, is a standard technique of the professional spy. Informants are often a rival's regular, temporary, or contractor employees, suppliers, vendors, or clients, plus wives, children, and friends. Also under the broad heading of informant are infiltrators and undercover operatives who penetrate the rival organization. Their activities can consist of recruiting and directing unsuspecting helpers, copying sensitive documents, intercepting communications, photographing, videotaping, and placing covert listening devices.

Volunteer. Volunteers motivated by an ideology or cause tend to be erratic, which requires careful treatment by their handlers.

Mole. A highly prized collector is the "mole" or operative-in-place. This individual is typically in a position of trust with access to highly sensitive information.

One of the best examples of a mole is Aldrich Ames, head of the CIA's counterintelligence branch who in 1983 began calling for the files on every important CIA operation involving Soviet spies. He sold the files to the Soviets in order to fund tastes not affordable by his salary. Dozens of U.S. operatives were exposed and many killed. Until his arrest and conviction for espionage in 1994, Ames received nearly $3 million for his treason.

Spies operate in a variety of ways. Following are examples:

The Set-Up. In this technique a smooth-talking con artist assumes a guise to entrap an innocent or ignorant insider. Using a pretext telephone call, the set-up agent calls an unsuspecting employee and pretends to be a vendor, such as for a company that prints architectural drawings, and elicits sensitive information by asking questions about a non-existent work order. A variation is the pretext letter. The letterhead bears the logo of a respected professional association. The letter invites the addressee, often a researcher, to submit a professional paper for publication.

Trespassing. The spy gains access to the facility by breaking and entering or by ruse. In the former, the trespasser enters by stealth and either steals or copies files, documents, computer

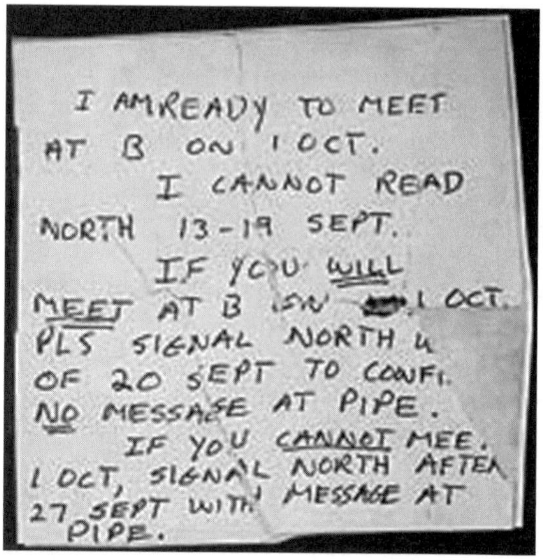

Figure 36. With this note, Aldrich Ames communicated with his Soviet handlers.

tapes, etc. In the latter, the trespasser presents false credentials that permit access to the facility and/or to restricted areas within.

Covert Listening. An eavesdropper uses sophisticated wiretap and bugging devices to capture conversations or simply overhear conversations at employee hangouts.

Stalking. Surveillance is made of personnel of interest, looking always for the hook—a personal indiscretion, a contact of questionable character, or any shortcoming that may be exploited to extort information.

Polling. Using phony questionnaires that ask apparently innocuous questions, the pollster obtains information useful in itself or useful in confirming an organization's activities such as developing a new product or moving into a new market.

The Finance Ploy. In this approach the spy gains access to a company executive by outlining an enticing proposition. In a one-on-one situation and subsequent telephone calls, the wizard spews attractive numbers that lead the executive to reveal sensitive proprietary information. Once the information is obtained, the wizard calls off the deal. The executive may not even discover he/she had been hoodwinked.

Blind Advertising. An employment ad encourages interested persons to mail their resumes to a post office box. If a resume indicates that the applicant is employed by a company of interest, the spy makes a follow-up telephone call or meets the applicant over lunch or cocktails. During discussion of the job, the spy says that a hiring decision cannot be made in the absence of specific (and sensitive) information about the applicant's job duties.

Reverse Engineering. The reverse engineer may be the spy or a person employed by the spy. Proprietary information that has been obtained about a product or process is broken down into examinable components. The engineer creates or synthesizes a clone of the product or process.

Soliciting. A dupe is recruited by deception or by rewarding a desire or satisfying a need. The recruit is connected in some way to the targeted organization: employee, vendor, delivery or repair person, customer, contractor, et al. The solicitor asks for certain types of information and to the extent the information is delivered, the solicitor satisfies the dupe's desire or need.

Spy Technology

The techniques of industrial espionage are assisted by an array of technological equipment:

- Miniaturized cameras and microphones that can be installed almost anywhere, inside telephones, furniture, walls, ceilings, and floors
- Microphones that can hear conversations from great distances
- Wireless devices for tapping into telephone lines
- Devices that can record and translate into useful information the naturally occurring electronic emissions of computers and communication equipment
- Photographic devices operated from aircraft and satellites

The same technological principles, if not the devices themselves, are applicable to counter-measures. The advantage, however, rests with the spy. Only after a spying technique has been detected can a countermeasure be put into effect. The spy, then, is always one step ahead of the counter spy.

Technical security countermeasures (TSCM) is the term for an inspection and monitoring technique that uses sophisticated electronic devices to detect the presence of covertly planted listening devices that vary widely in type and sophistication. The traditional devices are the telephone bug, line tap, hidden microphone, and parabolic microphone (such as that used on the sidelines of a televised football game to capture bumps and grunts).

Companies that use TSCM regard their proprietary information as a key asset, if not the very lifeblood of their business. These companies usually operate in a highly competitive industry and know that information leakage can adversely affect their market positions. The really large companies usually retain TSCM specialists on staff; others contract for the services.

The first step in TSCM is the inspection. If an objective is to "sneak up" on a covert listener, the inspection will feature non-alerting techniques such as monitoring the radio frequency (RF) spectrum and scanning electric power and telephone lines. If done carefully, a physical inspection can be done in a non-alerting manner. Examples include standing on a stepladder and looking above the lift-out tiles in a false ceiling, looking behind air conditioning vents and electrical wall plates, and checking the mouthpieces of telephones.

After the non-alerting techniques have been applied, the TSCM specialist transitions to a sweep using electronic tools. The term "sweep" derives from a tool resembling a vacuum sweeper. The specialist examines everything in the area (typically an office suite or a conference room) and everything entering the area such as power lines for telephones, fax machines, desktop computers, and modems.

The next step is monitoring. It involves some of the same tools used in inspecting. Think of monitoring in two forms. One has the TSCM specialist remaining at the site for one or two days listening and watching. This approach is often used when the sweep is intended to ster-ilize a room where sensitive conversations are planned to be held such as at a strategy meeting of senior executives. The monitoring can pre-cede and continue throughout the duration of the meeting.

A second form of monitoring has the TSCM specialist returning to the site periodically, say once per month on a random basis.

Competitive Intelligence

The aim of competitive strategy is not to kill or cripple the competition, but to build a position of sustainable competitive advantage. Indeed, it is possible to argue that every organization needs competitors, as without them there would be less incentive for creative thinking, and a ten-dency for the organization to become sleepy and less considerate of user needs.

Competitive intelligence is the gathering of information from overt sources; it is legal to do and is not the same as spying. Collecting infor-mation without skullduggery is both necessary and proper. Competitive intelligence becomes industrial espionage when it crosses the line between right and wrong.

Sources of Information

Perhaps the most "legitimate" source from which confidential information can be obtained is the federal government, which for regulatory and contractual purposes requires public corpora-tions—and even many private companies—to make extensive disclosures regarding their prod-ucts, finances, and operations. Hence, various agencies of the government are repositories of considerable confidential information, knowledge of which can be useful to business competitors.

There is nothing in law that prohibits studying a rival's products or services, analyz-ing advertisements, annual reports, published articles, public records, and conversing with knowledgeable consultants, customers, and suppliers. Some companies that regularly collect information about the competition assign the task to an in-house team committed to the pur-pose exclusively. Often, the team is a committee or task force made up of specialists in marketing, sales, product development, product manage-ment, and one or two members in the executive lineup.

Other companies hire outside vendors with expertise in competitive intelligence. A tacitly understood rationale for using a third party is the defense that a company can put up if the third party crosses the line separating legitimate information gathering from illicit economic spying. More and more security firms and private investigative agencies are moving into twin fields: collecting competitive intelligence for clients and preventing or detecting competitive intelligence and industrial espionage.

The rules of the game require the owner of the information to take reasonable steps to protect the information, e.g., by limiting its distribution and keeping it locked up when not in use. The information also has to be not known generally, not readily ascertainable, and of a nature to confer a competitive advantage upon its owner. A crime is committed when such information is obtained by improper means, such as theft or misrepresentation, and when the obtained information has been used to the disadvantage of the owner.

In the United States, competitive intelligence has been practiced by claim jumpers, cattle rustlers, and oil scouts. The modern era practitioner is the respected businessman. The importance and value of competitive intelligence has led some business leaders to mobilize their entire workforces to actively seek information from industry peers, for example with peers over lunch, on the phone, and at trade shows, professional conferences, and seminars.

Use of Computer Technology

The biggest of new twists is the constantly expanding variety of technological tools. Many information technology devices can be automatically programmed to constantly surf the Internet in search of significant keywords and to download industry-specific news of mergers, personnel movements, and product research and development, all of which is legal to do. The line is crossed when such tools are used to open gateways to protected domains such as a competitor's intranet or e-mail system or a confidential database of the industry's regulatory agency.

Competitive intelligence is both a product and a process. As a product, it is information with use and value that can be applied by decision makers to the organization's particular purposes or goals. As a process, it is the ethical and legitimate collection of information.

Industrial espionage, which is often viewed as the dark underbelly of competitive intelligence, is the collection of information in a manner and for purposes not entirely legitimate or which involve the use of a legitimately developed intelligence product to achieve an illegal end.

Many sources of business information are open and publicly available. They include information presented by the news media, public records, government reports, and reports issued by business competitors such as annual reports and stock offerings. On the gray fringe are the competitors' internal newsletters, proposals to prospective clients, and similar documents that are usually not confidential and which would be impossible for the authoring organizations to control in any meaningful way.

For the user of open information, the caveat is extreme caution because the data are often a potpourri of fact, half-truths, and wishful thinking. The challenge to the collector of publicly available information is to ferret out the factual portions and combine them with data obtained from other sources.

Some spokespersons in the field of corporate investigations oddly reject the claim that the Internet has made the quest for competitive intelligence any easier. They boast that the real meat is in the analysis and can only be achieved through exhaustive quantitative analysis of "the numbers." But nothing could be further from the truth. The fact is, the business world is filled with quantitative analysts who can run "the numbers," but there are many fewer professionals who can make reasoned judgments by bringing together a combination of investigative know-how and business experience.

Conclusion

In recent years, information has come to be valued on a par with equipment, materials, and capital. This utilitarian view emerges from evidence that the possession and use of information can increase profits and improve the ways that people work and think.

John J. Fay

RISK ASSESSMENT AND PREVENTION STRATEGIES FOR THE CHEMICAL INDUSTRY

The first step in constructing a solid security program is to conduct a risk assessment—in other words, to take stock of the assets that need to be protected, the threats that may be posed against those assets, and the likelihood and consequences of attacks against those assets. The chemical industry is unique in its approach to risk assessment because the security risks and needs of individual companies, and even those of individual facilities, can vary greatly from one to the next. Still, it is important to remember that attacks against chemical assets can hold greater consequences for the community than attacks on the assets of some other industries.

Assets

In security terms, assets are broadly defined as people, information, and property. At a chemical facility, the people include employees, visitors, contractors, haulers, nearby community members, and others. Information includes trade secrets (such as recipes, formulas, prices, and processes), other confidential business information, employee information, computer passwords, and other proprietary information. The range of property that a security effort might wish to protect includes the following:

- Buildings
- Vehicles
- Production equipment
- Storage tanks and process vessels
- Control systems
- Telephone and data lines
- Raw materials
- Finished product
- Electrical power lines
- Backup power systems
- Automated production equipment, such as digital control systems and programmable logic controllers
- Hazardous materials
- Boilers
- Water supply
- Sewer lines
- Waste treatment facilities and equipment
- Natural gas lines
- Rail lines
- Office equipment
- Supplies
- Tools
- Personal possessions

Threats, Vulnerabilities, and Consequences

Once assets have been evaluated, a security manager may want to consider which assets may be vulnerable. This procedure helps identify and prioritize likely targets and save companies from expending resources where the likelihood of attack is remote. For example, companies involved in certain polymer markets may produce a suspension in which a powdered polymer is suspended in solution. Even if this product is made in significant quantities, it is an unlikely candidate for a terrorist target. Therefore, expending resources to counter a terrorist threat against that target would not be wise.

How, then, do companies assess the likelihood that an asset would be a desirable target? Since chemical companies routinely perform many different evaluations and assessments, this guidance attempts to build on those existing practices to provide a tiered approach to risk-based assessment. A tiered, risk-based approach is the most effective and efficient way to evaluate, identify, and prioritize potential targets. A tiered approach is nothing more than starting with simple evaluation techniques, usually qualitative in nature, and identifying areas in which more information would be useful to reach a risk-based conclusion.

A common type of assessment in the chemical industry is a chemical hazards evaluation, in which the hazards of a chemical are compared with the potential for exposure or potentially dangerous conditions. This comparison helps answer whether a given chemical is likely to cause harm. The comparison can begin with a simple, qualitative description of how and under what circumstances a chemical is manufactured and used. The assessor can then analyze the physical and chemical properties of the substance and quickly weed out less hazardous scenarios before prioritizing on the likelihood of the scenarios.

In addition to a chemical hazards evaluation, companies routinely perform a process hazard analysis (PHA). A PHA analyzes the potential causes and consequences of fires, explosions, releases, and major spills of chemicals. The PHA focuses on equipment, instrumentation, human actions, and external factors. These considerations help managers determine the hazards and potential failure points or failure modes in a process. This type of analysis could easily be adapted to a vulnerability assessment.

Another type of assessment used in the chemical industry is a security risk assessment. Security risk assessment focuses specifically on whether a company's security management program is adequate for protecting its assets. Physical and geographical factors, too, should be evaluated in the context of vulnerability.

One approach is described below that could be used by companies that want to perform a vulnerability assessment. Many practices performed by companies on a regular basis could easily be incorporated into this approach. This is not a prescriptive approach; instead, it is a suggested flow of thought and information. It is entirely conceivable that one or more steps would not apply to certain chemicals. It is up to the assessor to use professional judgment and determine the appropriate areas to be addressed.

Chemical Hazards Evaluation. Chemical hazards evaluations are routinely performed in the chemical industry. They are often done in the context of the Responsible Care® Product Stewardship Code. Although they can and do differ in methodology, chemical hazards evaluations are designed to answer this two-part question: How likely is a chemical release, and how harmful would it be? These evaluations can easily be incorporated into a vulnerability assessment. Doing so augments the assessment of a given facility and helps in evaluating whether it might be considered an attractive target.

Process Hazard Analysis (PHA). PHAs are often done in the context of the Responsible Care Process Safety Code and are considered good practice in the chemical industry. PHAs may be a good place to begin a vulnerability assessment for chemicals and processes of security concern. A PHA is designed to highlight areas of potential vulnerability, which, upon further study, may also be a potential target of an adversary.

Consequence Assessment. Although it may be convenient to use worst-case scenarios and err

on the side of safety, that approach is not practical for assessing all threats and appropriate countermeasures. Economics and common sense dictate that potential threats and consequences (as well as the actions to counter them) be prioritized.

Physical Factors Assessment. After assessing the hazards and the likelihood that something could cause harm, it may be useful to address the physical factors that could affect the attractiveness of a potential target. These factors can potentially be used to reduce the likelihood that an object or location might be chosen as a target. Some questions that can be asked include these:

- What size and type of container is it?
- Where is it located?
- Are the containers side-by-side, stacked, isolated?
- What surrounds the plant site, and at what distance?

Mitigation Assessment

The information in risk management and emergency response plans can help managers assess factors that could mitigate the effects of a chemical release. The presence of effective risk management and emergency response plans may affect the likelihood that a facility is chosen as a potential terrorist target. For example, anhydrous ammonia is readily absorbed and controlled by a water fog. This reduces the likelihood that anhydrous ammonia will spread in its gaseous state to large areas, and thus could reduce its attractiveness as a target for terrorism.

Security Assessment/Gap Analysis. After identifying potential vulnerabilities, threats, and countermeasures, the manager could then turn to a security assessment. This assessment helps identify whether the security policies and measures in place are appropriate for meeting the potential threat. Security audits are often performed to help determine whether protective measures are adequate. The person responsible for security at a company, if he or she is not primarily a security professional, may want to consider consulting with security professionals for this part of the vulnerability assessment. Professional judgment is an integral part of the security assessment. The following list identifies some of the potential threats that a chemical facility may wish to address:

- Loss of containment
- Sabotage
- Cyber attack
- Workplace violence
- Theft
- Fraud
- Product contamination
- Infiltration by adversaries
- Attack on a chemical plant as part of chemical and biological terrorism
- Assault
- Trespassers committing vandalism or setting fires for fun
- Thieves looking for precursor chemicals to use in illegal drug manufacture; break-in can also result in valves being left open, causing a chemical release
- Protesters disrupting plant operations through trespassing, vigils, assemblies, rallies, intimidation of employees, chaining selves to plant, or blocking traffic
- Bomb threats
- Workplace drug crime
- Theft of confidential information
- Hacking into information systems to disrupt computer-controlled equipment, causing an unplanned release of chemicals
- Product tampering
- "Hands-off" threats, such as cutting off electricity, telephone, or computer network, or else contaminating or cutting off water
- Vandalism of control rooms and equipment, and destruction of system documentation to make repair more difficult
- Disruption of cooling systems for electronic equipment rooms
- Creation of destructive or hazardous conditions through modification of fail-safe mechanisms or tampering with valves (done in person or electronically from a distance)

There is no one-size-fits-all approach to a vulnerability assessment, nor is there a one-size-fits-all approach to security. A multidisciplinary approach may benefit companies performing an overall vulnerability assessment. The professional judgment of security personnel, combined with environmental health and safety employees, process safety engineers, and process operators, can yield a comprehensive approach without draining scarce resources.

Source American Chemistry Council. 2006. <www.chlorineinstitute.org/Files/PDFs/SecurityguidanceACC1.pdf>

RISK MANAGEMENT AND VULNERABILITY ASSESSMENT

This article describes how to identify the vulnerabilities of an installed Physical Protection System (PPS) and propose effective upgrades if needed. This is the basis of all vulnerability assessments (VAs) conducted by Sandia National Laboratories (SNL) during the last 30 years for a wide spectrum of customers including the U.S. Department of Energy (DOE), U.S. Department of Defense (DoD), North Atlantic Treaty Organization (NATO), U.S. Department of State (DOS), Government Services Administration (GSA), dam and water systems, prisons, schools, communities, and chemical companies.

A VA is a systematic evaluation in which quantitative or qualitative techniques are used to predict PPS component performance and overall system effectiveness by identifying exploitable weaknesses in asset protection for a defined threat. After the VA identifies weaknesses, it is used to establish the requirements for an upgraded PPS design. In addition, a VA is also used to support management decisions regarding protection system upgrades. Risk assessment and VA are closely related activities, to the point that many security professionals use the terms interchangeably. This may not present a huge problem in practice, but it does hinder communication between and among security service providers and customers.

This article is concerned with vulnerability assessment of a PPS, but the concepts can be applied to cyber protection, personnel protection, and overall security protection at a facility or across an enterprise. For the sake of clarity, an enterprise includes organizations, companies, agencies, governments, or any other entity with the need to manage security risks. Assets include people, property, information, or any other possession of an enterprise that has value.

It is important to differentiate security from safety when discussing vulnerability assessment. Safety is defined as the measures (people, procedures, or equipment) used to prevent or detect an abnormal condition that can endanger people, property, or the enterprise. These include accidents caused by human carelessness, inattentiveness, and lack of training or other unintentional events. Security, on the other hand, includes the measures used to protect people, property, or the enterprise from malevolent human threats. This includes civil disturbances, sabotage, pilferage, theft of critical property or information, workplace violence, extortion, or other intentional attacks on assets by a human. A good security VA will consider safety controls because some safety measures will aid in detection and response to security events (sprinklers will fight fires regardless of the cause), but some attacks require additional detection and response capability. For example, a disgruntled employee can sabotage critical manufacturing equipment and reduce production to a significant extent. Without security controls, it could be difficult to determine quickly enough whether this is an intentional act of sabotage and prevent a significant loss of revenue.

Risk Management

Risk management is the set of actions an enterprise takes to address identified risks and includes avoidance, reduction, spreading, transfer, elimination, and acceptance options. Good risk management programs will likely include a combination of these options. Risk avoidance is accomplished by removing the source of the risk. For example, a company may choose to buy a critical component from another company, rather than manufacture it. This removes the production line as a sabotage target. Risk reduction is achieved by taking some actions to lower risk to the enterprise to reduce the severity of the loss. This is the goal of many security programs—lower risk by implementing at least some security measures. Risk can also be spread among multiple locations, perhaps by having similar production capability at more than one enterprise facility. Then, loss of capability at one site may be managed by increasing production at the other locations. Another example of risk spreading is the distribution of

assets across a large industrial facility. By separating the assets, fewer assets may be at risk during any given adversary attack. Risk transfer is the use of insurance to cover the replacement or other costs incurred as a result of the loss. This is an important tool in many security systems. Risk acceptance is the recognition that there will always be some residual risk. The key is in knowingly determining an acceptable level, rather than unwitting acceptance. In security risk management, these decisions are based on the consequence of loss of the asset, the defined threat, and the risk tolerance of the enterprise. A tradeoff analysis must be performed to ensure that the dollars spent on physical security provide a cost-effective solution to security issues. If other risk management options provide equal or better results at lower cost, the use of a PPS may not be justified.

Security is only one facet of risk and therefore must be considered in the context of holistic risk management across the enterprise, along with other categories such as market, credit, operational, strategic, liquidity, and hazard risks. The relationships among risk management, risk assessment, and vulnerability assessment are shown in Figure 37.

To frame the relationship between risk assessment and risk management, consider definitions provided by Kaplan and Garrick (1981), who state that in risk assessment, the analyst attempts to answer the three questions: What can go wrong? What is the likelihood that it would go wrong? What are the consequences? The answers to these questions help identify, measure, quantify, and evaluate risks. Then, risk management builds on risk assessment by answering a second set of questions: What can be done? What options are available? What are their associated tradeoffs in terms of costs, benefits, and risks? What are the impacts of current management decisions on future options? The answer to the last question provides the optimal solution. Total risk management results from this process, where total risk management is defined as a systematic, statistically based, holistic process that builds on a formal risk assessment and management by answering the two sets of questions and addressing the sources of system failures.

A security risk assessment is the process of answering the first three questions using threat, likelihood of attack, and consequence of loss as their benchmarks. A thorough security risk

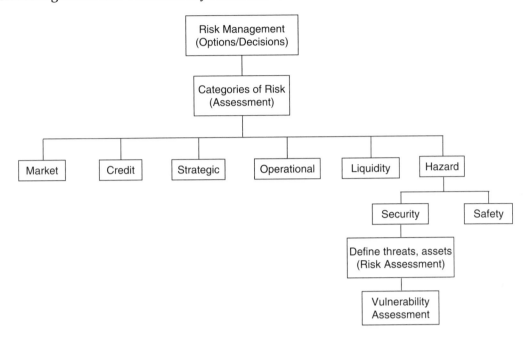

Figure 37. Risks across an enterprise must be managed holistically, and those that are identified as being above an acceptable level must be addressed. Vulnerability assessment is one of the constituent pieces of security risk assessment and is used to support risk management decisions. From *Vulnerability Assessment of Physical Protection Systems* by Mary Lynn Garcia, p. 3. Butterworth-Heinemann, 2006. Reprinted by permission.

assessment would consider risks in the component parts of a security system (cyber, executive, transportation protection, etc.) to facilitate informed risk decisions across the enterprise. As applied to the VA of a PPS, risk assessment is an evaluation of the PPS supported by a number of analysis methodologies, including:

- Threat analysis
- Consequence analysis
- Event and fault tree analysis
- Vulnerability analysis

Risk Assessment and the Vulnerability Assessment Process

Most facilities or enterprises routinely conduct risk assessments of their security systems to verify that they are protecting corporate assets and to identify areas that may need additional attention. These assessments are defined differently for different enterprises, but in general

they include consideration of the likelihood of a negative event, in this case a security incident and the consequence of that event.

Security risk can be measured qualitatively or quantitatively through the use of the following equation:

$$R = P_A^{\,*}(1-P_E)^{\,*}C$$

where

R = Risk to the facility (or stakeholders) of an adversary gaining access to, or stealing, critical assets. Range is 0 to 1.0, with 0 being no risk and 1.0 being maximum risk. Risk is calculated for a period of time, such as 1 year or 5 years.

P_A = Probability of an adversary attack during a period of time. This can be difficult to determine, but generally there are records available to assist in this effort. This probability ranges from 0 (no chance at all of an attack) to 1.0 (certainty of attack). Sometimes in the calculation of risk, we assume that there will be an attack, which mathematically sets P_A = 1.0. This is called a conditional risk, where the condition is that the adversary attacks. This does not mean that there will absolutely be an attack, but that the probability of attack is unknown or the asset is so valuable that it will be protected anyway. This approach can be used for any asset but is generally reserved for the most critical assets of a facility, where the consequence of loss is unacceptably high, even if P_A is low. For these assets, a PPS is generally required.

$P_E = P_I^* P_N$, where P_I is the probability of interruption by responders, and P_N is the probability of neutralization of the adversary, given interruption. P_N can include a range of tactics from verbal commands up through deadly force. The appropriate response depends on the defined threat and consequence of loss of the asset. P_E represents the vulnerability of the PPS to the defined threat.

C = Consequence Value. This is a value from 0 to 1 that relates to the severity of the occurrence of the event. This is a normalizing factor, which allows the conditional risk value to be compared to other risks across the facility. A consequence table of all events can be created which covers the loss spectrum, from highest to lowest. By using this consequence table, risk can be normalized over all possible events. Then, limited PPS resources can be appropriately allocated to ensure that the highest consequence assets are protected and meet an acceptable risk.

Using probabilistic risk assessment is more formal, scientific, technical, quantitative, and objective when compared to risk management, which involves value judgment and heuristics, and is more subjective, qualitative, societal, and political. Ideally, the use of probabilities is based on objective likelihoods, but in security it is common to use more subjective likelihoods based on intuition, expertise, partial, defective, or erroneous data and occasionally, dubious theories. This is important because these are major sources of uncertainty, and uncertainty is a major element of risk. Additionally, these measures can reduce the credibility of the security risk assessment for senior management, who are used to seeing documented data in standard analysis models. In security systems, this uncertainty is even larger than normal, owing to the lack of dependable (that is, quantifiable) data for all types of adversary attacks.

An additional use of the risk equation is that the security risk lifecycle can be viewed

in context. When considering security systems and the attack timeline, the attack can be broken into three discrete phases: pre-attack, which is the time the adversary takes to plan the attack; the attack phase, when the adversary actually shows up to attack the facility and the attack has started; and post-attack, when the adversary has completed the attack, and the consequences of a successful attack occur. If the problem is approached this way, each term in the equation is of primary importance during different phases of the attack. As such, P_A is most useful during the pre-attack phase. This is where intelligence agencies and deterrence have their biggest effect. Intelligence agencies gather information concerning threats and provide assessments about their likelihood of attack. These agencies may even develop enough information to disrupt an attack by collecting enough legal evidence to arrest the adversary, through tips from inside sources, or by alerting targeted enterprises, allowing them to increase security protection. All of these activities will have an effect on P_A. Heightened security responses to intelligence assessments indicating potential attacks on Citibank and the stock exchange in New York, and the World Bank in Washington DC, are examples of pre-attack influences.

If a quantitative approach is used, the P_A and C terms can be calculated using historical data and consequence criteria, respectively. In a qualitative analysis, these terms can be represented using descriptors such as likely, very likely, or not likely for P_A, and critical, severe, or minimal for the C term. This determination is based on the capability of the threat and the consequence of loss of the asset. If the likelihood of attack is high, but the consequence is low (think about shoplifting at one store in an enterprise), the problem to be solved is easier than if both P_A and C are high. (This ignores the cumulative effects of shoplifting across the enterprise. Many thefts of low-value items can add up to a high overall impact and this is part of the analysis.) There are times when either approach is appropriate, and the choice should be driven by the consequence of loss. This is based on the assumption that assets with a higher consequence of loss will attract more capable and motivated adversaries (threats), which in turn will require a PPS that is correspondingly more effective. Figure 38 represents the transition from qualitative to quantitative analysis, using consequence as the discriminator.

Some terms that are used in risk assessments, particularly with respect to the probability of attack by an adversary, may be used differently by some enterprises. Probability is a number that is, by definition, between 0 and 1, and may or may not be time dependent. (As an example, the probability of snow on any given day in Ohio may be .25, but the probability of snow in Ohio is 1.0 over the next year.) Although probability of attack is routinely cited as a threat measure, it is important to note that there frequently is not enough data to support a true probability. For example, there is no statistical data to support the probability of terrorist attacks. That fact, however, has not prevented the massive expenditure of dollars by governments and commercial enterprises to increase security at airports, seaports, critical infrastructures, and other facilities since 9/11. This is a good example of high-consequence, low-probability events and the use of conditional risk. For some assets, the consequence of loss is unacceptably high, and measures are taken to prevent successful adversary attacks, regardless of the low likelihood of attack. Frequency refers to how many times an event has happened over a specified time and is also called a rate. Annual loss exposure (ALE) is an example of a frequency often used in security risk assessments. Likelihood may be a frequency, probability, or qualitative measure of occurrence. This is more of a catch-all term and generally implies a less rigorous treatment of the measure. Haimes has written a thorough discussion of risk modeling, assessment, and management techniques that can be used in security or general risk applications.

Statistics and Quantitative Analysis

In any discussion of quantitative security system effectiveness, the subject of statistics of security performance arises. For many, statistics is a subject that arouses suspicion and even dread; however, there are a few fairly simple concepts that form the basis of statistical analysis of security effectiveness. Most of these concepts are related to the possible outcomes of a security event. A security event occurs when a security component (people, procedures, or equipment) encounters a stimulus and performs its intended

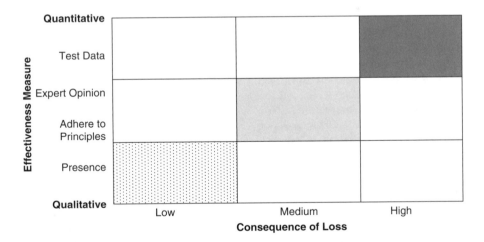

Figure 38. Qualitative analysis uses presence of PPS components and adherence to PPS principles as system effectiveness measures. A quantitative analysis uses specific component performance measures derived from rigorous testing to predict overall system effectiveness. At any given facility, either or both techniques may be used depending on the consequence of loss of the asset. Relative value of PPS components based on expert opinion is another form of analysis of system effectiveness; however, the outcome depends heavily on the knowledge and experience of the expert. From *Vulnerability Assessment of Physical Protection Systems* by Mary Lynn Garcia, p. 6. Butterworth-Heinemann, 2006. Reprinted by permission.

task, for example when something, such as a human or small animal, enters the detection envelope of an intrusion sensor. There are four possible outcomes of this event:

1. The sensor successfully detects a human-size object.
2. The sensor fails to detect a human-size object.
3. The sensor successfully ignores a smaller-than-human size object.
4. The sensor fails to ignore a smaller-than-human size object.

The successes and failures are related such that when a human-size object is presented there are two complementary results and when a smaller-than-human size object is presented there are also two complementary results. Sensors are the example used here, but this principle applies to any probability. The success or failure of a PPS component or the system in performing its intended task can be measured.

Most statistical analysis of security performance is based on these four possible outcomes. The rate at which a sensor successfully detects objects is described as the detection rate. For example, if a sensor successfully detects a human-size object nine times out of ten events the detection rate for that group of ten events is 0.9 or 90 percent. This is a statistic but is not yet a probability. The detection rate can be turned into a probability when coupled with a confidence level. A confidence level is established based on the number of events that are analyzed; the more data available, the more confidence there is in the probability. This is easily understood when considering a common example. If a person tosses a coin and the outcome is heads, it would be unwise to assume that every coin toss will result in heads. However, if that person tosses a coin 100 times and 49 results are heads and 51 results are tails, there is a fairly high confidence that the outcomes will be about 50/50. If the experiment is continued to include 1,000 trials, the confidence in the estimate of the likely results is even higher. At this point the rate can be estimated with some statistical confidence and this estimate is a probability. In other words, a probability is an estimate of predicted outcomes of identical trials stated with a confidence level. If 100 percent confidence is required, an infinite number of tests are required. In reality, when

designing performance tests, a confidence level is chosen that requires performance of a reasonable number of trials.

It is not the intent here to teach readers how to calculate the statistics of security component effectiveness but, rather, to familiarize them with the terminology and underlying concepts as applied to a PPS. For example, if a metal detector is tested by carrying a gun through it 20 times and it detects all 20 times, the probability of detection can be calculated at a specified confidence level. Often the confidence level used for security component testing is 95 percent. Using this confidence level, the probability calculated for the metal detector based on the 20 trials is 0.85 (it is often said that the probability is 85 percent but in proper statistical terminology a probability is always a number between zero and 1). In simpler language, there is a 95 percent confidence that the metal detector will detect the gun at least 85 percent of the time. The actual detection rate may be higher, but this is what can be supported given the amount of data collected. If the metal detector is tested 30 times at the same 95 percent confidence, the probability is now 0.9. Again restating into simple language, there is a 95 percent confidence that the metal detector will detect the gun at least 90 percent of the time.

Sometimes it is more useful to classify PPS component performance into error rates rather than probabilities. These error rates are the mathematical complement of the success rates, which is the number of trials minus the number of successes (i.e., the number of failures). The error rates are stated as false accept and false reject rates. In the preceding sensor example, not detecting the human-size object is a false accept and detecting a smaller-than-human size object is a false reject. This example is used to show that these are the same possible outcomes; however, error rates are seldom used when describing the performance of detection sensor devices. Error rates are much more useful when characterizing the performance of entry control devices, particularly when evaluating the performance of biometric identity verification devices. These devices measure some biological feature, such as a fingerprint, to verify the identity of an individual. In this case, false acceptance of a fingerprint from someone who should not be allowed into a security area and false rejection of someone who should be allowed to enter a secured area are a useful way to view the data.

Other factors of interest in security component evaluation include discrimination and susceptibility to noise. Discrimination describes a sensor's ability to ignore an object that is of the appropriate magnitude but is not the intended target. Often, this is beyond the technical capability of the device. In the preceding sensor example, a human-size object may or may not have specific characteristics that allow the sensor to discriminate between a human and a human-size animal like a small deer or large dog. When the sensor does not have the ability to discriminate between stimuli of equal magnitude, another statistic, the nuisance alarm rate, is used. A nuisance alarm is caused when the sensor detects an object that is of sufficient magnitude but benign in nature. Anyone who has had a belt buckle cause an alarm in an airport metal detector has experienced a nuisance alarm (assuming that person was not also carrying a gun!). The sources of nuisance alarms are easy to identify when the alarm is assessed by direct human observation or by viewing an image using a video camera. Understanding the causes of nuisance alarms is important in both design and analysis of a PPS. Installing a sensor that has low discrimination to an object or condition that is continually present in the sensor's operating environment will lead to a high nuisance alarm rate, thus lowering confidence in the system. In this scenario, human operators eventually discount alarms and may not pay sufficient attention to a real alarm when it occurs.

Some technologies are also susceptible to noise. Noise in the sensor includes sound, electromagnetic, or even chemical sources. This noise can be present in the background or internal to the system. Whenever a sensor alarms on external or internal noise, this is defined as a false alarm. In the same way that nuisance alarms reduce system effectiveness, false alarms also reduce system effectiveness. Indeed, false alarms can further erode confidence in the PPS because there is no observable alarm source present.

Throughout the discussions of security component performance, it is important to remember that the four possible outcomes of any event should be considered. This information, together with the concepts of discrimination and susceptibility to noise, form the basis of almost all security component performance evaluation.

Mary Lynn Garcia

Sources

Grose, V. 1947. *Managing Risk: Systematic Loss Prevention for Executives.* Arlington, VA: Omega Systems Group.

Haimes, Y. 2004. *Risk Modeling, Assessment, and Management, 2nd Edition.* Hoboken: Wiley and Sons.

Kaplan, S. and Garrick, B. 1981. "On the Quantitative Definition of Risk." *Risk Analysis,* Vol. 1, No. 1, pp. 11–27.

VULNERABILITY ASSESSMENT PROCESS

The evaluation techniques of the vulnerability assessment (VA) process use a system performance-based approach for meeting physical protection system (PPS) objectives. The primary functions of a PPS are detection, delay, and response. These functional subsystems can be evaluated by both quantitative and qualitative methods. Quantitative techniques are recommended for facilities with high-consequence loss assets; qualitative techniques can be used if there is no quantitative data available or if the asset value is much lower.

When performing a VA, the general purpose is to evaluate all components of the PPS to estimate their performance as installed at the facility. Once this is done, an estimate of overall system performance is made. The key to a good VA is accurately estimating element performance. When using a quantitative approach, this is done by starting with a tested performance value for a particular PPS component, such as a sensor, and degrading its performance based on how the device is installed, maintained, tested, and integrated into the overall PPS. For qualitative analysis, performance of each component is degraded based on the same conditions, but the performance of the device is assigned a level of effectiveness, such as high, medium, or low, rather than a number. In addition, component performance must be evaluated under all weather conditions, facility states, and considering all threats.

Planning the Vulnerability Assessment

Before a VA can be performed at a facility, a certain amount of preliminary work must be done.

The use of common project management principles and techniques provides a structure and a well-accepted method of approaching the technical, administrative, and business aspects of a VA.

Project Management

Project planning starts with understanding what the customer wants or needs. This stage of the project normally involves meetings with the customer to discuss what problems they are having or want to avoid, discuss why they are motivated to do this now, and discover any specific constraints they may have. Defining the project includes determining the scope of work, as well as what needs to be done, over what period of time, and the cost of the final product.

The actual work can begin after the project has been approved, the customer has sent funding, the project team has been identified, and other administrative issues have been set. Managing the project includes providing customer support; following the project plan; resolving major and minor project issues on a timely basis; and keeping the project on schedule, within budget and scope, and performing as expected.

Form the Vulnerability Assessment Team

The functional responsibilities of a VA team require a project leader and appropriate subject matter experts (SMEs). Many VA teams will use only a few personnel to serve these roles. Each team member may perform multiple functions, but all appropriate functions must be performed for a thorough VA. The major roles and responsibilities of the VA team include:

- Project Lead
- Systems Engineer
- Security System Engineer
- Subject Matter Expert (SME)—Sensors
- SME—Alarm Assessment
- SME—Alarm Communication and Display (AC&D)
- SME—Entry Control
- SME—Delay
- SME—Response
- SME—Communication Systems
- SME—Analyst
- SME—On-site Personnel

Project Kick-Off Meetings

Before starting the VA, it is helpful to have kick-off meetings with the project team and the customer. The project team kick-off meeting is meant to familiarize all team members with the project scope, deliverables, schedule, funding, and to answer any questions. This meeting is also the time to start planning the VA. An overview of the facility layout, geography, weather, and operations can be presented, along with information concerning threats and targets.

Another important aspect of the VA project is a briefing to senior management of the facility that will be evaluated. The better the purpose of the VA is communicated to management, the easier the evaluation will be, with few objections to team activities. This briefing should be clear about the goals and objectives of the VA, how it will be used, when it will be completed, and how the results will be communicated.

Protection Objectives

To successfully complete a good VA, it is critical that protection system objectives are well understood. These objectives include threat definition, target identification, and facility characterization. Each enterprise defines vulnerability assessment and risk assessment differently, and as result some facilities may not have defined threats or identified assets. At facilities where the threat and assets have not already been defined, this task must be included as part of the VA project. This will likely add cost and time to the project; therefore, it is critical to understand this before finalizing these details in the project plan.

Knowing the threat is one of the required inputs to a VA because the threat establishes the performance that is required from the PPS. We would not evaluate a PPS protecting an asset from vandals the same way that we would for a system protecting an asset from terrorists. By describing the threat, the assumptions that were made to perform the assessment are documented and linked to the decisions that are made regarding the need for upgrades. As such, threat definition is a tool that helps facility managers understand how adversary capabilities impact asset protection and helps PPS designers understand the requirements of the final PPS.

In addition to threat definition, the VA team must also have an understanding of the assets to be protected at the facility.

Facility Characterization

The major part of a VA is facility characterization, which consists of evaluating the PPS. The goal of a VA is to identify PPS components in the functional areas of detection, delay, and response and gather sufficient data to estimate their performance against specific threats. The PPS is characterized at the component and system level, and vulnerabilities to defeat by the threat are documented. Data collection is the core of PPS characterization; accurate data are the basis for conducting a true analysis of the ability of the PPS to meet its defined objectives. Accuracy, however, is only one of several factors to consider. The data gathered must be appropriate to the purpose and scope of the VA, and the quantity and form of the data must be sufficient based on available resources and desired confidence in the results.

A facility tour is usually conducted early in a VA. During the initial facility tour, the VA team begins to gather information regarding the general layout of the facility, the locations of key assets, information about facility operations and production capabilities, and locations and types of PPS components. Review of key documents and selected records are two important PPS characterization activities. These are useful in the evaluation of the effectiveness of a PPS and may begin during the planning phase of a VA. This step of a VA will also include interviews with key facility personnel.

Detection

The detection function in a PPS includes exterior and interior intrusion sensors, alarm assessment, entry control, and the alarm communication subsystem all working together. Intrusion detection is defined as knowledge of an unauthorized entry into a protected area by a person able to initiate a response. An effective PPS must first detect an intrusion, generate an alarm, and then transmit that alarm to a location for assessment and appropriate response.

Intrusion Sensors

Exterior sensors are grouped into three application types: freestanding, buried line, or fence associated sensors. Interior sensors are grouped as boundary penetration, interior motion, and proximity sensors.

The goal of the VA in evaluating the exterior sensor system is to estimate its effectiveness against defined threats. Factors that will cause performance degradation include nuisance alarm rate and ease of defeat of the sensor through bypass or spoofing.

Interior sensors are used to aid detection of intrusions inside buildings or other structures. Unlike exterior sensors, interior sensors are commonly used at all types of commercial, private, and government facilities. The most common interior sensors are balanced magnetic switches (BMS), glass-break sensors, passive infrared sensors (PIR), interior monostatic microwave sensors, video motion detectors (VMDs), and combinations of sensors, usually PIR and microwave sensors, in dual technology devices.

Interior boundary penetration sensors should detect someone penetrating the enclosure or shell through existing openings (doors, windows, and ventilation ducts) or by destroying walls, ceilings, and floors. Early detection gives more time for the response team to arrive; detection should occur during entry rather than afterward.

Volumetric detection uses sensors to detect an intruder moving through interior space toward a target. The detection volume is usually an enclosed area, such as a room or hallway. Most interior volumes provide little delay other than the time required to move from the boundary to the target. Common sensors used for volumetric sensing are microwave and passive infrared radiation. Point sensors, also known as proximity sensors, are placed on or around the target to be protected. In a high-security application, point sensors usually form the final layer of protection. Capacitance proximity, pressure, and strain sensors are commonly used for point protection.

Alarm Assessment

After an alarm is generated it must be assessed to determine the cause and decide what, if any, response is needed. The detection function is not complete without alarm assessment. There are two purposes of assessment. The first is to determine the cause of each alarm, which includes deciding whether the alarm is due to an adversary attack or a nuisance. The second purpose of assessment is to provide additional information about an intrusion that can be provided to responders. This information includes specific details such as who, what, where, and how many. The best assessment systems use video cameras to automatically capture images that show the cause of an alarm and then display these images to an operator who can assess the alarm.

Entry Control

The entry control subsystem includes all the technologies, procedures, databases, and personnel that are used to monitor movement of people and materials into and out of a facility. An entry control system functions in a total PPS by allowing the movement of authorized personnel and material through normal access routes and by detecting and delaying unauthorized movement of personnel and material.

The primary objective of exit control is to conduct searches of personnel, vehicles, and packages to ensure that assets are not removed without proper authorization. A secondary objective of entry and exit control is to provide a means of accounting for personnel during and after an emergency. There are several methods an adversary may use to defeat an entry control point. These include bypass, physical attack, deceit, and technical attacks.

Alarm Communication and Display

Alarm communication and display (AC&D) is the PPS subsystem that transports alarm and video information to a central location and presents the information to a human operator. The two critical elements of an AC&D subsystem are the speed of data transmission to specified locations and the meaningful presentation of that data. Most AC&D subsystems integrate the functions of detection and response, as well as other subsystems such as radio communications and entry control.

The AC&D communications system moves data from collection points (sensor and tamper alarms, video, self-test signals) to a central repository (database, server) and then to a control room and display. If the central repository is physically located in the control room, it may consist of multiple computers or displays, and the communication system may also move data throughout the repository and control room.

The control and display interfaces of the AC&D subsystem present information to an operator and enable the operator to enter commands. The ultimate goal of this subsystem is to promote the rapid evaluation of alarms. An effective control and display system presents information to an operator rapidly and in a straightforward manner.

The control and display system must be evaluated with the human operator in mind; therefore, operation under conditions not directly related to the AC&D subsystem must be observed during evaluations. A good human interface improves the mechanics of issuing commands and of deciphering the information presented.

Delay

The second function of an effective PPS is to slow down the adversary and allow time for assessment and response. Delay is effective only if it follows detection, which can take different forms. The most obvious form of detection is through the use of electronic sensor systems which relay information back to a monitoring station.

To aid alarm assessment and interruption of the adversary at predictable locations, consideration must be given to installing barriers and detection systems adjacent to each other so that the barrier is encountered immediately after the sensor. This delays the adversary at the point of an alarm, increases the probability of accurate assessment, and allows for an effective response.

It is quite often easier to defeat a barrier via stealth or other means than it is to penetrate it. Most security barriers at industrial facilities are designed to deter or defeat sporadic acts of vandalism, inadvertent entry, or casual thievery. For more motivated or capable threats, however, these barriers may present little deterrence or delay.

Response

Response is the third and final function of a PPS that is evaluated during a VA. There are many ways to respond to a security event. At any given facility, one or more response strategies may be in use, and this will affect data collection activities of the VA team. In addition to the response strategy, security communication is a critical part of any response function.

The two measures of an immediate response are the time for arrival and neutralization. The time to arrive is used to establish interruption; neutralization is a measure of response effectiveness. Interruption is a measure of the detection, delay, communication, and response functions of the PPS. Neutralization analysis looks at response force numbers, training, tactics, and use of weapons or equipment. In addition, the VA team must estimate the probability of communication, which is essential for an effective immediate response.

Response strategies include deterrence, denial, containment, and recovery. Deterrence is used to discourage low-level threats from attacking a facility by presenting the appearance of tight security, thereby suggesting that an attack would not be successful.

For some critical assets or production facilities, such as hazardous chemical, biological, and nuclear materials or toxic waste, where release of these agents into the environment through sabotage would cause many injuries, deaths, or contamination, a denial strategy is required. Denial refers to the protection of material by preventing adversary access to areas where materials are stored or to vital equipment used to process the material. For a successful sabotage event to occur, the adversary only has to complete the attack on the target and cause the release; capture of the adversary after a successful release does not prevent the consequence of the attack.

A containment strategy is generally used when the adversary goal is theft of an asset. Containment means that the adversary is not allowed to leave the facility with the asset; that is, the adversary is contained on-site and the theft attempt foiled. This strategy is usually reserved for facilities with high-value or high-consequence assets, such as reserve banks that store large quantities of currency.

In the event that deterrence or containment strategies fail, a backup approach is recovery of the stolen asset. For most facilities, there is an acceptance that assets may be lost for a period of time, and recovery of the assets at some point in the future is the primary response.

Recovery responses include investigation, tracking of assets, and follow-up using criminal prosecution.

Security communications consist of the people, procedures, and technology used to transmit communications among members of the response force. During normal operations, security communications may be required for conducting entry control, escort, patrols, and other routine security functions. During response to an attack, communications are essential for organizing responders, directing them to the scene of the emergency, and successfully interrupting or neutralizing the adversary.

Analysis

After all the appropriate data have been collected, analysis of the PPS can begin. There are two basic analysis approaches used in a VA: compliance and performance. Compliance-based approaches depend on conformance to specified policies or regulations; the metric for this analysis is the presence of specified equipment and procedures. Performance-based approaches actually evaluate how each element of the PPS operates and what it contributes to overall system effectiveness. The use of compliance (or feature-based) systems is only effective when loss of assets has a low consequence, or when cost-benefit analyses indicate that physical protection measures are not the most cost effective risk management option.

Performance-based analysis can use either qualitative or quantitative techniques. When conducting either a qualitative or quantitative performance-based analysis, the following six-step process is used:

1. Create an adversary sequence diagram (ASD) for all asset locations
2. Conduct a path analysis.
3. Perform a scenario analysis.
4. Complete a neutralization analysis, if appropriate.
5. Determine system effectiveness.
6. Develop and analyze system effectiveness upgrades, if system effectiveness is not acceptable.

An ASD is a functional representation of the PPS at a facility and is used to describe the specific protection elements present. It illustrates the paths that adversaries can follow to accomplish sabotage or theft goals.

A path analysis determines whether a system has sufficient detection and delay to result in interruption.

A scenario analysis determines whether the system has vulnerabilities that could be exploited by adversaries using varying tactics, resulting in lower effectiveness of the PPS. Scenario analysis considers specific tactics along the path, as well as attacks on the PPS itself or on the response force. These tactics include stealth, force, and deceit, and they may be used individually or combined during a scenario.

Neutralization analysis is performed only at facilities where an immediate response can result in a face-to-face confrontation with adversaries. Neutralization analysis provides information about how effective the response function will be under different scenarios and is a measure of response force capability, proficiency, training, and tactics.

System effectiveness can be calculated using qualitative or quantitative techniques. If the baseline analysis of the PPS shows that the system does not meet its protection objectives, the VA team can suggest upgrades that will address these issues. Usually, these upgrades are not specific technical recommendations, but are functional improvements that can be achieved by increasing performance at certain locations.

The analysis is then repeated using these performance increases to estimate the overall increase in the ability of the system to meet its objectives. These results are provided to security system designers who determine which specific equipment or other upgrades will provide the required performance. Once the analysis is completed, it is important to present both the baseline and upgrade analyses to establish the need for improvements and show the return on investment in upgrades.

Reporting and Using the Vulnerability Assessment

After analysis of facility data is complete, the VA team reports the results in a manner that is useful to the managers at the facility. The goal of the report is to provide accurate, unbiased information that clearly defines the current effectiveness of the PPS, along with potential solutions if the current system is not effective. The VA informs facility management of the state of the PPS and supports upgrade decisions.

Reporting can be formal or informal, verbal or written, and may take the form of a short overview, or a longer more detailed approach. The choice of reporting form and content is an aspect of the project agreement and generally follows the conventions of the customer or facility being evaluated. Regardless of how reporting is presented and documented, certain content must be included to make the report understandable and useful. By its very nature, a VA report is a powerful document and should not be shared indiscriminately. Protection of the final report, as well as the appropriate distribution, should be defined as part of the master project agreement.

Once the VA report is completed, a variety of responses or next steps can take place. By far, the most common approach is for the facility to pursue improving the PPS and following the recommendations of the VA team.

Mary Lynn Garcia

Sources

Flynn, S. 2004. *America the Vulnerable*. New York: HarperCollins.

Garcia, M. 2001. *The Design and Evaluation of Physical Protection Systems*. Boston: Butterworth-Heinemann.

IX: Security Fields

ARCHITECTURAL SECURITY: INTEGRATING SECURITY WITH DESIGN

The "form follows function" tenet of 20th century architecture holds that the specific functional requirements of a building should determine design criteria. A structure must permit efficient job performance, meet the needs of the user, and protect the user from safety hazards and criminal acts. In practice, however, the tenet is often reversed when design is focused on form rather than on function. Aesthetics, preferences for construction materials, and harmony with surroundings have predominated at the expense of the activities planned to occur within the structure.

Throughout history people have sought to control their physical environment. In the 21st century, the creation of new cities and expansion of existing large cities, the further industrialization of labor, and a growth in lawlessness have led to an interest in crime prevention controls that operate at the fundamental levels of societal life. Among these is the concept of crime prevention through environmental design or CPTED.

Architects worry about the fortress mentality of security professionals while security professionals are concerned about the failure of architects to include security elements in the design of buildings from the ground up. The conflict is not over whether to include security equipment in the building design; rather, the conflict lies between a building's openness on the one hand and the reasonable control of access to it on the other.

Making a building secure when it was not originally designed to be secure is an expensive proposition. Architects have to sacrifice much more of a building's openness in retrofitting for security than would be the case had the building been designed for security from the outset. Protection and operating expenses are greater than they need to be because of a lack of forethought during the design of a facility. This condition is particularly evident in many of today's buildings, where modern design and materials can result in facilities and infrastructure that are especially vulnerable.

Theoretical Background

Oscar Newman's concept of "defensible space" focused on the vulnerability of urban housing environments to crime because of poor design. Research has shown that criminals do not move about randomly through their environment looking for a target but use a spatial search process to try to find victims or targets that match their perceptual generalizations. When a match occurs, crime is likely to occur.

Deciding to commit a crime can be seen as a process of selecting a crime target and determining a crime method by taking cues from the environment.

Paul and Pat Brantingham's model of crime site selection is based on the following four propositions.

- Individuals who are motivated to commit specific crimes vary in character, strengths, and resources.
- The commission of an offense is the result of a multistage decision process that seeks out and identifies, within the general environment, a target or victim positioned in space and time.
- The environment emits many signals or cues about its physical, spatial, cultural, legal, and psychological characteristics.
- An individual motivated to commit a crime uses cues learned from experience and observed in the environment to locate and identify victims and targets.

Crowe, Saville, Sorenson, Atlas, and others have written extensively about CPTED and designing security into the built environment. Crime Prevention Through Environmental Design is a crime-environment theory based on the proposition that the appropriate design and application of the built and surrounding environment can improve the quality of life by deterring crime and reducing the fear of crime. Security and crime prevention practitioners should have a thorough understanding of CPTED concepts and applications in order to work more effectively with local crime prevention officers, security professionals, building design authorities, architects and design professionals, and others when designing new or renovating existing buildings.

Practical Realities

Theory holds, then, that altering the conditions that provide the opportunities for criminal behavior can curb crime. While this may be eminently sensible, great financial resources are required to alter the conditions. After a building has been constructed and put into use, the anticipated cost of physically changing it tends to overwhelm the anticipated benefits of crime reduction. Even in new construction projects, owners and investors are reluctant to commit the extra funds required to incorporate the physical features called for in the crime prevention through environmental design theory.

Reluctance to design for security is related to more than dollars. Modern buildings strive to attain openness and free-flowing movement. Design ideas that constrain and restrict are not on the agendas of the owners and not in the minds of the architects. Security features are often seen as obtrusive and lacking in aesthetical value. It seems to not matter that the world is an increasingly less safe place to work and live.

For a building to be made truly crime-resistant, security considerations must be in the architectural drawings from the very beginning. The drawings should reflect a comprehensive security perspective, one that takes into account the interrelationships between electronic security equipment, security officer services, and, most importantly, the routine and exceptional activities of the users of the building.

A common mistake, for example, is to establish an intrusion detection system without at the same time ensuring that intrusion alarms will be evaluated by a trained individual and that responses to alarms will be prompt, appropriate, and consistent with the needs of the building occupants.

We often see in facilities not designed for security a menu of problems associated with the control of human movement. These problems include vehicles backed up in and around garages and exterior entrances, employees bottle-necked at electronically controlled doors, criminal opportunists roving the stairwells in search of victims, and robberies at public service counters that were not installed with security in mind.

We also discover that electronic sensing devices do not function properly because someone failed to notice that a hanging ceiling or a wall extension would interrupt the sensing function.

The use of glass and foliage, which enhance the feeling of openness, can cause false alarms because sunlight will affect infrared detectors and motion detectors will activate when plants and trees are moved by air currents of the cooling system. Microwave detectors will react to cables moving in elevator shafts, vibration detectors will go off when the mail cart passes, and the fire department will be on the way when a cigar is lit under a smoke alarm.

False alarms cannot be taken lightly because they undermine confidence in the entire security program and they place an unnecessary burden on the response units. Also, when the false alarm rate is high, the building occupants tend to develop symptoms of the "cry wolf" syndrome and, as a result, may not react quickly and properly when an alarm is warning them of a true life-threatening condition.

In addition to the loss of life and property consequences that can flow from an improperly designed electronic system, there is the prospect of being held liable, both criminally and civilly. The governmental agencies that hold regulatory authority in matters affecting public safety are increasingly under pressure from society, generally to seek criminal prosecution when violations result in death or injury. Next, the extremely litigious nature of the security industry poses great potential loss in terms of compensatory and punitive awards and loss of reputation. A property owner or manager who makes security-sensitive design decisions without the input of a competent security professional is taking on a very large risk.

Security as a Design Requirement

Architects and designers can make the greatest contribution to meeting a project's security objectives. Architects generally make the basic design decisions about circulation, access, building materials, fenestration, and many other features that can support or thwart overall security aims.

Building clients and design professionals are not the only ones concerned about security during the design process. Many jurisdictions require a security review by the police as part of the building permit approval process, much the same as with fire safety requirements. Inspectors evaluate the plans for obvious spots where assaults, mugging, break-ins, and other crimes of opportunity may exist. Many jurisdictions have security ordinances that require certain lighting levels, and secure door and window designs and hardware. All federal government buildings must comply with the GSA Security Standards from 1995, and relates the many security classifications of government buildings.

If security is treated as one of the many design requirements, then the implementation and costs for such measures will be no more a burden to the project owners than fire safety features or landscaping requirements. The basic premise of security design is that proper design and effective use of the built environment can lead to a reduction in the incidence and fear of crime, and to an increase in the quality of life. The environmental design approach to security recognizes the space's designated or re-designated use—which defines the crime problem—and develops a solution compatible with that use. Good security design enhances the effective use of the space at the same time it prevents crime.

The emphasis in security design falls on the design and use of space, a practice that deviates from the traditional. The traditional approach focuses on denying access to a crime target through physical or artificial barriers, such as locks, alarms, fences, and gates. This approach tends to overlook opportunities for natural access control and surveillance. Sometimes the natural and normal uses of the environment can replace or work in harmony with mechanical hardening and surveillance techniques. An intelligent use of the environment will present three basic strategies: access control, surveillance, and territorial reinforcement.

Access Control. This strategy embraces the tried and true custom of utilizing security guard forces, and the less understood and infrequently applied strategy of making use of terrain and spatial characteristics and natural circulation patterns. Access control can be augmented by mechanical safeguards such as locks and card key systems. The central objectives of an access control strategy are to deny access to a crime target and to create in the mind of the criminal a belief that an attack on the target will present personal risk.

Surveillance. A strategy based on surveillance is directed at detecting intrusion attempts,

keeping an intruder under observation, and launching a response to an intrusion or an attempt at intrusion. A surveillance strategy can take advantage of terrain features, such as landscaping; building features, such as raised entrances; organized methods, such as patrolling; and electronic supplements, such as closed-circuit television.

Territorial Reinforcement. The thrust of this strategy is that physical design can create or extend the sphere of influence naturally exercised by the users of the territory. The idea is that an individual's sense of proprietorship concerning a place of work or domicile can be enhanced and extended by conscious individual action and by cooperating with others in a variety of crime-suppressing activities.

In a residential setting, individual actions can include installing lights, fences, locks, and alarms; cooperative actions can include neighborhood watch and patrol programs; and confronting suspect criminals who enter the neighborhood can combine individual and cooperative action. Territorial reinforcement communicates to criminals a message that they don't belong, that they are at risk of being identified, and that criminal behavior will not be tolerated by the residents.

The Architect Is the Key

The architect is the key to opening the opportunities inherent in the crime prevention through environmental design approach (CPTED). The architect is the essential element in creating a structure that will work in tandem with the various CPTED strategies. However, to be effective in this regard, the architect must be skilled in three areas.

Determining Requirements. Security needs must be determined early in the project's programming and problem-defining stage. The design team should analyze the designated purpose of how the space or building will be used. The designated purpose will be clear when designers examine the cultural, legal, and physical definitions of what the prescribed, desired, and acceptable behaviors are for that space. The space can then be designed to support desired behaviors and the intended function of the space. The design team should inquire about existing policies and practices, so that this information will be integrated in the programming process.

Knowing the Technology. Rapid and substantial advances in the technology of security systems make keeping up-to-date a challenge. Many construction projects, even those that may be seen as routine, will require the services of an architect knowledgeable in security principles and applications. An important competency is to understand and bring into existence the expressed needs of the security professionals representing a building's owner or manager. Within this competency is the ability to know when an expressed security need cannot be filled by a particular design idea and how to lead the security professional to an alternate idea.

Construction management, usually for reasons of economy, will sometimes invite an electronic security system vendor to act as an unpaid security consultant in matters involving major design decisions. The problem in such an arrangement is that the vendor's expertise will be in manufacturing and selling a product, not in providing an unbiased consulting service. The vendor's design recommendations are likely to reflect what will be best for the vendor in the short term without regard for the building occupants in the long term. Experience has shown this to be a primary reason underlying the poor performance of electronic security systems.

This is not to say that vendors should be excluded from contributing to the design, only that their contributed ideas should be critically examined by the design team for practicality and efficiency. Good sense dictates that all ideas, irrespective of source, be looked at from every perspective. The architect's best contribution to a project may be in providing a constructively critical analysis of security design concepts.

Understanding the Implications. Designs must integrate the complicated and sometimes conflicting goals of security and safety. The tendency to want to lock out the undesirables can create serious safety drawbacks in situations that require quick and unhampered egress. Space and function are variables that must also be brought into balance with security objectives.

Security and safety needs can be integrated in a five-stage approach. First is the problem statement, which explores the users' needs and leads to the development of functional requirements. Second is developing the scope of work from the problem statement, client expectations, and staff available. This stage should lead to a signed contract. Third is the design and documentation of the building and systems. It is at this stage that most architects go through schematic design, design development, and construction documents. Stage four is the administration and supervision of construction, and stage five involves acceptance testing, training, and setting up the building for occupancy.

Design Planning

Whenever possible, security planning should begin during the site selection process. The greatest opportunity for achieving a secure operation begins with locating a site that meets architectural requirements and also provides security advantages. The security analysis in site planning should begin with an assessment of conditions on-site and off-site, taking into account topography, vegetation, adjacent land uses, circulation patterns, sight lines, areas for concealment, location of utilities, and existing lighting. Other key factors for site security planning are off-site pedestrian circulation, vehicular circulation, access points for service vehicles and personnel, employee access and circulation, and visitor access and circulation. Site analysis is a starting point in security defense planning. It considers the perimeter and grounds of the facility, including walls, plantings, fences, berms, ditches, lighting, and natural topographic separations.

The next security level is the perimeter or exterior of the building. The building shell and its openings represent a crucial line of defense against intrusion and forced entry. The area being protected should be thought of as having four sides as well as a top and bottom. The principal points of entry to be considered are the windows, doors, skylights, storm sewers, roof, floor, and fire escapes. Doors are by nature among the weakest security links of a building because they inherently provide poor resistance to penetration. Attention must be paid to the door frame, latches, locks, hinges, panic hardware, the surrounding wall, and the door leaf. Window considerations for secure design include the type of glazing material, the window frame, the window hardware, and the size of the opening. The building shell itself is a security consideration for the simple reason that the type of construction will determine the level of security. Most stud walls and metal deck roof assemblies can be easily and rapidly compromised with common hand tools. Non-reinforced concrete block walls can be broken quickly with a sledgehammer or by impact of a motor vehicle. The architect's challenge is to provide security that is attractive and unobtrusive, while providing balanced and effective deterrence to unauthorized access.

Finally, the architect should design for internal space protection and specific internal point security. These security features may be necessary for the areas within a facility that warrant special protection. The level of protection may be based on zones, with access to the zones limited to persons with the required level of security clearance.

Zoning

Application of the zoning concept means control of human movement. The idea is to allow employees, visitors, vendors, and others to reach their destinations without hindrance, and at the same time prevent them from entering areas where they have no business. Controlling access to each department inside a building will screen out undesirable visitors, reduce congestion, and help employees spot unauthorized persons.

Zoning design goals are accomplished through the use of unrestricted zones, controlled zones, and restricted zones. Some areas of a facility should be completely unrestricted to persons entering the area during the hours of designated use. The design of unrestricted zones should encourage persons to conduct their business and leave the facility without entering controlled or restricted zones. Unrestricted zones might include lobbies, reception areas, snack bars, and public meeting rooms. Controlled zone movement requires a valid purpose for entry. Once admitted to a controlled area, persons may travel from one department to another without severe restriction. Controlled zones might include administrative offices, staff dining rooms, security offices, office working areas, and loading docks.

Restricted zones are essentially limited to designated staff. Particularly sensitive areas within restricted zones frequently require additional access control. These might contain classified records, chemicals, drugs, cash, and the like. Security zoning is a standard design feature of hospitals, jails, courthouses, laboratories, and industrial plants.

Electronic Systems

Devices intended to detect building intrusions is a major element of security design. The performance of a security device should be measured in terms of its probability of detecting an intruder, its vulnerability to intentional defeat, and its nuisance alarm rate. With this understanding, an architect can design and specify site intrusion detection devices, building penetration sensors, motion and volume sensors for key interior areas, access control systems, personnel identification systems, and security central control stations.

The architect should take steps to assure generous wiring in tamperproof conduit and provide a backup, uninterruptible power supply system.

Much has changed in security technology. Today's alarm systems work differently than systems of only a few years ago. Devices, like CCTV cameras, are much smaller and less costly, making them useable and affordable in many more situations. An interesting advance is the verified or dual technology technique used with interior motion-detection systems. Infrared detectors feel the change in temperature as a target crosses a zone, while microwave or ultrasonic detectors sense motion. Both technologies must be triggered to cause an alarm.

Architecture Making a Difference

Security planning is aimed at preventing crime in the built environment. The architect plays a key role in the shaping of the environment and of the cues and signals that the building sends to the user and visitors. Whether the building turns out to be safe, secure, and comfortable is a factor of how well the architect understands the intended uses. However, good architecture cannot prevent all misdeeds. The crimes that a building environment can deter by natural, mechanical, and organized means are usually external. That is, crimes from outsiders breaking in, robbery, or assault. These stranger-to-stranger crimes produce the greatest fear but not the greatest economic losses.

Internal crime represents the greatest potential loss. Terrorism of the future may not be bomb attacks on buildings but theft and destruction of assets within buildings. Can architecture make a difference in preventing internal crime? Possibly, for if a living or working environment is perceived as defensible, the occupants are likely to take greater responsibility in protecting their individual and common territories. Designing the next generations of buildings and infrastructure to be resistant to criminal attacks, or acts of workplace violence, or terrorism is incumbent upon the coordination of the design professional and the security director or consultant. Our future as a society depends on the ability to live, work, or play in buildings that are safe and secure.

Randall I. Atlas

Sources

Anderson, D. and McGowan, M.T. 1987. Untitled. *Progressive Architecture*, March, 1987.

Atlas, Randy. 2004. "Safeguarding Buildings Against Attacks from Terror and Crime with CPTED." AIA 2004 National Convention on Continuing Education.

Behrends, J. 1987. "Designing for Security." *Progressive Architecture*, March, 1987.

Brantingham, P. 1977. *A Theoretical Model of Crime Site Selection*. Dallas: American Society of Criminology.

Crowe, T. 2000. *Crime Prevention through Environmental Design, 2nd Edition*. Boston: Butterworth-Heinemann.

Keller, S. 1988. "Designing for Security." *Building Design and Construction*, March, 1988.

Krupat, E. and Kubzansky, P. 1987. "Designing to Deter Crime." *Psychology Today*, October, 1987.

Newman, O. 1973. *Defensible Space: Crime Prevention Through Urban Design*. New York: MacMillan.

Repetto, T. 1974. *Residential Crime*. Cambridge: Ballinger.

Sorensen, S. L., Maurizi, S. K. and Walsh, E. M. 1996. "Crime Prevention Through Environmental Design in Public Housing." *Technical Assistance and Training Workbook*.

Saville, G. and Gerry, C. 2003. "Introduction to 2nd Generation CPTED." *CPTED Perspectives*. Vol. 6 (2), pp. 3–7.

Vonier, T. 1987. "General Building Design Guides." *Progressive Architecture*.

Walters, J. 1984. "Design and Deterrence." *Security Management*.

CHEMICAL INDUSTRY SECURITY

Security of industrial chemicals has been a focus of concern since the attack on the United States in September of 2001, because just as the adversary transformed an element of commercial business—an airplane—into a bomb, so too, may an adversary transform hazardous materials into a weapon. Across the country from crowded urban centers to rural backwaters, hazardous chemicals are manufactured, used, and stored. These materials are deadly and, if used by a terrorist, may cause an unthinkable level of casualties.

Prior to September 11, these same poisons were viewed by many as a security deterrent. By and large, criminals steered clear of industrial chemicals because of the danger posed by them. Indeed, industrial facilities in high crime areas have been somewhat of an oasis of crime prevention. While criminal activity surrounds the enterprise, poisonous chemicals have isolated the property from harm. Consequently security within the industrial world has focused on internal types of exposures such as petty theft, embezzlement, and such.

September 11, however, changed the landscape. A new threat—the armed assailant seeking to access hazardous materials for use as a weapon—had to be addressed. Confronting exposures and addressing evident vulnerabilities, however, is a costly proposition. For an industry not known for its altruism, expenditures on new systems and personnel that are not revenue enhancement expenditures had little chance of being embraced by chemical industry management.

As a consequence, several years after the attack in 2001, chemical manufacturers, users, and transporters have done little to address obvious vulnerabilities. Those investments that have been made may be categorized as window dressing of little substantive value.

Security for a hazardous material facility, albeit a manufacturer of chemicals or a user of their products, requires the application of physical security measures aimed at preventing an adversary from reaching the target before response forces can intervene. Techniques for accomplishing this have been tried and tested many times and do not need to be reinvented. The processes and tools are readily available; the stewards of hazardous materials merely need to apply them.

What is unique about a hazardous material facility is the impact on emergency response protocols. To be sure, first responders—facility security officers, public law enforcement, fire officials, and hazmat teams—need to adapt traditional response protocols to the special conditions of a hazardous material facility.

The emergency response infrastructure across the nation is primarily structured for response to an industrial level accident, usually involving a leak of material or a spill. In some cases it will involve an explosion resulting from improper handling or mixing of materials. These procedures, however, are not applicable to a criminal attack involving a terrorist, because such an event will be of a magnitude much greater than an accident. Whereas procedures for an accident are structured for leaking vessels, the procedures for a terrorist attack must be structured for a ruptured vessel. This is the key distinction: For an accident, first responders must be trained to plug a leak or contain a spill, for a ruptured vessel there are no leaks to plug or spills to contain; the material is released instantaneously in a worst case scenario.

First responders must be prepared with Personal Protection Equipment (PPE) or be exposed as casualties. The cold zone perimeter will be unstable and will progressively spread over an area that will outstrip the capacity of the first response community to establish and maintain a perimeter.

Discharging a weapon in a hazardous material facility may be extremely dangerous as most vessels are not designed to withstand a bullet penetration. The consequence can be deadly.

Establishing detailed response procedures by private and public authorities is absolutely essential for a strategic response to be implemented. Rushing to the scene may not be advisable.

Developing a security plan for a hazardous material facility requires three distinct plans that complement and support each other.

1. Prevention: Defining and implementing the physical security systems required to delay an attacking adversary from reaching the target before response forces can intervene
2. Response Force Protocols: Procedures and training for on-site security personnel to intervene and stop an adversary
3. Public Agency Response Protocols: Protocols for communication and response by public authorities

Clearly a distinction is made between the on-site security personnel and the public authorities because it is not plausible for public authorities to respond rapidly enough to intervene before an adversary reaches the target. An adversary may reach the target and successfully complete the attack, despite the efforts of on-site security personnel, causing the public authorities to respond to a contaminated environment.

In the wake of 9/11, public agencies invested considerably in training and planning for terrorism. Unfortunately in the rush to be responsive much effort has been expended training the wrong people in the wrong material, and planning efforts, by and large, have failed to contemplate the magnitude of an attack.

Public authorities have been taught physical security concepts, even though they do not have the authority to impose physical security requirements on private businesses, nor do they have the background in physical security to do so, if they had the authority. Moreover, response planning has been constructed within the parameters of the industrial accident paradigm, not within the context of a terrorist attack. Indeed, the implications of a ruptured vessel containing toxic gas have yet to be recognized. When it is recognized, authorities may have to face the bitter reality that there is nothing they can do, but wait for the toxin to dissipate. In any event, failing to prepare adequately may simply result in first responders being added to the casualty list.

Securing hazardous material facilities requires application of physical security systems and practices that are well established. More importantly it requires cognizance of the need for response procedures within a contaminated environment.

Sal DePasquale

HOSPITAL SECURITY: BASIC CONCEPTS

Although hospitals are big business, they have generally lagged behind other business, industry, education, and government institutions in developing management policies and techniques for the non-medical functions of the organization. Included in these functions are the areas of accounting, inventory control, auditing, and security services. These deficiencies, which have been cited in the literature for many past decades, remain valid today. They persist in part because many hospitals have treated security as a short-term situation rather than a long-range objective for protecting the organization's total assets. Another reason is that healthcare facilities pose special protection problems that are not normally encountered in other organizations. It has been said that more quick decisions and rapid reactions are required in hospitals for more reasons than in almost any other type of business.

Contributing to the overall lack of long-term security planning are recent changes in healthcare facilities that have escaped the attention of administrators and have failed to alter their views of protection needs. Chief among these changes is the community's perception of the healthcare facility. Society, as a whole, has come to view the healthcare facility as another big business that is exploiting them. This perception of exploitation has increasingly led to acts of retaliation against the healthcare organization.

The healthcare facility, and in particular the hospital, the largest and most visible segment of the healthcare delivery system, is no longer as isolated as it was in the past. Hospital administrators must realize that they are no longer sheltered from the strife and anxieties of society. Nowhere is this more evident than in hospital emergency departments where violence continues to escalate each year. This escalation, which shows no sign of abating, is due in part to the lack of funding for mental health care and the epidemic use and misuse of both legal and illegal drugs.

Another area of major change for healthcare security systems is the increasing number of outside organizations that have a degree of control over the outcomes of a healthcare security program. These organizations include regulatory agencies such as state health departments, the Drug Enforcement Administration, Centers for Medicare/Medicaid, the Occupational, Safety and Health Administration, fire departments, accreditation agencies, the National Center for Missing and Exploited Children, International Association for Healthcare Security and Safety, National Fire Protection Association, and state/federal legislatures.

Too many hospital boards and chief executive officers have failed to recognize these changes in society, and the ways they affect the security of their organizations. This failure has resulted in substandard protection measures and subjected the organizations to valid criticism, economic losses, suffering, regulatory sanctions, undue litigation, and adverse community relations.

Crime and other negative behavior continue to increase as inner personal restraints on behavior are weakened. Our society has increasingly accepted impulsive behavior, and thus the individual has experienced a diminution of feelings of guilt and shame for inappropriate conduct. The same phenomenon coexists with an extremely high crime rate.

In addition to facing an increasing crime rate, healthcare facilities are becoming larger and exhibiting new characteristics. These facilities include hospitals, building physician office buildings adjacent to hospitals or attached to the main facilities, and satellite structures. New and enlarged outpatient treatment facilities are commonplace, as are large parking decks and daycare centers. The protection system must be modified to manage new environmental characteristics that create unique protection situations and attract an increasing number of people to healthcare facilities. As the number of people in a given area increases, so do the number of negative interactions.

The products used in healthcare facilities are also changing. The high use of disposable products has created more items vulnerable to theft, and the problem of safely disposing of these products is a new area for risk management. Even equipment design provides more opportunity for loss. The lightweight, collapsible wheelchair has become a major loss item for most organizations.

Continued changes in the U.S. criminal justice system have also had a significant impact on the protection needs of all organizations, including those in the healthcare field. The emphasis on individual rights has resulted in less protection for society as a whole. Those who are inclined toward criminal acts have found these times to be particularly lucrative. Shrinking law enforcement resources place increasing emphasis on organizational security self-reliance.

The September 11, 2001 terrorist attacks on the United States have had little impact on improving healthcare security programs. Despite the massive amount of spending on homeland security, virtually no money has been allocated to the security protection of hospitals. One impact of this tragic event has been a closer integration of hospital security and emergency management. A greater community awareness of the importance of medical treatment as part of the required infrastructure in the event of a terrorist event has promoted increased interaction between hospitals and public safety agencies.

Defining Hospital Security

The term security or protection for healthcare facilities might seem vague and elusive. It is in fact a relatively ill-defined concept that has taken on different connotations in different settings. Healthcare facilities continue to be defined as a system of safeguards designed to protect the physical property of the facility and to achieve relative safety for all people interacting with the organization and its environment.

This definition, of course, leaves the problem of defining relative safety. What is safe today may not be safe tomorrow. It is a difficult task to evaluate the environment of a particular facility to determine if safety has in fact been achieved. Protection, or security, is intended to reduce the probability of detrimental incidents, not to eliminate all risks. Security, then, is not static and cannot be viewed as a state or condition that fluctuates within a continuum. As environmental and human conditions change, so does the status of protection. It is this phenomenon that requires constant reevaluation of any system of protection.

Many persons providing healthcare security services attempt to view security too strictly or too definitively. The organization being served is the entity that provides the ultimate definition of the security system; after all, the organization provides the funding. This is not to say that the protection program and the philosophy and objectives of the principal security administrator do not have a strong influence on molding the organizational definition. In this respect, all organizations should prepare and maintain a current security mission statement, and continually evaluate their security programs in relation to the goals and objectives of the mission statement.

A common error for hospital organizations is to view security as being closely aligned with the law enforcement function. Although some common ground may exist between security and law enforcement, their respective activities are different in more ways than they are similar. A balanced perspective will view security as internal protection for the organization as a single unit of society, and view law enforcement as external protection that attempts to uphold the law for all of society.

Unique Aspects of Hospitals

A hospital operates 24 hours a day. Service, or in the language of the industrial complex, production, cannot be shut down at 5:00 p.m. and resume again at 7:00 a.m. the next work day. The facility must remain open to admit the sick and injured at any hour, to permit the patient to see visitors, and to carry on normal business, including gift shops, cashiers, the pharmacy, physicians' offices, and the like. With people entering and exiting through numerous entrances at all hours, it is extremely difficult to determine who belongs and who does not.

Hospital patients and visitors present unique problems not found in most other social settings. Patients are involuntary consumers, because they generally have no desire to be in the hospital or to undergo major treatment.

With the proliferation of health maintenance organizations (HMOs), preferred provider organizations (PPOs), and the like an increasing number of patients are being told which hospital they must use. Patients directly or indirectly pay the bills, and their wants must be considered. This is no simple matter because patients are presumed to be somewhat impaired due to illness or injury. Many patients are helpless. The newborn child, for example, is certainly in a helpless state, and pediatric patients can also be classed as helpless in many situations, either because they are non-ambulatory or because they are unable to define a clear course of action in situations that affect their welfare and safety.

Similar considerations can be applied to hospital visitors. When a member of the family or a close friend is ill, the visitor's actions and reactions to management practices may not always be completely rational. Thus, tolerance for abnormal behavior resulting from stress must be a major consideration in any hospital protection program.

Rationale for Hospital Security

The first of several basic reasons for providing a protection system is moral responsibility. Every organization, especially those serving the public, has an obligation to manage its environment in such a way that it minimizes the possibility of injury or death to all people on the premises. It is also the organization's moral and business responsibility to take reasonable steps to preclude the destruction, misuse, or theft of property so that the physical facility remains intact to carry on its mission without undue interruption.

A second justification for providing protection services is legal responsibility. The hospital corporation has a duty to exercise care and skill in the day-to-day management of corporate affairs. Specific examples of this general obligation are the duty to preserve its property by correcting fire and safety hazards and the duty to protect people from the actions of others.

The hospital's obligation to its patients is contractual in that the hospital assumes certain responsibilities toward them. The duty of protection becomes even greater when patients are unable to take care of themselves, as in the case of the critically ill, the elderly, infants, and children.

The issue of liability in the management of patient care facilities has become more acute in recent years. A hospital may be held liable for the negligence of an individual employee under the doctrine of *respondeat superior* or for corporate negligence. In terms of employee negligence, two general factors are requisite for imposing liability on the corporation. An employer-employee relationship must exist, and the employee's act or failure to act must occur within the scope of his or her employment.

Corporate negligence occurs when the hospital maintains its building and grounds in a negligent fashion, furnishes defective supplies or equipment, hires incompetent employees, or in some other manner fails to meet accepted standards. Such failure can result in harm or injury to a person to whom the hospital owes a duty.

The award of punitive damages is one aspect of the legal rationale and is of growing concern for hospitals. Jury awards that punish hospitals for not taking appropriate security measures are increasing in frequency and size. An added concern is that in many cases punitive damage awards are not covered by insurance and must be paid from the hospital's funds. And lastly, insurance deductibles are going higher and higher, requiring more organizational funds to be expended for litigation purposes.

A third important reason for maintaining a safe and secure environment is the responsibility of complying with requirements imposed by an increasing number of oversight organizations.

The fourth rationale for providing a protection system is to maintain a sound economic foundation for the organization. In this regard, healthcare has faced mounting criticism, especially in regard to the rapidly escalating costs of delivering quality medical care. Critics often cite the lack of cost-containment measures that in part relate to preventing theft and the waste of supplies and equipment. Authorities estimate that between 3 percent and 20 percent of hospital expenditures could be saved if proper security controls were implemented. Yet in most cases, the protection budget for healthcare facilities is generally less than 2 percent of the total operating budget.

It would seem that the economic stimulus of increased profits would be especially important to proprietary hospitals. Yet as a group they go no further than public hospitals in providing adequate loss prevention and protection systems.

Last, a safe and secure environment is required to maintain good public and employee relations. Although this reason does not appear to be as important as the others, it has probably been responsible for providing more funds for the security budget than the other four justifications combined. Hospital administrators that face bad media coverage relative to a security problem, or restless employees threatening to walk out over a security incident, somehow find the money to make necessary adjustments in the protection plan. Unfortunately, these quick solutions are generally not cost-effective and may actually be counterproductive.

Russell L. Colling

LODGING SECURITY

Security at a place of lodging is typically focused on providing a safe and secure environment for guests and employees. Protective measures vary from place to place according to the nature of threat; protective measures also range from none to barely adequate.

Places of lodging can be categorized: hotels without convention facilities, hotels with convention facilities, motels, and bed-and-breakfasts. All categories have certain security and safety problems in common and each category has its own unique set of problems.

Common Problems

Lodging security is directed at (1) care of the guest, (2) care of the staff, and (3) care of the physical site. In all cases, owners and managers must deal with the fact that they are serving a transient clientele, about which little is known. Lodging employees tend to know very little about the guests and the guests know nothing about employees that have access to their rooms. In large places of lodging, such as major hotels, the employees rarely know who is or who is not a guest.

Little or nothing is known about what occurs in guest rooms. For example:

- Prostitution
- Illegal gambling
- Surreptitious meetings among dangerous persons such as Mafia figures, terrorists, and drug dealers
- Arson
- Fires and explosions caused by materials and equipment such as those used in the manufacture of methamphetamine
- Illness and accidents such as by food poisoning and smoking in bed
- Room invasions
- Sexual assault
- Substance abuse
- Suicide and murder
- Theft of guest and lodging property

Also, lodging employees must be protected against verbal abuse, violence, and infectious disease contracted while cleaning the facility.

Loss and damage are common because the lodging business deals with transient customers that may be thieves, vandals, and drunkards. Civil liability results when guests are assaulted, raped and robbed, or have their property stolen.

Hotel Problems

Hotels tend to be multi-storied, which causes a delay in responding to serious incidents.

Large hotels host large parties, weddings, reunions, conventions, conferences, seminars, sales meetings, and the like. Employees, especially the event planner, regularly face a myriad of crime- and security-related incidents. Identification of unwelcome individuals, such as criminal opportunists, is nearly impossible. Exhibitor property, as well as hotel property, is at risk.

Motel Challenges

Single-storied motels provide easy access, both to guests and non-guests. Access is often possible through unlocked entrances, and movement in hallways is difficult to monitor. CCTV cameras and intrusion sensors are almost always non-existent. Some motels, as well as other lodging facilities, will channel entering persons through the lobby, which has the crime-deterring effect of direct observation. The same effect can be possible when a uniformed security officer is stationed in the lobby.

Bed and Breakfast (B&B) Facilities

A B&B is often located inside a private home and operates on the principle of trust. Because guests have a false sense of security, they are less careful in protecting themselves and their property.

Room keys can be primitive at best. Frequently, exterior entrances are either left unlocked or the locks can be easily defeated. Ground-floor windows tend to be unlocked or equipped with faulty locks, and shrubbery can provide concealment for burglars. Parking areas for guests are often on a street or in an unlit driveway.

TABLE 8.   Crimes Vary According to Places of Lodging

Common and Unique Problems in Places of Lodging			
	Hotel	**Motel**	**Bed and Breakfast**
Primary types of keys used	Standard or electronic	Standard or electronic	Standard or electronic
Security of room	Ranges from good to poor	Ranges from good to poor	Tends to be poor
Conventions at the place of lodging	High probability	Low probability	No
Staff knows guests	Usually not	Usually not	Yes
Location well known	Yes	Yes	Often no
Security staff on premises	Yes, in the larger hotels	Rarely	Never
Staff trained in matters of security	Often	Rarely	Almost never
Secure parking	Often	Often	Almost never
Large number of people registered	Yes	Yes	No
Secure access to room	Often	At times	Rarely
Lobby	Yes	Often	Parlor may serve as lobby during awake hours

The above chart demonstrates how difficult it is to classify place of lodging crimes. Many of these security issues depend on the management's attention to detail and its concern for the safety and security of its guests.

Peter E. Tarlow

MUSEUM SECURITY

"Museum security" is a general term applied to the protection of a variety of sites that fall loosely under the category of "museum." Museums might include museums of a classical sense—the type of building containing art or artifacts—but they might also include "house museums," where the building itself is as much of an artifact as the objects it contains. Museums might also include historic sites such as the Statue of Liberty or Mount Vernon, or facilities with other types of specimens more reminiscent of national parks than museums with walls. There are many types of museums, each posing different security problems.

It has been said that "We are born and we die. In between we wander. Museums are places where the marks of our wanderings are preserved." More specifically, museums are places where we collect and maintain (including protect) art, artifacts, and anything else that society deems important. Museum security, by its nature, is really museum "protection," as the role of the modern museum security practitioner involves aspects of safety, fire prevention and protection, and conservation, as well as classical security concerns. This description, however, concentrates on the "security" aspects of museum protection.

Museums differ from other facilities and institutions in that they do not lock their assets away in vaults. They hang them on the walls. In fact, they invite everyone to approach and sometimes even touch them. Museums are primarily educational institutions and the educational mission often comes into conflict with the protective mission in so far as the need to display objects that might best be protected by being locked in a safe is concerned.

Museums also have a concern for conservation of the displayed object. While it might seem to be a conflict for a museum to display a $100 million work of art on the wall and not place it safely in a vault each night out of concerns that moving it might cause harm, this is the type of conflict that constantly exists in the museum setting. Security practitioners who intend to work in the museum security field must reconcile this conflict if they are to be successful, for there is one reality in providing security for a museum. The reality is that the security practitioner will often have to adapt his or her protective measures to the "rules of the game," and the rules of the game for working in a museum say that museum objects *WILL* be displayed, studied, shipped, and placed in jeopardy as part of the museum's mission. The most frequent reason for failure of museum security managers is the insistence upon protecting the museum by conventional means and an inability to work within the framework of a museum setting.

It is as though the museum's governing board says to the security manager:

"Our objects are precious and valuable. But they are only valuable if we can use them for education and enjoyment. If we lock our objects away in a vault and display reproductions, their true value will be lost and they will be wasted. The artist or creator of the object intended them to be seen and enjoyed. So it is worth the risk to place these often irreplaceable objects on display. Now you go out there and don't let anything happen to them!"

The task of the museum security manager is to make every effort to work within the framework of the museum where objects will, by their nature, be in jeopardy. A good museum practitioner will provide creative solutions to museum security problems so that the precious objects are protected.

There are the other rules of the game, too. Often, museum security managers face problems unique to museums. Recommendations to place precious paintings behind protective glazing may be met with objections that doing so will change the color balance of light, affect the scholarly study of the object, or result in intolerable glare to the viewer. Recommendations to affix a sensor to the back of a picture will surely result in objections based on conservation principles universal worldwide, as it is common museum practice to not touch even the canvas backing on a picture with anything other than an acid-free white cotton glove. Recommend running wires to each picture for an alarm system and you soon learn that most museums are "changing environments" and the whole row of pictures will move 3 feet to the left, only to move

4 feet to the right a month later as new works are hung. Practitioners who recommend alarming or sprinklering a historic house museum soon learn the realities of "aesthetics" or "historic fabric." More than one major national historic site will not allow any exterior lights at night so as not to disturb the authentic feel of life in the 18th century without electricity. Many lack electricity to power alarms. Most will not allow holes to be drilled for alarm wires—even when the holes are in attics or closets, out of public view. Attics and closets are just as historic to the preservationist as walls and ceilings. Surface running of wires is also out of the question due to the impact on historic fabric, or how the house appears visually. Even in modern museums, the building is often a work of art created by a contemporary architect master. The placement of motion detectors or cameras is often unacceptable.

The security practitioner faces many problems and he or she must overcome them if security is to be provided. While the basic principles of security apply to museums, how they are applied and what tools are used to solve security problems will depend upon the skills and creativity of the practitioner. In one museum you may have to develop an expertise for protecting objects in display cases, while in another you protect two-dimensional works hung on walls. Move to a new job and you may find that your "collection" is stored in specimen jars containing alcohol. Now even your collection has become a fire hazard to your building! In another type of museum like the huge Smithsonian Institution you will protect everything from the Hope Diamond to animal specimens roaming a game preserve. In addition to classical museums, many libraries and archives have museum collections and displays. Even corporations are developing corporate art collections, often without any consideration to specialized security.

It is not unusual for major art museums to display a quarter-billion dollars in value in only one gallery. The largest art theft in U.S. history involved 12 objects valued at $200 million, probably carried out of the building in one load by two men. A recent art exhibit in Europe easily topped a billion dollars in value. The entire contents of the exhibit could have fit inside a mini-van.

There are about 6,500 museums listed in the directory of the leading museum professional association, the American Association of Museums. Of these, only about 500 have a security professional above the guard level in charge of their security and on-site. Many have a non-professional such as a registrar or building manager in charge of security, but most of the major museums do have full-time professional security management.

The American Society for Industrial Security (ASIS) has a Standing Committee on Museums, Libraries, and Archives. The American Association of Museums (AAM) has a security committee, as well. The leading conference on museum security is the *National Conference on Museum and Cultural Property Security* sponsored by the Smithsonian Institution in Washington, DC, and it is held each February. While there are no "standards" on museum security, the leading publication to guide museums in establishing a security program is *The Suggested Guidelines in Museum Security* (published by ASIS), which was adopted by both of the previously mentioned committees in 1989–1990 and are requirements of many museum insurers. The guidelines are intended to be a "minimum common denominator" of security for all museums in North America. Such a de facto standard is necessary because museums regularly borrow and lend valuable objects to one another, and it is desirable to have a measure of security when engaging in such activity.

The major elements of good museum security are: access control, parcel control, and internal security. If you can control who comes and goes and where they go once inside, and if you can control what is carried in and what is carried out, and if you can hire honest employees and keep them honest, your museum will be relatively secure.

Museum access control is often difficult. It involves admitting individuals with different levels of security clearance to different areas of the building. Access is also controlled by time of the day. For example, a conservator (the person in charge of protecting the physical well-being of the collection from such hazards as humidity, temperature, dirt, etc.) may find it necessary to have access to storage 24 hours per day, while the access for the curator (the person actually in charge of the collection) can be restricted to business hours. Problems with access control come when museums are requested to provide access to visiting scholars who wish to study for long periods of time in collection storage. The tendency of the museum is to grant such

scholarly requests because sooner or later every museum needs such access to the collection of another museum, but a substantial portion of museum thefts have occurred as a result of dishonest scholars or staff (including several dishonest security officers), so such unrestricted access can no longer be permitted. Access control is maintained via conventional methods such as locks, alarms, sign-in procedures, identification (ID) cards, visitor badges, and guards. Museums often have extensive alarm systems using saturation or near saturation motion detection. This is due to the fact that the best way to "break in" to a museum is not to break in at all, but to come in during normal operating hours and stay behind after closing. Museums using extensive motion detection can pick up the movement of a "stay behind" immediately.

Museum parcel control not only involves the removal of collection objects in employee lunch boxes, museums are also equally concerned about the razor blades or spray paint that can come into the museum, since vandalism is a serious problem in most museums. Parcel control is maintained by conventional means such as restrictions on the size and number of parcels that can be carried into the museum, alarms on objects and display cases, and parcel searches upon departure from the building.

Internal security is somewhat conventional, as well. Employees must be pre-screened and steps must be taken to keep them honest—or identify those who have become dishonest since being hired.

To protect a museum it is important to know how a museum operates. For example, if you do not understand how museum objects are cataloged and tracked on paper, you cannot know how they can be stolen by manipulation of the paper trail. The easiest way for an employee to steal from a museum is to simply manipulate the records. Therefore, safeguards need to be worked into the registration system to avoid this, particularly as museums computerize their collection records.

Since the security manager is often responsible for other aspects of protection, he or she often serves as a "troubleshooter," looking for problems before they occur. Since museums are constantly in a state of change due to the changing nature of exhibits, he or she must know how construction and renovation will impact on security and fire protection. It is not unusual for security managers to review new construction blueprints, for example, to look for water mains running through high-value collection storage or phone or electrical panels, which might require regular service access, located inside high-security storage rooms.

Museum security practitioners need to know about the following specialty areas of security: display cases, burglar and fire alarms, motion detection, key control and retrieval, line security between the museum and the central station, fire protection and suppression (said to be the most devastating threat to museums), historic fabric, museum aesthetics, wireless technology (used increasingly to alarm objects), how art and collection thefts occur, museum conservation, disaster planning, training, and policy development. The limited resources of many museums results in the security manager being a "one-man band." He or she will not have a training officer or a technician except in the larger institutions, so these skills are important.

Museum thefts are primarily crimes of opportunity but there are a growing number of thefts that are well-planned daylight thefts. One recent theft involved a team of criminals using an electric screwdriver to dismantle a case and remove many large objects in broad daylight. While night-time break-ins are relatively rare, as are daylight robberies, they do occur. The threat from visiting scholars and employees is very real.

Most museum objects of low value, such as historic artifacts, are never recovered and are stolen by "collectors" or souvenir hunters. Lower-value art is most often stolen for re-sale, while masterpieces are stolen for the purpose of extorting the insurer to get the object back. Most museum vandalism involves several categories of damage. They are: damage to historic buildings and artifacts by collectors who want a piece of the "real object," such as a piece of Babe Ruth's uniform or a chip of Plymouth Rock; damage to modern art that is not understood or appreciated by the viewer; damage to art that is irresistibly touchable, such as acrylic or textiles; damage to sexually explicit art (some people can't resist drawing in body parts on nudes); or the signing of pictures by individuals who, for some strange reason, find it interesting to do so. "Political art and artifacts" are always in jeopardy. During the Iranian hostage crisis a traveling exhibit of Persian objects was in danger, and during the Polish hostilities and

while a Vatican collection under the control of a Polish Pope traveled in the U.S., special precautions were taken. When a title card on an object in the Alexander the Great exhibition incorrectly referred to Alexander as being Greek, nationalists in his Macedonian homeland threatened the museum showing the art.

Whether you are protecting a museum containing baseball cards or Rembrandts, it is a good idea for the museum security professional to learn about the collection being protected. There is a tendency in the museum field for museum "professionals," as museum staff call themselves, to look closely at the credentials of anyone lacking a PhD in art history, anthropology, history, botany, or whatever degree best serves the institutions. Museums are academic institutions and many entry-level PhDs earn about the same as senior security guards, so senior staff expect a great deal from their "overpaid" security managers. There is a tendency to expect security personnel to move about "gracefully" within this environment if one is to be successful. Having a basic knowledge of the impressionist school of painting would not be a bad idea for a museum security manager in an art museum with an impressionist collection. Since museums are academic institutions, practitioners are required, more so than in other industries, to communicate effectively both verbally and in writing.

Museums often sponsor and stage special events. It is not unusual for museums to offer evening viewing hours, hold formal wine and cheese openings (opening night parties to kick off fund-raising events or new exhibits), or to hold lectures in their auditoriums. Many larger museums are affiliated with or actually house schools and colleges, and some house professional theaters or performing arts centers. Many museum buildings have faculty or staff offices requiring after-hour access. Some even find it necessary to hold lectures or college classes in high-value, high-density collection storage. The mixed use of space provides another dimension to the problems museum security managers face.

The changing nature of museums and the seasonal aspects of exhibit staging make it necessary to employ a large and changing staff of security guards. Many museums operate with a core of full-time professionals and supplement gallery protection with part-time seasonal personnel. This compounds the training, scheduling, and recruitment aspects of museum security, and is a constant drain on security management and support resources.

Probably the most creative aspect of museum security involves the ability of the security manager to adapt technology not intended for museum protection to suit his or her needs. The museum market is small and not directly targeted by manufacturers of security products. Few, for example, make alarms specifically for protecting pictures or motion detectors attractive enough for use in an historic house museum. Successful museum security managers will keep up with the market and with technology, and will be able to adapt equipment to solve their unique problems. While there are strict rules governing what we may and may not do in protecting museums, all of the problems are surmountable. All we have to do is think creatively.

Steven R. Keller

RESTAURANT SECURITY

Principles

While the principles of loss prevention are applicable in many working environments, they are particularly appropriate to restaurant operations.

Crime Is Preventable. Crime is never inevitable and always preventable. Support for this proposition is founded on the observation that a criminal usually selects a target based on three expectations: the fruits of the crime will be worthwhile, the criminal act will succeed, and the act will proceed with not much difficulty.

A restaurant management can assess its crime risk by comparing the three expectations against crime-sensitive conditions, such as geographic location, ease of access to and from the premises, police support, characteristics of the clientele and the employees, hours of operation, amount of cash on the premises, and the adequacy of electronic/physical safeguards and procedural controls.

A crime-sensitive condition that deserves close scrutiny is the characteristics of the restaurant's workforce. Dishonest employees commit internal theft and attract dishonest customers, poor supervisors and managers provide

opportunities for crime and are seen by criminals as easy targets, inadequately trained employees fail to exercise controls that guard against crime, and drug-abusing employees steal to support their addictions and make mistakes that open the door to crime.

Cash Attracts Thieves. Another sensitive condition is cash. Cash attracts thieves. Robbers who target restaurants want money. The best deterrent to robbery is to reduce the amount of cash available to the minimum amount necessary to conduct business. This means making frequent "bleeds" from the cash drawer and timely transfers of cash to the bank.

It Can Happen to You. Inattention to procedures is an open invitation to robbery. Many managers and employees who have been victims admit having violated one or more anti-robbery procedures. The rationale was that they believed it would not happen to them.

Trust but Verify. Misplaced trust leads to theft. The greatest threat to loss of money and inventory is from employee theft. Employees see and remember everything a manager does wrong or fails to do. Eventually, one or more of them may take advantage of these failures. While most employees are honest and trustworthy, at least a few are not. The dishonest employee is not easily identified and frequently goes to great lengths to appear reliable and trustworthy in order to take advantage of a careless or naive manager. The solution is to protect money, inventory, and other assets, and enforce controls in a fair and consistent manner.

Conventional wisdom says that 10 percent of the people are totally honest, 30 percent will steal if given the opportunity, and the remaining 60 percent may be tempted to steal under the right circumstances. Our experience tells us also that three elements contribute to the commission of a crime: the need or desire of the criminal, availability to the criminal of the skills and tools needed to commit the crime, and the opportunity to act.

The first two are difficult to control. Managers can attempt to control the desire to commit a crime by hiring honest people, but social and economic pressures can cause normally honest individuals to succumb to temptation.

It is also beyond management's control to deny individuals the skills or tools that may be used to commit a crime. The only remaining recourse is to influence the opportunity to commit the crime.

Controls Are Necessary. Physical safeguards, procedures, and accountability are necessary controls in reducing the opportunity to commit crime, especially internal theft. Studies have shown that internal theft rests on three conditions: the employee feels a need (real or imagined) to steal, the employee sees an opportunity to steal, and the employee rationalizes the stealing.

Loss can be considerable even when only one employee takes advantage of an opportunity to steal. It is virtually impossible for a manager to absolutely ensure that every employee will be so personally honest that theft will not occur. Neither can the manager control employee rationalizations about theft because rationalizing is very human and to be expected. The manager can, however, exercise a great deal of leverage in eliminating the opportunity to steal.

Management Attitudes Affect Security. The concern of supervisors and managers for protecting the employer's assets is expressed in a multitude of actions that include orienting new employees concerning expectations of honest behavior, providing employees with initial and refresher training designed to prevent crime, insisting on strict adherence to loss control procedures, and most of all, in personal behavior that reflects integrity.

Integrity means more than just being honest. It means doing the right thing and this applies to the quality of work as much as it does to the protection of assets. It should be no surprise that there is often a strong correlation between a smoothly operated restaurant and a respect for assets. When food is properly cooked and customers properly served in a clean, well-maintained setting, the odds are fairly high that the manager has a positive attitude toward security and that his or her subordinates emulate that attitude.

Employee Involvement Is Essential. The key to successful crime prevention is employee involvement. Employees need to be empowered to help in protecting assets in much the same way they are empowered to improve customer service. Despite the demanding work schedules typical of restaurant operations, management must set time aside for educating employees in crime prevention and allowing them to contribute their ideas and efforts.

Employees who are members of an opening or closing team need to be made aware of the robbery risks, they need to understand why it is necessary to leave as a group, and to appreciate that their individual safety is ensured when doors are locked and entry access is controlled during non-serving hours.

Theft at Work Affects Everyone. A myth continues that honest employees will come forward and report theft because they do not wish to work in a dishonest environment. The reality is that honest employees will usually just quit without explaining why. When management actively involves employees in efforts to rid the workplace of crime in all its forms, crime decreases and workers gain both the satisfaction of being contributors to the common effort and the ease of mind that comes with working in a safe and secure environment.

Crime Prevention Is Cost-Effective. Research findings suggest that over half of the businesses that fail do so because of employee dishonesty. Loss from theft is paid from net profits and has a great impact on restaurant profitability. In the restaurant business it is fair to say that for each dollar lost through theft the restaurant must generate $4 in new sales to compensate for the loss at the bottom line. As a practical matter, it is not possible in a short period of time to recover from a significant theft loss, such as the disappearance of a day's receipts, because the nature of the business does not provide opportunities for rapid and large increases in sales. Because recovery from the setback is difficult, if not impossible, the logical alternative is to keep the loss from occurring in the first place.

Crime Prevention Improves Employee and Customer Safety and Security. In addition to internal theft are the many loss-producing outcomes associated with robbery, burglary, vandalism, and personal injuries and property damage suffered by employees and customers. The value of a crime prevention program is impressive when its costs are weighed against the costs of loss and the severe impact of such losses on profit. Employees and managers working together can significantly reduce their exposure to crime and make their workplace safer and more secure.

Richard L. Moe

RETAIL SECURITY SYSTEM DESIGN

A large retail store or shopping center provides a unique challenge to the security system designer. Because customers, employees, and vendors are allowed relatively free access to areas within a building, the integrity of a security system is often compromised. An effective security system design must be flexible enough to work within the framework of the retail sales environment, as well as during after-hours cleaning and maintenance, and survive endless changes in management philosophy. It must function efficiently during special events and the Christmas season sales crunch with its sudden influx of customers and temporary employees. The security design should anticipate system upgrades and be expandable, while not being totally dependent upon minimum security staffing levels to manage the operation.

Design for Three Modes of Operation

Most large retail department stores have three primary modes of operation that require different levels of security. It is important to recognize this practical aspect of the retail business and design the security system accordingly. The initial security system concept must be flexible enough to accommodate daily retail sales and related activity while being capable of providing maximum security after hours.

Sales Mode. The first mode of operation is daily sales. During this period, merchandise is on display with relatively free access by customers, employees, and vendors. Most alarm systems are deactivated, and most common area doors are unlocked. The security emphasis during this period is primarily loss prevention: shoplifting, employee and vendor theft, robbery, and fraud. Customer safety is also a concern.

Non-Sales Mode. The second mode of operation involves activity just before and just after normal business hours when the store is

prepared and repaired for the day ahead. With the public excluded, perimeter doors are secured with the exception of the employee entrance and possibly the receiving and loading dock areas. Certain stockroom areas and sensitive areas can be secured, and access controls activated. Employees and vendors still have access to certain interior areas. The security emphasis during this period is access control of authorized persons and theft by employees and vendors.

After-Hours Mode. The third mode of operation involves the after-hours period when the store is vacated. The security emphasis is to ensure that all remaining personnel have exited and then to completely lock down and secure the store. The primary concern is burglary prevention and perimeter intrusion detection. A secondary concern is internal intrusion detection for the customer or employee who may hide inside the vacated store, burglarize it, and break out. Because most city fire codes require unrestricted egress from a building, early detection of lock-ins is an important task in retail security design. Fire detection and life safety are also important, but will not be discussed in detail here.

Because of these contrasts in facility usage, retail security design must be multi-functional to accommodate each mode of operation. The most cost-effective security design will integrate intrusion and activity detection, life safety, video surveillance, access control, and theft deterrence devices.

Common Design Flaws

The most common reason why retail security systems fail to function effectively is because hardware and equipment has been installed without understanding how the system will be utilized or supported. Another problem develops if a security designer, with a limited initial budget, focuses on perimeter intrusion detection only, without consideration for use of the same sensors and wiring for interior activity detection while the building is occupied. The most costly errors occur when a security designer fails to plan for system growth, future integration, and for hardware and software compatibility. Retail security will always be plagued by budget fluctuations; that is why systems should be designed modularly so that they can be built upon year after year.

A Typical Example

Take for example, a large retail department store located in a four-story building that intends to operate the first three floors for retail sales; the top floor for management offices and credit/cashier functions; and the basement for shipping/receiving, main stockrooms, and support staff operations. The store is part of a new regional mall with three public access points at ground level and interior access from the mall side at three levels.

In this example, the anticipated business hours are 9:00 a.m. to 9:00 p.m., 6 days per week, and 9:00 a.m. to 5:00 p.m. on Sundays. Cleaning crews access the facility at 6:00 a.m. each day. Management and employees may arrive as early as 6:00 am and may remain on the premises as long as 2 hours after closing. Occasional special events such as inventory, stocking, and promotions can extend facility usage into the night. Facility maintenance of escalators, elevators, and heating and air conditioning usually occur after hours as well.

Since the store's security needs vary depending on the time of day, the system components are designed to serve equally well during each period. The heart of the security system is housed in an intelligently designed console; a single security operator can monitor access control systems, alarm and video functions, and perform dispatcher duties as well. This proprietary system is designed to capture alarm data and video signals after hours, even though monitored remotely by a central station.

The security console incorporates a computer-based access control system to monitor card reader data and alarm status via a graphic interface of each floor plan. The video surveillance cameras are monitored by a high-speed, multi-format, system controller that has digital record/playback capability for 16 camera inputs, captured on a hard-drive with output to DVD capability. The system operator is able to view multiple color cameras on a single 25-inch color monitor, either in compressed mode or by calling up individual cameras to full screen size after receiving external alarm input annunciations. A second video system is installed in the security manager's private office to view and record hidden pinhole surveillance cameras in addition to views of the main system.

While the store is closed and vacated, traditional intrusion-detection methods are applied. These are designed to suit the particular retail environment. Perimeter alarm protection includes the standard door contacts with redundant interior motion sensors and photo-electric reflectors as backup. The store's glass doors and windows will be shaken, have faces pressed against them, and have police flashlights shone through them, all of which may activate poorly placed internal motion or heat sensors. The security designer must anticipate these occurrences and plan accordingly.

A combination of detection devices and physical barriers is designed into the store's interior protection scheme. Interior motion sensors and door alarm contacts are zoned separately, so they can report the location and path traveled by an intruder. A design strategy of lockable back hallway doors and basement recall capability for the elevators forces a "lock-in" intruder to use either the fire stairs or the escalators to move from floor-to-floor. This design tactic forces the intruder to move through the protected area allowing the motion sensors to electronically track him throughout the store while the color video cameras record the event. A burglar's location can be pin-pointed to the precise point within a store and his escape route can be easily predicted.

During after-hours maintenance, a flexible security system is designed to allow for specific detection device shunting allowing continuous monitoring of the remaining square footage. While the store is occupied, but closed to the public, the same devices are designed to monitor access to sensitive areas. The proprietary alarm and video system is supervised by on-site security personnel during this period.

Janitorial staff and employees are issued programmable ID keycards to limit and track access to their respective work areas and stockrooms. The access control software captures the data from each card-reader for review by security personnel.

The fine jewelry and cashier areas will have an alarm controller sub-system installed with robbery, panic, and redundant safe alarms. These specialty departments use a combination of a programmable keycard and a digital keypad to operate the alarm function. This method provides for dual supervision by the security staff and specialty department management.

Motion activated multi-camera record/ playback capability of the video controller is particularly beneficial as employees approach these sensitive departments. Pre-programmed function keys allow the console operator to monitor activity in all sensitive areas simultaneously at the push of button, while still recording the remaining camera locations on one digital recorder. Similarly, when the receiving dock raises the roll-up doors each morning, local alarm annunciation at the console alerts the guard to call up the camera to full screen mode to view this area. Since all 16 cameras are being recorded automatically, one guard can effectively monitor all areas.

During business hours, strict access control is neither reasonable nor desirable in a retail store. Most perimeter and interior alarm sensors will be deactivated. However, security has daytime monitoring capability for sensitive stockroom areas in the basement and can monitor the loading dock doors when not in operation.

All fire doors and emergency exits are monitored along with holdup and panic alarms for the jewelry department and cashier. The management offices have separate duress alarms installed under each desk, which report to the security console in an emergency or hostile customer.

Video surveillance cameras are heavily relied on during business hours because of expected security staff fluctuations. Each floor has six color camera domes installed and pre-wired for pan-tilt-zoom capabilities. Only three domes per floor contain cameras; the pre-wire allows for movement to any drone location. The basement level, employee entrance, loading dock, and shipping areas all have domes with cameras installed. The fourth floor cashier and management office area also have live cameras and domes.

The sophisticated, multi-camera, video controller system is designed to fit the current aggressive management policy regarding employee theft and shoplifting. However, this design will accommodate other, more passive philosophies in the future as well. The current design technology will allow a single console operator to follow a shoplifter from camera-to-camera and from floor-to-floor, while automatically recording the entire event on the digital hard drive and dispatching undercover security personnel.

The system design takes advantage of two lockable electrical utility closets located at opposite ends of each floor. Much of the video cable is routed through these rooms down to the security console. Break-out boxes are installed in each electrical room to facilitate maintenance of the video cables and to allow for cost-effective modifications.

The covert video surveillance system is designed to interface partially with the installed dome system. Additional coaxial cable is pulled during the construction phase branching out from each dome location to all appropriate areas for use with pinhole surveillance applications. Other coaxial cable is pulled independent of the dome installations as well.

This design shortcut requires some coaxial cable switching at dome sites, at break-out boxes, or at the security console, but saves hundreds of hours and thousands of dollars when system growth is desired.

The covert video surveillance inputs are routed separately to the security manager's office for privacy. The manager's office is also wired for video and audio recording and playback on a large color monitor capability in case of employee integrity interviews, theft interrogation, or for training purposes.

Vendor Support Can Affect Design Decisions

Local support from access control and video surveillance vendors often affects which design path to follow. Each component of a fully integrated security system must be able to operate independently, should other components fail or need repair. The access control computer and video controller will require rapid local repair service and replacement capability, should they go down. The use of exotic system components is not recommended without solid local vendor support and service capabilities.

Plan for System Growth

Another important design consideration is to plan for manual backup systems for both alarm and video systems. Also, during construction, specify 3/4- or 1-inch conduit when pulling video and data cables, instead of 1/2-inch, to allow for additional cable in the future.

A good retail security system design anticipates the human factors and supplies the main console area with excellent ventilation and ergonomics for the long hours of service by security officers. The expensive equipment has needs too including adequate cooling of the electronic components and an adequate power supply with back up capability.

The business of retail sales has not changed much over the years, but thanks to technology, controlling losses is becoming more manageable with a well-designed, integrated security system.

Chris E. McGoey

Source   Crime Doctor. 2006. <www.crimedoctor.com>

SECURING THE BUDGET MOTEL

Most hotels and motels are concerned with security and have measures in place to prevent crimes against patrons. At the same time, however, hotels and motels continue to be targeted by criminal elements.

The Budget Motel

According to the American Hotel & Motel Association, the budget motel typically provides no frills, has one to three stories with 20 to 125 rooms, and makes up 80 percent of the total domestic lodging community. Security in the lodging environment presents a wide range of challenges if only because the lodging business is in operation every hour of the day, every day of the year. At a budget motel the challenges are especially difficult. Why is this the case? Part of the answer lies in the observation that a budget motel usually has:

- Exterior entries to rooms, some with sliding doors
- Numerous remote entries and exits
- Parking right outside each room's door
- Exterior entries to rooms, some with sliding doors
- Limited staff with few or no security personnel

- Little or no physical security
- Limited capital resources

Inexpensive safeguards can usually be implemented at a budget motel, but the more significant and costly safeguards tend to be put on the back burner. Unfortunately, it is the absence of the significant safeguards that leads to litigation. On the one hand, budget motel management may recognize the need to upgrade security and appreciate the attendant liability risk, but on the other hand, may lack the financial resources to do anything about it. Even with new construction or retrofitting for expansion or other non-security purposes, management may be unable to find enough capital to fund needed security improvements.

With the exception of safe deposit boxes at the front desk, which limit a motel's exposure to property loss, no codes or laws require a motel to provide physical security. Courts across the nation have mandated that motels must merely take "reasonable" precautions to protect their guests from physical harm.

The public has become more educated concerning personal safety. In the last few years, for example, guests have insisted on sprinkler systems and 24-hour security. In an over-built lodging market with heavy competition and fewer people traveling, hotel and motel owners are responding to their customers' concerns about personal safety.

Six Basic Steps

Six very fundamental security steps that involve time but little cost can be implemented at the budget motel. These include:

Step 1.   Managing by walking around (MBWA) involves getting into the trenches and seeing what's going on in the business, and getting close to customers and employees. The really small "Mom and Pop" motels practiced MBWA before Tom Peters put a label on the concept. The larger, multi-unit motel chains are often lacking in this valuable practice.

MBWA is a caring attitude that is imparted to employees and guests alike. Many security professionals emphasize having a written policy and program, and although written materials can be helpful, they cannot engender the caring attitude and genuine concern that must be projected for security to succeed.

Step 2. A background investigation that includes contacting prior employers and making criminal records checks should be conducted before employees are hired. This is important because applicants may falsify prior employment information in order to conceal personal defects that make them unsuitable for assignment to high-trust jobs.

The value of background checking is apparent at the budget motel where only one or two employees are present in the evening hours. At stake are the care and custody of the motel and its assets, and the protection of the patrons and their valuables. These are awesome responsibilities that cannot be placed into the hands of people about whom little is known.

Step 3. Employees need to be involved in security. One way to promote involvement is to make employees aware of security risks, how the risks affect the motel, the staff and the patrons, and what the staff can do to offset risks. The American Hotel & Motel Association offers a series of training video workshops on the basics of lodging security. Workshops cover everything from awareness to handling disturbances.

Another consideration is to motivate employees to carry out their security responsibilities, especially with respect to emergency response procedures. Programs that provide rewards, such as a deserved thank you from a supervisor, a certificate of appreciation, recognition by co-workers, a day off or a merit bonus, can go a long way to building a security program.

It is not unusual in the lodging industry for an employer to pay for performance as opposed to paying for time spent on the job. Quality and quantity of work, especially work that is central and essential to the business, is recognized as having a higher value than hours spent at the workplace. Incentive programs can include financial rewards for excellence in security.

Step 4. Having a liaison with local law enforcement is crucial to the small property operator. Without adequate police protection, the budget motel is at extreme risk. The property management can contact the local crime prevention unit to identify the criminal threats confronting the motel and to learn what the police and the

management can do to improve security at the property. At a minimum, the local management needs to know the nature of the police services that are available, the manner in which those services are performed, and the officers who deliver the services.

Step 5. The motel manager needs to communicate with neighbors. The idea is to share information about crime in the neighborhood and to look out for each other's interests with respect to spotting and reporting suspicious activity. Neighbors can also share details of their successes and failures in setting up countermeasures to local crime. These are the kinds of activities that defend against allegations that the motel management was negligent by not recognizing crime risks that can impact its patrons and by not having a security program at least equal to that of nearby competitors.

The motel manager should be active in the local business organizations, especially with organizations that serve the lodging industry, such as the local chapter of the American Hotel & Motel Association. The contacts and information obtained through networking can be invaluable.

Step 6. Patrolling of the premises should be done during the hours of darkness and whenever crime presents a threat to property or people. Patrolling can be handled on a proprietary basis by designating in-house employees to perform the patrol (as full-time or add-on duties) or patrolling services can be handled on a contract basis with a security guard company.

Whatever the approach, four considerations are important. First, screen the persons to be selected for patrolling. Ensure they are drug-free, psychologically stable, trustworthy, and possess the physical ability to meet the rigors of constant movement in an outdoor environment. Second, provide the selected persons with the knowledge and skill to do their jobs effectively. Teach them how to look for the indicators of crime and hazardous conditions, and how to respond when the indicators are present; make sure they understand the limits of their lawful authority; and motivate them to convey an interested and caring attitude in their dealings with people. Third, give them the proper tools to carry out their jobs. Distinctive uniforms, inclement weather gear, flashlights, and a means of communication are essential. Fourth, give them plenty of supervision and lots of positive guidance.

This article has presented only a few of the elements of a fully developed motel security program. The key message is that the budget motel management, constrained and driven by cost imperatives, is often unable to provide a full range of security measures. Although the risks may be well understood, management lacks the necessary financial resources to implement what the prudent security professional would consider to be an adequate, reasonable security program.

There are nonetheless certain basic security steps that can be taken with only a modest expenditure of funds. These are: (1) manage by walking around (MBWA); (2) screen job applicants, at least those who will be in positions of trust; (3) make security a responsibility of all employees; (4) work with local law enforcement; (5) communicate with neighboring businesses; and (6) patrol the premises.

Robert L. Kohr

Sources

Boyer, J. 1988. "Get Back to Basics With Security." *Lodging*.

Ellis, R.C. Jr. 1988. *Security and Loss Prevention Management*. East Lansing: The Educational Institute of the American Hotel & Motel Association.

Kohr, R. 1991. *Accident Prevention for Hotels, Motels, and Restaurants*. New York: Van Nostrand Reinhold.

SECURITY CONSULTING

The term "security consultant" means different things to different people. In a broad sense, the term can apply to anyone offering security products, services, advice, or expertise. In a narrow sense, it refers to a branch of the security profession in which individuals and firms with special knowledge and skills provide independent, non-product-affiliated consultation to clients on a fee plus expense basis or similar arrangement.

The International Association of Professional Security Consultants (IAPSC) is the leading professional association specifically for this group of security practitioners, representing both the member consultant and the consumer.

The IAPSC imposes a strict code of ethics upon members, and its view of the security consultant role carries a great deal of weight in defining the profession. The IAPSC says that security consultants are independent, non-product-affiliated individuals or firms that offer security management, technical, or forensic consultation. This definition also includes professional security educators and trainers.

The IAPSC says that security consultants have nothing to sell but their expertise and advice, although it permits members to publish and produce consulting products such as books, manuals, training programs, and other information sources that are extensions of the consulting practice. Generally, these consulting products offer advice and expertise. Members may not represent or sell security products or other services such as guard or humanpower services, nor may they engage in certain types of private investigations. The goal is to reduce the possibility of a conflict of interest so that the advice of a security consultant is totally independent and free of conflict or the appearance of conflict of any type.

Security consultants fall into specialized areas and it is rare for one consultant to offer services in all areas. Even a single specialty will require many years of education, training, and practical experience before the practitioner reaches a level of marketable competency. Some consulting firms will offer a variety of specialized services, using a combination of in-house staff and outside associates. Associates are often part-timers who work on an as-needed, project-by-project basis. Some consulting firms will affiliate with other firms in order to expand the range of services. Of course, a senior security practitioner of the caliber and with the experience one would expect of a security consultant probably came up through the ranks in several industries and gained a range of skills. Therefore, few consultants offer only one specialized service, but consumers should beware of the jack of all trades consultant who is an expert in everything. He is either a true Renaissance man or someone who can't make a living in his specialty and finds it necessary to move into other fields to make ends meet. One sign of a true expert in the consulting field is that he or she is successful as a specialist rather than as a generalist.

Security management consultants offer "pro-active" advice such as preventive surveys, humanpower and cost reduction audits, and evaluations designed to improve the overall management and efficiency of the security operation. Most often they conduct security surveys that look at the management aspects of security for a client.

Technical security consultants offer a range of technical services from value surveys designed to ascertain if there are cost savings in redefining the alarm system service or maintenance agreement with the vendor to highly technical electronic system designs. Many technical security consultants work on projects under contract with architects and engineers. In this capacity they advise the architect on physical security design, lighting, alarms, closed-circuit television (CCTV), access controls, and related matters. They are closely involved with security codes and standards such as the standards of Underwriters Laboratories as they relate to alarm and electronic systems. They often advise on foreseeability issues as well. They often produce bid documents such as system design or performance specifications, blueprints, device and hardware schedules, bid forms, requests for proposals, detail drawings, etc. They provide project management during the installation of the electronic system or a construction project. Technical security consulting is highly specialized and involves considerable risk to the consultant due to the possibility of error and omission lawsuits.

Forensic security consultants are often referred to as "expert witnesses" but it is not necessary to testify in court to provide forensic consultation. Forensic consultants in the security specialty advise clients before, during, and after litigation. They advise on how to properly secure premises to avoid litigation and they advise the court during litigation on various aspects of the case in question. This is done through research reports submitted to the attorneys or the court, through depositions, testimony, or other means. Forensic consultation requires constant research on the part of the consultant to keep up with the current state of the art in security and current case law. This aspect of security is highly specialized and requires great attention to detail on the part of the expert advising the court or clients. While any security "expert" can testify in court, those who make testifying a profession had better be good at it because there will always be opposing experts.

Security educators and trainers are individuals who teach security and loss prevention subjects at a college level or who provide training services on a consulting basis to clients. Some provide evaluations of corporate loss prevention or of law enforcement training programs and give advice on improvements. Some offer training seminars and programs.

While the previous categories of security consultant cover most of the consulting activity, there are other specialized services offered as well. They might include executive recruitment of security managers for a client, or consultation to insurers and law enforcement on matters that they do not encounter frequently enough to gain their own expertise, such as recovery of stolen art or stamp collection theft investigation. Generally, consultants who engage in "high-level," special investigation do so as advisors, turning their cases over to law enforcement or to private investigators before arrests are made. The hourly rate for consultants is typically twice that of private investigators, precluding them from involvement in investigative activities of a routine nature.

Most security consultants are "niche consultants," that is, they specialize in one or more of the many security-sensitive industries, or they have unique qualifications in a fairly narrow security discipline. For every work activity having a security implication, there will be one or more persons who possess or claim to possess special knowledge and skill. Complementing these are technical experts who provide electronic countermeasures that protect against covert listening devices, experts who design access control systems, and so on. Add to these the many experts in forensic matters, such as questioned document examinations, tool marks, fingerprints, and biological fluids. Don't forget also the area consultants who understand security as it is practiced in certain geographic regions such as the Caribbean, South America, or the Middle East, where language, politics, and culture are important concerns.

Security consultants are usually independent contractors who own their own businesses, but many work for larger firms as staff consultants. It has been estimated by the IAPSC that fewer than 1,000 full-time non-product-affiliated security consulting firms operate in the United States and Canada, but there are hundreds more individuals who engage in security consulting on a part-time basis.

Security consulting is a rewarding profession for the practitioner who has become recognized in his or her specialty or in the security profession as a whole. While compensation for the more successful security consultants is about equal to the top compensation packages of security managers in the same specialty of security, many choose security consulting because they prefer the independence of working for themselves. Each year 10–15 percent of individuals who hang out their shingles give up consulting. This is due in part to lack of preparation and capitalization. Because it usually takes at least 1 full year to build even a modest consulting practice, the fledgling consultant needs to have a well-researched business plan and be prepared financially to carry out the plan during the start-up period.

The ranks of consultants will swell when employers cut back and will shrivel when employers are in a hiring mode. During a down trend, many of the displaced security professionals will turn to consulting, and most of these will be among the first to leave consulting during an up trend. Those that leave consulting often do so because they find the work and travel schedule to be intolerably demanding. Successful security consultants, not unlike their counterparts in the corporate environment, put in long, hard hours to reap the rewards.

Security consultants generally charge an hourly or daily fee about equal to that charged by general management consultants to industry, with technical and forensic security consultants commanding slightly more. They pay their own benefits and taxes, and devote a considerable amount of time to non-billable functions. For example, a security consultant who works steadily at a rate of 40 hours per week may find at the end of the year that the billable time will total about 1,100 hours, with non-billable time in the range of 1,000 hours. The billable hours were spent working directly for clients while the non-billable time was spent marketing one's services and performing a variety of administrative functions.

Consumers can often find qualified consultants by contacting the IAPSC or other professional associations that screen their members prior to admitting them to membership. The associations often provide referrals or directories to consumers. Or the consumers can search the Internet using a specific specialty identifier such as "bank security consultant" to find a list of consultants advertising their services. The next step would be to check professional credentials and references.

The use of security consultants has been growing steadily in the United States and Canada in recent years, but the trend has been for consumers to use the services of the more recognized experts. Security practitioners that are widely published, for example, find it less difficult to break into the profession. A client tends to want to contract with an individual who is immediately recognizable as an expert. High visibility is often equated with excellence, at least in the mind of the client.

The client also wants a consultant who knows security and knows the nature of the client's line of business. It is not sufficient, for example, to know how to detect embezzlement without at the same time knowing the arena of the suspected embezzlement. Success in detection will depend on a solid understanding of the client's industry and the client's unique business operations. In the area of electronic equipment, security consultants are increasingly expected to be on the leading edge of the technology and to be proficient in related scientific areas such as computer-assisted design techniques.

To the client, a security consultant can be an attractive alternative to carrying a professional on the regular payroll. The major incentive is the money that can be saved by not having to pay fringe benefits, such as medical insurance and paid holidays. A minor incentive is having to pay for security services only when needed. While thoughtful employers will not favor this type of band-aid approach, many small and mid-size employers have no other choice.

Steven R. Keller

THE SECURITY CONSULTANT

In-House Versus Outside Advice

Many companies call on outside consultants to perform studies, make evaluations, and offer recommendations for implementing or improving their security programs. Some companies have benefited from the experience and knowledge that consultants can bring to bear on problems encountered during surveys. Other companies have not benefited. Disappointments are a result of a number of factors. For one thing, employees sometimes regard an outsider as an interloper, a stranger, one who has no real feeling for the company or its employees. Rank-and-file employees as well as supervisors and line managers may be resentful and secretive, thus preventing the "outsider" from obtaining a full understanding of problems as they presently exist within the company. No matter how experienced the consultant may be, his or her first task, and it is often a difficult and time-consuming one, is to learn the intricacies of the company, its ingrained processes, procedures, and methods of operation. This is often referred to as the corporate culture. Absent a full understanding of the corporate culture, the consultant's recommendations, usually seen first by line managers in the form of a written report, may produce a less than positive reaction. Some line managers may spend more time defending the status quo than implementing what may be valid recommendations for improving their operations. Employees generally know that outside consultants charge large fees for work that may well be done, at substantially less cost, using inside resources. Additionally, some so-called security consultants represent manpower or hardware firms and are salespeople in the truest sense of the word and not consultants at all. The title of consultant has been misused perhaps more in the security field than in any other profession. The result of using a salesperson who is not a qualified consultant is that the client often ends up paying for more "security" (manpower or hardware) than is actually needed.

Security consultants can and do provide valuable services to their clients, provided the client does a reasonably good job of selecting the right consultant in the first place. As a one-time professional security consultant, one who earned his living by plying this trade, I would caution prospective users of consulting services to use the same solid business judgment and standards in selecting a security consultant that one would in selecting any other type of consultant. In order to do that, perhaps a brief look into the historical development of the security consultant will be a worthwhile journey.

The field of protection consulting is relatively new, perhaps not more than 70 years old. Protection consulting had its origins in the insurance industry, principally with regard to property (fire) protection. The field then grew, as a natural extension, into accident prevention (casualty) and safety consulting. Last, but certainly not least, came security (crime prevention) consulting.

Security consulting probably got its start just before the United States entered World War II, with the development of the defense industry and its secret and top secret projects. Originally the emphasis was on perimeter protection, access control, and document classification as the principal means to protect defense secrets. The requirements for a security program of some sort were contractual in nature; that is to say, adequate protection was deemed to be necessary before the facility would be considered safe for secret or top secret defense projects. It was only when an obvious flaw or hole in the security was detected that an outside inspector came in and analyzed the situation. The inspector's job was to make recommendations to improve the security sufficiently for the facility to retain its clearance for secret or top secret production.

It is probably safe to say that most security consulting assignments then were based on problems that had already occurred. Little, if any, thought was given to prevention. It was during the 1970s that professional security consulting came into existence. It was also about this time that enlightened developers, owners, and managers began to recognize that to increase efficiency and reduce cost, security had to be built into facility design and not added onto a building project as an afterthought. Today, it is not uncommon for architects to seek the services of qualified protection consultants to ensure that their final designs take into account the security requirements for the buildings or project under consideration. As such, we now see security consultants specializing in the business of design engineering.

Working with architects and engineers on complex design and construction projects is not a task to be assigned to an apprentice security consultant. Clearly a combination of education and experience leading to professional maturity is needed here. It is said that a wise man knows his limitations. In the consulting field, mistakes can be costly. One's professional reputation can suffer if one takes on a project for which one is not fully qualified, and fails. Huge industrial complexes, such as nuclear power generating facilities or a large hospital, will probably require the services of a team of consultants, because of the multifaceted and varied disciplines required to survey such complicated environments. In the team approach, consultants are selected because of their expertise in the particular fields or specialty for which their talents will be utilized, recognizing that no one consultant can be expert in all fields of endeavor having to do with security or any other discipline.

Using the team approach to consulting assignments can reduce time and expenses for most large projects. Often it is the only way some large projects can be managed, because of the many specialty areas encountered in these environments. No one security consultant should be expected to be an expert in all phases of security management, procedure, hardware, and electronics—though most, by necessity, have a general idea of the proper application of the various security systems that may be used under specific conditions.

Considerations

Why Use Outside Security Consultants? The question concerning when to use the services of an outside consultant does frequently arise. Some of the more common questions regarding the use of outside versus inside resources to do a security survey or consulting job are as follows.

Why Do I Need Outside Advice? An independent consultant can furnish objective opinions without prejudice and without regard to internal pressures or politics. The consultant can, in effect, "let the chips fall where they may."

More often than not, a competent security director or manager knows what his problems are and has even defined the solutions. In these cases, the outside consultant can furnish a "second opinion" to reinforce the initial opinion, especially regarding cost-effective solutions to complicated problems.

When one seeks outside advice and assistance, one will surely seek help from a professional with a high degree of experience in dealing with the problems at hand. As mentioned earlier, the second opinion technique is common practice among other professions and disciplines. Yet in the security field, we find a great reluctance on the part of some professionals to admit to their obvious limitations.

Unlike manpower or hardware salesmen, the truly independent security professional has only one concern—the best interest of his client.

Manpower and hardware consultants (read salespeople) are generally limited in scope and are understandably biased toward their own products or services. Their first loyalty is to the company that employs them, and rightfully so. Nevertheless, security professionals have little reluctance in accepting proposals for service from contract security salespeople. The very same security professional will agonize over the prospect of recommending an outside security consultant to do a comprehensive security survey of his entire operation, including procedures, manpower, and hardware.

How Can I Justify the Cost of a Consultant on a Limited Budget? One must not lose sight of the fact that most security surveys are full-time propositions. Assuming that the in-house professionals are fully employed at their day-to-day occupations (and who in this business will admit that they are not?), where will they find the time to conduct a meaningful audit or survey?

Professional consultants usually have available to them library and research assistance unavailable to the average security practitioner. The library resources have been collected, catalogued, and indexed over a period of many years. Admittedly, with the advent of the Internet, this is less critical today than in the past.

Few security professionals, however, have developed the depth of knowledge necessary to do risk assessment in a multi-disciplined environment. Most professionals tend to become specialists in certain fields—government, finance, utilities, hospitals, and retail, to name a few. It is not that most professionals are not capable of broadening their scope, it is just a fact of life that few of us do, preferring the "comfort" of our own field of expertise or practice.

An outside consultant can investigate the financial aspects of the necessary manpower and hardware solutions and then negotiate these cost factors with corporate management. Not every in-house security professional is schooled in the financial and negotiating techniques necessary to sell program changes. Most consultants, however, are.

Will an Outside Consultant Provide Assistance in Setting Up the Recommended Program? This touches on a very common fear—that the consultant will make broad-brush recommendations and then walk off into the sunset, counting his or her excessive fee, leaving a difficult job for those who have to implement the consultant's recommendations. In actuality, consultants can continue to be employed to the extent that they and management feel is necessary to achieve the level of protection required to solve the problems identified during the survey. Risk assessment is at best a matter of opinion, with much uncertainty. The continued presence of the consultant with input at the implementation or installation stages can materially contribute to the final success of the project. And, physical presence is not always necessary. As we tell all our clients, "Night or day, we are only a telephone call away."

Most consultants do not provide contract services. Instead, they usually recommend several reliable firms in the immediate geographical vicinity that have reputations for providing quality service. The consultant then assists the client by drawing up minimum specifications and requirements, which the client furnishes to several firms, requesting that each submit a written bid. After the bids are returned to the client, the consultant can assist the client in reviewing the bids and selecting the service that meets the client's requirements at the best (not necessarily the lowest) cost. Once the service is accepted, the consultant can inspect, guide, provide administrative oversight, and critique the implementation or installation of the service.

This same procedure is applicable whether the product is security manpower, hardware, or electronics. But, as with all other phases of the survey, the consultant's key role is to function as the client's representative. Successful consultants function in the best interest of their clients at all times. This means scrupulously avoiding even the mere impression of a conflict of interest.

Security Proposals (Writing and Costing)

A security survey can range from a simple telephone call, to a 1-day on-site review with verbal conclusions and recommendations, to a full field study. The last would encompass a comprehensive review of all risks, complete with a fully documented report detailing the entire security effort. Consulting assignments may also include plan development and review of blueprints and purchase specifications for access control and anti-intrusion alarm systems and other sophisticated security hardware and equipment.

To avoid misunderstanding the parameters of the task to be performed, both client and consultant should establish at the outset the specifications of the tasks to be performed. Probably the best way to accomplish this is with a written proposal.

Before a client asks for, or a consultant begins to prepare, a proposal, it is important that each have a basic understanding of the problems in need of being solved. This can be tricky. Often clients have only a limited idea of their problems and may not be able to articulate their needs. Some clients have not made a realistic appraisal of their problems and thus may not have realistic expectations regarding the solutions. The only way to ensure that both parties understand exactly what is to be accomplished is by outlining the issues in a written proposal.

Written proposals can take many forms, but five basic elements are common to most. They are the introduction, proposal, management, cost, and summary.

Introduction. The introduction identifies the client, geographical location, and problem in very broad terms. It also identifies the consultants and the firm that is submitting the proposal.

Proposal. The proposal must clearly state the need to be fulfilled, most often expressing it as a statement of work or scope. It sets forth in very specific terms both the problem and the proposed review or study that will be undertaken to gather the data necessary to solve the problem and meet the client's needs. It will also later serve as a general planning outline for the consultant doing the work. Following are examples of items that may be included in the proposal:

- Security Objectives
- Losses
- Security Organization
- Security Regulations and Procedures
- Guard Force
- Personnel Security
- Physical Security Conditions

- Utilities
- Construction of Security Facilities
- Security Hardware
- Alarm Systems
- Communications
- Surveillance
- Security and Fire Safety Hardware
- Procurement

Management. The management section of the proposal will identify and fully describe the consulting organization, its experience, its personnel, and if necessary, a sampling of client companies that may be used as references. In any event, management, administration resources, logistics involved, and capabilities should be spelled out in some detail and should fully qualify the consultant and firm for the task at hand. Usually included in this part of the proposal are biographical sketches of the consultants who will actually be performing the survey.

Cost. Cost figures are the best-guess estimate of the consultant doing the job. They are only a yardstick and are subject to change if the scope of the inquiry changes when the job is underway. Nevertheless, the client is entitled to a reasonably accurate estimate of the cost and to prompt notification when the job is underway if the scope (and thus the cost) is going to change. Some clients specifically outline the task to be accomplished and send the outline out for several firms to bid on, and then accept the return proposal with the lowest figure. This technique, found most often in government entities, is called a request for proposal (RFP). It is also used by large multinational corporations with well-structured purchasing departments.

Summary. The summary is used to highlight the details of the proposal, as set forth in the previous four sections. It also contains the total cost of the proposed project. This section should identify the benefits the survey hopes to accomplish in terms that even the most recalcitrant, bottom line–oriented, bean-counting executive can understand. It must leave the reader with the positive feeling of having just read a proposal prepared in a timely, efficient, and professional manner. A late, poorly prepared, and disjointed proposal is a reflection of what the future holds

regarding the primary task. Don't expect more or less from a consultant's proposal than you would expect to receive for the principal task.

James F. Broder

Source Broder, J. 2006. *Risk Analysis and the Security Survey*. Boston: Butterworth-Heinemann.

TOURISM SECURITY

Tourism Security is the name often given to the field that seeks to protect the world's tourism industry. The field has grown considerably since the terrorism attacks of September 11, with a tremendous emphasis on terrorism and tourism.

Tourism Security is often divided between the criminal side of the field and the terrorism side of the field. These two aspects of tourism security are often very different from each other. Tourism crimes tend to be crimes of opportunity. A partial listing would include hotel/motel invasions, crimes of distraction such as the stealing of luggage and pick-pocketing, and site defacement. Criminals often establish a parasitic relationship with the industry and are dependent on the industry's success in order to "succeed." Terrorism, on the other hand, often seeks to destroy or do great damage to the tourism industry. Its goals tend to be mass casualties, economic destruction, and publicity. In reality there is no such thing as total tourism security.

Although many disciplines make a clear distinction between security and safety, tourism scientists and professionals do not. Security is often seen as protection against a person or thing that seeks to do others harm. Safety is often defined as protecting people against unintended consequences of an involuntary nature. For example, a case of arson is a security issue while a spontaneous fire is a safety issue. In the case of the travel and tourism industry, both a safety and a security mishap can destroy not only a vacation but also the industry. It is for this reason that the two are combined into the term "tourism surety." Tourism surety is the point where safety, security, reputation, and economic viability meet. Another example of this interfacing between safety and security is in the issue of health related matters. Visitors are capable of carrying diseases from one part of the world to another. Visitors are also subjects of poor health standards in food preparation and the transferal of health problems from local tourism employees to visitors. Terrorists are also very much aware of this fact.

Tourism security/surety experts divide the field into six component parts or challenges. These are:

- Visitor Protection. Tourism seeks to protect visitors from locals who might seek to do them harm, from other visitors who may be in transit for the purpose of committing crime, and less than honest staff members. The visitor protection component also touches upon the need to protect visitors from tourism professionals who commit fraud or sell them a product or tour package that does not deliver what it promises.

- Protection of Staff. Often tourism employees are subjected to abuse or even forms of sexual and physical assault. A second aspect of a tourism surety is the assurance that honest staff members can work in an environment that is crime free and not hostile.

- Site Protection. A third component of tourism security is site protection. The term site can mean anything from a place of lodging to an attraction site. While in an age of terrorism there are people whose purpose it is to destroy or harm a specific site, site protection must also take into account the careless traveler. Travelers may also seek to "take" a part of a site home as a souvenir. Another aspect of site protection is assuring that the industry's property is not

mishandled. Tourism surety also takes into account the needs of cleaning staffs and hotel engineers and seeks to assure that site environment is both attractive and as secure/safe as possible.

- Ecological and Health Management. Closely related to and yet distinct from site security is the protection of the area's ecology. No tourism entity lives in a vacuum. The care of a locale's streets, lawns, and internal environment has a major impact on tourism surety. Ecology also involves the cultural ecology. When cultures tend to die, crime levels may tend to rise. Protecting the cultural ecology along with the physical ecology of a locale is a major preventative step that tourism surety professionals can do to lower crime rates and to assure a safer and more secure environment.

- Economic Protection. Around the world tourism is a major generator of income. As such it is open to attack from various sources. Tourists and visitors do not distinguish between the treatment they are afforded by the local travel and tourism industry and by people living and working in the community. As such, tourism security professionals have a special role in protecting the economic viability of a locale.

- Reputation Protection. Tourism crimes and acts of terrorism against tourism entities receive a great deal of media attention. As such, tourism security/surety develop clear risk management strategies in order to avoid need for a major marketing effort to counteract the negative reputation.

Peter E. Tarlow

X: Security Principles

CONVERGENCE OF PHYSICAL SECURITY AND IT

Convergence relating to security is occurring at two levels: technology and management. At the technology level is the convergence of digital information technology (software, computers, databases, networks, wireless communications, etc.) with electronic security systems. This level is part of a much larger adaptation of digital technology that is transforming nearly every facet of business from simple office administration to complex manufacturing operations. In the case of automobiles alone, digital technology is an element of computerized systems that monitor tire pressure, check the status of engine components, provide lane-change warnings, invoke skid prevention, and deploy air bags. In the security realm, the advances have been no less dramatic. Physical security systems now have capabilities to command and control, identify emergency conditions and initiate response, communicate globally, share information, and perform routine workflow tasks.

At the security management level, convergence is the integration of physical security functions, information security functions (also known as IT security), and security risk management. In many organizations that integrated the functions, a job position was created to manage the functions. The position title is usually Chief Security Officer (CSO).

The dictionary uses action verbs to define convergence:

- To tend toward or approach an intersecting point
- To come together from different directions; meet
- To tend toward or achieve union or a common conclusion or result

All three apply to security convergence.

Four Key Aspects of Convergence

There are four key aspects of the convergence process in security:

- Combining physical security and IT security
- Bringing physical security functions in line with business systems functions
- Bundling physical security tasks and IT security tasks
- Managing all of the above

Holistic Security, Integrated Security Management, and Enterprise Security Risk Management are variously used when referring to the fourth key aspect.

Combining Physical Security and IT Security

Methods of protection in the IT domain are distinctly different than protective methods in the physical security domain, which means that the protection managers in each domain have different knowledge and skill sets. Today's security systems require knowledge that goes beyond physical security's traditional domain. The procurement, deployment, and maintenance of security systems are functions that need close coordination with IT operations personnel regarding networking, especially for networked video systems, and also regarding network security and computer security for the security systems themselves.

IT Knowledge and Skills. Physical security system projects require close collaboration with IT operations personnel regarding networking, especially for networked video systems, and also regarding network security and computer security for the security systems themselves.

Internetworking of Physical Security and Business Systems

Internetworking is the connecting of two or more networks together. The use of access control systems for time and attendance involves integration of the access control system with a human resources or payroll computer system. The use of security video cameras and recordings for business operations (such as for quality control supervision, operations management, and training follow-up) involves sharing video information over the standard business network. Thus there are new stakeholders throughout the organization, whose use of security systems requires extending their information technology elements and infrastructure for non-security purposes. This means that non-security personnel must be involved early in the planning process regarding the design, deployment, and utilization of security systems. Fortunately, the user of security systems for additional non-security purposes increases the ROI for security systems, sometimes significantly.

There must be dialog between the physical security and IT operations groups so that IT can support the intended information sharing across the corporate network, and account for the additional load that it may place on the business network. Security precautions must be taken on both sides, because the security network must protect itself against intrusion from the business network, and vice versa.

Integration of Physical and IT Security Systems

Security can be strengthened by the integration of physical and IT security systems. A common example given is the integration of access control systems, so that a person cannot log on to a computer in a particular room, unless that person has already used the physical access control system to gain entry to the room and has not yet exited. This particular application helps prevent the fraudulent use of stolen computer logon names and passwords. An alarm generated by this attempted breach of security can alert security officers as well as IT security monitoring staff to the physical presence and location of someone attempting to breach information security.

Integration of Physical and IT Security Management

In recent years security interest and responsibility has been elevated to Senior Management and the Board of Directors, partly because new regulatory penalties exist for corporate officers who fail to establish and maintain integrity and security for corporate finances, and for failing to provide adequate protection of information subject to privacy restrictions, such as personal customer information. The existence of regulations requiring disclosure of privacy security breaches means that failures

to establish sufficient security can have a significant impact on the price of corporate stock or the willingness of customers to continue to do business.

For CEOs, CFOs, Boards of Directors, and corporate risk managers to evaluate, approve, and actively support security programs and security initiatives, there must be some means of relating security to the overall corporate risk picture and financial picture. A unified perspective is required that incorporates physical, information and human asset protection in a comprehensive risk treatment plan. Traditionally separate plans for physical, IT, and corporate security do not provide a way to prioritize security expenditures across the security domains, or to evaluate security risks relative to one another. An overall risk treatment plan and a corresponding cost/benefit analysis of risk treatment options is required to give senior level decision makers the ability to make informed decisions.

To help security practitioners and their organizations address these issues, in 2005 the Alliance for Enterprise Security Risk Management (AESRM) was established by three leading international security organizations: ASIS International, ISACA (the Information Systems Audit and Control Association) and ISSA (the Information Systems Security Association). The alliance is dedicated to providing guidance regarding the convergence, or integration, of traditional and information security in organizations throughout the world, to the end of helping address the significant increase and complexity of security-related risks to international commerce from terrorism, cyber attacks, Internet viruses, theft, fraud, extortion, and other threats.

Although some organizations have found that they can improve effectiveness and efficiency by combining the physical and IT security groups, for many organizations this is not practical or advisable. Nor is it necessary to establish a unified security perspective. By establishing a single corporate security executive, such as a CSO, and by establishing a corporate security steering committee or corporate risk council, security risks can be effectively mitigated throughout the enterprise without having to combine the physical and IT security groups.

Ray Bernard

CRIME CONTROL THEORIES

While the average security practitioner, in reviewing security literature, will read about Crime Prevention Through Environmental Design, or CPTED, as it is more commonly referred to, there are a host of other theories offering as much or more insight into crime control. If one wishes to implement any host of new security applications he or she should start with the "why" and "what" questions such as "Why do offenders choose to commit their offenses in this particular location? What is it that allows offenders to feel comfortable about committing their offenses at this location?" Learning the answers and applying a theory will not be enough to discover the magic solution but can allow one to make an informed judgment. Once an understanding is attained of the "why" and "what," the security practitioner is able to penetrate deeper to learn if rational choice made by the offenders plays a role (as Cornish and Clarke would believe) and/or if the absence of a capable guardian is a contributing factor (as Felson and Cohen would theorize). A deeper understanding of the offense allows the security professional to make keener and more analytical choices about how to reduce or eliminate the offenses.

Rational Choice Theory (Cornish and Clarke)

Rational Choice Theory was first fully presented by Ronald V. Clarke and Derek B. Cornish in 1986 in *The Reasoning Criminal: Rational Choice Perspectives on Offending*. The rationale behind the theory is that people will commit a crime if it is in their own best interests to do so. Basically the offender uses a decision-making process whereby the positive and negative aspects of committing a particular act are weighed. If the perception is that there are more reasons for proceeding, regardless of the existing security barriers, then at the very least the individual will make an attempt. If a crime opportunity presents itself, there is a benefit to be had, and there is little likelihood of being apprehended, the individual will commit the crime. Inherent in the criminal's decision is an assessment of the potential benefit, not unlike a businessman's assessment of the potential return on investment. Further, these decisions made by the offender, whether basic or sophisticated, are affected by time, skill level, and access to timely and relevant information.

It is up to the security practitioner to convince the potential criminal that it is not in his or her best interests to carry out the act. In other words, influence the potential criminal's choice to act or not act. To the extent that the influence is effective, crime is prevented. Influence takes the form of practical techniques (Clarke, 1997: 18) that make it more difficult for the criminal to commit the crime, increase the risks of being caught, reduce the anticipated rewards, and remove the excuses.

The security practitioner makes it more difficult for the criminal to commit the crime by use of physical equipment, such as intrusion detection and access control systems, and psychological deterrents such as lights, fences, and guards.

The techniques of Situational Crime Prevention are laid out in the following table.

A number of observations can be made concerning the principles of rational choice theory:

- In many cases criminal opportunists are average people.
- People will weigh the pros and cons of committing the crime.
- Choice is centered on the specifics of the target.
- If the reward is high enough, deterrents will not work.
- Situational Crime Prevention works best with the amateur and least with the professional. The least skilled opportunist will be deterred by or unable to defeat standard crime prevention techniques and is likely to be caught in the attempt; the skilled and determined opportunist will not be deterred and may succeed in committing the act.

In a later section, discussion will be made of two related factors: displacement and diffusion of benefits.

In a second-generation classification of the sixteen situational crime prevention techniques, Wortly stated, "the new classification is based upon the argument that there are two distinct situational forces acting upon potential offenders—the perceived costs and benefits of intended criminal acts [the basis for Clarke's classification] and factors that may induce individuals to commit crimes that they would not have otherwise considered [the basis of the present classification]" (Wortly, 2001: 63).

Wortly's views are reflected in the following chart.

TABLE 9. Sixteen Situational Crime Prevention Techniques

Increasing Perceived Effort	Increasing Perceived Risks	Reducing Anticipated Rewards	Removing Excuses
1. Target hardening Slug rejecter device Steering locks Bandit screens	5. Entry/Exit Screening Automatic ticket gates Baggage screening Merchandise tags	9. Target removal Removable car radio Women's refuges Phone cards	13. Rule setting Customs declaration Harassment codes Hotel registration
2. Access control Parking lot barriers Fenced yards Entry phones	6. Formal surveillance Red light cameras Burglar alarms Security guards	10. Identifying property Property marking Vehicle licensing Cattle branding	14. Stimulating conscience Roadside speedometers "Shoplifting is stealing" "Idiots drink and drive"
3. Deflecting offenders Bus stop placement Tavern location Street closures	7. Surveillance by employees Pay phone location Park attendants CCTV systems	11. Reducing temptation Gender neutral listings Off street parking rapid repair	15. Controlling Disinhibitors Drinking age laws Ignition interlock V-chip
4. Controlling facilitators Credit card photo Gun controls Caller-ID	8. Natural surveillance Defensible space street lighting Cab driver ID	12. Denying benefits Ink merchandise tags PIN for car radios Graffiti cleaning	16. Facility compliance Easy library checkout Public lavatories Trash bins

These techniques were developed by R. V. Clarke and R. Homel (Clarke, 1997: 18)

TABLE 10. Sixteen Opportunity-Reducing Techniques Within Four Components of Situational Crime Prevention

Controlling Prompts	Controlling Pressures	Reducing Permissibility	Reducing Provocations
Controlling triggers	Reducing inappropriate conformity	Rule setting	Reducing frustrations
Gun control	Dispersing gang members	Harassment codes	Inmate control of comfort settings
Pornography restrictions	Screening children's associates	Staff inductions	Improved wet playtimes
Environmental self-management	Bolstering independence	"Shoplifting is stealing" signs	Efficient road design
Providing reminders	Reducing inappropriate obedience	Clarifying responsibility	Reducing crowding
Warning signs	Support for whistle blowers	Server intervention	Limiting nightclub patron density
Symbolic territorial markers	Participatory management	Assigning discrete tasks	Regulating nightclub patron overflow
Litter bins	Semi-independent units	Encouraging sense of ownership	Use of color, windows, light, etc.
Reducing inappropriate imitation	Encouraging compliance	Clarifying consequences	Respecting territory
Rapid repair of vandalism	Persuasive signs	Copyright messages	Identifiable territories for residents
Controls on television content	Fairness of request	Public posting	Privacy rooms for residents
Supervisors as exemplars	Participation in rule making	Vandalism information brochures	Avoiding intrusions into inmates' cells
Setting positive expectations	Reducing anonymity	Personalizing victims	Controlling environmental factors
Pub gentrification	Restricting uniform use (perpetrators)	Victim co-operation	Irritants
Domestic prison furniture	School dress code	Humanizing conditions for prisoners	Smoke-free nightclubs
Fixing "broken windows"	Low-profile crowd management	Concern for employee welfare	Air conditioning
			Noise control

Routine Activities Theory

In 1979 Larry Cohen and Marcus Felson (Bottoms and Wiles, 1997: 320) introduced a theory that revolves around three factors:

- Potential offender
- Suitable target
- Absence of a capable guardian

Whether in areas of work, play, or leisure, all three factors must come together in order for criminal activity to be realized. Routine Activities Theory is consistent with the Rational Choice Theory and with Situational Crime Prevention. Target hardening, an element of Situational Crime Prevention, becomes important in the absence of a capable guardian, which is an element of the Routine Activities Theory.

As in any theory, the Routine Activities Theory is open to criticism. A prime criticism is that criminals are rational in their decision-making; security practitioners, who are also rational, look at the same situations differently. The crime prevention measures put in place by the security practitioner may play no part in the criminal's decision to act. A criminal may not even be aware of or care about deterrents or physical safeguards; for example, a criminal under the influence of alcohol or drugs.

Crime Pattern Theory (Paul and Patricia Brantingham)

Crime Pattern Theory is a rather complex amalgamation of Rational Choice Theory and Routine Activities Theory, with an added touch of socio-cultural, economic, legal, and environmental cues. The premise is that crime does not occur randomly in time, place, social group cohesiveness, or other aspects. Crime is more complex than that. Crime prevention must take a multi-disciplinary approach tailored for the situation. One must consider criminal opportunity, the readiness and willingness of the criminal, and how they are impacted by socio-cultural, economic, legal, and environmental factors. Crime Pattern Theory is hard to understand and even harder to put into practical use.

Defensible Space: Crime Prevention Through Urban Design (Oscar Newman)

This concept was borne out of a need to prevent crime in the public housing environment. It was the forerunner of Crime Prevention Through Environmental Design (CPTED), an approach for reducing crime through the use of natural surveillance, natural access control, and territorial concern.

Oscar Newman wrote many influential pieces on this concept, some of which are, *Architectural Design for Crime Prevention*, published in 1971 through the U.S. Department of Justice, *Defensible Space* published in 1972, and *Creating Defensible Space* published in 1996 by the U.S. Department of Housing and Urban Development.

Newman proposes that crime prevention measures can be effective when they:

- Serve to define spheres of influence in which occupants can easily adopt proprietary attitudes.
- Improve the natural capability of residents to survey both the interior and exterior of the residential space.
- Enhance the safety of adjoining areas such as communal facilities.
- Reduce the perception of peculiarity such as vulnerability, isolation, and stigma attached to housing projects and their residents.

Similarities between Defensible Space and CPTED are obvious. Both concepts address legitimate users versus illegitimate users, proper and effective utilization of natural and man-made surveillance opportunities, and safe havens.

Displacement and Diffusion

The displacement concept holds that when criminals are deterred at one location, they will move to different, less-protected locations. The concept does not say that crime is prevented; it is simply displaced to "criminal-friendly" locations.

Tyska and Fennelly have identified five aspects of displacement:

1. Time of day
2. Activities occurring at a targeted location

3.   Location of the target
4.   Technique of the criminal
5.   Type of victim or property targeted by the criminal

Displacement will occur or not occur relative to any of the five aspects. For example, a robber in search of money (the target) decides to rob a bank. He can only commit the robbery when a bank is open for business (time of day). The robber stakes out a bank and observes that it is continuously crowded and that a security guard is at the door (activities occurring at the targeted location). The robber goes to a different bank but it happens to be next door to a police station (location of the target). Finally, the robber finds a "robber-friendly" bank. Because the robber knows that the punishment for robbery with use of a gun is much more severe than robbery without a gun, the robber decides he will not carry a gun into the bank but will give a note to a teller that says he is carrying a gun (technique of the criminal).

Diffusion

Diffusion relates to benefits that occur when security measures taken at one place overlap to adjacent places so that crime in the immediate area is reduced overall.

Displacement and diffusion are opposite sides of the same coin. Displacement does not prevent crime because the criminal moves on to an easier or more vulnerable target. But with diffusion, especially diffusion that takes place in a large geographical area, crime is prevented to some degree. As Pease states in reference to both issues: "…the fact that displacement has been long debated, and that diffusion of benefits has been neglected suggests that displacement is dominant not because it reflects a real attempt to understand crime flux, but because it serves as a convenient excuse for doing nothing ("'Why bother? It will only get displaced.'") (1997: 978).

A somewhat controversial point to displacement is that there may be a benefit to displacing certain kinds of crime. For example, drug and prostitution control may be made easier or more tolerable when it is away from residential neighborhoods or concentrated in one locale (Pease, 1997: 979).

Understanding crime control theories can help security practitioners make the best decisions possible in a variety of situations.

Glen Kitteringham

Sources

Applied Crime Management: Unit 3: Crime Pattern Analysis. 2000. Leicester: The Scarman Centre for Public Order, University of Leicester. pp. 113–168.

Bottoms, A. and Wiles, P. 1997. "Environmental Criminology." *The Oxford Handbook of Criminology, 2nd Edition*. Oxford: Clarendon Press. pp. 305–359.

Center for Problem-Oriented Policy. 2006. <http://www.popcenter.org/learning/pam/help/theory.cfm.>

Clarke, R. 1997. *Situational Crime Prevention: Successful Case Studies, 2nd Edition*. Albany: Harrow and Heston.

Crime Prevention 2: The Situational Approach. 1999. Leicester: The Scarman Centre for Public Order, University of Leicester. pp. 305–344.

Criminological Theory 2: Rational Choice Theory. 1999. Leicester: The Scarman Centre for Public Order, University of Leicester. pp. 277–304.

Criminological Theory. 2006. <http://home.comcast.net/~ddemelo/crime/routine.html>

Newman, O. 1971. *Architectural Design for Crime Prevention*. National Institute of Law Enforcement and Criminal Justice.

Pease, K. 1997. "Crime Prevention." *The Oxford Handbook of Criminology, 2nd Edition*. Oxford: Clarendon Press. pp. 963–995.

Tayler, Ian. 1997. "The Political Economy of Crime." *The Oxford Handbook of Criminology, 2nd Edition*. Oxford: Clarendon Press. pp. 265–303.

Tyska, L. and Fennelly, L. 1998. *150 Things You Should Know about Security*. Boston: Butterworth-Heinemann.

Wortly, R. 2001. "A Classification of Techniques for Controlling Situational Precipitators of Crime." *Security Journal, Vol. Fourteen Number 4*. Perpetuity Press. pp. 63–82.

CRIME PREVENTION: A COMMUNITY APPROACH

A community approach to crime prevention starts with the notion that law enforcement agencies have a central, but not necessarily dominant, role in protecting citizens from crime.

Traditional law enforcement methods, although response-oriented, do in fact cause criminals to perceive personal risk and thus play an important role in preventing crime; but the larger role belongs to the citizens themselves.

Citizens typically are limited in the actions they are able to take to thwart crime because of their inability to effectively exercise full control over their environments. (The environments referred to here are those of the victim, not of the criminal.) This does not mean that a citizen is powerless because, even in the most limited sense, a potential victim can reduce criminal motivation by minimizing the opportunity of the criminal to succeed. Empirically, we observe that the absence of opportunity results in less crime, and theoretically we hope that the absence of opportunity will lessen the chances that an otherwise honest person will develop criminal habits.

We observe also that crime prevention activities in some communities have been both a cause and an effect of efforts to overcome severe crime problems, and that a successful outcome seems to hinge on the harmonious involvement of many skills and interest groups. Successful outcomes that were comprehensive and lasting appeared in many cases to result from a willingness to innovate and experiment. The doctrine of crime prevention, if such can be said of this emerging quasi-science, is interdisciplinary in nature, amenable to an ongoing process of discovery and change, and useful to the extent that it is applied and successes shared. Strategies and tactics in successful programs often were not carved in stone. What worked in one situation at one point in time did not always work later in other situations.

Strategies

A fundamental strategy of crime prevention is to simultaneously promote public awareness of crime problems and to inform citizens of their options and the resources available to them. The strategy naturally embraces a two-pronged approach. First, to broadly mobilize the public against crime in general, and second, to develop specific courses of action for dealing with crime that has been directed at specific neighborhoods, businesses, and organizations.

The principal actions often include the provision of teaching and counseling services,

especially those that give particular attention to key groups that hold leadership positions in the community. This approach naturally leads to group projects that harness collective efforts. One of the more unique and promising projects of a group nature has occurred in some municipalities where city officials, such as planners and code administrators, have joined with architects and builders to design into new construction projects physical security features that encourage active citizen involvement in their neighborhoods and which at the same time discourage deviant behavior.

Crime Prevention Through Environmental Design, or CPTED, is a name often assigned to group projects like these. A central tenet of CPTED is the concept of informal social control, which holds that crime in a small community or neighborhood can be reduced through:

- Intensified use by residents of streets, parks, and land around the structures in which they live.
- Increased watchfulness of residents for intruders who manifest unacceptable behavior.
- An increased tendency of people to look out for the property and well-being of their neighbors, and to interact with law enforcement.
- An enhanced ability to discriminate between outsiders and residents, and an ability to communicate by actions that deviant behavior will not be allowed.
- A strong sense of shared interests in improving and maintaining the quality of life in the physical environment and social climate of the area.

Neighborhood Watch

An example of a strategy founded on informal social control is Neighborhood Watch. This program and others like it encourage citizens to watch for crime and report observations to the police. The usual tactics include:

- Making open areas easily observable and increasing human activity in them.
- Establishing workable relationships between residents, businesses, and police for the common purpose of eradicating crime.

- Promoting a neighborhood identity, developing social cohesion, and attracting new financial investments.
- Conducting no-cost security surveys to residents and businesses, and providing guidance for implementing survey recommendations.
- Holding public meetings, creating special interest groups concerned with reducing particular crimes, and setting up community-operated response units such as crisis hot line, rape crisis center, rumor control, rap line, child abuse center, and block parent groups.
- Seeking to improve the quality of police patrol operations by creating a dialogue between the police and community leaders.
- Encouraging residents to report crimes and criminals.

A Model Community-Centered Program

Every program created from a model will have unique characteristics that require it to be different in some respects from the model it emulates. The reader will find in the following model a range of flexibility sufficient to meet the particular needs of programs operating within a neighborhood, a cluster of neighborhoods, or a community.

Obtain and Analyze Data Relating to the Neighborhood. Types of data worthy of analysis include crime and loss patterns, police patrol deployments, census tracts, terrain and topography descriptions, socioeconomic and demographic patterns, and political infrastructures. The purpose of the analysis is to identify major crime locations, trends, sources of crime, cultural strengths, and weaknesses of residents *vis-á-vis* the presence of crime; evaluate police effectiveness and efficiency; define perceptions by the police and of the police; identify leaders and leadership groups in the community; identify resources that exist and that need to be acquired; and assess the divisiveness and/or cohesiveness of the neighborhood.

Analysis of the obtained data is directed at determining what crimes are likely to impact particular targets, the criminals likely to commit the crimes, how the crimes are likely to occur, and when they are likely to occur. The process of analysis typically includes the collection and processing of data related to crime rate by opportunity; the varieties and preferences of attack methods; the preferred times of attacks by day, week, month, and other time variables; the characteristics of suspects; the targets preferred by criminals; and losses by type and value.

A consideration at this point is to look forward in time to when an accounting will be made of the program's effectiveness. The administrators of the program could identify a comparable neighborhood not planned to be covered under the program and use the comparable neighborhood as a control area or baseline against which success or failure can be measured.

Establish Goals and Objectives. A program's goals and objectives will vary according to the interests it serves. A community-centered program can operate at one or a combination of three levels. At the client or individual level, the overall goal is to design crime risk management systems that meet the needs of homes, businesses, institutions, and other entities that are owned or managed by one or a few individuals.

At the multiple-client level, the goal is to design crime risk management projects through which many citizens in neighborhoods, shopping centers, industrial areas, and similar localities can collectively work together to improve security. At the public-policy level, the goal is to design crime risk management activities that units of government can carry out to improve security within a large jurisdiction and across jurisdictional lines. The program's objectives will reflect tangible, measurable, and realizable outcomes that fall within the overall goal. The objectives are the milestones for progress and the indicators for efficiency and effectiveness.

Establish Criteria for Participation in the Program. What percentage of the neighborhood's population should be involved? What residents should be invited to perform organizing roles? What should those roles be? What kinds of projects are appropriate and likely to succeed, especially as first ventures? What kind of resistance can be expected? How can resistance be turned to advantage? These are questions to be answered at this stage in the development of the program.

Approach Neighborhood Leaders. Those who have been identified as having significant influence should be approached first. The local leaders should be invited to participate in the development of strategy and to act as a sounding board for program effectiveness. The program must be perceived as a neighborhood effort, with neighborhood involvement and direction.

Educate Residents through a Wide Variety of Programs. Work through the neighborhood leaders and the groups they lead. Generate interest, support, and an awareness of the program. The basic goal is to build a foundation for citizens and police to work together. This implies that police officials, from top on down, also need to be educated concerning program objectives.

Provide Feedback to Residents and Police. The residents need to know how the program is working (e.g., arrests made, convictions obtained, property recovered, and victims assisted) and the police need to know how the residents regard the work they are performing (e.g., timeliness of responses, courtesy, and visibility).

Formulate Crime-Specific Tactics Based on Accumulating Experiences. Ongoing analyses of crime data in the neighborhood will reveal times, places, and methods of criminal attack. Preventive and response tactics can be inferred from the analyses.

Implement Crime-Specific Tactics as They Are Developed. Existing tactics will call for modification, new tactics will emerge, and combinations of tactics can be attempted. Whatever tactics are selected, they should be applied comprehensively so that criminals will simply not move to another location and carry on as before.

Assess Performance and Evaluate the Program. Periodically look objectively at the successes and failings of the program's organizers, the residents, and the police. The purpose is not to pass final judgment but to determine what modifications are necessary to improve operation of the program. This means identifying weak and strong points of program operations and deriving suggestions for changes. Periodic assessments will focus on efficiency indicators as opposed to effectiveness indicators, which are measured in an overall program evaluation.

At a pre-established point in time (e.g., 2 years after start-up), an overall evaluation will examine the impact of the program on reducing crime. The data obtained in the first and second stages of the model, such as crime rates and objectives, can serve as baselines for measurement.

The impact of a crime prevention program can be evaluated by measuring the degree of progress made in meeting specific objectives set for the program and progress toward the general goal of crime reduction. This involves comparing initial program assumptions against assumptions derived from the realities of program operations. An overall evaluation can suggest new approaches, techniques, and human and physical resources.

John J. Fay

Sources

Jeffrey, C. 1977. *Crime Prevention Through Environmental Design*. Beverly Hills: Sage Publications.

National Crime Prevention Institute. 1986. *Understanding Crime Prevention*. Boston: Butterworth-Heinemann.

CRIME PREVENTION THROUGH ENVIRONMENTAL DESIGN

Crime prevention through environmental design (CPTED) alters the internal and/or external environment of a facility to increase crime deterrence and the likelihood of apprehension and detection of criminals. Landscape planners, architects, developers, and security professionals use CPTED to secure built structures and to improve the image of the individuals or companies that own them. And, as the National Crime Prevention Institute says, "The proper design and effective use of the built environment can lead to a reduction in the fear of crime and incidence of crime, and to an improvement in quality of life."

The Origin of CPTED

Architect Oscar Newman developed the initial and most recognized documentation of CPTED in 1972 in his book *Defensible Space*. The core components of the design strategy allow for a balanced security presence by taking into account physical security—in this case referring to architectural components like doors, walls, fencing, and landscaping—technical security, which includes alarms, access control technologies and CCTV, and operational security—that is, the policies and procedures that govern the security program.

CPTED uses these components of balanced security to create a built environment that facilitates the deterrence and delay of criminals and increases the likelihood of detection of criminal activities. Here we'll explore a few examples of CPTED strategies security directors should keep in mind if they're participating in new structure design.

Strategies for Physical Security

Compartmentalization. Compartmentalization means designing the facility to include layers of security starting from the outer perimeter and moving inward to the highest-security area of the building.

Natural Surveillance. Natural surveillance includes the placement of windows, open areas, and clear lines of sight to minimize built-in hiding places for criminals. It can be complemented by CCTV, but not replaced by it. Natural surveillance should also provide adequate clear space between the access points to the property and the actual exterior of the facility. Properly designed, clear sight lines will prevent potential ambush and hiding areas and should extend beyond the building's façade.

Activity Support. In the movies, the hero often tells the villain that he will meet him in a public space, anticipating that the villain won't pull any tricks in a highly visible area. The hero is using the concept of activity support to enhance the concept of natural surveillance. It is easy to establish public venues to support and enhance security. These will become part of the natural surveillance system, which will deter criminal activity.

If you know of areas that could provide cover for ambush, place vending machines, telephones, and other public interest points nearby. An ambush will be less likely in an area that is well traveled by multiple potential witnesses.

Territorial Enforcement. Territorial enforcement relates to the natural progression from public to private space. Clearly defining the boundaries between public and private areas of the campus or building through landscaping, architecture, and technology establishes a sense of ownership and pride and sends a message that the private area is off limits. This pride or psychological ownership is also perceived by visitors and pedestrian traffic. Therefore, territorial enforcement is likely to encourage increased subliminal perception of an area as secured or inaccessible.

Territorial enforcement can also be used to direct pedestrian and vehicle traffic and can define where the property begins, sending a clear message to visitors, tenants, and staff.

For instance, most buildings are directly accessible from driveways or roads. In some cases, those roads are straight. This could allow a vehicle to approach the facility at a high rate of speed, providing the opportunity for deliberate or accidental vehicular ramming. The costs to provide supplementary vehicle arresting equipment to offset this threat in a real-world application could be in the hundreds of thousands of dollars. Using the strategies of CPTED, however, you could instead design a winding road that provides areas for landscaping and natural access control, thereby preventing the opportunity for a high-speed vehicular ram attack.

Lighting. Nighttime permits the best opportunity for a criminal to approach a building undetected. The Illumination Engineering Society of North America (IESNA) has published a guideline that will likely become an American National Standard. It is entitled "Guideline for Security Lighting for People, Property, and Public Spaces." The guideline cites the work of Painter and Farrington, who determined in 1999 that "lighting does have an impact on crime prevention." Effective lighting inhibits crime because the behavior is more likely to be observed.

Operational Security

Maintenance. James Q. Wilson and George Kelling's Broken Window Theory suggests that uncorrected decay, such as accumulated trash, broken windows, and deteriorated building exteriors, will facilitate additional crime and cause people who live and work in the area to feel more vulnerable and withdraw to more desirable conditions. People become more fearful and less willing to address physical signs of deterioration or to intervene to maintain public order. For example, they're less likely to attempt to break up groups of rowdy teens loitering on street corners.

Sensing this, criminals and other offenders become bolder and intensify their harassment and vandalism. People become yet more fearful and withdraw further from community involvement and upkeep, thereby beginning a linear and upward progression of criminal activity.

In the same way that territorial enforcement encourages a psychological ownership of a facility or a secured area, the perceived psychological ownership of a facility can be enhanced by the proper maintenance and upkeep of the site and building. Lack of maintenance reduces psychological ownership and reduces the opportunity of detection and deterrence, which increases the "psychological opportunity" in a person who has subversive intentions.

To avoid this, facility designers and planners should take into consideration opportunities to reduce maintenance issues. For instance, consider using anti graffiti paint on the building's exterior.

In addition, planning should take into account lighting, camera placement, and landscaping. Planners should identify vegetation and tree growth to anticipate if camera and lighting placement will be effective for the future, which would prevent unneeded maintenance.

Upkeep is extremely important to the overall property. Fencing should be repaired if damaged. Vegetation and refuse should be removed from fencing areas. Broken windows should be repaired. Failure to provide these types of maintenances will have negative effects on the area and encourage opportunistic crime.

Policies and Procedures. Accurate policies and procedures should identify areas and time of patrol and determine appropriate responses to security incidents.

Technical Security

The application of technical security should complement physical security. Specifically, camera placement should be coordinated with way-finding and territorial enforcement. By using soft barriers (shrubs, bushes, etc.) we can anticipate avenues of foot or vehicle travel. Cameras should be located in areas where foot or vehicle travel intersects or at choke points where physical attributes of the building or way-finding force individuals into the camera view. It will be obvious to an operator if someone is trying to avoid a camera, thereby providing an opportunity for detection.

Traditionally, cameras were mounted at 10 to 11 feet, which provides undesirable views. Technology advancements have now provided the capability for smaller, more powerful cameras to be mounted at lower heights. Consider mounting cameras lower, so accurate facial characteristics can be documented.

Implementing CPTED

To implement CPTED, according to Timothy Crowe in his book *Crime Prevention Through Environmental Design*, we need to consider the designation, definition and design of the facility.

Designation

1. What is the purpose of this space?
2. For what was it originally intended to be used?
3. How well does the space support its current and future uses?

Definition

1. How is the space defined?
2. Is it clear who owns it?
3. Where are its borders?
4. Are there social or cultural definitions that affect how the space is used?
5. Is there adequate signage?
6. Is there a conflict or confusion between the designated purpose and definition?

Design

1. How well does the physical design support the intended function?
2. How well does the physical design support the definition of the desired or accepted behavior?
3. Does the physical design conflict with the productive use of the space?

CPTED is a proactive approach to security. Its byproduct is a decrease in crime and an increase in the perception of safety by visitors, employees, patrons, or tenants. This approach is the most cost effective method to developing a proactive, rather than reactive, security program.

Sean A. Ahrens

Source   Reprinted in part from *Security Technology and Design (ST&D)* magazine.

CPTED THEORY EXPLAINED

Probably the most well known of the environmental crime control theories is Crime Prevention Through Environmental Design (CPTED), a theory first expounded upon by Dr. C. Ray Jeffery in 1971. To quote Tim Crowe, a proponent, CPTED "expands upon the assumption that the proper design and effective use of the built environment can lead to a reduction in the fear of crime and the incidence of crime, and to an improvement in the quality of life" (Crowe, 1991: 1).

The Use of Natural Surveillance

Natural surveillance is obtained through increasing the ability of residents to see further and wider and decreasing the ability of criminals to hide until the time is right for them to carry out their activities. An example of the use of natural surveillance would be in an underground parking lot. As users leave their cars and head toward an elevator lobby or staircase, it is often not possible for them to see what lies ahead. Natural surveillance can be increased by the use of glass partitions instead of cinderblock walls. Drivers can now see directly into the vestibule area instead of guessing what lies ahead. Also, it is difficult for a criminal to stay for long in an easily scrutinized area.

The Use of Natural Access Control

This concept falls under the definition of spatial definition. An example of natural access control may be normal place-users being encouraged to use the area for legitimate purposes, and unwanted uses being discouraged. However this is accomplished is up to the particular location and imagination of the property manager. For example, if unwanted visitors are remaining in an area because of a design feature such as a wall or barrier, the recommendation is that the feature, unless required, could be removed thereby reducing the attractiveness of the area. Another example is thieves using a particular building for their activities because of the hidden concealment areas for conducting surveillance as they wait for opportunities to commit crime. This undesirable activity can be eliminated by designing out hidden areas.

Territorial Behavior

This concept is key to reclaiming an area that has been taken over by illegitimate users. If design features have made a haven for illegitimate users and have frightened off legitimate users, then one of the most important actions required is for the space to be reclaimed. Initially, this may take the form of enhanced security patrols. With the illegitimate users kept away, the area is seen as desirable once again for legitimate users. This in turn will keep the illegitimate users away because an increase in the number of normal space users will act as a deterrent. In the previous example, an area had practically been taken over by criminals for their activities including drug dealing, car prowling, breaks and enters, assaults, and petty thefts. Several simple design features and enhancing the security officer presence returned the area to its rightful users, and as the number of rightful users increased, the number of crimes decreased. While the problem did not completely go away, it decreased the problem to the extent that the quality of life improved for the legitimate users.

CPTED planners should employ three security strategies. First is to use human resources such as security or police officers or some other type of official guardian to watch for undesirable behavior and intervene as necessary. The second strategy is to incorporate mechanical methods such as CCTV, locks, access control systems, fences, and other barriers. The third, and probably most important strategy, is to use natural features, such as windows and front porches, to increase the surveillance opportunities of the building residents and enlist their help in looking for and reporting the presence of criminals. It is important to start with the natural methods of enhancing security and then augmenting with organized and mechanical methods.

There is, of course, far more to the concept of CPTED, and readers are encouraged to read Tim Crowe's book, *Crime Prevention Through Environmental Design, 2nd Edition,* as well as review material provided by a host of CPTED-related organizations.

Glen Kitteringham

Sources

Crowe, T. 1991. *Crime Prevention Through Environmental Design,* Boston: Butterworth-Heinemann.

National Crime Prevention Institute. 2001. *Understanding Crime Prevention, 2nd Edition,* Boston: Butterworth-Heinemann.

ENVIRONMENTAL CRIME PREVENTION AND SOCIAL CRIME PREVENTION THEORIES

Environmental Crime Prevention Theory

A short and simple explanation of the environmental crime control theory is that practitioners focus their attention and energies upon potential locations of criminal activity. Locks, doors and other barriers, CCTV equipment, and patrolling security officers are examples of tools used to control environmental crime.

There are several distinct models within the environmental crime control theory. While Crime Prevention Through Environmental Design (CPTED), and to a lesser extent, Defensible Space are probably best known to North American audiences, and are U.S.-based, there are others such as Geometry of Crime Theory and Pattern Theory (Canadian) and Routine Activities Theory and Rational Choice Theory (British).

Environmental crime control grew from work completed at the University of Chicago in the 1920s. It was there that attention was paid not to the people who committed the criminal acts but the places where the acts were committed. However, this area of study fell dormant for several decades. In 1961 the theory was given new life by the influential writer and social commentator, Jane Jacobs, author of *The Death and*

Life of Great American Cities. Her work inspired C. Ray Jeffery and Oscar Newman. Jeffery wrote *Crime Prevention Through Environmental Design* and Newman wrote *Defensible Space.* In turn, others were inspired such as Paul and Patricia Brantingham, Tim Crowe, Ronald V. Clarke, and Marcus Felson.

The theories of Crime Prevention Through Environmental Design and Defensible Space have much in common with:

- Routine Activities Theory
- Rational Choice Theory
- Situational Prevention
- Geometry of Crime
- Pattern Theory

An examination of the various theories suggests considerable overlap, most probably due to researchers drawing upon the work of previous researchers.

Social Crime Prevention Theory

Social crime prevention focuses upon the criminal and accompanying social programs, education, employment creation, welfare, unemployment insurance, corrections, and other after-the-fact follow-up programs. Social crime control has been practiced in one form or another for hundreds of years.

This theory holds that crime can be countered by positive community institutions, improved social conditions, and recreational, educational, and employment opportunities. The objective is to improve the lives of people and remove conditions conducive to criminal activity. The central tenet is that people are not born as criminals but some become criminals because that is what their environment has taught and shaped them to be, e.g., a child raised by thieves and a teenager that lives in a drug-infested neighborhood.

The theory assumes that a person's potential for criminality can be reduced by ridding his or her exposure to negative influences, such as a neighborhood's graffiti and garbage, drug users and dealers, pimps and prostitutes, and thugs and thieves, and by replacing the negatives with nurturing influences such as churches, schools, and recreational facilities. Another assumption is that crime is reduced when income from

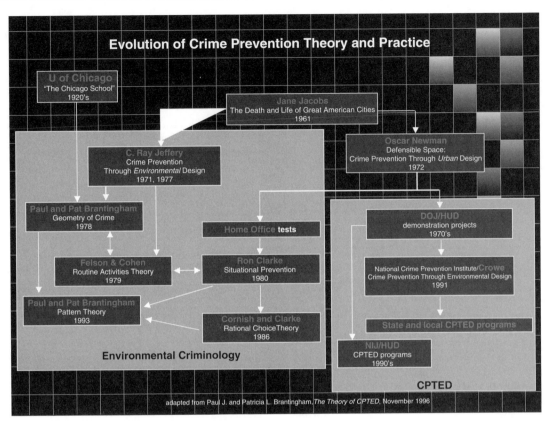

Figure 39.   CPTED has a rich and interesting history.

honest employment satisfies basic needs such as food and a place to live. When offered a choice between a life of crime and a life of honest work, a person will choose the latter.

Social crime prevention proponents believe that it is the responsibility of government to engineer removal of the negatives and give support to programs that channel people away from crime. Critics point to contradictory evidence; that despite billions of dollars spent on social crime prevention programs, crime remains largely unabated. Critics ask, "If employment meets a person's basic needs, why do gainfully employed persons commit crimes? Why do they steal from their employers, why do they shoplift, why do they rob and burglarize?"

The social crime control theory, like the environmental crime control theory, is overarching.

Within both are models that espouse some principles and not others.

Glen Kitteringham

Sources

Architecture,Virginia Technical Institute. 2006. <http://www.arch.vt.edu/crimeprev/pages/hdevbody.html>

Crowe, T. 2000. *Crime Prevention Through Environmental Design, 2nd Edition*. Boston: Butterworth-Heinemann.

Introduction to Security and Crime Risk Management. 2000. Leicester, UK: University of Leicester.

Jacobs, J. 1992. *The Death and Life of Great American Cities*. London: Vintage Publishing.

Newman, O. 1972. *Defensible Space: Crime Prevention Through Urban Design*. New York: MacMillan.

INCIDENT CAUSATION MODEL

The use of accident causation models is a standard approach in the safety field for identifying the causal factors of serious accidents. Generally, a model will force a consideration and careful examination of each circumstance related to the accident. The model recommended here is called the Incident Causation Model and is based on the International Loss Control Institute (ILCI) Loss Causation Model put forth by F.E. Bird, G.L. Germain, and R.G. Loftus.

The objectives of the Incident Causation Model are to determine why a security-related loss occurred, who was responsible, and what needs to be done to keep it from happening again. In the security field, we have not yet applied causation modeling in any substantive way to the analysis of causes underlying security violations.

The model can be used by security professionals to examine actual and potential loss-producing incidents. A loss-producing incident in the sense used here is an undesired event that results in harm to people or loss to property or process. It is usually the result of a violation of law, regulation, policy, procedure, or work rule. For example, in terms of harm to people, the violation may be aggravated assault; in terms of property, it may be theft; and in terms of process, the violation may be malicious disruption of work, such as sabotage, setting off a false fire alarm, or making a bomb threat.

The Incident Causation Model can be conceptualized as a structure; in this case, the structure is a pyramid. At the top is the loss. Below it in descending order are the incident (i.e., the violation), opportunities, and management failures.

Loss

The loss is the observable and often measurable impact upon people, property, or process. It is the direct and indirect fallout of the security incident and can take many forms.

Lost Time. A security incident involving violence will, for example, create time lost by employees who are injured or affected as the result of the misconduct. Time will be lost by co-workers who assist the injured and clean up of the incident scene, and by supervisors who restore work activities, investigate the incident, prepare reports, and testify at fact-finding proceedings. Then there are the time losses associated with employees generally due to upset, shock, diverted attention, and lowered morale.

Increased Operating Costs. These are losses that result from medical claims and escalated medical insurance premiums; legal expenses associated with hearings and liability claims; penalties, fines, and awards; recruiting, selecting, and training people to fill in for employees displaced by the incident; and acquiring interim equipment (*Supervisors Safety Manual*, 1985: 9).

Property Losses. Theft, misappropriation, and malicious damage or destruction involve property losses. In addition, they often require expenditure of supplies and equipment while dealing with the incident or compensating to overcome the immediate effects of a property loss.

Loss of Business. In this category of loss are the missed opportunities during downtime, deterioration of employee and customer goodwill, and adverse publicity.

Incident

The event that precipitates the loss is the incident. It is often rooted in a combination of violations. A theft, for example, is a violation of law, of the employer's policy, and of a work rule, and the same can be said for other violations. In many cases, an incident will consist of conduct that is prohibited in several venues.

Addressing the incident in terms of conduct helps to channel thinking to the means for controlling unacceptable conduct. Developing control measures that prevent incidents and minimize resultant losses is a fundamental responsibility of the chief security officer, and in this sense the Incident Causation Model has value in two respects: it can be used as a proactive tool for establishing preventive safeguards, and as a responsive tool for analyzing incidents to prevent recurrence and fix responsibility.

The incident and the loss are amenable to fairly easy examination. However, the opportunities of the incident to occur are not easily discerned.

Opportunities

The opportunities for an incident are the circumstances present in a situation at or immediately prior. In the chief security officer's parlance, opportunities are non-secure situations. In managerial parlance, they are deviations from standards. The term "standard" implies a minimum expectation, a basis for assessing performance against the expectation, and a means for correcting and upgrading unacceptable performance.

Standards. Workplace standards have at least two dimensions. First are standards that we may call practices and they relate to human performance. Second are standards that we may call conditions and these relate to the work environment such as the physical setting and the tools of the work.

When practices are substandard, they usually appear as human failures; for example, failure to control access, to lock things away, to enforce security rules, to make proper use of security resources, and to recognize and act upon the early warning signals of a violation in the making.

Substandard conditions often appear as inadequacies, such as inadequate physical safeguards, inadequate security personnel, inadequate warning systems and responses, inadequate security equipment, inadequate protections against fire and other hazards, and inadequate empowerment of security personnel to enforce security rules.

Identifying the existence of substandard practices and conditions is one thing; understanding why they exist is another. For corrective actions to be effective, the deviations must be clearly seen and fully understood.

The whys of the hidden causes fall into two groups: personal factors and job factors (Bird and Loftus, 1989). Personal factors are the characteristics of the job incumbents and job factors have to do with the work itself. Substandard personal factors can include lack of knowledge, skill, or motivation and lack of physical mobility, stamina, or mental capability.

Job factors pertain to the physical nature of the workplace and of the processes through which the work takes place. Physical aspects of the job include things like building structure and layout, utilities, machinery, equipment, and supplies. Process aspects reflect the manner in which the work is carried out.

To illustrate, a failure to control access to the company's stock of blank checks (an opportunity) occurred when the stock clerk left the blank checks cabinet unattended because no one trained him to the contrary (a substandard practice resulting from a deficiency in knowledge); or the opportunity for loss was the absence of a lock on the cabinet (a substandard condition resulting from poor physical construction), or that the accounting manager did not make access control to blank checks an element in the routine work processes of the department (a substandard condition resulting from the absence of a policy or directive). Many hidden causes are possible for each substandard practice and condition. Understanding the causes is essential to removing them.

As one might expect, the Incident Causation Model can be applied everywhere within an organization, including the Security Department. The substandard practices and conditions often found in security operations include:

- Poor and infrequent supervision
- Poor security program and procedures
- Poor selection of security applicants
- Poor initial and refresher training
- Poor assignment and utilization of personnel
- Poor team-building and interpersonal communications
- An absence of regularly conducted internal assessments
- Excessive physical and psychological stresses

The opportunities for a loss-producing incident can be tracked down without too much difficulty, but the reasons for them are not always apparent and not always fully understood. More significantly, they tend to be controversial because they point fingers at responsible managers. Patience and persistent probing are needed to get at the root causes and to expose them to rational examination. When brought to light, they will suggest changes in management that are needed.

Management Failures

The connection between underlying causes and management action is analogous to the connection between diseases and preventive medicine.

The causes are the diseases that produce the symptoms (the opportunities) and ill effects (loss-producing incidents). The diseases exist because the patient failed to maintain personal health (a lack of management control).

In the Incident Causation Model, the principal focal point for analysis and corrective action is at the base of the pyramid. The errors of management, whether large or small and whether committed by line supervisors or senior executives, form the foundation for the deficiencies that lead to loss. The errors occur at the upper level in the promulgation of policy and work rules, and especially in the setting of standards. Errors at the lower levels occur in the normal course of planning, organizing, leading, and controlling (Bird and Loftus, 1989).

It does not matter if the manager's work is directed at production, quality control, cost accounting, or security, and it does not matter where the manager sits on the organizational totem pole. The simple fact is that every person in a supervisory or managerial position has an obligation to protect the employer's assets and that even the most routine tasks of management involve the use of assets.

Another simple fact is that in the rush of meeting other priorities, managers tend to push their assets-protecting obligation into the background, and even when they are not so rushed, they have no idea how to go about meeting the obligation.

Using the Model

When using the model as a tool for fact finding and preventing repetition of an incident, the chief security officer starts with an examination of the incident and works downward through the pyramid. The amount of detail increases almost geometrically as the inquiry moves from incident to opportunities and then to management failures. A single incident is likely to result from the presence of 5 to 10 substandard practices and conditions, and each practice or condition is sure to be rooted in a like number of hidden causes.

A proactive use of the model is to prevent an incident or reduce its negative effects. In this approach, sometimes called the critical incident technique (*Accident Prevention Manual for Industrial Operations*, 1988:48–49), the chief security officer starts at the bottom of the pyramid and works upward. The idea is to identify the causes of an incident and take preventive steps before the incident can happen. A logical start is to examine policies that relate to the use and care of assets. One such policy would be the security policy. Does such a policy exist? Is it in writing? Has it been communicated throughout the organization? Is it understood, followed, and enforced?

Next to be examined would be the various programs for carrying out policies. Several func-

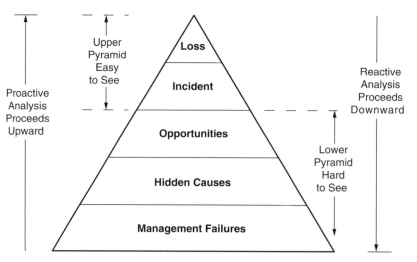

INCIDENT CAUSATION MODEL

Figure 40.   Post-incident analysis moves from top to bottom in search of why the incident happened. Incident prevention analysis moves from bottom to top in search of conditions that produce incidents.

tional areas of interest to the chief security officer should come to mind: internal audit, safety, and some aspects of human resources, such as pre-employment screening and drug testing. Program activities will vary among organizations.

The function of security should certainly be looked at closely. Program activities may include physical safeguards, security officer operations, protection of proprietary information, investigations, security awareness, and so forth. Each program component will be operated according to well-defined standards, e.g., fences will be constructed to certain heights with certain features, and proprietary information will be marked in certain ways and stored in certain containers.

The security professional sets the standards, implements standards that fall within his or her exclusive purview, and communicates the standards to managers in order to help them carry out their security responsibilities. Finally, the security professional evaluates compliance with the established standards.

The Incident Causation Model crosses many boundaries. Although it has particular application to the chief security officer's domain, it reaches into all levels of the organization. In principle, the management of security is a responsibility assigned to every person performing supervisory or managerial duties. Responsibility for protecting assets entrusted to a manager is assigned to the manager, and while a security professional may assist by setting up protections, the bottom line responsibility stays with the manager.

A loss-producing incident does not happen without warning. It will be preceded by signs that are detectable. The incident will have multiple causes and will develop through a sequence of errors. The sequence moves upward from management failures to opportunities. At the opportunities level, the incident is just waiting to be triggered.

John J. Fay

Sources

Bird, F. 1988. *Management Guide to Loss Control*. Loganville: International Loss Control Institute.

Bird, F. and Germain, G. 1988. *Practical Loss Control Leadership*. Loganville: International Loss Control Institute.

Bird, F. and Loftus, R. 1989. *Loss Control Management*. Loganville: International Loss Control Institute.

OPERATIONS SECURITY

Operations security (OPSEC) is the process of identifying critical friendly information and analyzing friendly actions to identify whether the information or actions can be observed and used by an adversary; and, subsequently developing actionable measures to eliminate or mitigate to an acceptable level the friendly vulnerabilities to adversary exploitation. It is important to understand that OPSEC is not intended to be a security system that protects highly classified information, but instead it is intended to protect general information of a sensitive nature. While it is up to a company to determine what information or actions it deems sensitive, an example might include employees' names and personal information. Whereas a release of this information might not be directly damaging or harmful to the company, it could prove devastating to the individual employee and indirectly affect the company.

In *History of the Peloponnesian War*, Thucydides wrote, "He passes through life most securely who has least reason to reproach himself with complaisance toward his enemies." This statement is no less true today as we negotiate a world full of individuals and organizations intent on using our own information and actions against us. Security managers in all industries must be prepared as terrorist organizations increasingly target public and private facilities; unscrupulous business competitors steal proprietary information; and foreign governments target American technology for economic or worse reasons. Technology transfer has become a pandemic problem and it will continue to remain a major concern in the future. The question, therefore, is how do we avoid the complaisance about which Thucydides wrote? Developing a strong OPSEC program is one answer.

It is also essential to recognize that OPSEC is a process and is not necessarily tied to a confining set of rules or instructions that can be applied in every situation or circumstance. The process of identifying information and actions to be protected and subsequently developing measures to do so is cyclic in nature and consists of the following steps:

Apply appropriate countermeasures (OPSEC measures). In business/corporate settings OPSEC measures fall predominately under two categories—prevention and deception. Preventive measures focus on preventing

Identify the critical information and actions that must be protected. Personnel at all levels should adopt an "adversarial" mindset to assist in identifying questions that an adversary might ask regarding friendly intentions, capabilities, and activities. The list of critical information and actions may change regularly to reflect changing circumstances, as specific information may only be critical for a specific period of time.

Analyze threats. Current and updated threat information is extremely important to developing effective OPSEC measures. Use all sources (open, law enforcement reports, etc.) to identify adversaries and answer the following questions:

Who are adversaries and what are their goals?

• What are the capabilities of the adversary and how might the adversary gather information?
• What does the adversary already know?
• What actions might an adversary take with the information it has?

Analyze vulnerabilities. The identification of vulnerabilities is crucial to developing mitigation measures. Identify OPSEC indicators—friendly actions and open-source information that can be interpreted or pieced together by an adversary to derive critical information. What indicators will the adversary be able to use? The list of indicators that an adversary might seek is vast and can vary greatly depending upon industry. Examples of possible OPSEC indicators might include the following among others:

• Daily schedules
• Access rosters
• Standard and emergency operations plans
• Communications plans or sudden changes in communications plans
• Volume and priority of requisitions
• Budget information

Assess risk. Risk assessment involves an estimate of an adversary's capability to exploit a weakness, the potential effects such as exploitation will have on operations, and a cost-benefit analysis of possible methods to control the availability of critical information to the adversary. In order for there to be a risk both a threat and vulnerability must exist. Using a matrix, determine the probability of an adversary gathering the information compared to the criticality of the loss of the information. Is it likely that the adversary can gather the information and would the gathering of this information be catastrophic to the friendly operations? If the answer to these questions is yes, this is a vulnerability that must be protected using physical security measures. If, on the other hand, the answer to either or both of these questions is no, there may be other options. Perhaps the purchase of an insurance policy is sufficient or perhaps nothing needs to be done at all.

adversary detection by masking and controlling friendly actions while deceptive measures involve providing adversaries with alternative interpretations to indicators in an attempt to confuse the adversary's ability to interpret the information. Keeping in mind that it is impossible to protect all information, carefully weigh the effects of applying OPSEC measures to mitigate vulnerabilities. What are appropriate measures? Do the measures have legal ramifications? Are the measures cost effective when measured with the likelihood of an adversary gathering indicators?

Development of an effective OPSEC program is dependent on a number of factors. First, an OPSEC manager/officer should be identified and given the required authority to fulfill his or her responsibilities. Dependent on the size of the organization, this individual may also be the security manager. Regardless, the OPSEC manager should be proficient in developing policy, interpreting higher authority guidance regarding OPSEC, conducting OPSEC training, and working with other professionals to obtain accurate information pertaining to OPSEC planning.

Once an individual is designated to oversee the program, he or she must develop the OPSEC plan. With a thorough understanding of the OPSEC process, the OPSEC manager should conduct a survey to determine the organization's current OPSEC posture. This survey might follow any one of many varying models, but it will generally include a planning phase, a field survey phase, and an analysis and reporting phase. In the planning phase the OPSEC manager will determine the scope of the survey, select team members, familiarize team members with the survey procedures and ensure they understand the operation or activity to be surveyed, conduct a threat assessment and determine preliminary vulnerabilities. During the field survey the OPSEC manager might conduct an in-briefing to individuals to be involved in the survey, collect data, and make an exit brief. And finally, in the analysis and reporting phase the OPSEC manager will correlate collected data, identify additional vulnerabilities based on the field survey, and prepare a final report. The final report does not have to follow a specific format, but at a minimum it should include findings, analysis and discussion, and most importantly, recommendations.

Based on recommendations from the OPSEC manager, senior-level management should decide what OPSEC measures to establish, if any. These might include preventive or deceptive measures. At a minimum, managers should seriously consider OPSEC awareness training and guidance to employees at all levels. This awareness training should explain what OPSEC is, why it is important, and how individual employees can contribute to an effective OPSEC program. All new employees should receive initial orientation training that might orient them to the threat facing the organization and specific measure that they might use to prevent inadvertent disclosure of sensitive information, and employees should receive annual training to reemphasize the importance of OPSEC. Periodic updates of policies and procedures might also be disseminated to employees as necessary when OPSEC threats and vulnerabilities change due to circumstances.

If Thucydides was correct, then only through vigilant effort can organizations and individuals be more secure in protecting their information—information that can become intelligence used against them. Security managers must stress the importance of an effective OPSEC program as an essential element of this vigilant effort. Most security systems are not completely infallible and it is unfortunate when a system fails. More unfortunate than this, however, is when the failure of a system can be blamed on complaisance.

Sidney W. Crews

SECURITY EXPERTISE

How did security-related activities and skills emerge in the modern managerial environment? Do they constitute matters that truly may be termed "expert" or involve "expertise"? And how have "security experts" informed civil and criminal litigation in the United States? Security is common sense, but how much more than common sense is it?

Conceptually and in actuality, no organized process can long survive or thrive without adequate security. The importance of security is based on the premise that vulnerability eventually is exploited or results in systematic declension. The British historian Boris (Leo) Brasol wrote: "Naturally, safeguarding society against criminality is the foremost duty of the state." The same could be argued for protection of assets from loss: "Naturally, safeguarding organizations against loss is the foremost duty of executives and managers." Persistent losses—even small—erode needed profit for growth and return to the capital providers putting the underlying capital investment at risk of being diminished or lost entirely.

Since World War II, American industry has evolved slowly to recognize security as a separate, bureaucratic management entity. Organizational spending for security has grown for contract and proprietary expenditures in real and absolute terms for over half a century. The usual reason given for the growth in security services and expenditures is because of "increased crime." But crime doesn't always increase; it can decrease and yet security services and systems continue to grow. Indeed, security services have importantly aided the recent decline in crime beginning approximately 1990. However, even if crime rates dropped substantially below their lowest point in the past century, solid requirements for security measures would still exist. These include such factors as meeting legal regulations; insurance coverage necessity; industry expectations; cost controls; terrorism; and safety of employees and the public. Indeed, when new management needs surface in an organization, the chief security officer (CSO) frequently is given the responsibility for organizing the program. A few examples can be cited: ethical programs; pre-employment screening measures; financial or governmental compliance requirements; risk management strategy and purchase of insurance; emergency and disaster planning, mitigation, and response; contingency planning; and IT security in its broadest forms. Other routine matters like guarding have taken on new significance in such diverse ways as first responder expectations, supply chain management, intellectual property protection, executive protection, and safeguarding global operations. Investigations are other routine matters conducted or supervised by security practitioners and these, too, have grown in scale and significance in diversified organizations.

In the past half century security management has moved from being a guard at a gate to a suit in a suite. This transformation has evolved as security practitioners have recast their tasks as efforts that protect, facilitate, and enhance all operations, current and projected. To accomplish this, security planners think of their responsibilities as positive, integral components in the success of the enterprise. This has been achieved partially by security practitioners learning and practicing the same methodology as that of academically trained managers in other fields.

Security services, systems, and products reached about $70 billion in expenditures within the United States in 2004. Billions more are allocated by organizations to manage and operate their own programs internally. But this impressive expenditure—representing 0.60 percent of the gross domestic product of the nation in 2000—does not by itself meet the inherent test of being an activity that necessarily requires deep expertise beyond the common sense of a reasonable person. But this contribution does argue that security practices meet the tests of expertness.

Security management has a theoretical basis. While many protective practices seem like common sense, and are, management decisions increasingly are guided by theoretical principles that may be tested by experimental research activities. The distinctive underpinning for theoretical constructs is related to precepts of situational crime prevention. An early exponent was an architect, Oscar Newman, who studied territoriality, surveillance, image, and environment as linked factors that affected crime rates in public housing. The means of reducing crime through design, changes in procedures, and modifications in image and environment created the principles of Crime Prevention Through Environmental Design (CPTED). From this basis a loosely inter-linked series of concepts emerged in the early 1980s from the work of Paul Brantingham and Patricia Brantingham, Ronald V. Clarke, L.E. Cohen, Marcus Felson, George Kelling, and others who argued that crime was a learned behavior characterized by repetition that could be mitigated often by simple, testable methods that often cost little to implement.

A precept of reduction of risk and loss is that vulnerability or negligence eventually results in the decline of value of assets. Security measures and management represent primary sources for mitigating losses.

Loss can refer to crime or other related decline in the value of assets to an organization. Opportunity reflects the chance to gain assets. The desire to amass assets is omnipresent, universal, cross-cultural, and insatiable. Controls represent the regulators or moderators to opportunity that can affect loss depending on the significance and pertinence of such controls. In short, losses rise when controls decline because the pull of opportunity never yields. The converse is also true.

Protection theory is supported by research and experimental design. As discussed above, the propounded theories have been tested by scores of experiments, particularly since the early 1980s. Since its inception in 1989, *Security Journal*, for example, has published well over 300 papers, many of them specifically reporting on experimental results of situational crime prevention research. Additionally, research concerning this field has appeared in criminology, police studies, and social science journals. Some of this research has been supported wholly or partially by government funds. In particular, the National Institute of Justice is a research leader in this nation.

Yet, much of the research base has been developed outside of the United States. Important contributions have been made in Australia, Canada, the Netherlands, and the United Kingdom, where research has been supported on a national level by federal authorities there. Not much federal, state, institutional, or corporate research is allocated for protection issues in the United States; still, the trend is positive and it all adds to a sense of growing expertise in the discipline.

The field or discipline has developed extensive distinctive practices. For the past half century a cadre of managers has evolved exclusively dealing with protection of assets from loss as broadly defined. Proof of this is in the emergence of professional and trade organizations which have arisen during this time. Such groups exist for social, political, educational, and economic reasons; additionally, they thrive to support sharing of tradecraft in the field: the opportunity to impart successful knowledge-based practices and to seek the solutions to problems faced by practitioners on a daily basis.

The number of security and security-related organizations is long and dynamic. A few organizations eschew public identification because the industry they involve is small and concerned with sensitive loss issues that need not involve participants outside of their immediate concerns. However, most security and security-related organizations are open, helpful, expansive, and professionally managed to help new and old practitioners in the field find their ways. Examples of this include ASIS International (formerly American Society for Industrial Security) founded in 1955; the Security Industry Association, 1967; the National Council of Investigation and Security Services, 1975; and the International Security Management Association, 1976. Additionally, scores of organizations—specific to industry and region—aid the field in sharing, critiquing, and developing effective practices. This is a mark of a mature, distinct expert endeavor.

Security has created a body of knowledge. The combination of industry-specific research and practices over the past generation has created a corpus of learning that is available to inform current and future researchers and practitioners.

Research results are published and open for all to consider; practices may be published in trade periodicals or newsletters or shared informally among those engaged in the field. The reality of a body of knowledge was demonstrated by James D. Calder who broadly surveyed the literature for security management, categorizing his findings into functional categories. Thus, a manager interested in finding case histories, technical findings, or "benchmark studies" may avail herself or himself to databases where such information resides.

Security expertise has been recognized in court. Because of the knowledge deriving from the vocation of security through education, special skills, and managerial experience, security practitioners have been recognized as experts in civil and criminal activities. Recognition of this expertise sets the expert apart from other men and women who do not possess this knowledge or skill. The means by which security experts have appeared in litigation has changed. In the 1950s through the 1970s, specialists appeared to testify in security-related actions involving art, biology and chemistry, handwriting, questioned documents, and technical matters. While these specialties continue to offer expertise in courts of law, since the 1970s tort and contract plaintiffs' actions have spurred the involvement of security experts on a continuous and constantly evolving basis. Texts have been published in the field.

Commentaries on appellate level decisions are available. College courses on the topic are taught. Services that supply experts to plaintiffs' and defense counsels search for security experts who can evaluate matters before the court for litigants.

In an increasingly complex world, authority plays a greater role in society. Thomas L. Haskell observes: "Sometimes consulting experts is not only prudent, but morally and legally obligatory. Anyone with fiduciary responsibilities could make himself [or herself] liable for severe legal penalties by failing to consult appropriate authorities about the treatment of assets under his [or her] care." Yet the public and the courts themselves have never been comfortable with the concept of expertness and appeal to authority even in measures involving scientific testimony. Sheldon Rampton and John Stauber observe: "Science, far from being merely a way to study the physical world, has undergone a dramatic transformation.... Science had ceased to be merely a methodology and had become an ideology as well." Still it is precisely with scientific material that testimony deriving from expertise, including security-related legal actions, is particularly contentious.

In 1923, the United States Supreme Court set down the admissibility of scientific evidence in Frye vs. United States. Frye was tried for second-degree murder. His defense attorneys requested the court to permit a polygraph examination of their client and then admit the finding as evidence. The court denied the application finding that a polygraph examination was not "generally accepted" in the scientific community. The Frye Test had stood the test of time and remains a legal standard in about half the jurisdictions in the nation. But what exactly "accepted science" is cannot always be answered with precision.

In the early 1990s, a class action tort involving use of a prescription drug, Bendectin, manufactured by Merrell Dow Pharmaceuticals, provided an additional basis for establishing standards for admissibility of scientific evidence in federal courts. The seminal case was Daubert vs. Merrell Dow Pharmaceuticals, Inc. decided in 1993. The decision reasoned that relevance and veracity of all evidence and testimony must be vetted by the court, including evidence that is scientific, medical, technical, or in some cases managerial in nature. The court may examine the expert's qualifications and methodology used to reach her or his opinions. Data presented may be subject to scrutiny. Additionally, the court may evaluate if the probative value exceeds the prejudicial effect of admitting a particular piece of evidence. Before Daubert, the expert might had opined on factual issues to be decided by the court. Now the plausibility of an expert's opinion could, under federal law, be the basis of setting aside a jury verdict if a post-trial motion is brought by the loser seeking a new trial and is granted by the court. Daubert has forced experts to think more analytically about their methodology, findings, and testimony. Civil and criminal actions involving security matters are not exceptions.

In recent decades managerial precepts and training from academic management programs have infused the ideology and strategy of security practitioners. But the discipline continues to produce distinctive learning and expertise on its own. Optimal security programs and practices are characterized by the application of such expertise. Well informed managers in other fields and private citizens are not likely to possess such expertise. Yet when security experts propound on such matters in the years to come, dispassionate scientific tests likely will be required for such views to be binding on legal decisions.

Robert D. McCrie

Source McCrie, R. 2004. "The History of Expertise in Security Management Practice and Litigation." *Security Journal*, vol. 17, no. 3.

TARGET ANALYSIS

As a simple definition, target analysis is the detailed examination of all information pertaining to a given target (asset) to determine its vulnerability to attack. Some security managers tend to use a vulnerability assessment methodology that is solely reactive in nature and, often times, not the appropriate approach to take. This is particularly true if it is not coupled with a more adversarial approach. By looking at vulnerabilities from a strictly defensive point of view it is easy to miss an adversary's probable attack method. This is a mistake if we remember that an adversary's intended target is most likely our vulnerability because it makes little sense for the adversary to attack a target that is not vulnerable. It is crucial, therefore, to put on "the bad guy hat" and conduct a good target analysis to better understand what an adversary perceives your vulnerabilities to be. For security managers, a good target analysis of assets, coupled with an understanding of an adversary's capabilities, can help define the appropriate protective strategy.

Militarily defined, a target is anything of military, economic, psychological, or political value designated for attack for purposes of destruction, degradation, removal, or surveillance. This is a comprehensive definition that serves well in the private sector of corporate America. A target system consists of a diverse and synchronized apparatus that provides a specific service over a wide geographical area and may be comprised of many target subsystems, complexes, or components. It is critical to ensure that a target system cannot be neutralized by the destruction of a single component. When this occurs, the component is called a "single point of failure." Any such component has to be regarded as highly critical to the operation of the system.

The most vital part of a system or a system component is the critical damage point, and the weakest part of the critical damage point is the target stress point. Target analysis includes a technique for identifying these two points and for developing a scheme to protect them. The technique is called The CARVER Matrix. CARVER is the acronym for Criticality, Accessibility, Recuperability, Vulnerability, Effect, and Recognizability. Private and public organizations have increasingly turned to using the CARVER matrix to assess vulnerabilities since the attacks on the Twin Towers in 2001. The CARVER matrix is not new; since 1952 it has been used by military special operations forces (SOF) to evaluate the relative merit of striking a particular target and in allocating the needed resources. In a corporate setting, CARVER can be a valuable tool for security managers to use—but in a reverse way. Instead of thinking about the destruction of a target and what is needed for that purpose, the security manager can think about protecting a target and the protection resources needed. To use the matrix in this way requires an understanding of it and how it can be applied in a corporate setting.

Criticality

Criticality is the importance of a system, subsystem, complex, or component and the primary consideration in targeting (and thus identifying vulnerabilities). Criticality is related also to the effect on the overall functioning of a system that would follow the destruction of a subcomponent such as people, property, or process. A target is critical when degradation of it would significantly impact an organization's ability to operate. When assessing criticality, an asset should always be viewed in relation to other components of the system. This holistic approach allows all components to be seen in the proper perspective. For example, while power generation at a wastewater treatment plant is critical, it may be secondary to having intact sludge separators. Generators are easily replaced, but specialized components might not be readily available. Only through thorough understanding of the system in its entirety can you understand the criticality of individual components. Protection of critical assets is of utmost impor-

tance, and redundancy of critical assets should be a goal when possible and practical.

Accessibility

Accessibility is the ease with which an asset can be reached, and both traditional and non-traditional access portals must be considered. Access to an asset can come in the form of direct physical access, direct access with standoff systems, or various forms of indirect access. Any target is accessible when an adversary can infiltrate the target area. Conventional assessments of accessibility have tended to focus on both ingress and egress routes to and from the asset. This is a parochial view, however, given the asymmetric nature of threat tactics today. The ability of an attacker to escape following an attack is beside the point when the attacker expects or even wants to die.

Recuperability

Recuperability is the effort and amount of time it will take to repair, replace, or bypass the damage done to an asset. Security managers should consider damage to both tangible and intangible assets. Damage to an intangible asset, such as employee dedication, can be costly and require a long time to repair. In the corporate environment, recuperability is the principal issue in business continuity planning.

Vulnerability

Vulnerability is a measure of the ability of an adversary to damage an asset. An asset is considered vulnerable if an adversary has the capability to adversely affect it. And, again, it is absolutely necessary to fully understand the nature of the asset to fully understand its vulnerabilities. For example, a steel vault can reduce the vulnerability of cash but has no value in protecting a trade secret in the mind of an employee.

Effect

Effect pertains to the consequences of an attack. A large effect is possible even when the damage is slight. Effect is not always limited to the organization; it can spill over to the surrounding neighborhood, the community, a region, or the nation. Effect can result from a force other than physical force. For example, a minute amount of a chemical contaminant released into a water storage tank would have little physical effect on consumers, but the psychological effect could be devastating. Instantly, the integrity of the water supply system is put into question. Millions of dollars and countless man hours could be spent to protect an already reasonably secure system.

Recognizability

Recognizability is the adversary's ability to understand a critical target without confusion. The adversary knows what it is and what it is not; what it looks like; and where it is. The security manager seeks to limit recognizability. The usual countermeasures are concealment and control of information.

The CARVER Rating System

When there are multiple potential targets, a numerical rating system is used to rank order them. The objective is to identify potential targets according to criticality. Later, in devising a protective scheme, high priorities are given to high-value targets.

The rating scale can be whatever you care to make it, e.g., it can be a straight scale, such as 1 to 5, or a weighted scale such as 8 for one factor, 13 for another, and so on. The chart below is an example of the CARVER matrix (which can be found in FM 3-05.232, *Special Forces Group Intelligence Operations*, table 4.4.) In this example, a straight five-point scale is used, with 5 being high and 1 low. The rated targets are functional areas of a bulk electric power plant.

The rater in the example used an arbitrary value of 22 as a cut-off level. Any target rated at 22 or higher was determined to have high criticality and a high potential for attack. With this information in hand, the rater was ready to begin development of a protective strategy.

The Office of the Joint Chiefs of Staff issued a document on target analysis. It is called *Doctrine for Joint Urban Operations*, and it sums up target analysis by saying, "... neither art nor science, [but] a combination of the two that systematically examines the components and relationships of potential military, political, or economic systems to establish their criticality and vulnerability to attack." Although related to operations in the military sector, the words hold meaning for security operations in the private sector.

Sidney W. Crews

TABLE 11. Using target analysis with an adversarial mind set can lead a security manager to uncover vulnerabilities that might not otherwise be seen, and using the CARVER matrix can help identify targets that deserve more security than others

Target Component	C	A	R	V	E	R	TOTAL
Water intake	3	5	1	1	5	4	19
Water filters and pumps	5	4	5	4	5	3	26*
Ion filter	2	1	1	1	5	1	11
Preheater and pumps	5	2	4	3	5	2	21
Air intake	2	1	1	1	5	1	11
Blowers	2	2	1	1	5	1	12
Barges	1	5	1	1	4	5	17
Docks and oil pumps	3	5	2	3	1	4	18
Storage tanks	1	4	1	4	1	5	16
Preheaters and pumps (fuel)	5	4	4	3	5	4	25*
Boiler	5	4	5	3	5	4	26*
Turbine	5	3	5	4	5	5	27*
Transformers	3	4	2	4	5	4	22*
Powerlines	5	1	1	1	1	1	10
Switching station	2	1	1	2	1	1	8

*Indicates targets suitable for attack.

XI: Terrorism

AGROTERRORISM

Agroterrorism can be defined as the deliberate introduction of a disease agent into animal or crop production systems before or during harvest, or post-harvest into the human food chain, with the purpose of causing political or economic damage, fear and/or human casualties. Agriculture and the general food industry are highly important to the social, economic, and political stability of the U.S. Agriculture in the U.S. accounts for 13 percent of the current Gross Domestic Product (GDP) and provides employment for 15 percent of the population. These numbers represent only a fraction of the total value of agriculture to the country, as they do not take into account allied services and industries such as suppliers, transporters, retail distributors, and restaurant chains. Despite its importance, agriculture is currently one of the sectors of the U.S. economy most vulnerable to terrorist attacks. A terrorist incident targeting one of the major U.S. agricultural commodities or the food processing industry could have catastrophic consequences for the economy of the country and the rest of the world, and will affect not only farmers and ranchers, but also farm suppliers, the transportation industry, grocery stores, restaurants, equipment distributors, tourism, and in the end the American consumer. Furthermore, because some of the animal disease agents that could be used as weapons of mass destruction (WMD) also affect humans, and because biological, chemical, or radiological agents could be introduced into agricultural products after they are harvested, terrorist attacks targeting any of the sectors of the human food chain could result in substantial human suffering and casualties.

Brief History of Agricultural Terrorism

Agroterrorism has been documented as far back as the sixth century B.C., when the Assyrians poisoned their enemies by contaminating wells with rye ergot, a fungus blight which can cause convulsions, delusions, and cardiovascularz problems that can result in death. The Greeks polluted their enemies' drinking water with animal corpses in 300 B.C.; and later, the Romans and Persians adopted the same strategy. During the twentieth century nine countries, including Canada, France, Germany, Iraq, Japan, South Africa, United Kingdom, United States, and the former Soviet Union, had documented agricultural bioweapons programs. During WWI, the German secret service mounted a covert biological campaign, using glanders and anthrax to infect draft animals, horses, and mules to be used by the Allies for the war effort in Europe. At the height of the Russian bioweapons programs after WWII, the Soviet military was manufacturing more than a thousand metric tons of disease agents each year, some of which, such as anthrax, bubonic plague, glanders, and tularemia, can infect both humans and animals. Probably the best known recent terrorist incident involving the human food chain in the U.S. is the deliberate contamination in 1984 of salad bars in Oregon with Salmonella by the Rajneeshee cult. More recently, an anonymous letter claiming that feed products at National By-Products Inc. had been tainted with a pesticide was received by the police of Berlin, Wisconsin in late December 1996, resulting in the company having to stop the shipment of 300 tons of feed. A multitude of similar incidents can be found in the scientific literature and the popular press. With the advancement of scientific knowledge about infectious agents and disease vectors, biological agents can be modified using relatively inexpensive means and with potentially devastating effects.

Potential Weapons of Mass Destruction (WMD) in Agroterrorist Attacks

Biological, chemical, and radiological WMD are the most likely agents that could be used in an agroterrorist attack. Throughout the world, there are many livestock and crop disease agents readily available in nature, from low-security laboratories, and even from commercial sources, that require little effort or risk to smuggle in. Foot and mouth disease (FMD), bovine spongiform encephalopathy (BSE), and highly pathogenic avian influenza have received a great deal of attention in the press. However, over one hundred lethal and contagious diseases, such as rinderpest, contagious bovine pleuropneumonia, Rift Valley fever, sheep and goat pox, classical swine fever, African swine fever, African horse sickness, and velogenic Newcastle disease, could be used to target the U.S. livestock industry. For plants, the list of agents that might be used is nearly endless, although some, such as Wheat Smut, Soybean rust, or Rice Blast, appear more harmful than others. For the food processing industry, food-borne and waterborne infectious diseases, such as salmonellosis, shigellosis, vibriosis, and campylobacteriosis, are major concerns. Also critical are toxins, such as botulinum and ricin, and chemical agents including mercury, arsenic, lead, and pesticides.

Impact of an Agroterrorist Attack in the U.S.

The potential economic, social, and environmental impact of an agroterrorist incident in the U.S. is difficult to determine. Based on estimates from natural outbreaks of FMD in other countries, it has been calculated that an outbreak of this disease in the U.S. would cost the livestock industry between $2 billion to $25 billion, depending on the extent of the outbreak. To this, the costs of depopulating infected and exposed herds, disinfecting premises, quarantines, surveillance, remediation of the environment, and the resulting higher prices of meat would have to be added. The deliberate contamination of human food by chemical, biological, or radionuclear agents for terrorist purposes is a real and current threat. Its potential impact on human health is difficult to determine, but can be estimated by extrapolation from examples of unintentional outbreaks of food-borne and waterborne-disease. Estimates from the Centers of Disease Control (CDC) and Prevention show that unsafe food in U.S. results in 76 million illnesses, 325,000 hospitalizations, and 5,000 deaths per year. For instance, a natural outbreak of salmonellosis due to contaminated pasteurized milk in U.S. in 1985 resulted in 170,000 people affected. Probably the most deadly incident of unintentional food contamination occurred in Spain in 1981. In this case, 800 people died and 20,000 people were injured, some permanently, due to the contamination of cooking oil by a chemical agent. An orchestrated terrorist attack on the human food chain would be devastating and could result in large numbers of deaths in humans. Some of

the social impacts, such as psychological diseases among affected farmers, are likely to be felt for considerably longer than duration of impact itself and may outlive the more obvious financial impacts of the outbreak. The need for carcass or crop destruction at the quarantine site is a major concern because of the potential underground and surface water contamination and air pollution. The public confidence in government could be eroded if authorities appear unable to prevent or rapidly control an agroterrorist attack or to protect the population's food supply.

Vulnerability of the U.S. Agriculture

The vulnerability of the U.S. agriculture is particularly high due to the size and diversity of the industry, the long borders shared with Canada and Mexico, and the number of international seaports and airports. Protection of critical agricultural infrastructure in the U.S. presents a big challenge because agricultural production is geographically disbursed in unsecured environments and thousands of animals are often concentrated in open-air pens that are difficult to secure from intruders. Live animals, grain, and processed food products are routinely transported and commingled in the production and processing system. The level of agroterrorism awareness among ranchers, farmers, agricultural workers, and agricultural extension agents, who may be the first ones to be confronted with animal and plant diseases related to terrorist events, varies but in general is considered to be low. In the food industry sector, the U.S. imports 33 percent of all fresh fruits and 55 percent of all seafood from other countries, making the nation's food supply highly vulnerable to contamination prior to importation. The food processing and packing plants tend to lack uniform security and safety preparedness measures, particularly those that have proliferated at the lower and medium end of the production spectrum. Particularly some small-scale operations do not keep accurate records of distribution, making it impossible to trace a tainted food item back to its original source of production. Ultimately, the magnitude of the damage in an agroterrorist incident will depend on the rapidity with which the disease is discovered and the response plans are implemented.

Response to an Agroterrorist Incident

Because of the great diversity of the U.S. agricultural industry, it is not possible to produce a model contingency plan that will be a perfect fit for all agroterrorist threats under all situations and circumstances in different jurisdictions or states. When responding to an agroterrorist incident, local, state, and federal governments and their industry partners in the private sector will have to respond in a coordinated, mutually supportive manner that is based on the Incident Command System (ICS). Most states have plans for preventing, responding, and remediating an agroterrorist attack. These plans are mostly based on an outbreak of FMD, but there is no standardization in the protocols and the response capability throughout the country. Veterinarians and other public health and agricultural professionals will play a major role in the response by establishing a quarantine area around the outbreak, vaccinating and/or slaughtering all infected herds and other herds that have been in close contact with infected animals, disposing of slaughtered animals; cleaning and disinfecting properties, compensating stock owners for the livestock slaughtered; and carrying out clinical inspection and surveillance to ensure the disease does not spread to other areas. Other emergency response disciplines, including law enforcement, fire services, hazardous material, emergency medical services, emergency management, health care, public works, and public safety communications also will play a crucial role in activities such as conflict resolution, criminal investigation, disinfection and decontamination, treatment of in-site related injuries, mental health support, establishment of telecommunications, road traffic control, carcass disposal, and many others.

Conclusions

The terrorist threat against the U.S. agricultural sector is serious and real. If the nation's agricultural products and food supply are to remain safe, federal and state authorities need to work in coordination with the agricultural commodity representatives to develop accurate terrorist risks and vulnerability assessments, response plans, and short- and long-term recovery strategies. No country can by its own efforts alone make itself invulnerable to today's terrorist threats. The development of better instruments for universal and national counter-terrorism cooperation is an essential component of a comprehensive response to agroterrorism. A priority of agricultural counter-terrorism planning should be to enhance the awareness level and preparedness against potential agroterrorist attacks among commodity owners, agricultural workers, agricultural extension agents, port inspectors, and first responders. Also important should be to heighten the States' animal and plant disease surveillance and diagnostic capabilities. Tabletop and full blown exercises that emphasize the decision-making, coordination, and logistic process execution are an essential part and should be conducted regularly at the regional and tri-national level, the latter between the U.S., Canada, and Mexico. The various sectors of the agricultural industry need to implement biosecurity measures, including isolation and infection control, traffic control, sanitation, and facility security. Finally, research is needed in areas such as devising environmentally-friendly carcass disposal methods, developing early and rapid disease detection and identification systems, including the recognition of bioengineered organisms, and in the areas of vaccine and therapeutics development.

Andrés de la Concha Bermejillo

CHEMICAL AND BIOLOGICAL WEAPONS

Chemical Weapons

By definition, a chemical warfare agent is any chemical substance, whether gaseous, liquid, or solid, which might be employed because of its direct toxic effects on man, animals, and plants. A toxic chemical can kill, injure, or incapacitate any living process. Included within the definition of a chemical warfare agent are dispersal mechanisms such as ammunition, projectiles, and aerosolizing devices.

Toxins

Thousands of toxic substances exist but only a few are amenable to chemical warfare. This is because a number of rigorous demands must be met before a toxic substance can be used as a chemical warfare agent. Mainly, these are:

- The agent cannot be so toxic as to affect the persons preparing to use it.
- The agent must be capable of being stored for a long period without degradation and without corroding the packaging material.
- The agent must be relatively resistant to atmospheric water and oxygen so that it does not lose effect when dispersed.
- The agent must withstand heat that is generated during dispersal.

Chemical warfare agents, at least the way they are produced today, are liquids or solids of which a certain amount is in a volatile form. Both solid and liquid substances can be dispersed in the air in an aerosolized form. As such, they enter the human body through the respiratory organs. Some chemical warfare agents can also penetrate the skin. The penetration of a solid substance is slow except when it is mixed with a penetrating solvent.

To achieve good ground coverage when dispersed from a high altitude, a chemical warfare agent must be in the form of droplets sufficiently large to ensure they fall within the target area. This can be achieved by making the agent viscous by the addition of polymers. In this form, the chemical warfare agent lasts longer and complicates decontamination.

Nerve Agents

Nerve agents are so called because they affect the transmission of nerve impulses in the nervous system. Nerve agents are stable and easily dispersed, highly toxic, and have rapid effects both when absorbed through the skin and inhaled into the lungs. Nerve agents can be manufactured by means of fairly simple chemical techniques. The raw materials are inexpensive and generally readily available.

In 1936, Dr Gerhard Schrader, a chemist at IG Farben, developed a phosphorus compound for use as an insecticide. Named tabun, the compound was later adapted for use as a nerve agent. In 1938, Schrader produced a second nerve agent called sarin, and in 1944 a third agent called soman. These three compounds are known as G agents.

In 1958, discovery was made of an even more effective nerve agent known by its U.S. Army code name VX. This is a persistent substance that can remain on material, equipment, and terrain for long periods. Penetration is mainly through the skin but also through inhalation when dispersed as a gas or aerosol.

VX is the deadliest nerve agent ever created. It is a clear, colorless liquid with the consistency of motor oil. A fraction of a drop of VX, absorbed through the skin, can kill by severely disrupting the nervous system. Although a cocktail of drugs can serve as an antidote, VX acts so quickly that victims would have to be injected with the antidote almost immediately to have a chance at survival. VX is the only significant nerve agent created since World War II.

The use of VX by terrorists is unlikely but possible. Synthesizing the agent is complicated and extremely dangerous. It requires the use of toxic and corrosive chemicals and high temperatures in a sophisticated chemical laboratory. Still, the Japanese doomsday cult Aum Shinrikyo, which recruited trained chemists from Japanese universities, managed to synthesize small quantities of VX to use for assassinations. Terrorists lacking access to trained organic chemists might be more likely to steal a weapon containing VX from a poorly guarded chemical weapons depot in a country such as Russia.

If terrorists obtained or produced a significant quantity of VX without killing themselves in the process, they might try to spread VX over a large area, such as a city. But experts say that because of the hazards involved in handling VX, terrorists might turn first to other forms of attack.

Mustard Agent

Mustard agent is often called a "blistering agent" because the wounds it causes resemble burns and blisters. It also causes severe damage to the eyes, respiratory system, and internal organs.

Mustard agent was produced in 1822 but its harmful effects were not discovered until 1860. It was first used as a chemical warfare agent during the latter part of World War I and caused lung and eye injuries to a very large number of soldiers.

During the war between Iran and Iraq in 1979–88, Iraq used large quantities of chemical agents. About 5,000 Iranian soldiers were reportedly killed, 10–20 percent of them by mustard agent, plus 40,000 to 50,000 injured.

Hydrogen Cyanide

Hydrogen cyanide is usually included among the chemical warfare agents, but there is no solid proof it has been used in chemical warfare. Iraq is suspected, however, of using hydrogen cyanide in its war against Iran and against Kurds in northern Iraq. During World War II, a form of hydrogen cyanide (Zyklon B) was used in Nazi gas chambers.

Chlorine

Chlorine is widely used in industry and found in some household products. As a gas, it can be converted to liquid form by pressurizing and cooling. In liquid form it can be shipped and stored. When liquid chlorine is released, it quickly turns into a gas that is heavier than air. In this form, it stays close to the ground and spreads rapidly. Chlorine is recognizable by its pungent, irritating odor, which is like the odor of bleach. The strong smell may provide warning to people that have been exposed.

Phosgene is an industrial chemical similar to chlorine. Both are transported in multi-ton shipments by road and rail. Rupturing a transport container can easily disseminate these gases over a fairly wide area. For this reason, these gases while in transit can have particular appeal to terrorists because the transport vehicle is a weapon in itself.

Biological Weapons

Discussion of the possible use of bio-weapons by terrorists began even earlier than September 11, 2001, during the break-up of the Soviet Union. The specter of Russia's biological agents covertly migrating into the weapons inventory of terrorist groups moved the issue from discussion to prevention and response.

Biological weapons are mysterious, unfamiliar, indiscriminate, uncontrollable, inequitable, and invisible—all characteristics associated with heightened fear. To the extent terrorists believe that a bio-attack would help their cause, the greater the likelihood of it.

A case can be made for anticipating the use of a bio-weapon. At some point the magnitude of terrorist attacks using conventional weapons will plateau. The next logical step in escalation will be the use of chemical and bio-weapons. Unlike conventional weapons, biological agents would be effective in destroying crops, poisoning foods, or contaminating pharmaceutical products. Terrorists might use biological agents to attack corporations perceived to be national icons such as Coca-Cola and Gerber. In addition to the fear factor, such an act would place enormous demands on the medical system, require large clean-up expenditures, and damage the economy.

On the other side of the coin, a terrorist group contemplating use of a bio-weapon will face several problems:

- Formidable political risk and loss of private support
- Acquisition or construction of a dispersal device
- The ability to deliver or disperse the agent covertly
- The risk of infection to themselves and to others they do not wish to infect

Biological agents with a potential for use by terrorists can be placed into three groups and their sub-groups:

- Bacteria
  - Anthrax
  - Plague
- Viruses
  - Smallpox
  - Viral Hemorrhagic Fevers
- Toxins
  - Botulism
  - Ricin

Bacterial Agents

Bacterial agent is a general term. In the current context it means any bacteria that has been or can be used by terrorists to kill people. Lethal bacteria are numerous. In this section we will address those that are amenable to use as a weapon of mass destruction.

Anthrax. Anthrax is an acute, specific, infectious, febrile disease of animals, including humans, and is caused by an organism that under certain conditions will form highly resistant spores capable of persisting and retaining their virulence in contaminated soil or other material for many years. The anthrax bacterium is often found naturally in the soil of rural Texas and Oklahoma and in areas near the Mississippi River. It is also produced in research laboratories—but not easily. Significant scientific training is needed.

Probably because so little is known about anthrax, opinions of it as a terrorist weapon vary widely. On the one hand, it is touted as the terrorist's preferred biological warfare agent because a single gram of anthrax material is believed capable of producing 100 million lethal doses and that a single dose is 100,000 times deadlier than the deadliest chemical warfare agent. It is also considered a silent, invisible killer because the symptoms of infection mimic non-lethal ailments. This view also holds that the barriers to production of anthrax are minimal because production costs are low; large quantities can be produced and stockpiled without great difficulty; and production know-how, although technical, is in the public domain. There is also little agreement on the extent of damage to human health if anthrax was introduced; for example, into an office building's ventilation system, a crowded bus, or a football stadium filled to capacity.

Among the experts is a shared belief that anthrax can be weaponized. Because anthrax is stable it can be stored almost indefinitely as a dry powder. When freeze-dried, it can be loaded into munitions, and with limited technology can be disseminated as an aerosol. With a little more expertise, the spores can be made smaller so they're easier to inhale and made lighter so they float in the air longer. Also, it is possible to alter the genetic makeup of the spore so that it is resistant to medical treatment.

Plague. This disease appears in two variants: bubonic and pneumonic. Bubonic plague is carried by rodents and transmitted to humans via flea bites; it cannot spread from person to person. This form of plague caused the Black Death that devastated China, the Middle East, and Europe in the fourteenth century, killing a larger proportion of the world's population than any single war or epidemic since.

During World War II, the Japanese army spread bubonic plague by dropping infected fleas over China with lethal results. In 1346, plague broke out in the Tartar army during its siege of Kaffa (now Feodosia in Crimea). Attackers hurled the corpses of plague victims over the city walls, causing an epidemic that forced the city to surrender. Some infected Kaffa residents who left the city may have inadvertently started the Black Death pandemic that raged all across Europe.

The pneumonic plague infects the lungs, travels through the air and is highly contagious. It's also rarer and more lethal than bubonic plague. If those infected do not receive treatment, their mortality rate can approach 100 percent. Pneumonic plague in an aerosolized form has a potential for use as a terrorist weapon.

Viruses

A virus is an extremely tiny infectious agent that is only able to live inside a cell. Basically, viruses are composed of just two parts. The outer part is a protective shell and the inner part is made of genetic material. A virus cannot reproduce by itself. To reproduce, a virus invades a cell within the body of a human or other creature, called the host. Each type of virus has particular types of host creatures and host cells that it will invade successfully. Once within the host cell, the virus uses the cell's own properties to produce more viruses. In essence, the virus forces the cell to replicate the virus' own genetic material and protective shell. Once replicated, the new viruses leave the host cell and are ready to invade others.

Smallpox. The most common and deadly form of smallpox is *variola major*. Smallpox is ancient; descriptions of the disease have been found dating from as far back as the 4th century A.D. in China.

The World Health Organization officially declared smallpox eradicated in 1979, after a painstaking vaccination campaign. Samples of the virus are kept for research purposes at the Centers for Disease Control and Prevention in Atlanta and in laboratories in Russia.

The use of smallpox as a weapon of war is not new. British forces in North America gave blankets used by smallpox patients to Native Americans during the French and Indian War of 1754–67. Some tribes lost up to half their populations. The threat of smallpox as a bioweapon greatly diminished when a vaccine was developed in 1796.

Smallpox is small enough to be inhaled, so it could be spread in an aerosol. The virus is very stable, which means it isn't easy to destroy, and it retains its potency for days outside a human host. Smallpox can be freeze-dried and stored at room temperature for months or years, and remain potent when revived with water. American scientists in the 1960s were able to turn dried smallpox into a fine powder and to create tiny aerosol generators that could disseminate the virus.

Viral Hemorrhagic Fever (VHF). The term "viral hemorrhagic fever" refers to a group of illnesses that are caused by several distinct families of viruses. In general, the term describes a severe syndrome that impairs the body's ability to regulate itself. These symptoms are often accompanied by hemorrhage or bleeding. With a few noteworthy exceptions, there is no cure or established drug treatment for VHF. Some viruses that cause hemorrhagic fever can spread from one person to another, once an initial person has become infected. Ebola, Marburg, Lassa, and Crimean-Congo hemorrhagic fever viruses are examples.

Compared to anthrax and smallpox, VHFs are less stable, more vulnerable to heat, light, and disinfectants, and once released into the air have shorter life spans than either anthrax or smallpox. Some experts, with good evidence, argue that terrorists would sooner turn to anthrax or smallpox than VHFs.

Toxins

Toxins are unusual because they are both chemical and biological agents.

Rapid development of gene technology during the 1970s stirred interest in creating bio-weapons using toxins, both natural and synthetic. Later research in cancer treatment discovered a way to target toxins to different body organs. Still, toxins are considered to be less suitable as a bio-weapon because they cannot be dispersed on a large scale; however, they could be used for sabotage of a specific location or assassination of specific persons.

Botulism. The botulinum nerve toxin is the single most toxic substance known to science. Its extraordinary potency has made it one of the most widely researched bio-weapons. If a lethal dose were administered to each person individually, a single gram of botulinum toxin would theoretically be enough to kill more than a million people.

Iraq, North Korea, Iran, and Syria are believed to have developed botulinum toxin as a weapon. After the 1991 Gulf War, Iraq told U.N. weapons inspectors that it had produced 19,000 liters of concentrated botulinum toxin, enough theoretically to kill everyone on earth three times over.

Botulinum toxin is the first biological toxin to be approved for medical treatment. It is used to treat neuromuscular disorders, lower back pain, and cerebral palsy. It is also an ingredient in Botox, a product that temporarily eliminates wrinkles by paralyzing the facial muscles.

Ricin. This toxin is found in the mash-like waste left over from the processing of castor beans, which are used to make castor oil. The ricin in the waste can be made into the form of a powder, pellet, or mist, and it can be dissolved in water or a weak acid. Ricin is only minimally affected by extreme temperature conditions and is stable in aerosolized form.

Ricin is produced easily and inexpensively, is highly toxic, and has no treatment or vaccine. When compared to some of the other biological agents that could be used to produce the desired effect of a weapon of mass destruction, ricin ranks relatively low. For example, to achieve the same damaging effect produced by one kilogram of anthrax would require four metric tons of ricin.

John J. Fay

Sources

Centers for Disease Control and Prevention. 2005. "Bioterrorism." <www.bt.cdc.gov/bioterrorism>

Centers for Disease Control and Prevention. 2005. "Chemical Emergencies." <www.bt.cdc.gov/chemical>

Fay, J. 2005. *Contemporary Security Management.* Boston: Butterworth-Heinemann.

WMD Threat and Risk Assessment. 2005. College Station: Texas A&M University System.

CRITICAL INFRASTRUCTURE PROTECTION (CIP)

Exactly thirty-five days after September 11, 2001, the President signed Executive Order 13231, "Critical Infrastructure Protection in the

Information Age," and established the President's Critical Infrastructure Protection Board. Now known as the National Infrastructure Advisory Council (NIAC), it is responsible to "provide the President through the Secretary of Homeland Security with advice on the security of the critical infrastructure sectors and their information systems." This Executive Order sparked the creation of The National Strategy for the Physical Protection of Critical Infrastructures and Key Assets—the subject of this article.

What are critical infrastructures and key assets? America's critical infrastructure sectors provide the foundation for our national security, governance, economic vitality, and way of life. The federal government lists critical infrastructure sectors as energy, water, public health, banking and finance, chemicals and hazardous materials, agriculture and food, emergency services, defense industrial base, telecommunications, transportation, and postal and shipping. Key assets and high profile events are individual targets whose attack in the worst case scenarios could result in not only large-scale human casualties and property destruction, but also profound damage to the national prestige, morale, and confidence. Key assets are listed as nuclear power plants, government facilities, dams, commercial key assets, and national monuments and icons.

The national strategy for CIP is based on three objectives.

1.   Identifying and assuring the protection of those infrastructures and assets that we deem most critical in terms of national-level public health and safety, governance, economic and national security, and public confidence consequences
2.   Providing timely warning and assuring the protection of those infrastructures and assets that face a specific, imminent threat
3.   Assuring the protection of other infrastructures and assets that may become terrorist targets over time by pursuing specific initiatives and enabling a collaborative environment in which federal, state, and local governments and the private sector can better protect the infrastructures and assets they control

This strategic national strategy was developed to counter the nation's greatest threat: terrorism. Terrorists will attack the critical infrastructure and key assets with the hopes of yielding one to three possible outcomes: direct infrastructure effects, indirect infrastructure effects, and exploitation of infrastructure. Direct infrastructure effects are defined as cascading disruption or arrest of the functions of critical infrastructures or key assets through direct attacks on a critical node, system, or function. Indirect infrastructure effects are defined as cascading disruption and financial consequences for government, society, and economy through public- and private-sector reactions to an attack. Exploitation of infrastructure is the exploitation of elements of a particular infrastructure to disrupt or destroy another target. The United States is so vast that terrorists will not have a problem selecting a vulnerable target.

The staggering number of facilities associated with the nation's critical infrastructure and key assets magnify the difficult challenge the United States faces in CIP. Here is a sample of those statistics by category with approximate numbers.

• Agriculture and food: 1,912,000 farms and 87,000 food-processing plants
• Water: 1,800 federal reservoirs and 1,600 municipal waste water facilities
• Public health: 5,800 registered hospitals
• Emergency services: 87,000 U.S. localities
• Defense industrial base: 250,000 firms in 215 distinct industries
• Telecommunications: 2 billion miles of cable
• Energy: 2,800 electrical power plants, 300,000 oil and natural gas producing sites
• Transportation: 5,000 public airports, 120,000 miles of major railroads, 590,000 highway bridges, 2 million miles of pipelines, 300 inland/coastal ports, and 500 major urban public transit operators
• Banking and finance: 26,600 FDIC insured institutions
• Chemical industry and hazardous materials: 66,000 chemical plants
• Postal and shipping: 137 million delivery sites
• Key assets include 5,800 historic buildings, 104 commercial nuclear power plants, 80,000 dams, 3,000 government owned/operated facilities, and 460 skyscrapers.

The paramount concept of the national strategy is cooperation. This involves all levels of government—federal, state, local, *and* the private sector. Without mutual cooperation between all these parties, the United States will fail at CIP and the nation will be at great risk. The Department of Homeland Security (DHS) is the lead agency for CIP. In this leadership role they are the primary liaison and facilitator for cooperation among federal agencies, state and local governments, and the private sector. Each category of critical infrastructure mentioned previously has an assigned federal department responsible for it. Even the Department of State is involved by facilitating international agreements with U.S. allies. The state and local governments are comprised of 87,000 jurisdictions that must interact with the federal government and the private sector to identify and secure the critical infrastructure and key assets they control. Finally, the private sector, which owns and operates most of the nation's critical infrastructure, should reassess and adjust their planning, assurance, and investment programs to better accommodate the increased risk presented by deliberate acts of violence. When the threat reaches a level that exceeds an organization's financial ability to mitigate then they should seek government assistance.

In light of the immense importance cooperation plays in the success of CIP, The National Strategy for the Physical Protection of Critical Infrastructures and Key Assets outlines five focus areas to address impediments to physical protection that significantly impact multiple sectors of the government, society, and economy. These are planning and resource allocation; information sharing and indication and warnings; personnel surety, building human capital and awareness; technology and research and development; and modeling, simulation, and analysis.

Planning and resource allocation involves eight initiatives.

1. Create collaborative mechanisms for government-industry critical infrastructure and key asset protection planning.
2. Identify key protection priorities and develop appropriate supporting mechanisms for these priorities.
3. Foster increased sharing of risk-management expertise between the public and private sectors.
4. Identify options for incentives for private organizations that proactively implement enhanced security measures.
5. Coordinate and consolidate federal and state protection plans.
6. Establish a task force to review legal impediments to reconstitution and recovery in the aftermath of an attack against a critical infrastructure or key asset.
7. Develop and integrate critical infrastructure and key asset geospatial database.
8. Conduct critical infrastructure protection planning with our international partners.

Information sharing and indications and warnings comprise six major initiatives.

1. Define protection-related information sharing requirements and establish effective, efficient information sharing processes.
2. Implement the statutory authorities and powers of the Homeland Security Act of 2002 to protect security and proprietary information regarded as sensitive by the private sector.
3. Promote the development and operation of critical sector Information Sharing Analysis Centers.
4. Improve processes for domestic threat data collection, analysis, and dissemination to state and local government and private industry.
5. Support the development of interoperable secure communications systems for state and local governments and designated private sector entities.
6. Complete implementation of the Homeland Security Advisory System.

Personnel surety, building human capital, and awareness also have six major initiatives.

1. Coordinate the development of national standards for personnel surety.
2. Develop a certification program for background-screening companies.
3. Explore establishment of a certification regime or model security training program for private security officers.

4. Identify requirements and develop programs to protect critical personnel.
5. Facilitate the sharing of public- and private-sector protection expertise.
6. Develop and implement a national awareness program for critical infrastructure and key asset protection.

Technology and research and development are comprised of four major initiatives.

1. Coordinate public- and private-sector security research and development activities.
2. Coordinate interoperability standards to ensure compatibility of communications systems.
3. Explore methods to authenticate and verity personnel identity.
4. Improve technical surveillance, monitoring, and detection capabilities.

Modeling, simulation, and analysis have six major initiatives.

1. Enable the integration of modeling, simulation, and analysis into national infrastructure and asset protection planning and decision support activities.
2. Develop economic models of near- and long-term effects of terrorist attacks.
3. Develop critical node/chokepoint and interdependency analysis capabilities.
4. Model interdependencies across sectors with respect to conflicts between sector alert and warning procedures and actions.
5. Conduct integrated risk modeling of cyber and physical threats, vulnerabilities, and consequences.
6. Develop models to improve information integration.

President George W. Bush summed it up best when he wrote: "The terrorist enemy that we face is highly determined, patient, and adaptive. In confronting this threat, protecting our critical infrastructures and key assets represents an enormous challenge. We must remain united in our resolve, tenacious in our approach, and harmonious in our actions to overcome this challenge and secure the foundations of our Nation and way of life."

Those wishing to keep up-to-date with the latest developments and news concerning CIP should sign up for the Department of Homeland Security Daily Open Source Infrastructure Report available by contacting dhsdailyadmin@mail.dhs.osis.gov. This daily brief is conveniently broken up into hyperlinked sections such as Production Industries, Service Industries, Sustenance and Health, Federal and State, and IT and Cyber.

Adolfo Meana, Jr. and James J. Zirkel

Sources
Charter of the National Infrastructure Advisory Council. Department of Homeland Security. Sep. 2005.
Department of Homeland Security. Jan. 2006. <http://www.dhs.gov/dhspublic/display?theme=31&content=5365>
The National Strategy for the Physical Protection of Critical Infrastructures and Key Assets. Feb. 2003.

CRITICAL NATIONAL INFRASTRUCTURE: ELECTRIC POWER

The electric power grid is a highly interconnected and dynamic system of over 3,000 public and private utilities and rural cooperatives. These utilities have incorporated a wide variety of information and telecommunications systems to automate the control of electric power generation, transmission, and distribution.

Physical destruction is the greatest threat facing the electric power infrastructure. Electronic intrusion represents an emerging but still relatively minor threat.

Insiders are considered to be the primary threat to information systems. Downsizing, increased competition, and the shift to standard protocols add to the potential sources of attacks, whether from inside, or outside, a utility.

Substations represent the most significant information security vulnerability in the power grid. Many of the automated devices used to monitor and control equipment within transmission and distribution substations are poorly protected against intrusion. Interconnections between control centers and corporate data networks, widespread use of dial-up modems, and use of public networks (PN) are other sources of vulnerabilities.

Utilities use a variety of mechanisms to protect the electric power grid from disruption, including contingency analysis, redundant control centers, dial-back modems, and firewalls. However, few utilities have an information security function for their operational systems, and the lack of convincing evidence of a threat has led senior managers to minimize information security investments. A major coordinated attack could disrupt activities at a national level.

Three trends increase the exposure of electric power control networks to attacks:

- The shift from proprietary mainframe control systems to open systems and standard protocols.
- Increasing use of automation, outside contractors, and external connections to reduce staff and operating costs.
- The requirement to provide open access to transmission system information dictated by the Federal Government.

The probability of a nationwide disruption of electric power through electronic intrusion short of a major coordinated attack is extremely low, but the potential for short-term disruptions at the regional level is not.

Overview of the Electric Power Industry

There are about 3,000 independent electric utilities in the United States. Each is interconnected with coordinated controls, operations, telecommunications networks, and sophisticated control centers. These utilities include investor-owned public utilities, government-owned systems, cooperatives, and manufacturing industries that also produce power. Nearly 80 percent of the nation's power generation comes from the approximately 270 investor-owned public utilities. The Federal Government generates another 10 percent of the nation's power, primarily through large facilities such as the Tennessee Valley Authority. However, the Federal Government owns few distribution facilities. The remaining power supply is generated by the cooperatives and manufacturing industries. There are approximately 1,000 cooperatives, which generally have limited power-generation capacity and focus primarily on transmission and distribution systems.

In addition, some manufacturing industries generate power for their own use but sell surplus power to utilities, accounting for a small portion of the industry total.

The basic structure of an electric power transmission and distribution system consists of a generating system, a transmission system, a sub-transmission system, a distribution system, and a control center. Power plant generation systems may include steam turbines, diesel engines, or hydraulic turbines connected to alternators that generate AC electricity.

Threats to the Electric Power Grid

A threat is any circumstance or event with the potential to cause harm to a system in the form of destruction, disclosure, modification of data, or denial of service. Generally speaking, threats can be placed into two broad categories: physical and electronic.

Physical Threat. Despite the growing concern about cyberspace attacks, the physical destruction of utility infrastructure elements is still the predominant threat to electric utilities. Physical threats to the infrastructure elements of an electric power utility fall under the general categories of accidental and deliberate events. Natural emergencies are the most significant accidental physical event to affect a utility and are the single greatest cause of outages in the electric power system. However, the impact of natural hazards on the power grid is the most manageable because utilities have years of experience with this threat and have designed facilities and infrastructure elements to minimize impact. Additionally, service providers design systems and operational procedures to allow them to respond to outages and restore service quickly. Most utilities have extensive experience with storms and other natural disasters and exercise their response systems periodically.

After natural hazards, deliberate physical attacks on utility infrastructure elements cause the most damage to the electric power grid. Transformers, microwave communications towers, and transmission substations can often be found in isolated, unpopulated areas. These pieces of equipment have proven to be popular targets for vandals, criminals, ecological terrorists, and amateur sharpshooters.

Electronic Threat. The electric power industry does not acknowledge a single incident of a power outage caused by an electronic intrusion. However, a majority of utility members agree that an electronic attack capable of causing regional or widespread disruption lasting in excess of 24 hours is technically feasible. The source for such an attack could come from within the utility or from an external source.

Insider Threat. Insiders can be employees, contractors, or anyone else with legitimate access to system components and/or premises. Generally, insiders are granted varying degrees of access to the software and databases and may compromise them using legitimately or surreptitiously acquired computer access privileges. The primary motives that drive an insider to exploit a system are usually financial gain or revenge.

Electric utility personnel believe that alienated employees pose the most significant insider security threat to information systems. Considering that the number of employees working for electric utilities has dropped significantly in recent years, there are many potentially bitter former utility employees with system knowledge who could attack the power grid.

Outsider Threat. An outsider is anyone not legitimately associated with the system in question. Outsiders could be rival companies, criminal elements, or foreign national intelligence agencies. Examples include technical hackers motivated by the challenge; terrorist groups motivated to inflict damage to systems for a variety of political, ideological, or personal reasons; or rival companies seeking competitive information.

While there have been instances of hackers breaking into electric utilities' business and support systems, the utilities have not encountered the full-scale attacks that the telecommunications services providers have experienced.

If an outside organization had goals beyond financial gain, a structured electronic attack targeting the utility's operations systems could be a way to cause widespread disruption to a given geographic region.

It is important to note that information systems do not just represent a way to directly attack the electric power grid. A large amount of information about infrastructure elements is readily available on the Internet and in public reading rooms.

The electric power industry clearly recognizes and has considerable experience in dealing with the risks to the energy infrastructure from physical threats. However, the implications of electronic intrusions are understood less well. Given the limited experience with electronic attacks, government efforts to identify and scope these threats are carried out with vulnerability assessments that produce guidelines for protection measures.

Threat Deterrents

A deterrent is an attempt to prevent or discourage an action before it is initiated generally through fear or doubt. The ability of law enforcement to investigate, prosecute, and convict is the principal deterrent to computer crime. Recent and pending legislation increases the jurisdiction of federal, state, and local law enforcement authorities over attacks on electric power control systems. However, the lack of effective reporting mechanisms, inconsistent use of logins, passwords, and warning banners, and a low probability of being detected, caught, and prosecuted hinder effective deterrence of potential attackers.

A number of factors tend to greatly reduce the effectiveness of deterrents. Most network and systems administrators lack efficient tools to detect intrusions reliably. Even when intrusions are detected, a majority of the organizations effected do not report the intrusions. The most common reason cited is the fear of negative publicity. For law enforcement to prove an offense, there must be a warning banner stating that computing activities may be monitored and that unauthorized use is a violation prosecutable under the law. Adding to the problem is widespread use of shared logins and weak passwords.

Vulnerability

An organization's systems are most vulnerable at the point where the connectivity is the greatest and the access control is the weakest. If someone opted to attack the electric power grid electronically rather than physically, he or she would have three prime targets to consider: the control center, the substation, and the communications infrastructure.

Control Center Vulnerabilities. There is no "standard" control center system configuration. A control center can range from an aged, isolated, in-house, mainframe-based system to a networked Unix client-server system tailored to unique needs. The industry trend is for utilities to procure "standard" vendor system products based on the distributed client/server technology so as to reduce schedule risk and minimize project costs. Control center systems are vulnerable to unauthorized access through several interfaces:

- Links to the corporate information system
- Links to other utilities or power pools
- Links to supporting vendors
- Remote maintenance and administration ports

Regardless of the access point, once in the control system network, the intruder may crash the system. A knowledgeable intruder can employ other, more subtle, options; for example, corruption of the databases and insertion of false commands that close relays and shut down lines.

Substation Vulnerabilities. A substation serves as a clearinghouse for power as it is stepped down from the high voltages used to transmit power across the service area and then to distribution systems for delivery to customers. A substation is likely to have digital programmable breakers, switches, relays, and other devices susceptible to electronic attack.

An electronic intruder that identifies the telephone line serving a digital programmable device is able to dial into an unprotected port and reset the breaker to a level of tolerance that would physically destroy the equipment it serves. The intruder could also set the device to be excessively sensitive, which would cause the system to shut down for self-protection.

A remote terminal unit (RTU) collects data and operates as a clearinghouse for control signals to transmission and distribution equipment. An intruder could dial into this port and issue commands to the substation equipment or report spurious data back to the control cen-

ter. Due to the highly networked nature of the power grid, knocking out an RTU can have a significant impact on "downstream" systems and customers.

Communications Vulnerabilities. Utilities rely on a mix of private microwave radio, private fiber, and the public networks for communications among control system elements. Any one of these mediums could be exploited in an electronic attack. In most cases, an attack on the communications infrastructure alone would constitute a nuisance attack. In such an event, most utilities would compensate with cellular phones and mobile radios. However, an attack on the communications infrastructure in conjunction with an attack on the electric power control system would be very serious. Restoring power would be extremely difficult and dangerous if all means of coordination were lost between the control center and generation and transmission elements.

Private Infrastructure Vulnerabilities. Microwave systems and aerial or buried fiber optics make up the majority of utility private communications networks. Utilities view their private communications network as a key asset, yet the communications infrastructures of private utilities are as vulnerable to intrusion and physical attack as the public network. Microwave communications can be intercepted or jammed quite easily using inexpensive microwave jamming units. Despite the apparent vulnerabilities, private sector utilities seem to believe that because their systems are isolated from the public networks, they are safe and secure.

Protection Measures

Electric utilities use a variety of mechanisms to protect the electric power grid from disruption. The most significant measure is a double contingency analysis system, which uses a real-time simulator to look for the two worst things that could happen to the grid at any instant and offers operators corrective actions to consider and initiate. These "security" systems are powerful; however, the system does not look at elements beyond the power grid and is only as accurate as the data it receives from the field. If the flow of information from the field is cut off, the effectiveness of the system is reduced drastically.

Beyond actively monitoring the status of the power grid, most utilities have taken measures to offset both physical attack and system failure. Practically all utilities have established back-up control centers equipped with uninterruptible power equipment and backup generators. Other utilities have installed completely redundant telecommunications facilities with their own telecommunications control center.

Typically, a utility will have a robust physical security department that conducts or contracts for security evaluations and audits. But these audits rarely extend into the operational elements.

Potential Consequence of an Attack

The electric power grid is a complex, highly networked entity, whose elements are highly interdependent. A by-product of the highly networked power grid is the potential for a cascading power failure. When transmission capacity is unexpectedly lost, generation must immediately be taken off-line; otherwise, the generator's output will reroute and overload remaining transmission lines. This creates "voltage oscillations" that ripple through the power grid. Unless corrective action is taken quickly, these oscillations can pull down significant portions of the electric power grid.

Conclusion

The greatest risk facing the electric power infrastructure of the United States remains physical damage and destruction. Compared to the threat posed by natural disasters and physical attacks on electric power infrastructure elements, electronic intrusion represents an emerging but still relatively minor threat. However, changes within the electric power industry and in technology are increasing the risk posed by electronic intrusion.

The security posture of electric power control networks and information systems varies widely from utility to utility. As the complexity of equipment and processes increase, electric power control networks will be exposed to a considerably wider range of attacks and potential attackers.

Source   Electric Power Risk Assessment, Information Assurance Task Force (IATF) of the National Security Telecommunications Advisory Committee (NSTAC). 2006. <www.aci.net/Kalliste/electric.htm>

CRITICAL NATIONAL INFRASTRUCTURE: THE NATIONAL INFRASTRUCTURE PROTECTION PLAN

Protecting the critical infrastructure of the United States is essential to the nation's security, public health and safety, economic vitality, and way of life. Attacks on the national critical infrastructure (NCI) could significantly disrupt the functioning of government and business alike and produce cascading effects far beyond the targeted sector and physical location of the incident. Direct terrorist attacks and natural, manmade, or technological hazards could produce catastrophic losses in terms of human casualties, property destruction, and economic effects, as well as profound damage to public morale and confidence. Attacks using components of the NCI as weapons of mass destruction could have even more devastating physical and psychological consequences.

The Department of Homeland Security (DHS) has developed the National Infrastructure Protection Plan (NIPP), a plan designed to:

- Prevent, deter, neutralize, or mitigate the effects of deliberate efforts by terrorists to destroy, incapacitate, or exploit NCI assets.
- Strengthen national preparedness.
- Provide timely response and rapid recovery in the event of an attack, natural disaster, or other emergency.

The NIPP provides the unifying structure for the integration of existing and future protection efforts into a single national program. The NIPP framework enables the prioritization of protection initiatives and investments across sectors to ensure that government and private sector resources are applied where they offer the most benefit for mitigating risk by lessening vulnerabilities, deterring threats, and minimizing the consequences of terrorist attacks and other manmade and natural disasters. The NIPP risk management framework recognizes and builds on existing protective programs and initiatives.

Protection includes actions to mitigate the overall risk to NCI assets, systems, networks, functions, or their interconnecting links resulting from exposure, injury, destruction, incapacitation, or exploitation. In the context of the NIPP, this includes actions to deter the threat, mitigate vulnerabilities, or minimize consequences associated with a terrorist attack or other incident. Protection can include a wide range of activities such as hardening facilities, building resiliency and redundancy, incorporating hazard resistance into initial facility design, initiating active or passive countermeasures, installing security systems, promoting workforce surety programs, and implementing cyber security measures.

Objectives

Achieving the NIPP goal requires actions to address a series of objectives that include:

- Understanding and sharing information about terrorist threats and other hazards.
- Building security partnerships to share information and implement CI/KR protection programs.
- Implementing a long-term risk management program.
- Maximizing efficient use of resources.

These objectives require a collaborative partnership between and among a diverse set of security partners, including the Federal Government; State, Territorial, local, and tribal governments; the private sector; international entities; and nongovernmental organizations. The NIPP provides the framework that defines the processes and mechanisms that these security partners will use to develop and implement the national program to protect NCI assets across all sectors over the long term.

Authority

The Homeland Security Act of 2002 provides the basis for Department of Homeland Security (DHS) responsibilities in the protection of the NCI. The act assigns DHS the responsibility

to develop a comprehensive national plan for securing NCI assets and for recommending "measures necessary to protect the key resources and critical infrastructure of the United States in coordination with other agencies of the Federal Government and in cooperation with state and local government agencies and authorities, the private sector, and other entities."

Risk Management

The cornerstone of the NIPP is a risk management framework that establishes the processes for combining consequence, vulnerability, and threat information to produce a comprehensive, systematic, and rational assessment of national or sector risk. The risk management framework is structured to promote continuous improvement to enhance NCI protection by focusing activities on efforts to: set security goals; identify assets, systems, networks, and functions; assess risk based on consequences, vulnerabilities, and threats; establish priorities based on risk assessments; implement protective programs; and measure effectiveness. The results of these processes drive risk-reduction and risk management activities. The framework applies to the strategic threat environment that shapes program planning, as well as to specific threats or incident situations.

DHS, in collaboration with other security partners, measures the effectiveness of protection efforts to provide constant feedback. This allows continuous refinement of the national protection program in a dynamic process to efficiently achieve NIPP goals and objectives.

The risk management framework is tailored and applied on an asset, system, network, or function basis, depending on the fundamental characteristics of the individual sectors. Sectors that are primarily dependent on fixed assets and physical facilities may use a bottom-up, asset-by-asset approach, while sectors (such as Telecommunications and Information Technology) with diverse and logical assets may use a top-down business or mission continuity approach. Each sector chooses the approach that produces the most actionable results for the sector and works with DHS to ensure that the relevant risk analysis procedures are compatible with the criteria established in the NIPP.

Organization

The enormity and complexity of the NCI, the distributed character of its associated protective architecture, and the uncertain nature of the terrorist threat and other manmade and natural disasters make the effective implementation of protection efforts a great challenge. To be effective, the NIPP must be implemented using organizational structures and partnerships committed to sharing and protecting the information needed to achieve the NIPP goal and supporting objectives.

The NIPP defines the organizational structures that provide the framework for coordination of protection efforts at all levels of government, as well as within and across sectors. Sector-specific planning and coordination are addressed through private sector and government coordinating councils that are established for each sector. DHS also works with cross-sector entities established to promote coordination, communications, and best practices sharing across NCI sectors, jurisdictions, or specifically defined geographical areas.

Information-sharing and information-protection processes that are based on mutually beneficial, trusted relationships help to ensure implementation of coordinated and integrated protective programs and activities. Information sharing enables both government and private-sector partners to assess events accurately, formulate risk assessments, and determine appropriate courses of action. The NIPP uses a network approach to information sharing that represents a fundamental change in how security partners share and protect the information needed to analyze risk and make risk-based decisions. A network approach enables secure, multidirectional information sharing between and across government and industry. The network approach provides mechanisms, using information protection protocols to support the development and sharing of strategic and specific threat assessments, threat warnings, incident reports, all-hazards impact assessments, and best practices. This information-sharing approach allows security partners to assess risks, conduct risk management activities, allocate resources, and make continuous improvements to the protective posture.

Sensitive Information

NIPP implementation relies on critical infrastructure information provided by the private sector. Much of this is sensitive business or security information that could cause serious damage to private firms, the economy, public safety, or security through unauthorized disclosure or access. The Federal Government has a statutory responsibility to safeguard NCI protection-related information. DHS and other federal agencies use a number of programs and procedures to ensure that security-related information is properly safeguarded. Relevant programs and procedures include Sensitive Security Information for Transportation Activities, Unclassified Controlled Nuclear Information, Classified National Security Information, Law Enforcement Sensitive Information, Federal Security Information Guidelines, Federal Security Classification Guidelines, among others.

The National Response Plan

The NIPP and the National Response Plan (NRP) together provide a comprehensive, integrated approach to the homeland security mission. The NIPP establishes the overall risk-based approach that defines the NCI steady-state protective posture, while the NRP provides the approach for domestic incident management. Increases in protective measures in the context of specific threats or that correspond to the threat conditions established in the Homeland Security Advisory System (HSAS) provide an important bridge between NIPP steady-state protection and incident management activities using the NRP.

The NRP is implemented to guide overall coordination of domestic incident management activities. NIPP partnerships and processes provide the foundation for the NRP and facilitating NRP threat and incident management across a spectrum of activities including incident prevention, response, restoration, and recovery.

Long-Term Mechanisms

To ensure an effective protection program over the long term, the NIPP relies on mechanisms that:

- Build national awareness.
- Enable education, training, and exercise programs.
- Conduct R&D and use available technology.
- Develop, safeguard, and maintain data systems.

This approach also includes mechanisms to involve private-sector partners in the planning process, and supports collaboration among security partners to establish priorities, define requirements, share information, and maximize the use of finite resources.

Source   Department of Homeland Security. 2006. <www.asisonline.org>

CRITICAL NATIONAL INFRASTRUCTURE: ROLE OF SCIENCE AND TECHNOLOGY

The Department of Homeland security (DHS) has designated the following sectors and key resources as critical national infrastructures:

- Agriculture
- Food
- Water
- Public Health
- Emergency Services
- Government
- Defense Industrial Base
- Information and Telecommunications
- Energy
- Transportation
- Banking and Finance
- Chemical Industry
- Postal and Shipping

Attacks on critical infrastructure (CI) could disrupt the direct functioning of key business and government activities, facilities, and systems, as well as have cascading effects throughout the nation's economy and society. A plan called The National Critical Infrastructure Protection Research and Development Plan addresses physical, cyber, and human elements of the critical infrastructure sectors. The Plan is structured around nine science, engineering, and technology themes that support all critical infrastructure sectors, encompass both cyber and physical concerns, and are strongly integrated in a layered security strategy. The themes are:

- Theme 1: Detection and Sensor Systems
- Theme 2: Protection and Prevention
- Theme 3: Entry and Access Portals
- Theme 4: Insider Threats
- Theme 5: Analysis and Decision Support Systems
- Theme 6: Response, Recovery, and Reconstitution
- Theme 7: New and Emerging Threats and Vulnerabilities
- Theme 8: Advanced Infrastructure Architectures and Systems Design
- Theme 9: Human and Social Issues

Theme 1: Detection and Sensor Systems

Effective protection of critical infrastructure (CI) requires increased innovation and development of advanced, intelligent detection and sensor systems for both physical and cyber aspects of CI. These sensor systems must rapidly and accurately locate and characterize threats against CI, such as acts of cyber or physical intrusion, or the presence of chemicals and/or explosives. The sensors can also be used to monitor and report the condition of the various nodes (such as power plants and industrial complexes) and links (such as transportation systems and utilities) that form CI networks. In addition to advanced sensing capabilities and increased reliability, sensors must communicate with each other and be deployed at many locations to form a robust network. The deployment platforms may be fixed locations, such as embedded in the construction materials of physical infrastructure, or mobile, such as unmanned aircraft, unmanned vehicles, unmanned submersibles, other types of robotics, or even animals.

In cyber systems, the sensors may take the form of intelligent autonomous software agents that can travel throughout a computing or communications network. These networked systems of sensors must be smart, self-organizing, self-healing, and capable of analysis and reporting. Sensors will need to be developed to cover all possible avenues of physical and cyber attack, and tailored to the environmental conditions under which they must operate. In the future, sensors must be able to either adapt to the environment of the attack, or be diverse enough to incorporate a different physical means of data collection to optimize performance.

Theme 2: Protection and Prevention

Effective protection of CI involves layers of defensive measures that deny successful attacks by deterring attackers, preventing entry beyond safe perimeters, providing back-up systems, stopping attackers in their tracks, inhibiting the use of weapons, rendering the CI elements resistant to these weapons, and using forms of deception to mislead terrorists.

Prevention and protection measures for physical and cyber CI evolve with each new threat, participant, and motivation. As better protective measures are developed, there is a concurrent need to prepare for developing or resorting to other tactics to overcome these measures by terrorists. Critical infrastructure protection and prevention R&D involves exploring techniques that would protect against a wide variety of threat tactics, be adaptable to new threats, and/or require the terrorist to expend an inordinate amount of time and effort in planning and executing an attack to overcome these measures.

The more time and planning required by the terrorists, the more telltale signs and patterns they will leave in their tracks, thus increasing the likelihood that intelligence efforts will discover and thwart the attack. Collaboration with intelligence communities and local law enforcement is essential to know beforehand if an attack is likely, to respond quickly and appropriately to alarms and warning signals, and to capture and deal with terrorists who attempt these attacks.

More effective and less costly critical infrastructure protection (CIP) can be achieved if we can develop a completely new way of working together in a collaborative leadership mode by sharing unified security systems across the many business and government entities that own and operate CI networks and sub-systems, including international allies. The Departments of Defense and Energy and other communities have investigated many kinds of threat and vulnerability, and developed significant depth and breadth of relevant expertise. Threats can come from the air, on land, on the water, underwater, underground, and via cyber routes. Robust yet affordable protection will need to be developed to include all these avenues of attack in addition to the wide variety of types of structural links, nodes, and system elements that form CI. Understanding the vulnerabilities of the critical infrastructures, and identifying and validating the threats to those CI networks, involves the use of in-depth knowledge about each CI network, the systems of assets of which they are comprised, and the interconnectivity of assets that are shared across multiple sectors, such as the interdependence of all sectors on energy and communications.

Threats against physical infrastructure and assets include:

- High explosive blast, projectile, and fire damage
- Chemical, biological, radiological and nuclear attacks
- Physical assaults and intrusions
- Failures caused by natural disasters, accidents, and other emergencies

The cyber infrastructure is threatened by:

- Infiltration of a network from the outside
- Disclosure, exposure, or corruption of stored data, or rendering stored data inaccessible
- Interception, interruption or redirection of data flows or communications
- Malicious software agents
- Compromised software applications or hardware components
- Local or widespread disruption of services
- Compromised or usurped (hijacked) machines

Theme 3: Entry and Access Portals

The physical and virtual doorways into the country and its critical infrastructure have taken on much greater importance with regard to homeland security, protection, and defense since September 11, 2001. The objects that pass through the nation's many portals on a daily basis include people, vehicles, goods, cargo and freight, electronic information, and communications. Adequately protecting critical infrastructure at the point of entry of people, materials, and information is a tremendous undertaking considering the wide variety of physical and electronic items that must be screened and in light of the variety of threats that may be present.

Entry and access portals are evolving from standard physical entryways (e.g., guarded doors, gates, airport screening areas, etc.) to complicated communication portals that may involve biometric identifiers, radio frequency (RF) tags, sensor data, and integrated information for automated analysis and decision support. Portal security will require robust and predictable operations under a variety of environmental conditions that provide identification and authentication of the people, materials, and information that pass through them.

Cyber portals for the exchange of critical data and information will require widely available and technologically advanced protections that are well beyond the basic password systems commonly used today. They also will require adaptation to attacks that are continuously changing and evolving.

Emerging security issues will require that physical portals (entryways, checkpoints) and cyber portals (network access, secure transmissions) manage increasingly similar scopes of information, to include accurate identification, authentication, data protection, and information exchange regarding people, material, or information. Future needs of both physical portals and cyber portals can benefit from similar ongoing applied R&D approaches, communication standards development, and engineering requirements.

The focus of this theme is the technology necessary for successful and robust protection of critical access portals, both physical and cyber:

- Identification
- Authentication
- Authorization
- Access Control
- Tracking
- Dynamic Situational Control

Each of these topics represents an area of active commercial development and fundamental research, but the current state of these interrelated technologies is limited for most entry and access portal scenarios. For example, there are many biometric identification systems being researched, or indeed on the market already, but persistent issues continue with these systems regarding reliability and performance, integration into a security system, and known approaches to circumvention. The pervasive lack of sufficient standards for security hardened hardware and tamperproof designs and for maintaining and communicating sensor data coupled with inconsistent methods for accurately characterizing the performance of these systems are also common deficiencies impeding broad-based adoption.

Theme 4: Insider Threats

One of the greatest threats to CI networks of nodes and links today is from the insider who performs actions that could destroy or degrade these systems and services. Insider threats originate from individuals or groups of people who have authorized physical or electronic access to information and infrastructure resources. These threats are among the most disturbing and difficult to guard against because potential insider threats are already inside our infrastructure, and worse, in our area of trust. Thus the threats require that we presume any insider could conduct unauthorized or rogue activities. These individuals and groups are opportunists who exploit vulnerabilities by choosing the time, place, and method of attack according to perceived weaknesses.

There is a fine line in depicting an individual's actions or behaviors as that of an insider threat. On one hand, if accusations are true, a significant threat has been stopped; on the other hand, if the accusations are false, there are potential legal ramifications including libel and character defamation. Understanding and abiding by privacy laws and civil boundaries when considering an individual to be an insider threat will reduce the risk of legal actions.

The Insider Threats Theme will discuss three focus areas for R&D that apply to both information-based and physical insider threats against CI networks and components:

- Intent
- Detection and Monitoring
- Protection and Prevention

These R&D focus areas link intelligence gathering capabilities to identify, measure, and verify threats.

Theme 5: Analysis and Decision Support Systems

Critical infrastructure protection requires a wide range of decision processes, many of which involve value systems with input data in different units and ranges. As an example, a decision process regarding CI assets in a risk analysis may take cultural, historical, monetary value, economic losses, and political factors into account. The factors themselves may have different weights in the decision process.

Other types of decision processes may involve some form of operations analysis employing engineering data such as queuing models used to model the flow of traffic in transportation networks, or deterioration and risk models to make investment trade-off decisions between maintaining or improving the security of existing systems versus replacing them with new, inherently more resilient systems. All of these systems and models involve uncertainties that also must be addressed.

The future R&D in analysis and decision support is critical due to the:

- Increasing size and complexity of the models under examination
- Vast size and complexity of the sectors being modeled
- Requirement to tightly couple or integrate multiple models across disciplines
- Requirement to tightly couple or integrate multiple models across sectors
- Absence of standardized analysis metrics and measures across sectors
- Need for more agile, robust, and high confidence systems

Advances in the fundamentals of analysis and decision support approaches, combined with improvements in graphical and computational capabilities and the ability to provide actionable decision information with improved communication capability, will potentially transform how analysis is performed and decisions are made.

Theme 6: Response, Recovery, and Reconstitution

This theme covers a broad timeframe beginning with the period before an event occurs, through immediate response, to temporary recovery measures, all the way to complete and permanent restoration of the CI sectors and elements that have been impacted. The National Response

Plan and supporting R&D from the Emergency Preparedness and Response community focus on saving lives and property, restoring order to the community, and meeting the specific needs of first responders.

Efforts for this topic are more narrowly focused on the critical infrastructure networks themselves, and getting these critical physical and cyber services restored or replaced quickly and efficiently. The National Critical Infrastructure and Protection (CIP R&D) Plan concentrates on technology in areas of response, recovery, and reconstitution particularly for infrastructure operators and owners, and not on training and needs of more traditional groups of emergency responders and civilians.

Within this theme, the focus areas are:

- Response—Saving Lives, Property, and CI Capabilities
- Recovery—Temporary Restoration of Services
- Reconstitution—Permanent Restoration Techniques

Theme 7: New and Emerging Threats and Vulnerabilities

These threats lead to changes in vulnerabilities and possible consequences. Just a few of the emerging technological threats would include:

- New explosives with almost no volatile release of trace chemicals.
- Proliferation of emerging infections.
- New toxins so unusual that there is no physical attribute or behavioral data available on them.
- Bioengineered genomic and proteomic substances related to biological threats.
- Electromagnetic, directed energy and pulse weapons which use no ammunition and are unrecognizable by most law enforcement personnel.
- Nano-delivery methods of infinitesimal but deadly materials.
- New software virus architectures that arrive in pieces and self-assemble later.
- New, more damaging network infestations which appear, perform, and self-destruct leaving no forensic trail.

Advances in technology are not the only threats. Advanced ingenuity and insight by adversaries about the American lifestyles and values can also be manifested as threats. For example, the September 11, 2001 attacks exemplified a high degree of sophistication and understanding of our weaknesses but used readily available commercial technology and training.

In an era where international commercial interests are in the forefront of many technological advancements and most critical infrastructure is privately owned, it is essential that the protection strategy against new and emerging threats includes multi-faceted and layered solutions, both technical and non-technical.

It must be assumed that all arenas of commercial and public endeavor may contain clues from which can be derived knowledge or envision target-rich vulnerabilities that should be addressed. The technology and methods to do this exist in some measure in the intelligence community, but the scale of such efforts will require significant expansion to deliver what is required.

This theme asks the critical question, "How well can we anticipate the next generation of threats or identify the next emerging or previously undetected vulnerability of our CI?"

The purpose is to propose research directions that will institute CIP-focused detection, analysis, and interpretation processes and capabilities to enable the country to have actionable intelligence for serious threats to complex interconnected CI sectors and to (1) anticipate and discover the formulation of threats that exploit existing technologies in innovative ways; and (2) anticipate and discover the formulation of threats that exploit new technologies while they are in the making or at least before they mature to a state where they can be reliably delivered by our enemies.

These advances will come primarily from the intelligence R&D community as many involve tools and methods the intelligence community is already addressing in the face of new and sophisticated adversaries. CIP relies on the intelligence community to provide information about threats and their likelihood for risk-based decision support analyses. This intelligence is critical to enact appropriate countermeasures, set investment priorities, and maximize the protection that can be achieved within limited budgets.

CIP R&D must work cooperatively with the intelligence community to communicate CIP vulnerabilities, consequences, and operational characteristics to assist the intelligence community as they seek and analyze indicators from massive amounts of data. Conversely, as new forms of infrastructure are being planned (e.g., nanotech manufacturing or biotech fabrication facilities), look at what they do, what they use or produce as materials, what they can accomplish, and dependency on their results and potential sources of new threats and vulnerabilities will be required.

Theme 8: Advanced Infrastructure Architectures and Systems Design

All three strategic goals of this plan require new computing architectures from the most fundamental level of the core of an operating system, to the definition of an interface, to new secure protocols far more advanced in security, processing speed, and efficiency than anything available today. It is not solely for these goals that the need exists to seek such advances as many were already being planned to support areas like next generation cyber security and new protective materials for buildings.

This theme discusses how far beyond simple product and system evolution is required to achieve security beyond current limits. It addresses the framework to develop next-generation infrastructural concepts, architectures, and systems, both physical and cyber and includes built-in security and better operation.

Fundamental science and engineering advances are needed to create the tools and methodologies to enable CI facilities, delivery systems, sensors and detectors, information systems, and systems of the future to have robust, new designs. These designs must be able to withstand, and automatically adjust to, events such as terrorist attacks and natural disasters and they must continue to perform reliably and safely, even if at somewhat diminished capacity during a short period of recovery.

As part of this theme, the following focus areas are addressed:

- Re-examination of Fundamental Theory behind Systems

- Legacy Systems Design and Architecture
- System Design Concepts for Next-Generation Critical Infrastructure
- Auto-Responsive and Self-Healing Systems
- Flexible, Robust, and High-Confidence Critical Infrastructure
- Platforms, Standards, and Technology Layers

From the context of current capabilities, and those to be produced by this R&D, many opportunities exist for greater distributed interconnection and networked cooperative operation among devices and systems to dramatically raise the level of security, operational reliability, and support better decision-making. A key challenge is the integration and interoperation of complex, networked systems. Ad hoc, patchwork attempts cannot achieve the same value as true integration, which incorporates design methods and enhancements produced by a full reexamination and reconstruction of the underlying technologies.

Theme 9: Human and Social Issues

This theme addresses the need for research and development in distinct areas of the human and social sciences. Critical infrastructure protection is concerned with the infrastructure operators, owners, the societal effects on the economy and market forces, effects on societal openness of security, and the communication between the government and private infrastructure sectors.

Other research and development groups, such as the social, economic, and behavioral R&D communities are interested in the processes of the human mind and the human motivations of terrorists.

The country's CI is composed of various human, cyber, and physical components that must work effectively together to sustain the reliable flow of goods, people, and information vital to quality of life. The relationship between people and their physical and cyber infrastructure is intimate and complex. People, as individuals and groups, invent, build, operate, and work within this environment.

The environment, like the people, is continually changing, in part as a result of the interaction of infrastructure with people and in part as a simple function of the passage of time.

Men and women of varying ages, experience, and expertise, coming from long-established American communities, including immigrant and migrant communities, are the ones who build where we live, determine how we travel, and put in place the lines that bring water and power to our homes, among many other things and services. These workers and their families also are the customers and users of the services delivered via critical infrastructure.

Policy- and decision-makers, both public and private, operate within domains shaped by their knowledge, experience, and connections to occupational and personal human and social networks. All of these shape and constrain how well infrastructure serves the public need.

Four categories of issues are the focus for this theme. These relate to both physical and cyber insults against critical infrastructure sectors:

- Communication and cooperation among government and private sectors
- User-centered designs
- Resiliency of commercial enterprises and the economy related to infrastructure
- Risk communication and management

Part of the challenge of infrastructure protection is how to take full advantage of human capabilities. The Social, Behavioral, and Economic (SBE) Working Group in the National Science and Technology Council (NSTC) is focused on scientific research in the areas of sensory, motor, cognitive, and adaptive capability of the human. Currently, the brain is unmatched by any technological system. The human brain is a semi-quantitative supercomputer that is pro-grammable and repro-grammable by explicit training, previous experience, and ongoing observations on a real-time, virtually instantaneous basis.

Human eyes are capable of high-resolution, stereo-optical vision with immense range, and, integrated with a highly plastic brain, make humans uniquely capable of discovery, integration, and complex pattern recognition.

Human hands constitute a dexterous, sensitive biomechanical system that, integrated with the brain and eyes, are unmatched by current and near-future robotic technologies.

Humans operate in groups synergistically and dynamically, adjusting perceptions, relationships, and connections as needed on a real-time and virtually instantaneous basis.

Human language capabilities exist and operate within a dimensional space that is far more complex and fluid than any known artificial architectures.

Conclusion

The long-term vision involves three strategic goals that drive requirements to assure future security of the nation's critical infrastructure. The goals involve creation of:

- A national common operating picture for critical infrastructure.
- A next-generation computing and communications network with security "designed-in" and inherent in all elements rather than added after fact.
- Resilient, self-diagnosing, and self-healing physical and cyber infrastructure systems.

By mapping the long-term over-arching goals to the nine science, engineering, and technology themes, R&D priorities were developed to achieve valuable shorter term results while adding knowledge and capability required to meet the longer-term strategic goals.

Source Office of Science and Technology Policy, Department of Homeland Security. 2004. <http://www.dhs.gov/dhspublic/theme_home5.jsp>

CRITICAL NATIONAL INFRASTRUCTURE: TRANSPORTATION

Recent events in the United States and in other parts of the world have focused considerable attention on the potential occurrence of major incidents of public terrorism. In our own country, such incidents have included the bombings of the World Trade Center in New York City, the Federal Building in Oklahoma City, and the Olympic Park in Atlanta. Throughout the rest of the world there have been bombings and chemical weapon attacks in Japan, Europe, the Middle East, South America, and Africa. The high level of concern about terrorism is reflected in the President's creation of a Presidential Commission on Critical Infrastructure Protection and a White House Commission on Aviation Safety and Security.

Historically, transportation is among the most visible and frequent targets of terrorist attacks, and recent terrorist incidents have reinforced that observation. Yet another security concern in transportation is cargo theft. Estimates place the losses resulting from such theft at over $13 billion a year.

Requirements

Assessing the potential threat to transportation facilities and the range of measures that can be taken to guard against them requires the participation and assent of all organizations, both public and private, involved in transportation operations and oversight. This includes numerous federal agencies with transportation, law enforcement, and threat-analysis responsibilities, as well as their State and local counterparts; transit and port authorities; and private transportation providers.

Among other topics, this partnership addresses the following:

- Physical security of terminals
- Security of vital communication and information systems
- Development and dissemination of information about security incidents, as well as assessments of the potential threats to transportation facilities and operators

In particular, this partnership supports the Transportation Subgroup of the NSTC Committee on Technology's Critical Infrastructure Protection R&D Interagency Working Group by identifying current and new R&D activities that are necessary to (1) protect the nation's transportation infrastructure, operators, and users against future acts of terrorism and crime, and (2) enable the transportation system to adapt rapidly to natural or intentional disruptions.

Strategy

An overall strategy is needed to meet the requirements.

Participants. At the federal level are DOT (FAA, FHWA, FRA, FTA, ITS Joint Program Office, MARAD, RSPA, USCG); DOD; DOJ (FBI, INS, NIJ); NSF; Treasury (U.S. Customs).

Others include state and local law enforcement agencies; port and airport authorities; transportation service providers (airlines, bus lines, transit agencies, trucking companies, ship lines, railroads, parcel, and freight companies).

Management. Partners undertake this initiative under the overall guidance of the NSTC, with each providing resources and support as required. In the case of freight terminals, the executive staff of the National Cargo Security Council has offered to collaborate closely with the initiative's partners.

Critical Technology Elements and Activities. This partnership is undertaking the following activities:

- Transportation Community Awareness and Understanding: This includes (1) outreach events on topics related to passenger and freight security, and (2) an ongoing program of system-level vulnerability assessments at major transportation terminals (air, rail, transit, port).
- Identification of Best Practices: This activity is assessing a number of operational concepts and designs for an integrated security approach, documenting those that have proven to be the most effective, and identifying where further technological or procedural improvements are needed. Future efforts will build on the May 1999 report, Intermodal Cargo Transportation: Industry Best Security Practices.
- Identify Key Technologies and Research Needs: This effort seeks to characterize the security technologies currently available, identify their potential application in an integrated security approach, and determine where further technology development is required.

Funding. Funding will be provided from a mix of federal, state, and local government and private sources. Federal funding will be determined through the annual budget process.

Technical Challenges and Implementation Issues

One of the most interesting technical challenges for this partnership is determining the best means of successfully implementing countermeasures originally developed for one mode or environment—for example, airports—in another mode or environment with different characteristics, operational procedures, and resource levels.

Moreover, a major non-technical issue is that transportation operations require the effective cooperation of a variety of institutions, some of which have differing or even conflicting perspectives and goals. Any major security feature must achieve at least the consent of these varying organizations to be implemented successfully.

Source   Threats and Protection, Department of Homeland Security. 2006. <http://www.dhs.gov/dhspublic/display?theme=31>

CRITICAL NATIONAL INFRASTRUCTURE: URBAN TRANSIT

Since September 11th, the Federal Transit Administration (FTA) has undertaken a series of major steps to help prepare the transit industry to counter terrorist threats. FTA has provided direct assistance to transit agencies through on-site readiness assessments, technical assistance teams, regional forums for emergency responders, grants for drills, training, and accelerating technology and research projects.

From this initial work, it is clear that it is critical to integrate security throughout every aspect of transit programs, operations, and infrastructure. The most important areas of focus should be employee training, public awareness, and emergency response planning.

Although the transit industry has made great strides to strengthen security and emergency preparedness, there is much more to do. FTA has developed a list of Security Program Action Items for transit agencies that are the most important elements transit agencies should incorporate into their System Security Program Plans. These top 20 items are based on good security practices identified through FTA's Security Assessments and Technical Assistance provided to the largest transit agencies. FTA is working with transit agencies to encourage them to incorporate these practices into their programs.

Transit is a critical, high risk, and high consequence national asset. Everyday transit provides mobility to millions of Americans in our most densely populated urban areas and serves the largest economical and financial centers in the nation. Every workday, transit moves more than 14 million passengers. In two weeks, transit moves more passengers than AMTRAK moves in year. In one month, transit moves more passengers than U.S. airlines move in a year. Transit systems are designed to provide not only open, easy access to passengers, but to run under or alongside our largest business and government buildings, intermodal transportation centers, and many of our nations most visible public icons. The U.S.D.O.T Office of Intelligence and Security estimated that in the 1990s transit was the target of 20 to 35 percent of terrorist attacks worldwide.

Transit is designed and operated as an open environment—it is by its very nature a high risk, high consequence target for terrorists. More than 9.5 billion passengers a year ride our transit systems. Some of the largest transit systems report that more than 1,000 people a minute enter their largest intermodal facilities during rush hour. Transit subways travel under key government buildings, business centers, and harbors. Worldwide, transit has been a frequent terrorist target, including bombings in the London and Paris subways, the sarin gas attack in Tokyo, and bus bombings in Israel.

Five-Point Security Initiative

The FTA has launched five initiatives:

1. Conduct threat and vulnerability assessments: Multi-disciplinary teams including experts in anti-terrorism, security, and transit operations assessed the readiness of the largest and highest risk transit agencies. Based on these assessments, FTA has provided specific feedback to individual agencies on how to improve their security systems and reduce vulnerabilities, as well as information on "best practices" to all transit agencies.

2. Deploy technical assistance teams: Emergency response planning and technical assistance teams are deployed to the top 50 to 60 transit agencies to help them to implement the major components of a systematic security program including current security and emergency response plans, training assessments, security awareness materials for transit employees and customers, etc.

3. Award grants for drills by emergency responders and transit agencies: Grants are awarded to conduct tabletop and full scale drills with regional emergency responders to test and improve their security and emergency response plans.

4. Accelerate technology deployment: FTA accelerated the deployment and testing of a system for chemical detection in subway systems.

5. Facilitate training and regional collaboration: A security awareness course for front line employees and supervisors is delivered nationwide along with regional forums to promote regional collaboration and coordination among fire, police, medical emergency, and transit system responders.

A Systems Approach

Research and policy leaders call for an integrated, systematic approach to security. The Transportation Research Board recommends layered security systems that are well integrated throughout transportation operations. Such security systems have interleaved and concentric features (e.g., fencing, security patrols, and closed circuit television), so a breach of any one layer will not defeat the entire system. Each layer provides backup for the others.

Fundamentally, security should be built into all aspects of transit operations as they are developed and created, rather than added as an afterthought. Given the age of most transit systems, FTA is having to play "catch up" with respect to security. Indeed, security is in its program infancy, just as safety was 10 to 15 years ago, before every agency dramatically increased its focus and resources to address the alarming number of transportation fatalities.

Next Steps

The FTA has added new initiatives to meet two critical needs identified in the Office of Homeland Security's national strategy:

Prevent Terrorist Attacks. Because of the openness of transit facilities, timely threat and intelligence information is critical for the transit agencies to strategically target resources based on real-time threat information. FTA is tapping into existing intelligence information and warning networks, and developing new intelligence sharing systems to provide two-way communication between the intelligence community and the transit industry. We are also launching a nationwide "transit watch" program with the transit industry that will draw upon more than 350,000 transit employees and millions of passengers to watch for and report suspicious activities.

Reduce America's Vulnerability to Terrorism. FTA is working with the transit industry to identify critical, high-risk assets and operations, and is developing a broad range of strategies to increase security. These strategies must become an integral part of daily transit operations and will include a special emphasis on training as well as technical assistance, guidelines, best practices, and testing of available technologies for intrusion detection, surveillance, and chemical and biological detection. As these strategies are formulated, new initiatives will be introduced.

Source   Transit Security, Federal Transit Administration. 2006. <http://transit- safety. volpe.dot.gov/Security/Default.asp>

CRITICAL NATIONAL INFRASTRUCTURE: VULNERABILITY ASSESSMENT OF WATER SYSTEMS

Vulnerability assessments help water systems evaluate susceptibility to potential threats and identify corrective actions that can reduce or mitigate the risk of serious consequences from adversarial actions (e.g., vandalism, insider sabotage, terrorist attack, etc.). Such an assessment for a water system takes into account the vulnerability of the water supply (both ground and surface water), transmission, treatment, and distribution systems. It also considers risks posed to the surrounding community related to attacks on the water system.

An effective vulnerability assessment serves as a guide to the water utility by providing a prioritized plan for security upgrades, modifications of operational procedures, and/or policy changes to mitigate the risks and vulnerabilities to the utility's critical assets. The vulnerability assessment provides a framework for developing risk reduction options and associated costs.

Water systems review their vulnerability assessments periodically to account for changing threats or additions to the system to ensure that security objectives are being met. Preferably, a vulnerability assessment is "performance-based," meaning that it evaluates the risk to the water system based on the effectiveness (performance) of existing and planned measures to counteract adversarial actions.

Six Common Elements

The common elements of vulnerability assessments are conceptual in nature and not intended to serve as a detailed methodology:

1. Characterization of the water system
2. Identification and prioritization of adverse consequences
3. Identification of critical assets
4. Assessment of the likelihood of malevolent acts
5. Evaluation of existing countermeasures
6. Analysis of current risk

The vulnerability assessment process ranges in complexity relative to the design and operation of the water system itself. The nature and extent of the vulnerability assessment will differ among systems based on a number of factors such as system size, potential population affected, source water, treatment complexity, and system infrastructure.

Security and safety evaluations also vary based on knowledge and types of threats, available security technologies, and applicable local, state, and federal regulations.

Characterization of the Water System

Answers to system-specific questions may be helpful in characterizing the water system:

What are the important missions of the system to be assessed? What high-priority services are provided by the utility and who are the utility's customers?

- General public
- Government

- Military
- Industrial operations
- Critical care facilities
- Retail operations
- Emergency response agencies

What are the most important facilities, processes, and assets of the system for achieving the mission objectives and avoiding undesired consequences?

- Utility facilities
- Operating procedures
- Management practices that are necessary to achieve the mission objectives
- How the utility operates (e.g., water source including ground and surface water)
- Treatment processes
- Storage methods and capacity
- Chemical use and storage
- Distribution system

In assessing those assets that are critical, consideration is given to critical customers, dependence on other infrastructures (e.g., electricity, transportation, other water utilities), contractual obligations, single points of failure (e.g., critical aqueducts, transmission systems, aquifers, etc.), chemical hazards and other aspects of the utility's operations, or availability of other utility capabilities that may increase or decrease the criticality of specific facilities, processes, and assets.

Identification of Critical Assets

The impacts that could substantially disrupt the ability of the system to provide a safe and reliable supply of drinking water or otherwise present significant public health concerns to the surrounding community are taken into account.

Water systems use the vulnerability assessment process to determine how to reduce risks associated with the consequences of significant concern. Ranges of consequences or impacts for each of these events are identified and defined. Factors to be considered in assessing the consequences may include:

- Magnitude of service disruption
- Economic impact (such as replacement and installation costs for damaged critical

assets or loss of revenue due to service outage)
- Number of illnesses or deaths resulting from an event
- Impact on public confidence in the water supply
- Chronic problems arising from specific events
- Other indicators of the impact of each event as determined by the water utility

Risk reduction recommendations at the conclusion of the vulnerability assessment are designed to prevent or reduce each of these consequences.

Identification of Critical Assets

What are the malevolent acts that could reasonably cause undesired consequences? Operation of critical facilities, assets, and/or processes and assessing what an adversary could do to disrupt these operations are considered, along with potential physical damage to or destruction of critical assets, contamination of water, intentional release of stored chemicals, interruption of electricity or other infrastructure interdependencies.

The Public Health Security and Bioterrorism Preparedness and Response Act of 2002 (PL 107 to 188) states that a community water system which serves a population of greater than 3,300 people must review the vulnerability of its system to a terrorist attack or other intentional acts intended to substantially disrupt the ability of the system to provide a safe and reliable supply of drinking water. A review includes the evaluation of:

- Pipes and constructed conveyances
- Physical barriers
- Water collection, pretreatment and treatment facilities
- Storage and distribution facilities
- Electronic, computer or other automated systems which are utilized by the public water system such as the Supervisory Control and Data Acquisition (SCADA) system
- The use, storage, or handling of various chemicals
- The operation and maintenance of such systems

Assessment of the Likelihood of Malevolent Acts

The possible modes of attack that might result in consequences of significant concern based on the critical assets of the water system are determined. Assessment is intended to move beyond what is merely possible and assess the likelihood of a particular attack scenario. This is a difficult task because often there is insufficient information to make a judgment with any degree of certainty.

The threat (the kind of adversary and the mode of attack) selected for consideration during a vulnerability assessment dictates risk reduction measures appropriate to countering the threat.

The vulnerability assessment methodologies refer to this approach as a Design Basis Threat (DBT). The DBT serves as the basis for the design of countermeasures. It should be noted that there is no single DBT or threat profile for all water systems in the United States. Many other factors will influence the threat(s) that need to be considered.

Water system managements consult with the local FBI and/or other law enforcement agencies, public officials, and others to determine the threats upon which their risk reduction measures are based.

Management is bound also to the Environmental Protection Agency's program called Baseline Threat Information for Vulnerability Assessments of Community Water Systems.

Accurate assessment is very difficult because of the differences in geographic location, size of the utility, and risks in the local area such as crime, flooding, severe weather, etc.

Evaluation of Existing Countermeasures

Some critical assets may already be sufficiently protected by existing countermeasures. Nevertheless, re-examination is made of current capabilities to detect, delay, and respond to malevolent acts. Detection capabilities include CCTV, intrusion detection systems, water quality monitoring, operational alarms, guard post orders, and employee security awareness programs.

Delay mechanisms are terrain, locks and key control, fencing, structure integrity, and vehicle access checkpoints.

Policies, plans, and procedures for evaluating and responding to intrusion and system malfunction alarms are important also. This category includes post orders, contingency plans, adverse water quality indicators, and cyber system detectors.

The existence of countermeasures is one thing; performance is another. Results of tests and practical exercises provide valuable guidance for revision of plans and training; equipping and reorganizing response personnel; and acquisition of supplies and equipment.

Among the elements that require performance measurement are SCADA and business-related computer information systems. Sub-elements include firewalls, modem access, Internet and other external connections, wireless data and voice communication, and equipment that conduct system diagnostics remotely.

Performance evaluation applies also to the quality and training of security officers, physical security safeguards, access control, and information security. An area that deserves close examination is the delivery of chemicals and other vendor deliveries, and the vendors themselves.

Analysis of Current Risk

Information gathered on threat, critical assets, water utility operations, consequences, and existing countermeasures are analyzed as a whole to determine the current level of risk. The utility's management then judges whether current risks are acceptable or whether additional risk control measures are needed. Implementation of additional measures usually proceeds from recommendations made in the vulnerability assessment. Although cost is a major decision factor, it should be shelved until recommended actions are thoroughly examined.

Both short- and long-term solutions should be considered. When a solution is achievable concomitant to renovation or new construction, an opportunity is presented to reach a security objective economically; retrofitting to improve security carries a higher cost than incorporating it with physical changes made for other purposes.

Generally, strategies for reducing vulnerabilities fall into three broad categories. First are sound business practices because they affect a wide range of security-related elements such as policies, plans, procedures, training, employee commitment to security, the culture of the work-force, and a positive relationship with external emergency response agencies. Second is to upgrade systems such as power, HVAC, water, waste removal, communication, and operational systems. Third is to upgrade security equipment and processes that enhance the capability to detect, delay, and respond to malevolent acts early and effectively.

Source Office of Water Management, Environmental Protection Agency. 2002. <www.epa.gov/ogwdw/security/index.html>

CYBERTERRORISM .

The threat posed by cyberterrorism has grabbed the attention of the mass media, the security community, and the information technology (IT) industry. Journalists, politicians, and experts in a variety of fields have popularized a scenario in which sophisticated cyberterrorists electronically break into computers that control dams or air traffic control systems, wreaking havoc and endangering not only millions of lives but national security itself.

Because most critical infrastructure in Western societies is networked through computers, the potential threat from cyberterrorism is, to be sure, very alarming. Hackers, although not motivated by the same goals that inspire terrorists, have demonstrated that individuals can gain access to sensitive information and to the operation of crucial services. Terrorists, at least in theory, could thus follow the hackers' lead and then, having broken into government and private computer systems, cripple or at least disable the military, financial, and service sectors of advanced economies. The growing dependence of our societies on information technology has created a new form of vulnerability, giving terrorists the chance to approach targets that would otherwise be utterly unassailable, such as national defense systems and air traffic control systems. The more technologically developed a country is, the more vulnerable it becomes to cyberattacks against its infrastructure.

Concern about the potential danger posed by cyberterrorism is thus well founded. That does not mean, however, that all the fears that have been voiced in the media, in Congress, and in other public forums are rational and reasonable. Some fears are simply unjustified, while others are highly exaggerated. In addition, the distinction between the potential and the actual damage inflicted by cyberterrorists has too often been ignored, and the relatively benign activities of most hackers have been conflated with the specter of pure cyberterrorism.

The Roots of Cyberterrorism

The roots of the notion of cyberterrorism can be traced back to the early 1990s, when the rapid growth in Internet use and the debate on the emerging "information society" sparked several studies on the potential risks faced by the highly networked, high-tech-dependent United States. As early as 1990, the National Academy of Sciences began a report on computer security with the words, "We are at risk. Increasingly, America depends on computers.... Tomorrow's terrorist may be able to do more damage with a keyboard than with a bomb." At the same time, the prototypical term "electronic Pearl Harbor" was coined, linking the threat of a computer attack to an American historical trauma.

The Fear of Cyberterrorism

Psychological, political, and economic forces have combined to promote the fear of cyberterrorism. From a psychological perspective, two of the greatest fears of modern time are combined in the term "cyberterrorism." The fear of random, violent victimization blends well with the distrust and outright fear of computer technology. An unknown threat is perceived as more threatening than a known threat. Although cyberterrorism does not entail a direct threat of violence, its psychological impact on anxious societies can be as powerful as the effect of terrorist bombs. Moreover, the most destructive forces working against an understanding of the actual threat of cyberterrorism are a fear of the unknown and a lack of information or, worse, too much misinformation.

After 9/11, the security and terrorism discourse soon featured cyberterrorism prominently. This was understandable, given that more nightmarish attacks were expected and that cyberterrorism seemed to offer al Qaeda opportunities to inflict enormous damage. But there was also a political dimension to the new focus on cyberterrorism. Debates about national security, including the security of cyberspace, always attract political actors with agendas that extend beyond the specific issue at hand.

What Is Cyberterrorism?

There have been several stumbling blocks to creating a clear and consistent definition of the term "cyberterrorism." First, much of the discussion of cyberterrorism has been conducted in the popular media, where journalists typically strive for drama and sensation rather than for good operational definitions of new terms. Second, it has been especially common when dealing with computers to coin new words simply by placing the word "cyber," "computer," or "information" before another word. Thus, an entire arsenal of words—cybercrime, infowar, netwar, cyberterrorism, cyberharassment, virtual warfare, digital terrorism, cybertactics, computer warfare, cyberattack, and cyber-break-ins—is used to describe what some military and political strategists describe as the "new terrorism" of our times.

Fortunately, some efforts have been made to introduce greater semantic precision. Most notably, Dorothy Denning, a professor of computer science, has put forward an admirably unambiguous definition in numerous articles and in her testimony on the subject before the House Armed Services Committee in May 2000:

> "Cyberterrorism is the convergence of cyberspace and terrorism. It refers to unlawful attacks and threats of attacks against computers, networks and the information stored therein when done to intimidate or coerce a government or its people in furtherance of political or social objectives. Further, to qualify as cyberterrorism, an attack should result in violence against persons or property, or at least cause enough harm to generate fear. Attacks that lead to death or bodily injury, explosions, or severe economic loss would be examples. Serious attacks against critical infrastructures could be acts of cyberterrorism, depending on their impact. Attacks that disrupt nonessential services or that are mainly a costly nuisance would not."

It is important to distinguish between cyberterrorism and "hacktivism," a term coined by scholars to describe the marriage of hacking with political activism. ("Hacking" is here understood to mean activities conducted online and covertly that seek to reveal, manipulate, or otherwise exploit vulnerabilities in computer operating systems and other software. Unlike hacktivists, hackers tend *not* to have political agendas.) Hacktivists have four main weapons at their disposal: virtual blockades; e-mail attacks; hacking and computer break-ins; and computer viruses and worms.

A virtual blockade is the virtual version of a physical sit-in or blockade: political activists visit a website and attempt to generate so much traffic toward the site that other users cannot reach it, thereby disrupting normal operations while winning publicity—via media reports—for the protesters' cause. "Swarming" occurs when a large number of individuals simultaneously access a website, causing its collapse. Swarming can also amplify the effects of the hacktivists' second weapon: e-mail bombing campaigns (bombarding targets with thousands of messages at once, also known as "ping attacks").

Many cyberprotesters use the third weapon in the hacktivists' arsenal: web hacking and computer break-ins (hacking into computers to access stored information, communication facilities, financial information, and so forth).

The fourth category of hacktivist weaponry comprises viruses and worms, both of which are forms of malicious code that can infect computers and propagate over computer networks. Their impact can be enormous. The Code Red worm, for example, infected about a million servers in July 2001 and caused $2.6 billion in damage to computer hardware, software, and networks, and the I LOVE YOU virus unleashed in 2000 affected more than twenty million Internet users and caused billions of dollars in damage. Although neither the Code Red worm nor the I LOVE YOU virus was spread with any political goals in mind (both seem to have been the work of hackers, not hacktivists), some computer viruses and worms have been used to propagate political messages and, in some cases, cause serious damage. During the NATO operation to evict Serbian forces from Kosovo, businesses, public entities, and academic institutes in NATO member-states received virus-laden e-mails from a range of Eastern European countries. The e-mail messages, which had been poorly translated into English, consisted chiefly of unsubtle denunciations of NATO for its unfair aggression and defenses of Serbian rights. But the real threat was from the viruses. This was an instance of cyberwarfare launched by Serbian hacktivists against the economic infrastructure of NATO countries.

In February 2000, the sites of Amazon.com, e-Bay, Yahoo, and a host of other well-known companies were stopped for several hours due to DoS attacks. On October 22, 2002, the *Washington Post* reported that "the heart of the Internet network sustained its largest and most sophisticated attack ever." A DoS attack struck the thirteen "root servers" that provide the primary road map for almost all Internet communications worldwide. It caused no slowdowns or outages because of safeguards built into the system, but a longer and more extensive attack could have inflicted serious damage.

Hacktivism, although politically motivated, does not amount to cyberterrorism. Hacktivists do want to protest and disrupt; they *do not* want to kill or maim or terrify. However, hacktivism does highlight the threat of cyberterrorism, the potential that individuals with no moral restraint may use methods similar to those developed by hackers to wreak havoc. Moreover, the line between cyberterrorism and hacktivism may sometimes blur, especially if terrorist groups are able to recruit or hire computer-savvy hacktivists or if hacktivists decide to escalate their actions by attacking the systems that operate critical elements of the national infrastructure, such as electric power networks and emergency services.

The Appeal of Cyberterrorism for Terrorists

Cyberterrorism is an attractive option for modern terrorists for several reasons.

- First, it is cheaper than traditional terrorist methods. All that the terrorist needs is a personal computer and an online connection. Terrorists do not need to buy weapons such as guns and explosives; instead, they can create and deliver computer viruses through a telephone line, a cable, or a wireless connection.
- Second, cyberterrorism is more anonymous than traditional terrorist methods. Like many Internet surfers, terrorists use online nicknames—"screen names"—or log on to a website as an unidentified "guest user,"

making it very hard for security agencies and police forces to track down the terrorists' real identity. And in cyberspace there are no physical barriers such as checkpoints to navigate, no borders to cross, and no customs agents to outsmart.
- Third, the variety and number of targets are enormous. The cyberterrorist could target the computers and computer networks of governments, individuals, public utilities, private airlines, and so forth. The sheer number and complexity of potential targets guarantee that terrorists can find weaknesses and vulnerabilities to exploit. Several studies have shown that critical infrastructures, such as electric power grids and emergency services, are vulnerable to a cyberterrorist attack because the infrastructures and the computer systems that run them are highly complex, making it effectively impossible to eliminate all weaknesses.
- Fourth, cyberterrorism can be conducted remotely, a feature that is especially appealing to terrorists. Cyberterrorism requires less physical training, psychological investment, risk of mortality, and travel than conventional forms of terrorism, making it easier for terrorist organizations to recruit and retain followers.
- Fifth, cyberterrorism has the potential to affect directly a larger number of people than traditional terrorist methods, thereby generating greater media coverage, which is ultimately what terrorists want.

Source U.S. Institute for Peace. 2006.

EXPLOSIVE, RADIOLOGICAL, AND NUCLEAR WEAPONS

Explosive Weapons

The most frequently used terrorist weapon is the explosive bomb. The materials for constructing a bomb are not difficult to obtain and the know-how of construction is relatively simple. For the totally uninformed potential bomber, do-it-yourself information is available on the Internet and in bookstores.

Explosion Dynamics

An explosion is an extremely rapid release of energy in the form of light, heat, sound, and a shock wave. The shock wave consists of highly compressed air that travels outward from the source at supersonic velocities. When the shock wave encounters a surface that is in line-of-sight of the explosion, the wave is reflected, resulting in a tremendous amplification of pressure.

Late in the explosive event, the shock wave is followed by a partial vacuum, which creates suction behind the shock wave. Immediately following the vacuum, air rushes in, creating a powerful wind or drag pressure. This wind picks up and carries flying debris in the vicinity of the detonation. In an external explosion, a portion of the energy is also imparted to the ground, creating a crater and generating a ground shock wave analogous to a high-intensity, short-duration earthquake.

Explosives are categorized as high and low. The primary distinguishing characteristic is the pressure wave. A high explosive detonation can produce a pressure wave ranging from 50,000 to 4 million pounds per square inch (psi) while a low explosive detonation will produce a pressure wave under 50,000 pounds psi.

Among the high explosives are military compositions 3, 4, and B, TNT, nitroglycerin, dynamite, RDX, semtex, amatol, ednatol, picric acid, pentolite, and tetrytol. The low explosives are fewer in number: black powder, ammonium nitrate, and the pyrotechnics.

Although not accurate technically, incendiaries are often considered explosives. An incendiary is any device used to start a fire; it is generally man-made, hand-held, and thrown or propelled a short distance. The Molotov Cocktail is an incendiary device, typically a glass bottle filled with gasoline. At the mouth of the bottle is a piece of gasoline-soaked cloth. The tip of the cloth is ignited and the bottle is thrown. The bottle breaks upon impact; the gasoline is dispersed and ignited by the flaming cloth.

Bomb-Related Structural Damage

From the standpoint of structural design, the vehicle bomb is the most important consideration for the chief security officer (CSO). Vehicle bombs are able to deliver a sufficiently large quantity of explosives to cause devastating structural damage. Security design intended to limit or mitigate damage from a vehicle bomb assumes that the bomb is detonated at a so-called critical location. The critical location is a function of the site, the building layout, and the security measures in place. The critical location is taken to be at the closest point that a vehicle can approach, assuming that all security measures are in place. This may be a parking area directly beneath the occupied building, the loading dock, the curb directly outside the facility, or at a vehicle-access control gate where inspection takes place, depending on the level of protection incorporated into the design.

Another explosive attack threat is the small bomb that is hand delivered. Small weapons can cause the greatest damage when brought into vulnerable, unsecured areas of the building interior such as the building lobby, mail room, and retail spaces. Events around the world make it clear that bombs will be delivered by persons who are willing to sacrifice their own lives. Hand-carried explosives are typically on the order of five to ten pounds of TNT equivalent. However, larger charge weights, in the 50 to 100 pounds TNT equivalent range, can be readily carried in rolling cases. Mail bombs are typically less than ten pounds of TNT equivalent.

In general, the largest credible explosive size is a function of the security measures in place. Each line of security may be thought of as a sieve, reducing the size of the weapon that may gain access. Therefore the largest weapons are considered in totally unsecured public space (e.g., in a vehicle on the nearest public street), and the smallest weapons are considered in the most secured areas of the building (e.g., in a briefcase smuggled past the screening station).

Two parameters define the design threat: the weapon size, measured in equivalent pounds of TNT, and the standoff. The standoff is the distance measured from the center of gravity of the charge to the component of interest (target). Historically, more building damage has been done by collateral effect than direct attack.

It is difficult to quantify the risk of terrorist-style bombings. However, qualitatively it may be stated that the chance of a large-scale terrorist attack occurring is extremely low. A smaller explosive attack is far more likely.

TABLE 12. Vehicle Bomb Explosion Hazard and Safe-Distance Range

Vehicle Type	Carrying Capacity	Lethal Blast Range	Safe-Distance Range
Compact car	500 pounds	100 feet	1,500 feet
Full-size car	1,000 pounds	125 feet	1,750 feet
Passenger van	4,000 pounds	200 feet	2,750 feet
Small cox van	10,000 pounds	300 feet	3,750 feet
Mid-size truck	30,000 pounds	450 feet	6,500 feet
Semi-trailer	60,000 pounds	600 feet	7,000 feet

The lethal blast range is a function of the amount of explosives and the type of vehicle carrying the explosives.

Radiological Weapons

A radiological dispersion device (RDD), commonly known as a dirty bomb, is a device that combines a radioactive material and a conventional explosive. The explosive is used to disperse the radiological material. The area of dispersal is conditioned by the type and amount of explosive, the nature of the container, the detonation height, and weather/wind factors such as rain, wind velocity, and air currents.

The harmful effects of an RDD include radiation burns, acute poisoning, and contamination of the environment. The tasks of first responders are complex and very much different in an RDD incident than a conventional bomb incident.

The radiological material in an RDD is not weapons-grade fissionable material such as that contained in a nuclear weapon. The more likely terrorist attack involving radiological material is by use of the RDD rather than a nuclear weapon. This is the case because construction of a nuclear weapon is enormously difficult whereas the RDD can be constructed simply and with types of radiological material that are routinely used in health care, research, metal structure evaluation, and a variety of industrial applications. These materials include cobalt, cesium, strontium, and others. CSOs at facilities that contain radiological materials are obligated to implement and enforce highly stringent security measures.

Nuclear Weapons

As already stated, a terrorist-attack scenario involving a nuclear weapon is less likely than one involving an RDD. Although relatively remote, the possibility does exist. In the case of a nuclear weapon being stolen or purchased by a terrorist group, the possibility rises to a very dangerous level. The doctrine of mutual assured destruction (MAD) becomes irrelevant when the adversary is a terrorist group. The MAD doctrine holds that a nuclear weapon attack by one nation state upon another nation state that also has a nuclear weapon capability would cause the defending state to launch a nuclear weapon counterattack, thus assuring the destruction of both states. MAD is therefore considered a deterrent to nuclear weapons warfare. The amorphous nature of terrorist groups renders MAD ineffective as a deterrent.

Loose Nukes

A loose nuke is a nuclear weapon that has left control of its original owner. The term can also refer to weapons-grade uranium and plutonium. Since the collapse of the Soviet Union in 1991, concern has been raised that unpaid and embittered nuclear scientists may have sold Russian nuclear weapons to terrorist or criminal groups. Also of concern is poor security at Russia's nuclear storage facilities and evidence that enriched uranium has been sold and purchased on Europe's black market. Evidence also exists that terrorist groups have attempted to acquire loose nukes.

Improvised Nuclear Device (IND)

A type of loose nuke is the improvised nuclear device (IND). It is constructed entirely of covertly obtained or manufactured components. The IND contains fissile material (highly enriched uranium or plutonium) and is designed to cause a nuclear explosion. The IND can be constructed

"from scratch" or with nuclear weapon components or an actual nuclear weapon that has been
modified.

If successfully detonated, a small nuclear
weapon would cause the sort of destruction seen
at Hiroshima or Nagasaki. With larger, more
modern weapons, which are hundreds to thousands of times more powerful, the results would
be much worse. Experts predict that human
casualties would vary dramatically depending on the bomb's yield, the height above the
ground at which it was detonated, and weather
conditions. One worst-case scenario simulation estimated that a one-megaton explosion in
Detroit could kill 250,000 people, injure half a
million more, and flatten all buildings within a
1.7 mile radius.

John J. Fay

Sources

Fay, J. 2005. *Contemporary Security
Management*. Boston: Butterworth-Heinemann.
Providing Protection to People and Buildings.
2002. Washington: Federal Emergency
Management Agency.
Terrorist Threats. 2003. Washington: Federal
Emergency Management Agency.
The Effects of Nuclear War. 2002.
Washington: United States Office of Technology
Assessment.
WMD Threat and Risk Assessment. 2005.
College Station: Texas A&M University System.

HOW THE FEDERAL GOVERNMENT RESPONDS TO A MAJOR DISASTER

Introduction

When the capabilities and resources of local and
State government are overwhelmed by a major
disaster event, the Governor requests from the
President of the United States a Presidential
Disaster Declaration. If the President approves a
Declaration, the National Response Plan (NRP)
is activated and the full resources of the Federal
Government are made available to support state
and local officials in responding to the disaster
and in helping individuals and communities to
recover.

This paper provides a brief history of the
genesis of the FRP and examines the structure of
the NRP, the federal departments and agencies,
and voluntary organizations that are signators
to the plan and the command structure that the
Federal Government puts in the field during a
major disaster event.

The Federal Response Plan

In 1992 the Federal Emergency Management
Agency (FEMA) developed the Federal
Response Plan (FRP). FEMA defined the FRP as,
a "Signed agreement among 27 federal departments and agencies, including the American
Red Cross, that provides the mechanism for
coordinating delivery of federal assistance and
resources to augment efforts of state and local
governments overwhelmed by a major disaster
or emergency, supports implementation of the
Robert T. Stafford Disaster Relief and Emergency
Assistance Act, as amended (42 U.S.C. 5121,
et seq.), as well as individual agency statutory authorities, and supplements other federal emergency operations plans developed to
address specific hazards."

The fundamental goal of the FRP was to
maximize available federal resources in support
of response and recovery actions taken by state
and local emergency officials. The FRP made
available the following types of assistance:

To deliver immediate relief:

- Initial response resources, including food,
  water, emergency generators
- Emergency services to clear debris, open
  critical transportation routes, provide mass
  sheltering and feeding

To speed return to normal and reduce damage
from future occurrences:

- Loans and grants to repair or replace damaged housing and personal property
- Grants to repair or replace roads and public buildings, incorporating to the extent
  practical hazard-reduction structural and
  nonstructural measures
- Technical assistance to identify and implement mitigation opportunities to reduce
  future losses
- Other assistance, including crisis counseling, tax relief, legal services, job placement

The National Response Plan

Following the absorption of FEMA into the Department of Homeland Security on February 18, 2003, President Bush signed Presidential Directive 5 (HSPD-5) "to enhance the ability of the United States to manage domestic incidents by establishing a single, comprehensive national incident management system." This action authorized the design and development of a National Response Plan (NRP) to "align Federal coordination structures, capabilities, and resources into a unified, all-discipline, and all-hazards approach to domestic incident management."

There are 32 Signatory Partners in the NRP. Each of these partners serves as a primary agency or support agency in one or more of the 15 Emergency Support Functions (ESF) in the NRP. FEMA defines primary and support agencies as follows.

Primary Agencies. A federal agency designated as an ESF primary agency serves as a federal executive agent under the Federal Coordinating Officer (or Federal Resource Coordinator for non-Stafford Act incidents) to accomplish the ESF mission. When an ESF is activated in response to an Incident of National Significance, the primary agency is responsible for:

- Orchestrating federal support within their functional area for an affected state.
- Providing staff for the operations functions at fixed and field facilities.
- Notifying and requesting assistance from support agencies.
- Managing mission assignments and coordinating with support agencies, as well as appropriate state agencies.
- Working with appropriate private-sector organizations to maximize use of all available resources.
- Supporting and keeping other ESFs and organizational elements informed of ESF operational priorities and activities.
- Executing contracts and procuring goods and services as needed.
- Ensuring financial and property accountability for ESF activities.
- Planning for short-term and long-term incident management and recovery operations.

- Maintaining trained personnel to support interagency emergency response and support teams.

Support Agencies. When an ESF is activated in response to an Incident of National Significance, support agencies are responsible for:

- Conducting operations, when requested by DHS or the designated ESF primary agency, using their own authorities, subject-matter experts, capabilities, or resources.
- Participating in planning for short-term and long-term incident management and recovery operations and the development of supporting operational plans, SOPs, checklists, or other job aids, in concert with existing first-responder standards.
- Assisting in the conduct of situational assessments.
- Furnishing available personnel, equipment, or other resource support as requested by DHS or the ESF primary agency.
- Providing input to periodic readiness assessments.
- Participating in training and exercises aimed at continuous improvement of prevention, response, and recovery capabilities.
- Identifying new equipment or capabilities required to prevent or respond to new or emerging threats and hazards, or to improve the ability to address existing threats.
- Nominating new technologies to DHS for review and evaluation that have the potential to improve performance within or across functional areas.
- Providing information or intelligence regarding their agency's area of expertise.

The National Response Plan Signatory Partners are:

- Department of Agriculture
- Department of Commerce
- Department of Defense
- Department of Education
- Department of Energy
- Department of Health and Human Services
- Department of Homeland Security

- Department of Housing and Urban Development
- Department of the Interior
- Department of Justice
- Department of Labor
- Department of State
- Department of Transportation
- Department of the Treasury
- Department of Veterans Affairs
- Central Intelligence Agency
- Environmental Protection Agency
- Federal Bureau of Investigation
- Federal Communications Commission
- General Services Administration
- National Aeronautic and Space Administration
- National Transportation Safety Board
- Nuclear Regulatory Commission
- Office of Personnel Management
- Small Business Administration
- Social Security Administration
- Tennessee Valley Authority
- U.S. Agency for International Development
- U.S. Postal Service
- American Red Cross
- Corporation for National and Community Service
- National Voluntary Organizations Active in Disaster

Emergency Support Functions (ESFs)

The NRP applies a functional approach that groups the capabilities of federal departments and agencies and the American Red Cross into Emergency Support Functions (ESFs) to provide the planning, support, resources, program implementation, and emergency services that are most likely to be needed during Incidents of National Significance. The federal response to actual or potential Incidents of National Significance is typically provided through the full or partial activation of the ESF structure as necessary.

The ESFs serve as the coordination mechanism to provide assistance to state, local, and tribal governments or to federal departments and agencies conducting missions of primary federal responsibility. ESFs may be selectively activated for both Stafford Act and non-Stafford Act incidents where federal departments or agencies request DHS assistance or under other circumstances as defined in HSPD-5.

Each ESF is composed of primary and support agencies. The NRP identifies primary agencies on the basis of authorities, resources, and capabilities. Support agencies are assigned based on resources and capabilities in a given functional area. The ESF structure provides a structure within which to mobilize the components necessary to best address the requirements of each incident. For example, a large-scale natural disaster or massive terrorist event may require the activation of all ESFs. A localized flood or tornado might only require activation of a select number of ESFs.

The scope of each ESF is summarized below.

ESF #1—Transportation
- Federal and civil transportation support
- Transportation safety
- Restoration/recovery of transportation infrastructure
- Movement restrictions
- Damage and impact assessment

ESF #2—Communications
- Coordination with telecommunications industry
- Restoration/repair of telecommunications infrastructure
- Protection, restoration, and sustainability of national cyber and information technology resources

ESF #3—Public Works and Engineering
- Infrastructure protection and emergency repair
- Infrastructure restoration
- Engineering services, construction management
- Critical infrastructure liaison

ESF #4—Firefighting
- Firefighting activities on federal lands
- Resource support to rural and urban firefighting operations

ESF #5—Emergency Management
- Coordination of incident management efforts
- Issuance of mission assignments
- Resource and human capital
- Incident action planning
- Financial management

ESF #6—Mass Care, Housing, and Human Services
• Mass care
• Disaster housing
• Human services

ESF #7—Resource Support
• Resource support (facility space, office equipment and supplies, contracting services, etc.)

ESF #8—Public Health and Medical Services
• Public health
• Medical
• Mental health services
• Mortuary services

ESF #9—Urban Search and Rescue
• Life-saving assistance
• Urban search and rescue

ESF #10—Oil and Hazardous Materials Response
• Oil and hazardous materials (chemical, biological, radiological, etc.) response
• Environmental safety and short- and long-term cleanup

ESF #11—Agriculture and Natural Resources
• Nutrition assistance
• Animal and plant disease/pest response
• Food safety and security
• Natural and cultural resources and historic properties protection and restoration

ESF #12—Energy
• Energy infrastructure assessment, repair, and restoration
• Energy industry utilities coordination
• Energy forecast

ESF #13—Public Safety and Security
• Facility and resource security
• Security planning and technical and resource assistance
• Public safety/security support
• Support to access, traffic, and crowd control

ESF #14—Long-Term Community Recovery and Mitigation
• Social and economic community impact assessment

• Long-term community recovery assistance to States, local governments, and the private sector
• Mitigation analysis and program implementation

ESF #15—External Affairs
• Emergency public information and protective action guidance
• Media and community relations
• Congressional and international affairs
• Tribal and insular affairs

Field-Level Organizational Structures: JFO Coordination Group

The field-level organizational structures and teams deployed in response to an Incident of National Significance include the following potential members of the Joint Field Office (JFO) Coordination Group:

Principal Federal Official (PFO). The PFO is personally designated by the Secretary of Homeland Security to facilitate federal support to the established Incident Command System (ICS) Unified Command structure and to coordinate overall federal incident management and assistance activities across the spectrum of prevention, preparedness, response, and recovery. The PFO ensures that incident management efforts are maximized through effective and efficient coordination. The PFO provides a primary point of contact and situational awareness locally for the Secretary of Homeland Security.

Federal Coordinating Officer (FCO). The FCO manages and coordinates federal resource support activities related to Stafford Act disasters and emergencies. The FCO:

• Assists the Unified Command and/or the Area Command.
• Works closely with the Principal Federal Official (PFO), Senior Federal Law Enforcement Official (SFLEO), and other Senior Federal Officials (SFOs).

In Stafford Act situations where a PFO has not been assigned, the FCO provides overall coordination for the federal components of the JFO and works in partnership with the State Coordinating Officer (SCO) to determine and satisfy state and local assistance requirements.

Senior Federal Law Enforcement Official (SFLEO). The SFLEO is the senior law enforcement official from the agency with primary jurisdictional responsibility as directed by statute, Presidential directive, existing federal policies, and/or the Attorney General. The SFLEO directs intelligence/investigative law enforcement operations related to the incident and supports the law enforcement component of the Unified Command on-scene. In the event of a terrorist incident, this official will normally be the FBI Senior Agent-in-Charge (SAC).

Federal Resource Coordinator (FRC). The FRC manages federal resource support activities related to non-Stafford Act Incidents of National Significance when federal-to-federal support is requested from DHS by another federal agency. The FRC is responsible for coordinating the timely delivery of resources to the requesting agency. In non-Stafford Act situations when a federal department or agency acting under its own authority has requested the assistance of the Secretary of Homeland Security to obtain support from other federal departments and agencies, DHS designates an FRC. In these situations, the FRC coordinates support through interagency agreements and memoranda of understanding (MOUs).

State/Local/Tribal Official(s). The JFO Coordination Group also includes state representatives such as:

- The State Coordinating Officer (SCO), who serves as the state counterpart to the FCO and manages the State's incident management programs and activities.
- The Governor's Authorized Representative, who represents the Governor of the impacted State.
- The JFO Coordination Group may also include local area representatives with primary statutory authority for incident management.

Senior Federal Officials (SFOs). The JFO Coordination Group may also include representatives of other federal departments or agencies with primary statutory responsibility for certain aspects of incident management. SFOs utilize existing authorities, expertise, and capabilities to assist in management of the incident working in coordination with the PFO, FCO, SFLEO, and other members of the JFO Coordination Group. When appropriate, the JFO Coordination Group may also include U.S. attorneys or other senior officials or their designees from Department of Justice (DOJ) to provide expert legal counsel.

Conclusion

The goal of the NRP is to ensure that the full resources of the federal government are made available to support state and local emergency managers in responding to a major disaster event. The Department of Homeland Security and the Federal Emergency Management (FEMA) have primary responsibility for managing the plan and coordinating plan driven activities. DHS and FEMA also manage the field personnel deployed during a major disaster event.

George D. Haddow

Source Department of Homeland Security. 2006. <www.dhs.gov/dhspublic/theme_home2.jsp>

INTELLIGENCE AND LOCAL LAW ENFORCEMENT

The intelligence function in the United States has traditionally remained a relative unknown. Work of the intelligence community was carried out by the military and various federal entities; very few argued that something was wrong in that community and that change was needed.

The main focus of intelligence activities were on international persons and groups that posed a danger to our national security. A lesser focus was on domestic intelligence and it was handled by the Federal Bureau of Investigation (FBI). Whether these separate systems functioned as intended is a topic for much debate. The events of September 11, 2001, suggest they were not functioning well at all. If they had been, the supposition is that the events would not have occurred because Al Qaeda's intentions would have been detected in the planning stage and effectively prevented.

The 9/11 events point out a number of problems: separate agencies failing to talk with one another, failing to share information, arguing about who had authority to do what, competing for funding, and working hard to outmaneuver each other in gaining Presidential and Congressional support. Perhaps the biggest negligence of all was the failure not to utilize the intelligence gathering capabilities of law enforcement departments nationwide. This article will focus on that issue.

A Brief History of Intelligence in the United States

To understand the benefit to be had from tapping into local law enforcement, it is first helpful to take a brief look at how U.S. intelligence gathering started and evolved. The earliest roots were in the Revolutionary War. Benjamin Franklin was essentially an intelligence agent. Under direction of the Colonial government, he set up an office in Paris and was given a twofold mission: obtain military and economic assistance from France, and establish a network of agents in London to track developments in the British government. Another operative in the same war was Nathan Hale. He was hanged by the British on a charge of spying.

From these humble beginnings, an American intelligence apparatus was created, and given its origins there should be no surprise that the great majority of intelligence activities since then were performed by the military. Each military branch gathered intelligence for their separate purposes; the Army for determining the enemy's battlefield strategy and the Navy for determining the same for operations on the high seas. This was the situation when the Japanese attacked Pearl Harbor. It became clear that the military intelligence services, while effective during warfare, were not effective in gauging the intentions of governments. As World War II progressed, the need for change grew. In 1947 Congress enacted The National Security Act, a law that dramatically reorganized the military services. In that law was a provision to create a centralized intelligence agency, which is now known as the Central Intelligence Agency (CIA).

A main problem with the National Security Act of 1947 was a failure to give the CIA authority to coordinate the activities of the intelligence units already in place. Pride, protection of turf, and competition for resources limited the CIA's effectiveness. Eventually, however, the CIA carved out a niche as the premier agency for

analyzing collected intelligence. The reports it generated caught the attention of upper-level government officials, including the President.

The Problems Remain

Despite the ascendancy of the CIA, the original problems plaguing the entire intelligence community remained uncorrected and failures resulted; for example, the invasion into South Korea by North Korea, the Bay of Pigs incident in Cuba, the Phoenix program in Vietnam, the Iran hostage crisis, and the Iran-Contra affair. In fairness, it stands to reason that the CIA engineered many successes. Unfortunately, those successes cannot be revealed.

A significant factor in the overall failure of the intelligence community to anticipate 9/11 was competitiveness between the CIA and the FBI. Agents on both sides spoke harshly of their counterparts, and given the chance would sabotage each other's efforts.

The CIA mission was to gather intelligence from outside of the United States. The FBI mission was to gather intelligence, but only within the United States. Coordination between the two groups was essential, but antipathy between them translated into a refusal to share information, even when it was apparent that terrorism has no borders. What occurs in a terrorist training camp in Afghanistan can have implications for terrorist acts inside our borders, and the movement of suspected terrorists in New York, for example, can have implications for activities in Afghanistan. Clearly, both agencies would have benefited from sharing information.

Local Law Enforcement

The events of September 11, 2001, changed the equation. The CIA and FBI were told to partner up whether they liked it or not. While retaining their separate identities, they joined forces and are apparently functioning very well as a team.

But along came a third member of the team, and it is that team which constitutes the thrust of this article. The third member is local law enforcement. Local means "grass roots." Local law enforcement is comprised mainly of municipal police departments and sheriff departments whose officers are in daily, routine contact with the public. The CIA and FBI and all of the other federal-level intelligence gathering agencies do not have daily, routine contact with the public. Terrorist cells and their supporters are hidden inside the body public. Local law enforcement can be the eyes and ears of the intelligence community. Doing so would be consistent with law enforcement's overall mission: "Serve and Protect."

Terrorists are criminals. Murder is a crime; planning to murder is a crime. Police officers are trained to deal with criminals. They are adept at noticing unusual activity, such as people taking photos of a chemical plant, finding persons in hiding, and taking suspicious persons into custody. Once in custody, the FBI might step into the picture.

Through day-to-day patrolling and other contacts with people, police officers can be gatherers of useful intelligence without ever really taking on an intelligence role. The average street cop knows far more at the local level than a highly skilled intelligence agent.

Local law enforcement officers are not bound by red tape and obstructed by multiple bureaucracies common at the federal level. By the time a federal agent is permitted to seek raw intelligence, the need for it has ended. For example, it is lawful to look through a trash barrel on a public street. If asked to do so, the police simply go to the barrel and look. For a federal agent to do the same, reams of paperwork and approvals are necessary.

Local law enforcement can do other things as well: spot the early signals of terrorist planning, detect vulnerabilities in the protection of critical assets, and help businesses reduce their exposures to terrorist acts. (The Department of Homeland Security is funding courses that teach police officers these very skills.)

Increased communication between the agencies of law enforcement and intelligence is essential. A law enforcement agency of size will have an intelligence unit. A police intelligence unit does many of the same functions performed by the CIA and FBI. The unit taps into a variety of overt sources, such as police officers on patrol and friendly witness, and covert sources such as informants and legally obtained wire taps. The collected information is compiled, collated, analyzed, placed in actionable formats, and distributed to the end users such as the head of the uniformed

division or the detective division. The user acts on the information such as placing a stakeout team at a convenience store likely to be visited by a robber or identifying the hiding place of a fugitive. The focus of the unit is criminal activity. It would be fairly simple to task criminal intelligence units with an intelligence collection function, leaving the analysis functions with the FBI.

Where a government clearance might be required, police officers have already been cleared by the use of polygraph examinations, drug testing, criminal records checks, and background investigations.

At present it is unclear as to the intelligence collecting role that will be played by law enforcement departments in coming years. We can reasonably expect, however, that the role will be extensive and important to national security. The Department of Homeland Security is calling for a partnership between the intelligence and police communities.

Summary

Federal-level intelligence units have a history of bickering among themselves, engaging in turf battles, and competing for the attention of national leaders. To become effective, there must be true cooperation and across-the-board communication among and between intelligence and law enforcement agencies. Developed and projected in the right way, the effort would be fully supported by the Congress and the American people. To be sure, the combined effort will require extensive authority to act, sufficient funding, and staffing by America's best and brightest.

Kathleen M. Sweet

Sources

Berkowitz, B. D. and Goodman, A. E. 1989. *Strategic Intelligence for American National Security*. Princeton, N.J.: Princeton University Press.

Holt, P. M. 1995. *Secret Intelligence and Public Policy: A Dilemma of Democracy*. Washington DC: Congressional Quarterly Press.

Johnson, L. K. 1989. *America's Secret Power: The CIA in a Democratic Society*. New York: Oxford University Press.

SUICIDE BOMBERS

Suicide as a demonstration of political will can be traced back to Samson, Cato, the Jewish Zealots, the Shi'a Ismaili Assassins, various 19th and 20th century anarchists, and World War II Kamikaze pilots. A suicide terrorist operation requires the perpetrator's death as a precondition of a successful attack. For example, a suicide bomber will purposefully approach targeted victims and detonate a bomb he or she is personally wearing or carrying at that moment he or she decides the greatest number of casualties will be inflicted. Because terrorism consists primarily of violence directed at innocent civilians in order to incite fear for political purposes, however, suicide missions directed at military targets do not constitute suicide terrorism.

Suicide bombers are not known to be psychotic or otherwise deranged. Although some may be emotionally disturbed, most destroy themselves and the innocents around them due to a fanatical combination of social, cultural, national, and religious loyalties. Others act more out of revenge for loss of a loved one or in an attempt to escape from a sense of guilt or shame. Particularly susceptible to participation in murder-suicide bombings are individuals holding radical religious beliefs who feel angered by a sense of relative deprivation occasioned by the convergence of rising social aspirations with diminishing realistic expectations, especially regarding civil liberties. A sense of personal and group humiliation also tends to fuel their anger. Since the 1980s suicide bombing campaigns have involved such disparate groups as the Tamil Tigers of Sri Lanka, Hezbollah in Lebanon, and Hamas in Israel. Chechen and Kurdish nationalistic terrorist groups have also engaged in suicide bombings. Al-Qaeda is responsible for murder-suicide bombings on several continents.

Some suicide bombings have been defined as "altruistic" suicides because they represent an extreme devotion to one's reference group. "Egoistic" suicide bombers, on the other hand, are motivated more by a desire to escape personal alienation and may seize upon suicide bombing as a way to establish a sense of worth, even at the cost of their lives and the lives of others. These terrorists may grow in number as disaffected members of European, American, and other Western societies are influenced by the mass media coverage of radical Muslim suicide bombings in war zones and other locations around the world.

Suicide bombings have become a tactical choice of terrorist groups for a number of reasons. These attacks have been successful in convincing democratic nations to withdraw troops from contested areas and in extracting other concessions from a militarily superior force. Suicide bombings are inexpensive, relatively easy to deliver to a prime target, and yield high civilian casualties at low personnel cost to the organization. Terrorist groups do not have to plan for the bomber's escape nor worry about his or her interrogation. Given that the ultimate goal of a terrorist act is to influence a wider audience, extensive media coverage generally accompanying a suicide bombing serves as a force multiplier for those groups fielding suicide bombers. Such attacks also help a terrorist group compete with other terrorist groups for money and recruits and tend to shore up the morale of its own members.

Although Western societies have not yet experienced ongoing murder-suicide campaigns, scattered suicide bomber attacks have served to put security managers on notice that soft targets, particularly which draw large masses of people, are at risk of suicide-bomber incidents. Sports stadiums, shopping centers, educational institutions, and mass transit systems are just a few of the venues which may be targeted for attack.

There is no single demographic or cultural profile of a suicide bomber which would not generate an unacceptably high rate of false positives. This is because bombing campaigns may be driven by differing nationalist or religious motivations, and involve participants ranging from the uneducated, unemployed youth to middle-class university graduates. Males and females ranging from teenagers to older adults have participated in these acts. Suicide bombings represent an organizational effort with many participants. Some terrorists will specialize in recruiting murder-suicide candidates, others focus on their training. Bomb makers, surveillance specialists, and even video technicians will be involved. Finally, some terrorists are skilled at delivering the bomber to his target area and may even detonate the bomb from a distance should the suicide bomber fail to do so at the ideal opportunity.

Security managers should train their personnel to profile behavior rather than demographic or cultural characteristics. The U.S. Department of Homeland Security advises security personnel to be on the lookout for such indicators of terrorist activity as surveillance, elicitation of information about a property, tests of existing security measures, acquiring supplies useful in an attack, suspicious persons out of place, trial runs, and the deployment of people and supplies into position to commit an attack.

Individual suicide bombers may be wearing bulky clothes to hide a Person-Borne Improvised Explosive Device (PBIED). They may appear nervous, avoid eye contact with venue staff, and walk quite purposefully toward a crowded or high-value target. The acronym A.L.E.R.T. has been proposed as a mnemonic aid for security personnel: Alone and nervous; Loose or bulky clothes inconsistent with weather conditions; Exposed wires, possibly through sleeves; Rigid midsection due to wearing a bomb; Tightened hands from holding a detonation device.

Since security personnel will often be the "first" first-responders, another acronym has been proposed by the Department of Homeland Security to guide their response: R.A.I.N. Security personnel should be trained to Recognize the hazard (including chemical and biological weapons); Avoid the hazard; Isolate the hazard area; and Notify the appropriate support. If a safe standoff distance cannot be realistically attained by potential victims, they should be directed to lie prone on the ground in order to reduce injuries from the blast pressure wave and attendant fragmentation. If gunfire is to be used against the suicide bomber, headshots are preferred so as to avoid inadvertently detonating a PBIED.

Military and police actions alone are unlikely to eradicate suicide bombings. An effective strategy would include three lines of defense. Through target hardening and scientific technology, terrorists may be blocked from hitting or destroying their targets. A second line of defense entails penetrating terror organizations and networks through a combination of intelligence and counterterrorist strikes. Finally, the root causes of terrorism must be understood and acted on in order to reduce the receptivity of potential recruits to the seductions of suicide bombing.

Daniel B. Kennedy

Sources

Atran, S. 2003. Genesis of Suicide Terrorism. *Science*, 299, 1534–1539.

Bloom, M. 2005. *Dying to Kill: The Allure of Suicide Terror*. New York: Columbia University Press.

Bunker, R. 2005a. *Training Key #581: Suicide (Homicide) Bombers: Part I*. Alexandria, VA: International Association of Chiefs of Police.

Bunker, R. 2005b. *Training Key #582: Suicide (Homicide) Bombers: Part II*. Alexandria, VA: International Association of Chiefs of Police.

Crenshaw, M. 1983. *Terrorism, Legitimacy, and Power*. Middleton, CT: Wesleyan University Press.

Hoffman, B. 1998. *Inside Terrorism*. New York: Columbia University Press.

Lester, D., Yang, B., and Lindsay, M. 2004. Suicide Bombers: Are Psychological Profiles Possible? *Studies in Conflict and Terrorism*, 27, 283–295.

Nunn, S. 2004. Thinking the Inevitable: Suicide Attacks in America and the Design of Effective Public Safety Policies. *Journal of Homeland Security and Emergency Management*, 1, No. 4, Article 401. Retrieved from http://www.bepress.com/jhsem/vol1/iss4/401.

Pape, R. A. 2005. *Dying to Win: The Strategic Logic of Suicide Terrorism*. New York: Random House.

Pedahzur. A. 2005. *Suicide Terrorism*. Malden, MA: Polity Press.

Sageman, M. 2004. *Understanding Terror Networks*. Philadelphia: University of Pennsylvania Press.

Silke, A. 1998. Cheshire-Cat Logic: The Recurring Theme of Terrorist Abnormality in Psychological Research. *Psychology, Crime and Law*, 4, 51–69.

Stern, J. 2003. *Terror in the Name of God: Why Religious Militants Kill*. New York: Harper Collins Publishers.

Victoroff, J. 2005. The Mind of the Terrorists: A Review and Critique of Psychological Approaches. *Journal of Conflict Resolution*, 49, 3–42.

TACTICS OF TERRORISTS

Historically, the prevailing view has been that terrorists stage their attacks to derive maximum propaganda value. Their attacks are deliberate and calculated to achieve goals: recruit new followers, obtain financial and in-kind support, influence public opinion, force political decisions, undermine a government, and demonstrate a capacity and resolve to act. Their targets have leaned to the symbolic and intended to deliver a message, usually political or religious.

The 9/11 attacks conformed to the prevailing view. They were staged, deliberate, and calculated; they influenced public opinion and demonstrated a capacity and resolve; they targeted symbols and delivered a message. Billions of people around the globe saw on television screens an impression that the United States was vulnerable.

But given the inhumanity of the 9/11 attacks, the prevailing view seems to have shifted: the primary objective, certainly of religion-based terrorist groups, may no longer be the attainment of propaganda value but the infliction of mass casualties.

Exploitation of the Media

There can be no doubt that terrorists use television, radio, newspapers, and web sites to deliver their messages. Neither can there be doubt that the media give to violent acts a high level of coverage, a circumstance that often encourages further violence. Benefits accrue to the terrorists, who want publicity, and to the media which thrive on sensational events. A further observation of news reporting organizations is that they are nearly always motivated by profits and rarely motivated by a sense of public service.

Not all experts agree, however. They point out that media reporting of a particularly horrendous act can alienate supporters, turn away sympathizers, and close off the flow of essential outside financing. Of equal or greater importance can be a garbling of the terrorist message. Instead of the act defining the cause, it can make the public see only the brutality of the act.

In extortive acts, such as kidnapping or the taking of hostages, media coverage can protect lives by building sympathy for the victims and antipathy for the captors. Conversely, the victims can suffer when the media report resistance to the extortion, the effect of which can induce the captors to carry out their threats because they do not want to be seen as weak or compromising.

Another negative effect of media reporting can be the pressure placed on the government (or corporation) to make a quick response

when caution is the better course. To round out the negatives, the media have a knack for ferreting out and exploiting inside sources that, with assurances of anonymity, may reveal an intended response such as a rescue attempt.

Kidnap and Assassination

Kidnapping can be labeled as political and criminal. In the former, the kidnappers' adversary is a government or a prominent government figure. The kidnapping victim may be one person, e.g., a prominent government figure or other noted government official, a diplomat of another nation, and sometimes a non-government celebrity revered by the governed. The kidnappers may choose to take several hostages, that may or may not be linked to the government or have celebrity status.

The typical motive behind a political kidnapping is attainment of a specific objective such as amnesty or release of prisoners. Money is not a common demand. The kidnappers communicate to the government through the news media and often use video tapes of the victims to elicit public sympathy and sow discord in the government. Because the government has no direct communication channel to the kidnappers, it must reply through the media. From a propaganda standpoint, the kidnappers benefit greatly.

If the kidnappers' demands are not met, the hostages are assassinated singly, in combinations, or all at once. Video taping of the murders are sent to the news media and over the Internet. (Note: Technically, an assassination is the murder of a politically important person or otherwise prominent individual. In recent days, the term is being applied to the murder of people, prominent or not, when the purpose is to advance a cause or extort money.)

The criminal form of kidnapping is motivated by criminal greed or by a terrorist group's need to procure operational funds. The target is usually a profitable business or wealthy family, the demand is for money, the kidnap victim is a sole figure, selection of the victim is made on the basis of economic value and vulnerability, and communications between the kidnappers and the business or family is direct and sometimes kept secret from the media and law enforcement.

Suicide Attack

Suicide terror has been around a long time. When the killing weapon was a knife, assassins of public figures rarely escaped with their own lives. The same held true for later assassins firing pistols at close range or throwing makeshift bombs. Today's suicide terrorists use explosive-laden trucks and themselves. While suicide terror has remained constant, the killing methods have kept pace with weapons technology.

A knife or a gun or a thrown bomb has a limit to the number of casualties, but this is not so with vehicle-laden bombs or biological, chemical, and radiological bombs. A single terrorist with a single weapon can cause mass casualties not ever known before. At the same time that weapon technology has evolved, the sophistication of terrorists has evolved. They are now at a level that enables them to construct rudimentary, but nonetheless effective, weapons of mass destruction. If the objective of the terrorist is to strike fear through the infliction of death and injury, the tools are at hand.

Suicide terrorism as we know it today began in 1983 when the Hezbollah blew up the Marine barracks in Lebanon. It has since been picked up by Hamas and other Palestinian groups in their attacks upon Israel. Al Qaeda used it effectively in attacks upon U.S. Embassies in Kenya and Tanzania and U.S. military living quarters in Saudi Arabia. We have seen the same in Afghanistan and Iraq.

The notion that suicide terrorists are insane is simply too simple and not at all conducive to coming to grips with the threat. Suicide terrorists see themselves as martyrs to be glorified and rewarded in the hereafter. This is not to suggest that we should empathize but to know who and what we are dealing with.

Early on, Middle East suicide terrorists tended to be male, young, uneducated, and impoverished. But like the change in weapon technology, so have the users changed. They are not always male or young or uneducated or impoverished. We saw this in the events of 9/11. The terrorists were mature, intelligent, at least moderately affluent, and knew they were going to die. Terrorist bombers in Israel have been young women and mothers, as was the case with Chechen terrorists.

A suicide terrorist rarely acts without encouragement and support from a larger organization. The decision to use this tactic, as well as to select the target, the time, and the place, rests not with the individual but with functionaries of the terrorist group. Moreover, the individual is often recruited, psychologically prepared, and trained well in advance. The idea that suicide terrorism is an individual act of uncontrolled rage is false. If the objective of the larger organization is to achieve dramatic results with minimum expenditure of resources, suicide terrorism is a good choice.

A question confronting the chief security officer is whether or not suicide terrorism can be prevented. The answer can be a yes—but only when preventive measures are in place. At a minimum, these would include a well-conducted vulnerability assessment followed by implementation of countermeasures designed to keep the suicide terrorist out of range of the target.

Vehicle Bomb Attack

Compared with other weapons, vehicle bombs are inexpensive, simple to assemble, and easy to use. The number of vehicle bomb attacks around the world supports the view that vehicle bombs are the weapon of choice. In the United States, where vehicles of all types are commonplace everywhere, it is extremely difficult, if not impossible, to differentiate between vehicles that are innocent and those that are lethal.

The challenge for the chief security officer is to establish procedures for keeping vehicles outside the blast zone of the protected facility. The blast zone is the area within which a high-explosive bomb will inflict death and serious injury. The size of the area is determined by the type of explosive and the carrying capacity of the vehicle.

High-Explosive versus Low-Explosive. An explosion is the conversion of a solid or liquid into a gas. The rate of conversion for a bomb constructed with high explosives is much higher than the rate of conversion for a low-explosive bomb. Rapid conversion creates a blast or shockwave. With a high explosive, the blast or shockwave can travel through air up to 27,000 feet per second; the shockwave of a low explosive moves at about 3,000 feet per second. Because blast or shockwave causes death, injury, and serious physical damage, the high-explosive bomb is the better choice for terrorists.

Types of high explosives:

- Military C-4
- PETN (pentaerythritol tetranitrate)
- TNT (trinitrotoluene)
- Dynamite
- Nitroglycerine
- ANFO (ammonium nitrate and fuel oil)

As of this date, the high explosive most often used by terrorists is ANFO, ammonium nitrate laced with diesel fuel. The ANFO-type bomb is inexpensive, easy to construct, and very effective.

A terrorist-controlled aircraft with a near-full gas tank is a type of vehicle bomb, as we saw on 9/11. The same can be true of other transport vehicles such as buses, trains, and ships.

A chief security officer of an organization owning or contracting for vehicles ought to consider making background checks of operators, using a global positioning system, and placing within easy reach of the operator a duress alarm that annunciates at a monitoring station, security control center, or a dispatcher's office when a vehicle is in jeopardy such as a hijacking. Another step would be an engine kill switch for land-based vehicles.

Direct Action Attack

Direct action refers to any effort that seeks to achieve an end directly and by the most immediately effective means. Public demonstrations, boycotts, and labor strikes are nonviolent forms. In terrorism, direct action typically takes the form of armed assault in which a group, as opposed to an individual, seeks to attain a well-defined objective. The objectives tend to be assassination of opposition leaders, armed assault of government buildings, and storming prisons to obtain release of group members.

An example of direct action occurred in Munich, Germany, on September 5, 1972, when five Black September terrorists wearing sweat suits and carrying gym bags climbed over a fence surrounding the Olympic Village. Inside the gym bags were assault rifles. Three more terrorists already inside the village joined them. They went to the dormitory housing Israeli athletes and knocked on the door of a room occupied by the wrestling team. Two

Israelis who resisted were shot and killed. Nine other Israeli athletes were taken captive to be used as bargaining chips in negotiating the release of Arab terrorists held in Israel and safe passage of the terrorists and their captives from Germany to Cairo, Egypt. The German government provided helicopters to transport the terrorists and their hostages to an airfield where German marksmen were in position. A fierce gunfight, followed by a second gunfight, ended with the deaths of all nine Israeli athletes, one policeman, five terrorists, and capture of three terrorists.

Preparation of Terrorists

An Al Qaeda training manual obtained in 2000 by United Kingdom authorities provides insights to terrorist preparation in targeted countries. The manual suggests that up to 80 percent of information useful to a terrorist group can be collected from public sources.

Information Gathering. Much of the collected information is downloaded from:

- The target's website where it may be possible to obtain the names of senior persons, their photographs, and biographies; physical addresses and photos of site locations and processes; phone numbers; and announcements of upcoming conferences and stockholder meetings
- Government web sites that contain public records
- Fact sheets and images discovered by Internet search engines
- Chat rooms and bulletin boards

Other open sources that are available and of possible interest to terrorists include:

- Records available to the public at federal, state and county agencies, with particular interest given to technical facts such as those that can be derived from maps, as-built plans, blue prints, and engineering schematics
- Public libraries
- News media
- People knowledgeable about the target site such as employees, ex-employees,

contractors, and vendors; and pretext interviews conducted on the phone and in person
- The target's trash bins

Surveillance. Operatives will reconnoiter the areas around the target site and travel routes to and from the site. They will look for police patrols to determine:

- Frequency and pattern
- The number of officers in a patrol unit
- The distance and time between the target site and the nearest police station

Operatives will stakeout the target site from several vantage points at various times: day and night, workdays and weekends, holidays, shift changes, and morning and afternoon rush hours. They will take photographs and make notes, sketches, and maps. Operatives will look for vulnerabilities such as poor or non-existent fencing and lighting, unlocked gates, and a guard service that may be stretched thin, poorly trained, or inadequately equipped.

Opportunities for surveillance are presented when the target site is open to the public such as during an open house or a seasonal party when access control measures are relaxed. The operatives will pay attention to sign-in procedures, security posts and patrols, security communications, access control devices, intrusion detection sensors, CCTV cameras, elevators, hallways, restrooms, and similar places where bombs can be planted. Also of interest will be the physical aspects of the interior plus the parking area and its proximity to people and on-site operations.

Photographs are highly prized by the planning cadre of the terrorist group. Operatives will be trained in photography and provided with cover identification such as a college student ID card or tourist visa.

Testing of Security. Operatives will want to determine the effectiveness of security at the target site. They may test security officers by attempting to gain entry using innocuous appearing ruses. They may rattle perimeter fences to determine if they are alarmed, measure response times to alarms, or break out security lights to see how long it will take for them to be replaced.

Acquisition of Needed Materials. The individuals that do the pre-attack preparation may or may not be the same individuals who carry out the attack. In either case, the attack party will acquire necessary materials; for example, firearms and ammunition, explosives and detonators, night-vision equipment, vehicles, communications gear, camouflaged clothing, counterfeit identification, and funds for escape. The attack party will make several dry runs in order to identify and correct flaws in the attack plan.

John J. Fay

Sources

Fay, J. 2005. *Contemporary Security Management.* Boston: Butterworth-Heinemann.

Jenkins, B. "Terrorism: Communicating with Kidnappers." *Encyclopedia of Security Management.* John J. Fay (Ed.). Boston: Butterworth-Heinemann. 712.

TERRORISM

Terrorism is a form of asymmetrical warfare, utilized by non-governmental actors to further their agendas through acts of violence or coercion directed against the populace.

Unlike traditional warfare, combatants do not meet on a battlefield and are not part of a recognized military force. Instead, terrorist organizations seek to cause fear among the populace by creating uncertainty. This uncertainty eventually undermines the target population's trust in the government, thus creating instability and, if left unchecked, eventually leading to a change in government or policies.

Terrorist Group Typologies

Terrorist organizations generally fall into one of three categories: Ideological/Political, Religious, or Single Issue.

The objective of the ideological/political terrorist organization is the establishment of a government structure that is in line with the political philosophies or separatist ideologies of the group. Examples of ideological/political terrorist organizations include left wing organizations such as Action Direct, the Red

Brigades, the Japanese Red Army, and the Tupac Amaru Revolutionary Movement, to name a few. Examples of right wing terrorist organizations include the Arizona Patriots, United Self Defense Forces of Venezuela, Fatherland and Liberty National Front, and the Anti-communist Command.

The objective of religious-based terrorist organizations is the fulfillment of their faith through violent means. Religious-based terrorist organizations are typically offshoots of mainstream religious beliefs that have come to believe that violence is the only way to accomplish what they see as their god's will on earth. Due to their zeal, religious-based terrorist organizations can be some of the most difficult to combat. Examples of religious-based terrorist organizations include Al Qaeda, Aum Shinri Kyo, Divine Wrath Brigades, and Hezbollah.

As the name of the last category suggests, the objective of the single-issue based terrorist organization is very specific. These issues may be social, political, environmental, economic, or any one of myriad other causes. Examples of single-issue terrorist organizations include Earth First, the Animal Liberation Front, Earth Liberation Front, and Revolutionary Cells Animal Liberation Brigade.

Terrorist Strategy

Terrorism is asymmetrical in that it involves the use of unorthodox techniques against undefended or lightly defended civilian targets. In other words, the operational cost of a terrorist act is minor when compared to the damage inflicted on the enemy and the subsequent influence generated for the group. Recent examples of terrorism clearly illustrate this return on investment.

The attacks of September 11th, 2001, involved 19 identified hijackers and most likely several dozen additional and unidentified support personnel. In return for this investment, Al Qaeda toppled the twin towers, damaged the Pentagon, and killed over three thousand people. Beyond the direct operational effects resulting from the attacks, Al Qaeda made further gains as well. The stock market fell precipitously, civil aviation temporarily ground to a halt, and the government of the United States conducted one of the largest departmental reorganizations in history. Most importantly, Al Qaeda became known, and in some places respected, throughout the world, thus generating a platform from which to advance its agenda.

The subsequent anthrax attacks and numerous "white powder" incidents provide yet another example of the effectiveness of this type of asymmetrical warfare. A small number of actual anthrax attacks created hysteria and tied up the federal, state and local law enforcement resources, as well as corporate security and fire personnel, for months.

The Madrid railway attacks of March 11th, 2004, also produced a significant return on investment for terrorists. By placing several bombs on commuter trains, the terrorists were able to influence the Spanish elections, effectively removing Spain from the U.S.-led coalition fighting in Iraq.

By engaging in seemingly random acts of violence, the terrorist organization can disrupt day-to-day life to such an extent that its cause is eventually placed on the nation's political agenda.

Government Responses

Targeted governments have traditionally responded to terrorist organizations by either capitulating to their demands or seeking to combat the terrorists through the use of police, security, intelligence, and military assets. When governments have capitulated, it has typically taken place after a long period of unsuccessful attempts to arrest or destroy the terrorist organization. The longer a government remains unsuccessful at stopping terrorist actions, the more credibility it loses. This process is exacerbated when attempts to crack down on terrorism result in prolonged encroachments on civil liberties and abuse of power by frustrated government forces.

Targeted governments who do not capitulate to terrorist demands typically go through a long period of low intensity conflict, involving a necessary increase in defensive and emergency response posture. This often also results in a temporary reduction of civil liberties, and internal criticism of government policies. Over time, the successful government will "win the hearts and minds" of the populace first, thus undermining the terrorist organization's ability to hide. Once this is accomplished, it will lead to solid intelligence that can be exploited by police and military forces.

Terrorist Tactics

The range of tactics employed by the terrorist organization is limited only by the resources and ingenuity of the leadership. Common tactics include, but are not limited to, kidnapping, assassination, armed assault, bombing, hijacking, and sabotage.

The success of a terrorist operation is dependent on pre-operational intelligence, internal security, and commitment by the members of the organization. Pre-operational intelligence may include detailed surveillance of the target for weeks, months, or even years at a time. It may also include the collection of both open source and privately held data. Terrorist operatives may attempt to infiltrate the target organization by securing employment, posing as an employee, or employing time-tested social engineering techniques.

The internal security employed by a terrorist organization is based on the same principles utilized by government, military, and corporate security professionals. Namely, the terrorist leadership recruits operatives over long periods of time, conducts background research, and gradually increases the recruit's responsibilities over time. Additionally, the terrorist organization is compartmentalized into a cellular structure in which one member of one cell may know only one member of another cell. This structure prevents the entire organization from being compromised should one member or a small group be arrested. In many cases, this structure is further divided by responsibilities in which one cell may be responsible for pre-operational surveillance, another for obtaining supplies, another to secure financing, and still another to carry out the attack.

The commitment of the terrorist organization's members is dependent on a wide variety of factors, including the cause itself, the leadership, and the actions of their adversaries.

The Security Professional and Terrorism

Terrorism represents a significant threat to the economic well-being of any organization. Even firms that are unlikely to be a direct target of a terrorist operation need to plan for collateral damage in the form of employee deaths, loss of vital information, damaged property, and sustained business interruption. In order to even begin to successfully mitigate the threat of terrorism, the security professional needs to employ a multi-disciplinary, all-hazards strategy. An understanding of terrorist organizations, risk and vulnerability assessment, physical security, crisis management, and the intelligence process are essential to securing a facility against terrorism.

When reviewing the security posture of a facility basic questions should be addressed:

1. Does senior management support the security program?
2. How does security fit in with the overall mission of the organization?
3. What are the specific risks and vulnerabilities of the particular operating environment?
4. What is the most effective means of allocating the organization's risk management budget?
5. What crisis management plans are in place?
6. Are the crisis management plans adequate?
7. How would management ensure the safety of employees?
8. Have the organization's emergency plans been exercised?
9. Do employees fully understand their roles?
10. Do the current emergency plans take into account organizational security and business continuity issues?

Proactive Observation and Awareness: The Key to Success

The following steps are common recommendations for recognizing a burgeoning terrorist operation before it reaches the attack stage:

1. Counter-Surveillance: Security personnel and employees need to be watchful for people conducting surveillance of the facility. Surveillance may include photographs, video, notes, drawings, or simply observation.

2. Social Engineering and Information Gathering: Security personnel and employees need to be wary of people trying to directly or indirectly solicit information on or demonstrating an unusual interest in building systems, security procedures, schedules, organizational structures, or similar information.

3. Probing: Security personnel and employees need to be wary for tests of security procedures. Hostile actors may attempt to gain surreptitious entry to a facility, leave unidentified parcels in common areas to observe the response of security, or otherwise find ways to compromise the integrity of the security program.

4. Obtaining Equipment: Merchants, security personnel, and employees should be aware of attempts to obtain explosives, weapons, or other material that may be utilized to carry out a terrorist incident.

5. Awareness: The organization that focuses on security personnel and employee awareness will more likely than not "fail" a terrorist organization's target selection criteria. While these steps may not prevent a terrorist attack from occurring, it may deflect or delay the attack to another facility, or increase the chance of intervention by law enforcement agencies.

While terrorist incidents don't happen every day, emergencies can and do happen anywhere, anytime, and anyplace. The successful security program will address all the aforementioned areas by implementing an all-hazards approach. Only by doing so, can an organization hope to be prepared to deal with the threat of terrorism.

Scott A. Watson

Sources

Answers.com at http://www.answers.com/topic/asymmetric-warfare

ASIS International at http://www.asisonline. org/toolkit/toolkit.xml

MIPT Terrorist Knowledge Base at http://www.tkb.org/Home.jsp

New York State Metropolitan Transportation Authority: Field Information-Seven Signs of Terrorist Activity.

TERRORISM: BOMB SCENE SEARCH

Bombing crime scenes, in spite of their massive destruction, must be searched on the theory that everything at the scene prior to the explosion is still in existence unless it has been vaporized by the explosion. Locating and identifying items is the problem. The often-used statement that so much is destroyed by the explosion that the cause must remain unknown is rarely true. Due to various factors the exact amount of explosives used cannot be determined based on an evaluation of the damage at the scene. The purpose of a bomb scene search is to determine what happened, how it happened, and gather evidence. The actual searching is conducted by specialists employed or acquired by the governmental agency having investigative jurisdiction.

Search Procedures

The following steps assist in the preparation, supervision, and evaluation of activity connected with the scene of a bombing.

Plan of Action. Formulate a plan adapted to the particulars of the bomb crime scene. This plan will include consideration of the creation of an on-scene command post; establishment of lines of supervision; assignment of various tasks such as photographing, fingerprint processing, crowd control, and collecting evidence; protecting the crime scene; obtaining necessary equipment; periodically evaluating progress; providing pertinent information to the public; safety; etc.

Command Post. Consider establishing an on-scene command post, particularly at a large bombing that may require days or weeks to complete the crime scene search. The command post should coordinate efforts among investigative personnel and between representatives of other agencies and utilities, as well as handle inquiries from sightseers, persons associated with the scene, relatives of victims, and the press.

One person should be in overall charge of the bombing investigation, another over the actual crime scene search, and another over the collection of the evidence. These three individuals must maintain close coordination and expeditiously exchange information on a continual basis. The evidence coordinator will report directly to the individual responsible for the overall bombing investigation.

Safety. Evaluate safety conditions at the outset of the crime scene search and on a continual basis throughout the search. Consider the possibility of a second bomb, a "jammed" bomb, or live explosives in the debris, as well as the safety of crowds, nearby residents, and personnel at the crime scene. Utilities, weakened walls, and the like that may create dangerous situations should also be considered.

Protection of the Crime Scene. Take adequate safeguards to protect the crime scene from fire, law enforcement, utility, and rescue personnel, as well as others such as sightseers, victims, and individuals with a personal interest in the property. Also, since most residues remaining after an initiation of an explosion are water soluble, the crime scene should, as much as possible, be protected against exposure to excessive moisture, be it from rain, snow, broken water pipes, or other sources.

Photographs. Take appropriate photographs to give a photographic presentation of the crime scene. These photographs should be made immediately before, periodically during, and at the completion of the crime scene activity. Properly identify each photograph, coordinate the photographs with diagrams and/or blueprints or maps, and consider the advisability of aerial photographs.

Bomb Scene Specialist. If without a specialist trained in handling and processing bomb scenes, make arrangements for obtaining such an individual. Although the basic principles of conducting a crime scene search apply in a bomb scene search, individuals with specialized

knowledge of explosives, improvised explosive devices, damage produced by explosive charges, and other facets associated with bomb scene searches are extremely valuable to the effective and efficient processing of the scene. These specialists need not be qualified bomb disposal specialists. They should be the first persons, if possible, to be selected for the evidence and crime scene search coordinator positions.

Equipment. Promptly make arrangements to obtain the necessary equipment to move the debris and material at the scene. Although the equipment needed at the scene varies, the following have been used:

- Shovels, rakes, brooms, boltcutters, wire cutters, sledgehammers, hammers, screwdrivers, wrenches, chisels, hacksaws, magnets, flashlights, knives, measuring tapes, and traffic wheel-measuring devices
- Screens for sifting debris, wheelbarrows, metal trash cans, power saws, cutting torch equipment, ladders, portable lighting equipment, metal detectors, large plastic sheets, photographic equipment, and a parachute harness with related rope and pulleys
- Truck, front-end loader, bulldozer, crane, and shoring materials
- Hard hats, safety goggles, gloves (work and rubber types), foul weather clothing, coveralls, and work shoes
- Crime scene processing kit containing equipment and supplies used for the collection, preservation, and identification of physical evidence

If the bombed target was a vehicle, bring an identical vehicle, if possible, to the scene for use as a model in identifying fragmented and mutilated items.

Search for Evidence

Bear in mind the search for evidence at a bombing crime scene is important because the crime scene may contain principal evidence that will lead to the identification of the bomber(s) and/or assist in the successful prosecution of the matter. The following guidelines are general in nature since the exact method of searching will depend on various uncontrollable factors:

- It is extremely important that the area be photographed before a search begins, and when evidence is located.
- Place one person in overall charge of the collection of the evidence from the various collectors as valuable evidence may not be admissible in court if a proper "chain of custody" cannot be established. Include the location where the items were found. A diagram of the crime scene is always useful.
- Do not stop the search after a few items of evidence have been found.
- Look for signs of safety fuse, detonating cord, blasting caps, electrical wire, dynamite wrappers, batteries, clock and timing devices, electronic and electrical components, metal end cap from a TNT block, plastic end cap from a C4 block, explosive residues, and unconsumed explosives.
- While searching for the previous items, avoid overlooking other valuable evidence, such as fingerprints, hair, fibers, soil, blood, paint, plastic, tape, tools, tool marks, metals, writing paper, printing, cardboard, wood, leather, and tire tread-shoe print impressions.
- Conduct a well-organized, thorough, and careful search to prevent the necessity of a second search. However, have a secure "dump" area for debris in the event a second search becomes necessary.
- Normally, initiation of the search should start at the site of the explosion and work outward. If the bomb crater is in earth, obtain soil samples from the perimeter of the crater as well as from the sides and bottom, making sure to dig into the substrata. If the crater is in another material, obtain similar samples.
- Sift small debris through a 1/4-inch wire screen onto an insect-type wire screen. Usually these screens are placed on 2-foot square wooden frames constructed from 2-inch by 4-inch lumber.
- X-ray the bodies of living and deceased victims who were in close proximity of the explosion site for possible physical evidence and, if possible, have the evidence removed. (Their clothing should be retained as it may contain explosive residues.)
- Search a greater-than-sufficient distance from the site of the explosion in order to have a chance at finding evidence that may have been widely scattered.
- Determine the possible flight paths of bomb components to prevent needless searching.
- Search trees, shrubbery, telephone poles, and the roofs, ledges, and gutters of buildings. Instances have occurred where physical evidence has been "carried away" on the tires of fire and rescue vehicles.
- Establish a search pattern for large areas. A line of searchers moving forward has been found to be a satisfactory method. A bomb scene specialist should follow the line of searchers to evaluate the items found, control the searchers, and furnish guidance. If a second search is desired, the positions of the searchers on the line should be rotated. Charting the area to be searched will ensure a thorough search pattern.
- Retain all items foreign to the scene and items that the searchers cannot identify after seeking the assistance of those familiar with the bombed target.

Source *The Handbook of Forensic Sciences*. 2003. Washington D.C.: Federal Bureau of Investigation, U.S. Department of Justice.

TERRORIST METHODS

Organizing for Terrorism

Because of the loose, flexible, transnational network structure of modern terrorist organizations, facilitated by modern technology, terrorists can work together on funding, sharing intelligence, training, planning, and executing attacks (US Government, 2003). For example, in 2001, three members of the Irish Republican Army were arrested by Columbian authorities for training the Revolutionary Armed Forces of Columbia (FARC) in how to operate an urban bombing campaign.

Terrorists operate on three levels:

- State level: Operate primarily within a single country and their reach is limited. Such a group may expand unless it is countered.

- Regional level: These groups operate regionally and transcend at least one international boundary.
- Global level: Their operations cover several regions and their ambitions can be transnational and even global.

Whatever level a terrorist group operates at, its structure follows basic, universal characteristics of legitimate (e.g., business or government) or criminal organizations. For example, division of labor means that tasks are divided among workers according to such factors as function and clientele. A terrorist organization may have members specialize in recruitment, training, planning, finance, surveillance, bomb making, and assassinations. Smaller groups or cells may require members to specialize in multiple tasks.

Chain of command refers to upward and downward communications within an organized hierarchy to maintain order and control among workers. Superiors communicate tasks to be accomplished to subordinates through the chain of command. For example, terrorist leaders may decide that a suicide bombing is the next plan of action, so a subordinate is contacted to execute the plan. The subordinate then contacts another group member to prepare for the mission and to contact the suicide bomber. If, for instance, a serious problem develops with the preparation for the mission, then the chain of command would be followed so word of the problem would reach the leaders. The chain of command also serves to insulate leaders, as is the case with organized crime. Terrorists may also be organized into cells and characterized by decentralized decision-making.

Organizations typically utilize manuals that are like "rule books" containing an organization's mission, philosophy, and policies and procedures. Manuals serve as training tools and assist individuals in learning how they can best serve the organization and its goals.

White (2003: 35–36) refers to the work of Fraser and Fulton (1984) to describe similarities in the organizational structure of terrorist groups. Fraser and Fulton divide the hierarchical structure of terrorist groups into four levels arranged as a pyramid:

- *Leadership* is at the top of the pyramid with command responsibilities.

- A *cadre* is at the second level and responsible for executing missions.
- *Active supporters* comprise the third level and they provide assistance through safe houses, weapons, and other logistics.
- *Passive supporters* provide political support without actually joining a terrorist group. They are difficult to identify and they may be used by terrorists without their knowledge.

From a law enforcement or military perspective, terrorist groups that follow universal characteristics of organizations generate evidence of terrorist activities that can assist in their arrest. Because a division of labor requires specialized tasks, members must communicate and coordinate their work within a chain of command. Authorities using surveillance equipment can intercept communications. When authorities confiscate terrorist manuals, such information can be valuable for investigations and counterterrorism.

Because of the threat from law enforcement, both transnational and homegrown terrorists are similar in their use of the cellular model of organization. This approach is decentralized, rather than centralized. A decentralized cell is characterized by more discretion, very little, if any, communication within a larger chain of command, more self-sufficiency, and greater pressure to be creative and resourceful. This approach has also been referred to as leaderless resistance. Because a cell consists of a few members, and they know each other well, infiltration by government agents is very difficult. Since communication within a centralized chain of command or between cells in unnecessary, the interception of telephone calls, e-mails, and other forms of communication are less of a risk. Example of successful cells with leaderless resistance is the al-Qaida network and the McVeigh-Nichols group that bombed the Murrah Federal Building in Oklahoma City.

Terrorist cells may be divided into various types according to functions. A *recruitment cell* serves to identify individuals who may be willing to join the cause. These cell members are active at houses of worship, institutions of higher education, and locations where radical ideas are being espoused. Since terrorists are very concerned about undercover agents infiltrating their cells, extreme caution and screening methods are employed to reduce this threat. A *support cell* provides aid to the mission by securing funds, training, transportation, travel documents, cover stories, disguises, safe houses, weapons, equipment, and so forth. An *intelligence cell* gathers a variety of information through surveillance, countersurveillance, investigation, careful interviewing, Web research, and other methods to increase security and secrecy and to help the mission succeed. A *sleeper cell* remains dormant, while blending into a community, until it is activated for a mission. Such cells present a serious threat and security concern to nations. An *operational cell* executes a mission. Since avoidance of detection is an extremely important objective of terrorists, the number of both cells and cell members is usually very limited. To increase security, a *multi-function cell* performs a variety of tasks while reducing the need to communicate and make contact with other cells.

Poland (2005) writes that al-Qaida has several traits:

- Long range planning of several years prior to attacks
- The ability to conduct simultaneous attacks
- Great emphasis on operational security (e.g., compartmentalized planning)
- Flexible, decentralized, command structure of diverse membership that cuts across ethnic, class, and national boundaries
- Attacks often follow these stages: intelligence and surveillance of a target; attackers rehearse the operation; a support team organizes safe houses, vehicles, forged documents, and weapons; and mission executed

Since the 9/11 attacks in 2001, a variety of sources have provided a description of al-Qaida operations. These sources include information from intelligence agencies, interrogation of captives, and documents from training camps and safe houses. One subject of interest is the selection of al-Qaida members (Caruso, 2002). To begin with, only Muslim men are considered in the rigorous screening process that covers background checks and interviews with family, friends, and the potential member. Since al-Qaida is acutely aware that government agents are seeking to infiltrate their group, a variety of coun-

termeasures are used, such as never accepting volunteers. Al-Qaida recruits young men (late teens to early 30s), who have patience and discipline, and are willing to follow orders to the point of dying for "the cause." Al-Qaida hand-picks recruits from Islamic centers, mosques, and schools. According to *Intelligence Digest* (2003), recruitment goes beyond the conflict areas of the Middle East, into Western countries, and essentially, it is worldwide.

A sworn oath of allegiance and code of silence is required by the group that, if broken, will result in a death sentence. Another method used to protect the group is to not reveal plans for attacks throughout the organization.

Once a prospect has been identified, they may be required to attend a religious or education center that is aligned with the al-Qaida perspective. Afghanistan was a prime location for al-Qaida basic training camps where recruits learned about al-Qaida ideology, weapons and explosives, identifying targets, and a broad range of techniques of terrorism. However, U.S. military action following 9/11 ended the Taliban regime in Afghanistan that supported the terrorist training camps in that country. Because of the global war on terrorism, training must be conducted under greater secrecy, in geographic areas that are isolated and under limited government control, or online.

During 2004, the Congressional commission investigating the 9/11 attacks heard testimony from the Central Intelligence Agency (CIA) about al-Qaida. The CIA noted that although al-Qaida lost some of its high-ranking members and a lot of its command structure, it is not a spent force. It is adaptable, agile, and capable of lethal attacks in the U.S. and elsewhere. Diverse, autonomous groups inspired by al-Qaida ideology and successes have replaced the cohesive network of pre-9/11 days. These diverse groups may or may not receive multinational network support for training, financing, and other logistics.

Educational Resources for Terrorists

Students studying to be terrorists have access to a wide assortment of readily available resources. The Web offers a huge volume of information on political groups, terrorist groups, targets, methods and tactics of terrorism, bomb making, homeland security, policing, the military, and so forth. For example, al-Qaida offers its on-line military magazine, Camp al-Battar, that contains a variety of instructions on terrorist methods. Publications used to instruct terrorists include *The Terrorist's Handbook*, *The Anarchist's Cookbook*, *The Turner Diaries*, and assorted al-Qaida and Cold War-era manuals. Libraries and bookstores are other sources of information. Writers from a variety of disciplines have published periodical articles and books on terrorism that can provide helpful information on planning, goals, and strategies of terrorism. It is hoped that legitimate counterterrorism publications do more to control terrorists than to help them.

Training for Terrorists

- State terrorism has a long history and it takes on many forms. During the last half of the twentieth century, the former Soviet Union, for instance, provided aid to terrorists through training camps and arms. It established training camps internally and in Eastern Europe, Cuba, and the Mideast. It also conspired with terrorist states, such as Libya, to supply arms and training to terrorists. Cuba was a popular Western training location for terrorists from Lain America, Africa, Palestine, and North America (e.g., Weather Underground). The Soviets tried to be discreet in their support of terrorists by arguing that they were supporting struggles for "liberation." By the 1990s, as the Soviet Union collapsed, this training network became too expensive, both financially and politically (Comb, 2003: 105–107). During the decades of Soviet power, the United States also played a role in supporting groups seeking "liberation." The methods of supporting terrorist groups have changed as Soviet-era support has declined and countries (e.g., Libya, Iran, and Syria) seek to distance themselves from terrorists because of the worldwide war on terrorism that is led by the U.S.
- Prior to 9/11, the Taliban in Afghanistan permitted Osama bin Laden to operate al-Qaida training camps until the Taliban fell to U.S. forces. Then, the training shifted to "home schooling," on-line training, and on-the-job training in Iraq during the occupation by coalition forces.

Al-Qaida Training

Following the 9/11 attacks and the war in Afghanistan, several terrorist publications (printed, electronic, and video) were seized from terrorist training camps in Afghanistan and from raids at terrorist residences worldwide. The information that follows is from an al-Qaida training manual that was located by the Manchester (England) Metropolitan Police during a search of an al-Qaida member's house. This manual was found in a computer file described as "the military series" related to the "Declaration of Jihad." The manual was retrieved from a U.S. Department of Justice Web site. The purpose of presenting this information is to improve counterterrorism, security, and investigations by studying the enemy. What follows are al-Qaida methods and tactics. Here are excerpts from the manual:

The Military Organization dictates a number of requirements to assist it in confrontation and endurance. These are:

- Military organization commander and advisory council
- The soldiers (individual members)
- A clearly defined strategy
- Forged documents and counterfeit currency
- Apartments and hiding places
- Communication means
- Transportation means
- Information
- Arms and ammunition

Missions Required of the Military Organization. The main mission of the Military Organization is to overthrow of the godless regimes and their replacement with an Islamic regime. Other missions:

- Gathering information about the enemy, the land, the installations, and the neighbors

- Kidnapping enemy personnel, documents, secrets, and arms
- Assassinating enemy personnel as well as foreign tourists
- Spreading rumors and writing statements that instigate people against the enemy
- Blasting and destroying places of amusement, bridges, embassies, and economic centers

Security precautions for forged documents:

- The photograph of the brother in these documents should be without a beard.
- When a brother is carrying a forged passport of a certain country, he should not travel to that country. It is easy to detect forgery at the airport, and the dialect of the brother is different from that of the people from that country.

Hiding Places. These are apartments, command centers, etc., in which secret operations are executed against the enemy.

- It is preferable to rent apartments on the ground floor to facilitate escape and digging of trenches.
- Prepare secret locations in apartments to hide documents, arms, etc.
- Rent apartments using false names, appropriate cover, and non-Moslem appearance.
- Rent apartments in newly developed areas where people do not know one another. In older quarters, people know one another and strangers are easily identified.
- Prepare special ways of knocking and signs to communicate, such as hanging out a towel or opening a curtain.
- Replace locks and keys with new ones.

Security Plan. This is a set of coordinated, cohesive, and integrated measures that are related to a certain activity and designated to confuse and surprise the enemy. The plan should be:

- Realistic and based on fact so it would be credible to the enemy before and after the work
- Coordinated, integrated, cohesive, and accurate, without any gaps
- Simple so that the members can assimilate it

- Creative
- Flexible
- Secretive

Traveling through an airport, the brother might be interrogated so he must be taught the answers to the following questions:

- What are the reasons for your travel?
- How did you get the money to travel?
- What will you be doing in the arrival country?
- Do you belong to a religious organization?
- With whom will you be staying?

When your true travel plans are discovered:

- Who trained you?
- On what weapons were you trained?
- Who are your contacts?
- What is your mission?

Security measures when gathering information:

- Walking down a dead-end street and observing who is walking behind you.
- Beware of traps.
- Casually dropping something out of your pocket and observing who will pick it up.
- Stopping in front of a store window and observing who is watching you.
- Agreeing with one of your brothers to look for whoever is watching you.
- Do not accept events at their face value.
- Do not overlook a quick friendship or an apparent dispute.
- Covert means of gathering information include surveillance, theft, interrogation, excitement, drugging, and recruitment.
- Collecting information from a military base should include fortifications, guard posts, lighting, numbers of soldiers, and sleeping and waking times. Start a friendship with soldiers by giving them rides to bus or train stations.

Many other topics were included in the manual such as gathering information, communications, transportation, meetings, weapons, assassinations, and guidelines for beating and killing hostages.

Terrorist Methods of Operation

Martin (2003: 252, G-17) writes about the New Terrorism of the twenty-first century and defines it as follows: "A typology of terrorism characterized by a loose cell-based organization structure, asymmetrical tactics, the threatened use of weapons of mass destruction, potentially high casually rates, and usually a religious or mystical motivation." He adds that advances in technology, information, and transnational interconnectivity today influence terrorism. Terrorists have easy access to cell phones, computers, and the opportunity to locate almost anything (e.g., weapons of mass destruction; target information) on the Web. They travel the globe, often use false documents, and establish small, decentralized cells.

Asymmetrical warfare offers terrorists, who are not a match against a powerful enemy in a conventional war, with unorthodox methods to strike unexpectedly at symbolic targets and cause high casualties for maximum propaganda. In the Israeli-Palestinian conflict of recent years, Palestinian suicidal martyrs, with bombs strapped to their bodies, reached Israel and boarded buses or entered restaurants and detonated their explosives. The carnage immediately became global news.

A modus operandi (MO) or method of operation may characterize a terrorist group or individual terrorist. Also known as "signature crimes," these terms refer to the characteristic way in which an act is committed. As examples, some terrorist groups commit suicide bombings to inflict mass casualties, while others target for assassination diplomats and military and police officials. During the 1970s and 1980s, the Red Brigades of Italy used "kneecapping" to cripple their enemies; essentially, firearms were aimed low to destroy a victim's knee joints and kneecaps. Terrorists and criminals may use multiple MOs, or vary their MOs, to mislead authorities.

Risk Management Solutions, Inc., refers to the evolving MO of al-Qaida attacks as "multiple, synchronized detonations of large scale bombs, carefully planned, rehearsed, and resourced over many months of preparation." Also, as al-Qaida switches from "hardened" targets (i.e., locations with increased security, such as military bases and government buildings) to "soft" targets (i.e., locations with minimal secu-rity, such as schools, housing complexes, and houses of worship), a developing MO is a pre-emptive armed assault (while using disguises) on security officers at access points to clear the way for the bomb run.

Terrorists follow a sequence of steps in an attack. Here is a generalization:

- *Step 1, Significant Event:* An enormous number of possible events can prompt a terrorist attack. Examples include an anniversary date, government action or inaction, violence against the terrorist group, and the availability of a particular target.
- *Step 2, Purpose:* This step has two parts: it delineates the message to be conveyed to the world once the attack is executed and media attention has focused on the attack; and the intended impact of the attack. The intended impact may force a government or corporation to change policies, but this may not occur.
- *Step 3, Target Selection, Research, and Surveillance:* Numerous targets are available to terrorists. The purpose of the attack influences the target. For instance, if terrorists in a particular country maintain a hatred for foreigners, tourists and international corporations may be subject to attack. Research and surveillance is an on-going process because it serves as a foundation for a change in plans or subsequent attacks.
- *Step 4, Planning the Attack:* Terrorists have tremendous advantages in timing an attack and methods of attack. Questions in planning include those that relate to financing, intelligence, security, communications, cover stories, documents, equipment, vehicles, weapons, safe houses, ploys, assignments, and escape (if needed).
- *Step 5, Attack:* At this point, following careful planning, the attack is executed. The results will vary depending on numerous factors.
- *Step 6, Evaluation of Immediate and Long-Term Impact:* Terrorists assess the immediate impact of their attack including casualties (victims and terrorists), property damage, media attention, and government and public reaction. The long-term impact can also include media attention, and government and public reaction. Over

a period of time, the policies of authorities may or may not change.

The list that follows contains terrorist strategies and tactics to illustrate the range of methods they employ and their cunning and creativity. A strategy means to plan and command forces to meet an enemy under advantageous conditions, whereas a tactic applies the most promising techniques of employing forces, weapons, and resources.

- Terrorists, such as al-Qaida, are often meticulous in their surveillance of potential targets and use disguises.
- They may communicate an anonymous threat to a potential target to monitor response and procedures.
- Terrorists often emulate military methods as they plan, train, and execute their attacks. They have a high level of concern for security of operations and they are in need of intelligence, weapons, communications equipment, and vehicles.
- They may use the identification, uniforms, or vehicles of delivery, utility, emergency, or other type of service to access a target. Or, dress as females to lower the perceived threat.
- Terrorists research the Web, libraries, and other sources for target intelligence. According to the al-Qaida training manual (discussed earlier), 80 percent of information about an enemy can be obtained legally through the Web.
- A terrorist may be planted in an organization as an employee to obtain information. The terrorist may work for a service or consulting firm to access many locations.
- Terrorists may attempt to detect surveillance by conducting dry runs of planned activities, using secondary roads and public transportation, employing neighborhood lookouts and tail vehicles, and establishing prearranged signals.
- Terrorists are keenly aware that counterterrorism analysts study terrorist groups, seek intelligence, and piece together information to anticipate terrorist plans and attacks. Studies of terrorist groups and their methods are available from many sources. Terrorists study these resources and, in a "cat and mouse game," seek to mislead analysts by releasing bogus infor-

mation to disrupt the intelligence process. Terrorists maintain an advantage over analysts because terrorists plot and analysts must seek to uncover the plot.
- Terrorists may employ economic warfare or target symbols of capitalism to harm an enemy. The airline industry and other businesses suffered economic hardship following the 9/11 attacks that included the World Trade Center. During 1997, the killing of several foreign tourists devastated the Egyptian tourist industry.
- Domestic right-wing terrorists are less organized than terrorists with links to the Middle East. The Christian Identify movement, with connections to the KKK, and World Church of the Creator members, are noted for limited planning and random violence by lone wolves. They justify their rage through twisted religious teachings.
- The Animal Liberation Front (ALF) and the Earth Liberation Front (ELF) commit arson through the use of improvised incendiary devices equipped with crude timing components. Members develop intelligence through surveillance of targets and reviews of industry publications. They may post details of their bombing devices and targets on their Web sites. ELF advocates "monkey wrenching," a euphemism for arson, tree spiking, and sabotage against industries perceived to be harming the environment.
- ALF and ELF, like al-Qaida, have a decentralized structure and operate in cells. ALF and ELF carry out direct action according to Web-posted guidelines. Each cell is autonomous and anonymous. Such a structure helps to maintain security and evade law enforcement
- The extremist animal rights group, People for the Ethical Treatment of Animals (PETA), has threatened researchers and calls for the violent destruction of animal industries. Their "Kids Campaign" includes distributing "unhappy meals" (boxes containing a toy bloody animal) at McDonald's restaurants and promoting "animals are your friends, not your food."
- Various terrorist groups publish manuals on tactics as a tool to advance their cause. Antiabortionists have written a manual to close down abortion clinics by squirting

Superglue into key holes so clinics cannot open, drilling holes into the low points of flat roofs, and placing garden hoses into mail slots and other openings to cause flooding.

Phillip P. Purpura

Sources

Caruso, J. 2002. Acting Assistant Director, Counter Terrorism, FBI, U.S. Senate Committee on Foreign Relations.

Combs, C. 2003. *Terrorism in the Twenty-First Century, 3rd Edition.* Upper Saddle River, NJ: Prentice-Hall.

Fraser, J. and Fulton, I. 1984. "Terrorism Counteraction. FC 100–37." Fort Leavenworth, KS: U.S. Army Command and General Staff College.

Intelligence Digest. 2003. "Al-Qaeda Influence Spreads." <www.janes.com/security>

Martin, G. 2003. *Understanding Terrorism: Challenges, Perspectives, and Issues.* Thousand Oaks, CA: Sage Pub.

Poland, J. 2005. *Understanding Terrorism: Groups, Strategies, and Responses, 2nd Edition.* Englewood Cliffs, NJ: Prentice Hall.

Purpura, P. 2006. *Terrorism and Homeland Security: An Introduction with Applications.* Boston: Butterworth-Heinemann.

U.S. Government. 2003. *National Strategy for Combating Terrorism.* (Mar).

White. J. 2003. *Terrorism: An Introduction, 4th Edition.* Belmont, CA: Wadsworth/Thomson Learning.

TERRORIST THREATS

Terrorism is the use of force or violence against persons or property in violation of the criminal laws of the United States for purposes of intimidation, coercion, or ransom. Terrorists often use threats to:

- Create fear among the public.
- Try to convince citizens that their government is powerless to prevent terrorism.
- Get immediate publicity for their causes.

Acts of terrorism include threats; assassinations; kidnappings; hijackings; bomb scares and bombings; cyber attacks (computer-based);

and the use of chemical, biological, nuclear, and radiological weapons.

High-risk targets for acts of terrorism include military and civilian government facilities, international airports, large cities, and high-profile landmarks. Terrorists might also target large public gatherings, water and food supplies, utilities, and corporate centers. Further, terrorists are capable of spreading fear by sending explosives or chemical and biological agents through the mail.

Explosion Threat

Terrorists have frequently used explosive devices as one of their most common weapons. Terrorists do not have to look far to find out how to make explosive devices; the information is readily available in books and other information sources. The materials needed for an explosive device can be found in many places including variety, hardware, and auto supply stores. Explosive devices are highly portable using vehicles and humans as a means of transport. They are easily detonated from remote locations or by suicide bombers.

Conventional bombs have been used to damage and destroy financial, political, social, and religious institutions. Attacks have occurred in public places and on city streets with thousands of people around the world injured and killed.

Biological Threat

Biological agents are organisms or toxins that can kill or incapacitate people, livestock, and crops. The three basic groups of biological agents that would likely be used as weapons are bacteria, viruses, and toxins. Most biological agents are difficult to grow and maintain. Many break down quickly when exposed to sunlight and other environmental factors, while others, such as anthrax spores, are very long lived. Biological agents can be dispersed by spraying them into the air, by infecting animals that carry the disease to humans, and by contaminating food and water. Delivery methods include:

- Aerosols: Biological agents are dispersed into the air, forming a fine mist that may drift for miles. Inhaling the agent may cause disease in people or animals.

- Animals: Some diseases are spread by insects and animals, such as fleas, mice, flies, mosquitoes, and livestock.
- Food and water contamination: Some pathogenic organisms and toxins may persist in food and water supplies. Most microbes can be killed, and toxins deactivated, by cooking food and boiling water. Most microbes are killed by boiling water for one minute, but some require longer. Follow official instructions.
- Person-to-person: Spread of a few infectious agents is also possible. Humans have been the source of infection for smallpox, plague, and the Lassa viruses.

Chemical Threat

Chemical agents are poisonous vapors, aerosols, liquids, and solids that have toxic effects on people, animals, or plants. They can be released by bombs or sprayed from aircraft, boats, and vehicles. They can be used as a liquid to create a hazard to people and the environment. Some chemical agents may be odorless and tasteless. They can have an immediate effect (a few seconds to a few minutes) or a delayed effect (2 to 48 hours). While potentially lethal, chemical agents are difficult to deliver in lethal concentrations. Outdoors, the agents often dissipate rapidly. Chemical agents also are difficult to produce.

A chemical attack could come without warning. Signs of a chemical release include people having difficulty breathing; experiencing eye irritation; losing coordination; becoming nauseated; or having a burning sensation in the nose, throat, and lungs. Also, the presence of many dead insects or birds may indicate a chemical agent release.

Nuclear Blast

A nuclear blast is an explosion with intense light and heat, a damaging pressure wave, and widespread radioactive material that can contaminate the air, water, and ground surfaces for miles around. A nuclear device can range from a weapon carried by an intercontinental missile launched by a hostile nation or terrorist organization, to a small portable nuclear devise transported by an individual. All nuclear devices cause deadly effects when exploded, including blinding light, intense heat (thermal radiation), initial nuclear radiation, blast, fires started by the heat pulse, and secondary fires caused by the destruction.

Hazards of Nuclear Devices. The extent, nature, and arrival time of these hazards are difficult to predict. The geographical dispersion of hazard effects will be defined by the following:

- Size of the device. A more powerful bomb will produce more distant effects.
- Height above the ground the device was detonated. This will determine the extent of blast effects.
- Nature of the surface beneath the explosion. Some materials are more likely to become radioactive and airborne than others. Flat areas are more susceptible to blast effects.
- Existing meteorological conditions. Wind speed and direction will affect arrival time of fallout; precipitation may wash fallout from the atmosphere.

Radioactive Fallout. Even if individuals are not close enough to the nuclear blast to be affected by the direct impacts, they may be affected by radioactive fallout. Any nuclear blast results in some fallout. Blasts that occur near the earth's surface create much greater amounts of fallout than blasts that occur at higher altitudes. This is because the tremendous heat produced from a nuclear blast causes an up-draft of air that forms the familiar mushroom cloud. When a blast occurs near the earth's surface, millions of vaporized dirt particles also are drawn into the cloud. As the heat diminishes, radioactive materials that have vaporized condense on the particles and fall back to Earth. The phenomenon is called radioactive fallout. This fallout material decays over a long period of time, and is the main source of residual nuclear radiation.

Fallout from a nuclear explosion may be carried by wind currents for hundreds of miles if the right conditions exist. Effects from even a small portable device exploded at ground level can be potentially deadly.

Nuclear radiation cannot be seen, smelled, or otherwise detected by normal senses. Radiation can only be detected by radiation monitoring devices. This makes radiological emergencies different from other types of emergencies, such as floods or hurricanes. Monitoring can project the fallout arrival times, which will be announced through official warning channels. However, any increase in surface build-up of gritty dust and dirt should be a warning for taking protective measures.

Electromagnetic Pulse. In addition to other effects, a nuclear weapon detonated in or above the earth's atmosphere can create an electromagnetic pulse (EMP), a high-density electrical field. An EMP acts like a stroke of lightning but is stronger, faster, and shorter. An EMP can seriously damage electronic devices connected to power sources or antennas. This includes communication systems, computers, electrical appliances, and automobile or aircraft ignition systems. The damage could range from a minor interruption to actual burnout of components. Most electronic equipment within 1,000 miles of a high-altitude nuclear detonation could be affected. Battery-powered radios with short antennas generally would not be affected. Although an EMP is unlikely to harm most people, it could harm those with pacemakers or other implanted electronic devices.

Radiological Dispersion Device. Terrorist use of an RDD—often called "dirty nuke" or "dirty bomb"—is considered far more likely than use of a nuclear explosive device. An RDD combines a conventional explosive device—such as a bomb—with radioactive material. It is designed to scatter dangerous and sub-lethal amounts of radioactive material over a general area. Such RDDs appeal to terrorists because they require limited technical knowledge to build and deploy compared to a nuclear device. Also, the radioactive materials in RDDs are widely used in medicine, agriculture, industry, and research, and are easier to obtain than weapons grade uranium or plutonium.

The primary purpose of terrorist use of an RDD is to cause psychological fear and economic disruption. Some devices could cause fatalities from exposure to radioactive materials. Depending on the speed at which the area

of the RDD detonation was evacuated or how successful people were at sheltering-in-place, the number of deaths and injuries from an RDD might not be substantially greater than from a conventional bomb explosion.

The size of the affected area and the level of destruction caused by an RDD would depend on the sophistication and size of the conventional bomb, the type of radioactive material used, the quality and quantity of the radioactive material, and the local meteorological conditions—primarily wind and precipitation. The area affected could be placed off-limits to the public for several months during cleanup efforts.

Source Federal Emergency Management Agency. 2006. <http://www.fema. gov/about/index.shtm>

THE MANY FACES OF TERRORISM

On September 11, 2001, terrorists hijacked four U.S. commercial passenger planes. Two crashed into the World Trade Center, a third crashed into the Pentagon, and the fourth, believed to have a target in or near Washington, D.C., crashed into a field in Pennsylvania. The World Trade Center was completely destroyed, the Pentagon substantially damaged, and nearly 3,000 people killed in a matter of a few hours. Thus began the greatest shift in security the world has ever seen.

People tend to think of terrorism as brutal and senseless. Brutal it is, but senseless it is not. Behind every terrorist act is a motive, if not a calculated strategy. While the nature of the acts vary widely—from the use of kidnapping and extortion to guns and bombs—they are neither spontaneous nor random.

The tactics of terrorists are intended to be spectacular. The greater the spectacle, the greater the fear, the greater the intimidation. "Terrorism is theater," says Brian Jenkins who is one of the world's leading authorities on terrorism.

In recent days Americans have begun to see terrorism in a clearer, yet differing, perspective. The organizations that exist to deal with terrorism have come up with several definitions.

In the Code of Federal Regulations, terrorism is said to be:

The unlawful use of force and violence against persons or property to intimidate or coerce a government, the civilian population, or any segment thereof, in furtherance of political or social objectives.

The FBI describes terrorism as either domestic or international, depending on the origin, base, and objectives of the terrorists.

Domestic terrorism is the unlawful use, or threatened use, of force or violence by a group or individual based and operating entirely within the United States or its territories without foreign direction committed against persons or property to intimidate or coerce a government, the civilian population, or any segment thereof, in furtherance of political or social objectives.

International terrorism involves violent acts dangerous to human life that are a violation of the criminal laws of the United States or any state, or that would be a criminal violation if committed within the jurisdiction of the United States or any state. These acts appear to be intended to intimidate or coerce a civilian population, influence the policy of a government by intimidation or coercion, or affect the conduct of a government by assassination or kidnapping. International terrorist acts occur outside the United States or transcend national boundaries in terms of the means by which they are accomplished, the persons they appear intended to coerce or intimidate, or the locale in which the perpetrators operate or seek asylum.

The State Department defines terrorism as:

Premeditated, politically motivated violence perpetrated against noncombatant targets by sub-national groups or clandestine agents, usually intended to influence an audience.

The Department of Defense definition of terrorism is:

The calculated use of violence or the threat of violence to inculcate fear; intended to coerce or to intimidate governments or societies in the pursuit of goals that are generally political, religious, or ideological.

Paul Pillar, formerly of the CIA's Counterterrorist Center, says that terrorism consists of four key elements. Paraphrasing Pillar, a terrorist act is:

- Premeditated and planned in advance; it is not an impulsive act of rage designed to change the existing political order; it is not violence like that used by common criminals.
- Aimed at civilians rather than military targets or combat-ready troops.
- Carried out by a sub-national group, not by the legitimate army of a country.

Motives of Terrorist Groups

Terrorist groups can be categorized in several ways, e.g., where they are from, where they operate, weapons and tactics they use, and the targets they attack. One categorization label that seems to work well is motivation. Terrorist groups can be seen to operate from one or any combination of politics, religion, and special interests.

Politics. Terrorist groups motivated by political considerations cover a lot of ground. First are terrorists that seek to form a separate state for their own group, which is often an ethnic minority. The group is likely to portray its activist followers as patriots struggling to achieve freedoms unjustly withheld by an oppressive government. Their appeal is to a world audience. They hope to win concessions at home, gain sympathy abroad, and obtain financial and logistical assistance from outside supporters.

Nationalist groups tend to calibrate their violent acts at a level high enough to maintain pressure on the established government but not so high as to alienate the group's members and outside supporters.

Among the many nationalist groups are the Irish Republican Army, the Palestine Liberation Organization, Basque Fatherland and Liberty, and the Kurdistan Workers' Party.

Also in the political arena are state-sponsored terrorist groups that are essentially nameless. They serve as the foreign policy tools of radical governments. What the state cannot achieve through diplomacy or conventional warfare, it hopes to achieve by intimidation. Behind the intimidation are violent acts, such as assassinations and bombings, and saber rattling such as the threatened use of nuclear weapons. Groups in this category operate covertly, often hire mercenaries, and enlist no-cost services of sympathizers. These groups are capable of carrying out large-scale attacks because they can call upon resources of the state: government intelligence and weaponry, diplomatic immunity, documents that permit cross-border travel, and a cloak of legitimacy.

Religion. Religious terrorists use violence to further what they see as divinely commanded purposes. Their playing field is global as opposed to national and their targets are wide-ranging. Some terrorist groups in this category are small and cult-like and a few exist on the ultra-radical fringe. The larger groups come from major religions and are almost always minorities within them.

One of the difficulties in assessing the intentions of religiously motivated terrorist groups is the vague and irrational statements of their leaders. For example, a leader will call for a jihad (holy war) but leave followers to use their own imagination in waging it, or leaders in subgroups will interpret the jihad in a variety of ways. By contrast, the politically motivated terrorist groups express less amorphous objectives: removal of a government or establishment of an independent nation. At least with the politically motivated groups, the protectors are able to somewhat more accurately assess the persons and groups they are dealing with, their likely targets, and the arenas of operation.

Special Interest. What the United States lacks in the way of political and religious terrorism, it makes up for in special interest terrorism. Many of the special interest groups are motivated by opposition to federal taxation and regulation, the United Nations, other international organizations, and the U.S. government generally. Much of the opposition comes from right-wing militia organizations, and depending on who's doing the estimates, the overall membership of these groups will range from 10,000 to 100,000. Even if the total numbers are high, the extremist core of the militia movement is quite small and often out of sync with the desires of the broad majority. A strategy exercised by the leaders of some groups is to endorse violence but leave the execution of it to hard-core individuals acting on their own. An example of this strategy in action was the bombing by Timothy McVeigh of the Alfred P. Murrah federal building in Oklahoma City. The mailing of anthrax letters to government officials may be another.

Then there are the hate groups that terrorize in the name of race or religion or both. The Ku Klux Klan, which used lynching to terrorize African-Americans following the Civil War, was a forerunner of today's Neo-Nazis, Skinheads, and so-called Christian Patriots. The Aryan Nation group embraces multiple issues: they hate anyone who is not white or is Jewish or is favorably disposed to the U.S. government. A similar group is the Aryan Brotherhood which is composed of present and former prison gang members.

Pro-life zealots have assassinated physicians and bombed abortion clinics but because these individuals appear not to be members of an organized group, the FBI has classified their attacks as criminal events rather than terrorist events.

The Animal Liberation Front (ALF) encourages individuals to take "direct action" against organizations that commit animal abuse such as the meat industry's practice of slaughtering cattle or the medical research industry's practice of vivisecting laboratory animals. ALF's call for action is believed to be connected to crimes that include arson, breaking and entering, and theft.

The Earth Liberation Front (ELF) is a loosely-knit eco-terrorist organization whose primary agenda is protection of the environment. ELF's likely targets are new construction projects, logging sites, petroleum drilling and production facilities, and mining operations. An allied organization with a similar agenda is Earth First.

It is most probably correct to believe that only a very few animal-rights and environmental activists would resort to activities that kill and maim. The troubling part of the belief is that the "very few" are alive and well and that law enforcement authorities have no way of knowing who they are before they act. Even more troubling is the reality that one person, a Timothy McVeigh for example, can bring about hundreds of deaths and injuries in a single act.

Policing Priorities

A consequence of 9/11 has been a nationwide shift in policing priorities. Police departments, especially those in major cities, are devoting increased resources to prevent and mitigate terrorist attacks, the effect of which is to reduce other law enforcement services. And then there is the cost of gearing up to meet extreme circumstances. Because police officers are almost always first to arrive at the scene of a disaster and first to begin rendering aid, they have to be specially trained and adequately equipped.

The shift in law enforcement priorities varies according to a community's perception of threat, its vulnerabilities, and resources available to law enforcement. Even where great variance exists, law enforcement departments in general have:

- Created new working relationships with other first-responder agencies such as fire departments and agencies responsible for delivering emergency medical treatment and hazardous materials containment.
- Acquired new communication equipment and revised their methods for communicating within and outside of the department.
- Refined their training programs and emergency response plans to address terrorist threats, including attacks with weapons of mass destruction.
- Given more patrol attention to potential target sites such as government buildings, ports of entry, transportation hubs, nuclear power plants, chemical plants, and other facilities of a symbolic or critical nature.
- Increased their presence at major public events.
- Reorganized and reassigned officers to perform counter-terrorism duties; major city departments have joined with federal agencies to form Joint Terrorism Task Forces.
- Employed new technologies in metal detection, X-ray scanning, and sensors for detecting the signals of chemical, biological, and radiological attacks.

Conclusion

Extraordinary measures have been taken since 9/11, both in the government and private sectors. The government's efforts have moved along two tracks: destroy terrorism wherever it exists and prevent further terrorist attacks on U.S. soil. The private sector has taken a serious look at its vulnerabilities to terrorism and in

substantial measure has turned to chief security officers for help.

Arising out of these efforts is a growing recognition that the public and private sectors must form a partnership and pool their separate resources and expertise. More than ever before, community leaders in law enforcement, firefighting, and emergency management are sitting down with chief security officers and chief executive officers of local businesses. Vulnerability assessments are being made, new and comprehensive emergency plans developed, mutual aid agreements signed, and likely scenarios rehearsed. Federal government funding for the purchase of emergency equipment and supplies is flowing to areas where public and private sector leaders have rationally assessed and reached agreement on actual needs. It is in this context that the chief security officer can be an important participant in the war against terrorism.

John J. Fay

Sources

Benton, W. 1968. *The Annals of America.* Chicago: Encyclopedia Britannica.

Council on Foreign Relations. Terrorism: Questions and Answers. 2006. <http://www.cfrterrorism.org>

Fay, J. 2005. *Contemporary Security Management.* Boston: Butterworth-Heinemann.

McCullough, D. 1992. *Truman.* New York: Simon and Schuster.

Patterns of Global Terrorism. 2003. Washington: United States Department of State.

U.S. Army. Field Manual 100–20, Stability and Support. 2006.<http://www.usmilitary.about.com/od/armymanuals>

WMD Threat and Risk Assessment. 2005. College Station: Texas A&M University System.

TRANSPORTATION INFRASTRUCTURE

Recent events in the United States and in other parts of the world have focused considerable attention on the potential occurrence of major incidents of public terrorism. In our own country, such incidents have included the bombings of the World Trade Center in New York City, the Federal Building in Oklahoma City, and the

Olympic Park in Atlanta. Throughout the rest of the world there have been bombings and chemical weapon attacks in Japan, Europe, the Middle East, South America, and Africa. The high level of concern about terrorism is reflected in the President's creation of a Presidential Commission on Critical Infrastructure Protection and a White House Commission on Aviation Safety and Security.

Historically, transportation is among the most visible and frequent targets of terrorist attacks, and recent terrorist incidents have reinforced that observation. Yet another security concern in transportation is cargo theft. Estimates place the losses resulting from such theft at over $13 billion a year.

Requirements

Assessing the potential threat to transportation facilities and the range of measures that can be taken to guard against them requires the participation and assent of all organizations, both public and private, involved in transportation operations and oversight. This includes numerous Federal agencies with transportation, law enforcement, and threat-analysis responsibilities, as well as their state and local counterparts; transit and port authorities; and private transportation providers.

Among other topics, this partnership addresses the following:

- Physical security of terminals.
- Security of vital communication and information systems.
- Development and dissemination of information about security incidents, as well as assessments of the potential threats to transportation facilities and operators.

In particular, this partnership supports the Transportation Subgroup of the NSTC Committee on Technology's Critical Infrastructure Protection R&D Interagency Working Group by identifying current and new R&D activities that are necessary to (1) protect the nation's transportation infrastructure, operators, and users against future acts of terrorism and crime, and (2) enable the transportation system to adapt rapidly to natural or intentional disruptions.

Strategy

An overall strategy is needed to meet the requirements.

Participants. At the Federal level are DOT (FAA, FHWA, FRA, FTA, ITS Joint Program Office, MARAD, RSPA, USCG); DOD; DOJ (FBI, INS, NIJ); NSF; Treasury (U.S. Customs).

Others include state and local law enforcement agencies; port and airport authorities; transportation service providers (airlines, bus lines, transit agencies, trucking companies, ship lines, railroads, parcel and freight companies).

Management. Partners undertake this initiative under the overall guidance of the NSTC, with each providing resources and support as required. In the case of freight terminals, the executive staff of the National Cargo Security Council has offered to collaborate closely with the initiative's partners.

Critical Technology Elements and Activities. This partnership is undertaking the following activities:

- Transportation Community Awareness and Understanding: This includes (1) outreach events on topics related to passenger and freight security, and (2) an ongoing program of system-level vulnerability assessments at major transportation terminals (air, rail, transit, port).
- Identification of Best Practices: This activity is assessing a number of operational concepts and designs for an integrated security approach, documenting those that have proven to be the most effective, and identifying where further technological or procedural improvements are needed. Future efforts will build on the May 1999 report, Intermodal Cargo Transportation: Industry Best Security Practices.
- Identify Key Technologies and Research Needs: This effort seeks to characterize the security technologies currently available, identify their potential application in an integrated security approach, and determine where further technology development is required.

Funding. Funding will be provided from a mix of federal, state, and local government and private sources. Federal funding will be determined through the annual budget process.

Technical Challenges and Implementation Issues

One of the most interesting technical challenges for this partnership is determining the best means of successfully implementing countermeasures originally developed for one mode or environment—for example, airports—in another mode or environment with different characteristics, operational procedures, and resource levels.

Moreover, a major non-technical issue is that transportation operations require the effective cooperation of a variety of institutions, some of which have differing or even conflicting perspectives and goals. Any major security feature must achieve at least the consent of these varying organizations to be implemented successfully.

Source Threats and Protection, Department of Homeland Security. 2006. <http://www.dhs.gov/dhspublic/display?theme=31>

URBAN TRANSIT: A CRITICAL NATIONAL INFRASTRUCTURE

Since September 11th, the Federal Transit Administration (FTA) has undertaken a series of major steps to help prepare the transit industry to counter terrorist threats. FTA has provided direct assistance to transit agencies through on-site readiness assessments, technical assistance teams, regional forums for emergency responders, grants for drills, training, and accelerating technology and research projects.

From this initial work, it is clear that it is critical to integrate security throughout every aspect of transit programs, operations, and infrastructure. The most important areas of focus should be employee training, public awareness, and emergency response planning.

Although the transit industry has made great strides to strengthen security and emergency preparedness, there is much more to do. FTA has developed a list of Security Program Action Items for transit agencies that are the most important elements transit agencies should incorporate into their System Security Program Plans. These top 20 items are based on good security practices identified through FTA's Security Assessments and Technical Assistance provided to the largest transit agencies. FTA is working with transit agencies to encourage them to incorporate these practices into their programs.

Transit is a critical, high risk, and high consequence national asset. Everyday transit provides mobility to millions of Americans in our most densely populated urban areas and serves the largest economical and financial centers in the nation. Every workday, transit moves more than 14 million passengers. In two weeks, transit moves more passengers than AMTRAK moves in year. In one month, transit moves more passengers than U.S. airlines move in a year. Transit systems are designed to provide not only open, easy access to passengers, but to run under or alongside our largest business and government buildings, intermodal transportation centers, and many of our nations most visible public icons. The U.S.D.O.T Office of Intelligence and Security estimated that in the 1990s transit was the target of 20 to 35 percent of terrorist attacks worldwide.

Transit is designed and operated as an open environment—it is by its very nature a high risk, high consequence target for terrorist. More than 9.5 billion passengers a year ride our transit systems. Some of the largest transit systems report that more than 1,000 people a minute enter their largest intermodal facilities during rush hour. Transit subways travel under key government buildings, business centers, and harbors. Worldwide, transit has been a frequent terrorist target, including bombings in the London and Paris subways, the sarin gas attack in Tokyo, and bus bombings in Israel.

Five-Point Security Initiative

The FTA has launched five initiatives:

1. Conduct threat and vulnerability assessments: Multi-disciplinary teams including experts in anti-terrorism, security, and transit operations assessed the readiness of the largest and highest risk transit agencies. Based on these

assessments, FTA has provided specific feedback to individual agencies on how to improve their security systems and reduce vulnerabilities, as well as information on "best practices" to all transit agencies.

2. Deploy technical assistance teams: Emergency response planning and technical assistance teams are deployed to the top 50–60 transit agencies to help them to implement the major components of a systematic security program including current security and emergency response plans, training assessments, security awareness materials for transit employees and customers, etc.

3. Award grants for drills by emergency responders and transit agencies: Grants are awarded to conduct tabletop and full scale drills with regional emergency responders to test and improve their security and emergency response plans.

4. Accelerate technology deployment: FTA accelerated the deployment and testing of a system for chemical detection in subway systems.

5. Facilitate training and regional collaboration: A security awareness course for front line employees and supervisors is delivered nationwide along with regional forums to promote regional collaboration and coordination among fire, police, medical emergency, and transit system responders.

A Systems Approach

Research and policy leaders call for an integrated, systematic approach to security. The Transportation Research Board recommends layered security systems that are well integrated throughout transportation operations. Such security systems have interleaved and concentric features (e.g., fencing, security patrols, and closed circuit television), so a breach of any one layer will not defeat the entire system. Each layer provides backup for the others.

Fundamentally, security should be built into all aspects of transit operations as they are developed and created, rather than added as an afterthought. Given the age of most transit systems, FTA is having to play "catch up" with respect to security. Indeed, security is in its program infancy, just as safety was 10 to 15 years ago, before every agency dramatically increased its focus and resources to address the alarming number of transportation fatalities.

Next Steps

The FTA has added new initiatives to meet two critical needs identified in the Office of Homeland Security's national strategy:

Prevent Terrorist Attacks. Because of the openness of transit facilities, timely threat and intelligence information is critical for the transit agencies to strategically target resources based on real-time threat information. FTA is tapping into existing intelligence information and warning networks, and developing new intelligence sharing systems to provide two-way communication between the intelligence community and the transit industry. We are also launching a nationwide "transit watch" program with the transit industry that will draw upon more than 350,000 transit employees and millions of passengers to watch for and report suspicious activities.

Reduce America's Vulnerability to Terrorism. FTA is working with the transit industry to identify critical, high-risk assets and operations, and is developing a broad range of strategies to increase security. These strategies must become an integral part of daily transit operations and will include a special emphasis on training as well as, technical assistance, guidelines, best practices, and testing of available technologies for intrusion detection, surveillance, and chemical and biological detection. As these strategies are formulated, new initiatives will be introduced.

Source　Transit Security, Federal Transit Administration. 21006. <http://transit-safety. volpe. dot.gov/Security/Default.asp>

VULNERABILITY TO CYBERTERRORISM

Black Ice: The Invisible Threat of Cyber-Terror, a book published in 2003 and written by *Computerworld* journalist and former intelligence officer Dan Verton, describes the 1997 exercise code-named

"Eligible Receiver," conducted by the National Security Agency (NSA). (The following account draws from "Black Ice," *Computerworld*, August 13, 2003.) The exercise began when NSA officials instructed a "Red Team" of thirty-five hackers to attempt to hack into and disrupt U.S. national security systems. They were told to play the part of hackers hired by the North Korean intelligence service, and their primary target was to be the U.S. Pacific Command in Hawaii. They were allowed to penetrate any Pentagon network but were prohibited from breaking any U.S. laws, and they could only use hacking software that could be downloaded freely from the Internet. They started mapping networks and obtaining passwords gained through "brute-force cracking" (a trial-and-error method of decoding encrypted data such as passwords or encryption keys by trying all possible combinations). Often they used simpler tactics such as calling somebody on the telephone, pretending to be a technician or high-ranking official, and asking for the password. The hackers managed to gain access to dozens of critical Pentagon computer systems. Once they entered the systems, they could easily create user accounts, delete existing accounts, reformat hard drives, scramble stored data, or shut systems down. They broke the network defenses with relative ease and did so without being traced or identified by the authorities.

The results shocked the organizers. In the first place, the Red Team had shown that it was possible to break into the U.S. Pacific military's command-and-control system and, potentially, cripple it. In the second place, the NSA officials who examined the experiment's results found that much of the private-sector infrastructure in the United States, such as the telecommunications and electric power grids, could easily be invaded and abused in the same way.

The vulnerability of the energy industry is at the heart of *Black Ice*. Verton argues that America's energy sector would be the first domino to fall in a strategic cyberterrorist attack against the United States. The book explores in frightening detail how the impact of such an attack could rival, or even exceed, the consequences of a more traditional, physical attack. Verton claims that during any given year, an average large utility company in the United States experiences about 1 million cyberintrusions. Data collected by Riptech, Inc.—a Virginia-

based company specializing in the security of online information and financial systems—on cyberattacks during the six months following the 9/11 attacks showed that companies in the energy industry suffered intrusions at twice the rate of other industries, with the number of severe or critical attacks requiring immediate intervention averaging 12.5 per company.

Deregulation and the increased focus on profitability have made utilities and other companies move more and more of their operations to the Internet in search of greater efficiency and lower costs. Verton argues that the energy industry and many other sectors have become potential targets for various cyberdisruptions by creating Internet links (both physical and wireless) between their networks and supervisory control and data acquisition (SCADA) systems. These SCADA systems manage the flow of electricity and natural gas and control various industrial systems and facilities, including chemical processing plants, water purification and water delivery operations, wastewater management facilities, and a host of manufacturing firms. A terrorist's ability to control, disrupt, or alter the command and monitoring functions performed by these systems could threaten regional and possibly national security.

According to Symantec, one of the world's corporate leaders in the field of cybersecurity, new vulnerabilities to a cyberattack are being discovered all the time. The company reported that the number of "software holes" (software security flaws that allow malicious hackers to exploit the system) grew by 80 percent in 2002. Still, Symantec claimed that no single cyberterrorist attack was recorded (applying the definition that such an attack must originate in a country on the State Department's terror watch list). This may reflect the fact that terrorists do not yet have the required know-how. Alternatively, it may illustrate that hackers are not sympathetic to the goals of terrorist organizations—should the two groups join forces, however, the results could be devastating.

Equally alarming is the prospect of terrorists themselves designing computer software for government agencies. In March 2000, Japan's Metropolitan Police Department reported that a software system they had procured to track 150 police vehicles, including unmarked cars, had been developed by the Aum Shinryko cult, the same group that gassed the Tokyo subway in 1995, killing 12 people and injuring 6,000 more. At the time of the discovery, the cult had received classified tracking data on 115 vehicles. Further, the cult had developed software for at least 80 Japanese firms and 10 government agencies. They had worked as subcontractors to other firms, making it almost impossible for the organizations to know who was developing the software. As subcontractors, the cult could have installed Trojan horses to launch or facilitate cyberterrorist attacks at a later date.

Despite stepped-up security measures in the wake of 9/11, a survey of almost 400 IT professionals conducted for the Business Software Alliance during June 2002 revealed widespread concern. (See Robyn Greenspan, "Cyberterrorism Concerns IT Pros," Internetnews.com, August 16, 2002.) About half (49 percent) of the IT professionals felt that an attack is likely, and more than half (55 percent) said the risk of a major cyberattack on the United States has increased since 9/11. The figure jumped to 59 percent among those respondents who are in charge of their company's computer and Internet security. Seventy-two percent agreed with the statement "there is a gap between the threat of a major cyberattack and the government's ability to defend against it," and the agreement rate rose to 84 percent among respondents who are most knowledgeable about security. Those surveyed were concerned about attacks not only on the government but also on private targets. Almost three-quarters (74 percent) believed that national financial institutions such as major national banks would be likely targets within the next year, and around two-thirds believed that attacks were likely to be launched within the next twelve months against the computer systems that run communications networks (e.g., telephones and the Internet), transportation infrastructure (e.g., air traffic control computer systems), and utilities (e.g., water stations, dams, and power plants).

A study released in December 2003 (and reported in the *Washington Post* on January 31, 2004) appeared to confirm the IT professionals' skepticism about the ability of the government to defend itself against cyberattack. Conducted by the House Government Reform Subcommittee on Technology, the study examined computer security in federal agencies over the course of a year and awarded grades. Scores were based on numerous criteria, including how well an agency

trained its employees in security and the extent to which it met established security procedures such as limiting access to privileged data and eliminating easily guessed passwords. More than half the federal agencies surveyed received a grade of D or F. The Department of Homeland Security, which has a division devoted to monitoring cybersecurity, received the lowest overall score of the twenty-four agencies surveyed. Also earning an F was the Justice Department, the agency charged with investigating and prosecuting cases of hacking and other forms of cybercrime. Thirteen agencies improved their scores slightly compared with the previous year, nudging the overall government grade from an F up to a D. Commenting on these results, Rep. Adam H. Putnam (R-Fl.), chairman of the House Government Reform Subcommittee on Technology, declared that "the threat of cyberattack is real.... The damage that could be inflicted both in terms of financial loss and, potentially, loss of life is considerable."

Such studies, together with the enormous media interest in the subject, have fueled popular fears about cyberterrorism. A study by the Pew Internet and American Life Project found in 2003 that nearly half of the one thousand Americans surveyed were worried that terrorists could launch attacks through the networks connecting home computers and power utilities. The Pew study found that 11 percent of respondents were "very worried" and 38 percent were "somewhat worried" about an attack launched through computer networks. The survey was taken in early August, before the major blackout struck the Northeast and before several damaging new viruses afflicted computers throughout the country.

Cyberterrorism Today and Tomorrow

It seems fair to say that the current threat posed by cyberterrorism has been exaggerated. No single instance of cyberterrorism has yet been recorded; U.S. defense and intelligence computer systems are air-gapped and thus isolated from the Internet; the systems run by private companies are more vulnerable to attack but also more resilient than is often supposed; the vast majority of cyberattacks are launched by hackers with few, if any, political goals and no desire to cause the mayhem and carnage of which terrorists dream. So, then, why has so much concern been expressed over a relatively minor threat?

The reasons are many:

• Cyberterrorism is novel, original, it is attention gaining.
• The mass media frequently fail to distinguish between hacking and cyberterrorism and exaggerate the threat of the latter by reasoning from false analogies such as the following: "If a sixteen-year-old could do this, then what could a well-funded terrorist group do?"
• Ignorance is a third factor. Many people, including most lawmakers and senior administration officials, do not fully understand cyberterrorism and therefore tend to fear it.
• A fourth reason is that some politicians, whether out of genuine conviction or out of a desire to stoke public anxiety about terrorism in order to advance their own agendas, have played the role of prophets of doom.
• A fifth factor is ambiguity about the very meaning of "cyberterrorism," which has confused the public and given rise to countless myths.

Verton argues that "al Qaeda [has] shown itself to have an incessant appetite for modern technology" and provides numerous citations from bin Laden and other al Qaeda leaders to show their recognition of this new cyberweapon. In the wake of the 9/11 attacks, bin Laden reportedly gave a statement to an editor of an Arab newspaper claiming that "hundreds of Muslim scientists were with him who would use their knowledge … ranging from computers to electronics against the infidels." Sheikh Omar Bakri Muhammad, a supporter of bin Laden and often the conduit for his messages to the Western world, declared in an interview with Verton, "I would advise those who doubt al Qaeda's interest in cyber-weapons to take Osama bin Laden very seriously. The third letter from Osama bin Laden … was clearly addressing using the technology in order to destroy the economy of the capitalist states."

"While bin Laden may have his finger on the trigger, his grandchildren may have their fingers on the computer mouse," remarked Frank Cilluffo of the Office of Homeland Security in a statement that has been widely cited. Future terrorists may indeed see greater potential for cyberterrorism than do the terrorists of today. Furthermore, the next generation of terrorists is now growing up in a digital world, one in which hacking tools are sure to become more powerful, simpler to use, and easier to access. Cyberterrorism may also become more attractive as the real and virtual worlds become more closely coupled. For instance, a terrorist group might simultaneously explode a bomb at a train station and launch a cyberattack on the communications infrastructure, thus magnifying the impact of the event. Unless these systems are carefully secured, conducting an online operation that physically harms someone may be as easy tomorrow as penetrating a website is today.

Paradoxically, success in the "war on terror" is likely to make terrorists turn increasingly to unconventional weapons such as cyberterrorism. The challenge before us is to assess what needs to be done to address this ambiguous but potential threat of cyberterrorism—but to do so without inflating its real significance and manipulating the fear it inspires. Terrorism experts conclude that, at least for now, hijacked vehicles, truck bombs, and biological weapons seem to pose a greater threat than does cyberterrorism. However, just as the events of 9/11 caught the world by surprise, so could a major cyberassault. The threat of cyberterrorism may be exaggerated and manipulated, but we can neither deny it nor dare to ignore it.

Source U.S. Institute for Peace. 2006. *www. usip.org/*

XII: Liaison

BUREAU OF ALCOHOL, TOBACCO, FIREARMS, AND EXPLOSIVES (ATF)

The Bureau of Alcohol, Tobacco, Firearms, and Explosives (ATF) is a principal law enforcement agency within the United States Department of Justice dedicated to preventing terrorism, reducing violent crime, and protecting our nation. The men and women of ATF perform the dual responsibilities of enforcing federal criminal laws and regulating the firearms and explosives industries. We are committed to working directly, and through partnerships, to investigate and reduce crime involving firearms and explosives, acts of arson, and illegal trafficking of alcohol and tobacco products.

ATF's complex tax collecting, regulatory, and enforcement missions are interwoven with unique responsibilities dedicated to reducing violent crime, collecting revenue, and protecting the public. ATF enforces the federal laws and regulations relating to alcohol, tobacco, firearms, explosives, and arson by working directly and in cooperation with other federal, state, and local law enforcement agencies.

For management and budgetary purposes, the Bureau combines all criminal and regulatory enforcement activities into four major program areas:

Firearms

ATF recognizes the role that firearms play in violent crimes and pursues an integrated regulatory and enforcement strategy. Investigative priorities focus on armed violent offenders and career criminals, narcotics traffickers, narco-terrorists, violent gangs, and domestic and international arms traffickers.

Sections 924(c) and (e) of Title 18 of the United States Code provide mandatory and enhanced sentencing guidelines for armed career criminals and narcotics traffickers as well as other dangerous armed criminals. ATF uses these statutes to target, investigate, and recommend prosecution of these offenders to reduce the level of violent crime and to enhance public safety. ATF also strives to increase state and local awareness of available federal prosecution under these statutes.

To curb the illegal use of firearms and enforce the federal firearms laws, ATF issues firearms licenses and conducts firearms licensee qualification and compliance inspections.

In addition to aiding the enforcement of federal requirements for gun purchases, compliance inspections of existing licensees focus on assisting law enforcement to identify and apprehend criminals who illegally purchase firearms.

The inspections also help improve the likelihood that crime gun traces will be successful, since inspectors educate licensees in proper record keeping and business practices. Compliance inspections target licensees likely to divert firearms from legitimate trade to criminal use and dealers with a history of poor compliance.

Arson and Explosives

As an integral part of the Bureau's overall violent crime reduction strategy, ATF's Explosives Program provides vital resources to local communities to investigate explosives incidents and arson-for-profit schemes. This program saves the insurance industry, and ultimately the American public, millions of dollars in fraudulent claims annually.

To investigate explosives incidents and arsons, ATF uses National Response Teams, International Response Teams, and Arson Task Forces. These teams consist of ATF special agents, auditors, technicians, laboratory personnel, and canines. Explosives regulation and enforcement programs are recognized to be vital to public safety, and ATF works to prevent both the criminal use and accidental detonations of explosives materials.

ATF's efforts require the combined use of resources for explosives and arson incidents, such as special agents, auditors, inspectors, and forensic and technical specialists, that no other federal agency can provide. The public safety is further protected by inspections to ensure that explosives are safely and securely stored and by issuing pen-nits and licenses.

ATF plays a lead role in the investigations of arson and bombing incidents directed at abortion clinics and is a member of the Department of Justice Task Force focused on addressing abortion clinic violence. ATF also provides expertise internationally in the areas of post-blast examination, and cause and origin determination.

An inherent function of the Bureau's Explosives Program is to maintain the Explosives Incident System. This system is a computerized repository for historical and technical data on national explosives.

Alcohol/Tobacco Programs

In the alcohol beverage industry, the Bureau regulates the qualification and operations of distilleries, wineries, and breweries, as well as importers and wholesalers in the industry. ATF has established mutually beneficial working relationships to minimize the regulatory burdens on businesses while still providing necessary government oversight and protecting consumer interests.

Consumers of alcohol beverage products are protected by several functions unique to ATF. The ATF National Laboratory Center is the premier tester of new products coming onto the market, as well as the facility that determines whether any products currently on the market pose a health risk to consumers. To ensure alcohol beverage labels do not contain misleading information and adhere to regulatory mandates, ATF examines all label applications for approval.

The goals of the alcohol program are to ensure the collection of alcohol beverage excise taxes; to provide for accurate deposit and accounting for these taxes; to prevent entry into the industry by criminals or persons whose business experience or associations pose a risk of tax fraud; and to suppress label fraud, commercial bribery, diversion and smuggling, and other unlawful practices in the alcohol beverage marketplace.

The goals of the tobacco program are to ensure the collection of tobacco excise taxes and to qualify applicants for permits to manufacture tobacco products or operate tobacco export warehouses. Tobacco inspections verify an applicant's qualification information, check the security of the premise, and ensure tax compliance. ATF special agents investigate trafficking of contraband tobacco products in violation of federal law and sections of the Internal Revenue Code.

Points of Contact

Bureau of Alcohol, Tobacco, Firearms and Explosives, 650 Massachusetts Avenue, NW, Washington, D.C. 20226. Telephone: 202-648-8010

Field Offices

Atlanta Field Division:
404-417-2600
Atlanta, GA (Group I)
404-417-1300
Atlanta, GA (Group II—Arson)
404-417-1300
Atlanta, GA (Group III)
404-417-1300
Atlanta, GA (Group IV)
404-815-4400
Atlanta, GA (Group V—Industry Operations)
404-417-2670
Atlanta, GA (Group VI)
404-417-2600
Atlanta, GA (Group VII)
404-417-1300
Augusta, GA (Satellite Office)
706-724-9983
Columbus, GA (Satellite Office)
706-653-3545
Macon, GA
478-474-0477
Macon, GA (Group II—Industry Operations)
478-474-0477
Savannah, GA
912-790-8326

Baltimore Field Division:

410-779-1700
Baltimore, MD (Group I—Arson)
410-779-1710
Baltimore, MD (Group II)
410-579-5011
Baltimore, MD (Group III)
410-779-1730

Baltimore, MD (Group IV)
410-779-1740
Baltimore, MD (Group V—Industry
   Operations)
410-779-1750
Hyattsville, MD
301-397-2640
Wilmington, DE (Criminal Enforcement)
302-252-0110
Wilmington, DE (Industry Operations)
302-252-0130

Boston Field Division:

617-557-1200
Boston, MA (Group I Arson)
617-557-1210
Boston, MA (Group II)
617-557-1220
Boston, MA (Group III)
617-557-1326
Boston, MA (Group IV)
617-557-1240
Boston, MA (Group V—Industry Operations)
617-557-1250
Burlington, VT
802-951-6593
Hartford, CT (Industry Operations)
860-240-3400
Manchester, NH
603-471-1283
New Haven, CT
203-773-2060
Portland, ME
207-780-3324
Providence, RI
401-528-4366
Providence, RI (Satellite Office—Industry
   Operations)
401-528-4366
Springfield, MA (Satellite Office)
413-785-0007
Worcester, MA
508-793-0240

Charlotte Field Division:

704-716-1800
Asheville, NC (Satellite Office)
828-271-4075/4076
Charleston, SC
843-763-3683

Charlotte, NC (Group I)
704-716-1810
Charlotte, NC (Group II)
704-716-1820
Charlotte, NC (Group III—Industry
   Operations)
704-716-1830
Charlotte, NC (Group IV)
704-716-1840
Charlotte, NC (Violent Crime Task Force)
704-716-1850
Columbia, SC
803-765-5723
Columbia, SC (Satellite Office—Industry
   Operations)
803-765-5722
Fayetteville, NC
910-483-3030
Fayetteville, NC (Satellite Office—Industry
   Operations)
910-483-3030
Florence, SC (Satellite Office)
843-292-0179
Greensboro, NC (Group I)
336-547-4224
Greensboro, NC (Group II—Industry
   Operations)
336-547-4150
Greenville, SC
864-282-2937
Greenville, SC (Satellite Office—Industry
   Operations)
864-282-2937
Raleigh, NC
919-856-4366
Wilmington, NC
910-343-6801

Chicago Field Division:

312-846-7200
Chicago, IL (Group I)
312-846-7230
Chicago, IL (Group II)
312-846-7250
Chicago, IL (Group III)
312-846-7270
Chicago, IL (Group IV)
312-846-8850
Chicago, IL (Group V)
312-846-8870
Fairview Heights, IL
618-632-9380

Fairview Heights, IL (Satellite Office—
   Industry Operations)
618-632-0704
Downers Grove, IL (Group I)
630-725-5220
Downers Grove, IL (Group II—Arson &
   Explosives)
630-725-5230
Downers Grove, IL (Group III—Industry
   Operations)
630-725-5290
Peoria, IL (Satellite Office—Industry
   Operations)
309-671-7108
Rockford, IL (Satellite Office)
815-987-4310
Rock Island, IL (Satellite Office)
309-732-0636
Springfield, IL (Group I—Criminal
   Enforcement)
217-547-3650
Springfield, IL (Group II—Industry
   Operations)
217-547-3675

Columbus Field Division:

614-827-8400
Cincinnati Field Office
513-684-3354
Cincinnati II IO Office
513-684-3351
Cleveland I Field Office
216-522-3080
Cleveland II Field Office
216-522-3786
Cleveland III IO Office
216-522-3374
Columbus I Field Office
614-827-8450
Columbus II Intel Group
614-827-8430
Columbus IO Satellite
614-827-8470
Fort Wayne Field Office
260-424-4440
Indianapolis I Field Office
317-226-7464
Indianapolis II IO Office
317-248-4002
Merrillville Field Office
219-755-6310

Toledo Field Office
419-259-7520
Youngstown Field Office
330-707-2300

Dallas Field Division:

469-227-4300
Dallas, TX (Group I)
469-227-4350
Dallas, TX (Group II Arson)
469-227-4370
Dallas, TX (Group III)
469-227-4395
Dallas, TX (Group IV)
972-915-9570
Dallas, TX (Group V—Industry
   Operations)
469-227-4415
El Paso, TX
915-534-6449
El Paso, TX (Satellite Office—Industry
   Operations)
915-534-6475
Fort Worth, TX
817-862-2800
Fort Worth, TX (Industry
   Operations)
817-862-2850
Lubbock, TX (Group I)
806-798-1030
Lubbock, TX (Satellite Office—Industry
   Operations)
806-798-1030
Oklahoma City, OK (Group I—Industry
   Operations)
405-297-5073
Oklahoma City, OK (Group II)
405-297-5060
Tulsa, OK
918-581-7731
Tyler, TX
903-590-1475

Detroit Field Division:

313-259-8050
Ann Arbor
734-741-2456
Detroit, MI (Group I)
313-259-8110

Detroit, MI (Group II)
313-259-8120
Detroit, MI (Group III —Arson)
313-259-8140
Detroit, MI (Group IV)
313-259-8320
Detroit, MI (Group V—Industry
  Operations)
313-259-8390
Detroit, MI (Group VI)
313-259-8760
Flint, MI
810 341-5710
Flint, MI (Satellite Office—Industry
  Operations)
810 341-5730
Grand Rapids, MI (Group I)
616-301-6100
Lansing, MI (Satellite Office)
517-337-6645
Grand Rapids, MI (Group II—Industry
  Operations)
616-301-6100

Houston Field Division:

281-372-2900
Austin, TX
512-349-4545
Beaumont, TX
409-835-0062
Beaumont, TX (Satellite Office—Industry
  Operations)
409-835-0062
Corpus Christi, TX
361-888-3392
Houston, TX (Group I)
281-372-2990
Houston, TX (Group II)
281-372-2960
Houston, TX (Group III—
  Arson)
281-372-2930
Houston, TX (Group IV)
281-372-2980
Houston, TX (Group V)
281-372-3010
Houston, TX (Group VI—Industry
  Operations)
281-372-2950
McAllen, TX
956-687-5207

San Antonio, TX (Group I)
210-805-2727
San Antonio, TX (Group II—Industry
  Operations)
210-805-2777
Waco, TX (Satellite Office)
254-741-9900

Kansas City Field Division:

816-559-0700
Cape Girardeau, MO (Satellite Office)
573-331-7300
Cedar Rapids, IA (Satellite Office)
(covered by Des Moines Field
  Office)
319-393-6075
Davenport, IA
(covered by Des Moines Field Office)
309-732-0636
Des Moines, IA
515-284-4372
Des Moines, IA (Satellite Office—Industry
  Operations)
515-284-4857
Kansas City, MO (Group I)
816-559-0710
Kansas City, MO (Group II)
816-559-0720
Kansas City, MO (Group III—Industry
  Operations)
816-559-0730
Kansas City, MO (Group IV)
816-746-4962
Kansas City, MO (Group V)
816-559-0850
Kansas City, MO (Group VI—Industry
  Operations)
816-559-0730
Omaha, NE
402-952-2605
Omaha, NE (Satellite Office—Industry
  Operations)
402-952-2635
Sioux City, IA
(covered by Omaha, NE Field
  Office)
712-255-9128
Springfield, MO
417-837-2100
St. Louis, MO (Group I)
314-269-2200

St. Louis, MO (Group II)
314-269-2200
St. Louis, MO (Group III—Industry
Operations)
314-269-2250
Wichita, KS
316-269-6229

Los Angeles Field Division:

213-534-2450
Los Angeles, CA (Group I—Metro)
213-534-1050
Los Angeles, CA (Group II)
213-534-1070
Los Angeles, CA (Group III Arson)
213-534-6480
Los Angeles, CA (Group IV—Industry
Operations)
213-534-2430
Los Angeles, CA (Group V)
213-534-5050
Riverside, CA
909-276-6031
San Diego, CA (Group I)
858-966-1010
San Diego, CA (Group II)
858-966-1020
San Diego, CA (Group III—Industry
Operations)
858-966-1030
Santa Ana, CA (Group I)
714-246-8210
Santa Ana, CA (Group II—Industry
Operations)
714-246-8252
Santa Maria, CA (Enforcement)
805-348-1820
Santa Maria, CA (Industry Operations)
805-348-0027
Van Nuys, CA
818-756-4350
Van Nuys, CA (Satellite Office—Industry
Operations)
818-756-4364

Louisville Field Division:

502-753-3400
Ashland, KY
606-329-8092

Bowling Green, KY
270-393-4755
Bowling Green, KY (Satellite Office—
Industry Operations)
270-781-1757
Charleston, WV (Charleston I)
304-347-5249
Charleston, WV (Satellite Office—Industry
Operations)
304-347-5172
Lexington, KY (Lexington I Field
Office)
859-219-4500
Lexington, KY (Group II—Industry
Operations)
859-219-4508
London, KY (Satellite Office)
606-878-3011/3012
Louisville, KY (Group I)
502-753-3450
Louisville, KY (Group II—Industry
Operations)
502-753-3500
Louisville, KY (Group III)
502-753-3550
Wheeling, WV
304-232-4170
Wheeling, WV (Satellite Office—Industry
Operations)
304-232-4170

Miami Field Division:

305-597-4800
Fort Lauderdale, FL
954-453-6001
Fort Lauderdale, FL HIDTA
954-888-1661
Fort Pierce, FL (Satellite Office)
561-835-8878
San Juan, PR (Group I—HIDTA)
787-766-5084
San Juan, PR (Group II)
787-766-5084
San Juan, PR (Group III—Industry
Operations)
787-766-5584
Mayaguez, PR (Satellite Office—Industry
Operations)
787-344-8636
Miami, FL (Group I)
305-597-4910

Miami, FL (Group II)
305-597-4920
Miami, FL (Group III)
305-597-4930
Miami, FL (Group IV)
305-597-4940
Miami, FL (Group V—HIDTA)
305-597-2056
Miami, FL (Group VI—Industry Operations)
305-597-4960
St. Croix, VI (Satellite Office)
340-719-4799
St. Thomas, VI
340-774-2398
West Palm Beach, FL
561-835-8878

Nashville Field Division:

615-565-1400
Birmingham, AL (Group I)
205-583-5920
Birmingham, AL (Group II—Industry
  Operations)
205-583-5950
Birmingham, AL (Group III)
205-583-5970
Chattanooga, TN
423-855-6422
Huntsville, AL (Satellite Office)
256-539-0623
Jackson, TN (Satellite Office)
731-265-4258
Johnson City, TN (Satellite
  Office)
423-283-7262/7104
Knoxville, TN
865-545-4505
Memphis, TN
901-544-0321
Mobile, AL
251-405-5000
Mobile, AL (Satellite Office—Industry
  Operations)
251-405-5000
Montgomery, AL
334-206-6050
Nashville, TN (Group I)
615-565-1400
Nashville, TN (Group II—Industry
  Operations)
615-565-1420

Nashville, TN (Group III)
615-565-1430

New Orleans Field Division:

985-246-7000
Baton Rouge, LA
225-819-4314
Biloxi, MS
Phone Numbers Pending
Fort Smith, AR
501-709-0872
Jackson, MS
601-292-4000
Jackson, MS (Group II—Industry
  Operations)
601-292-4025
Little Rock, AR
501-324-6181
Little Rock, AR (Satellite Office—Industry
  Operations)
501-324-6457
New Orleans, LA (Group I)
985-246-7100
New Orleans, LA (Group II)
985-246-7140
New Orleans, LA (Group III—Industry
  Operations)
985-246-7120
New Orleans, LA (Group IV)
985-246-7160
New Orleans V (Arson/Explosives)
(985) 893-8333
Oxford, MS (Group I)
662-234-3751
Shreveport, LA
318-424-6850
Shreveport, LA (Satellite Office—Industry
  Operations)
318-424-6861

New York Field Division:

718-650-4000
Albany, NY (Criminal)
518-431-4182
Albany, NY (Satellite Office)
518-431-4188
Bath, NY (Satellite Office—Industry
  Operations)
607-776-4549

Buffalo, NY (Group I—Criminal)
716-853-5070
Buffalo, NY (Group II—Industry Operations)
716-853-5160
Jersey City, NJ (Satellite Office)
201-547-6821
Long Island, NY (Satellite Office—
Industry Operations)
631-694-8372
Mellville, NY
631-694-8372
New York, NY (Group I)
718-552-1610
New York, NY (Group II)
718-552-1620
New York, NY (Group III—Arson)
718-896-6400
New York, NY (Group IV)
718-650-4040
New York, NY (Group V)
718-650-4050
New York, NY (Group VI—Industry
Operations)
718-650-4060
New York, NY (Group VII)
718-650-4070
Rochester, NY (Satellite Office)
716-263-5720
Syracuse, NY (Criminal)
315-448-0889
Syracuse, NY (Satellite Office—Industry
Operations)
315-448-0898
West Patterson, NJ (NJ Group I)
973-247-3010
West Patterson, NJ (NJ Group II—Arson)
973-247-3020
West Patterson, NJ (NJ Group III—Industry
Operations)
973-247-3030
White Plains, NY
914-682-6164
White Plains, NY (Satellite Office—
Industry Operations)
914-682-6164

Philadelphia Field Division:

215-717-4700
Atlantic City, NJ (Satellite Office)
609-487-2110
Camden, NJ

856-488-2520
Erie, PA (Satellite Office)
814-456-1200
Harrisburg, PA
717-231-3400
Harrisburg, PA (Group II—Industry
Operations)
717-231-3400
Lansdale, PA (Industry Operations)
215-362-1840
Philadelphia, PA (Group I—Violent Crime
Impact Team)
215-446-9610
Philadelphia, PA (Group II—Arson &
Explosives)
215-446-7860
Philadelphia, PA (Group III)
215-446-9680
Philadelphia, PA (Group IV—Industry
Operations)
215-446-7880
Philadelphia, PA (Group V—Intelligence
Group)
215-446-7840
Philadelphia, PA (Group VI—Ceasefire)
215-446-9640
Philadelphia, PA (Group VII)
215-446-9610
Pittsburgh, PA (Group I and Group II—
Arson)
412-395-0540
Pittsburgh, PA (Group III—Industry
Operations)
412-395-0600
Reading, PA
610-208-5200
Reading, PA (Satellite Office—Industry
Operations)
610-208-5200
Trenton, NJ (Arson and Explosives)
609-989-2155
Trenton, NJ (Satellite Office—Industry
Operations)
609-989-2142
Wilkes-Barre, PA (Industry Operations)
570-826-6551

Phoenix Field Division:

602-776-5400
Albuquerque, NM
505-346-6914

Albuquerque, NM (Satellite Office—
  Industry Operations)
505-346-6910
Cheyenne, WY
307-772-2346
Colorado Springs, CO
719-473-0166
Denver, CO (Group I)
303-844-7540
Denver, CO (Group II—Arson)
303-844-7570
Denver, CO (Group III—Industry
  Operations)
303-844-7545
Phoenix, AZ (Group I)
602-776-5440
Phoenix, AZ (Group II)
602-776-5460
Phoenix, AZ (Group III—Industry
  Operations)
602-776-5480
Phoenix, AZ (Group IV)
602-776-5500
Salt Lake City, UT
801-524-7000
Salt Lake City, UT (Satellite Office—
  Industry Operations)
801-524-7012
Tucson, AZ (Group I)
520-770-5100
Tucson, AZ (Group II)
520-770-5120
Tucson, AZ (Satellite Office—Industry
  Operations)
520-670-4804

Napa, CA (Satellite Office—Industry
  Operations)
707-224-7801
Oakland, CA (Group I)
510-267-2200
Oakland, CA (Satellite Office—Industry
  Operations)
925-479-7500
Redding, CA (Satellite Office)
530-224-1862
Reno, NV
775-784-5251
Sacramento, CA (Group I)
916-498-5100
Sacramento, CA (Group II—Industry
  Operations)
916-498-5095
San Francisco, CA (Group I)
415-436-8020
San Francisco, CA (Group II—Arson)
925-479-7520
San Francisco, CA (Group III—Industry
  Operations)
925-479-7530
San Francisco, CA (Group IV)
925-479-7540
San Jose, CA (Group I)
408-535-5015
San Jose, CA (Group II—Industry
  Operations)
408-535-5538
Santa Rosa, CA (Industry
  Operations)
707-576-0184

San Francisco Field Division:

925-479-7500
Bakersfield, CA (Satellite Office)
661-861-4420
Fresno, CA (Group I)
559-487-5393
Fresno, CA (Group II—Industry
  Operations)
559-487-5093
Las Vegas, NV
702-387-4600
Stockton, CA (Stockton I Satellite Office
  and Stockton II Satellite Office)
209-321-8878

Seattle Field Division:

206-389-5800
Anchorage, AK
907-271-5701
Anchorage, AK (Satellite Office—Industry
  Operations)
907-271-5701
Boise, ID
208-334-1160
Boise, ID (Satellite Office—Industry
  Operations)
208-334-1164
Hawaii County, HI
809-933-8139
Honolulu, HI
808-541-2670

Honolulu, HI (Satellite Office—Industry
 Operations)
808-541-2670
Mongmong, Guam
671-472-7129
Portland, OR (Group I)
503-331-7810
Portland, OR (Group II)
503-331-7820
Portland, OR (Group III)
503-331-7830
Seattle, WA (Group I)
206-389-6860
Seattle, WA (Group II—Industry
 Operations)
206-389-6800
Seattle, WA (Group III—Arson &
 Explosives)
206-389-6830
Seattle, WA (Group IV)
206-389-5870
Spokane, WA (Group I)
509-324-7866
Spokane, WA (Group II—Industry
 Operations)
509-324-7881
Yakima, WA
509-454-4403

St. Paul Field Division:

651-726-0200
Billings, MT (Group I)
406-657-6886
Fargo, ND (Group I)
701-293-2860
Fargo, ND (Group II—Satellite Office,
 Industry Operations)
701-293-2880
Helena, MT (Group I)
406-441-1100
Helena, MT (Group II—Satellite Office,
 Industry Operations)
406-441-1100
Madison, WI (Group I Field
 Office)
608-441-5050
Milwaukee, WI (Group I)
414-727-6170
Milwaukee, WI (Group II—Industry
 Operations)
414-727-6200

Missoula, MT (Satellite Office)
406-721-2611
Rapid City, SD (Satellite
 Office)
605-343-3288
Sioux Falls, SD (Group I)
605-330-4368
St. Paul, MN (Group I)
651-726-0300
St. Paul, MN (Group II—Industry
 Operations)
651-726-0220
St. Paul, MN (Group III)
651-726-0230
St. Paul, MN (Group IV)
651-726-0260

Tampa Field Division:

813-202-7300
Fort Myers, FL (Group I Satellite
 Office)
239-334-8086
Fort Myers, FL (Group II Satellite Office—
 Industry Operations)
239-334-8086
Gainesville, FL (Satellite Office)
352-378-8017
Jacksonville, FL
904-380-5500
Jacksonville, FL (Satellite Office—Industry
 Operations)
904-380-5500
Orlando FL
407-384-2411
Orlando FL II (Industry
 Operations)
407-384-2420
Panama City, FL (Satellite
 Office)
850-769-0234
Pensacola, FL
850-435-8485
Tallahassee, FL
850-942-9660
Tampa, FL (Group I)
813-202-7310
Tampa, FL (Group II—Industry
 Operations)
813-202-7320
Tampa, FL (Group III)
813-301-3650

Washington Field Division:

202-648-8010
Bristol, VA
276-466-2727
Charlottesville, VA (Satellite
  Office)
434-970-3872
Falls Church, VA (Group I—Arson)
703-287-1110
Falls Church, VA (Group II)
703-287-1120
Falls Church, VA (Group III—Industry
  Operations)
703-287-1130
Martinsburg, WV, LE
304-260-3400
Martinsburg, WV (Satellite Office—
  Industry Operations)
304-260-3400
Norfolk, VA
757-616-7400
Norfolk, VA (Satellite Office—Industry
  Operations)
757-441-3192
Richmond, VA (Group I)
804-200-4200
Richmond, VA (Group II—Industry
  Operations)
804-200-4141
Richmond, VA (Group III)
804-775-4200
Roanoke, VA
540- 983-6920
Roanoke, VA (Satellite Office—Industry
  Operations)
540-983-6944
Washington, DC (Group I) (HIDTA)
202-305-8189
Washington, DC (Group II) (Firearms
  Trafficking)
202-648-8105
Washington, DC (Group III) (VCIT—
  Violent Crime Impact Team)
202-648-8090
Washington, DC (Group IV)
  Intelligence/Regional Crime Gun
  Center
202-648-8100

Source Bureau of Alcohol, Tobacco, Firearms,
and Explosives (ATF). 2006. http://www.atf.
treas.gov/about/mission.htm

CENTRAL INTELLIGENCE AGENCY (CIA)

The Central Intelligence Agency (CIA) is an independent agency responsible for providing national security intelligence to senior U.S. policymakers. The Director of the Central Intelligence Agency (D/CIA) is appointed by the President with the advice and consent of the Senate. The Director manages the operations, personnel, and budget of the Central Intelligence Agency.

CIA's main job is to keep top U.S. officials aware of key intelligence issues. To do this is a very involved process. First, we have to identify a problem or an issue of national security concern to the U.S. government. In some cases, CIA is directed to study an intelligence issue—such as what activities terrorist organizations are planning, or how countries that have biological or chemical weapons plan to use these weapons—then we look for a way to collect information about the problem.

There are several ways to collect information. Translating foreign newspaper and magazine articles and radio and television broadcasts provides open-source intelligence. Imagery satellites take pictures from space and imagery analysts write reports about what they see, for example, how many airplanes are at a foreign military base. Signals analysts work to decrypt coded messages that other countries send. Operations officers recruit foreigners to give information about their countries to the U.S.

After the information is collected, the intelligence analysts pull together relevant information coming in from all available sources and assess what is happening, why it is happening, what might occur next, and what it means for U.S. interests. The result of this analytic effort is timely and objective assessments, free of any political bias, provided to senior U.S. policymakers in the form of finished intelligence products that include written reports and oral briefings. One of these reports is the President's Daily Brief (PDB)—an Intelligence Community product—which the U.S. President and other senior officials receive each day. It is important to know that CIA analysts only report the information and do not make policy recommendations. Making policy is left to the executive branch of the government, such as the State Department or the Defense Department.

These policymakers use the information that CIA provides to help them make U.S. policy toward other countries. It is also important to know that CIA is NOT a law enforcement organization. That is the job of the FBI. However, the CIA and the FBI cooperate on a number of issues, such as counterintelligence.

The CIA is divided into four directorates. They carry out "the intelligence cycle," the process of collecting, analyzing, and giving intelligence information to top U.S. government officials.

The Directorate of Intelligence (DI) analyzes all-source intelligence and produces reports, briefings, and papers on key foreign intelligence issues. The DI is responsible for timeliness, accuracy, and relevance of intelligence analysis that is of concern to national security policymakers and other intelligence consumers.

The Directorate of Operations (DO) has primary responsibility for the clandestine collection of foreign intelligence, including human source intelligence (HUMINT). Domestically, the DDO is responsible for the collection of foreign intelligence volunteered by individuals and organizations in the United States.

The Directorate of Science and Technology (DS&T) is responsible for applying technology and technical expertise to the most critical intelligence problems. The DS&T engages in the full range of technology activities: from applied research and development to the design, development, and operational deployment of specialized intelligence systems.

The Directorate of Support (DS) provides the foundation critical to the Agency's mission. This foundation encompasses a wide range of services that include protection of Agency personnel, information, facilities, technology, communications, logistics, training, financial management, medical services, human resources, records management and declassification, and information technology.

The Director of the Central Intelligence Agency (D/CIA) has several staffs directly subordinate to him that deal with public affairs, protocol, congressional affairs, legal issues, information management, and internal oversight.

Point of Contact

Central Intelligence Agency, Office of Public Affairs, Washington, D.C. 20505

Office: (703) 482-0623 from 7:00 a.m. to 5:00 p.m., US Eastern time
Fax: (703) 482-1739 from 7:00 a.m. to 5:00 p.m., US Eastern time

Source   The Central Intelligence Agency (CIA). 2006. <https://www.cia.gov/>

DEFENSE SECURITY SERVICE

The Defense Security Service (DSS) is a Department of Defense (DoD) agency. The Under Secretary of Defense for Intelligence provides authority, direction and control over DSS. DSS headquarters is located in Alexandria, Va., with field offices throughout the United States.

DSS provides the Secretary of Defense, the DoD Components, federal government defense contractors, and other authorized recipients, with a full range of security support services, as permitted by law and Executive Order.

As part of its security mission, DSS administers the National Industrial Security Program and the Security Education, Training and Awareness (SETA) program on behalf of DoD.

National Industrial Security Program

DSS administers and implements the defense portion of the National Industrial Security Program pursuant to Executive Order 12829. Approximately 285 Industrial Security Representatives are spread across the U.S. in four geographic regions. They provide oversight and assistance to cleared contractor facilities and assist the organization's management and Facility Security Officers in ensuring the protection of national security information. DSS has responsibility for approximately 11,000 cleared contractor facilities.

Collaborative Adjudication Services (CAS)

The DSS Counterintelligence (CI) Office, the Defense Industrial Security Clearance Office

(DISCO) and the Clearance Liaison Office (CLO) are organizations under CAS.

DISCO, located in Columbus, Ohio, processes requests for industrial personnel security investigations and provides eligibility or clearance determinations for cleared industry personnel under the NISP. There are approximately 800,000 cleared contractor personnel under the NISP.

The CI office provides support to DSS programs; infusing CI experience and expertise to our workforce, increasing CI awareness throughout DSS and cleared industry and assisting customers in recognizing and reporting suspected foreign intelligence collection activities.

The CLO provides liaison and support to the Office of Personnel Management (OPM) in the conduct of personnel security investigations for DoD.

The DSS Counterintelligence (CI) Office

The DSS Counterintelligence (CI) Office provides counterintelligence support to the DSS mission. The DSS CI Office provides direct support to the Industrial Security Program (ISP) and Collaborative Adjudication Services which also encompasses the Defense Industrial Security Clearance Office (DISCO), and the Defense Office of Hearings and Appeals (DOHA). In accordance with the DSS mission, as well as the NCIX (National Counterintelligence Executive) and DoD CI strategies, the Counterintelligence Office provides CI support to the Research Technology Protection (RTP) Program, the Critical Infrastructure Protection (CIP) Program, the Anti-Terrorism/Force Protection (ATFP) Program, and the Insider Threat Program. The CI Office also provides support services to CI investigations, operations, collections, analysis, and production. The Office accomplishes its mission by providing early detection and reporting of foreign intelligence and non-state actor collection attempts against U.S. industry. The CI office supports 47 CI Working Groups and industrial security/CI training missions at the DSS Academy, the Joint Counter- Intelligence Training Academy (JCITA), and the FBI Academy. By working closely with the contractors cleared under the NISP, the CI Office is in a unique position to not only provide advice and assistance to industry but to also provide the DoD CI community with insight into the contractor community and how they can become active participants in the CI process. To accomplish its mission, the CI Office is task organized into four divisions: Field Operations, Analysis and Production, Issues, and Operations Support.

CI Objectives:

- Provide for the early detection and referral of potential espionage cases.
- Assist industry in the recognition and reporting of foreign intelligence and non-state actors' collection attempts.
- Develop security countermeasures and advise industry on their application.
- Support industry's growing involvement in the international market place as more U.S. production efforts are relocated to overseas locations.

Priorities:

- In coordination with the Industrial Security Program, design, develop, implement, and evaluate a DSS transformational initiative which provides for a pilot program allowing limited Defense SIPRNET (Secure Internet Protocol Router Network) To Industry (DSTI).
- Obtain additional resources to fund a CI Analyst at each Industrial Field Office, the Defense Joint Intelligence Operations Center (DJIOC), and the Foreign Supplier Assessment Center (FSAC).
- Provide threat awareness to industry through the annual publication of the DSS Technology Trends.
- Develop, publish, and update a DSS CI Functional Support Plan.
- Establish and maintain strong relationships with NCIX and CIFA RTP, CIP, ATFP, C3T, and IT Program Managers.
- Update the DSS CI classified and unclassified web pages.

Point of Contact

Defense Security Service, 1340 Braddock Place, Alexandria VA 22314. Office 703-325-9471. Fax: 703-325-6545

Source The Defense Security Service (DSS). 2006. <http://www.dss.mil/>

DRUG ENFORCEMENT ADMINISTRATION

The mission of the Drug Enforcement Administration (DEA) is to enforce the controlled substances laws and regulations of the United States and bring to the criminal and civil justice system of the United States, or any other competent jurisdiction, those organizations and principal members of organizations, involved in the growing, manufacture, or distribution of controlled substances appearing in or destined for illicit traffic in the United States; and to recommend and support non-enforcement programs aimed at reducing the availability of illicit controlled substances on the domestic and international markets.

In carrying out its mission as the agency responsible for enforcing the controlled substances laws and regulations of the United States, the DEA's primary responsibilities include:

- Investigation and preparation for the prosecution of major violators of controlled substance laws operating at interstate and international levels.
- Investigation and preparation for prosecution of criminals and drug gangs who perpetrate violence in our communities and terrorize citizens through fear and intimidation.
- Management of a national drug intelligence program in cooperation with federal, state, local, and foreign officials to collect, analyze, and disseminate strategic and operational drug intelligence information.
- Seizure and forfeiture of assets derived from, traceable to, or intended to be used for illicit drug trafficking.
- Enforcement of the provisions of the Controlled Substances Act as they pertain to the manufacture, distribution, and dispensing of legally produced controlled substances.
- Coordination and cooperation with federal, state, and local law enforcement officials on mutual drug enforcement efforts and enhancement of such efforts through exploitation of potential interstate and international investigations beyond local or limited federal jurisdictions and resources.
- Coordination and cooperation with federal, state, and local agencies, and with foreign governments, in programs designed to reduce the availability of illicit abuse-type drugs on the United States market through non-enforcement methods such as crop eradication, crop substitution, and training of foreign officials.
- Responsibility, under the policy guidance of the Secretary of State and U.S. Ambassadors, for all programs associated with drug law enforcement counterparts in foreign countries.
- Liaison with the United Nations, Interpol, and other organizations on matters relating to international drug control programs.

Points of Contact

Drug Enforcement Administration headquarters, 2401 Jefferson Davis Highway, Alexandria, VA 22301. Telephone: (800) 882-9539

Field Offices

Atlanta Division	(404) 893-7000
Boston Division	(617) 557-2100
Caribbean Division	(787) 775-1815
Chicago Division	(312) 353-7875
Dallas Division	(214) 366-6900
Denver Division	(303) 705-7300
Detroit Division	(313) 234-4000
El Paso Division	(915) 832-6000
Houston Division	(713) 693-3000
Los Angeles Division	(213) 621-6700
Miami Division	(305) 994-4870
New Jersey Division	(973) 776-1100
New Orleans Division	(504) 840-1100
New York Division	(212) 337-3900
Philadelphia Division	(215) 861-3474
Phoenix Division	(602) 664-5600
San Diego Division	(858) 616-4100
San Francisco Division	(415) 436-7900
Seattle Division	(206) 553-5443
St. Louis Division	(314) 538-4600
Washington DC Division	(202) 305-8500

Source Drug Enforcement Administration (DEA). 2006. <http://www.dea.gov/>

FEDERAL AIR MARSHAL SERVICE

The TSA Office of Law Enforcement directs all TSA law enforcement activities and related critical incident management functions. It includes the Federal Air Marshal Service and the TSA National Explosives Detection Canine Program.

Federal Air Marshals serve as the primary law enforcement entity within the Transportation Security Administration and are deployed on flights around the world and in the United States. While their primary mission of protecting air passengers and crew has not changed much over the years, Federal Air Marshals have an ever expanding role in homeland security and work closely with other law enforcement agencies to accomplish their mission. Currently, air marshals staff several positions at different organizations such as the National Counterterrorism Center, the National Targeting Center, and on the FBI's Joint Terrorism Task Forces. In addition, they are also distributed among other law enforcement and homeland security liaison assignments during times of heightened alert or special national events.

The Federal Air Marshal Service has twenty-one field offices strategically located near our nation's airports. Assistant Federal Security Directors for Law Enforcement are stationed directly at airports across the country. There are also Federal Air Marshals attached to each of the fifty-six FBI Joint Terrorism Task Forces nationally.

History

In the late 1960s, a rash of hijackings of U.S. flagged commercial air carriers necessitated the creation of a program aimed at halting the increasing threat to passenger safety. In an agreement signed in October 1970 between the Departments of the Treasury and Transportation, the U.S. Customs Service was given the responsibility to establish an enforcement program aimed at eliminating this threat.

The result was the creation of the Customs Air Security Officers Program, more familiarly known as the "Sky Marshal Program." Starting in late 1970, 1,784 men and women completed intense, rigorous training at the U.S. Army's Fort Belvoir in Virginia.

Placed on American aircraft dressed as typical passengers, the Customs Air Security Officers were flying armed and ready to thwart an attempted hijacking at a moment's notice. This program ceased operations in June 1974 when x-ray screening equipment was introduced in the nation's airports.

In response to the hijacking of TWA Flight 847 in 1985, President Ronald Reagan directed the Secretary of Transportation, in cooperation with the Secretary of State, to explore expansion of the armed Sky Marshal program aboard international flights for U.S. air carriers. Congress responded by passing the International Security and Development Cooperation Act (Public Law 99-83), which provided the statutes that supported the Federal Air Marshal Service.

On September 11, 2001, the Air Marshal Program consisted of less than fifty armed marshals who, by statute, flew only on international flights flown by U.S. air carriers. The tragic events which unfolded that day demonstrated the need for an expanded law enforcement presence on board American carriers on both foreign and domestic flights.

Federal Flight Deck Officers

The September 11, 2001 terrorist attacks tragically demonstrated the need for a multi-layered approach to securing commercial airliners—and in particular the cockpit—from terrorist and criminal assault. In addition to improved security at airport checkpoints, the use of federal air marshals, and the hardening of cockpit doors, the Transportation Security Administration developed the Federal Flight Deck Officer program as an additional layer of security.

Under this program, eligible flight crew members are authorized by the Transportation Security Administration to use firearms to defend against an act of criminal violence or air piracy attempting to gain control of an aircraft. A flight crew member may be a pilot, flight engineer, or navigator assigned to the flight.

In December 2003, President George W. Bush signed into law legislation that expanded program eligibility to include cargo pilots and certain other flight crewmembers.

Federal Flight Deck Officers are trained on the use of firearms, use of force, legal issues, defensive tactics, the psychology of survival and program standard operating procedures. Flight crew members participating in the program are not eligible for compensation from the Federal Government for services provided as a Federal Flight Deck Officer.

Point of Contact

Federal Air Marshal Service,
   Transportation Security Administration,
   601 South 12th Street, Arlington, VA
   22202-4220. TSA Contact Center: 1-866-
   289-9673.

Source   Federal Air Marshal Service. 2006.
<http://www.tsa.gov/lawenforcement/>

FEDERAL BUREAU OF INVESTIGATION

 The mission of the Federal Bureau of Investigation (FBI) is to protect and defend the United States against terrorist and foreign intelligence threats, to uphold and enforce the criminal laws of the United States, and to provide leadership and criminal justice services to federal, state, municipal, and international agencies and partners. FBI priorities are:

- Protect the United States from terrorist attack.
- Protect the United States against foreign intelligence operations and espionage.
- Protect the United States against cyber-based attacks and high-technology crimes.
- Combat public corruption at all levels.
- Protect civil rights.
- Combat transnational/national criminal organizations and enterprises.
- Combat major white-collar crime.
- Combat significant violent crime.
- Support federal, state, local, and international partners.
- Upgrade technology to successfully perform the mission.

As of March 31, 2006, the FBI had a total of 30,430 employees. That includes 12,515 special agents and 17,915 support staff, such as intelligence analysts, language specialists, scientists, information technology specialists, and other professionals.

Budget and Strategic Plan

In fiscal year 2005, the FBI's total budget was approximately $5.9 billion, including $425 million in net program increases to enhance counterterrorism, counterintelligence, cyber crime, information technology, security, forensics, training, and criminal programs.

Locations

The FBI works literally around the globe. Along with its Headquarters in Washington, D.C., the FBI has 56 field offices located in major cities throughout the U.S., more than 400 resident agencies in smaller cities and towns across the nation, and more than 50 international offices called "Legal Attaches" in U.S. embassies worldwide.

Points of Contact

The Federal Bureau of Investigation, 601
   4th Street, N.W., Washington, D.C.
   20535-0002. washingtondc.fbi.gov. (202)
   278-2000

Field Offices

FBI Albany
200 McCarty Avenue
Albany, New York 12209
albany.fbi.gov
(518) 465-7551

FBI Albuquerque

4200 Luecking Park Ave. NE
Albuquerque, New Mexico 87107
albuquerque.fbi.gov
(505) 889-1300

FBI Anchorage

101 East Sixth Avenue
Anchorage, Alaska 99501-2524
anchorage.fbi.gov
(907) 276-4441

FBI Atlanta

Suite 400
2635 Century Parkway, Northeast
Atlanta, Georgia 30345-3112
atlanta.fbi.gov
(404) 679-9000

FBI Baltimore

2600 Lord Baltimore
Baltimore, Maryland 21244
baltimore.fbi.gov
(410) 265-8080

FBI Birmingham

1000 18th Street North
Birmingham, Alabama 35203
birmingham.fbi.gov
(205) 326-6166

FBI Boston

Suite 600
One Center Plaza
Boston, Massachusetts 02108
boston.fbi.gov
(617) 742-5533

FBI Buffalo

One FBI Plaza
Buffalo, New York 14202-2698
buffalo.fbi.gov
(716) 856-7800

FBI Charlotte

Suite 900, Wachovia Building
400 South Tyron Street

Charlotte, North Carolina 28285-0001
charlotte.fbi.gov
(704) 377-9200

FBI Chicago

2111 West Roosevelt Road Chicago,
   IL 60608-1128
chicago.fbi.gov
(312) 421-6700

FBI Cincinnati

Room 9000
550 Main Street
Cincinnati, Ohio 45202-8501
cincinnati.fbi.gov
(513) 421-4310

FBI Cleveland

Federal Office Building
1501 Lakeside Avenue
Cleveland, Ohio 44114
cleveland.fbi.gov
(216) 522-1400

FBI Columbia

151 Westpark Blvd
Columbia, South Carolina 29210-3857
columbia.fbi.gov
(803) 551-4200

FBI Dallas

One Justice Way
Dallas, Texas 75220
dallas.fbi.gov
(972) 559-5000

FBI Denver

Federal Office Building, Room 1823
1961 Stout Street, 18th Floor
Denver, Colorado 80294-1823
denver.fbi.gov
(303) 629-7171

FBI Detroit

26th. Floor, P. V. McNamara FOB
477 Michigan Avenue
Detroit, Michigan 48226
detroit.fbi.gov
(313) 965-2323

FBI El Paso

660 S. Mesa Hills Drive
El Paso, Texas 79912-5533
elpaso.fbi.gov
(915) 832-5000

FBI Honolulu

Room 4-230, Kalanianaole FOB
300 Ala Moana Boulevard
Honolulu, Hawaii 96850-0053
honolulu.fbi.gov
(808) 566-4300

FBI Houston

2500 East TC Jester
Houston, Texas 77008-1300
houston.fbi.gov
(713) 693-5000

FBI Indianapolis

Room 679, FOB
575 North Pennsylvania Street
Indianapolis, Indiana 46204-1585
indianapolis.fbi.gov
(317) 639-3301

FBI Jackson

Room 1553, FOB
100 West Capitol Street
Jackson, Mississippi 39269-1601
jackson.fbi.gov
(601) 948-5000

FBI Jacksonville

Suite 200
7820 Arlington Expressway
Jacksonville, Florida 32211-7499
jacksonville.fbi.gov
(904) 721-1211

FBI Kansas City

1300 Summit
Kansas City, Missouri 64105-1362
kansascity.fbi.gov
(816) 512-8200

FBI Knoxville

Suite 600, John J. Duncan FOB
710 Locust Street
Knoxville, Tennessee 37902-2537
knoxville.fbi.gov
(865) 544-0751

FBI Las Vegas

John Lawrence Bailey Building
700 East Charleston Boulevard
Las Vegas, Nevada 89104-1545
lasvegas.fbi.gov
(702) 385-1281

FBI Little Rock

#24 Shackleford West Boulevard
Little Rock, Arkansas 72211-3755
littlerock.fbi.gov
(501) 221-9100

FBI Los Angeles

Suite 1700, FOB
11000 Wilshire Boulevard
Los Angeles, California 90024-3672
losangeles.fbi.gov
(310) 477-6565

FBI Louisville

Room 500
600 Martin Luther King Jr. Place
Louisville, Kentucky 40202-2231
louisville.fbi.gov
(502) 583-3941

FBI Memphis

Suite 3000, Eagle Crest Bldg.
225 North Humphreys Blvd.
Memphis, Tennessee 38120-2107
memphis.fbi.gov
(901) 747-4300

FBI Milwaukee

Suite 600
330 East Kilbourn Avenue
Milwaukee, Wisconsin 53202-6627
milwaukee.fbi.gov
(414) 276-4684

FBI Minneapolis

Suite 1100
111 Washington Avenue, South
Minneapolis, Minnesota 55401-2176
minneapolis.fbi.gov
(612) 376-3200

FBI North Miami Beach

16320 Northwest Second Avenue
North Miami Beach, Florida 33169-6508
miami.fbi.gov
(305) 944-9101

FBI Mobile

One St. Louis Centre
200 N. Royal Street
Mobile, Alabama 36602
mobile.fbi.gov
(251) 438-3674

FBI New Haven

600 State Street
New Haven, Connecticut 06511-6505
newhaven.fbi.gov
(203) 777-6311

FBI Newark

11 Centre Place
Newark, New Jersey 07102-9889
newark.fbi.gov
(973) 792-3000

FBI New Orleans

2901 Leon C. Simon Dr.
New Orleans, Louisiana 70126
neworleans.fbi.gov
(504) 816-3000

FBI New York

26 Federal Plaza, 23rd. Floor
New York, New York 10278-0004
newyork.fbi.gov
(212) 384-1000

FBI Norfolk

150 Corporate Boulevard
Norfolk, Virginia 23502-4999
norfolk.fbi.gov
(757) 455-0100

FBI Oklahoma City

3301 West Memorial Drive
Oklahoma City, Oklahoma 73134
oklahomacity.fbi.gov
(405) 290-7770

FBI Omaha

10755 Burt Street
Omaha, Nebraska 68114-2000
omaha.fbi.gov
(402) 493-8688

FBI Philadelphia

8th. Floor
William J. Green Jr. FOB
600 Arch Street
Philadelphia, Pennsylvania 19106
philadelphia.fbi.gov
(215) 418-4000

FBI Pittsburgh

3311 East Carson St.
Pittsburgh, PA 15203
pittsburgh.fbi.gov
(412) 432-4000

FBI Phoenix

Suite 400
201 East Indianola Avenue
Phoenix, Arizona 85012-2080
phoenix.fbi.gov
(602) 279-5511

FBI Portland

Suite 400, Crown Plaza Building
1500 Southwest 1st Avenue
Portland, Oregon 97201-5828
portland.fbi.gov
(503) 224-4181

FBI Richmond

1970 E. Parham Road
Richmond, Virginia 23228
richmond.fbi.gov
(804) 261-1044

FBI Sacramento

4500 Orange Grove Avenue
Sacramento, California 95841-4205
sacramento.fbi.gov
(916) 481-9110

FBI St. Louis

2222 Market Street
St. Louis, Missouri 63103-2516
stlouis.fbi.gov
(314) 231-4324

FBI Salt Lake City

Suite 1200, 257 Towers Bldg.
257 East, 200 South
Salt Lake City, Utah 84111-2048
saltlakecity.fbi.gov
(801) 579-1400

FBI San Antonio

Suite 200
U.S. Post Office Courthouse Bldg.
615 East Houston Street
San Antonio, Texas 78205-9998
sanantonio.fbi.gov
(210) 225-6741

FBI San Diego

Federal Office Building
9797 Aero Drive
San Diego, California 92123-1800
sandiego.fbi.gov
(858) 565-1255

FBI San Francisco

450 Golden Gate Avenue, 13th. Floor
San Francisco, California 94102-9523
sanfrancisco.fbi.gov
(415) 553-7400

FBI San Juan

Room 526, U.S. Federal Bldg.
150 Carlos Chardon Avenue
Hato Rey
San Juan, Puerto Rico 00918-1716
sanjuan.fbi.gov
(787) 754-6000

FBI Seattle

1110 Third Avenue
Seattle, Washington 98101-2904
seattle.fbi.gov
(206) 622-0460

FBI Springfield

900 East Linton Avenue
Springfield, Illinois 62703
springfield.fbi.gov
(217) 522-9675

FBI Tampa

5525 West Gray Street
Tampa, Florida 33609
tampa.fbi.gov
(813) 253-1000

Source The Federal Bureau of Investigation. 2006. <http://www.fbi.gov/quickfacts.htm>

IMMIGRATION AND CUSTOMS ENFORCEMENT

Created in March 2003, Immigration and Customs Enforcement (ICE) is the largest investigative branch of the Department of Homeland Security (DHS). The agency was created after 9/11, by combining the law enforcement arms of the former Immigration and Naturalization Service (INS) and the former U.S. Customs Service, to more effectively enforce our immigration and customs laws and to protect the United States against terrorist attacks. ICE does this by targeting illegal immigrants: the people, money, and materials that support terrorism and other criminal activities. ICE is a key component of the DHS "layered defense" approach to protecting the nation.

The ICE mission is to protect America and uphold public safety. They fulfill this mission by identifying criminal activities and eliminating vulnerabilities that pose a threat to our nation's borders, as well as enforcing economic, transportation, and infrastructure security. By protecting our national and border security, ICE seeks to eliminate the potential threat of terrorist acts against the United States.

Before 9/11, immigration and customs authorities were not widely recognized as an effective counterterrorism tool in the United States. ICE changed this by creating a host of new systems to better address national security threats and to detect potential terrorist activities in the U.S. ICE targets the people, money, and materials that support terrorist and criminal activity.

Operation Community Shield

Operation Community Shield, launched in March 2005, is ICE's comprehensive law enforcement initiative targeting violent criminal street gangs nationwide. Initially, the focus of the effort was the Mara Salvatrucha organization, commonly referred to as "MS-13," one of the most violent and rapidly growing of these street gangs.

In May 2005, ICE expanded Operation Community Shield to include all criminal street gangs that pose a risk to public safety and a concern to national security, putting into motion an aggressive law enforcement action with the goal to investigate, arrest, and prosecute any violent street gang members, leaders, and/or associates of MS-13, as well as other gangs such as Sureños, 18th Street gang, Latin Kings, Vatos Locos, Mexican Mafia, La Raza gang, Border Brothers, Brown Pride, Norteno, Florencia 13, Tiny Rascal, Asian Boyz, and Jamaican Posse, that routinely seek to exploit or engage in violent criminal activities.

In these efforts, ICE focuses on a single goal: dismantling gang organizations by targeting its members, seizing its financial assets, and disrupting its criminal operations.

Worksite Enforcement

Worksite enforcement plays an important role in the fight against illegal immigration and in protecting the homeland. ICE has developed a comprehensive worksite enforcement strategy that promotes national security, protects critical infrastructure, and ensures fair labor standards.

The Worksite Enforcement Unit's mission encompasses enforcement activities intended to mitigate the risk of terrorist attacks posed by unauthorized workers employed in secure areas of our nation's critical infrastructure. In order to fulfill this mission, ICE special agents apply risk assessment principles to their critical infrastructure and worksite enforcement cases in order to maximize the impact of limited resources against the most significant threats and violators.

Though worksite enforcement efforts are focused on investigations related to critical infrastructure and national security, these efforts and resources are also extended to other places of employment. Unauthorized workers employed at sensitive sites and critical infrastructure facilities—such as airports, seaports, nuclear plants, chemical plants, and defense facilities—pose serious homeland security threats.

Worksite enforcement investigations often involve egregious violations of criminal statutes by employers and widespread abuses, and by uncovering such violations ICE can send a strong deterrent message to other employers who knowingly employ illegal aliens. These worksite enforcement cases often involve additional violations such as alien smuggling, alien harboring, document fraud, money laundering, fraud, or worker exploitation.

ICE agents use many tools to conduct these worksite enforcement investigations, among them a Forensic Documents Laboratory, which determines the authenticity of documents used to establish employment eligibility. ICE also works with the private sector to educate employers about their responsibilities to hire only authorized workers and how to accurately verify employment eligibility.

Illegal workers frequently lack the employment protections afforded those with legal status. and are less likely to report workplace safety violations and other concerns. In addition, unscrupulous employers are likely to pay illegal workers substandard wages or force them to endure intolerable working conditions. In addition to alleviating the potential threat

posed to national security, these efforts prohibit employers from taking advantage of illegal workers. The Worksite Enforcement Unit also helps employers improve worksite enforcement of employment regulations. The unit is currently engaged in developing automated mechanisms that will enable security agencies controlling access to sensitive facilities to verify immigration status independently before granting access to new employees.

Identity and Benefit Fraud

Immigration fraud poses a severe threat to national security and public safety because it creates a vulnerability that may enable terrorists, criminals, and illegal aliens to gain entry to and remain in the United States. A concentrated national effort to combat immigration fraud aids many other programs in accomplishing their goals and objectives. Identity and benefit fraud are elements of many immigration-related issues such as human smuggling and trafficking, critical infrastructure protection, worksite and compliance enforcement, and national security investigations. Immigration fraud is also a component of other types of fraud involving state drivers' licenses, state-issued public assistance, and Social Security fraud. The IBFU also coordinates its efforts with other ICE entities such as the Office of Intelligence and other components of the Department of Homeland Security such as U.S. Customs and Border Protection and U.S. Citizenship and Immigration Services (USCIS), as well as other federal agencies such as the Department of State and Department of Labor.

Benefit Fraud

Benefit Fraud is the willful misrepresentation of material fact on a petition or application to gain an immigration benefit. Benefit fraud is an extremely lucrative form of white-collar crime that is complex and challenging to investigate, often involving sophisticated schemes and multiple co-conspirators that take years to investigate and prosecute. Benefit fraud has serious consequences, because the perpetrator gains an immigration benefit even though it was obtained fraudulently.

Identity Theft

Also known as document fraud, identify theft is the manufacturing, counterfeiting, alteration, sale, and/or use of identity documents and other fraudulent documents to circumvent immigration laws or for other criminal activity. Identity fraud does not itself confer lawful status upon the perpetrator. Identity fraud often underlies or supports the crime of benefit fraud. Identity fraud in some cases also involves identity theft, a crime in which an imposter takes on the identity of a real person (living or deceased) for some illegal purpose.

Document and Benefit Fraud Task Forces

As of this writing, the Department of Homeland Security, Department of Justice, Department of Labor, Department of State, and other agencies plan to create Document and Benefit Fraud Task Forces in 10 major U.S. cities. These are Atlanta, Ga.; Boston, Mass.; Dallas, Texas; Denver, Colo.; Detroit, Mich.; Los Angeles, Calif.; New York, N.Y.; Newark, N.J.; Philadelphia, Pa.; and St. Paul, Minn.

Led by ICE, the task forces will build on existing partnerships to bring investigators together from a variety of agencies with expertise in different aspects of document and benefit fraud. These agents will partner with U.S. Attorney's Offices to formulate a comprehensive approach in targeting criminal organizations as well as the ineligible beneficiaries. Any case in which a sufficient nexus to terrorism is discovered will be referred to the Joint Terrorism Task Forces.

Participants in the task forces include ICE, the Department of Justice, U.S. Citizenship and Immigration Services (USCIS), Department of Labor Office of Inspector General, Social Security Administration Office of Inspector General, State Department Office of Inspector General, State Department Bureau of Diplomatic Security, U.S. Postal Inspection Service, U.S. Secret Service, and various other state and local law enforcement agencies. The task forces will primarily target two types of crimes:

Document Fraud. This crime refers to the manufacture, sale or use of counterfeit identity documents, such as fake drivers' licenses, birth certificates, social security cards, or passports, for immigration fraud or other criminal activity. Document fraud also includes efforts to obtain genuine identity documents through fraudulent means. These activities have helped illegal aliens, criminals and even terrorists evade detection and embed themselves in our society. Document fraud often supports the crime of benefit fraud.

The threat posed by document fraud is exemplified by the fact that at least seven of the 9/11 hijackers obtained genuine Virginia identity documents by submitting fraudulent Virginia residency certificates. Using these ID cards, the hijackers were able to clear airport security and board aircraft for the attacks.

Benefit Fraud. This crime refers to the misrepresentation or omission of material facts on an application to obtain an immigration benefit one is not entitled to—such as U.S. citizenship, political asylum, or a valid visa. Because these benefits give one the ability to freely enter, work, or reside in this country, they are prized by illegal aliens, criminals, and terrorists who may be willing to pay substantial fees for them. As a result, the criminal organizations that help individuals fraudulently obtain immigration benefits reap enormous profits.

Illegal Trade

Working with U.S. Customs and Border Protection (CBP), ICE plays an integral role in protecting the American public from international terrorism. One of the ways ICE achieves this mission is through initiatives such as Project Shield America—part of ICE's strategy to prohibit illegal exporters, foreign countries, terrorist groups, and international crime organizations from trafficking in weapons of mass destruction (WMD) and the various components, licensable commodities, technologies, conventional munitions, and firearms that are part of WMD.

There has been a need for an initiative such as Project Shield America since World War II, as adversaries of the U.S. began to acquire U.S. and Western technology by both legal and illegal means. Nuclear, chemical, and biological weapons and their components are more widely available to terrorists and rogue nations now than at any other time in our history.

Project Shield America works in concert with a three-pronged effort:

1. CBP inspectors stationed at high-threat ports selectively inspect suspect export shipments.
2. ICE special agents deployed throughout the country initiate and pursue high-quality cases that result in the arrest, prosecution, and conviction of violators of various acts and statutes that prohibit illegal export and trading.
3. ICE attaché offices enlist the support of their host governments to help initiate new investigative leads based on information provided by their foreign contacts, and to develop information in support of ongoing domestic investigations.

ICE recommends that industry partners implement an export management system (EMS), consisting of several elements that can facilitate export control. These elements include:

- A policy statement demonstrating senior management's commitment to export control.
- Identification of persons within the company who are responsible for export control.
- An up-to-date training program for employees with export responsibilities.
- A program for maintaining records in compliance with export regulations.
- Periodic internal review of the EMS.
- A procedure for dealing with violations or noncompliance of exports regulations.
- A strict policy of reporting suspicious orders or inquiries to ICE.

Human Trafficking and Human Smuggling

Human trafficking and human smuggling represent significant risks to homeland security. Would-be terrorists and criminals can often access the same routes and utilize the same methods being used by human smugglers. The Human Smuggling and Trafficking Unit of ICE works to identify criminals and organizations involved in these illicit activities.

Human Trafficking. Recruitment, harboring, transportation, provision, or obtaining of a person for labor or services, through the use of force, fraud or coercion for the purpose of subjection to involuntary servitude, peonage, debt bondage, or slavery is human trafficking. Sex trafficking occurs when a commercial sex act is induced by force, fraud, or coercion, or when the person induced to perform such acts has not attained 18 years of age.

Human Smuggling. The importation of people into the country via the deliberate evasion of immigration laws is human smuggling. This offense includes bringing illegal aliens into the United States as well as the unlawful transportation and harboring of aliens already in the country illegally.

Some smuggling situations may involve murder, rape, and assault. The perpetration of violent crime in itself does not constitute human trafficking, because its elements remain fraud or coercion for commercial sex or forced labor.

ICE has developed initiatives that focus on attacking the infrastructure that supports smuggling organizations as well as the assets that are derived from these criminal activities. This includes seizing currency, property, weapons, and vehicles.

One of the new tools that helps ICE fight human smuggling and trafficking is the Civil Asset Forfeiture Reform Act (CAFRA). The Act requires that notices be given to property owners whose properties have been identified as being used to facilitate smuggling or harboring aliens. This is an important tool because many employers turn a blind eye to the facilitation of criminal activity on their properties.

National Fugitive Operations Program

Congress passed the landmark USA PATRIOT Act in response to 9/11. Pursuant to the war on terrorism, and in support of this act, several measures were taken to protect the homeland. The Absconder Apprehension Initiative was established, making the apprehension of absconders, or fugitives, a priority within the Department of Homeland Security. On February 25, 2002, the National Fugitive Operations Program (NFOP) was officially established under the auspices of the Office of Detention and Removal.

The primary mission of NFOP is to identify, locate, apprehend, process, and remove fugitive aliens from the United States, with the highest priority placed on those fugitives who have been convicted of crimes. Furthermore, NFOP's goal is to eliminate the backlog of fugitives and ensure that the number of aliens deported equals the number of final orders of removal issued by the immigration courts in any given year.

The NFOP Fugitive Operations Teams strategically deployed around the country work solely on those cases identified as fugitives, and attempt to locate and apprehend those persons, who will ultimately be removed from the United States.

The NFOP serves as a resolution unit, assisting in the preparation of cases for entry into the National Crime Information Center (NCIC) database. NFOP also serves as a clearinghouse for all leads regarding fugitive aliens. Through the use of command centers, NFOP forwards "hot leads" (information identifying the possible locations of these absconders) to the appropriate Fugitive Operations Team for resolution. These "hot leads" are based on information from other law enforcement entities, both internal and external, as well as on information gathered through internal intelligence assets.

Most Wanted Criminal Aliens

The ICE Most Wanted Criminal Aliens list is focused on foreign nationals from around the globe who have been convicted of committing serious crimes in the United States and served their time. Each of these criminal aliens have been issued orders of removal, commonly referred to as deportation orders, but have eluded law enforcement, thereby posing a continuing threat to public safety.

Training

The NFOP training course is conducted at the ICE Academy located at the Federal Law Enforcement Training Center (FLETC), providing the ICE officer with the tools necessary to locate and apprehend fugitive aliens. A major focus of the course is to enable participants to effectively utilize Internet, database, and other sources of information to locate where a fugitive lives, visits, and/or works.

Liaison Activities

ICE's Office of Detention and Removal (DRO), and in particular the NFOP, liaise with all federal, state, and local law enforcement agencies. One of the ways that outside law enforcement agencies can assist the NFOP is by participating in local Joint Fugitive Task Forces. Task forces already exist in several areas, with ICE officers participating.

Financial and Trade Investigations

Terrorist and other criminal organizations constantly seek diverse ways to finance their illicit operations and avoid detection by law enforcement. Recognizing the need to adapt and adjust to this fluid environment, ICE established the Cornerstone Initiative program. It seeks to detect and close down vulnerabilities within U.S. financial, trade, and transportation sectors that could be exploited by these criminal networks. Criminal organizations use many methods to earn, move, and store illicit funds:

- Bulk cash smuggling (BCS) continues to be a major method utilized by criminal organizations to move illicit funds.
- Alternative financing mechanisms are often used to launder illicit proceeds.
- Money service businesses, financial institutions, and international trade and transportation sectors are often utilized by criminal organizations to accomplish their goals.
- Common highly profitable cross-border crimes include commercial fraud, IPR violations, immigration violations, identity

and benefits fraud, contraband and alien smuggling, and human trafficking.

Money Laundering

Money laundering is the legitimization of proceeds from illegal activity. To make a profit, illicit proceeds of crimes must be introduced (laundered) into the world's legitimate financial systems. Criminal organizations transform illicit monetary proceeds into funds derived from an apparent legal source. Three primary stages of money laundering are:

1. Placement of illegal funds into financial systems.
2. Layering funds through a series of mechanisms, such as wire transfers, designed to complicate the paper trail.
3. Integrating the laundered funds back into the legitimate economy through the purchase of real estate, businesses, and other investments.

Money laundering has devastating social consequences. It is estimated to introduce hundreds of billions of illegal dollars into the world's economy every year. If left unchecked, it can erode the integrity of financial institutions, and in some cases threaten a nation's very sovereignty. Money laundering extends beyond hiding narcotics profits. Trade fraud, alien smuggling and human trafficking, organized crime, arms smuggling, child pornography, and other criminally defined offenses all contribute to a money-laundering epidemic that knows no borders.

Commercial Fraud

Commercial fraud investigations focus on commercial importations involving false statements and deceptive business practices. Fraud investigations are important components of an overall trade strategy whereby ICE concentrates on enforcing revenue protection and non-revenue (e.g., trademark, quota, health) protection laws and regulations. Successful cases produce significant seizures, civil penalties, and/or criminal prosecutions.

The Financial and Trade Investigations Division of ICE oversees several programs aimed at stopping predatory and unfair trade practices that threaten our economic stability, restrict the competitiveness of U.S. industry in world markets, and place the public health and safety of the American people at risk. These programs include NAFTA/trade agreements, in-bond diversion, textile fraud, anti-dumping/countervailing duties, forced labor (child/prison), tobacco, public health/safety and environmental crimes, and endangered species trafficking. Combating commercial fraud is the basis of important links to the international trade community, and more importantly, to the war on terrorism. Fraud investigations have identified systems shortfalls, which could facilitate the illegal importation of weapons of mass destruction and chemical/biological agents. They also have shown how fraudulent importations may generate illegal revenues for organizations engaged in international organized crime.

Counterfeit merchandise not only represents a billion dollar industry at the expense of American companies, it also represents a public safety hazard when the merchandise involves medicines, auto and aircraft parts, as well as inferior hardware that could potentially be used in the construction of buildings, bridges, and other major structures. ICE, along with the FBI, run the National Intellectual Property Rights Coordination Center (IPR Coordination Center) based in Washington. It serves as a collection point for IPR intelligence, and a national point of contact for IPR-related matters.

In-Bond Diversion

In-bond diversion occurs when an importer brings merchandise through the U.S., allegedly intended only for export. Once in the U.S., the importer doesn't move the merchandise out of the country thereby illegally circumventing duty payments, quota and visa restrictions and sometimes introducing restricted or prohibited merchandise into this country.

In-bond diversion is probably the biggest single commercial fraud threat. To address this problem, the Commercial Fraud and IPR Unit has partnered with CBP to target high-risk commodities such as textiles, tobacco, and liquor for intensive inspection and surveillance. This initiative has led to an increase in seizures, penalties, ,and arrests for fraud.

National Intellectual Property Rights Coordination Center

As the largest investigative arm of the Department of Homeland Security, ICE plays a leading role in targeting criminal organizations responsible for producing, smuggling, and distributing counterfeit products. Some of these products, such as pharmaceuticals and counterfeit merchandise, are protected by IPR.

In many cases, the enormous profits realized from the sale of counterfeit goods are used by international organized crime groups to bankroll other criminal activities, such as the trafficking in illegal drugs, weapons, and other contraband.

In recent years, counterfeiting, piracy, and other IPR violations have grown in magnitude and complexity, costing U.S. businesses billions of dollars in lost revenue and often posing health and safety risks to U.S. consumers.

The growth in IPR violations has been fueled in part by the spread of enabling technology allowing for simple and low-cost duplication of copyrighted products, as well as by the rise in organized crime groups that smuggle and distribute counterfeit merchandise for profit. ICE investigations focus not only on keeping counterfeit products off U.S. streets, but also on dismantling the criminal organizations behind this activity.

ICE agents use a variety of assets and resources to combat the counterfeiting problem, including the National Intellectual Property Rights Coordination Center (IPR Center), the ICE Cyber Crimes Center, and attaché offices overseas.

The IPR Center is staffed with agents and analysts from ICE, U.S. Customs and Border Protection, and the FBI. The Center coordinates the U.S. government's domestic and international law enforcement attack on IPR violations. ICE agents in the United States and abroad work closely with the Cyber Crimes Center in detecting IPR violations committed via the Internet. Attaché offices around the globe coordinate IPR investigative efforts with host nation law enforcement.

Located in Washington, DC, the IPR Center is a multi-agency organization responsible for coordinating a unified U.S. government response regarding IPR enforcement issues. Investigative personnel provide core staffing from ICE and the FBI. Particular emphasis is given to investigating major criminal organizations and those using the Internet to facilitate IPR crime.

The IPR Center's responsibilities include:

- Coordinating U.S. government domestic and international law enforcement activities involving IPR issues.
- Serving as a collection point for intelligence provided by private industry, as well as a channel for law enforcement to obtain cooperation from private industry (in specific law enforcement situations).
- Integrating domestic and international law enforcement intelligence with private industry information relating to IPR crime.
- Disseminating IPR intelligence for appropriate investigative and tactical use.
- Developing enhanced investigative, intelligence, and interdiction capabilities.
- Serving as a point of contact for U.S. government agencies, the Executive Department, Congress, and media outlets.

Telemarketing Fraud

Every year U.S. consumers lose millions of dollars through telemarketing and other consumer-related mail and wire frauds. These frauds include fictitious lottery winnings, phony inheritances, and bogus investment opportunities or credit offers. ICE investigates this cross-border crime, which frequently targets the elderly and other vulnerable segments. Since 1998, ICE has been a member of Project Colt, an international, multi-agency task force based in Montreal, Canada. It was created to combat Canadian-based telemarketing fraud.

Federal Protective Service

Federal Protective Service (FPS) protects federal buildings and the employees within them through measures such as risk assessment, security and surveillance support, and safety education. In addition, FPS performs several roles that assist the general public. One of these roles is to keep the public safe while in a federal building. This includes training federal building employees on procedures to follow in emergencies.

Code Adam

On April 30, of the year it was conceived, the Code Adam Act of 2003 became a law. The act is named in the memory of six-year-old Adam Walsh, whose abduction from a Florida shopping mall and murder in 1981 helped to bring the horror of child abduction to national attention.

The Code Adam Alert requires that the designated authority for a public building establish procedures for a child missing in a federal facility. On November 1 of 2003, the Department of Homeland Security Federal Protective Service (FPS) implemented a policy nationwide that established procedures for locating a missing child in federal facilities. The General Services Administration administers the program in both owned and leased federal facilities.

Coordinating available resources during the first few minutes a child is missing is critical to a positive outcome. Regardless of where a child is reported missing, FPS instructs the following:

1. Alert a store or building employee, manager, or administrator with as detailed a description of the child as possible.
2. Contact local police authorities, and in the case of a federal building, the FPS or facility contract security guards.
3. Act immediately when the child is believed missing.

Operation Predator

ICE works with both local and international law enforcement agencies in a collaborative effort to combat crimes against children. Fifty-six attaché offices overseas and field offices around the U.S. provide technical support, particularly on child pornography over the Internet, and work closely with locals to ensure those who are deportable are deported.

Programs that fight these crimes are Internet Crimes Against Children Task Forces (ICACs) and the Virtual Global Task Force (VGTF).

Internet Crimes Against Children Task Forces (ICACs)

There are numerous ICACs around the country, providing forensic, investigative, training, technical support, victim services, and community education to state and local law enforcement agencies to help them develop an effective response to cyber enticement and child pornography cases.

Virtual Global Task Force (VGTF)

The VGTF is an international alliance of law enforcement agencies from the U.S., U.K., Australia and Canada, working together to make the Internet a safer place; to identify, locate and help children at risk; and to hold those who commit on-line child abuse appropriately accountable. On-line child abuse includes activities such as searching for, sharing, and downloading images of children being physically and sexually abused and engaging children in chat rooms with the intention of committing sexual abuse both on- and off-line. The VGT delivers innovative crime prevention and crime reduction initiatives to prevent and deter individuals from committing on-line child abuse.

ICE also partners with several Non-Governmental Organizations (NGOs), including the National Center for Missing & Exploited Children, Netsmartz, World Vision, and Rape, Abuse and Incest National Network.

The C3 Section

This section investigates the trans-border dimension of large-scale producers and distributors of images of child abuse, as well as individuals who travel in foreign commerce for the purpose of engaging in sex with minors. Within C3 is the Child Exploitation Section (CES). It employs the latest technology to collect evidence and track the activities of individuals and organized groups who sexually exploit children through the use of websites, chat rooms, newsgroups, and peer-to-peer trading. These investigative activities are organized under Operation Predator. The CES also conducts clandestine operations throughout the world to identify and apprehend violators, assists ICE field offices, and routinely coordinates major investigations. The CES works closely with law enforcement agencies from around the world because the exploitation of children is a matter of global importance.

A full range of computer and forensic assets work together in a single location to deal with such Internet-related crimes as:

- Possession, manufacture, and distribution of images of child abuse
- International money laundering and illegal cyber-banking
- Illegal arms trafficking and illegal export of strategic/controlled commodities
- Drug trafficking (including prohibited pharmaceuticals)
- General smuggling (including the trafficking in stolen art and antiquities; violations of the Endangered Species Act, etc.)
- Intellectual property rights violations (including music and software)
- Immigration violations
- Identity and benefit fraud

C3 is actually an umbrella organization. It consists of four sections, three of which provide cyber technical and investigative services, the Cyber Crimes Section (CCS), the Child Exploitation Section (CES), and the Digital Forensic Section (DFS). The fourth section, the Information Technology and Administrative Section (ITAS), provides the technical and operational infrastructure services necessary to support the other three C3 sections. The center is a co-location of special agents, intelligence research specialists, administrative staff, and contractors, all of which are instrumental in operational and technical continuity. Within each section, there are various program managers assigned to certain programmatic areas. These program managers are responsible for supporting Internet investigations through the generation and the dissemination of viable leads. Program managers are available to provide guidance and training to field agents as well as to other law enforcement agencies, both foreign and domestic.

Cyber Crimes Section

The Cyber Crimes Section (CCS) is responsible for developing and coordinating investigations of Immigration and Customs violations where the Internet is used to facilitate the criminal act. The CCS investigative responsibilities include fraud, theft of intellectual property rights,

money laundering, identity and benefit fraud, the sale and distribution of narcotics and other controlled substances, illegal arms trafficking, and the illegal export of strategic/controlled commodities and the smuggling and sale of other prohibited items such as art and cultural property.

The CCS is involved in the development of Internet undercover law enforcement investigative methodology, and new laws and regulations to strengthen U.S. Cyber-Border Security. C3 supports the ICE Office of Investigation's (OI) domestic field offices, along with ICE foreign attachés offices with cyber-technical, and covert online investigative support.

Forensic Document Laboratory

The Forensic Document Laboratory (FDL) dedicates its services exclusively to detecting travel and identity fraud. FDL's staff assists ICE, the Department of Homeland Security, and other federal, state, and local law enforcement agencies by providing support such as forensic examination of handwriting and documents, training and technical assistance in detection of fraudulent documents, document intelligence alerts, and other operational support.

Digital Forensics Section (DFS)

Digital evidence has become prevalent in every ICE investigative case category. Digital evidence is quickly replacing documentary evidence as the "smoking gun" in investigations. Evidence can be vital when it is recovered from electronic devices. ICE special agents often access information stored on personal computers, complex business networks, personal digital assistants (PDA), cellular telephones, and multifunction communications devices.

Digital forensics serve as the primary source for technical forensic support issues, conduct research and development on new and emerging technologies, and develop and deliver training to field agents.

The DFS operates a state of the art laboratory that processes "strange and large" digital evidence and evidence resident on "non-standard" hardware or too voluminous for a field office to process.

The DFS also provides ICE with advanced data exploitation capabilities. Digital evidence submitted by field offices can be imported onto the DFS Lab network, indexed, and searched using advanced data exploitation tools. Large volumes of unrelated data can quickly and efficiently be mined for evidence of criminal activity.

Law Enforcement Support Center

The Law Enforcement Support Center (LESC) serves as a national enforcement operations center by providing timely immigration status and identity information to local, state, and federal law enforcement agencies on aliens suspected, arrested, or convicted of criminal activity. The LESC operates 24 hours a day, 7 days a week assisting law enforcement agencies with information gathered from 8 DHS databases, the National Crime Information Center (NCIC), the Interstate Identification Index (III), and other state criminal history indices.

In addition to providing real time assistance to law enforcement agencies that are investigating, or have arrested, foreign-born individuals involved in criminal activity, the LESC also performs investigative functions in concert with:

- National Crime Information Center (NCIC). The LESC administers and controls immigration related cases in this nationwide law enforcement consortium and criminal database for ICE.
- Investigative Services Branch. The LESC provides support to a host of on-going multi-agency investigative initiatives. Working in concert with ICE field units, task forces and other local, state, and federal investigators the Center gathers, analyzes, and responds to thousands of offline query requests.
- Federal Bureau of Investigation National Instant Criminal Background Check System (NICS). Every foreign-born firearm applicant is screened by the LESC for immigration status before being authorized to purchase or possess a weapon. The LESC also handles queries and field responses relating to national security employment issues (Bio-Terrorism, CDL with Haz-Mat endorsement, Nuclear Industry, etc.).

The LESC Communications Center serves the law enforcement community with NCIC hit confirmation information as well as ICE Special Agents and Deportation Officers nationwide with after-hours telephonic enforcement support via digitally recorded duty lines confirmed by Personal Identification Numbers.

Summary

As the second largest federal law enforcement contributor to the Joint Terrorism Task Force, ICE:

- Dismantles gang organizations by targeting their members, seizing their financial assets, and disrupting their criminal operations through Operation Community Shield.
- Investigates employers and targets illegal workers who have gained access to critical infrastructure worksites (like nuclear and chemical plants, military installations, seaports, and airports) through the Worksite Enforcement Initiative.
- Helps to identify fraudulent immigration benefit applications and fraudulent illegal document manufacture and target violators through the Identity and Benefit Fraud Program.
- Investigates the illegal export of U.S. munitions and sensitive technology through the Project Shield America Initiative.
- Combats criminal organizations that smuggle and traffic in humans across our borders through the Human Smuggling and Trafficking Initiative.
- Ensures that every alien who has been ordered removed departs the U.S. as quickly as possible through the National Fugitive Operations Program.
- Seeks to destroy the financial infrastructure that criminal organizations use to earn, move, and store illicit funds through our Cornerstone Initiative.
- Provides law enforcement and security services to more than 8,800 federal buildings that receive nearly one million visitors and tenants daily through the Federal Protective Service.

- Plays a leading role in targeting criminal organizations responsible for producing, smuggling, and distributing counterfeit products through the National Intellectual Property Rights Coordination Center.
- Supports the law enforcement community through three units dedicated to sharing information and providing investigative support: the Law Enforcement Support Center, Forensic Document Laboratory, and the Cyber Crimes Center.

Offices of Investigation

The Special Agent-in-Charge (SAC) Offices are responsible for the administration and management of all enforcement activities within the geographic boundaries of the Office. The SACs develop, coordinate, and implement enforcement strategies to ensure conformance with national policies and procedures and to support national intelligence programs. In addition, SACs supervise all administrative responsibilities assigned to the Office and ensure a responsive Internal Controls Program is developed.

Each SAC office is responsible for subordinate field offices, which support the enforcement mission. These subordinate field offices, Resident Agent-in-Charge (RAC) and Resident Agent Offices (RAOs), are responsible for managing enforcement activities within the geographic boundaries of the Office. RACs are responsible for ensuring all enforcement activities are conducted pursuant to national policies and procedures and contribute to the development and implementation of national and SAC level enforcement strategy.

Points of Contact

Atlanta
1691 Phoenix Boulevard, Suite 250
Atlanta, GA 30349
Main (770) 994-4200
Fax (770) 994-2262

Baltimore
40 South Gay Street, 3rd Floor
Baltimore, MD 21202
Main (410) 962-2620
Fax (410) 962-3469

Boston
10 Causeway Street, Room 722
Boston, MA 02222-1054
Main (617) 565-7420
Fax (617) 565-7422

Buffalo
1780 Wehrle Drive, Suite D
Williamsville, NY 14221
Main (716) 565-2039
Fax (716) 565-9509

Chicago
1 North Tower Lane, Suite 1600
Oakbrook Terrace, IL 60181
Main (630) 574-4600
Fax (630) 574-2889

Dallas
125 E. John Carpenter Freeway, Suite 800
Irving, TX 75062
Main (972) 444-7300
Fax (972) 444-7461

Washington, DC
22685 Holiday Park Drive, Suite 10
Dulles, VA 20166
Main (703) 709-9700
Fax (703) 709-8082

Denver
5445 DTC Pkwy, Suite 600
Englewood, CO 80111
Main (303) 721-3000
Fax (303) 721-3003

Detroit
477 Michigan Avenue, Suite 1850
Detroit, MI 48226
Main (313) 226-3166
Fax (313) 226-6282

El Paso
4191 N. Mesa
El Paso, TX 79902
Main (915) 231-3200
Fax (915) 231-3227

Honolulu
595 Ala Moana Boulevard
Honolulu, HI 96850
Main 808-532-3746
Fax 808-532-4689

Houston
4141 N. Sam Houston Parkway East #300
Houston, TX 77032
Main 281-985-0500
Fax 281-985-0505

Los Angeles
501 West Ocean Boulevard, Suite 7200
Long Beach, CA 90802-4213
Main (562) 624-3800
Fax (562) 590-9604

Miami
8075 N.W. 53rd Street
Miami, FL 33166
Main (305) 597-6000
Fax (305) 597-6227

New Orleans
1250 Poydras Street, Suite 2200
New Orleans, LA 70113
Main (504) 310-8800
Fax (504) 310-8900

New York
601 W. 26th Street, 7th Floor
New York, NY 10001
Main (646) 230-3200
Fax (646) 230-3255

Newark
620 Frelinghuysen Avenue
2nd Floor
Newark, NJ 07114
Main (973) 776-5500
Fax (973) 776-5650

Philadelphia
220 Chestnut Street, Room 200
Philadelphia, PA 19106
Main (215) 597-4305
Fax (215) 597-4200

Phoenix
400 North 5th Street
11th Floor
Phoenix, AZ 85004
Main (602) 364-7830
Fax (602) 514-7790

San Antonio
10127 Morocco, Suite 180
San Antonio, TX 78216
Main (210) 541-7200
Fax (210) 541-7285

San Diego
185 West F Street, Suite 600
San Diego, CA 92101
Main (619) 744-4600
Fax (619) 557-7275

San Francisco
1500 Broadway, 2nd Floor
Oakland, CA 94612
Main (510) 267-3800
Fax (510) 267-3870

San Juan
Capitol Office Building, 12th Floor
800 Ponce de Leon Avenue
Santurce, PR 00908
Main (787) 729-5151
Fax (787) 729-6646

Seattle
1000 Second Avenue, Suite 2300
Seattle, WA 98104
Main (206) 553-7531
Fax (206) 553-0826

Minneapolis/St. Paul
2901 Metro Drive, Suite 100
Bloomington, MN 55425
Main (952) 853-2940
Fax (612) 313-9045

Tampa
2203 North Lois Avenue
Suite 600
Tampa, FL 33607
Main (813) 348-1881
Fax (813) 348-1871

Tucson
7400 N. Oracle Road, Suite 242
Tucson, AZ 85704
Main (520) 229-5100
Fax (520) 229-5160

Main Contact Point
U.S. Immigration and Customs
Enforcement, Department of
Homeland Security, 1300 Pennsylvania
Avenue, NW, Rm. 3.5A, Washington,
DC 20229. Phone: (202) 344-2410 1-866-
IPR-2060, or 1-866-477-2060. Fax: (202)
344-1920

Source   U.S. Immigration and Customs
Enforcement. 2006.

INTERNAL REVENUE SERVICE CRIMINAL INVESTIGATION

Criminal Investigation (CI) serves the American
public by investigating potential criminal violations of the Internal Revenue Code and related
financial crimes in a manner that fosters confidence
in the tax system and compliance with the law.

CI is comprised of approximately 4,400
employees worldwide, approximately 2,800 of
which are special agents whose investigative
jurisdiction includes tax, money laundering,
and Bank Secrecy Act laws. While other federal
agencies also have investigative jurisdiction for
money laundering and some bank secrecy act
violations, IRS is the only federal agency that
can investigate potential criminal violations of
the Internal Revenue Code.

Compliance with the tax laws in the United
States relies heavily on self-assessments of what
tax is owed. This is called voluntary compliance.
When individuals and corporations make deliberate decisions to not comply with the law, they
face the possibility of a civil audit or criminal
investigation which could result in prosecution
and possible jail time. Publicity of these convictions provides a deterrent effect that enhances
voluntary compliance.

As financial investigators, CI special
agents fill a unique niche in the federal law
enforcement community. Today's sophisticated
schemes to defraud the government demand
the analytical ability of financial investigators
to wade through complex paper and computerized financial records. Due to the increased use
of automation for financial records, CI special
agents are trained to recover computer evidence.
Along with their financial investigative skills,
special agents use specialized forensic technology to recover financial data that may have been
encrypted, password protected, or hidden by
other electronic means.

Criminal Investigation's conviction rate is
one of the highest in federal law enforcement.
Not only do the courts hand down substantial
prison sentences, but those convicted must also
pay fines, civil taxes, and penalties.

Strategic Priorities

The Criminal Investigation strategic plan is comprised of three interdependent programs:

- Legal Source Tax Crimes
- Illegal Source Financial Crimes
- Narcotics Related Financial Crimes

These three programs are mutually supportive,
and encourage utilization of all statutes within CI's
jurisdiction, the grand jury process, and enforcement techniques to combat tax, money laundering, and currency crime violations. Criminal
Investigation must investigate and assist in the
prosecution of those significant financial investigations that will generate the maximum deterrent
effect, enhance voluntary compliance, and promote public confidence in the tax system.

Point of Contact

Internal Revenue Service Criminal Investigation,
1111 Constitution Ave NW, Room 2501,
Washington, DC 20224

Source   Internal Revenue Service Criminal
Investigation. 2006. <http://www.irs.gov/>

NATIONAL DRUG INTELLIGENCE CENTER

Threat assessments are
the primary intelligence
products of the National
Drug Intelligence Center
(NDIC). These products
provide policymakers and
counter-drug executives
with reports of the threat
posed by illicit drugs in
the United States.

The National Drug Threat Assessment

NDIC's major intelligence product is a comprehensive annual report on national drug trafficking and abuse trends within the United States. The assessment identifies the primary drug threat to the nation, monitors fluctuations in consumption levels, tracks drug availability by geographic market, and analyzes trafficking and distribution patterns. The report highlights the most current quantitative and qualitative information on availability, demand, production and cultivation, transportation, and distribution, as well as the effects of a particular drug on abusers and society as a whole.

Intelligence Division

The Intelligence Division consists of two branches: the Domestic Strategic Branch and the National Issues Branch. The Domestic Strategic Branch monitors the drug situation in U.S. geographic regions in search of drug trends. The National Issues Branch coordinates the collection and analysis of current counter-drug intelligence and focuses on particular issues of the drug trade such as gang activity and money laundering.

Under these two branches are four regional units and six specialized units. The four regional units examine drug threats in each state and in U.S. territories. Specialized units include Collections; Current Intelligence; Money Laundering; Organized Crime and Violence; and Drug Trends Analysis. Outputs from these units are the main working material of the National Drug Threat Assessment and the National Interdiction Support Unit. Intelligence analysts in many of these specialty units interact with counterparts in the intelligence community as well as law enforcement and demand personnel throughout the country.

Field Program Specialists

NDIC created the Field Program Specialist initiative in January 2001 to encourage information sharing with federal, state, and local law enforcement. Field Program Specialists are independent contractors who support the program through the exchange of information on drug-related issues with local law enforcement personnel across the country. Field representatives assigned to this program typically have more than 30 years' experience in federal, state, or local drug law enforcement.

Document Exploitation Division

The Document Exploitation Division deploys teams of intelligence analysts to federal agency field offices or other sites to expedite the exploitation of information seized in major federal drug investigations. Document Exploitation teams use a state-of-the-art computer database developed at NDIC know as Real-time Analytical Intelligence Database (RAID) to quickly collect, collate, and label large volumes of information from seized documents and computers. The team then subjects this material to detailed analysis to help identify hidden assets, previously unknown associates, and other leads for further investigation.

National Drug Intelligence Library

NDIC maintains an extensive library of intelligence publications from the counter-drug community. The repository includes books, journals, magazines, and numerous counter-narcotics reports and studies. Services include specialized searching of the Internet and other online databases, web development, document retrieval, and interlibrary loan.

Collaborating Agencies

NDIC collaborates with other agencies such as the DEA, FBI, U.S. Coast Guard, Bureau of Alcohol, Tobacco and Firearms, the Bureau of Prisons, and the Office of National Drug Control Policy (ONDCP). NDIC is one of four national intelligence centers: El Paso Intelligence Center (EPIC); U.S. Department of the Treasury's FinCEN; and Director of Central Intelligence Crime and Narcotics Center (CNC). NDIC also works closely with the High Intensity Drug Trafficking Areas (HIDTAs) and Organized Crime Drug Enforcement Task Force (OCDETF).

Points of Contact

NDIC, 319 Washington Street, 5th Floor, Johnstown, PA 15901-1622. Telephone: 814-532-4601 and by fax at 814-532-4690. E-mail: NDIC.Contacts@usdoj.gov.

Office of Policy and Interagency Affairs, United States Department of Justice, Robert F. Kennedy Building (Room 1335), 950 Pennsylvania Avenue NW, Washington, DC 20530. Telephone: (202) 532-4040

Source   National Drug Intelligence Center. 2006. <http://www.usdoj.gov/ndic/index.htm>

NATIONAL SECURITY AGENCY/CENTRAL SECURITY SERVICE

The mission of the National Security Agency/Central Security Service is direct and simple:

"The ability to understand the secret communications of our foreign adversaries while protecting our own communications—a capability in which the United States leads the world—gives our nation a unique advantage."

Executive Order 12333, dated December 4, 1981, describes the responsibility of the National Security Agency and the Central Security Service (NSA/CSS) in more detail. The resources of NSA/CSS are organized for the accomplishment of two national missions:

- The Information Assurance mission provides the solutions, products, and services, and conducts defensive information operations, to achieve information assurance for information infrastructures critical to U.S. national security interests.
- The foreign signals intelligence or SIGINT mission allows for an effective, unified organization and control of all the foreign signals collection and processing activities of the United States. NSA is authorized to produce SIGINT in accordance with objectives, requirements, and priorities

established by the Director of Central Intelligence with the advice of the National Foreign Intelligence Board.

Information Assurance

The NSA/CSS is America's cryptologic organization. It coordinates, directs, and performs highly specialized activities to protect U.S. government information systems and produce foreign signals intelligence information. A high technology organization, NSA is on the frontiers of communications and data processing. It is also one of the most important centers of foreign language analysis and research within the government.

Signals Intelligence (SIGINT)

SIGINT is a unique discipline with a long and storied past. SIGINT's modern era dates to World War II, when the U.S. broke the Japanese military code and learned of plans to invade Midway Island. This intelligence allowed the U.S. to defeat Japan's superior fleet. The use of SIGINT is believed to have directly contributed to shortening the war by at least one year. Today, SIGINT continues to play an important role in keeping the United States a step ahead of its enemies.

As the world becomes more and more technology-oriented, the Information Assurance (IA) mission becomes increasingly challenging. This mission involves protecting all classified and sensitive information that is stored or sent through U.S. government equipment. IA professionals go to great lengths to make certain that government systems remain impenetrable. This support spans from the highest levels of U.S. government to the individual war-fighter in the field.

NSA conducts one of the U.S. government's leading research and development (R&D) programs. Some of the Agency's R&D projects have significantly advanced the state of the art in the scientific and business worlds.

NSA's early interest in cryptanalytic research led to the first large-scale computer and the first solid-state computer, predecessors to the modern computer. NSA pioneered efforts in flexible storage capabilities, which led to the development of the tape cassette. NSA also made ground-breaking developments in semiconductor technology and remains a world leader in many technological fields.

NSA employs the country's premier cryptologists. It is said to be the largest employer of mathematicians in the United States and perhaps the world. Its mathematicians contribute directly to the two missions of the Agency: designing cipher systems that will protect the integrity of U.S. information systems and searching for weaknesses in adversaries' systems and codes.

Technology and the world change rapidly, and great emphasis is placed on staying ahead of these changes with employee training programs. The national Cryptologic School is indicative of the Agency's commitment to professional development. The school not only provides unique training for the NSA workforce, but it also serves as a training resource for the entire Department of Defense. NSA sponsors employees for bachelor and graduate studies at the nation's top universities and colleges, and selected Agency employees attend the various war colleges of the U.S. Armed Forces.

Most NSA/CSS employees, both civilian and military, are headquartered at Fort Meade, Maryland, centrally located between Baltimore and Washington, DC. Its workforce represents an unusual combination of specialties: analysts, engineers, physicists, mathematicians, linguists, computer scientists, researchers, as well as customer relations specialists, security officers, data flow experts, managers, administrative officers, and clerical assistants.

Point of Contact

National Security Agency, 9800 Savage Road, Suite 6740, Fort Meade, MD 20755-6740. Phone: (410) 854-6091

Source National Security Agency/Central Security Service. 2006. <http://www.nsa.gov>

U.S. AIR FORCE OFFICE OF SPECIAL INVESTIGATIONS

The Office of Special Investigations for the Air Force (AFOSI) is a field operating agency with headquarters at Andrews Air Force Base, Maryland. It has been the Air Force's felony-level investigative service since August 1, 1948. The agency reports to the Inspector General, Office of the Secretary of the Air Force.

Mission

AFOSI provides investigative service to commanders of all Air Force activities. It identifies, investigates, and neutralizes criminal, terrorist, and espionage threats to Air Force and Department of Defense personnel and resources. The command focuses on four priorities:

- Detect and provide early warning of worldwide threats to the Air Force.
- Identify and resolve crime impacting Air Force readiness or good order and discipline.
- Combat threats to Air Force information systems and technologies.
- Defeat and deter fraud in the acquisition of Air Force prioritized weapons systems.

Personnel and Resources

AFOSI has 2,533 active-duty, Reserve and civilian personnel. Of this number, approximately 1,935 are federally credentialed special agents, who are drawn from all segments of the total force. There are 363 active-duty officers, 791 active-duty enlisted, 402 civilians, and 379 are reservists.

Organization

In addition to the command's headquarters AFOSI has eight field investigations regions. Seven of the regions are aligned with Air Force major commands: Region 1 with Air Force Materiel Command, Region 2 with Air Combat Command, Region 3 with Air Mobility Command, Region 4 with Air Education and Training Command, Region 5 with U.S. Air Forces in Europe, Region 6 with Pacific Air Forces, and Region 8 with Air Force Space Command.

While the regions serve the investigative needs of those aligned major commands, all AFOSI units and personnel remain independent of those commands, and their chains of command flow directly to AFOSI headquarters. Such organizational independence ensures unbiased investigations.

The single region not aligned with a major command is Region 7, the mission of which is to provide counterintelligence and security-program management for special-access programs under the Office of the Secretary of the Air Force.

At the regional level are subordinate units called field investigations squadrons, detachments, and operating locations. In sum, AFOSI owns more than 160 units worldwide.

Operations

Threat Detection. AFOSI manages offensive and defensive activities to detect, counter, and destroy the effectiveness of hostile intelligence services and terrorist groups that target the Air Force. These efforts include investigating the crimes of espionage, terrorism, technology transfer, and computer infiltration. This mission aspect also includes providing personal protection to senior Air Force leaders and other officials, as well as supervising an extensive antiterrorism program in geographic areas of heightened terrorist activity.

Criminal Investigation. The vast majority of AFOSI's investigative activities pertain to felony crimes including murder, robbery, rape, assault, major burglaries, drug use and trafficking, sex offenses, arson, compromise of Air Force test materials, black market activities, and other criminal activities.

Economic Crime Investigation. A significant amount of AFOSI investigative resources are assigned to fraud (or economic crime) investigations. These include violations of the public trust involving Air Force contracting matters, appropriated and nonappropriated funds activities, computer systems, pay and allowance matters, environmental matters, acquiring and disposing of Air Force property, and major administrative irregularities. AFOSI uses fraud surveys to determine the existence, location, and extent of fraud in Air Force operations or programs. It also provides briefings to base and command-level resource managers to help identify and prevent fraud involving Air Force or DOD resources.

Information Operations. The Air Force is now countering a global security threat to our information systems. Our role in support of Information Operations recognizes future threats to the Air Force, and our response to these threats, will occur in cyberspace. AFOSI's support to Information Operations comes in many facets. AFOSI's computer crime investigators provide rapid worldwide response to intrusions into Air Force systems.

Technology Protection. The desires of potential adversaries to acquire or mimic the technological advances of the U.S. Air Force have heightened the need to protect critical Air Force technologies and collateral data. The AFOSI Research and Technology Protection Program provides focused, comprehensive counterintelligence and core mission investigative services to safeguard Air Force technologies, programs, critical program information, personnel, and facilities.

Specialized Services. AFOSI has numerous specialists who are invaluable in the successful resolution of investigations. They include technical specialists, polygraphers, behavioral scientists, computer experts, and forensic advisers.

Defense Cyber Crime Center. AFOSI is the DOD executive agent for both the Defense Computer Forensics Laboratory and the Defense Computer Investigations Training Program, which together comprise the Defense Cyber Crime Center. The forensics laboratory provides counterintelligence, criminal, and fraud computer-evidence processing, analysis, and diagnosis to DOD investigations. The investigations training program provides training in computer investigations and computer forensics to DOD investigators and examiners.

Antiterrorism Teams. Created out of a need to meet the increasing challenges presented by worldwide terrorism, AFOSI antiterrorism teams are maintained around the globe. These teams stand ready on a moment's notice to deploy globally to provide antiterrorism, counterintelligence information collections, and investigative services to Air Force personnel and units.

Points of Contact

Air Force Office of Special Investigations, 1535 Command Drive, Suite C-309, Andrews AFB, MD 20762-7002. Phone 240 857-0989.

Air Force Office of Special Investigations. 2006. <http://www.af.mil/factsheets/factsheet.asp?fsID=145>

U.S. ARMY CRIMINAL INVESTIGATION DIVISION

The Army's Criminal Investigation Division (CID) conducts criminal investigations in which the Army is, or may be, a party of interest. Headquartered at Fort Belvoir, Virginia, and operating throughout the world, the CID conducts criminal investigations that range from death to fraud, on and off military reservations, and, when appropriate, with local, state, and other federal investigative agencies. The CID supports the Army through the deployment, in peace and conflict, of highly trained soldier and government service special agents and support personnel, the operation of a certified forensic laboratory, a protective services unit, computer crimes specialists, polygraph services, criminal intelligence collection and analysis, and a variety of other services normally associated with law enforcement activities.

Using modern investigative techniques, equipment and systems, CID concerns itself with every level of the Army throughout the world in which criminal activity can or has occurred. Unrestricted, CID searches out the full facts of a situation, organizes the facts into a logical summary of investigative data, and presents this data to the responsible command or a United States attorney as appropriate.

Source   U.S. Army Criminal Investigation Division. 2006. <http://www.globalsecurity.org/military/agency/army/cid.htm>.

U.S. COAST GUARD OFFICE OF LAW ENFORCEMENT

The United States Coast Guard is the nation's leading maritime law enforcement agency and has broad, multi-faceted jurisdictional authority. The specific statutory authority for the Coast Guard Law Enforcement mission is given in 14 USC 2, "The Coast Guard shall enforce or assist in the enforcement of all applicable laws on, under and over the high seas and waters subject to the jurisdiction of the United States." In addition, 14 USC 89 provides the authority for U.S. Coast Guard active duty commissioned, warrant, and petty officers to enforce applicable U.S. law. It authorizes Coast Guard personnel to enforce federal law on waters subject to U.S. jurisdiction and in international waters, as well as on all vessels subject to U.S. jurisdiction (including U.S., foreign, and stateless vessels).

Drug Interdiction

The Coast Guard is the lead federal agency for maritime drug interdiction and shares lead responsibility for air interdiction with the U.S. Customs Service. As such, it is a key player in combating the flow of illegal drugs to the United States. The Coast Guard's mission is to reduce the supply of drugs from the source by denying smugglers the use of air and maritime routes in the Transit Zone, a six million square mile area, including the Caribbean, Gulf of Mexico, and Eastern Pacific. The Coast Guard coordinates closely with other federal agencies and countries within the region to disrupt and deter the flow of illegal drugs. In addition to deterrence, Coast Guard drug interdiction accounts for nearly 52 percent of all U.S. government seizures of cocaine each year.

Alien Migration Control

As the United States' primary maritime law enforcement agency, the Coast Guard is tasked with enforcing immigration law at sea. The Coast Guard conducts patrols and coordinates with other federal agencies and foreign countries to interdict undocumented migrants at sea, denying them entry via maritime routes to the United States, its territories and possessions. Thousands of people try to enter this country illegally every year using maritime routes, many via smuggling operations. Interdicting migrants at sea means they can be quickly returned to their countries of origin without the costly processes required if they successfully enter the United States.

Point of Contact

Commandant (G-OPL), U.S. Coast Guard, 2100 2nd St. SW, Washington, DC 20593-0001

Source   U.S. Coast Guard Office of Law Enforcement. 2006. <http://www.uscg.mil/hq/g-o/g-opl/>.

U.S. CUSTOMS AND BORDER PROTECTION

The Department of Homeland Security incorporates U.S. Customs and Border Protection (CBP). The priority mission of the CBP is preventing terrorists and terrorist weapons, including weapons of mass destruction, from entering the United States. Border Patrol Agents patrol nearly 6,000 miles of international land border with Canada and Mexico and nearly 2,000 miles of coastal border.

The CBP maintains a presence at 317 official ports of entry in the United States and 14 preclearance offices in Canada and the Caribbean. CBP personnel are the face at the border for most cargo and visitors entering the United States; they enforce the import and export laws and regulations of the U.S. federal government, and conduct immigration policy programs. CBP port personnel also perform agriculture inspections to detect carriers of animal and plant pests or diseases that could cause serious damage to America's crops, livestock, pets, and the environment.

Over 800 canine teams conduct inspections that look for indications of a variety of crimes such as terrorist activities, drug trafficking, money laundering, and smuggling in general, including the smuggling of humans.

The CBP operates 70 Deferred Inspections Sites throughout the United States and the outlying territories where incoming aliens are referred when documentation requires additional review and/or possible correction.

CBP operations are linked to an anti-terrorism intelligence office that gathers, processes, and disseminates intelligence on emerging risks.

Point of Contact

U.S. Customs and Border Protection, Department of Homeland Security, 1300 Pennsylvania Avenue, NW, Washington, D.C. 20229. Telephone (202) 354-1000.

Source   U.S. Customs and Border Protection. 2006. <http://www.cbp.gov/>

U.S. MARSHALS SERVICE

Court Security

Senior inspectors, deputy marshals, and contracted court security officers (CSOs) provide security inside federal court facilities in each of the 94 federal judicial districts and the District of Columbia Superior Court. The Marshals Service (USMS) protects more than 2,000 sitting judges plus other court officials at more than 400 court facilities throughout the nation.

Explicit threats against the judiciary, U.S. attorneys and other court officers are assessed to determine the level of danger. On average, about 600 threats/inappropriate communications against judicial officials are logged each year, some of which result in round-the-clock protective details.

Marshals Service court security personnel provide the latest in state-of-the-art protective techniques and equipment in all phases of court proceedings, threat situations, and judicial conferences, thus ensuring quick and safe responses in emergency situations as well as unobtrusive surveillance and protection during routine operations.

Fugitive Program

The U.S. Marshals Service has been designated by the Department of Justice as the primary agency to apprehend fugitives who are wanted by foreign nations and believed to be in the United States. Also, the Marshals Service is the primary agency responsible for tracking and extraditing fugitives who are apprehended in foreign countries and wanted for prosecution in the United States. The U.S. Marshals Service, which has statutory responsibility for all international, federal, and state extraditions, sees to it that there is no safe haven for criminals who flee the territorial boundaries of the United States.

The USMS established the 15 Most Wanted Fugitive Program in 1983 to prioritize the investigation and apprehension of high-profile offenders who are considered to be some of the country's most dangerous fugitives. These offenders tend to be career criminals with histories of violence or whose instant offense(s) pose a significant threat to public safety. Current and past fugitives in this program include murderers, sex offenders, major drug kingpins, organized crime figures, and individuals wanted for high-profile financial crimes.

The Marshals Service is the federal government's lead agency for conducting investigations involving: escaped federal prisoners; probation, parole and bond default violators; and fugitives based on warrants generated during drug investigations.

The U.S. Marshals have the authority to make an arrest on all federal warrants.

The USMS has a long history of providing assistance and expertise to other federal, state, and local law enforcement agencies in support of their fugitive investigations. The USMS is the lead agency for 102 interagency fugitive task forces located throughout the United States, including five congressionally funded regional fugitive task forces. These task forces, staffed by federal, state, and local law enforcement agencies, target the most dangerous fugitives.

Major Cases

The USMS established its Major Case Fugitive Program in 1985 to supplement the successful 15 Most Wanted Fugitive Program. Much like the 15 Most Wanted Fugitive Program, the Major Case Fugitive Program prioritizes the investigation and apprehension of high-profile offenders who are considered to be some of the country's most dangerous individuals. These offenders tend to be career criminals with histories of violence or whose instant offense(s) pose a significant threat to public safety. Current and

past fugitives in this program include murderers, sex offenders, major drug kingpins, organized crime figures, and individuals wanted for high-profile financial crimes. All escapes from custody are automatically elevated to Major Case status.

Technical Operations

Deploying the most sophisticated technologies available, the Technical Operations Group provides investigative and intelligence support for the U.S. Marshals and U.S. Marshals-led fugitive task forces. Technical Operations also provides assistance when requested by other federal, state, and local law enforcement agencies to solve complex criminal investigations or crimes of violence.

Criminal Information Branch

The Criminal Information Branch provides investigative research and analysis in support of various Marshals Service operations and provides oversight of special law enforcement information systems used by the Marshals Service and management of data sharing projects with other agencies.

The Witness Security Program was authorized by the Organized Crime Control Act of 1970 and amended by the Comprehensive Crime Control Act of 1984. Since its inception, more than 7,500 witnesses and over 9,500 family members have entered the Program and have been protected, relocated, and given new identities by the Marshals Service.

The successful operation of this program is widely recognized as providing a unique and valuable tool in the government's war against major criminal conspirators and organized crime. Since the program's inception, it has obtained an overall conviction rate of 89 as a result of protected witnesses' testimonies.

Final determination that a witness qualifies for Witness Security protection is made by the Attorney General. The decision is based on recommendations by U.S. Attorneys assigned to major federal cases throughout the nation. In a state court case, the determination is based on a request from a State Attorney General through the appropriate U.S. Attorney's office.

After the witness receives a pre-admittance briefing by Marshals Service personnel and agrees to enter the program, the procedure usually involves the immediate removal of the witness and his/her immediate family members from the danger area and their relocation to a secure area selected by the Marshals Service.

Witnesses and their families typically get new identities with authentic documentation. Housing, medical care, job training, and employment can also be provided. Subsistence funding to cover basic living expenses is also provided to the witnesses until they become self-sufficient in the relocation area.

The Marshals Service provides 24-hour protection to all witnesses while they are in a high threat environment, including pre-trial conferences, trial testimonials, and other court appearances.

In both criminal and civil matters involving protected witnesses, the Marshals Service cooperates fully with local law enforcement and court authorities in bringing witnesses to justice or in having them fulfill their legal responsibilities. A recidivism study found that less than 17 percent of protected witnesses with criminal histories are arrested and charged after joining the Program.

Points of Contact

United States Marshals Service District Offices
    Northern District of Alabama (N/AL)
    1729 N. 5th Avenue, Room 240
    Birmingham, AL 35203
    (205) 776-62 00

Middle District of Alabama (M/AL)

Frank M. Johnson Federal Building
15 Lee Street, Room 224
Montgomery, AL 36104
(334) 223-7401

Southern District of Alabama (S/AL)

U.S. Courthouse
113 St. Joseph Street, Room 413
Mobile, AL 36602
(205) 690-2841

District of Alaska (D/AK)

U.S. Courthouse
222 W. 7th Avenue, Room 189
Anchorage, AK 99513
(907) 271-5154

District of Arizona (D/AZ)

Sandra Day O'Connor U.S. Courthouse
401 W. Washington St., SPC 64, Suite 270
Phoenix, AZ 85003-2159
(602) 382-8767

Eastern District of Arkansas (E/AR)

U.S. Courthouse
600 W. Capitol Avenue, Room 445
Little Rock, AR 72201
(501) 324-6256

Western District of Arkansas (W/AR)

Judge Isaac C. Parker Federal Building
30 S. 6th Street, Room 243
Fort Smith, AR 72901
(501) 783-5215

Northern District of California (N/CA)

U.S. Marshal: Federico L. Rocha
U.S. Courthouse/Phillip Burton Building
450 Golden Gate Avenue, Room 20-6888
San Francisco, CA 94102
(415) 436-7677

Eastern District of California (E/CA)

U.S. Courthouse
501 I Street
Sacramento, CA 95814
(916) 930-2030

Central District of California (C/CA)

U.S. Courthouse
312 N. Spring Street, Room G-23
Los Angeles, CA 90012
(213) 894-6820

Southern District of California (S/CA)

U.S. Courthouse
940 Front Street, Room LL B-71
San Diego, CA 92189
(619) 557-6620

District of Colorado (D/CO)

U.S. Courthouse
1929 Stout Street, Room C-324
Denver, CO 80294
(303) 844-2801

District of Connecticut (D/CT)

U.S. Courthouse
141 Church Street, Room 323
New Haven, CT 06510
(203) 773-2107

District of Columbia (DC/DC)

U.S. Courthouse
3rd & Constitution Avenue, N.W., Room
   1103
Washington, DC 20001
(202) 353-0600

District of Columbia (Superior Court)

H. Carl Moultrie Courthouse
500 Indiana Avenue, N.W., Room C-250
Washington, DC 20001
(202) 616-8600

District of Delaware (D/DE)

U.S. Courthouse
844 King Street, Room 4311
Wilmington, DE 19801
(302) 573-6176

Northern District of Florida (N/FL)

U.S. Marshal: Dennis A. Williamson
U.S. Courthouse

111 N. Adams Street, Room 277
Tallahassee, FL 32301
(850) 942-8400

Middle District of Florida (M/FL)

U.S. Courthouse
801 N. Florida Avenue, 4th Floor
Tampa, FL 33602-4519
(813) 274-6401

Southern District of Florida (S/FL)

Federal Courthouse Square
301 N. Miami Avenue, Room 205
Miami, FL 33128
(305) 536-5346

Northern District of Georgia (N/GA)

U.S. Marshal: Richard Vaughn Mecum
Federal Building
75 Spring Street, S.W., Room 1669
Atlanta, GA 30303
(404) 331-6833

U.S. Marshal: Theresa A. Rodgers

U.S. Courthouse
3rd & Mulberry Street, Room 101
Macon, GA 31201
(912) 752-8280

Southern District of Georgia (S/GA)

U.S. Courthouse
125 Bull Street, Room 333
Savannah, GA 31401
(912) 652-4212

District of Guam (D/GU)

344 U.S. Courthouse
520 West Soledad Avenue
Hagatna, Guam 96910
011-671-477-7827

District of Hawaii (D/HI)

U.S. Courthouse
300 Ala Moana Boulevard, Room C-103
Honolulu, HI 96850
(808) 541-3000

District of Idaho (D/ID)

U.S. Courthouse
550 W. Fort Street, MSC-10, Room 777
Boise, ID 83724
(208) 334-1298

Northern District of Illinois (N/IL)

219 S. Dearborn Street, Room 2444
Chicago, IL 60604
(312) 353-5290

Central District of Illinois (C/IL)

U.S. Marshal: Steven Deatherage
600 E. Monroe Street, Room 333
Springfield, IL 62701
(217) 492-4430

Southern District of Illinois (S/IL)

U.S. Courthouse
750 Missouri Avenue, Room 127
East St. Louis, IL 62201
(618) 482-9336

Northern District of Indiana (N/IN)

Federal Building
204 S. Main Street, Room 233
South Bend, IN 46601
(574) 236-8291

Southern District of Indiana (S/IN)

U.S. Courthouse
46 E. Ohio Street, Room 227
Indianapolis, IN 46204
(317) 226-6566

Northern District of Iowa (N/IA)

Federal Building
101 First Street, S.E., Room 320
Cedar Rapids, IA 52401
(319) 362-4411

Southern District of Iowa (S/IA)

U.S. Courthouse
123 E. Walnut Street, Room 208
Des Moines, IA 50309
(515) 284-6240

District of Kansas (D/KS)

Federal Building
444 S.E. Quincy, Room 456
Topeka, KS 66683
(785) 295-2775

Eastern District of Kentucky (E/KY)

Federal Building
Barr & Limestone Streets, Room 162
Lexington, KY 40507
(859) 233-2513

Western District of Kentucky (W/KY)

U.S. Courthouse
601 W. Broadway, Room 162
Louisville, KY 40202
(502) 588-8000

Eastern District of Louisiana (E/LA)

U.S. Courthouse
500 Camp Street, Room C-600
New Orleans, LA 70130
(504) 589-6079

Middle District of Louisiana (M/LA)

U.S. Courthouse
777 Florida Street, Room G-48
Baton Rouge, LA 70801
(225) 389-0364

Western District of Louisiana (W/LA)

U.S. Courthouse
300 Fannin Street, Suite 1202
Shreveport, LA 71101
(318) 676-4200

District of Maine (D/ME)

156 Federal Street, 1st Floor
Portland, ME 04101
(207) 780-3355

District of Maryland (D/MD)

U.S. Courthouse
101 W. Lombard Street, Room 605
Baltimore, MD 21201
(410) 962-2220

District of Massachusetts (D/MA)

John Joseph Moakley Courthouse
1 Courthouse Way, Suite 1-500
Boston, MA 02210
(617) 748-2500

Eastern District of Michigan (E/MI)

U.S. Courthouse
231 W. Lafayette Street, Suite 300
Detroit, MI 48226
(313) 234-5600

Western District of Michigan (W/MI)

Federal Building
110 Michigan Avenue, N.W., Room 544
Grand Rapids, MI 49503
(616) 456-2438

District of Minnesota (D/MN)

U.S. Courthouse
300 South Fourth Street
Minneapolis, MN 55415
(612) 664-5900

Northern District of Mississippi (D/MS)

Federal Building
911 Jackson Avenue, Room 348
Oxford, MS 38655
(601) 234-6661

Southern District of Mississippi (D/MS)

James O. Eastland Courthouse Building
245 E Capitol Streets, Suite 305
Jackson, MS 39201
(601) 965-4444

Eastern District of Missouri (E/MO)

Thomas Eagleton Courthouse
111 S. 10th Street, Room 2.319
St. Louis, MO 63102-1116
(314) 539-2212

Western District of Missouri (W/MO)

U.S. Courthouse
400 E. 9th St., Room 3740
Kansas City, MO 64106
(816) 512-2000

District of Montana (D/MT)

Federal Building
215 1st Avenue N., Room 307
Great Falls, MT 59401
(406) 453-7597

District of Nebraska (D/NE)

Roman L. Hruska–United States
  Courthouse
111 South 18th Plaza–Suite B06
Omaha, NE 68102
(402) 221-4781

District of Nevada (D/NV)

U.S. Courthouse
300 Las Vegas Boulevard S., Room 448
Las Vegas, NV 89101
(702) 388-6355

District of New Hampshire (D/NH)

Federal Building
55 Pleasant Street, Room 409
Concord, NH 03301
(603) 225-1632

District of New Jersey (D/NJ)

U.S. Courthouse
50 Walnut Street
Newark, NJ 07102
(973) 645-2404

District of New Mexico (D/NM)

U.S. Courthouse
333 Lomas Boulevard, N.W., Suite 180
Albuquerque, NM 87101
(505) 346-6400

Northern District of New York (N/NY)

227 Federal Building
Federal Station
Syracuse, NY 13261
(315) 448-0341

Eastern District of New York (E/NY)

U.S. Courthouse
225 Cadman Plaza
Brooklyn, NY 11201
(718) 260-0400

Southern District of New York (S/NY)

500 Pearl Street
Suite 400
New York, NY 10007
(212) 331-7100

Western District of New York (W/NY)

U.S. Courthouse
68 Court Street, Room 129
Buffalo, NY 14202
(716) 551-4851

Eastern District of North Carolina (E/NC)

Federal Building
310 New Bern Avenue, Room 744
Raleigh, NC 27611
(919) 856-4153

Middle District of North Carolina (M/NC)

U.S. Courthouse
324 W. Market Street, Room 234
Greensboro, NC 27402
(336) 333-5354

Western District of North Carolina (W/NC)

401 West Trade Street
P.O. Box 34247
Charlotte, NC 28234
(704) 344-6234

District of North Dakota (D/ND)

Old Federal Building
655 1st Avenue N., Room 317
Fargo, ND 58108
(701) 297-7300

District of the Northern Mariana Islands (D/MP)

Horiguchi Building, 1st Floor
Garpan, Saipan, MP 96950
011-670-234-6563

Northern District of Ohio (N/OH)

U.S. Courthouse
801 West Superior Avenue, Suite 1200
Cleveland, OH 44113
(216) 522-2150

Southern District of Ohio (S/OH)

U.S. Courthouse
85 Marconi Boulevard, Room 460
Columbus, OH 43215
(614) 469-5540

Northern District of Oklahoma (N/OK)

U.S. Courthouse
333 W. 4th Street, Room 4557
Tulsa, OK 74103
(918) 581-7738

Eastern District of Oklahoma (E/OK)

U.S. Courthouse
111 N. 5th Street, Room 136
Muskogee, OK 74401
(918) 687-2523

Western District of Oklahoma (W/OK)

U.S. Courthouse
200 N.W. 4th Street, Room 2418
Oklahoma City, OK 73102
(405) 231-4206

District of Oregon (D/OR)

Mark O. Hatfield U.S. Courthouse
1000 S.W. 3rd Avenue, Room 401
Portland, OR 97204
(503) 326-2209

Eastern District of Pennsylvania (E/PA)

U.S. Courthouse
601 Market Street, Room 2110
Philadelphia, PA 19106
(215) 597-7273

Middle District of Pennsylvania (M/PA)

Federal Building
Washington Avenue & Linden Street,
    Room 231
Scranton, PA 18501
(570) 346-7277

Western District of Pennsylvania (W/PA)

U.S. Courthouse
7th Avenue & Grant Street, Room 539
Pittsburgh, PA 15219
(412) 644-3351

District of Puerto Rico (D/PR)

Federal Building
150 Carlos Chardon Avenue, Room 200
Hato Rey, PR 00918
(787) 766-6000

District of Rhode Island (D/RI)

Kennedy Plaza
Fleet Center, Suite 300
Providence, RI 02901
(401) 528-5300

District of South Carolina (D/SC)

U.S. Courthouse
901 Richland Street, Suite 1300
Columbia, SC 29201
(803) 765-5821

District of South Dakota (D/SD)

Federal Building
400 S Phillips Avenue
Room 216
Sioux Falls, SD 57104
(605) 330-4351

Eastern District of Tennessee (E/TN)

Federal Building
800 Market Street, Suite 2-3107
Knoxville, TN 37902
(865) 545-4182

Middle District of Tennessee (M/TN)

Estes Kefauver Federal Building
110 9th Avenue S., Room A750
Nashville, TN 37203
(615) 736-5417

Western District of Tennessee (W/TN)

Federal Building
167 N. Main Street, Room 1029
Memphis, TN 38103
(901) 544-3304

Northern District of Texas (N/TX)

Federal Building
1100 Commerce Street, Room 16F47
Dallas, TX 75242
(214) 767-0836

Eastern District of Texas (E/TX)

Federal Building
300 Willow Street, Room 329
Beaumont, TX 75702
(409) 839-2581

Southern District of Texas (S/TX)

U.S. Courthouse
515 Rusk Avenue, Room 10130
Houston, TX 77002
(713) 718-4800

Western District of Texas (W/TX)

U.S. Courthouse
655 E. Durango Boulevard, Room 235
San Antonio, TX 78206
(210) 472-6540

District of Utah (D/UT)

U.S. Post Office & Courthouse
350 S. Main Street, Room B-20
Salt Lake City, UT 84101
(801) 524-5693

District of Vermont (D/VT)

11 Elmwood Avenue
Suite 601
Burlington, VT 05401
(802) 951-6271

District of the Virgin Islands (D/VI)

U.S. Courthouse
Veteran's Drive, Room 371
St. Thomas, VI 00801
(340) 774-2743

Eastern District of Virginia (E/VA)

401 Courthouse Square
Alexandria, VA 22314
(703) 837-5500

Western District of Virginia (W/VA)

247 Federal Building
210 Franklin Road SW
Roanoke, VA 24009
(540) 857-2230

Eastern District of Washington (E/WA)

U.S. Courthouse
920 W. Riverside Avenue, Room 888
Spokane, WA 99201
(509) 353-2781

Western District of Washington (W/WA)

700 Stewart Street, Suite 9000
Seattle, WA 98101-1271
(206) 370-8600

Northern District of West Virginia (N/WV)

U.S. Courthouse
500 W. Pike Street
P.O. Box 2807
Clarksburg, WV 26302
(304) 623-0486

Southern District of West Virginia (S/WV)

300 Virginia Street East, Suite 3602
Charleston, WV 25301
(304) 347-5136

Eastern District of Wisconsin (E/WI)

U.S. Courthouse
517 E. Wisconsin Avenue, Suite 38
Milwaukee, WI 53202
(414) 297-3707

Western District of Wisconsin (W/WI)

U.S. Courthouse
120 N. Henry Street, Room 440
Madison, WI 53703
(608) 661-8300

District of Wyoming (D/WY)

Joseph C. O'Mahoney Federal Center
2120 Capitol Avenue, Room 2124
Cheyenne, WY 82001
(307) 772-2196

Source U.S. Marshals Service (USMS). 2006.
<http://www.usmarshals.gov/>

U.S. NAVAL CRIMINAL INVESTIGATIVE SERVICE

The U.S. Naval Criminal Investigative Service (NCIS) is the law enforcement and counterintelligence arm of the United States Department of the Navy. It works closely with other local, state, federal, and foreign agencies to counter and investigate the most serious crimes: terrorism, espionage, computer intrusion, homicide, rape, child abuse, arson, procurement fraud, and more.

NCIS is the Navy's primary source of security for the men, women, ships, planes, and resources of America's seagoing expeditionary forces worldwide.

NCIS' three strategic priorities are to prevent terrorism, protect secrets, and reduce crime.

Prevent Terrorism

The Combating Terrorism Directorate directs NCIS support for efforts aimed at detecting, deterring, and disrupting terrorism against Department of Navy personnel and assets worldwide. Offensively, from the counterterrorism side, NCIS conducts investigations and operations aimed at interdicting terrorist activities. Defensively, from the antiterrorism side, NCIS supports key Department of Navy leaders with protective services and performs vulnerability assessments of military installations and related facilities—including ports, airfields, and exercise areas to which naval expeditionary forces deploy.

Protect Secrets

Presidential Executive Order 12333 defines counterintelligence as "information gathered and activities conducted to protect against espionage, other intelligence activities, sabotage or assassinations conducted for or on behalf of foreign powers, organizations or persons or international terrorist activities."

Within the Department of the Navy, NCIS has exclusive investigative jurisdiction in non-combat matters involving actual, potential, or suspected terrorism, sabotage, espionage, and subversive activities.

Reduce Crime

NCIS investigates all major criminal offenses (felonies)—those crimes punishable under the Code of Military Justice by confinement of more than one year—within the Department of the Navy. The primary categories in the reduce crime mission include Felony Criminal Investigations, Law Enforcement, and Investigative Support.

Points of Contact

U.S. Naval Criminal Investigative Service,
Washington Navy Yard, 716 Sicard
Street, S.E., Washington, D.C. 20388-5380

NCIS Hotlines	
Most Wanted Fugitives	1-877-579-3648
Computer Crime	1-800-278-9917
Espionage	1-800-543-6289
DoD Inspector General	1-703-604-8569
Inspector General of the Marine Corps	1-866-243-3887
Navy Matters	1-800-522-3451

Source U.S. Naval Criminal Investigative Service. 2006. <http://www.ncis.navy.mil/>

U.S. SECRET SERVICE (USSS)

The United States Secret Service (USSS) is mandated by statute and executive order to carry out two significant missions: protection and criminal investigations. The Secret Service protects the President and Vice President, their families, heads of state, and other designated individuals; investigates threats against these protectees;

protects the White House, Vice President's Residence, Foreign Missions, and other buildings within Washington, D.C.; and plans and implements security designs for designated National Special Security Events. The Secret Service also investigates violations of laws relating to counterfeiting of obligations and securities of the United States; financial crimes that include, but are not limited to, access device fraud, financial institution fraud, identity theft, computer fraud; and computer-based attacks on our nation's financial, banking, and telecommunications infrastructure.

Authorization

Today, the Secret Service is authorized by law to protect:

- The President, the Vice President (or other individuals next in order of succession to the Office of the President), the President-elect and Vice President-elect.
- The immediate families of the above individuals.
- Former Presidents, their spouses for their lifetimes, except when the spouse remarries. In 1997, Congressional legislation became effective limiting Secret Service protection to former Presidents for a period of not more than 10 years from the date the former President has left office.
- Children of former presidents until age 16.
- Visiting heads of foreign states or governments and their spouses traveling with them, other distinguished foreign visitors to the United States, and official representatives of the United States performing special missions abroad.
- Major Presidential and Vice Presidential candidates, and their spouses within 120 days of a general Presidential election.

Protective Methods

Certain Secret Service protective methods are generally the same for all individuals protected. Permanent protectees, such as the President and the First Lady, have details of special agents assigned to them. Temporary protectees, such as candidates and foreign dignitaries, have details

of special agents on temporary assignment from Secret Service field offices.

The Secret Service does not discuss methods or means in any detail, however generally speaking, the advance team surveys each site to be visited. From these surveys, the members determine manpower, equipment, hospitals, and evacuation routes for emergencies. Fire, rescue, and other public service personnel in the community are alerted. A command post is established with full communications facilities. The assistance of the military, federal, state, county, and local law enforcement organizations is a vital part of the entire security operation.

Before the protectee's arrival, the lead advance agent coordinates all law enforcement representatives participating in the visit. Personnel are posted and are alerted to specific problems associated with the visit. Intelligence information is discussed, identification specified, and emergency options outlined. Prior to the arrival of the protectee, checkpoints are established, and access to the secured area is limited.

Investigative Mission

The Secret Service was established as a law enforcement agency in 1865. While most people associate the Secret Service with Presidential protection, its original mandate was to investigate the counterfeiting of U.S. currency—which is still done. Today the primary investigative mission is to safeguard the payment and financial systems of the United States. This has been historically accomplished through the enforcement of the counterfeiting statutes to preserve the integrity of United States currency, coin, and financial obligations. Since 1984, USSS investigative responsibilities have expanded to include crimes that involve financial institution fraud, computer and telecommunications fraud, false identification documents, access device fraud, advance fee fraud, electronic funds transfers, and money laundering.

Counterfeiting

The Secret Service has exclusive jurisdiction for investigations involving the counterfeiting of United States obligations and securities. This authority to investigate counterfeiting is derived from Title 18 of the United States Code, Section 3056. Some of the counterfeited United States obligations and securities commonly dealt with by the Secret Service include U.S. currency and coins; U.S. Treasury checks; Department of Agriculture food coupons and U.S. postage stamps. The Secret Service works closely with state and local law enforcement agencies, as well as foreign law enforcement agencies, to aggressively pursue counterfeiters.

Financial Crimes

The Financial Crimes Division (FCD) plans, reviews, and coordinates criminal investigations involving Financial Systems Crimes, including bank fraud; access device fraud; telemarketing; telecommunications fraud (cellular and hard wire); computer fraud; automated payment systems and teller machines; direct deposit; investigations of forgery, uttering, alteration, false personation, or false claims involving U.S. Treasury Checks, U.S. Savings Bonds, U.S. Treasury Notes, bonds, and bills; electronic funds transfer (EFT) including Treasury disbursements and fraud within Treasury payment systems; fraud involving U.S. Department of Agriculture Food Coupons and Authority to Participate (ATP) cards; Federal Deposit Insurance Corporation investigations; Farm Credit Administration violations; fraud and related activity in connection with identification documents and fraudulent commercial, fictitious and foreign securities. The Division also coordinates the activities of the U.S. Secret Service Organized Crimes Program, and oversees money laundering investigations.

Forensics

Forensic examiners in the Secret Service Forensic Services Division (FSD) provide analysis for questioned documents, fingerprints, false identification, credit cards, and other related forensic science areas. Examiners use both instrumental and chemical analysis when reviewing evidence. FSD also manages the Secret Service's polygraph program nationwide. The division coordinates photographic, graphic, video, and audio and image enhancement service, as well as the Voice Identification

Program. In addition, FSD is responsible for handling the Forensic Hypnosis Program. Much of the forensic assistance the Secret Service offers is unique technology operated in this country only by FSD.

As part of the 1994 Crime Bill, Congress mandated the Secret Service to provide forensic/technical assistance in matters involving missing and sexually exploited children. FSD offers this assistance to federal, state, and local law enforcement agencies, the Morgan P. Hardiman Task Force, and the National Center for Missing and Exploited Children (NCMEC).

Points of Contact

U.S. Secret Service Headquarters, 245 Murray Drive, Building 410, Washington, DC 20223. Telephone 202-406-5800.

Field Offices

Alabama
  • Birmingham 205-731-1144
  • Mobile 251-441-5851
  • Montgomery 334-223-7601
Alaska
  • Anchorage 907-271-5148
Arizona
  • Phoenix 602-640-5580
  • Tucson 520-670-4730
Arkansas
  • Little Rock 501-324-6241
California
  • Fresno 559-487-5204
  • Los Angeles 213-894-4830
  • Riverside 951-276-6781
  • Sacramento 916-930-2130
  • San Diego 619-557-5640
  • San Francisco 415-744-9026
  • San Jose 408-535-5288
  • Santa Ana 714-246-8257
  • Ventura 805-339-9180
Colorado
  • Denver 303-866-1010
Connecticut
  • New Haven 203-865-2449
Delaware
  • Wilmington 302-573-6188
District Of Columbia
  • Washington, D.C. 202-406-8000

Florida
- Fort Myers 239-334-0660
- Jacksonville 904-296-0133
- Miami 305-863-5000
- Orlando 407-648-6333
- Tallahassee 850-942-9523
- Tampa 813-228-2636
- West Palm Beach 561-659-0184

Georgia
- Albany 229-430-8442
- Atlanta 404-331-6111
- Savannah 912-652-4401

Guam
- 671-472-7395

Hawaii
- Honolulu 808-541-1912

Idaho
- Boise 208-334-1403

Illinois
- Chicago 312-353-5431
- Springfield 217-726-8453

Indiana
- Indianapolis 317-226-6444

Iowa
- Des Moines 515-284-4565

Kansas
- Wichita 316-267-1452

Kentucky
- Lexington 859-223-2358
- Louisville 502-582-5171

Louisiana
- Baton Rouge 225-389-0763
- New Orleans 504-589-4041

Maine
- Portland 207-780-3493

Maryland
- Baltimore 443-263-1000

Massachusetts
- Boston 617-565-5640

Michigan
- Detroit 313-226-6400
- Grand Rapids 616-454-4671
- Saginaw 989-497-0580

Minnesota
- Minneapolis 612-348-1800

Mississippi
- Jackson 601-965-4436

Missouri
- Kansas City 816-460-0600
- Springfield 417-864-8340
- St. Louis 314-539-2238

Montana
- Billings 406-245-8585

Nebraska
- Omaha 402-965-9670

Nevada
- Las Vegas 702-388-6571
- Reno 775-784-5354

New Hampshire
- Concord 603-626-5631

New Jersey
- Atlantic City 609-487-1300
- Newark 973-971-3100
- Trenton 609-989-2008

New Mexico
- Albuquerque 505-248-5290

New York
- Albany 518-436-9600
- Buffalo 716-551-4401
- JFK 718-553-0911
- Melville 631-293-4028
- New York 718-840-1000
- Rochester 585-232-4160
- Syracuse 315-448-0304
- White Plains 914-682-6300

North Carolina
- Charlotte 704-442-8370
- Greensboro 336-547-4180
- Raleigh 919-790-2834
- Wilmington 910-815-4511

North Dakota
- Fargo 701-239-5070

Ohio
- Akron 330-761-0544
- Cincinnati 513-684-3585
- Cleveland 216-706-4365
- Columbus 614-469-7370
- Dayton 937-222-2013
- Toledo 419-259-6434

Oklahoma
- Oklahoma City 405-810-3000
- Tulsa 918-581-7272

Oregon
- Portland 503-326-2162

Pennsylvania
- Harrisburg 717-221-4411
- Philadelphia 215-861-3300
- Pittsburgh 412-395-6484
- Scranton 570-346-5781

Puerto Rico
- San Juan 787-277-1515

Rhode Island
- Providence 401-331-6456

South Carolina
- Charleston 843-747-7242
- Columbia 803-772-4015

• Greenville 864-233-1490
South Dakota
   • Sioux Falls SD 605-330-4565
Tennessee
   • Chattanooga 423-752-5125
   • Knoxville 865-545-4627
   • Memphis 901-544-0333
   • Nashville 615-736-5841
Texas
   • Austin 512-916-5103
   • Dallas 972-868-3200
   • El Paso 915-533-6950
   • Houston 713-868-2299
   • Lubbock 806-472-7347
   • Mcallen 956-630-5811
   • San Antonio 210-308-6220
   • Tyler 903-534-2933
   • Waco 254-741-0576
Utah
   • Salt Lake City 801-524-5910
Vermont
   • Burlington 802-651-4091
Virginia
   • Norfolk 757-441-3200
   • Richmond 804-771-2274
   • Roanoke 540-857-2208
Washington
   • Seattle 206-220-6800
   • Spokane 509-353-2532
West Virginia
   • Charleston 304-347-5188
Wisconsin
   • Madison 608-264-5191
   • Milwaukee 414-297-3587
Wyoming
   • Cheyenne 307-772-2380

Overseas USSS Offices: Listed By City

Brazil
   • Brasilia 011-55-613-312-7523
Bulgaria
   • Sofia 011-35-92-958-5461
Canada
   • Montreal 1-514-398-9488
   • Ottawa 1-613-688-5461
   • Vancouver 1-604-689-3011
Colombia
   • Bogota 011-571-315-1318
China
   • Hong Kong 011-852-2841-2524
Europol
   • The Hague 011-3170-353-1533
France
   • Paris 011-331- 4312-7100
Germany
   • Frankfurt 011-49-697-535-3763
Romania
   • Bucharest 011-40-21-316-4052
Interpol 011-334-7244-7198
Italy
   • Milan 011-39-02-290-35-447
   • Rome 011-390-64-674-2736
Mexico
   • Mexico City 011-210-472-6175
Russia
   • Moscow 011-7-095-252-2451
South Africa
   • Pretoria 011- 2-712-342-3380
United Kingdom
   • London 011-44-207-894-0846

Source   The U.S. Secret Service. 2006. <http://www.secretservice.gov/field_offices.shtml>

A

AAM. *See* American Association of Museums
Abduction, 369–370
ABFDE. *See* American Board of Forensic
    Document Examiners
Abrasion collar, 203
Accelerant indicators, 127–128
Acceptance testing, 253–255
Access control, 255–258
    architectural security with, 447
    CCTV for, 276
    chemical industry using, 345–346
    electronic systems for, 256–257
    levels of, 346–348
    materials, 257–258
    in museum security, 458
    natural, 487
    people and, 255–256
    traffic, 257
    wireless, 313
Access portals, 518–519
Accessory, 223
Accountability, 120
Accusatory interrogation, 184
AC&D. *See* Alarm communications and display
ACFE. *See* Association of Certified Fraud
    Examiners
Active detectors, 344
Active infrared sensors, 281, 284
Active sensors, 278, 282
Active sonic sensors, 286
ADA. *See* Americans with Disabilities Act
ADEA. *See* Age Discrimination in Employment
    Act
Administrative false positive, 361–362
Administrative law, 208–209
Admissibility, 139
The advance, 371
Advance team, 381
Advanced fee schemes, 195
Adversaries, 101
A&E. *See* Architect and engineer
AESRM. *See* Alliance for Enterprise Security
    Risk Management
Affidavits, 239–240
Affirmative action, 210
Affirmative defenses, 33
AFOSI. *See* Air Force Office of Special
    Investigations
After-action report, 382

After-hours mode, 462
Age Discrimination, 1–2
Age Discrimination in Employment Act
    (ADEA), 1, 28–29
Age of technology, 38
The Age of Unreason (Handy), 16
Aggressor, 405, 407
Agroterrorism, 501–503
    impact of, 502
    U.S. vulnerability to, 502–503
    WMDs and, 501–502
Air Force Office of Special Investigations
    (AFOSI), 606–607
Alarm assessment system, 277, 441–442
Alarm communications and display (AC&D), 442
Alarm points, 259
Alarm system management, 258–261
    alarm points in, 259
    communication/display in, 259–260
    history files in, 260–261
    human component of, 258–259
Alarm zones, 328
Alcohol abuse, 30
Alcohol testing, 348–349
ALE. *See* Annual loss exposure
ALF. *See* Animal Liberation Front
Alien migration control, 608
Alliance for Enterprise Security Risk
    Management (AESRM), 476
Alligator effect, 127
Alternate question, 186
Alternate site, 107
American Academy of Forensic Sciences, 176
American Association of Museums (AAM), 458
American Board of Forensic Document
    Examiners (ABFDE), 176
American law sources, 207
American National Standards Institute (ANSI),
    314
American Polygraph Association, 172
American Society for Industrial Security (ASIS),
    458, 464
American Society of Questioned Document
    Examiners, 176
Americans with Disabilities Act (ADA), 25,
    33–34, 52, 238, 388
Ames, Aldrich, 427, 428f
Animal Liberation Front (ALF), 557, 562
Annual loss exposure (ALE), 437
Anonymous letter file, 151
ANSI. *See* American National Standards
    Institute
Antenna design, 285f

Anthrax, 505–506
Antiterrorism teams, 607
Antitrust laws, 12, 16
Anti-virus, 107
Aperture, 168
Apprenticeship programs, 1
Architect and engineer (A&E), 254
Architectural design, 452
Architectural Design for Crime Prevention
    (Newman), 480
Architectural security, 445–450
  design planning for, 448–449
  zoning concept in, 449
Architecture, 521–522
Armstrong, Lance, 372
Arraignment, 213–214
Arrest law, 205–207
  probable cause in, 205–206
  search incidental to, 240–241
  searches in, 206
  suspect questioning in, 206–207
Arson, 127–130
  accelerant indicators in, 127–128
  checklist for, 128–130
  gas chromatography used in, 144
Artis v. Wayside Baptist Church, 233
Aryan Brotherhood, 562
ASIS. *See* American Society for Industrial Security
ASIS International, 86, 391, 497
Assassinations, 543
Assertiveness, 184
Asset protection, 272–273, 308, 431–432
Association of Certified Fraud Examiners
    (ACFE), 364
Association of Threat Assessment Professionals
    (ATAP), 402
Asymmetric Cryptography, 108
Asymmetrical warfare, 546, 547, 556
ATAP. *See* Association of Threat Assessment
    Professionals
ATF. *See* Bureau of Alcohol, Tobacco, Firearms
    and Explosives
Attacks, 525–526, 544–545
Attempt, 224
Attendance sheets, 228
Audio detection sensors, 330–331
Audit, 7
Authentication, 349–351
Authentication/authorization/cryptography,
    349–351
  FIPS 201 and, 350–351
  identity management in, 350
  RBAC in, 351

Authenticity determination, 141
Authorization, 6, 349–351
Automobile paints, 148
Awareness program, 115

B

BAC. *See* Blood alcohol content
Background checks. *See* Background screening
Background investigation, 472
Background screening, 233, 234
  credential verification in, 386
  FCRA and, 374–375
  legal issues of, 386–387
  pre-employment, 384–387
  public/private records used in, 385–386
Backup systems, 464–465
Bacterial agents, 505–506
Baggage team, 381–382
BAI. *See* Behavior Analysis Interview
Bait and switch, 196
Balance magnetic switch (BMS), 441
Balanced protection, 306
Bank Robbery film, 151
Bank Robbery Note file, 151
Barrier (penetration) detectors
  in interior intrusion detection, 338–339
  sensors in, 331–333
Barriers, 22–24
Bed and breakfast facilities, 455–456
Behavior Analysis Interview (BAI), 130–132
Behavioral changes, 406
Behavioral competence, 54
Behavioral investigative analysis, 401
Benchmarking, 352
Benefit fraud, 592–593
Best practices, 2–5
  achieving, 5
  challenging assumptions of, 2–3
  continuous loop of, 352–353
  corporate security using, 18
  discrimination reduced with, 50
  guard operations using, 351–354
  organizations using, 22–23
  pursuing, 4
  quality in, 5
  staffing allocations for, 3
  technical knowledge with, 62
BFOQ. *See* Bona fide occupational
    qualifications
BIA. *See* Business impact analysis

Bid-rigging, 198
bin Laden, Osama, 554, 569
Biological weapons, 505–507
  as bacterial agents, 505–506
  threat of, 558–559
  as toxins, 507
  as viruses, 506–507
Biometric identification systems, 519
Bird, F.E., 490
Bistatic microwave sensors, 281
Black Ice: The Invisible Threat of Cyber-Terror
    (Verton), 566
Blind specimen testing, 362
Blood alcohol content (BAC), 348
Blood examinations, 142
Blood testing, 349
BMS. *See* Balance magnetic switch
Body language, 161–167
Body movements, 165–166, 165t
BOMA. *See* Building Owners and Managers
    Association
Bomb scene, 549–551
Bomb threat management, 65–70
  bomb threat evaluation in, 66–67
  prevention activities in, 65–66
  responses in, 67f
  search considerations in, 68–69
  search/evacuation in, 67–68
  suspicious objects in, 69–70
  training in, 66
Bombs, 532–533
Bona fide occupational qualifications (BFOQ), 1
Botulism, 507
Boundary-penetration sensors, 283
Bovine spongiform encephalopathy (BSE), 501
Brain problem syndrome, 62
Branham, F. Leigh, 395
Brannigan, Francis L., 88, 89
Brannigan, Maureen, 89
Brantingham, Paul/Pat, 445, 488, 496
Breath tests, 349
Broken Window Theory, 485–486
BSE. *See* Bovine spongiform encephalopathy
Bubonic plague, 506
Budget motel, 465–467
Budget planning, 8–9, 9t
Budgeting, 5–8
  cost-benefit ratio in, 8
  stages of, 6–7
  zero-based, 7
Budgets, 471
Building Construction for the Fire Service
    (Brannigan), 88

Building materials, 150–151
Building Owners and Managers Association
    (BOMA), 96
Bullets, 146
Burden of proof, 139, 201–202, 236
Bureau of Alcohol, Tobacco, Firearms and
    Explosives (ATF), 571–581
  field offices of, 572–581
  firearms/explosives and, 571–572
Burglary, 132–133, 153
Buried-line sensors, 261–262, 279–280
  exterior intrusion detection with, 333–334
  geophone transducers and, 261
  piezoelectric transducers and, 261–262
  strain/magnetic, 262
Bush, George W., 510, 585
Business conduct, 10, 19
Business continuity planning, 70–74
  components of, 72–73
  disaster recovery planning synonymous
    with, 70
  process of, 71
  recovery strategies in, 73–74
Business ethics, 9–15
  antitrust laws and, 12
  classified information used in, 12–13
  code of ethics in, 10
  conflicts of interest in, 12
  political contributions and, 11
  prohibited investments in, 12–13
  sample policies of, 11–15
  violations of, 14
Business ethics policy, 15–19
Business impact analysis (BIA), 71, 409–411
  conducting, 72
  methodology of, 410–411
  risk analysis and, 409–410
Business intelligence, 99–100
Business law, 207–209
Business opportunity schemes, 195–196
Business systems, 475–476
"But for" defense, 216
Buy-busts, 192–193

C

CA. *See* Certificate Authority
CAI. *See* Computer-assisted instruction
Calder, James D., 497
Call-for-service record, 418
Camera scanning functions, 263

Camera system, 272f
Canine breeds, 379
Capacitance proximity detectors, 310–311
Capacitance proximity sensors, 287–288
Capacitance sensors, 284
Capacity defense, 214–215
Card system, 69
Career development, 61
CARVER Matrix, 499, 500t
CAS. *See* Collaborative Adjudication Services
Case law, 208, 224
Cash, theft and, 460
CBP. *See* Customs and Border Protection
CBT. *See* Computer-based training
CCD. *See* Charge coupled device
CCI. *See* Competitive counterintelligence
CCS. *See* Cyber Crimes Section
CCTV. *See* Closed-circuit television
CDC. *See* Centers of Disease Control
Centers of Disease Control (CDC), 502
Central heating, ventilating and air
    conditioning (HVAC), 86
Central Intelligence Agency (CIA), 539, 581–582
Central nervous system (CNS), 358
Central Security Service (CSS), 605–606
Certificate Authority (CA), 109
Certificate revocation list (CRL), 109
Certification, for dogs, 404
Certified Protection Professional (CPP), 42
CES. *See* Child Exploitation Section
Chain of command, 94
Chain of custody, 139
Chain Referral schemes, 195
Charge coupled device (CCD), 263, 267
Charge Transfer Device (CTD), 264
Charity fine program, 61
Charity fraud, 199
Check kiting, 199
Checkwriter standards, 146
Chemical examinations, 144
Chemical false positive, 361
Chemical industry
    access control in, 345–346
    mitigation assessment in, 432
    perimeter protection in, 345–346
    PHA in, 432
    potential threats to, 433
    prevention strategies for, 431–433
    risk assessment in, 431–433
    security assessments in, 432–433
    security for, 450–451
    security officers in, 346
Chemical threats, 559

Chemical weapons, 503–505
    as chlorine, 505
    as hydrogen cyanide, 505
    as mustard agent, 504
    as nerve agents, 504
    as toxins, 503–504
Chief Security Officer (CSO), 40, 258
    change adaptation of, 16
    major accident and, 92
    security group services and, 393
    spokesperson duties of, 90–91
    strategic planning and, 57
    suspicious object notification to, 69–70
    training responsibilities of, 382–383
Child Exploitation Section (CES), 599
Chlorine, 505
CI. *See* Competitive intelligence;
    Counterintelligence office; Criminal
    Investigation
CIA. *See* Central Intelligence Agency
CID. *See* Criminal Investigation Division
Cilluffo, Frank, 569
CIP. *See* Critical Infrastructure Protection
CIS. *See* Comprehensive Information services
Civil actions, 248–249
Civil courts, 389
Civil law, 224
Civil litigation, 225
Civil Rights Act, 388
    Title VII of, 29, 40–41, 47–55
    violations of, 59–60
Clarke, Ronald V., 477, 488, 496
Classified information, 12–13, 17
Clean desk policy, 115
Clear zones, 301
Clinton Administration, 110
Closed-circuit television (CCTV), 257, 380
    access control from, 276
    asset protection from, 272–273
    camera scanning functions in, 263
    color cameras used in, 266
    covert techniques using, 266–271
    emergency/disaster plan with, 273
    employee training using, 274
    false security from, 413
    fiber-optic lenses in, 270
    fire and safety with, 275
    format sizes in, 265
    lenses used with, 268
    low-light sensors in, 265
    resolution of, 264–265
    for security, 262–266
    security roles of, 271–276

security surveillance from, 275–276
sensor types in, 263–264
single camera system of, 272f
small cameras used in, 268–269
solid-state sensors in, 264
special configurations of, 270–271
sprinkler head pinhole lens used in, 269–270, 269f
stand-by power and, 273
system, 262f
wall hiding, 267f
wireless transmission in, 271
CMOS. *See* Complementary metal-oxide device
CMT. *See* Crisis management team
CNS. *See* Central nervous system
Co-analysis counseling, 19
Code Adam Act, 598
Code of ethics, 10
CODEC (compression/decompression), 291, 292
Codes, 328–329
Cohen, Larry, 480, 496
Collaborative Adjudication Services (CAS), 582–583
Color cameras, 266
Color discrimination. *See* Race discrimination
Command and control, 70
Commercial bribery, 198
Commercial buildings, 96–98
Commercial fraud, 596
Commercial property, 416–420
Commodity syndrome, 351–352
Common law, 224
Communications, 106, 121
alarm systems and, 259–260
vulnerabilities to, 513
Community approach, 481–484
Community-centered program, 483–484
Compensation, 50
Compensation discrimination, 28–29, 50
Compensation, of security officers, 395–396
Compensatory damages, torts, 250–251
Competitive counterintelligence (CCI), 99, 100–101, 101f
Competitive intelligence (CI), 99, 102–104, 103f, 429
The complainant, 159–160
Complementary metal-oxide device (CMOS), 263
Complementary sensors, 300
Compliance, 77–78
Compliancy policy, 243
Compliancy programs, 244
Component failure, 306

Comprehensive Information services (CIS), 233
Computer revolution, 87
Computer security, 104–107
data gathering in, 105–106
disaster recovery and, 104–107
emergency plans in, 105
Computer software, 567–568
Computer systems
protecting, 158
protecting information on, 121
Computer technology, 430
Computer-assisted instruction (CAI), 354
Computer-based training (CBT)
advantages of, 355–356
interactivity types in, 356–357
organizational considerations in, 357
security professionals with, 354–357
Computer-controlled equipment, 38
Computer-related fraud, 198
Condonation defense, 215
Confession, 140, 237
Confidentiality agreement, 115–116
Conflict of interest, 12, 16
Consent defense, 215
Conspiracy, 224
Constitutional law, 208
Consumer credit reports, 373–374
Consumer Report (CRA), 238
Contact switches, 298
Containment strategy, 443
Contemporary threats, 294–295
Continuous quality improvement (CQI), 21
barriers removed in, 22–24
warranties instead of, 27–28
Contraband, 240
Contract force, 376
Contract law, 249–250
Contractors, 16
Contracts, 21, 377–378
Contributory negligence, 209–210
Control center vulnerabilities, 513
Control vector, 402
Convergence, 475
Cookies (computer), 107–108
Copyrights, 116, 220
Cornish, Derek B., 477
Corporate environment, 56–57
Corporate security, 15–19
Corporations
compliancy policy of, 243
compliancy programs for, 244
probation for, 244
sentencing guidelines for, 242–244

Corpus Delicti, 221
Corrective action, 194
Cosmetics, 148
Cost-benefit ratio, 8
Cost-effectiveness, 353
Counseling, 19–20
Counterintelligence office (CI), 583
Countermeasures, 102, 135
Countersurveillance, 371
Courts
    indigent defendants in, 211
    plea negotiations in, 212
    state court prosecutions in, 211–213
Cover story, 191–192
Covered individuals, 52
Covert sensors, 278, 282–283
Covert techniques, 266–271
CPP. *See* Certified Protection Professional
CPTED. *See* Crime Prevention Through
    Environmental Design
CQI. *See* Continuous quality improvement
CRA. *See* Consumer Report
Creating Defensible Space (Newman), 480
Credential verification, 386
Credential-reading locks, 312
Credit card fraud, 198–199
Credit header, 374
Credit information, 375
Credit reports, 373–374
Crime analysis, 133–136
    countermeasures assessed in, 135
    threat assessments in, 133–134
Crime control theories, 477–481
    crime pattern, 480
    defensible space, 480
    diffusion in, 481
    displacement concept in, 480–481
    rational choice, 477, 488
    routine activities, 480
Crime of force, 183
Crime pattern theory, 480
Crime prevention
    community approach to, 481–484
    community-centered program in, 483–484
    through environmental design, 484–488
    environmental/social, 488–489
    neighborhood watch for, 482–483
    restaurant security and, 460, 461
Crime Prevention Through Environmental Design
    (CPTED), 445, 477, 480, 482, 484–488, 489f
    implementing, 486–487
    operational security in, 485–486
    territorial behavior and, 487–488

Crime Prevention Through Environmental Design
    (Crowe), 486, 488
Crime record research, 416–417
Crime scene, 169
Crime statistics, 417
Crime-environment theory, 445
Crime-specific tactics, 484
Criminal aliens, 595
Criminal courts, 389
Criminal defenses, 214–216
Criminal history data, 212
Criminal information branch, 610–611
Criminal intent, in security law, 221–224
Criminal Investigation (CI), 603
Criminal Investigation Division (CID), 608
Criminal justice, 213–214
Criminal law, 224
Criminal records, 388–389
Crisis management team (CMT), 368
Crisis situations, 89–92
Critical assets, 527–528
Critical elements, 101
Critical functions, 72–73
Critical incident technique, 492
Critical Infrastructure Protection (CIP),
    507–510, 583
Critical national infrastructure
    access portals in, 518–519
    advanced architectures/designs in, 521–522
    decision support systems in, 519–520
    of electric power, 510–514
    NRP and, 516
    protection plan for, 514–517
    protection/prevention of, 518
    recovery/restitution in, 520
    risk management in, 515
    science/technology in, 517–523
    sensor systems in, 517
    social issues in, 522–523
    threats/vulnerabilities in, 520–521
    of transportation, 523–524
    of urban transit, 524–526, 565–566
    water system vulnerabilities in, 526–529
Critical technology, 564
Criticality, 499
CRL. *See* Certificate revocation list
Cross-examination, 246, 247–248
Crowe, Timothy, 486, 488
Cryptography, 108–109, 349–351
CSO. *See* Chief Security Officer
CSS. *See* Central Security Service
CTD. *See* Charge Transfer Device
Curtain walls, 87

Customer intelligence, 104
Customers, 58
Customs and Border Protection (CBP), 593, 609
Cutoff levels, drug testing, 363–364
Cyber Crimes Section (CCS), 599
Cyber offenses, 422
Cyber portals, 519
Cybercrime, 75
Cyberterrorism, 529–531
   future of, 568–569
   vulnerability to, 566–569

D

Dam failure, 79
Data gathering, 105–106
Data protection, 116–117
Data systems, 73
Database management, 75
Data-driven incident management, 74–79
Data-driven security myths, 77
Date stretching, 233–234
Daubert v. Merrell Dow Pharmaceuticals, 498
DBT. *See* Design Basis Threat
DEA. *See* Drug Enforcement Agency
The Death and Life of Great American Cities (Jacobs), 488
Debt consolidation schemes, 197
Decentralized cells, 552–553
Deceptive behaviors, 163, 166t
Deceptive signals, 165–167
Decision makers, 135–136
Decision matrix, 412–413, 413t
Decision support systems, 519–520
Decision-makers, 99f
Defense cyber crime center, 607
Defense Industrial Security Clearance Office (DISCO), 583
Defense Office of Hearings and Appeals (DOHA), 583
Defense Security Service (DSS), 582–583
Defenses
   capacity, 214–215
   criminal, 214–216
   specific, 215–216
Defensible space, 480
Defensible Space (Newman), 480, 488
Delay (components), 305, 305f, 442
Delivery system, security, 231

Deming, W. Edwards, 20–25
   employee troubleshooting and, 21
   leadership/training promoted by, 21–22
   quotas counterproductive from, 26–27
   Seven Deadly Sins from, 22–23
   statistical methods of, 20
Denials, 185, 406
Denning, Dorothy, 530
Department of Defense (DOD), 113
Department of Health and Human Services (DHHS), 360
Department of Homeland Security (DHS), 79, 509, 514, 517
Deposition, 216–217
   expert witness and, 219–221
   as witness testimony, 216–217
Depth of field, 168
Design
   elements, 307
   of perimeter sensor systems, 299–302
   planning, 448–449
   in PPS, 303–304
   security system flaws in, 462–464
Design Basis Threat (DBT), 528
Detection, 277, 304, 304f
Detention, 221–223
Deterrents, 310
DFS. *See* Digital Forensic Section
DHHS. *See* Department of Health and Human Services
DHS. *See* Department of Homeland Security
Diffusion, 481
Digital certificates, 108–109
Digital components, 291t
Digital Forensic Section (DFS), 599–600
Digital signatures, 108–109
Digital video, 289–291, 291–292
Digital video multiplexer/recorder (DVMR), 290
Digital video recorders (DVR), 266, 267, 290, 291
Digressions, 182
Diminished capacity, 216
Direct examination, 246
Direct witness, 159
Directive counseling, 19
Dirty bomb, 560
Disability discrimination, 25
Disaster(s)
   plans for, 273
   recovery from, 104–107
   recovery planning, 70
   response equipment for, 106
   types of, 79–83
Disciplinary action, 194

Discipline, 26–28
  clear instructions in, 27
  principles of, 26–27
  self-discipline and, 27–28
  in supervision, 26–28
DISCO. *See* Defense Industrial Security
    Clearance Office
Discrimination
  age, 1–2
  best practices reducing, 50
  compensation, 28–29, 50
  disability, 25
  national origin based, 40–41
  pregnancy, 55, 59
  race/color, 49–51
  religious, 51
  retaliation, 51–53
  sex-based, 54–55
Displacement concept, 480–481
Display, 259–260
District offices, 611–618
Divided-attention psychophysical tests, 359
DNA analysis, 136–138
  functions of, 138
  methodologies of, 136–137
  PCR in, 137–138
  RFLP in, 137
  violent crime using, 144
Documents
  forensics examination of, 144–146
  formal, 106
  fraud, 593
Documents, questioned, 174–177
DOD. *See* Department of Defense
Dog handler, 404. *See also* Working dogs
DOHA. *See* Defense Office of Hearings and
    Appeals
Domestic terrorism, 561
Door locks
  electronic hotel, 312
  Kaba PowerLever, 314
  network systems and, 313–314
  revolution in, 312–314
Doppler, Christian, 344
Doppler shift, 285, 341, 342
Double billing, 197
Double contingency analysis system, 513
Double jeopardy, 216
Driving histories, 389
DRO. *See* Office of Detention and Removal
Drucker, Peter, 75
Drug abuse, 30, 398–401
Drug dealers, 399

Drug Enforcement Agency (DEA), 398, 584
Drug interdiction, 608
Drug recognition process, 358–359
Drug testing, 360–362
  cutoff levels for, 363–364
  passive inhalation in, 362
  urinalysis in, 361–362
  urinalysis technologies in, 362–364
Drug type, false positive rates, 363f
DSS. *See* Defense Security Service
Dual-channel motion detectors, 287
Dual-technology sensors, 282, 287
Due diligence, 232–235
Due process, 201
Dumpster diving, 111, 157
DVMR. *See* Digital video multiplexer/recorder
DVR. *See* Digital video recorders
Dying declaration, 236

E

EAP. *See* Employee assistance program
Earth Liberation Front (ELF), 557, 562
Earthquakes, 79–80, 82–83
Eavesdropping, 428
Economic espionage, 109–111
Economic Espionage Act, 110
Economic protection, 474
Education verification, 390
Educational resources, 553–554
EEOC. *See* Equal Employment Opportunity
    Commission
EIA. *See* Electronic Industry Association
Electret cable transducer, 336–337
Electric field/capacitance sensors, 281, 334
Electric power
  as critical national infrastructure, 510–514
  protection of, 513–514
  threats to, 511–512
  vulnerabilities of, 512–513
Electric-field sensors, 299
Electromagnetic pulse (EMP), 560
Electromechanical sensors, 283–284
Electromechanical transducers, 335–336
Electronic hotel door locks, 312
Electronic Industry Association (EIA), 265
Electronic recording, 180
Electronic security systems, 253, 325
Electronic systems
  access control with, 256–257
  security design using, 449

Electrophoresis, 137
ELF. *See* Earth Liberation Front
E-mail, 158
Emergency
    at nuclear power plants, 81–82
    planning zones in, 81
    search, 241
Emergency management planning, 83–84
Emergency plans, 273
    in computer security, 105
    management's authority in, 106
Emergency response protocols, 84
Emergency Support Functions (ESF), 95, 535–537
EMIT. *See* Enzyme multiplied immunoassay
    test
EMP. *See* Electromagnetic pulse
Employee assistance program (EAP), 406
Employee Assistance Society of North America,
    348
Employee hotlines, 364–367
    legal mandates of, 365
    system selection for, 367
    warning signs for, 365–366
Employee Polygraph Protection Act (EPPA),
    171, 172, 388
Employees
    CCTV training, 274
    enriching lives of, 60–63
    five-step plan for, 408
    keeping good, 395
    loyalty of, 4
    prosecution of, 192
    troubleshooting by, 21
    upward feedback process and, 63f
Employers
    polygraph test guidance for, 172–173
    polygraph test requirements on, 174
    reasonable accommodations required by, 25
    religious practices and, 55
    substance abuse and, 398–401
    wage factors of, 28–29
Employment verification, 390
EMS. *See* Export Management System
Encoders/decoders, 292
Encryption, 425
Energy industry, 567
Engineering section, 141–142
Entrapment, 203, 215
Entry control, 442
Environmental crime prevention, 488–489
Environmental design, 484–488
Environmental Protection Agency (EPA), 106
Enzyme multiplied immunoassay test (EMIT), 363

EP. *See* Executive protection
EPA. *See* Environmental Protection Agency
EPPA. *See* Employee Polygraph Protection Act
Equal Employment Opportunity Commission
    (EEOC), 28, 238, 388
Equal pay. *See* Compensation discrimination
Equal Pay Act, 28
Equipment rental, 73–74
ESF. *See* Emergency Support Functions;
    Emergency support functions
Espionage, 222–223
Ethics
    of business, 9–15
    in business law, 209
Evacuation, bomb threat management, 67–68
Evaluation criteria, 2, 67
Evaluation, training, 227–228
Evidence
    bomb scene with, 550–551
    chain of custody, 139
    exclusion rules in, 140
    hearsay, 236
    identification, 139
    physical, 138–139
    rules of, 139–140, 235–237
    search and seizure and, 240
    types of, 138–140
Evidentiary testing, 349
Examiners, document, 176–177
Examiners, polygraph test, 173, 174
Exclusion rules, 140
Exclusionary rule, 206
Execution, 6
Executive kidnapping, 368–370
Executive protection (EP), 370–373
    advance information in, 371
    countersurveillance in, 371
    security awareness training in, 372–373
    threat assessment for, 370–371
    travel risk reduction in, 371–372
Exemplars, 174, 175
Expert witness, 219–221
Explosion dynamics, 532
Explosion threat, 558
Explosive weapons, 531–532, 544–545
Explosives, 146, 571–572
Export Management System (EMS), 594
Exposure assessment, risk, 415–416
Exterior intrusion detection, 333–334, 441
Exterior intrusion sensors, 276–282
    buried-line, 279–280
    fence-associated, 280–281
    freestanding, 281

Exterior intrusion sensors (*Continued*)
  performance characteristics of, 277–278
  sensor classification for, 278–279
  types of, 279t
Extreme heat, 80
Eye contact, 131
Eye management, 162

F

FAA. *See* Federal Aviation Administration
Facial expressions, 166–167, 166t
Facility characterization, 441
Factory Acceptance Test (FAT), 254
Factory system, 36–37
Fair Credit Reporting Act (FCRA), 234, 373–375,
    387–388, 390
  background checks and, 374–375
  credit reports and, 373–374
  inaccurate information and, 375
False alarms, 326
False positive errors, 171
False positive rates, 363f
False security, 413
Farrington, 485
FAT. *See* Factory Acceptance Test
Fayol, Henri, 37
FBI. *See* Federal Bureau of Investigation
FBOs. *See* Fixed-base operators
FCC. *See* Federal Communications Commission
FCO. *See* Federal Coordinating Officer
FCRA. *See* Fair Credit Reporting Act
FDL. *See* Forensic Document Laboratory
Federal Air Marshall Service, 585–586
Federal Aviation Administration (FAA), 106
Federal bankruptcy court, 389
Federal Bureau of Investigation (FBI), 176, 368,
    538, 586–591
  field offices of, 586–591
  forensic services of, 140–153
Federal Communications Commission (FCC),
    340, 344
Federal Coordinating Officer (FCO), 537
Federal Emergency Management Agency
    (FEMA), 79, 106, 534
Federal government, 534–538
Federal offenses, 222–223
Federal Personal Identity Verification program.
    See FIPS 201
Federal Protection Service (FPS), 597
Federal Resource Coordinator (FRC), 538

Federal Response Plan (FRP), 534–535
Federal Sentencing Guidelines, 244
Federal Trade Commission (FTC), 155, 234
Federal Transit Administration (FTA), 524, 525,
    565–566
Felonies, parties to, 223
Felson, Marcus, 480, 488, 496
FEMA. *See* Federal Emergency Management
    Agency
Fence disturbance detection
  electret cable transducer in, 336–337
  electromechanical transducers in, 335–336
  geophone transducers in, 336
  piezoelectric transducers in, 336
  sensors in, 334–337
  taut-wire switches in, 337
Fence disturbance sensors, 333
Fence-associated sensors, 280–281
Fences, 309
FFL. *See* Fixed focal length
Fiber/hair examinations, 147–148
Fiber-optic cable sensors, 280, 284
Fiber-optic lenses, 270
Field interviews, 419
Field of view, 169, 267
Field offices
  of ATF, 572–581
  of FBI, 586–591
Field-level organizational structures, 537–538
Fifth amendment, 206–207
Financial crimes, 620
Financial institutions, 30
Financial investigations, 595–596
Financial Services Modernization Act. *See*
    Gramm-Leach-Bliley Act
Fingerprint identification, 140–141
FIPS 201 (Federal Personal Identity Verification
    program), 109, 350–351
Fire, 80
Fire and safety, 275, 295
Fire detection systems, 89
Fire Life Safety, 85–89
Fire Protection Handbook (Holmes), 88
Firearms, 146–147, 372, 571–572
Firewall protection, 107, 425
Fischer, Robert J., 85
Five-step incident management cycle, 78f
Five-step plan, 408
Fixed focal length (FFL), 269
Fixed-base operators (FBOs), 372
Flagging, 157
Flexible labor force, 16
Flood, 80

FMD. *See* Foot and mouth disease
Focal length, 268
Focal points, 421
Follow-through, 13–14, 19
Food stamp frauds, 198
Foot and mouth disease (FMD), 501
Forecasting, budget planning, 9
Foreign intelligence services, 110
Foreign nationals, 41
Forensic Document Laboratory (FDL), 599
Forensics, 620
    documents examined in, 144–146
    explosives examinations in, 146
    FBI services in, 140–153
    firearms examined in, 146–147
    hair/fibers examined in, 147–148
    materials analysis in, 148–149
    metallurgy examined in, 149–150
    mineralogy and, 150–151
    photographic examinations in, 151
    security consultants in, 468
    serology, 142–143
    shoe print/tire tread evidence used by, 152
    tool mark identification by, 152–153
    toxicological examinations in, 144
Forgery, 145
Formal organizations, 41
Fourth Amendment, 237
FPS. *See* Federal Protection Service
Franklin, Benjamin, 539
Fraser, J., 552
Fraud, document, 593
FRC. *See* Federal Resource Coordinator
Free-enterprise system, 11
Freestanding sensors, 281
Fringe benefits, 48
FRP. *See* Federal Response Plan
Frye v. United States, 498
FTA. *See* Federal Transit Administration
FTC. *See* Federal Trade Commission
Fugitive program, 609–610
Fulton, I., 552

G

Gallium arsenide light-emitting diode, 332
Gantt chart, 37
Gantt, Henry L., 37
Garrick, B., 434
Gas chromatography technique, 144, 360, 363
General Auditor, 14, 19

Geometry of Crime Theory, 488
Geophone transducers
    buried line sensors and, 261
    in Fence disturbance detection, 336
Germain, G.L., 490
Gestures, 130–131, 162, 166
Gilbreth, Lillian/Frank, 37
Glass breakage detectors, 338
Glass fractures, 150
Glass-break sensors, 283
GLBA. *See* Gramm-Leach-Bliley Act
Good character defense, 214
Gorman, Mark, 87, 88
Grading systems, 49
Gramm-Leach-Bliley Act (GLBA), 29–31
Green, Gion, 85
Group typologies, 546–547
Guard operations, 375–378
    benchmarking improving, 352
    best practices used in, 351–354
    contracts in, 377–378
    cost in, 353
    expectations/realities in, 353–354
    propriety/contract choices in, 376
    RFP in, 376–377
Guilt, 179–180
Guilt complex reactor, 164
Gunshot residue, 147
Gunshot wounds, 203–204

H

Hackers, 530–531
Hacktivists, 530–531
Hair/fiber examinations, 147–148
Hale, Nathan, 539
Hall, Brandon, 355
Hall effect switch, 283
Hamas, 541
Handwriting analysis, 145
Handy, Charles, 16
Hardware, 346
Haskell, Thomas L., 497
Hazardous materials, 80, 451
Health insurance, 48
Health maintenance organizations (HMOs), 453
Healthcare security systems, 452
Hearsay evidence, 236
Heat sensors, 338–339
Hezbollah, 541
Hiding places, 555

Hierarchy of needs, 39f
High security, 347
High-rise buildings
    commercial, 96–98
    fire life safety in, 85–89
    infrastructure capabilities of, 97
    security hazards in, 86–87
High-tech companies, 49
Hiring, 50, 232–235
Historical perspective, 155–156
Historical roots, 36–38
History files, 260–261
History of the Peloponnesian War (Thucydides), 493
HMOs. *See* Health maintenance organizations
Hoenig, Christopher, 56
Holmes, Wayne D., 88
Home improvement schemes, 197
Home solicitation schemes, 197
Homeland Security Presidential Directive/ HSPD-5, 93, 95
Homicides, 294–295
Horizontal-gaze nystagmus, 359
Hospital security
    concepts for, 452–454
    moral responsibilities in, 454
    unique aspects of, 453–454
Hostility, 50, 154
Hot site, 77
Hotel security, 455
Human component, 258–259
Human factors, in interviewing, 153–155
Human memory, 154
Human relations era, 37
Human resources, 352, 366
Human smuggling, 594
Human trafficking, 594
Hurricanes, 80–81
HVAC. *See* Central heating, ventilating and air conditioning
Hydrogen cyanide, 505

I

IAP. *See* Incident action plans
IAPSC. *See* International Associations of Professional Security Consultants
ICACs. *See* Internet Crimes Against Children Task Forces
ICE. *See* Immigration and Customs Enforcement

ICRs. *See* Investigative consumer reports
ICS. *See* Incident Command System
Identity management, 350
Identity theft, 155–159, 593
    historical perspective of, 155–156
    methods of, 156–157
    prevention of, 157–158
    terminology of, 157
IESNA. *See* Illumination Engineering Society of North America
ILCI. *See* International Loss Control Institute
Illegal trade, 593–594
Illumination Engineering Society of North America (IESNA), 485
IMI. *See* Interactive multimedia instruction
Immigration and Customs Enforcement (ICE), 591–603
    benefit fraud and, 592–593
    financial investigations and, 595–596
    human trafficking/smuggling and, 594
    illegal trade and, 593–594
    IPR enforced by, 597
    LESC and, 600
    NFOP and, 594–595
    operation community shield from, 591
Immunity defense, 215
Immunoassays, 360–361, 364
Improvised nuclear device (IND), 533–534
In-Bond diversion, 596
Incident action plans (IAP), 95
Incident causation model, 490–493
    loss incidents in, 490–491
    management failures in, 491–492
    post-incident analysis using, 492f
    using, 492–493
Incident Command System (ICS), 93–95, 503, 537
Incident management, 80f
    data-driven, 74–79
    five-step cycle in, 78f
    knowledge in, 76f
    national structure of, 92–93
    security departments and, 76–77
IND. *See* Improvised nuclear device
Indictment, 213
Indigent defendants, 211
Indirect approach, 179
Indirect witness, 159
Individual protection, 1–2
Industrial espionage, 111–112
    computer technology in, 430
    five stages of, 426
    risk assessment and, 425–428

spies in, 426–428
technology in, 428–429
Industrial revolution, 36–37
Industrial Security Program (ISP), 583
Informal organizations, 41–42
Informant, 427
Information
    CI cycle of, 103f
    classification of, 114–115
    collection/processing of, 102–103
    computer systems and, 121
    finding/protecting, 75–76
    inaccurate credit, 375
    industrial espionage and, 426
    integrated business intelligence cycle
        processing, 99f
    in knowledge-based decisions, 76f
    managing sensitive, 112–117
    protection policy for, 422
    security management finding, 79–80
    security of, 113–114
    sources of, 429–430
Information Systems Audit and Control
    Association (ISACA), 476
Information Systems Security Association
    (ISSA), 476
Information technology (IT), 117, 290, 475–476,
    529
Information Technology and Administrative
    Section (ITAS), 599
Infrared detectors, 340–341
Infrared sources, 207
Infrasonic sensors, 284
Infrastructure, 563–565
Infrastructure capabilities, 97
In-house security consultants, 469–471
In-house security reports, 418
Insanity defense, 215
Insider threats, 519
Inspections
    of packages, 257–258
    TSCM protection, 123–125
Instructions, 27
Instructor standards, 228–229
Instructors, training, 228–229
Insurance, 191
Insurance fraud, 198
Integrated business intelligence cycle, 99f
Integrated security system, 275f, 327–329
Integration considerations, 327–329
Intellectual property rights (IPR), 220–221, 597
Intelligence agencies, 539
Intelligence function, 538–540

Intelligent video processing, 290
Intentional torts, 251
Interactive listening, 22
Interactive multimedia instruction (IMI), 354
Interactivity types, 356–357
Interior barrier detectors, 339
Interior boundary penetration sensors, 441
Interior intrusion detection
    barrier penetration detectors in, 338–339
    operable opening switches in, 339
    sensors in, 337–339
    volumetric motion detectors in, 337–338
Interior intrusion sensors, 282–289
    boundary-penetration, 283
    classification of, 288t
    electromechanical, 283–284
    proximity, 287–289
    volumetric/line detection, 283
Internal Revenue Service (IRS), 603
International Associations of Professional
    Security Consultants (IAPSC), 467
International Loss Control Institute (ILCI),
    490
International Security Management
    Association, 497
International terrorism, 75, 561
Internet
    risk assessment and, 422–425
    website blocking software for, 125–126
Internet Crimes Against Children Task Forces
    (ICACs), 598
Internet protocol video (IP), 289–293
    advantages of, 290
    evolution of, 290–291
    implementation of, 292–293
    new products for, 291–292
    switching in, 292
Internetworking, 475–476
Internship programs, 32–34
    advantages/disadvantages of, 33
    joining, 33–34
    for security manager's apprentice, 32–33
Interpersonal skills, 39
Interrogation
    interview v., 181–182
    kinesics and, 163–164
    nine steps of, 184–187
    room preparation for, 166
Interruption, 305
Interstate commerce, 226
Interview
    human factors in, 153–155
    interrogation v., 181–182

Interview *(Continued)*
   perception in, 153–154
   resentment in, 154–155
   of security administrator, 397–398
   undercover investigations with, 193
   witness, 159–161
Interviewing witnesses, 159–161
   the complainant and, 159–160
   direct/indirect witnesses and, 159
Intoxication defense, 215
Intranet, 424–425
Introduction to Security (Fischer/Green), 85
Intruder types, 293–295
Intrusion detection, 251, 463
   architectural design with, 452
   contemporary threats for, 294–295
   exterior sensors for, 276–282
   intruder types for, 293–295
   maintenance department and, 295–296
   possible outcomes of, 438
   sensors in, 441
   system design coordination for, 295–296
   traditional threats for, 293–294
Intrusion torts, 251
Invasion of privacy, 203
Investigations
   labor unions involved in, 202
   methods of, 201
   photography in, 167–169
   in pre-employment background screening,
      387–388
   in workplace, 199–203
Investigative consumer reports (ICRs), 373–
   374
Investigative techniques, 188–189
Investments, prohibited, 12–13, 17
Invisible barrier detector
   infrared detectors and, 340–341
   microwave detectors and, 340
   sensors in, 339–341
Invisible barrier detectors, 333
IP. *See* Internet protocol video
IPR. *See* Intellectual property rights
Irresistible impulse defense, 216
IRS. *See* Internal Revenue Service
ISACA. *See* Information Systems Audit and
   Control Association
ISP. *See* Industrial Security Program
ISSA. *See* Information Systems Security
   Association
IT. *See* Information technology
ITAS. *See* Information Technology and
   Administrative Section

J

Jacobs, Jane, 488
Jamb peeling, 133, 297
JCITA. *See* Joint Counter-intelligence Training
   Academy
Jeffery, C. Ray, 488
Jenkins, Brian, 560
JFO. *See* Joint Field Office
JIT. *See* Just-in-time production
Job requirements, 54
Job Task Analysis, 34–36
Joint Counter-intelligence Training Academy
   (JCITA), 583
Joint Field Office (JFO), 95, 537
Joint Terrorism Task Force, 600
Jury trial, 212
Just-in-time production (JIT), 38

K

Kaba PowerLever lock, 314
Kaplan, S., 434
Kelling, George, 485, 496
Key cards, 256
Kidnapping, 543
Kinesics
   body language studied in, 161–167
   deceptive signals in, 165–167
   interrogation and, 163–164
   physiological roots of, 164–165
Kingsbury, Arthur A., 85
Knife wounds, 203–204
Knowledge
   in incident management, 80f
   pyramid, 104f
Knowledge-based decisions, 75, 76f
Ku Klux Klan, 562

L

Labor unions, 202
LAN. *See* Local area network
Land schemes, 197
Landslide (mudslide), 81
Larceny, 218, 221
Lateral blasts, 83
Lava flow, 83

Law enforcement agencies
  dogs working for, 403
  intelligence function of, 538–540
  polygraph used by, 170
  terrorism and, 562–563
  undercover investigations and, 191–192
Law enforcement records, 417–418
Law Enforcement Support Center (LESC), 600
Laws, 224–225
Lawsuits, 225–226, 231
Leadership
  Deming promoting, 21–22
  interpersonal skills in, 39
  terrorist groups with, 552–553
LED. See Light-emitting diode
Lee, John, 31
Legal counsel, 352
Legal issues, 386–387
Legal mandates, 365
Legislative intelligence, 103–104
Lens mounts, 266
Lenses, CCTV, 268
LESC. See Law Enforcement Support Center
Liabilities, 454
Life safety threats, 86
Light-emitting diode (LED), 270, 332
Lighting, 169
Lighting, photography, 169
Line detection sensors, 278–279, 283
Line of demarcation, 128
Line-of-sight sensors (LOS), 278
Litigation, avoiding, 202
LLL. See Low-light level
Local area network (LAN), 112
Locks. See also Door locks
  burglary and, 132–133, 153
  credential-reading, 312
  types of, 296–298
Lodging security, 455–456, 456t
Loftus, R.G., 490
LOS. See Line-of-sight sensors
Loss incidents, 490–491
Low security, 347
Lowballing, 197
Low-light level (LLL), 267
Low-light level sensors, 265

M

MAD. See Mutual assured destruction
Magnetic buried line sensor, 262

Magnetic field sensors, 280
Magnetostrictive transducers, 343
Maintenance department, 295–296
Major accident, 92
Major disaster response, 534–538
Malcolm Baldrige process, 49
Malice, 222
Management
  of budget planning, 8–9
  emergency plan authority in, 106
  historical roots of, 36–38
  incident causation model and, 491–492
  interactive listening needed by, 22
  minimum layers of, 59
  mobility of, 24
  proprietary information and, 121–122
  restaurant security and, 461
  risk analysis and, 415
  science era of, 37–38
  sensitive information, 112–117
Managers, 53–54, 57–58
Mara Salvatrucha organization, 591
Martin, G., 556
Maslow, A.H., 39–40, 39f
Mass spectrometry, 360, 363
Materials access control, 257–258
Materials analysis, 148–149
Mayo, Elton, 37
MCP. See Micro-channel plate
MCRENDERS, 164
McVeigh, Timothy, 562
Mean-time-between-failure (MTBF), 328
Mean-time-to-repair (MTTR), 328
Mechanical impression examination, 145
Mechanical inertia switches, 335
Mechanical vibration transducers, 311
Media, 543
Media control, 89–92
Medical fraud, 197
Medical review officer (MRO), 361
Medium security, 347
Mental illness, 398
Merchandising schemes, 196
Mercury switches, 335
Merit rating, 44–45
Metallurgy examination, 149–150
Methodologies of DNA analysis, 136–137
Micro-channel plate (MCP), 265
Microwave detectors, 340
Microwave motion detector, 341–342
Microwave sensors, 285, 285f
Microwave systems, 513
Microwave transmission systems, 271

Military, 403
Mineralogy, 150–151
Mini-lenses, 268
Miranda rights, 206, 213
Miranda v Arizona, 206
Misconduct litigation, 225
Mitigation assessment, 432
Mitigation inspections, 76
MO. *See* Modus operandi
Modes of operation, 462
Modus operandi (MO), 556
Mole, 427
Molotov cocktails, 532
Money laundering, 596
Monostatic microwave sensors, 281
Moral responsibilities, 454
Mortgage loan schemes, 197
Motel security, 455
Motivation, 40–42, 405
Motivation, Maslow's theory of, 39–40
Motivational controls, 17–18
Motive, 222, 561–562
MPEG4, 292
MRO. *See* Medical review officer
MTBF. *See* Mean-time-between-failure
MTTR. *See* Mean-time-to-repair
Mugging, 187–188
Muhammad, Omar Bakri, 569
Museum security, 456–460
    access control in, 458
    thefts and, 459
Mustard agent, 504
Mutual assured destruction (MAD), 533

N

NAANF. *See* National Automobile Altered
    Numbers File
NAPBS. *See* National Association of
    Professional Background Screeners
NAR. *See* Nuisance Alarm Rate
National Association of Professional
    Background Screeners (NAPBS), 235
National Automobile Altered Numbers File
    (NAANF), 141
National Center for Missing and Exploited
    Children (NCMEC), 620
National Council of Investigation and Security
    Services, 497
National Crime Information Center (NCIC),
    235, 595, 600

National Crime Survey (NCS), 416, 417
National Drug Intelligence Center (NDIC),
    603–605
National Drug Intelligence Library, 604
National Explosives Detection Canine Program
    (NEDCP), 378–379
National Fire Protection Association (NFPA), 96
National Fraudulent Check file, 151
National Fugitive Operations Program (NFOP),
    594–595
National Household Survey on Drug Abuse,
    398
National incident command system
    organization, 92–93
National Incident Management System (NIMS),
    93–95
National Industrial Security Program (NISP),
    33, 120, 582
National Infrastructure Advisory Council
    (NIAC), 514
National Infrastructure Protection Plan (NIPP),
    514
National Institute on Drug Abuse (NIDA), 363,
    398
National Motor Vehicle Certificate of Title, 151
National origin, discrimination of, 40–41
National Response Plan (NRP), 516, 534–536
National Response Plan (NSP), 79, 95–96
National Science and Technology Council
    (NSTC), 522
National Science Foundation of America (NSF),
    355
National Security Act, 539
National Security Agency (NSA), 605–606
National Stolen Art file, 151
National Stolen Coin file, 151–152
National structure, 92–93
National Television System Committee (NTSC),
    263, 265
National Vehicle Identification Number
    Standard File (NVSF), 141
Natural access control, 487
Natural surveillance, 485, 487
Naval Criminal Investigation Service (NCIS),
    618
NCIC. *See* National Crime Information Center
NCIS. *See* Naval Criminal Investigation Service
NCMEC. *See* National Center for Missing and
    Exploited Children
NCS. *See* National Crime Survey
NDIC. *See* National Drug Intelligence Center
NEDCP. *See* National Explosives Detection
    Canine Program

Negligence
    cases in, 231
    concepts in, 209–210
    hiring and, 232–235
    in premise design, 229–232
Negligence liability, 225–229
Negligent hiring, 210
Negligent training, 225–229
Neighborhood watch, 482–483
Nerve agents, 504
Nervous system, 164f
Network access control systems, 313
Network issues, 292
Network systems, 313–314
Network video recorder (NVR), 291, 292
Neutralization analysis, 444
Newman, Oscar, 445, 480, 488
NFOP. *See* National Fugitive Operations
    Program
NFPA. *See* National Fire Protection Association
NGOs. *See* Non-Government Organizations
NIAC. *See* National Infrastructure Advisory
    Council
NIDA. *See* National Institute on Drug Abuse
NIMS. *See* National Incident Management
    System
NIPP. *See* National Infrastructure Protection Plan
NISP. *See* National Industrial Security Program
NLRB v. Weingarten Inc., 202
Noble v. Sears, Roebuck & Co., 202
Non-competition agreement, 116
Non-compliance, 14, 18
Non-directive counseling, 19
Non-disclosure agreement, 118f, 122
Non-evacuation method, 69
Non-Government Organizations (NGOs), 598
Non-linear junction detector, 124
Nonpublic personal information (NPI), 30
Non-sales mode, 462
Nonsecretors, 143
Nonverbal behavior, 130–131
Non-verbal communication, 161, 167
Nordstrom's golden rule, 61
Note taking, 180
NPI. *See* Nonpublic personal information
NRC. *See* Nuclear Regulatory Commission
NRP. *See* National Response Plan
NSA. *See* National Security Agency
NSF. *See* National Science Foundation of
    America
NSP. *See* National Response Plan
NSTC. *See* National Science and Technology
    Council

NTSC. *See* National Television System Committee
Nuclear blast, 559
Nuclear power plants, 81–82
Nuclear Regulatory Commission (NRC), 81
Nuclear weapons, 531–534, 559
Nuisance Alarm Rate (NAR), 277–278
Nuisance alarms, 326–327
NVR. *See* Network video recorder
NVSF. *See* National Vehicle Identification
    Number Standard File

O

OAT. *See* Operational Acceptance Test
Objections, overcoming, 185
Observational tests, 349
Occupational Safety and Health Administration
    (OSHA), 106, 405
Ocean floor movement, 82–83
OCSP. *See* Online certificate status protocol
Office of Detention and Removal (DRO), 595
Older Workers Benefit Protection Act
    (OWBPA), 1
Olfactory fatigue, 127
Ongoing System Operational Test (OSOT), 255
Online certificate status protocol (OCSP), 109
On-scene functions, 91–92
Open competition, 11
Open-door policy, 15, 19
Operable opening switches, 339
Operable openings, 309–310
Operating practices, 3–4
Operation community shield, 591
Operation methods, 556–558
Operational Acceptance Test (OAT), 255
Operational environment, 325–326
Operational security, 485–486
Operations, 84
Operations Security (OPSEC), 113–114, 493–495
Operative extraction, 193–194
OPSEC. *See* Operations Security
Oral confessions, 186–187
Organizational chart, 41, 51
Organizations, 5, 20–23, 45–46
    best practices approach in, 22–23
    CBT considerations in, 357
    formal, 41
    informal, 41–42
    relationships in, 45–47
    vulnerabilities in, 101–102

Organized Crime Control Act, 610
Original documents, 176
OSHA. *See* Occupational Safety and Health
    Administration
OSOT. *See* Ongoing System Operational Test
Overt act, 222
OWBPA. *See* Older Workers Benefit Protection Act

P

Packages
    control of, 458
    inspecting, 257–258
Painter, 485
Panel Interface Module (PIM), 313
Parcel control, 458
The Paris Convention, 116, 221
Parking ramp security, 379–380
Passive detectors, 344
Passive infrared sensors (PIR), 281, 286–287,
    286f, 441
Passive inhalation, 362
Passive mood, 186
Passive sensors, 278, 282
Passive sonic sensors, 284
Password cracking, 158
Patents, 116, 220
Paternity, 138
Path analysis, 444
Patient care facilities, 454
Pattern recognition, 302
Pattern Theory, 488
PBIED. *See* Person-Borne Improvised Explosive
    Device
PCP. *See* Phencyclidine
PCR. *See* Polymerase Chain Reaction
PD. *See* Probability of detection
Penetration testing, 102
People, access control of, 255–256
People v. Zelinsky, 206
Perception, 153–154
Performance appraisals, 42–45
    continuous process of, 44f
    cycles in, 43–44
    merit ratings in, 44–45
    objectives in, 42–43
    reviews in, 43
Performance characteristics, 277–278
Performance reviews, 24
Performance-based analysis, 443–444
Perimeter protection

in chemical industry, 345–346
    electric-field sensors for, 299
    infrared detectors in, 340–341
Perimeter sensor systems
    clear zones in, 301
    combinations in, 301
    complementary sensors in, 300
    design concepts/goals of, 299–302
    pattern recognition in, 302
    priority schemes in, 300–301
    site-specific system in, 301–302
Personal defenses, 184
Personal Identity Verification (PIV), 109, 350–351
Personal improvement schemes, 197
Personal protection equipment (PPE), 451
Personal security mission, 380–382
Personality conflicts, 155
Person-Borne Improvised Explosive Device
    (PBIED), 542
PHA. *See* Process hazard analysis
Phencyclidine (PCP), 358
Phishing, 157
Photocopier examinations, 145
Photoelectric detectors, 332
Photography
    forensic examinations of, 151
    in investigations, 167–169
    lighting for, 169
    techniques of, 168–169
Physical barriers, 308–310
Physical environment, 325
Physical evidence, 138–139
Physical protection systems (PPS), 433, 439
    characteristics of, 306
    concepts of, 302–307
    design/evaluation criteria of, 307
    designs in, 303–304
    functions of, 303f, 304–306
Physical security, 475–476, 485
Physical security design, 307–310
    asset protection through, 308
    deterrents in, 310
    hardware used in, 346
    physical barriers in, 308–310
Physical security systems
    acceptance testing of, 253–255
    FAT of, 254
    OAT of, 255
    OSOT of, 255
    SAT of, 254
    scenario-based testing in, 253
    SWAT of, 254–255
    video surveillance in, 289

Physiological roots (kinesics), 164–165
Pickard, James, 117
Piezoelectric transducers, 261–262, 336, 343
Pillar, Paul, 561
PIM. *See* Panel Interface Module
Ping-ponging, 197
Pinhole lenses, 268
PIO. *See* Public Information Office
PIR. *See* Passive infrared sensors
PIV. *See* Personal Identity Verification
PKI. *See* Public Key Infrastructure
Plague, 506
Planned bankruptcy schemes, 196
Planning coordinator, 72, 106
Planning tool, budgeting, 5–8
Planning zones, 81
Plastics, 148
Plea negotiations, 212
Pneumonic plague, 506
Point sensors, 311
Policies, corporate environment, 56–57
Political contributions, 11, 15
Polling, 428
Polygraph test, 170–174
    critics of, 170
    employer requirements for, 174
    employers guidance from, 172–173
    examiners of, 173, 174
    false positive/negative errors in, 171
Polymerase Chain Reaction (PCR), 137–138
Polymers, 148
Ponzi schemes, 195
Pornographic Materials file, 152
Pornographic websites, 125–126
Ported coaxial cable sensors, 280
Position description, 46f
Position evaluation, 45–47
Positive confrontation, 185
Post, Richard S., 85
Post-evacuation method, 69
Post-incident analysis, 492f
Posture, 130
PPE. *See* Personal protection equipment
PPOs. *See* Preferred provider organization
PPS. *See* Physical protection systems
Pre-employment background screening, 384–391
    criminal records and, 388–389
    investigations in, 387–388
    prior employment verification in, 390
    search strategies for, 389–390
    statutory prohibitions in, 388
    vendor selection for, 390–391
Pre-employment test accuracy, 170–171

Pre-evidentiary testing, 348
Preferred provider organization (PPOs), 453
Pregnancy discrimination, 55, 59
Prejudice, 154
Preliminary offenses, 223–224
Premise design, 229–232
Preparation, 6
Presentation, 9t
Pressure mats, 311
Pressure sensors, 279–280, 288
Pressure switches, 311
Pre-trial motions, 214
Pre-trial preparation, 245
Prevention activities, 65–66
Prevention strategies, 431–433
Principles of Scientific Management (Taylor), 37
Prior employment verification, 390
Priority schemes, 300–301
Private key pair, 108
Private law, 207
Private protections, 30–31
Private sector employers, 174
Private sector police, 249
Private security, 85
Proactive awareness, 548–549
Probability of detection (PD), 277, 326
Probable cause, 205–206, 213, 239
Probation, for corporations, 244
Process hazard analysis (PHA), 431, 432
The Process of Investigation phases, 200
Procurement, 13–14, 18
Production rescheduling, 74
Profits, 27
Progress reviews, 48
Project management, 440
Project Shield America, 594
Proof-of-life code, 369
Property, 258
Proposals, security consultants, 472–473
Proprietary force, 376
Proprietary information, 116–123
    administering program for, 120–123
    classification of, 119–120
    management protecting, 121–122
    protection of, 117–119, 125
    storage for, 122–123
Prosecution
    of employees, 192
    report writing increasing, 391–392
Protected activity, 52–53
Protected opposition, 57
Protection objectives, 440–441
Protection of Assets Manual (ASIS International), 86

Protection plan, 514–517
Protection policy, information, 422
Protection requirements, 101f, 564
Protection theory, 496–497
Protection-in-depth, 306, 326
Provisioning, 350
Proximity detectors, 339
Proximity sensors, 287–289, 310–311
Public agency response protocols, 451
Public Health Security and Bioterrorism
   Preparedness and Response Act, 527
Public Information Office (PIO), 90, 91–92
Public Key Infrastructure (PKI), 109
Public key pair, 108
Public records, 389
Public relations, 106
Public safety authorities, 92–93
Public security, 85
Public/private records, 385–386
Punitive damages, 225, 250–251
Putnam, Adam H., 568
Pyramid schemes, 195

Q

Al-Qaeda, 541, 545–547, 552–555, 569
Quality
   improving, 31, 58
   pursuing, 31–32
   in security management, 64–67
   thriving for, 60–63
Quality assurance, 48–49, 321
Quantitative analysis
   PPS principles and, 437f
   statistics in, 437–439
Questioning suspects, 177–181
   Fifth amendment and, 206–207
   kinesics in, 161–167
   location for, 177–178
   sessions of, 178–180, 182–183
Questioning techniques, 181–183
Quick-ship agreements, 74
Quotas, 22, 26–27

R

RAC. See Resident Agent-in-Charge
Race discrimination, 49–51
Radio frequency identification (RFID), 256

Radioactive materials, 81–82, 559–560
Radioimmunoassay test (RIA), 363
Radiological dispersion device (RDD), 533, 560
Radiological weapons, 533
RAGE-V. See Risk Assessment Guide Elements
   for Violence
RAID. See Real-time Analytical Intelligence
   Database
Rampton, Sheldon, 497
RAOs. See Resident Agent Offices
Rape cases, 143, 183–184
Rational choice theory, 477, 488
RBAC. See Role-based access control
RDD. See Radiological dispersion device
Reagan, Ronald, 585
Real-time Analytical Intelligence Database
   (RAID), 604
Reasonable accommodations, 25
Reasonableness, 240
The Reasoning Criminal: Rational Choice Perspectives
   on Offending (Clarke/Cornish), 477
Reciprocal agreements, 73
Records, training, 228
Recoveries, from theft, 193
Recovery strategies, 73–74
Recovery/restoration, 71
Red Brigades, 556
Reference checks, 386
Regulations, 328–329
Regulatory intelligence, 104
Reid, John E., 184
Religion, 562
Religious discrimination, 51
Religious practices, 55
Remote terminal units (RTU), 513
Report writing, 391–392
Reputation protection, 474
Request for proposal (RFP), 376–377
Requirement analysis, 316–318, 317f
Research Technology Protection (RTP), 583
Resentment, 154–155
Resident Agent Offices (RAOs), 601
Resident Agent-in-Charge (RAC), 601–603
Resident team, 381
Resolution, 264–265
Resource allocation, for CIP, 509
Resources, 74
Respondeat superior, 237, 249
Response, 442–443
Response (components), 305, 305f
Response equipment, 106
Response force protocols, 451
Restaurant security, 460–462

Restitution, 520
Restoration/recovery, 71
Restriction Fragment Length Polymorphism (RFLP), 137, 144
Resume, 396–397
Resumption, 71
Retail security system design, 462–465
    backup system planning in, 464–465
    design flaws in, 462–464
    modes of operation for, 462
Retaliation, 55
Retaliation discrimination, 51–53
Return on Investment (ROI), 78
Reverse engineering, 428
Reviews, 47–48
RFID. *See* Radio frequency identification
RFLP. *See* Restriction Fragment Length Polymorphism
RFP. *See* Request for proposal
RIA. *See* Radioimmunoassay test
Ricin, 507
Risk analysis, 414–416, 494
    BIA and, 409–410
    commercial property with, 416–420
    crime record research in, 416–417
    crime statistics in, 417
    exposure assessment in, 415–416
    field interviews in, 419
    in-house security reports in, 418
    law enforcement records in, 417–418
    managements role in, 415
Risk assessment
    chemical industry with, 431–433
    computer technology in, 430
    consensus in, 421–422
    cyber offenses and, 422
    focal points in, 421
    industrial espionage and, 425–428
    information in, 429–430
    internet and, 422–425
    model of, 420f
    sensitive information and, 420–430
    spy technology in, 428–429
    for violence, 401–402
    vulnerability assessment process in, 435–437
Risk Assessment Guide Elements for Violence (RAGE-V), 402
Risk equation, 435–436
Risk Identification, 58, 72
Risk management, 77–78, 366
    in critical national infrastructure, 515
    vulnerability assessment and, 433–439, 435f
Risk potential, 411–413

Robbery, 187–189
    investigative techniques in, 188–189
    types of, 187–188
Robert T. Stafford Disaster Relief and Emergency Assistance Act, 534
ROI. *See* Return on Investment
Role-based access control (RBAC), 351
Room preparation, interrogation, 166
Routine activities theory, 480, 488
RTP. *See* Research Technology Protection
RTU. *See* Remote terminal units
Rules of evidence, 245–246
Rules of exclusion, 236–237

S

SAC. *See* Special Agent-in-Charge
Safe hiring, 384–387
Safe insulation, 150–151
Safety, 85
Sales mode, 462
Saliva, 143
Saliva tests, 349
Sandria National Laboratories (SNL), 433
SARA. *See* Spousal Assault Risk Assessment Guide
SARAH, 63
Sarbanes Oxley Act, 74, 364–366
SAT. *See* Site Acceptance Test
SCADA. *See* Supervisory control and data acquisition
Scenario analysis, 444
Scenario-based testing, 253
Schrader, Gerhard, 504
Science and technology, 517–523
Science era, 37–38
Scientific management era, 37
SCO. *See* State Coordinating Officer
Seabrook, John, 88
Search(es), 206
    bomb threat management with, 67–68
    considerations for, 68–69
    and rescue, 403
    strategies of, 389–390
    warrants for, 238–239
Search and seizure, 237–242
    affidavits in, 239–240
    incriminating evidence in, 240
    search consent in, 241
    search warrants in, 238–239
Secretors, 143

Security, 403
  analysis, 438
  architecture and, 445–450
  assessment, 432–433
  awareness training, 372–373
  budget motel, 465–467
  CCTV used in, 262–266, 271–276
  for chemical industry, 450–451
  decision makers, 135–136
  delivery system, 231
  detail, 380–381
  environment, 41–42
  expertise, 495–498
  group, 10
  group services, 392–393
  hazards, 86–87
  of information, 113–114
  initiatives, 525, 565–566
  laws influencing, 224–225
  levels of, 346–347
  as measurable, 353
  negligence cases in, 231
  problems in, 16–17
  program development, 329–330
  requirement analysis/system definition in,
      317f
  risk equation for, 435–436
  screens, 339
  services, 53–54
  staff, 59
Security administrator
  interviewing, 397–398
  qualifications required of, 396
  resume/job application of, 396–397
  selecting, 396–398
*Security and Administration: An Introduction to
    the Protective Services* (Post/Kingsbury), 85
Security consultants, 467–469
  in-house v. outside, 469–471
  proposals by, 472–473
Security departments
  incident management and, 76–77
  substandard practices in, 491
Security design
  codes/regulations in, 328–329
  considerations in, 323–329
  electronic systems used in, 449
  integration considerations in, 327–329
  operational environment in, 325–326
  physical environment in, 325
  process of, 324
  protection-in-depth in, 326
  system objectives in, 323–324

system performance in, 326
system selection in, 324–325
Security design and integration, 314–323
  implementation, 320–321
  integration in, 319f
  objectives of, 315
  requirements analysis in, 316–318
  system engineering in, 318–320
  system operation in, 321–323
Security Education, Training and Awareness
    (SETA), 582
Security Industry Association, 497
Security law
  concepts in, 221–224
  federal offenses in, 222–223
  preliminary offenses in, 223–224
Security management, 37
  information finding in, 79–80
  new age of, 77–78
  quality in, 64–67
  strategies for, 55–60
  technical knowledge in, 57–58
  theoretical basis of, 496
Security managers
  evaluation criteria of, 2
  internship programs and, 32–33
  obstacles met by, 24
Security officers
  in chemical industry, 346
  compensation of, 395–396
  turnover rates of, 393–396
Security professionals, 232
  computer-based training for, 354–357
  obligations of, 229–230
Security Risk Analysis, 83
Security surveillance, 275–276
Security system
  implementation of, 321, 321f
  integration of, 275f
  logical stages of, 315f
  operation/evaluation of, 322f
  technology, 448
Segregation, 50–51
Seismic sensors, 279–280
Self-defense, 216
Self-discipline, 27–28
Self-esteem, 39–40
Semen, 143
Senior Federal Law Enforcement Official
    (SFLEO), 538
Senior management, 67–68
Sensitive information, 112–117
  classification of, 114–115

data protection and, 116–117
proprietary information and, 116
protecting, 123–125
risk assessment and, 420–430
Sensors
    audio detection of, 330–331
    barrier detectors with, 331–333
    classification of, 278–279
    exterior intrusion detection, 333–334
    fence disturbance detection, 334–337
    fences with, 280–281
    interior intrusion detection, 337–339
    intrusion detection with, 441
    invisible barrier detector, 339–341
    microwave motion detector, 341–342
    photoelectric detector, 332
    sonic motion detector, 342
    systems with, 517
    trip-wire device, 332–333
    types of, 263–264
    ultrasonic motion detection, 342–344
    volumetric motion detection, 344
Sentencing guidelines, 242–244
Sentencing Reform Act, 242
Serology, forensic, 142–143
Service and repair schemes, 196–197
Service Level Agreement (SLA), 255
Service sector, 38
Service-level agreements, 78
SETA. *See* Security Education, Training and
    Awareness
Seven Deadly Sins, 22–23
Sex-based discrimination, 54–55
Sexual harassment, 54–55
Sexual offenses, 237
SFLEO. *See* Senior Federal Law Enforcement
    Official
The Shamrock Organization, 16–18
    four leaves of, 20–21
    motivational controls in, 17–18
    security problems in, 16–17
Sherman, Lawrence, 231
Shoe print examination, 146, 152
Shoplifting, 221–223
Short weighing, 196
Short-term profits, 28
Shotshell casings, 146–147
Shunting, 182
SIGINT. *See* Signals Intelligence
Signal analysis, 141
Signals Intelligence (SIGINT), 605–606
Single camera system, 272f
Site Acceptance Test (SAT), 254

Site protection, 474
Site-specific system, 301–302
Situational crime prevention, 477, 478t, 479t
Sixth Amendment, 212
Skimming, 157
Skinheads, 562
Sky Marshall Program, 585
SLA. *See* Service Level Agreement
Slight negligence, 209
Slip-knifing, 133
Small cameras, covert, 268–269
Smallpox, 506–507
SME. *See* Subject matter expert
Smith, Adam, 36
SNL. *See* Sandria National Laboratories
Social crime prevention, 488–489
Social isolation, 398
Social issues, 522–523
SOF. *See* Special operations forces
Soil, 150
Solid-state sensors, 264
Solis v. Southern Cal. Rapid Transit Dist., 202
Sonic motion detector, 342
Sound recordings, 141
Spalling, 128
Speaker identification, 141
Special Agent-in-Charge (SAC), 601–603
Special operations forces (SOF), 499
Spectrum analyzer, 124
Spies, 426–429
Spokesperson, 90–91
Spontaneous declaration, 140, 237
Spoof protection, 256, 278
Spousal Assault Risk Assessment Guide
    (SARA), 402
Sprinkler head pinhole lens, 269–270, 269f
Spy technology, 428–429
Spyware blockers, 107–108
Staff resources, 3
Stairwells, 88
Stalking, 428
Stand-by power, 273
Stare decisis, 208
State Coordinating Officer (SCO), 537, 538
State courts, 211–213
Statistical methods, 20
Statistics
    quantitative analysis with, 437–439
    security analysis using, 438
Statute of limitations, 215
Statutory law, 208
Statutory prohibitions, 388
Stauber, John, 497

Stimuli, 164f
Sting operations, 192
Storage, 122–123
Strain buried line sensor, 262
Strategic planning, 55–60
Structural damage, 532–533
Stulb, David L., 156
Subject matter expert (SME), 440
Subjects, 186
Substance abuse, 398–401
Substandard conditions, 491
Substandard practices, 491
Substantive law, 207
Substation vulnerabilities, 513
The Suggested Guidelines in Museum Security
    (ASIS), 458
Suicide bombers, 541–542, 544
Supervision
    counseling function in, 19
    discipline in, 26–28
    self-discipline in, 27–28
Supervisory control and data acquisition
    (SCADA), 567
Suppliers, 58–59
Supplier/vendor intelligence, 104
Surveillance, 201, 447, 546
Suspects
    assessing, 178
    identifying, 138
    questioning, 161–167, 177–181, 206–207
Suspended ceilings, 87–88
Suspicious objects, 69–70
SWAT. *See* System-wide acceptance test
Switches, 292
    balance magnetic, 441
    balanced magnetic, 298
    contact, 298
    hall effect, 283
    mechanical inertia, 335
    mercury, 335
    operable opening, 298, 339
    pressure, 311
    taut-wire, 337
Sympathetic function, 164–165
Sympathetic technique, 179
System definition, 317f
System design coordination, 295–296
System engineering, 318–320, 318f
System engineering and design, 318–320
System objectives, 323–324
System operation, 321–323
System performance, 326
System Security Program Plans, 524

System selection, 324–325, 367
System-level training, 321
System-wide acceptance test (SWAT), 254–255

T

Tallahassee Furniture Co. Inc. v. Harrison, 233
Tamil Tigers, 541
Tape duplications, 141
Tape enhancements, 141–142
Target analysis, 498–500, 500t
Task statements, 34–35
Tasks
    analysis of, 226
    characteristics of, 34–35
    duties making up, 35f
    rating, 35–36
Taut-wire switches, 337
Taylor, Frederick W., 37
Teamwork, 58, 64
Technical competence, 53
Technical knowledge
    best practices with, 62
    in security management, 57–58
Technical security, 486
Technical security consultants, 468
Technical Security Countermeasures (TSCM),
    429
Technical Services Division, FBI, 140–142
Technical Surveillance Countermeasures
    (TSCM), 123–125
Technology
    best practices use of, 3
    in industrial espionage, 428–429
    making use of, 59
    security system, 448
Telecommunications, 73
Terrain-following sensors, 278
Territorial behavior, 487–488
Territorial enforcement, 485
Territorial reinforcement, 447
Terrorism, 540
    anti, teams, 607
    bomb scene search from, 549–551
    domestic/international, 75, 561
    group typologies in, 546–547
    kidnapping/assassinations from, 543
    law enforcement priorities fighting, 562–563
    many faces of, 560–563
    methods/tactics of, 542–546, 551–558
    preparations for, 545–546

preventing attacks of, 525–526
proactive awareness fighting, 548–549
strategies of, 547–548
suicide bombers in, 541–542, 544
tourism security and, 473–474
vehicle bomb attacks from, 544–545
vulnerability reduced against, 566
Terrorist groups, 552–553
computer software and, 567–568
educational resources for, 553–554
hiding places of, 555
motives of, 561–562
operation methods of, 556–558
threats from, 558–560
Testifying, 245–248
cross-examination in, 247–248
pre-trial preparation for, 245
rules of evidence and, 245–246
witness stand and, 246–247
Testing techniques, 255
"The Master Planner" (Hoenig), 60
Theft, 218
cash and, 460
museum security and, 459
reducing, 271–272
Theme development, 185
Thermal imaging equipment, 124
Thin layer chromatography (TLC), 363
Third-party manufacturing, 73
Threat analysis, 293–294, 494
Threat assessment, 133–134, 370–371
Threat management, 406–408
Threats
of biological weapons, 558–559
bomb threat management, 65–70
chemical, 559
to chemical industry, 433
contemporary, 294–295
in critical national infrastructure, 520–521
to electric power, 511–512
explosion, 558
insider, 519
for intrusion detection, 293–295
life safety, 86
from terrorist groups, 558–560
traditional, 293–294
Thunderstorms, 82
Time domain reflectometer, 124
Tire tread examination, 146, 152
Title I of ADA, 25
Title VII, of Civil Rights Act, 29, 40–41, 47–55
TLC. *See* Thin layer chromatography

Tool mark identification, 152–153
Tornados, 82
Tort law, 209, 248–250
civil actions in, 248–249
contract law and, 249–250
Torts, 250–251
intentional/intrusion, 251
private sector police and, 249
punitive/compensatory damages in, 250–251
Tourism security, 473–474
Toxicological examinations, 144, 359
Toxins, 503–504, 507
Trade secrets, 116, 220–221
Trademarks, 116, 220
Traditional threats, 293–294
Traffic access control, 257
Trainers, 383–384
Training
in bomb threat management, 66
CCTV used for, 274
CSO responsible for, 382–383
Deming promoting, 21–22
essential elements of, 383–384
evaluation in, 227–228
executive kidnapping prevention, 369–370
instructor standards in, 228–229
keeping records for, 228
NEDCP, 378–379
negligence liability in, 225–229
planning/organizing, 382–384
specifications in, 226–227
validation in, 226
working dogs, 403–404
Training courses, 229
Transportation, 523–524
critical technology elements of, 564
infrastructure of, 563–565
protection requirements of, 564
Transportation Security Administration (TSA), 378
Travel risk reduction, 371–372
Trespassing, 427–428
Trip-wire device, 332–333
Troubleshooting, 21
TSA. *See* Transportation Security Administration
TSCM. *See* Technical Security Countermeasures; Technical Surveillance Countermeasures
Tsunami, 82–83
Tuneable receiver, 124
Turnover rates, 393–396
Typewriter examination, 146

U

UCR. *See* Uniform Crime Report
Ultrasonic motion detection, 342–344
Ultrasonic sensors, 285–286
Unaccustomed writing hand, 175
Undercover investigations
  cover story for, 191–192
  Interviews in, 193
  operative extraction in, 193–194
  process of, 190–191
  recoveries in, 193
  in workplace, 189–194
Uniform Crime Report (UCR), 416, 417
Union contracts, 249
United States (U.S.), 502–503
United States Coast Guard, 608–609
United States Secret Service (USSS), 618–622
Unity of command, 94
Upward feedback process, 63–64, 63f
Urban design, 480
Urban transit, 524–526, 565–566
Urinalysis, 361–362
Urinalysis technologies, 362–364
Urine, 143
U.S. *See* United States
U.S. Army, 608
U.S. Citizenship and Immigration Services
  (USCIS), 592
U.S. Marshals Service (USMS), 609–618
  criminal information branch of, 610–611
  district offices of, 611–618
  fugitive program of, 609–610
USA PATRIOT Act, 594–595
USCIS. *See* U.S. Citizenship and Immigration
  Services
USMS. *See* U.S. Marshals Service
USSS. *See* United States Secret Service

V

VA. *See* Vulnerability assessment
Validation, 226
VCR. *See* Video cassette recorder
VDMs. *See* Video motion detection sensors
Vehicle bomb attack, 544–545
Vehicle bomb explosion hazard, 533t
Vehicle Identification Number (VIN), 141
Vendor selection, 390–391

Vendors, 21
Verbal behavior, 130–131
Verton, Dan, 566, 569
VGTF. *See* Virtual Global Task Force
VHF. *See* Viral hemorrhagic fever
Vibration sensors, 283
Video cassette recorder (VCR), 267, 272
Video decoders, 292
Video encoders, 292
Video motion detection sensors (VDMs), 282,
  287, 441
Video recording, 180
Video security system, 293
Video surveillance, 289
VIN. *See* Vehicle Identification Number
Violations, of business ethics, 14, 18
Violence
  motivation toward, 405
  risk assessment for, 401–402
  workplace preventing, 404–408
Violence Risk Appraisal Guide (VRAG), 402
Violent crime, 144
Viral hemorrhagic fever (VHF), 507
Virtual Global Task Force (VGTF), 598
Virtual matrix switching, 292
Viruses, 506–507
Visitor protection, 474
Volcano, 83
Volumetric detection, 441
Volumetric motion detection, 344
Volumetric motion detectors, 337–338
Volumetric sensors, 278–279, 283
VRAG. *See* Violence Risk Appraisal Guide
Vulnerability analysis, 330, 494
Vulnerability assessment (VA), 302, 439–444
  AC&D in, 442
  alarm assessment in, 441–442
  facility characterization in, 441
  performance-based analysis in, 443–444
  process of, 435–437
  project management in, 440
  protection objectives in, 440–441
  response in, 442–443
  risk management and, 433–439, 435f
  using, 444
  water systems and, 526–529

W

Wage factors, 28–29
Walls, 309

WAN. *See* Wide area network
War on terror, 569
Warning signs, 365–366
Warranties, 24, 27–28
Warrants, 239, 240
Water system, 526–529
Watermark standards, 146
Waterspouts, 82
Watt, James, 117
WBT. *See* Web-based training
The Wealth of Nations (Smith), 36
Weapons, explosive, 531–532
Weapons of Mass Destruction (WMDs), 501–
    502, 593
Web bugs, 107
Web-based training (WBT), 354
Website blocking software, 125–126
Welfare fraud, 197–198
Whistleblowers, 365
White balance, 266
White, J., 552
White-collar crime, 74, 194–199
    nature of, 194–195
    types of, 195–199
Wide area network (WAN), 289
Wild fire, 80
Wilson, James Q., 485
Wireless access control, 313
Wireless sensors, 288–289
Wireless transmission, 271
Withdrawal defense, 215
Witness stand, 246–247
Witness testimony, 216–217. *See also* Expert
    witness
Witnesses, 159–161

WMDs. *See* Weapons of Mass Destruction
Workforce management, 73
Working conditions, 28–29
Working dogs
    history of, 402–403
    specialties of, 403
    training of, 403–404
Workplace
    homicides at, 294–295
    hostility in, 50
    investigations in, 199–203
    substance abuse in, 398–401
    undercover investigations in, 189–194
    violence prevention/intervention in,
        404–408
Worksite enforcement, 591–592
World-class organization, 5
Wounds, 203–204
Writing instrument analysis, 145
Written confessions, 187
Written examination, 227
Written statements, 180

X

X.509 certificates, 109

Z

Zero-based budgeting, 7
Zoning concept, 449